WOLF LESLAU

CONCISE AMHARIC DICTIONARY

CONCISE

AMHARIC DICTIONARY

Amharic - English

English - Amharic

by

WOLF LESLAU

UNIVERSITY OF CALIFORNIA PRESS
Berkeley and Los Angeles

The research reported herein was performed pursuant to a contract with the United States Department of Health, Education, and Welfare, Office of Education, Institute of International Studies.

For the United States, Canada, and the Philippine Islands:
University of California Press
Berkeley and Los Angeles, California
ISBN: 0-520-20501-4
Library of Congress Catalog Card Number: 73-90668

2 3 4 5 6 7 8 9

The paper used in this publication is both acid-free and totally chlorine-free (TCF).
It meets the minimum requirements of American Standard for Information Sciences—
Permanence of Paper for Printed Library Materials, ANSI Z39.48-1984. ⊚

TABLE OF CONTENTS

TO THE MEMORY OF

MARCEL COHEN

TEACHER AND FRIEND

PREFACE

The oldest dictionary of Amharic, the national language of Ethiopia, is that of H. Ludolf, *Lexicon Amharico-Latinum*, 1698. The latest Amharic dictionaries of scientific character are: I. Guidi, *Vocabolario Amarico-Italiano*, Rome, 1901 (an Amharic-Italian dictionary); J. Baeteman, *Dictionnaire amarigna-français*, Dire-Daoua, 1929 (an Amharic-French dictionary); E. Gankin, *Amkharsko-Russkii Slovar*, Moscow, 1969 (an Amharic-Russian dictionary). The only Amharic-English dictionary is that of C.H. Armbruster, *Initia Amharica*, Part III. Cambridge, 1920. This dictionary, however, is incomplete; indeed, it contains only the first five letters of the alphabet.

The dictionaries from foreign languages into Amharic are: a French-Amharic index in the above-mentioned work by J. Baeteman; an Italian-Amharic dictionary by L. Fusella and A. Girace, *Dizionario pratico e frasario per conversazione italiano-amarica*, Napoli, 1937; a Russian-Amharic dictionary by E. Gankin, *Russko-Amkharskii Slovar*, Moscow, 1965. English-Amharic dictionaries are: C. H. Armbruster, *Initia Amharica*, Part II, 1910; C. H. Walker, *English-Amharic Dictionary*, 1920; Amsalu Aklilu and G. P. Mosback, *English-Amharic Dictionary* (Addis Ababa, 1973); and W. Leslau, *English-Amharic Context Dictionary* (Otto Harrassowitz, Wiesbaden, 1973).

Since the publication of the oldest dictionaries, Amharic has developed considerably. Progress in the field of education, literary works of the last 50 years, expansion of technology, contact with the Western world, and natural development within the language itself have all contributed greatly not only to the enrichment of the language but also to numerous changes within the existing vocabulary. A few examples taken from Armbruster's dictionary will illustrate such changes in expression. Thus "address" is rendered by Armbruster as ምልክት against the present-day አድራሻ; "bank" ግምጃ ፡ ቤት as against ባንክ; "bicycle" የሰይጣን ፡ ፈረስ as against ቢሲክሌት; "cigarette" በወረ ቀት ፡ የተጠቀለለ ፡ ትምባሆ as against ሲጃራ; "general" ደጃዝማች as against ጄኔራል; "story of a house" ደርብ as against ፎቅ, and many more.

Needless to say, in Armbruster's time there was no need for expressions such as "United Nations, Trusteeship Committee, Security Council, control tower, book review, agenda, airlines, basketball, elevator," and so on.

Likewise in the Amharic-foreign language dictionaries (with the exception of the Amharic-Russian dictionary), one will not find the expressions or idioms used in everyday writing or speech. Thus, while the root ዘረዘረ is mentioned in the dictionaries of Baeteman and Guidi, the common usage of ዝርዝር "list, detail", በዝርዝር "minutely, item by item" is not mentioned. Likewise, even though the roots are found in the dictionaries, one will not find in the above-mentioned works expressions of everyday usage such as ኃላፊ "responsible, head of a firm"; ሒሳብ "arithmetic"; ለመል "barely"; መልመጃ "exercise (in a textbook)"; አስተያየት "opinion, point of view"; በተለይ "especially, in particular"; ከሞላ ፡ ጐደል "by and large, more or less"; መልስ "change (in money)"; ማመልከቻ "application (request)"; መረቀ "inaugurate, dedicate"; ሥልጣኔ "civilization"; ስብሰባ "session, assembly, conference," and many more. As a result of the inadequacy of the existing dictionaries, the student is greatly handicapped in his studies. The present dictionary is intended to remedy this situation. Since this is only a concise dictionary — particularly the Amharic-English section — there is no need to stress the fact that the remedy can be only partial. There is still an urgent need for a complete Amharic-English dictionary.

ORTHOGRAPHY

As is well known, the Amharic alphabet has various letters that are identical in the pronunciation. This is a case of ኣ and ዐ, both letters being vowel carriers and no longer consonants; ሀ, ሐ and ኀ pronounced *h*; ስ and ሠ pronounced *s*; ጸ and ፀ pronounced *ṣ*. As a result of the merging of these letters, there is considerable lack of consistency in the Amharic spelling. The principle adopted in this dictionary is that of etymologies. In the case of ኣ and ዐ, Geez as well as Tigre and Tigrinya and the other Semitic languages could be used as sources for correct spelling. In the case of ሀ (*h*), ሐ (*ḥ*), ኀ (*h*), only Geez (and Arabic) could be used as a guide since Tigre and Tigrinya kept only ሀ and ሐ, this last sound representing a merger of ሐ and ኀ. Likewise for ስ and ሠ as well as for ጸ and ፀ, Geez alone could serve as a source of information, since in both Tigre and Tigrinya, ስ and ሠ are represented as ስ, and ጸ and ፀ have merged into ጸ. It is on the basis of this principle that I adopted spellings such as ዐወቀ "know" (Geez ዐቀ), ዐሥር "ten" (G. ዐሥር), እኅት "sister" (G. እኅት), ሦስት "three" (G. ሠለስቱ), ሕፃን "baby" (G. ሕፃን), እቃ "things, package" (Tigrinya ኣቅሐ), and so on. Less generally accepted spellings are those of ዐጠፈ "double", ዐጨደ "mow", ዕንጨት "wood", but here again the spelling with ዐ was adopted because these roots have an ዐ as first radical in Geez: ዐጠፈ, ዐጸደ, and ዕዕ respectively.

Etymological spelling is also used in Arabic loanwords. Thus, ሐሳብ "bill", Arabic حساب; ሐኪም "doctor", Arabic حکیم; ዒላማ "aim", Arabic علامة; ጋላማ "object, purpose", Arabic علامة, and so on.

The standardization of spelling through etymology is not intended to disregard the actual pronunciation of a lexeme. Thus, for instance, the verb "he went out" is pronounced *wäṭṭa*, with final *ṭ*, and is therefore written ወጣ (with ጣ), and not ወጸ as it would be if one adhered strictly to the origin of the verb, namely Geez ወጽአ. Likewise, the expression "he is" is pronounced *allä*, with an initial *a*. It is therefore written ኣለ and not ሀለ, as it might be if one were to consider the origin of the verb, namely Geez ሀለወ. Or, the adjective "new" is pronounced *addis* with an initial vowel *a*. It is therefore written ኣዲስ and not ሐዲስ as it was originally in Geez.

In roots for which there is no corresponding Ethiopic or Semitic etymology, I have adopted ኣ for an initial vowel, ሀ for *h* (except in ውኃ "water"), ስ for *s*, and ጸ for *ṣ*.

There is no consistency concerning the representation of the vowel *a* after a laryngeal or velar. Thus ኃይል and ኃይል are written, both pronounced *hayl*; or ሀብት and ሃብት, both pronounced *habt*.

The labiovelars are normally kept; thus ቈረጠ (and not ቆረጠ). However, there are occasional inconsistencies as in the verb ኩመጠጠ with the labiovelar (ኩ), but the adjective ኩምጣጣ, with ኩ, from the same root.

The combination of a vowel followed by አ or እ has been treated in several different ways. In some instances I have retained the አ or እ in the Amharic script (as in የአየር) while in others I have eliminated it (as in የጅ for የእጅ). Similarly in the transcription I have followed the pronunciation, eliminating one of the vowels in certain cases (as in *yayyär*, written የአየር), retaining it in others (as *läakalä*, written ለአከለ), and in still other instances retaining both vowels and inserting ' representing አ or ዐ (as in *sä'at*, written ሰዓት). This last representation is in fact not transcription, but transliteration. In few examples only is the symbol ' to be pronounced as a glottal stop, as in *a'məro*, written አእምሮ.

OBSERVATIONS ON THE ARRANGEMENT AND THE DEFINITIONS

The order of the entries is alphabetical by consonant, and not in regard to the vowel of the first consonant. However, if the consonants of any two entries are identical, they are arranged according to the traditional order of the Amharic vocalic system. Thus, for instance, ለት is placed before ላት, and ላት before ሌት.

Verbs are entered in the form of the perfect, 3rd masculine, singular. They are translated by the English infinitive without "to".

The subentries in the English-Amharic section are in alphabetical order. For example "end" (p. 356) has the subentries "bring to an end; come to an end; no end; put an end to", in that order.

An impersonal verb is indicated by placing the third masc. sing. object suffix pronoun in parentheses after it; e.g. ራበ(ው) "be hungry, starve"; ገባ(ው) "understand"

Only derived stems whose meaning cannot automatically be deduced from the basic stem are given in the dictionary. Thus, for instance, no ት-stem is given if its meaning is that of the passive of the basic transitive verb. Therefore ተለከ is not given as a derived stem of ለከ "measure", since the student knows that ተለከ means "be measured", passive of the transitive verb ለከ "measure". On the other hand, ተሰበረ is given since outside of its passive meaning "be broken", it also means "break" (intransitive).

All the verbal and nominal derivations are given under the root. Thus, under ሳበ, for instance, the derived stem ተሳበ and the nominal derivations ስበት and መሳቢያ are given; or under አዘዘ, the derived stem ታዘዘ and the nominal derivations አዛዥ, ትእዛዝ and ታዛዥ are given. Wherever the derived form may not be easily recognizable or has idiomatic expressions, it is taken up in the appropriate alphabetical order. Thus, መሳቢያ "drawer" is given under መሳቢያ with the indication that its root is ሳበ; or አዛዥ is also given as an independent entry under አዛዥ since it is used in idiomatic expressions such as አዛዥ ፡ መኩኑን ; ምክትል ፡ አዛዥ; and ዋና ፡ አዛዥ.

The English words in parentheses restrict the meaning of the entry. Thus ተማገተ "argue (in court)", ሞግዚት "nurse (one who takes care of children)", በከለ "contaminate (with sewage)".

In the English-Amharic section, likewise, the expression in parentheses more specifically defines the main entry. Normally, an adjective as a main entry is explained by another adjective, as in "able" (capable), or (competently done); or by a noun preceded by ～, as in "coarse" defined by (～cloth), or (～sand). A noun or a verb is defined by another noun or verb; see "accent" defined by "stress", or "special way of pronouncing"; or the verb "check" is defined by "examine", or "mark with a check". A transitive verb as a main entry is further defined by giving a direct object after ～ ; see "beat" defined by (～the woods); "charge" defined by (～money), or (～battery).

The expression "of" followed by a noun indicates that the noun is the subject of the verb. Thus *ነፈነፈ, አነፈነፈ "scent (of a dog)" indicates that "scent" refers to the dog as the subject. Or, in the entry "come" (of time) or (of holiday) in the English-Amharic section, the element "of" indicates that "time" or "holiday" are subjects of the verb "come". In entries consisting of "be" followed by an adjective, the subject is not always preceded by "of"; e.g. "lumpy, be" (flour), that is "flour" is the subject of "be lumpy".

The part of speech is indicated wherever there is ambiguity; e.g. አዎንታ "affirmative" (n.), but የአዎንታ "affirmative" (adj.). If in a group of definitions, some are not ambiguous but others may be, the part of speech is not indicated. Thus, in አቤቱታ "complaint, petition, plea, appeal", "petition" and "appeal" may be nouns or verbs. However, since "complaint" and "plea" are not ambiguous, it is evident that all of these words are nouns and thus there is no need to indicate the part of speech.

The abbreviation (vt.) after the transcription indicates that all of the verbs of the English definition are transitive, e.g. አነቃነቀ annäqannäqä (vt.) "jar, budge, loosen". The same principle applies to the abbreviation (vi.) as in ታነቀ tannäqä (vi.) "strangle, choke, suffocate", all the verbs being intransitive.

The abbreviation (n.) following the transcription indicates that all the following words are nouns. Thus, አበባ abäba (n.) "flower, bloom".

The choice of the entries in the Amharic-English section is subjective since there exists no study on word frequency in Amharic.

LIST OF ABBREVIATIONS

adj.	=	adjective	pl.	=	plural
adv.	=	adverb	prep.	=	preposition
conj.	=	conjunction	resp.	=	respect
fem.	=	feminine	sg.	=	singular
intr.	=	intransitive	v.	=	verb
masc.	=	masculine	vi.	=	intransitive verb
n.	=	noun	vt.	=	transitive verb

B indicates type B of verbs. A verb without the symol (B) is of type A. The type is indicated only in the Amharic-English section. For the features of type B, see the existing grammars.

SYMBOLS

The symbols are †, ~, *

† indicates a derived form (noun or verb) that also has subentries. The form is mentioned twice, first under its root and then in the appropriate alphabetical order. Thus, አብዛኛ derived and placed under በዛ is preceded by †. It is given independently under አብዛኛ with its subentries.

~. This symbol is used only in the English-Amharic section. It tells the reader to substitute the entry. This is frequent in the case of a transitive verb specified by a direct object, as in "draft (~ a bill)" to be read "draft a bill"; or of an adjective specified by a noun as in "congenial (~ roommate)" to be read "congenial roommate".

* indicates that the basic stem does not occur. The root is then followed by the actual stem. Thus, *መስገነ, አመሰገነ "thank, be grateful"; *ደረገ, አደረገ "make, do". In the English-Amharic section the verb is given in the actual stem without indicating the root. Thus "ascertain" is rendered by አረጋገጠ or አጣራ. The reader who is familiar with the verb structure will know that the root of አረጋገጠ is ረጋጠ, and that ጣራ is the root of አጣራ.

PRONUNCIATION OF PHONETIC SYMBOLS

The consonants that have approximately the same pronunciation as in English are: *b*, *p*, *m*, *f*, *w*, *s* (as in "sun"), *z*, *y*, *g* (as in "go"), *k* and *h*.

č corresponds to *ch* as in "church".
š corresponds to *sh* as in "shoe".
ǧ corresponds to *j* as in "joke".
ž corresponds to *s* as in "pleasure".
ñ corresponds to *ni* as in "onion".
d and *t* in Amharic are of the dental type, that is, the tip of the tongue touches the upper part of the teeth.
l is like the English *l* at the beginning of a word (as in "light").
r is a flap, as in Spanish and Italian.
' corresponds to the pronunciation of the sound of English "uh-uh" as a negation, or "oh-oh" as an expression of surprise.

ṭ, *č̣*, *p*, *q* and *ṣ* These are sounds that are characteristic of Amharic and are not found in English. These sounds are called "glottalized" or "ejectives". In the pronunciation of the glottalized consonants, the stream of air coming from the lungs is shut off by closure of the glottis while the air above it is forced out through a stricture formed in the various vocal organs. This stricture is at the lips for *p*, at the teeth for *ṭ*, *ṣ*, at the palate for *č̣*, and at the velum for *q*.

The slightly raised ^{w} as in k^w, g^w, q^w indicates that the consonant is pronounced with a rounding of the lips.

A repeated letter indicates a long consonant; e.g. *säbbärä*.

The pronunciation of the vocalic symbols is as follows:
i like 'ee' in "feet"
e like 'a' in "state"
a like the English exclamation "ah"
o like 'o' in "nor"
u like 'oo' in "boot"
ä is pronounced like the sound one makes in hesitating in speaking and which is represented in writing by "uh"
ə has a pronunciation approximatety like the 'e' in "roses".

In the Amharic-English section the transcription is given only for the main entry or for the subentry if it is not taken up elsewhere. If the subentry is taken up elsewhere, the transcription is given in the appropriate place. Thus, ዐወጅ *awwäğä*, ዐዋጅ *awağ*, but for ዐዋጅ ፡ ነጋሪ the transcription for ነጋሪ is found under ነገረ, ነጋሪ *nägari*.

In the English-Amharic section all the entries are transcribed.

THE ORDER OF THE ALPHABET

The letters that have the same sound in present-day Amharic are placed together. The order is as follows:

ሀ—ሐ—ኀ, ለ, መ, ረ, ሠ—ሰ, ሸ, ቀ (ቄ), በ, ተ, ቸ, ነ, ኘ, አ—ዐ, ከ (ኩ, ኸ), ወ, ዘ, ዠ, የ, ደ, ጀ, ገ (ጕ), ጠ, ጨ, ጸ, ፀ—ፀ, ፈ, ፐ

I wish to express my thanks to Chahriman and Vartkes Tchakerian of Commercial Printing, Addis Ababa, who performed the task of printing with professional skill, diligence, and wholehearted devotion.

Los Angeles, May, 1975   Wolf Leslau

AMHARIC-ENGLISH

ሀ ሐ ኀ

ሆዬ *hohe* sound, letter (alphabet)

ሁሉ *hullu* every, all, everybody
ሁሌ *hulle* always, all the time
ሁሉ ፡ ሰው ፤ ሰው ፡ ሁሉ everybody, everyone
ሁሉ ፡ ቀን ፤ ሁልቀን *hulləqän* daily
ሁሉ ፡ ነገር everything
ሁልጊዜ *hulgize* always, every time, perpetually, all the time
ሁሉም *hullum* all of them, everything
ሁሉም ፡ ሆኖ all in all
ሁሉም ፡ ቦታ everywhere
ሁለመናው, see below
[See also እንደ, ፊት]

ሃሌ *halle* halleluiah
ሃሌ ፡ ሉያ *halleluya* halleluiah

ኋላ *hʷala* behind, in the back, later, afterwards
እ - - - ኋላ ፤ ከ - - - ኋላ behind, in the back of, after
በኋላ later, later on, afterwards, then (after that), behind
ከ - - - በኋላ behind, after (place, time)
ከ + perfect + በኋላ after (conj.)
ከኋላ behind
ከኋላ ፡ በኩል in the rear
በስተኋላ *bästähʷala* behind, from behind, from the back, after
ወደ ፡ ኋላ backward, backwards, behind, in the back
ከ - - - ወደ ፡ ኋላ from behind
የኋላ (adj.) hind, back, rear
የኋላ ፡ ኋላ in the long run, sooner or later, finally
የኋሊት *yähʷalit* back (adv.), backward, in the back, on the back
ኋለኛ *hʷaläňňa* (adj.) latter, posterior
የኋለኛ *yähʷaläňňa* (adj.) posterior, latter, rear

ሕልም *həlm* dream, fancy (see አለመ)

ሁለመናው *hullämänaw* all over (the body); see ሁሉ

ሁለት *hulätt* two
ሁለት + (suffix pronoun) two of . . . , both of . . .
ሁለቴ *hulätte* twice
ሁለቴም *hulättum* both
ሁለት ፡ ሰዓት eight o'clock
ሁለት ፡ ጊዜ twice
ሁለተኛ *hulättäňňa* second, another time, again
ሁለተኛ ፡ ደረጃ ፡ ትምህርት ፡ ቤት high school
የሁለተኛነት *yähulättäňňannät* second (prize)
አንድ ፡ ሁለት a couple of (dollars)

ኅሊና *həllina* conscience, mind, reason
ዐይነ ፡ ኅሊና imagination

ህልውና *həlləwənna* being (the fact of being), existence

ኅልዮ *halləyo* theory

ኅላፊ *halafi* one who passes, transient, transitory, ephemeral (see አለፈ)
ኅላፊ ፡ አግዳሚ passer-by
ኅላፊ ፡ ጊዜ (n.) past, past tense

ኅላፊ *halafi* one in charge of something, responsible, curator, head (of a firm); see also አላፊ
ኅላፊ ፡ ሆነ account for
ኅላፊነት *halafinnät* responsibility, charge (responsibility)

ሐምሌ *hamle* July

ሕመም *həmäm* illness, ache, sickness, disease, ailment (see አመመ)
የሕመም ፡ ፈቃድ sick leave
ሕሙም *həmum* sick, ill
ሕመምተኛ *həmämtäňňa* sick, ill, patient

ሐመር *hamär* ark

ሐምራዊ *hamrawi* pink, purple

ጎሙስ *hamus* Thursday (see also አሙስ, አምስት)

ጎምሳ *hamsa* fifty (see also አምሳ, አም
ስት)
የጎምሳ : አለቃ sergeant

ኃምስ *haməs* fifth order (*e*) of the Amharic vocalic system (see አምስት)

ሐሜት *hamet* (n.) slander, calumny (see
አማ)

ሐሞት *hamot* bile, gall (see also አሞት)
ሐሞቱ : ፈሰሰ his courage failed, he
lost courage
የሐሞት : ፊኛ gall bladder

ሆመጠጠ *homäṭṭäṭä* be acid, be tart, be
sour, turn sour (see also ኰመጠጠ)
ሆምጣጣ *homṭaṭṭa* sour, acid, tart

ሐር *harr* silk
የሐር silken
የሐር : ትል silkworm

ሐሩር *harur* intense heat (of weather);
see አረረ
የሐሩር : አውራጃ tropics

ሐርነት, see አርነት

ሐራጅ *harağ* auction

ሐረግ *haräg* shoot, kind of creeping ivy,
vine; phrase, line of a poem, clause
in a sentence; design (of rug)

ሐሳብ *hassab* opinion, point of view,
idea, notion, thought, concept, stand
(position), mind (opinion), proposal,
proposition, motion (proposal),
worry, concern (see አሰበ)
ሐሳብ : አቀረበ move, make a motion
(proposal), suggest (see ቀረበ)
ሐሳብ : የወለደው *hassab yäwällädäw*
imaginary
ሐሳብ : ቈራጥ determined, resolute
ሐሳብ : ቀና straightforward
ሐሳብ : ግትር headstrong, bull-head-
ed, intransigeant, willful, opinionated

ሐሳብ : ጽኑነት consistency
በሐሳብ : ናወዘ daydream
ከሐሳብ : አሳረፈ. put someone's mind
at rest (see አረፈ.)
መሪ : ሐሳብ leading idea, motif (see
መሪ.)
ቁርጥ : ሐሳብ decision, determination

ሒሳብ *hisab* arithmetic, mathematics,
calculation, figure (number), bill (account), check (bill), account (report
of money spent), checking account
ሒሳብ : ባዋቂ accountant (see ባወቀ)
ሒሳብ : ያዥ bookkeeper (see ያዘ)
የሒሳብ : መዝገብ accounts
ሒሳብተኛ *hisabtäňňa* accountant

ሐሰት *hassät* falsehood, lie (see also
አሰት)
በሐሰት : የመሰከረ perjuror (see መሰ
ከረ)
የሐሰት fraudulent, fake (adj.), false
የሐሰት : ስም alias
ሐሰተኛ *hassätäňňa* untruthful, false
(friend)

ሆስፒታል *hospital* hospital
ሆስፒታል : ገባ be hospitalized
ሆስፒታል : ተኛ be hospitalized, be
in the hospital

ሐቅ *haqq* truth
ሐቀኛ *haqqäňňa* just (righteous),
true, truthful, honest, straight (in
business), square (deal)
ሐቀኝነት *haqqäňňənnät* honesty (fair-
ness), integrity, probity
የሐቀኝነት ethical (behavior)

ሀቅ : አለ(ው) *həqq alä(w)* have the
hiccups
ሀቅ : ስርቅ : አለ(ው) *həqq sərq alä(w)*
have the hiccups

ሐብሐብ *habhab* melon, watermelon

ሐብል *habl* necklace, chain worn around
the neck

ገብር *həb(ə)r* combination (see also ገብ
ረት, ማገናበር, አበረ)

ጉብረ ፡ ሰብ society
(የጉብረ ፡ ሰብ social)
ጉብረ ፡ ትምህርት social studies
ጉብረ ፡ ኮከብ constellation
የጉብር ፡ አነጋገር pun (see ነገረ)

ጉብረት *həbrät* alliance, unison, coalition, harmony, union, cooperation, solidarity (see also ጉብር, አበረ)
ጉብረተ ፡ ሰብ society (all the people)
በጉብረት hand-in-hand, in concert
የጉብረት communal
የጉብረተ ፡ ሰብ social
የጉብረተ ፡ ድርጅት cooperative

ሐበሻ *habäša* Ethiopian, Abyssinian (see also አበሻ)

ሀብት *habt* wealth, riches, fortune (wealth), property, possessions, affluence, treasure, produce (of a country), resources (wealth)
ባለሀብት *balähabt* owner (see ባለ)
ምጣኔ ፡ ሀብት economics
የተፈጥሮ ፡ ሀብት natural resources (see ተፈጥሮ)
ሀብታም *habtam* rich, wealthy, well-to-do

ሆታ *hota* cheering, acclaim, shout

ሆቴል *hotel* hotel

ሐተታ *hatäta* commentary, version (account); see አተተ
ሐተታ ፡ ሰጭ commentator (see ሰጠ)

ሆነ *honä* be, become, happen, turn out, turn into
ሆነ(ለት) *honä(llät)* it suits him
ሆነ(በት) *honä(bbät)* he has to, he must
(በዚህም ፡ ሆነ ፡ በዚህ one way or another; see -ዚህ)
(የም ፡ ሆነ ፡ ይሁ in any case, somehow or other)
ሆኖም *honom* anyhow, yet (however), and yet, nevertheless
ሆን ፡ ብሎ *hon bəlo* intentionally, deliberately, purposely, consciously
መሆን *mähon*, in ለመሆኑ by the way

ቢሆን *bihon*, in ምንም ፡ ቢሆን in any event, whatever happens, on any condition
(አሁንም ፡ ቢሆን even now)
ቢሆንም still (nevertheless), notwithstanding, all the same, anyway
ባይሆን *bayhon* at least
አይሆንም *ayhonəm* it is inappropriate, it is unsuitable
ከሆነ *kähonä* granted that, if it (he) is
(እንዲህ ፡ ከሆነ if that is the case)
(ካልሆነም *kalhonäm* otherwise)
(ካልሆነ ፡ በቀር outside of, unless (he) it is)
(እንደ + pronoun or noun + ከሆነ according to, as in እንዴ ፡ ከሆነ according to me)
የሆነ ፡ ሆኖ *yähonä hono* nevertheless, anyway
የሆነ ፡ ያልሆነ *yähonä yalhonä* unimportant, all sorts of things
የሆነው ፡ ሆኖ be that as it may
የሆነ ፡ ቢሆን whatever happens, in any event
ያልሆነ inappropriate
ይሁን ፡ አለ *yəhun alä* agree
ይሁን ፡ እንጂ *yəhun ənǧi* nevertheless, but on the other hand, however, be that as it may
ይሆናል *yəhonal* it is possible, conjecture (n.), about (approximately)
ይሆናል preceded by the imperfect "probably" (as in ይመጣ ፡ ይሆናል he will probably come)
(ይህ ፡ ይሆናል this will do)
የማይሆን *yämmayhon* impossible, inappropriate
ሁኔታ, see below
ሁነኛ, see below
አኳኋን, see below

ሁኔታ *huneta* circumstance, way (condition), state of affairs, status, situation (condition, state), event, attitude, position, manner, mood, air (see ሆነ)
የአየር ፡ ሁኔታ weather conditions

ሁነኛ *hunäňňa* reliable, trustworthy, dependable (see ሆነ)

ህንድ *hənd* India, Indian

ሕንጻ *hənṣa* structure, edifice, building
የሕንጻ ፡ አሠራር architecture (style of building)
የሕንጻ ፡ ጥበብ architecture (art of designing buildings)

ሐኪም *hakim* physician, doctor (see አከመ)
ሐኪም ፡ ቤት hospital
ሕክምና *həkmənna* medicine (science), medical treatment
የሕክምና medical (school)
የሐኪምነት *yähakimənnät* medical (profession)

ሁከት *hukät* violence, insurrection, disturbance, agitation, furor, uproar, clamor, trouble, riot (see also ሁካታ)

ሁካታ *hukata* uproar, turbulence, racket, tumult, commotion (see also ሁከት)

ሀዋ *həwa* atmosphere

ሐዋላ *hawwala* money order, draft (bank)

ሐውልት *hawəlt* monument, statue, obelisk, stele
መታሰቢያ ፡ ሐውልት memorial (n.)

ሐዋርያ *hawarya* (pl. ሐዋርያት *hawaryat*) apostle

ሕዋስ *həwas* (pl. ሕዋሳት *həwasat*) sense (such as sight, touch)
ረቂቅ ፡ ሕዋሳት germs

ሕዝብ *həzb* (pl. አሕዛብ, ሕዝቦች) population, people, community, public (n.), crowd, mob
የሕዝብ secular (court), public (adj.), popular, national (holiday)
የሕዝብ ፡ መዝሙር national anthem
ተራ ፡ ሕዝብ crowd (common people), masses

ሕዝባዊ *həzbawi* public (adj.), civic (duty), civil (liberties)

ሐዘን *hazän* sadness, compassion, sorrow, grief, affliction (see አዘነ)
ሐዘኑን ፡ ገለጸ(ለት) commiserate
የሐዘን mournful
ሐዘኔታ *hazäneta* pity
ሐዘንተኛ *hazäntäňňa* mourner, grieving

ሀያ ፤ ሃያ *haya* twenty

ሆይ *hoy* oh !

ኀይል *hayl* power, force, strength, might, impetus, intensity, vehemence, action (effect)
በኀይል vehemently, strongly, furiously
የባሕር ፡ ኀይል navy
የአየር ፡ ኀይል air force
የጦር ፡ ኀይል armed forces
ኀያል *hayyal* omnipotent, almighty, powerful
ኀያልነት *hayyalənnät* omnipotence
ኀይለኛ *hayläňňa* powerful, mighty, strong, terrific, violent, intense, vehement, ardent, severe (judge, weather), sharp (pain), extreme (heat), high (fever), harsh (words), heavy (drinker)
ኀይለኛነት *hayläňňannät* vehemence, strength, potency

ሃይማኖት *haymanot* faith, belief, religion
ሃይማኖት ፡ ቢስ irreligious
የሃይማኖት religious, sectarian (dispute)
ሃይማኖተኛ *haymanotäňňa* religious, pious, devout
ሃይማኖተኛነት *haymanotäňňannät* piety

ሐይቅ *hayq* lake
ሐይቅ ፡ ባሕር lagoon

ሕያው *həyaw* immortal (adj.), alive, living, animate
ሕያውነት *həyawənnät* immortality (see also ሕይወት)

ሕይወት *həywät* life, existence (see ሕየው)
ሕይወቱን ፡ ሳተ lose consciousness, faint
ሕይወቱን ፡ አሳለፈ give one's life (see አለፈ)
በሕይወት ፡ ቆየ keep alive (intr.)
በሕይወት ፡ አለ ——*allä* be alive
የሕይወት ፡ ታሪክ biography, memoirs, record (of one's life)
የሕይወት ፡ ዋስትና life insurance
ዘለዓለማዊ ፡ ሕይወት eternity, eternal life

ሄደ *hedä* go, depart, leave, go away
አሄደ *ahedä* thresh grain with animals
አስኬደ *askedä* allow to go, drive away, lead (of a way, of a road)
አካሄደ *akkahedä* manage, administer, conduct (affairs), run (a business), handle (affairs), operate (a factory)
ተካሄደ *täkahedä*, passive of the preceding; get on (of work)
መሄድ *mähed* departure
አካሄድ *akkahed* manner of walking, gait, procedure, way an affair or project develops
አስኪያጅ, see below

ሆድ *hod* stomach, belly, abdomen
ሆድ ፡ አደረቀ constipate (see ደረቀ)
ሆደ ፡ ባሻ susceptible (sensitive), easily insulted, easily hurt
የሆድ abdominal
(የ)ሆድ ፡ ቁርጠት colic, stomach ache (see ቄረጠ)
(የ)ሆድ ፡ እቃ entrails, guts
(የ)ሆድ ፡ ድርቀት constipation
ሆዳም *hodam* glutton, big eater, corpulent
ሆዳምነት *hodamənnät* gluttony

ኅዳር *hədar* November

ሐዲድ *hadid* rail (of railroad)
የሐዲድ ፡ መንገድ railroad

ሁዳዴ *hudade* Lent (see also ኩዳዴ)

ኅዳግ *həddag* margin (of page)

ሕግ *həgg* (pl. ሕግጋት *həggəgat*) law, rule (of law, of grammar), legislation, dogma, doctrine (of church), measure (legislative enactment)
ሕግ ፡ አስከበረ enforce the law (see ከበረ)
ሕግ ፡ አስከባሪ prosecutor, attorney for the prosecution (see ከበረ)
ሕግ ፡ አወጣ legislate, draw up rules (see ወጣ)
ሕግ ፡ አውጪ *həgg awči* lawgiver, legislator, lawmaker (see ወጣ)
ሕግ ፡ የለሽ lawless
ሕግ ፡ መሠረት charter
ሕግ ፡ መንግሥት constitution
ሕግ ፡ ወጥ illegal, irregular, outlaw (see ወጣ)
ሕግ ፡ ወጥነት lawlessness
ሕግ ፡ ፍልስፍና jurisprudence (see ፈለሰፈ)
በሕግ rightfully, lawfully
በሕግ ፡ አምላክ in the name of the law
ከሕግ ፡ ውጭ ፡ የሆነ illegal, unlawful
የሕግ legal, legislative, judicial (reform)
የሕግ ፡ መምሪያ ፡ ምክር ፡ ቤት Chamber of Deputies
የሕግ ፡ ሚስት first-time wife
የሕግ ፡ መወሰኛ ፡ ምክር ፡ ቤት Senate
የሕግ ፡ ረቂቅ bill (in law), draft
የሕግ ፡ ባለሥልጣን magistrate
የሕግ ፡ ተርጓሚ ፡ ሥልጣን judicial power
(ዋና ፡ የሕግ ፡ አስፈጻሚ chief executive)
(የ)ሕግ ፡ ዐዋቂ jurist, lawyer (see ዐወቀ)
(የ)ሕግ ፡ አውጪ ፡ ክፍል legislature
ወታደራዊ ፡ ሕግ martial law
የታወጀ ፡ ሕግ *yätawwäǧä həgg* act (law)
የወንጀል ፡ ሕግ ፡ ፍልስፍና criminal jurisprudence
ጠቅላይ ፡ ዐቃቤ ፡ ሕግ attorney general
ሕጋዊ *həggawi* legitimate, rightful, lawful, legal, juridical, valid (will)
ሕጋዊ ፡ ወራሽ legal heir
ሕጋዊነት *həggawinnät* legality

ሀገር *hagär* country; see also አገር
አህጉር *ahəgur* continent

የሀገር (adj.) native, national
የሀገር ፡ ተወላጅ native (n.)
ክፍለ ፡ ሀገር region, area

ኃጥእ *haṭəʾ* sinner (see ኃጢአት)

ኃጢአት *haṭiʾat* evil (n.), sin, sinful act
(see ኃጥእ)
ኃጢአት ፡ ሥራ sin (v.)
ኃጢአተኛ *haṭiʾatäňňa* sinful man,
sinner, evil (adj.)

ሕፃን *həṣan* (pl. ሕፃናት *həṣanat*) baby,
infant, child
ሕፃንነት *həṣanənnät* childhood, babyhood
የሕፃንነት ፡ ጊዜ infancy
[See also ማሕፀን]

ኀፍረት *hafrät* disgrace, shame (see አፈረ)
ኀፍረት ፡ ሥጋ genitals
ኀፍረት ፡ ቢስ brazen

ለ

ለ *lä* to, for; (with object suffix pronouns) in behalf of, in the interest of
(መሬት ፡ ለመሬት along the ground)
(መሃል ፡ ለመሃል right in the middle)
(ቁም ፡ ለቁም lengthwise)
ለምን *lämən* why?, for what? (see
ምን)

ለ *lə* + (imperfect) in order that, in
order to, so that
ለ + imperfect + ነው he is about
to (as in ሊሄድ ፡ ነው he is about
to leave)
ለ + imperfect + ነበር he was
about to

ለሀጭ *lähač* (n.) drivel, spit, spittle,
saliva, foam (on the mouth of a dog)
ለሀጩን ፡ አዝረከረከ drool (see ዘረክ
ረክ)

ሉል *lul* pearl; knob (on the top of the
flagpole), globe

ላላ *lalla* be slack (rope), slacken (vi.),
be loose, loosen (vi.), be lax, relent
አላላ *alalla* soften, slacken (vt.),
loosen (vt.), relax
ልል, see below
ልልነት, see ልል

- ሌለ *-lellä* (preceded by a particle)
he is not, it is not (as in የሌለ *yälellä*
who is not; በሌለበት ፡ ጊዜ *bälelläbbät*
gize when he is not around)
- ሌለው *-lelläw* (preceded by a particle) he does not have (as in የሌለው
yälelläw who does not have)

ሌላ *lela* other, another, different,
further (adj.), any more, some more
ሌላ ፡ ሰው anybody else, someone
else
ሌላ ፡ ቦታ anywhere else, elsewhere
ሌላ ፡ ነገር anything else
ሌላጋ *lelaga* elsewhere, somewhere
else (see ጋ)
ሌላጋ ፡ የት where else?
ከ - - - ሌላ aside from, outside of,
besides (prep.), other than, in addition to
ከዚህ ፡ ሌላ beside this
ከዚያም ፡ ሌላ besides (adv.), moreover

ልል *ləl* loose, soft, lax, lenient, indulgent, permissive (see ላላ)
ልልነት *lələnnät* lenient attitude,
lenience

ሎሌ *lole* vassal, servant

ሌሊት *lelit* night (see also ሌት)
እኩለ ፡ ሌሊት midnight
የሌሊት nocturnal
የሌሊት ፡ ወፍ bat
ዛሬ ፡ ሌሊት last night

ልልነት, see ልል

ለማ *lämma* be fertile (ground), be
productive (ground), be verdant,
prosper, thrive (see also ለመለመ)
አለማ *alämma* render fertile, render
productive, cultivate (trees), develop

(land), make to prosper, make to flourish
ለም, see below
ለምነት, see below
ልማት, see below

ለም *läm* fertile, rich (soil), productive (soil), verdant, prosperous (see ለማ)

ላመ *lamä* be pulverized, be powdery, be tender
አላመ *alamä* reduce to fine powder

ላም *lam* cow

ሎሚ *lomi* lime (fruit), lemon
የጉልበት ፡ ሎሚ *kneecap*

ላመል *lamäl* a touch of, barely (see እመ ል)

ለመለመ *lämällämä* send forth leaves, be verdant, be green, be fertile (see also ለማ)
አላመለመ *alämällämä* make verdant
ለምለም *lämläm* green (leaves), tender (leaves), lush (grass), fertile, verdant
ልምላሜ *lämällame* fertility, exuberant vegetation

ልምምድ , see ለመደ

ሌማት *lemat* wickerwork basket

ልማት *lämat* development (of land), prosperity (see ለማ)

ለመነ *lämmänä* (B) beg, beseech, pray (ask), entreat, supplicate, petition, adjure, invoke, implore, plead, appeal (request), urge, request
ልመና *lämmäna* begging, entreaty, request, supplication, plea
ለማኝ *lämmaň* beggar, mendicant

ለምን *lämən* why? (see ለ, ምን)

ላሙና *lamuna* specimen, sample (see also ናሙና)

ለምነት *lämännät* fertility (of soil); see ለማ

ለምንድር *läməndər* why? (see ምንድር)

ለምንድን *läməndən* why? (see ምንድን)

ለማኝ *lämmaň* beggar, mendicant (see ለመነ)

ለመደ *lämmädä* be accustomed, adopt habits, get into the habit, be habituated, be used to, adapt to, acclimate, learn (get used to)
ተለመደ *tälämmädä* be customary, be usual
አስለመደ *aslämmädä* accustom
ተላመደ *tälammädä* adjust oneself, adapt oneself, get accustomed
አላመደ *allammädä* accustom, familiarize, acquaint, domesticate
ተለማመደ *tälämammädä* familiarize oneself, be acquainted (with a task), practice, rehearse (a play)
አለማመደ *allämammädä* accustom, acclimatize, exercise, vt. (horses)
ለማዳ *lämmada* tame, tamed, accustomed, domesticated
ለማዳ ፡ አደረገ *domesticate*
ለማዳ ፡ እንስሳ *pet*
ልማድ *ləmad* custom, habit, usage, practice, routine, way (custom), manners, convention
ልምድ *ləmd* habit, experience
ልምድ ፡ ያለው *seasoned* (troops), experienced
ልምምድ *ləmämməd* exercise (military), experience, practice, drill, maneuvers (of army)
ልምምድ ፡ አደረገ *train* (v.)
ልማዳዊ *ləmadawi* habitual
ልማደኛ *ləmadäňňa* chronic, habitual
ልምደኛ *ləmdäňňa* hardened (criminal)
መልመጃ *mälmäǧa* school exercise
ተለማማጅ *tälämamaǧ* apprentice
የተለመደ *yätälämmädä* accustomed, habitual, familiar, customary, usual, ordinary, characteristic (habitual), common, normal (temperature), natural (voice), regular (price)
ያልተለመደ *yaltälämmädä* extraordinary, anomalous, unusual, abnormal (behavior)

እንደተለመደው *əndätälämmädäw* as a matter of course, as is usual, as is customary
ከተለመደው ፡ የወጣ *kätälämmädäw yäwätta* irregular, unusual

ለምድ *lämd* kind of cloak worn by boys and made of sheepskin, mantle of cloth or lion skin worn in battle

ለመጠ *lämmätä* (B) grease, smear, polish, daub
ተለmeas.ጠ *tälämmätä* be limber (branch)
አላመጠ *allammätä* chew (gum), munch (on a cookie), masticate
ተለማመጠ *tälämammätä* coax, entreat
ልሙጥ *ləmmut* smooth, polished, plain (embroidery)
ተለማጭ *tälämmač* flexible (stick)
ተለማማጭ *tälämamač* subservient, obsequious
የሚለመጥ *yämmillämmät* limber (branch)

ለምጥ *lämt* leprosy
ለምጣም *lämtam* leper

ላምፉ, see ላንፉ

ላሰ *lasä* lick
ላስ ፡ አደረገ *lass adärrägä* lap up
† ምላስ *məlas* tongue

ለሰለሰ *läsälläsä* be soft, be smooth, become supple, be mild (see ለሰስ ፡ አለ)
አለሰለሰ *aläsälläsä* soften, loosen (the soil), smooth, mellow (the character)
ለሰለሰ ፡ አለ *läsläss alä* be moderate (reply), be soft (sound)
ለስላሳ *läslassa* soft (cushion, ground), smooth (stone, disposition), supple, sleek, mild (tobacco, drink), tender (meat), delicate, dainty (dress), fluffy (pillow)
ለስላሳ ፡ መጠጥ *məttät* soft drinks
ልስላሴ *ləsəllase* delicateness (delicate quality)
ልስልስ *ləsləs* soft, mild, delicate

ለሰስ ፡ አለ *läsäss alä* be mild, be gentle, be soft (see ለሰለሰ)

ሊስትሮ *listro* shoeshine boy

ላስቲክ *lastik* elastic, rubber band, tube, garter, garden hose

ለሰነ *lässänä* (B) plaster, coax
ልስን *ləssən* plaster (n.)

ልሳነ ፡ ንጉሥ *ləssanä nəgus* Amharic (lit. the language of the king)

ሊቅ *liq* (pl. ሊቃውንት *liqawənt*) scholar, expert, learned person (see ላቀ)
ሊቀ ፡ መላእክ *mälaʾk* archangel
ሊቀ ፡ መንበር *mänbär* chairman
ሊቀ ፡ መንበርነት *mänbärənnät* chairmanship
ሊቀ ፡ ካህናት *kahənat* head priest (see ካህን)
ሊቀ ፡ ጳጳስ *papas* archbishop
ሊቅነት *liqənnät* distinction (excellence), scholarship (possession of knowledge)

ላቀ *laqä* be pre-eminent, be more than, be ahead of, excel, be superior, exceed
(ልቆ *ləqo*, in ከሁሉም ፡ ልቆ more than anything)
አላቀ *alaqä* increase, raise
የላቀ *yälaqä* foremost, eminent
ሊቅ, see above
ሊቅነት, see ሊቅ
ይልቅ, see below
ትልቅ, see below

ልቅ *ləqq* stray (cattle), loose (see ለቀቀ)

ለቀለቀ *läqälläqä* smear, soil, stain, whitewash, rinse (clothes)
አለቀለቀ *aläqälläqä* rinse (dishes), clothes), wash (clothes)

ለቀመ *läqqämä* collect, gather (wood), pick (fruit), pick up, peck (of bird pecking grain), pasture
አለቀመ *aläqqämä* take to pasture, make to graze
ለቃ°ማ *läqäma* gleaning, gathering

*ለቀሰ፣ አለቀሰ *aläqqäsä* weep, cry, lament, wail, bewail, mourn a dead person
ለቅሶ *läqso*, ልቅሶ *ləqso* lamentation, wail, crying, mourning
ለቀስተኛ *läqqästäňňa* mourner
አልቃሽ *alqaš* professional mourner

ለቀቀ *läqqäqä* let go, let free, let out, let loose, emit (a scream), release, give up, abandon, leave, desert (vt.), quit (a job), free (a prisoner), relinquish, vacate (an apartment), cede, fade (of color), come out (of stain), come loose, be driven out (ሥራውን ፡ በፈቃዱ ፡ ለቀቀ resign)
(ቤት ፡ ለቀቀ move (change residence)
(በነጻ ፡ ለቀቀ let free, set free)
ተለቀቀ *täläqqäqä* be discharged, be deserted (village), be free (room, bird)
አስለቀቀ *asläqqäqä* drive out, dislodge, dispossess, make go away, make someone let go, release, remove (stains)
አላቀቀ *allaqqäqä* extricate, separate two people who are fighting, disengage, disjoin, help to get rid of
ልቅ *ləqq* stray (cattle), loose

ሊቅነት, see ሊቅ

ለብ ፡ አለ *läbb alä* be lukewarm, be tepid

*ላበ, አላበ *alabä* make to sweat
አላበው *alabäw* he perspired, he sweated
ላብ *lab* sweat, perspiration

ላባ *laba* feather of bird

ሌባ *leba* thief
ሌባ ፡ ጣት index finger
ሌባና ፡ ፖሊስ *lebanna polis* tag (children's game)
ሌብነት *lebənnät* theft, larceny

ልብ *ləbb* heart, intelligence
ልብ ፡ አለ *ləbb alä* pay attention to,
be mindful of, notice (pay attention), take notice of
ልብ ፡ ብሎ ፡ አዳመጠ pay attention, listen attentively
ልብ ፡ አደረገ take note, notice, make sure, pay attention
ልብ ፡ አጣ lose one's head
ልብ ፡ ገዛ acquire good sense, be sensible
ልብ ፡ ሙሉ presumptuous, daring, confident
ልብ ፡ ሙሉነት confident manner
ልብ ፡ ቅን kindhearted, straightforward
ልብ ፡ አልባ *ləbb alba* forgetful
ልብ ፡ ወለድ fiction, imagination
ልብ ፡ ወለድ ፡ ታሪክ novel
ልብ ፡ ወለድ ፡ መጽሐፍ novel
በሙሉ ፡ ልብ wholeheartedly, unreservedly, actively
በግማሽ ፡ ልብ half-heartedly
እንደልብ *əndäləbb* at will, freely, without restriction
ከልብ *käləbb* heartily, truly, warmly, sincerely
ከልብ ፡ የሆነ sincere
ከልብ ፡ ያልሆነ feigned, insincere
የልብ cardiac, inmost (desire), inner, staunch (friend), cordial
ልባም *ləbbam* intelligent, attentive
ልቡና, see below
ልባዊ *ləbbawi* cordial

ለበለበ *läbälläbä* singe, scorch
በርበሬ ፡ ለበለበኝ pepper burns me

ልብልብ *ləbbalba* embroidered silk, trousers worn by a lady of rank

ልባም *ləbbam* intelligent, attentive (see ልብ)

ለበሰ *läbbäsä* wear, put on a dress, get dressed, cover oneself up, dress (vi.)
አለበሰ *aläbbäsä* dress (vt.), clothe someone
ለባበሰ *läbabbäsä* be dressed up
ልባስ *ləbas* covering, cover (of book)
ልብስ, see below
ለባሽ, see ነጭ

ልብስ *ləbs* garment, clothes, dress, costume, gown, robe, apparel (see ለበሰ)
ልብስ ፡ ሰፊ *ləbs säfi* tailor
ልብስ ፡ አጣቢ ፡ ቤት laundry
ሙሉ ፡ ልብስ suit
ብርድ ፡ ልብስ blanket
የውስጥ ፡ ልብስ slip (undergarment), underclothing
የልጋ ፡ ልብስ bedspread, bedding, linen (see አልጋ)
የከት ፡ ልብስ suit worn on holidays or on special occasions, Sunday clothes, finery
(የ)ዝናብ ፡ ልብስ raincoat
የደንብ ፡ ልብስ uniform
የጠረጴዛ ፡ ልብስ tablecloth

ልባብ *ləbab* bit (of bridle), harness

ልቡና *ləbbuna*, **ልቦና** *ləbbona* perspicacity, consciousness, intellect, reason (see ልብ)
ልቦና ፡ ይስጥህ bear up!, be patient ! (lit. may He give you perspicacity)

ሌብነት *lebənnät* theft, larceny (see ሌባ)

ልባዊ *ləbbawi* cordial (see ልብ)

ለበደ *läbbädä* (B) sew a strip of leather around the edge or the bottom of a basket, make a cover for a book

ልብድ *ləbd* horse blanket

ለት *lät* day (see also ዕለት)

ላት *lat* fleshy sheep's tail

ሌት *let* night (see also ሌሊት)
ሌት ፡ ተቀን night and day, around the clock
የሌት ፡ ወፍ bat

ለተመ *lättämä* (B) butt (of sheep), ram something, quarrel (of men)
ተላተመ *tälattämä* lock together, vi. (of arms)
ከ --- ጋር ፡ ተላተመ crash into

ሊትር, **ሊተር** *litro, litär* liter

ሎተሪ *lotäri* lottery

ልታይ ፡ ልታይ ፡ አለ *ləttay ləttay alä* give oneself airs, show off (see አየ)

ሊኖ *lino* linen

ላንቃ *lanqa* roof of the mouth, palate of mouth

ላንፋ *lanfa* husk (n.); see also ላምፉ

ልዑል *lə'ul* prince
ልዕልት *lə'əlt* princess
ልዑልነታቸው *lə'ulännätaččäw* His Highness, Her Highness

ለካ *läkka* (B) measure, gauge, time
ልክ, see below
መልካ, see below
መለኪያ, see below

ለካ *läkka* particle indicating surprise of discovery

ለኮ *läko* halter, rope for leading a horse or mule

ሉክ *luk*, **ሉኽ** *luh* legal size paper

ላከ *lakä* send, remit, ship off
ተላላከ *tälalakä* send to one another, run errands
(ደብዳቤ ፡ ተላላከ correspond)
ላኪ *laki* exporter, sender
ተላላኪ *tälalaki* messenger, messenger boy, errand boy, page
መላክ, see below
መልእክት, see below

ልክ *ləkk* (n.) measure, measurements, size, proportion, extent, the right amount (see ለካ)
ልክ (adj., adv.) precise, exact, correct, right (correct), fitting; sharp (time), at the precise moment, precisely, promptly, exactly, just (exactly), on the dot
ልክ ፡ ስ+ (imperfect) just as
ልክ ፡ በሰዓቱ right on the dot
ልክ ፡ ነው that's right
ልክ ፡ ይሁንም ፡ አይሁን rightly or wrongly

ልክ ፡ የሌለው immeasurable, awful
በልክ exactly, with moderation, properly
በ - - - ልክ in keeping with
በዚያው ፡ ልክ to the same extent,
in that very amount, correspond-
ingly
ከልክ ፡ ያለፈ inordinate (see አለፈ)
የዕድሜ ፡ ልክ lifelong
የፍጥነት ፡ ልክ speed limit
[See also ዕድሜ]

ለኩሰ läkkʷäsä (B) light (pipe, cigarette), set fire to, ignite, scald (by
water or steam)

*ለከሰከሰ, ተልከሰከሰ tälkäsäkkäsä mess
around, be disorderly, be dissolute
in one's conduct, act in an unseemly
way
ልክስክስ ləkəskəs disorderly, wanton
(behavior), loose (conduct), unseemly (conduct), promiscuous

ሉካንዳ lukanda butcher shop
ሉካንዳ ፡ ነጋዴ butcher

ለከከ lakkäkä smear, anoint, grease,
shift the blame on someone, pin a
crime on someone

ለከፈ läkkäfä touch with one's nose,
sniff, annoy, infect
ተለከፈ täläkkäfä be infected
ልክፍት ləkkəft infection

ለወሰ läwwäsä (B) knead flour for
bread, mix powder and liquid to
make a paste
ተላወሰ tälawwäsä move to and fro,
stir (vi.), budge

ለውዝ läwz nut, almond

ለወጠ läwwäṭä (B) change (vt.), exchange, shift, transform, alter,
permute, switch (direction), trade
(exchange), barter, convert, cash (a
check)
ተለወጠ täläwwäṭä be changed,
change (vi.), mutate

ለዋወጠ läwawwäṭä vary (vt.),
change completely
ተለዋወጠ täläwawwäṭä vary (vi.), exchange mutually (vt.), interchange
(vi.), rotate (take turns), fluctuate,
be in flux, be diversified
ለውጥ läwṭ change, alteration, exchange (see also መሡረት)
ለውጥ ፡ የማይፈልግ läwṭ yämmay-
fälləg reactionary
ልውጥ ləwwəṭ changed, altered
ልውውጥ ləwəwwəṭ exchange (n.)
ልዋጭ ləwwač in return, thing given
in return
መለዋወጥ mälläwawäṭ (n.) change, interchange, reshuffle
መለወጫ mälläwäča, in የዘመን ፡ መለ
ወጫ New Year
መለዋወጫ , see below
ተለዋዋጭ täläwawač variable, inconsistent, changeable, volatile, unstable, spotty (work)
የማይለወጥ yämmayəlläwwäṭ immu-
table, invariable, unchanging
የማይለዋወጥ yämmayəlläwawwäṭ stable (currency)

ለዛ läzza speak in a captivating
fashion
ለዛ läzza charisma in speaking,
attractiveness
ለዛ ፡ ቢስ unattractive in speech or
looks
ለዛ ፡ ያለው läzza yalläw graceful
(dancer, speech), charismatic speaker, fascinating (talker)
የጨዋታ ፡ ለዛ fascinating conversation

ለዘላለም läzälaläm, ለዘላዓለም läzälä'aläm
forever (see ዓለም)

ለዘበ läzzäbä (B) be tender, be smooth,
be soft, be supple, be gentle (breeze),
be finely ground
አለዘበ aläzzäbä make to be smooth,
polish, refine
ለዝብ ፡ ያለ läzäbb yalä gentle
(breeze), soft (voice)

ልዝብ *ləzzəb* smooth, soft, gentle (breeze)

ለየ *läyyä* (B) distinguish, discern, differentiate, discriminate, assort, dissociate, disentangle, separate, divide (separate), recognize, identify (ፊደል ፡ ለየ master the alphabet)
ተለየ *täläyyä*, passive of the preceding; part company, differ, be different
ለያየ *läyayyä* sort, classify, spread apart, break up, separate, decompose (vt.), dismantle (a bookcase), detach, disconnect
ተለያየ *täläyayyä* differ, be different, diverge (of opinion), separate (vi.), be divided (opinion), part (vi.), come apart, disintegrate, be at variance, disjoin (vi.), decompose (vi.), contrast (vi.), branch off, bifurcate, adjourn (vi.)
አለያየ *alläyayyä* take apart, detach, part (separate), estrange, alienate, differentiate
ለይቶ *läyyəto* exactly, precisely (see also በወቀ)
ልዩ, see below
ልዩነት, see below
መለያ, see below
መለዩ, see below
በተለይ ፤ በተለየ, see below
የተለየ *yätäläyyä* peculiar, different, special, strange, particular (special), characteristic (special); see also ተፈጥሮ
የተለያየ *yätäläyayyä* varied, different, dissimilar, variant (adj.)
የማይለይ *yämmayəlläyy* indistinct, indistinguishable

ላይ *lay* on, upon, above, north
ላይኛ *layəñña* upper, top (adj.)
ላይ ፡ ላዩን superficially, externally
ላይና ፡ ታች ፡ አለ *layənna tačč alä* march up and down, go hither and thither
በ+ noun +ላይ on, on top of, in addition to, over, about (in connection with)

በ + verbal noun +ላይ ፡ ነው he is in the process (or, act) of
በላይ up there
በ - - - ላይ up, about (concerning)
በዚህም ፡ ላይ in addition to this
እ - - - ላይ at, on, on top of
አንድ ፡ ላይ together, at the same time
እዚህ ፡ ላይ there (in that matter), at this point
ከላይ on top
ከ - - - በላይ above, upwards, beyond, more than, in addition to, besides, outside of
ከመጠን ፡ በላይ to excess, too much, unusually, beyond measure
ከዚህ ፡ ላይ at this point
ከዚህ(ም) ፡ በላይ furthermore, moreover, besides, again (moreover)
ወደ - - - ላይ upwards, toward the top, up to
የላይ upper
የበላይ, see below
በላይነት, see below

ልዩ *ləyyu* special, specific, different, separate, strange, eccentric, distinctive, private (special), extra, extraordinary (special); see ለየ
ልዩ ፡ ልዩ distinct, various, separate
ልዩ ፡ መልእክት special delivery
ልዩ ፡ መልእክተኛ envoy extraordinary
ልዩ ፡ ጸሐፊ private secretary
ልዩነት, see below

ለይስሙላ *läyəsmulla* only for show, pose (see ስም)

ልዩነት *ləyyunnät* difference, divergence, distinction, division, discrimination, discrepancy, variation, conflict (of opinion), gap (difference); see ለየ, ልዩ
የዘር ፡ ልዩነት discrimination

ልደት *lədät* birth, Christmas, Nativity (see ወለደ)
የልደት ፡ ቀን birthday
መልካም ፡ ልደት happy birthday!

ልደታ *lədäta* first of the month, payday, birth of the Virgin
በልደታ on the first

ልጅ *ləǧ* child, boy, honorific title (see ወለደ)
ልጅ ፡ እግር young man
ልጅ ፡ እግር ፡ ሴት young woman
ልጅ ፡ እግሮች young people
የልጅ ፡ ልጅ grandchild, granddaughter, grandson
የልጅ ፡ ሚስት daughter-in-law
ሴት ፡ ልጅ daughter
(የሴት ፡ ልጅ rude, unmannerly child)
አራስ ፡ ልጅ new-born baby
ወንድ ፡ ልጅ son
የሙት ፡ ልጅ orphan
የሰው ፡ ልጅ person of good family, mankind
የአጎት ፡ ልጅ nephew, niece
የአባት ፡ ልጅ half-brother, half-sister
የእናት ፡ ልጅ half-brother, half-sister, genuine brother
የአጐት ፡ ልጅ cousin
የወንድም ፡ ልጅ nephew, niece
የጡት ፡ ልጅ adoptive son
[See also ልጅነት, ልጃገረድ]

ልጅነት *ləǧənnät* infancy, childhood, boyhood (see ልጅ, ወለደ)

ልጃገረድ *ləǧagäräd* girl (see ልጅ, ገረድ)

ለጋ *lägga* (B) hit (the ball), bat
አለጋ *allagga* dash, vt. (the waves dashing the boat)
መለጊያ *mäläggiya* curved stick used as a bat

ለጋ *läga* fresh (butter)
ለጋ ፡ ሾምበቆ bamboo shoot
ለጋ ፡ ቅርንጫፍ new shoot

ላጋ *lagä* plane (a board)
መላጊያ *mälagiya* plane (carpenter's tool)
ያልተላጋ *yaltälagä* rough (plank)

ለጋሀር *lägähar*, ላጋር *lagar* railway station in Addis Ababa

ለጋመ *läggämä* (B) work with ill will and badly, be lazy, be inactive

ለጋሞ ፡ ቆም *läggəmo qomä* balk
ልግመኛ *ləgmäňňa* recalcitrant (cattle), refractory (ox), one who works with an ill will, resentful worker

ለጐመ *läggʷämä* (B) bridle (a mule), put on the bit; trim with leather
ልጓም *ləgʷam* bridle, rein
ለጓሚ *läggʷami* muleteer, one who takes care of the stable

ላጋር, see ለጋሀር

ለገሰ *läggäsä* (B) be generous, be charitable
ለጋስ *läggas* generous (donor), liberal, bountiful
ልግስና *ləggəsənna* charity, munificence, open-handedness
ልግስነት *ləggəsənnät* generosity
ለጋስነት *läggasənnät* generosity, liberality, magnanimity, largess

ለጋሲዮን *lägasiyon* legation

*ለገጠ, አለገጠ *allaggäṭä* mock, deride, make fun of

ለጥ ፡ አለ *läṭṭ alä* bow, bend down low, duck, stretch out (vi.); see also ለጠጠ
ለጥ ፡ ብሎ *läṭṭ bəlo* low (adv.)
ለጥ ፡ ብሎ ፡ ተኛ lie outstretched
ለጥ ፡ ያለ flat (roof, plain), broad (expanse), level

ሊጥ *liṭ* dough, batter

ላጠ *laṭä* peel (vt.), skin, scrape, strip, abrade, bark (a tree), rub (the skin), shell (eggs), pare (an apple)
ተላጠ *tälaṭä*, passive of the preceding; peel (vi.)
ላጥ *laṭ* (n.) bark, peel
ላጣጭ *laṭṭač* rind, bark, peel, parings

ሌጣ *leṭa* without a saddle, bareback, unburdened (horse or mule)
ሌጣ ፡ ፈረስ ፡ ጋለበ ride bareback
በሌጣው barebacked

ልጥ, see ላጠ

ለጠጠ *läṭṭäṭä* (B) stretch (a hide), distend (see also ለጥ ፡ አለ)

ልጣጭ, see ላጠ

ለጠፈ *läṭṭäfä* (B) paste, patch, glue, affix (a label), stick (a stamp on the envelope)
ልጥፍ *ləṭṭəf* patch (on the tire)

ሉጫ *luččа* smooth hair

ላጨ *laččä* shave (vt.)
ተላጨ *tälaččä* shave (vi.)
ምላጭ *məlaččə* razor, razor blade, trigger (of gun)

ላጲስ *lappis* eraser

ለፋ *läffa* toil, make an effort, work much, grow tired, wear oneself out; grow soft
(ለፍቶ ፡ የተገኘ *läfto yätägäňňa* hard-earned (money)
አለፋ *aläffa* soften, tan (hide), tire out, exhaust
ልፍ *ləf* soft, pliant
ልፋት , see below

ለፈለፈ *läfälläfä* chatter, talk too much, talk nonsense, babble
ለፍላፊ *läflafi* talkative, loquacious, chatterbox, chatty
ልፍለፋ *ləfläfa* (n.) chatter, prattle

ለፈስፈስ *ləfəsfəs* languid, flabby, limp (cardboard)
ለፍስፍስነት *ləfəsfəsənnät* lethargic condition

ልፋት *ləfat* hard work, toil, labor, exertion, weariness, softness (see ለፋ)

መ

- ም - *m* as to, with regard to, also, too, and

- ም ፡ --- ም (with negative verb) neither ... nor

መሃል *mähal* middle, center, central part, among (see አከለ, መኸል, መሀከል)
መሃል ፡ ለመሃል right in the middle
በ --- መሃል amid, amidst
በመሃሉ in the meantime
የመሃል interior (adj.)

መሐላ *mähalla* oath, vow, pledge (see ማለ)
መሐላ ፡ ገባ be under oath, take an oath
የመሐላ ፡ ቃል ፡ ገባ pledge allegiance
ቃለ ፡ መሐላ pledge of allegiance

ምሁር *məhur* erudite (man), learned, intellectual (see *ማረ)
የምሁር erudite (lecture), scholarly (lecture)

መሐረብ *mäharräb* handkerchief

ምሕረት *məhrät* pity, pardon, mercy, compassion, forgiveness, amnesty, remission of taxes (see ማረ)
ምሕረት ፡ አደረገ show mercy, be gracious to, amnesty (v.)
ዓመተ ፡ ምሕረት Year of Grace (i.e. Ethiopian year)
ያለ ፡ ምሕረት *yalä məhrät* ruthlessly

ማሕበር *mahbär* association, society, monthly gathering in honor of a saint, organization, corporation, congregation, guild, league (see ማበር, አበረ)
ማሕበር ፡ ጠጣ participate in the monthly gathering
የዓለም ፡ መንግሥታት ፡ ማሕበር League of Nations
ማሕበርተኛ *mahbärtäňňa* member of an association
ማሕበራዊ *mahbärawi* social

ማህተም *mahtäm* stamp (seal), rubber stamp, seal (see አተመ)

መሃንዲስ *mähandis* engineer

መሀከል *mähakkäl* center, middle (see አከለ, መሃል, መኻል, መከከል)
በ - - - መሀከል among, amongst, between
መሀከለኛ *mähakkäläñña* average, middle (adj.), medial, mean, adj. (halfway between two extremes)

ምሕዋር *məhwar* orbit

መሃይም *mähayyəm*, see መሃይምን

መሃይምን *mähayyəmən* layman, illiterate (see also መሃይም)
መሃይምነት *mähayyəmənnät* illiteracy

ማኅደር *mahdär* folder, leather book case (see አደረ)

ማሕፀን *mahṣän* womb, uterus (see ሕፃን)

መላ *mäla* (n.) scheme, guess, idea for solving a problem
መላ : መታ make a guess
መላ : ምት hypothesis, guess, conjecture
መላ : ቅጡን : አጣ be at a loss
በመላ : በወቀ guess (v.)

መላ *mälla* be full (see ሞላ)

መላ *mälla* whole, entire (see ሞላ)
በመላ entirely
በመላው all over

ሙሉ *mulu* whole, full, complete, plenary, active (member), solid (hour), even (number); see ሞላ
ሙሉ : በሙሉ completely, entirely, fully, wholly, full blast, throughout, absolutely
ሙሉ : ልብስ suit
ሙሉ : ቀን full time (work), all day long, favorable day
በሙሉ fully, in full, throughout, all over, completely, in all
በሙሉ : ልብ wholeheartedly, unreservedly, actively

ማለ *malä* swear, vow, take a vow, take an oath

† መሐላ *mähalla* oath, vow, pledge

ሞላ *molla* fill (vt., vi.), be filled, fill out, fill up, be full of, be plentiful, abound, flood (vi.), overflow (vi.), rise (of river), charge (the battery), wind (a watch); see also መላ
(ሞላ(ለት) *molla(llät)* it is suitable for him)
(ሞልቷል there is plenty of it, it exists in abundance)
ተሞላ *tämolla* be filled, swell, vi. (with joy), be alive with
አሞላ *ammʷalla* make complete, complement, supplement, fill (a need)
ተሞላ *tämʷalla* be complete, be done completely
† መላ *mälla* whole, entire
ሙሉ , see above
ሞላ *molla* spring (of watch)
(በሞላ *bämolla* entirely)
(ከሞላ : ጐደል by and large, approximately, roughly, on the average, more or less)
ሙላት , see below
ሙሉነት , see below
ማሞያ *mammʷaya* complement (n.)
የተሞላ *yätämʷalla* exhaustive, adequate, full, complete, whole
ያልተሞላ *yaltämʷalla* fragmentary, imperfect, inadequate (diet)
አሟልቶ abundantly

ሟል , in ባለሟል *balämʷal* favored, favorite, courtier
ባለሟልነት *balämʷalənnät* favor, grace (favor)

መልሕቅ *mälhəq* anchor (n.)
መልሕቅ ፣ ጣለ anchor (v.), drop the anchor

*ማለለ, ተማለለ *tämallälä* implore, beg pressingly

ሞላላ *molala* oblong, oval

መለመለ *mälämmälä* pick out, hew off (a branch), prune a tree, enlist, recruit (into the army)

ምልምል *məlməl* picked out, conscript
ምልምል ፡ ወታደር recruit
መመልመል *mämälmäl*, in በግዴታ ፡
መመልመል conscription

*ጥለጥለ , አጥለጥለ *amolämmolä* roll
dough into oblong shapes

መልመጃ *mälmäǧa* school exercise (see
ለመደ)

መለሰ *mälläsä* (B) return (vt.), bring
back, hand back, give back, put
back, render (give back), recoup
(regain), repulse (repel), restore,
repay, reply, answer, respond
(ብድር ፡ መለሰ retaliate, requite; see
በደረ)
(ወደ ፡ ኋላ ፡ መለሰ keep back)
ተመለሰ *tämälläsä* be returned, return (vi.), come back, go back, revert,
retrogress, be answered
አስመለሰ *asmälläsä* redeem (pay
back), make give back, recover (gain
back)
(አስመለሰ(ው) throw up, vomit)
መላለሰ *mälalläsä* repeat several times,
answer casually
ተመላለሰ *tämälalläsä* go to and fro;
commute (between places), shuttle
between, answer one another
አመላለሰ *ammälalläsä* take back and
forth, transport
መልስ , see below
መለስ *mälläs*, in ከ - - - መለስ on the
side of, beyond
መልሶ *mälləso* again
መላልሶ *mälalso* time and again,
repeatedly
ምላሽ , see below
መመለሻ , see below
ማመላለሻ *mammälaläša* means of
transportation
ተመላላሽ , see below

መልስ *mäls* answer, response, reply,
return visit of bride to her parents
some time after the wedding, change
(in money); see መለሰ
መልስ ፡ ሰጠ answer, talk back

ደርሶ ፡ መልስ ፡ ቲኬት round-trip ticket
ከ - - - መልስ after (time)

ምላስ *məlas* tongue (see ላሰ)
ምላሰኛ *məlasäñña* sharp-tongued
person

መለስተኛ *mällästäñña* second-class, medium sized
መለስተኛ ፡ ደረጃ ፡ ያለው second-rate

ምላሽ *mällaš* (n.) answer, reply (see
መለሰ)

*ጥለቀቀ , አጥላቀቀ *ammolaqqäqä* spoil
(pamper), coddle (pamper), indulge
ጥልቃቃ *molqaqqa* spoiled (child)

ማለቂያ *maläqiya* end (see አለቀ)
ማለቂያ ፡ የሌለው endless, everlasting,
interminable

ሙላት *mulat*, ምላት *məlat* abundance
(see ሞላ)
የውኃ ፡ ሙላት flood

ማለት *malät* to say, that is, that is to
say, namely, it means (see አለ)
ይህ ፡ ምን ፡ ማለት ፡ ነው what does
this mean?

ሙሉነት *mulunnät* fullness (see ሞላ)
ልብ ፡ ሙሉነት confident manner

መልአክ *mäl'ak* (pl. መላእክት *mäla'əkt*)
angel (see ላከ , and መላክ)
መልአካዊ *mäl'akawi* angelic
ሊቀ ፡ መልአክ archangel

መልእክት *mäl'əkt* message, mission,
errand, communication (message);
see ላከ
ልዩ ፡ መልእክት special delivery
የአየር ፡ መልእክት air letter, airmail
መልእክተኛ *mäl'əktäñña* messenger,
emissary, courier, delegate, envoy,
representative
መልእክተኞች *mäl'əktäññočč* delegation
ልዩ ፡ መልእክተኛ envoy extraordinary

*መለከ, አመለከ amälläkä worship, idolize, deify, adore (worship)
(ጣዖት ፡ አመለከ practice idolatry)
†መለኮት mäläkot divinity
አምላከ , see below
አምልኮ amləko cult

መላክ mälak angel (see መልአከ)

መልከ mälka ford

መልክ mälk form, looks, shape, appearance (aspect), air (appearance), feature, complexion, right side (of coat, cloth); see ለከ
መልከ ፡ መልካም handsome, good-looking
መልከ ፡ ቀና mälkä qänna handsome, good-looking
መልከ ፡ ቢስ ugly
መልከ ፡ ጥፉ ugly (see ጠፉ)
በመልኩ ፡ በመልኩ in every respect
መልካም, see below

መልካም mälkam beautiful, good, nice, all right, well (see መልከ)
መልከ ፡ መልካም handsome, good-looking

*መለከተ, ተመለከተ tämäläkkätä look, look on, look at, view, watch, consider, give consideration, take into consideration, observe, notice, take into account, consult (a dictionary), refer to, pertain (relate), have bearing on, respect (concern), regard (concern)
አመለከተ amäläkkätä signify, signal, give evidence, show, indicate, notify, report, hint, denote, point out, observe, stand for (represent), submit an application, appeal (submit an appeal)
ተመለካከተ tämäläkakkätä survey, skim through (a book)
መልከት ፡ አደረገ mälkätt adärrägä cast a glance
ምልክት mələkkət indication, sign, gesture, signal, cue, symptom, mark, check, marker, phenomenon, expression, trace

(የንግድ ፡ ምልክት trade mark)
ተመልካች tämälkač observer, onlooker, spectator, audience (of television)
†አመልካች amälkač one who indicates, applicant, petitioner
ማመልከቻ, see below

መለከት mäläkät long trumpet, horn (instrument)

መለኮት mäläkot divinity (see *መለከ)
መለኮትነት mäläkotənnät divinity

ምልክት, see *መለከተ

መለኪያ mäläkkiya measure (unit), scale (measure), gauge, index (measure), means of measuring, criterion; small glass (see ለከ)
የትኩሳት ፡ መለኪያ thermometer

መለዋወጫ mäläwawäča something which helps to transform or to change (see ለወጠ)
መለዋወጫ ፡ እቃ spare parts
ኮረንቲ ፡ መለዋወጫ transformer

መለወጫ, see ለወጠ

መለያ mälläyya characteristics, feature (see ለየ)

መለዮ mälläyyo distinguishing feature, attribute, singularity, characteristics, insignia, badge, hallmark (see ለየ)

ሚሊዮን miliyon million

*ማለደ, አማለደ ammallädä intercede, intervene (for someone)
አማላጅ ammalaǧ intercessor, mediator
አማላጅነት ammalaǧənnät intercession, intervention, good services

ማለደ mallädä rise early
ማልዶ ፡ ተነሣ maldo tänässa get up early
ማለዳ maläda early (in the morning), early morning, at daybreak

መለጊያ, see ለጋ

መላጊያ , see ላጐ

መለጠ *mälläṭä* bark (a tree), depilate, skin, fall out (hair)
ተመለጠ *tämälläṭä* lose the hair, become bald
አመለጠ *amälläṭä* escape, break out (escape), break loose, slip from the hand
አመለጠ(ው) *amälläṭä(w)* miss
(ለጥቂት ፡ አመለጠ have a narrow escape)
መላጣ *mälaṭa* bald
ማምለጫ *mamläča* escape (n.)

*ሟለጠ, አሟለጠ *amʷalläṭä* be slippery, slip from the hand, escape (see also *ሟለጨ)

*ሟለጨ , አሟለጨ *amʷalläčä* be slippery, slip from the hand, escape (see also ሙልጭልጭ)
ሙልጭ *mulləčč* slippery
ሙልጭ ፡ አለ *mulləčč alä* be slippery, slip from the hands, slip away, be completely used up
ሙልጭ ፡ አድርጐ *mulləčč adrəgo* completely

ምላጭ *məlačč* razor, razor blade, trigger (of gun); see ላጨ

ሙልጭልጭ ፡ አለ *mulačləčč alä* be slippery (see *ሟለጨ)

ማለፊያ *maläfiya* passage, good, fine (see አለፈ)

ማሞ *mammo* baby boy
ማሚቱ *mammitu* baby girl
[See also ማሚቴ , ማሚቶ]

ሟሟ *mʷammʷa* be dissoluble, dissolve, vi. (of salt in water), melt, vi. (in a liquid), thaw, vi. (of ice)
አሟሟ *amʷammʷa* dissolve (vt.), melt, vt. (sugar in water)
መሟሟት *mämʷamʷat* the dissolving (of sugar, of salt in water)

መምህር *mämhər* (pl. መምህራን *mäm-*

həran) professor, master (teacher), head of a monastery (see *ማረ)
የመምህራን ፡ ማሠልጠኛ ፡ ትምህርት ፡ ቤት —*masälṭäňňa* Teachers' Training School
መምህርነት *mämhərənnät* teaching profession

ማመላለሻ *mammälaläša* means of transportation (see መለሰ)

መመለሻ *mämmäläša*, in የመመለሻ ፡ ቲኬት return ticket (see መለሰ)

ማመልከቻ *mamälkäča* application (request), official letter (see *መለከተ)
የተማሪ ፡ ማመልከቻ report card

መማሪያ *mämmariya* teaching aid (see *ማረ)
የመማሪያ ፡ መጽሐፍ textbook

መምሪያ *mämriya* guideline, directive, instructions, formula, manual, guidebook (see መራ)
የሕግ ፡ መምሪያ ፡ ምክር ፡ ቤት Chamber of Deputies
የምግብ ፡ መምሪያ recipe
ያሠራር ፡ መምሪያ recipe (see ሠራ)
ጠቅላይ ፡ መምሪያ headquarters (of army, police)
(ፖሊስ ፡ ጠቅላይ ፡ መምሪያ police headquarters)

ማማሰያ *mammasäya* stirring rod, stirrer (see መሰለ)

ማሚቴ *mammite* servant who takes care of the children or who cooks (see ማሞ)

ማሚቱ *mammitu* baby girl (see ማሞ)

ማሚቶ *mammito*, in የገደል ፡ ማሚቶ echo (see ማሞ)

መመኪያ *mämmäkiya* means for boasting, object of pride, credit (good reputation), reliance, dependence (see *መከ)

ማሟያ *mammʷaya* complement (n.); see ሟላ

ማምጠጫ *mamṭäča* blotter (see መጠጠ)
ማምጠጫ ፥ ወረቀት absorbent paper

መራ *märra* lead, guide, be ahead,
march at the head of, head, direct,
administer, conduct (an orchestra),
pilot (a ship), steer (a ship)
ተመራ *tämärra* follow the lead, be
guided, be governed (guided), be
ruled by, be destined for (bound for),
be intoned (chant)
አመራ *amärra* lead toward, head
toward, make for
መሪ *märi* guide, leader, leading
spirit, pilot, head (of government),
conductor (of orchestra), steering
wheel (see also መኪና)
መሪ ፥ ሐሳብ leading idea, motif
መሪ ፥ ቃል directive
መሪነት *märinnät* leadership, guidance, direction (guidance)
መመሪያ *mämmäriya* motto
መምሪያ, see above
አመራር, see below

መሮ *märo* chisel (n.)

ማረ *marä* pardon, forgive, have mercy,
have pity, have compassion, release
(from a promise, from a debt), grant
remission (of debts)
እግዚአብሔር ፥ ይማርዎ — *yamarwo*
may the Lord make you well! (used
when wishing health to a sick person)
[See also ምሕረት]

*ማረ, ተማረ *tämarä* learn, study, receive an education, take a course in,
be accentuated (rhythm)
አስተማረ *astämarä* teach, instruct,
educate, hold classes, give lessons,
send to school
†ተማሪ *tämari* student, pupil
†አስተማሪ *astämari* teacher, instructor
ተስተማሪ *tästämari* beginner
†መማሪያ *mämmariya* teaching aid
ማስተማሪያ, see below
የተማረ *yätämarä* learned, literate,
educated

ተምሮ ፥ ማስተማር *tämaro mastämar*
literacy campaign
[See also ምሁር, መምህር, ትምህርት]

ማር *mar* honey

*ምር, የምር *yämärr* serious, implacable (enemies), seriously (see መረረ)
የምርህን ፥ ነው ? *yämärrəhən näw*
are you serious?, do you really mean
it?
የምሩን *yämärrun* seriously
የምሩን ፥ ነው he is serious about it,
he means business
ከምሩ *kämərru* seriously

ሞራ *mora* animal fat, subcutaneous
fat covering the ventral region

ሞራል *moral* morale, morals

ማርመላታ *marmälata* marmalade, jam

መረመረ *märämmärä* investigate, examine (of doctor), inspect, test (the
blood), prove, question (seek information), interrogate, do research,
check (the bill), study (a problem)
ተመረመረ *tämärämmärä*, passive of
the preceding; reason (think logically), inquire, be reflective
ምርመራ *mərmära* research (n.), investigation, diagnosis, inquiry, probe,
examination (of a witness), interrogation (of suspects), inquisition,
analysis (testing), review (of events),
check-up
ምርምር *mərəmmər* reason, logic
ተመራማሪ *tämäramari* inquisitive

መረረ *märrärä* taste bitter, be sour
(green fruit)
ተመረረ *tämärrärä* be bitter about, be
embittered, be angered, get irritable
አመረረ *amärrärä* render bitter, embitter
አማረረ *ammarrärä* complain, be-
moan
መራራ *märara* bitter
ምሬት *mərrät* bitterness
*ምር, see above

ተማሮ *tämarro* bitterly
አምሮ *amərro* bitterly
የመረረ *yämärrärä* violent
የተማረረ *yätämarrärä* deadly (enemies)
የሚያስመርር *yämmiyasmärrər* acrimonious

ማረረ *marrärä* gather, pick up, glean

ማረሻ *maräša* plough (n.); see አረሰ

ማርሽ *marš* military music

ማርሽ *marš* gear (of car)
ማርሽ ፡ አገባ put in gear

መረቀ *märräqä* (B) leave in possession of, bless, give benediction, inaugurate, dedicate (an installation, a facility)
(መረቀ(ለት) *märräqä(llät)* give a bit extra (usually grain or legumes)
(መርቆ ፡ ከፈተ *märrəqo käffätä* dedicate a facility or an installation)
ተመረቀ *tämärräqä*, passive of the preceding; graduate (vi.)
አስመረቀ *asmärräqä* cause to bless, graduate, vt. (of school)
ምረቃ *mərräqa* blessing, inauguration
(የምረቃ ፡ ሥነ ፡ ሥርዓት inauguration)
(የምረቃ ፡ በዓል commencement (graduation exercises)
ምሩቅ *mərruq* blessed, graduate (n.)
ምርቃት *mərrəqat* blessing, benediction, compliment
ተመራቂ *tämärraqi* graduate (n.)

መረቅ *märäq* broth, gravy

ምራቅ *məraq* saliva, spittle
ምራቅ ፡ ተፋ expectorate
ምራቁን ፡ የዋጠ serious, judicious person, poised, grave

መረብ *märäb* fisherman's net
የመረብ ፡ ኳስ volleyball

መረተ *märrätä* be cleaned and threshed (grain)

አመረተ *amärrätä* clean and thresh grain, reap, harvest, raise (crops), produce (wheat, coffee)
ምርት *mərt* crop, yield, product (of farm)

መሬት *märet* earth, ground, soil, terrain, land, lot (of land), tract of land, bottom (of lake)
የመሬት terrestrial
የመሬት ፡ አያያዝ land holding
የመሬት ፡ ዝላይ broad jump
የመሬት ፡ ይዞታ land tenure
ባለመሬት landowner (see ባለ)
ከመሬት ፡ ተነሥቶ without rhyme or reason (see ነሣ)
ድንግል ፡ መሬት virgin soil

ምራት *mərat* daughter-in-law, sister-in-law

መሪነት , see መሪ

ማረከ *marräkä* take prisoner in war, capture, captivate, beguile (charm), attract (win the attention), magnetize (attract), fascinate, bedazzle, absorb (take up the attention), appeal (be attractive)
ማራኪ *maraki* attractive, captivating
ማራኪነት *marakinnät* lure, attraction
ምርኮ *mərko* captivity, loot, booty, trophy
ምርኮኛ *mərkoňňa* captive, prisoner of war
ምርኮኛነት *mərkoňňannät* captivity
የሚማርክ *yämmimarrək* ravishing, attractive

ማርክ *mark* grade (in an exam)

መርከብ *märkäb* vessel (ship), boat, ship
የመርከብ ፡ ምሰሶ mast
የመርከብ ፡ ሸራ sail (n.)
የጦር ፡ መርከብ warship
ጫኝ ፡ መርከብ freighter (see ጫነ)
መርከበኛ *märkäbäňňa* sailor, seaman

መርካቶ *märkato* Mercato (the market in Addis Ababa)

ምርኮኛ, see ማረከ

*መረኰዘ, ተመረኰዘ tämäräkk^wäzä lean on a stick, be based
ምርኩዝ mərkuz walking stick, crutch, stilts

መረዘ märräzä (B) envenom, poison, contaminate, infect, pollute
መርዝ, see below
መመረዝ mämmäräz inflammation (of eye)

መርዝ märz poison, venom (see መረዘ)
መርዝ ፡ አበላ poison someone
መርዝ ፡ አደረገ(በት) poison (food)
የመርዝ ፡ ጢስ poison gas
መርዛም märzam poisonous, venomous
መርዘኛ märzäňňa poisonous, venomous, pestilent (disease)

መርዶ märdo announcement of death of a relative (see ረዳ-ው)

ሞረደ morrädä (B) file, rasp
ሞረድ moräd file (tool), rasp (n.)

መረዳዳት, see ረዳ

መረጃ märräğa proof, evidence, information, intelligence (secret information), fact (see *ረዳ)
መረጃ ፡ ክፍል information desk

መራጃ märraǧa sledgehammer

መረገ märrägä plaster (a wall with mud)
ምርጊት mərgit mud or dung used for plastering

ማራገቢያ marragäbiya fan (n.); see *ረገበ

ማርገብገቢያ margäbgäbiya fan (n.); see *ረገበገበ

ምርጊት, see መረገ

መርገጫ märgäča pedal (see ረገጠ)
የቀለም ፡ መርገጫ inkpad

ማረጋገጫ, see ረገጠ

መረጠ märräṭä choose, select, pick out, elect, screen (choose), opt for, vote, prefer, have preference for
አማረጠ ammarräṭä compare two objects in order to choose, choose carefully
ምርጥ mərṭ select (adj.), best, superior, choicest, choice (adj.), chosen, picked
ምርጥነት mərṭənnät excellence (of food)
መራጭ märač choosy, voter
ምርጫ mərča choice, selection, preference, option, election, voting
(የምርጫ ፡ ድምፅ vote)
አማራጭ ammarač alternative (adj.)

ምርጫ, see መረጠ

መርፌ märfe needle, injection, shot (injection), syringe
መርፌ ፡ ወጋ give an injection
መርፌ ፡ ቄልፍ safety pin
የወረቀት ፡ መርፌ pin, paper clip

ማረፊያ maräfiya accommodation, hostel, haven, resting place (see አረፈ)
ማረፊያ ፡ ክፍል waiting room
የእንግዳ ፡ ማረፊያ lounge
የእንግዳ ፡ ማረፊያ ፡ ቤት lounge (in a hotel)
የአውሮፕላን ፡ ማረፊያ airport

ማሰ masä dig a hole for planting
ማሳ, see below

ማሳ masa farm, field, land which has been tilled (see ማሰ)

ማስ mas tanned hide

ምሳ məsa lunch, midday meal

መሰለ mässälä (A) be like, look like, resemble, liken, simulate, seem, appear
መሰለ mässälä (B) speak in parables, speak in proverbs
መሰለ(ው) mässälä(w) think, judge, suppose, feel, have a feeling
ተመሰለ tämässälä be compared, be represented, be restored

አስመሰለ *asmässälä* make believe, pretend, imitate, mimic, feign, assume (feign), act (make believe)
አማሰለ *ammassälä* cause to resemble one another, agitate (shake), stir (a liquid)
ተመሳሰለ *tämäsassälä* look alike, be alike, be similar, resemble one another, be identical, be homogeneous, correspond (be alike), be parallel
አመሳሰለ *ammäsassälä* compare, draw an analogy
መሰል *mässäl* analogous, similar, peer, congenial
ምሳሌ , see below
ምስል *məsəl* likeness, image, effigy, figure (picture)
ምስለኔ , see below
መመሳሰል *mämmäsasäl* resemblance, similarity, analogy
ማማሰያ *mammasäya* stirring rod, stirrer
መሳይ, see below
ተመሳሳይ, see below
ተመሳሳይነት, see below
አምሳል *amsal* image
አምሳይ, see below
ልምስል ፡ ባይ ፡ ሁኔታ *ləmsäl bay huneta* affectation
የማይመስል *yämmaymäsəl* improbable, unlikely
የይምሰል *yäyəmsäl* sham, supposition

መሳል *mäsal* whetstone (see ሳለ)

ምሳሌ *məssale* example, proverb, allegory, maxim, parable, pattern (example), figure (image), symbol, saying, instance (example), epitome (see መሰለ)
ለምሳሌ *ləmsale* for instance, for example

መሰላል *mäsälal* ladder

መስለል *mäsläl* paralysis (see ሰለለ)

ምስለኔ *məsläne* deputy, substitute of a magistrate (see መሰለ)

ማሳለፊያ *masalläfiya*, in የጊዜ ፡ ማሳለፊያ pastime (see አለፈ)

መስማማት *mäsmamat* agreement, settlement, conformity (see ሰማ)
አለመስማማት *alämäsmamat* misunderstanding

መሥመር *mäsmär* line, busline, circuit (of telephone), stripe (see *ሠመረ)
ባለ ፡ መሥመር lined

ምስማር *məsmar* nail

ማሥመሪያ *masmäriya* ruler (for drawing lines); see *ሠመረ

ማሰሮ *masäro* small earthen pot used for cooking or storing food

ምሳር *məssar* large ax

ምስር *məssər* lentil

መሰርሰሪያ *mäsärsäriya* drill (n.); see ሰረሰረ

ምሥራቅ *məsraq* east, Orient (see ሠረቀ)
የምሥራቅ oriental, eastern
ምሥራቃዊ *məsraqawi* east (adj.), eastern, oriental

መሠረተ *mäsärrätä* base, found (base), lay the foundation of a house, establish
ተመሠረተ *tämäsärrätä*, passive of the preceding; rest (be based), depend on, be subject to, be conditioned, hinge on, be contingent (dependent)
መሠረት, see below
መሥራች *mäsrač* founder (n.)

መሠረት *mäsärät* foundation, base, cornerstone, basis, pivot (base), essence, origin (base), keystone (see መሠረተ)
መሠረት ፡ ጣለ lay the foundation
መሠረት ፡ ሐሳብ principle
መሠረት ፡ ቢስ groundless, baseless, irrational
የመሠረት ፡ ድንጋይ cornerstone
ሕግ ፡ መሠረት charter
(በሕጉ ፡ መሠረት as a matter of principle, according to the law)

በ - - - መሠረት according to, in accordance with, in concordance with,
in conformity with, in answer to, in
compliance with, in keeping with,
on the basis of
በመሠረቱ substantially, basically, essentially, in principle
በዚያ ፡ መሠረት accordingly
እንደ + verbal noun + መሠረት on
the principle, on the basis
መሠረታዊ *mäsärätawi* fundamental,
basic, radical (basic), primary (of
meaning)
መሠረታዊ ፡ ለውጥ revolution
መሠረታዊ ፡ ደንብ principle

ምሥራች, see የምሥራች

መሣሪያ *mässariya* tool, instrument,
implement, appliance, building material, mechanism, equipment, arms
(see ሥራ)
የመሣሪያ ፡ ፋብሪካ arms factory
ከባድ ፡ መሣሪያ artillery, heavy artillery
የጦር ፡ መሣሪያ weapon, armament
(የጦር ፡ መሣሪያ ፡ ያዘ bear arms)
የጽሕፈት ፡ መሣሪያ writing material,
stationery

መሥሪያ *mäsriya*, in መሥሪያ ፡ ቤት
office, department (of government);
see ሥራ

ማሰሪያ *masäriya* something to tie with
(string, chain), thong, strap (of sandals), band (for watch), leash (for
the dog); see እሰረ
የጫማ ፡ ማሰሪያ shoelace, shoestring

ማስረጃ *masräǧǧa* evidence, proof, explanation, demonstration, instance
(see *ረዳ)

ምሰሶ *məsässo* pillar, post, pole, central pillar of the round Ethiopian
house
የመርከብ ፡ ምሰሶ mast

ሟሰሰ *mʷassäsä* wipe, rub, wipe away
(tears)

*መሰቀለ, አመሳቀለ *ammäsaqqälä* mix
up (cards), confuse, tangle up, put
in the shape of a cross (denominative
from መስቀል "cross")
ተመሳቀለ *tämäsaqqälä*, passive of the
preceding; intersect, be intertwined,
be placed crosswise
ተመሰቃቀለ *tämäsäqaqqälä* be in disorder, be disheveled
አመሰቃቀለ *ammäsäqaqqälä* upset (put
in disorder), turn inside out, snarl
(vt.)
[See also መስቀል , ምስቅልቅል]

መስቀል *mäsqäl* cross, the feast of the
cross celebrated on the 27th of September (see ሰቀለ and *መሰቀለ)
የመስቀል ፡ አበባ flower that blos-
soms about the time of the *mäsqäl*
feast
የመስቀል ፡ ወፍ kind of bird
ቀይ ፡ መስቀል Red Cross
መስቀለኛ ፡ መንገድ *mäsqäläñña mängäd* crossroad, intersection
መስቀለኛ ፡ ጥያቄ cross-examination

ምስቅልቅል *məsqəlqəl* mess, mix-up,
clutter, chaotic condition (see *መሰ
ቀለ)
ምስቅልቁሉን ፡ አወጣ go on a rampage, ransack, leave in a shambles,
turn upside down, turn topsy turvy

ማስቀመጫ, see *ቀመጠ

መሰቅሰቂያ *mäsäqsäqiya* spatula (see
ሰቀሰቀ)

መስቀያ *mäsqäya* hanger, hook (of telephone receiver); see ሰቀለ
የልብስ ፡ መስቀያ clothes hanger
የባንዴራ ፡ መስቀያ flagpole, flagstaff

ማስቀመጫ, see *ቀመጠ

መሶብ *mäsob* a round footed basket
of woven straw serving as a table
upon which food is placed
መሶብ ፡ ወርቅ decorated *mäsob*

ምስባሕ *məsbah* kind of rosary

መሳቢያ *mäsabiya* drawer (see ሳበ)
ባለመሳቢያ ፡ ቁም ፡ ሣጥን chest of drawers

ሚስት *mist* wife, spouse (see also ምሽት)
ሚስቱ ፡ የሞተችበት ፡ ሰው *mistu yä-motäččəbbät säw* widower
ለሚስት ፡ ደረሰ he is old enough for marriage

ማስተማሪያ *mastämariya* instruction material (see *ማረ)
ማስተማሪያ ፡ መጽሐፍ textbook
የማስተማሪያ ፡ ቋንቋ language of instruction

ማስተባበያ, see አበለ

መስተንግዶ *mästängədo* hospitality (see ነገደ)

መስተአምር *mästä'ammər* article (in grammar)
የተወሰነ ፡ መስተአምር definite article
ያልተወሰነ ፡ መስተአምር indefinite article

መስቲካ *mästika* chewing gum

ማስተካከያ *mastäkakäya* adjustment, alteration (see አከለ)

ማስታወሻ *mastawäša* remembrance (gift), souvenir, token of remembrance, reminder, memorandum, memento, note (see አወሰ)
በማስታወሻ with regard to, regarding
በማስታወሻ ፡ ያዘ keep notes on, make a note on
የማስታወሻ ፡ ደብተር notebook
የቀን ፡ ማስታወሻ diary
የግርጌ ፡ ማስታወሻ footnote (see እግርጌ)

ማስታወቂያ *mastawäqiya* notice, public notice, bulletin, announcement, advertisement (see ዐወቀ)
የማስታወቂያ ፡ ሚኒስቴር Ministry of Information
የማስታወቂያ ፡ ሰሌዳ bulletin board
የንግድ ፡ ማስታወቂያ advertisement

ማስታወት *mastawät*, መስተዋት *mästawat* glass, pane of glass, mirror

መስተዋድድ *mästäwadəd* preposition

መስተፃምር *mästäṣamər* conjunction (in grammar); see *ጠመረ

መስተፋቅር *mästäfaqər* love philtre (see *ፈቀረ)

መሲና *mäsina* sterile (cow)

መስኖ *mäsno* irrigation channel
በመስኖ ፡ አጠጣ irrigate

ማሰነ *massänä* lose strength (from illness or excessive work)

መሲንቆ *mäsinqo*, መስንቆ *mäsənqo*, ማሲንቆ *masinqo* one-stringed violin
ማሲንቆ ፡ መታ play the violin

* መሰኳ, አመሰኳ *amäsäkkʷa* ruminate, chew the cud

መስክ *mäsk* meadow, field, pasture, field (of activity, of study)

መሰከረ *mäsäkkärä* testify, bear witness, attest, certify
(በሐሰት ፡ የመሰከረ perjuror)
መሰከረለት *mäsäkkärällät* bear witness on behalf of
መሰከረበት *mäsäkkäräbbät* bear witness against
የተመሰከረለት *yätämäsäkkärällät* true (scholar)
ምስክር *məsəkkər* witness, testimony
የምስክር ፡ ወረቀት certificate, diploma

መስከረም *mäskäräm* September

መስኮብ *mäskob* Russia
መስኮብኛ *mäskobəñña* Russian (language)
መስኮባዊ *mäskobawi* Russian (person)

መስኮት *mäskot* window
የመስኮት ፡ መስተዋት windowpane

ምስኪን *məskin* poor (miserable), indigent, poor devil, destitute, wretch, wretched, hapless, miserable

መሰኪያ *mäsäkkiya* electric socket (see ሰካ)
የኮረንቲ ፡ መሰኪያ plug, outlet

መሥዋዕት _mäswa'ət_ sacrifice (n.); see ሠዋ
መሥዋዕት ፡ አቀረብ sacrifice (v.)

መሠዊያ _mäsäwwiya_ altar (see ሠዋ)

መሳያ _mäsaya_ grindstone, whetstone, sharpener (for knives); see ሳለ

መሳይ _mäsay_ sort of, kind of, similar (see መሰለ)

*መሰገነ , አመሰገነ _amäsäggänä_ thank, be grateful, appreciate (be grateful), compliment, approve (speak well), commend, praise, glorify
ተመሰገነ _tämäsäggänä_ be praised, get the credit, take credit for
አስመሰገነ _asmäsäggänä_ cause to praise, cause to be praised, reflect credit on
ምስጋና _məsgana_ thanks, praise, compliment, appreciation (gratitude), glory (praise)
ምስጋና ፡ አቀረብ say the blessing, thank (see ቀረበ)
ምስጋና ፡ አደረሰ say grace (see ደረሰ)
ምስጋና ፡ ቢስ ungrateful
የምስጋና grateful (letter)
የተመሰገነ _yätämäsäggänä_ noted (scholar), celebrated
አስመስጋኝ _asmäsgañ_ meritorious
እግዜር ፡ ይመስገን _əgzer yəmmäsgän_ thank you! (in answer to greetings)

መስጊድ _mäsgid_ mosque

መሰጠ _mässäṭä_ (B) enthrall, enrapture, enchant
ተመሰጠ _tämässäṭä_ be absorbed (one's attention), be rapt, be lost (in a book), be ravished, be engrossed in, be fascinated
ተመስጦ _tämästo_ abstraction (absence of mind), rapture, enchantment

ሚስጥ _misṭ_, ምስጥ _məsṭ_ termite

መሰጠረ _mäsäṭṭärä_ plot secretly
ተመሳጠረ _tämäsaṭṭärä_ intrigue (scheme secretly), connive

ምስጢር , see below

ምስጢር _məsṭir_ secret, secrecy, mystery, enigma, hidden meaning (see መሰጠረ)
ምስጢር ፡ ቋጠረ keep a secret
ምስጢር ፡ አየ be admitted into the Holy of Holies (is said of deacon)
ምስጢር ፡ ጠበቀ keep a secret
በምስጢር confidentially
የምስጢር clandestine, intimate (details), covert
ምስጢረኛ _məsṭiräñña_ confidant
ምስጢራዊ _məsṭirawi_ secret (message, place), secretive, confidential (report), enigmatic

ማስጠንቀቂያ _masṭänqäqiya_ warning, notice (see *ጠነቀቀ)

መስጫ _mäsča_, in ቤንዚን ፡ መስጫ accelerator (see ሰጠ)

መስፍ _mäsf_ anvil

መስፈሪያ _mäsfäriya_ measure (for liquids); see ሰፈረ

ማሳፈሪያ _massafäriya_ carfare (see ሰፈረ)

መስፍን _mäsfən_ duke, prince (see ሰፈነ)
መሳፍንት _mäsafənt_ aristocracy, hereditary nobility
የመስፍን ፡ ግዛት dukedom

መስፊያ _mäsfiya_ instrument for sewing (see ሰፋ sew)
ወረቀት ፡ መስፊያ stapler

መሸ _mäššä_ become evening, get dark, it is late
(መሽ(በት) _mäššä(bbät)_ he was overtaken by night)
(ምድር ፡ መሸ become evening)
አመሸ _amäššä_ spend the evening, stay up late, be late in the evening, do something in the evening
እንዴት ፡ አመሸህ good evening!
አምሸቶ _amšəto_ late in the evening, at a late hour
አምሽቶ ፡ መጣ come late in the evening

ምሽት *məššət* evening

ሙሾ *mušo* dirge
ሙሾ ፡ ጣሪ professional mourner

ማሸላ *mašəlla* white sorghum, millet
የበሕር ፡ ማሸላ maize

መሿለኪያ *mäššʷaläkiya* subway, tunnel, underpass (see ሿለከ)

ሙሽራ *mušərra* groom, bride, bridegroom
ሙሽሮች *mušərročč* couple, newly married couple
የሙሽራ bridal

መሻሻያ, see *ሻለ

መሽቆልቆል *mäšqolqol* downward swoop (of birds); see *ቆለቆለ

መሸታ ፡ ቤት *mäšäta bet* tavern

ምሽት *məššət* evening (see መሸ)

ምሽት *məšt* spouse, wife (see also ሚስት)

መሽከርከሪያ *mäškärkäriya* pivot (see *ሽከረከረ)

መሸገ *mäššägä* (B) build a fort, fortify, entrench oneself
ምሽግ *məššəg* citadel, fort, fortification, stockade

መሻገሪያ, see *ሻገረ

መሸጫ *mäšäča* place where one sells (see ሸጠ)
ቲኬት ፡ መሸጫ ticket office

መቃ *mäqa* reed, rush

ሙቅ, see ሞቀ

ሞቀ *moqä* be warm, be heated, get hot, feel hot, pick up, vi. (of business)
(ሞቀ(ው) warm oneself, be warm (feel warm)
(እሳት ፡ ሞቀ warm oneself by the fire)
(ፀሐይ ፡ ሞቀ warm oneself in the sun, sun oneself)

አሞቀ *amoqä* warm (vt.), warm up, keep warm, heat, heat up

ተሟሟቀ *tämʷamʷaqä* boom (of business)

ሞቅ ፡ አለ *moqq alä* be astir, be lively (cheerful)

ሞቅ ፡ አለ(ው) he felt high (from drinking)

ሙቅ *muq* hot, warm

ሙቀት *muqät* heat, warmth

የሞቀ *yämoqä* warm (adj.), cozy (home)

የተሟሟቀ *yätämʷamʷaqä* animated, full of good cheer

ሞቃት, see below

መቅለጫ ፤ ማቅለጫ, see ቀለጠ

መቄለፊያ ፡ ጋን *mäqʷälläfiya gan* lock (see ቄለፈ)

መቆሚያ *mäqomiya* stop, place where one halts (see ቆመ)
አውቶቡስ ፡ መቆሚያ bus stop

መቋሚያ *mäqʷamiya* prayer stick (see ቆመ)

መቀመጫ *mäqqämäča* seat (see *ቀመጠ)

መቅረዝ *mäqräz* oil lamp

መቅረጫ *mäqräča* pencil sharpener (see ቀረጸ)

መቁረጫ *mäqʷräča* clippers (see ቄረጠ)

ማቁረጫ, see ቄረጠ

መቀስ *mäqäs* scissors, clippers

መቅሠፍት *mäqsäft* calamity, catastrophe, disaster, scourge, affliction, plight, misfortune (see ቀሠፈ)

ማቀቀ *maqqäqä* languish (in prison)

መቃብር *mäqabər* grave, tomb, sepulcher, cemetery, funeral (see ቀበረ)
የመቃብር ፡ ሥነ ፡ ሥርዓት burial ceremony
የመቃብር ፡ ቦታ burial grounds
የመቃብር ፡ ድንጋይ tombstone

መካነ : መቃብር cemetery, graveyard

ሙቀት *muqät* heat, warmth (see ሞቀ)

ሞቃት *moqqat* warm (climate), warm weather, hot, inebriation (see ሞቀ)
ሞቃት : አገሮች tropics

መቀነት *mäqännät* belt, girdle (see ቀነተ)
መቀነት : ታጠቀ wear a girdle
የምድር : መቀነት equator

መቄንጠጫ *mäqʷänṭäča* tongs, pliers (see ቄነጠጠ)

*መቀኘ , ተመቀኘ *tämäqäňňä* feel envy toward, begrudge, wish someone harm due to envy
ሞቀኛ *məqqäňňa* envious, spiteful
ሞቀኛነት *məqqäňňannät*, ምቀኝነት *məqqäňňənnät* envy, spite

መቅዘፊያ *mäqzäfiya* paddle, oar, rudder (see ቀዘፈ)

ማቀዝቀዣ *maqäzqäža* refrigerator, freezer (see ቀዘቀዘ)
የሞተር : ማቀዝቀዣ radiator (of car)

መቆያ *mäqoyya* snack (see ቆየ)

መቅድም *mäqdäm* foreword, preface, prologue (see ቀደመ)

መቅደስ *mäqdäs* sanctuary (see ቀደሰ)
ቤተ : መቅደስ temple, sanctuary

መቍጠሪያ *mäqʷṭäriya* chaplet, rosary, dial (see ቈጠረ)
(የ)ቀን : መቍጠሪያ calendar

ማቀጣጠያ *maqqäṭaṭäya* tinder, lighter (for cigarettes); see *ቃጠለ

መቀጫ *mäqqäča*, መቀጮ *mäqqäčo* penalty, fine (see ቀጣ)

ሙቀጫ *muqäčča* mortar for pounding (see ወቀጠ)

መብል *mäbəl* food (see በላ)
መብል : ቤት dining room

ማበር, see ማኅበር

ማብራሪያ, see በራ

መብረቅ *mäbräq* lightning, stroke of lightning, thunder bolt (see በረቀ)

መብራት *mäbrat* lamp, light (see በራ)

ማብሪያ *mabriya* light switch (see በራ)

ማብረጃ *mabräǧa* big jar for keeping liquid cool, pitcher (see በረደ)

ማብሰያ *mabsäya* cooking utensil (see በሰለ)

መብት *mäbət* right (privilege), title (privilege), liberty (privilege)
ልዩ : መብት privilege

ማበጠሪያ *mabäṭṭäriya* comb (v.); see *በጠረ

መታ *mätta* beat, hit, strike, spank, smite, thrash, knock (hit), hammer in, drive in (a nail), pluck (a guitar), play (the drum, violin)
(መላ : መታ make a guess)
(ቤት : መታ rhyme, v.)
(ድል : መታ defeat)
ተማታ *tämatta* come to blows, fight
አማታ *ammatta* cause to hit one another, complicate, muddle, confuse, confound, falsify (accounts), flutter (the wings)
መታ : መታ : አደረገ *mäta mäta adärrägä* tap
ምት *mət* (n.) blow, stroke, beat (see also መላ)
ምች, see below
ምታት, see below

መቶ *mäto* hundred
መቶ : በመቶ decidedly, fully, wholly
መቶ : አለቃ lieutenant
መቶ : ዓመት century
በመቶ percent, percentage
ከመቶ percent, percentage
ከመቶ---እጅ percent, percentage
የመቶ platoon
መቶኛ : ዓመት *mätoňňa amät* centennial
መቶኛ : ዓመት : በዓል centenary

ማታ mata evening
ማታ ፡ ማታ every evening, evenings
ማታ ፡ ተማሪ ፡ ቤት night school
የማታ ፡ ማታ late at night
ትላንትና ፡ ማታ last night
ዛሬ ፡ ማታ this evening, tonight

ማት, see መዓት

ሞተ motä die, be dead, be deceased, be killed
ሙት mut, ይሙት yəmut sure!, really!, lit. die!, let him die!
(አባቴ ፡ ይሙት I give you my word of honor, lit. may my father die)
ይሙት ፡ በቃ ፡ ፍርድ capital punishment
ሙት mut (pl. ሙታን mutan) dead, inactive (volcano)
የሙት ፡ ልጅ orphan
† ሞት mot death
ሟች, see below
መሞት mämot decease, death
መሞቻ mämoča demise
የሞተ yämotä dead
[See also ሙትት ፡ አለ]

ሞት mot death (see ሞተ)
ሞት ፡ ያስከተለ fatal (accident); see *ከተለ
የሞት ፡ ቅጣት death penalty
የሞት ፡ ፍርድ death sentence
የሞት ፡ ፍርድ ፡ ፈረደበት he sentenced him to death

መተላለሪያ, see አለፈ

ማታመኛ mättamäñña evidence, credentials (see አመነ)

ማተሚያ, in ማተሚያ ፡ ቤት mattämiya bet printing press (see አተመ)
ማተሚያ ፡ መኪና printing press

መተረ mättärä slice (meat), chop, mince, cut into small pieces

ሜትር metər meter

ሞተር motär engine, motor

መተርኮሻ mätärkʷäša ashtray (see[e] ተረኰሰ)

ሙትረየስ mäträyyäs machine gun

መታሰቢያ mättasäbiya souvenir, remembrance, memento, memorial, commemoration (see አሰበ)
መታሰቢያ ፡ ሐውልት monument
መታሰቢያ ፡ ቀን memorial day
የመታሰቢያ memorial (adj.)
የመታሰቢያ ፡ ጸሎት memorial service

*ማተበ, አማተበ amattäbä cross oneself, make the sign of the cross
ማተብ matäb cord worn around the neck by Christians

መተባባር mättäbabär solidarity (see አበረ)

መተት mätät (n.) magic, spell
መተት ፡ አደረገበት bewitch (of witch)
በመተት ፡ አሰረ cast a spell

ሙትት ፡ አለ mutətt alä fall dead (see ሞተ)
ሙትት ፡ ብሎ ፡ ደከመ be dead tired
ሙትት ፡ አደረገ exhaust, v. (tire very much)

ምታት mətat stroke, blow (see ማተ)
(የ)ራስ ፡ ምታት headache

ሙታንታ, in ሙታንታና ፡ ካናቴራ mutantanna kanatera underwear
ሙታንቲዎች trunks

ምትክ mətəkk alternate (n.), substitute, replacement, makeshift, restitution, surrogate (see ተካ)
በ - - - ምትክ instead of

መታወሻ mättawäša remembrance (see አወሰ)

መታወቂያ mättawäqiya identification (see ዐወቀ)
መታወቂያ ፡ ወረቀት identification card

መተዳደሪያ mättädadäriya livelihood, manner of making a living, maintenance (see አደረ)

መታጠቢያ, in መታጠቢያ ፡ ቤት mättaṭäbiya bet bathroom (see አጠበ)
የመታጠቢያ ፡ ልብስ bathrobe
የገላ ፡ መታጠቢያ bath

የገላ : መታጠቢያ : ገንዳ bathtub

መታጠፊያ mättaṭäfiya corner, bend in the road (see ዐጠፈ)

*መቸ, ተመቸ tämäččä(B), አመቸ amäč-čä be convenient, be comfortable, be suitable, fit, suit, be opportune
ተመቸ(ው) it is convenient for him
ምቹ mäčču suitable, opportune, prop-er, fit, advantageous (favorable), appropriate, comfortable, expedient, convenient, handy (convenient)
ምቹ : ወምበር armchair, easy chair
ምቹት mäččot luxury, ease, comfort, conveniences, ameniities
ምቹት : የጕዲለ rough (life)
የሚያመቸ yämmiyamäčč favorable (opportunity)
የማይመቸ yämmayəmmäčč inoppor-tune (time), inconvenient

መቸ mäčä, መቼ mäče when?
መቸም ፤ መቼም well! (interj.), of course, after all, at any rate, any-way; (with negative verb) never
መቸስ mäčäss well!
ከመቸ : ጀምሮ since when?
ከመቼውም kämäčewəm (more) than ever before

ምቼ, see *መቸ

ምች mäčč sudden and violent illness (see መታ)
የሳምባ : ምች pneumonia

ሟች mʷač deceased, departed, late (who died), mortal (see ሞተ)
ሟችነት mʷačənnät mortality

ምቹት, see *መቸ

መና mäna useless, worthless

ማን man (pl. ማን : ማን man man or እነማን ənnäman) who?
ማን : አለብኝ : ባይ man alläbbäňň bay despot
ማንም, see below
ማንን mannən whom?
የማን yäman whose?

ማናቸው mannaččäw who of two or more?, whoever?
† ማንኛውም mannəňňawəm every, any, anyone, whatever
ማንነት, see below

ምን mən what?, which?
ምን : አለበት mən alläbbät what does it matter?
ለምን what for?, why?
ስለምን why?
በምን : ጊዜ when?
[See also ምኑም, ምንም, ምናም, ምን ነት, ምንኛ, ምነው, እንደምን]

ምናልባት mənalbat perhaps, probably, possibly, maybe, presumably, sup-position
ለምናልባት for exigencies, for emer-gencies, for any eventuality

ማንም mannəm any, any man, anyone, everyone (see ማን)
ማንም + (negative verb) no one, nobody, not anything, not anyone

ምኑም mənum none of (see ምን)

ምንም mənəm whatever, any, anything, something (see ምን)
ምንም + (negative verb) none, noth-ing, not any, not a thing
ምንም : ብ + (imperfect) no matter what
ምንም : ቢሆን on any condition, in any case
ምንም : እንኳ : ብ + (simple imper-fect) even if, even though
ምንም : አይል mənəm ayəl so-so, it is all right, it is not bad (see አለ)
ምንም : አይደል don't mention it!
ምንም : ያህል + (negative verb) hard-ly any more
ምንም : ያህል : ሰው + (negative verb) hardly anyone
[See also እንደምን]

መነመነ mänämmänä be emaciated, waste away (of a person), wither (of hope), fade (of hope), be attenuated (of body), dwindle

አመነመነ *amänämmänä* emaciate, make gaunt

የመነመነ *yämänämmänä* faint (hope), gaunt

ምናምን *mənamən* something, something or other, anything, worthless, rubbish (worthless); see ምን

መኖሪያ *mänoriya* means of living, residence, living quarters, domicile, lodgings, abode, habitat (see ኖረ)
መኖሪያ ፡ ቤት dwelling
የመኖሪያ residential

ሚኒስቴር *minister* ministry

ሚኒስትር *ministər* minister

መንሳፈፊያ *mänsafäfiya* raft, float (see *ሰፈፈ*)
የመንሳፈፊያ ፡ ትጥቅ life belt, life vest

መነሻ *mänäššä* winnow with a hay fork
መንሽ *mänš* pitchfork

መነሻ *männäša* departure, point of departure, starting point, root of the matter, motive, cause, background, reason, origin (see ነሣ)
በምን ፡ መነሻ in what connection?
ባዕድ ፡ መነሻ prefix
የመነሻ starting (adj.)

መነሾ *männäšo* heart (of a quarrel), source (of trouble), origin (of war, quarrel); see ነሣ

መንሻ *mänša*, in እጅ ፡ መንሻ gift, bribe (see ነሣ)

መንሽ, see መነሻ

መነቀረ *mänäqqärä* tear up (ground), dig up, plow up

ማንቄርቄሪያ *manqʷärqʷäriya* pitcher (see *ቄረቄረ*)

ማንቁርት *manqurt* Adam's apple, larynx

መንቀጥቀጥ *mänqäṭqäṭ*, in የመሬት ፡ መን ቀጥቀጥ earthquake (see *ቀጠቀጠ*)

ማኑቬል *manuvel* crank (of car)

መንበር *mänbär* seat, chair, altar (see ነበረ)
ሊቀ ፡ መንበር chairman
መንበርነት *mänbärənnät*, in ሊቀ ፡ መንበርነት chairmanship

ምንባብ *mənbab* excerpt, passage from a book (see *ነበበ*)

*አመነታ, አመነታ *amänätta* hesitate, be undecided, waver, debate with oneself, feel dubious
ማመናታት *mammänatat* ambivalence
[See also መንታ]

መንታ *mänta* twin, fork (in a road), double (door); see *አመነታ*
መንታ ፡ ሆነ divide, vi. (of road)
መንታ ፡ መንገድ crossroad
መንቲያ *mäntiyya*, መንትያ *mäntəyya* one of a pair of twins, double, n. (person who looks alike)

መነተፈ *mänättäfä* snatch
ኪስ ፡ መነተፈ pick pockets

ምንቸት *mənčät* pot

መነነ *männänä* (B) retire from the world, renounce the world
መናኝ *männañ* ascetic, recluse, hermit

ማንነት *mannənnät* identity (individuality), personality (see ማን)

ምንነት *mənənnät* worth (n.); see ምን

መናኛ *mänañña* inferior (cloth), of poor quality, of low grade, shoddy, cheap (inferior), roughly made, crude

መናኝ, see መነነ

ምንኛ *mənəñña* how much!, what!, how! (see ምን)

ማንኛውም *mannəññawəm* every, any, anyone, whatever (see ማን)
ማንኛውም ፡ ሰው anybody
ማንኛውም ፡ ነገር everything
ለማንኛውም in any case

ማንካ *manka* spoon (see also ማንኪያ)

መንኩራኩር *mänkʷärakʷər* wheel, rocket
ሰው ፡ ሥራሽ ፡ መንኩራኩር satellite (of
space)

መንከሪያ *mänkäriya* dye (see ነከረ)

መነኮሰ *mänäkkʷäsä* become a monk
መነኩሴ *mänäkʷse* (pl. መነኮሳት *mä-
näkʷäsat*) monk
መነኩሲት *mänäkʷsit* nun
ምንኩስና *mänkʷəsənna* monastic life,
monkhood

ማንኪያ *mankiya*, ማንካ *manka* spoon
የሾርባ ፡ ማንኪያ tablespoon
የሻይ ፡ ማንኪያ teaspoon
የጫማ ፡ ማንኪያ shoehorn

ምነው *mənnäw* why? (for ምን ፡ ነው)

መነዘረ *mänäzzärä* become dissolute
አመነዘረ *amänäzzärä* commit adultery
የመነዘረች ፡ ሴት *yamänäzzäräčč set*
adulteress
ምንዝረኛ *mənzəräňňa* dissolute
አመንዝረኛ *amänzəräňňa* adulterer

መነዘረ *mänäzzärä* exchange money,
convert money, cash (a check)
ምንዛሪ *mənəzzari* change (in money),
exchange
የምንዛዛሪ ፡ ዋጋ rate of exchange
የገበያ ፡ ምንዛሪ stock exchange
የገንዘብ ፡ ምንዛሪ exchange (of foreign
money)

*አመነዠከ, አመነዠከ *amänäžžähä* ruminate, chew cud
ምንዣኪ *mənəžžaki* cud

መንደር *mändär* village, town, hamlet,
neighborhood
መንደርተኛ *mändärtäňňa* villager, resident of a particular section or neighborhood of the town

ምንድር *məndər* what?, what thing? (see
also ምንድን)
ለምንድር why?

መንዳሪን *mändärin* tangerine

ምንድን *məndən* what?, whatever? (see
also ምንድር)
ለምንድን why?

መንጃ ፡ ፈቃድ *mänǧa fäqad* driver's
license (see ነዳ , ፈቀደ)

መንጋ *mänga* herd, flock, swarm (of
bees)

መንግሥት *mängəst* kingdom, government, reign, state (government), regime (government); see ነገሠ
መንግሥትነት *mängəstənnät* nationhood
መንግሥት ፡ ሰማያት heaven, kingdom
of heaven
የመንግሥት official (seal)
የመንግሥት ፡ ሠራተኛ civil servant,
government employee
ሕገ ፡ መንግሥት constitution
ቤተ ፡ መንግሥት royal residence, palace, court (royal family)
ዘመነ ፡ መንግሥት reign, rule
የተባበሩ ፡ መንግሥታት United Nations
(see አበረ)

መናገሻ *männagäša*, in የመናገሻ ፡ ከተማ
capital city (see ነገሠ)

ማንጋቻ *mangäča* suspenders (see አነገተ)

ምንጊዜም, see ጊዜ

መንገድ *mängäd* road, route, way, street,
journey, stretch, means, possibility,
fashion
መንታ ፡ መንገድ crossroads
እግረ ፡ መንገዱን on one's way
የአየር ፡ መንገድ airlines
(የ)እግር ፡ መንገድ sidewalk, footpath,
path, trail, track
መንገደኛ *mängädäňňa* traveler, passenger, traveling, passer-by
[See also አቋራጭ]

መንጋጋ *mängaga* jawbone, molar tooth

ማንጠልጠያ *manṭälṭäya* handle (of suitcase), hook (for coat); see *ጠለጠለ

መነጠረ *mänäṭṭärä* clear (the forest), log (cut down trees), deforest
ምንጥር *mänṭər* clearing

መነጥር *mänäṭṭər*, see መነጽር

መነጠቀ *mänäṭṭäqä* carry off suddenly and with violence, wrench

መንጠቆ *mänṭäqqo* hook (for lamp), fishhook

ምንጣፍ *mänṭaf* rug, mat, carpet (see *ነጠፈ)

መነጨ *mänäččä* gush, issue, vi. (of water from a spring), stem (orig- inate), emerge
አመነጨ *amänäččä* secrete (nectar), exhale (give off), think up (a plan), conceive (a plan)
ምንጭ *mänč* source, spring (of water), fountain, head (of river), headwa- ters, root (source), mine (source), genesis, well (of information)

መናጫ *mänača* churn (n.); see ናጠ

ምንጭ, see መነጨ

መነጨቀ *mänäččäqä* jerk (out of the hand), snatch

መነጽር *mänäṣṣər* spectacles, eyeglasses (see also መነጥር)
ማጉሊያ ፡ መነጽር magnifying glass
የፀሐይ ፡ መነጽር sunglasses

መንፈስ *mänfäs* spirit, feeling, frame of mind, will, demon (see ነፈሰ)
መንፈስ ፡ ቅዱስ Holy Ghost
የመንፈስ ፡ ልጅ confessional child
እርኩስ ፡ መንፈስ evil spirit
የርጋታ ፡ መንፈስ poise (see እርጋታ)
መንፈሳዊ *mänfäsawi* spiritual, devo- tional, devout
መንፈሳዊ ፡ ትምህርት theology
መንፈሳዊነት *mänfäsawinnät* spiritual merit, spirituality

መናፈሻ *männafäša*, መናፈሻ ፡ ቦታ *männafäša bota* park (n.); see ነፈሰ

መናፍቅ *mänafəq* heretic (see ኑፋቄ)
መናፍቅነት *mänafəqənnät* heresy

መንፈቅ *mänfäq* middle, half a year
መንፈቀ ፡ ሌሊት middle of the night

*መኘ, ተመኘ *tämäňňä* desire, wish, be desirous of, covet, aspire to
ምኞት *mäňňot* wish, desire, ambition, aspiration

*ሞኘ, አሞኘ *amoňňä* deceive, fool, cheat, make a fool of someone, bluff, outwit
ሞኝ *moňň* foolish, fool, silly
ሞኝነት *moňňənnät* foolishness

መኝታ ፡ ቤት *mäňňəta bet* bedroom, dormitory (see ተኛ)

ምኞት, see *መኘ

ምእመን *mä'əmän* worshipper, true believer, faithful (see አመነ)
ምእመናን *mä'əmänan* laity

ምዕራብ *mä'ərab* west, occident
በስተምዕራብ toward the west, westerly
ምዕራባዊ *mä'ərabawi* western, West- erner
የምዕራብ west (adj.), westerly, oc- cidental

ማዕረግ *ma'əräg* series, order, rank, dignity, position, title, class (rank); see ዐረገ
የማዕረግ ፡ እድገት promotion
ባለ ፡ ማዕረግ high-ranking official

ምዕራፍ *mä'əraf* chapter, episode, phase, event

ማዕበል *ma'əbäl* wave, storm

መዓት *mä'at* calamity, disaster, wrath, many, loads of, a lot, stream (of words), flood (of words)

ማዕከላዊ *ma'əkälawi* central, middle (adj.), average (adj.); see አከለ

ማእከላይ *ma'əkälay* mean (halfway between two points); see አከለ

መዓዛ *mä'aza* fragrance, odor (of perfume), scent (of roses), aroma
መዓዛ ፥ አለው *mä'aza alläw* smell, vi. (of roses), lit. it has fragrance

ማእዘን *ma'əzän* corner, angle
ሦስት ፥ ማእዘን triangle
አራት ፥ ማእዘን square, quadrangle, rectangle
ማእዘናዊ *ma'əzänawi* angular

ማእድ, see ማድ

ማዕድን *ma'ədən* mineral, mine (of coal or gold)
የማዕድን ፥ ቴፋሪ *yäma'ədən qʷäffari* miner

*መካ, ተመካ *tämäkka* boast, be proud of, rely on
ትምክሕት, see below
መመኪያ, see above

መሻል, see መያል

መከላከያ *mäkkälakäya* resistance, defense, defensive measure, safeguard, protection, prevention, preventive measure, repellent (see ከለከለ)
መከላከያ ፥ የሌለው defenseless
የመከላከያ defensive (weapon)
(የ)መከላከያ ፥ ሚኒስቴር Ministry of Defense
የግጥት ፥ መከላከያ buffer

መከረ *mäkkärä* advise, counsel, warn (advise), enjoin (advise)
ተማከረ *tämakkärä* take counsel together, consult each other, deliberate, confer
አማከረ *ammakkärä* consult with someone, advise, give advice
ተመካከረ *tämäkakkärä* take counsel, seek advice, consult, deliberate, confer
ምክር, see below
ምክክር *məkəkkər* consultation, conference
አማካሪ *ammakari* advisor, advisory, counselor

መከራ *mäkära* hardship, misery, trouble, misfortune, affliction, adversity, tribulation, plight
መከራ ፥ ጠራ court disaster

መከር *mäkär*, መኽር *mähär* autumn, harvest, crop

ሙከራ *mukkära* (n.) test, experiment, attempt, trial (testing); see ሞከረ

ምክር *məkər* advice, counsel, precept, consultation (see መከረ)
ምክር ፥ ያዘ hold a council
ምክር ፥ ቤት parliament, Congress, council
የሕግ ፥ መምሪያ ፥ ምክር ፥ ቤት Chamber of Deputies
የሕግ ፥ መወሰኛ ፥ ምክር ፥ ቤት Senate

ሞከረ *mokkärä* (B) try, test, try on, try out, give a trial, make an attempt, experiment
ሙከራ, see above

መኩሪያ *mäkuriya* glory (see ኩራ)

መክሰስ *mäksäs* snack

ማክሰኞ *maksäňňo* Tuesday
ሰኞ ፥ ማክሰኞ hopscotch

ሞክሼ *mokše* namesake

መከተ *mäkkätä* (B) fend off, parry, ward off a blow with a shield
መከታ *mäkäta* (n.) barricade, support

ሞከተ *mokkätä* (B) castrate
ሙክት *mukkət* castrated animal

ምክትል *məkəttəl* deputy, vice- (see *ከተለ)
ምክትል ፥ ሚኒስትር deputy minister
ምክትል ፥ አዛዥ second in command, deputy commander
ምክትል ፥ ወረዳ sub-district

ማክተሚያ *maktämiya* climax (see ከተመ)

መክተቻ *mäktäča* receptacle, container (see ከተተ)

መከነ *mäkkänä* be sterile (woman, cattle)
መካን *mäkan,* መኻን *mähan* barren (woman, cattle), sterile (woman, cattle)

መኪና *mäkina* auto, car, machine
በመኪና ፡ ጻፈ type (v.)
የመኪና ፡ መሪ steering wheel
የጭነት ፡ መኪና truck, lorry
የጽሕፈት ፡ መኪና typewriter

መካን ፤ መኻን, see መከነ

መካን *mäkan* place
መካን ፡ መቃብር graveyard, cemetery

መኰንን *mäkʷännən* governor, noble person of high rank, officer (in the army), dignitary, gentleman (see ኩነነ)
መኳንንት *mäkʷanənt* appointive nobility, noble, nobleman, aristocracy, gentry
እጮቄ ፡ መኰንን cadet

መካኒክ *mäkanik* mechanic

ምክንያት *məknəyat* cause, reason (cause), pretext, excuse, justification, ground (reason), motive (see *መከነ)
ምክንያቱም because
በ - - - ምክንያት on account of, because of, due to, owing to
በምን ፡ ምክንያት on what account?, for what reason?, why?
በምንም ፡ ምክንያት + (negative verb) in no case, on no account

*መከነ, አመከነ *ammäkaňňä* use as an excuse or pretext, blame something on someone
ተመከነ *tämäkaňňä* be offered as an excuse, be used as an excuse
ምክንያት, see above

መካከል *mäkakkäl* center, middle, midst (see መሃል, መሀከል, አከለ)
በ - - - መካከል between, among
በመካከሉ in the interim
በመካከል ፡ ገባ intervene
እ - - - መካከል between, in the middle of, in the center of, among

እስከ - - - መካከል up to the middle of, up to the center of
መካከለኛ *mäkakkäläňňa* average, middle, medial, mean (halfway between two extremes), medium (adj.), mild (climate), moderate (political views)
መካከለኛ ፡ ምሥራቅ Middle East
መካከለኛ ፡ ዘመን Middle Ages

መኳኳያ *mäkkʷakʷaya* toilet articles, cosmetics (see ኳለ)

መከዳ *mäkkädda* couch, pillow (for a chair)

መክደኛ *mäkdäňňa* lid, cover (see ከደነ)

መክፈቻ *mäkfäča* key (see ከፈተ)

መወልወያ *mäwälwäya* mop (see ወለወለ)

መወርወሪያ *mäwärwäriya* latch, shuttle (n.); see ወረወረ

መውቂያ *mäwqiya* flail (see ወቃ)

መውቀጫ *mäwqäča* pestle (see ወቀጠ)

መወተፊያ *mäwättäfiya* stopper (see ወተፈ)

መዋዕል , see ዜና

መዋያ , see ዋለ

መወጠሪያ , see ወጠረ

መዋጮ *mäwwaço* contribution (in money), fund, drive to collect money (see ወጣ)

መውጫ *mäwča* exit, way out, issue (see ወጣ)
መውጫ ፡ የሌለው dead end

ማውጫ *mawča* index (of a book), directory (see ወጣ)
የመጽሐፍ ፡ ማውጫ table of contents
የስም ፡ ማውጫ directory

ሙዝ *muz* banana

ሙዝ, in አፈሙዝ barrel (of gun)

ሚዜ *mize* best man, one of the groom's three companions

ግልገል ፡ ሚዜ junior best man

መዝሙር mäzmur canticle, hymn, psalm
(see ዘመረ)
መዝሙረ ፡ ዳዊት Psaltery
የመዝሙር ፡ ጓድ choir, chorus
የሕዝብ ፡ መዝሙር national anthem
ደቀ ፡ መዝሙር disciple

ማዞሪያ mazoriya telephone operator
(see ዞረ)

ሙዚቃ muziqa music
የሙዚቃ musical
የሙዚቃ ፡ ሸክላ record (of music,
songs)
የሙዚቃ ፡ ክበብ glee club
የሙዚቃ ፡ ደራሲ composer
የሙዚቃ ፡ ጓድ orchestra, band (musicians)
ሙዚቀኛ muziqäňňa musician

መዘበረ mäzäbbärä ravage, devastate

መዘነ mäzzänä (B) weigh, balance,
measure (the importance of a thing),
estimate, calculate
ተመዘነ tämäzzänä weigh oneself
አመዘነ amäzzänä give weight to, be
preponderate
(ከ - - - አመዘነ outweigh)
ተመዘዘነ tämäzazzänä have an equal
weight, balance one another, be in
equilibrium
አመዛዘነ ammäzazzänä evaluate, appraise (estimate the quality), take
into account, consider both sides of
a question, compare, weigh two
things to compare the weight
ሚዛን, see below
መመዘኛ mämäzzäňňa weight (object
used to balance a scale), criterion
ተመዛዘኝ tämäzazaň symmetrical,
equivalent
ተመዛዘኝነት tämäzazaňňannät ratio
አመዛዘኝ ammäzazaň judicial (mind),
judicious (person)
ሚዛን mizan scales, balance, weight,
equilibrium (see መዘነ)

ሚዛን ፡ ተጫወተ seesaw (v.); see
*ጫወተ

መዝናኛ, see *ዘና

መዘውር mäzäwwar pulley (see ዞረ)

መዘዘ mäzzäzä draw the sword from
the sheath, uproot a plant
ተመዘዘ tämäzzäzä grow tall

መዘገበ mäzäggäbä register (vt.), keep
a record, have on file, enroll (vt.),
note down, catalog (record)
ተመዘገበ tämäzäggäbä register (vi.),
be registered, be listed, enroll (vi.),
sign up
አስመዘገበ asmäzäggäbä have something registered, declare (goods at
customs)
መዝገብ, see below
ምዝገባ registration
መመዝገቢያ mämäzgäbiya register
(n.)
መመዝገቢያ mämmäzgäbiya registration

መዝገብ mäzgäb roster, ledger, record,
register (see መዘገበ)
መዝገብ ፡ ያዘ keep books, keep re-
cords
መዝገብ ፡ ቤት ፤ ቤተ ፡ መዝገብ ar-
chives, record office, registry
መዝገበ ፡ ቃላት vocabulary, lexicon,
dictionary
የሒሳብ ፡ መዝገብ accounts

መዝጊያ mäzgiya door, gate (see ዘጋ)

ማዘጋጃ, in ማዘጋጃ ፡ ቤት mazzägaǧa
bet municipality, city hall (see *ዘጋጀ)
የማዘጋጃ ፡ ቤት ፡ ሹም mayor

ማዠት mažät, in የዓይን ፡ ማዠት ፡
ሕመም conjunctivitis (see አዠ)

መዥገር mäžgär cattle tick

ሙያ muya, ሞያ moya skill, craft
(skill), task, professional specialty,
achievement, deed, virtue

ሙያ : የሌለው *muya yälelläw* inept, unskilled
ባለሙያ *balämuya* skillful, handy, expert, handyman, craftsman
ባለሙያ : ሚስት a good housewife
የሙያ professional (ethics), vocational
የሙያ : ትምህርት : ቤት vocational school
የቀን : ሙያ daily work
የጀግንነት : ሙያ heroism
ሙያተኛ *muyatäñña* laborer
ሟያተኛነት *moyatäñňannät*, in የሟያተ ኛነት : ሥራ manual labor

ሟያ *mʷaya* day's pay
ሟያተኛ *mʷayatäñña* day laborer

ማይል *mayl* mile

ሚያዝያ *miyazəya*, ሚያዚያ *miyaziya* April

መያዣ *mäyaža* means for holding, holder, bolt, clasp, frame (of glasses), mortgage, security, deposit (pledge), pawn, hostage (see ያዘ)

ሚዶ *mido* comb (n.)

ማድ *mad* table laid with bread for a meal (see also ማእድ)
ማድቤት kitchen, cook house
ማድ : ተነሣ the table is cleared (see ነሣ)

ማዶ *mado* the other side, the beyond
ከ - - - ማዶ across, on the far side of
ባሕር : ማዶ overseas
እዚያ : ማዶ yonder, over there
ወዲህ : ማዶ on this side
ወዲያ : ማዶ beyond (adv.)

ሜዳ *meda* plain (n.), field, court (of tennis), course (for golf)
ሜዳ : ወጣ defecate (lit. he went out to the field)
የሜዳ wild (horse)
የሜዳ : አህያ zebra
የሜዳ : ፍየል antelope, mountain goat

የጦር : ሜዳ battlefield
ጇን : ሜዳ race course at Addis Ababa
ሜዳማ *medamma* flat (country)

ሞድ *mod* mode, fashion, style (of clothing)
ሞድ : አወጣ design (v.); see ወጣ

መድኃኔ *mädhane* savior (see ዳነ, መድ ኃኒት, መድኅን)
መድኃኔ : ዓለም savior of the world

መድኃኒት *mädhanit* remedy, cure, medicine, medicament, drug, poison (see ዳነ, መድኃኔ, መድኅን)
መድኃኒት : ቀማሚ druggist, pharmacist (see ቀመመ)
(የ)መድኃኒት : ቤት pharmacy, drugstore
የሚያስተኛ : መድኃኒት *yämmiyastäñña mädhanit* anesthetic (see ተኛ)
መድኃኒተኛ *mädhanitäñña* healer

ሞዴል *model* model, design

ሜዳማ *medamma* flat (country); see ሜዳ

መደመደ *mädämmädä* level, make level, flatten

መደምደሚያ *mädämdämiya* conclusion (see ደመደመ)

ምድር *mədər* earth, land, region
ምድር : ቤት basement, cellar, ground floor
(እምድር : ቤት downstairs)
ምድረ : በዳ desert (n.)
ምድረ : ግቢ compound (of school), campus
የምድር : ባቡር railway, railroad
የምድር : ዋልታ pole
የምድር : ወገብ equator
የምድር : ጦር ground forces
ምድራዊ *mədrawi* terrestrial, earthly

መድረሻ *mädräša* arrival, time or place of arrival, destination (see ደረሰ)
ባዕድ : መድረሻ suffix

መድረክ *mädräk* stage, platform, tribune, rostrum, podium, reviewing stand, pier

ማደሪያ, see አደረ

መደርደሪያ *mädärdäriya* shelf (see ደረ ደረ)

መዶሻ *mädoša* hammer (n.)

ሚዳቋ *midaqq^wa* kind of antelope

መደበ *mäddäbä* (B) assign, set aside, reserve (set apart), designate, allocate, appropriate (allot), detach (send away on special duty), consign, station, classify (students), rank (arrange in a row), group, detail (set apart)
ለየብቻ ፡ መደበ segregate, put in categories, classify (see ብቻ)
[See also መደብ, ምድብ]

መደብ *mädäb* stand (on the market), stall for merchandise, (flower) bed, lot (of ground), bench made of earth, platform (for sitting or sleeping), post (station), person (in grammar); see መደበ
መደበኛ *mädäbäñña* basic, regular, fixed, ordinal (number), standard (adj.)

መዳብ *mädab* copper, brass

ምድብ *mäddəb*, in ምድብ ፡ ተውላጠ ፡ ስም personal pronoun (see መደበ)

መደብር *mädäbbər* store, seller's booth, bazaar, department store
የምግብ ፡ መደብር grocery store
የመጽሐፍ ፡ መደብር book store

ማድቤት *madbet* kitchen, cook house (see ማድ)

መደበኛ, see መደብ

መድን *mädən* immunity, recovery, bail, security (see ዳነ)
መድን ፡ ወጣ give immunity

መደወያ *mädäwwäya* button of door bell (see ደወለ)

ሙዳይ *muday* small basket or box for keeping personal possessions

ማያያ *maddäya*, in ቤንዚን ፡ ማያያ gas station, filling station (see ዐደለ)

ሜዳይ *meday* medal

መዳዳ *mädäda* row, city block
መዳዳ ፡ በመዳዳ one after another, in single file
መዳዳወን *mädädawən* consecutively
በመዳዳው at one stretch, in a row

ምድጃ *mədəǧǧa* furnace, stove, hearth, oven, fireplace (see ነደደ)

መዳፍ *mädaf* palm (of hand), paw

መድፍ *mädf* cannon, gun (cannon)
መድፈኛ *mädfäñña* gunner
መድፈኞች *mädfäññočč* artillery

መጅ *mäǧ* upper millstone; corn (on toe), callus
መጅ ፡ አበቀለ be callused (hand); see በቀለ

መጀመሪያ *mäǧämmäriya* start, beginning, first, front (see ጀመረ)
መጀመሪያ ፡ ነገር first of all
በመጀመሪያ at first, first (adv.), originally
የመጀመሪያ front (adj.), original (idea, inhabitant)

ማጅራት *maǧrat* nape of neck

ማጋ *magä* drink in sips, sip

ማግ *mag* weft, woof

መጋለ *mäggälä* suppurate, discharge pus
መግል *mägəl* pus
መግል ፡ ያዘ fester

ማጕሊያ *mag^wliya* that which serves to magnify (see ጕላ)
ማጕሊያ ፡ መነጽር magnifying glass
የድምፅ ፡ ማጕሊያ loudspeaker

መግለጫ *mägläča* explanation, reference, statement, declaration, communiqué, bulletin, information, report, account, demonstration (explanation), manifestation, sign, expression (see ገለጠ)

ማገረ *maggärä* put cross-pieces in building a house wall
ማገር *magär* wall of poles fastened in the ground, horizontal pieces of wood holding the uprights of a wall together

ማጐሪያ *magg^wäriya* enclosure, pen (for a donkey); see አጐረ

መጋረጃ *mäggaräǧa* curtain, blind for windows (see ጋረደ)
መጋረጃ : ጋረደ draw the curtain
መጋረጃ : ጣለ draw the curtain, put up a curtain
የሽራ : መጋረጃ shade (for the window)

***ሞገሰ, አሞገሰ** *amoggäsä* (B) glorify, pay a compliment, sing someone's praise, laud, extol, celebrate
ሙገሳ *muggäsa* praise, glorification
ሞገስ *mogäs* dignified aspect, dignified countenance, majesty
ሞገስ : ያለው *mogäs yalläw* solemn (festivity)

ማግስት *magəst* the following day, the next day, the day after
በማግስቱ the following morning, the next day, on the morrow

መገበ *mäggäbä* (B) nourish, feed
መጋቢ *mäggabi* steward, administrator, quartermaster
ምግብ, see below
አመጋገብ *ammägagäb* alimentation
ያመጋገብ : ዘዴ nutrition

ምግብ *məgəb* food, aliment, nourishment, comestible, repast, sustenance, meal, diet (see መገበ)
ምግብ : ሻጭ grocer (see ሸጠ)
ምግብ : ቤት restaurant, dining room

ምግብ : ነጋዴ grocer
ምግብ : አሠራር cooking (see ሠራ)
የምግብ : መምሪያ recipe (see መራ)
የምግብ : መደብር grocery store
የምግብ : ዝርዝር menu, bill of fare
የምግብ : ዘይት edible oil
ዋና : ምግብ staple

ምግባር *məgbar* practice, act (see ገበረ)

መግባባት, see ገባ

መጋቢት *mäggabit* March

መግቢያ *mägbiya* entrance, admission, gateway, introduction, preface, prelude, preamble (see ገባ)
የመግቢያ introductory, prefatory

ሞገተ *moggätä* (B) quarrel, litigate, bring a person to court
ተሟገተ *täm^waggätä* litigate, argue (in court), plead in a court case
ተሟጋች *täm^wagač* litigant, litigious, campaigner
ሙግት *muggət* lawsuit, legal case, litigation, controversy

ማግኔት *magnet* magnet

መገናኛ, see *ገኘ

መገናኘት, see *ገኘ

መጋዘ *mäggäzä* (B) saw
መጋዝ *mägaz* saw (n.)
በመጋዝ : ቆረጠ saw (v.)

ሞግዚት *mogzit* nurse (who takes care of children), nursemaid, tutor, guardian (appointed by law to take care of a minor), trustee
ሞግዚትነት *mogzitənnät* guardianship, trusteeship

መጋዘን *mägazän* warehouse, storeroom, storage

ማጉያ *mag^wya*, in የማጉያ : መነጽር microscope (see ጐላ)
ድምፅ : ማጉያ loudspeaker, amplifier

ማገዶ *magädo* firewood, fuel

ሞጋድ *mogäd* wave, tide; riot, violence
ሞጋደኛ *mogädäñña* revolutionary (leader)

ማገኛ *maggäǧa* embargo, barrier, interdiction, sanction (see አ፡ደ)
የማገኛ ፡ ድምፅ veto

መጋገሪያ *mägagäriya*, in የዳቦ ፡ መጋገሪያ oven (see ጋገረ)

ማገጣጠሚያ *maggäṭaṭämiya* joint (of body, of chair); see ገጠመ

መጣ *mäṭṭa* come
(ይዞ ፡ መጣ bring along)
አመጣ *amäṭṭa* bring, bring about
(እንዳመጣለት *ǝndamäṭṭallät* by chance)
(ዘመን ፡ አመጣሽ *zämän amäṭṭaš* contemporary (culture), newfangled)
አስመጣ *asmäṭṭa* import (v.)
መጥ *mäṭṭ*, in አዲስ ፡ መጥ newcomer
መጢ *mäṭṭe* newcomer, recent arrival
መጪ *mäči* future (adj.)
አስመጪ *asmäčči* importer
መምጣት *mämṭat* advent
የመጣው ፡ ይምጣ *yämäṭṭaw yəmṭa* come what may!
የሚመጣ *yämmimäṭa* next (week, month)
አማጭ, see below
[See also ምጽአት]

*ማጠ, አማጠ(ች) *amaṭä(čč)* suffer labor pains
ምጥ, see below

ማጥ *maṭ* mire
ማጥ ፡ የበዛበት *maṭ yäbäzzabbät* miry

ምጥ *mǝṭ* labor pains, birth pangs, childbirth (see *ማጠ)

መጠለያ *mäṭṭäläya* shelter, shed (see *ጠለለ)

ማጥለያ *maṭläya* strainer made of woven grass, filter, funnel (see ጠለለ)

መጣጠምር *mäṭṭamär* conjunction (see *ጠመረ and መስተፃምር)

መጠምዘዣ, see ጠመዘዘ

መጠመጠ *mäṭämmäṭä* suck (milk); see also መጠጠ

ሚጥሚጣ *miṭmiṭṭa* a kind of fiery pepper

ምጥማጥ *mǝṭmaṭ* skunk

*ሞጠመጠ, አሞጠመጠ *amoṭämmäṭä* round (the lips)

ማጠራቀሚያ *maṭṭäraqämiya* reservoir (see *ጠረቀመ)
የውሃ ፡ ማጠራቀሚያ cistern, water reservoir
የፖስታ ፡ ማጠራቀሚያ ፡ ሣጥን letter box, mailbox

መጥረቢያ *mäṭräbiya* hatchet, ax, adze (see ጠረበ)

መጣጠሪያ *mäṭṭäriya* term (expression), appellation (see ጠራ call)
መጠሪያ ፡ ስም the name by which one calls, given name

መጥሪያ *mäṭriya* summons, citation (see ጠራ call)
የስም ፡ መጥሪያ roll, record of attendance

ማጣሪያ *maṭṭariya* filter (n.); see ጠራ 'be pure'

መጥረጊያ *mäṭrägiya* broom, sweeper (see ጠረገ)

*መጠቀ, አመጠቀ *amäṭṭäqä* propel (a rocket), launch (rocks)

መጠቅለያ *mäṭäqläya* wrapper, package (see ጠቀለለ)
መጠቅለያ ፡ ወረቀት wrapping paper

መጥበሻ *mäṭbäša* roasting pan, frying pan, toaster (see ጠበሰ)

ማጠቢያ *maṭäbiya*, in ማጠቢያ ፡ ቤት *maṭäbiya bet* washroom (see አጠበ)
ልብስ ፡ ማጠቢያ ፡ ቤት laundry

መጠነ *mäṭänä* (B) measure out the right amount, apportion, practice moderation

መጣጠነ *mäṭaṭṭänä* test one's strength

ተመጣጠነ *tämäṭaṭṭänä* be suited (appropriate), be proportionate, be commensurate with, be in keeping with, bear relation to, be of similar capacity, be comparable, be equivalent, be equal

መጠን, see below

ምጣኔ, see below

ምጥን, see below

ተመጣጣኝ *tämäṭaṭañ* equivalent, equal, commensurate

መጠን *mäṭän* amount, measure, size, magnitude, norm, proportion (size), extent, limit (extent), dosage, range (see መጠነ)

መጠን ፡ የሌለው inordinate

በ - - - መጠን according to (in proportion to), to the extent that

በመጠኑ in some measure, within limit, with moderation, moderately, relatively, to a certain extent, to a certain degree, fairly

እንደ + verb + መጠን inasmuch as

ከመጠን ፡ በላይ beyond measure, to excess, too much, unusually, profusely

ከመጠን ፡ በላይ ፡ የሆነ excessive

ከመጠን ፡ አለፈ overdo, exceed the limit

በተቻለ ፡ መጠን *bätäčalä mäṭän* as much as possible

አካል ፡ መጠን manhood

መጠነኛ *mäṭänäñña* medium-sized, normal, proportionate, moderate, modest (income, drinker), reasonable (amount), fair (knowledge)

*ማጠነ, ተማጠነ *tämaṭṭänä* appeal for protection, plead for something, enter a plea for asylum, commit oneself to someone's care, propitiate [See also *ማጸነ, የሙጥኝ]

ምጣኔ *mäṭṭane* measure, meter (in a poem); see መጠነ

ምጣኔ ፡ ሀብት economics

ምጥን *mäṭṭən* measured out, exact (see መጠነ)

እጥር ፡ ምጥን ፡ ያለ *əṭṭər mäṭṭən yalä* concise, succinct, compact (report); see አጠረ

ሙጥኝ, see የሙጥኝ

ምጣድ *mäṭad* griddle, disc (of iron or clay) on which bread is made (see ጣደ)

የሸህላ ፡ ምጣድ clay griddle

የብረት ፡ ምጣድ iron griddle

መጠጊያ *mäṭṭägiya* source of protection, shelter, refuge (see ጠጋ)

መጠጊያ ፡ አሳጣ leave homeless (see አጣ)

መጠጠ *mäṭṭäṭä* absorb (suck up), imbibe (see also መጠመጠ)

አመጠጠ *amäṭṭäṭä* sop up (water), blot up

ማምጠጫ *mamṭäča* blotter

መጠጥ *mäṭäṭṭ* drink (n.), beverage, strong drink, liquor (see ጠጣ)

መጠጥ ፡ ቤት tavern, saloon

ለስላሳ ፡ መጠጥ soft drink

ሚጠጠ *mʷaṭṭäṭä* scrape, scratch with the nails or claws

መጣጢስ *mäṭaṭis* sweet potato (see also በጣጢስ)

መጣፍ *mäṭaf* book (see መጽሐፍ)

መጥፎ *mäṭfo* bad, evil, wicked, foul (weather), repugnant (odor), miserable (meal), harsh (climate); see ጠፋ

መጣፊያ *mäṭafiya* patch (see ጣፈ)

ማጠፊያ *maṭäfiya* hinge (of door); see አጠፈ

ሙጫ *mučča* glue, resin

ሚጨረ *mʷaččärä* (B) scratch

ተሚጨረ *tämʷaččärä* be marred

ሞጫጨረ *močaččärä* mark (scratch)

መጨረሻ *mäčärräša* end (n.), conclusion
(see ጨረሰ)
በመጨረሻ at last, lastly, eventually,
finally, in conclusion
እስከ : መጨረሻው for good, as far
as it would go
የመጨረሻ (adj.) terminal, last, latest, late, ultimate, final, extreme
(limit), youngest (child), maximum

መጫኛ *mäčañña* strap of leather used
in fastening a load, thong (see ጫነ)

መጫወቻ *mäččawäča* toy, plaything,
game (see *ጫወተ)
መጫወቻ : ሜዳ playground

ማጭድ *mačəd* sickle, clavicle (see
በጨደ)

መጽሔት *mäshet* journal, magazine,
periodical (journal), bulletin
ሳምንታዊ : መጽሔት weekly, n. (magazine)
ዓመታዊ : መጽሔት annual, n. (magazine)

መጽሐፍ *mäshaf* (pl. መጻሕፍ ኮ *mäsa-
həft*) book, tome (see ጻፈ, መጣፍ)
መጽሐፍ : ቅዱስ Scripture, Bible
ቤተ : መጻሕፍት library

ምጸት *məssät* irony
የምጸት ironical
ምጸታዊ : ትችት *məssätawi təččət* satire

*ማጸነ, see *ማጠነ

ማጽናኛ *masnañña* consolation, comfort, sympathy (see ጸና)

ምጽአት *məs'at* Advent of Christ (see
መጣ)

መጸው *mäsäw* season after the summer rains

መጸወተ *mäsäwwätä* give alms
ምጽዋት *məswat* charity, alms

ሞፈር *mofär* beam of plough

መፋቂያ *mäfaqiya* stick of a particular
tree serving to brush the teeth (see
ፋቀ)

መፈቀፈቂያ *mäfäqfäqiya* scraper (see
ፈቀፈቀ)

መፍትሔ *mäftəhe* solution, remedy
(solution); see ፈታ

መፍቻ *mäfča* key (see ፈታ)
(የ)ጠመንጃ : መፍቻ screwdriver

ማፈኛ *maffäñña* gag (see አፈነ)

ማፍያ *mafəya* pot, kettle (see ፈላ)

ረ

ርኅሩኅ *rəhruh* kindhearted, tenderhearted, soft-hearted, compassionate,
clement, sympathetic, humane (see
ራራ)
ርኅራኄ *rəhrahe* pity, leniency, clemency, goodness, quarter (mercy)
ያለ : ርኅራኄ *yalä*—mercilessly

ረኅብ *rähab* hunger, famine, starvation
(see ራበ)
ረኅብተኛ *rähabtäñña* starving

ረመሰ *rämmäsä* mix several things together
ተረመሰ *tärammäsä* snarl, vi. (of
traffic), be muddled up
ትርምስ, see below
[See also *ረመሰመሰ]

*ረመሰመሰ, ተረመሰመሰ *tärmäsämmäsä*
squirm (of a worm); see ረመሰ
ትርምስምስ, see below

ሮማን *roman* pomegranate

*ረመደ, ተራመደ *tärammädä* tread,
walk, take steps, take measured
steps, stride, progress, advance
(ከ - - - ጋራ : ተራመደ keep abreast)
(ወደ : ፊት : ተራመደ advance)
አራመደ *arrammädä*, causative of the
preceding; adapt
ተራማጅ *täramaǧ* radical, adj. (in
political beliefs), progressive (in politics)

አረጓመድ *arrämamäd* gait, walk (gait)
እርምጃ, see below

ረመጥ *rämäṭ* hot ashes, cindᵊr

ራራ *rarra* be merciful, be compassionate, feeᆯ for (see also ርኅሩኅ)
አራራ *ararra* soften (the heart)

ረሳ *rässa* forget, be oblivious
ተረሳ *tärässa* be forgotten, pass into obscurity, fall into oblivion
ተረሳ(ው) *tärässa(w)* slip one's mind

ራሰ *rasä* be wet, be damp, be moist, be soggy, get soaked
አራሰ *arasä* drench, dampen, moisten, soak (of rain soaking the ground)

ራስ *ras* head (n.), top, summit, Ras (Ethiopian title), bulb (of onion), ear of corn (see also ርእስ)
ራሱ *rasu* he himself, by himself, in person, he personally, oneself
(የ)ራስ ： ምታት headache (see ምታ)
ራስጌ *rasge* the head part (especially of a bed)
ራሱ ： ዞረ be dizzy
ራሱን ： ሳተ faint, lose consciousness
ራሱን ：ቻለ be independent, come into one's own, be self-supporting, fend for oneself
ራሱን ： ችሎ ： ኖረ be on one's own, fend for oneself
ራሱን ： በወቀ recover consciousness, come to
ራሱን ： ወዳድ selfish
ራሱን ： ገታ control oneself
የራስ personal, own (as in የራስ፡ጉዳይ personal affairs)
የራስ ： ቅል skull
የራስ ： ወርቅ diadem

ሬሳ *resa* cadaver, corpse, carcass, body (corpse)
የሬሳ ： ሣጥን casket, coffin

*ርስ, in የርስ ： በርስ *yärs bärs* mutual

ርስት *rᵊst* estate (landed property), property, inheritance, family land, land, domain (land owned by a person); see ወረስ
ርስትና ： ንብረት estate (possession)
ሰምርስት *sᵊmärᵊst* deed (legal document); see ስም
ባለ ： ርስት landowner
ርስተኛ *rᵊstäñña* landowner, owner of *rᵊst* land

ሬስቶራንት *restorant* restaurant

ሩሲያ *rusiya* Russia

ራስቬ, see ራስ

ረሽ *räš* shotgun

ረሽነ *räššänä* (B) gun down, execute by shooting

ራሽን *rašᵊn* ration

ሩቅ, see ራቀ

ራቀ *raqä* be far, be farthest, be distant, be remote, deviate
አራቀ *araqä* remove to a distance, make far, make remote, estrange, keep away
ተራራቀ *täraraqä* be far apart
ራቅ ： አለ *raqq alä* stay away
ራቅ ： ያለ *raqq yalä* outlying, far, long (journey)
ሩቅ *ruq* far, remote, far off, distant, afar, far away
ርቀት *rᵊqät* distance, remoteness
መራራቅ *märraraq* lag (distance)
አርቆ *arᵊqo* far (adv.)

ረቀቀ *räqqäqä* be fine, be thin, be refined, be subtle
አረቀቀ *aräqqäqä*, causative of the preceding; draft (a bill), draw up (a constitution)
ተረቀቀ *täraqqäqä* be adept in
የረቀቀ *yäräqqäqä* subtle, refined
የተረቀቀ *yätäräqqäqä* intricate (design), complicated, drafted (of a letter)
ረቂቅ, see below

ረቂቅ *räqiq* fine, subtle, abstract, elaborate (structure), minute (adj.); draft (of bill), outline (see ረቀቀ)
ረቂቅ ፡ ሕዋሳት germs (see ሕዋስ)
ረቂቅ ፡ ነፍሳት microbe
የሕግ ፡ ረቂቅ bill (in law), draft
ረቂቅነት *räqiqənnät* exactitude, minuteness, abstraction (abstract idea)

*ራቄተ, ተራቄተ *täraqqʷätä* be naked, be barren, be bare, be too poor to buy clothing
አራቄተ *arraqqʷätä* denude, despoil, lay bare
ራቁት *raqut* + (suffix pronouns) naked, nude, bare (naked)
ራቁቱን ፡ ነው he is naked
[See also ዕርቃን]

ርቀት, see ራቀ

ረቡ *räbu* Wednesday (see also ሮብ, ረቡዕ)

ረባ *räbba* be profitable, be advantageous, be useful, be fertile (cattle), breed, vi. (cattle)
አረባ *aräbba* breed, vt. (cattle), raise (cattle), decline (in grammar), conjugate, inflect (in grammar)
ተራባ *tärabba* breed, vi. (of rabbits), multiply, vi. (of rabbits, of family)
ርቢ *rəbbi* fecund, giving birth several times a year, animal husbandry
አርቢ *arbi*, in ከብት ፡ አርቢ cattleman
አረባብ *arräbab* inflection (in grammar), conjugation
እርባታ *ərbata* declension, conjugation; husbandry (animal)
መራባት *märrabat* fertility (of rabbits)
መርቢያ *märbiya* breeding ground
አይረባም *ayräbam* he (it) is no good, he is good for nothing, it is not worth it
የረባ *yäräbba* decent (meal)
የሚረባ *yämmiräba* worthwhile
የማይረባ *yämmayräba* senseless, worthless, useless, irrelevant, foolish (behavior), idle (rumor), poor (excuse), crazy (idea), a no-good (man), light-headed
የማይረባ ፡ ነገር nonsense, trifle

ሩብ *rub* quarter, fourth part (see አራት)

ራበ(ው) *rabä(w)* be hungry, starve
(እንጀራ ፡ ራበኝ I am hungry for bread)
ተራባ *tärabä* starve (vi.), go hungry
የተራባ *yätärabä* starving, hungry, famished
ራብ *rab* hunger
ራኀብ *rähab* hunger, famine, starvation

ሮብ *rob* Wednesday (see also ረቡ, ረቡዕ)

ረበረበ *räbärräbä* pile up

*ረበረ, አረበረ *aräbärräbä* spray, sprinkle lightly

ርብራብ *rəbrab* lattice, joist, framework, scaffold (see also እርብራብ)

ረበሸ *räbbäšä* (B) disturb, make trouble
ተራበሸ *tärabbäšä* brawl
ረብሻ *räbša* riot, brawl, disorder (riot), uprising, upheaval
ረብሻኛ *räbšäňňa* rioter, riotous (conduct)
የተራበሸ *yätärabbäšä* riotous (crowd)

ሪቬት *rivet* rivet

*ረበተበተ, ተርበተበተ *tärbätäbbätä* be filled with trepidation

ሪበን *ribän* ribbon

ረቡዕ *räbu'* Wednesday (see also ረቡ, ሮብ)

ራብዕ *rabə'* the 4th order of the Amharic vocalic system (vowel *a*); see አራት

ረባዳ *räbbadda* low place between rolling hills

*ረበደበደ, ተርበደበደ *tärbädäbbädä* be tremulous, get nervous

ሪታ *rätta* win (in court)

ተረታ *tärätta* lose the case, lose a lawsuit, yield (give in)

ራት *rat* supper, dinner (see also እራት)

ርቱዕ *rətu'*, in አንደበተ ፣ ርቱዕ eloquent
ርቱዕ ፣ ተሳቢ. direct object
ኢ.ር.ቱዕ ፣ ተሳቢ. indirect object

ርችት *rəččət* fireworks, shots fired in succession (as a signal or an expression of joy)

ሬንዥ *renž* asphalt, tar (for the road), pitch

ርእስ *rə'əs* heading (see also ራስ and አርእስት)
ርእስ ፣ ምድር cape (point of land)
ርእስ ፣ አንቀጽ leading article, editorial

ራእይ *ra'əy* revelation, vision (see also ትርእይት, አርአያ)

ረካ *räkka* be satisfied (of needs), be sated from drinking, be complacent
አረካ *aräkka* satiate with drink, quench (thirst), supply (the demand), satisfy, gratify (satisfy)
(ራሱን ፣ አረካ content oneself)
(ፍላጎት ፣ አረካ appease)
የማይረካ *yämmayräka* insatiable

ሬኮማንዴ *rekomande* registered letter

ረከሰ *räkkäsä* be impure, be defiled, be contaminated, be cheap (price)
አረከሰ *aräkkäsä* desecrate, profane, contaminate, defile, debase (gold), cheapen
ርኩስ *rəkus* unclean, impure, contaminated (see also እርኩስ)
ርካሽ, see below

ርካሽ *rəkkaš* cheap, inexpensive (see ረከሰ)

*ረከበ, ተረከበ *täräkkäbä* take over (a business), take possession, be turned over (weapons)
አስረከበ *asräkkäbä* deliver (merchandise), turn over (weapons), surrender (arms), hand in, hand over

ራኬት *raket* racket

*ረከፈከፈ, አርከፈከፈ *arkäfäkkäfä* spray, sprinkle (water)
ተርከፈከፈ *tärkäfäkkäfä* be sprayed, be sprinkled
ውኃ ፣ አርከፈከፈ dampen (clothes)

*ረወጠ, see ርጠ

ሩዝ *ruz* rice

ሪዝ *riz* beard, mustache, whiskers

ረዘመ *räzzämä* become long, lengthen (vi.), extend (vi.)
አረዘመ *aräzzämä* lengthen (vt.), extend (a visa)
አስረዘመ *asräzzämä* elongate, heighten
አራዘመ *arrazzämä* prolong, draw out
ርዝመት *rəzmät* length, height (of building)
(ርዝመት ፣ ያለው long)
ርዚም, see below
ርዡም, see below

ርዚም *räžžim*, ርዡም *räžžəm* high, tall, long, lengthy, extensive (see ረዘመ, ርዡም)

ርዘራዥ *rəzərraž* trace (of dwelling), survival (of a custom), remnant
የቦምብ ፣ ርዘራዥ fallout from a bomb

ረዳ *rädda* aid, help, help out, be helpful, lend a hand, assist, be cooperative, be of service, accommodate (help), be conducive to
ተረዳ *tärädda* be helped, get help
ተረዳዳ *tärädadda* cooperate, give mutual aid
ረዳእ *rädə'* assistant
ረዳት *räddat* helper, assistant, aide (assistant), auxiliary, adjutant, orderly
መረዳዳት *märrädadat* cooperation, mutual help
እርዳታ, see below

*ረዳ, ረዳ(ው) *rädda(w)* realize (be aware)
ተረዳ(ው) *tärädda(w)* understand, acquaint oneself (with facts), inform

oneself of, sense, apprehend (perceive), remark (notice), judge (conclude), take cognizance, find out,
conceive, deduce, be convinced,
realize (be aware), be informed of the
death of a near relative
(በስሕተት ፡ ተረዳ misconstrue)
አረዳ arädda break the news of someone's death
አስረዳ asrädda describe, enlighten,
explain, put across, define (make
clear), inform, delineate (a plan),
demonstrate, prove, convince, persuade
መረጃ , see above
ማስረጃ , see above
መርዶ märdo announcement of death

ራዳ radä tremble with fright, shake

ረዳት , see ረዳ

ረድእ rädə' assistant (see ረዳ)

ራዲዮ radiyo, ራዲዮን radiyon radio

ረድፍ räd(ə)f column (of figures, of
troops), row (of seats), line (of people), queue

ረጂም räǧǧim, ረጅም räǧǧəm high, tall,
long, lengthy, extensive (see ረዘመ,
ረዥም)

ረጋ rägga coagulate, curdle, congeal,
be condensed (milk), clot (of blood),
freeze, vi. (of water), become stagnant (water), solidify, vi. (of butter),
be calm, be composed
አረጋጋ arrägagga calm (vt.), soothe
(a frightened child), pacify, compose
one's thoughts
ረጋ ፡ አለ räga alä compose oneself,
be poised, calm down, vi. (of an
angry man), be impassive
ረጋ ፡ ያለ räga yalä sober (opinion),
sedate (child), solemn (aspect),
poised, unexcitable (person)
የረጋ yärägga calm, adj. (voice, sea),
smooth (surface), still (water, air),
stagnant (water), frozen (water),

stolid (face), impassive, stable (government)
የረጋ ፡ መንፈስ poise
እርጋ , see below
እርጋታ , see below

ረገመ räggämä rue, curse
ተራገመ täraggämä swear (curse)
ርጉም rəgum cursed
እርግማን , see below
የተረገመ yätäräggämä accursed

*ረገረገ , አረገረገ arägärrägä be shaky
(bridge), be unsteady

ረግረግ rägräg marsh, marshland,
marshy swamp
የረግረግ swampy

*ረገበ , አራገበ arraggäbä fan (v.)
ማራገቢያ marragäbiya fan (n.)
[See also *ረበበ]

ርግብ rəgb turtledove, pigeon (see also
እርግብ)
ዓይነ ፡ ርግብ veil (lit. pigeon's eye)

*ረገበገበ , ተረገበገበ tärgäbäggäbä trill
(of voice), tremble (of voice), be
tremulous (of voice), vibrate (of a
guitar string), quaver, twitch (of
eyelids), flutter (of eyelids); see also
*ረበበ
አረገበገበ argäbäggäbä wave (a handkerchief, the hand), blink (the eye),
flap
ማርገብገቢያ margäbgäbya fan (n.)

*ረገዘ, ተረገዘ täräggäzä be conceived
አረገዘ(ች) aräggäzä(čč) become pregnant, be with child
እርጉዝ ərguz pregnant

ረገድ rägäd order, class, extent
በማንኛውም ፡ ረገድ in every respect
በዚህ ፡ ረገድ in this instance, in this
manner, in this respect

ረገጠ räggäṭä kick, trample, step on,
tread on
ረጋገጠ rägaggäṭä trample, trample
down

ተራገጠ *täraggäṭä*, in ወደ ፡ ኋላ ፡ ተራ
ገጠ recoil (of gun)
መርጋጫ *märgäča* pedal
መረጋጋጫ *märrägagäča* foothold,
footing
እርግጫ , see below

*ረገጠ , አረጋገጠ *arrägaggäṭä* assure,
make sure, reassure, make certain,
substantiate, prove, affirm, confirm,
convince, validate (a story), acknowledge, verify, certify, ascertain, give
assurance, circumstantiate, corroborate, warrant (guarantee)
ማረጋገጫ *marrägagäča* assurance,
confirmation, verification, warrant
(guarantee), pledge (sign of good
will), acknowledgment
እርግጥ , see below
የተረጋገጠ *yätärägaggäṭä* secured
(future), sure, confirmed

ረገፈ *räggäfä* drop, vi. (of fruit), fall
to the ground (of fruit, leaves), fall
out (of teeth)
አራገፈ *arraggäfä* discharge (cargo),
shake out (dusty rug), brush off (dust),
unpack (the horses), empty out (a
bag), unload, unsaddle, unharness

ሮጠ *roṭä* run
ተሯሯጠ *tärʷarʷaṭä* scurry, run about
(ወዲያ ፡ ወዲህ ፡ ተሯሯጠ run about)
ሩጫ , see below
ሯጭ *rʷač* runner

ረጠበ *räṭṭäbä* be wet, get wet, be damp,
be moist
አረጠበ *aräṭṭäbä* wet, vt. (hands,
clothes), moisten, dampen
እርጥብ *ərṭəb* wet, damp, moist
ርጥበት *rəṭbät*, እርጥበት *ərṭəbät* dampness, moisture

ረጨ *räčča* sprinkle, spray, spatter (with
mud), splash, spend profusely
(ውኃ ፡ ረጨ spray, splash, vt.)
ተረጨ *täräčča* splash (vi.)

ሩጫ *ručča* race, running (see ሮጠ)
የሩጫ ፡ ውድድር race

ረፈረፈ *räfärräfä* litter, strew plenti-
fully, lay flat, beat down (of rain
beating down the grass)

ረፈተ *räffätä* (B) discharge (from the
army)

ረፈደ *räffädä* be midmorning, become
late in the morning
(ጊዜ ፡ ረፍዷል *gize räfdʷal* it is late)
አረፈደ *aräffädä* spend the morning,
do something late in the morning,
be late in the morning
(አርፍዶ ፡ መጣ *arfədo mäṭṭa* come
late in the morning)
(ተኝቶ ፡ አረፈደ he overslept)
ረፋድ *räffad* midmorning

ራፖር *rapor*, ሪፖርት *riport* report

ሠ ሰ

ስ *sə* + (imperfect) while, when, by the
time
ስ + (verb) because, since, as (reason)
ስ + (negative imperfect) before
(conj.), without (conj.), unless
ስ + negative imperfect + አይቀርም
be apt to

-ስ -*ss* what about ?, as for

ስሕተት *səhtät* mistake, fault, error,
blunder, slip (mistake); see ሳተ, ስተት
ስሕተተኛ *səhtätäňňa* faulty, wrong
(adj.)

ሳህን *sahən* plate, dish
ዝርግ ፡ ሳህን plate, platter
የሸዋላ ፡ ሳህን china, porcelain
ጐድጓዳ ፡ ሳህን bowl, basin

*ሰላ , አሰላ *asälla* figure (reckon), figure
out, calculate (the costs); see also
*ሰለሰለ

ሰላ *sälla* prosper, succeed, be in good
condition
አሰላ *asälla* cause to succeed

ሰላ *sälla* be sharp (see also ሳለ)
አሰላ *asälla* sharpen
የሰላ *yäsälla* sharp, acute (angle),
shrill (voice)
ስል *səl* acute (angle), sharp (edge),
keen (edge)

ሣለ *salä* paint (a painting), draw (a
picture), portray
ሠዓሊ *sä'ali* painter, illustrator
ሥዕል , see below

ሳለ *salä* cough (v.)
ሳል *sal* cough (n.)

ሳለ *salä* sharpen (a knife), grind
(sharpen); see also ሰላ
ስለት , see below
መሳል *mäsal* whetstone
መሳያ , see above

*ሳለ , ተሳለ *täsalä* vow (make a vow
to give an offering)
ስለት *səlät* vow (n.), votive offering

ሳሌ *salle* crock

ስለ *səlä* because of, regarding, on account of, concerning, about, of
(about), with regard to, in consideration of, for the sake of, on behalf of
ስለ + (verb) because, since (because),
as
ስለሆነም therefore, because of this
ስለምን why? (see ምን)
ስለዚህ *səläzzih* therefore, because of
this (see -ዚህ)

ሶል *sol* sole (bottom of shoe)
ሶል ፡ አገባ sole the shoes

ሰለለ *sällälä* (B) spy, scout out
ስለላ *səlläla* espionage, reconnaissance
ሰላይ *sällay* spy, secret agent

ሰለለ *sällälä* be paralyzed, atrophy, be
thin (voice)
ሰላላ *sälala* paralyzed, crippled
መስለል *mäsläl* paralysis
የሰለለ *yäsällälä* thin (voice), strained
(voice)

*ሰለመ , ተሳለመ *täsallämä* kiss the
door or the wall of a church or holy
place, make a pilgrimage, go to
church
ተሳላሚ *täsalami* pilgrim
መሳለም *mässaläm* pilgrimage
[See also ሰላም , ሰላምታ]

ሰላም *sälam* peace, tranquillity, safe
(peaceful), greetings! (see *ሰለመ)
የሰላም *yäsälam* pacific, amicable (friendly)
የሰላም ፡ ጓድ Peace Corps
ሰላማዊ *sälamawi* secure (life), peaceful, civilian
ሰላማዊ ፡ ሰልፍ demonstration (political)

ሰላምታ *sälamta* salutation, salute, greeting, regards, respects, compliments
(greeting); see *ሰለመ , ሰላም
ሰላምታ ፡ ሰጠ greet, salute
ሰላምታ ፡ አቀረበ greet (see ቀረበ)

ስለምን *sälämən* why? (see ስለ, ምን)

ሠላሳ *sälasa* thirty (see ሦስት)

ሣልስ *saləs* the 3rd order of the Amharic vocalic system (vowel *i*); see
ሦስት
ሣልሳዊ *salsawi* Third (in the title
of a king)

ሥላሴ *səllase* Trinity (see ሦስት)

ስልሳ *sälsa* sixty (see also ስድሳ, ስድስት)

*ሰለሰለ , አሰላሰለ *assälassälä* ponder
(think over carefully), contemplate,
deliberate, muse (see also *ሰላ)

ሰለቀ *sälläqä* (B) grind (grain) a second
time

*ሰለቀ , ተሳለቀ *täsalläqä* laugh at,
ridicule, jest
መሳለቂያ *mässaläqiya* laughing stock,
source of amusement

ሰለበ *sälläbä* emasculate, castrate (a
person)
ስልብ *sälb* eunuch

ሰልባቦት *səlbabot* cream which forms on milk

ሰለት *səlät* fine edge, cutting edge, blade of knife (see ሳለ)
ስለታም *səlätam* sharp

ሰለት *səlät* vow (n.), votive offering (see *ሳለ)

ስልት *səlt* mode, manner, way, style, device, liturgical chant
የቋንቋ ፡ ስልት dialect
የጦር ፡ ስልት strategy, tactics

ሰለቸ *säläččä* be tedious, be tiresome
ሰለቸ(ው) *säläččä(w)* be tired of, feel disgust, be bored, be weary of
ተሰለቸ *täsäläččä* be dull (boring), be disgusted with
አሰለቸ *asäläččä* bore (vt.), weary, nag, excite disgust
አሰልቺ *asälči* boring, wearisome
መሰልቸት *mäsälčät* boredom
የሚያሰለች *yämmiyasäläčč* irksome

ስልቻ *səlləčča* bag made of animal skin

ሰሌን *sälen* mat made of palm leaves

ሳሎን *salon* living room

ስልክ *səlk* telephone, phone (n.)
ስልክ ፡ ደወለ phone (v.)
ስልከኛ *səlkäñña* telephone operator
የስልክ ፡ ማዘሪያ telephone exchange
የስልክ ፡ ቁጥር telephone number

ሰልከከ ፡ አለ *sälkäkk alä* be svelte, be delicate (features)
ሰልካካ *sälkakka* clean-cut (features)

ስለዚህ *səläzzih* therefore, because of this (see ስለ , -ዚህ)

ሰላይ *sällay* spy, secret agent (see ሰለለ)

ሰሌዳ *säleda* tablet, board, chart, sign (inscribed board), license plate
ማስታወቂያ ፡ ሰሌዳ bulletin board
የትምህርት ፡ ቤት ፡ ሰሌዳ schedule
ጥቁር ፡ ሰሌዳ blackboard

ሰሊጥ *säliṭ* sesame

ሰላጣ *sälaṭa* salad, lettuce

ሰላጤ *sällaṭe* channel (geographical)
የባሕር ፡ ሰላጤ bay, gulf

ሠለጠነ *säläṭṭänä* be proficient in, be skillful, become trained, become acculturated
ተሠለጠነ *täsäläṭṭänä* be trained, be civilized
አሠለጠነ *asäläṭṭänä* train (make skillful by teaching), civilize
ሥልጡን *səlṭun* civilized
ሥልጣን , see below
ሥልጣኔ *sələṭṭane* civilization, modern culture
አሠልጣኝ *asälṭañ* trainer, coach (of a team)
የሠለጠነ *yäsäläṭṭänä* civilized, trained
(በእጅ ፡ ሥራ ፡ የሠለጠነ skilled (laborer)

ሥልጣን *səlṭan* power, authority (power), capacity (authority), jurisdiction, authorization, prerogative (see ሠለጠነ)
ሥልጣን ፡ ሰጠ authorize
ባለ ፡ ሥልጣን dignitary, official (n.), executive (n.)
ባለ ፡ ሥልጣኖች authorities
ባለሙሉ ፡ ሥልጣን plenipotentiary

*ሰለፈ., ተሰለፈ *täsälläfä* (B) fall in line, form a line, parade, align (vi.), align oneself, be placed in battle formation
አሰለፈ *assälläfä* line up (vt.), align (vt.)
ሰልፍ , see below

ሰልፍ *sälf* parade, demonstration, order of battle, review, procession, line (row of persons), line-up, queue (see *ሰለፈ.)
ሰልፍ ፡ ወጣ file out
በሰልፍ ፡ ጐበኘ pass in review (vt.)
ሰላማዊ ፡ ሰልፍ demonstration (showing feelings by a parade)
ሰላማዊ ፡ ሰልፍ ፡ አደረገ demonstrate (show feelings by a parade)

ሰላማዊ ፡ ሰልፈኛ *sälamawi sälfäñña* demonstrator

ሰማ *sämma* hear, listen, take heed, understand (a language)
ተሰማ *täsämma* be heard, be listened to, be perceptible, be heeded
ተሰማ(ው) *täsämma(w)* sense (v.), feel, appreciate (be sensitive of), be sensitive to
አሰማ *assämma* announce, voice, utter (a cry), broadcast (on the radio), convey (information, advice)
ተስማማ *täsmamma* get along, correspond (agree), consent, harmonize (vi.), go well together, be consistent with, be consonant with, conform, concur, be suited, befit, coincide, adapt oneself, be in accord, agree (also of food), go together, see eye to eye
አስማማ *asmamma*, causative of the preceding; accommodate, reconcile, harmonize (vt.), conform (vt.)
†ስምም *sämämm* agreement
ስሜት , see below
ስሞታ *sämota* complaint
ስምምነት , see below
ተስማሚ *täsmami* agreeable (suitable to), compatible, convenient, congruous, fit (time), right (appropriate), acceptable (fitting), suitable
ተስማሚነት *täsmaminnät* suitability, appropriateness
ተሰሚነት *täsäminnät* influence
መስማማት , see above
የሚስማማ *yämmismamma* favorable, fitting, appropriate, sensible (clothing)
አይስማማም *ayəsmammam* it is incongruous
የመስሚያ *yämäsmiya* acoustic
የሰሚ ፡ ሰሚ *yäsämi sämi* hearsay (adj.), at second hand
ለይስሙላ *läyəsmulla* only for show, pose

ሰም *säm* wax, beeswax
ሰምና ፡ ወርቅ *sämənna wärq* expression, phrase, or sentence in prose or poetry with a latent and patent meaning, hand in glove
ሰምና ፡ ወርቅ ፡ ሆነ dovetail

ሳመ *samä* kiss (v.), give a kiss
ቤት ፡ ክርስቲያን ፡ ሳመ go to church
ማርያም ፡ ሳመችው *maryam samäččəw* he has a birthmark (lit. Mary kissed him)

ስም *səm* name, noun, reputation
ስሙ ፡ ማን ፡ ነው? what's his name?
ሲም ፡ አወጣ name (a child); see ወጣ
ስም ፡ አጠፋ ruin one's reputation, blacken one's name (see ጠፋ)
ስም ፡ ጠራ call the roll
ስመ ፡ ርስት ፤ ስመርስት deed (legal document)
ስመ ፡ ጥሩ ፤ ስመ ፡ ጥር famous, reputable, prestigious, eminent, celebrity
ለስሙ ፡ ያህል skimpy (meal)
የስም ፡ መጥሪያ record of attendance
የሐሰት ፡ ስም alias
የተጸውዖ ፡ ስም *yätäṣäw'o səm* proper noun, given name
የወል ፡ ስም common noun, general term
[See also አስገታት]

ስምም *sämämm* agreement (see ሰማ)
ስምም ፡ ናቸው *sämämm naččäw* they agree among each other

ስምምነት *sämämmənnät* harmony, settlement, agreement, consent, accord, treaty, conciliation, concord, consensus (see ሰማ)
የስምምነት ፡ ንግግር negotiations

ሠመረ *sämmärä* go well with, be successful, turn out all right, be pleasing
አሠመረ *asämmärä* arrange well, prepare well

*ሠመረ, አሠመረ *asämmärä* rule (paper), line, draw (a line)
(ከሥር ፡ አሠመረ underline)
መሥመር , see above
ማሥመሪያ , see above

*ሰግራ, ተሰግራ *täsämarra* pasture, graze (vi.), browse, engage (in an activity, profession), practice (a profession), head for
አሰግራ *assämarra* graze (vt.), lead to pasture, deploy (an army)
ማሰግሪያ, in ከብት ፡ ማሰግሪያ *käbt massämariya* cattle range

ሰመርስት *sämärəst* deed (legal document); see ሰም, ርስት

ሶመሰመ *somässomä* trot (vi.)
ሶምሶማ *somsomma* trot (n.)

ሳምባ *samba* lung (see also ሳንባ)
የሳምባ pulmonary
የሳምባ ፡ በሽታ pleurisy, pneumonia
የሳምባ ፡ ነቀርሳ tuberculosis
ፊቱ ፡ ሳምባ ፡ መሰለ turn red (from embarrassment or rage)

ስሜት *səmmet* feeling, emotion, excitement, stir (excitement), impulse (emotion), attention, passion, sensation, sense (sensation), sentiment (see ሰማ)
ስሜት ፡ ሰጠ appeal (v.)
ስሜት ፡ አሳደረ give the impression (see አደረ)
ስሜትን ፡ የሚቀሰቅስ *səmmetən yämmiqäsäqqəs* exciting, stirring, moving (see ቀሰቀሰ)
ስሜትን የሚነካ *səmmetən yämminäka* emotional (speech), fervid (see ነካ)
ብሔራዊ ፡ ስሜት nationalism
ያለ ፡ ስሜት *yalä*—impassive, unfeeling
የጋለ ፡ ስሜት ardor, enthusiasm, excitement, animation

ስሞታ *səmota* complaint (see ሰማ)

ሰሜን *sämen* north
የሰሜን ፡ ዋልታ North Pole
ሰሜናዊ *sämenawi* northern

ሰሞን *sämon* few days (3-4 days)
በዚህ ፡ ሰሞን *bäzzih sämon* during this week, one of these days

ሰሞኑን one of these days, lately, recently, currently

ሳሙና *samuna* soap
የሳሙና ፡ አረፋ lather
ኪሎ ፡ ሳሙና bar of soap
የጥርስ ፡ ሳሙና toothpaste

ሰሙኒ *səmuni* quarter (of a dollar)

ሲሚንቶ *siminto* cement, mortar, concrete

ሳምንት *sammənt* week (see ስምንት)
ባለ ፡ ሳምንት one whose turn it is to give the monthly gathering (called mahbär)
ሳምንታዊ *samməntawi* weekly (adj.)

ስምንት *səmmənt* eight
ስምንት ፡ ሰዓት two o'clock
ስምንተኛ *səmməntäňňa* eighth
[See also ሳምንት, ሰሞን, ሰማንያ]

ሰማንያ *sämanya* eighty, the 80th day memorial service; civil marriage, marriage contract (see ስምንት)

ሰማዕት *säma'ət* (pl. ሰማዕታት *säma'ə-tat*) martyr
ሰማዕትነት *säma'ətənnät* martyrdom

ሴማዊ *semawi* Semite

ሰማይ *sämay* (pl. ሰማያት *sämayat*) sky, heavens, firmament
ሰማይ ፡ ወጣ be sky-high (prices)
የሰማይ heavenly, celestial
የሰማይ ፡ ዝላይ high jump
መንግሥተ ፡ ሰማይ heaven, kingdom of heaven

ሰመጠ *sämmäṭä* sink, go down (see also ሰጠመ)

ሠራ *särra* make, work, do, repair, be employed, build, weave, function, implement, manufacture, operate, take effect, act upon, have an effect (of medicine), be applicable, be in use
(ምን ፡ ይሠራል what's the use?, what good will it do?)

(ሰው ፡ ሠራሽ *säw särraš* man-made,
artificial)
ሥራ, see below
ሠራተኛ, see below
አሠሪ *assärri* employer, foreman
አሠራር, see below
መሥሪያ, see above
መሥሪያ ፡ ቤት *mäsriya bet* office,
department (of government)

ሱሪ *surri* pants, trousers, drawers
ጠባብ ፡ ሱሪ breeches

ሣር *sar* grass, straw
ሣር ፡ ቅጠል vegetation
የሣር ፡ ሜዳ prairie
የሣር ፡ ክዳን ፡ ጣሪያ thatched roof

*ሴረ, አሴረ *aserä* (v.) intrigue, conspire,
plot
ሴራ *sera* intrigue, conspiracy, plot
ሴረኛ *seraňňa* plotter, conspirator

ሥራ *sara* work, job, labor, occupation,
career, function, task, act, deed,
action, performance, employment,
position (job), business, vocation
(see ሠራ)
ሥራ ፡ በዛ(በት) *sara bäzza(bbät)* he
is busy, he is too busy
ሥራ ፡ ያዘ be busy, be engaged in a
task
ሥራ ፡ ገባ go to work
ሥራ ፡ ፈታ be idle, be out of work
ሥራ ፡ ፈት idle, unemployed, jobless
በሥራ ፡ ላይ ፡ አለ be in commission
በሥራ ፡ ላይ ፡ ዋለ be in operation, go
into force, be implemented, materialize
በሥራ ፡ ላይ ፡ አዋለ put into practice,
invest (money); see ዋለ
ከሥራ ፡ ውጭ ፡ ሆነ be out of commission, be out of order
የሥራ ፡ ቀን weekday
የሥራ ፡ ጓደኛ colleague
የሥራና ፡ የመገናኛ ፡ ሚኒስቴር Ministry
of Communication and Public Works
የቤት ፡ ሥራ housework, homework
የእጅ ፡ ሥራ ፤ የጅ ፡ ሥራ handicraft

ሥር *sar* root, bottom, under, beneath,
at the foot of; vein, artery, nerve,
tendon
ሥር ፡ ሰደደ root (vi.), take root,
entrench oneself
ሥር ፡ የሰደደ entrenched, ingrained,
chronic
ሥር ፡ ያልሰደደ abortive (not developed properly), tentative, provisory
(see ሰደደ)
ሥረ ፡ ነገር subject (substance), bottom
(of a matter)
በ - - - ሥር ፤ እ - - - ሥር ፤ ከ - - - ሥር
under, beneath, below, at the bottom
of, at the foot of
ከሥር below
ከሥር ፡ ሥር from beginning to end
ከሥር ፡ ያለ underlying
ቀይ ፡ ሥር radish (lit. 'red root')
የደም ፡ ሥር vein, artery, blood vessel
ሥረኛ *säräňňa* bottom (adj.)
ሥርጭ, see below

ሰረረ *särrärä* mount a horse, mount,
climb; cover (of stallion, bull)

*ሰራራ, አንሰራራ *ansärarra* experience
a revival, recoup (after a disaster),
recover (of a country)
ማንሰራራት *mansärarat* revival, re-
birth

ሰረሰረ *särässärä* bore (a hole), pierce,
undermine (a wall), drill
ሰርሳሪ *särsari* sapper
ሰርሳሪ ፡ ሌባ burglar
የቤት ፡ ሲሳሪ burglar
መሰርሰሪያ *mäsärsäriya* drill, n. (tool)

ሠረቀ *särräqä* rise, appear (star)
ምሥራቅ *masraq* east, Orient

ሰረቀ *särräqä* steal, rob
ስርቆ ፡ አየ *särqo ayyä* take a peep
ስርቆት *sarqot* theft, robbery
በስርቆሽ *bäsarqoš* stealthily

ስርቅ *sarq*, in ሀቅ ፡ ስርቅ ፡ አለ have
the hiccups
†ስርቅታ *saraqta* hiccups

ስርቆሽ , see ሰረቀ

ስርቅታ *sərəqta* hiccups (see ስርቅ)
ስርቅታ ፡ ያዘ(ው) have the hiccups

ሱረት *surrät* snuff

ሥራት , see ሥርዓት

ሠራተኛ *särratäňňa* workman, worker, laborer, working man, employee, functionary (see ሥራ)
የመንግሥት ፡ ሠራተኛ public servant, civil servant
የዕለት ፡ ሠራተኛ daily laborer

ሥርቻ *sərəčča* nook along the wall (see ሥር)
በየሥርቻው *bäyyäsərəččaw* high and low

ሴረኛ *seräňňa* plotter, conspirator (see *ሴረ)

ሥረኛ *səräňňa* bottom (adj.); see ሥር

ሥርዓት *sər'at* procedure, formality, regulation, ceremony, ordinance, principle, manners, order, statute, system, rule, discipline
ሥርዓት ፡ አጣ be disorganized, be unsystematic
ሥርዓት ፡ ያለው *sər'at yalläw* methodical
ሥርዓተ ፡ ቅስና holy orders
ሥርዓተ ፡ ቢስ unmannerly
ሥርዓተ ፡ ትምህርት curriculum, syllabus
ሥርዓተ ፡ ነጥብ punctuation
ሥርዓተ ፡ የጠበቀ orderly (class)
በሥርዓት properly, systematically
ሥን ፡ ሥርዓት , see ሥን

ሰርክ *särk* often, frequently
የሰርክ for everyday

ሰርከስ *särkäs* circus

ሥርው *sərrəw*, in ሥርወ ፡ መንግሥት dynasty
ሥርወ ፡ ቃላት derivation of words (see ቃል)

ሰራዊት *särawit* army, military (n.)
የጦር ፡ ሰራዊት army
የፊደል ፡ ሰራዊት literacy campaign

ሰረዘ *särräzä* (B) cross out, delete, rub out, strike out, cancel (a stamp), revoke (a concession), call off, dismiss (a complaint), withdraw (a charge)
ሰረዘ(ለት) *särräzä(llät)* he absolved him (from a promise)

ሰረዝ *säräz* punctuation mark
ንኡስ ፡ ሰረዝ comma
ነጠላ ፡ ሰረዝ semi-colon
ድርብ ፡ ሰረዝ colon (see ደረበ)

*ሰረየ , ተሰረየ *täsärräyä* be absolved, be pardoned, be forgiven
አስተሰረየ *astäsärräyä* obtain absolution
ስርየት *səryät* absolution

ሰረገ *särrägä* sink, go down
ሰርጎ ፡ ገባ *särgo gäbba* infiltrate
ሰርጎ ፡ ገብ infiltrator

ሰርግ *särg* nuptials, wedding
ሰርገኛ *särgäňňa* member of the group which accompanies the bridegroom to the bride's house

ሰረገላ *särägälla* carriage, wagon, coach, chariot

ሰረጐደ *särägg"ädä* mark by pressure, pierce through, make a dent
ሰርጓጅ ፡ መርከብ *särg"ağ märkäb* submarine

*ሰራጨ , ተሰራጨ *täsäraččä* diffuse (vi.), spread (vi.), splash (vi.), leak out (of secret), circulate (of news), be widespread (view), be disseminated, branch out (of business)
አሰራጨ *assäraččä* circulate (news), disseminate, emit (of sun emitting light), propagate (news), spread (a new method)
የተሰራጨ *yätäsäraččä* common (disease)

ሱስ *sus* addiction (for coffee, smoking, etc.)
ሱሰኛ *susäñña* addict
(የአልኮል ፡ ሱሰኛ alcoholic)

ሢሦ *siso* one-third (see ሦስት)

ሳሳ *sassa* be thin, be sparse, be threadbare (coat)
አሳሳ *asassa* thin out (plants)
ስስ *səs* thin, fine (cloth), sheer (silk)

ሠሣ *sassa* become greedy, be insatiable
† ሥሥት *səssət* greed, cupidity

ሦስት *sost* three
ሦስት ፡ ሰዓት nine o'clock
ሦስቴ *soste* thrice
ሦስተኛ *sostäñña* third, thirdly
ሦስትየ *sostəyya* one-third
[See ሠላሳ, ሢሶ, ሣልስ, ሥላሴ]

ሥሥት *səssət* greed, cupidity (see ሠሣ)
ሥሥታም *səssətam* greedy, miserly
ሥሥታምነት *səssətamənnät* parsimony

ሲሳይ *sisay* good fortune, plenty

ሶሲዮሎጂ *sosiyoloği* sociology

ሶሺያሊዝም *sošiyalizm* socialism

ሱቅ *suq* store, shop
ሱቅ ፡ በደረቴ peddler (see ደረት)
ባለሱቅ *baläsuq* shopkeeper

ሲቃ *siqa* sob (n.); see *ሰቀሰቀ

ሣቀ *saqä* laugh
አሣቀ *assaqä* amuse (cause to laugh), evoke a laugh
ሣቅ ፡ አለ *saqq alä* smile, chuckle
ሣቅ ፡ ሣቅ ፡ አለ *saqq saqq alä* gurgle happily (of a baby), smile slightly
ሣቅ *saq* laughter
ሣቂታ *saqqitta* jocund
አሥቂኝ *assəqiñ* laughable, humorous, funny, comic, amusing
(አሥቂኝ ፡ ተዋናይ clown)
የሚያሥቅ *yämmiyassəq* ridiculous

ስቅ ፡ አለ *səqq alä* have the hiccups

ሰቀለ *säqqälä* hang (vt.), hang out, hang up, suspend, raise up, hoist (a flag), crucify
ተሰቀለ *täsäqqälä*, passive of the preceding; fly, vi. (of flag)
ስቅለት, see below
መስቀል, see above
መስቀያ, see above

ሰቀላ *säqäla* large rectangular shed

ስቅለት *səqlät* hanging, Crucifixion (see ሰቀለ)
ስቅለት ፡ ዓርብ Good Friday
የስቅለት ፡ ዕለት Good Friday

ሰቀሰቀ *säqässäqä* scrape off
መስቅሰቂያ *mäsäqsäqiya* spatula

*ሰቀሰቀ, ተንሰቀሰቀ *tänsäqässäqä* sob
ስቅስቅ ፡ ብሎ ፡ አለቀስ *səqsəqq bəlo aläqqäsä* he cried his heart out (see also ስቅቅ ፡ አለ)
ሲቃ *siqa* sob (n.)

ሰቀቀ, አሰቀቀ *assäqqäqä* (B) shock (of behavior), appall, horrify
ተሰቀቀ *täsäqqäqä*, in ሰውነቱ ፡ ተሰቀቀ it made his flesh creep
አሰቃቂ *assäqqaqi* frightful, disastrous, shocking, dreadful, awful, abominable, abject, hideous (crime), execrable, outrageous (crime), atrocious, cruel (war), miserable (life), gruesome
አሰቃቂነት *assäqqaqinnät* enormity (of crime)

ስቅቅ ፡ አለ *səqəqq alä*, in ስቅቅ ፡ ብሎ ፡ አለቀስ bawl (see also *ሰቀሰቀ)

ሣቂታ *saqqitta* jocund (see ሣቀ)

*ሠቀየ, ተሠቃየ *täsäqayyä* (also ተሣቀየ) be afflicted, be plagued, be in misery, be in torment, be in agony, suffer
አሠቃየ *assäqayyä* torment, torture, distress, afflict, plague, excruciate, persecute, martyrize
ሥቃይ *səqay* torture, torment, agony, distress, affliction, ordeal, suffering, pain, horror, discomfort

ሰባ *säba* seventy (see ሰባት)

ሡባ *säbba* be fat (animal)
አሡባ *asäbba* fatten
ሥብ *səb* grease, fat

ሰብ *säb*, in ቤ.ተ ፡ ሰብ family
ጉብረት ፡ ሰብ society (all the people)
የጉብረ ፡ ሰብ social
[See also ሰብእዊ]

ሳበ *sabä* drag, pull, lead (a horse), suck
(air into the lungs), draw (pull),
attract (of magnet, of personality),
appeal (be attractive)
ተሳበ *täsabä*, passive of the preceding; creep (of vine), crawl, grav-
itate
ስበት, see below
† መሳቢያ *mäsabiya* drawer
ተሳቢ, see below

ሰብል *säbəl* crop, productivity (agricul‐
tural)
ዋና ፡ ሰብል staple

ሲቪል *sivil* civil (service), civilian (n.)

ሰበረ *säbbärä* break, burst (vt.), fracture
(ዜማ ፡ ሰበረ sing false notes)
(ሰብሮ ፡ ከፈተ *säbro käffätä* break
open)
(ሰብሮ ፡ ገባ break into a house)
ተሰበረ *täsäbbärä* be broken, break
(vi.), crash (vi.)
ሰባበረ *säbabbärä* shatter, smash,
wreck (a machine), break up
ስባራ *säbara* broken, broken down
ስባሪ *səbbari* chunk (of stone), broken
piece
ስብራት *səbbərat* fracture (n.)
ስብርባሪ *səbərbari* chip (n.), broken
piece, fragment
ተሰባሪ *täsäbbari* breakable, fragile
አሳባሪ ፡ መንገድ *assabari mängäd*
short cut

ሰበሰበ *säbässäbä* gather (vt.), assemble (vt.), collect, convene (vt.), concentrate (collect), harvest (wheat)

(ሸሚዙን ፡ ሰበሰበ gather the sleeves,
roll up the sleeves)
ተሰበሰበ *täsäbässäbä* meet (of an assembly), gather (vi.), convene (vi.),
get together (vi.), congregate (vi.),
assemble (vi.)
ሰብሳቢ *säbsabi* chairman of a society
where collecting of money is involved
ስብሰባ *səbsäba* session, assembly,
meeting, gathering, conference, congress, convention (meeting), rally
ስብሰባ ፡ አደረገ hold a conference
ስብሰባ ፡ ያዘ sit (of parliament)
ስብስብ *səbsəb* collection
ስብስብ ፡ ብለው together
የስብስብ together (in a group)

*ሰበቀ , አሳበቀ *assabbäqä* tell on, tattle
on, inform on, denounce
አሳባቂ *assabaqi* informer, tattle-tale

*ሰበበ , አሳበበ *assabbäbä* rationalize, excuse
ሰበብ *säbäb* pretext, pretense, cause,
reason

ሰባት *säbatt* seven
ሰባት ፡ ሰዓት one o'clock
ሰባተኛ *säbattäñña* seventh
[See ሰባ, ሱባዔ, ሳብዕ]

ስበት *səbät* gravity, gravitation (see ሳበ)

ሱባዔ *suba'e* kind of spiritual retreat
(see ሰባት)

ሳብዕ *sabə'* seventh order of the Amharic vowel system (vowel *o*); see
ሰባት

ሰብእዊ *säb'awi* human (rights), humane
(see ሰብ)

ሰበከ *säbbäkä* preach, advocate, make
propaganda, propagandize, seek to
convince by indoctrination or propaganda
ሰባኪ *säbaki* preacher
ስብከት *səbkät* sermon, preaching,
propaganda
መስበኪያ ፡ ስገነት *mäsbäkiya sägännät* pulpit

ሲባጎ *sibago* string, twine, cord

ሳተ *satä* be mistaken, make a mistake, miss (not find), miss the target, lose (the way), err
(ራሱን ፡ ሳተ faint, lose consciousness)
ተሳተ *täsatä* be wrong, be mistaken, be missed
ተሳሳተ *täsasatä* be mistaken, make a mistake, err, be wrong, be in the wrong, blunder, have faults
አሳሳተ *assasatä* misguide, mislead, lead astray, seduce
ስተት *sətät* mistake, error, blunder
አሳሳች *assasač* deceptive, misleading
የተሳሳተ *yätäsasatä* mistaken, faulty, wrong, fallacious, false, erroneous
የማይሳሳት *yämmayəssasat* infallible
[See also ስሕተት]

ሳት, see ሰዓት

ሴት *set* woman, female, lady
ሴቶች *setočč* women folk
ሴቴ *sete* negative (electric charge)
ሴት ፡ ሐኪም woman doctor
ሴት ፡ ልጅ daughter, girl
(የሴት ፡ ልጅ rude, unmannerly child)
ሴታ ፡ ሴት effeminate
የሴት effeminate, feminine (adj.)
ሴትኝ ፡ አዳሪ, see below
ሴትነት, see below

ስተት, see ሳተ

ሴትነት *setənnät* womanly qualities (see ሴት)
የሴትነት feminine

ሴትኛ ፡ አዳሪ *setəňňa adari*, ሴትኛ አዳሪ *setäňňa adari* prostitute, whore (see ሴት)

*ሰተፈ, ተሳተፈ *täsattäfä* participate, take part in, partake of
ሱታፌ *sutafe* participation

ሰኔ *säne* June

ሲኒ *sini*, ስኒ *səni* cup, porcelain cup

*ሳነ, ተሳነ *täsanä* not be possible, be impossible

ተሳነ(ው) *täsanä(w)* not be able, not succeed, be powerless, be impotent

ሥን *sən* beauty
ሥን ፡ ምግባር ethical behavior, etiquette
(የሥን ፡ ምግባር ፡ ትምህርት ethics)
ሥን ፡ ሥርዓት ceremony, procedure, proprieties, rite, ritual, routine, discipline, etiquette, standard
ሥን ፡ ሥርዓት ፡ ተከተለ be formal (in etiquette); see *ከተለ
ሥን ፡ ሥርዓት ፡ ያለው — *yalläw* ceremonial
ሥን ፡ በዓል festivity
ሥን ፡ ተፈጥሮ evolution
ሥን ፡ ጥበብ fine arts
ሥን ፡ ጽሑፍ literature, letters
ሥን ፡ ፍጥረት science
የሥን ፡ ልቦና ፡ ትምህርት psychology
የሥን ፡ ጽሑፍ literary
የጸሎት ፡ ሥን ፡ ሥርዓት religious service

ሲኔማ *sinima* cinema, movie

ሰንሰለት *sänsälät* chain

ሳንሱር *sansur* censorship
የሳንሱር ፡ ሹም censor

ሰነቀ *sännäqä* take provisions for the road, pack provisions, furnish provisions
ሥንቅ *sənq* provisions for a journey, food supply
ትጥቅና ፡ ሥንቅ *təṭqənna sənq* supplies (military)

ሳንቃ *sanqa* lumber, board (of wood), plank, leaf of door, door

ሳንባ, see ሳምባ

ሰንበሌጥ *sänbäleṭ* kind of grass

ሰንበር *sänbär* stripe (from stroke with a whip), bruise (n.)
ሰንበር ፡ አወጣ bruise (v.); see ወጣ

ሰነበተ *sänäbbätä* stay a certain time, reside a week, dwell, spend some days

(እንደምን ፡ ሰነበቱ? how have you been?)
(ደኅና ፡ ሰንብት dähna sänbət farewell!)
አሰነበባተ asänäbbätä make last, make stay long
ተሰናበተ täsänabbätä make adieus, bid farewell, take leave of one another, be dismissed, be fired, be discharged (from the army)
አሰናበተ assänabbätä dismiss, fire a worker
ሰንበት sänbät Sabbath, Sunday
ሰንበቴ sänbäte weekly gathering in the church in which food is distributed to the poor
ሰንብት sənəbbət leave, leave of absence
የመሰናበቻ ፡ ወረቀት yämässänabäča wäräqät discharge (from the army)

ስንት sənt how many?, how much?
ስንቱ sənte how often?, how long?
ስንት ፡ ሰዓት ፡ ነው? what time is it?
ስንት ፡ ጊዜ? how often?, how long?
በስንት ፡ ሰዓት? when?, at what time?
ከስንት ፡ አንዴ once in a great while, once in a blue moon

ሳንቲም santim penny

ስንኳ sənkʷa even (adv.); see እንኳ

ሰነከለ sänäkkälä hobble (tie the legs), tie the foot of the animal to its neck, disable, cripple
ተሰነከለ täsänakkälä stumble over, hit a snag, break down (of car, machine)
አሰነከለ assänakkälä hamper, prevent, hinder, cripple (disable)
ስንኩል sənkul invalid (adj.), crippled, disabled
(አካለ ፡ ስንኩል disabled, cripple, invalid)
መሰናክል mäsänakəl obstacle, bar (obstacle), hurdle, impediment, interference (hindrance), handicap, roadblock, barricade

መሰናከያ mässänakäya obstruction, handicap, roadblock
ስንክሳር sənkəsar encyclopedia
ሰነዘረ sänäzzärä launch a blow, raise the arm as if to hit, strike (a ball), direct a remark toward someone, level (criticism)
ተሰነዘረ täsänäzzärä be aimed at (of a remark), be intended for (a remark)
ሰነዘረ sänäzzärä measure by spans
ስንዝር sənzər span
ሰነድ sänäd document, declaration (statement of goods)
*ሰነዳ, ተሰናዳ täsänadda be prepared, be put in order, be arranged, be ready
አሰናዳ assänadda prepare, put in order, make ready, arrange
ሰነዱ sənäddu prepared, ready, arranged
መሰናዶ mässänado arrangement, preparation
ስንዴ sənde wheat
ሰንደቅ ፡ ዓላማ sändäq alama flag
ሳንዱቅ sänduq box, chest (box)
ሳንጃ sanǧa bayonet
ሰንጋ sänga steer, castrated
ሰንጢ sänṭi pocket knife, penknife
ሰነጠረ sänäṭṭärä break into splinters
ስንጥር sənṭər splinter, sliver of wood, strip of bamboo
ስንጣሪ sənəṭṭari sliver of wood
ሰንጠረዥ sänṭäräž chess, schedule
ሰነጠቀ sänäṭṭäqä splinter, split (vt.), crack (vt.), cleave, dissect (an animal)
ተሰነጠቀ täsänäṭṭäqä crack (vi.), split (vi.)
ሰነጣጠቀ sänäṭaṭṭäqä split asunder, chap (the skin)
ስንጣቂ sənəṭṭaqi splinter, chip of wood, split-off piece

ስንጥቅ *sənṭəq* split, rift, fissure, crack, flaw (in a glass), crevice

ሰነፈ *sännäfä* be indolent, be feeble, be lazy, become idle
ሰነፍ *sänäf* lazy, indolent, feeble, idle
ስንፍና *sənfənna* laziness, idleness, inaction, indolence

ሰነፈጠ *sänäffäṭä* be hot (mustard)
የሚሰነፍጥ *yämmisänäffəṭ* pungent (odor of sauce)
ሰናፍጭ, see below

ሰናፍጭ *sänafəčč* mustard (see ሰነፈጠ)

ሳንፔር *sanper*, in ዕንቁ ፡ ሳንፔር sapphire

*ሰነ, አሰነ *assäňňä* name, nominate, designate, make to be called; used as causative with composite verbs
አሰነ(ው) *assäňňä(w)* he feels like, he feels up to

ሰኞ *säňňo* Monday
ሰኞ ፡ ማክሰኞ hopscotch

ሠዓሊ *sä'ali* painter, illustrator (see ሣለ)

ሲኦል *si'ol* hell, perdition

ሥዕል *sə'əl* painting, picture, drawing, portrait, illustration, plate (in a book); see ሣለ
ሥዕላዊ *sə'əlawi* pictorial

ሰዓት *sä'at* hour, clock, watch, o'clock, time (see also ሳት)
ሰዓት ፡ ቁጥር *hour hand* (see ቁጠር)
ሰዓት ፡ እላፊ overtime, curfew (see አለፈ)
ስንት ፡ ሰዓት ፡ ነው what time is it?
በሰዓቱ just at the right moment, on time
በሰዓት at noon
በየሰዓቱ *bäyyäsä'atu* hourly (adv.), from time to time
ከሰዓት ፡ በኋላ afternoon
(ዛሬ ፡ ከሰዓት ፡ በኋላ this afternoon)
ከሰዓት ፡ በፊት before noon

ሰካ *säkka* (B) string (beads), pin (a flower on the dress), thread (beads), plug in (make electric connection), stick into, insert, drive a nail into the wall
ተሰካ *täsäkka*, passive of the preceding; stick, vi. (of a nail in the tire)
ተሳካ *täsakka* turn out well, be successful, be a success, be coherent (sentence)
ተሳካ(ለት) *täsakka(llät)* succeed, have success in, get ahead
የተሳካ *yätäsakka* coherent (sentence), successful
ሳይሳካ ፡ ቀረ *sayəssakka qärrä* fail
መሳካት *mässakat* success
መሰኪያ *mäsäkkiya* electric socket

ሰከረ *säkkärä* become drunk, be intoxicated
አሰከረ *asäkkärä* intoxicate, inebriate
ስካር *səkar* drunkenness
ሰካራም *säkkaram* drunk (n.), drunkard

ሱኳር *sukkʷar*, ስኳር *səkkʷar* sugar

ሰካሰከ *säkässäkä* stuff, cram

ሰኰና *säkʷäna* animal's foot, hoof (see also ሽኰና)

ሴኮንድ *sekond* second (n.)

ሠዋ *säwwa* (B) sacrifice, offer sacrifice
መሥዋዕት *mäswa'ət* sacrifice (n.)
መሠዊያ *mäsäwwiya* altar

ሰው *säw* man, person, personage, human (n.), mankind, fellow, gentleman, individual, people, anybody, anyone, someone
ሰውዬ *säwəyye* individual
ሰውዬው *säwəyyew* the man, this fellow
ሰው ፡ ሠራሽ man-made, artificial (see ሠራ)
የሰው human (adj.), belonging to someone else
የሰው ፡ ልጅ person of good family, freeman, human race, mankind, human, humanity

የሰው ፡ አገር foreign country
ሁሉ ፡ ሰው everybody
ተራ ፡ ሰው layman, ordinary person
ሰውነት, see below

ሰወረ *säwwärä* (B) hide, conceal
ስውር *səwwər* secret (hiding place),
hidden, implicit, occult, surreptitious
(በስውር secretly)
(ዓይነ ፡ ስውር blind)
የተሰወረ *yätäsäwwärä* secret (plan)

ሰዋስው *säwasəw* grammar

ሰውነት *säwənnät* body, figure (body),
constitution (of a person), personality (see ሰው)
ሰውነቱ ፡ ተሰቀቀ it made his flesh
creep (see ሰቀቀ)
ሰውነቱ ፡ ጕጐለ ache all over
የሰውነት bodily (adj.)
የሰውነት ፡ ማጠንከሪያ gymnastics (see
ጠነከረ)

ስዊድን *swidən* Sweden

ሠየመ *säyyämä* (B) designate (appoint),
give the title of, call (name)
ሥዩም *səyyum* appointed
ሥዩም ፡ እግዚአብሔር designated by
God, elect of God
ሥያሜ *səyyame* naming, name-giving,
appelation, designation

ሳይንስ *sayəns* science
የሳይንስ scientific
የሳይንስ ፡ ሊቅ scientist

ሰይጣን *säyṭan* devil, demon, Satan
ሰይጣኔ ፡ ይመጣል it makes me angry

ሰያፍ *säyyaf* diagonal, slant (adj.)

ሰይፍ *säyf* sword

ስድ *sədd* wandering freely, undisciplined, vulgar, uncouth (see ሰደደ)
ስድ ፡ ንባብ prose
ስድ ፡ አደግ impertinent, bold (impolite), boor, vulgar, impudent, insolent

ስድነት *səddənnät* vulgarity, insolence,
impertinence

ሰደሪያ *sädäriyya* vest

ሳድስ *sadəs* sixth order of the Ethiopian
vowel system (vowel *ə* or *zero*); see
ስድስት

ስድሳ *sədsa* sixty (see ስድስት, ስልሳ)

ስድስት *səddəst* six
ስድስት ፡ ሰዓት twelve o'clock
ስድስተኛ *səddəstäñña* sixth
[See also ሳድስ, ስድሳ]

ሰደቃ *sädäqa* table

ሰደበ *säddäbä* insult, abuse, call someone names, revile
ተሳደበ *täsaddäbä* curse
ስድብ *sədəb* (n.) insult, abuse (insulting language)

ስደት *sədät* immigration, emigration,
exile (see ሰደደ)
ስደተኛ *səddätäñña* refugee, immigrant, emigrant

ሰደደ *säddädä* send away, dispatch,
chase away, banish, exile, shoot (an
arrow), strike (roots), put roots into
the ground
(ሥር ፡ ሰደደ root (v.), take root, entrench oneself)
(ሥር ፡ የሰደደ entrenched, chronic,
ingrained)
(ሥር ፡ ያልሰደደ abortive (not developed properly), tentative, provisory)
ተሰደደ *täsäddädä* be sent away, emigrate, go into exile
አሳደደ *assaddädä* chase, pursue
ስድ, see above
(የ)ሰደድ ፡ እሳት (*yä*)*sädäd əsat* wildfire
ስደት, see above

ሰደፍ *sädäf* stock (of rifle), butt (of
rifle)

ሲጃራ *siǧara* cigarette, cigar

ሲጃራ፡ አጨስ smoke cigarettes (see ጨስ)

ሰጋ sägga be apprehensive, fear, be anxious, be fearful, worry
አሰጋ asägga cause apprehension, threaten (be a cause of possible harm), menace, alarm
ስጋት, see below
አስጊ, see below
የማያሰጋ yämmayasäga secure (hiding place)

ሥጋ səga meat, flesh, pulp
ሥጋ፡ ሻጭ butcher (see ሻጠ)
ሥጋ፡ በል carnivorous (see በላ)
ሥጋ፡ ወደም· Holy Communion
የሥጋ carnal
የሥጋ፡ ዘመድ blood relative
ኀፍረተ፡ ሥጋ genitals
ጥሬ፡ ሥጋ raw meat
ሥጋዊ səgawi fleshy, carnal, material, secular (education)

ስጎ səgo, ሱጎ sugo sauce

ሰገረ säggärä amble, trot (vi.)
አሰገረ asäggärä trot, vt. (a mule), make to amble

ሰገራ sägära latrine
የሰገራ፡ ቤት outhouse, latrine

ሲጋራ sigara cigar

ሰገባ sägäba sheath

*ሰገበገበ, ተሰገበገበ täsgäbäggäbä be greedy, be avid, gobble (food)
ተስገብግቦ täsgäbgəbo voraciously, greedily
ስግብግብ səgəbgəb ravenous, stingy, greedy

ስጋት səgat dread, anxiety, alarm, apprehension, fear, calamity, worry, care (worry), spectre (of war); see ሰጋ
ስጋት፡ የሌለበት səgat yälelläbbät secure (old age)

ሰጉን sägʷän ostrich

ሰገነት sägännät gallery, grandstand, balcony
መስበኪያ፡ ሰገነት pulpit (see ሰበከ)

ሥጋዊ, see ሥጋ

ሰገደ säggädä genuflect, prostrate oneself in prayer, bow down, worship
ስግደት səgdät adoration, devotion
[See also ስጋጃ]

ስጋጃ səgagga rug, carpet, tapestry (see ሰገደ)

ሰጠ sättä give, grant, afford, provide, accord
(እጅ፡ ሰጠ surrender, give in, yield, capitulate)
(ድምፅ፡ ሰጠ vote, v.)
(አብሮ፡ ይስጠን abro yəstän don't mention it!)
(እግዚር፡ ይስጥልኝ əgzer yəstəllänn thank you!)
(ጤና፡ ይስጥልኝ tena yəstəllänn goodbye!, hello!)
የሰጠ yäsättä ideal (place)
ስጦታ, see below
ተሰጥዖ ፤ ተሰጥኦ, see below
መስጫ, see above

*ሰጣ, አሰጣ asätta spread out (cloth or grain to dry)

ሰጠመ sättämä go under (of boat), drown, sink, flounder (of boat); see also ሰመጠ
አሰጠመ asättämä drown (vt.), sink (vt.)

ስጦታ sətota gift, endowment, present, aptitude, facility (talent); see ሰጠ

ሣጥን satən coffer, case (box), chest (box), locker
የሬሳ፡ ሣጥን casket, coffin (see ሬሳ)
ያስከሬን፡ ሣጥን coffin (see አስከሬን)
(የ)ቁም፡ ሣጥን wardrobe (closet), cupboard, cabinet

ሲጢጥ፡ አለ sititt alä squeak, screech, creak (of door), jar (of brakes)

ሰፊ *säfi* tailor (see ሰፋ sew)
ልብስ ፡ ሰፊ dressmaker, tailor, seam-stress
ጫማ ፡ ሰፊ shoemaker, cobbler

ሰፊ *säffi* broad, wide, spacious, wide-spread, large, extensive, all-out (see ሰፋ become broad)
በሰፊው *bäsäffiw* extensively, abun-dantly, widely, at length

ሰፋ *säffa* be (become) broad, become wide, widen (vi.), broaden (vi.), dilate (vi.)
አሰፋ *asäffa* widen (vt.), broaden (vt.), enlarge, spread out, dilate (vt.), stretch (shoes)
ተስፋፋ *täsfaffa* enlarge (vi.), expand (vi.), be widespread, develop (vi.), flourish, grow (of business)
አስፋፋ *asfaffa* develop (vt.), ex-pand (vt.), extend, promote, foster (develop), diffuse (vt.), spread
ሰፋ ፡ ያለ *säfa yalä* roomy, wide-spread
ሰፊ, see above
ስፋት *səfat* width, breadth, size (of room), area (surface), extent

ሰፋ *säffa* sew, sew up, stitch, seam
ተሰፊ *säfi* tailor
ስፌት, see below
ወስፌ, see below
መስፊያ, see above

ሱፍ *suf* wool
ሱፍ ፡ ልብስ *suf ləbs* woolens

ሱፍ *suf* sunflower

ሳፋ *safa* tub

ሶፋ *sofa* sofa, couch

ሰፈረ *säffärä* measure (grain, area)
ስፍር ፡ ቁጥር ፡ የሌለው *səfər qutər yälelläw* numberless, myriads of
መስፈሪያ *mäsfäriya* measure (n.)

ሰፈረ *säffärä* encamp, camp, settle (vi.)
ተሳፈረ *täsaffärä* be on board, go

aboard, board (a train), embark
አሳፈረ *assaffärä* take on passengers
ሰፈር, see below
ሰፋሪ *säfari* settler
ስፍራ *səfra* place, site, area, spot, seat, position, post (position), role
ተሳፋሪ *täsafari* passenger
መሳፈሪያ *mässafäriya* fare (for bus, train)

ሰፈር *säfär* section (of town), neigh-borhood (section of city), settlement, quarters, camp, barracks, base (sta-tion); see ሰፈረ encamp
የጦር ፡ ሰፈር camp, military base

ስፋት, see ሰፋ 'become broad'

ስፌት *səfet* basketwork, needlework, sewing, seam (see ሰፋ sew)
የስፌት ፡ መኪና *yäsəfet mäkina* sew-ing machine

ሰፈነ *säffänä* (B) be dominant, prevail, reign (prevail), pervade (of feeling)
መስፍን *mäsfən* (pl. መሳፍንት *mäsa-fənt*) duke, prince

ሰፍነግ *säfnäg* sponge (n.)
በሰፍነግ ፡ ወለወለ sponge (v.)

ሰፈፍ *säfäf* scum, film (of oil); see *ሳፈፈ

*ሳፈፈ, ተንሳፈፈ *tänsaffäfä* float, be afloat, soar, hover, drift (of logs in the river)
አንሳፈፈ *ansaffäfä* get afloat, float (vt.)
መንሳፈፍ *mänsafäf* floating
የመንሳፈፍ ፡ ኃይል buoyancy
መንሳፈፊያ *mänsafäfiya* raft, float (n.)
መንሳፈፊያ ፡ ትጥቅ life belt
ሰፈፍ, see above

ስፖርት *sport* sport (see also እስፖርት)
ስፖርተኛ *sportäñña* athlete, sports-man

ሽ

ሺ. *ši* thousand (see also ሺህ)

ሻ *ša* want, wish
አሻ *ašša* be necessary
አሻ(ው) *ašša(w)* choose, wish
ያሻል *yaššal* it is necessary

ሺህ *ših* thousand (see also ሺ.)

ሾህ *šoh* thorn, spine (see also ሾክ, እሾክ)

ሽሀላ, see ሽክላ

ሱል *šul* pointed, sharp (point); see ሾል

*ሻለ, ተሻለ *täšalä* be better, improve (vi.), be preferable, be advisable
ተሻለ(ው) *täšalä(w)* be well, get well, feel better, prefer
(የተሻለ *yätäšalä* better, best)
(ምን ፡ ይሻላል *mən yəššalal* what should be done?)
አሻለ *aššalä* improve (vt.), relieve (reduce the pain), ameliorate
ተሻሻለ *täšašalä* improve (vi.), ameliorate (vi.), be amended
አሻሻለ *aššašalä* ameliorate (vt.), improve (vt.), remedy, revise (the constitution, a story), amend, reform
መሻሻል *mäššašal* advance (progress), advancement (improvement), betterment, reform, progress, revision (of the constitution, of a story)
ማሻሻያ *maššašaya* means of ameliorating
የማሻሻያ ፡ ሓሳብ amendment

ሽል *šəl* foetus, embryo

ሾለ *šolä* be pointed, be sharpened (a point)

አሾለ *ašolä* sharpen
ሹል *šul* pointed, sharp (point)
የሾለ *yäšolä* pointed

ሾላ *šola* kind of sycamore

ሻለለ *šällälä* (B) chant war songs
ሽለላ *šəlläla* war song

ሸለመ *šällämä* (B) decorate (give a medal), award, adorn
ሽልማት, see below

ሽልማት *šəlləmat* reward, award, decoration (medal), prize (medal), medal (see ሸለመ)
የሽልማት ፡ ድርጅት Prize Trust

ሸለቆ *šäläqo* valley
የወንዝ ፡ ሸለቆ river basin

ሻለቃ *šaläqa* major (in the army), battalion

ሸለቀቀ *šäläqqäqä* husk, strip off the husk

ሸለብታ *šäläbta* nap (n.)

ሸለተ *šällätä* (B) shear

ሾለከ *šolläkä* slip away, slip through, creep through, sneak out
አሾለከ *ašolläkä* slide through (vt.), slip (under the door), let slip through
ሹልክ ፡ አለ *šulləkk alä* slip away
ሹልክ ፡ ብሎ ፡ ወጣ slip out, slip away, sneak out, glide out, steal away
ሹልክ ፡ ብሎ ፡ ገባ sneak in, steal into, insinuate oneself into
አሾለኮ ፡ አየ *ašolləko ayyä* peek
መሿለኪያ *mäšš"aläkiya* underpass, tunnel

ሸለፈት *šäläfät* foreskin
የብልት ፡ ሸለፈት foreskin

*ሻመ, ተሻመ *täšamma* scramble, struggle to obtain something desirable
አሻመ *aššamma* make scramble, make ambiguous

አሻሚ *aššami* ambiguous
ሽሚያ *šəmmiya* (n.) scramble, struggle (to obtain something desirable)

ሻማ *šamma* Ethiopian toga-like national dress

ሹም *šum* (pl. ሹማምንት *šumamənt*) chief, official, officer (of a club); see ሾመ
(የ)ሹም ፡ ሽር dismissal from office, reshuffling of offices
ጭቃ ፡ ሹም village headman

ሻማ *šama* candle, candlelight

ሾመ *šomä* nominate, appoint to an office, promote, invest with an office
ሹም, see above
ሹመት, see below

ሻምላ *šamla* sabre

ሸመል *šəmäl* bamboo, cane

ሸመቀ *šämmäqä* (B) hide, conceal

ሸመቀቀ(ው) *šämäqqäqä(w)* have a cramp
ተሸመቀቀ *täšämäqqäqä* wince, crawl (of flesh)
አሸማቀቀ *aššämaqqäqä* cramp (vt.)
ተሸማቀቀ *täšämaqqäqä* double over (with pain), cringe

ሻምበል *šambäl* captain (of army), company (military unit); see አምበል

ሽምብራ *šəmbəra* chickpea

ሻምበቆ *šämbäqqo* bamboo, cane, reed
ለጋ ፡ ሻምበቆ bamboo shoot

ሸመተ *šämmätä* (B) buy grain or other cereals, sell grain

ሹመት *šumät* office (job), appointment (to office), promotion (to a higher office); see ሾመ

ሻማኔ *šämmane* weaver
የሻማኔ ፡ እቃ loom

ሸሚዝ *šämiz* shirt, blouse
ሸሚዙን ፡ ሰበሰበ gather the sleeves, roll up the sleeves

ሽሚያ, see ሽማ

ሸመደደ *šämäddädä* cram (learn hurriedly)

ሸመገለ *šämäggälä* become old, arbitrate, reconcile
አሸመገለ *ašämäggälä* age (vt.)
ሸማግሌ *šəmagəlle* old man, old gentleman, elder (n.), respectable person, arbiter
ሽምግልና *šəmgələnna* old age, arbitration

ሻምፒዮን *šampiyon* champion (in a game)

ሸራ *šära* canvas
ሸራ ፡ አልጋ cot
የመርከብ ፡ ሸራ sail (n.)

ሻረ *šarä* annul, abrogate (a law), dismiss (from office), abolish, rescind, nullify, cancel, override, repeal, reverse (a decision), invalidate, demote; heal (of a wound), be cured
አሻረ *ašarä* act as a laxative, cure (vt.)
ሽር *šər*, in (የ)ሹም ፡ ሽር dismissal from office, reshuffling of offices
መሻር *mäššar* demotion
የማይሻር *yämmayəššar* irrevocable
የማይሻር ፡ የማይለወጥ *yämmayəššar yämmayəlläwwäṭ* hard and fast (rule)

ሽር, see ሻረ

ሽሮ *šəro*, ሹሮ *šuro* mush made of peas

ሸርሙጣ *šärmuṭa* prostitute

ሸረሪት *šärärit* spider
የሸረሪት ፡ ድር cobweb, spiderweb

ሸረሸረ *šäräššärä* erode, undermine (a house), wear away (of water wearing away the rocks)

*ሸረሸረ, ተንሸራሸረ *tänšarraššärä* promenade, walk around, take a walk; be digested (food)
ሸርሸር *šərrəšərr* walk, excursion, stroll, hike, picnic, outing
መንሸራሸር *mänšärašär*, in የምግብ ፡ መንሸራሸር digestion
(በመኪና ፡ መንሸራሸር drive, n. (by car)

ሹሩባ *šurrubba* braided hairdo

ሹራብ *šurrab* sweater
የእጅ ፡ ሹራብ glove
የእግር ፡ ሹራብ sock, stocking
የእግር ፡ ሹራብ ፡ አደረገ wear stockings

ሾርባ *šorba* soup, broth

*ሸረተተ, ተንሸራተተ *tänšärattätä* glide, slide (vi.), slip, skid
ሸርታቴ *šärtätte* slide (surface for sliding)

ሸርካ *šərka*, ሸሪክ *šärik* partner, associate
ሸርክና *šərkənna* partnership

ሸርጥ *šärrəṭ* apron
ሸርጥ ፡ አሸረጠ *šärrəṭ ašärräṭä* wear an apron

ሸርጣን *šärṭan* crab

ሸረፈ *šärräfä* chip (vt.), notch, break something at the edge, change money (from bills to coins)
ሸራረፈ *šärarräfä* wear away (vt.)
ተሸራረፈ *täšärarräfä* chip (vi.), become chipped

ሹሮፕ *šurop* syrup

ሸሸ *šäššä* flee, run away, avoid, shrink from, recede, shirk, ebb
አሸሸ *ašäššä* put to flight, spirit away
ሸሺ *šäši*, ሸሽ *šäš* fugitive
ሸሽት, see below
መሸሻ *mäšäša* refuge

ሻሽ *šaš* gauze, muslin, kerchief (worn on the head)
ሻሽ ፡ አሰረ wear a headdress

ሸሽት *šəššət* flight, rout (see ሸሸ)

ሸሸገ *šäššägä* (B) hide, conceal, dissimulate, hold back, vt. (hide)
ተሸሸገ *täšäššägä* hide (vi.), be hidden
መሸሸጊያ *mäššäšägiya* haven (for fugitives), hideout

*ሸቀበ, አሸቀበ *aššaqqäbä* ascend a slope, look up
ሸቅበ *šäqqəb* upward
ሸቅብ ፡ ሸቅብ ፡ አደረገ *šäqqəbb šäqqəbb adärrägä* dandle (a baby on the knees)

ሸቀጥ *šäqäṭ* merchandise
ሸቀጣ ፡ ሸቀጥ *šäqäṭa šäqäṭ* merchandise, goods

ሸባ *šäba* lame (leg, man), crippled (leg, man)
ሸባ ፡ ሆነ be paralyzed
ሸባ ፡ አደረገ paralyze

ሸቦ *šäbo* wire, stitch (made by a doctor)
የሸቦ ፡ ቤት cage
የሸክ ፡ ሸቦ barbed wire

ሻቦላ *šabola*, in የሻቦላ ፡ ግጥሚያ fencing (sport)

*ሸበለለ, ተሸበለለ *täšäbällälä* curl, vi. (of parchment)

ሸብለቅ *šäbəlləq* wedge

*ሸበረ, ተሸበረ *täšäbbärä* be excited, be panic-stricken, be alarmed, feel jittery, be appalled
አሸበረ *aššäbbärä* agitate (excite), fill with panic, terrorize, alarm, upset (of bad news), reduce to chaos
ሸብር *šäbbər* panic, excitement, commotion, unrest, riot, revolution, furor
የሚሸብር *yämmiššäbbär* excitable

*ሽበረቀ, አሽበረቀ *ašäbärräqä* be resplendent, sparkle (with decorations),
glitter, glisten, blaze (with light), be
flashing, be illuminated, be elegant
(dress)

ሽበሽበ *šäbäššäbä* wrinkle (v.)
ሽብሽብ *šəbšəb* wrinkle, n. (in the
forehead)

ሽበተ *šäbbätä* (B) turn white (hair),
turn gray, have white hair
ሽበት *šəbät* gray hair, white hair
የደንጊያ : ሽበት moss (on rocks)
ሽበቶ *šäbbätto* gray-haired

ሽታ, see ሽተተ

ሽቶ, see ሽተተ

ሽተተ *šättätä* smell (vi.), give off an
odor, putrefy, stink
ሽተተ(ው) *šättätä(w)* smell (vt.)
አሽተተ *ašättätä* smell (vt.), sniff
ሽታ *šätta* odor, smell, aroma, stink
ሽቶ *šätto* perfume, scent

ሾተል *šotäl* sword

*ሽተተ, ተንሻተተ *tänšattätä* slip down,
slide

ሽና *šänna* urinate
ሽንት *šənt* urine

ሽነሽነ *šänäššänä* pleat, gather in (the
skirt)
ሽንሽኖ : አካፈለ *šänšəno akkaffälä*
parcel out
ሽንሽን *šänšən* pleat (n.), gathering
at the waist

ሻንቅላ *šanqəlla* Negro

ሽንት *šənt* urine (see ሽና)
ሽንት : ቤት toilet, lavatory
የሴቶች : ሽንት : ቤት ladies' room
የወንዶች : ሽንት : ቤት men's room

ሽንተረር *šäntärär* mountain chain,
mountain range

ሽንኩር : አገዳ *šänkʷär agäda* sugar
cane stalk

ሽንኩርት *šənkurt* onion
ቀይ : ሽንኩርት onion
ነጭ : ሽንኩርት garlic

ሽንጎ *šängo* forum, council, assembly
of elders
ሽንጎ : ያዘ hold an assembly

ሽነገለ *šänäggälä* flatter
ተሽነገለ *täšänäggälä* feel flattered
ሽንገላ *šəngäla* flattery

ሽንጐበት *šängʷäbät* chin, beard

ሻንጣ *šanṭa* suitcase, valise, trunk

ሽንጥ *šänṭ* hip, flank (side of body)

*ሽነፈ, አሽነፈ *aššännäfä* (B) conquer,
win a battle, win a game, be victorious, defeat, overcome, overpower,
prevail, get the upper hand
ተሽነፈ *täšännäfä* lose (a game), suffer
defeat
አሽናፊ *aššännafi* winner, victor, victorious
አሽናፊነት *aššännafinnät* champion-
ship

ሻኘ *šäññä* (B) accompany, see off,
escort

ሻኛ *šäñña* hump (of cattle)

ሹካ *šukka* fork

ሹክ *šukk* tip (secret information); see
also *ሿከሿከ
ሹክ : አለ *šukk alä* whisper, tip
off (give secret information)
ሹክክ : ያለ *šukəkk yalä* furtive
(manner)

ሽክ : አለ *šəkk alä* be all dressed up,
be well dressed

ሾክ *šok* thorn, spine (see also ሾህ, አሾክ)
የሾክ : ሽቦ barbed wire

ሽክላ *šäkla* clay, pottery, pot, earthenware, record (for music); see also
ሽሀላ
ሽክላ : ማጫወቻ *šäkla maččawäča*

phonograph, record player
ሽክላ ፡ ሠሪ potter
የሽክላ porcelain (adj.)
(የ)ሽክላ ፡ ምጣድ clay griddle
የሽክላ ፡ ሳሕን china, porcelain
የሽክላ ፡ እቃ earthenware
የሙዚቃ ፡ ሽክላ record (of music,
songs)

*ሽከሞ, ተሽከሞ täšäkkämä (B) carry,
bear (carry), sustain (weight), be
loaded
አሽከሞ aššäkkämä put a load on,
help to carry
ሽክም šäkəm load, charge, burden
ተሽካሚ täšäkkami porter

ሻከረ šakkärä be rough, be harsh, be
strained (relations), turn sour (friendship)
አሻከረ ašakkärä roughen, strain
(relations)
ሻካራ šakara rough (fur, surface),
coarse (cloth, table), harsh (soap)

*ሽኮረሞም, አሽኮረሞም aškorämmämä
court (v.)
የሚያሽኮረምም yämmiyaškorämməm
suitor (who is courting a woman)

*ሽከረከረ, ተሽከረከረ täškäräkkärä ro-
tate (vi.), turn, vi. (rotate), revolve,
pivot, swivel, spin (vi.), whirl
around, roll along
አሽከረከረ aškäräkkärä twirl, spin
(a top)
መሽከርከር mäškärkär revolution (of
the earth)
መሽከርከሪያ mäškärkäriya pivot
ተሽከርካሪ täškärkari vehicle

ሽከሸከ šäkäššäkä pound grain

*ሾካሾከ, አንሾካሾከ anšokaššokä whisper
(v.); see ሹ-ክ
ሹክሹክታ šukšukta whisper (n.)

ሻኩና šäkʷäna foot of a beast, hoof
(see also ሰኩና)

*ሽካካ, አሽካካ aškakka neigh, snort
(of horses)
(The root is perhaps ካካ with the
morpheme አሽ-)

ሹከከ ፡ አለ šukəkk alä be furtive
(manner); see ሹ-ክ

ሽኮኮ šəkokko squirrel

ሾዋ šäwa Shoa

ሾ ፡ አለ šəww alä shoot ahead (see
also ሾ-ሾ-)
ሾ- ፡ ብሎ ፡ አለፈ flash by, roar
past, whiz
ሾ-ታ, see below

ሾ-ረ-ረ- šäwrarra cross-eyed

ሾ-ሾ ፡ አደረገ šäwwəšäww adärrägä
swish (see ሾ- ፡ አለ)

ሾ-ታ šäwwəta whiff (of air); see ሾ- ፡
አለ
የነፋስ ፡ ሾ-ታ breeze

ሻይ šay tea

ሽያጭ šəyyač sale (see ሻጠ)

*ሻገረ, ተሻገረ täšaggärä cross (a river),
clear (a ditch), traverse
አሻገረ aššaggärä make cross, take
across
(እንኳን ፡ ከዘመን ፡ ወደ ፡ ዘመን ፡
አሻገረም Happy New Year!)
ሻገር ፡ ብሎ šagärr bəlo just across
መሻጋገር mäššägagär transition
ማሻገሪያ maššagäriya ferry, ford,
thing used to cross a river, fording
place, place where one crosses over
መሻጋገሪያ mäššägagäriya gangplank
ተሻጋሪ täšagari transitive (verb)
አሻግሮ aššagro across
አያሻግርም ayaššaggərəm impassable
የማይሻጋር yämmayəššaggär intransitive (verb)
ከ - - - ባሻገር kä - - - baššaggär
beyond (prep.), across

ሻገተ šaggätä be moldy, be covered
with mildew

ሽጋታ *šagata* mildew

ሽጕጠ *šäggʷäṭä* (B) tuck (put away out of sight)
ሽጕጥ ፡ ብሎ ፡ ቆም *šägguṭṭ bälo qomä* hide by crouching
ሽጕጥ, see below

ሽጕጥ *šägguṭ* pistol, revolver (see ሽጕጠ)
ሽጕጥ ፡ ታጠቀ —*taṭṭäqä* wear a gun, strap on a pistol

ሽጠ *šäṭä* sell, sell out
ሻጭ *šač* seller, salesman, vendor, clerk (who waits on customers)
ሽያጭ *šəyyač* sale
አሻሻጭ *aššašač* salesclerk, salesman
መሽጫ, see above

ሽጥ ፡ አደረገ *šäṭṭ adärrägä* slip (into the pocket)

ሾጥ ፡ አደረገ *šoṭṭ adärrägä* flick (with a whip)

ሻጭ, see ሽጠ

ሽፍ ፡ አለ *šäff alä* have a rash (see also ችፍ ፡ አለ)
ሽፍታ *šäffəta* rash

*ሾፈ, አሾፈ *ašofä* tease, poke fun, make fun of, be facetious, mock, deride

ሽፈል *šəfal* eyebrow

*ሽፈረ, see አሻፈረ

ሾፌር *šofer* chauffeur

ሽፈሽፍት *šəfašəft* eyebrow

ሽፈተ *šäffätä* (B) become a rebel, become an outlaw
ሽፍታ *šəfta* outlaw, bandit, brigand, rebel

ሽፍታ *šäffəta* rash (see ሽፍ ፡ አለ)

ሽፈነ *šäffänä* (B) cover, hide (vt.), conceal, enshroud, veil (of fog)
(ዓይን ፡ ሽፈነ blindfold)
ሽፈፈነ *šäfaffänä* gloss over, cover slightly

ሽፈን *šäfan* cover (of book), wrapping, casing
(የዓይን ፡ ሽፈን eyelid)
መሽፈኛ *mäšäffäňňa* cover, lid

ሽፈጠ *šäffäṭä* (B) deny falsely, deceive, dupe
ሽፍጥ *šäfṭ* perfidy, fraud
ሽፍጠኛ *šäfṭäňňa* perfidious
ሽፋጭ, see below

ሽፋጭ *šäffač* dishonest (person); see ሽፈጠ

ቀ

ቀላ *qälla* redden, become red
አቀላ *aqälla* inflame (make red hot)
ቀላ ፡ ያለ *qäla yalä* reddish, pink
†ቀይ *qäyy* red

ቀላ *qälla* decapitate

ቂል *qil* fool, silly, simple-minded, imbecile

ቃል *qal* (pl. ቃላት *qalat*) word, sound, term (expression), text, statement (in court)
ቃል ፡ በቃል verbatim, word for word, literally
ቃል ፡ ሰጠ promise, make a promise, pledge
ቃል ፡ ገባ promise, make a promise, pledge, make a commitment, guarantee
ቃል ፡ አቀባይ spokesman, reporter, correspondent (of a newspaper)
ቃል ፡ ኪዳን agreement, pact, pledge, promise, covenant, treaty, vows (marital)
ቃል ፡ ኪዳን ፡ ገባ make a pledge
ቃለ ፡ መሐላ pledge of allegiance
ቃለ ፡ አጋኖ exclamation (see ገነነ)
ቃለ ፡ ጉባኤ minutes (of a meeting)
በቃል by rote, by heart, from memory, orally, verbally
በቃል ፡ አጠና memorize, learn by heart (see ጠና)

በቃል ፡ ወጣ recite
በቃል ፡ ያዘ learn by heart
ከቃል ፡ ወጣ disobey
የቃል verbal, oral
የቃል ፡ አገባብ context
የቃል ፡ ጥያቄ interview
ዐሥርቱ ፡ ቃላት ፡ ኦሪት the Ten Commandments
ክፍለ ፡ ቃል syllable

ቅል qəl gourd
የራስ ፡ ቅል skull (see ራስ)
እየቅሉ əyyäqəlu individually

ቄላ qʷälla wag (the tail)

ቄላ , ቆላ qʷälla, qolla parch, roast (grain, coffee)
(ረኃብ ፡ ቄላው· hunger tormented him)
ቆሎ qolo roasted grain, parched grain

ቄላ , ቆላ qʷälla, qolla low country, lowland (between sea level and 5000 ft. elevation)
የቄላ ፡ ቁስል ulcer (external)
ቆላኛ qolläñña inhabitant of the lowland

ቀለህ qäläh rifle shell, cartridge case, empty cartridge

ቀለለ qällälä be light (of weight), be easy, lack discretion
አቀለለ aqällälä make easy, make lighter, lighten, simplify
ተቃለለ täqallälä ease up, be lightened, be dishonored
አቃለለ aqqallälä simplify, facilitate, ease, relieve, alleviate (distress), mitigate, allay, minimize, belittle, despise
ቀላል qällal easy, simple, light (weight, duty), mild (punishment), minor (injury)
በቀላሉ bäqällalu easily, lightly, simply

ቄለለ qʷällälä (B) pile (vt.), heap up
ቁልል qulləl (n.) heap, pile

ቀለም qällämä (v.) dye, stain
ማቅለሚያ maqlämiya pigment, dye

ቀለም , see below

ቀለም qäläm (pl. ቀለማት qälämat) color, paint, dye, stain, polish, ink, learning, education
ቀለማት decoration
ቀለም ፡ ነከረ dye (v.)
የቀለም ፡ ልዩነት discrimination
የቀለም ፡ መርገጫ inkpad
የቀለም ፡ ትምህርት academic training
የቀለም ፡ ጓደኛ school companion
የቀለማት ፡ ስሕተት spelling errors
የከንፈር ፡ ቀለም lipstick

ቋሊማ qʷalima sausage

*ቀለሸለሸ , አቅለሸለሸ aqläšälläšä nauseate, make feel nauseous
አቅለሸለሸ(ው·) aqläšälläšä(w) be overcome by nausea

*ቀለቀለ , ተንቀለቀለ tänqäläqqälä blaze (of fire), be restless

ቀላቀለ qälaqqälä mix, blend together, combine, mingle, annex (a conquered territory)
ተቀላቀለ täqälaqqälä be mixed, mingle (vi.), be added, merge (vi.), affiliate, join with others, associate (vi.)
አቀላቀለ aqqälaqqälä mix (vt.), mingle (vt.), combine (mix), aggregate
ቅልቅል qələqqəl mixture, mixed, mash (a mixture of various kinds of food)

ቁልቁል , ቁልቁለት , see ቄለቄለ

ቁልቋል qulqʷal euphorbia, cactus

*ቄለቄለ , አቁለቄለ aqʷäläqqʷälä slope down, decline (slope down), lower, vi. (of sun)
ተቄለቄለ täqʷäläqqʷälä descend a slope
ቁልቁል qulqul downward
ቁልቁል ፡ ሲል downhill
ቁልቁለት qulqulät downhill slope, descent (slope)
ቁልቁለቱን qulqulätun downhill

ቄልቄለቱን ፡ ወረደ go downhill
መሸቆልቆል, see above

ቀለበ *qälläbä* catch in midair (ball or a
falling object)

ቀለበ *qälläbä* (B) feed (oxen), provide
support, nourish
ቀለብ *qälläb* food supplies, rations,
stipend
የቤት ፡ ቀለብ supplies (of food)
የቤት ፡ ቀላቢት *yäbet qällabit* housekeeper

ቀልብ *qälb* mind, intelligence, power of
reasoning
ቀልበ ፡ ቢስ scatterbrain
ቀልባም *qälbam* prudent

ቃሊብ *qalib* mold (casting)

ቀለበሰ *qäläbbäsä* turn down (the collar)

ቀለበት *qäläbät* ring (finger ring), loop
የቀለበት ፡ ጣት ring finger

ቃልቻ *qalläčča* magician

ቆለኛ, see ቄላ

ቀላዋጭ *qälawaç* one who goes from
house to house to get food, parasite

ቀለደ *qällädä* (B) joke, have fun, play
a joke on, make fun of, trifle, kid,
tease
ተቃለደ *täqallädä* joke with each
other, joke with people
ቀልድ, see below

ቀላድ *qälad* rope serving to measure
land, land that is measured

ቀልድ *qäld* joke, fun, jest, mockery,
farce, wit, humor (see ቀለደ)
ቀልደኛ *qäldäñña* joker, witty, jocular
ቀልደኛ ፡ ነህ no kidding, are you
kidding?
ቀልደኛነት *qäldäññannät* sense of humor

ቀለጠ *qällätä* melt, vi. (of butter, of

metal), liquefy, vi. (of butter), be
animated (applause), to be in quantity (of an item)
አቀለጠ *aqällätä* liquefy, vt. (butter),
smelt (ore), melt (vt.), thaw (the ice),
cause to resound
የቀለጠ *yäqällätä* molten (metal)
የቀለጠ ፡ ሀብታም very rich
ማቅለጫ *maqläça* melting pot
መቅለጫ *mäqläça*, in የብረት ፡ መቅ
ለጫ foundry

ቅልጠም *qältäm* marrow, shin, shin-
bone, shank

ቀለጠፈ *qälättäfä* hasten (vi.), hurry
(vi.), make haste, be quick in doing
something
አቀለጠፈ *aqälättäfä* make to hasten,
hasten (vt.)
ቀልጣፋ *qältaffa* quick, rapid, fast,
swift, supple, deft, nimble (acrobat),
agile, dexterous, handy, skillful,
efficient, expeditious, facile (writer)
ቅልጥፍና, see below
አቀላጠፈ *aqqälatfo* fluently
የቀለጠፈ *yäqälättäfä* limber (piano
player)

ቅልጥፍና *qältəfənna* dispatch (promptness), dexterity, efficiency, skill (facility); see ቀለጠፈ
ቅልጥፍና ፡ ጐደለው be clumsy
በቅልጥፍና skillfully

ቁልጭ ፡ ቁልጭ ፡ አለ *qulləčč qulləčč
alä* light up (of eyes); see *ቄለጨለጨ

*ቄለጨለጨ, ተቀ°ለጨለጨ *täqʷläčälläčä*
blink repeatedly (of eyes); see ቁልጭ

*ቀላፋ, እንቀላፋ *anqälaffa* doze, fall
asleep
እንቅልፍ *ənqəlf* sleep (n.)

ቁልፍ *qulf* key, button, snap (of dress);
see ቄለፈ
ቁልፍ ፡ ሠራተኛ locksmith
ቁልፍ ፡ ያዥ custodian, guard (see
ያዘ)

የቁልፍ ፡ ቀዳዳ keyhole
የቁልፍ ፡ እናት lock
የቁልፍ ፡ ጋን lock
መርፌ ፡ ቁልፍ safety pin
የእጅጌ ፡ ቁልፍ cuff link

ቄሰፈ *q*ʷ*älläfä* (B) lock (vt.), close with a key, buckle, button, hook (a dress), fasten
ተቄሰፈ *täq*ʷ*älläfä*, passive of the preceding; lock (vi.)
ተቄሳሰፈ *täq*ʷ*älalläfä* be locked together (bumpers)
አቄሳሰፈ *aqq*ʷ*älalläfä* interlace (vt.), couple together (two cars)
ቁልፍ, see above
መቄሰፈያ ፡ ጋን *mäq*ʷ*älläfiya gan* lock

ቀማ *qämma* (B) rob, take by force, carry away by force, snatch from the hand
†ቀማኛ *qämmañña* brigand, robber

*ቀማ, አቅማማ *aqmamma* falter (hesitate), play with the idea of doing something

ቁም *qum*, see ቆመ
ቁም ፡ ለቁም lengthwise
ቁም ፡ ሣጥን cupboard, cabinet, wardrobe (closet)
(ባለመሳቢያ ፡ ቁም ፡ ሣጥን chest of drawers)
ቁም ፡ ነገር worthwhile thing, important matter, significance, serious matter, basic thing, essential thing
ቁም ፡ ነገር ፡ አለው carry weight
ቁም ፡ ነገረኛ trustworthy (person), dutiful (person)
ቁም ፡ ጸሐፊ scribe, calligrapher
(የ)ቁም ፡ ጽሕፈት calligraphy
በቁሙ in his lifetime
በቁሙ ፡ ቀረ be unchanging, be constant

ቂም *qim* resentment, grudge, rancor, ill feeling, revenge (see *ቀየመ)
ቂም ፡ በቀል vengeance, feud
ቂም ፡ ያዘ nurse a grudge

ቂመኛ *qimäñña* vindictive, person who holds a grudge

ቃመ *qamä* swallow without chewing, eat powdery things (roasted grain, sugar) from the hand

ቆመ *qomä* stop (vi.), be erected, stand, stand up, halt (vi.), come to a halt, cease, land (of a ship), be under way (of market)
(ቆማ ፡ ቀረች she is an old maid)
አቆመ *aqomä* stand something up, erect (a monument), raise, bring to rest, arrest (stop), put an end to, stop (vt.), bring to a stop, halt (vt.), park (a car), settle (an argument)
ተቃወመ *täqawwämä* be against, oppose, be opposed to, hinder, protest, resist, object, raise an objection, contradict, dissent, disapprove, take issue with, defy (the authority)
ተቋቋመ *täq*ʷ*aq*ʷ*amä* be established, be founded, be set up, be constituted, come into being, withstand (oppose), defy, resist, fight against, counter, cope with, come to grips with (a problem)
አቋቋመ *aqq*ʷ*aq*ʷ*amä* establish, set up (a business), situate, build (a factory), found (a bank), organize (a committee)
ቆም ፡ አለ *qomm alä* pause (v.)
ቁም, see above
ቋሚ *q*ʷ*ami* permanent, steady (work), salaried (employee), skeleton (of building)
(ቋሚ ፡ ሥራ career)
(ቋሚ ፡ ንብረት immovable property)
ቁመት, see below
አቋም *aq*ʷ*am* stand (position), standpoint, approach (attitude), structure (of human body, of organization), makeup, framework, bearing (manner)
ተቃዋሚ *täqawami* opponent, dissident
ተቃውሞ *täqawmo* opposition, ob-

jection, protest, resistance, disapproval (expression against)
(ካላንዳች ፡ ተቃውሞ unopposed; see አንዳች)
መቃወም *mäqqawäm* opposition
(በመቃወም against, in opposition)
መቋቋም *mäqqʷaqʷam*, in የመቋቋም ፡ ኃይል resistance (power of resisting)
መቋሚያ *mäqʷamiya* prayer stick
መቆሚያ, see above

ቀመለ *qämmälä* be filled with lice; (B) remove lice
ቅማል *qəmal* louse

ቀመመ *qämmämä* (B) add condiments, add spices, season (v.)
ቀማሚ *qämmami*, in መድኃኒት ፡ ቀማሚ druggist, pharmacist
ቅመም, see below

ቅመም *qəmäm* spice, condiment, seasoning (see ቀመመ)
ቅመማ ፡ ቅመም *qəmäma qəmäm* all kinds of spices, ingredients, seasoning
ቅመም ፡ የሌለው bland (food)
ቅመም ፡ የበዛበት —*yäbäzzabbät* spicy

ቀመረ *qämmärä* reckon (time)

ቁማር *qumar* gambling, game of chance
ቁማር ፡ ተጫወተ gamble (v.); see *ጫወተ
ቁማርተኛ *qumartäňňa* gambler

ቀመሰ *qämmäsä* taste, take a taste, eat a little
(ኑር ፡ ቀመሰ experience life)
አቀመሰ *aqämmäsä* give someone something to taste

ቀሚስ *qämis* gown, dress (of woman)
ጉርድ ፡ ቀሚስ skirt

ቀመቀመ *qämäqqämä* hem (v.)
ቅምቅማት *qəmqəmat* hem (n.)

ቀምበር, see ቀንበር

ቁመት *qumät* size (of a person), height (of man), stature (see ቆመ)

ቀማኛ *qämmaňňa* robber, brigand (see ቀማ)
ቀማኛነት *qämmaňňannät* robbery
ቂመኛ, see ቂም

*ቀመጠ, ተቀመጠ *täqämmäṭä* (B) sit, sit down, seat oneself, settle (vi.), sojourn, mount (a horse, mule), ascend (the throne), be put away (set apart), be set aside
አስቀመጠ *asqämmäṭä* place, seat, make to sit, lay, set apart, set aside, save, put aside, keep (reserve), store, deposit, purge (of medicine)
የቅምጥ *yäqəmmәṭ* sitting, seated
መቀመጫ *mäqqämäča* seat
ማስቀመጫ *masqämmäča* container, depository, repository, saucer
ተቀማጭ, see below
ተቀማጭ *täqämmač* resident, reserve (saved money), savings deposit
አቀማመጥ *aqqämamäṭ* manner of sitting, seating, location, placement, situation (position), layout
የሚያስቀምጥ ፡ መድኃኒት *yämmiyasqämmәṭ mädhanit* purgative

ቁምጣ *qumṭa* shorts, short trousers

ቆመጥ *qomäṭ* cudgel

ቆማጣ *qomaṭa*, ቁማጣ *qʷämaṭa* leper, leperous, maimed by leprosy
ቁምጥና *qumṭәnna* leprosy

ቀረ *qärrä* be left, remain, be missing, be absent, absent oneself, stay away, be cancelled (meeting), be omitted, be no longer in existence, go out of use, die out (of custom), be called off
(ኋላ ፡ ቀረ stay behind)
(ወደ ፡ ኋላ ፡ ቀረ be slow (of watch), be backward, lag)
(እንደወጣ ፡ ቀረ he never returned, he is still missing)

አስቀረ *asqärrä* make remain, leave, leave out, abolish, exclude, cancel, omit (details), deprive, prevent (keep from happening), keep out (vt.), keep aside (vt.), hold back (vt.), put an end to, waive
(ወደ ፡ ኋላ ፡ አስቀረ cause to lag behind)
ቀርቶ *qärto* let alone, leaving aside
(ሌላው ፡ ቀርቶ to say nothing of others)
ቢቀረው *biqäräw*, in እንድ ፡ ቀን ፡ ቢቀ ረው one day before
ቢቀር *biqär*, in ሌላው ፡ ቢቀር let alone
ሳይቀር *sayqär*, in እንድም ፡ ሳይቀር without exception
ቀሪ *qäri* balance, remainder, residual
ቀሪ ፡ ገንዘብ balance
ቅሪት, see below
የቀረ *yäqärrä* absent (adj.), extinct, rest (remaining), remnant
የቀረው ፡ ቢቀር at least, at worst
የማይቀር *yämmayəqär* unavoidable
ል + imperfect + ምንም ፡ አልቀረውም come to the point of doing something, almost, nearly
ስ + negative imperfect + አይቀርም be liable to, most probably (as in ሳይመጣ ፡ አይቀርም he will most probably come, he may come)
[See also በቀር, በተቀር, በስተቀር, ይቅር, ይቅርታ]

*ቀራ, see ቀራራ

ቁራ *qura* crow, raven

ቁር *qur*, in የራስ ፡ ቁር helmet

ቃር *qar* heartburn

ቄራ *qera* slaughterhouse

ቅር ፡ አለ(ው) *qərr alä(w)* be discontented, be disappointed, be sore (vexed), feel amiss, have misgivings, have ill will
ቅር ፡ አሰኘ *qərr assäňňä* disappoint, be disappointing, dissatisfy, hurt one's feelings, irk, make gloomy,

slight, chagrin, depress, make resentful
ቅር ፡ ተሰኘ *qərr täsäňňä* be dissatisfied, be disenchanted, feel aggrieved, be chagrined, be resentful
ቅሬታ, see below

ቃረመ *qarrämä* glean, pick up (information)

*ቀራራ, አቅራራ *aqrarra* sing a battle song
ቀራርቶ *qärärto* war cry, battle song

ቄርስ, see ቄረስ

ቅርስ *qərs* heritage, heirloom, legacy, relic

ቄረስ *qʷärräsä* tear off a portion (of bread and other things), cut bread
ቁርስ *qurs* breakfast
ቁራሽ *qurraš* piece (of bread)

*ቀረሸ, አቀረሸ *aqäräššä* regurgitate

ቁራሽ, see ቄረስ

ቅርሽም ፡ አለ *qəršəmm alä* crack, vi. (of branch)

ቀረቀረ *qäräqqärä* bolt (the gate), bar (the gate)
ተቀረቀረ *täqäräqqärä* be wedged, be lodged (be caught), get stuck (get caught), be jammed

ቄረቄረ *qʷäräqqʷärä* found (a city), establish (a city)

ቄረቄረ *qʷäräqqʷärä* cause discomfort (e.g. lumpy bed)

*ቄረቄረ, ተንቄረቄረ *tänqʷäräqqʷärä* exude, pour down (of sweat)
አንቄረቄረ *anqʷäräqqʷärä* pour water in a thin stream, decant
ማንቄርቄሪያ *manqʷärqʷäriya* pitcher

ቆርቆሮ *qorqorro* tin, tin can, corrugated iron
ቆርቆር ፡ መክፈቻ can opener
ቆርቆር ፡ ቤት house with tin roof

በቆርቆር ፡ አሽን can (food)
የቆርቆር ፡ ምግብ canned food

ቀረቀበ *qäräqqäbä* join two packs into a single load before putting them on the pack animal, tie up a load
ቅርቃብ *qərqab* load, pack

ቅራቅንቦ *qəraqənbo* odds and ends

ቄቄዘ *q*ʷ*äräqq*ʷ*äzä* fail to grow (of grain), be dwarfed, be stunted
አቄቄዘ *aq*ʷ*äräqq*ʷ*äzä* dwarf, vt. (of diet), stunt

ቀረበ *qärräbä* approach, come close, come near, be near, appear (stand before an authority), come forward, be presented to, be served (food), be submitted (bill, resolution)
አቀረበ *aqärräbä* present, offer, bring near, put forward, serve (dinner), convey (greetings), introduce (a bill), submit (a proposal), bring to the attention of (see also ሐሳብ)
ተቃረበ *täqarräbä* near (vi.), come near, approach, approximate
አቃረበ *aqqarräbä* bring together
ተቀራረበ *täqärarräbä* be in close vicinity, be about the same
አቀራረበ *aqqärarräbä* bring together, cause to come to a rapprochement
†ቅርብ *qərb* near (adj.), shallow
መቀራረብ *mäqqäraräb* affinity
ማቅረቢያ *maqräbiya* tray, serving tray
አቀራረብ *aqqäraräb* presentation
አቅራቢያ, see below

ቅርብ *qərb* near (adj.), shallow (see ቀረበ)
በቅርብ recently, close by, closely
በቅርቡ before long, recently, lately, shortly, soon, closely
በቅርብ ፡ ጊዜ recently, shortly, soon
ከቅርብ ፡ ጊዜ ፡ ወዲህ lately, recently
የቅርብ recent, close (friend), intimate (friend)
(የ)ቅርብ ፡ ዘመድ close relative
የቅርብ ፡ ጊዜ recent
ቅርብነት *qərbännät* neighborhood (nearness), vicinity

ቄረበ *q*ʷ*ärräbä* receive holy communion
አቄረበ *aq*ʷ*ärräbä* administer the communion
ቁርባን, see below

ቁርበት *qurbät* tanned hide used as a sleeping mat

ቁርባን *qurban* holy communion, eucharist (see ቄረበ)
የቁርባን ፡ ሥነ ፡ ሥርዓት sacrament of communion

ቅርብነት, see ቅርብ

ቅሪት *qərrit* remainder (see ቀረ)
ቅሪት ፡ አካል fossil

ቅሬታ *qərreta* discontent, resentment, displeasure, disappointment, chagrin, grievance, breach (in friendship); see ቅር ፡ አለ
የቅሬታ reproachful

*ቀረነ, ተቃረነ *täqarränä* go against, clash (of stories), be irreconcilable, contradict, conflict with
ተቃራኒ *täqarani* opponent, opposite, contrary (term), conflicting, converse, inverse, reverse, counterpart, antipode, antithesis
ተቃራኒነት *täqaraninnät* contradiction, opposition, discrepancy (between two accounts)
መቃረን *mäqqarän* contradiction

ቅርንጫፍ *qərənčaf* bough, branch (of tree, of a company), subsidiary (of a company), chapter (of an association)

ቅርንፉድ *qərənfud* clove
የቅርንፉድ ፡ ምስማር screw

ቄረኘ *q*ʷ*äräňňä* bind, attach, shackle
አቄራኘ *aqq*ʷ*äraňňä* tie (prisoner to guard), bind (to a job)
ተቄራኘ *täq*ʷ*äraňňä* be tied (prisoner to guard)
(በካቴና ፡ ተቄራኘ be shackled)
(ከአልጋ ፡ ተቄራኘ be bedridden)

ቄራኛ *quraňňa*, in በዓይን ፡ ቄራኛ ፡ ተመለከተ keep an eye on በዓይን ፡ ቄራኛ ፡ ጠበቀ keep under surveillance
የመጽሐፍ ፡ ቄራኛ bookworm
የአልጋ ፡ ቄራኛ bedridden

ቀርከሻ *qärkäha* wicker cane (plant)

ቃሬዛ *qareza* stretcher, litter (stretcher)

ቃሪያ *qariya* green pepper, immature (person)

ቀረጠ *qärräṭä* tax (v.), make pay custom duties
ቀረጥ, see below

ቀረጠ, see ቀረጸ

ቀረጥ *qäräṭ* tax, taxation, tariff, custom duties (see ቀረጠ)
ቀረጥ ፡ ጣለ tax (v.)
ቀረጥ ፡ ተቀባይ tax collector

ቁርጥ *qurṭ* cut, definite, decided, explicit, just like (see ቀረጠ)
ቁርጥ ፡ ሐሳብ resolution, determination, decision
ቁርጡን ፡ ቃል ፡ ልንገርህ let me tell you once and for all
ቁርጠኛ *qurṭäňňa* definite, resolute

ቁርጥ ፡ ቁርጥ ፡ አለ *qurräṭṭ qurräṭṭ alä* come in gasps (breath), be abrupt (speech, words); see ቀረጠ
ቁርጥ ፡ ያለ *qurräṭṭ yalä* decisive, downright (answer), firm (price), terse, positive, categorical

ቈረጠ *qʷärräṭä* cut, cut down, chop (wood), chop off, hew (logs), cut loose, clip, amputate, disconnect, slice (bread, onions), rupture, determine, decide, fix, make a resolution, make up one's mind, be determined
(ሆዱን ፡ ቈረጠ gripe (of unripe fruit)
(ሐሳቡን ፡ ቈረጠ set one's mind, decide on, resolve)
(ተስፋ ፡ ቈረጠ despair, give up hope, be discouraged, be disheartened)

(ቲኬት ፡ ቈረጠ sell tickets)
(ቆርጦ ፡ ተነሣ *qʷärṭo tänässa* set oneself to, have one's mind set on)
(በነፍሱ ፡ ቆረጠ at the risk of his life)
አስቈረጠ *asqʷärräṭä*, causative of the preceding
(ተስፋ ፡ አስቈረጠ discourage, deject, dishearten)
(ቲኬት ፡ አስቈረጠ buy a ticket)
ተቈረጠ *täqʷarräṭä* discontinue (vi.), be interrupted, cease (vi.), go dead (of telephone)
እቈረጠ *aqqʷarräṭä* cut off, break off (relations), cut short (interrupt), discontinue, cease, sever (relations), terminate, cross (a street, border), take a short cut, cut across (a field), traverse
ቈራረጠ *qʷärarräṭä* mutilate
ቁርጥ, see above
ቈራጥ *qʷärraṭ* resolute, strongminded, determined (person), firm (attitude)
(ሐሳብ ፡ ቈራጥ determined, resolute)
ቈራጥነት, see below
ቁርጠት, see below
ቈራጭ *qʷäraç* one who cuts
(ቲኬት ፡ ቈራጭ ticket seller)
ቁራጭ *qurraç* piece, slice, slab, stub (of pencil), slip (of paper), clipping, butt
ማቈረጥ *maqqʷaräṭ* interruption
(ያለማቈረጥ *yalämaqqʷaräṭ* perpetually, continuously, regularly, on and on)
መቀረጫ *mäqʷräča* clippers
ማቈረጫ *maqqʷaräča* crossing
ማቈረጫ ፡ ስፍራ crosswalk
ተቈራጭ *täqʷaraç*, in ሥራ ፡ ተቈራጭ contractor
እቈራጭ *aqqʷaraç* cutoff, short cut
የማይቈረጥ *yämmayəqqʷarräṭ* constant (ceaseless), continual, perpetual (clatter), persistent
ሳይቈረጥ *sayəqqʷarräṭ* constantly, steadily, regularly, without interruption

[See also ቁርጥራጭ]

ቄረጠመ *qʷäräṭṭämä* chew hard food and make noise, munch (on parched grain)
ቄረጣጠመ *qʷäräṭaṭṭämä* crunch, gnaw
[See also ቁርጥማት]

ቁርጥማት *qurṭəmat* rheumatism (see ቄረጠመ)

ቁርጥራጭ *quraṭračč* slip (of paper), piece, scrap (see ቄረጠ)

ቁርጠት *qurṭät*, in (የ)ሆድ ፡ ቁርጠት stomach ache, colic (see ቄረጠ)
የቁርጠት ፡ ሕመም bellyache

ቄራጠነት *qʷärraṭənnät* resolve (determination), will power, decisive manner (see ቄረጠ)

ቁርጠኛ *qurṭäňňa* definite, resolute (see ቁርጥ)

ቀረጠፈ *qäräṭṭäfä* pinch (of door pinching the finger)

ቁራጭ, see ቄረጠ

ቄራጭ, see ቄረጠ

ቁርጭምጭሚት *qurčəmčəmit* ankle

ቅርጫት *qərčat* kind of basket
የቅርጫት ፡ ኳስ basketball

ቀረጸ *qärräṣä* engrave, carve, incise, cast (a statue), inscribe, impress, sharpen (a point)
ቅርጽ, see below
መቅረጫ *mäqräča* pencil sharpener

ቅርጽ *qərṣ* sculpture, engraving, shape, form, figure (form), outline (of a mountain), contour, features (of face); see ቀረጸ
ቅርጸ ፡ ቢስ shapeless
ቅርጽ ፡ አውጪ sculptor

ቀረፈ *qärräfä* peel off, bark, remove the bark, skin off, decorticate
ተቀረፈ *täqärräfä* peel, vi. (of paint, skin)

ቅርፊት *qərfit* peel, bark (of tree), hull, skin (of apple), scales (of fish), scab, crust, shell
ቅርፍራፊ, see below

ቀረፋ *qäräfa* cinnamon

ቅርፍራፊ *qərəfrafi* flake (of soap); see ቀረፋ

ቅርፊት, see ቀረፋ

ቄረፈደ *qʷäräffädä* be chapped (skin by cold), become horny (skin)
አቄረፈደ *aqʷäräffädä* chap (of cold chapping the skin)
ቄርፈዳ *qʷärfadda* horny (hands)

ቀስ ፡ አለ *qäss alä* slow down, be slow, do something slowly
ቀስ ፡ ብሎ lightly, softly, slowly
ቀስ ፡ በቀስ little by little, step by step, gradually, by degrees, slowly, gently
ቀስታ, in በቀስታ *bäqässəta* slowly, softly
[See also ቅስስ ፡ አለ]

ቄስ *qes* (pl. ቀሳውስት *qäsawəst*) priest (see ቀሰሰ)
ቅስና, see below

ቁስል *qusəl* wound, injury, lesion, sore (see ቄሰለ)
የቆላ ፡ ቁስል ulcer (external)
ቁስለኛ *qusläňňa* wounded man, wounded, injured

ቄሰለ *qʷässälä* be wounded, be injured, have a sore
አቄሰለ *aqʷässälä* wound, injure, make sore
የቄሰለ *yäqʷässälä* wounded, injured
ቁስል, see above

ቁስለኛ, see ቁስል

ቀሰመ *qässämä* gather nectar (of bees), acquire (knowledge), absorb (knowledge), be acquisitive (of ideas), assimilate (customs)
ወሬ ፡ ቀሰመ snoop

ቅስም *qəs(ə)m* physical stamina, power
ቅስሙን ፡ ሰበረው fill with dismay,
crush one's spirit, break the back of
one's resistance

ቀሰሰ *qässäsä* be ordained priest, become a priest
[See ቄስ , ቀሲስ , ቅስና]

ቀሲስ *qäsis* presbyter (see ቀሰሰ)

ቅሰስ ፡ አለ *qəsəss alä* be faint (noise);
see ቀስ ፡ አለ
ቀሰስተኛ *qäsästäñña* low (voice)

ቀሰቀሰ *qäsäqqäsä* awaken, wake up,
awake, arouse, stimulate (interest),
activate, stir up, excite, inspire, provoke (incite), bring about
(ስሜትን ፡ ቀሰቀሰ excite)
ተቀሰቀሰ(በት) *täqäsäqqäsä(bbät)* recur (of disease)
ተንቀሳቀሰ *tänqäsaqqäsä* budge (vi.),
move slightly, be animated
አንቀሳቀሰ *anqäsaqqäsä* stir, stimulate, animate (put into action),
move (vt.), operate (a machine), ma-
neuver, manipulate (a tractor), ruffle
(the surface of a lake)
ተንቀሳቃሽ *tänqäsaqaš* movable (property)
እንቅስቃሴ , see below
የሚንቀሳቀስ ፡ ንብረት *yämminqäsaqqäs nəbrät* movable property
የማይንቀሳቀስ ፡ ንብረት *yämmayənqäsaqqäs nəbrät* immovables, realty,
real estate, reserve funds

ቀሰቀሰ *qäsäqqäsä* search, rummage

ቄሰቄሰ *qʷäsäqqʷäsä* stir up the fire,
poke (the fire), stoke
ጠብ ፡ ቄሰቄሰ provoke an argument

ቀስታ , see ቀስ ፡ አለ

ቀስት *qäst* bow, arrow
ቀስተ ፡ ዳመና rainbow

ቃሰተ *qassätä* breathe with difficulty,
have asthma, moan

አቃሰተ *aqassätä* groan, moan
አስቃሰተ *asqassätä* make sigh

ቅስት *qəssət* arc, arch

ቅስና *qəssənna* ministry (of priest); see
ቄስ
የቅስና priestly, pastoral (of priest)
ሥርዓተ ፡ ቅስና holy orders

ቀሠፈ *qässäfä* castigate
መቅሠፍት , see above

ቄሸሸ *qʷäššäšä*, ቆሸሸ *qoššäšä* (B) be
filthy, be dirty, be soiled
አቄሸሸ *aqʷäššäšä*, አቆሸሸ *aqoššäšä*
(vt.) dirty, soil, litter, stain
ቄሸሽ ፡ ያለ *qʷäšäšš yalä* dingy, squalid, stained
ቆሻሻ *qošaša*, ቄሻሻ *qušaša* dirt, filth,
trash, garbage, waste, rubbish, scum
(of water), refuse, dirty, unclean,
impure

*ቋሸሸ , አቋሸሸ *aqʷaššäšä* show contempt, belittle
አንቋሸሸ *anqʷaššäšä* show contempt,
belittle, disdain, scorn

*ቃቃ , ተንቃቃ *tänqaqqa* creak (of stairs)

ቆቅ *qoq* partridge

ቀቀለ *qäqqälä* (B) boil in water, cook
in water
ተቀቀለ *täqäqqälä* be boiled (meat)
ቅቅል *qəqqəl* boiled in water, cooked
in water
ያልተቀቀለ *yaltäqäqqälä* raw (vegetables)

*ቋቋም , ተቋቋም , አቋቋም , see ቆም

ቀባ *qäbba* (B) anoint, paint (a house),
spread (butter, honey), grease, smear
(the wall, the hair)
(ሐሰት ፡ ቀባ slander, v.)
ተቀባ *täqäbba*, passive of the preceding; smear oneself with
ቀባባ *qäbabba* embroider (a story),
embellish (a story)
ቅባ , see below

ቅቤ *qəbe* butter
ቅብ *qəb* finish (of surface)
ቅባት, see below

ቅባ ፥ ኑግ *qəba nug* nug oil (see ቀባ)

ቅቤ *qəbe* butter (see ቀባ)

ቆብ *qob* skull cap, hood, headgear
  ቆብ ፥ ጫነ don the hood
  የዓይን ፥ ቆብ eyelid

*ቀበለ, ተቀበለ *täqäbbälä* (B) accept,
receive, greet (receive), meet (receive),
welcome, grant (a request), approve,
absorb (assimilate), admit (accept),
embrace (a religion), say in refrain,
join in a song or in cries of mourning
  አቀበለ *aqäbbälä* hand, hand over,
pass around, make to accept
  አቀባበለ *aqqäbabbälä* cock (a gun)
  ቅብብል *qəbəbbəl*, see እሽቅድድም
  አቀባበል *aqqäbabäl* manner of receiving, welcome, reception
  አቀባይ, see below
  ተቀባይ, see below
  ተቀባይነት, see below

ቀበሌ *qäbäle* district, area, precinct,
section of city or country, region
  የቀበሌ regional

ቀበረ *qäbbärä* bury, entomb
  ቀብር *qäbər* burial, funeral
  (የቀብር ፥ ሥነ ፥ ሥርዓት burial ceremony)
  ቀባሪ *qäbari* one who attends a funeral, one who buries
  መቃብር, see above

ቀበሮ *qäbäro* jackal, fox

ቀበቶ *qäbätto* belt of hide
  አደጋ ፥ (የ)መከላከያ ፥ ቀበቶ safety belt,
seat belt

ቁብታ *qubbəta* cupola

ቅባት *qəbat* ointment, grease, cream,
lotion, lubricant, coating (see ቀባ)

ቀብኛ *qäbäňňa*, in የመጽሐፍ፥ ቀብኛ bookworm, voracious reader

ቀባዠረ, see ቀባጀረ

ቀብድ *qäbd* down payment

ቀባጀረ *qäbaǧǧärä* ramble, talk nonsense, be delirious (see also ቀባዠረ)

ቀበጠ *qäbbäṭä* act heedlessly, disregard proprieties

ቀበጥ *qäbäṭ* brat

ቀባጠረ *qäbaṭṭärä* bluster
  የቆጡን ፥ የባጡን ፥ ቀባጠረ ramble on,
talk off the top of one's head

*ቃተ, አቃተ *aqatä* be difficult
  አቃተ(ው) *aqatä(w)* find it hard, not
be able to do
  (ከ --- አቃተው he failed to)

ቃታ *qata* asthma (see ቃተተ)
  ቃታ ፥ ያዘኝ I have asthma, I am out
of breath

ቀትር *qätər* noon, midday
  ከቀትር ፥ በኋላ afternoon

ቃተተ *qattätä* gasp
  አቃተተ *aqattätä* wheeze
  ቃታ *qata* asthma

ቀና *qänna* be straight (road), be straightforward, be upright, be correct, be
successful, be fortunate, prosper
  (ይቅናህ *yəqnah* may it go well with
you!, good luck!)
  አቀና *aqänna* straighten, put straight,
cause to prosper, raise (the head),
unbend, settle (a country), colonize
(a country)
  ተቃና *täqanna* be straight, be
straightened, be in order, succeed
(be successful), turn out well, work
out (vi.)
  አቃና *aqqanna* straighten (a rod),
straighten out, balance
  ቀና ፥ አለ *qäna alä* straighten up (vi.),
be uplifted, look up
  ቀና ፥ አደረገ hold up (the head), lift
up (one's eyes), hold erect

ቀና ፡ ብሎ ፡ ተቀመጠ sit up, sit up
straight
ቀና ፡ ብሎ ፡ አየ look up
ቀና qänna, in መልክ ፡ ቀና handsome,
good looking
(ሐሳብ ፡ ቀና straightforward, genuine)
ቅን, see below
ቀናነት, see below
ቅንነት, see ቅን
ቅኝ, see below
ቀኝ, see below
አቅኚ aqñi, in የአገር ፡ አቅኚ colonizer
መቃናት mäqqanat, in የዕድል ፡ መቃ
ናት success
ያልተቃና yaltäqanna adverse (unfavorable)

ቀና qänna be envious, be jealous, be
zealous, begrudge
ቅናት, see below
[See also ቀናኢ.]

ቀን qän (pl. ቀናት qänat) day, date,
daytime, weather
ቀን ፡ በቀን daily, day by day, day
after day, in broad daylight
ቀን ፡ አለፈ(በት) be out of date
ቀን ፡ ወጣ(ለት) it has seen its day (see
ወጣ)
ቀን ፡ አወጣ(ለት) put in the ascend-
ant (see ወጣ)
ቀኑ ፡ የርሱ ፡ ነበር he was successful,
he got the upper hand
የቀን daily (adj.)
(የ)ቀን ፡ መቁጠሪያ calendar (notebook); see ቁጠረ
የቀን ፡ አቆጣጠር calendar (counting
of days); see ቁጠረ
ሁልቀን ፤ ሁሉ ፡ ቀን hullu qän daily
በቀን daily
በየቀኑ bäyyäqänu every day, day after day, day by day
ከቀን ፡ ቀን day after day
ከቀን ፡ ወደ ፡ ቀን by the day, from
day to day
አንድ ፡ ቀን one of these days, some
day
እኩለ ፡ ቀን noon, midday

ቁና qunna measure for grain (about
5 liters)

ቁና ፡ ቁና ፡ ተነፈሰ qunna qunna tänäffäsä pant, utter a sigh, breathe hard,
puff

ቅኔ qəne sacred hymn, religious poetry
(see *ቀኘ)
ቅኔ ፡ ማኀሌት outermost corridor of
the church
የቅኔ ፡ ቤት qəne school
ባለ ፡ ቅኔ poet

ቅን qən earnest, sincere, candid, honest,
veracious, dutiful (service); see ቀና
be straight
ቅን ፡ ያልሆነ devious
ልብ ፡ ቅን sincere, upright
ቅንነት qənənnät sincerity, benevolence, veracity, constancy, good
nature

ቀነሰ qännäsä (B) decrease (vt.), deduct, diminish, lessen, abate, reduce,
lower (rent), subtract, dim (light),
drop, vi. (of temperature), decline
(vi.), be slashed (prices), fall off
(of receipts)
(ክብደት ፡ ቀነሰ lose weight)
ተቀነሰ täqännäsä be reduced, fail (of
health), diminish (vi.), decrease (vi.)
ቅነሳ qənnäsa decrease, diminution
(የጦር ፡ መሣሪያ ፡ ቅነሳ disarmament)
ቅናሽ qənnaš discount, rebate, deduction, reduction
የመቀነስ yämäqännäs minus, adj.
(sign)

ቆንሲል qonsil consul

ቆንስላ qonsəla consulate

ቅናሽ, see ቀነሰ

ቋንቋ qʷanqʷa language, tongue, speech
የቋንቋ ፡ በዋቂ linguist (see በዋቀ)
የእናት ፡ ቋንቋ native speech, native
tongue

*ቀነቀነ, ተቀናቀነ täqänaqqänä be a rival

ተቀናቃኝ *täqänaqañ* rival, contender

*ቀነበረ, አቀናበረ *aqqänabbärä* interrelate, combine, organize (work), link, coordinate
ቀንበር, see below
ቅንብር *qənəbbər* coherence, coordination
አለመቀነባበር *alämäqqänäbabär* discord (in music)

ቀንበር *qänbär* yoke, burden (responsibility); see *ቀነበረ, ቀምበር

ቀንባጥ *qänbäṭ* twig, shoot

ቀነተ *qännätä* (B) harness up a beast of burden
መቀነት *mäqännät* belt, girdle

ቅናት *qənat* envy, jealousy (see ቀና be envious)

ቀናተኛ *qännatäñña* envious, jealous (see ቀና be envious)

ቀናነት *qännannät* simplicity (of a plan); see ቀና be straight

ቅንነት, see ቅን

ቀናኢ. *qäna'i* zealot, zealous (see ቀና be envious)
ቅንአት *qən'at* zeal

ቀንድ *qänd* horn, antler
ቀንድ ፡ አውጣ *qänd awṭa* snail
የቀንድ horny
የቀንድ ፡ ከብት cattle, horned cattle
የአፍሪካ ፡ ቀንድ Horn of Africa
ቀንደኛ *qändäñña* horned, ringleader
የተንኮል ፡ ቀንደኛ ringleader

ቅንድብ *qəndəb* eyelash, eyebrow

*ቀነጀ, አቀናጀ *aqqänaǧǧä* borrow an ox to make up the pair needed for ploughing, yoke together oxen

ቆንጆ *qonǧo* pretty, beautiful, handsome
ቆነጃጅት *qonäǧaǧət* young girls
†ቁንጅና *qunǧənna* beauty

ቋንጃ *qʷanǧa* hock

ቁንጅና *qunǧənna* beauty (see ቆንጆ)
የቁንጅና ፡ ሳሎን beauty parlor

*ቀነጣ, ተቀናጣ *täqänaṭṭa* dress well, be haughty, put on airs, flirt
ቄንጥ *qenṭ* fashion
ቄንጠኛ *qenṭäñña* stylish (clothing), braggart, boaster

ቋንጣ *qʷanṭa* dry strips of meat

ቌነጠረ *qʷänäṭṭärä* take a pinch (of roasted grain, etc.), pick up crumbs, peck
ተቌነጠረ *täqʷänäṭṭärä* be fidgety

ቀነጠሰ *qänäṭṭäsä* string (beans)

ቀነጠበ *qänäṭṭäbä* cut off (a tip of a cigar, piece of meat)
ቅንጣቢ. *qənäṭṭabi* a cutoff piece

ቅንጣት *qənṭat* grain taken separately, particle, a bit

*ቌነጠነጠ, ተቋነጠነጠ *täqʷnäṭännäṭä* wriggle (of child), twitch impatiently, fidget, get restless, be nervous
ቁንጥንጥ *qunəṭnəṭ* restless

ቄንጠኛ, see *ቀነጣ

ቌነጠጠ *qʷänäṭṭäṭä* pinch, sting (of insect)
መቌንጠጫ *mäqʷänṭäča* tongs

(የ)ቆንጠጰስጤ ፡ በዓል *(yä)qonṭäpäsṭe bä'al* Pentecost (see also ጰንጠቆስጤ.)

ቁንጫ *qunəčča* flea

ቁንጮ *qunčo* lock of hair on the shaved head of a child, tuft, crest of bird, elite
የሴት ፡ ቁንጮ ፡ ናት she is a model housewife

ቅንፍ *qənnəf* brackets, parentheses

ቀኝ *qäññ* right hand, right (side); see ቀና be straight
ቀኝ ፡ ዙሪ ፡ ዙር about face!

ቀኛዝማች, see below

*ቀኘ, ተቀኘ *täqäññä* (B) compose a hymn
ቃኘ *qaññä* tune musical instruments
ተቁኒ religious poetry, sacred hymn

ቃኘ *qaññä* glance about, reconnoiter, scout (v.)
በዓይኑ ፡ ቃኘ scan
ቃኝ ፡ ጓድ *qaññ g*ʷ*add* patrol
መቃኘት *mäqqañät* reconnaissance

ቅኝ, in ቅኝ ፡ አገር *qəññ agär* colony (see ቀና, አገር)
ቅኝ ፡ ገዢ colonizer (see ገዛ)
ቅኝ ፡ ግዛት colony, settlement (colony)
ቅኝ ፡ ግዛት ፡ አደረገ colonize
የቅኝ ፡ አገዛዝ *yäqəññ aggäzaz* colonization, colonialism, colonial rule (see ገዛ)

ቀኛዝማች *qäññazmač* commander of the right (title of distinction); see ቀኝ, አዝማች

*ቀወለለ, ተንቀዋለለ *tänqäwallälä* roam, loiter, wander, fool around
ቀውላላ *qäwlalla* tall

*ቀወመ, ተቃወመ, see ቆመ

*ቀወሰ, ተቃወሰ *täqawwäsä* be confused, be intertwined, be interlaced, be at fault
አቃወሰ *aqqawwäsä* upset, mess up (plans), disorganize
ቀውስ *qäws* confusion

ቀዘቀዘ *qäzäqqäzä* cool (vi.), be cold (water), drop off (of business), be slow (of market), be lifeless (of town)
ቀዘቀዘ(ው) *qäzäqqäzä(w)* feel cold
አቀዘቀዘ *aqäzäqqäzä* cool (vt.), cool off, chill (vt.), depress (press down, lower), damp (enthusiasm), dampen (joy)
ቀዝቀዝ ፡ ያለ *qäzqäzz yalä* cool (adj.), soft (breeze), slack (business)
ቀዝቃዛ *qäzqazza* cold, adj. (water, food), cool, chilly, frigid (climate, reception)

ቅዝቃዜ *qəzəqqaze* cold (n.)
ማቀዝቀዣ, see above
የቀዘቀዘ *yäqäzäqqäzä* dead (of party), lacking luster

ቀዘነ *qäzzänä* have diarrhea, defecate
ቅዘን *qəzän* diarrhea

ቀዘዝ ፡ አለ *qäzäzz alä* feel dismal

ቀዘፈ *qäzzäfä* row, paddle
መቀዘፊያ *mäqzäfiya* paddle, oar, rudder

ቃዠ *qažžä* have a nightmare, rave, see things
አቃዠ(ው) *aqqažžä(w)* become delirious, have a nightmare
ቅዠት *qəžät* nightmare

ቀይ *qäyy* red, reddish, light complexioned (Europeans); see ቀላ
ቀይ ፡ መስቀል Red Cross
ቀይ ፡ ሥር radish
ቀይ ፡ ሽንኩርት onion

ቈየ *q*ʷ*äyyä*, ቆየ *qoyyä* (B) last, be late, wait, await, linger, stay, remain (stay)
አቆየ *aqoyyä* delay, detain, make wait, keep waiting, keep in (detain), spare (put aside), preserve
ቆይቶ *qoyyəto* late, later, a little later, for a while
(ቆይተን ፡ ገባን we arrived late; ሲሄድ ፡ ቆይቶ walking on for a while)
ቆይታ, see below
መቆያ *mäqoyya* snack
የቆየ *yäqoyyä* long-standing, hardened (criminal), old (food, model, history), ancient
(ሲሠራበት ፡ የቆየ *sissärrabbät yäqoyyä* which was in use for quite a while)

*ቀየመ, ተቀየመ *täqäyyämä* (B) harbor desire for revenge, resent, take offense, hold a grudge
አስቀየመ *asqäyyämä* offend, hurt one's feelings, scandalize

አስቀያሚ *asqäyyami* grotesque, ugly, offensive
ቅያሜ *qəyyame* grudge, rancor, resentment, ill-feeling, revenge
ቂም, see above

ቀየረ *qäyyärä* (B) change (shirt, residence, etc.), move (from the place of residence), relieve (change)
አቀያየረ *aqqäyayyärä* interchange (vt.), rotate
ተቀያሪ *täqäyyari* relief (release from a post)

ቀየሰ *qäyyäsä* (B) measure land, make a survey of land, outline
ቅየሳ *qəyyäsa* survey (measurement)
ቀያሽ *qäyyaš* surveyor
አቀያየስ *aqqäyayäs* layout

ቆይታ *qoyyəta* secret conference, huddle (see ቆየ)

ቀየደ *qäyyädä* (B) tie, entangle, hobble

ቀየጠ *qäyyäṭä* (B) blend (vt.), compound (mix)
ቅይጥ *qəyyəṭ* blend, alloy, heterogeneous

ቀዳ *qädda* draw (water), pour, drip (water from a spring); imitate, copy, mimic, reproduce, record (on tape) (ወሬ ፡ ቀዳ gossip, v.)
ቅጂ ፤ ቅጇ, see below
ቅዳ, see below

ቅዳ *qəda*, in ደም ፡ ቅዳ artery (see ቀዳ)

ቆዳ *qoda* skin, raw hide, leather, pelt, peel (of orange)
ቆዳማ *qodamma* leathery

ቀደመ *qäddämä* precede, advance, be first, be ahead of, go ahead, be anterior, come before, be in advance, lead (be first), anticipate (do in advance), be fast (of watch)
ተቀደመ *täqäddämä* be put before, be put in front
አስቀደመ *asqäddämä* anticipate, cause to precede

ቀደም ፡ አለ *qädämm alä* be early, come early
ቀደም ፡ ያለ *qädämm yalä* prior, previous, former, early (adj.)
ቀደም ፡ አደረገ *qädämm adärrägä* advance (vt.), make earlier
ቀደም ፡ ሲል *qädämm sil* previously, before
ቀደም ፡ ብሎ *qädämm bəlo* earlier, in advance, sooner, previously, ahead of time, prior to, in front
ቀዳም *qäddäm*, in በቀደም ፡ ዕለት the other day
ቀዳሚ *qädami* preceding, previous, primary
ቀድሞ *qädmo* formerly, before, ahead of, previously, early times (በቀድሞ ፡ ዘመን once, in former days) (የቀድሞ earlier, former)
ቅዳሚ, see below
ቅድም *qəddəm* some time ago, earlier, a little while ago (see also አያት)
(በ)ቅደም ፡ ተከተል *(bä)qədäm täkkätäl* in proper order, in sequence, one after the other
ቀደምትነት *qäddämtənnät* priority
ቀዳሚነት *qädaminnät* precedence, lead, priority
ቀዳማዊ, see below
ቀዳማይ, see below
ቅድሚያ, see below
ተቀዳሚ *täqäddami* first (in rank)
ተቀዳሚነት *täqäddaminnät* priority, precedence
መቅደም, see above
አስቀድሞ *asqäddəmo* beforehand, in advance, previously, already (ከሁሉ ፡ አስቀድሞ first of all)
[See also ተሽቀዳደመ]

ቅዳሜ *qədame* Saturday, Sabbath (see ቀደመ)

ቀዳማዊ *qädamawi* First (in the title of a king); see ቀደመ

ቀዳማይ *qädamay* First (in the title of a king), pommel (see ቀደመ)

ቅድሚያ *qədmiya* precedence (see ቀደመ)
በቅድሚያ *bäqədmiya* ahead, in advance
በቅድሚያ ፡ ሰጠ advance (money)
የቅድሚያ ፡ መንገድ right of way

ቀደሰ *qäddäsä* (B) sing Mass, celebrate Mass, sanctify
ተቀደሰ *täqäddäsä* be hallowed
አስቀደሰ *asqäddäsä* worship, attend Mass
ቅዳሴ, see below
ቅዱስ *qəddus* (pl. ቅዱሳን *qəddusan*, fem. sg. ቅድስት *qəddəst*) saint, holy, blessed, sacred
(ቅዱስ ፡ ዮሐንስ *qəddus yohannəs* St. John's Day, New Year)
(መጽሐፍ ፡ ቅዱስ Bible)
ቅድስተ ፡ ቅዱሳን *qəddəstä qəddusan* holy of holies
ቅድስና *qəddəsənna* piety, righteousness
ቅዱስነት *qəddusənnät* sanctity, holiness
መቅደስ *mäqdäs* sanctuary
(ቤተ ፡ መቅደስ temple)
የተቀደሰ *yätäqäddäsä* sacred, venerable

ቅዳሴ *qəddase* church service, Mass, liturgy (see ቀደሰ)
ቅዳሴ ፡ ወጣ the Mass is over
ቅዳሴ ፡ ገባ celebrate Mass

ቀደደ *qäddädä* tear (vt.), tear open, tear up, slit, cut open, rip (cloth), make a hole in
(ጐህ ፡ ሲቀድ *gʷäh siqädd* at dawn)
ተቀደደ *täqäddädä* tear (vi.)
ቀዶ ፡ ጥገና *qäddo ṭəggäna* operation, surgery
ቀዶ ፡ ጥገና ፡ አደረገ operate (perform surgery)
ቀዶ ፡ ጠጋኝ ፡ ሐኪም *qäddo ṭäggaň hakim* surgeon
ቀዳዳ *qädada* tear (n.), opening, hole, slit, leak, loophole, gap (in a hedge), eye (of a needle)
የቁልፍ ፡ ቀዳዳ keyhole

ቅጇ *qəǧǧi*, ቅጅ *qəǧǧ* copy, imitation, reproduction, print (copy of a painting); see ቀዳ
ሁለት ፡ ቅጅ duplicate

ቋጕሜ *qʷagʷme* intercalary month (5-10 September); see also ጳጕሜ

ቀጣ *qäṭṭa* punish, penalize, chastise, discipline, impose a fine, correct (punish)
ተቀጣ *täqäṭṭa* be punished, be penalized, receive punishment
ቃጣ *qaṭṭa* threaten (make the movement of hitting), raise a hand against someone, make as if, brandish, feint, be about to
ቅጣት, see below
መቀጫ *mäqqäča*, መቀጮ *mäqqäčo* penalty, fine

ቀጥ ፡ አለ *qäṭṭ alä* be straight (line), stand straight, be perpendicular, be upright, be steep (stair, hill), be bold (cliff)
ቀጥ ፡ ብሎ *qäṭṭ bəlo* straight (adv.)
ቅጥ, see below
ቀጥታ, see below

ቁጡ, see *ቄጣ

ቁጣ *quṭṭa* anger, wrath (see *ቄጣ)
ቁጠኛ *quṭṭäňňa* quick-tempered
የቁጣ *yäquṭṭa* angry

ቂጣ *qiṭṭa* unleavened bread

ቂጥ *qiṭ* buttock, anus

ቅጥ *qəṭ* arrangement, order, rule (see ቀጠ ፡ አለ)
ቅጥ ፡ አጣ be disorderly, be abnormal, be in disarray
ቅጥ ፡ ያጣ abnormal, disorderly (see አጣ)
ቅጥ ፡ አሳጣ clutter, derange (see አጣ)
ቅጥ ፡ የሌለው shapeless
መላ ፡ ቅጡን ፡ አጣ go haywire, go berserk
መላ ፡ ቅጡ ፡ ጠፋው he did not know what to do, he was at a loss
በቅጡ *bäqəṭu* properly, correctly

ያለ ፥ ቅጥ tremendously, greatly, infinitely, grossly, immoderately, immeasurably

ቆጥ *qoṭ* loft, perch
የቆጡን ፥ የባጡን ፥ ቀባጠረ ramble on, talk off the top of one's head

*ቄጣ, ተቄጣ *täqʷäṭṭa* be (become) angry, lose one's temper, erupt (of skin), be irritable (of skin)
አስቄጣ *asqʷäṭṭa* anger (vt.), enrage, irritate (the skin)
ቁጡ *quṭṭu* enraged, ill-tempered, angry, quick (temper), sensitive(skin)
ቄጣ, see below
መቄጧት *mäqqʷäṭat* eruption (of skin)
የሚያስቄጣ *yämmiyasqʷäṭṭa* inflammatory

ቀጠለ *qäṭṭälä* (B) proceed, go on, continue, join, add, follow, resume, carry on, persist, connect (the telephone)
ቀጥሎ *qäṭṭəlo* next (adv.), afterwards, later on, subsequently, then
(ከ - - - ቀጥሎ next to)
ቀጥሎ ፥ ያለው *qäṭṭəlo yalläw* adjacent
ቅጣይ, see below
ቅጥይ, see below
ተቀጥይ, see below
የሚቀጥል *yämmiqäṭṭəl* next, following, adjoining
የተቀጣጠለ *yätäqäṭaṭṭälä* cursive (script)

*ቃጠለ, ተቃጠለ *täqaṭṭälä* burn (vi.), be on fire (of house), burn oneself, be destroyed by fire, burn down, burn out (of light bulb), blow out (of fuse)
አቃጠለ *aqqaṭṭälä* set fire to, set on fire, burn (vt.), burn down (vt.), scorch, bite (of pepper), smart (of alcohol)
ተቀጣጠለ *täqäṭaṭṭälä* be on fire, burn, catch fire, be aflame, light (vi., of wood)
አቀጣጠለ *aqqäṭaṭṭälä* ignite, vt. (twigs), light a cigarette, set fire to

ቃጠሎ *qaṭälo* fire, blaze
ማቃጠጫ, see above
የማይቃጠል *yämmayəqqaṭṭäl* incombustible

ቅጠል *qəṭäl* leaf, foliage
ቅጠል ፥ አወጣ send out leaves (see ወጣ)
ቅጠላ ፥ ቅጠል *qəṭäla qəṭäl* vegetables, herbs
እህል ፥ ቅጠል ፥ አይልም it tastes flat (of food)

ቀጠማ *qeṭäma* reed

ቀጠረ *qäṭṭärä* employ, engage (a servant), hire (a worker); give an appointment, adjourn (put off)
ተቀጠረ *täqäṭṭärä* be hired, take service with, have an engagement, be put off (by having another date set for the meeting)
ቀጠር, see below
ቀጣሪ *qäṭari* employer
ቅጥር, see below

ቀጠረ *qäṭṭärä* encircle, make a fence around
ቅጥር, see below

ቀጠሮ *qäṭäro* appointment (date), engagement (appointment), hearing (in court); see ቀጠረ employ
ቀጠር ፥ አከበረ keep an appointment (see ከበረ)
ቀጠር ፥ አፈረሰ not keep an appointment (see ፈረሰ)
በቀጠር ፥ አቆየ hold in abeyance (see ቆየ)

ቁጥር *quṭər* number, figure (number), numeral, arithmetic (see ቄጠረ)
ቁጥር ፥ ስፍር ፥ የሌለው innumerable
ቁጥር ፥ የሌለው countless, innumerable
ሙሉ ፥ ቁጥር even number
መደበኛ ፥ ቁጥር ordinal number
ብዙ ፥ ቁጥር plural
ተራ ፥ ቁጥር cardinal number
ነጠላ ፥ ቁጥር singular (in grammar)

የስልክ ፡ ቁጥር *yäsəlk quṭər* telephone number
ጉደሎ ፡ ቁጥር odd number
በ + verb + ቁጥር each time that, every time (conj.), whenever

ቅጥር *qəṭər* encircled, enclosure, compound (see ቀጠረ encircle)
ቅጥር ፡ ግቢ compound

ቅጥር *qəṭär* hired (see ቀጠረ employ)
ቅጥር ፡ ወታደር mercenary

ቄጠረ *qʷäṭṭärä* count (vt.), reckon, enumerate, number, calculate, regard (consider), rank
(ሰዓት ፡ ቄጠረ tell time)
(ሰዓት ፡ ቄጣሪ *sä'at qʷäṭari* hour hand)
(ፊደል ፡ ቄጠረ master the alphabet)
ተቄጠረ *täqʷäṭṭärä*, passive of the preceding; be branded (considered), amount (be equivalent)
ተቄጣጠረ *täqʷäṭaṭṭärä* control, keep track of, supervise, inspect, oversee, regulate (control), handle (control)
ቁጥር, see above
ቄጠራ, see below
ቁጥጥር, see below
ተቄጣጣሪ *täqʷäṭaṭari* inspector, controller, supervisor, superintendent, overseer, auditor (who examines the accounts)
ተቄጣጣሪነት *täqʷäṭaṭarinnät* direction (supervision)
መቀጠሪያ, see above
መቄጣጠር *mäqqʷäṭaṭär* surveillance
መቄጣጠሪያ *mäqqʷäṭaṭäriya* check (control), valve
አቄጣጠር, see below

ቄጠራ *qʷäṭära* count (n.); see ቄጠረ
ኮከብ ፡ ቄጠራ astrology
የሕዝብ ፡ ቄጠራ census

ቋጠረ *qʷaṭṭärä* make a knot, knot, tie (a knot)
ምስጢር ፡ ቋጠረ keep a secret, be discreet

ውኃ ፡ ቋጠረ form blisters
ግምባር ፡ ቋጠረ frown (v.)
ፊት ፡ ቋጠረ frown (v.)
ቋጠሮ *qʷaṭäro* knot (n.)
መቋጠር *mäqʷaṭär* furrow (of brow)
የተቋጠረ ፡ ውኃ *yätäqʷaṭṭärä wəha* puddle

ቅጥራን *qəṭran* tar
በቅጥራን ፡ መረገ caulk

ቀጠቀጠ *qäṭäqqäṭä* beat repeatedly, castrate by crushing the testicles, crush, pulverize, powder, hammer, pound, forge
ቀጥቃጭ *qäṭqač* blacksmith

*ቀጠቀጠ, ተንቀጠቀጠ *tänqäṭäqqäṭä* shiver, tremble, quake, shudder, vibrate, shake (vi.), be unsteady (of hand), wobble (of steering wheel), be convulsed (with pain)
አንቀጠቀጠ *anqäṭäqqäṭä*, causative of the preceding; shake (vt.)
አንቀጠቀጠ(ው) *anqäṭäqqäṭä(w)* shiver (v.)
መንቀጥቀጥ, see above
እንቅጥቃጤ *ənqəṭəqqaṭe* trembling, shudder

ቁጥቋጦ *quṭqʷaṭo* shrub, bush, underbrush, undergrowth (see ቄጠቄጠ)
የቁጥቋጦ ፡ አጥር hedge

ቄጠቄጠ *qʷäṭäqqʷäṭä* smart (of a bee sting or salt on wound), prune, lop off branches
አቄጠቄጠ *aqʷäṭäqqʷäṭä* sprout new leaves, send out fresh shoots
ቁጥቋጦ, see above

ቄጥቋጣ *qʷäṭqʷaṭṭa* parsimonious, tight-fisted, stingy

ቀጥቃጭ *qäṭqač* blacksmith (see ቀጠቀጠ)

ቄጠበ *qʷäṭṭäbä* (B) be economical, economize, be thrifty, save (money, strength), spare (efforts), lay aside
(ከ) ---- ተቄጠበ *(kä)* --- *täqʷäṭṭäbä* abstain, refrain

ቂጣቢ *q^wäṭṭabi* economical, thrifty, saving (adj.), frugal (saving)
ቁጠባ *quṭṭäba* economy, saving (n.) (በቁጠባ sparingly)
ያልተቂጠበ *yaltäq^wäṭṭäbä* unsparing (effort), constant, all-out (effort)

ቀጥታ *qäṭṭəta* straight, direct (see ቀጥ ፡ አለ)
በቀጥታ directly, straight ahead
ቀጥተኛ *qäṭṭətäňňa* direct, straight (answer), straightforward

ቅጣት *qəṭat* punishment, penalty, fine (see ቀጣ)
የቅጣት *yäqəṭat* disciplinary
የሞት ፡ ቅጣት death penalty

ቀጠነ *qäṭṭänä* slim down, be thin, be fine
አቀጠነ *aqäṭṭänä* make slim, dilute with water, weaken (tea), adulterate (beer with water)
ቀጭን, see below

ቂጠኝ *qiṭṭəň* syphilis

ጮጠኝ *q^waṭəňň* rock, boulder

ቅጣይ *qəṭṭay* epilogue (see ቀጠለ)

ቅጥያ *qəṭṭəyya* annex, extension (of a house), addition (to a building); see ቀጠለ
የቅጥያ additional

ቀጠጠ *qäṭṭäṭä* cut (grass, bushes), shear (sheep)
አስቀጠጠ *asqäṭṭäṭä* set one's teeth on edge(of scraping on a blackboard)

ቁጢጥ ፡ አለ *quṭiṭṭ alä* squat

ቁጥጥር *quṭəṭṭər* supervision, discipline, control (see ቆጠረ)
ያለ ፡ ቁጥጥር freely

ቀጠፈ *qäṭṭäfä* pick (flowers, leaves), pluck (fruit)

ቀጣፊ *qäṭafi* swindler, cheat, rogue, rascal
ቅጥፈት *qəṭfät* cheating

ቀጨ *qäččä* cut, cut down (grass), nip (of frost nipping flowers), cut short (see also *ቀጨጨ)
ተቀጨ *täqäččä* be struck down (by illness), strain oneself

ቁጭ ፡ አለ *qučč alä* sit down, settle down
ቁጭ ፡ ብሎ *qučč bəlo* merely

ቃጫ *qačča* fiber, sisal, jute

ቄጨ(ው) *q^wäččä(w)* begrudge (money), feel chagrined

*ቃጨለ, ተቃጨለ *täqaččälä* clank
አቃጨለ *aqqaččälä* clink
ተንቃጨለ *tänqaččälä* tinkle
አንቃጨለ *anqaččälä* jingle, vt. (keys), ring a small bell
መቃጨል *mäqqačäl* jingle (n.)
ቃጨል *qačəl* small bell
[See also *ቀጨለቀጨለ]

*ቀጨለቀጨለ, ተቀጨለቀጨለ *täqčäläččälä* jingle, vi. (of bells), clink, vi. (of coins); see also *ቃጨለ
የሚቀጨለቀጨል ፡ መጫወቻ *yämmiqčäläččäl mäččawäča* rattle (toy);

ቀጨቀጨ *qäčäqqäčä* break with the teeth, shake something while holding it in the teeth (e.g. dog)
ተንቀጫቀጨ *tänqäčaqqäčä* chatter (of teeth)

ቀጭን *qäččən* thin (ribbon, man, voice), slender, skinny, fine (point), narrow (lane), lean, high (voice), tenuous (web), weak (tea); see ቀጠነ
ቀጭኔ *qäččəne* giraffe

*ቀጨጨ, አቀጨጨ *aqäččäčä* stunt (plants), constrain the growth (see also ቀጨ)
ቀጫጫ *qäčača* scrubby (tree)
ያልቀጨጨ *yalqäččäčä* fleshy (peach)

ቅጽ *qəṣ* volume (book)
የመሳፈሪያ ፡ ቅጽ *yämässafäriya qəṣ* boarding pass (see ሰፈረ)

ቅጽል *qəṣṣəl* adjective
የቅጽል ፡ ስም nickname, epithet

ቅጽበት *qəṣbät* wink (n.)
ከመቅጽበት *kämäqəṣbät* a split second, in a flash, in a moment

ቀፎ *qäfo* hive, beehive
ቀፎ ፡ ነው be hollow

ቋፍ *qʷaf*, in በቋፍ ፡ ላይ ፡ ነው come to a head

ቈፈረ *qʷäffärä* (B) dig, excavate
ቈፍሮ ፡ አወጣ *qʷäffəro awäṭṭa* dig up, excavate, exhume (see ወጣ)
ቁፈራ *quffära* excavation
መቈፈሪያ *mäqʷäffäriya* pickaxe

ቀፈፈ *qäffäfä* trim the edge with hide

ቀፈፈ *qäffäfä* beg from door to door
ቀፋፊ *qäfafi* vagrant

ቀፈፈ(ው) *qäffäfä(w)* feel repulsion for, feel miserable, feel uneasy, feel gloomy
ቅፍፍ ፡ አለ(ው) *qəfəff alä(w)* look glum
ቀፋፊ *qäfafi* repulsive, gloomy (day), cheerless, dreary, dismal, bleak (weather)
የቀፈፈ *yäqäffäfä* nasty

በ

በ *bä* with (by means of), in, on, by, at, against, through, on the occasion of, due to
በ + perfect + ጊዜ when

ብ + (simple imperfect) when, if
ብ + imperfect + ም ፡ እንኳ(ን) in spite of, although, even though
ብ + imperfect + (ቅሉ) though
[See also ቁጥር]

ቡሆ *buho* fermented dough to make bread (see ቦካ, ቡሀቃ, ቦኻቃ)

ባህል *bahəl* culture, tradition, convention, custom
የባህል cultural, traditional
ባህላዊ ፡ ዘፈን *bahlawi zäfän* folk song

ባሕር *bahər* sea
ባሕር ፡ ማዶ overseas
የባሕር marine (adj.), maritime
የባሕር ፡ ኀይል navy
የባሕር ፡ ኀይል ፡ ዋና ፡ አዛዥ admiral
የባሕር ፡ ሰላጤ bay, gulf
የባሕር ፡ ወሽመጥ channel
(የ)ባሕር ፡ ዛፍ eucalyptus
ሐይቀ ፡ ባሕር lagoon

ብሔር *bəher*, in ፍትሐ ፡ ብሔር civil code
የፍትሐ ፡ ብሔር ፡ ሕግ civil code, civil law
[See ብሔራዊ]

ብሔራዊ *bəherawi* territorial (army), national (adj.), nationalist (adj.); see ብሔር
ብሔራዊ ፡ ስሜት nationalism
ብሔራዊ ፡ በዓል national holiday
ብሔራዊ ፡ ጦር militia

ባሕሪይ *bahriy* nature (human), character, temperament, essence, personality, trait, attribute, characteristic (n.), disposition (nature)

ቡሀቃ *buhaqa* kneading trough (from ቡሆ ፡ እቃ; see also ቦኻቃ)

ባሕታዊ *bahtawi* anchorite, hermit
ብሕትውና *bəhtəwənna* celibacy

በላ *bälla* eat, consume
ተበላ *täbälla* be eaten, wear away (vi.), corrode
አበላ *abälla* feed, give to eat, provide food
አብላላ *ablalla* study a problem thoroughly so a solution can be found
በል *bäll*, in ሥጋ ፡ በል carnivorous, carnivore

በሊ.ታ, see below
†መብል *mäbəl* food

በል, በለው, see አለ *alä*

ቢላ *billa* knife (see also ቢላዋ)

ባለ *balä* used in composition. For the pronunciation and details in meaning, see the noun following ባለ- (see also ባል)
ባለሀብት owner
ባለሟል courtier, favorite, favored
ባለሟልነት grace, favor
ባለመሬት landowner
ባለሙያ skillful, handy, expert
ባለ : ርስት landowner
ባለ : ሥልጣን official, dignitary, executive
ባለ : ሥልጣኖች authorities
ባለሱቅ shopkeeper
ባለቅኔ poet
ባለቤት proprietor, owner, master of the house, patriarch of family, lady of the house, husband, spouse, wife, subject (in grammar)
ባለቤትነት ownership
ባላባት nobleman, squire, patriarch, chief, tribal notable
ባለ : ታሪክ hero (in a book), character (in a play)
ባለትዳር married couple
ባላንብረት owner, proprietor
ባለ : ዕዳ debtor
ባለ : እጅ skilled, artisan, craftsman, blacksmith
ባለጌ ill-mannered, impudent, insolent, unmannered, rude, vulgar, rough (manner)
ባላገር country (countryside), countryman, rustic (see አገር)
ባለጋራ ፤ ባላጋራ opponent, adversary in a lawsuit
ባለ : ግርማ majestic
ባለ : ጉዳይ person who has a case in court or a problem to take up with an official
ባለ : ጥቅም partner
ባለጸጋ rich, well-to-do, affluent

ባለ : ፋብሪካ manufacturer
-ባለ, in ተባለ *täbala* be said (see አለ)

ባላ *balla* fork of a branch, wooden pole with forked top

ባል *bal* husband, master (see also ባለ)
ባልና : ሚስት *balənna mist* couple
ባል : አልባ *bal alba* an unmarried woman who has been married before
ባ. : የሞተባት : ሴት *balwa yämotäbbat set* widow
የባል *yäbal* marital
ባልትና, see below

ባል *bal* holiday, festival, celebration (see also በዓል)

ብል *bəl* cloth eating vermin

ብሎ, see አለ *alä*

ብልህ *bələh* clever, ingenious, bright (person), expert, intelligent, wise, sage, keen, sharp (lawyer), judicious (remark)
ብልሃት *bəlhat* tact, finesse, guile
ብልሃተኛ *bəlhatäňňa*, same meanings as ብልህ
ብልህነት *bələhənnät* intelligence, ingenuity, acumen

ቦላሌ *bolale* long trousers

ባላምባራስ *balambaras* honorific title

በለስ *bäläs* fig tree

ባሌስትራ *balestra* spring (of truck)

*በላሽ, ተበላሸ *täbälaššä* spoil (vi.), be spoiled, deteriorate, go wrong, get worse, be ruined, perish (fruit), break down (machinery)
አበላሸ *abbälaššä* spoil (vt.), ruin, corrupt, deface, deform, wreck (a business), destroy, pervert, damage, waste (a chance)
የተበላሸ *yätäbälaššä* corrupt, defective, imperfect
ብልሹ *bələššu* corrupt (adj.)
ብልሹ : አደረገ corrupt (v.)

ብልሽት *bələššət* corruption, breakdown (of machinery)
የማይብላሽ *yämmayəbbälašš* imperishable
[See also ብላሽ]

ብላሽ *bəlaš* damaged, useless, valueless (see *በላሽ)
በብላሽ *bäbəlaš* free of charge, gratis, at no cost, for nothing

ቡልቅታ *bulləqta* jet (of water)

ብልቃጥ *bəlqaṭ*, ቢልቃጥ *bilqaṭ* small glass container for perfume or the like

*በለበለ, ተንበለበለ *tänbäläbbälä* blaze up, burn with flames, be alight (fire)
አንበለበለ *anbäläbbälä*, in በቃሉ ፡ አን በለበለ rattle off.
ነበልባል *näbälbal* flame

ባልቦላ *balbola* fuse (n.)

ባለቤት *baläbet* proprietor, owner, master of the house, lady of the house, husband, spouse, wife, subject (in grammar); see ባለ, ቤት
ባለቤትነት *baläbetənnät* ownership

ባላባት *balabbat* nobleman, squire, tribal notable, patriarch, chief (from ባለ ፡ አባት)
የባላባት feudal (system)

በሊታ *bällitta* one who is always eating (see በላ)
አደራ ፡ በሊታ embezzler

ብላታ *blatta*, abbreviated form of ብላ ቴንጌታ (see below)

ብልት *bəllət* part of the body, part, cut of meat, genitals
የብልት ፡ ሽለፈት foreskin
የብልት ፡ ፍሬ testicle

*ቧለተ, አቧለተ *ab^wallätä* joke (v.)
ቧልታ *b^walta* joke, levity, frivolous manner, trivial talk
ቧልተኛ *b^waltäñña* frivolous, trivial

ባልቴት *baltet* elderly woman, elderly lady

ባልትና *baltənna* good housekeeping, feminine accomplishments, housewifely skills (see ባል)
(የ)ቤት ፡ ባልትና home economics

ብላቴንጌታ *blattengeta* honorific title (usually given for achievement in learning); see also ብላታ

ቢልተኛ, see *ቢለተ

ቡሎን *bulon* screw, nut (of metal)

ብሌን *bəlen* pupil of the eye
የዓይን ፡ ብሌን pupil of the eye

ባልንጀራ *balənǧära* companion, friend (from ባል ፡ እንጀራ)

ቡሉኮ *bullukko* heavy hand-made blanket made of cotton

ቢላዋ *billawa* knife (see also ቢላ)

ብሉይ ፡ ኪዳን *bəluy kidan* Old Testament

በላይነት *bälayənnät* mastery, upper hand, superiority, higher authority (over something); see ላይ
የበላይነት *yäbälayənnät* dominion, superiority, mastery

ባልዲ *baldi* pail, bucket

ባልደራስ *baldäras* groom (who is in charge of horses)

ባልደረባ *baldäräba* intermediary in one's relations with a person of high authority, member of a military unit

በልግ *bälg* season of small rains in Ethiopia

ባለገ *ballägä* misbehave, be naughty, be rude, be unrefined
ባለጌ *baläge* ill-mannered, impudent, insolent, unmannered, rude, rough (manner), vulgar (see ባለ, ጌ)

ብልግና *bəlgənna* bad manners, rudeness, indecent behavior, impudence, insolence, impertinence
የብልግና *yäbəlgənna* disrespectful, indecent, boorish, profane (language)

ባለጋራ *balägara*, ባላጋራ *balagara* opponent, adversary in a lawsuit (see ባለ, ጋራ)

ባላጋር *balagär* country (countryside), countryman (man from the country), rustic (see ባል, አገር)

ብልግና, see ባለገ

በለጠ *bälläṭä* surpass, excel, be more than, exceed, outdo, get the better of someone
(በዕድሜ ፡ በለጠ be older than)
አበለጠ *abälläṭä* increase
ተበላለጠ *täbälalläṭä* be unequal in status (people), vary, not be of the same age, not be of the same height
አበላለጠ *abbälalläṭä* make a great difference, favor
አበላለጥ *abbälaläṭ* favor (n.), superiority, advantage
ብልጥ, see below
ብልጫ, see below
አብልጦ *abləṭo* more, best (adv.)
(ከሁሉ ፡ አብልጦ best (adv.))
ቢበልጥ *bibälṭ* at the most
የበለጠ *yäbälläṭä* best (adj., adv.)
(ከሁሉ ፡ የበለጠ more than)
ይበልጥ, see below
የሚበልጥ *yämmibälṭ* more
አበላላጭ ፡ ደረጃ *abbälalač däräǧa* superlative

ብልጥ *bəlṭ* shrewd, sly, smart, tricky, cunning, clever, astute, crafty (see በለጠ)
ብልጣ ፡ ብልጥ *bəlṭa bəlṭ* sly (fox)
ብልጣት *bəlṭät* trickery

ብልጫ *bəlča* superiority, excess, advantage, plurality (of votes); see በለጠ

ብልጭ ፡ አለ *bälläčč alä* shine, twinkle, glitter, sparkle, dazzle, flash

ብልጭ ፡ ድርግም ፡ አለ *bälläčč dərgəmm alä* flicker, wink (of light), go on and off (light)
ብልጭ ፡ ድርግም ፡ አደረገ blink (the flashlight), turn on and off
ብልጭታ *bəlləčta* gleam, dazzling light, flash
[See also *በለጨለጨ]

*በለጨለጨ, ተበለጨለጨ *täbläčälläčä* glitter, sparkle (of eyes), lighten, vi. (flash with lightning); see ብልጭ ፡ አለ
አብለጨለጨ *abläčälläčä* have a shine, make sparkle
ብልጭልጭ *bäläčläč* flamboyant, flashy, gaudy, showy, fanciful, fancy (adj.)

ባልጩት *balčut* flint, obsidian

ብልጭታ, see ብልጭ ፡ አለ

በለጸገ *bäläṣṣägä* get rich, prosper, flourish, develop, vi. (of a country)
አበለጸገ *abäläṣṣägä* enrich, make wealthy, develop (a country), render prosperous
ባለጸጋ *baläṣägga* rich, well-to-do, affluent (see ባለ, ጸጋ)
ብልጽግና *bəlṣəgənna* wealth, prosperity
የበለጸገ *yäbäläṣṣägä* prosperous, abundant (rich)

ቢላፎን *bilafon*, ብላፎን *blafon* ceiling

ቦምብ *bomb* bomb
በቦምብ ፡ ደበደበ bomb, bombard
የቦምብ ፡ ድብድባ bombardment (see ደበደበ)

ቧምቧ *bʷambʷa* hose, pipe (for water), water pipe, faucet
የቧምቧ ፡ መክፈቻ faucet
ቧምቧ ፡ ሠራተኛ plumber
የቧምቧ ፡ ውኃ running water
የውኃ ፡ ቧምቧ hose

በራ *bära* bald on the top of the head
በራ ፡ ሆነ become bald, lose the hair

ራስ ፡ በራ bald

በራ *bärra* burn, vi. (of light), be alight, be lit, light up, gleam (of eyes)
አበራ *abärra* be aglow, shine, vi. (of eyes, sun), be bright, gleam (of eyes), blaze (of face with joy), light up, glow vi. (of hot metal); also transitive: turn on the light, light (a lamp), light up (the face), burn (a candle), illuminate
አባራ *abarra* clear up, vi. (of weather) (ዝናቡ ፡ አባራ the rain stopped)
አብራራ *abrarra* explain, expound, clarify, amplify (enlarge on), expand on, illustrate, throw light on, elucidate
ብራ *bərra* clear weather, bright weather
መብራት *mäbrat* lamp, light
ማብራሪያ *mabrariya* illumination (explanation), illustration, explanation, annotation
ማብሪያ *mabriya* light switch
[See also ብሩህ, ብርሃን]

በሬ *bäre* ox, bull
አውራ ፡ በሬ bull
የበሬ ፡ ሥጋ beef

በር *bärr* gate, entrance, doorway, goal (in soccer)
በረኛ *bärränña* gatekeeper, doorman, janitor
በራፍ *bärraf* doorway (see አፍ)

ቢራ *bira* beer

ቢሮ *biro* office, bureau
የጉዞ ፡ ቢሮ travel bureau

ብራ *bərra* clear weather (see በራ)

ብር *bərr* silver, dollar, money, banknote
የብር silver (adj.)

በረሃ *bäräha* wild region, wilderness (see also በረኻ)
በረሃማ *bärähamma* deserted

ብሩህ *bəruh* bright (sunshine), glowing light (color), radiant (smile), lucid, clear (see በራ)

ብርሃን *bərhan* light, glow, flame (of candle); see በራ, ብሩህ
ብርሃነ ፡ ልደት *bərhanä lədät* Christmas (used in greeting)
እንኳን ፡ ለብርሃነ ፡ ልደት ፡ አቃዋት Happy Christmas! (see ቃ)

ብርሌ *bəralle* small flask with a long neck used for drinking mead, crystal

በርሚል *bärmil*, በርሜል *bärmel* barrel, tank (container for liquid), drum (container for liquid)

በረረ *bärrärä* fly (vi.), run fast
አባረረ *abbarrärä* drive away, chase away, repel, keep off (chase away)
(ከሥራ ፡ አባረረ dismiss, fire)
በረራ *bärära* flight (of bird, of plane)
በራሪ *bärari* express, adj. (bus), rush (order)
በራሪ ፡ ኮከብ meteor
ተባራሪ ፡ ጥይት *täbarari ṭəyyət* stray bullet
መባረር *mäbbarär* expulsion

በራሮ *bäräro* cockroach

በርስ, see እርስ

ቦርሳ *borsa* wallet, portfolio, bag, pocketbook, briefcase, purse

በረሸ *borräšä* brush (v.)
ብሩሽ *bruš* brush (n.)

በረቀ *bärräqä* lighten, shine, scintillate
ብራቅ *bəraq* thunderbolt
መብረቅ, see above
[See also *በረቀረቀ]

ባረቀ *barräqä* go off accidentally (of a gun)

ብርቅ *bərq* scarce, rare, scant (rare), precious, singular (unusual), something uncommon, uniqueness

ብርቅዩ *bərqəyye* pet (child)

በረቀ *bʷarräqä* bound (of deer through the woods), prance about, gambol, frolic
ቡረቃ *burräqa* merriment

*በረቀረቀ, አብረቀረቀ *abräqärräqä* glisten, have a sheen, sparkle (see also በረቀ)
የሚያብረቀርቅ *yämmiyabräqärrəq* shiny

በረበረ *bäräbbärä* search carefully, clean out, fumble, rummage, burrow
አንበረበረ *anbäräbbärä,* አምበረበረ *ambäräbbärä* ransack

በርበሬ *bärbärre* Ethiopian red pepper

ቡራቡሬ *burraburre* spotted (animal), multi-colored

ቡርቡር, see ቦረቦረ

ቢራቢሮ *birrabirro* butterfly
የቢራቢሮ ፡ ቅርጽ *bow of ribbon

ቦረቦረ *boräbbora* hollow out, cut a groove, channel its way (of a river)
የተቦረቦረ ፡ ጥርስ *yätäboräbbora ṭərs* cavity (of tooth)
ቦረቦር *boräbor* hole (in a road)
ቡርቡር *burbur* groove

በረታ *bärätta* be strong, prevail (against)
አበረታ *abärätta* strengthen, intensify (heat), encourage, invigorate
አበረታታ *abbärätatta* encourage, hearten, foster, cheer up (vt.), promote
በርታ *bärta* cheer up!
ብርቱ, see below
ብርታት, see below
በርተቶ *bärtəto* hard (adv.), intensely
ማበረታታት *mabbärätatat* encouragement

በረት *bärät* fenced enclosure for cattle, corral, stall, pen

ብረት *brät* iron, cast iron, shell (of cannon), metal, rifle

ብረታ ፡ ብረት *bräta brät* metals
ብረት ፡ ሠሪ *smith (see ሠራ)
የብረት ፡ አፈር iron ore, ore
(የ)እንግር ፡ ብረት shackles, fetter, chains

ብረት *brät,* in የዓይን ፡ ብረት pupil (of eye)

ብርቱ *bərtu* strong, powerful, industrious, vigorous, severe (punishment), important, active, arduous, difficult (book); see በረታ
ብርቱ ፡ ነዎት? are you all right?

ብርታት *bərtat* strength, vigor, endurance, rigor (of heat); see በረታ

ብርቱካን *bərtukan* orange

ብራና *bəranna* parchment, vellum
የብራና ፡ መጽሐፍ manuscript

በርኖስ *bärnos* long black mantle

ባርነት *barənnät* slavery, servitude, bondage (see ባሪያ)

በረንዳ *bärända* veranda, terrace, porch, raised platform in front of a building
በረንዳ ፡ አዳሪ tramp

ብርንዶ *bərəndo* red raw meat to be eaten as such

ባርኔጣ *barneṭa* hat
ባርኔጣ ፡ አደረገ put on a hat
ባርኔጣ ፡ ደፋ put on a hat

በረኛ, see በር

ባረከ *barräkä* bless (of priest), give benediction, sanctify
ቡራኬ *burake* blessing, benediction
ቡሩክ *buruk* blessed

ብራኳ *bərakʷa* shoulder blade

ብርክ *bərk* hysteria

በረከተ *bäräkkätä* wear (last), be durable (clothes, shoes), stand up (clothes), be plentiful, be numerous

አበረከተ *abäräkkätä* increase in number, make a present of, give as a gift, wear one garment a long time
ከ - - - ይልቅ ፡ አበረከተ *abäräkkätä* outlast, outwear
በረከት *bäräkät* plentifulness, blessing, gift
(ገጸ ፡ በረከት gift, present)
በርከት ፡ ያለ *bärkätt yalä* a number of, quite a few, several, a good many, numerous, copious, substantial, considerable, large (number)
በርካታ *bärkatta* big (meal)

*በረከከ, ተንበረከከ *tänbäräkkäkä* kneel, genuflect, drop on one's knees, bend the knees
አንበረከከ *anbäräkkäkä* bring to one's knees, make kneel

በረኸ *bäräha* wild region, wilderness (see also በረሃ)
በረኸኛ ፡ ዓረብ *bärähäñña aräb* Bedouin

በረዘ *bärräzä* (B) dilute honey in water to make *bärz*, dilute with water
ብርዝ *bärz* a non-alcoholic drink made of honey and water

ባሪያ *bariya*, ባርያ *baräya* slave
ባሪያ ፡ ፈንጋይ slave dealer, slave trader
የባሪያ ፡ በሽታ epilepsy
ባርነት *barännät* slavery, servitude, bondage

በረደ *bärrädä* cool down (vi.), cool off, be cold (drink), be cool (coffee), quiet down (of excitement), burn down (of fire), be quiescent (volcano)
በረደ(ው) *bärrädä(w)* feel cold
አበረደ *abärrädä* make cool, cool off (vt.), appease (anger), calm down (vt.), soothe
በረድ ፡ አለ *bärädd alä* let up (of storm)
በረዶ, see below
በራድ *bärrad* cold, adj. (coffee)

ብርድ, see below
ማብረጃ, see above

በረዶ *bärädo* hail, snow, ice (see በረደ)
በረዶ ፡ ሆነ freeze, be frozen solid
በረዶ ፡ ጣለ (v.) snow, hail
ድንጋይ ፡ በረዶ ፡ ሆነ be frozen stiff

ባሩድ *barud* powder, gunpowder

ብርድ *bärd* chill (n.), cold (n., adj.); see በረደ
ብርድ ፡ ልብስ blanket
ብርዳም *bärdam* cold (wind)
ብርዳማ *bärdamma* cold (month), glacial

ቦርድ *bord* board (committee)

ብርዳም, ብርዳማ, see ብርድ

በርጋታ, see እርጋታ

በረገደ *bäräggädä* burst open, vt. (the door), fling open, vt. (the door)
(ሰብሮ ፡ በረገደ smash open)
ተበረገደ *täbäräggädä* fly open, blow open (vi.)

በረገገ *bäräggägä* be startled, apprehend danger
አበረገገ *abäräggägä* cause to start

ቦርጭ *borč* paunch
ቦርጭ ፡ አወጣ have a paunch (see ወጣ)
ቦርጫም *borčam* obese
ቦርጫምነት *borčamännät* obesity

በርጩማ *bärčumma* stool

ብርጭቆ *bärčäqqo* drinking glass

በራፍ *bärraf* doorway (see በር, አፍ)

በሳ *bässa* perforate, puncture, pierce, drill a hole

በሶ *bässo* type of food made usually from roasted barley flour

ቢስ *bis* (in compound) without, devoid of, un-; ex. ፍሬ ፡ ቢስ devoid of results, fruitless, ዕድል ፡ ቢስ unfortunate, መልክ ፡ ቢስ ugly (see ባሰ)

ባሰ *basä* be bad, be worse, worsen
(vi.), deteriorate, be worse off; serves
also to express a heightened situation
(as in ጀግንነቱ ፡ እየባሰ ፡ ሄደ his courage
hardened)
አባሰ *abasä* worsen (vt.), make
worse, aggravate
አባሰ(በት) *abasä(bbät)* aggravate
(make worse), exacerbate
(የባሰ *yäbasä* worse, worst (modify-
ing a negative quality, state or condition)
የባሰ(በት) *yäbasä(bbät)* awful (liar)
አብሶ *abəso* especially
[See also ቢስ, በሽታ]

ቢሳ *besa* coin, penny

በሰለ *bässälä* be ripe (fruit), ripen
(vi.), be cooked, age (of wine), reach
maturity, be mature
አበሰለ *abässälä* ripen (vt.), cook (vt.)
ብሱል *bəsəl* cooked, mature
የበሰለ *yäbässälä* ripe, mature (mind)
ያልበሰለ *yalbässälä* unripe, immature
ማብሰያ *mabsäya* cooking utensil

*በሰረ, አበሰረ *abässärä* announce good
news, herald (v.), announce
አብሳሪ *absari* herald (n.), bearer
of good tidings
ብስራት, see below

ብስራት *bəsrat* good news (see *በሰረ)

በሰበሰ *bäsäbbäsä* be wet, be drenched,
get soaked, be soggy, rot, be rotten,
spoil (vi.), decay (of fruit), putrefy
አበሰበሰ *abäsäbbäsä* soak, vt. (of
rain soaking clothes), drench, spoil
(vt.), decay (vt.)
መበስበስ *mäbäsbäs* decay (n.), caries
የበሰበሰ *yäbäsäbbäsä* spoiled, bad
(apple), rotten

በስተ *bästä* toward, to
በስተኋላ toward the back, from
behind
በስተቀኝ on the right-hand side of
በስተግራ toward the left

በስተ - - - በኩል in the direction of,
on the - - - side
[See also በስተቀር]

በስተቀር *bästäqär* except, besides
(prep.), furthermore, moreover,
otherwise, nonetheless (see በስተ, ቀረ)
ከ - - - በስተቀር except for, besides,
with the exception of, save (prep.),
aside from, apart from

ቢሲክሌት *bisiklet* bicycle

ብስኩት *bəskut* cookie

*በሳጨ, ተበሳጨ *täbäsaččä* be annoyed,
be irritated, be in a bad temper, be
cross, be peevish
አበሳጨ *abbäsaččä* irritate, annoy,
upset, vex, exasperate, frustrate
ብስጩ *bəsəčču* moody, sour (bad-
tempered), peevish, irritable, miserable (unhappy)
ብስጭት *bəsəččət* vexation, irritation,
frustration, aggravation, fit of depression, disappointment

ቡሽ *buš* cork, stopper

ባሻ *baššä*, in ሆዱ ፡ ባሻ susceptible (to
slights), easily insulted, easily hurt,
emotional

ብሽሽት *bəšəššät* groin

በሽታ *bäššəta* sickness, disease (see ባሰ)
ተላላፊ ፡ በሽታ epidemic (see አለፈ)
የሚጥል ፡ በሽታ *yämmiṭəl bäššəta*
epilepsy, fit (see ጣለ)
የባሪያ ፡ በሽታ epilepsy
የእንቅልፍ ፡ በሽታ sleeping sickness
በሽተኛ *bäššətäňňa* diseased (organ),
sick, ill, sickly person, patient (sick)

ባሻገር *baššagär*, in ከ - - - ባሻገር beyond,
across (see *ሻገረ)

በቄ, see በቃ

በቃ *bäqqa* suffice, be sufficient, be
enough, be qualified, be competent;
renounce the world

(በቃ enough!)
(ለአገሩ ፡ በቃ he finally returned to
his native land)
አበቃ *abäqqa* qualify (make competent), terminate (vi.), finish (vt.),
bring to an end, cease to exist, be
consummated, be adjourned, be
lifted (finished)
(እንኳን ፡ ለብርሃነ ፡ ልደቱ ፡ አበቃዎት
Joyous Christmas! Happy Christmas!)
(የሱ ፡ ነገር ፡ አበቃ he is finished, it's
all over with him)
አባቃ *abbaqqa* make ends meet
አብቃቃ *abqaqqa* offset (make up
for), make both ends meet
በቃኝ *bäqqaňň* I have enough
በቃኝ ፡ የማይል *bäqqaňň yämmayəl*
exacting, demanding (lit. who does
not say 'I have enough')
በቃኝ ፡ ባይ *bäqqaňň bay* contented
(lit. who says 'I have enough')
የበቃ *yäbäqqa*, in በአእምሮ ፡ የበቃ
one who has come of age
በቂ *bäqi* sufficient, enough, adequate
(sufficient), decent (grades), ample
(enough), satisfactory (reason)
በቂ ፡ ያልሆነ deficient, inadequate,
insufficient
ብቁ *bəqu* adequate (competent),
qualified (person), competently done,
able (speech)
ብቁ ፡ ሆነ become competent, measure up
ብቃት, see below
ብቁነት *bəqunnät* competence, adequacy
የሚበቃ *yämmibäqa* sufficient
አይበቃም *aybäqam* be inadequate
ማብቂያ *mabqiya* end

ቡቃ *buqa* hernia
ቡቃ ፡ ወረደው he has hernia

ብቁ, see በቃ

ብቅ ፡ አለ *bəqq alä* appear, emerge,
come into view, drop by, drop in,
pop in, come around, put in an
appearance

በቀለ *bäqqälä* sprout (vi.), shoot up,
germinate, flourish, grow, vi. (of
plant)
አበቀለ *abäqqälä* sprout, vt. (of
rain sprouting beans), grow, vt. (of
soil growing wheat), produce (of a
farm)
ብቅል *bəqəl* malt
በቆልት *bäqqolt* sprout
ቡቃያ, see below

*በቀለ, ተበቀለ *täbäqqälä* (B) seek vengeance, take vengeance, revenge,
avenge, retaliate
በቀል *bäqäl* revenge, vengeance
የበቀል vindictive (punishment)
ቂም ፡ በቀል vengeance, feud
የደም ፡ በቀል vendetta

በቅሎ *bäqlo* mule

በቆሎ *bäqqollo* corn, maize

ባቄላ *baqela* bean

ብቅል *bəqəl* malt (see በቀለ)

በቆልት *bäqqolt* sprout (see በቀለ)

በቀር *bäqär* except, outside of (see ቀረ)
ከ - - - በቀር outside of
ከ + negative verb + በቀር unless

በቀቀን *bäqäqän* parrot

በቅበቃ *bäqbäqqa* parakeet

ብቃት *bəqat* life of withdrawal from
the world, ascetic life, immaculate
life (see በቃ)
የብቃት *yäbəqat* ascetic

ብቁነት *bəqunnät* competence, adequacy
(see በቃ)

ቡቃያ *buqayya* sprouting grain, seedling, bud, shoot (see በቀለ)

ባባ *babba* be afraid

ባቡር *babur* train, locomotive, railroad
የባቡር ፡ ሐዲድ railroad, railway,
railroad tracks, rail(s)

(የ)ባቡር ፡ ጣቢያ railroad station
የምድር ፡ ባቡር railway, railroad

ብብት bəbbət armpit

ባት bat calf (of leg)

ቤት bet house, verse (a single line of
poetry)
ቤቶች betočč people (family), folks
ቤተኛ betäňňa friend of the family
ቤት ፡ መታ rhyme (v.)
(የቤት ፡ መምቻ, n. rhyme)
ቤት ፡ ለቤት around the house
በ - - - ቤት according to
ከቤት ፡ ቤት from door to door,
from house to house
ቤተ ፡ መቅደስ temple, sanctuary
ቤተ ፡ መንግሥት royal residence,
palace, capitol
ቤተ ፡ መዘክር museum (see ዘከረ)
ቤተ ፡ መጻሕፍት library (see መጽሐፍ)
ቤተ ፡ ሰብ parentage, family, house
(family), household
ቤተ ፡ ሰቦች folks
ቤተ ፡ ንጉሥ circular hut
ቤተ ፡ ክህነት clergy (see ካህን)
ቤተ ፡ ክርስቲያን church
ቤተ ፡ ዘመድ relations, kin, family
የቤት ፡ ሥራ housework, homework
የቤት ፡ እመቤት lady of the house
የቤት ፡ እቃ furniture
የቤት ፡ ጫማ slippers
መሥሪያ ፡ ቤት office
መብል ፡ ቤት dining room
መኝታ ፡ ቤት bedroom
ምክር ፡ ቤት parliament, Congress,
council
መዝገብ ፡ ቤት archives, record office
ማዘጋጃ ፡ ቤት municipality
ማድ ፡ ቤት kitchen, cook house
ምድር ፡ ቤት ground floor
ምግብ ፡ ቤት restaurant
ሽንት ፡ ቤት toilet
ባለቤት proprietor, owner, master
of the house, lady of the house, husband, spouse, wife, subject (in grammar)
ባለቤትነት ownership

ቡና ፡ ቤት coffee house, bar
ትምህርት ፡ ቤት school
ተማሪ ፡ ቤት school
እስር ፡ ቤት prison (see እሰረ)
እቃ ፡ ቤት vestry, storehouse
ወጥ ፡ ቤት kitchen, cook
ወፍጮ ፡ ቤት mill
የሰገራ ፡ ቤት latrine, outhouse
የወፍ ፡ ቤት cage, nest
ግምጃ ፡ ቤት treasury
ጠጅ ፡ ቤት bar where Ethiopian
drinks are served

ቦታ bota place, spot (place), space,
area, site, point (place), status (position), role, part (in a play)
ቦታ ፡ ያዘ reserve a place, book passage, play a part
በየቦታው bäyyäbotaw everywhere, all
over, throughout
ከየቦታው käyyäbotaw from all over
አንድ ፡ ቦታ somewhere

ቦት bot, in ቦት ፡ ጫማ high boot
ተደራቢ ፡ ቦት galoshes (see ደረበ)

በተለይ bätäläyy, በተለየ bätäläyyä, በተ
ለይም bätäläyyəm chiefly, specially,
especially, specifically, in particular,
particularly (see ለየ)

በትር bättər, ብትር bəttər stick, club,
cudgel
በትረ ፡ መንግሥት scepter

ባትሪ batri battery, flashlight

በተረፈ bätärräfä besides, apart from,
otherwise (see ተረፈ)
በተረፈም moreover
ከ - - - በተረፈ except, outside of

በተቀር bätäqär except, otherwise, besides, in that case (see ቀረ)
ከ - - - በተቀር except, besides, apart
from

ቡትቶ butətto rags, tatters, tattered
clothes
ቡቱቷም bututʷam ragged (beggar)

በታች, see ታች

በተነ *bättänä* (B), vt. disperse, disband, scatter, dissipate, break up (a meeting), demobilize, adjourn, dispel, strew (flowers, leaflets)
ተበተነ *täbättänä* (vi.) disperse, be scattered, disband, dissipate, adjourn, break up (of a meeting)
በታተነ *bätattänä* (vt.) scatter about, disperse, dissipate
ተበታተነ *täbätattänä* scatter in all directions (vi.), be dispersed
[See also ብትንትን]

ብትንትን *bətəntən*, in ብትንትን ፡ አወጣ blow to bits (see በተነ, ወጣ)

ቤተኛ *betäňňa* friend of the family (see ቤት)

ቢትወደድ *bitwäddäd* a senior honorific title

ብቻ *bəčča* only (adj., adv.), the only one, alone, merely, solely, exclusively, but, however
(ቆይ ፡ ብቻ just wait, I will show you)
ብቻ ፡ ለብቻ alone
ብቻውን *bəččawən* by himself, he alone, in itself
ለብቻ in private, separately
ለብቻ ፡ ለብቻ separately
ለብቻው he alone, of his own
ለየብቻ *läyyäbəčča* separately, apart
ብቸኛ, see below

ቡችላ *buččəlla* puppy, whelp

ብቸኛ *bəččäňňa* lone, lonesome, solitary (see ብቻ)
ብቸኛነት *bəččäňňannät*, ብቸኝነት *bəččäňňannät* loneliness
የብቸኛነት solitary (life), secluded (life), lonely (life)

ቡና *bunna* coffee, coffee bean
ቡና ፡ ቤት coffee house, bar
የቡና ፡ ቁርስ any food taken with coffee in the morning
ቡናማ *bunnamma* brown

ቡን ፡ አለ *bunn alä*, ብን ፡ አለ *bənn alä* rise (of dust), be blown by the wind into the air, fly up in the air (see also

በነነ, ቦነነ)
አመዱ ፡ ቡን ፡ አለ be flabbergasted

ባና *bana* woolen blanket

ብን ፡ አለ, see ቡን ፡ አለ

ቡናማ *bunnamma* brown (see ቡና)

በንተ *bäntä* for the sake of

በነነ *bännänä*, ቦነነ *bonnänä* be blown away, blow (of dust), rise here and there (of smoke, dust); see ቡን ፡ አለ
ባነነ *bannänä* wake up with a start
ብናኝ, see below

ብናኝ *bənnaň* particle of dust, flurry (of snow); see በነነ
የአሸዋ ፡ ብናኝ grit

ባንክ *bank* bank (credit firm)
ባለ ፡ ባንክ banker

ባንኮ *banko* counter (in a café)

ቤንዚን *benzin* gasoline, petrol
ቤንዚን ፡ መስጫ accelerator (see ሰጠ)
ቤንዚን ፡ ቀጂ gas station attendant (see ቀዳ)
(የ)ቤንዚን ፡ ማደያ filling station, gas station

ባንዴ *bande* at a glance, at once, at one time (see አንድ)

ቦንዳ *bonda* iron strap

ባንዴራ *bandera* flag
የባንዴራ ፡ መስቀያ flagpole

ባንድነት *bandənnät* in a body (see አንድነት)

ባንዳፍታ *bandafta* in no time (from በ+አንድ+አፍታ)

ባኞ *baňňo* bathtub

በዓል *bä'al* holiday, festival, anniversary (see also ባል)
በዓል ፡ አከበረ celebrate a holiday (see ከበረ)
የበዓል ፡ አከባበር celebration
የነጻነት ፡ በዓል Liberation Day

የዕለት ፡ በዓል festival
የዓመት ፡ በዓል anniversary

ብዕር *bəʼər* pen, fountain pen

ባዕድ *baʼəd* one who is an outsider to the family, one who has no blood relations to one, alien (adj.)
ባዕድ ፡ መነሻ prefix
ባዕድ ፡ መድረሻ suffix
የባዕድ foreign
የባዕድ ፡ አገር foreign country, foreign

ቡኮ *bukko* puncture (of tire)

ቡኮ *buko* fermented dough to make bread (see በካ, ቡሶ)
ቡኮ ፡ እቃ trough (see also ቡሀቃ, ቦሃቃ)

በካ *bokka* ferment (of dough), be rancid (butter)
አበካ *abokka* make to ferment, knead, make dough
ቡኮ, see above
የበካ *yäbokka* rancid (butter)
ያልበካ *yalbokka* unleavened (dough)
[See also ቡሶ, ቡሀቃ, ቦሃቃ]

በከለ *bäkkälä* (B) contaminate (with sewage), pollute (water), defile (make filthy), taint (spoil), corrupt (a judge)
በደም ፡ ተበከለ *bädäm täbäkkälä* be bloody

በኩል *bäkkul*, in በ - - - በኩል as regards, with regard to, in respect of, as for, in the matter of, in the direction of, on the side of, along, by means of, by way of, in care of, on the part of (see እኩል)
በኔ ፡ በኩል, or በበኩሌ for my part, as far as I am concerned
በንዱ፡በኩል in one respect
በንድ ፡ በኩል ... በሌላ ፡ በኩል on the one hand ... on the other hand
በየት ፡ በኩል which way?, in which direction?, in which respect?
በዚህ ፡ በኩል this way

ከ - - - በኩል from the direction of, on the part of, up to
ወደ - - - በኩል toward - - - side, in the direction of

በከራ *bäkära* spool, bobbin

በኩር *bäkʷər* first-born
የበኩር ፡ ልጅ eldest, first-born
ብኩርና *bəkʷrənna* primogeniture, primacy

በከተ *bäkkätä* die (animal) without being ritually slaughtered (hence unfit to eat)
በክት *bäkt* dead animal which has not been ritually slaughtered

ቡኮን *bukkän* coward

ባከነ *bakkäna* be dissipated (wealth), go to waste (of food), stray (of thoughts)
(በሕሳብ ፡ ባከነ daydream)
አባከነ *abakkänä* dissipate (money), be prodigal (with money), waste, idle away, squander, divulge (a secret)
ብኩን *bəkun* dissipated (life)
አባካኝ *abakaň* wasteful, lavish, spendthrift
አባካኝነት *abakaňənnät* waste (n.)
(ገንዘብ ፡ አባካኝነት extravagance)
የባከነ *yäbakkäna* wasted (time)

ቦሃቃ *bohaqa* kneading trough (from ቦሃ ፡ እቃ); see ቡሀቃ, በካ, ቡሶ

ብው ፡ አለ *bəww alä* pop (balloon)

በወን *bäwən* in actual fact, actually (see እውን)

በውነት *bäwnät* indeed, in fact, truly, actually (see እውነት)

በወዘ *bäwwäzä* (B) shuffle (cards)

ባውዛ *bawza* spotlight, searchlight

በዛ *bäzza* be abundant, be numerous, increase (vi.), be much, be too much, multiply (vi.), be frequent, be full of

(በዛበት *bäzzabbät*) it is too much for
him)
(ሥራ ፡ በዛበት he has a lot to do)
አበዛ *abäzza* increase (vt.), multiply
(vt.), do something in great quantity
(አብዝቶ ፡ በላ *abzəto bälla* he ate a
lot)
ተባዛ *täbazza* multiply (vi.), propagate themselves, reproduce (vi.)
አባዛ *abbazza* multiply (vt.), duplicate
(copies)
በዛ ፡ ያለ *bäza yalä* considerable
ብዙ, see below
ብዛት, see below
ቢበዛ *bibäza* at the most
እምብዛም, see below
አብዛኛ, see below
የሚበዛው *yämmibäzaw* most
የሚበዛውን ፡ ጊዜ *yämmibäzawən gize*
most of the time
ይብዛ ፡ ይነስ *yəbza yənäs* more or
less

ቪዛ *viza* visa

ቤዛ *beza* ransom
የጣት ፡ ቤዛ thimble

ብዙ *bəzu* abundant, much, numerous,
many, a great many, plenty of, a
great deal, a lot of (see በዛ)
ብዙ ፡ ሰው crowd
ብዙ ፡ ጊዜ a long time, many times,
often, oftentimes, frequently, normally
ብዙውን ፡ ጊዜ *bəzuwən gize* commonly, most of the time
በብዙ a great deal, in plenty, abun-
dantly
ከብዙ ፡ ጊዜ ፡ በፊት long ago

ቦዝ ፡ አንቀጽ *boz anqäṣ* gerund

በዚህ *bäzzih* here, in this way, in
this (see -ዚህ)

ባዝራ *bazra* mare

ባዜቃ *bazeqa* mercury, quicksilver

ባዘቱ *bazäbotu* usually (see አዘቱ)

በዘበዘ *bäzäbbäzä* sack (v.), pillage,
despoil, make a raid on

ብዛት *bəzat* abundance, totality, multitude, quantity, prevalence (see በዛ)
በብዛት *bäbəzat* in large numbers,
in large quantities, frequently
በጊዜ ፡ ብዛት in the course of time

ቦዘነ *bozzänä* loaf, leave off working,
be idle

በዚያ *bäzziya* there, that way, in that
(see -ዚያ)

በየ *bäyyä* each, every (as in በየሌሊቱ
nightly; በየቀኑ every day, daily;
በየወሩ monthly; በየጊዜው occa-
sionally; በየዓሙቱ yearly)
በያለበት *bäyyalläbbät* everywhere
(from በየ-አለ-በት)

ብይ *bəyy* marbles

ቦይ *boy* small irrigation channel, drain-
age canal, trench

በየት *bäyät* where? (from በ-የት)
በየትም ፡ በታ any place, everywhere

በየነ *bäyyänä* (B) decide (of judge),
decree, resolve
ብይኔ *bəyyane* decision, definition

ቢያንስ *biyans* at least (see አነሰ)
ቢያንስ ፡ ቢያንስ at least

በየደ *bäyyädä* (B) weld, solder
በያጅ *bäyyağ* welder

በየፋ *bäyəfa* publicly, openly, straight
out (see ይፋ)
በይፋ ፡ ታወቀ become public (see
ወቀ)

በዳ *bäda* desolate (adj.), desolate and
deserted
ምድረ ፡ በዳ desert

ቡዳ *buda* evil eye, one who kills or
casts a spell with the evil eye

ባዶ *bado* empty, vacant, bare, unoccupied (house, seat), free (empty, available), naked (eye), blank (sheet of

paper, space, bullet), coffee or tea served without cream and/or sugar ባዶውን *badowən* with empty stomach, empty-handed
ባዶውን ፡ አስቀረ denude
ባዶ ፡ እጁን penniless, empty-handed (see እጅ)
ባዶ ፡ እግሩን barefoot (see እግር)
ባዶ ፡ ኪሱን ፡ ነው he is broke

በደለ *bäddälä* (B) wrong, do wrong, harm, mistreat, treat ill, commit an injustice
በደል *bädäl* ill-treatment, harm, wrong, injustice

*በደረ, ተበደረ *täbäddärä* (B) borrow (money or grain)
አበደረ *abäddärä* lend (money or grain)
ብድር *bəddər* loan (of money), credit
ብድር ፡ መለሰ pay back, get even with, retaliate
ተበዳሪ *täbäddari* debtor
አበዳሪ *abäddari* creditor

በድን *bädən* corpse, cadaver, dead matter
በድን ፡ ሆነ be frozen to the spot, be half dead, be lifeless, be petrified (with fear)
በድን ፡ አደረገ petrify

ቡድን *budən* team
የቡድን ፡ አባት team captain
የፖለቲካ ፡ ቡድን political party

ብድግ ፡ አለ *bədəgg alä* rise, get up, stand up

በጀ *bäǧǧä* (B) be good (for), turn out well, suit, be fitting
ተበጀ *täbäǧǧä* be well made
አበጀ *abäǧǧä* prepare, repair, do well, arrange, fix, mend, produce (form), develop (habits)
(ወዳጅ ፡ አበጀ make friends)

ባጀት *baǧät* budget

በጋ *bäga* dry season

በግ *bäg* sheep, ram
የበግ ፡ ጠቦት lamb
የበግ ፡ ጠጉር wool
ሴት ፡ በግ ewe

በጎ *bäggo*, ቦጎ *boggo* good (adj.), well (adv.)
በጎ ፡ አድራጊ charitable, benevolent (person)
በጎ ፡ አድራጎት welfare, charity
የበጎ ፡ አድራጎት charitable
የሕዝብ ፡ በጎ ፡ አድራጎት social welfare

ቦግ ፡ አለ *bogg alä* flare, flare up, flame quickly

*በገረ, ተበገረ *täbäggärä* (B) give in, yield
አልበገርም ፡ አለ *aləbbäggärəmm alä* remain defiant, remain unyielding
የማይበገር *yämmayəbbäggär* invincible, invulnerable (fortress), impregnable, immovable (stubbornness), unflinching, unyielding, obstinate (fever)
አለመበገር *alämäbbägär* defiance

ቡጉር *bugur* pimple

*ቦገቦገ, ተንቦገቦገ *tänbogäbbogä* be ablaze

በገና *bägäna* harp-like musical instrument
በገና ፡ ደረደረ play the harp

ቡጉንጅ *bugunǧ* boil (n.)
ቡጉንጅ ፡ ወጣበት *bugunǧ wäṭṭabät* he has a boil

ቢጋፈ *bigäfa* at most (see ጋፈ)

በጣ *bäṭṭa* make a cut in the flesh with a sharp instrument (to draw blood), lance a boil, make an incision, slit open

ቡጢ *buṭṭi* fist, blow with the fist, punch
በቡጢ ፡ አለው *bäbuṭṭi aläw* he hit him with his fist
በቡጢ ፡ መታ (v.) punch, box, sock

ቡ.ጢ.ኛ *buṭṭiňňa* boxer, pugilist

ቢ.ጢ *biṭe*, ብጤ *bəṭe* kind of, sort of, of sorts
የኔ ፡ ቢ.ጢ pauper, indigent

ባጥ *baṭ* beam that supports the roof of a small house
የባጡን ፡ የቆጡን ፡ ቀባጠረ ramble on, talk off the top of one's head

በጣም *bäṭam* very, greatly, much, considerably, too (much, very), quite, highly (very); see ጣም

*በጠረ, አበጠረ *abäṭṭärä* (B) comb, winnow, clean grain by throwing it into the air
ማበጠሪያ *mabäṭṭäriya* comb (n.)

በጠሰ *bäṭṭäsä* (B) break a string or the like, detach (a button), snip (thread)
ተበጠሰ *täbäṭṭäsä* snap, vi. (of string), come off (of a button), give way (of a rope)
ብጣሽ, see below

ብጣሽ *bäṭṭaš* cut-off piece, strip of paper, clipping, scrap (of cloth); see በጠሰ

በጠበጠ *bäṭäbbäṭä* shake something in a pot, beat a liquid, disturb, create commotion, upset, disrupt (a conference)
በጣበጠ *bäṭabbäṭä* mix slightly, stir
ብጥብጥ *bəṭəbbəṭ* confusion, rebellion, upheaval, revolution, crisis, violence, discord
ብጥብጥ *bəṭbəṭ* mixed with water, dissolved
በጥባጭ *bäṭbač* unruly, trouble maker, mischievous

ቡ.ጢ.ኛ, see ቡ.ጢ.

ቧጠጠ *bʷaṭṭäṭä* lacerate, scratch (with the fingernails), prick (with claws)

በጣጢስ *bäṭaṭis* sweet potato (see also መጣጢስ)

ብጫ *bəča*, ቢ.ጫ *biča* yellow
ብጫ ፡ ወባ yellow fever

ቧጨረ *bʷaččärä* scratch, mar
በጫጨረ *bočaččärä* scribble
ተበጫጨረ *täbočaččärä* be scarred (of face)

በጨቀ *boččäqä* tear
በጫጨቀ *boččaččäqä* tear to shreds
ብጫቂ *bäččaqi* scrap (of paper), shred

ብጹዕ *bäṣu'* His Holiness
ብጹዕነታቸው *bäṣu'ənnätaččäw* His Grace

ተ

ተ, variant of ከ

ታህሣሥ *tahsas* December

ትሑት *təhut* humble, polite, courteous, modest, affable
ትሕትና *təhtənna* humility, modesty, politeness, civility, courtesy

ትኋን *təhʷan* bug, bedbug (see also ትኺን)

ተላ *tälla* be worm-eaten, be putrid, be rotten (see ትል)

ትል *təl* worm, earthworm, insect, bug (see ተላ)
ትል ፡ በላው be worm-eaten
የሐር ፡ ትል silkworm

ቶሎ *tolo* soon, quickly, at once, early (adv.)
ቶሎ ፡ ቶሎ rapidly, fast, quickly
በቶሎ promptly, quickly, in a minute, fast
ቶሎ ፡ አለ *tolo alä* be quick, hurry
ቶሎ ፡ በል hurry!, come on!
ቶሎ ፡ ብሎ quickly

*ታለለ, አታለለ *attallälä* deceive, cheat, trick, get the best of someone, beguile, bluff, elude (see *አለለ)
ተታላይ *tätalay* dupe, credulous

አታላይ , see below
ማታለል *mattaläl* deceit, cheating

ትልልቅ *tələlləq* big, large (used for plural); see ትልቅ

ተላላኪ. , see ላከ

ተላላፊ. , see አለፈ.

ተለመ *tällämä* furrow (v.)
ትልም *təlm* furrow, ridge (of soil)

ተለማማጅ *tälämamaǧ* apprentice (see ለመደ)

ታላቅ *tallaq* elder (adj.), older, great, large, big (important), grand (palace), mighty, significant (see ትልቅ)
ታላቅነት *tallaqənnät* grandeur, greatness, glory

ትልቅ *tälləq* huge (box), big, great (in size); see ላቀ , ታላቅ
ትልልቅ , see above
ትልቅነት *təlləqənnät* size (of a city), importance

ተልባ *tälba* flax, linseed

ትላንት *tälant* yesterday (see also ትላንትና , ትናንት , ትናንትና)

ትላንትና *tälantənna* yesterday (see also ትላንት , ትናንት , ትናንትና)

ቴሌግራም *telegram* cable (n.), wire, telegram

ትምህርት *təmhərt* lesson, training, schooling, learning, study, education, discipline (field of learning), academic subject (see *ማረ)
ትምህርት : ቤት school
ትምህርተ : ምድር geography
ትምህርተ : አለት geology
የትምህርት *yätəmhərt* scholastic
የትምህርት : ሚኒስቴር Ministry of Education
የትምህርት : ጓደኛ fellow student
ሁለተኛ : ደረጃ : ትምህርት : ቤት secondary school, high school
ኅብረ : ትምህርት social studies

አንደኛ : ደረጃ : ትምህርት : ቤት primary school
የቀለም : ትምህርት academic training

ተመላላሽ *tämälalaš*, in ተመላላሽ : ተማሪ day student (see መለሰ)
ተመላላሽ : በሽተኛ outpatient
ተመላላሽ : የሚበዛበት *tämälalaš yämmibäzabbät* busy (street); see በዛ

ተማመነ , see አመነ

ተማሪ *tämari* student, pupil (see *ማረ)
ተማሪ : ቤት school
ተማሪ : ቤት : ገባ start school
ተመላላሽ : ተማሪ day student

ተምር *tämr* date (fruit), date palm

ተምሮ : ማስተማር *tämro mastämar* literacy campaign (see *ማረ)

ታምር *tammər* miracle, marvel (see also ተአምር)

ተመሳሳይ *tämäsasay* parallel, similar, akin, comparable, analogous, synonym (see መሰለ)
ተመሳሳይነት *tämäsasayənnät* parallelism, agreement, identity, similarity, correspondence (identity)

ተመስጦ *tämästo* abstraction (absence of mind), rapture, enchantment (see መሰጠ)
በተመስጦ in complete oblivion, with rapture, rapturously
የተመስጦ abstracted (absent-minded)

ቴምቢ. , see ቴንቢ.

ትምባሆ *təmbaho* tobacco
ትምባሆ : ጠጣ smoke (v.)

ታምቡር *tambur* drum (n.)
ታምቡር : መታ drum (v.), pulse, v. (of heart)

ቴምብር *tembər* postage stamp

ቲማቲም *timatim* tomato

ተመነ *tämmänä* (B) price, put a price on

ተተመነ *tätämmänä* be priced
የተተመነ ፡ ዋጋ *yätätämmänä waga* list price
ተመን *tämän* estimate (n.)
ትመና *təmmäna*, in ያስተያየት ፡ ትመና poll (expression of opinion)

ታማኝ *tammaňň* loyal, honest, faithful, trustworthy, dependable, devoted, reliable (see እመነ)
ታማኝነት *tammaňňənnät* loyalty, allegiance, honesty, rectitude, devotion
ታማኝነት ፡ የጉደለው disloyal

ትምክሕት *təmkəhət* boast, bragging, false pride (see *መከ)
ትምክሕተኛ *təmkəhətäňňa*, ትምክተኛ *təmäktäňňa* snob

ተራ *tära* turn, order, rank, line, section, stall (of merchandise), series; common (man), plain (adj.), mediocre, ordinary (mechanic), private (citizen)
ተራ ፡ ጠበቀ take turns, wait one's turn
ተራ ፡ በተራ in turns
(በተራ ፡ በተራ in turns)
ተራ ፡ ሕዝብ masses, crowd
ተራ ፡ ሰው layman, ordinary person
ተራ ፡ ቁጥር cardinal number
ተራ ፡ ክፍል ward (of hospital), prison
ተራ ፡ ወታደር enlisted man, private (soldier)
ከተራ ፡ የተወለደ lowly, of humble birth (see ወለደ)
የተራ everyday, ordinary, lay (person)
ባለተራ one whose turn it is
ተረኛ *täräňňa* person whose turn it is
ተረኛ ፡ ነው be on duty, be on call (doctor)
[See also ተርታ]

ትር ፡ ትር ፡ አለ *tərr tərr alä* pulsate (of heart), flutter (of heart)
ትርታ *tərrəta*, in የልብ ፡ ትርታ pulse, heartbeat

ትራም *tram* streetcar

ተርሞሜትር *tärmometər* thermometer (for weather)

ተርምስ *tərəmməs* disarray, confusion, hustle and bustle, fuss (see *ረመሰ, ትርምስምስ)
የትርምስ ፡ ቤታ madhouse

ተርምስምስ *tərməsməs* chaos, disorder, confusion (see ትርምስ)
ተርምስምስ ፡ አለ *tərməsməss alä* be in an uproar, be chaotic

ተራራ *tärara* mount, mountain
ተራራማ *täraramma* mountainous

*ተራሰ, ተንተራሰ *täntärasä* be put under the head to serve as a pillow
ትራስ, see below

ትራስ *təras* cushion, headrest, pillow (see *ተራሰ)
ትራስ ፡ ተንተራሰ sleep on a pillow
የትራስ ፡ ልብስ pillowcase

ቱሪስት *turist* tourist
የቱሪስት ፡ ድርጅት tourist office

ተራቢ *tärrabi* clown

ተርብ *tärb* hornet, wasp
የተርብ ፡ እንጀራ wasp nest

ተረተ *tärrätä* (B) tell a story, speak in parables
ተረት *tärät* story, fable, fairy tale, parable, anecdote
ተረትና ፡ ምሳሌ *tärätənna məssale* folklore

ተርታ *tärta* single line, row (line), queue, order
[See also ተራ]

ትርታ, see ትር ፡ ትር ፡ አለ

ተረተረ *tärättärä* unravel, rip (seams), untwist, break up, split open

ተራተር *tärätär* ridge (chain of hills)

ትርንን *tərəngo* kind of citrus fruit

ተረኛ, see ተራ.

ትርእይት *tər'əyt*, ትርኢት *tər'it* exhibition, fair, performance, exhibit, scenery, sight, view
የሥዕል ፡ ትርእይት picture exhibition
[See also ራእይ, አርአያ]

ቱርክ *turk* Turk
የቱርክ ፡ ዶሮ turkey

ታሪክ *tarik* tale, history, story, marvel
ታሪክ ፡ ጸሐፊ historian
ልብ ፡ ወለድ ፡ ታሪክ novel, fiction
ባለ ፡ ታሪክ hero (of a story), protagonist
አፈ ፡ ታሪክ tradition, legend, myth, mythology
ዜና ፡ ታሪክ annals
የሕይወት ፡ ታሪክ biography, memoirs, record (of one's life)
የአፍ ፡ ታሪክ fable, legend
ታሪካዊ historic, historical

ትርኪ ፡ ምርኪ *tərki mərki* stuff, hodgepodge, junk, rubbish, nonsense

ተረኩሰ *täräkkʷäsä* put out a cigarette
መተርኩሻ *mätärkʷäša* ashtray

ተረከዝ *täräkäz* heel (of foot, of shoe)

ታረዘ *tarräzä* be without clothes (from *አረዘ)

ተራዳ *tärada* tent pole

ትርጁማን *tərǧuman* interpreter

ታርጋ *targa* license plate, license number

ተረጐመ *täräggʷämä* translate, render (translate), interpret
ተርጓሚ *tärgʷami* translator
(የሕግ ፡ ተርጓሚ ፡ ሥልጣን judicial power)
ትርጓሜ *tərgʷame* translation, interpretation
ትርጉም *tərgum* translation, interpretation, meaning, sense (of word)
ትርጉም ፡ የሌለው *tərgum yälelläw* meaningless (words)

ትርጉም ፡ ያለው *tərgum yalläw* meaningful, expressive
አስተርጓሚ *astärgʷami* translator, interpreter

ተረፈ *tärräfä* be left, be left over, remain, be in excess, be superfluous, survive, be spared (saved)
(ከደጋ ፡ ተረፈ be out of danger; see አደጋ)
አተረፈ *atärräfä* make a profit, earn, gain (strength, popularity), make remain, preserve, leave, save, rescue, win (reputation), bring forth, generate
ተራፊ *tərrafi* leftover, reject
ትርፍ, see below
በተረፈ *bätärräfä* besides, apart from, moreover, otherwise
የተረፈ *yätärräfä* remains, survivor

ትርፍ *tərf* profit (in business), gain, remainder, excess, remnant, residue, spare (time, tire), saving, extra (adj.); see ተረፈ
ትርፍ ፡ ከፈለ overpay, pay extra
ትርፍ ፡ እቃ surplus goods
ትርፍ ፡ አንጀት appendix (anatomy)
(የትርፍ ፡ አንጀት ፡ በሽታ appendicitis)
ትርፍ ፡ ጊዜ leisure, free time

*ተረፈረፈ, ተትረፈረፈ *täträfärräfä* overflow, be present in abundance, abound, be copious

ትራፊክ *trafik* traffic, traffic police
ትራፊክ ፡ የሚበዛበት busy (street)

ተስማሚ, see ሰማ

ተስማሚነት, see ሰማ

ተሳሰረ, see አሰረ

ተሳቢ *täsabi* object (in grammar); see ሳበ
ርቱዕ ፡ ተሳቢ direct object
እ.ር.ቱዕ ፡ ተሳቢ indirect object

ተሰቦ *täsəbo* typhoid, typhus

ተስተካከለ, see አከለ

ተሰጥኦ *täsäṭ'o*, ተሰጥዎ *täsäṭwo* ability, talent, gift (natural talent), affinity (natural attraction); see ሰጠ
ተሰጥዎ ፡ ያለው *täsäṭwo yalläw* gifted, talented

ተስፋ *täsfa* hope, promise, prospect
ተስፋ ፡ ሰጠ promise (v.)
ተስፋ ፡ ቈረጠ despair, be discouraged, be disheartened, lose hope
ተስፋ ፡ አስቈረጠ discourage, deject, dishearten, be a discouragement
ተስፋ ፡ አለ(ው) be hopeful
ተስፋ ፡ አደረገ hope, promise (v.)
ተስፋ ፡ አጣ despair (v.)
ተስፋ ፡ ጣለ(በት) he placed his hopes on him
ተስፋ ፡ ቢስ desperate
ተስፋ ፡ የሚጣልበት *täsfa yämmiṭṭaləbbät* promising (see ጣለ)
ምድረ ፡ ተስፋ Promised Land

ቱሽ ፡ አለ *tušš alä* hiss (of air in a leak)

ተሸቀዳደም *täšqädaddämä* race (vi.); see ቀደም

ተሸካሚ *täšäkkami* porter (see *ሸከመ)

ተሸከርካሪ *täškärkari* vehicle (see *ሽከረ ከረ)
ተሸከርካሪ ፡ ወምበር swivel chair

ተሿጋሪ *täšagari* transitive (verb); see *ሻገረ

ተቅማጥ *täqmaṭ* diarrhea, dysentery (see *ቀመጠ)
የተቅማጥ ፡ በሽታ dysentery

ተቀማጭ *täqämmač* resident, reserve (saved money), savings deposit (see *ቀመጠ)
ተቀማጭ ፡ ሒሳብ account (in a bank), savings account
ተቀማጭ ፡ ገንዘብ savings, savings account

ተቀባይ *täqäbbay* one who welcomes, refrain singer, one who gives the response in singing (see *ቀበለ)

ተቀባይነት *täqäbbayənnät* acceptance, receiving (see *ቀበለ)
ተቀባይነት ፡ አገኘ find acceptance, be accepted, be acceptable, be approved, be admissible, be carried (of a motion), gain ground
ተቀባይነት ፡ አጣ be unacceptable, fail to get a hearing or obtain acceptance
እንግዳ ፡ ተቀባይነት hospitality

ተቃውሞ, see ቆም

ተቀጥያ *täqäṭṭəyya* offshoot (of a plant); see ቀጠለ

ተቄጣጣሪ, see ቄጠረ

ቱቦ *tubbo* tube, pipe
የቱቦ ፡ ሜዳፍ nozzle

ተባለ *täbalä* be called, be named, be said (see አለ)

ተባበለ, see አበለ

ተባባረ, see አበረ
የተባበሩት ፡ መንግሥታት *yätäbabbärut mängəstat* United Nations
ተባባሪ *täbabari* associate, ally
ትብብር *təbəbbər* co-operation, coordination

ተባት *täbat* male, masculine (see also ተባዕት)

ታቦት *tabot* Ark of the Covenant, altar stone of the Ethiopian church, patron saint
ታቦት ፡ ነገው take the *tabot* in procession around the church
[See also ኪዳን]

ተበተበ *täbättäbä* twist, tie (baggage), wind around
(በአስማት ፡ ተበተበ enchant (of witch), cast a spell on)
ተተበተበ *tätäbättäbä* be fouled up (rope)

*ተበተበ, ተንተባተበ *täntäbattäbä* stammer, stutter, lisp, falter (stammer)

መንተብተብ *mäntäbtäb* (n.) stutter, stuttering, stammering
ተብታባ *täbtabba* stammerer

ተባዕት *täba'ət* male (see also ተባት)
ተባዕታይ ፡ ጾታ *täba'ətay ṣota* masculine (gender)

ተባይ *täbay* vermin, insect

ታበየ *tabbäyä* be haughty, be arrogant, be vain (see *በበየ, በቢይ)
ትዕቢት, see below

ትቢያ *təbbiya* dust
ከትቢያ ፡ ተነሣ rise from obscurity (see ነሣ)

ታታ *tatta* interlace, intertwine

ተታላይ, see *ታለለ

ታታሪ *tatari* industrious, dynamic, energetic, enterprising, ambitious

ተቸ *täččä* (B) comment (v.)
ተቺ *täčči* critic, commentator
ትችት, see below

ታች *tačč* below, down there
በታች below
ከ - - - ታች below, under
ከ - - - በታች under, below (prep.)
ከታች ፤ ከበታች beneath (adv.)
ከዚህ ፡ በታች below (adv.)
ወደ ፡ ታች downwards
ታችኛ *taččəňňa* lower (adj.)
የበታች, see below

ትችት *təččət* comment, criticism (making of judgments), critical opinion (see ተቸ)
ምጸታዊ ፡ ትችት satire

ተነ- *tännä-*, variant of ከነ-

ተን *tänn* evaporation (see ተነነ)

ተኒስ *tänis* tennis

ትንሣኤ *tənsa'e* resurrection, reincarnation (see ነሣ)

ታናሽ *tannaš* small, younger (brother); see also ትንሽ, አነሰ

ትንሽ *tənnəš* little, small, meager, some of, a bit, a few, a while, a little while, a moment (see also ታናሽ, አነሰ)
ትንሽ ፡ ትንሽ just a little
ትንሽ ፡ በትንሽ bit by bit
ትንሽም in the least
በትንሹ just a little, not too much, easily
በትንሽ ፡ ጊዜ shortly

ተንቀሳቃሽ *tänqäsaqaš* movable, mobile (property); see *ቀሰቀሰ

ትንቅንቅ *tənəqnəq* (n.) struggle, fight (see አነቀ)

ቱንቢ *tunbi* plumb line

ትንቢት *tənbit* prophecy, prediction, forecast (see *ነበየ)
የትንቢት ፡ ጊዜ future tense
ትንቢተኛ *tənbitäňňa* seer, soothsayer
ትንቢታዊ ፡ ጊዜ *tənbitawi gize* future tense

ተነተነ *tänättänä* treat (discuss), analyze
ትንተና *təntäna* analysis
ተንታኝ *täntaň* analyst

ተነነ *tännänä* (vi.) evaporate, vaporize
አተነነ *atännänä* evaporate (vt.)
ተን *tänn* evaporation

ተናነቀ *tänannäqä* grapple (see አነቀ)

ትናንት *tənant* yesterday (see also ትናንትና, ትላንት, ትላንትና)

ትናንትና *tənantənna* yesterday (see also ትናንት, ትላንት, ትላንትና)
ትናንትና ፡ ማታ last night
ከትናንትና ፡ ወዲያ the day before yesterday

ትንኝ *tənəňň* gnat, mosquito
የወባ ፡ ትንኝ mosquito

ታኒካ *tanika* tin can

ታንክ *tank* tank (armored vehicle)

ታንኳ *tankʷa* reed boat

*ተነከለ, ተተናከለ *tätänakkʷälä* attack, (of a dog), go at (attack, of dog, of snake), excite (a dog); see ተንኮል

ተንኮል *tänkʷäl* trick, ruse, subterfuge, devious ways, guile, foul play, malice, mischief (see *ተነከለ)
ተንኮል ፡ ያዘለ *tänkʷäl yazzälä* malicious (see አዘለ)
የተንኮል insidious, vicious (rumor)
የተንኮል ፡ መሪ ringleader
የተንኮል ፡ ቀንደኛ ringleader (see ቀንድ)
ተንኮለኛ *tänkʷäläňňa* crafty, sly, sneaky, foxy, malicious

ትናግ *tənag* palate

ትንግርት *təngərt* trick (feat of skill)
ለትንግርት amazingly

ተነፈሰ *tänäffäsä* breathe, exhale, deflate (vi.), expire, blow on the hands (see ነፈሰ); this verb is treated as a quadriradical
ጎማው ፡ ተነፈሰ(በት) he had a flat tire
ትንፋሽ, see below

ትንፋሽ *tənfaš* respiration, breathing, breath, puff of air (see ተነፈሰ)
ትንፋሹ ፡ አጠረ(ው) he is out of breath
ባንድ ፡ ትንፋሽ in one gulp

ተኛ *täňňa* (B) sleep, be asleep, fall asleep, go to bed, stay in bed, slumber, get flat (tire), be stagnant (water)
(ተኛቶ ፡ አረፈደ *täňňəto aräffädä* oversleep)
(ሆስፒታል ፡ ተኛ he was in the hospital)
(ጎማህ ፡ ተኛቷል you have a flat tire)
አስተኛ *astäňňa* make sleep, put to bed, make lie down
የሚያስተኛ ፡ መድኃኒት *yämmiyastäňňa mädhanit* anesthetic
የተኛ *yätäňňa* stagnant (water)
መኝታ ፡ ቤት *mäňňəta bet* bedroom, dormitory

ተአምር *tä'ammər* (pl. ተአምራት *tä'am-mərat*) miracle, marvel (see also ታምር)
ተአምራዊ *tä'ammərawi* miraculous
ትእምርት *tə'əmərt* sign, miraculous sign
ትእምርት ፡ ጥቅስ quotation mark

ትዕቢት *tə'əbit* pride, arrogance, conceit, haughtiness (see ታበየ)
ትዕቢተኛ *tə'əbitäňňa* arrogant, haughty, conceited, proud

ትእዛዝ *tə'əzaz* order, command, commandment, directive, instruction (see አዘዘ)
ትእዛዝ ፡ አንቀጽ imperative (n.)
ጸሐፊ ፡ ትእዛዝ Minister of the Pen

ትዕይንት *tə'əyənt* view (scenery), scene (part of act), display

ትዕግሥት *tə'gəst*, ትግሥት *təgəst* patience, resignation (see ታገሠ)
ትዕግሥተኛ *tə'gəstäňňa* patient (adj.), calm

ተካ *täkka* (B) substitute, supersede, replace, succeed (in an office), take the place of, refund
ተተካ *tätäkka*, passive of the preceding; succeed, vt. (in an office), be made up (of losses)
በ - - - እግር ፡ ተተካ take the place of
ተተኪ *tätäki* successor, replacement
የማይተካ *yämmayəttäkka* irreplaceable
ምትክ, see above

ተከሀኖ *täkəhəno*, in ልብሰ ፡ ተከሀኖ priestly vestments (see ካህን)

ተከለ *täkkälä* plant (flowers, trees), pitch (a tent), fix (the eyes on something), establish, sew on (a button)
ተክል *täkl* plant, orchard
[See also አታክልት, አትክልት]

ተኩላ *täkʷla* jackal

ተክሊል *täklil* sacrament of indissoluble marriage, church wedding

በተክሊል ፡ አገባ marry in church
ሥርዓተ ፡ ተክሊል marriage service

ተከላካይ, see ከለከለ

ተኮሬ *täkkʷärä* (B) look, stare threateningly
አተኮሬ *atäkkʷärä* stare fixedly
አተኩሮ ፡ ተመለከተ *atäkkʷəro tämäläkkätä* peer, gaze, give an intent look (see *መለከተ)

ተኮሰ *täkkʷäsä* (B) cauterize, brand (animals), iron (clothes), press (clothes), shoot, fire a gun
አተኮሰ(ው) *atäkkʷäsä(w)* have fever, run a fever
ተኩስ *täkʷs* shot, shooting
ተኳሽ *täkkʷaš* shot (one who shoots)
ትኩስ, see below
ትኩሳት, see below

ታክሲ *taksi* taxi

ትኩስ *təkkus* warm (roast), fresh (eggs, meat, news); see ተኮሰ
ትኩስ ፡ ወሬ latest news

ተከሳሽ *täkässaš* accused, defendant (see ከሰሰ)

ትኩሳት *təkkusat* fever, temperature (fever); see ተኮሰ
የትኩሳት ፡ መለኪያ thermometer

ትከሻ *təkäšša* shoulder
በትከሻው ፡ ኖረ depend on someone else, live off someone else's labor

ቲኬት *tiket* ticket, coupon
ቲኬት ፡ ቄረጠ sell tickets
ቲኬት ፡ አስቄረጠ buy tickets
ቲኬት ፡ መሸጫ ticket office, box office (see ሸጠ)
ቲኬት ፡ ቄራጭ ticket seller, conductor (of bus); see ቄረጠ
ደርሶ ፡ መልስ ፡ ቲኬት roundtrip ticket

ታከተ(ው) *takkätä(w)* be tired, be bored, tire of, wear oneself out, become weary

የማይታክት *yämmayətakkət* tireless (worker), indefatigable

*ተከተከ, ተንተከተከ *täntäkättäkä* simmer

ትክትክ *təkkəttəkk* whooping cough

ተከታይ, ተከታታይ, see *ከተለ

ቴክኒሺያን *teknišiyan* technician

ቴክኒክ *teknik* technique

ተካከለ, see አከለ

ትክክል *təkəkkəl* straight, proportional, equal, uniform, correct, accurate, just, even, level (see አከለ)
በትክክል fairly, evenly, exactly, equally, precisely, accurately
ትክክለኛ *təkəkkəläňňa* correct, right (correct), exact, accurate, precise, fair (judge), equitable, honest (weight)
ትክክለኛነት *təkəkkəläňňannät* precision, equity, accuracy, correctness

ተከዘ *täkkäzä* (B) be sad, be pensive, be thoughtful
ትካዜ *təkkaze* melancholy, sadness
መተከዝ *mätäkkäz* gloom

ተካፋይ *täkafay* participant (see ከፈለ)

ትኋን *təhʷan* bug, bedbug (see also ትኳን)

ተወ *täwä* let go, give up, leave, leave off, cast away, quit, desist, abandon, stop doing something, relinquish, forbear, drop (the subject), dismiss (a matter)
ተው! *täw* is it really so?, be quiet!
ተው ፡ እባክህ come now!

ተዋሕዶ *täwahdo* monophysitism, profession of faith regarding the unitary nature of Christ (see *ወሐደ)

ትውልድ *təwlədd* race, generation, descent (see ወለደ)
የትውልድ native (land)

(የ)ትውልድ ፡ አገር motherland, native country, homeland, birthplace, ancestral home

ተወላጅ *täwällağ* descendant, native of a particular place (see ወለደ)

ተውላጠ ፡ ስም *täwlaṭä səm* pronoun

ታወረ, see *በወረ

ቴዎሪ *tewori* theory

ትውስት *təwəst*, in (የ)ትውስት ፡ ቃል loanword (see *ዋሰ)

ተውሳከ ፡ ግስ *täwsakä gəss* adverb

ተዋናይ *täwanay* actor, performer

ተዋወቀ, see በወቀ

ተወያየ, see *ወየ

ተወዳዳሪ *täwädadari* rival, contestant, competitor, candidate, opponent (in election); see ወደረ
ተወዳዳሪ ፡ የሌለው peerless
የንግድ ፡ ተወዳዳሪ competitor (in business)

ተወዳጅ, see ወደደ

ታዛ *taza* porch, eaves

ትዝ ፡ አለ(ው) *təzz alä(w)* remember, recall, think of
ትዝታ *təzzəta* remembrance, remembering, memoirs, memory, recollection, reminiscence

ታዘበ *tazzäbä* (B) make critical observations, observe, watch (look at); see *አዘበ
ታዛቢ *tazzabi* observer
ትዝብት *təzzəbt* observation, disapproving observation

ትዝታ, see ትዝ ፡ አለ

ተዘናና, see *ዘና

ተዝካር *täzkar* commemoration of a dead person by a religious service and banquet, memorial service held on the 40th day after death (see ዘከረ)

ታዛዥ *tazzaž* obedient, docile, subordinate, dutiful (see አዘዘ)
ታዛዥነት *tazzažənnät* obedience

ቲያትር *tiyatər* theater, drama, play (drama)
ቲያትር ፡ ደራሲ playwright
ቲያትር ፡ አሳየ put on a play (see አየ)

ትይይ *təyəyy* opposite (see አየ)
የ --- ትይይ opposite
በ --- ትይይ ፡ ነው face (v.)

ተድላ *tädla* pleasure, delight (see *ደላ)

ትዳር *tədar* livelihood, existence, married life, marriage (married life), home life (see ዳረ)
ትዳር ፡ ያዘ get married, start a home
በትዳር ፡ ኖረ get married
ባለትዳር married couple (see ባለ)

ታዲያ *tadiya* so!, so then!, well then!, now then
ታዲያስ *tadiyass* how about it?
ታዲያስ ፡ ምን ፡ ይሁን so what?

ተዳደረ, see አደረ

ታደገ *taddägä* save, spare (deliver)
ታዳጊ *taddagi* patron saint
ታዳጊ ፡ መልአክ guardian angel

ቱጃር *tuğar* rich man, wealthy man

ተጋ *tägga* be diligent, persevere, be assiduous
ትጉ *təgu* diligent, attentive, assiduous, vigilant, conscientious
ትጋት *təgat* diligence, perseverance [See also ትጉህ]

ቱግ ፡ አለ *tugg alä* explode with rage, flare up (in anger)
በንዴት ፡ ቱግ ፡ አለ fly into a fury

ትጉህ *təguh* diligent, attentive, assiduous, conscientious, vigilant (see ተጋ)

ታገለ *taggälä* wrestle, strive, struggle, scuffle (see *በገለ)

ትግል *təgəl* struggle (n.), wrestling, conflict, campaign (to combat crime), effort
ትግለኛ *təgläňňa* wrestler

ታገሠ *taggäsä* (B) tolerate, be patient, endure, bear (endure); see *ዐገሠ አስታገሠ *astaggäsä* make to endure, alleviate (pain), ease (pain), allay, soothe (of ointment), relieve, lull (a suspicion), calm (a person)
ትዕግሥት, ትግሥት, see above
ታጋሽ, see below

ታጋሽ *taggaš* patient (see ታገሠ)
ታጋሽነት *taggašənnät* patience, longanimity

ተገቢ, see ገባ

ተግባር *tägbar* action, duty, work, task, occupation, activity, behavior, deed, office (duty), function (see ገበረ)
በተግባር practically
ተግባረ ፡ እድ ፡ ትምህርት ፡ ቤት vocational school
ተግባራዊ *tägbarawi* applied (science)

ተግባቢ, see ገባ

ትጋት, see ተጋ

ተገን *tägän* shelter, cover (protection)
ተገን ፡ ያዘ seek shelter, take cover

ተጋድሎ *tägadlo* crusade, campaign (to fight crime), battle, mortification of flesh (see ገደለ)

ተጋዳይ *tägaday* champion (see ገደለ)

ታጠቀ *taṭṭäqä* wear a belt, put on a belt (for fighting), gird oneself (usually for fighting or doing a difficult task), put around the waist, arm (vi.), be equipped (soldier), fold the *šämma*-dress as a mark of respect (see *ዐጠቀ)
አስታጠቀ *astaṭṭäqä* arm (vt.), equip
ሽጉጥ ፡ ታጠቀ wear a gun, strap a pistol
ትጥቅ, see below

ትጥቅ *təṭq* gear, equipment (of soldier), outfit (see ታጠቀ)
ትጥቅና ፡ ሥንቅ *təṭqənna sənq* (military) supplies, ammunition
የመንሳፈፊያ ፡ ትጥቅ life belt, life vest

ተጠባባቂ *täṭäbabaqi*, in ተጠባባቂ ፡ ሚኒስትር acting minister (see ጠበቀ)
ተጠባባቂ ፡ ጎማ spare tire
ተጠባባቂ ፡ ገንዘብ reserve funds

ታጣፊ *taṭafi*, in ታጣፊ ፡ ወምበር folding chair (see ዐጠፈ)

ተጽዕኖ *täṣə'əno* influence, pressure (in politics)
ተጽዕኖ ፡ አለው influence (v.), affect (have influence)

ተጸውዖ *täṣäw'o*, in የተጸውዖ ፡ ስም proper noun, given name

ተፋ *täffa* spit, spit out, vomit, disgorge (of volcano), belch (of volcano); see also እትፍ ፡ አለ
ትፍ ፡ አለ *təff alä* spit
ትፍታ *təffəta* sputum, saliva

ተፍ ፡ አለ, in ተፍ ፡ ብሎ ፡ ተነሣ *täff bəlo tänässa* jump, rise suddenly

ቱፋ *tufa* apple (see also ቱፋሕ)

ታፋ *tafa* thigh, rump

ቶፋ *tofa* small jar

ቱፋሕ *tufah* apple (see also ቱፋ)

ትፍታ *təffəta* sputum, saliva (see ተፋ)

ተፋጥሮ *täfäṭro* natural state, nature (see ፈጠረ)
በተፈጥሮ naturally (by nature)
ከተፈጥሮ ፡ የተለየ abnormal (see ለየ)
የተፈጥሮ native (ability), natural (talent, resources), innate, inherent, inborn, physical (laws)
የተፈጥሮ ፡ ሀብት natural resources
ሥነ ፡ ተፈጥሮ evolution

ቴፕ *tep* tape

ቸ

ቸል ፡ አለ *čäll alä* neglect, disregard,
be careless, ignore (see also ችላ ፡ አለ)
ቸል ፡ ባይነት *čäll bayənnät* negligence, neglect
ቸልታ, see below

ቻለ *čalä* have the ability to, be able,
can, be capable, defray, endure,
withstand (endure), be in a position,
know how, have a command of (a
language)
(ራሱን ፡ ቻለ be self-supporting, be
independent, fend for oneself)
(ራሱን ፡ ችሎ ፡ አደረ *rasun čəlo addärä* shift for oneself)
(አማርኛ ፡ ትችላለህ? *amarəñña təčəlal-
läh* can you speak Amharic?)
ተቻለ *täčalä* be possible
የማይቻል *yämmayəččal* impossible,
intolerable (heat), unbearable
አስቻለ *asčalä* enable, make possible,
sit (of court)
(ችሎት ፡ አስቻለ hold court)
ቻይ, see below
ችሎታ, see below

ችላ ፡ አለ *čəlla alä* neglect, be careless,
be neglectful, not mind, disregard,
take no notice of, not pay attention,
ignore, slack off, be slack (see also
ቸል ፡ አለ)

ቸልታ *čälləta* negligence, neglect (not
caring for), carelessness (see ቸል ፡ አለ)
ቸልተኛ *čällətäñña* negligent, careless,
derelict (in duty), slack
ቸልተኝነት *čällətäññannät* negligence,
carelessness, laxity

ችሎታ *čəlota* ability, skill, qualification,
proficiency, capacity, capability, caliber, mastery (skill); see ቻለ

ችሎታ ፡ ያለው *čəlota yalläw* competent, able, capable
ችሎታ ፡ የሌለው *čəlota yälälläw* incompetent, unqualified

ችሎት *čəlot* assembly, law court, tribunal, session of court
ችሎት ፡ ቻለ sit in court
ችሎት ፡ አስቻለ hold court

ቸልተኛ, see ቸልታ

ቸረ *čärä* give to charity, be generous
ቸር *čär*, ቼር *čer* good, generous, magnanimous
ችሮታ, see below
ችርነት, see below

ችሮታ *čərota* charity, bounty, philanthropy, beneficence (see ቸረ)
ችሮታ ፡ አደረገ be charitable, endow
(with money)
የችሮታ philanthropic

ቸረቸረ *čäräččärä* sell at retail, retail (v.)
ችርቻሪ *čärčari* retail dealer, retailer
ችርቻሮ *čərəččaro* retail (in trade)

ችርነት *čärənnät* bounty, kindness (see
ቸረ)

ችርኬ *čärke* rim (of tire)

ቸቦ *čəbbo* kind of torch

ቸነከረ *čänäkkärä* nail (boards), rivet
(boards)
ችንካር *čənkar* peg

ቸነፈር *čänäfär* pestilence, plague

ቸከ *čäkä* be persistent, be importunate,
be stubborn, be obstinate (see also
ችክ ፡ አለ, ቸከቸከ)
ቸከ(በት) *čäkä(bbät)* get sick and
tired of
ችኮ *čəkko* obstinate, stubborn, willful, heavy-handed, tiresome, vexatious
የቸከ *yäčäkä* monotonous, dull

ቼክ *ček* check, n. (money)
የቼክ ፡ ደብተር checkbook

ችክ ፡ አለ *čəkk alä* be importunate, be persistent, insist, be stubborn, be obstinate (see also ቸኸ)

ቸከለ *čäkkälä* (B) drive a peg into the ground, plant (posts)
ችካል *čəkal* peg, post (peg)

ቸኰለ *čäkkʷälä* (B) hurry, be in a hurry, hasten (vi.), rush (vi.)
አቸኰለ *aččakkʷälä* rush, vt. (a job)
ችኩል *čəkkul* hasty, hurried, rapid, quick, impetuous, impulsive
ችኰላ *čəkkʷäla* haste, hurry, precipitation
(በችኰላ hastily)
(የችኰላ hasty, not thought out)
ችኩልነት *čəkkulənnät* rashness, urgency, hastiness
አስቸኳይ *asčäkkʷay* urgent, pressing
የሚያስቸኩል *yämmiyasčäkkʷəl* emergency (adj.)

ቸኮላታ *čäkolata* chocolate

ቸከቸከ *čäkäččäkä* nag, pester (see ቸኸ)

ቻይ *čay* tolerant, patient, enduring (see ቻለ)

ቻይና *čayna* China
የቻይና ፡ ሰው Chinese (n.)

ቸገረ *čäggärä* (B) be in difficulty, be in need of something, have a need for, lack, be in distress
(ምን ፡ ቸገረኝ why should I care?, I don't care!)
ቸገረ(ው) *čäggärä(w)* he is poor, he is in need
ተቸገረ *täčäggärä* bother (vi.), be bothered, be hard put, go to any bother, go to any trouble, inconvenience oneself, be disturbed
አስቸገረ *asčäggärä* give trouble, trouble, disturb, bother (vt.), make difficulties, worry (vt.), encumber, inconvenience
አስቸገረ(ው) *asčäggärä(w)* he found it hard

ችጋር *čəggar* famine, hunger, deprivation, affliction
ችግር, see below
አስቸጋሪ *asčäggari* difficult, troublesome, harsh (life), hard (question)

ችግር *čəggər* trouble, disturbance (nuisance), annoyance, difficulty, distress, inconvenience, misery, want, bother, need, encumbrance, problem, hardship (see ቸገረ)
ችግር ፡ ላይ ፡ ጣለ get one in trouble
በችግር scarcely, hardly
የችግር ፡ ጊዜ hard times
የለችግር *yaläčəggər* easily
ችግረኛ *čəggəräñña* needy, poor, afflicted

ችግኝ *čəggəñ* shoot which is transplanted, seedling

ቸፈ *čəfe* eczema

ችፍ ፡ አለ *čəff alä* have a rash (see also ሽፍ ፡ አለ)

ነ

ነ *na* come! (fem. ነይ, pl. ኑ)

ነ - *nna* and; (combined with certain verb forms) since, because

*ነሀለለ, እነሀለለ *anähollälä* stupefy, bewitch (of beauty)

ነሐሴ *nähase* August

ነሐስ *nähas* copper, brass, bronze

ነላ *nala* brain
ነላው ፡ ዞረ he lost his head (got excited)

ነሙና *namuna* specimen, sample (see also ላሙና)

ኑሮ *nuro* living, existence, subsistence, life (see ኖረ)
የኑሮ ፡ ሁኔታ living conditions

የኑሮ ፡ ውድነት living costs
የኑሮ ፡ ደረጃ standard of living, station of life

ዋሬ *norä* live, reside, dwell, lead a life, inhabit, exist, lead an existence
(ይኖርበታል *yənorəbbätal* he must, he has to)
አኖረ *anorä* place, maintain, keep, put, lodge, house
ኖር *nor* form of welcome to someone who joins a group
ኑር, see above
ነዋሪ *näwari*, ኗሪ *n*ʷ*ari* inhabitant, resident, dweller
መኖር *mänor* presence, existence
(አለመኖር *alämänor* absence)
መኖሪያ, see above
አኗኗር *ann*ʷ*an*ʷ*ar* way of life, living

ኖራ *nora* lime (from limestone), whitewash (n.)
ኖራ ፡ ቀባ whitewash (v.)

ነርስ *närs* nurse

ነሳ *nässa* deprive of, take away, hold back
(ልቡን ፡ ነሳው he took it badly)
(እጅ ፡ ነሳ bow down to greet, curtsy, pay one's respects, pay homage)
(እንቅልፍ ፡ ነሳ not let sleep, keep awake)
(ድል ፡ ነሳ win a victory)
(ፊት ፡ ነሳ give someone the cold shoulder, act distant against someone, show disfavor to)
ተነሳ *tänässa* be removed, be lifted, rise, arise, get up, wake up, be resurrected, originate, stand up, start, vi. (of fire, of car), break out (of war, of disease), leave (of bus, of train), come up (of a discussion)
(ክርስትና ፡ ተነሳ receive baptism, become Christian)
አነሳ *anässa* lift up, raise, pick up (from the floor), clear away (the dishes), move (the table), remove (take off), bring up (a subject),

make allusion to, allude, make reference to, mention (a name)
(በክፉ ፡ አነሳ speak ill of)
(ፎቶግራፍ ፡ አነሳ take a picture)
አስነሳ *asnässa* wake (vt.), rouse, give rise to, start (a motor), touch off (an argument)
ተነሳሳ *tänäsassa* rise one against the other, be excited, be aroused, be inspired, be stirred up
አነሳሳ *annäsassa* provoke, stir (to revolt), stir up, agitate, prompt, foment, urge, instigate, incite, clear (dishes from the table)
አንስቶ *ansəto*, in ከ - - - አንስቶ beginning from, starting from, ranging from
ተነስቶ *tänästo*, in ከመሬት ፡ ተነስቶ without rhyme or reason
የተነሳ *yätänässa*, in በ - - - የተነሳ ፤ ከ - - - የተነሳ on account of, because of
አነሳሽ *annäsaš* agent (agent provocateur), instigator
አነሳሽነት *annäsašənnät* instigation
መነሳሳት *männäsasat* agitation
መነሻ, see above
መንሻ, see above
መንሻ, see above
ትንሣኤ *tənsa'e* resurrection, reincarnation

ንስሐ *nəssəha* penance, penitence, confession (made to the priest)
ንስሐ ፡ ገባ do penance, go to confession, confess, atone
ንስሐ ፡ አስገባ confess (of priest); see ገባ
የንስሐ ፡ አባት father confessor

ነሰረ(ው) *nässärä(w)* have a nosebleed

ንስር *nəsər* hawk, eagle

ነሰነሰ *näsännäsä* sift (flour on cake), sprinkle (sugar, straw), scatter (straw on floor), twitch (the tail)

ኒሻን *nišan* medal

ነሸጠ *näššäṭä* (B) animate
ተነሸጠ *tänäššäṭä* be animated

ነቃ *näqqa* awake (vi.), wake up (vi.)
አነቃ *anäqqa* awaken, wake up (vt.),
rouse
አነቃቃ *annäqaqqa* lift one's spirits,
stimulate (of coffee), perk up (vt.),
foster, exhilarate (of weather), revive
(restore), refresh
ነቃ ፡ አለ *näqa alä* feel fresh (feel well),
lift, vi. (of spirits), liven up, feel lively,
feel alert
ነቃ ፡ ብሎ *näqa bəlo* with alacrity
ንቁ, see below
ንቃት *nəqat* vigilance, liveliness, alertness, pep
የተነቃቃ ፡ መንፈስ *yätänäqaqqa mänfäs* exuberance
ማነቃቂያ *mannäqaqiya* stimulation

ነቃ *näqqa* crack (v.); see also ነቀነቀ
ንቅ *nəq* split, crack, crevice
ንቃቃት *nəqaqat* crack, n. (in the wall)

ናቀ *naqä* despise, scorn, frown upon,
look down upon someone, disdain,
deprecate, belittle, abnegate
(ዓለም ፡ የናቀ unworldly)
አስናቀ *asnaqä* overshadow, outshine,
outclass, put to shame
ንቀት, see below

ንቁ *nəqu* wide-awake, watchful, vigilant, alert, keen (mind), lively, active, agile (lively), acute (see ነቃ
awake)
ንቁ ፡ ሆነ be on the alert, be awake to
ንቁነት *nəqunnät* activity, alertness

ንቅ, see ነቃ crack

ነቀለ *näqqälä* dig up, uproot, pull out,
pull up (weeds), extract, eradicate,
remove (a tooth), disconnect (phone)
ነቃቀለ *näqaqqälä* uproot

ነቀርሳ *näqärsa* scrofula
የነቀርሳ ፡ በሽታ cancer
የሳምባ ፡ ነቀርሳ tuberculosis
ያንገት ፡ ነቀርሳ scrofula (see አንገት)

ነቀሰ *näqqäsä* comb the hair, remove
(thorn from foot), deduct, tattoo
ንቅሳት *nəqqəsat* tattoo (n.)

ንቃቃት, see ነቃ crack

ንቀት *nəqät* contempt, scorn, disdain,
belittling (see ናቀ)
የንቀት *yänəqät* contemptuous, scorn-
ful
በንቀት ፡ ተመለከተ sneer at (see *መለ
ከተ)

ንቃት, see ነቃ awake

ነቀነቀ *näqännäqä* shake, make a movement, rock, jar (shake); see also
ነቃ
ተነቃነቀ *tänäqannäqä* move
አነቃነቀ *annäqannäqä* (vt.) jar (shake),
budge, loosen
ንቅናቄ *nəqənnaqe* movement (physical, political), motion
ንቅንቅ ፡ የማይል *nəqnəqq yämmayəl*
inflexible (law), adamant

ንቁነት, see ንቁ

ነቀዘ *näqqäzä* be worm-eaten, be spoiled by vermin
ነቀዝ *näqäz* worm, moth
የነቀዘ *yänäqqäzä* wormy

ነቍጥ *näqʷṭ* the four dots at the end
of the sentence

ነቀፈ *näqqäfä* blame, criticize, be critical of, disapprove, denounce, scold
ነቀፋ *näqäfa* criticism, blame, scold-
ing
ነቀፌታ *näqäfeta* rebuke, criticism,
disapproval

*ነባ, ተነባ *tänäbba* prophesy (see also
*ነብየ)

ንብ *nəb* bee
የንብ ፡ እንጀራ honeycomb
የንብ ፡ አውራ queen bee

ነበልባል *näbälbal* flame, flare (see *በለ
በለ)

ነበረ *näbbärä*, ነበር *näbbär* he was, he
was present
(ነበረው he had)
(ነበረ(በት) he had to)
አነባበረ *annäbabbärä* heap, pile up,
accumulate, place one atop the other
አስተናበረ *astänabbärä* usher (v.), be
a good host, take charge of
ንብረት, see below
መንበር *mänbär* seat, chair, altar
ወምበር ፤ ወንበር, see below
አስተናባሪ *astänabari* usher (n.)

ነብር *näbər* leopard, tiger

ንብረት *nəbrät* belongings, possessions,
property, assets, estate (see ነበረ)
ባለንብረት *balänəbrät* ownership (see
ባለ)
ጽሚ ፡ ንብረት immovable property
የሚንቀሳቀስ ፡ ንብረት *yämminqäsaqqäs
nəbrät* movable property (see ቀሰቀስ)
የአየር ፡ ንብረት climate, weather

*ነበበ, አነበበ *anäbbäbä* read
†ንባብ *nəbab* reading
አንባቢ *anbabi* reader (one who reads)
አናባቢ *annababi*, in ድምፅ ፡ አናባቢ
vowel
ተናባቢ *tänababi* consonant (n.)
ምንባብ, see above

ንባብ *nəbab* reading (see *ነበበ)
የንባብ ፡ መጽሐፍ reader (book)
ስድ ፡ ንባብ prose
ዐውደ ፡ ንባብ primer

*ነበነበ, አነበነበ *anäbännäbä* gabble (of
child), mumble, hum (of a fan), drone
(of a bee)

*ነበየ, ተነበየ *tänäbbäyä* prophesy, divine, foretell, predict (see also *ነባ)
ነቢይ *näbiyy* prophet
ትንቢት, see above

ኖታ *nota* notation (musical), note (musical)

ነታረከ *nätärräkä* trouble, annoy with
harsh words, nag

ተነታረከ *tänätarräkä* squabble (v.)
ንትርክ *nətərrək* squabble, altercation, controversy, quarrel, nagging

ነተበ *nättäbä* be ragged (sleeve), be
frayed

ንኡስ *nə'us* small
ንኡስ ፡ ሰረዝ comma
ንኡስ ፡ ደርግ subcommittee
ንኡስ ፡ ጭረት hyphen

ነካ *näkka* touch, reach (the top of the
wall), involve (affect), bear upon,
impinge on
(ምን ፡ ነካህ what's the matter?, what
ails you?)
ተነካ *tänäkka* be touched, be affected, be abridged (e.g. rights of a
citizen)
ነካካ *näkakka* tinker
ነክ ፡ የሆነ *näkk yähonä* concerning,
what is of . . . . type, what is of . . .
nature
ንክ *nək* touched (mentally)
የሚነካ *yämminäka* derogatory (remark)
እንካ *ənka* take! (fem. እንኪ; pl. እንኩ)

ነከረ *näkkärä* immerse, soak, dip (in
water), dye, plunge, steep (tea in water), plate (with gold)
መንከሪያ *mänkäriya* dye

ነከሰ *näkkäsä* bite (a person or a
thing but not food), deduct a sum
from a total, clench the teeth in pain,
be engaged (of gear, of clutch), jam
(be blocked), stick (be blocked)
(ጥርሱን ፡ ነከሶ patiently)
ተነከሰ *tänakkäsä* (used only in the
imperfect and participle) have the
habit of biting, fight (of dogs)
ተነካሽ *tänakaš* vicious (dog), fierce
ንክሻ *nəkša* bite (n.)

*ነኮሰ, ተነኮሰ *tänäkkʷäsä* pick on
(tease)

ንክሻ *nəkša* bite (n.); see ነከሰ

ነኩተ *näkkʷätä* break, smash

ነኳኩ፦ተ *näkʷakkʷätä* smash (dishes)

ነው *näw* he is, it is

*ነወረ, አስነዋሪ *asnäwwari* immodest, scandalous
ነውር, see below

ነዋሪ ፤ ናሪ, see ዋረ

ነውር *näwər* disgrace, dishonor, infamy, scandal
ነውር ፤ ነው it is rude
ነውረኛ *näwränna* depraved, indecent

ናወዘ *nawwäzä* be restless, be unable to sit still, wander about
በሕሳብ ፤ ናወዘ daydream

ነወጠ *näwwäṭä* (B) shake, agitate, disturb, upset
ተናወጠ *tänawwäṭä* be rough (sea), be turbulent (air), be upset (stomach)
አናወጠ *annawwäṭä* agitate, make choppy (the lake), disrupt (the surface of the water), disturb, derange, stir up violently, ruffle (one's composure), shake (one's confidence)
ነውጥ *näwṭ* disturbance, rebellion, commotion
ነውጠኛ *näwṭänna* militant
ደም ፤ ነውጠኛ revolutionary

ነወጸ, see ነወጠ

ነዛ *näzza* spread (a rumor), scatter, diffuse, disseminate
(ጉራ ፤ ነዛ boast, brag, show off, put on airs, talk big)
ተነዛ *tänäzza* spread, vi. (of news, of rumor, of dust), buzz (with news)

ነዘነዘ *näzännäzä* bother, nag, importune, harass, pester
ተነዛነዘ *tänäzannäzä* fuss, make a fuss
ነዝናዛ *näznazza* shrew, querulous, nag
ንዝንዝ *nəzənnəz* nagging

ናዘዘ *nazzäzä* hear confession, confess (of priest)

ተናዘዘ *tänazzäzä* confess (to a priest), leave a will, make one's will
ኑዛዜ *nuzaze* will, last will, bequest, testament, confession
የኑዛዜ ፤ ቃል last will

ነዳ *nädda* drive (a car, a herd to pasture), fly (a plane), steer (a car)
ተነኚ *näği* driver
(የ)መንኚ ፤ ፈቃድ driver's license

ናዳ *nadä* make to collapse, demolish
ተናዳ *tänadä* collapse, crumble (of wall), give way (of bridge)
ናዳ *nada* slide (of rocks), landslide

ነደለ *näddälä* poke a hole in, bore, pierce

ንዴት, see ነደደ

ነደደ *näddädä* burn, vi. (of wood), kindle (vi.), catch fire, ignite
አነደደ *anäddädä* make to burn, kindle, vt. (a fire), light (a fire)
ተናደደ *tänaddädä* get angry, get mad, be indignant
አናደደ *annaddädä* anger, irritate, infuriate, enrage
ንዴት *nəddet* anger, rage, fury
ነዳጅ, see below
የተናደደ *yätänaddädä* irate, furious
ምድጃ, see above

ነዳጅ *nädağ* fuel, inflammable, combustible (see ነደደ)
የነዳጅ ፤ ማደያ ፤ ጣቢያ fueling station
የነዳጅ ፤ ዘይት motor oil

ነደፈ *näddäfä* sting, vt. (of bee), bite (of poisonous snake), infect, card (cotton), make a sketch, outline (a drawing)
ተነደፈ *tänäddäfä*, passive of the preceding
(በፍቅር ፤ ተነደፈ be enamored)
ንድፍ *nədf* carded (cotton), sketch, design, blueprint, outline (of a drawing), pattern (for dress)
በንድፍ ፤ አነሣ sketch (v.); see ነሣ

ነጂ *näǧi* driver (see ነዳ)
አውሮፕላን ፡ ነጂ pilot (of a plane)
የመርከብ ፡ ነጂ pilot (of a boat)

ነገ *nägä* tomorrow (see ነገ)
ነገ ፡ ጧት tomorrow morning
ለነገ ፡ የማይል *länägä yämmayəl* unsparing
ከነገ ፡ (ተነገ) ፡ ወዲያ the day after
tomorrow

ነጋ *nägga* dawn (v.), become morning
አነጋ *anägga* remain until dawn
ነጋ ፡ ጠባ *nägga ṭäbba* day in, day
out, persistently
ተነገ *nägä* tomorrow
ነጋ *näga*, in በበነጋው *bäbänägaw* on
the morrow, the following day
ንጋት *nəgat* dawn (n.)

*ነጋ, አናጋ *annagga* dislocate, rock
(shake), shatter, disrupt
መናጋት *männagat* concussion

ኑግ *nug* kind of leguminous plant with
oily seeds
ቅባ ፡ ኑግ nug oil (see ቅባ)

ነገረ *näggärä* say, tell, speak, inform
ተነገረ *tänäggärä* be announced, be
said, be told, be notified
(የሚነገርለት ፡ አይደለም *yämminnäggä-
rəllät aydälläm* nothing to speak of)
ተናገረ *tänaggärä* speak, tell, speak
to, talk, converse, discuss, address
(speak to), make a remark
አናገረ *annaggärä* talk to someone,
make someone speak
ተነጋገረ *tänägaggärä* talk, speak to
one another, be on speaking terms,
have a word with, have a conversation, discuss, converse
አነጋገረ *annägaggärä* talk to, converse
ነጋሪ *nägari* one who tells
(በዋጅ ፡ ነጋሪ herald)
ነገር, see below
ንግግር, see below
ነጋሪት, see below
ተናጋሪ *tänagari* speaker, orator, lecturer, (radio) announcer

አነጋገር *annägagär* manner of speaking, speech, statement, account,
diction, accent

ነገር *nägär* word, thing, affair, matter,
item, subject, fact (see ነገረ)
ነገር ፡ ግን but
የነገር ፡ አባት arbiter
ለነገሩ by the way
በነገሬ ፡ ላይ in passing, by the way,
while I'm on the subject
በነገራችን ፡ ላይ *bänägäraččən lay* by
the way, incidentally
እንደነገሩ with indifference, crudely,
after a fashion, poorly, so-so
ነገረኛ *nägäräňňa* one who has a sharp
tongue, quarrelsome, troublemaker
(ቃም ፡ ነገረኛ trustworthy (person),
dutiful (person))
ነገርተኛ *nägärtäňňa* litigant, party
(to a lawsuit), client (of lawyer)

ነጋሪት *nägarit* kind of drum (see ነገረ)
ነጋሪት ፡ ጋዜጣ official gazette

ነገርተኛ, see ነገር

ነገረኛ, see ነገር

ነገሠ *näggäsä* become king, reign, rule
አነገሠ *anäggäsä* make king
ንጉሥ, see below
ንግሥት, see below
መንግሥት, see above
የመናገሻ ፡ ከተማ capital city

ንጉሥ *nəgus* (pl. ነገሥት *nägäst*) king,
sovereign; chapter (in Psalms); see
ነገሠ
ንጉሠ ፡ ነገሥት emperor
የንጉሥ kingly (crown), royal
የንጉሠ ፡ ነገሥት imperial
ቤት ፡ ንጉሥ circular house
ንጉሥነት *nəgusənnät* royalty
ንጉሣዊ *nəgusawi* kingly, regal, royal

ንግሥት *nəgəst* queen (see ነገሠ)
ንግሥት ፡ ነገሥታት empress

ንጉሥነት *nəgusənnät* royalty (see ንጉሥ)

ንጉሣዊ, see ንጉሥ

ንጋት *nəgat* dawn (n.); see ነጋ

ነገደ *näggädä* (B) trade in, deal in
አስተናገደ *astänaggädä* treat (customers), handle (customers), wait on (customers), entertain (guests), show hospitality
አስተናጋጅ *astänagaǧ* host, steward (of boat), hostess (on plane), receptionist
አስተናጋጅ ፡ መንግሥት host government
አስተናጋጅነት *astänagaǧənnät* hospitality
አስተናጋጅነት ፡ የጐደለው inhospitable
ማስተንግዶ *mastängədo* hospitality
ነጋዴ *näggade* merchant, dealer, businessman, trader
ንግድ , see below

ነገድ *nägäd* tribe

ነጋዴ , see ነገደ

ነጐደ *näggʷädä* (v.) thunder, roar
ነጐድጓድ , see below

ንግድ *nəgd* business, commerce, trade, deal, traffic (business); see ነገደ
የንግድ mercantile, commercial
የንግድ ፡ ምልክት trademark
የንግድ ፡ ድርጅት enterprise
የንግድ ፡ ጉዳይ deal

ነጐድጓድ *nägʷädgʷad* thunder, thunderstorm (see ነጐደ)

ንግግር *nəgəggər* speech, oration, address (speech), lecture, talks (negotiations); see ነገረ
ንግግር ፡ አደረገ give a lecture, make a speech

ነጣ *nätta* be white
አነጣ *anätta* whiten
ነጣ ፡ ያለ *näta yalä* blond
ንጡ *nətu* white
†ነጭ *näčč* white, white man
[See also ንጹሕ]

ናጠ *natä* churn, rock (a baby)
መናጫ *mänača* churn (n.)

ነጠለ *nättälä* (B) detach, separate, sever, cut off, make single
ነጣጠለ *nätattälä* detach
ነጠል ፡ አለ *nättäll alä* keep apart (vi.)
ተነጠሎ *tänättälo* all alone
ተነጣይ ፡ ጓድ *tänättay gʷadd* squad, (detachment)
ነጠላ , see below

ነጠላ *nätäla* kind of shawl-like garment which is made of a single layer of cloth, single (not doubled), singular (in grammar); see ነጠለ
ነጠላ ፡ ሰረዝ comma
ነጠላ ፡ ቁጥር singular (in grammar)
ነጠላ ፡ ጫማ sandal

ነጠረ *nättärä* bounce, vi. (of ball)
አነጠረ *anättärä* bounce a ball

ነጠረ *nättärä* be clarified, be purified (butter), be melted
አነጠረ *anättärä* clarify, purify, distill, melt (butter, gold), prove the truth of a matter
ንጥር *nətr* melted, purified
ጥንት ፡ ንጥር element (single substance, pure substance)
አንጥረኛ *antəräñña* metal worker, silversmith

*ነጠረ , አነጣጠረ *annätattärä* aim, take aim
አነጣጣሪ *annätatari* marksman
አነጣጥሮ ፡ ተኳሽ sharpshooter

ነጥር *nätr* pound (measure)

ነጠቀ *nättäqä* snatch away, take away violently, wrest, revoke (a license)
ተነጠቀ *tänättäqä* be dispossessed of, be deprived of

ነጠበ *nättäbä* drop, fall drop by drop (see ነጥብ , ነጠብጣብ)

ነጥብ *nätəb* punctuation mark, the two dots separating the words in the Ethiopian alphabet, dot, point (item), score (record of points); see ነጠበ
ሥርዓት ፡ ነጥብ punctuation

አራት ፡ ነጥብ full stop, period (in punctuation)

ነጠብጣብ *näṭäbṭab* drop (n.), dot (see *ጠባጠበ , ነጠበ)
የነጠብጣብ dotted (line)

ነጠፈ(ች) *näṭṭäfä(čč)* stop giving milk, be dry (of cow, or woman)

*ነጠፈ , አነጠፈ *anäṭṭäfä* spread (a rug), pave (the road)
(አልጋ ፡ አነጠፈ make the bed)
ተነጠፈ *tänäṭṭäfä* be spread out (mat), be paved (road)
የተነጠፈ ፡ መንገድ *yätänäṭṭäfä mängäd* pavement, paved road
ምንጣፍ *mənṭaf* rug, mat, carpet

ነጨ *näččä* pull out, tear off, tear (the hair), pluck (chicken), pluck out (hair), nip off, scratch (the face)

ነጭ *näčč* white, white man (see ነጣ)
ነጭ ፡ ለባሽ irregular (soldier), militia man (see ለበሰ)
ነጭ ፡ ሽንኩርት garlic
ነጭ ፡ ጋዝ kerosene

*ነጨነጨ , ተነጫነጨ *tänäčannäčä* complain, be grouchy, be fussy, be in ill humor
ነጭናጫ *näčnaččä* cranky, grouchy

ነጻ *näṣa* free, freeborn, independent, autonomous, exempt, free of charge, gratuitous
ነጻ ፡ ሰው freeman
ነጻ ፡ አደረገ (v.), exempt, free, absolve (acquit)
ነጻ ፡ ወጣ be freed, be emancipated
ነጻ ፡ አወጣ liberate, emancipate (see ወጣ)
በነጻ free of charge, for nothing
በነጻ ፡ ለቀቀ free (an accused), acquit, set free (a prisoner)
ከ --- ነጻ innocent of, free from
ነጻነት , see below

ንጹሕ *nəṣuh* clean, pure, neat, tidy, fresh (air), sanitary (place), innocent

(not guilty), sound (free of disease), chaste (see ነጣ)
ንጽሕና *näṣhənna* cleanliness, purity, innocence, blamelessness, tidiness, sanitation
የልብስ ፡ ንጽሕና ፡ መስሪያ cleaner, laundry (cleaner)

*ነጸረ , አነጻጸረ *annäṣaṣṣärä* compare, contrast, draw a parallel, put one opposite another
ተነጻጸረ *tänäṣaṣṣärä* be compared with one another, contrast with
ንጽጽር *näṣəṣṣər* comparison
ተነጻጻሪ *tänäṣaṣari* simile, comparable, counterpart
ማነጻጸር *mannäṣaṣär* comparison
የማነጻጸር ፡ ደረጃ comparative (in grammar)
እነጸር , see below

ነጸብራቅ *näṣäbraq* glare (n.); see *ጸበረቀ

ነጻነት *näṣannät* freedom, liberty, independence, sovereignty (of a country); see ነጻ
ነጻነት ፡ ያለበት *näṣannät yalläbbät* free (country)
የነጻነት ፡ በዓል Independence Day (holiday)

ንጽጽር , see ነጸረ

ነፋ *näffa* blow, inflate, play (the flute), blow up, vt. (the tire)
ተነፋ *tänäffa* blow the fire with the bellows
አናፋ *anaffa* bray
ወናፍ *wänaf* bellows

ነፋ *näffa* sift
ወንፊት *wänfit* sieve, sifter, grate

ነፈረ *näffärä* boil, vi. (of water), boil with anger
ንፍሮ *nəfro* mush (of cornmeal), dish of boiled cereals

ነፈሰ *näffäsä* blow (of wind), be in the air (of rumor), circulate (of rumor)

(ግራም ፡ ነፈስ ፡ ቀኝ sooner or later, be that as it may)

(ትምህርት ፡ ነፈሰበት *təmhərt näffä-säbbät* he had a smattering of education)

ተነፈሰ *tänäffäsä* breathe, exhale, expire (breathe), blow (on the hands), leak (of a tire)

(የተነፈሰበት *yätänäffäsäbbät* trite, commonplace)

አነፈሰ *anäffäsä* winnow, throw the grain up into the wind

አስተነፈሰ *astänäffäsä* deflate (vt.), let the air out

ተናፈሰ *tänaffäsä* take fresh air, take a walk in the open

አናፈሰ *annaffäsä* aerate, air out, ventilate

†ነፋስ *näfas*, ንፋስ *nəfas* wind

†ነፍስ *näfs* soul, life

†ነፍሳት *näfsat* insect

ነፋሻ *näffaššа* windy, airy

መንፈስ, see above

መተንፈስ *mätänfäs* inspiration (breathing in)

መናፈሻ *männafäša*, or መናፈሻ ፡ ቦታ park

ትንፋሽ, see above

እስትንፋስ *əstənfas* breath, breathing

የመተንፈሻ *yämätänfäša* respiratory

ነፋስ *näfas*, ንፋስ *nəfas* wind (see ነፈሰ)

ነፋስ ፡ መስጫ fan (n.)

ነፋስ ፡ የሚገባው *näfas yämmigäbaw* airy (see ገባ)

0ውሎ ፡ ነፋስ whirlwind, gale, tornado

ነፍስ *näfs* soul, life (see ነፈሰ)

ነፍሱን ፡ ሳተ faint, lose consciousness, be senseless (person)

ነፍሱ ፡ ተመለሰ regain consciousness, come to (see መለሰ)

ነፍስ ፡ 0ወቀ reach the age of reason, be mature

ነፍሱን ፡ 0ወቀ recover consciousness, come to

ነፍሱን ፡ አጣ faint, lose consciousness

ነፍስ ፡ ዘራ come to life, regain consciousness, revive

ነፍስ ፡ ገዳይ murderer, assassin

ነፍስ ፡ ገዳይነት murder, manslaughter

ነፍስ ፡ ጡር pregnant

በነፍስ ፡ እንዲደርስ in the nick of time

የነፍስ ፡ ወከፍ individual, per capita

በነፍሱ ፡ ደረሰ he came to his rescue just in time

የነፍስ ፡ አባት father confessor

ነፍሳት *näfsat* insect (see ነፈሰ)

ረቂቅ ፡ ነፍሳት microbe

ጥገኛ ፡ ነፍሳት parasite

ነፋሻ *näffaššа* windy, airy (see ነፈሰ)

ኑፋቄ *nufaqe* heresy

መናፍቅ *mänafəq* heretic

ናፈቀ *naffäqä*, ናፈቀ(ው) *naffäqä(w)* yearn, languish for, be lonesome for, be homesick

ናፍቆት *nafqot* yearning, longing for affection

*ነፈነፈ, አነፈነፈ *anäfännäfä* sniff, nose about (of dog), scent (of dog), root (of pig)

ነፈገ *näffägä* be stingy, be miserly, stint, hold back on, deny (refuse one the opportunity)

ንፉግ *nəfug* miserly, stingy, avaricious

ንፉግነት *nəfugənnät* avarice, stinginess

*ነፈጠ, ተናፈጠ *tänaffäṭä* blow one's nose

ንፍጥ *nəfṭ* mucus

ንፍጡን ፡ ጠረገ sniffle, wipe one's nose

ነፍጥ *näfṭ* gun, rifle, musket

ነፍጠኛ *näfṭäñña* rifleman, armed retainer

አ ፡ 0

አ *ə* in, to, at
አ + perfect + ድረስ as long as, so
long as
አ + noun + ድረስ up to, as far as

እህል *əhəl* grain, cereal, crops, food
እህል ፡ ቅጠል ፡ አይልም it tastes flat
(of food)
እህል ፡ ውኃ sustenance, food and
drink
እህል ፡ ውኃ ፡ አይልም be tasteless

እኅት *əhət* (pl. እኅቶች *əhətoččə*, እኅትማ
ማች *əhətəmmamaččə*) sister
የእኅት ፡ ልጅ nephew, niece
[See also እት]

አሁን *ahun* now, at present, presently,
shortly, right now, soon
አሁንም even now, still, yet (still)
አሁንም ፡ አሁንም constantly
አሁንም ፡ ሆነ ፡ ሌላ ፡ ጊዜ sooner or
later
አሁኑኑ right away, here and now,
at once, immediately
አሁን ፡ ከሁን at any moment
አሁን ፡ ገና just now, just this moment
ላሁኑ just this once
ባሁን ፡ (ባሁኑ) ፡ ጊዜ nowadays, currently
እስከሁን up to now, to date, as yet,
by now, thus far, still (adv.)
ከሁን ፡ ጀምሮ from now on
ያሁን present (adj.)
ያሁኑ (adj.) present, current
ያሁን ፡ ጊዜ present, n. (time), present tense
ገና ፡ አሁን just, adv. (a moment ago)

አህያ *ahəyya* donkey, ass
የአህያ ፡ ኪንታሮት hemorrhoids
እናቲት ፡ አህያ she donkey

ወይል ፡ አህያ he donkey, jackass
የሜዳ ፡ አህያ zebra

እሑድ *əhud* Sunday
እሑድና ፡ ቅዳሜ weekend

አህጉር, see ሀገር

አኅጽሮተ ፡ ቃል *ahṣərotä qal* abbreviation
አኅጽሮተ ፡ ቃል ፡ አደረገ abbreviate

አለ *alä* say, call, name (imperfect ይል,
jussive ይበል, imperative በል, gerund
ብሎ, participle ባይ, infinitive ማለት)
ተባለ *täbalä* be said, be called, be
named, be termed
ተባባለ *täbabalä* say to each other
አለ preceded by a repeated noun
means 'it has the taste of, it gives
the sensation of' (as ማር ፡ ማር ፡
ይላል it has the taste of honey)
አባባል *abbabal* expression, statement, pronunciation, formula (way
of saying something)
በል *bäl* come on!, well then!, so
then!
በለው *bäläw* hit him!, let him have it!
ብሎ *bəlo* saying, thinking
ተማለት *malät* that is, that is to say,
namely, it means
ለ - - - ብሎ *lä - - - bəlo* for the sake
of
ለ - - - ሲል *lä - - - sil* for the sake of,
for the benefit of
ል + imperfect + ሲል be on the
point of
ምንም ፡ አይል *mənəmm ayəl* so-so, mediocre
(በልቡ ፡ ምንም ፡ አይል he has his
heart in the right place)
ሲል ፡ ሲል *sil sil* little by little
ሳይል *sayəl* without reflecting, without regard to
እንበል *ənnəbäl* let's suppose
ማን ፡ ልበል? *man ləbäl* who is speaking? (when picking up the telephone), may I ask what your name is?
የተባለ *yätäbalä* alleged
የሚባል *yämmibbal* presumed

ይባላል yəbbalal it is said, it is presumed

ምን ፡ ይባላል what's its name?, what is it called?

ይህ ፡ ነው ፡ የማይባል yəh näw yämmayəbbal indescribable, fabulous, unspeakable

ይህ ፡ ነው ፡ ሊባል ፡ አይቻልም yəh näw libbal ayəččaləm it is beyond description

እገሌ፡ከእገሌ፡ ሳይባሉ əgäle kägäle sayəbbalu people from all ranks of life, without distinction

[See also ይሉኝታ]

አለ allä he is, he is present, he is around, he exists, there is

አለ(ው-) allä(w) he has, he owns, he possesses

አለሁ allähu I am all right, I am getting along

አለሁ ፡ አለሁ ፡ ባይ pretentious, show-off

አለበት alläbbät he has to, he must

አለብኝ alläbbəňň, in ማን ፡ አለብኝ ፡ ባይ despot

(ምን ፡ አለብኝ what business is it of mine?)

በሌለበት bälelläbbät behind his back, when he is away, in his absence

በያለበት (=በ+እየ+አለበት) bäyyalläbbät everywhere, throughout (all over), all around

ከያለበት(=ከ+እየ+አለበት)käyyalläbbät from far and near, from all over

እንዳለ əndallä, as in ደሞዙን ፡ እንዳለ his whole salary

ያለ ፡ የሌለው- yallä yälelläw in full force, all possible (kinds of), all imaginable (things)

አለ alä (with verbal noun) without, except, not-, un- (as in አለመድረሱ his not coming, አለማመን unbelief); see also ያለ, አሉታ

ኤሊ. eli tortoise, turtle

እልህ əlləh obstinacy, stubbornness

†እልኸኛ əlləhäňňa stubborn, obstinate

*አለለ , see ታለለ

እልል ፡ አለ ələll alä ululate, utter cries of joy

እልልታ ələlta ululation, cries of joy

አለመ allämä (B) dream (v.)

ሕልም həlm (n.) dream, fancy

እልም əlm dream (n.)

ዐለመ allämä (B) sight (aim a gun)

ዒላማ , ዓላማ, see below

ዒላማ ilama target, aim (direction aimed at); see ዐለመ

ዓለም aläm world, planet, eternity

ዓለማት alämat universe

ዓለም ፡ አየ he enjoyed life

ዓለም ፡ አቀፍ universal, international, global

ክፍለ ፡ ዓለም hemisphere

ዓለማዊ alämawi worldly, temporal, secular, profane (literature)

ዓለማዊነት alämawinnät worldliness

ለዘለዓለም läzälä'aläm forever, eternally

ለዘላለም läzäläm forever, eternally

የዘላለም yäzälaläm eternal

ዓላማ alama goal, aim, purpose, target, objective, object (purpose), mission (purpose), intent, concern, design (plan), motif, destiny (see ዐለመ)

ያላንዳች ፡ ዓላማ aimlessly (see እንዳች)

ሰንደቅ ፡ ዓላማ flag

እልም፡ አለ əlləmm alä vanish, disappear

እልም ፡ ያለ əlləmm yalä out-and-out (scoundrel), deep (sleep, forest)

አልማዝ almaz diamond

አለቀ alläqä end (vi.), come to an end, be over, terminate (vi.), finish (vi.), wear out (vi.), perish, be used up, be consumed, be destroyed, lapse (end)

እልቂት əlqit holocaust, slaughter, massacre, carnage

†ማለቂያ *maläqiya* end (n.)
ያለቀ *yalläqä* shabby (cloth), worn-out, threadbare
የማያልቅ *yämmayalq* inexhaustible, interminable (chatter)

አለቃ *aläqa* chief, leader, boss, head (of a gang), superior of monastery, title borne by a learned man, vicar (of church)
(የ)ሻለቃ major, battalion
የነምሳ ፡ አለቃ sergeant
(የ)መቶ ፡ አለቃ lieutenant
, የሠር ፡ አለቃ corporal (see በሠC)

አልቃሽ *alqaš* professional mourner (see *ለቀሰ)

አልቅት *alqət* leech

አልቄት , see አለቀ

አለበ *alläbä* milk (v.)

አለባ ፡ ገለባ *aläba gäläba* usufruct

አልባ *alba* anklet

አለባባሌ *aləbbale* humble (home), cheap (person), not worthy of considera-tion

አሉባልታ *alubalta* gossip, hearsay

አለበለዚያ *aläbäläzziya* otherwise, or else, if not (see also አለዚያ)
ያለበለዚያ *yaläbäläzziya* otherwise, else, or else

እልባት *əlləbat* bookmark

አለት *alät* hard stone, rock

አሉታ *aluta* negation, negative (n.); see አለ without
የአሉታ negative (adj.)

ዕለት *əlät* (pl. ዕለታት *əlätat*) day (see also ለት)
ዕለት ፡ ዕለት day after day
ዕለት ፡ በዕለት day by day
ዕለቱ ፡ ምጽአት *əlätä məṣ'at* Judg-ment Day
በዕለቱ ፡ ቀኑ on the same day

በየዕለቱ *bäyyä'əlätu* daily (adv.)
ከዕለታት ፡ አንድ ፡ ቀን once upon a time
የዕለት daily (adj.)
የ(ዕ)ለት ፡ (ዕ)ለት the same day, ex-actly that day
በቀደም ፡ (ዕ)ለት the other day
ዕለታዊ *əlätawi* daily (adj.)

አለንጋ *alänga* small whip

አለኝታ *alläňňəta* backing (support), moral support (see አለ he is)

አልኮል *alkol* liquor, alcohol, spirits
የአልኮል ፡ ሱሰኛ alcoholic (n.)
አልኮልነት ፡ ያለው *alkolənnät yalläw* alcoholic (drink)

ኤሌክትሪክ *elektrik* electricity

እልኸኛ *əlləhäňňa* stubborn (see እልህ)
እልኸኝነት *əlləhäňňannät* stubborn-ness

አለዚያ *aläzziya* otherwise, or else, or if not (see also አለበለዚያ)

አልጀብራ *alǧebra* algebra

አልጋ *alga* bed, throne
አልጋ ፡ አነጠፈ make the bed (see *ነጠፈ)
አልጋ ፡ ወራሽ Crown Prince (see ወረሰ)
ያልጋ ፡ ልብስ bedding, bedspread, linen
ያልጋ ፡ ቂራኛ bedridden (see *ቂረኝ)
ሽራ ፡ አልጋ cot
የሕፃን ፡ አልጋ cradle, crib
የፉሚሊ. ፡ አልጋ double bed

አልጫ *alləčča* stew made without *bär-bärre*-pepper, but may have green pepper

አለፈ *alläfä* go beyond (the limits), exceed, expire (of time), pass (vi.), go by, pass by, elapse, get by, overlook (a mistake), allow for (make conces-sions)

(ጊዜ ፡ አለፈ(በት) *gize alläfä(bbät*) be antiquated, be outmoded, be obsolescent

አሳለፈ *asalläfä* pass (vt.), cause to pass, let through, let by, make way for, shift, while away (time), spend (time), serve (food or drink)

(ሕይወቱን ፡ አሳለፈ give one's life)

(ሕይወቱን ፡ አሳልፎ ፡ ሰጠ he sacrificed himself)

(የገዛ ፡ ሕይወቱን ፡ አሳለፈ he took his own life)

(አሳልፎ ፡ ሰጠ *asallǝfo säṭṭä* betray, deliver (hand over), extradite, forbear (a claim)

ተላለፈ *tälalläfä* pass (go from one to another), pass (elapse), transgress, break (the law), intersect, be forwarded, be remitted, be handed down, be postponed, be deferred, be transmitted (disease), be contagious

አስተላለፈ *astälalläfä* let pass, transmit, transfer, forward (a request), pass around, relay (a message), circulate, conduct (of electricity), deliver, convey (transfer), carry (transmit), communicate (a disease), defer, delay, put off, postpone

አልፎም *alfom* and further, moreover

አልፎ ፡ አልፎ *alfo alfo* every so often, now and again, intermittently, every once in a while, occasionally, infrequently, from time to time, here and there

አላፊ *alafi* one who passes

አላፊ ፡ አግዳሚ passer-by

እልፍ ፡ ብሎ *ǝllǝff bǝlo* a little further

እላፊ *ǝllafi*, in ሰዓት ፡ እላፊ overtime, curfew

አሳላፊ *asallafi* waiter

ተላላፊ *tälalafi* contagious, communicable, transgressor

ማለፊያ ; see above

ማሳለፊያ *masalläfiya*, in የጊዜ ፡ ማሳለፊያ pastime

መተላለፊያ *mättälaläfiya* passage, hall, hallway, corridor, lobby, vestibule, aisle, communication (passageway)

ያለፈ *yalläfä* past (adj.)

(ያለፈ ፡ ሳምንት past week, last week)

የሚታለፍ *yämmittalläf* excusable

የይለፍ ፡ ወረቀት *yäyǝläf wäräqät* pass, laissez - passer, visa, permit, passport, safe conduct

አላፊ *alafi* responsible (see also ኃላፊ)

እልፍ *ǝlf* innumerable

እልፍኝ *ǝlfǝňň* interior room used for privacy, reception house

እልፍኝ ፡ አስከልካይ chamberlain, who is in charge of the visitors by either letting them in or keeping them away (see ከለከለ)

አማ *amma* calumniate, slander, backbite, malign, talk behind one's back, libel

አሜት *amet* slander, calumny

[See also ሐሜት]

እም *ǝmmǝ* + (imperfect) who, that, which (relative); see also የም —

እግሆይ *ǝmmahoy*, appelation for a nun

አመል *amäl* character, conduct (behavior), habit (usually with a negative connotation), bad temper

ላመል *lamäl* barely, touch of

አመለኛ *amäläňňa* one who has a bad character

አሞሌ *amole* salt bar used as currency

አምላክ *amlak* (pl. አማልክት *amalǝkt*) god, deity (see መለከ)

በሕግ ፡ አምላክ in the name of the law (said when one forbids someone to do something illegal)

አምላክነት *amlakǝnnät* divinity

አምልኮ *amlǝko* cult (see መለከ)

የጣዖት ፡ አምልኮ idolatry

አመልካች *amälkač* one who indicates, applicant, petitioner (see *መለከተ)

አመልካች ፡ ተውላጠ ፡ ስም demonstrative pronoun

አምላክነት *amlakənnät* divinity (see አም
ላክ)

አማላጅ *ammalaǧ* intercessor, mediator
(see *ማለደ)

አመመ *ammämä* be painful, be sore,
hurt
አመመ(ው) *ammämä(w)* feel pain in,
have a pain in, be ill, be ailing
ታመመ *tammämä* be sick, feel ill,
fall ill
አሳመመ *asammämä* make sick, upset
አስታመመ *astammämä* take care of
a sick person, nurse a sick person
አስታማሚ *astamami* nurse (n.)
እመም *əmäm* illness, ache, sickness,
disease, ailment (see also ሕመም)

እማማ *əmmamma* mamma!, address to
a mother or to an elderly woman

አማረ *amarä* look handsome, look
good, be pleasing, be beautiful, be
good (of results)
አማረ(ው) *amarä(w)* he liked, he felt
like, he had the desire for
(የማረ *yamarä* handsome, beautiful)
አሳመረ *asammärä* embellish, pretty
up, make beautiful, adorn, grace
(decorate), make attractive, improve
(the character)
አሳምሮ *asamməro* beautifully, to advantage, well
የሚያምር *yämmiyamər* attractive
(pretty), handsome, beautiful

አማራ *amara* name of a region of
Ethiopia, Amhara
አማርኛ *amarəñña* Amharic

አሞራ *amora* kind of large bird, bird
of prey
ጆፌ ፡ አሞራ vulture

አመራር *ammärar* management (handling), direction (management), guidance, conduct, policy, leadership
(see መራ)

አማርኛ *amarəñña* Amharic (see አማራ)

አሜሪካ *amerika* America
አሜሪካዊ *amerikawi* American
አሜሪካን *amerikan* American

አሙስ *amus* Thursday (see also ነሙስ)

አምሳ *amsa* fifty (see also ነምሳ)

እምስ *əms* vulva, vagina

አምሳል, see መሰለ

አምስት *amməst* five
አምስት ፡ ሰዓት eleven o'clock
አምስተኛ *amməstäñña* one-fifth; quin-
tessence
[See also አምሳ, ነምሳ, ኃምስ, አሙስ,
ነሙስ]

አምሳያ *amsayya* copy, reproduction,
likeness, image, imitation (see መሰለ)

አመቀ *ammäqä* (B) compress (cotton
into balls), squeeze, force by pressing,
cram
አምቆ ፡ ያዘ *ammәqo-yazä* suppress
(one's feelings)

አምባ *amba* a flat-topped mountain
used formerly as a fortress, village
አምባ ፡ ገነን *amba gännän* self-ap-
pointed ruler who has arrogated
power to himself, dictator
[See also አምባ ገነን]

እምቢ *əmbi* no
እምቢ ፡ አለ *əmbi alä* refuse, give a
refusal, disobey
†እምቢታ *əmbita* refusal

እምቧ ፡ አለ *əmbʷa alä* low (of a cow)

አምበል *ambäl* captain (of a team)
[See also ሻምበል]

አምቡላ *ambulla* dregs (of mead)

አምቡላንስ *ambulans* ambulance

እምቢልታ *əmbilta* flute

አምቦልክ *ambolәkk* envelope (see also
አንቦልክ)

አምባር *ambar* anklet, bracelet (worn by women)

እምብርት *əmbərt* navel, center (see also እንብርት)

ኤምባሲ *embasi* embassy

እምቦሳ *əmbossa* calf (1-3 months after birth)
ቤት ፡ ለእምቦሳ may it be a house of prosperity! (said to someone who built a new house)

አምባሳደር *ambasadär* ambassador

እመቤት *əmmäbet* mistress (of the house), lady of the house; shortened into እሜቴ (see እመት)
እመቤታችን *əmmäbetaččən* Our Lady, the Virgin Mary
የቤት ፡ እመቤት housewife
የእመቤትነት *yäəmmäbetənnät* aristocratic

እምቢታ *əmbita* refusal (see እምቢ)
የእምቢታ negative (answer)
እምቢተኛ *əmbitäñña* recalcitrant, refractory, disobedient
እምቢተኝነት *əmbitäññännät* refusal
የእምቢተኝነት *yäəmbitäññannät* resistant (nature)

እምብዛም *əmbəzam* + (negative verb) seldom, rarely, hardly, scarcely, hardly ever (see በዛ)
እምብዛም ፡ ነው it does not amount to much, it is negligible

አምባጓሮ *ambagʷaro* free-for-all, row, quarrel, brawl, conflict (see አምባ)

እምቡጥ *əmbuṭ* (n.) bud, bloom
እምቡጥ ፡ ያዘ (v.) bud, bloom

ዓመት *amät* year, age
ዓመተ ፡ ምሕረት (written ዓ ፡ ም) year of Grace (Ethiopian year)
መቶ ፡ ዓመት century
ስንት ፡ ዓመቱ ፡ ነው? how old is he?
በያመቱ *bäyyamätu* yearly (adv.), annually, year by year

በውደ ፡ ዓመት turn of the year (e.g. festival of New Year or of St. John)
ከዓመት ፡ ዓመት year in, year out; the year round
ከዓመት ፡ እስከ ፡ ዓመት year in, year out
የዓመት (adj.) yearly, annual
(የ)ዓመት ፡ በዓል holiday, anniversary
ዓመታዊ *amätawi* annual (adj.)

አማት *amat* mother-in-law, father-in-law

አሜት , see አማ

አሞት *amot* bile, gall (see also ሐሞት)
አሞት ፡ የሌለው coward

እመት *əmmät*, እሜት *əmmet*, እሜቴ *əmmete* madame!, yes (in reference to a summons by a woman); see እመቤት

አማች *amač* father-in-law, son-in-law, brother-in-law
አማቾች *amačočč* in-laws

አመነ *ammänä* believe, trust, have confidence, have faith, profess (declare one's belief in), confess (admit), concede (admit)
ታመነ *tammänä* be faithful, be trusted, be loyal, rely, count on, be accepted (believed)
አሳመነ *asammänä* persuade, convince, indoctrinate, convert (to another religion), extort a confession
ተማመነ *tämammänä* trust (rely on), depend on, rely on, count on, confide in, have confidence in, be confident, be convinced of
አሜን *amen* Amen, so be it!
እሙን *əmun* faithful, sure, certain
እምነት , see below
አማኝ *amañ* believer
እማኝ *əmmañ* witness
ታማኝ , see above
ምእመን , see above
መታመኛ *mättamäñña* evidence, credentials
መተማመኛ *mättämamäñña* evidence

መተማመን *mättämamän*, in በራስ ፡
መተማመን self-assurance
የታመነ *yätammänä* reliable (source)
የሚታመን *yämmittammän* veracious
(report)
የማይታመን *yämmayəttammän* unbelievable, inconceivable, fantastic,
dishonest
የሚያስተማምን *yämmiyastämammən*
safe (reliable)

አሜን *amen* Amen, so be it! (see አሚን)

ዓምና *amna* last year
†አቻምና *aččamna* year before last

ኢምንት *imənt* nothing

እምነት *əmnät* faith, belief, confidence,
creed, fidelity, conviction (belief),
confession (in court), trust, reliance,
assurance (see አመነ)
እምነት ፡ አገኘ be trustworthy (see
*ገኘ)
እምነት ፡ አጉደለ abuse one's trust
(see ጎደለ)
እምነት ፡ ጣለ count on, place confidence or trust in
እምነተ ፡ ቢስ faithless
እምነተ ፡ ጎደሎ dishonest
የእምነት ፡ ቃል confession (of criminal)

እማኝ *əmmaň* witness (see አመነ)

አማካኝ *ammakaň* mean (average)

አማካይ *ammakay* mediator, moderate,
mean (n.), central, middle, average
(n., adj.); see አከለ
አማካይ ፡ ክፍል nucleus
አማካይነት *ammakayənnät* agency
(means)
(በ - - አማካይነት through the good
offices of, by means of, through the
mediation)

አመድ *amäd* cinder, ashes
አመድ ፡ ሆነ be burnt to ashes
አመድ ፡ ለበሰ be livid, be pale
አመድ ፡ አደረገ wreck, turn to rubble

አሚዶ *amido* starch (n.)
አሚዶ ፡ አደረገ(በት) starch (v.)

ዓምድ *amd* column, pillar

አመዳይ *amäday* hoarfrost

አማጭ *ammač* matchmaker, go-between
(in arranging marriage); see መጣ

እመጫት *əmmäçat* nursing mother, woman who has recently given birth,
cow with calf

አመጸ *ammäṣä* (v.) revolt, rebel
አመፅ *amäṣ* mutiny, insurgency, rebellion, uprising insurrection
የአመፅ subversive
አመፀኛ *amäṣäňňa* rebel, insurgent,
terrorist

አምፑል *ampul* electric bulb

ኧረ *ärä* why!, why! (exclamation of
surprise when something unexpected
happens); see also ኧረጋ
ኧረ ፡ ለመሆኑ how on earth!

አራ *arra* defecate
አር *ar* excrement

እሪ *ərri* yell, a cry for help
እሪ ፡ አለ *ərri alä* cry for help
እሪ ፡ ብሎ ፡ አለቀሰ he cried his head
off (see *ለቀሰ)

አረመ *arrämä* (B) weed, correct, redress, mark (examination papers),
grade (papers), prohibit
አረም *aräm* weed, weeding
እርም *ərm* prohibited, taboo, anathema
እርማት *ərrəmat* correction
የታረመ *yätarrämä* expurgated
(book), fine (manners)
ያልታረመ *yaltarrämä* common (manners), coarse (language, behavior),
unrefined

አርማ *arma* insignia, symbol, emblem,
badge, slogan

አርምሞ armǝmo, in በአርምሞ ፡ ተቀበለ
acquiesce in

እርማት, see አረም

አረማኒ arämäne pagan, infidel, unbeliever, wild (tribe), savage (n.)

አረማዊ arämawi pagan

እርምጃ ǝrmǝǧǧa step, pace, stride, action (step), move (step), measure
(step), progress (see *ረመደ)

አረረ arrärä be scorched (food), burn
(of food), turn green (with envy)
አሳረረ asarrärä char (meat)
አሩር arur intense heat (see also ሐሩር)

አሬራ arera buttermilk

አረሰ arräsä plow, till the land, cultivate land, farm
አራሽ araš farmer, cultivator
እርሻ, see below
ማረሻ maräša plow (n.)

አራስ aras woman in childbed
አራስ ፡ ልጅ newborn baby

እርሱ ǝrsu he (see also እሱ)
የርሱ yärsu his

እርስ, in እርስ ፡ በርሳቸው ǝrs bärsaččäw
each other, with each other, among
- - - selves
የርስ ፡ በርስ yärs bärs one against
the other, each other, among -, mutual, reciprocal, internecine

እርሷ ǝrsʷa she (see also እሷ)
የርሷ yärsʷa her, hers

እርሳስ ǝrsas pencil, lead

እርሳቸው ǝrsaččäw He (respect); see
also እሳቸው

እርሳዎ ǝrsäwo, እርስዎ ǝrsǝwo You
(resp.); see also እስዎ
የርስዎ yärsǝwo Your, Yours (resp.)

አራሽ, see አረሰ

እርሻ ǝrša farm, plantation, cultivated
field, farming, agriculture (see አረሰ)
የእርሻ ፤ የርሻ agricultural, agrarian
እርሻ ፡ ሚኒስቴር Ministry of Agriculture
የእርሻ ፡ ተግባር agriculture

እርሾ ǝršo leaven, yeast, ferment

ዐረቀ arräqä (B) straighten out (an
affair, branches), train, mold (the
character)
ታረቀ tarräqä be straightened, make
peace (vi.) be reconciled, patch up a
quarrel (vi.)
አስታረቀ astarräqä (vt.) reconcile,
conciliate, make peace, arbitrate
ዕርቅ ǝrq conciliation, reconciliation, peace
ዕርቅ ፡ አወረደ establish peace
አስታራቂ astaraqi conciliator, con-
ciliatory, arbiter, mediator, go-between

ዐረቄ aräqe, ዐረቂ aräqi anise (liquor),
arrack

ዕርቃን ǝrqan nakedness
ዕርቃኑን ፡ ቆመ he was naked

ዐረብ aräb Arab
ዐረብ ፡ ሱቅ Arab store
ዐረብ ፡ ብረት steel
የዐረብ ፡ አገር Arabia
ዐረብኛ aräbǝñña Arabic

አርባ arba forty, memorial service for
a dead person on the fortieth day after his decease (see አራት)

ዓርብ arb Friday

እርብራብ ǝrǝbrab lattice, joist, framework, scaffolding (see also ርብራብ)

እርባታ, see ረባ

አርበኛ arbäñña patriot (during the
Italian invasion), partisan

አራት aratt four
አራት ፡ ሰዓት ten o'clock

አራተኛ *arattäñña* fourth
[See also አርባ, ሩብ, ራብዕ]

እራት *ərat* supper, dinner (see also ራት)
የራት ፡ ግብገ *yärat gəbža* banquet,
formal dinner
የእሳት ፡ እራት moth

ኦሪት *orit* Mosaic law, Pentateuch

ኤርትራ *erətra* Eritrea

አርቲስት *artist* artist

አርነት *arənnät* freedom (see also ሐር
ነት)
አርነት ፡ ወጣ become free
አርነት ፡ አወጣ free (a slave), emancipate, deliver from slavery (see ወጣ)

አረንጓዴ *aräng^wade* green, moss (on
water)

ሃረኛ *ərräñña* shepherd, cowherd, herdsman
የእረኛ ፡ አነጋገር vulgar expression

አርእስት *ar'əst* subject (of a play), subject matter, topic, title, heading (see
ርእስ)
አርእስተ ፡ ነገር main subject
አርእስተ ፡ ዜና headline(s)
አርእስተ ፡ ጉዳይ outline (of a lecture)
ከአርእስት ፡ ውጭ beside the question
ዋና ፡ አርእስት lead article

አርአያ *ar'aya, araya* example, model,
embodiment
አርአያ ፡ ነው exemplify
አርአያነት ፡ ያለው *ar'ayannät yalläw*
exemplary
[See also ራእይ, ትርእይት]

እርኩም *ərkum* stork

እርኩስ *ərkus* unclean (ritually), impure,
contaminated (see ረከሰ, ርኩስ)

እርካብ *ərkab* stirrup

አርኬዎሎጂ *arkewoloǧi* archeology

አራዊት *arawit* beasts (see አውሬ)

የአራዊት ፡ መጠበቂያ zoo
የዱር ፡ አራዊት wild animal

*አረዘ, see ታረዘ

አረደ *arrädä* slaughter, butcher, cut the
animal's throat
እርድ *ərd* slaughtering, butchering

አራዳ *arada* market area

እርዳታ *ərdata* (n.) help, aid, assistance,
grant, donation (see ረዳ)
የመማሪያ ፡ እርዳታ fellowship (for
studies)
የመጀመሪያ ፡ እርዳታ ፡ ሕክምና first
aid
የመጀመሪያ ፡ እርዳታ ፡ መድኃኒት first
aid kit

አረጀ *aräǧǧä* grow old, get older, grow
older, age (vi.), be worn out (articles, clothes)
እርጅና, see below

እርጅና *ərǧənna* old age (see አረጀ)
በስተ ፡ ጅና *bästärǧənna* in old age

ዐረገ *arrägä* go up into heaven
አሳረገ *asarrägä* make go up, offer a
final prayer
ዕርገት, see below
ማዕረግ, see above

እረግ *äräg* why! why! (exclamation of
surprise when something unexpected happens); see also እረ

አሮጌ *aroge* ancient, old (thing), secondhand (book)
አሮጊት *arogit* old woman
አረጋዊ, see below

እርጎ *ərgo* curds, yogurt, coagulated
milk (see ረጋ)
የእርጎ ፡ ዝምብ meddlesome

እርግማን *ərgəman* malediction, curse,
imprecation (see ረገመ)

እርግብ *ərgəb* turtle-dove, pigeon (see
also ርግብ)

አርጊት, see አርጊ

ዕርገት *ərgät* Ascension (of Christ), Feast of the Ascension (see ዐረገ)

እርጋታ *ərgata* calm (n.), composure (see ረጋ)
በእርጋታ ፤ በርጋታ calmly, leisurely, gently
የርጋታ ፤ መንፈስ poise

አረጋዊ *arägawi* venerable (appearance), honorable person, old man (see አርጊ)

እርጉዝ *ərguz* pregnant (see ረገዘ)
እርግዝና *ərgazənna* pregnancy

እርግጥ *ərgaṭ* sure, certain, definite (sure); see *ረገጠ
በእርግጥ, በርግጥ positively, in reality, really, for certain, definitely, surely
እርግጠኛ *ərgaṭäňňa* positive, sure, certain, definite
እርግጠኛነት *ərgaṭäňňannät* confirmation (verification), certainty

እርግጫ *ərgəčča* kick, recoil (of gun); see ረገጠ

አራጣ ፤ አበዳሪ *araṭa abäddari* usurer
በአራጣ ፤ ማበደር *baraṭa mabäddär* usury

እርጥብ *ərṭəb* moist, damp, wet (see ረጠበ)
እርጥበት *ərṭəbät* dampness, moisture
እርጥበት ፤ ያለው—*yalläw* humid
እርጥበት ፤ የበዛበት—*yäbäzzabbät* humid (see በዛ)

አርጩሜ *arčumme* switch (slender stick), rod, thin and flexible stick

አረፈ *arräfä* rest (vi.), be quiet, land, vi. (of a plane), alight, stay (dwell), be housed, be centered on, make a stop (stay); die, pass away
አሳረፈ *asarräfä* bring to rest, let rest, land (a plane); see also ሐሳብ
(አስተያየት ፤ አሳረፈ set down one's views in writing)

ዕረፍት, see below
ማረፊያ, see above

አረፋ *aräfa* froth (on milk, on the mouth), lather, foam, bubble, suds
አረፋ ፤ ወጣ foam (v.)
አረፋ ፤ ደፈቀ foam at the mouth
የሳሙና ፤ አረፋ lather

እራፊ *ərrafi* patch (on the trousers)

እርፍ *ərf* plow handle

ዓረፍተ ፤ ነገር *aräftä nägär* sentence (in grammar)

ዕረፍት *əräft* rest, repose, recess, vacation, pause, interval, death (see አረፈ)
ዕረፍት ፤ ነሣ not be restful (lit. 'deprive of rest')
ዕረፍት ፤ አደረገ take a break
የዕረፍት ፤ ጊዜ recess, vacation
ዜና ፤ ዕረፍት obituary

አሣ *asa* fish
አሣ ፤ ነባሪ *asa näbari* whale
አሣ ፤ አጥማጅ fisherman (see *ጠመደ)

እሱ *əssu* he (see also እርሱ)
እሱ ፤ ላይ in that respect
የሱ *yässu* his
እሱነት *əssunnät* personality, identity

እሷ *əssʷa* she (see also እርሷ)
የሷ *yässʷa* her, hers

እስላም *əslam* Muslim, Islam
እስልምና *əsləmənna* Islam

አሳማ *asama* wild boar, pig, hog, sow
ያሳማ ፤ ሥጋ pork

አስማ *asma* asthma

አስማት *asmat* magic, black magic, magical spell, sorcery, witchcraft, charms (see ስም)
በአስማት ፤ ተበተብ enchant (of witch), cast a spell on
አስማተኛ *asmatäňňa* magician, sorcerer, wizard, witch

አሰረ *assärä* tie, bind, attach, lash together, lace, imprison, put in jail

ተሳሰረ *täsassärä* be interconnected, be knit together, be tied together, be linked
(ምላሱ ፡ ተሳሰረ he was tongue-tied)
አስተሳሰረ *astäsassärä*, causative of the preceding
እስር *əsər* knot, bundle, imprisonment
እስር ፡ ቤት *əsər bet* jail, prison
እስራት, see below
እስረኛ *əsräňňa* prisoner
ማሰሪያ, see above

አሠሪ *assärri* employer, foreman (see ሠራ)

አሠር *asär* dregs

ዐሥር *assər* ten
ዓሥር ፡ አንድ ፤ ዓሥራንድ *asrand* eleven
ዐሥራ ፡ ሁለት *asra* — twelve
ዐሥራ ፡ ሦስት thirteen
ዐሥራ ፡ አራት fourteen
ዐሥራ ፡ አምስት ፤ ዐሥራምስት fifteen
ዐሥራ ፡ ስድስት sixteen
ዐሥራ ፡ ሰባት seventeen
ዐሥራ ፡ ስምንት eighteen
ዐሥራ ፡ ዘጠኝ nineteen
ዐሥር ፡ ሰዓት four o'clock
ዐሥራ ፡ አንድ ፡ ሰዓት five o'clock
ዐሥራ ፡ ሁለት ፡ ሰዓት six o'clock
ዐሥር ፡ ዓመታት *assər amätat* decade
የዐሥር ፡ አለቃ corporal
ዐሥረኛ *assəräňňa* tenth
[See also ዐሥራት, ዐሠርቱ]

አሠራር *assärar* construction, workmanship, execution, function (see ሠራ)
ያሠራር ፡ መምሪያ recipe

ዐሥራት *asrat* tithe, tenth of agricultural product paid in cash or in kind (see ዐሥር)

ዐሠርቱ ፡ ቃላት ፡ አሪት *assärtu qalata orit* the Ten Commandments (see ዐሥር)

እስራት *əssarat* imprisonment, confinement, arrest (see አሰረ)

የዕድሜ ፡ ልክ ፡ እስራት life imprisonment
ጽኑ ፡ እስራት hard labor

ዐሥረኛ *assəräňňa* tenth (see ዐሥር)

እስረኛ *əsräňňa* prisoner (see አሰረ)

አሰሰ *assäsä* (B) scan, scour (the town), grease (a griddle)
አሳሽ *assaš* explorer, scout

እስስት *əsəst* chameleon, two-faced person, fickle

አሳሽ, see አሰሰ

አስቃቄ, see *ሰቀቀ

አሠቄኝ, see ሣቀ

አሰበ *assäbä* (B) think, imagine, be considerate, have in mind, meditate, contemplate, have concern for, take into consideration, intend, conceive an idea, reckon, plan, calculate, worry (vi.), be concerned (worry)
አሳሰበ *asassäbä* remind, call attention to, suggest, connote, recommend, worry (vt.), concern (worry)
አሳብ *assab* thought, idea, opinion, intention, contemplation, proposal (legislature)
አሳቢነት *assabinnät* consideration
አሳሳቢ *asassabi* serious (situation), grave, alarming, critical (situation), weighty (problem)
አሳሳቢነት *asassabinnät* seriousness or gravity (of the situation), thoughtfulness, concern
አስተሳሰብ, see below
መታሰቢያ, see above
ሳይታሰብ *sayəttassäb* unexpectedly, accidentally, without warning
ያልታሰበ *yaltassäbä* sudden, unexpected
[See also ሐሳብ]

አሰት, see ሐሰት

እሳት *əsat* fire
እሳት ፡ ጫረ get fire from a neighbor

እሳተ ፡ ገሞራ volcano
(የእሳተ ፡ ገሞራ volcanic)
(የእሳተ ፡ ገሞራ ፡ አናት crater)
የእሳት incendiary
የእሳት ፡ እሪ ት moth
የእሳት ፡ አደጋ fire hazard
የእሳት ፡ አደጋ ፡ መኪና fire engine
የእሳት ፡ አደጋ ፡ ተከላካይ fireman
የእሳት ፡ አደጋ ፡ ተከላካይ ፡ ጓድ fire
brigade
(የ)ሰደድ ፡ እሳት wildfire

እስተ, see እስከ

እስቲ *əsti* come now!, so then!, let
me!, please!

አስታማሚ *astamami* nurse (see አመመ)

አስተማሪ *astämari* teacher, instructor
(see *ማረ)
አስተማሪነት *astämarinnät* teaching,
teaching profession

አስተርጓሚ *astärgʷami* translator, interpreter (see ተረጐመ)

አስተሳሰብ *astäsasäb* way of thinking, idea, opinion, notion, suggestion, reasoning, mentality (see አሰበ)

አስተባበለ, see አበለ

አስተባበረ, see አበረ

አስተናባሪ *astänabari* usher (see ነበረ)

አስተናገደ, see ነገደ

አስተናጋጅ, see ነገደ

እስትንፋስ *əstənfas* breath, breathing
(see ነፈሰ)

አስተከከለ, see አከለ

አስተካካይ *astäkakay*, in ጠጉር ፡ አስተከ
ካይ hairdresser, barber (see አከለ)

አስተዋለ *astäwalä* pay attention, be
attentive, look at, take note of (see
ዋለ and አስተዋይ)

አስታወሰ, see አወሰ

አስታወቀ, see ወወቀ

አስተወወቀ, see ወወቀ

አስተዋይ *astäway* observant, attentive,
prudent, wise, intelligent, thoughtful,
perspicacious, perceptive, reasonable (see አስተዋለ)
አስተዋይነት *astäwayənnät* judgment
(ability to form opinions), soundness
of judgment, prudence, perspicacity
አስተዋይነት ፡ የጐደለው imprudent

አስተያየ *astäyayyä* compare (see አየ)

አስተያየት *astäyayät* opinion, judgment
(opinion), point of view, notion, outlook, attitude, contention, remark,
observation, perspective (see አየ)
አስተያየት ፡ አደረገ take into consideration
መልካም ፡ አስተያየት favor (n.)
በኔ ፡ አስተያየት in my view, in my
opinion

እስታድዮም *əstadyom* stadium

አስተዳደረ, see አደረ

አስተዳደር *astädadär* administration,
management (see አደረ)
ያስተዳደር executive (adj.), administra-
trative

አስተዳዳሪ *astädadari* manager, executive, administrator (see አደረ)
አስተዳዳሪዎች *astädadariwočč* management (persons who handle a business)

አስተዳደግ *astädadäg* breeding, upbringing (see አደገ)

አስቸኳይ *asčäkkʷay* urgent, pressing
(see ቸኩለ)
አስቸኳይ ፡ ሁኔታ emergency, state of
emergency
አስቸኳይ ፡ ጊዜ emergency, state of
emergency
ባስቸኳይ urgently
አስቸኳይነት *asčäkkʷayənnät* urgency,
exigency

እሳቸው *əssaččäw* He (respect); see also እርሳቸው

አሳንሰር *asansär*, አሳንሱር *asansur* lift, elevator

እሱነት *əssunnät* personality, identity (see እሱ)

እስከ *əskä* until, up to, till, as far as, even (see also እስተ)
እስከ + noun + ድረስ up to, till, until (prep.), as far as
እስከ + perfect + ድረስ as long as, so long as
እስካሁን *əskahun* so far, up to now (see አሁን)
እስከነ *əskännä* including, inclusive of (እስከነጥራሹ for good (as in 'he came back for good'; see ጥራሽ)
እስከዚህ *əskäzzih* so far, that far, so (that much), all that (see -ዚህ)
እስከዚያ *əskäzziya* meanwhile (see -ዚያ)

እስኪ *əski* may I?, let me!, please!

እስከ + imperfect + ድረስ to the point of

አስኳል *ask{}^wal* egg yolk

አስከልካይ, see እልፍኝ

አስከሬን *askären* corpse, body (corpse), skeleton
ያስከሬን ፡ ሣጥን coffin

እስክስታ *əskəsta* kind of dance in which the shoulders are shaken
እስክስታ ፡ አስነካ (or ወረደ) perform the *əskəsta* (see ነካ)

እስከነ *əskännä* including, inclusive of (see እስከ)

እስካውት *əskawt* scout, boy scout

አስኪያጅ *askiyağ* administrator, director, manager (see ሄደ, *ኬደ)
ሥራ ፡ አስኪያጅ manager

እስኳድሮን *ask{}^wadron* squadron

አስከሬ, see ከፉ

አሳዛኝ, see አዘነ

እሰይ *əssäy*, exclamation of joy

እስያ *əsya* Asia

አሲድ *asid* acid (n.)

አስጊ *asgi* critical (condition), serious (condition), dangerous (disease), alarming, risky (see ሰጋ)
አስጊ ፡ ሁኔታ crisis
አስጊነት *asginnät* gravity, seriousness (of condition)

አስፋልት *asfalt* asphalt, asphalt road, paving
አስፋልት ፡ ፈሰሰ be paved
አስፋልት ፡ አፈሰሰ lay down a coat of asphalt

እስፒል *əspil* pin

እስፖርት *əsport* sport (see also ስፖርት)

አሸ *aššä* rub, scrub, massage
አሻሸ *ašaššä* pat, stroke

እሺ *əšši* yes, all right, O.K.
እሺ ፡ አለ consent, comply, accept (agree), acquiesce
እሺ ፡ ባይ submissive, compliant
†እሺታ *əššəta* consent

እሽ *əšš* hush!, silence!
እሽ ፡ አለ *əšš alä* shoo (the flies)

እሾህ *əšoh* thorn, spine (see also ሾክ, ሾህ, እሾክ)
እሾህማ *əšohəmma* thorny, prickly

አሸመ *aššämä* (B) braid (the hair)

አሻሚ *aššami* ambiguous (see *ሸማ)
አሻሚነት *aššaminnät* ambiguity

አሽሙር *ašmur* sarcasm, veiled insult

አሻር ፡ ባሻር *ašär bašär* poor (food)

አሹራ *ašura* land sale tax

አሻራ *ašara* fingerprint
የጣት ፡ አሻራ fingerprint

እሹሩሩ *əššururu* lullaby
እሹሩሩ ፡ አለ sing a lullaby, lull by
singing softly

አሻሻጭ *aššašač* salesclerk, salesman
(see ሸጠ)

እሽቅድምድም *əšqədəmdəm* race, racing
(see ቀደም, ተሽቀዳደመ, እሽቅድድም)
የፈረስ ፡ እሽቅድምድም horse race

እሽቅድድም *əšqədəddəm* racing, race
(see also እሽቅድምድም)
የዱላ ፡ ቅብብል ፡ እሽቅድድም relay race
የፈረስ ፡ እሽቅድድም horse race

እሽት *əšät* grain before it matures

እሽታ *əššəta* consent (n.); see እሺ
የእሽታ positive (affirmative)

አሸንዳ *ašända* gutter, spout (of roof)

አሻንጉሊት *ašangullit* toy, doll

እሾክ *əšok* thorn, spine (see also ሾህ,
ሾክ, እሾህ)

አሽከር *aškär* servant, domestic

አሽካካ *aškakka* neigh (see *ሽካካ)

አሸዋ *ašäwa* sand
አሸዋማ *ašäwamma* sandy

አሸገ *aššägä* (B) seal (close tightly),
glue
በቆርቆሮ ፡ አሸገ can (food)
በቆርቆሮ ፡ የታሸገ *bäqorqorro yätaš-
šägä* conserve, n. (preserved food)
በጣሳ ፡ አሸገ can (food)

አሻግሮ *aššagro* across (see *ሻገረ)

አሻፈረ(ኝ) *ašaffärä(ññ)* absolutely not,
definitely not, I won't do it (see *ሸፈረ)
አሻፈረኝ ፡ አለ revolt (not accept the
authority), refuse flatly
አሻፈረኝ ፡ አልሄድም I will definitely
not go

እቃ *əqa* things, object, utensil, baggage,
goods, stuff, effects, article (object)

እቃ ፡ አስገባ furnish (an apartment);
see ገባ
እቃ ፡ ማጠቢያ sink (n.)
እቃ ፡ ቤት vestry, storehouse
እቃ ፡ አዟሪ peddler (see ዞረ)
ትርፍ ፡ እቃ surplus goods
(የ)ሆድ ፡ እቃ entrails, guts
የሸክላ ፡ እቃ earthenware
የቤት ፡ እቃ furniture
ጥሬ ፡ እቃ raw material

ዓቅም *aqəm* strength, means, power,
capacity, ability
ዓቅም ፡ አጣ be powerless
ዓቅመ ፡ ሔዋን *aqmä hewan* puberty
(of woman), maturity (of woman),
adulthood (of woman)
ዓቅመ ፡ ቢስ weakling
ዓቅመ ፡ አዳም puberty (of man), maturity (of man), adulthood (of man)
ለዓቅመ ፡ ሔዋን ፡ ደረሰች be of age
(woman), reach puberty (woman)
ለዓቅመ ፡ አዳም ፡ ደረሰ be of age (man),
come of age, reach puberty (man)
እንደ ፡ ዓቅሙ as much as he can

አቋም, see ቆመ

አቀማመጥ, see *ቀመጠ

አቆማዳ *aqomada* leather bag

አቅራቢያ *aqrabbiya* immediate neighborhood, vicinity (see ቀረበ)
በአቅራቢያ ፡ የሚገኝ nearby (adj.)
በ - - - አቅራቢያ near (prep.)

አቋራጭ *aqʷarač* crosscut, cutoff (see
ቋረጠ)
አቋራጭ ፡ መንገድ short cut

አቃቂር *aqaqir* review (of a book)
አቃቂር ፡ ጻፈ review (a book)

አቃቢ *aqqabi* custodian, guardian
አቃቢ ፡ ሕግ prosecutor
አቃቢ ፡ መጻሕፍት librarian
ጠቅላይ ፡ አቃቢ ፡ ሕግ attorney general

ዕቁብ *əqqub* mutual aid association,
credit association

በቀበት *aqäbät* upward slope, ascent
በቀበቱን uphill (adv.)

ዕቁባት *əqqubaṭ* concubine

አቀባይ *aqäbbay*, in ቃል ፣ አቀባይ correspondent (of a newspaper), reporter, spokesman (see *ቀበለ)
ወሬ ፣ አቀባይ informer
ዜና ፣ አቀባይ reporter

አቅኚ *aqñi* pioneer (see ቀኚ)
ያገር ፣ አቅኚ colonizer (see አገር)

አቀደ *aqqädä* (B) plan, make plans, devise a plan, project, design (plan out), conceive a plan
የታቀደ *yätaqqädä* intended, designed
አቅድ *aqd*, እቅድ *əqqəd* plan, project, scheme, setup
ያለ ፣ አቅድ haphazardly

አቈጣጠር *aqqʷäṭaṭär* way of counting, computation, reckoning (see ቈጠረ)
የቀን ፣ አቈጣጠር calendar (counting of days)

አቅጣጫ *aqṭaččä* direction, drift (of wind), course (of river), bearings
ከያቅጣጫው *käyyaqṭaččäw* from all sides
ከሁሉም ፣ አቅጣጫ from all angles, from all directions
ዋነኛ ፣ አቅጣጫ cardinal point

እቅጩን *əqqəččun* the naked truth
እቅጩን ፣ ተናገረ hit the nail on the head (see ነገረ)

አቀፈ *aqqäfä* embrace, hug, hold close, take in one's arms
ታቀፈ *taqqäfä* hold in one's arms, brood (of hen, of eggs)
†እቅፍ *əqqəf* armful
አቃፍ *aqqäf*, in ዓለም ፣ አቃፍ international, universal, global

እቅፍ *əqqəf* armful (see አቀፈ)
እቅፍ ፣ አደረገ hug, squeeze (hug), press (embrace)

እቅፍ ፣ ሙሉ armful, armload
የአበባ ፣ እቅፍ bouquet

አባ *abba* Father (title of priests), appelation for monks, reverend (see አቡን); is also used in personal names and noms de guerre
አባ ፣ ጨጓራ caterpillar

አብ *ab* (pl. አባው *abäw*, አበይት *abäyt*) elder, forefather, Eternal Father

አበለ *abbälä* break one's promise, promise falsely, make believe
ተባበለ *täbabbälä* be false, be untrue
አባበለ *ababbälä* entice with promises, cajole, coax, placate, conciliate (coax), hush (a baby)
አስተባበለ *astäbabbälä* deny (a report), disavow (disclaim), refute
አባይ *abay* fake (n.)
እብለት *əblät* deceit, lie, falsehood
ማስተባበያ *mastäbabäya* denial, refutation

አበል *abäl* means of existence, stipend, allowance, alimony, annuity, wages
የቀን ፣ አበል per diem
የጡረታ ፣ አበል social security, pension

አባል *abal* member (of a board)
አባል ፣ ዘር genitals
አባሎች *abaločč* staff (group assisting a chief)
አባልነት *abalənnät* membership

አቦል *abol* first boiling of coffee

እብለት, see አበለ

አበረ *abbärä* join up, stand with, collaborate, be united, conspire against
ተባበረ *täbabbärä* unite (vi.), be united, be allied, ally oneself, be aligned, confederate, be in association, join forces, cooperate, coalesce
አስተባበረ *astäbabbärä* unite (vt.), coordinate, combine (efforts)
አብሮ *abro*, አብረው *abräw* together, along with

(አብሮት ፡ መጣ he came along with
him)
(አብራችሁ ፡ ሂዱ abraččəhu hidu go
together!)
አቢር abbär, in ግብረ ፡ አቢር collaborator, accomplice, confederate, partner in crime
አባሪ abari associate, enclosure (something enclosed)
ተባባሪ täbabari associate, ally
ተባብረው täbabräw in unison
መተባበር mättäbabär solidarity
ትብብር təbəbbər cooperation, coordination
የተባበረ yätäbabbärä concerted
[See also ጉብር, ጉብረት, ማጉበር]

አቢራ abʷara dust (n.); see also አዋራ
አቢራማ abʷaramma dusty

እብሪት əbrit conceit, vanity (conceit),
arrogance
እብሪተኛ əbritäňňa arrogant

ዕብራይስጥ əbrayəsṭ Hebrew language

አበሰ abbäsä (B) wipe, clean, rub in
(e.g. butter)

አበሳ abäsa misfortune, sin

አብሶ abəso especially (see ባሰ)

አበሱዳ abäsuda kind of spice

አበሻ abäša Ethiopian, Abyssinian (see
also ሐበሻ)

አብሽ abəš fenugreek

እብቅ əbbəq chaff

አበበ abbäbä (B) flower, bloom, blossom (see አበባ)

አበባ abäba (n.) flower, bloom (see አበበ)
ያበባ ፡ ማስቀመጫ vase
ያበባ ፡ እቅፍ bouquet
ያበባ ፡ ጉንጉን wreath, garland
አበባማ abäbamma flowery

አባባ abbabba daddy!, papa! (see አባት)

እባብ əbab snake, serpent

አባባል, see አለ say

አባት abbat father
አባቶች abbatočč forefathers, ancestors
አባትና ፡ እናት abbatənna ənnat parents
ያባት ፡ ስም patronymics
ያባት ፡ አባት paternal grandfather
ማን ፡ አባቱ man abbatu bastard!
(lit. who is his father?)
ምን ፡ አባቱ what the devil!
የንስሐ ፡ አባት father confessor
የእንጀራ ፡ አባት stepfather
የአደራ ፡ አባት guardian, trustee
የክርስትና ፡ አባት godfather
የጡት ፡ አባት protector (formal relationship)
አባታዊ abbatawi fatherly, paternal
አባባ abbabba daddy!, papa!
አባዬ abbayye daddy!

አቤት abet yes, Sir!, at your service!,
present!
አቤት ፡ አቤት, expression of surprise;
my! my!; justice, justice!
አቤት ፡ አለ abet alä complain, appeal, petition
[See also አቤቱታ]

እበት əbbät fresh dung (of cow)

አቤቱታ abetuta complaint, petition,
plea, appeal (see አቤት)
አቤቱታ ፡ አቀረብ complain, submit
a petition

አቡን abun, አቡነ abunä, title of a
bishop, title of the head of the
Ethiopian Church (see አባ)

እብን ፡ በረድ əbnä bäräd marble

አበናት abənnät model, pattern, doctrine

እባክህ əbakkəh please! (sg. masc.)
እባክሽ əbakkəš please! (sg. fem.)

አበወ, see አብ

አብዛኛ abzaňňa bulk (see በዛ)
አብዛኞች abzaňňočč majority

አብዛኛው *abzaňňaw* chiefly, mostly, large proportion of, majority
አብዛኛውን most
አብዛኛውን ፡ ጊዜ in the main, mainly, usually, commonly, most of the time, mostly, often

ዐበየ, see ታበየ

ዐቢይ *abiyy* cardinal (adj.), capital (adj.), leading (thought), important, grandiose
ዐቢይ ፡ ጽሑፍ leading article
[See also ዐባይ, ታበየ, ትዕቢት]

አባዬ *abbayye* daddy! (see አባት)

አባይ *abay* fake (n.); see አበለ

ዐባይ *abbay* Blue Nile
(feminine of ዐቢይ, see above)

አበደ *abbädä* go mad, be insane, be crazy
አሳበደ *asabbädä* madden, drive crazy
እብድ *əbd* mad, crazy, lunatic, insane, rabid (dog)
እብደት *əbdät* madness, lunacy, insanity

አቡጃዲ *abuğädi*, አቡጃዲድ *abuğädid* calico

አበጠ *abbäṭä* swell (vi.), be swollen, swell up
አሳበጠ *asabbäṭä* cause to swell, cause a swelling, bulge (vt.)
አባጣ ፡ ጕርባጣ *abaṭa gʷärbaṭṭa*, አባጣ፡ ጕባጣ *abaṭa gʷäbaṭa* bumpy, broken (terrain)
እብጠት *əbṭät* bump, swelling, tumor
አባጭ, see below

እባጭ *əbbač* swelling, abscess (see አበጠ)

አቶ *ato* Mister, title of respect

እት *ət* (pl. እቶች *ətočč*, እትማማች *ətəmmamačč*) sister
[See also እኅት]

አተላ *atäla* coffee grounds, dregs, lees

አታላይ *attalay* swindler, cheat, cheater, deceitful, dishonest, doublefaced (see ታለለ)
አታላይነት *attalayənnät* duplicity

አተመ *attämä* (B) print, stamp, seal, coin (pennies)
ታተመ *tattämä*, passive of the preceding; go to press
አሳተመ *asattämä* publish, get something printed
አታሚ *attami* printer
አሳታሚ *asattami* publisher
እትም *əttəm* printing, typography, issue of a magazine, edition
ማተሚያ ፡ ቤት *mattämiya bet* printing press
ማኅተም *mahtäm* rubber stamp, seal

አታሞ *atamo* small drum

እትማማች *ətəmmamačč* sisters (see እት)

አተር *atär* pea

እትብት *ətəbt* umbilical cord

አተተ *attätä* (B) comment, make a commentary, report (of a newspaper)
ሐተታ, see above

አታክልት *atakəlt* garden, vegetables (see ተከለ)
አትክልት *atkəlt* fruit, vegetables
ያትክልት ፡ ቦታ garden
አትክልተኛ *atkəltäňňa* gardener

እትዬ *ətəyye*, address to a young woman by her juniors

ኢትዮጵያ *ityoppəya* Ethiopia
ኢትዮጵያዊ *ityoppəyawi* (pl. ኢትዮጵያ ውያን) Ethiopian

እቴጌ *ətege*, title of queen, sovereign's consort

እትፍ ፡ አለ *əttəff alä* spit (see also ተፋ)

አቻ *ačča* equal, peer, of the same rank, of the same status
አቻ ፡ ለአቻ being of the same age, being of the same status, matching pair

ያላቻ ፡ ጋብቻ *yalačča gabəčča*, አላቻ ፡ ጋብቻ *alačča gabəčča* misalliance

አቾሎኒ *oččoloni* peanut

አቻምና *aččamna* year before last (see ዓምና) ካቻምና *kaččamna* year before last

እና *ənnä*, marker of plurality (as in እነ ማን who? (plural), እነዚህ these, እነ ዚያ those, እናንተ you (pl.), እነሱ they); also, 'those with, the followers of' as in እነራስ ፡ ዮሐንስ the followers of Ras Yohannes

እኔ *əne* I የኔ *yäne* my, mine

ኦና *ona* deserted (house), abandoned (house); see also ወና

እናሆ *ənnäho* here is!, behold!

እኚህ *ənnih* these, this (respect); see also እኒህ

እነማን *ənnäman* who? (plural); see እነ, ማን

አነር *anär* panther

እነርሱ *ənnärsu* they (see also እነሱ) የነርሱ *yännärsu* their, theirs

አነሰ *annäsä* be less, be insufficient, diminish (vi.), decrease, be too little, be small, shrink, flag (of strength) አነሰ(ው) *annäsä(w)* he lacks in, he is short of, he has little of, (something) is not enough for him አሳነሰ *asannäsä* lessen, diminish (vt.), decrease አነስ ፡ ያለ *anäss yalä* light (sentence), scant (small) አነስተኛ *anästäñña* lesser, little (matter), small, minimum, few, minor (change), spare (scanty), slender (income), insignificant ያነሰ *yannäsä* less ቢያንስ *biyans* at least ቢያንስ ፡ ቢያንስ *biyans* at least, a minimum of

ማነስ *manäs* paucity, small number, lack, shortage ትንሽ, see above ታናሽ, see above

እነሱ *ənnässu* they (see also እነርሱ) የነሱ *yännässu* their, theirs

አንሶላ *ansola* sheet, bedsheet

እንስራ *ənsəra* water jug

እንስሳ *ənsəsa* (pl. እንስሳት) animal እንስሳት *ənsəsat* fauna የቤት ፡ እንስሳ domestic animal

አንስት *anəst*, እንስት *ənəst* female (see also አንስታይ)

አንሥቶ *ansəto*, in ከ - - - አንሥቶ beginning from, starting from (see ነሣ)

እንስት *ənsät* false banana

አነስተኛ, see አነሰ

አንስታይ ፡ ጾታ *anəstay şota* feminine (n.), feminine gender (see አንስት)

እንሽላሊት *ənšəlalit* lizard

አነቀ *annäqä* choke (vt.), strangle, suffocate, seize by the neck, attack (of a leopard) ታነቀ *tannäqä* (vi.) strangle, choke, suffocate ተናነቀ *tänannäqä* grapple አንቆ ፡ ገደለ *anqo gäddälä* throttle, strangle (kill by squeezing the throat) ትንቅንቅ *tənəqnəq* (n.) struggle, fight

ዕንቍ *ənq*[w] precious stone, jewelry ዕንቍ ፡ ሳንፔር sapphire

እንቍላል *ənqulal* egg እንቍላል ፡ ጣለ(ች) lay an egg የእንቍላል ፡ አስኳል yolk

እንቅልፍ *ənqəlf* (n.) sleep, slumber (see *ቀለፉ) እንቅልፉ ፡ መጣ he is sleepy (lit. the sleep came) እንቅልፍ ፡ ነሣ not let sleep, keep awake

እንቅልፍ ፡ እንቅልፍ ፡ አለው he is sleepy
እንቅልፍ ፡ ወሰደው he fell asleep
እንቅልፍ ፡ ያዘው he fell asleep
የእንቅልፍ ፡ በሽታ sleeping sickness
የእንቅልፍ ፡ እጦት insomnia
እንቅልፋም ənqəlfam sleepy

እንቁራሪት ənqurarit frog, toad

እንቅርት ənqərt goiter
እንቅርት ፡ አወጣ have a goiter (see
ወጣ)

እንቅስቃሴ ənqəsəqqase movement (political), activity (movement), motion
(movement); see *ቀሰቀሰ
የመኪናዎች ፡ እንቅስቃሴ traffic
የሰውነት ፡ እንቅስቃሴ gesture, exercise
(physical)

እንቆቅልሽ ənqoqəlləš riddle, puzzle

እንቅብ ənqəb kind of platter serving
as a measure

እንቁጣጣሽ ənqʷəṭaṭaš New Year's celebration, New Year season

እንቀጽ anqäṣ article (section of document), paragraph, clause, stipulation, term (of treaty), provision (of
law), predicate
ርእሰ ፡ አንቀጽ editorial, lead article
ትእዛዛ ፡ አንቀጽ imperative
የግጥም ፡ አንቀጽ strophe

እንቅፋት ənqəfat stumbling block, hindrance, obstacle, pitfall, encumbrance, drawback, impediment
እንቅፋት ፡ መታው he bumped into
something, he stumbled

እንባ ənba tear (from the eye)
እንባ ፡ አዘለ be teary, be tearful

እንቦልክ anboləkk envelope (see also
አምቦልክ)

ኤንቬሎፕ envelop envelope

እንብርት ənbərt navel, center (see also
እምብርት)

እንበሳ anbässa lion, brave, courageous

እንበጣ anbäṭa locust

አናት anat summit, crown of the head,
head (of page, of staircase), bolt
በ - - - አናት ፤ ከ - - - አናት on the
top of, on the summit of

አንተ antä you (sg. masc.)
ያንተ yantä your, yours (sg. masc.)

እናት ənnat mother
እናትና ፡ አባት parents
እናትና ፡ አባት ፡ የሌለው orphan
የእናት maternal
የእናት ፡ ቋንቋ native speech, native
tongue, mother tongue
የቁልፍ ፡ እናት lock
(የ)እንጀራ ፡ እናት stepmother
የክርስትና ፡ እናት godmother
እናትነት ənnatənnät motherhood

እንተ əntä, in በእንተ ፡ ስማ ፡ ለማርያም
in the name of Mary

እንቶ ፡ ፍንቶ ənto fənto junk

አናቶሚ anatomi anatomy

እናቲት ənnatit, in እናቲት ፡ አህያ she
donkey; እናቲት ፡ ዶሮ mother hen

አንቴና antena antenna

እንተን əntän, እንትና əntəna what's-his-
name (when one cannot remember
the name of a person or wishes to
avoid mentioning it)
እንትን əntən what's the name (when
one cannot remember the name of a
thing)

እንትፍ ፡ እንትፍ ፡ አለ əntəff əntəff alä
splutter

አንቺ anči you (sg. fem.)
ያንቺ yanči your, yours (sg. fem.)

አኗኗር annʷanʷar way of life, life style,
living (see ኗሪ)

እናንተ ənnantä you (pl.)
የናንተ yännantä your, yours (pl.)

እንጄህ *ənnäňňih* these

እንካ *ənka* take!, here! (fem. እንኪ *ən-ki,* ንንቺ *ənči,* pl. እንኩ *ənku*); see ነካ
በእንካ ፡ ስላንቲያ ፡ ተያያዙ engage in recrimination (see የሀ)

እንኳ *ank*ʷ*a* even (adv.)
እንኳ + (simple imperfect) even if, even though, although
ምንም ፡ እንኳ ፡ ብ + (simple imperfect) despite, even though, although
[See also እንኳን, ስንኳ]

አንኳር *ank*ʷ*ar* cube (of sugar), lump (of sugar)

እንኩሮ *ənkuro* dish made of flour of parched barley and sorghum which has been mixed with water

አነከሰ *anäkkäsä* limp, be lame
አንካሳ *ankassa* lame (person), one who limps

እንክብል *ənkəbəll* round, spherical, tablet (of aspirin), pill (see *ከባለለ)

እንክትክት ፡ አለ *ənkətkətt alä* go to pieces (see ከተከተ)
እንክትክት ፡ አደረገ wreck (v.)

እንከን *ənkän* defect, spot (stain), blemish (of reputation), flaw
እንከን ፡ የሌለበት (or የሌለው) *ənkän yälelläbbät* (or *yälelläw*) flawless, blameless, immaculate, impeccable
እንከን ፡ የማይወጣለት *ənkän yämma-yəwäṭallät* perfect (without defect)

እንኳን *ank*ʷ*an* even (adv.)
እንኳን + (negative verb) not even
ምንም ፡ እንኳን ፡ ብ + (imperfect) even if
ብ+ imperfect + እንኳን even if, even though
እንኳን is also used in formulas for wishing well, as in እንኳን ፡ ደኅና ፡ ገባህ welcome home! (see ገባ); እንኳን ፡ ደስ ፡ ያለህ congratulations!; እንኳን ፡

ከዘመን ፡ ወደ ፡ ዘመን ፡ አሸጋገረህ Happy New Year! (see *ሻገረ)
እንኳን ፡ ደስ ፡ ያለህ ፡ አለ congratulate, felicitate
ሁሉም ፡ እንኳን ፡ አለ everyone said that he had it coming
[See also እንኳ]

እነዚህ *ənnäzzih* these (adj., pr.) from እነ, -ዚህ

እንዝርት *ənzərt* spindle, axis

እነዚያ *ənnäzziya* those (adj., pron.) from እነ, -ዚያ

አንዱ ፡ ጋ *anduga* somewhere (see አንድ)

አንዴ *ande* once, at once (see አንድ)
አንዴ ፡ ሁለቴ a few times
በአንዴ at a glance, at once, overnight
ካንዴም ፡ ሁለቴ more than once
ከዓመት ፡ አንዴ rarely, very seldom, once in a blue moon

አንድ *and* (fem. አንዲት *andit*) one, a, an, single, a certain, the same, about (approximately)
አንድ ፡ ሁለት a couple
አንድ ፡ ላይ together
አንድ ፡ ሰዓት seven o'clock
አንድ ፡ ሰው somebody, someone
አንድ ፡ ቀን some day
አንድ ፡ ቦታ some place
አንድ ፡ በንድ singly, point by point, one by one, one at a time
አንድ ፡ ነገር something
አንድ ፡ አደረገ unify
አንድ ፡ ጋ together
አንድ ፡ ጊዜ sometime, once
አንድ + (suffix pronoun + negative verb) none of
አንዱ ፡ ጋ somewhere
አንዴ, see above
በአንድ together
በአንድ ፡ ጊዜ at once
አንዳም either
አንዳም + (negative verb) neither
አንድም also, or
አንድም + (negative verb) nobody, not a single

እንድም ፤ ነገር + (negative verb) not
a thing
አንዳች, see below
አንድነት, see below
አንደኛ, see below
አንዳንድ, see below
አንዳፍታ, see below

እንደ əndä like, as, according to, in
accordance with, instead of
እንደ+(perfect) if, even as, as, as
soon as, just as, whether, once (conj.)
እንደ + perfect + ወዲያው as soon as
እንደ + (perfect or relative imperfect)
that (conj.)
እንደ + (relative imperfect) as far as
(conj.), as (conj.)
እንደ + verb + ሁሉ just as, just like,
as though
እንደኔ to my mind, according to
me
እንደኔ ፤ ከሆነ to my mind, according
to me
[እንደ is the first element of እንደምን,
እንዲህ, ኡንደሆን, and so on]

እንደ ənde what!, how!, why! (exclamation of surprise)
እንደው əndew suddenly
እንደውም əndewəm in any case, as
a matter of fact

እንድ əndə + (imperfect) in order
that, in order to, so that; serves also
for the expression of the infinitive

እንዲህ əndih such, such a, like this,
so, thus (from እንደ-ይህ)
እንዲሁ əndihu thus, likewise
እንዲሁም əndihəm, እንዲሁም əndihum
like this, likewise, thus

እንደሆነ əndähonä, እንደሆን əndähon if,
whether (see እንደ)

አንዱም ፤ አንድም, see እንድ

እንደምን əndämən how? (see እንደ, ምን)
እንደምንም əndämənəm anyhow, somehow

እንደምንም ፤ ብሎ anyhow, somehow
or other, barely, after a fashion

እንደራሴ əndärase deputy, representative, vice-, stand-in (see እንደ, ራስ)
የሕዝብ ፤ እንደራሴ deputy (in parliament)
እንደራሴነት əndärasennät regency

ኢንዱስትሪ industri industry

አንደበት andäbät tongue
አንደበተ ፤ ርቱዕ eloquent
አንደበተ ፤ ርቱዕነት andäbätä rətu'ənnät eloquence

አንዲት andit one (fem.); see አንድ

እንደታ əndeta and how!, certainly!,
surely!, of course!, naturally!

እንደት əndet how?, how!, how much!
ኡንደት ፤ እንደ + (verb) how
እንደት ፤ ያለ such a!

አንዳች andačč any, anything (see አንድ)
አንዳችም andaččəm + (negative verb)
nothing, not anything
ከአንዳች ፤ ተቃውሞ unopposed (see
ቆመ)

አንድነት andənnät union, unity, solidarity, integrity (territorial); see አንድ
በአንድነት in a body, together, in
unison

አንዳንዴ andande sometimes, at times
(from አንድ-አንዴ)

አንዳንድ andand some, certain, several
(see አንድ)
አንዳንዶች andandočč several, some
አንዳንዶቹ several (pron.)
አንዳንድ ፤ ጊዜ sometimes, at times
እያንዳንድ əyyandand each, every
እያንዳንዱ ፤ ሰው everyone

እንደነገሩ, see ነገር

አንደኛ andäňňa first, firstly, unique,
of excellent quality, first-class (see
አንድ)

አንደኛ ፡ ደረጃ ፡ ትምህርት ፡ ቤት
primary school, elementary school
አንደኛው· either
አንደኛነት andäňňannät champion-ship, primacy, top rank (in class)

እንዴው, see እንዴ

እንዴውም, see እንዴ

እንደዚህ ǝndäzzih this way, like this, thus, such a
እንደዚሁ· ǝndäzzihu likewise, the same way
እንደዚህ ፡ ከሆነ in this case

እንደዚያ ǝndäzziya that way, thus
እንደዚያው as before

እንዲያ ǝndiya that way, thus
እንዲያው ǝndiyaw to no purpose, for nothing, just (merely), without result, purely
እንዲያውም as a matter of fact, in fact, for that matter, rather, in any case

እንደገና ǝndägäna again, anew

እንዳጋጣሚ, see አጋጣሚ

አንዳፍታ andafta at one gulp(from አንድ, አፍታ)
በንዳፍታ at one stroke

አንጎ angǒ tough (meat)

እንጃ ǝnǧa I wouldn't know!

እንጂ ǝnǧi but, on the contrary, except that
እንጂ (preceded by the jussive) even though
ይሁን ፡ እንጂ nevertheless

እንጀራ ǝnǧära Ethiopian bread (is made from a batter and is cooked like a pancake)
እንጀራ ፡ ወጣልኝ ǝnǧära wättallǝňň I made a good living
የእንጀራ ፡ ልጅ stepchild, stepdaugh-ter, stepson
(የ)እንጀራ ፡ አባት stepfather

(የ)እንጀራ ፡ እናት stepmother
የእንጀራ ፡ አባቱ ፡ ልጅ stepbrother
የእንጀራ ፡ እናቱ ፡ ልጅ stepbrother
የተርብ ፡ እንጀራ wasp nest

እንጆሪ ǝnǧorre raspberry, strawberry

አንጀት anǧät intestine, entrails, bowels, guts
አንጀቱ ፡ ተቄረጠ he was mortally offended (see ቄረጠ)
አንጀት ፡ የለሽ heartless
ያንጀት yanǧät intestinal
ያንጀት ፡ ሕመም colic
ያንጀት ፡ ወዳጅ close friend
ትርፍ ፡ አንጀት appendix
የትርፍ ፡ አንጀት ፡ በሽታ appendicitis

አንጓ angʷa joint (of bamboo)
የእጅ ፡ አንጓ wrist

አንጎል angʷäl brain
የአንጎል cerebral

እንግሊዝ ǝngliz Englishman
እንግሊዝኛ ǝnglizǝňňa English (lan-guage)
እንግሊዛዊ ǝnglizawi Englishman

አንተርተሮ, see *ጉረጉረ

አነገተ anäggätä shoulder (a gun), sling over the shoulders, wear on the neck
ማንገቻ mangäča suspenders
አንገት, see below

አንገት angät neck (see አነገተ)
አንገቱን ፡ ብቅ ፡ አደረገ lean forward
ካንገት ፡ በላይ ፡ የሆነ insincere, forced, strained (not natural)
ያንገት ፡ ልብስ shawl, scarf
ያንገት ፡ ነቀርሳ scrofula
ያንገት ፡ ፎጣ scarf

እንግዳ ǝngǝda stranger, guest, visitor, strange, odd, queer, weird, unusual, new (unusual)
እንግዳ ፡ ቤት sitting room
እንግዳ ፡ ተቀባይ host, hospitable (see *ቀበለ)

እንግዳ ፡ ተቀባይነት hospitality (see
*ቀበለ)
እንግዳ ፡ ነገር oddity
እንግዳ ፡ አትሁን make yourself at
home! (see ሆነ)
የእንግዳ ፡ ማረፊያ lounge
ቤት ፡ ለእንግዳ make yourself at
home!
እንግዳነት əngədannät peculiarity

እንግዴ əngəde, in የእንግዴ ፡ ልጅ placen-
ta, afterbirth

እንግዲህ əngədih therefore, for that reason, now (thus), so, in any case
ከእንግዲህ hereafter
ከእንግዲህ ፡ ወዲህ henceforth, from
this time forward
ከእንግዲህ ፡ ወዲያ any longer, any
further

እንጉዳይ ənguday mushroom

እንግዲያ əngədiya therefore, well then
እንግዲያውም əngədiyawəmma then
(if that is so)
እንግዲያስ əngədiyass then, so then

አንጋፋ angaffa first-born son

አናጢ anaṭi carpenter, mason (see also
አናጺ)

እንጥል əntəl uvula, tonsil

አንጥረኛ antəräñña metal worker, silversmith (see ነጠረ)

አነጠሰ anäṭṭäsä sneeze
አስነጠሰ asnäṭṭäsä cause to sneeze

ዕንጨት ənčät wood, timber, peg, stake
የዕንጨት wooden

አነጸ annäṣä build, form (the character)
አናጺ carpenter, mason (see also
አናጢ)

አንጻር anṣar direction (line of action),
aspect, facing (see *ነጸረ)
አንጻር ፡ ለአንጻር against each other
ከ - - - አንጻር ፤ በ - - - አንጻር opposite
(prep.), against, in contrast to

እንፋሎት ənfalot vapor, steam

ኢንፍሉዌንዛ influwenza flu, grippe

እኛ əñña we
የኛ yäñña our, ours

እኒህ əññih this (respect); see also እዚህ

አኘከ aññäkä (B) chew, masticate

አእምሮ a'məro reason (ability to think),
mind (intellect), consciousness, intelligence
አእምሮ ፡ ዐወቀ he has reached the
age of reason
አእምሮ ፡ ያለው rational (being)
አእምሮ ፡ ደካማ feeble-minded
የአእምሮ mental, intellectual (adj.)
የአእምሮ ፡ ሕመምተኛ insane
የአእምሮ ፡ ሐኪም psychiatrist
የአእምሮ ፡ ሕክምና psychiatry

ኡኡታ u'uta a call for help

አዕዋፍ a'waf fowl (see ወፍ)

እኮ əkko yes, indeed!; well then!, of
course!, after all!, really!

አከተ, see ታከተ

አኳኋን akkʷahʷan manner of being,
essence, condition, state of affairs,
position, fashion, style (see ሆነ)
በምንም ፡ አኳኋን by all means

አካሄድ, see ሄደ

አከለ akkälä be equal, equal, be like,
amount to, be worth
አከለ(ለት) akkälä(llät) add, contribute
ተካከለ täkakkälä be equal, be uniform, be even
አስተካከለ astäkakkälä make equal,
equalize, make uniform, even out,
adjust, regulate, set (a watch), smooth
out (the mortar), trim, cut (hair),
balance, straighten, level, rectify
ተስተካከለ tästäkakkälä be level, be
equal, be straight, be regular
(feature)
እኩል, see below

እኩልነት *əkkulənnät* equality, equivalence
እኩሌታ *əkkuleta* half, equal part
እኩይ, see below
መሃል, see above
መhalhል, see above
ማስተካከያ, see above
ማእከላዊ, sec above
ማእከላይ, see above
መካከል, see above
ትክክል, see above
አማካይ, see above
አስተካካይ, see above
ይሀል, see below

አካል *akal* (pl. አካላት *akalat*) body, body (of water), organ, member
አካላት members of the body
አካል ፥ መጠን manhood, full growth
አካል ፥ መጠን ፥ የደረሰ grown (man)
አካል ፥ ስንኩል disabled, cripple, invalid
አካል ፥ ጉዱሎ invalid (adj.), crippled, maimed
አካል ፥ ጉዱሎ ፥ አዱረገ cripple (v.)
አካል ፥ ጉዱሎነት *akalä gʷädälonnät* deformity
ቅሪት ፥ አካል fossil
የሰው ፥ አካል ፥ ጥናት physiology
አካላዊ *akalawi* physical (activity), bodily

እከሌ *əkäle* such-and-such, so-and-so

እኩል *əkkul* equal, even, evenly, alike, uniform, half, middle (see አካለ)
ከ - - - እኩል as, like
እኩል ፥ ሌሊ.ት midnight
እኩል ፥ ቀን noon
እኩል ፥ አዱረገ equate
እኩሌታ *əkkuleta* half, equal part
እኩልነት *əkkulənnät* equality, equivalence, parity
[See also በኩል]

አክሊል *aklil* crown

አካላት *akalat* members of the body (see አካል)

እኩሌታ, see እኩል

እኩልነት, see እኩል

አከመ *akkämä* (B) attend (treat), treat medically, doctor (v.); see also ሐከም

አከምባሎ *akəmbalo* cover of the griddle on which እንጀራ-bread is made (see also አክንባሎ)

አከርካሪ *akärkari* spinal column, spine, vertebra, backbone

አክስት *akəst* aunt
ያክስት ፥ ልጅ cousin

አክሲዮን *aksiyon* stock, share

ኤክስፖዚሲዮን *ekspozisiyon* exposition

አክብሮት *akbərot* respect, deference, homage (see ከበረ)
አክብሮት ፥ የጎዱለው irreverent, disrespectful
በአክብሮት respectfully

አካባቢ *akkababi* surrounding area, surroundings, environment, outskirts, zone, region (see ከበበ)
በካባቢው nearby
በ - - - አካባቢ around

አክታ *akkəta* spittle, phlegm

ኤኮኖሚክስ *ekonomiks* economics

አክንባሎ, see አከምባሎ

አከከ *akkäkä* have an itch, scratch
ታከከ *takkäkä* scratch oneself
አሳከከ *asakkäkä* itch (vt.), make to scratch
እከክ *əkäk* itch (n.)

እኩይ *əkkuya* equal, of the same age, of the same size, peer (see አካለ)

አካዳሚ *akadami* academy

አካፋ *akafa* shovel, spade
በአካፋ ፥ ዛቀ shovel (v.)

አዎ *awo* yes (see also አዎን)

በውሎ ፥ ነፋስ *awlo näfas* whirlwind, gale, tornado

አውላላ *awlalla* vast (plain)
አውላላ ፡ ሜዳ open field,

አወላዋይ *awwälaway* hesitant, irre.
(see ወላወለ)

አዋላጅ *awwalaǧ* midwife (see ወለደ)

*በወረ, ታወረ *tawwärä* (B) go blind,
lose one's sight
አሳወረ *asawwärä* blind (vt.)
ዕውር *əwwər* blind (adj.)
ዕውርነት *əwwərənnät* blindness

አዋራ *awwara* dust (n.); see also አቧራ

አውራ *awra* male (of animals), head
(of family), important, chief
አውራ ፡ በሬ bull
አውራ ፡ ዶሮ rooster
አውራ ፡ ጎዳና highway
አውራ ፡ ጣት thumb
አውራ ፡ ፍየል he-goat
የንብ ፡ አውራ queen bee

አውሬ *awre* beast, wild animal, carnivorous animal, brute
አውሬነት, see below
[See also አራዊት]

አውራሪስ *awraris* rhinoceros

አውሬነት *awrennät* ferocity, wild state,
savagery (see አውሬ)
የአውሬነት bestial

ዕውርነት *əwwərənnät* blindness (see
*በወረ)

አውራጃ *awraǧǧa* district, sub-province

አውራጅ *awraǧ* song leader (see ወረደ)

አውሮፓ *awroppa*, አውሮጳ *awroppa*
Europe

አውሮፕላን *awroplan* plane, aircraft
(see also አይሮፕላን)
አውሮፕላን ፡ ጣቢያ airport
አውሮፕላን ፡ ማረፊያ airport

አወሰ *awwäsä* (B) reflect, ponder,
remember, recall
ታወሰ(ው) *tawwäsä(w)* think of, recollect, remember

አስታወሰ *astawwäsä* remind, call
to mind, refer, remember, retain a
memory of, commemorate
ማስታወሻ, see above
መታወሻ *mättawäša* remembrance

በወቀ *awwäqä* know, be familiar with,
be acquainted with, recognize, learn
(the truth), discover (find out), be
cognizant of, realize, notice
(በመላ ፡ በወቀ guess, v.)
(ነፍስ ፡ በወቀ reach the age of reason, be mature)
(ነፍሱን ፡ በወቀ recover consciousness, come to)
(አያውቅም *ayawqəm* (preceded by
the gerund) never (e.g. ሰምቶ ፡ አያው-
ቅም he never heard)
(ለይቶ ፡ በወቀ diagnose; see ለየ)
ታወቀ *tawwäqä* be known, be famous, manifest itself, be found out
አሳወቀ *asawwäqä* acquaint, inform
አስታወቀ *astawwäqä* let know, inform,
announce, notify, declare, give notice, report (inform), proclaim
ተዋወቀ *täwawwäqä* be acquainted
with one another, make the acquaintance
አስተዋወቀ *astäwawwäqä* make get
acquainted, familiarize, introduce
(people)
በዋቂ *awaqi* intelligent, wise, knowledgeable, expert, full-grown, adult
(አላዋቂ *alawaqi* ignorant person)
በውቆ *awqo* knowingly, by design,
on purpose, intentionally, deliberately, by itself (without any help)
ዕውቅ *əwq* known, reputed
ዕውቀት *əwqät* knowledge, understanding, comprehension, cognizance,
erudition
በዋቂነት *awaqinnät* knowledge
አላዋቂነት *alawaqinnät* ignoranc e
ዕውቂያ *əwqiya* acquaintance
ማስታወቂያ, see above
መታወቂያ *mättawäqiya* identification

አለማወቅ *alämawäq* innocence (ignorance), misconception
የታወቀ *yätawwäqä* famous, outstanding, noted, notorious, renowned

ዕውቀት, see ዐወቀ

አውታር *awtar* string of a musical instrument; beam (of wood), framework (of bridge)
የድምፅ ፡ አውታሮች *yädəmṣ awtaročč* vocal cords

አውቶቡስ *awtobus* bus
አውቶቡስ ፡ መቆሚያ bus stop

አዎን *awon* yes (see also አዎ, አዎንታ)

እውን *əwən*, in በእውን, በውን in real life, in actual fact, actually

አዎንታ *awonta* affirmative (n.); see አዎን
የአዎንታ affirmative (adj.)

እውነት *əwnät* truth, reality
እውነትህ ፡ ነው you are right
እውነትም certainly, indeed
በእውነት ፤ በውነት indeed, actually, in fact, truly, honestly, really
እንደ ፡ እውነቱ ፡ ከሆነ as a matter of fact
እውነተኛ *əwnätäňňa* true, truthful, actual, real, rightful, genuine, authentic
እውነተኛነት *əwnätäňňannät* truthfulness

አወከ *awwäkä* (B) cause a disturbance, disturb, upset, agitate, mar
አስታወከ(ው) *astawwäkä(w)* vomit, throw up
አዋኪ *awwaki* unruly, mischievous
መታወክ *mättawäk* failure (of health)
የታወከ *yätawwäkä* (mentally) disturbed

አወደ *awwädä* (B) perfume, vt. (of roses)

ዐውድ *awd* rotation, cycle, circuit
ዐውደ ፡ ንባብ primer

ዐውደ ፡ ዓመት turn of the year (e.g. festival of New Year's or of St. John)
ዐውደ ፡ ጥበብ encyclopedia
የዐውደ ፡ ፀሐይ ፡ ዓመት solar year

አውድማ *awdəmma* threshing floor

አወጀ *awwäǧä* (B) edict, issue a decree, proclaim, promulgate
አዋጅ *awaǧ* proclamation, decree
አዋጅ ፡ ነጋሪ herald (n.)

አውጫጭኝ *awčačəňň* investigation sponsored by a community for apprehending or identifying a wrongdoer (see ወጣ)

አዞ *azzo* crocodile

እዛ *əzza* there

እዚህ *əzzih* here, over here (see -ዚህ)
እዚህ ፡ ጋ over here

አዘለ *azzälä* carry on the back, bear (e.g. letter bearing a threat), contain
ትምህርት ፡ ያዘለ—*yazzälä* didactic
እንባ ፡ ያዘለ teary, tearful
ጥላቻ ፡ ያዘለ hostile, inimical

አዝማሚያ *azmamiya* current (trend, direction), drift (trend); see ዘመም

አዝመራ *azmära* crop, harvest

አዝማሪ *azmari* singer, minstrel (see ዘመረ)

አዝማች *azmač* commander (military), refrain of a song (see ዘመተ)
አዝማች ፡ ጦር vanguard
ቀኝዝማች commander of the right (title of distinction); see ቀኝ
ደጃዝማች honorary title (see ደጅ)
ግራዝማች commander of the left (honorific title); see ግራ

አዝሙድ *azmud* thyme

አዝማድ, see ዘመድ

አዛማጅ ፡ ተውላጠ ፡ ስም *azzamaǧ täwlaṭä səm* relative pronoun (see ዘመደ)

አዝራር *azrar* button (of shirt)

አዙሪት *azurit* whirlpool (see ዞረ, አዝ ዋሪት)

*ዐዘበ, see ታዘበ

እዛብ *əzab* reins (see also ዛብ)

አዘቦት *azäbot* working day
አዘቦት ፡ ቀን working day
ባዘቦቱ *bazäbotu* usually

አዘነ *azzänä* be sad, be sorrowful, grieve, mourn, have regrets, deplore, be in low spirits
አዘነ(ለት) *azzänä(llät)* feel for, have pity on, feel sympathy for
አሳዘነ *asazzänä* sadden, grieve someone, depress, move to pity, arouse compassion
አሳዛኝ *asazzañ* sad (news), deplorable, grievous (news), distressing, pitiful, tragic
የሚያሳዝን *yämmiyasazzən* appalling, deplorable, regrettable
ያሳዝናል *yasazzənal* what a shame! [See also ሐዘን, ሐዘንተኛ]

አዝዋሪት *azwarit* whirlpool (see ዞረ, አዙሪት)

አዛውንት *azawənt* respected elder, notables

አዘዘ *azzäzä* order, command, prescribe, enjoin, instruct, charge someone to do something
ታዘዘ *tazzäzä* receive orders, obey, be compliant
(ምን ፡ ልታዘዝ *män ləttazäz* what can I do for you?)
አዛዥ, see below
ትእዛዝ, see above
ታዘዘ, see above
ማዘዣ *mazäža*, in የመድኃኒት ፡ ማዘዣ prescription
(የፍርድ ፡ ቤት ፡ ማዘዣ warrant)

አለመታዘዝ *alämättazäz* insubordination, disobedience
የማይታዘዝ *yämmayəttazzäz* insubordinate, disobedient, recalcitrant

አዛዥ *azzaž* commander, chief (see አዘዘ)
አዛዥ ፡ መኰንን commanding officer
ምክትል ፡ አዛዥ second-in-command, deputy commander
ዋና ፡ አዛዥ commander in chief

እዚያ there, over there (from እ-ዚያ)
እዚያ ፡ ላይ in this respect
እዚያ ፡ ማዶ over there
እዚያ ፡ ጋ over there

አዣ *ažžä* ooze out
ማዠት, see above

አጀንስ *ažans* agency (see also አጃንስ)

አየ *ayyä* see, look, look at, notice, witness, watch (a game or play), regard, consider, try (a case), hear (of judge hearing a case), treat, test (the brakes), check (oil in a car)
(እንዳላየ ፡ አየ *əndalayyä ayyä* close one's eyes to something, ignore)
ታየ *tayyä* be visible, be seen, be shown, appear, be apparent, seem (to someone), be in evidence, be on display, show (vi.)
አሳየ *asayyä* show (vt.), display, exhibit, demonstrate, depict (demonstrate), present (a play), point out
ተያየ *täyayyä* see one another
(ከሱ ፡ ጋር ፡ እንተያያለን *kässu gar ənnəttäyayyallän* I have an account to settle with him)
አስተያየ *astäyayyä* compare
አስተያየት, see above
መታየት *mättayät* display, appearance (act of appearing)
ትትይይ *təyəy* opposite
የሚታይ *yämmittayy* visible, apparent
†(የ)እዩልኝ *(yä)əyulləññ* pretentious
ልታይ ፡ ልታይ ፡ አለ *ləttay ləttay alä* give oneself airs, show off, be ostentatious, be pompous

[See also አየት ፡ አደረገ]

አዮ aye, expression of disbelief

እየ əyyä (with perfect) while, all the time that; (with noun) every, each (see also በየ)

አይሁድ ayhud Jews
አይሁዳዊ ayhudawi Jew

አየለ ayyälä (B) overpower, predominate, be powerful, be prevalent, preponderate, get the upper hand, prevail, be overwhelming
አያሌ ayyale several, many, numerous, much, in great quantity, a lot
ባያሌው in big quantities

አይል ayəl, in ምንም ፡ አይል it is tolerable, so-so (see አለ)
በልቡ ፡ ምንም ፡ አይል he has his heart in the right place

እዮልኝ əyulləňň, የእዮልኝ pretentious, lit. 'see for me' (see አየ)
እዮልኝ ፡ አለ make a parade of
ለእዮልኝ for effect

አየር ayyär air, atmosphere, climate, weather
አየር ፡ ወለድ airborne
አየር ፡ ወለድ ፡ ወታደር paratrooper
የአየር ፡ ሁኔታ weather conditions
የአየር ፡ ኃይል Air Force
የአየር ፡ መልእክት airletter, airmail
የአየር ፡ መንገድ airline
የአየር ፡ ንብረት climate
የአየር ፡ ወረራ air raid (see ወረረ)
የአየር ፡ ጠባይ climate, weather
የአየር ፡ ፖስታ airmail

አይሮፕላን ayroplan airplane (see also አውሮፕላን)

ኢየሱስ iyyäsus Jesus

አይብ ayəb cheese, curds

ኢዮቤልዩ iyobelyu jubilee
(የ)ኢዮቤልዩ ፡ ቤተ ፡ መንግሥት Jubilee Palace

አየት ፡ አደረገ ayätt adärrägä cast a glance (see አየ)

አያት ayat grandfather, grandmother
አያት ፡ ቅድም ፡ አያት ayat qədmä ayat ancestor
ሴት ፡ አያት grandmother
ቅድም ፡ አያት qədmä ayat ancestor, progenitor
ቅድም ፡ አያቶች qədmä ayatočč antecedents, ancestry
ወንድ ፡ አያት grandfather
የሴት ፡ ቅድም ፡ አያት great-grandmother
የወንድ ፡ ቅድም ፡ አያት great-grandfather

ዓይን ayn eye, sight, knot (in a board)
ዓይን ፡ ለዓይን face to face
ዓይን ፡ ምድር human excrement
ዓይን ፡ ርግብ veil
ዓይን ፡ ስውር blind (see ሰወረ)
ዓይን ፡ አውጣ ፤ ዓይናውጣ impudent, forward (bold); see ወጣ
ዓይን ፡ አፋር ፤ ዓይናፋር coy, shy, bashful (see አፈረ)
ዓይን ፡ አፋሪነት ayn afarinnät shyness
ዓይን ፡ የሌለው out-and-out (lie)
ለዓይን ፡ ሲይዝ in the dusk (see ያዘ)
የዓይን ፡ ቆብ eyelid
የዓይን ፡ ብሌን pupil of the eye
በንድ ፡ ዓይን ፡ አየ treat alike

ዓይነት aynät kind, sort, species, type, nature (kind), quality, make (of merchandise)
በምንም ፡ ዓይነት at all costs
በምንም ፡ ዓይነት ፡ ቢሆን by all means, in any way, in any fashion
በያይነቱ bäyyaynätu of various kinds
ዓይነተኛ aynätäňňa typical, characteristic (adj.), classic, important, integral (essential), principal

ዓይናውጣ, see ዓይን

እያንዳንድ, see አንዳንድ

ዓይናፋር, see ዓይን

አይዞህ *ayzoh* come on!, cheer up!, take heart!

አያያዝ *ayyayaz* grip, grasp, hold, treatment, handling, management (see ያዘ)
የመሬት ፡ አያያዝ landholding
የቤት ፡ አያያዝ housekeeping

አየደ *ayyädä* (B) determine, define

አይደለም *aydälläm*, አይዶለም *aydolläm* he is not, it is not, no, not so
ምንም ፡ አይደለም it does not matter

እያደረ *əyyaddärä*, እያደር *əyyaddär* little by little, by and by, gradually, eventually (see አደረ)

አይጥ *ayṭ* mouse, rat

ዕዳ *əda* debt
ዕዳ ፡ ገባ make debts, get into debts
ባለ ፡ ዕዳ creditor, debtor
ባለ ፡ ዕዳ ፡ (ባለዳ) ፡ ሆነ owe money

ዐደለ *addälä* (B) distribute (mail), allot, hand out, dispense, issue
ታደለ *taddälä* be distributed, receive one's share, be lucky, be in luck, be fortunate
ዕድል, see below
ማደያ, see above

ዕድል *əddəl* luck, fortune, destiny, lot, chance, odds, fatality (fate), opportunity, success (see ዐደለ)
ዕድል ፡ ቢስ unlucky, unfortunate
መጥፎ ፡ ዕድል misadventure, misfortune, bad luck
እንደ ፡ ዕድል ፡ ሆኖ fortunately
የሚያጋጥመው ፡ ዕድል *yämmiyaggaṭṭəmäw əddəl* opportunity
ያርባ ፡ ቀን ፡ ዕድል predestination
ዕድለኛ *əddəläñña* fortunate, lucky

አድልዎ *adləwo* bias, favoritism (see *ደላ)
አድልዎ ፡ የሌለበት impartial

አደመ *addämä* (B) plot, conspire, intrigue, strike (stop working)

አድማ *adma* conspiracy, plot, strike, boycott, coup d'etat
አድመኛ *admäñña* conspirator, plotter, mutinous

ዕድሜ *ədme* age, lifetime
ዕድሜህ ፡ ስንት ፡ ነው? how old are you?
ዕድሜ ፡ ለሱ thanks to him
ዕድሜ ፡ ለንጉሡ ፡ ነገሥት long live His Imperial Majesty!
ዕድሜ ፡ ልኩን for the duration of his life, for life
ዕድሜ ፡ የሌለው he is short-lived
ዕድሜ ፡ ይፍታህ life imprisonment (see ፈታ)
በዕድሜ ፡ ገፋ get on in years
በዕድሜ ፡ የገፋ elderly
የዕድሜ ፡ ልክ lifelong
ዕድሜ ፡ ልክ ፡ እስራት life imprisonment
የዕድሜ ፡ አፍላ prime of life

አድማስ *admas* horizon

አድማጭ *admač* hearer, listener, auditor, audience (see *ደመጠ)

አደረ *addärä* spend the night, stay overnight, live, dwell, enter someone's service, be devoted to
(አደረበት *addäräbbät* it developed in him, it came over him, it befell him)
(ሥርቶ ፡ አደረ earn a living; see ሠራ)
(ውሎ ፡ አደረ stay somewhere for a long time; see ዋለ)
(ውጭ ፡ አደረ stay out at night)
(እንዴት ፡ አደርህ good morning!, sg. mas.)
(ደህና ፡ እደር *dähna ədär* good night!, sg. masc.)
(ያደረ ፡ መሬት *yaddärä märet* fallow land)
(ለእግዚአብሔር ፡ ያደረ devout)
አሳደረ *asaddärä* give lodging, cause to pass the night, inculcate, instill, arouse (stir up), let lie fallow (a plot of land)
ተዳደረ *tädaddärä* be governed, make a living, manage (vi.), earn one's livelihood

(በ - - - ሥር ፥ ተዳደረ be under the care of)

አስተዳደረ astädaddärä administer, manage, provide for one's family, keep (house)

አድሮ adro finally

(ውሎ ፥ አድሮ eventually, in the long run; see ዋለ)

አዳሪ adari boarder

አዳሪ ፥ ትምህርት ፥ ቤት boarding school

አዳሪ ፥ ተማሪ boarding student

(ሴትኛ ፥ አዳሪ prostitute)

(በረንዳ ፥ አዳሪ tramp, vagabond)

(ዱር ፥ አዳሪ tramp, vagabond, brigand)

አዳር ፥ አደረገ adar adärrägä make an overnight stop

አድር ፥ ባይ adər bay obsequious, opportunist, servile

አድር ፥ ባይነት adər bayənnät servility

†እዳሪ əddari fallow land

ማደሪያ madäriya place where one spends the night, habitation, lodging; military service land

መተዳደሪያ, see above

አስተዳደር, see above

አስተዳዳሪ, see above

እያደር, see above

አደራ adära trust, deposit, custody, safekeeping, care

(የልጄን ፥ ነገር ፥ አደራ please, look after my son!)

አደራዎ please!

አደራ ፥ ሰጠ trust to someone's care, confide to the care, entrust, consign (to a guardian)

አደራ ፥ ተሰጠ be in one's charge

አደራ ፥ አለ recommend, implore

አደራ ፥ በላ embezzler

የአደራ ፥ አባት guardian, trustee

ለ - - አደራ in one's care

ባለ ፥ አደራ person to whom something is entrusted, trustee

እዳሪ əddari fallow land (see አደረ)

እዳሪ ፥ ወጣ defecate

እድር əddər mutual aid society, burial society

እድርተኛ əddərtäñña member of a burial society

እድርተኛ ፥ ቀባሪ burial society funeral attendant

አዳራሽ addaraš hall, auditorium, reception room

የከተማ ፥ አዳራሽ town hall

አድራሻ adrašša address (see ደረሰ)

እድርተኛ, see እድር

አድራጎት adragot dealings, doings, action, activity (see *ደረገ)

በጎ ፥ አድራጎት welfare, charity

አደሰ addäsä (B) renew, renovate, restore, amend

አሳደሰ asaddäsä renew (the lease), renovate

አዲስ, see below

እድሳት əddəsat restoration (of a building), renovation

አዲስ addis new, newly, novel (adj.), recent (see አደሰ)

አዳዲስ adaddis new (plural)

አዲስ ፥ አበባ Addis Ababa (capital of Ethiopia)

አዲስ ፥ ከተማ Mercato (the market section of Addis Ababa)

አዲስ ፥ ኪዳን New Testament

አዲስ ፥ ወሬ latest news

አዲስ ፥ ገብ (or መጥ) newcomer (see ገባ, መጣ)

አደበ addäbä behave well, show restraint

አድባር adbar tree or trees consecrated to spirits (people make sacrifices to them), guardian spirit

አደባባይ addäbabay public place, city square, open space between houses, public view

አደባባይ ፥ ወጣ a public assembly is conducted

በደባባይ publicly, in public

ዐደት *udät* cycle, circuit (of sun), procession of the *tabot* around a church

አደነ *addänä* (B) hunt, go hunting
አደን *adän* hunting, the hunt
አዳኝ *addañ* hunter

አድናቆት *adnaqot* astonishment, admiration, feeling of awe, appreciation, acclamation, fervor, interest (see ደነቀ)

አደንጓሬ *adäng"arre* bean

አዱኛ *adduñña* happiness coming from good fortune
አዱኛ ፡ ከዳ(ው) meet with reverses (see ከዳ)

አደይ *adäy* Mäsqäl flower

አዳዲስ, see አዲስ

አደገ *addägä* grow, vi. (of child, of tree), grow up, develop physically, rise (from ranks)
አሳደገ *asaddägä* make to grow, bring up a child, raise a child, grow (a beard), enlarge (a photograph), advance (promote), augment (the income)
አደግ *addäg*, in አብሮ ፡ አደግ childhood friend
(ስድ ፡ አደግ impertinent, bold, boor)
እድገት, see below
አሳዳጊ *asaddagi* foster father
አሳዳጊ ፡ እናት foster mother
አስተዳደግ *astädadäg* breeding, upbringing
እጅግ, see below

አደጋ *adäga* peril, danger, accident, hazard, mishap
አደጋ ፡ ጣለ attack by surprise, strike a blow
አደጋ ፡ ላይ ፡ ጣለ expose to danger, venture, vt. (risk), imperil, jeopardize
አደጋን ፡ ተጋፈጠ court danger (see *ገፈጠ)
የአደጋ ፤ ያደጋ emergency, adj. (brakes)

(የ)እሳት ፡ አደጋ fire hazard
አደገኛ *adägäñña* dangerous, perilous, unsafe, hazardous, disastrous, malignant

እድገት *ədgät* growing, growth, raising, development, raise (in rank), promotion (see አደገ)
የማዕረግ ፡ እድገት promotion
የሥራ ፡ እድገት promotion

አዳጋች *adagač* hard (difficult), formidable (task); see *ዳገት

አደፈ *addäfä* be dirty, be soiled, be polluted, be stained, menstruate
አሳደፈ *asaddäfä* pollute
አደፍ *adäf* menstruation
አደፍ ፡ ወረዳት menstruate (see ወረደ)
እድፍ *ədəf* dirt, filth, stain

አጃ *ağğa* oats, rye

እጅ *əğğ* hand, arm, paw (of animal), portion, - fold (as in tenfold)
(አራት ፡ እጅ four times as much)
እጅና ፡ እግር limbs, members of body
እጅና ፡ እግሮች extremities
እጅ ፡ መለሰ pay in kind
እጅ ፡ ሰጠ give in, give oneself up, yield (vi.), surrender, capitulate
እጅ ፡ ነሣ bow down to greet, curtsy, pay one's respects, pay homage
እጅ ፡ እንዳመጣ indiscriminate (bombing); see መጣ
እጅ ፡ መንሻ gift, bribe
እጅ ፡ ከፍንጅ ፡ ተያዘ be caught redhanded
እጅ ፡ ጠባብ narrow-sleeved Ethiopian shirt
የእጅ ፡ ሥራ ፤ የጅ ፡ ሥራ handicraft, handiwork
የእጅ ፡ ሰዓት wristwatch
የእጅ ፡ ሹራብ glove
የእጅ ፡ ቦምብ grenade
የእጅ ፡ ጥበብ handicraft
የእጅ ፡ ጽሕፈት penmanship, handwriting

የእጅ ፡ ፎጣ napkin
ባለ ፡ እጅ ፤ ባለጅ skilled, craftsman,
artisan, blacksmith
በገዛ ፡ እጅ by one's own self
እጅታ, see below
እጅጌ əǧǧəge sleeve

ዐጀበ aǧǧäbä (B) accompany, escort
ዐጀብ aǧäb escort, retinue, attendance
ዐጀቢ aǧǧabi bodyguard, escort
ዕጅብ ፡ ያለ əǧǧəbb yalä bushy (eye-
brows), thick (beard)
ዕጅብ ፡ ብሎ in clusters, in masses

ዐጀብ aǧäb oh dear!

እጅታ əǧǧäta handle, haft (of spear),
knob, ear (of pitcher); see እጅ

አጃንስ aǧans agency (see also አገንስ)

አጀንዳ aǧända agenda

እጅጌ əǧǧəge sleeve (see እጅ, ጌ)
እጅጌ ፡ ጉርድ short-sleeved
የእጅጌ ፡ ቁልፍ cuff link

እጅግ əǧǧəg much, very, exceedingly,
enormously (see አደገ)
እጅግ ፡ በጣም extremely
እጅግም rare, rarely

እጀጠባብ əǧǧäṭäbbab narrow-sleeved
Ethiopian shirt (see እጅ, ጠበበ)

*ዐገለ, see ታገለ

አጐል, see አጐለ

አጐለ aggʷälä (B) suspend, hold someone up in his work, put off, keep
(a meeting) from taking place
አስታጐለ astaggʷälä hinder (hold
back), interrupt (work)
አጐል agul undecided, foolhardy,
false (pride), awkward (place), mis-
guided
አጐል ፡ እምነት superstition, superstitious belief

እገሌ əgäle (fem. እገሊት əgälit) so-and-
so

እገሌ ፡ ከገሌ ፡ የምለው ፡ የለም əgäle
kägäle yämmələw yälläm I will make
no exceptions

አገልግል agälgəl basket with lid

አገልግሎት agälgəlot service, benefit
(see *ገለገለ)

አገልጋይ agälgay servant, aid, attendant (see *ገለገለ)

አገመ aggämä draw blood with a suck-
ing cup, cup (bleed)
ዋገምት waggämt cup for drawing
blood (medical treatment)

አጋማሽ aggamaš middle (n.), half,
halfway (see ገመሰ)
የዓለም ፡ አጋማሽ hemisphere

አጋሚዶ agamiddo armed bandit (politi-
cally motivated)

አገረ aggärä (B) impede, stop

አገር agär country, nation, territory,
(region, land), district, state, land
(country, fatherland)
አገሬ agäre native (n.), people of a
particular country
አገር ፡ ቤት countryside
(ያገር ፡ ቤት rustic)
አገረ ፡ ገዥ governor
ያገር ፡ ልጅ compatriot
ያገር ፡ ውስጥ local, domestic (as
opposed to foreign)
ያገር ፡ ግዛት ፡ ሚኒስቴር Ministry of
Interior
ያገር ፡ ፍቅር patriotism
ቅኝ ፡ አገር colony
ባላገር country (countryside), countryman
ውጭ ፡ አገር abroad
(የውጭ ፡ አገር ፡ ሰው foreigner)
የሰው ፡ አገር foreign country
(የ)ትውልድ ፡ አገር native country

አጐረ aggʷärä (B) huddle, herd,
bundle (clothes), confine, close with
a bar, pen up (livestock)

ማጕሪያ *magʷäriya* enclosure (for donkeys), pen (for donkeys)

እግር *əgər* foot, leg
እግር ፡ አው-ጪኝ ፡ አለ *əgər awčiňň alä* take to one's heels
እግረ ፡ መንገዱን on one's way, along the way, en route to
የእግር ፡ መንገድ sidewalk, footpath, path, trail, track
የእግር ፡ ሹራብ sock, stocking
(የ)እግር ፡ ብረት shackles, fetter, chains
የእግር ፡ ኳስ soccer
የእግር ፡ ጣት toe
ልጅ ፡ እግር young man
ባዶ ፡ እግሩን barefooted
እጅና ፡ እግር limbs, members of body
ውስጥ ፡ እግር sole (bottom of foot)
†እግረኛ *əgräňňa* pedestrian
እግርጌ, see below

እግረኛ *əgräňňa* pedestrian (see እግር)
የእግረኛ ፡ መሄጃ sidewalk (see ሄደ)
የእግረኛ ፡ ጦር infantry

እግርጌ *əgərge* at the foot, on the bottom, below, beneath, foot of the bed (see እግር,ጌ)
የግርጌ ፡ ማስታወሻ footnote

*ዐገሠ, see ታገሠ

አጋሰስ *agasäs* packhorse
አጋሰስ ፡ በቅሎ baggage mule

አጒበር *agʷäbär* canopy

አገባብ *aggäbab*, አግባብ *agbab* propriety, proper conduct, correct procedure; syntax, context (see ገባ)
አግባብ ፡ አለው —*alläw* be relevant, have jurisdiction over (of authority)
አግባብ ፡ ያለ(ው) — *yallä(w)* proper (appropriate), relevant, competent (authority)
አላግባብ *alagbab*, ያለ ፡ አግባብ *yalä agbab* unfairly, unjustly
ያለ ፡ አግባብ ፡ (ያላግባብ) ፡ ተጠቀም abuse, misuse

አግባብነት *agbabənnät* application (relevance to)
አግባብነት ፡ አለው apply, be relevant, be applicable (law)
አግባብነት ፡ የለውም be irrelevant

አጒት *aggʷät* uncle
የአጒት ፡ ልጅ cousin

አጓት *aggʷat* whey

አጋኖ *agganno*, in ቃለ ፡ አጋኖ exclamation (see ቃል, ገነነ)

አጋንንት *aganant* evil spirits, demons (see ጋኔን)

አገዘ *aggäzä* (B) help, aid, assist, lend a hand

አጒዛ *agʷäza* sheepskin

እግዜር *əgzer* God (short form of እግዚአ ብሔር)
እግዜር ፡ ይመስገን *əgzer yämmäsgän* thank you! (see *መሰገነ)
እግዜር ፡ ይስጥልኝ *əgzer yəsṭəlläňň* thank you! (see ሰጠ)

አጋዘን *agazän* kind of antelope, gazelle, deer, stag

እግዚአብሔር *əgziabəher* God (see also እግዜር)
ስለ ፡ እግዚአብሔር ፡ ብለህ for heaven's sake
በእግዚአብሔር for goodness' sake

አገደ *aggädä* (B) stop, vt. (obstruct), bar, ban (a book), check (stop), block, congest (of traffic), constrict, confine (hold back), keep off, impede, prevent, restrain, halt (the advance of the enemy), suspend (from one's job); watch over (of guard), pasture herds
አገዳ *əggäda* proscription, ban, prohibition, sanction
ማገጃ, see above

አገዳ *agäda* stalk (of sugar cane, of maize)
ሸንኮር ፡ አገዳ sugar cane stalk

አግዳሚ *agdami* horizontal, transverse, standing at right angles (see * ጋደመ, አግድም)
አግዳሚ ፡ ወምበር bench
አላፊ ፡ አግዳሚ passer-by

አግድም *agdəm* across, horizontal, transverse (see * ጋደመ)
በ - - - አግድም across (a path)

አጓዳኝ *aggʷadaň* parallel

አጋጣሚ *aggaṭami* coincidence, strange or curious circumstance, opportunity, experience (what has happened to one), adventure, incident, fortuitous, circumstantial (see ገጠመ)
አጋጣሚ ፡ ነገር opportunity, coincidence
አጋጣሚ ፡ ጊዜ suitable moment, convenient opportunity
እንዳጋጣሚ *əndaggaṭami* by accident, accidentally, incidentally, by coincidence, by chance, as it happened, it so happens

አገጭ *agäč* chin, jaw

አጋፋሪ *aggafari* usher, one who introduces guests, supervisor at a banquet

አጣ *aṭṭa* lack, be lacking, miss, not find, be without something, lose, not get
አሳጣ *asaṭṭa* causative of the preceding; bereave, deprive of
እጦት, see below
መታጣት *mättaṭat* lack of

አጤ, see አጼ

እጢ *əṭi* gland

ዕጣ *əṭa* lot, chance (of lottery), destiny, fate
ዕጣ ፡ አወጣ toss a coin (see ወጣ)
ዕጣ ፡ ከዳው he had bad luck, it was his misfortune (see ከዳ)
ዕጣ ፡ ደረሰው he drew the winning lot (see ደረሰ)
ዕጣ ፡ ጣለ cast lots

እጥላስ *aṭlas* velvet, satin

ኢጣልያ *iṭalya* Italy
ኢጣልያን *iṭalyan* Italian (person)

አጠረ *aṭṭärä* fence in, make a fence around something, enclose (with a fence or hedge)
አጥር *aṭər* fence (n.)
አጥር ፡ ግቢ compound, courtyard

አጠረ *aṭṭärä* be short, be shorter, be brief, shrink
አጠረ(ው) *aṭṭärä(w)* he is short of (ቃል ፡ አጠረው words failed him)
አሳጠረ *asaṭṭärä* shorten, cut short, abridge, abbreviate, contract (shorten), abstract (make a summary)
ያጠረ *yaṭṭärä* abridged
እጥረት *əṭrät* shortage, deficiency, lack, dearth, scarcity, deficit
አጭር, see below
[See also እጥር]

እጥር ፡ ምጥን ፡ ያለ *əṭər məṭṭən yalä* concise, succinct, compact (report), few and terse (see አጠረ, መጠነ)

አጠራር *aṭṭärar* appelation (see ጠራ call)

እጥረት, see አጠረ be short

* ዐጠቀ, see ታጠቀ

አጥቂ *aṭqi* aggressor (see * ጠቃ)
አጥቂነት *aṭqinnät* aggression

አጠቃላይ *aṭṭäqalay* inclusive, comprehensive (review); see ጠቀለለ

አጠብ *aṭṭäbä* wash (dishes, clothes, a person), bathe (vt.), develop (a film)
ታጠብ *taṭṭäbä* be washed, take a bath, wash up, wash (hands, face), wash oneself
አጣቢ *aṭabi* laundry man
(ልብስ ፡ አጣቢ cleaner)
(ልብስ ፡ አጣቢ ፡ ቤት laundry)
መታጠብ *mättaṭäb* ablution
ማጠቢያ ፡ ቤት *maṭäbiya bet* washroom

†መታጠቢያ ፡ ቤት *mättaṭäbiya bet* bathroom

አጥብቆ *aṭbəqo* very much, greatly, tightly, strongly, emphatically (see ጠበቀ)

አጥቢያ *aṭbiya* vicinity, parish, congregation
አጥቢያ ፡ ዳኛ Justice of the Peace

አጥቢያ *aṭbiya* dawn (see ጠባ)
ያጥቢያ ፡ ኮከብ morning star

እጦት *əṭot* lack, loss, want (lack); see አጣ

ዐጠነ *aṭṭänä* perfume with incense, fumigate, smoke, vt. (a beehive)
ዕጣን *əṭan* incense, perfume (n.)

አጠና *aṭäna* pole (of fence), post (for a fence)

አጥንት *aṭənt* bone
አጥንት ፡ ሰበረ have great effect
አጥንት ፡ ሰባራ *aṭəntä säbara* of defective lineage
አጥንት ፡ የሚሰብር—*yämmisäbər* piercing (wind); see ሰበረ
አጥንት ፡ የሚነካ—*yämminäka* biting (remark); see ነካ
አጥንቱ ፡ የወጣ he is skin and bones (see ወጣ)
አጥንታም *aṭəntam* bony, of good parentage

አጠገብ *aṭägäb* nearness, closely, close to
አጠገቡ near him
በ - - - አጠገብ by, near, beside
እ - - - አጠገብ by, near, beside

ዐጠፈ *aṭṭäfä* double (vt.), fold, bend (vt.), retract (a statement), break (one's word)
ታጠፈ *taṭṭäfä* be folded, bend (vi.), be bent, fold up (of folding chair), curve (of road)
ዐጣጠፈ *aṭaṭṭäfä* fold (clothes), fold up (a letter), roll up (the blanket)

ዕጥፍ *əṭəf* double, -fold, portion, share, times
(አምስት ፡ ዕጥፍ five times, five-fold, quintuple)
ዕጥፍ ፡ ሆነ double, vi. (become twice as much)
ዕጥፍ ፡ አደረገ double, vt. (make twice as much)
ዐጣፈታ *aṭäfeta* double (twice as much), twofold
ዕጥፋት *aṭṭəfat* crease (n.)
ዕጥፈት *aṭfät* fold (n.)
ታጣፊ ፡ ወምበር *taṭafi wämbär* folding chair
የሚተጣጠፍ *yämmittäṭaṭäf* pliant (vine)
ማጠፊያ *maṭäfiya* hinge (of door)
መታጠፊያ *mättaṭäfiya* corner, bend in the road

አጨ *aččä* be engaged (to marry), be affianced, recommend (to a position)
ታጨ *taččä* be betrothed, be a candidate for office
አሳጨ *asaččä* betroth (speaking of the father)
†እጩ *əčču* betrothed, candidate
†እጮኛ *əččoňňa* fiancé, fiancée
መታጨት *mättaččät* engagement (to marry)
መተጫጨት *mättäčaččät* engagement
የታጨ *yataččä* destined

እጩ *əčču* betrothed, candidate (see አጨ)
እጩ ፡ መኮንን cadet (of air force or army)

እጭ *əč* larva

አጭር *aččər* short, brief, low (in height); see አጠረ
አጭር ፡ ታሪክ short story
አጭር ፡ ጽሕፈት shorthand
ባጭሩ *baččəru* in short, in brief, briefly, to sum up

አጨቀ *aččäqä* (B) stuff (push, thrust), cram
እጭቅ ፡ ብሎ *əččəqq bəlo* in a compact bundle

እርጮኛ *əččoňňa* fiancé, fiancée (see እጮ) እርጮኞች *əččoňňočč*, እርጮኛሞች *əččoň-ňamočč* engaged couple

በጨደ *aččädä* mow, cut with a sickle
ማጭድ *mačəd* sickle

እጮጌ *əčäge* head of the Ethiopian monks

አጼ *aṣe* sovereign, title of the emperors of Ethiopia

ዕፅ *əṣ* plant, herb
ዕፅዋት *əṣäwat* flora

ዐፅም *aṣəm* skeleton, remains (dead body)

ዓጽቅ *aṣq* joint (of finger, of bamboo), knuckle

ዕጹብ ፡ ድንቅ *əṣub dənq* magnificent, gorgeous, marvel, wonder

ዐፃፋ *aṣäfa* reprisal, retaliation, things done in return
ዐፃፋ ፡ መለስ *aṣäfa mäläs* retaliate, counterattack, reciprocate
ዐፃፋ ፡ ተውላጠ ፡ ስም pronominal affix
ዐፃፋውን *aṣäfawən* in reprisal, in retaliation

አፍ *af* mouth, language, beak, rim (of glass), entrance
አፍ ፡ አወጣ become brash (see ወጣ)
አፉ ፡ ተያዘ be dumbfounded, halt (in speech); see ያዘ
አፍ ፡ እንዳመጣ casual (remark), off-hand (see መጣ)
አፉ ፡ እንዳመጣለት offhandedly, brashly, casually (see መጣ)
†አፈ ፡ ሙዝ barrel of gun
አፈ ፡ ታሪክ myth, mythology, legend, tradition
አፈ ፡ ንጉሥ president of the Supreme Court
አፈ ፡ ጮሌ smooth talker, glib
ባፍ ፡ ጢሙ ፡ ተደፋ he fell on his face

እንዲያው ፡ ለአፉ ፡ ነው it's only a bluff
ያፍ ፡ ታሪክ fable, legend
አፋፍ, see below
በራፍ *bärraf* doorway (see በር)

እፍ ፡ አለ *əff alä* blow, blow on the fire

አፍላ *afla* prime, moment when something is in full vigor
አፍላ ፡ እሸት period when practically all the crop is ripe
የሕይወት ፡ አፍላ prime of life
የዕድሜ ፡ አፍላ prime of life
አፍለኛ *afläňňa* unleavened (bread)

አፈላማ ፡ ያዘ *afälama yazä* impound (straying cattle)

አፍለኛ, see አፍላ

አፈሙዝ *afämuz* barrel of gun (see አፍ, ሙዝ)
(የ)አፈሙዝ ፡ ስፋት caliber

አፈረ *affärä* be ashamed, be shy, be embarrassed, be abashed, be modest, blush, be respectful
አሳፈረ *asaffärä* bring shame to, put to shame, abash, embarrass, disgrace, shock (of language), be disgraceful
አፋር *affar* shy, bashful, timid, modest
እፍረት, see below
አሳፋሪ *asaffari* shameful, scandalous, embarrassing, ignominious (act), dishonorable
አሳፋሪ ፡ ነገር scandal
ዓይን ፡ አፋር ፡ ዓይናፋር, see ዓይን
ነፍረት, see above

አፈር *afär* soil, earth, dirt
አፈር ፡ ይብላኝ *afär yəblaňň*, exclamation of admiration or of compassion (lit. 'may the earth eat me')
አፈር ፡ ብላ *afär bəla* go to hell! (lit. 'eat earth!')
የብረት ፡ አፈር iron ore, ore

አፈርሰታ *afärsäta* investigation imposed on a community for apprehending or identifying a wrongdoer

አፍሪቃ *afriqa* Africa (see also አፍሪካ)

እፍረት *əfrät* shame, shyness, humiliation (see አፈረ)
እፍረተ ፡ ቢስ shameless, brazen

አፍሪካ Africa (see also አፍሪቃ)

አፈሰ *affäsä* take a fistful of grain with two hands, scoop up dry grainy material with the hand

አፍታ, in አንዳፍታ *andafta* at one gulp
በንዳፍታ at one gulp, instantly, in no time, at one stroke
ላንድ ፡ አፍታ for a moment

አፎት *afot* sheath

አፈነ *affänä* (B) suffocate, choke, smother, muffle (the noise), put a gag into the mouth, kidnap, invade (of smell of cooking)
ታፈነ *taffänä* suffocate (vi.), be choked, be muffled, be gagged
አፍኖ ፡ ወሰደ *affəno wässädä* kidnap, abduct
አፍኖ ፡ ያዘ *affəno yazä* suppress (a smile)
አፍኖ ፡ ገደለ *affəno gäddälä* smother
ማፈኛ *maffäñña* gag (n.)
የታፈነ *yätaffänä* stuffy (hall)

አፈነ *affänä* (B) take a fistful of earth or grain with the two hands open
እፍኝ *əffəñ* handful, fistful

አፍንጫ *afənča* nose, snout
የአፍንጫ, ያፍንጫ nasal

እፍኝ *əffəñ* handful, fistful (see አፈነ)

እፉኝት *əffuññət* viper

አፊያ *əffiya* lid (of box), cover (of pan)

እፎይ ፡ አለ *əffoyy alä* feel relief, be relieved, take a rest, sigh in relief
እፎይታ *əffoyta* relief

አፈገ *affägä* be cramped
ታፈገ *taffägä* be stuffy (room), be stale (air), be huddled (in a corner)
የታፈገ *yätaffägä* stagnant (air)
መተፋፈግ *mättäfafäg* (traffic) jam
[See እፍግፍግ, below]

እፍግፍግ ፡ ብለው ፡ ተቀመጡ *əfəgfəgg bəläw täqämmäṭu* they huddled together (see አፈገ)

አፋፍ *afaf* edge of a cliff, hilltop, crest of hill (from አፍ-አፍ)
በ - - - አፋፍ ፡ ላይ on the verge of, on the brink of

አፐራሲዮን *operasiyon* surgery

አፓርተማ *apartäma* apartment

ከ

ከ *kä* at, out of, from (origin, place, descendence), more than
ከ + (perfect) if, when, since
ከ + (negative verb) unless
ከቦታ ፡ ቦታ from place to place

ካህን *kahən* (pl. ካህናት *kahənat*) pastor, priest, churchman, clergyman
ካህናት priestly class
ሊቀ ፡ ካህናት head priest
ክህነት *kəhənät* priesthood
ቤተ ፡ ክህነት clergy

ከሐዲ *kähadi* traitor, renegade, perfidious (see ካደ)

*ካሄደ, in አካሄደ, ተካሄደ, see ሄደ

ክሕደት *kəhdät* betrayal, treachery, treason, unbelief, atheism (see ካደ)
ከሓዲነት *kähadinnät* treachery, treason

ከላ *källa* hinder, impede, prevent (see also ከለከለ)

ከል *käll* cheap blue-black dye in which garments are dipped for mourning, mourning clothes

ከል ፡ ለበሰ he is in mourning

ኩሊ. *kuli* porter, coolie

ኩል *kul* antimony dust, kohl (see ኳለ)

ኪሎ *kilo* kilo

ኬላ *kella* toll station
የኬላ ፡ ቀረጥ toll

ኳለ *k^walä* put kohl (on the eyes)
ተኳለ *täk^walä* wear makeup
ኩል *kul* antimony dust, kohl
መኳኳያ *mäkk^wak^waya* toilet articles,
cosmetics

ከለለ *källälä* (B) stake out (a plot of
land), demarcate, appropriate, delimit a boundary, delineate, define
(the limits), shut out the view, conceal from view, screen
ተከለለ *täkällälä*, passive of the preceding; be sequestered, take shelter
under
ከለላ *käläla* (n.) cover, screen (afford-
ing concealment)
ከልል *källäl* limits, confines, boundary, enclosure, zone, precincts (of
the town)
መከለያ, see above

ኩለል ፡ አለ *k^wäläll alä* stream (of tears),
roll, vi. (of tears)

ኩላሊት *kulalit* kidney

ኪሎሜትር *kilometər* kilometer

ከለር *kälär* crayon
ከለር ፡ ቀባ color (v.)

ከለሰ *källäsä* (B) dilute a strong drink,
review (a lesson)
ከላለሰ *kälalläsä* brush up (on a language)
ከለሳ *källäsa* review (of a lesson)

ከልስ *källəs* half-caste, half-breed

*ኩላሸ, አኩላሸ *ak^wälaššä* castrate (animals)

ኮሌታ *kolletta* collar, lapel

*ኮላተፈ, ተኮላተፈ *täk^wälattäfä* lisp,
stutter
ኮልታፋ ፡ አነጋገር *koltaffa annägagär*
lisping

ኮሎኔል *kolonel* colonel

ክሊኒክ *klinik* clinic

ከለከለ *käläkkälä* (with noun, or with
እንደ + negative verb) prevent, prohibit, forbid, hinder, impede, deprive, bar (forbid); see also ከላ
ተከላከለ *täkälakkälä* oppose one
another, resist, withstand, prevent,
fend off, ward off, defend (protect),
counteract, fight (a disease, fire),
combat, protect (shelter), shield
ከልክል *kəlkəl* forbidden, prohibited
መከላከል *mäkkälakäl* defensive (n.)
መከላከያ, see above
ተከላካይ *täkälakay* defense, anything that protects
አስከልካይ, see እልፍኝ

ኮሌጅ *kolleǧ* college

ከመ, see ከመቅጽበት

ከመረ *kämmärä* (B) pile in a heap,
accumulate, stack, amass
ክምር *kəmmər* heap, pile, mound

ከምሱር *kämsur* capsule

ኬሚስትሪ *kemistri* chemistry

ኮሚስዮን *komisyon* commission (group
of persons, percentage of a selling
price paid as a fee to a salesman)

ከመቅጽበት *kämäqəṣbät* in a breath,
in a moment, in no time, in a split
second (from ከመ and ቅጽበት)

ኩምቢ, see ኩንቢ.

ኮሚቴ *komite* committee
ንኡስ ፡ ኮሚቴ sub-committee

*ኮማተረ, አኮማተረ *akk^wämattärä*
shrink (vt.), contract (shrink), furrow
the brow, distort (rage distorting
the face)

ተኮማተረ *täkʷämattärä* shrink (vi.), shrivel

*ከማቸ, አከማቸ *akkämaččä* heap up, store, store up, amass, hoard, accumulate (vt.), concentrate
ተከማቸ *täkämaččä* accumulate (vi.), be gathered, be concentrated, be stored
ክምችት *kəməččət* heap, congregation (gathering), batch, hoard
ማከማቻ *makkämača*, in የውኅ ፡ ማከ
ማቻ reservoir

ከሙን *kämun* cumin

ከመንዳሪያ *kämändariya* inner tube

ካሚዮን *kamiyon* truck

ኮመዲኖ *komädino* night stand

ኮመጠጠ *kʷämäṭṭäṭä* be acid, be sour, turn sour (of milk); see also ሟመጠጠ
ኮምጣጣ *komṭaṭṭa* acid, sour
ኮምጣጤ *komṭaṭṭe* vinegar

ካምፕ *kamp* camp (military)

ኮምፓስ *kompas* compass

ኩሩ *kuru* proud, vain (see ኮራ)

ኩሬ *kure* pond, pool

ካራ *karra* kitchen knife

ካሬ *kare* square (meter)

ከር *kərr* thread, wick, ribbon (for typewriter); see ከረረ

ኮር ፡ ዲፕሎማቲክ *kor diplomatik* diplomatic corps

ኮራ *kʷärra* be proud, show off
ኩሩ *kuru* proud, vain
ኩራት *kurat* pride, vanity
የሚያኮራ *yämmiyakʷära* honorable, glorious
መኩሪያ *mäkuriya* glory

ከረመ *kärrämä* spend the rainy season, spend the year, spend a certain time

(እንደምን ፡ ከረምክ *əndämən kärrämk* how have you been?, how have you spent the rainy season?)
(እንደምንም ፡ ከረም scrape by)
አከረመ *akärrämä* let lie fallow (the field) for a while
(ለ)ከርሞ for next year, for the next season
ከረምት, see below

ኮርማ *korma* bull (not castrated)

ከረሜላ *kärämella* candy, caramel, sweets

ከረምት *krämt* rains, rainy season (from July to September); see ከረመ

*ኮራመተ, ተኮራመተ *täkʷärammätä* double over (with pain), be shrunk up
ኩርምት ፡ ብሎ ፡ ተኛ *kurmət bəlo täňňa* cuddle up

ከረረ *kärrärä* be taut (tied string, rope, etc.), twist threads together to make a strong thread, be acute (crisis), be intense (quarrel)
ተካረረ *täkarrärä* come to a head (of quarrel)
የከረረ *yäkärrärä* fierce (enemy)
ከር, see above

ኩሩሩ *kururu* stumpy

ከራር *krar* six-stringed lyre
ከራር ፡ መታ play the *krar*

ክርስቶስ *krəstos* Christ

ክርስትና *krəstənna* Christianity, baptism, christening
ክርስትና ፡ አነሣ christen (of godparents); see ነሣ
ክርስትና ፡ ተነሣ receive baptism, be christened (see ነሣ)
የክርስትና ፡ ስም baptismal name
የክርስትና ፡ አባት godfather
የክርስትና ፡ እናት godmother

ክርስቲያን *krəstiyan* Christian
ቤት ፡ ክርስቲያን church

ኩርሽም ፡ አለ *kuršəmm alä* be crisp
(bread)

ከርበ *kärbe* myrrh

ኪሩቤል *kirubel* cherub

ክራቫት *kravat* tie, necktie

ኮረብታ *koräbta* hill
ኮረብታማ *koräbtamma* hilly

ካርቦን *karbon* carbon
የካርቦን ፡ ወረቀት carbon paper

ኩራት *kurat* pride, vanity (see ኩራ)

ካርታ *karta* map, chart, playing cards

ካሮት *karot* carrot

ኳረት *kʷärät*, ኮረት *korät* gravel

ካርታስ *kərtas* folder, cardboard

*ካራተተ, ተንካራተተ *tänkärattätä* wander off, wander from place to place,
roam

ካርቶን *karton* cardboard

ኮርቻ *korəčča* saddle
ኮርቻ ፡ ሥሪ saddler (see ሥራ)
የኮርቻ ፡ ፈረስ mount

ካርኒ *karni* receipt

ከርን *kərn* elbow

ኮረንቲ *korränti* electric current, electricity
ኮረንቲ ፡ መለዋወጫ transformer (see
ለወጠ)

ክራንቻ *kranča* canine tooth
የክራንቻ canine (animal)
የውሻ ፡ ክራንቻ canine tooth

ከረከመ *käräkkämä* prune (fruit trees)

ኳረከመ *kʷäräkkʷämä* rap on the head
with the knuckles
ኩርኩም *kurkum* a blow with the
knuckles

ከረከረ *käräkkärä* be acrid (sharp, stinging)

ተከራከረ *täkärakkärä* argue (give
reason for or against), debate, haggle,
bargain, quibble, protest, contend
(maintain as true), contest (challenge),
defend (of a lawyer)
(በዋጋ ፡ ተከራከረ bargain, haggle)
ክርክር, see below
አከራካሪ *akkärakari* controversial,
polemic, moot (point), contender
ተከራካሪ *täkärakari* advocate (who
argues for), defender
የሚያከራክር *yämmiyakkärakkər* debatable
የሚከራከር *yämmikäräkkər*, in አፍ
ንኜ ፡ የሚከራከር acrid

ከርካሮ *kärkärro* wild boar

ክርክር *kərəkkər* argument, debate, dispute, polemics (see ከረከረ)

ኳረኳረ *kʷäräkkʷärä* spur (prick with
spurs), dig one's spurs into, tickle;
clean the ears of wax

ኳራኳንች *kʷäräkʷänč* rough (road),
rocky (path)

ኩራዝ *kurraz* small kerosene lamp

*ከራየ, ተከራየ *täkärayyä* rent (take on
hire), be rented, lease, hire (a boat,
a house)
አከራየ *akkärayyä* rent out (lease),
let (rent)
ኪራይ *kiray*, ከራይ *kəray* lease, rent,
rental
ተከራይ *täkäray* tenant, lodger

ካርድ *kard* post card

ኳረዳ *kʷärädda*, ኮረዳ *korädda* adolescent (female)
ኮረዳንነት *koräddannät* adolescence (of
female)

ከርዳዳ *kärdadda* kinky, curly (hair),
coarse (cloth)

ከረጢት *kärätit* pouch, bag

ከረፋ *käräffa* have an unpleasant smell,
stink, reek

ከርፋት *kərfat* bad smell, stench

ኰረፈ *kʷärräfä* foam, v. (of beer)
አኰረፈ *akʷärräfä* sulk, snore
አንኳረፈ *ankʷarräfä* purr
ኩርፊያ *kurfiya* snore (n.)
ኩርፍተኛ, see below

ኩርፍተኛ *kurrəftäňňa* temperamental
(see ኰረፈ)

ኩርፊያ *kurfiya* snore (n.); see ኰረፈ

ከሳ *kässa* become thin, lose weight,
be skinny, be emaciated
አከሳ *akässa* render skinny, make be
emaciated
ከሲታ *kässitta* skinny

ኩስ *kus* excrement (of bird)

ኪስ *kis* pocket

ካሳ *kasä* compensate, pay damages, in-
demnify
ካሳ *kasa* damages (paid someone),
indemnity, compensation, recompense, amends, restitution
የጦር ፡ ካሳ war reparations

ከስ *kəss* legal charge, complaint (in
court), accusation, prosecution, suit
(in law court), indictment (see ከሰሰ)
ከስ ፡ አቀረብ bring charges (against
someone)

ኮሶ *koso* anthelmintic medicine, name
of a tree from which the anthelmintic medicine is made, tapeworm
ኮሶ ፡ ታየኝ *koso tayyäňň* I have a
tapeworm (see አየ)
ፊቱን ፡ ኮሶ ፡ አስመሰለ make a horrible face, make a grimace (see መሰለ)

ኳስ *kʷas* ball
የመረብ ፡ ኳስ volleyball
የቅርጫት ፡ ኳስ basketball
የእግር ፡ ኳስ soccer

ከሰለ *kässälä* become charcoal
አከሰለ *akässälä* color, v. (fever color-
ing the cheeks)
ከሰል, see below

ከሰል *käsäl* charcoal, coal (see ከሰለ)
የድንጋይ ፡ ከሰል coal

ካስማ *kasma* stake (for tent), tent peg

ከሰረ *kässärä* be bankrupt, go broke,
lose money
አከሰረ *akässärä* ruin (bring into
bankruptcy), bankrupt
ኪሳራ *kisara* deficit, loss (of money),
bankruptcy, expenses, costs
(የንግድ ፡ ኪሳራ bankruptcy)
መክሰር *mäksär* bankruptcy

ከሰሰ *kässäsä* accuse, bring an accusation against, indict, bring suit, sue,
prefer charges
ከስ, see above
ከሳሽ, see below
ተከሳሽ *täkässaš* accused, defendant

ኰሰሰ *kʷässäsä* (B) grow emaciated,
be thin
አንኳሰሰ *ankʷassäsä* belittle, deprecate, disparage
ኰሳሳ *kʷäsasa*, ኮሳሳ *kosasa* skinny

ከሳሽ *käsaš* accuser, plaintiff (see ከሰሰ)

ከሲታ *kässitta* skinny (see ከሳ)

ኰሰተረ *kʷäsättärä*, in ፊት ፡ ኰሰተረ
frown the forehead, wrinkle
ፊቱን ፡ አኰሰተረ *fitun akʷäsättärä*
make a grimace, be grim
ፊቱ ፡ ኰስተር ፡ አለ *fitu kʷästärr alä*
have a solemn face (of judge)
ኰስተር ፡ ያለ *kʷästärr yalä* stern (expression), somber-faced, grim-faced
ኰስታራ *kʷästarra* serious (person),
composed (person), austere (look),
grave (person), reserved (in behavior)

ከሰከሰ *käsäkkäsä* break up (the clods
of earth), dash to bits

ኰሰኰሰ *kʷäsäkkʷäsä* itch (of wool
shirt), cause discomfort (of cloth)

ከሽ ፡ ከሽ ፡ አለ *käšš käšš alä* crunch,
vi. (of broken glass); see also *ኰሽ
ኰሽ

ኬሻ *keša* straw, straw mat, cloth bag
የኬሻ straw, adj. (hat)

*ኮሻኮሽ, ተንኮሻኮሸ *tänkʷäšakkʷäšä*
rustle (vi.), crunch, vi. (of dry grass,
leaves); see also ከሽ ፡ ከሽ ፡ አለ
አንኮሻኮሸ *ankʷäšakkʷäšä* (vt.)
rustle, rattle

ከሸፈ *käššäfä* fail to go off (of gun),
fail (of intrigue), misfire (of gun, of
plan), abort (of plan)
አከሸፈ *akäššäfä* foil, frustrate

ኩብ *kub* cubic

ከበ *kabä* build a dry wall of stone or
bricks
ከብ *kab* dry wall (made of stones
without mortar)

ከባ *kabba* mantle, cloak, cape

ካብ, see ከበ

ከብ *kəbb* round, circular, spherical (see
ከበበ)

ኮባ *koba* false banana

ኩበለለ *kʷäbällälä* run away (leave
home), abscond, elope
የኩበለለ *yäkʷäbällälä* runaway

*ከባለለ, ተንከባለለ *tänkäballälä* roll, vi.
(of a ball), tumble (in the grass),
wallow
አንከባለለ *ankäballälä* roll, vt. (a marble, a log)
እንክብል, see above

ከበረ *käbbärä* be precious, become
honored, be respected, get rich, be
wealthy
ተከበረ *täkäbbärä* be venerated, command respect, be celebrated, be
observed (holiday)
አከበረ *akäbbärä* respect, hold in
respect, honor, esteem, venerate,
commemorate (a victory), celebrate,
observe (the holidays, a code)
(ቃሉን ፡ አከበረ he kept his word)

አስከበረ *askäbbärä* dignify, enno-
ble, esteem, uphold (the law), enforce (the law), make rich
ከቡር *kəbur* respectful, His Honor,
Excellency
ከቡራት *kəburat* ladies
ከቡራን *kəburan* gentlemen
ከብር, see below
ከብርቴ *käbbärte* wealthy
ከብረት, see below
†ከብርና *kəbrənna* virginity
†አክብሮት *akbərot* respect, deference, homage
የከበረ *yäkäbbärä* precious (stone), respectable (person)
የከበረ ፡ ድንጋይ gem, precious stone
የተከበረ *yätäkäbbärä* respected, respectable
አክባሪ *akbari*, in ቀጠሮ ፡ አክባሪ punctual
አስከባሪ *askäbbari*, in ሕግ ፡ አስከባሪ
prosecutor
አከባበር *akkäbabär* ceremony, celebration, the way it is celebrated

ከበሮ *käbäro* drum
ከበሮ ፡ መታ play the drum, palpitate
(of heart), thump (of heart)

ከብር *kəbər* respect, honor, dignity,
prestige, distinction (honor), glory
(see ከበረ)
ከብር ፡ በዓል celebration, holiday
ከብር ፡ ወሰን record (in sports)
የክብር honorary, honored
የክብር ፡ ልብስ regalia
የክብር ፡ በዓል ceremonial
የክብር ፡ ዘበኛ Imperial Bodyguard

ከብርቴ *käbbärte* wealthy (see ከበረ)

ካቦርት *kabbort* coat, overcoat (see also
ካፖርት)

ከብረት *kəbrät* wealth, riches (see ከበረ)

ከብሪት *kəbrit* match

ከብርና *kəbrənna* virginity (see ከበረ)
ከብርና ፡ ያላት *kəbrənna yallat* virgin

ከበበ *käbbäbä* cluster around, crowd around, surround, encircle, envelop, encompass, enclose, besiege, beleaguer
ክብ *kəbb* round, circular, spherical
ክብነት *kəbbənnät* roundness
ከበብ , see below
መከበብ *mäkkäbäb* siege (being besieged)
መክበብ *mäkbäb* siege (laying siege)
አካባቢ , see above

ከበብ *kəbäb* enclosure, circumference, circle, club (organization), zone (see ከበበ)
የከበብ ፡ አጋማሽ semicircle
የሙዚቃ ፡ ከበብ glee club

ከብት *käbt* livestock, wealth, riches
የቀንድ ፡ ከብት cattle, bovines
የጋማ ፡ ከብት equines (horses, donkeys, mules)
የጭነት ፡ ከብት pack animal

ኩበት *kubät* dried cow dung used as fuel

ካቢኔ *kabine* cabinet (of ministers)

ክብነት *kəbbənnät* roundness (see ከበበ)

ኩባንያ *kubbanəyya* company, firm

*ከከበ, አንከባከበ *ankäbakkäbä* coddle, cherish (treat with affection), yield to the wishes of, indulge, see to the comfort of, take under one's wings
አንከባክቦ ፡ አቀፈ *ankäbakbo aqqäfä* cuddle

ኩባያ *kubbayya* cup, mug (of metal)

ከበደ *käbbädä* be heavy, be difficult, be honored, be pregnant (animal), be serious (mistake), be severe (punishment), be hard-fought (battle)
ከበድ ፡ ያለ *käbädd yalä* solemn (voice)
ከባድ *käbbad* difficult, hard, heavy, pregnant, serious (mistake), grave, harsh (times), gross (mistake), severe (wound), impressive

ክብድ *kəbd* pregnant (cow)
†ክብደት *kəbdät* weight
ከባደننት *käbbadənnät* heaviness, seriousness, gravity

ክብደት *kəbdät* weight (see ከበደ)
ክብደት ፡ ቀነሰ lose weight
ክብደት ፡ ጨመረ gain weight, put on weight

ከት ፡ አለ *kätt alä*, in ከት ፡ ብሎ ፡ ሣቀ burst into laughter, roar (with laughter); see *ከትከተ

ከቶ *kätto* fully, completely, absolutely (see ከተተ)
ከቶ + (negative verb) never, at all

ኩታ *kuta* large *šamma*-dress with embroidered stripe on each end

ከት *kətt* stored, put away (because used on special occasions); see ከተተ
የከት ፡ ልብስ finery, suit worn on holidays or special occasions

ኮቴ *kotte* foot, hoof (of horse), print of foot, track (of an animal)
የእግር ፡ ኮቴ footstep

ኮት *kot* coat
ጉርድ ፡ ኮት jacket

*ከተለ, ተከተለ *täkättälä* (B) follow, result from, ensue
አስከተለ *askättälä* make follow, give rise to, lead to, result in, bring about, bring on, evoke, provoke (bring about), cause
ተከታተለ *täkätattälä* go after, keep track of, trail, pursue, keep up with, follow in succession, happen in succession
ተከታይ *täkättay* follower, following, attendant, continuation, sequel
ተከታዮች *täkättayočč* suite, following
ተከታታይ *täkätatay* consecutive, successive
ተከታታይነት *täkätatayənnät* coherence, sequence
ምክትል , see above

ኩተለቲ *kotälati* cutlet

ካቶሊክ *katolik* Catholic

ከተመ *kättämä* (B) found a city, be ended
ተከተመ *täkättämä* be built up (area)
አከተመ *akättämä* be finished, be ended, finish
(የሱ ፡ ነገር ፡ አከተመ he is finished, it's all over with him)
†ከተማ *kätäma* city, town
ማከተሚያ *maktämiya* climax

ከተማ *kätäma* town, city (see ከተመ)
የከተማ urban
አዲስ ፡ ከተማ market section of Addis Ababa, also called Mercato
ዋና ፡ ከተማ capital city
የመንገሻ ፡ ከተማ capital city
ከተሜ *kätäme* city folk, city dweller
ከተመኛ *kätämäñña* city dweller

ከተራ *kätära* eve of Epiphany

ኬትሮንስ *ketrons* latitude

ከተበ *kättäbä* vaccinate
ተከተበ *täkättäbä* be inducted into the army, be vaccinated
ከታብ *kətab* charm (amulet), talisman
ክትባት *kəttəbat* vaccination, vaccine, inoculation

ከተተ *kättätä* gather, bring together, mobilize (troops), put (into the pocket), tuck away, put in storage, put into, insert, involve (in debt)
አስከተተ *askättätä* mobilize, raise (troops, army)
ከት ፡ አለ *kätt alä* mobilize
†ክታት *kətät* mobilization
ከቹ, see above
ከት, see above
መከተቻ *mäktäča* receptacle, container

ክታት *kətät* mobilization (see ከተተ)
የክታት ፡ (ሰራዊት) ፡ ትእዛዝ mobilization

የክተት ፡ ሰራዊት ፡ ወዋጅ call to the colors

ካቴና *katena* handcuff (n.)
በካቴና ፡ ተቄራኘ be handcuffed
በካቴና ፡ አሰረ handcuff (v.)

ካቲካላ *katikala* kind of strong drink

ከተከተ *kätäkkätä* cut in little pieces, mince
ተንከታከተ *tänkätakkätä* crush
[See also እንክትክት ፡ አለ]

*ከተከተ, ተንከተከተ *tänkätäkkätä* giggle, be convulsed (with laughter)
በሣቅ ፡ ተንከተከተ *bäsaq tänkätäkkätä* howl with laughter
[See also ከት ፡ አለ]

ኰተኰተ *kʷätäkkʷätä* cultivate (plants), hoe

ከተፈ *kättäfä* hash, cut in little pieces, chop up, mince (meat, onions)
ክትፎ *kətfo* chopped meat, hash

ከነ *kännä* including, along with (from ከ, እነ)
ከነ - - - ጋር including, along with
ከነሕይወቱ ፡ ተማረከ he was captured alive

ኪነ ፡ ጥበብ *kinä ṭəbäb* art, work of art

*ከነበ, ተከናነበ *täkänannäbä* cover one's head with the *šämma* or with a veil, pull (a blanket) over one's head

ኩንቢ *kunbi* trunk (of elephant); see also ኩምቢ

ከንቱ *käntu* useless, vain, futile, idle (talk), false (hope)
ከንቱ ፡ ሆነ come to naught, fail, vi. (of efforts)
ከንቱ ፡ አደረገ bring to naught, discredit
በከንቱ in vain, without success, to no avail
የከንቱ ፡ ውዳሴ flattery
ከንቱነት *käntunnät* vanity

ኩንታል _kuntal_ quintal (100 kilos)

ካናቴራ _kanatera_ undershirt

ኪንታሮት _kintarot_ wart, tumor
የአህያ ፡ ኪንታሮት hemorrhoids

*ኮኑናተረ, ተኮኑናተረ _täkʷänattärä_ make a contract
ኮንትራት, see below

ኮንትሮባንድ _kontroband_ contraband
የኮንትሮባንድ ፡ ነጋዴ smuggler
የኮንትሮባንድ ፡ እቃ contraband

ኮንትራት _kontrat_ lease, contract (see *ኮኑናተረ)

ከንቲባ _käntiba_ mayor (of Addis Ababa or Gondar)

ኮንታክት _kontakt_ short circuit

ኪኒን _kinin_ pill (medical)

ኮነነ _kʷännänä_ (B) damn, punish, condemn
ኵናኔ _kʷənane_ damnation of the soul
መኮንን, see above

ከነከነ _känäkkänä_ irritate, tickle, irk

*ከናወን, አከናወን _akkänawwänä_ perform, accomplish, discharge (duties), prosecute (a plan), carry out
ተከናወን _täkänawwänä_ be carried out, be well made, be arranged, be executed, be accomplished successfully
ከነውን _kənäwwən_ achieved
የሥራ ፡ ከነውን achievement, performance of a job

ከነዳ _känädda_ measure by cubits
አስከነዳ _askänädda_ top (be first), excel
ከንድ, see below

ከንድ _kənd_ cubit, arm, forearm (see ከነዳ)
የከንድ ፡ ጡንቻ biceps

ካንዴላ _kandella_ spark plug

ከንፍ _kənf_ wing, fin (of fish)

ከንፈር _känfär_ lip, edge
የከንፈር labial
የከንፈር ፡ ቀለም lipstick
የከንፈር ፡ ወዳጅ boy friend, girl friend

ካዕብ _ka'əb_ second order of the Amharic vowel system (the vowel _u_)

ከከ _käkka_ (B) grind coarsely
ከክ _kəkk_ coarsely ground

ኩክ _kuk_ earwax

*ካካ, አስካካ _askakka_ cluck (of hens), cackle, neigh
ተንካካ _tänkakka_ cluck
ካካታ _kakata_ (n.) burst of laughter, cackle

ኬክ _kek_ cake

ክክ, see ከከ

ኮክ _kok_ peach

ኳኳ ፡ አለ _kʷakʷa alä_ (vi.) rattle, clatter
አንኳኳ _ankʷakkʷa_ (vt.) clatter, rattle, knock
ተንኳኳ _tänkʷakkʷa_ rattle (vi.)
በሩን ፡ አንኳኳ knock
ኳኳታ _kʷakʷata_ clatter (n.)

ኬክሮስ _kekros_ longitude

ኮከብ _kokäb_ (pl. ከዋክብት _käwakəbt_) star, horoscope, fortune (destiny)
ኮከብ ፡ ቆጠራ astrology
ኮከብ ፡ ቆጣሪ fortuneteller, astrologer
የኮከብ ፡ ምልክት asterisk
ነብር ፡ ኮከብ constellation
በራሪ ፡ ኮከብ meteor
ተወርዋሪ ፡ ኮከብ shooting star, falling star
ጅራታም ፡ ኮከብ comet (see ጅራት)

ካካታ, see *ካካ

ኳኳታ, see ኳኳ

ከው ፡ አለ _kəww alä_ be stunned, be aghast, be shocked
ከው ፡ አደረገ jar, vt. (of shock)
ከው ፡ ብሎ ፡ ቀረ be stupefied

ከው ፡ ብሎ ፡ ደነገጠ be aghast

ከውያ *kawəyya* iron (for clothes)

ከዚህ *käzzih* here, from here (see ከ,
-ዚህ)
ከዚህ ፡ በኋላ after this
ከዚህ ፡ ወዲያ starting from here, since,
ever since

ከዘራ *käzära* stick, cane

ከዝና *kazna* safe (n.)

ከዚያ *käzziya* there, from there (see ከ,
-ዚያ)
ከዚያ ፡ በኋላ after that

ከይሲ *käysi* dragon
አንተ ፡ ከይሲ you little mischief!

ኪያቬ *kiyave* wrench

ከዳ *kädda* betray, desert, abandon
አዳኝ ፡ ከዳው he met with reverses
ከዲ traitor
ክዳት, see below
ከዳተኛ, see below

ካደ *kadä* deny, abjure, disown, recant,
repudiate (a statement), renounce
የማይካድ *yämmayəkkad* irrefutable
[See also ከሐዲ, ክሕደት, ከሐዲነት]

*ኬዳ, አስኬዳ *askedä* drive away (see
ሄደ)

ኮዳ *kodda* canteen (leather bottle)

ክዳት *kədat* betrayal, denial, deser-
tion, apostasy, atheism (see ከዳ)

ከዳተኛ *käddatäňňa* traitor, deserter,
renegade (see ከዳ)
ከዳተኛነት *käddatäňňannät* treachery

ከደነ *käddänä* thatch a house with
grass, cover with a lid
ክዳን *kədan* thatch, covering, cover,
lid, flap (of pocket), cap (of pen)
መክደኛ *mäkdäňňa* lid, cover

ኪዳን *kidan* pact, treaty, covenant (Bib-
lical)

ኪዳን ፡ ገባ make a pact
የኪዳን ፡ ታቦት Ark of the Covenant
ቃል ፡ ኪዳን agreement, pact, pledge,
promise, covenant, treaty, vows (marital)
ብሉይ ፡ ኪዳን Old Testament
አዲስ ፡ ኪዳን New Testament

ኩዳዬ *kudade* Lent (see also ሁዳዬ)

ከዲ *käǧi* traitor (see ከዳ)

ከጀለ *käǧǧälä* (B) covet, feel like doing
something or having something

ከፋ *käffa* be bad, be worse
ከፋ(ው) *käffa(w)* feel low, be in a bad
humor, look gloomy, be morose
(ምን ፡ ከፋኝ *mən käffaňň* I don't
mind)
(አይከፋም *aykäfam* not bad, satis-
factorily)
አስከፋ *askäffa* displease, cause to dislike
ከፉ, see below
ክፋት, see below
አስከፊ *askäffi* deplorable (condition), morbid (thought), depressing,
abominable, infamous, reprehensible,
hideous, detestable, offensive (passage), mean (remark)
የከፋ *yäkäffa* unhappy
የሚያስከፋ *yämmiyaskäffa* offensive
(behavior, words)

ከፍ ፡ አለ *käff alä* be high, be elevated,
rise
ከፍ ፡ አደረገ raise (in rank), elevate
(in rank), increase (productivity),
boost
ከፍ ፡ ዝቅ ፡ አለ heave, vi. (of waves),
undulate
ከፍ ፡ ያለ *käff yalä* high, elevated,
major (important), keen (interest),
enormous, eminent (services)
ከፍታ, see below

ኩፍ ፡ አለ *kuff alä* rise (of dough)

*ካፋ, አካፋ *akaffa* (v.) drizzle, sprinkle
ካፊያ *kaffiya* (n.) shower (rain),
sprinkle, drizzle

ከፉ *kəfu* evil, bad, wicked, vicious, mean, hard (times), sinister (look); see ከፋ
ከፉ ፡ ቀን misfortune, hard times
ከፉኛ *kəfuňňa* bad, gravely, awfully, badly, seriously, severely
ከፉነት *kəfunnät* villainy

ከፈለ *käffälä* divide, pay, pay out
ተካፈለ *täkaffälä* take part, take a share, partake, participate with one another, share with one another, split (profit)
አካፈለ *akkaffälä* divide (a total), distribute, impart (one's ideas)
አስከፈለ *askäffälä* charge an amount of money, require payment
ከፋፈለ *käfaffälä* divide, divide up, partition, disunite, classify
ተከፋፈለ *täkäfaffälä* be segmented, be divided, branch off, share
አከፋፈለ *akkäfaffälä* apportion, portion out
ከፊል *käfil* partial, portion
(በከፊል partially, in part, up to a certain point, to some extent)
ከፍል, see below
ከፋይ *käfay* one who pays
ከፋይ *kəffay* segment
ከፍያ, see below
ማከፈል *makkafäl* division (in arithmetic)
መከፋፈል *mäkkäfafäl* schism, fission
ተካፋይ *täkafay* participant
[See also ከፍልፋይ]

ከፍል *kəfəl* part, share, room, classroom, grade (class in school), department, compartment, region, fragment, division (section), unit, category, chamber (of congress); see ከፈለ
ከፍል ፡ ገባ take a class in, enter . . . . grade
ከፍለ ፡ ሀገር region
ከፍለ ፡ ቃል syllable
ከፍለ ፡ ዓለም hemisphere
ከፍለ ፡ ዘመን century
ከፍለ ፡ ጊዜ session (in class), period (in class)

ከፍለ ፡ ጦር division (army unit)
የከፍል ፡ ጓደኛ classmate, roommate
የጦር ፡ ከፍል army unit

ከፍልፋይ *kəfəlfay* fraction (see ከፈለ)

ከፈተ *käffätä* open (vt.), unlock
ተከፈተ *täkäffätä* open (vi.), be opened
ከፍት *kəft* open (adj.), vacant (position)
መክፈቻ *mäkfäča* key

ከፍታ *käffəta* height (of mountain), elevation, altitude (see ከፍ ፡ አለ)
የከፍታ ፡ ዝላይ high jump
ከፍተኛ *käffətäňňa* high, lofty, advanced (course), important (matter), extreme (very great), utmost, maximum, considerable (skill)
ከፍተኛነት *käffətäňňannät* magnitude, amplitude, extent

ከፋት *kəfat* evil (n.), spite, wickedness (see ከፋ)
ከፋቱ *kəfatu* unfortunately

ከፍተኛ, see ከፍታ

ከፈነ *käffänä* (B) wrap up a corpse for burial
ከፈን *käfän* shroud

ከፉነት, see ከፉ

ኩፍኝ *kuffəňň* smallpox, chicken pox, measles

ከፉኛ, see ከፉ

ከፈከፈ *käfäkkäfä* compact the thatch well, pat down the hair
ከፍ ፍ ፡ አደረገ *käfkäff adärrägä* flatten

ከፈይ *käfay* velvet

ካፊያ *kaffiya* (n.) shower, sprinkle, drizzle (see *ካፋ)

ከፋይ *kəffay* segment (see ከፈለ)

ከፍያ *kəfəyya* pay, payment, division, partition, share (see ከፈለ)

ኮፍያ *kofəyya*, ኮፊያ *kofiyya* round cap
ኮፍያ ፡ ደፋ put on a cap

ከፈፈ *käffäfä* (B) edge, trim with
leather
ተከፈፈ *täkäffäfä* be edged, be trimmed (with leather), be bordered
ክፈፍ *kəfäf* rim (of glasses), brim
(of hat), sash (of window), frame (of
picture), molding

ካፖርት *kapport* overcoat (see also ካፐ
ርት)

ካፒቴን *kapiten* captain (of plane, ship)

ወ

ውሃ *wəha* water, juice (of a plant), sap
(of a plant)
ውሃ ፡ ውሃ ፡ አለ *wəha wəha alä* taste
flat (of beer)
ውሃ ፡ ሆነ his courage evaporated
ውሃ ፡ ቋጠረ form blisters
ውሃ ፡ አጠጣ water (flowers); see ጠጣ
ውሃ ፡ ወረደ fetch water
የውሃ ፡ ማጠራቀሚያ water reservoir
(see *ጠረቀም)
የውሃ ፡ ጉድጓድ well (of water)
እህል ፡ ውሃ food and drink, sustenance
የቧምቧ ፡ ውሃ running water
ፍል ፡ ውሃ hot springs (see ፈላ)
ውሃማ *wəhamma* watery

ወህኒ *wähni*, ወህኒ ፡ ቤት *wähni bet* jail,
penitentiary
የወህኒ ፡ ቤት ፡ አለቃ warden

*ወሐደ, ተዋሐደ *täwahadä* be united,
merge, vi. (of companies), amalgamate (vi.), fuse, mix (vi.), be digested.
አዋሐደ *awwahadä* amalgamate, unite, digest (food), merge (vt.), consolidate, integrate
ውሑድ *wəhud* compound (combination)

መዋሐድ *mäwwahad* agglutination,
fusion
ተዋሕዶ, see above

ወል *wäl*, in የወል ፡ ስም common noun,
general term
የወል ፡ ጾታ common gender

ዋለ *walä* spend the day, spend time,
spend the time at home, be observed
(of holiday), be held (of market)
አዋለ *awalä* cause to spend the day,
invest (time, money), devote (time,
one's life), dedicate (one's life)
አስተዋለ *astäwalä* pay attention, be
attentive, do something carefully,
look at, take note of, perceive
from ዋለ ፡
እንዴት ፡ ዋልክ how are you?, good
afternoon! (lit. how did you spend
the day?)
ቤት ፡ ዋለ stay home
በሥራ ፡ ላይ ፡ ዋለ go into effect, be
effective, be in practice, materialize
(vi.), be implemented
ደኅና ፡ ዋል be well!, have a good day!
ውሎ ፡ አደረ *wəlo addärä* stay somewhere for a long time
ውሎ ፡ አድሮ ultimately, eventually,
in the long run, sooner or later
ያልዋለ ፡ ያላደረ *yalwälä yaladdärä*
fresh (vegetables); see አደረ
መዋል *mäwal* association (being
with)
መዋያ *mäwaya* way of spending the
day, time when a festival occurs,
means of celebrating a holiday
from አዋለ ፡
በሙሉ ፡ አዋለ concentrate
በሥራ ፡ ላይ ፡ አዋለ apply, put into
practice, adopt, execute (a plan),
invest (money)
እቤት ፡ አዋለ keep at home
ጥረቱን ፡ ሁሉ ፡ አዋለ apply oneself,
devote one's efforts to
ጥቅም ፡ ላይ ፡ አዋለ put into use
from አስተዋለ ፡
አስተዋይ *astäway* observant, attentive, prudent, wise, intelligent,

thoughtful, reasonable, sensible, perspicacious
ማስተዋል *mastäwal* concentration (of mind), discrimination (discernment)

*ዋለ, ተዋዋለ *täwawalä* make an agreement, transact a deal, negotiate, commission (e.g. a painting), be drawn up (of a contract)
ተዋዋይ *täwaway* contracting party
ውል, see below

ዋለ *wala* chamois

ውል *wəl* contract, pact, treaty, agreement, deal (in business); see *ዋለ

ውል *wəl*, in ውል ፡ አገኘ disentangle (a rope)
በውል closely (from close, attentively)

ወለል *wäläl* floor
የባሕር ፡ ወለል sea bottom

ወለል ፡ አደረገ *wäläll adärrägä* light up, vt. (flashlight lighting up the woods)
ወለል ፡ አድርጎ ፡ ከፈተ *wäläll adrəgo käffätä* open wide

ዋለለ *wallälä* vacillate, roll, vi. (of a ship), drift (of people, clouds), run around
ተዋለለ *täwallälä* rock, vi. (of a boat)
የሚዋልል *yämmiwalləl* erratic (wind), fluid (situation)

ወለም ፡ አለ *wälämm alä* be dislocated (bone), be sprained
ወለም ፡ አለ(ው) *wälämm alä(w)* sprain, dislocate, wrench
ወለምታ *wälämta* sprain (n.)

ወለቀ *wälläqä* be out of joint (finger), be dislocated, fall off (tooth, ring from finger), slip off (vi.), be knocked out
አወለቀ *awälläqä* slip off, vt. (shoes), take off (a coat), undress, remove

(the hat), dismantle, deal a hard blow (on the chin)
ወላለቀ *wälalläqä* fall apart (of stool)
አወላለቀ *awälalläqä* dismantle (a machine), take apart, strip off (clothes)
ኪስ ፡ አውላቂ *kis awlaqi* pickpocket

*ወለበለበ, ተወለበለበ *täwläbälläbä* fly in the breeze, flutter, wave, vi. (of flags), flap, vi. (of shutters)
አውለበለበ *awläbälläbä* wave (vt.), fly, vt. (a kite)
ውልብልቢት *wələbləbit* propeller

ዋልታ *walta* center piece of the roof of a round house
የምድር ፡ ዋልታ pole
የሰሜን ፡ ዋልታ North Pole
የደቡብ ፡ ዋልታ South Pole

ውለታ *wəläta* gratitude, favor, kindness (favor), good turn, pact, obligation
ውለታ ፡ ዋለ do a favor
ውለታ ፡ ቢስ ingrate, ungrateful
ውለታ ፡ ቢስነት *wəläta bisənnät* ingratitude
ባለውለታ *baläwəläta* one who has one's gratitude
ባለውለታው ፡ ነው he is obligated to him, he is under an obligation to him, he is indebted to him, he is thankful

ወላንዳ *wälanda* kite

ወለወለ *wäläwwälä* wipe (dishes, table, floor), mop (the floor), polish, shine, clean (windows), rub
በሰፍነግ ፡ ወለወለ sponge (v.)
መወልወያ *mäwälwäya* mop (n.)

ወላወለ *wälawwälä* hesitate, be undecided
አወላወለ *awwälawwälä* waver, vacillate, feel uncertain, be of two minds, hesitate, falter
ወላዋይ, see below
አውላዋይ, see above
የማያወላውል *yämmayawwälawwəl* grim (determination)

ወላዋይ _wälaway_ hesitant, irresolute
(see ወላወለ)

ዋልያ _walya_ ibex

ወለደ _wällädä_ engender, bear, give
birth to, have a baby, accrue interest
ተወለደ _täwällädä_ be born, be a
descendant
ተዋለደ _täwallädä_ multiply (of family,
flock), reproduce (vi.)
አዋለደች _awwallädäčč_ she delivered
the baby (speaking of a midwife),
she assisted in childbirth, she acted
as a midwife
ወለድ _wälläd_ interest (money paid
for the use of money)
(ልብ ፡ ወለድ fiction, imagination)
(አየር ፡ ወለድ airborne)
ወላድ _wällad_ fecund, prolific, fertile
(cattle)
ወልድ _wäld_ son (only used in compound proper names)
†ወላጅ _wälağ_ parent
ተወላጅ _täwällağ_ descendant, native
አዋላጅ _awwalağ_ midwife
ትውልድ, see above
ልደት, see above
ልጅ, see above
ልጅነት, see above

ወላጅ _wälağ_ parent (see ወለደ)
ወላጅነት _wälağǝnnät_ parenthood

ወምበር _wämbär_ chair, seat, chief judge
(see also ወንበር)
ሞላላ ፡ ወምበር bench
አግዳሚ ፡ ወምበር bench
የ - - - ወምበር ፡ ገፉ sit at the feet of

ወምበዬ, see ወንበዬ

*ወራ, አወራ _awärra_ announce, report,
tell news, narrate, relate, gossip,
talk
ወሬ, see below
ወረተኛ, see below
ወረኛ ፤ ወሬኛ, see below

ወሬ _wäre_ news, tidings, rumor, conversation, information, gossip (see
*ወራ)

ወሬ ፡ ቀሰመ snoop
ወሬ ፡ ቀዳ gossip (v.)
ወሬ ፡ ነዛ spread news
ወሬ ፡ አቀባይ informer (see*ቀበለ)
የወሬ ፡ ቋት an old gossip
የወሬ ፡ ወሬ various rumors
ምን ፡ ወሬ ፡ አለ? what is new?
ትኩስ ፡ ወሬ latest news
አዲስ ፡ ወሬ latest news
[See also ወረኛ, ወረተኛ]

ወር _wär_ month
የወር monthly (adj.)
በየወሩ _bäyyäwäru_ monthly (adv.)
[See also ወርሃት]

ወርኃዊ _wärhawi_ seasonal (rains)

ወረረ _wärrärä_ invade, raid, pillage,
plunder, swarm over (of ants), overrun, storm (of soldiers)
ወረራ _wärära_ invasion, incursion,
attack
(የአየር ፡ ወረራ air raid)
ወራሪ _wärari_ invader
አውራሪ, in ፊት ፡ አወራሪ ፤ ፊታው
ራሪ _fitawrari_ general of the vanguard
(see ፊት)
[See also ወረርሽኝ, ወርበላ]

ወረርሽኝ _wärräršǝňň_ plague (lit. you
invaded me); see ወረረ
ወረርሽኝ ፡ በሽታ plague

ውርርድ, see ወረደ

ወረሰ _wärräsä_ inherit, succeed in office,
accede to (the throne), confiscate
(speaking of governmental authority)
አወረሰ _awärräsä_ bequeathe, give an
inheritance
ውርስ _wǝrs_ bequest, inheritance, con-
fiscated
(ውርስ ፡ አደረገ confiscate)
ወራሽ, see below
ርስት, see above

ዋርሳ _warsa_ sister-in-law, brother-in-
law

ወራሽ _wäraš_ heir, successor (see ወረሰ)

ሕጋዊ ፡ ወራሽ legal heir (see ሕግ)
አልጋ ፡ ወራሽ Crown Prince

ወርቅ *wärq* gold (n.)
ወርቅ ፡ ሠሪ goldsmith (see ሠሪ)
የወርቅ gold (adj.), golden
የወርቅ ፡ ልብስ cloth embroidered
with gold
የወርቅ ፡ ጥላ umbrella embroidered
with gold
መሶብ ፡ ወርቅ decorated *mäsob*
ወርቅማ *wärqəmma* golden
ወርቃማ *wärqamma* gilded
[See also ሰም]

ወረቀት *wäräqät* paper, letter, document
የወረቀት ፡ መርፌ pin
የምስክር ፡ ወረቀት certificate, report
card
የይለፍ ፡ ወረቀት pass, passport,
laissez-passer, visa, permit, safe conduct (see አለፈ)
የፈቃድ ፡ ወረቀት license

ወሮበላ *wärrobälla* vagabond, ruffian,
gangster (lit. having raided he consumed); see ወረረ, በላ

ወራት *wärat* time, season (see also ወር)

ወሮታ *wärrota* benefit, favor, gratitude,
reward
ወሮታ ፡ ከፈለ reward (v.)

ወረተኛ *wärätäňňa* fickle, turncoat,
giddy (girl); see *ወረ

ወርች *wärč* front leg of animal

ወረንጦ *wärränṭo* tweezers, pincers

ውርንጭላ *wərənčəlla* young donkey
የፈረስ ፡ ውርንጭላ colt, foal

ወራኛ *wäräňňa*, ወሬኛ *wäreňňa* one who
tells news, who tells gossip, who has
a loose tongue (see *ወረ)

ወርካ *wärka*, ዋርካ *warka* sycamore

ወራወረ *wäräwwärä* throw, hurl, flip
(a coin), fling, pitch (a ball), toss
away, shoot (an arrow)

ወርወር ፡ አደረገ *wärwärr adärrägä*
interject
(ዓይኑን ፡ ወርወር ፡ አደረገ cast a
glance)
መወርወሪያ *mäwärwäriya* latch, shuttle
ተወርዋሪ *täwärwari* dynamic (force
of water)
ተወርዋሪ ፡ ኮከብ shooting star, falling star

ወረደ *wärrädä* descend, go down, come
down, get off, dismount, disembark,
drop (come down)
አወረደ *awärrädä* put down, bring
down, set down, unload, hand
down, lower, recite (verses)
አስወረደ *aswärrädä* cause to bring
down, expiate (sins)
(አስወረዳት she miscarried)
ተዋረደ *täwarrädä* be disgraced, be
humiliated, be humbled, be handed
down
(ሲወርድ ፡ ሲዋረድ *siwärd siwwarräd*
hereditary)
አዋረደ *awwarrädä* humiliate, debase, degrade, dishonor, bring shame
on, affront, abuse
ወራረደ *wärarrädä* recite
ተወራረደ *täwärarrädä* wager, bet,
make a bet
ወራዳ *wärradda* lowly (occupation),
mean (ignoble), sordid (business)
ውርደት *wərdät* disgrace, dishonor,
humiliation, degradation, affront
ውርርድ *wərarrəd* wager, bet
ወራጅ, see below
ውራጅ *wərraǧ* worn-out, shabby
አውራጅ *awraǧ* song leader
አዋራጅ ፡ ሆነ *awwaraǧ honä* be a
discredit to
የወራዳነት *yäwärraddannät* dissolute
(life)
[See also ውርጅብኝ]

ወረዳ *wäräda* province, district (administrative), subdivision of an
awraǧǧa
ምክትል ፡ ወረዳ sub-district

ውርድ, in ውርድና ፡ ስፋት *wərdənna səfat* dimensions (see ሰፋ be wide)

ውርደት, see ወረደ

ወራጅ *wäraǧ* one who goes down (see ወረደ)
ወራጅ ፡ ውኃ torrent

ውራጅ *wərraǧ* worn-out, shabby (see ወረደ)

ውርጅብኝ *wərǧəbbəňň* stream of invectives (see ወረደ)

ውርጭ *wərč* frost

*ወሳ, አወሳ *awässa* bring to mind, remind, refer to something, deal (have to do with)

*ዋሰ, ተዋሰ *täwasä* borrow an object that has to be returned specifically, loan an object, vouch, be a bondsman, be a guarantor
(በሕይወት ፡ ተዋሰ risk one's life)
አዋሰ *awasä* lend an object, give surety, give bail
ዋስ, see below
ዋስትና, see below
ትውስት, in የትውስት ፡ ቃል *yätəwəst qal* loanword

ዋስ *was* surety, guarantor, guarantee, bail (see *ዋስ)
የገንዘብ ፡ ዋስ bail

ወስላታ *wäslatta* rascal, rogue, cheat

*ወሰሰ, ወሳሰበ *wäsassäbä* tangle
ተዋሳሰበ *täwäsassäbä* become involved, be complicated, be interwoven, become tangled up
የተወሳሰበ *yätäwäsassäbä* complicated, complex, involved, intricate (idea)
ያልተወሳሰበ *yaltäwäsassäbä* simple (design)
[See also ውስብስብ]

ውስብስብ *wəsəbsəb* intricacy, complicated (see *ወሰሰ)

ውስብስብነት *wəsəbsəbənnät* complexity

ዋስትና *wastənna* guarantee, security, bail, warranty, insurance (see *ዋስ)
ዋስትና ፡ ሰጠ guarantee (v.)
ዋስትና ፡ አስገባ insure
የሕይወት ፡ ዋስትና life insurance

ወሰነ *wässänä* (B) delimit, delineate, confine, define, determine, decide, regulate, resolve, circumscribe, fix (a time), set (a date), specify, assign
ተወሰነ *täwässänä*, passive of the preceding; confine oneself, be limited, be restricted
ተዋሰነ *täwassänä* border, be bordered, adjoin, share a common border
ወሰን *wäsän* border, boundary, limit, frontier
ወሰን ፡ የሌለው boundless, limitless, unlimited
ውሳኔ *wəssane* decision, resolution, conclusion, definition
ወሰንተኛ *wäsäntäňňa* man who owns territory adjoining someone's land
የተወሰነ *yätäwässänä* limited, strict (diet), specific, definite
የማይወሰን *yämmayəwwässän* infinite, indefinite, unrestricted
መወሰኛ *mäwässäňňa*, in የሕግ ፡ መወሰኛ ፡ ምክር ፡ ቤት Senate

ወሰወሰ *wäsäwwäsä* baste (in sewing)

ወሰደ *wässädä* take, take away, haul away, carry off, carry away, remove, lead (of a road)

ውስጥ *wəsṭ* interior, inside, core (of apple)
ውስጥ ፡ ውስጡን inwardly, secretly
ውስጥ ፡ ለውስጥ inside, secretly
ውስጥ ፡ እግር sole (bottom of foot)
ውስጠ ፡ ደንብ bylaw
በውስጥ (adv.) inside, within
እውስጥ inside (adv.)
ከውስጥ (adv.) within, underneath
የውስጥ inside (adj.), internal
በ - - - ውስጥ (prep.) in, inside, within, into, in the course of, through

እ - - - ውስጥ inside (prep.), in
ከ - - - ውስጥ from, from within, out
of
ወደ - - - ውስጥ into
ውስጣዊ wəsṭawi internal, inward,
inner, inside (adj.), intrinsic
የውስጠኛ yäwəsṭäñña inner

ወስፈ wäsfe awl, large needle used for
basketwork (see ሰፋ sew)

ወስፋት wäsfat hookworm

ወስፈንጥር wäsfänṭər arrow

ዋሸ waššä lie, tell a lie, falsify
ዋሾ waššo mendacious, liar
†ውሸት wəšät lie
ዋሽነት waššonnät mendacity

ዋሻ wašša cave, cavern, den
ዋሻ ፡ የበዛበት wašša yäbäzzabbät
cavernous

ውሻ wəšša dog

ወሸላ wäšäla uncircumcized

ውሻል wəššal wedge

ወሻሚ wäššami adulterer
ውሸማ wəšəmma adultery

ወሽመጥ wäšmäṭ, የባሕር ፡ ወሽመጥ yäbahər wäšmäṭ strait, channel

ውሸት wəšät lie (n.); see ዋሸ
የውሸት yäwəšät false, counterfeit
የውሸት ፡ ጥይት blank (bullet), blank
cartridge
ውሸታም wəšätam liar
ውሸተኛ wəšätäñña liar

ዋሽንት wašənt three-holed pipe, flute
ዋሽንት ፡ ነፋ play the flute

ዋሽነት waššonnät mendacity (see ዋሸ)

ውሽንፍር wəšənfər rain accompanied
by strong wind gusts

ወቃ wäqqa thresh, beat grain with
a stick

ውቂያ wəqqiya threshing
መውቂያ mäwqiya flail

ወቀረ wäqqärä incise, chisel, pit (a
grinding slab to make it grind better)

ወቀሰ wäqqäsä blame, reprimand, reproach, scold, reprehend, rebuke,
chide
ወቀሳ (n.) wäqäsa reproach, rebuke,
blame, criticism

ውቃቢ wəqabi, ውቃቤ wəqabe protective
spirit, guardian spirit
ውቃቢ ፡ አምላክ guardian angel
ውቃቢ ፡ የራቀው unappealing person, unattractive person
ውቃቢው ፡ አልወደደኝም wəqabiw al-
wäddädäñňəm he took a dislike to me

ወቄት wäqqet 28 grams

ወቅት wäqt season, time, semester,
occasion
ወቅቱ ፡ አይደለም it is untimely
በየወቅቱ bäyyäwäqtu periodically

ውቂያ wəqqiya threshing (see ወቃ)

ውቅያኖስ wəqyanos ocean

ወቀጠ wäqqäṭä grind (coffee, spices),
pound, crush in a mortar, castrate
by crushing the testicles
ሙቀጫ muqäčča mortar for pounding
መውቀጫ mäwqäča pestle

ወባ wäba malaria
የወባ ፡ ትንኝ mosquito
ብጫ ፡ ወባ yellow fever

*ዋበ, ተዋበ täwabä be beautiful
ውብ wəb beautiful, pretty, gorgeous, scenic
ውበት wəbät beauty, splendor, charm,
glamor, attractiveness

ውብ, see ዋበ

ወበቀ wäbbäqä (B) be sticky (weather),
be humid (air)
ወበቅ wäbäq humidity

ውብት, see *ዋበ

ወትሮ wätro always, continually, as in the past (see *ዘወተረ)
እንደ ፡ ወትሮው as usual, as always
እንደ ፡ ወትሮው ፡ ነው he is himself
ያለወትሮው፡ ነው yaläwätrow näw he is acting strange, he is not himself

ወተት wätät milk, sap (of tree)
የዱቄት ፡ ወተት powdered milk

ወተወተ wätäwwätä importune

ወታደር wättaddär soldier
የወታደር military, adj. (uniform, camp)
ተራ ፡ ወታደር enlisted man, private (soldier)
ወታደራዊ wättaddärawi military, adj. (rule), soldierly (bearing)
ወታደራዊ ፡ ሕግ martial law
ወታደርነት wättaddärənnät condition of being a soldier

ወተፈ wättäfä (B) stuff, plug up, cork, obstruct, clog
ውታፍ wətaf stopper, plug
መወተፊያ mäwättäfiya stopper

ወና wäna abandoned (house); see also አና

ወኔ wänne zeal, ardor

ዋና wanna principal (adj.), essential, chief, important, main, prime, primary, major (adj.), real (reason), original (as opposed to copy)
ዋና ፡ ዋና essential (adj.), principal
ዋና ፡ አዛዥ commander in chief
ዋና ፡ ከተማ capital city
ዋና ፡ ዲሬክተር director-general
ዋና ፡ ገንዘብ capital, n. (money), principal, n. (money)
ዋና ፡ ጎዳና thoroughfare, main road
ዋና ፡ ጸሐፊ secretary general
ዋነኛ, see below

ዋና wana swim, swimming (see ዋኘ)
የዋና ፡ ልብስ bathing suit
ዋናተኛ wanatäňňa swimmer

ወንበር, see መምበር

ወንባዴ wänbäde brigand, robber (see also መምበዴ)
ውንብድና wənbədənna banditry, brigandage

ዋነኛ wannäňňa principal (adj.); see ዋና
ዋነኛ ፡ አቅጣጫ cardinal point

ወንዝ wänz river, stream
ወንዝ ፡ ወረደ go to the river to fetch water
የወንዝ ፡ ሸለቆ river basin

ወንዴ wände positive (electric charge); see ወንድ

ወንድ wänd male, man, boy, brave, masculine (in grammar)
ወንድ ፡ ልጅ son
ወንዴ positive (electric charge)
ወንዳ፡ ወንድ manly
የወንድ masculine (adj.), manly (sport), mannish
የወንዶች yäwändočč male (adj.)
ወንድነት wändənnät manhood
[See also ወንደላጤ, ወንድም]

ወንደላጤ wändälaṭṭe bachelor (see ወንድ)

ወንድም wändəmm (pl. ወንድሞች wändəmmočč, ወንድማማች wändəmmamačč) brother
የወንድም ፡ ልጅ nephew, niece
ታላቅ ፡ ወንድም elder brother
ወንድማማችነት wändəmmamaččənnät brotherhood (of man), fraternity
የወንድምነት yäwändəmmənnät fraternal

ወንድነት wändənnät manhood (see ወንድ)

ወነጀለ wänäǧǧälä charge with a crime, ወንጀል, see below

ወንጀል wänǧäl violation, penal offense, delinquency, crime, criminal act (see ወነጀለ)
ወንጀል ፡ መርማሪ detective
(በሞት ፡ የሚያስቀጣ ፡ ወንጀል —yämmiyasqäṭṭa—capital crime)

(የሚያስቀጣ ፡ ወንጀል criminal offense)
የወንጀል ፡ ሕግ ፡ ፍልስፍና criminal
jurisprudence
ወንጀለኛ wänǧäläňňa criminal, felon,
culprit, convict
የወንጀለኛ ፡ መቅጫ ፡ ሕግ penal code

ወንጌል wängel Gospel

ዋንጫ wanča drinking horn, tumbler

ወንጭፍ wänčǝf sling

ወናፍ wänaf bellows (see ነፋ blow)

ወንፈል wänfäl communal labor

ወንፊት wänfit sieve, sifter, grate (see
ነፋ sift)

ዋኘ waňňä swim, take a swim
†ዋና wana swim, swimming
መዋኛ mäwaňňa swimming pool

ወከለ wäkkälä (B) act for, substitute,
delegate, commission
ወኪል wäkkil agent, representative

*ዋከበ , አዋከበ awwakkäbä harry, harass

ውካታ wǝkkata commotion, uproar

ወከፍ wäkäf, in በነፍስ ፡ ወከፍ per capita, individual

ወዛ wäzza perspire, sweat
ወዝ wäz perspiration, sweat, sheen,
glossy complexion

*ዋዛ , ተዋዛ täwazza make jokes, joke,
mock one another
ዋዛ waza joke, mockery
ዋዛ ፡ ፈዛዛ aimless pursuit

ዋዜማ wazema vigil (the day and night
before church festivities), eve of
holiday, eve, prelude

ወዘተ wäzätä etc. (abbreviated from
Geez ወዘተረፈ)

ወዘወዘ wäzäwwäzä shake, make to
move, brandish, agitate, turn something this way and that

ተወዛወዘ täwäzawwäzä be shaky (of
table), tremble (of leaves), swing, vi.
(of the pendulum), dangle, sway
(of trees in the wind), rock (in the
chair)
አወዛወዘ awwäzawwäzä shake (the
leaves), sway (vt.), wave (the hand),
swing (vt.), rock (the cradle), dangle
(the legs)
ውዝዋዜ wǝzǝwwaze rhythm
ተወዛዋዥ täwäzawaž pliant (branch)

ወዘፈ wäzzäfä (B) put off
(በግማሹ ፡ ወዘፈ leave half finished)
ውዝፍ wǝzzǝf something which is put
aside, unfinished, which is in arrears

*ወየ, ተወያየ täwäyayyä converse, dis-
cuss with one another
ውይይት, see below

*ወየ, አወየ awwayyä tell another one's
misfortunes
ወዮ wäyyo alas!, woe!
ወይኔ wäyne alas!, woe to me!
ወዮው wäyyäw oh dear!

ወይ wäy or; at the end of the sentence
it expresses a question
ወይም wäyǝm or, either ... or
ወይም - - - ወይም either ... or
ወይስ wäyǝss or (in a question)

ወይም, see ወይ

ወይራ wäyra wild olive tree
(የ)ወይራ ፡ ዘይት olive oil
የወይራ ፡ ፍሬ olive

ወይስ wäyǝss or (in a question); see
ወይ

ወይና ፡ ደጋ wäyna däga temperate
zone (at intermediate altitude); see
ወይን, ደጋ

ወይኔ wäyne alas!, woe to me! (see *ወየ)

ወይን wäyn grape, vine
ወይን ፡ ጠጅ wine
[See also ወይና ፡ ደጋ]

ወይንስ *wäyənəss* or (in a question);
see ወይ

ወይዘሮ *wäyzäro* (pl. ወይዛዝር *wäyzazər*,
ወይዛዝርት *wäyzazərt*) madam, lady,
Mrs.
ወይዘሪት *wäyzärit* mademoiselle, Miss

ወየው *wäyyäw* oh dear! (see *ወየ)

ውይይት *wəyəyyət* discussion, dialogue,
deliberation (see *ወየ)

ወይድ *wäyəd* go away!, beat it! (see also
 መግደ)

ወይፈን *wäyfän* young bullock

ወደ *wädä* toward, to, into, around,
about, approximately (with numer-
als)
ወደ ፡ ኋላ backwards
ወደ ፡ ላይ upwards
†ወደዚህ *wädäzzih* here, toward
here, somewhere around here
†ወደዚያ *wädäzziya* there, toward
there, beyond
ወደ ፡ ጎን sideways
ወደ ፡ ፊት, see ወደፊት
[See also ወዲህ, ወዴት, ወዲያ]

ወዶ *wäddo* willingly (see ወደደ)

ውድ *wədd* costly, expensive, dear
(beloved, expensive), precious, high
(in price); see ወደደ
በውድ at high price
በውድም ፡ በግድም *bäwəddəm bägəddəm* willy-nilly
በውድም ፡ ሆነ ፡ በግድ *bäwəddəm
honä bägədd* willy-nilly

ወዲህ *wädih* hither, here, toward here,
somewhere around here (from ወደ-
ይህ)
ከ - - - ወዲህ since (prep.), on this
side of
ከ+ perfect +ወዲህ since (conj.)
ከቅርብ ፡ ጊዜ ፡ ወዲህ lately
ከእንግዲህ ፡ ወዲህ henceforth
ከዚህ ፡ ወዲህ *käzzih wädih* since (adv.)
ከዚያ ፡ ወዲህ *käzziya wädih* thereafter

ወደል *wädäl*, in ወደል ፡ አህያ jackass,
he-donkey

*ወደለደለ, አውደለደለ *awdäläddälä* be
idle, loaf

ወደመ *wäddämä* be demolished, be lev-
eled to the ground
አወደመ *awäddämä* devastate, ravage,
demolish, put an end to
ውድም, see below

ውድም *wədəmma* uninhabited, deserted
place, threshing floor (see ወደመ)

ወደረ *wäddärä* (B) hobble (the hind
legs of a cow)

ወደረ *wäddärä* (B) bet against
ተወዳደረ *täwädaddärä* compete, rival, contend (compete), vie, compare (vi.), be compared, run for
office
ወደር *wädär* equal (n.)
ወደር ፡ የሌለው *wädär yälelläw* incomparable, unrivalled, exceptional,
champion (adj.), abysmal
ውድድር, see below
ተወዳዳሪ, see above

ወደሰ *wäddäsä* (B) praise, glorify
አወደሰ *awäddäsä* hallow, exalt
(በከንቱ ፡ አወደሰ flatter)
ውዳሴ *wəddase* glory, praise
ከንቱ ፡ ውዳሴ flattery

ወደቀ *wäddäqä* fall, fall down, fall off,
drop out, fail (exams), decline, drop
(of price)
ውዳቂ *wəddaqi* reprobate, refuse, rubbish, litter
ውድቅ *wədq* corrupt (manners)
ውድቅ ፡ ሆነ be defeated (a motion),
fail, vi. (of experiment), be a failure,
be invalid (document)
ውድቅ ፡ አደረገ defeat (a bill), demolish
ውድቀት *wədqät* downfall, collapse,
crash (in business), fall, failure, decadence, turpitude
ውድቅት, see below

ውድቀት, see ወደቀ

ውድቅት wəddəqt midnight (see ወደቀ)
በውድቅት in the dead of the night,
late (at night)
በዚህ ፡ ውድቅት at this ungodly hour

ወደብ wädäb port, harbor

ወዴት wädet where?, whither? (from
ወደ-የት)
ከወዴት whence?

ውዴታ wəddeta will (desire), willingness (see ወደደ)
በውዴታ willingly
ያለ ፡ ውዴታ involuntarily

ወደዚህ wädäzzih hither, this way,
toward here (from ወደ, -ዚህ)
ከ - - - ወደዚህ on this side of

ወደዚያ wädäzziya toward there (from
ወደ-ዚያ)
ከ - - - ወደዚያ beyond

ወዲያ wädiya there, toward there, on
the other side of, beyond (see ወደ)
ወዲያና ፡ ወዲህ back and forth
ወዲያና ፡ ወዲህ ፡ አለ walk about,
pace, go around here and there, get
about, ramble, fiddle around, hang
around
ከ - - - ወዲያ beyond
ከትናንትና ፡ ወዲያ the day before
yesterday
ከነገ ፡ ወዲያ the day after tomorrow
ከዚህ ፡ ወዲያ starting from here,
from now on
ወዲያኛ, see below
ወዲያው, see below

ወዲያኛ(ው) wädiyaňňa(w) the one over
there (see ወዲያ)
በወዲያኛው in the next world
የወዲያኛ farther (adj.)

ወዲያው wädiyaw suddenly, instantly,
forthwith, immediately, right away,
very soon after, shortly afterwards,
then and there (see ወዲያ)

ወዲያውኑ wädiyawnu immediately,
right away, soon after, suddenly, on
the spot, outright, promptly

ወደደ wäddädä love, desire, like, have
a liking for, become enamored of
ተወደደ täwäddädä be in favor, be
loved, be liked, be expensive, be
popular
አስወደደ aswäddädä cause to be
loved, boost (prices), heighten (the
value)
ወዶ wäddo willingly
ወዶ ፡ ዘማች volunteer, n. (see ዘመተ)
ውድ, see above
ውዴታ, see above
ወዳድ wäddad, in ራሱን ፡ ወዳድ selfish; ሰው ፡ ወዳድ friendly
ወዳጅ, see below
ወዳጅነት, see below
ተወዳጅ täwäddağ one who is loved,
amiable, popular, dear (loved), congenial (host)
ተወዳጅነት täwäddağənnät popularity,
desirability
እወደድ ፡ ባይ əwwäddäd bay toady,
obsequious person
የተወደደ yätäwäddädä popular

ውድድር wədəddər contest, competition,
campaign, tournament (see ወደደ)
ውድድር ፡ ያለበት wədəddər yalläbbät
competitive
(የ)ሩጫ ፡ ውድድር race (running)

*ወዳጀ, ተወዳጀ täwädağğä fraternize,
be on friendly footing (denominative
of ወዳጅ)

ወዳጅ wädağ friend, lover, beloved (see
ወደደ)

ወዳጅነት wädağənnät amity, friendly
relations (see ወደደ)
የወዳጅነት amicable, friendly, genial

ወደፊት ፤ ወደ ፡ ፊት wädäfit onward,
in the future, later on, further on,
ahead, forwards
ለወደፊት next time

ለወደፊቱ፡ in the future
የወደፊት prospective, future (adj.)

ወጋ wägga pierce, stab, prick, gore,
jab, stick (vt.), make war on, thrust
ተዋጋ täwagga fight, be in combat,
struggle
ወጋጋ wägagga poke
ወጋ ፡ ወጋ ፡ አደረገ wäga wäga adärrägä prod (an ox)
ውጋት wəgat pain, stinging pain,
sharp pain (in chest, stomach)
ውጊያ, see below

*ወጋ, አወጋ awägga talk (chat), narrate,
tell stories
ወግ, see below

ወግ wäg narrative, talk, lore, usage,
traditional customs, wit (see *ወጋ)
ወግና ፡ ልግድ form (ceremony)
በወግ properly

ዋጋ waga cost, price, rate, value, fee,
reward
ዋጋ ፡ ቢስ worthless, useless, null
and void, void (agreement), of no
account, trivial (remark)
ዋጋ ፡ ሰጠ appreciate
ዋጋ ፡ አለው waga alläw be important,
be worthwhile, carry weight, count
(possess value)
ዋጋ ፡ ያለው worthy
ዋጋ ፡ የለውም waga yälläwəm be null,
be null and void, it is of no consequence
ዋጋ ፡ አጣ become a dead letter (of
law), be discredited (a theory)
ዋጋ ፡ አሳጣ put to shame, discredit
(see አጣ)
የዋጋ ፡ ዝርዝር invoice
ምንም ፡ ዋጋ ፡ የለውም there is no
point in (doing something)
በምንም ፡ ዋጋ at any price
የጉልበት ፡ ዋጋ labor cost

ዋገምት waggämt cup for drawing
blood (see አገመ)

ወገረ wäggärä knock someone unconscious with a stone

ተወገረ täwäggärä, in በድንጋይ ፡ ተወገረ
be stoned to death

ወጌሻ wägešša local medical practi-
tioner

ወገብ wägäb back of waist, loin, hip,
haunch, flank, trunk (of human
body)

ውጋት, see ወጋ

ወገን wägän side (of a place), flank
(side), clan, group, kin, faction, sect,
party, people on the same team,
partisans

*ወገዘ, አወገዘ awäggäzä excommuni-
cate, proscribe, decry (condemn),
denounce, fulminate against
ውግዘት wəgzät excommunication,
anathema

ውጊያ wəggiya battle, fighting, combat, attack (see ወጋ)
የጨበጣ ፡ ውጊያ hand-to-hand combat

ወገደ wäggädä (B) quit, go away
ተወገደ täwäggädä be avoided, be
eliminated, be fired (from work)
አስወገደ aswäggädä eliminate (difficulties), discard, smooth away
(objections), dispel, put an end to,
get rid of, overcome (difficulties)
ወገድ wägəd get out of the way! (see
also ወይድ)

ውጋጋን wəgagan beam of light, reflection of light

ወጣ wätta go out, be out, come out,
exit, be fired, be expelled, leave (a
place), go up, mount, surmount,
climb, rise (of sun), appear, be published
(ወጣው wättaw it came out of him,
as in ጥሩ ፡ ሐኪም ፡ ይወጣዋል he
will make a good doctor)
ተወጣ täwätta surmount (obstacles),
overcome (difficulties)

(ተወጣለት *täwäṭṭallät* it came off well for him)
አወጣ *awäṭṭa* make go out, expel, take out, bring out, put out, raise (one's head), spend (money), issue (a coin, magazine), publish, produce, remove, extract, reveal (secrets), withdraw, devise (a plan)
(አወጣ ፡ አወረደ ponder, meditate, play with the idea, deliberate)
(ባወጣ ፡ ያውጣ *bawäṭṭa yawṭa* hit or miss (method), gamble (n.)
(ባወጣ ፡ ያውጣው ፡ አለ take a chance)
(አውጥተው ፡ አውርደው ፡ ተነጋገሩ *awṭaṭäw awrdäw tänägaggäru* they discussed thoroughly)
(ይህ ፡ እህል ፡ ምን ፡ ያወጣል how much does this grain cost ?)
አስወጣ *aswäṭṭa* eliminate, evict, eject, expel
አዋጣ *awwaṭṭa* help to bring out, contribute (money), take up a collection
ወጣ ፡ አለ *wäṭa alä* stick out, step out
ወጣ ፡ ገባ *wäṭṭa gäbba* rugged (terrain), uneven (ground), jagged (coastline), irregular
ወጣ ፡ ገባ ፡ አደረገ warp
ውጣ *wäṭa*, in የዋጋ ፡ ውጣ ፡ ውረድ haggling
ውጣ ፡ ውረዱን ፡ ተከራከረ haggle, bargain
ወጥ *wäṭṭ*, in ሕገ ፡ ወጥ illegal, irregular, outlaw
ወጥነት, see below
ውጤት, see below
ወጭ, see below
ውጭ, see below
መውጣት *mäwṭat* ascension, ascent
መውጫ, see above
ማውጫ, see above
መዋጮ, see above
የወጣለት *yäwäṭṭallät* accomplished (adj.), successful, sensational (player), excellent
የሚያዋጣ *yämmiyawwaṭṭa* profitable, successful (business)

አውጫኞኝ, see above
አውጪኝ, in እግረ ፡ አውጪኝ ፡ አለ *ǝgre awčiňň alä* take to flight

ወጥ *wäṭ* stew, curry-type sauce
ወጥ ፡ ሠራ prepare stew
ወጥ ፡ ቤት kitchen, cook
ዶሮ ፡ ወጥ stew made with chicken

ዋጠ *waṭä* swallow, absorb, engulf, take medicine
(ሣቁን ፡ ዋጠ hold back a laugh, suppress one's laughter)
ተዋጠ *täwaṭä* be swallowed, be lost (in thought), be deeply involved (in debt), be possessed (by an idea), be overcome with (fright, joy)
ዋጠ ፡ አደረገ *waṭṭ adärrägä* gulp down
ዋጠ ፡ ዋጠ ፡ አደረገ gobble

ወጥመድ *wäṭmäd* trap for animals, snare (see *ጠመደ)

ወጠረ *wäṭṭärä* (B) stretch (a string, hide), make taut, distend, strain at (chains)
ተወጠረ *täwäṭṭärä*, passive of the preceding; expand, vi. (of balloon), bulge, vi. (of bag), be puffed
የተወጠረ *yätäwäṭṭärä* taut (rope)
መወጠሪያ *mäwäṭṭäriya* frame (for stretching a hide, etc.)

ወጣት *wäṭṭat* youth (young man), adolescent, youngster
የወጣት juvenile
የወጣትነት *yäwäṭṭatǝnnät* youthful (appearance)

ውጤት *wǝṭṭet* result, outcome, conclusion, mark (in an examination), output, effect (see ወጣ)
የሥራ ፡ ውጤት accomplishment

ወጠነ *wäṭṭänä* (B) begin, commence
ውጥን *wǝṭṭǝn* project, undertaking, scheme
ጥንት, see below

ውጥንቅጥ *wǝṭǝnqǝṭ* medley, jumble, mess

ወጥነት *wäṭṭənnät*, in ሕገ ፡ ወጥነት lawlessness

ወጠጤ *wäṭäṭe* fresh kid, young goat

ወጪ *wäči* costs, expenditure, expense (see ወጣ)

ውጭ *wəčč*, ወጪ *wəčči* exterior, outside, outdoors (see ወጣ)
ውጪ ፡ መሆን exception
ውጪው outside (adv.)
ውጭ ፡ አገር abroad, overseas
የውጭ exterior (adj.), outside (adj.), external, outward, foreign
የውጭ ፡ አገር foreign
የውጭ ፡ አገር ፡ ሰው foreigner
የውጭ ፡ ጉዳይ foreign affairs
የውጭ ፡ ጉዳይ ፡ ሚኒስቴር Ministry of Foreign Affairs, foreign office
ከ - - - ውጭ out, outside of, besides (prep.)
ከሕግ ፡ ውጭ ፡ የሆነ illegal, unlawful
ወደ ፡ ውጭ outward (adv.)

ወጨፎ *wäčäfo* driving rain

ወፍ *wäf*, ዎፍ *wof* (pl. አዕዋፍ) bird
ወፍ ፡ ዘራሽ *wäf zärraš* wild (flower); see ዘራ
የወፍ ፡ በሽታ jaundice
የወፍ ፡ ቤት nest, cage
የወፍ ፡ ጎጆ nest
የወፍ ፡ ጥርስ milk tooth
የወፍ ፡ ጫጩት fledgling
የሌሊት ፡ ወፍ ፤ የሌት ፡ ወፍ bat

ወፈረ *wäffärä* (B) be fat, be thick, get stout
አወፈረ *awäffärä* fatten, thicken, increase the consistency (of soup), concentrate (juice)
ውፍሬ *wəffare* fatness
ውፍረት *wəfrät* thickness, fatness
ወፍራም *wäfram* fat (adj.), thick, stout, obese, deep (voice), strong (tea), heavy (cloth)

ወፍራም, see ወፈረ

ውፍረት, see ወፈረ

ወፍጮ *wäfčo* grinding slab, mill (see ፈጨ)
የወፍጮ ፡ ቤት mill
እናት ፡ ወፍጮ lower millstone
የነፋስ ፡ ወፍጮ windmill

ወፋፈ *wäfäffe* touched (slightly crazy), crank

ዘ

-ዚህ *-zzih* a demonstrative element combined with a preposition as በዚህ 'here', ስለዚህ 'therefore', እስከዚህ, 'so far', and so on (see also -ዚያ)

ዘሆን *zəhon* elephant
የዘሆን ፡ ጥርስ ivory
የዘሆን ፡ ጆሮ ፡ ይስጠኝ ፡ አለ — *yəsṭäňň alä* lend a deaf ear

ዛለ *zalä* be stiff (legs)
የዛለ weary (feet, from exertion)

ዛላ *zala* bearing, carriage

ዘለለ *zällälä* jump, leap, climb over, skip, skip over (a word), hop
ዘለል ፡ ዘለል ፡ አለ *zäläll zäläll alä* hop about, hop around
ዘሎ ፡ ገባ *zällo gäbba* burst into, plunge into
ዘሎ ፡ ብድግ ፡ አለ spring to one's feet
†ዝላይ *zəllay* (n.) leap, jump

ዘለላ *zäläla* bunch (of bananas, grapes, etc.), strand (of hair)

ዘላለም *zälaläm* forever (see ዓለም and also ዘለዓለም)

ዘለቀ *zälläqä* go through, complete (course of study), penetrate, continue, percolate (of water), permeate, go beyond, get ahead, proceed, get by (manage), have endurance, last
ዘላቂ *zälaqi* perpetual, staunch (friend), lasting

ዘለቄታ *zäläqeta* perpetuity, permanence
ዘለቄታ ፡ አለው *be lasting*
ለዘለቄታታው in perpetuity, permanently, forever, in the long run
ዘላቂነት *zälaqinnät* permanence
ዘላቂነት ፡ ያለው perennial

ዘለበት *zäläbät* key ring, collar of dog, buckle (of belt)

ዘላን *zällan* nomad

ዘለዓለም *zälä'aläm* forever (see also ዘላ ለም and ዓለም)
ለዘለዓለም forever
የዘለዓለም everlasting, lasting
ዘለዓለምነት *zälä'alämənnät* eternity
ዘለዓለማዊ *zälä'alämawi* eternal
ዘለዓለማዊ ፡ ሕይወት eternity

ዘለዘለ *zäläzzälä* cut meat into strips
ዘልዛላ *zälzalla* meat cut in strips

ዝላይ *zəllay* (n.) jump, leap (see ዘለለ)
የመሬት ፡ ዝላይ broad jump
የሰማይ ፡ ዝላይ high jump
የከፍታ ፡ ዝላይ high jump

ዝልግልግ *zələgləg* slimy, sticky (juice)

ዘለፈ *zälläfä* (v.) rebuke, reproach, blame, criticize, insult
ዘለፋ *zäläfa* (n.) reproach, rebuke, insult, blame
የዘለፋ abusive

*ዘለፈለፈ, ተዘለፈለፈ *täzläfälläfä* go limp
አዝለፈለፈ *azläfälläfä* cause languor, fill with languor
ተዝለፍልፎ ፡ ወደቀ *täzläfləfo wäddäqä* collapse

ዘማ *zämma* fornicate, commit adultery
ዝሙት *zəmmut* fornication, adultery, lust

*ዜመ, አዜመ *azemä* intone, chant
ዜማ *zema* chant, church song, tune
ዜማ ፡ ሰበረ sing false notes
ዜማ ፡ አወረደ sing a song (see ወረደ)

ዝም ፡ አለ *zəmm alä* be quiet, keep quiet, hold still, remain silent, shut up, hush
ዝም ፡ አሰኘ *zəmm assäňňä* quiet (vt.), silence (vt.)
ዝም *zəmm* be silent!
ዝም ፡ ብሎ *zəmm bəlo* motionless, quietly, just so (without purpose), merely, continuously
ዝም ፡ ብሎ ፡ ይሠራል he keeps on working, he simply goes on working
ዝም ፡ ማለት silence (n.)
†ዝምታ *zəmməta* silence (n.)

ዘመመ *zämmämä* lean, vi. (bend), sag (of wall), hang down
አዝማሚያ, see above

ዘመረ *zämmärä* (B) sing (of birds), sing a song, chant, intone
ዝማሬ *zəmmare* intonation, singing
መዝሙር, see above
አዝማሪ *azmari* singer, minstrel

ዘምብ *zəmb* fly (n.); see also ዝንብ
የእርን ፡ ዝምብ meddlesome (see እርን)

ዘምቢል *zämbil* basket of woven palm leaves

ዘምባባ *zämbaba* palm tree

ዘመተ *zämmätä* make a military expedition, make a raid, go on a mission
ተዘመተ *täzammätä* be rampant (disease), spread, vi. (of news, fire, disease)
አዛመተ *azzammätä* spread (news), propagate
ዘመቻ, see below
ዘማች *zämač* raider
(ወደ ፡ ዘማች volunteer; see ወደደ)
†አዝማች *azmač* commander (military), refrain
የተዘመተ *yätäzammätä* popular (belief), widespread (belief)

ዝሙት *zəmmut* fornication, adultery, lust (see ዘማ)

ዝምታ *zəmməta* silence (see ዝም ፡ አለ)
ዝምተኛ *zəmmətäňňä* silent (boy), taciturn, reticent

ዘመቻ *zämäča* campaign, raid, military expedition, fight (against disease); see ዘመተ
ዘመቻ ፡ አደረገ wage a campaign

ዘመን *zämän* (pl. ዘመናት *zämänat*) period, epoch, era, date
ዘመን ፡ አመጣሽ *zämän amäṭṭaš* contemporary (culture), newfangled (see መጣ)
ዘመን ፡ ያለፈ(በት) *zämän yalläfä-(bbät)* out-of-date, obsolete (see አለፈ)
ዘመን ፡ የገፋ *zämän yägäffa* advanced in age (see ገፋ)
ዘመነ ፡ መንግሥት (n.) reign, rule
ዘመነ ፡ ዮሐንስ leap year
በዘመኑ at present
የዘመን modern
ለብዙ ፡ ዘመናት in ages, for a long time
ክፍለ ፡ ዘመን century
ዘመናዊ *zämänawi* modern, up-to-date, contemporary (furniture), popular (song)
ዘመናይ *zämänay* parvenu, excessively modern (in dress, behavior); see also ዘበናይ

*ዘመደ, ተዛመደ *täzammädä* be related to one another, be akin, associate (vi.), be linked
አዛመደ *azzammädä* relate (connect), correlate, associate (vt.)
ዘመድ, see below
ዝምድና *zəmdənna* relationship, family relationship, kinship, affiliation
አዛማጅ ፡ ተውላጠ ፡ ስም *azzamaǧ*— relative pronoun
የሚዘመድ *yämmizzammäd* cognate, allied
የተዛመደ *yätäzammädä* kindred (adj.)

ዘመድ *zämäd* (pl. ዘመዶች *zämädočč*, አዝማድ *azmad*) relative, relation (relative), kin, kinsman, family, friend (see *ዘመደ)
ዘመደ ፡ አዝማድ relatives
(የ)ቅርብ ፡ ዘመድ close relative

ቤተ ፡ ዘመድ relations, kin, family
ዘመዶች *zämädočč* kindred (n.), folks

ዝምድና, see *ዘመደ

ዘራ *zärra* sow, seed, plant (wheat), grow (wheat, cotton)
(ነፍስ ፡ ዘራ regain consciousness, come to)
(ወፍ ፡ ዘራሽ *wäf zärraš* wild (flower)
(ጠብ ፡ ዘራ sow dissension)
አዘራ *azärra* winnow (grain), sift grain letting it fall little by little
ዘር, see below
ዝርያ, see below

ዘር *zär* seed, descent (origin), offspring, line, lineage, issue (descent), species, race (of human species); see ዘራ
ከዘር ፡ ተላለፈ be hereditary, be congenital (see አለፈ)
የዘር racial, ancestral
የዘር ፡ ልዩነት discrimination
የዘር ፡ አወራረድ genealogy (see ወረደ)
የዘር ፡ ግንድ genealogy, pedigree

ዙር *zur* race (in a contest), round (section of a game); see ዘራ

ዛሬ *zare* today
ዛሬ ፡ ነገ ፡ አለ stall (v.)
ዛሬም still
ዛሬም ፡ አለ survive (continue to exist)
ዛሬ ፡ ሌሊት last night
ዛሬ ፡ ማታ tonight, this evening
ዛሬ ፡ ጧት this morning
ዛሬውኑ *zarewnu* this very day
በዛሬ ፡ ጊዜ nowadays
እስከዛሬ *əskäzare* to date
(እስከዛሬ ፡ ወር a month from today)
የዛሬ ፡ ሳምንት ፡ ሄደ he left a week ago today
የዛሬ ፡ ሳምንት ፡ ይሄዳል he will leave a week from today

ዛር *zar* kind of spirit, possession by a spirit
ዛር ፡ ያዘው he was possessed by a spirit

ዜሮ *zero* zero, naught

ዞረ *zorä* go around, get around, turn around, revolve, circle, rotate
(ራሱ ፡ ዞረ be dizzy)
አዞረ *azorä* turn (vt.), make giddy, make dizzy
ዘወረ *zäwwärä* (B) change around
ተዛወረ *täzawwärä* move to another place, be transferred, transfer (vi.), be transplanted (population)
አዛወረ *azzawwärä* transfer from place to place, transplant (a heart), hand over, assign (property)
ዛዋወረ *zäwawwärä* move around, go here and there, get about
ተዛዋወረ *täzäwawwärä* wander, roam, get about, rove, move around (vi.), circulate, cruise, travel about, be transferred
አዛዋወረ *azzäwawwärä* make move around, move (vt.), shuttle (vt.), shift (several things or persons)
ዞር ፡ አለ *zorr alä* turn around, turn away, step aside, look back
ዞር ፡ አደረገ swerve (the car), move
ዞር ፡ በል step aside!, scram!
ዞሮ ፡ ዞሮ *zoro zoro* finally, in the end, eventually
ዙሮ, see above
†ዙረት *zurät* turning (n.)
ዙሪያ, see below
ዛዋሪ *zäwari* wanderer, vagabond
ዘውውር *zäwəwwər* transfer
ዛወርዋራ *zäwärwarra* roundabout (way)
ተዘዋዋሪ *täzäwawari* errant, itinerant, migrant, migratory, mobile, one who goes back and forth
ተዘዋዋሪ ፡ የሚበዛበት *täzäwawari yämmibäzabbät* busy (street)
መዛወር *mäzäwwər* pulley
ማዞሪያ *mazoriya* telephone operator
አዛዋሪ *azwari*, in እቃ ፡ አዛዋሪ peddler
አዙሪት *azurit* whirlpool
አዝዋሪት *azwarit* whirlpool
የሚያዞር *yämmiyazor* giddy (height)

ዛረረ *zärrärä* stretch one out (on the ground), topple
ተዛረረ *täzärrärä* lie stretched out, fall flat, stretch full length, be laid prostrate
መዛረር *mäzzärär* knockout

ዙረት *zurät* turning (n.); see ዞረ
ዙረት ፡ ሄደ ramble

*ዘረከረከ, ተዘረከረከ *täzräkärräkä* be littered up, be cluttered, be strewn
አዘረከረከ *azräkärräkä* drop things carelessly everywhere, strew about
(ለሀጩን ፡ አዘረከረከ drool)
ዝርክርክ *zərəkrək* sloppy, messy
መዝረክረክ *mäzräkräk* disorder

ዘረዘረ *zäräzzärä* itemize, list, enumerate, put everything in detail, outline (a plan), discuss in detail, change money into small denominations
ተዘረዘረ *täzäräzzärä* have a run (stockings)
ዘርዘሮ *zärzəro* one by one
ዝርዝር, see below

ዝርዝር *zərzər* list, detail, detailed, minute (adj.), small change, inventory, catalog (see ዘረዘረ)
ዝርዝር ፡ ገንዘብ change, n. (money)
በዝርዝር *bäzärzər* minutely, one by one, item by item, in detail, thoroughly
በዝርዝር ፡ ጻፈ list (v.)
የምግብ ፡ ዝርዝር menu, bill of fare
የዋጋ ፡ ዝርዝር invoice

ዙሪያ *zuriya* circuit, circumference, surrounding area, environs, all the way around (see ዞረ)
በ - - - ዙሪያ around
እ - - - ዙሪያ around
ዙሪያውን *zuriyawən* all around, around in a circle
በዙሪያው around it

ዝርያ *zərrəyya* offshoot, offspring, progeny (see ዘራ)

ዘረጋ *zärägga* spread, spread out, stretch out (the arms, the hand), extend, stretch (a rope), unroll (a carpet)
ተዘረጋ *täzärägga* be spread out, stretch, vi. (of a road), sprawl, extend (vi.)
ዝርግ, see below

ዝርግ *zərg* flat (dish), plain (surface), shallow (dish); see ዘረጋ
ዝርግ ፡ ሳሕን plate, platter, tray

ዘረፈ *zärräfä* rob, pillage, loot, plunder, rustle (cattle)
ዘረፋ *zäräfa* robbery, plunder, pillaging
ዘራፊ *zärafi* robber, plunderer, rustler
ዘራፊነት *zärafinnät* robbery, rapacity

ዘርፍ *zärf* fringe, ruffle (of skirt), border, offshoot, branch (of office)

*ዘረፈፈ, ተንዘረፈፈ *tänzäräffäfä* hang loose, droop (of pants)
ዘርፋፋ *zärfaffa* drooping, droopy

ዛቀ *zaqä* scoop up (dung)

ዝቅ ፡ አለ *zəqq alä* be low, drop (vi.), decline, be inferior, sink (of prices)
ዝቅ ፡ አደረገ demote, degrade, depreciate, vt. (currency), devalue
ዝቅ ፡ አድርጎ ፡ ገመተ underestimate
ዝቅ ፡ ያለ low (voice), small, little
ዝቅታ, see below

ዝቅታ *zəqqəta* lowering, depression, condescension (see ዝቅ ፡ አለ)
ዝቅተኛ *zəqqətäňňa* low (mark, income, position), humble (origin, occupation), inferior (position), minor (official), menial (task)

ዘቀዘቀ *zäqäzzäqä* turn upside down, hold upside down, overturn
ተዘቀዘቀ *täzäqäzzäqä* hang upside down (vi.)
አዘቀዘቀ *azäqäzzäqä* go down (of sun), be low (of sun)
ዘቅዘቅ ፡ አለ *zäqzäqq alä* slope, v. (of field)

ዘቅዘቅ ፡ ያለ gentle (slope)
የዝቅዝቅ *yäzəqzəq* upside down

ዝቃጭ *zəqqač̣* sediment, residue (of oil), sludge

ዘባ *zäbba* be warped, be bent
አዘባ *azzabba* garble, twist (someone's words), distort (the meaning of words), slant (news), pervert (facts)
የተዛባ *yätäzabba* colored (report), distorted, twisted

ዘብ *zäb* act of guarding, guard, sentry
ዘብ ፡ ጠበቀ be on guard duty
የክብር ፡ ዘብ *yäkəbər zäb* guard of honor
ዘበኛ, see below

ዛብ *zab* reins (see also እዛብ)

ዘባረቀ *zäbarräqä* talk nonsense, ramble on, confuse an issue (in talking)
አዘባራረቀ *azzäbärarräqä* mess up (papers)
[See also ዝብርቅርቅ ፡ አለ]

ዝብርቅርቅ ፡ አለ *zəbrəqrəqq alä* be messy (see ዘባረቀ)
ዝብርቅርቅ *zəbrəqrəq* mess

ዘቢብ *zäbib* dried grape, raisin, sacramental wine

ዘበት *zäbät* absurdity, absurd

ዘበናይ *zäbänay* parvenu, extreme in one's behavior (in attempting to be modern); see also ዘመን, ዘመናይ

ዘበኛ *zäbäňňa* guard, guardian, watchman, keeper (see ዘብ)
የክብር ፡ ዘበኛ Imperial Bodyguard

ዛቢያ *zabiya* haft (of axe), axe handle

ዝባድ *zəbad* civet, musk

ዘበጠ *zäbbäṭä* dip, vi. (slope downward)
አዘበጠ *azäbbäṭä* depress (press down)

ዛተ *zatä* threaten, launch threats, menace
ዛቻ, see below

ዛቻ *začčä* threat, menace (see ዛተ)

*ዘና, ተዝናና *täznanna* feel at ease, relax, feel comfortable, lounge
እንዲዝናና ፡ አደረገ *əndiznanna adärrägä* put at ease
መዝናኛ ፡ ክፍል *mäznaña kəfəl* lounge (n.)

ዜና *zena* news
ዜና ፡ መዋዕል *zena mäwa'əl* chronicle
ዜና ፡ ታሪክ annals
ዜና ፡ ዕረፍት obituary
ዜና ፡ አቀባይ reporter
ዜና ፡ አጠናቃሪ *zena aṭṭänaqari* correspondent (for a newspaper), reporter (see *ጠነቀረ)
አርእስተ ፡ ዜና headline(s)

ዝና *zənna* fame, renown, repute, reputation
ዝነኛ, see below

ዘነመ *zännämä* rain (v.); see also ዘነበ
ዝናም *zənam* rain (n.); see also ዝናብ

ዝናር *zənnar* cartridge belt

ዘነበ *zännäbä* rain (v.); see also ዘነመ
ዝናብ, see below

ዝናብ *zənab* rain (n.); see ዘነበ, ዝናም
ዝናብ ፡ አባራ it stopped raining (see *በራ)
ዝናብ ፡ ጣለ rain (v.)
ዝናብ ፡ ልብስ raincoat
የዝናብ ፡ መለኪያ rain gauge

ዝንብ *zənb* fly (n.); see also ዝምብ

*ዘነበለ, አዘነበለ *azänäbbälä* bend, vi. (of tree), incline (vi.), slant, lean, vi. (show preference)
ተዘነበለ *täzänäbbälä* be bent, be inclined
ዘንበል ፡ ያለ *zänbäll yalä* slanted (roof)
ዝንባሌ *zənəbbale* inclination, tendency, partiality, leaning (preference), trend

ዝነኛ *zənnäñña* famous, eminent, renowned, celebrated (see ዝና)

ዝነኛ ፡ ሰው celebrity

ዘነዘና *zänäzäna* pestle

ዘንድ *zänd* near, beside, by (near); (following a verb in the simple imperfect) in order that, so that
በ - - - ዘንድ by, among
እ - - - ዘንድ close to, near to
ከ - - - ዘንድ close to, near to; in-asmuch as, in view of the fact that

ዘንዶ *zändo* python

ዘንድሮ *zändəro* this year, the current year

ዝንጀሮ *zənǧäro* monkey, ape

ዝንጅብል *zənǧəbəl* ginger

ዘነጋ *zänägga* forget, lose sight of, be absent-minded
ዝንጉ *zəngu* forgetful, absent-minded
ዝንጉነት *zəngunnät* forgetfulness

ዘንግ *zäng* rod, staff (stick), axis, shaft (of spear), goad
ሹል ፡ ዘንግ prod (n.)

ዝንጉርጉር *zəngurgur* variegated, multicolored, speckled, spotted, striped (see also ዝጉርጉር)

ዘንጋዳ *zängada* kind of small red sorghum

ዘነፈ *zännäfä* make crooked, make a cutting remark, insult in veiled terms
አዛነፈ *azzannäfä* distort, warp, cause to overlap in folding
ተዛነፈ *täzannäfä* be of uneven length, be folded unevenly

ዙኦሎጂ *zuoloǧi* zoology

ዘኬ *zäkke* food collected by students from begging, meal eaten at church after Sunday mass, a commemorative meal for priests and poor donated by well-to-do people

ዘከረ *zäkkärä* commemorate a saint's day with a feast, give alms to a beggar
ዝክር *zəkər* commemoration of a saint (usually with a banquet in his honor)
ዝክረ ፡ ነገር *zəkrä nägär* memorabilia
መዘከር *mäzäkkər*, in ቤተ ፡ መዘከር museum
ተዝካር, see above

ዘው ፡ አለ *zäww alä* enter abruptly, enter unexpectedly

ዘወረ *zäwwärä* (B) change around (see ዞረ)
For the other derived forms, see ዞረ

ዘወርዋራ *zäwärwarra* roundabout (way); see ዞረ

*ዘወተረ, አዘወተረ *azäwättärä* have the habit of doing something frequently, frequent (a place), always do something
ዘወትር *zäwätər* as a rule, frequently, usually, constantly, regularly, all the time
የዘወትር constant, steady (customer), normal, everyday, adj. (for every ordinary day)
ለዘወትር always
አዘውትሮ *azäwtəro* frequently, constantly, always
[See also ወትር]

ዘውውር, see ዞረ

ዘውድ *zäwd* crown (n.)
ዘውድ ፡ ደፋ be crowned
ዘውድ ፡ ጫነ wear a crown, be crowned
ዘውድ ፡ ጫነ(ለት) *zäwd čanä(llät)* crown (v.)
ዘውድ ፡ አማካሪ counselor of the emperor
የዘውድ ፡ በዓል coronation anniversary

-ዚያ *-zziya* a demonstrative element combined with a preposition, such as በዚያ there, in that way

ዘይ *zəyy*, ዘዪ *zəyyi* goose
ወንድ ፡ ዘይ gander

ዘይበ *zäyəbe* figure of speech, expression, phrase

ዘይት *zäyt* olive, oil, petroleum
ወይራ ፡ ዘይት olive oil
የምግብ ፡ ዘይት *yäməgəb zäyt* edible oil
የነዳጅ ፡ ዘይት motor oil

ዛዴ *zäde* method, plan, scheme, trick (the best way of doing something), ways and means, tactics, system, strategy, device, formula
በዛዴ carefully, methodically
የጦር ፡ ዛዴ strategy
ዛዴኛ *zädeňňa* tactful, diplomatic, resourceful, adroit, artful, cagey

ዘጋ *zägga* close, bar, barricade, block, shut off, obstruct
ተዘጋ *täzägga* be closed, close (vi.)
ዝግ *zəg* closed
መዝጊያ *mäzgiya* door, gate

ዛገ *zagä* corrode, rust (vi.)
አዛገ *azagä* rust (vt.)
የዛገ *yäzagä* rusty
ዝገት *zəgät* rust (n.)

*ዛጋ, አዛጋ *azzagga* yawn

ዜጋ *zega* national (n.), subject, citizen
የውጭ ፡ አገር ፡ ዜጋ foreign national
ዜግነት, see below

ዝግ ፡ አለ *zəgg alä* be slow, slow down, crawl
ዝግ ፡ አደረገ slow down (vt.)
ዝግታ *zəggəta* slowness
በዝግታ *bäzəggəta* at a slack pace, slowly
ዝግተኛ *zəggətäňňa* slow-flowing, slow-moving

ዛጉል *zagʷäl* coral, shell

*ዘገመ, አዘገመ *azäggämä* make slow headway, plod, trudge

*ዘጉረጉረ, ተዘጉረጉረ *täzgʷäräggʷärä*
become multicolored, become striped
ዝጉርጉር *zəgurgur* multicolored,
speckled, spotted, striped
[See also ዠንጉርጉር]

ዝግባ *zəgba* kind of cedar tree

ዝጋት *zəgät* rust (n.); see ዛገ

ዝግታ, see ዝግ ፡ አለ
ዝግተኛ, see ዝግ ፡ አለ

ዘገነ *zäggänä* take a handful (of grain,
ashes), scoop up, cup the hands

ዝግን *zəgən* dish of minced meat cooked in butter

ዜግነት *zegənnät* nationality, citizenship (see ዜጋ)
የዜግነት civic (duties)
ዜግነት ፡ የሌለው stateless

ዘገየ *zägäyyä* be late, do something
late, be delayed, be tardy
አዘገየ *azägäyyä* delay (vt.), detain,
postpone, retard, put off, hold off
ዘግይቶ *zägəyto* late (adv.)
ዘግይቶ ፡ መጣ he was late
ዘግይቶ ፡ ደረስ he was late
መዘግየት *mäzägyät* delay (n.), lateness
ቢዘገይ ፡ ቢዘገይ *bizägäyy* at the latest

*ዘጋጀ, አዘጋጀ *azzägaǧǧä* put in order,
make ready, prepare, arrange, process, compile, equip, edit
ተዘጋጀ *täzägaǧǧä* be ready, be
prepared, be outfitted (with furniture)
ዝግጁ *zəgəǧǧu* ready, prepared
ዝግጅት *zəgəǧǧət* preparation, arrangement, preparedness, organization
ዝግጅት ፡ አደረገ make arrangements
አዘጋጅ *azzägaǧ* editor
ማዘጋጃ ፡ ቤት *mazzägaǧa bet* municipality, city hall

ዘጠና *zäṭäna* ninety (see ዘጠኝ)

ዘጠኝ *zäṭäňň* nine (see ዘጠና)
ዘጠኝ ፡ ሰዓት three o'clock

ዘጠነኛ *zäṭänäňňa* ninth

ዛፍ *zaf* tree
ባሕር ፡ ዛፍ eucalyptus

ዞፍ *zof* white of egg

ዘፈቀ *zäffäqä* immerse in water

ዝፍት *zəft* tar

ዘፈነ *zäffänä* sing, dance and sing
ዘፈን *zäfän* melody, song, dance
ዘፋኝ *zäfaň* singer

ዙፋን *zufan* throne
ዙፋን ፡ ለቀቀ abdicate
ዙፋኑን ፡ ወረሰ succeed to the throne

ዘፈዘፈ *zäfäzzäfä* infuse (tea leaves),
steep (flax in water), soak

*ዘፈዘፈ, ተንዘፈዘፈ *tänzäfäzzäfä* writhe
(in pain), palpitate (with terror)

ዚፐር *zipär* zipper
ዚፐር ፡ ዘጋ zip up

ዠ

[See also ጀ]

ዠመረ *žämmärä* (B) begin (see also
ጀመረ)

ዠማት *žəmmat* tendon (see also ጅማት)

ዠራት *žärat* tail (see also ጅራት)

*ዠረገገ, ተንዠረገገ *tänžäräggägä* flow
down (of hair), hang down (of hair)

*ዠበበ, አንዠበበ *anžabbäbä* soar (of
hawk), hover

ዠንጉርጉር *žängurgur* motley, striped
(see also ዠጉርጉር)

ዠንጠላ *žanṭəla* umbrella, parasol (see
also ጃንጥላ)

*ዠገመገመ, አዠገመገመ *ažgämäggämä*
glide (of kite)

እግራ- *žəgra* guinea fowl (see also ጀግራ)

እጉርጉር *žəgurgur* dapple, striped, speckled, spotted (see also እሥንጉር ጉር)

የ

የ *yä* of
የ+(perfect) who, that, what, which (relative)

ያ *ya* that (demonstrative, masc.), the one; when preceded by a preposition it is -ዛ.ያ
ያም ፡ ሆነ ፡ ይህ *yam honä yəh* in any case, at any rate, anyway, be that as it may
ያም ፡ ቢሆን even at that
[See also ያን, ያኛው, ያው]

ይህ *yəh* this (masc.), this one; when preceded by a preposition, it is -ዛ.ህ
ይህም ፡ ሆነ *yəhəm hono* be that as it may
ይህኛው *yəhəňňaw* this one

ያህል *yahəl* about, nearly, around (approximately), roughly, approximately (see አከለ)
ለምሳሌ ፡ ያህል just for an example
ምን ፡ ያህል how much?
ምን ፡ ያህል ፡ ጊዜ how soon?, how long?
ምንም ፡ ያህል + (negative verb) hardly, hardly any
እንደ + negative perfect + ያህል just as though
የ + perfect + ያህል as much as, as long as
ይህን ፡ ያህል *yəhən yahəl* this much, such as, so long, so much
ይህን ፡ ያህል ፡ ጊዜ so long
የቱን ፡ ያህል to what degree?, to what extent?
ያን ፡ ያህል that long, that much
ያንኑ ፡ ያህል *yannənu yahəl* the like amount

የዚያን ፡ ያህል *yäzziyan yahəl* as much, that many times

ይህች *yəhəčč*, ይህቺ *yəhəčči* this (fem.), this one (see also ይች)

ይሁን ፡ አለ *yəhun alä* agree (see ሆነ)

ይህኛው *yəhəňňaw* this one (see ይህ)

ይሁዲ *yəhudi* Jew

የለ *yällä* + suffix pronouns + ም not have
(የለኝም *yälläňňəm* I don't have)

ያለ *yalä* without, except (see also አለ and ያለዚያ)
ያለ ፡ ስፍራው out of place
ያለ ፡ ጊዜው prematurely, untimely

የሌለ *yälellä* who is not
የሌለው *yälelläw* one who does not have

የለም *yälläm* there is not, he is not, he is not around, no
የለበትም *yälläbbätəm* he (it) should not

የለሽ *yälläš*, in ሕግ ፡ የለሽ lawless; ግድ ፡ የለሽ careless, unconcerned; አንጀት ፡ የለሽ heartless

ይልቅ *yələq* more, farther (see ላቀ)
ይልቁንም *yəlqunəm* especially, rather, on the contrary
ይልቅስ *yələqəss* rather, on the contrary
ከ - - - ይልቅ more than, rather than
ከሁሉም ፡ ይልቅ above all

ያለበለዚያ *yaläbäläzziya* otherwise, or else, else (see also አለበለዚያ)

ይሉኝታ *yəluňňəta* sensitivity to opinions of others, regard for others' feelings, concern about public opinion, sense of the proprieties
ይሉኝታ ፡ የለ(ውም) he is unscrupulous

ያለዚያ *yaläzziya* otherwise (see ያለ, -ዚያ)

የም *yämmə* + (imperfect) who, that, which (relative); see also እም-

ያም , see ያ

የምc , see ምc

የምስራች *yäməssərač* hurrah!, glad tidings, good news
የምስራች ፡ አለ congratulate, felicitate

የሙቶ *yämäto* platoon (see ሙቶ)

የሚጥል ፡ በሽታ *yämmiṭəl bäššəta* epilepsy (see ጣለ)

የሙጥኝ *yämuṭṭəňň* I am under your protection, I seek refuge with you (see *ማጠነ)
የሙጥኝ ፡ አለ be a client of someone rich or influential, appeal for protection

ያርድ *yard* yard, yardstick

የሰሚ ፡ ሰሚ *yäsämi sämi* hearsay (adj.), at second hand (see ሰማ)

ይስሙላ *yəsmulla* pose (see ሰማ)
ለይስሙላ only for show, just a pose

ይቅር ፡ አለ *yəqər alä* forgive, pardon (see ቀረ)
ይቅር ፡ ባይ *yəqər bay* magnanimous (ከኔ ፡ ይቅር ፡ ከኔ ፡ ይቅር ፡ የሚል ፡ ስምምነት compromise)
ይቅርታ, see below

ይቅርታ *yəqərta* pardon, apology, forgiveness, sorry!, excuse me! (see ይቅር, ቀረ)
ይቅርታ ፡ ለመነ apologize
ይቅርታ ፡ አደረገ forgive, excuse
ይቅርታ ፡ ጠየቀ excuse oneself, apologize

ይቅናህ *yəqnah* good luck! (see ቀና)

የበላይ *yäbälay* superior (in rank, office); see ላይ
የበላይነት *yäbälayənnät* dominion, superiority, mastery (upper hand)

ይበልጥ *yäbälṭ* more, best (adv.), increasingly (see በለጠ)

ይበልጡ *yəbälṭu* mostly, the major part
ይበልጡን(ም) especially, particularly, mainly
ይበልጥ ፡ ጊዜ most of the time
በይበልጥ more (adv.), better, by far the best
ከሁሉ ፡ ይበልጥ the most
ከሁሉም ፡ ይበልጥ above all

የብስ *yäbs* mainland, dry land

የበታች *yäbätačč* lower (in office), inferior, subordinate, junior (clerk, officer); see ታች

የቱ *yätu* (fem. የቷ) which?
የቱን ፡ ያህል *yätun yahəl* to what degree?, to what extent?
[See የት, የትም, የትኛው]

የት *yät*, ዬት *yet* where?
በየት where?
ከየት from whence?, from where?, from which?
ወዴት, see above
[See also የቱ, የትም, የትኛው]

የትም *yätəm* anywhere, any place, somewhere, wherever; (with a negative verb) nowhere; see የት
የትም ፡ ቦታ wherever; (with a negative verb) nowhere
በየትም everywhere
በየትም ፡ ቦታ wherever
በየትም ፡ ያለ universal
ከየትም (with a negative verb) nowhere

የተነሣ *yätänässa*, in በ - - - የተነሣ ፤ ከ - - - የተነሣ on account of, because of (see ነሣ)
በምን ፡ የተነሣ for what reason?

የትኛው *yätəňňaw* which?, which one? (see የት)
የትኛውም ፡ ቢሆን whichever

ያች *yačč*, ያቺ *yačči* that (fem.), that one (see also ያችኛዋ)

ይች *yəčč*, ይቺ *yəčči* this (fem.); see also ይህች

ያችኛዋ *yaččənñawa* that one (fem.); see ያች

የኔ ፡ ቢጤ *yäne biṭe* pauper (see እኔ, ቢጤ)

ያኔ *yanne* then, by then, at that moment, thereupon
[See also ያኔውኑ)

ያን *yan* that (direct object); see ያ
ያን ፡ ጊዜ then, at that time

ዩኒቨርሲቲ *yunivärsiti* university

ያኔውኑ *yannewnu* in the same breath, immediately, outright (adv.); see ያኔ

ያኛው *yaññaw* that there, that one (masc.); see ያ

የካቲት *yäkkatit* February

ይኸው *yəhäw* behold!, here it is!
ይኸውልህ *yəhäwəlləh* here it is!, behold!
ይኸውም *yəhäwəm* namely

ያው *yaw* the same (see ያ)
ያው ፡ ነው it is the same, all the same

የዋህ *yäwwah* meek, innocent (simple), frank, ingenuous
የዋህነት *yäwwahənnät* meekness, ingenuousness, innocence (simplicity)

ያዘ *yazä* catch, hold, seize, carry, keep, grasp, take hold of, possess, contain, handle (people), make an arrest, embrace (include), comprehend (include), assimilate (a lesson), retain, reserve (a seat), begin (when preceded by a verb or a verbal noun)
(ያዘው he has an access of [fever, headache])
(ይዞ *yəzo* with, including)
(ይዞ ፡ ጠፋ run off with)
(ጉዳይ ፡ ይዞኛል *gudday yəzoňňal* I am busy with something)
ተያዘ *täyazä*, passive of the preceding; be under arrest, be impounded, be filled (position), be occupied (country, seat), be busy (telephone)
አስያዘ *asyazä* help arrest someone, mortgage, pawn, impound
ተያያዘ *täyayazä* be connected, be held together, be linked, be tied up, catch fire, be on fire, be lit (a cigarette)
(በእሳት ፡ ተያያዘ be in flames, be on fire)
(ሲያያዝ ፡ መጣ it came down from ancient times)
አያያዘ *ayyayazä* unite, assemble, attach (fasten, jam), connect, link, clip together, append, join together, handle people, kindle, vt. (grass)
(እሳት ፡ አያያዘ start a fire)
ይዞታ, see below
መያዝ *mäyaz* arrest (n.)
መያዣ, see above
ተያዥ *täyaž* bail, bond, guarantor
አያያዝ, see above
የተያያዘ *yätäyayazä* connected, coherent
ያልተያያዘ *yaltäyayazä* disconnected, disjointed

የዘላለም *yäzälaläm* eternal (see ዓለም)

ይዞታ *yəzota* content, volume, capacity, control of something, dealings (commercial), situation, position (of army in a battlefield), state (situation); see ያዘ
የመሬት ፡ ይዞታ land tenure
የምድር ፡ ይዞታ landholding

የይለፍ ፡ ወረቀት *yäyəläf wäräqät* permit, passport, pass, visa, laissez-passer, safe conduct (see አለፈ, ወረቀት)

የይምሰል *yäyəmsäl* sham (n.); see መሰለ
ለይምሰል ፡ ነው it is just a gesture, it is a pretense

የይፉ, see ይፉ.

የግል, see ግል

የጋራ *yägara* collective, common, joint, reciprocal, mutual (see ጋራ)

የጋራ ፣ ጸጥታ collective security

የጋርዮሽ *yägarəyyoš* collective, joint, collectively (see ጋራ)

ይግባኝ *yəgbaňň* (n.) appeal in court, petition (see ገባ)
ይግባኝ ፣ አለ appeal (v.)
ይግባኝ ፣ ጠየቀ appeal (v.)

ይገባኛል ፣ ማለት *yəggäbbaňňal malät* claim (n.); see ገባ
ይገባኛል ፣ ባይ *yəggäbbaňňal bay* claimant

ይፋ, in በይፋ *bäyəfa* officially, openly, publicly, straight out
በይፋ ፣ ታወቀ become public
የይፋ *yäyəfa* official (visit)

የፊጥኝ ፣ (የፍጥኝ) ፣ አሰረ *yäfiṭṭəňň* (*yäfəṭṭəňň*) *assärä* tie the hands behind the back

ይ

ዳ ፣ አለ *da alä* be tardy
ዳተኛ *datäňňa* tardy

ድሃ ፤ ድጋ, see ድኻ

ደኅና *dähna* good, safe, well, fairly well, fine, all right, fair (price); see ዳነ
(በደኅና safely, in good health, well)
(በደኅና ፣ ያግባህ bon voyage!, may you arrive safely!; see ገባ)
ደኅና ፣ ነኝ I am fine
ደኅና ፣ ሁን goodbye!
ደኅና ፣ እደር *dähna ədär* good night! (lit. spend the night well!, sg. masc.)
ደኅና ፣ ዋል be well!, have a good day! (sg. masc.); see ዋለ
ደኅንነት *dähnənnät* safety, welfare, well-being, good state, salvation

ደላ *dälla* be comfortable
አደላ *adälla* make feel better
ተደላ, see above
ድሎት, see below

*ደላ, አደላ *adälla* be partial, show favor, favor, give preference, be biased, lean toward
አድልዎ *adləwo* bias, favoritism
የማያደላ *yämmayadäla* fair-minded, impartial
ያድላዊነት *yadlawinnät* preferential

ዱላ *dulla* club, cudgel
በዱላ ፣ አለ *bädulla alä* hit with a stick
ከዱላ ፣ አደረሰ lead to blows (see ደረሰ)
የዱላ ፣ ቅብብል ፣ እሽቅድድም relay race
ዱለኛ *dulläňňa* quarrelsome, prone to fighting

ዳሌ *dalle* hips (of woman)

ድል *dəl* victory, triumph
ድል ፣ ሆነ be conquered, be defeated
ድል ፣ መታ vanquish
ድል ፣ ተነሣ lose the battle (see ነሣ)
ድል ፣ ነሣ be victorious, win a victory, defeat
ድል ፣ አደረገ be victorious, win a victory, defeat, triumph

ድልህ, see ድልኽ

ደለለ *dällälä* (B) cajole, flatter, entice
በጉቦ ፣ ደለለ bribe (v.)
ድለላ *dəlläla* flattery, illusion
ድልል *dəlləl* gullible, dupe

ደለል *däläl* sediment, layer (of mud, of sand), deposit of mud, silt

ደላላ *dällala* broker, middleman, jobber

ደለበ *dälläbä* get fat (of ox)
አደለበ *adälläbä* fatten (oxen)
ድልብ *dəlb* fat (ox)

ዱለት, see ዶለት

ድሎት *dəlot* opulence, luxury (see ደላ)

ዶለተ *dollätä* (B) scheme, plot, conspire, intrigue
ዱለት (n.) *dulät* plot, conspiracy, scheme, intrigue

ዱለኛ, see ዱላ

ድልኸ *dəlləh* sauce made of pepper, roasted onion, garlic and salt

ደለደለ *däläddälä* level (the ground), level off, even out, flatten, smoothen, divide in equal parts, arrange, assign to a series of places (e.g. children to classes)
ተደላደለ *tädäladdälä* be well proportioned, be settled (in a house), be apportioned, be balanced (economy), be even (disposition), be allotted
አደላደለ *addäladdälä*, causative of the preceding
ደልዳላ *däldalla* level, adj. (ground), even, flat (place), well-proportioned
ድልድል *dəldəl* even, smooth
ድልድል *dələddəl* assignment, classification, distribution (arrangement) (የደረጃ ፡ ድልድል rating)

ዶለዶመ *doläddomä* become blunt (point), be dull (pencil)
ዱልዱም *duldum* blunt (pencil), dull
የዶለዶመ *yädoläddomä* pointless (pencil)

ድልድይ *dəldəy* bridge

ዳለጠ *dalläṭä* slip, slide
አዳለጠ *adalläṭä* make to slip, be slippery
አዳለጠ(ው) *adalläṭä(w)* he slipped

ደማ *dämma* bleed (vi.)
አደማ *adämma* draw blood
ደም , see below

ደም *däm* blood, complexion (see ደማ)
ደም ፡ መሰለ turn red (from anger)
ደም ፡ አፈሰሰ shed blood (see ፈሰሰ)
ደም ፡ ወረዳት *däm wärrädat* (or በደም ፡ ናት) she had her menses (see ወረደ)
ደም ፡ ቅዳ artery (see ቀዳ)
ደም ፡ መላሽ *däm mälläš* avenger (see መለሰ)
ደም ፡ ነውጠኛ revolutionary (n.); see ነወጠ
የደም ፡ መበቀል *yädäm mäbbäqäl* vendetta (see *በቀለ)

የደም ፡ ሥር blood vessel, vein, artery
(የ)ደም ፡ ግባት good complexion
ሥጋ ፡ ወደሙ· Holy Communion
ባለ ፡ ደም one whose duty is to avenge his kinsman
ደመኛ *dämäñña* mortal enemy, one who is engaged in the vendetta

ደሞ *dämmo* also, too, again (see also ደግሞ)

ዳማ *dama* bay (color)

ዳማ *dama* checkers

ዶማ *doma* pick (for digging), pickax, hoe

ደማም *dämam* effervescent
ደማም ፡ ናት she has a lovely color
ደማምነት *dämamənnät* charm

ደማሚት *dämamit* explosives, dynamite

ደማምነት *dämamənnät* charm (see ደማም)

ደመረ *dämmärä* (B) sum up, add, total up
ድምር *dəmmər* addition, sum, total (ጠቅላላ ፡ ድምር grand total, sum; see ጠቀለለ)
መደመር *mädämmär* addition

ዳመራ *damära*, ደመራ *dämära* large heap of poles placed on end so as to form a tall pile on the eve of the *mäsqäl*-feast, the entire ceremony itself

ደመሰሰ *dämässäsä* stamp out, crush (an uprising, a rebellion), exterminate, destroy, obliterate, efface (writing), wipe out
ደምሳሽ , see below

ደምሳሽ *dämsaš* destroyer (see ደመሰሰ)

ደመቀ *dämmäqä* be bright (color), be loud (color), become lively (game, party), warm up (become animated), be in abundance
አደመቀ *adämmäqä* enliven, brighten

ደማቅ *dämmaq* gay (color), loud (color), bright (color), rich (color)
ድምቀት *dəmqät* gaiety (bright appearance), dash (gaiety), brightness, luster, zest
ድምቀት ፡ ሰጠ animate (make lively)

ደምብ , see ደንብ

ድምበር , see ድንበር

ደምበኛን *dämbäžan* jug

ድመት *dəmmät* cat
የድመት ፡ ግልገል kitten

ደመነ *dämmänä* (B) be cloudy
ደመና , see below

ደመና *dämmäna*, ዳመና *dammäna* cloud
(see ደመነ)
ቀስተ ፡ ደመና rainbow
ደመናማ *dämmänamma* cloudy, nebulous

ደመኛ , see ደም

ደሞዝ *dämoz* salary, wages, pay
ደሞዝተኛ *dämoztäňňa* salaried worker

ደመደመ *dämäddämä* end, finish, terminate, wind up (a speech), conclude (a speech)
ተደመደመ *tädämäddämä* culminate, conclude (vi.)
መደምደሚያ *mädämdämiya* conclusion

*ደመጠ, አደመጠ *adämmäṭä* listen, pay attention, heed
አዳመጠ *addammäṭä* listen, pay attention, heed
አደማጭ , see above
ማድማጫ *madmäča*, in የጆር ፡ ማድማጫ earphone
ድምፅ , see below

ዳመጠ *dammäṭä* smash flat, crush cotton to separate the seeds, crush (with a roller)
[See ዳምጠው and ድምጥምጥ]

ድምጥምጥ, in ድምጥምጡን ፡ አጠፋ *dəməṭmäṭun aṭäffa* annihilate, raze (destroy); see ጠፋ, ዳመጠ

ዳምጠው *damṭäw* steam roller (lit. crush it); see ዳመጠ

ድምፅ *dəmṣ* voice, sound, tone, vote (see *ደመጠ)
ድምፅ ፡ ሰጠ vote (v.)
ድምፅ ፡ ማጉያ loudspeaker, amplifier
የድምፅ ፡ አናባቢ vowel (see *ነባ)
የድምፅ ፡ አውታሮች vocal cords

ደራ *därra* be in full swing, be bustling (market), be animated
(ተዳሩ ፡ ደርቷል *tədaru därtʷal* his marriage is successful)
ተዳራ *tädarra* flirt

ዱር *dur* woods, forest
ዱር ፡ አዳሪ vagabond, tramp, brigand, outlaw
የዱር ፡ አራዊት wild animal
ዱርዬ, see below

ዶር , see ድር

ዳራ *darä* give in marriage (on the part of parents), marry, marry off
የተዳረች *yätädaräčč* married (woman)
ያልተዳረች *yaltädaräčč* single (woman), lit. she who did not marry
ትዳር, see above

ዳሩ ፡ ግን *daru gən* nonetheless, but

ዳር *dar* edge, border (of lake), bank (of river), extremity, periphery, outskirts (see also ዳርቻ)
ዳር ፡ ዳር ፤ ዳር ፡ ዳሩን along
ዳር ፡ ዳሩን ፡ ሂዶ skirt (a city)
ዳር ፡ ዳር ፡ አለ beat around the bush
እ - - - ዳር ፤ ከ - - - ዳር ፤ በ - - - ዳር
on the edge of, along
ከዳር ፡ እስከ ፡ ዳር from start to finish, throughout
ከዳር ፡ ዳር from all sides
የባሕር ፡ ዳር seashore

ድሪ *dəri* necklace, string (of pearls)
ያንገት ፡ ድሪ necklace (see አንገት)

ድር *dər* warp, web
የሸረሪት ፡ ድር spider web

ድሮ *dəro* formerly, previously, in olden times, in the past, at one time, long ago, already (see also ዱሮ)
የድሮ *yädəro* previous, old, olden, old-fashioned, former
የድሮ ፡ ሰው ancient (n.)

ዶሮ *doro* chicken, hen, poultry
ዶሮ ፡ ወጥ stew made with chicken
ዶሮ ፡ ሲጮኸ *doro siçoh* early morning, lit. when the cock crows (see ጮኸ)
ሴት ፡ ዶሮ hen
አውራ ፡ ዶሮ cock, rooster

ድራማ *drama* drama
የድራማ dramatic

*ደረመሰ, ተደረመሰ *tädärämmäsä* collapse (bridge), cave in

ደረሰ *därräsä* arrive, reach (a place), happen, be ready (food), reach maturity
ደረሰ(ለት) *därräsä(llät)* he came to his help
ደረሰ(በት) *därräsä(bbät)* learn (find out), surprise someone, approach (come within the range for comparison), catch up with, come upon, befall
(የደረሰ grown-up)
(ለማስት ፡ ደረሰ he is old enough to marry)
(ለጋብቻ ፡ ደረሰች she is old enough for marriage)
(የልቡ ፡ አልደረሰለትም *yäləbbu aldärräsällätəm* he did not receive satisfaction)
አደረሰ *adärräsä* make reach, deliver (a package), bring forward (a message), lead to, result in
ድረስ, see below
ደርሶ ፡ መልስ ፡ ቲኬት *därso mäls tiket* round-trip ticket (see መለሰ)

ደረሰኝ *därräsäňň* receipt, voucher
ደራሽ ፡ ውኃ *däraš wəha* flash flood
ድርሻ, see below
መድረስ *mädräs* arrival
መድረሻ, see above
አድራሻ *adrašša* address (n.)

ደረሰ *därräsä* compose (poetry, a book, a symphony), write novels
ደራሲ, see below
ድርሰት, see below
ድርሳን *dərsan* homily

ደራሲ *därasi* author, writer, composer (see ደረሰ)
ቲያትር ፡ ደራሲ playwright
የሙዚቃ ፡ ደራሲ composer

ድረስ *dəräs* until, till, up to, as far as (see ደረሰ)
እ - - - ድረስ up to, until, as far as
እስከ - - - ድረስ (prep., conj.) till, until, up to

ድርሰት *dərsät* essay, treatise, composition (see ደረሰ compose)

ድርሳን *dərsan* homily (see ደረሰ compose)

ደረሰኝ *därräsäňň* receipt, voucher (see ደረሰ arrive)

ድርሻ *dərša* share, dues, stake (in business), portion (see ደረሰ arrive)

ደረቀ *därräqä* dry (vi.), be dry, dry out, dry up, be stiff (collar), be stubborn, be persistent, get strong (of wine), harden (vi., cement)
አደረቀ *adärräqä* make dry, drain (marshland), harden (vt., cement)
(ሆድ ፡ አደረቀ constipate)
ድርቅ ፡ አለ *dərrəqq alä* insist, be insistent
ድርቅ ፡ ያለ *dərrəqq yalä* curt, flat (refusal), dry (report), crisp (manner), stiff
ድርቅ ፡ ብዬ *dərrəqq bəyye* perverse (willful, evil)

ደረቅ *däräq* dry, dried, stubborn, persistent, stiff (collar), fat-free, strong (coffee)
ድርቅ *dərq* drought, dry (weather)
ድርቀት, see below
ድርቆሽ, see below

ድርቆሽ *dərqoš* fodder, hay (see ደረቀ)

ድርቀት *dərqät* dryness, aridity, dry spell, drought (see ደረቀ)
(የ)ሆድ ፡ ድርቀት constipation

ደረበ *därräbä* (B) put something atop of something, pile up, put on a blanket, wrap oneself in something, double a cloth
ደራረበ *därarräbä* cross (the legs), pile in layers one over the other
ተደራረበ *tädärarräbä* overlap, be concurrent
ደረብ ፡ አደረገ *därräbb adärrägä* throw on (a coat)
ድርብ *dərrəb* double, doubled
ድርብ ፡ ሰረዝ *dərrəb säräz* semicolon
ተደራቢ *tädärrabi* complementary, layer (of paper)
የሚደረብ ፡ ልብስ *yämmiddärräb ləbs* cover (for the bed)
[See also ድርብርብ]

ድርብርብ *dərəbrəb* stratum (see ደረበ)

ደረት *därät* chest (human), bosom, bust, breast
ደረቱን፡ነፋ he plucked up his courage
በደረቱ ፡ ተኛ lie prone
ሱቅ ፡ በደረቱ peddler

ድሪቶ *dərrito* patch, patched material

ዳርቻ *daräčča* extremity, end, limit, edge, shore, bank (of river); see also ዳር
የባሕር ፡ ዳርቻ seaside, shoreline, beach
በ - - - ዳርቻ alongside

ዲሬክተር *diräktär* director, principal (of school)
ዋና ፡ ዲሬክተር director general

ደርዘን *därzän* dozen

ዱርዬ *durrəyye* hoodlum, hooligan (see ዱር)

ደረደረ *däräddärä* assemble in a row, put in order one beside the other, range, align (objects), arrange in order, display (wares), enumerate
(ሰላም ፡ ደረደረ negotiate peace)
ድርድር *dərəddər* negotiation, terms (conditions), offer (for peace or reconciliation), display (of wares)
ድርድር *dərdər* orderly arrangement
መደርደሪያ *mädärdäriya* shelf

ደረደረ *däräddärä*, in በገና ፡ ደረደረ play the harp

ደረጃ *däräǧǧä* be built up, acquire strength, develop physically, be organized
አደራጃ *addäraǧǧä* arrange, put in order, array, organize, prepare, make ready, develop, further, outfit, build up (an army, industry)
ተደራጃ *tädäraǧǧä* get ready, be arranged
ድርጅት, see below

ደረጃ *däräǧa* step, stairs, stairway, rank (level), grade, degree, stage (degree), standard, social status, standing
ሁለተኛ ፡ ደረጃ ፡ ትምህርት ፡ ቤት high school
አንደኛ ፡ ደረጃ ፡ ትምህርት ፡ ቤት primary school
አበላላጭ ፡ ደረጃ *abbälalač däräǧa* superlative (see በለጠ)
የኑሮ ፡ ደረጃ standard of living, station in life

ድርጅት *dərəǧǧət* organization, installation, firm (concern), foundation (institution), institute (agency); see ደረጃ
የኅብረት ፡ ድርጅት cooperative
የንግድ ፡ ድርጅት firm (n.)

*ደረገ, አደረገ *adärrägä* make, do, act, wear (a hat), put on (glasses, shoes); it is also used in composite verbs

for the expression of the causative (as in ብቅ ፡ አደረገ cause to appear, as against ብቅ ፡ አለ appear)
ተደረገ tädärrägä be done, be made, come to pass, happen
ድርጊት dərgit action, doing, undertaking, event, episode, happening, incident
አድርጎ adrəgo combined with an adjective serves as an adverbial expression, as in ደኅና ፡ አድርጎ well, ግልጥ ፡ አድርጎ frankly
አድራጊ adragi active (verb), agent (grammar)
አድራጎት, see above

ደርግ därg committee
ንኡስ ፡ ደርግ subcommittee

ድርጎ dərgo gift of hospitality offered strangers, allowance of food

ደረገመ däräggämä shut fast (a door), slam (the door)
ድርግም ፡ ብሎ ፡ ተዘጋ dərgəmm bəlo täzägga snap shut
ብልጭ ፡ ድርግም ፡ አለ flicker, wink (of light)

ድርጊት, see *ደረገ

ደስ ፡ አለ däss alä be charming, be pleasing
ደስ ፡ አለ(ው) däss alä(w) rejoice, be delighted
ደስ ፡ አሰኘ däss assäňňä make happy, afford pleasure, please, gladden
ደስ ፡ ብሎት däss bəlot happily, gladly, with open arms
ደስ ፡ የሚል däss yämmi! charming, pleasant, lovely
እንኳን ፡ ደስ ፡ አለህ best wishes!, congratulations!
ደስታ, see below
[See also *ደሰተ, and ደስደስ ፡ አለ]

ዳስ das booth, hut made from poles and covered with leaves and branches

ደሳሳ däsasa squalid, sordid, shabby
ደሳሳ ፡ መኖሪያ slum

ደሳሳ ፡ ጎጆ hovel, shanty, miserable shack

ዳሰሰ dassäsä touch, feel (cloth), grope one's way, rub (massage), stroke

*ደሰተ, ተደሰተ tädässätä (B) enjoy, enjoy oneself, be satisfied, rejoice (vi.), take pleasure, be content, be glad, be pleased, be interested in (see ደስ ፡ አለ)
አስደሰተ asdässätä make happy, amuse, delight, rejoice (vt.), divert (amuse), please, entertain (amuse), interest (of a book)
አስደሳች asdässač delightful, agreeable, pleasing, lovely, pleasant, cheerful, exciting (news), enjoyable, bright (smile)
የሚያስደስት yämmiyasdässət pleasing, charming, glad (news), amusing, gay, joyful, exciting, interesting
የተደሰተ yätädässätä amused. happy
ደስታ, see below
መደሰቻ mäddäsäča place of amusement

ደሴት däset island
የደሴት insular

ደስታ dässəta joy, happiness, pleasure, delight, amusement (see ደስ ፡ አለ)
በደስታ happily, gladly, with open arms
በደስታ ፡ የተሞላ exuberant (see ሞላ)
በደስታ ፡ ሮጐጠ cheer (v.)
የደስታ festive
ደስተኛ dässətäňňa joyful, happy, merry

ድስት dəst saucepan, casserole

ደስተኛ, see ደስታ

ዴስክ desk desk

ደስደስ ፡ አለ(ው) dässədäss alä(w) be pleased (see ደስ ፡ አለ)
የደስደስ yädässədäss joy, charm
የደስደስ ፡ አላት she is charming
የደስደስ ፡ ያለው lovable, charming

ደቅ ፡ መዝሙር *däqqä mäzmur* disciple

ደቃ *däqqa* beat (the breast)

ዶቃ *doqa* bead of glass

ዳቀለ *daqqälä* crossbreed, fuse
ዲቃለ, see below

ዲቃለ *diqala* bastard, illegitimate child,
hybrid, cross (mixing of breeds);
see ዳቀለ

ደቄሰ *däqqʷäsä* (B) crush to a fine
powder, pulverize (salt, pepper)

ደቀቀ *däqqäqä* be fine, be thin, be
skinny, be minute
አደቀቀ *adäqqäqä* make fine, pulverize, grind (meat with teeth), mash
(ሰውነቱን ፡ አደቀቀ leave one exhausted)
ድቅቅ ፡ ያለ *dəqəqq yalä* decrepit
ደቂቅ *däqiq* fine, minute (adj.), delicate
ደቃቃ *däqaqa* fine (sand), powdered,
flimsy (boat)

ደቂቃ *däqiqa* minute (n.)

ዱቄት *duqet* flour, powder
(የ)ዱቄት ፡ ወተት powdered milk
ያበባ ፡ ዱቄት pollen (see አበባ)
የፉርኖ ፡ ዱቄት white flour
የፊት ፡ ዱቄት powder (for the face)

ዲቁና *diqqunna* deaconship, rank of
deacon (see ዲያቁን)

ደቀደቀ *däqäddäqä* stamp (earth with
one's foot), pound (clay, ground)

*ደባ, አደባ *adäbba* sneak, prowl, creep
stealthily, lurk, stalk

ደቦ *däbo* communal labor

ዱባ *dubba* pumpkin, squash

ዱቤ *dube* credit, n. (delayed payment),
goods bought on credit
በዱቤ ፡ ገዛ buy on credit

ዱብ ፡ ዱብ ፡ አለ *dubb dubb alä* trickle (of
tears), tumble down, thud

ዳቦ *dabbo* bread (made of wheat), loaf
of raised bread (as opposed to እንጀራ)
ዳቦ ፡ ቆሎ *dabbo qolo* small round
dough balls which have been roasted
until they are dry and brittle
ዳቦ ፡ ደፋ make bread

ድብ *dəbb* bear (n.)

ደበለ *däbbälä* (B) room with someone
ተደበለ *tädabbälä* room with someone, double up in a room, be associated
አደበለ *addabbälä* let someone room
with someone, mingle
ደባል *däbbal* roommate, boarder

ደበለለ *däbällälä* throw down (in wrestling)

*ደበለለ, ተንደባለለ *tändäballälä* wallow,
roll, vi. (in the dust)

ደበለቀ *däballäqä* mix (vt.), mix up, confuse, confound
ተደበለቀ *tädäballäqä* mingle (vi.),
intermingle (vi.), merge, be mixed,
be associated
አደበላለቀ *addäbälalläqä* mix up, intermingle (vt.), agglomerate, amalgamate
ድብልቅ *dəbəlləq* mixed, mixture, confused, amalgamation, compound
[See also ድብልቅልቅ]

ደብልቅልቅ *dəbləqləq* confusion (see
ደበለቀ)

*ደቦለቦለ, አድቦለቦለ *adboläbbolä* round
(make round), roll (dough)
ድቡልቡል *dəbulbul* round, spherical

ደብር *däbr* (pl. አድባራት *adbarat*) mountain, sanctuary, parish, church served
by married priests
የደብር ፡ ሕዝብ parishioners
የደብር ፡ አለቃ vicar

ዳበረ *dabbärä* thrive (business)
አዳበረ *adabbärä* fertilize, enrich
(the soil), build up (a business), develop (the muscles, natural resources),

cultivate (one's mind), advance (further), promote, consolidate (gains)
ማዳበር *madabär* culture (physical)
ማዳበሪያ *madabäriya*, in የመሬት ፡ ማዳበሪያ fertilizer

ደበሰ *dabbäsä* touch lightly, grope, feel (touch), feel one's way, stroke
ደባበሰ *däbabbäsä* palpate, caress, pat (a child), stroke, fondle

*ደበሰበሰ, አድበሰበሰ *adbäsäbbäsä* dodge, cloud (an issue), evade (a question)
አድብስብሶ ፡ አለፈ *adbäsbəso alläfä* hedge (avoid giving a direct answer)

ደበቀ *däbbäqä* (B) conceal, hide (vt.), shelter (hide), cover up, disguise, mask
ተደበቀ *tädäbbäqä* hide (vi.), remain under cover
†ድብቅ *dəbbəq* hidden
መደበቂያ *mäddäbäqiya* hideout
ድብብቆሽ, see below

ድብቅ *dəbbəq* hidden (see ደበቀ)
በድብቅ secretly, on the sly, furtively
በድብቅ ፡ አስገባ smuggle into

ደቡብ *däbub* south
የደቡብ ፡ ዋልታ South Pole
ደቡባዊ *däbubawi* southern, southerly

ድባብ *dəbab* large processional umbrella for the ark

ድብብቆሽ *dəbəbbəqoš* hide-and-seek (game); see ደበቀ

ደብተራ *däbtära* unordained member of the clergy who is well educated in the Ethiopian church rituals, literature and the scriptures
የደብተራ ፡ አማርኛ refined Amharic

ደብተር *däbtär* notebook, register

ደበነ *däbbänä* be tight (knot)
ድብን ፡ ያለ *dəbbənn yalä* heavy (sleep), sound (sleep), tight (knot)

ደበዘዘ *däbäzzäzä* tarnish, vi. (lose luster)

አደበዘዘ *adäbäzzäzä* fade, vt. (a curtain), blot (a page), blur (a page)
ደብዛዛ *däbzazza* subdued (light), dim, blurred (print), indistinct (shape), nebulous (idea)
ደብዛዝ ፡ ያለ *däbzäzz yalä* quiet (color), somber (color), dull (color), pale (star)

ደበደበ *däbäddäbä* attack, beat, assault, rap (the table), pound (on the door), slam (the fist on the table)
(በቦምብ ፡ ደበደበ bombard)
(በጥይት ፡ ደበደበ execute by shooting)
ተደባደበ *tädäbaddäbä* come to blows, beat each other up
ድብደባ *dəbdäbä* beating, assault
(የቦምብ ፡ ድብደባ bombing)

ደብዳቤ *däbdabbe* letter, epistle, dispatch
የሹመት ፡ ደብዳቤ letter of accreditation (diplomatic)

ድብዳብ *dəbdab* sheep or goat skin serving as pack saddle

ዳተኛ *datäñña* tardy (see ዳ ፡ አለ)
ዳተኛነት *datäññannät* tardiness

ደን *dänn* forest, woods
ደን ፡ አለበሰ afforest
ደን ፡ የለበሰ bushy (land), forested

ዳነ *danä* be saved, be spared, heal (vi.), be cured, recover, recuperate, get well again
አዳነ *adanä* save, rescue, cure, heal (vt.), redeem (save)
[See ደኅና, መድን, መድኃን, መድኃኒት]

ደነሰ *dännäsä* (B) dance (European style)
ዳንስ *dans* European-style dance
ደናሽ *dännaš* dancer
ዳንሰኛ *dansäñña* dancer

ደነቀ *dännäqä* be admirable, be wonderful, be marvelous, astonish, surprise, evoke admiration

ተደነቀ *tädännäqä* be surprised, be astonished, wonder, marvel at, be admired

አደነቀ *adännäqä* admire, applaud (praise), esteem, cheer

አዳነቀ *addannäqä* exaggerate

አስደነቀ *asdännäqä* astonish, surprise, impress, awe, amaze, be amazing

ድንቅ *dənq* marvel, wonder, astonishment, astonishing, wonderful, marvelous, admirable, brilliant (speaker)

አድናቆት, see above

አስደናቂ *asdännaqi* wonderful, admirable, impressive, magnificent, brilliant (performance)

አስደናቂነት *asdännaqinnät* magnificence

የሚደነቅ *yämmiddännäq* admirable, remarkable, impressive

የሚያደንቅ *yämmiyadänq* admirer

የሚያስደንቅ *yämmiyasdännəq* admirable, amazing, exciting

ደነቈረ *dänäqqʷärä* be deaf, be stupid

አደነቈረ *adänäqqʷärä* deafen

ደንቆሮ *dänqoro* deaf, ignorant, stupid

ድንቁርና *dənqurənna* deafness, ignorance, stupidity

*ደነቀፈ, ተደናቀፈ *tädänaqqäfä* falter, stumble, stagger, trip (vi.)

አደናቀፈ *addänaqqäfä* make to stumble, trip (vt.), hamper the movement

ደንብ *dänb* rule, principle, statute, regulation, established procedure, ordinance, provision (see also ደምብ)

የደንብ ፡ ልብስ uniform (n.)

ለደንብ ፡ ያህል ፡ ነው- it is a pure formality, it is a matter of form

በደንብ as it should be, in accordance with the rule, properly, perfectly, thoroughly, pretty well, nicely

እንደ ፡ ደንቡ- accordingly, as is the rule

ውስጠ ፡ ደንብ bylaw

ደንበኛ *dänbäñña* regular, correct, a person with whom one has regular

business dealings, customer, patron, client (in a shop, of a lawyer)

ደንበኛ ፡ ነው- patronize

ደነበረ *dänäbbärä* jump (be startled), shy (v.), flee in fright, bolt, startle (vi.)

አስደነበረ *asdänäbbärä* stupefy (astound), stun, take by surprise

ድንበር *dənbär* border, borderline, boundary, limit, frontier (see also ድምበር)

ደንበኛ, see ደንብ

ደንታ ፡ የለኝም *dänta yälläññəm* I don't care

ድንች *dənnäčč* potato

ድንክ *dənk* dwarf, midget

ድንኳን *dənkʷan* tent

ድንኳን ፡ ተከለ pitch a tent

ደነዘ *dännäzä* (B) become blunt (knife, blade), lose the edge, be dull (of intellect), be slow to understand

ደነዝ *dänäz* blunt (knife), dull (knife)

ደነዘዘ *dänäzzäzä* grow numb (part of the body), become stiff, be in a stupor, lose sensation, be dull

ደነዘዘ(ው-) *dänäzzäzä(w)* be asleep (foot)

አደነዘዘ *adänäzzäzä* deaden (of drug), benumb, make insensitive, stupefy (dull the senses)

ደንዛዛ *dänzazza* numb, rigid, stiff

ዶኒያ *doniyya* bag, sack (see also ጆኒያ)

ደነደነ *dänäddänä* be fat, be plump (big and fat)

ደንዳና *dändanna* fat (ox), fleshy, plump

ድንጉላ *dəngula* stallion

ድንግል *dəngəl* celibate, virgin

ድንግል ፡ መሬት virgin soil

ድንግል ፡ ማርያም Virgin Mary

ድንግልና *dəngələnna* chastity, virginity

*ደነገረ, ተደናገረ *tädänaggärä* be perturbed, be uneasy, be perplexed
አደናገረ *addänaggärä* perplex, perturb, mix one up (confuse), disconcert, confuse, puzzle (perplex)

ድንገት *dəngät* surprise, accident, sudden, suddenly, unexpected, by chance, in case, perhaps
በድንገት all of a sudden, accidentally, unexpectedly
ድንገተኛ *dəngätäňňa* abrupt (sudden), sudden, unexpected, emergency (adj.)

ደንጊያ *dängiya*, ድንጋይ *dəngay* rock, stone
የደንጊያ ፡ ከሰል coal
ልብ ፡ ድንጋይ hard-hearted
የከበረ ፡ ድንጋይ gem
ጥቁር ፡ ድንጋይ slate
ድንጋያማ *dəngayamma* stony, rocky

ደነገገ *dänäggägä* decree (v.), institute (law), regulate, formulate, define (laws)
ድንጋጌ *dənəggage* legislative decree, ordinance, decree, regulation

ደነገጠ *dänäggäṭä* be alarmed, startle (vi.), be taken aback, be unpleasantly surprised, be terrified, be shocked, be frightened
ተደነገጠ *tädänäggäṭä* be scared, be dismayed
አስደነገጠ *asdänäggäṭä* appall, scare (vt.), startle (vt.), terrify, frighten, shock
ድንግጥ ፡ አለ *dəngəṭṭ alä* start (make a sudden movement of shock)
ድንጉጥ *dəngguṭ* shy (animal), timid (animal), frightened
ድንጋጤ *dənəggaṭe* shock, fright, alarm, dismay, consternation

ደንጓጡር *dängäṭur* bridesmaid, lady-in-waiting

ደነፋ *dänäffa* brag, boast, raise hell, bluster, be enraged
ድንፋታ *dənfata* bragging, boom (of cannon)

ዳኘ *daňňä* arbitrate, judge (v.)
ዳኛ *daňňa* judge, umpire
ዳኝነት *daňňənnät* judgeship, arbitration, judgement (ability to judge something)
የዳኝነት judicial (system)

ደኝ *dəňň* sulphur

ዳኝነት, see ዳኘ

ዱካ *duka* footprint, imprint, trace, trail, track

ድኵላ *dək*ʷ*la* antelope

ደከመ *däkkämä*, ደከመ(ው) *däkkämä(w)* get tired, be failing, fatigue (vi.), be weak, strive, endeavor, concern oneself with
አደከመ *adäkkämä* weaken, tire (vt.), fatigue (vt.), debilitate, exhaust
ተደከመ *tädakkämä* weaken (vi.), be exhausted, be tired out, flag (of a horse)
ደካማ *däkkama* tired, weary, infirm, weak, feeble, frail
ድካም *dəkam* fatigue, weakness, feebleness, exertion, exhaustion, effort, toil, pains (effort), hard work
ደካማነት *däkkamannät* frailty, weakness
አድካሚ *adkami* tiresome, tiring, strenuous, laborious (job)
የደከመ *yädäkkämä* feeble, tired, weary

ዶክተር *doktär* doctor, physician

ዳክዬ *dakəyye* duck (n.)

ዳኸ *dahä* crawl, creep, walk on all fours like a baby

ድኻ *dəha* poor (see ድኸየ)
ከድኻ ፡ ቤተሰብ of humble family

ከድኻ ፡ የተወለደ of mean birth (see ወለደ)
የእግዜር ፡ ድኻ poor creature

ድኽነት dəhənnät poverty, penury, humble circumstances (see ደኸየ)

ደኸየ dähäyyä be poor, be impoverished, be indigent
አደኸየ adähäyyä impoverish
†ድኻ dəha poor
ድኽነት, see above

ደዌ däwe disease, illness, sickness

ደወለ däwwälä (B) ring a bell, strike (of a clock), call up, call on the telephone, dial
ደወል däwäl bell.
መደወያ mädäwwäya button of doorbell

ዳውላ dawəlla measure of 20 qunna (or 100 kg)

*ደወረ, አዳወረ adawwärä wind on the spool
ድውር dəwər spool
ማዳወሪያ madawäriya distaff

ዳዊት dawit Psalter

ዲያቆን diyaqon (pl. ዲያቆናት diyaqonat) deacon
ዲቁና diqqunna deaconship, rank of deacon

ዲዳ dida, ድዳ dəda mute, dumb (one who does not hear), idiot

ድድ dədd gum (of teeth)

ደደቀ däddäqä (B) hit, pound hard

ደደብ däddäb idiot, stupid, obtuse

ደጅ däǧǧ doorway, entrance, outside, outdoors, out of doors
ደጅ ፡ ሰላም the eastern door of the church, gateway of church compound
ደጅ ፡ ወጥ out of doors
ደጅ ፡ ጠና wait at someone's door for favors, court favor

እደጅ outside (adv.)
ደጃፍ, see below
[See also ደጃች, ደጃዝማች]

ደጃች däǧǧač, abbreviated form of ደጃዝማች

ደጀን däǧän rear guard

ደጃዝማች däǧǧazmač honorary title (see ደጅ, አዝማች and ደጃች)

ደጃፍ däǧǧaf front of house, doorstep, doorway, entrance (see ደጅ and አፍ)

ደጋ däga highland (about 5000 feet up)
ወይና ፡ ደጋ temperate zone (at intermediate altitude); see ወይን
ደጋኛ dägäňňa highlander

ደግ dägg kind, good, gentle, nice, gracious, good-hearted
ደግ ፡ አድራጊ virtuous
በደግ ፡ ተመለከተ view with favor
ደግነት, see below

ድግ dəg long body band (worn wrapped tightly around the middle of the body)

ድጓ dəggʷa Geez hymn book with musical notations

ደገመ däggämä repeat, do again, recite prayers, review a lesson, give a second time
ተደገመ tädäggämä happen again, be repeated
ደጋገመ dägaggämä reiterate, repeat again and again
ደገማ dägäma recitation
ደግሞ dägmo furthermore, besides, moreover, also, once more, again, too (see also ደሞ)
ዳግም dagəm second
ድግማ dəggäma repetition, second serving
ደጋግሞ dägagmo repeatedly, time after time, again and again
ድግምት, see below
ዳግማዊ, see below
ዳግመኛ, see below

የተደጋገመ *yätädägaggämä* frequent (adj.)
ድግግሞሽ, see below

ድግምት *dəgəmt* incantation, charm (see ደገመ)

ዳግመኛ *dagmäňňa* second, another time, again (see ደገመ)

ዳግማዊ *dagmawi* second (numerator preceding the name of a king); see ደገመ

ዲግሪ *digri* degree (diploma)

ደገሰ *däggäsä* (B) give a feast, make preparations for a banquet
ተደገሰ *tädäggäsä* the banquet is prepared, be in store (of trouble)
ድግስ *dəggəs* festive meal, feast, banquet
ድግስ ፡ አበላ give a feast

ደጐሰ *däggʷäsä* (B) make designs on leather, decorate the book cover

ዳጉሳ *dagussa* small millet

*ደገተ, አዳገተ *addaggätä* climb a mountain, tire, fatigue (of an ascent), be difficult, be hard
አዳገተ(ው) he is unable, he has difficulty in doing something
አዳጋች *addagač* formidable (task), difficult
ዳገት, see below

ዳገት *dagät* uphill road, slope, ascent (see *ደገተ)
ዳገቱን uphill (adv.)

ደገነ *däggänä* (B) point (a gun, a hose)

ዳጋን *dägan* bow for carding wool or cotton

ደግነት *däggənnät* kindness, goodness, bounty, virtue (see ደግ)
ደግነቱ luckily, happily, fortunately
የደግነት generous (act), benevolent, kind, kindly (adj.)

ደገኛ *dägäňňa* highlander (see ደጋ)

*ደገደገ, አደገደገ *adägäddägä* bring the *šämma* down over the shoulder and tuck it around the waist as a sign of respect

ድግግሞሽ *dəgəggəmoš* frequency (of the radio); see ደገመ

ደገፈ *däggäfä* (B) support (vt.), sustain, prop up, hold up, favor (support), rally to, second (a motion), be in favor of, side with, back, stand by one
ተደገፈ *tädäggäfä*, passive of the preceding; rest against, lean on, prop oneself against
አስደገፈ *asdäggäfä* rest, vt. (lean)
ደገፍ ፡ አለ *dägäff alä* lean, vi. (rest against something for support)
ደጋፊ *däggafi* partisan, adherent, backer, support, sponsor, benefactor
ደገፍ, see below
ድጋፍ *dəgaf* support, endorsement, auspices, backing
ደጋፊነት *däggafinnät* adherence (attachment)
መደገፊያ *mäddägäfiya* brace (n.), buttress, arm (of chair), bracket, railing
የሚደግፍ *yämmidäggəf* favorable (report)

ደገፍ *däggəf*, in ጆሮ ፡ ደገፍ mumps (see ደገፈ)

ዳጠ *daṭä* run over (vt.), roll ove something, mash (e.g. cooked vegetables), crush
አዳጠ *adaṭä* cause to slip
አዳጠ(ው) he slipped on something

ዳፋ *däffa* turn downwards, bend (the neck), overturn, tip over (a glass), overturn (a lamp), spill (milk), empty out (a container), dump (coffee grounds), make someone fall flat on his face, put on (a cap)
(በአፉ ፡ ዳፋ turn upside down (a glass)
(አንገቱን ፡ ዳፋ he dropped his eyes, he hung his head)

(ዘውድ ፡ ደፋ be crowned)
(ዳቦ ፡ ደፋ bake bread)
ተደፋ tädäffa fall upside down, fall
flat, pore over (a book)
(በፊት ፡ ጢሞ ፡ ተደፋ fall on one's
face, fall upside down)
(ተደፍቶ ፡ ተኛ tädäfto tänna lie prone)
ደፋ ፡ ቀና ፡ አለ däfa qäna alä bustle
about
ደፋ ፡ ቀና ፡ አደረገ nod (the head),
incline
ድፎ, see below

ደፍ däf doorsill

ድፎ dǝfo large wheat bread cooked
with fire above and below (see ደፋ)
ድፎ ፡ ዳቦ baked bread

ዶፍ dof heavy rain, downpour, cloud-
burst

ደፈረ däffärä be bold, dare, be impudent, be audacious, be disrespectful,
venture (dare), violate
ተዳፈረ tädaffärä take liberties with,
get too familiar, treat with impudence
አደፋፈረ addäfaffärä encourage, exhort (give courage), embolden
ደፋር däffar bold, intrepid, daring,
fearless, venturesome, adventurous,
impudent, audacious
ደፋርነት däffarǝnnät temerity, boldness
ድፍረት, see below

ደፈረሰ däfärräsä become turbid (water), get muddy (liquid)
ድፍርስ dǝfrǝs muddy, turbid

ድፍረት dǝfrät audacity, boldness, in-
trepidity, impudence (see ደፈረ)
የድፍረት heroic (measure)

ደፋርነት, see ደፈረ

ደፈቀ däffäqä dip, dunk, immerse,
pound grain to get the kernels out;
foam

ደፈነ däffänä fill up (hole in the
ground), stop a leak, clog, plug up,
block up, close (eyes), cover (fire)

ድፍን dǝfǝn stopped up, solid (not
hollow), entire, all of it
ድፍን ፡ ዓለም the whole world, everybody
በደፈናው bädäfänaw in generalities,
wholly
የተዳፈነ yätädaffänä latent

*ደፈጠ, አደፈጠ adäffäṭä lurk, lie in
wait for, lie in ambush
አድፍጦ ፡ ጠበቀ adfǝṭo ṭäbbäqä lie in
wait
ደፈጣ däfäṭa ambush (n.)
የደፈጣ ፡ ተዋጊ (yä)däfäṭa täwagi guerilla
የደፈጣ ፡ አደጋ ፡ ጣይ one who lies in
ambush

ዲፕሎማት diplomat diplomat

ጀ

[See also ገ]

ጀል ǧǝl fool, imbecile, silly, stupid,
foolish (chatter)
ጀልነት ǧǝlǝnnät stupidity, silliness,
folly, absurdity

ጀልባ ǧälba small boat
የማመላለሻ ፡ ጀልባ ferry

ጀልቦ ǧǝlbo top (toy)

ጅምላ ǧǝmla wholesale
በጅምላ bäǧǝmla wholesale (adv.),
in bulk

ጀመረ ǧämmärä (B) commence, start
(vt., vi.), begin (vt., vi.), set about
(see also ገመረ)
ተጀመረ täǧämmärä begin (vi.)
ጀማሪ ǧämmari beginner
ከ - - - ጀምሮ kä - - - ǧämmǝro since
(prep.), beginning from
ከ + perfect + ጀምሮ since (conj.)
†መጀመሪያ mäǧämmäriya start, beginning, first, front

ጀምበር *ğämbär* disc of sun (see also ፀሐይ ጀምበር)

ጅማት *ğəmmat* sinew, nerve, tendon (see also ሥርማት)

ጅምናስቲክ *ğəmnastik* physical exercise
ጅምናስቲክ ፡ ሠራ exercise (v.)

ጆሮ *ğoro* ear, handle (of cup)
ጆሮ ፡ ደግፍ mumps
ጆሮ ፡ ጠቢ informer, tattler (see ጠባ)
(የ)ጆሮ ፡ ግንድ area of the head around the ears

ጀርመን *ğärmän* German
(የ)ጀርመን ፡ አገር (*yä*)*ğärmän agär* Germany
ጀርመንኛ *ğärmänəňňa* German (language)

ጀርባ *ğärba* back (part of body), loin, reverse (of coin), rear (back); behind (prep.)
ከ - - - ጀርባ ፤ እ - - - ጀርባ ፤ ወደ - - - ጀርባ behind
በስተጀርባ in the back
ከ - - - በስተጀርባ in the rear of, in the background

ጃርት *ğart* porcupine

ጅረት *ğərät* brook, creek, tributary (river), confluent

ጅራት *ğərat* tail (see also ሥራት)
ጅራተ ፡ ቀጭን giraffe
ጅራታም ፡ ኮከብ comet

ጅራፍ *ğəraf* whip (used mainly by plowmen when plowing)

ጌሶ *ğesso* plaster cast

ጅብ *ğəb* hyena

ጀበና *ğäbäna* coffee pot, kettle
የሻይ ፡ ጀበና teakettle

ጀብዱ *ğäbdu* act of bravery, adventure, exploit, valor

ጀብዱ ፡ የበዛበት *ğäbdu yäbäzzabbät* adventurous
የጀብዱ heroic, valorous
የጀብዱ ፡ ሰው adventurer
ባለ ፡ ጀብዱ hero

ጅን *ğin* spirit, genie

ጃን ፡ ሜዳ *ğan meda* race course at Addis Ababa

ጃኖ *ğano* kind of *näṭäla*-dress with wide red stripes

ጃንሆይ *ğanhoy*, title used in addressing the Emperor

ጄኔራል *ğeneral* general

ጀንበር *ğänbär* sun (see also ጀምበር)

*ጀነነ, ተጀነነ *täğännänä* (B) swagger

ጁንያ *ğunəyya*, ጁኒያ *ğuniyya*, ጆንያ *ğonəyya* sack, bag (see also ዶኒያ)

ጀንደረባ *ğändäräba* eunuch

ጃንጥላ *ğanṭəla* umbrella, parasol, parachute (see also ጥንጥላ)

ጃንፎ *ğänfo* iron counterbalance on the butt of the spear

ጂኦሎጂ *ğioloği* geology

ጂኦግራፊ *ğiografi* geography

ጃኬት *ğakket* jacket

ጀውጀው *ğäwwäğäw* swing, trapeze
ጀውጀው ፡ ተጫወተ swing, vi. (play on the swings); see *ጫወተ

ጃጀ *ğağğä* be senile

ጅጌ *ğəge* communal labor

ጅግራ *ğəgra* guinea hen (see also ሥግራ)

ጀግና *ğägna* valiant, brave, gallant, hero, courageous
ጀግንነት, see below

ጀግንነት *ğägnənnät* bravery, valor, courage (see ጀግና)

የጀግንነት heroic, valiant (deed)
የጀግንነት ፡ ሙያ heroism

ጀፈ ፡ አሞራ ǧoffe amora vulture

ጃፓን ǧapan Japan

ጋ

ጋ ga by (near), near to, close to
እ - - - ጋ close to, near to
ሌላ ፡ ጋ ፤ ሌላጋ somewhere else, elsewhere
ሌላ ፡ ጋ ፡ ዬት where else?
እንዱ ፡ ጋ somewhere
እንድጋ together
እዚህ ፡ ጋ əzzih ga over here
እዚያ ፡ ጋ əzziya ga there, over there

*ጌ -ge, in ራስጌ rasge the head part
(especially in a bed), እግርጌ əgərge,
ግርጌ gərge at the foot of, እጅጌ əǧǧəge sleeve

ጎህ goh, ጉህ gʷäh dawn, daybreak
ጎህ ፡ ሲቀድ at dawn, at daybreak
(see ቀደደ)

ገሃነም gähannäm hell, Gehenna

ገላ gäla body
ገላ ፡ ታጠብ take a bath (see አጠብ)

ጉሎ gulo castor bean plant
የጉሎ ፡ ፍሬ castor bean
ጉሎ ፡ ዘይት castor oil

ጋለ galä be red-hot, be burning, be
red from heating (metal), heat up
የጋለ hot (pan), fervid (feeling), fierce
(attack), fiery (speech), warm (welcome), heated (argument)
የጋለ ፡ ስሜት animation, ardor, enthusiasm
ግለት gəlät intensity (of anger)

ግል gəll, in የግል personal (matter,
property), private, individual, exclu-
sive, one's own (see ገለለ)

በግል individually, alone, in private
በየግል bäyyägəll individually
ግለኛ gəlläñña individualistic
ግላዊ gəllawi personal
ግላዊነት gəllawinnät individuality

ጐላ gʷälia be magnified, be clear, stand
out
አጐላ agʷälla make clear, magnify,
accentuate, amplify, emphasize
ጐልቶ gʷälto clearly, sharply
ጐላ ፡ ያለ gʷäla yalä prominent, conspicuous
ማጐሊያ, see above
ማጐያ, see above
[See also ጉልህ]

*ጐላ, አጐላላ agʷlalla mistreat, inflict
hardship on
ማጐላላት harsh treatment

ጓል gʷal lump (of earth), clod turned
up in plowing

ጉልህ guləh evident, visible, obvious,
conspicuous, noticeable, plain (clear),
flagrant, gross (error), vivid (description), loud (voice); see ጐላ
በጉልህ plainly

ገለለ gällälä cut (wood, grass); retire, withdraw (vi.), stand aside, get
out of the way
ተገለለ tägällälä keep apart (vi.), withdraw (from society), be isolated, be
separated
(ተገሎ ፡ ቆመ tägällo qomä stand aloof)
አገለለ agällälä keep in the background (vt.), withdraw (vt.)
(ራሱን ፡ አገለለ seclude oneself)
ገለል ፡ አለ gäläll alä give way, move
aside
ገለል ፡ አደረገ part (vt.), make give
way, segregate
ገለልተኛ, see below
ግል, see above

*ጋለለ, ተንጋለለ tängallälä lie down, lie
on one's back, lie back (in an armchair)

ጉልላት *gullǝlat* clay pot put on the top of an Ethiopian house, cupola, dome

ገለልተኛ *gälältäñña* secluded, detached, aloof, solitary, isolated (house), lonely, neutral (see ገለለ)
ገለልተኛነት *gälältäññannät* neutrality, life of retirement, detachment (aloofness), seclusion

ጉለመሰ *gʷälämmäsä* mature, vi. (of a person), become physically developed
አጉለመሰ *agʷälämmäsä* mature (the character), elevate (the mind)
ጉልማሳ *gʷälmassa* one who has reached the age of young adulthood, vigorous, virile, robust
የጉልማሶች ፡ ትምህርት *yägʷälmassočč tämhǝrt* adult literacy
ጉልምስና *gʷälmǝssǝnna* adolescence

ጋለሞታ *galämota* prostitute, dissolute woman

ገላመጠ *gälammäṭä* look at disapprovingly, glare at

ገለሸጠ *gäläššäṭä* skin (scrape)

ገለባ *gäläba* straw, chaff, hull (of peanut)

ጋለበ *galläbä* gallop (vi.), set at a gallop, make to gallop, ride a horse
ግልቢያ *gǝlbiya* gallop (n.), galloping, horse riding

ግልብ *gǝlb* shallow

ጉልበት *gulbät* knee, strength, might, vigor, energy, effort
የጉልበት physical
የጉልበት ፡ ሎሚ kneecap
የጉልበት ፡ ሥራ physical labor
የጉልበት ፡ ዋጋ labor cost
የኤሌክትሪክ ፡ ጉልበት electric power, electric energy

ግልቢያ, see ጋለበ

ገለበጠ *gäläbbäṭä* turn upside down, overturn, pour liquid from one con-

tainer to another, overthrow, turn over (a page), copy, upset, subvert
ተገለበጠ *tägäläbbäṭä* passive of preceding; capsize (of a boat), tip over (vi.)
አገለበጠ *aggälabbäṭä* leaf through (a book), turn this way and that
ግልባጥ *gǝlbaṭ* inversion
ግልባጭ, see below

ግልባጭ *gǝlǝbbač* copy (of book, of letter); see ገለበጠ

*ገላታ, አንገላታ *angälatta* toss (throw about), maltreat, handle roughly

ጉልት *gult* land given by a ruler to an individual or to a religious institution as an endowment, fief

ግለት *gǝlät* intensity (of anger); see ጋለ

ጉልቻ *gullǝčča* three stones or earthenware tripod on which the cooking pot rests above the fire
ጉልቻ ፡ አቆመ get married (see ቆመ)

ጋሎን *galon* gallon

ግለኛ *gǝlläñña* individualistic (see ግል)

ግላዊ *gǝllawi* personal (see ግል)
ግላዊነት *gǝllawinnät* individuality

*ጉላጅ, አንጉላጅ *angʷälaǧǧä* doze, drowse

ገልጃጃ *gälǧaǧǧa* awkward, clumsy

*ገለገለ, አገለገለ *agäläggälä* serve, be in use, be usable, render service, do duty as, be valid
ተገለገለ *tägäläggälä* make use of, adopt, employ
አገልጋይ *agälgay* servant, aide, attendant
አገልግሎት *agälgǝlot* service, benefit
ያገለገለ *yagäläggälä* used (book), secondhand
መገልገያ *mäggälgäya* agent (power that produces results)

ገላገለ *gälaggälä* separate two people who fight, relieve from danger, arbitrate, help to get rid of (እንኳን ፡ እግዚአብሔር ፡ አገላገለሽ, expression of congratulation on the birth of a child)
ተገላገለ *tägälaggälä* be separated when fighting, be relieved (of responsibility), get rid of, be clear of (debts), be independent of (ተገላገለች *tägälaggäläčč* she gave birth)
ግልግል *gələggəl* good riddance
ግልግል ፡ አደረገ compromise (vi.)
ገላጋይነት *gälagayənnät* intervention

ግልገል *gəlgäl* young of domestic animals (goat, sheep, horse, donkey), cub, kid
ግልገል ፡ ሚዜ junior best man

ገላጋይነት *gälagayənnät* intervention (see ገላገለ)

ገለጠ *gällätä* uncover, unveil, unfold (a map), reveal, expose, explain, interpret (a text); see also ገለጸ
ተገለጠ *tägällätä* be open to, be exposed, expose oneself
አጋለጠ *aggallätä* lay open, uncover, expose (a plot)
ገልጦ *gälto* openly
ገላጣ *gälata* open, clear, bare (space without trees)
ግልጥ, see ገለጸ, ግልጽ
ግልጥ ፡ አድርጎ *gällətt adrəgo* frankly
መግለጫ, see above

ገለጸ *gälläsä* reveal, disclose, divulge, explain, expose, show, express (an opinion), report, describe, depict, declare, manifest (see also ገለጠ)
ገለጻ *gäläsa* description, briefing (informing)
ግልጽ *gəls* visible, evident, apparent, clear, obvious, plain, manifest, lucid (explanation), straightforward
በግልጽ *bägəls* visibly, expressly, clearly, openly
አገላለጽ *aggälaläs* description

ግልፍ ፡ አለ *gəlləff alä* get mad, get sore
ግልፍተኛ *gəlləftäñña* short-tempered, irritable, one who has an abrupt manner, temperamental, hot-blooded
ግልፍተኛነት *gəlləftäññannät* violent temper

ገማ *gämma* be putrid, stink, smell bad, be rotten
ግም *gəm* fetid, stinking, vile (smell)
ግማት *gəmat* stink, bad smell, stench

ጉማ *guma* blood money

ጉሜ *gume* armband

ጉም *gum* fog, mist

ጋማ *gamma* mane (of a horse, mule)
የጋማ ፡ ከብት equines (horses, donkeys, mules)

ጋሜ *gamme* hairdo of girls

ጎማ *gomma* tire, rubber, wheel
ጎማ ፡ ተኛ have a flat tire
ጎማ ፡ ፈነዳ(በት) have a blowout
የጎማ ፡ ጫማ rubbers
ተጠባባቂ ፡ ጎማ spare tire (see ጠበቀ)

ግመል *gəmäl* camel

ገመምተኛ *gämämtäñña* convalescent (see *ገመመ)

ገሞራ *gämora*, in እሳተ ፡ ገሞራ volcano
የእሳተ ፡ ገሞራ volcanic
የእሳተ ፡ ገሞራ ፡ አናት crater

ጉማሬ *gumarre* hippopotamus

ጉምሩክ *gumruk* customs, customs office, custom house
የጉምሩክ ፡ መሥሪያ ፡ ቤት customs office
የጉምሩክ ፡ ቤት custom house

ገመሰ *gämmäsä* (B) divide into two, split, cleave, plow for the first time and hastily
ተጋመሰ *tägammäsä* be halfway finished
ገሚስ *gämis* half, some of

ግማሽ , see below
አጋማሽ , see above

ግማሽ *gəmmaš* half, portion of, some
of (see ገመሰ)
በግማሽ ፡ ልብ half-heartedly

ገምቢ *gämbi* mason, bricklayer (see
ገነባ)

ገምቦ *gämbo* clay pot (see also ገነቦ)

ግምብ *gəmb* stone wall, castle, tower
(see ገነባ)
ግምብ ፡ ቤት stone house, concrete
building
ግምበኛ *gəmbäñña* mason, bricklayer
የግምበኝነት ፡ ሥራ *yägəmbäññənnät
səra* masonry

ግምባር *gəmbar* brow, forehead, front
(military), forward part (of ship),
fortune, luck (see also ገንባር)
ግምባር ፡ ቀደም *gəmbar qäddäm* fore-
front, progressive (in politics)
ግምባሩን ፡ ቋጠረ frown
የጦር ፡ ግምባር front line

ጐምበስ , see ጐነበሰ

ገመተ *gämmätä* (B) estimate (v.), evaluate, rate, guess, value, size up, assess, gauge, appraise, characterize,
presume, assume, reckon
(ዝቅ ፡ አድርጎ ፡ ገመተ underestimate)
ግምት *gəmmət* estimate, esteem, esti-
mation, appraisal, approximation,
guess, hypothesis, reckoning, assumption
ግምት ፡ ጣለ form an opinion
በግምት *bägəmmət* roughly (approximately)

ግማት , see ገማ

*ጐመተመተ , አጐመተመተ *agwmätäm-
mätä* mumble

ጐመን *gwämmän*, ጎመን *gommän* greens
(e.g. turnip)
የፈረንጅ ፡ ጐመን cabbage

ጐመዘዘ *gwämäzzäzä* taste sour (wine)
ጐምዛዛ *gwämzazza* sour (wine)
ጐምዛዛነት *gwämzazzannät* acerbity
(of fruit)

ገመደ *gämmädä* make a rope, twist a
rope
ገመድ *gämäd* rope, measure of land

ጐመደ *gwämmädä* cut (meat, wood),
slice off, castrate
ጐማዳ *gwämada* cut, emasculated

ግምጃ *gəmǧa* silk or velvet cloth
ግምጃ ፡ ቤት storehouse, warehouse,
depot, treasury

ጐመጀ *gwämäǧǧä* desire eagerly, crave,
have an appetite for
አስጐመጀ *asgwämäǧǧä* tempt (of
candy)

ገመገመ *gämäggämä* evaluate (a book),
sound out (public opinion)

ገመጠ *gämmäṭä* take a bite of, bite off,
bite into (an apple), tear off a mouthful

*ጐመጠመጠ , ተጐመጠመጠ *tägwmäṭäm-
mäṭä* rinse (the mouth), gargle

ገራ *gärra* tame, train a beast, break in
(a horse), subdue
ገር *gär* tame, mild (person), meek,
gentle, simple-hearted, good-natured
ገራም *gärram* gentle (horse)
ያልተገራ *yaltägärra* wild (horse)
ገራገር *gäragär* naive

ገር , see ገራ

ጉራ *gurra* boast, boasting, bragging,
show-off
ጉራ ፡ ነዛ boast, brag, show off, put
on airs, talk big
ጉራውን ፡ ነፋ boast (v.)
ጉረኛ *gurräñña* braggart, pompous

ጋሪ *gari* carriage, horse-drawn car,
wheelbarrow
ባለጋሪ *balägari* carriage driver

ጋራ *gara* mountain

ጋራ *gara* with (in company of); see also ጋር

ከ - - - ጋራ with, together with, along with

ባላጋራ opponent (see ባለ)

ለጋራ among them, jointly

በጋራ in common

በጋራ ፡ አለ(ው) *bägara allä(w)* have in common

የጋራ, see above

የጋርዮሽ *yägarəyyoš* collective, joint, collectively

ጋር, see ጋራ with

ግራ *gəra, gra* left hand, left (direction)

ግራ ፡ ገባ(ው) be in difficulty, be confused, be at a loss, feel strange, be awkward

ግራ ፡ አጋባ perplex, puzzle, bewilder, baffle, disorient

ግራ ፡ ቢስ awkward (shape)

ግራ ፡ የሆነ bizarre

ግራም ፡ ነፈሰ ፡ ቀኝ sooner or later, be that as it may

በግራ ፡ በኩል on the left side

በስተግራ on the left-hand side

ግራኝ *graňň* left-handed

ግራዝማች *grazmač* commander of the left (title of distinction); see አዝማች

ጐራ ፡ አለ *gʷära alä* stop off, stop over, come around (for a visit), drop in

*ጐራ, አጓራ *agʷarra* bellow (of ox), boom (of cannons)

ጐሬ *gʷäre* hideout, den, lair, burrow, refuge

ጓሮ *gʷaro* backyard

ከቤት ፡ ጓሮ behind the house

ገረመ *gärrämä* be amazing, be wonderful, be extraordinary

ገረመ(ው) *gärrämä(w)* he is surprised, he is astonished, he is amazed

ተገረመ *tägärrämä* be surprised, be astonished, be impressed, be amazed

አስገረመ *asgärrämä* surprise, astonish, amaze, astound, impress

ገሩም *gərum* marvelous, wonderful, amazing, magnificent, splendid, superb

ግርማ, see below

ይገርማል *yəgärmal* it's strange, it's odd, it's interesting

ይገርምህ ፡ ብሎ *yəgräməh bəlo* to my surprise

አስገራሚ *asgärrami* exciting, startling

ገራም *gärram* gentle (horse); see ገራ

ግርማ *gərma* dignity, majesty, glory (see ገረመ)

ግርማ ፡ ያለው imposing, stately

ግርማ ፡ ሞገስ majestic appearance, grandeur, dignified bearing

ግርማ ፡ ሞገስ ፡ ያለው—*yalläw* august (ባለ ፡ ግርማ *balä gərma* majestic)

†ግርማዊ *gərmawi* majestic

*ጐረመረመ, አጐረመረመ *agʷrämärrämä*, ተጐረመረመ *tägʷrämärrämä* growl, grumble, grunt, rumble, mumble, mutter, murmur

ጉሩምሩም *gurumrum* (n.) murmur, mutter

ጐረምሳ *gʷärämsa* young man, robust young man, adolescent (male)

ግርምቢጥ *gərəmbiṭ* contrary (person)

ግርማዊ *gərmawi* majestic (see ግርማ)

ግርማዊ ፡ ሆይ Your Majesty!

ግርማዊ ፡ ንጉሠ ፡ ነገሥት His Imperial Majesty

ግርማዊነትዎ *gərmawinnätwo* Your Majesty!

ግርማዊነታቸው *gərmawinnätaččäw* His Majesty

ገረረ *gärrärä* be scorching (sun)

ጉrorro *gurorro*, ጓሮሮ *gʷərorro* throat

የጉrorro guttural

የዕለት ፡ ጉrorro daily consumption

ግራር *grar* kind of mimosa, acacia abessynica

ጕረስ *gʷärräsä* take a mouthful, take a morsel, chew (tobacco), be loaded (gun)
አጕረስ *agʷärräsä* give a mouthful, put food into someone's mouth, load (the gun)
ጉርስ *gurs*, in የዕለት ፡ ጉርስ daily bread
ጉርሻ , see below

*ገረሽ , አገረሽ *agäräššä* return (of illness)
አገረሽ(በት) *agäräššä(bbät)* relapse (after a recovery), suffer a relapse

ጉርሻ *gurša* mouthful, morsel, bonus, gratuity, tip for services (see ጕረስ)

ገርበብ ፡ አለ *gärbäbb alä* be ajar

*ጕረበተ , አጕራበተ *agʷärabbätä* be neighbors of one another, live in the neighborhood
ጕረቤት *gʷäräbet* neighbor, neighborhood
ጉርብትና *gurbətənna* neighborhood

ጕረበጠ *gʷäräbbäṭä* be uncomfortable because of being uneven
ጕርባጣ *gʷärbaṭṭa* uneven
[See also አበጠ]

ጉረኖ *guränno* enclosure (for sheep)

ጕረና *gʷäränna* taste burnt

ጕርናና *gʷärnanna* hoarse (voice), husky (voice), rough (voice), gruff, raucous

ጉረኛ *gurräñña* pompous, braggart (see ጉራ)

ግራኝ *graññ* left-handed (see ግራ)

ግሪክ *grik* Greece, Greek
የግሪክ ፡ ቋንቋ Greek (language)

ገረዘ *gärräzä* cut, circumcise (see also ገዘረ)
ግርዘት *gərzät* circumcision

ጉሬዛ *gureza* gureza monkey

ግራዝማች *grazmač* commander of the left (title of distinction); see ግራ, አዝማች

ጋራዥ *garaž* garage, hangar (see also ጋራጅ)

ገረድ *gäräd* housemaid, servant
ልጃገረድ girl

ጉርድ *gurd* stub (of ticket); see ጉረደ, ጉራጅ
ጉርድ ፡ ቀሚስ skirt
ጉርድ ፡ ኮት jacket

ጋረደ *garrädä* cover, conceal, veil, drape (the window), make a shelter, make shade, shield, screen, obstruct (the view), curtain off
†ግርዶሽ *gərdoš* awning, eclipse
መጋረጃ *mäggaräǧa* curtain, shutters for windows

ግርድ *gərd* chaff which is blown away by the wind

ጉረደ *gʷärrädä* cut off, chop off
ጉርድ *gurd* stub (of ticket)
(እጅጌ ፡ ጉርድ short-sleeved)
ጉራጅ *gurraǧ* stub (of ticket)

ጉራዴ *gʷärade* sword

ግርዶሽ *gərdoš* awning, eclipse (see ጋረደ)
የጨረቃ ፡ ግርዶሽ lunar eclipse
የፀሐይ ፡ ግርዶሽ solar eclipse

*ጉራደደ , ተንጉራደደ *tängʷäraddädä* amble (walk at a slow pace), pace up and down, strut

ገረደፈ *gäräddäfä* pound coarsely

ጉራጅ *gurraǧ* stub (of ticket); see ጉርድ, ጉረደ

ጋራጅ *garaǧ* hangar, garage (see also ጋራዥ)

ግርጌ *gərge* at the foot of, foot (of bed), at the bottom, lower part (see also እግር)
ከ - - - በስተግርጌ at the foot of

ግርግም *gərgəm* manger, place where the equines are fed

ገራገር *gäragär* naive (see ገራ)

ግርግር *gərrəgərr* hustle and bustle, panic, tumult, riot, anarchy, confusion, turmoil, excitement, disturbance
ግርግርታ *gərgərta* commotion
የግርግር *yägərrəgərr* hectic

ጐረጐረ *g^wärägg^wärä* search (a house, a person), look over through something, poke

*ጐረጐረ , አንጐራጐረ *ang^wäragg^wärä* grumble, mutter, complain, hum, recite poems of sorrow
እንጉርጉሮ *əngurgurro* muttering, murmuring
የሐዘን ፡ እንጉርጉሮ lament (n.)

ግርገዳ *gərgədda* wall (see also ግድግዳ)

ገረጣ *gärätta* become yellow due to ripening (said of crops), lose color, acquire a sickly hue (person), fade (color), be pale
የገረጣ *yägärätta* pale

ጉርጥ *gurt* kind of frog

ግራጫ *graččạ* gray, brown (usually donkey, mule)

ገረፈ *gärräfä* flagellate, whip, lash

ጐረፈ *g^wärräfä* flow by, flow in abundance, stream (of crowds), stream down (of torrent, of rain), gush (of tears)
ጐርፍ *g^wärf*, ጎርፍ *gorf* flood, torrent, torrential rain, deluge

ገሣ *gässa* belch
አገሣ *agässa* roar (of lion), burp, belch
ግሣት *gəsat* roar, n. (of lion)

ግስ *gəss* verb

ጐሳ *g^wäsa* ethnic group, tribe, subtribe

ግስላ *gəssəlla* panther

ገሰሰ *gässäsä* deprive of something, efface, obliterate, cancel, rape, wipe out

*ጐሳቀለ , አጐሳቀለ *agg^wäsaqq^wälä* treat harshly, treat roughly, misuse, abuse, render haggard (of disease, of suffering)
የተጐሳቀለ *yätäg^wäsaqq^wälä* haggard, drawn (face)
መጐሳቀል *mägg^wäsaq^wäl* discomfort, suffering

ግሣት *gəsat* roar, n. (of lion); see ገሣ

ገሰገሰ *gäsäggäsä* make a forced march, hurry, walk rapidly, leave early in the morning
ግስጋሴ *gəsəggase* forward march, rapid advance

ጐሰጐሰ *g^wäsägg^wäsä* cram, stuff (a pillow with feathers), devour

ገሠጸ *gässäsạ* (B) admonish, scold, reprimand, rebuke, reprove, lecture someone, censure
ግሣጼ *gəssasẹ* rebuke, reprimand, admonition, blame
ተግሣጽ *tägsasẹ* censure, admonition, reproof

ጉሽ *guš* unfiltered beer

ጋሻ *gašša* shield, bulwark, measure of land (ca. 40 hectares); see ጋሼ

ጋሼ *gašše* term of address to a male who is somewhat older than oneself (lit. my shield); see ጋሻ

ጌሾ *gešo* kind of plant the leaves of which are used like hops in making beer

ጐሽ *g^wäšš*, ጎሽ *gošš* buffalo

ጐሽ *g^wäšš*, ጎሽ *gošš* bravo!, well done!

ጐሸመ *g^wäššämä* (B) poke (in the ribs)

*ገሻገሽ , ተንገሻገሽ *tängäšaggäšä* have an aversion to, have enough of food because of dislike for it or because of having overeaten
አንገሻገሽ(ው) *angäšaggäšä(w)* loathe
የሚያንገሻግሽ *yämmiyangäšaggəš* distasteful

ገባ *gäbba* come in, go in, get home, enter, get in, meddle, set (sun), submit (of rebel to authority)
ገባ(ው) understand, comprehend, grasp (understand), follow (understand), catch on
ገባ(በት) *gäbba(bbät)* have a hand in, interfere, be involved in, meddle, deal with (a problem)
(ቃል ፡ ገባ , see **ቃል)**
(ግራ ፡ ገባ , see **ግራ)**
(እንደገባ ፡ ይውጣ it must run its course)
(ከዚህ ፡ ግባ ፡ የማይባል nonentity)
ተገባ *tägäbba* be legitimate, be advisable, be convenient, be proper, be appropriate, be suitable, be seemly
ተገባ(ው) *tägäbba(w)* deserve, he has to
አገባ *agäbba* bring in, make to enter, put into, insert, hand in, introduce, lead into (of a road), score (a goal), marry
(አላገባም *alagäbbam* he is single, lit. he did not marry)
(የላገባች ፡ ሴት *yalagäbbačč set* spinster, lit. a woman who did not marry)
አስገባ *asgäbba* insert, admit (let in), make enter, put in, let in, introduce, send in, intercalate
ተጋባ *tägabba* marry one another, intermarry, be catching (contagious disease); be empty, be emptied
አጋባ *aggabba* arrange a marriage, make a match, empty a container, clear (a plate), unpack (a suitcase), clear out (the closet)
አስተጋባ *astägabba* echo, parrot, reverberate, resound

አግባባ *agbabba* bring to reason, persuade, influence, lure into, win over, prevail on, induce
ተግባባ *tägbabba* understand each other, get along, agree, come to an understanding
ገባ ፡ አለ *gäba alä* be set back (a house, from the street), come inside a little way
ገቢ , see below
ገብ , see below
ግቢ , see below
ግብ , see below
ግባት , see below
†ጋብቻ *gabəčča* marriage, matrimony
ገብነት , see below
ተገቢ *tägäbi* proper, adequate, equitable, appropriate, right (person), reasonable (choice), fitting, pertinent, due (proper), apt (suitable), advisable
ተገቢነት *tägäbinnät* pertinence, propriety
ተግባቢ *tägbabi* suitable, agreeable
መግቢያ , see above
መጋቢያ *mäggabiya* threshold
መግባባት *mägbabat* accord, mutual understanding
(አለመግባባት *alämägbabat* disagreement, misunderstanding, cleavage, conflict of opinion)
ማስተጋባት *mastägabat* repercussion
አገባብ *aggäbab*, **አግባብ** *agbab*, see above
የሚገባ *yämmiggäbba* natural (normal), right, just, proper, appropriate
በሚገባ *bämmiggäbba* well, perfectly, rightly, duly, properly, appropriately, fittingly
በሚገባ ፡ ያዘ treat with consideration, treat fittingly
ከሚገባ ፡ በላይ *kämmiggäbba bälay* too much
የማይገባ *yämmayəggäbba* inappropriate, improper, objectionable
ይግባኝ , see above

ገቢ *gäbi* revenue, import, receipts, income (see **ገባ**)

ገብ *gäbb*, in አዲስ ፡ ገብ newcomer
(see ገባ)
ሁለ ፡ ገብ ፡ የሆነ versatile, all-around
ግብረ ፡ ገብ morals
ሰርጎ ፡ ገብ infiltrator (see ሰረገ)
የግብረ ፡ ገብ moral

ጐብ፡ አለ *gubb alä* heave, vi. (of ground)
ጐብጣ, see below

ጐቦ *gubbo* (n.) bribe, graft
ጐቦ ፡ በላ take bribes
በጐቦ ፡ ደለለ bribe (v.)

ጋቢ *gabi* thick *šämma*-dress put on in
the evening

ጋብ ፡ አለ *gabb alä* subside (storm),
let up (of rain)

ግቢ *gəbbi* enclosure, premises, grounds
(land), compound, palace (see ገባ)
ምድረ ፡ ግቢ compound (of school),
campus
አጥር ፡ ግቢ compound (of house);
see አጠረ

ግብ *gəb* objective, aim, score (in a
game), goal (in soccer); see ገባ
ግብ ፡ ጠባቂ goal keeper (see ጠበቀ)
ከግብ ፡ አደረሰ bring to maturity,
achieve the purpose, carry out a plan
(see ደረሰ)

ገበረ *gäbbärä* (B) pay tribute, pay tax
አገበረ *agäbbärä* compel, force
አስገበረ *asgäbbärä* subjugate, subject,
conquer, cause to pay tribute
ገበሬ, see below
ገባር, see below
ግቢር *gäbir* act (in a play), action,
practice
ግብር *gäbər* servant (used in personal names)
ግብር, see below
ግብርና *gəbrənna* farming, agriculture
ምግባር *məgbar* practice, act, conduct, behavior
ተገባር, see above

ገበሬ *gäbäre* farmer, peasant (see ገበረ)

ገበር *gäbär* lining of a garment

ገባር *gäbbar* tenant farmer, serf, bondsman, tributary (paying tribute); see
ገበረ
ገባር ፡ ወንዝ tributary (river)

ግብር *gəbər* tribute, tax; feast, banquet, reception; action, conduct,
function, activity, effect (see ገበረ)
ግብር ፡ አበላ feast (v.); see በላ
ግብረ ፡ ሥጋ *gəbrä səga* sexual relations
ግብረ ፡ አበር *gəbrä abbär* accomplice, confederate, collaborator, partner in crime
ግብረ፡አበር ፡ ሆነ work in collusion
ግብረ ፡ አበርነት *gəbrä abbärənnät*
complicity
ግብረ ፡ ገብ morals
ግብረ ፡ ገብነት morals, morality
የግብረ ፡ ገብ moral
ግብራዊ ፡ ስያሜ *gəbrawi səyyame* tech-
nical term

ግብርና *gəbrənna* farming, agriculture
(see ገበረ)

ግብራዊ, see ግብር

ገብስ *gäbs* barley

*ገበሰበሰ, አግበሰበሰ *agbäsäbbäsä* be acquisitive of (money)

ገበታ *gäbäta* large cup or bowl of
wood, basin for washing hands, table
made of bamboo
ገበታ ፡ ቀረበ the table is set
ገበታ ፡ ከፍ ፡ አለ the table is cleared
የገበታ ፡ ልብስ tablecloth
የገበታ ፡ እቃ tableware

ገበቴ *gäbäte* wooden bowl

ጐበት *gubbät* liver

ጐብጣ *gubbəta* hillock, mound, knoll,
bump (of road); see ጐብ ፡ አለ

ግባት *gəbat*, in የደም ፡ ግባት good complexion (see ገባ)

ጋብቻ *gabəčča* marriage, matrimony
(see ገባ)
የጋብቻ marital (vows), conjugal
የሰማንያ ፡ ጋብቻ civil marriage
የቃል ፡ ኪዳን ፡ ጋብቻ church marriage

ገብነት *gäbbənnät*, in ግብረ ፡ ገብነት morals, morality (see ግብር, ገባ)
ጣልቃ ፡ ገብነት intrusiveness

ጐበኘ *g^wäbäññä* visit, inspect (troops),
review (troops), tour (vi.)
አስጐበኘ *asg^wäbäññä* guide (tourists),
show around
ጐብኚ *g^wäbñi*, ጐብኝ *g^wäbəñ* tourist,
visitor
(የገር ፡ ጐብኝ visitor from abroad)
ጐብኝት *gubəññət* (n.) visit, tour

ጉባኤ *guba'e* assembly, congregation,
meeting, gathering, conference
ጉባኤ ፡ አደረገ hold a conference (see
*ደረገ)
ቃለ ፡ ጉባኤ minutes (of a meeting)
ትምህርታዊ ፡ ጉባኤ seminar
የሚኒስትሮች ፡ ጉባኤ cabinet meeting
ጠቅላላ ፡ ጉባኤ General Assembly (of
the UN); see ጠቀለለ

ገበዘ *gäbbäzä* (B) act with hypocrisy
ግብዝ *gəbbəz* hypocrite, false, vain
(conceited)
ግብዝና *gəbbəzənna* hypocrisy
ግብዝነት *gəbbəzənnät* hypocrisy, vanity (conceit)

ገበዝ *gäbäz* head of a church, vicar

ጋበዘ *gabbäzä* invite to a meal, give
a dinner, entertain (guests), treat to,
offer (a drink, cigarette)
ተጋበዘ *tägabbäzä* be offered hospitality, help oneself to food
ተጋበዘ(በት) threaten with a knife,
come at someone with a knife
ጋባዥ *gabaž* host, hostess
ግብዣ, see below
ተጋባዥ *tägabaž* guest for a meal

ጐበዘ *g^wäbbäzä* (B) be strong, be
brave, be smart

ጐበዝ *g^wäbäz* young man, fine young
man, manly (like a man), smart,
brilliant, clever, strong, brave, quite
a fellow
ጉብዝና *gubzənna* courage, virility,
manliness

ግብዝነት, see ገበዘ

ግብዣ *gəbža* reception, banquet, feast,
party, invitation (see ጋበዘ)
የእራት ፡ ግብዣ banquet, formal dinner

ገበየ *gäbäyyä* transact business in the
market, go marketing, shop, acquire
ተገበየየ *tägäbäyayyä* make a deal
ገበያ, see below
መገበያየት *mäggäbäyayät* deal (business arrangement), transaction

ገበያ *gäbäya* market, marketplace (see
ገበየ)
ገበያ ፡ ቆም the market is underway
ገበያ ፡ አቆም ፤ ገበያ ፡ ተበተነ the market is over (see ቆም, በተነ)
ገበያ ፡ አለው *gäbäya alläw* he makes
good business
ገበያ ፡ ደራ the market is in full
swing
ገበያተኛ *gäbäyatäñña* shopper

ገብጋባ *gäbgabba* stingy, parsimonious

ገበጣ *gäbäṭa* an Ethiopian game consisting of a board with a double row
of hollows and played with pebbles
or beans

ጐበጠ *g^wäbbäṭä* be bent (stick), be
humped, be hunchbacked, be curved
(back)
አጐበጠ *ag^wäbbäṭä* bend (vt.), bow,
curve
ጐባጣ *g^wäbaṭa* curved, bent, hunched,
hunchback
መጐብጥ *mäg^wbäṭ*, in የጀርባ ፡ መጐብጥ
hunch

ግብጽ *gəbṣ* Egypt

ጋታ *gätta* pull on the reins in order to make the horse go slower or stop, restrain, curb, constrain (temper), hold (temper), repress (laughter) (ራሱን ፡ ጋታ control oneself) ያልተጋታ *yaltägätta* intemperate (language)

ጉቶ *gutto* tree stump, short and stout person

ጌታ *geta* lord, master, owner ጌታችን *getaččən* our Lord ጌቶች *getočč* master (used in form of respect) የጌትነት *yägetənnät* aristocratic

ጋት *gət* udder

ጋትልትል *gətəltəl* long straggling line of people, or of people and animals

ጋተረ *gättärä* (B) stretch tight, pull tight, be stubborn ግትር *gəttər* obstinate, stubborn, refractory (child), unbending ሐሳበ ፡ ግትር intransigent, headstrong, opinionated, willful

ጐተራ *gʷätära* granary, grain storage, crib (for corn), storehouse (of information)

ጐተተ *gʷättätä* (B) drag, draw, pull, haul, tow, tug on, drawl (words), conjure up (spirits) ተጐተተ *tägʷättätä*, passive of the preceding; crawl (of work, of time), lag behind, drag (vi.), become slack (work) ተጓተተ *tägʷattätä* move slowly, drag on, be drawn out ጐታታ *gʷätata* slow (worker)

ጉትቻ *gutəčča* earring

ጉትዬ *guttəyye* crest (of bird)

ጋና *gäna* still, yet, but (still), just (merely) ጋና ፡ ነው it is not time yet ጋና ፡ አሁን just now

ጋና ፡ የመጣ ፡ ሰው newcomer ሰዓቱ ፡ ጋና ፡ ነው it is too early አሁን ፡ ጋና just now, just this moment እንደገና anew, again

ገና *gänna* Christmas, name of hockey-like game played on Christmas day

ጋን *gan* large pottery jar used in making beer, chamber (of gun) የቁልፍ ፡ ጋን lock

ግን *gən* however, but ነገር ፡ ግን but ዳሩ ፡ ግን but

ጐን *gʷänn* flank, side of body, by the side of, beside ጐን ፡ ለጐን side by side እ - - - ጐን beside ከ - - - ጐን alongside, beside, close to ወደጐን abreast, aside (as in ወደጐን ፡ አስቀመጠ lay aside)

ገነባ *gänäbba* build a wall with stones, cement or mortar ገንቢ , ግንብ , ግንበኛ , see ገምቢ, ግምብ

ጋንቦ *gänbo* clay pot (see also ገምቦ)

ግንባር , see ግምባር

ጐነበሰ *gʷänäbbäsä* be bent, bend (vi.) አጐነበሰ *agʷänäbbäsä* bend (vi.), bend down, stoop, bow, curve (vi.) ጐንበስ ፡ አለ *gʷänbäss alä* stoop, incline the head, hold one's head down, bend (to the ground) ጐንበስ ፡ ቀና ፡ አለ *gʷänbäss qäna alä* nod, bow down and rise again ጉንብስ *gunbəs* bent, curved

ግንቦት *gənbot* May

ገነት *gännät* paradise, garden

ጓንቲ *gʷanti* glove

ገነነ *gännänä* be abundant, be in large quantity (grass, trees), augment, increase, grow (of fame), be famous

አገነነ(ለት) *agännänä(llät)* add luster
to (one's renown)
አጋነነ *aggannänä* exaggerate, over-
state, emphasize, maximize, play
something up
ገናና *gänana* abundant, famous, illustrious
ቃል ፡ አጋኖ *qal agganno* exclamation

ገነነ , see አምባ

ጋኔን *ganen* (pl. አጋንንት *aganənt*) evil
spirit, demon

ግንኙነት *gənəññunnät* contact, bond
(relation), relationship, intercourse,
connection, association (companionship), communication (see *ገኝ)
ግንኙነት ፡ አደረገ associate, come into
contact, deal (with people)
ግንኙነት ፡ የለውም be irrelevant

ገነዘ *gännäzä* (B) wrap a corpse up in a
shroud, enshroud

*ገነዘበ , ተገነዘበ *tägänäzzäbä* remember,
recall, realize, perceive, be aware,
appreciate, note (make an observation), conclude
አስገነዘበ *asgänäzzäbä* hint, point out,
remind, draw attention, cause to
realize
አገናዛቢ ፡ ተውላጠ ፡ ስም *aggänazabi*—
possessive pronoun

ገንዘብ *gänzäb* money, currency, coin,
bank note, property
ገንዘቤ *gänzäbe* my dear!
ገንዘብ ፡ አጠፋ squander money (see
ጠፋ)
ገንዘብ ፡ አወጣ spend money (see ወጣ)
ገንዘብ ፡ ሰብሳቢ money collector,
chairman of a society where money
collecting is involved
ገንዘብ ፡ ቤት treasurer
ገንዘብ ፡ ተቀባይ cashier (see *ቀበለ)
ገንዘብ ፡ ከፋይ teller (see ከፈለ)
ገንዘብ ፡ ያዥ treasurer (see ያዘ)
በገንዘብ ፡ በኩል financially
የገንዘብ pecuniary, financial, monetary

የገንዘብ ፡ ሚኒስትር Finance Minister
የገንዘብ ፡ ሥራ ፡ ባዋቂ financier
የገንዘብ ፡ ይዞታ finances
ቀሪ ፡ ገንዘብ balance (see ቀረ)
ተጠባባቂ ፡ ገንዘብ reserve fund (see
ጠበቀ)
ዋና ፡ ገንዘብ capital, n. (money),
principal, n. (money)
ጥሬ ፡ ገንዘብ cash, hard cash

ገንዳ *gända* trough, font
የገላ ፡ መታጠቢያ ፡ ገንዳ bathtub

ግንድ *gənd* trunk of a tree, log, stump,
block (of wood), stem (of flower)
የዘር ፡ ግንድ genealogy, pedigree
የጆሮ ፡ ግንድ area of head around
the ears

ጉንድል *gundəl* capon

ገነደሰ *gänäddäsä* topple (vt.)

ጉንዳን *gundan* kind of black ant

ጐነጐነ *gʷänäggʷänä* (v.) braid, plait
(threads, hair)
ጉንጉን *gungun* (n.) braid, plait
ያበባ ፡ ጉንጉን garland, wreath (see
አበባ)

ጊንጥ *gint* scorpion

ገነጠለ *gänäṭṭälä* cut by tearing, tear
off, tear out, break off (branches),
rip off (a cover), detach (the stub)
ተገነጠለ *tägänäṭṭälä* secede, diverge
(of paths), branch off
ገነጣጠለ *gänäṭaṭṭälä* cut up in
pieces (chicken, ox), disjoint, disas-
semble, dismantle (car), disintegrate
(vt.), blow down (of wind blowing
down trees)
ተገነጣጠለ *tägänäṭaṭṭälä* fall to pieces
(book)

*ጐነጨ , ተጐነጨ *tägʷänäččä* take a gulp,
sip
አስጐነጨ give a mouthful of drink
ጉንጭ , see below

ጉንጭ *gunč* cheek (see *ጐነጨ)

ገነፋ *gänäffa* boil over

ገንፎ *gänfo* porridge (of wheat, barley, oats)

ገናፈለ *gänäffälä* boil over

ጉንፋን *gunfan* common cold, cough
ጉንፋን ፡ ያዘ(ው) catch cold

*ገኘ, አገኘ *agäññä* find, earn, gain, meet, obtain, get, discover, come across, acquire, win, procure
ተገኘ *tägäññä* be found, be situated, exist, attend (be present), assist (be present), be on hand, be available, occur, be common
አስገኘ *asgäññä* bring in (money), result in, produce, provide, give forth
ተገናኘ *tägänaññä* have a rendezvous, meet one another, come together, be together, converge, join, contact, get in touch, communicate, interconnect (vi.), get a connection (on the telephone), be connected, be linked
አገናኘ *aggänaññä* bring together, reunite (vt.), connect, join, introduce people
ግንኙነት, see above
ማግኘት *magñät* achievement (attainment), acquisition
መገኘት *mäggäñät* attendance, discovery
መገናኛ *mäggänaña* junction, communication, intersection, confluence, rendez-vous, place where one meets, the coming together
(የሥራና ፡ የማገናኛ ፡ ሚኒስቴር Ministry of Communications and Public Works)
መገናኘት *mäggänaññät* juncture, concurrence (coming together)

ግዑዝ *gə'uz* inanimate, inert

ግዕዝ *gə'əz* Geez (liturgical language of Ethiopian church); first order of the Ethiopian vowel system (*ä*)

ገውዝ *gäwz* nut

ገዛ *gäzza* buy, purchase, own, possess, govern, rule over, dominate, hire (a lawyer)
ተገዛ *tägäzza*, passive of the preceding; submit (yield to), be subject to
የገዛ *yägäzza* own (adj.), one's own
የገዛ ፡ ራሴ I myself
(በገዛ ፡ እጁ *bägäzza əǧǧu* by himself, on his own)
(በገዛ ፡ ፈቃዱ on his own accord, voluntarily)
ገዥ ፤ ገሮ, see below
ግዢ *gəžži* (n.) buy, bargain, purchase
ግዛት, see below
ተገዥ *tägäž* subject (under the control of)
ተገዥነት *tägäžənnät* subjection (submission)
አገዛዝ *aggäzaz* manner of governing, reign (rule), domination
(የቅኝ ፡ አገዛዝ colonialism, colonial rule)

ጉዞ *guzo* march, trip, itinerary, travel, journey, voyage, peregrination, caravan (of traders); see *ጎዘ

ጊዜ *gize* time, period, occasion, moment, weather
ጊዜያት *gizeyat* tense, n. (in grammar)
ጊዜ ፡ አለፈ expire
ጊዜ ፡ አለፈ(በት) be antiquated, be outmoded, be obsolete
ጊዜው ፡ አይደለም be unseasonal
ጊዜ ፡ የወለደው *gize yäwällädäw* haphazard (thing), transitory
የጊዜ current, contemporary (event)
የጊዜ ፡ ቤት multiplication table
ሁልጊዜ *hulgize* always, every time, all the time
ለጊዜው at the moment, for the time being, for a while, for a short period, temporarily
ምንጊዜ *mängize* when?, at what time?
ምንጊዜም always, all along, ever, at any time; (with negative verb) never

(ለምንጊዜውም in perpetuity, at any time whatever)
ስ + imperfect + ጊዜ when
ስንት ፥ ጊዜ how many times?
በ + verb + ጊዜ when, by the time
በጊዜ on time, early
በጊዜው on time, in due course, regularly
በየጊዜው *bäyyägizew* every so often, occasionally, constantly, many times, from time to time, regularly, momentarily
ባሁኑ ፥ ጊዜ nowadays (see አሁን)
በቅርብ ፥ ጊዜ *bäqərb gize* shortly
በዛሬ ፥ ጊዜ nowadays
ብዙውን ፥ ጊዜ most of the time
ትርፍ ፥ ጊዜ leisure
አብዛኛውን ፥ ጊዜ most of the time
አንድ ፥ ጊዜ once, just a moment
(ባንድ ፥ ጊዜ immediately)
ከቅርብ ፥ ጊዜ ፥ ወዲህ *käqərb*—in recent times
ክፍለ ፥ ጊዜ session (in class), period (in class)
ያለ ፥ ጊዜ prematurely, untimely, inopportunely
ያን ፥ ጊዜ then (see ያ)
ጥቂት ፥ ጊዜ a while
ጊዜያዊ *gizeyawi* interim, provisional, tentative, transient

ጋዘ *gazä* banish
ተጋዘ *tägazä* be imprisoned (for a long time), be under house arrest
አጋዘ *agazä* exile, banish, carry away
ግዞት *gəzot* banishment to an area which one cannot leave without permission, house arrest, confinement

ጋዝ *gaz* kerosene, petroleum, gas
ነጭ ፥ ጋዝ kerosene

*ዝ ,ተዝ *tägʷaza* depart, travel, go on a trip, cover a distance, journey, migrate, move (travel), sail (of ship)
አዝ *agʷazä* transport (v.)
አዝዝ *aggʷagʷazä* convey (passengers), transport, move (transport)

ጉዞ, see above
ዝ *gʷaz* baggage, luggage, belongings (which one transports)
መንዝ *mäggʷaz* expedition
መንዝዝ *mäggʷagʷaža* locomotion, transportation (being transported)

ገዘረ *gäzzärä* circumcise (see also ገረዘ)
ግዝረት *gəzrät* circumcision

ገዘተ *gäzzätä* (B) anathematize, place under a ban or sanction
ግዝት *gəzzət* (n.) ban, sanction

ግዛት *gəzat* possession (territory under the rule of a country), area of jurisdiction, domain (dominion), realm (see ገዛ)
የንጉሥ ፥ ነገሥት ፥ ግዛት empire
የአገር ፥ ግዛት ፥ ሚኒስቴር Ministry of Interior
ጠቅላይ ፥ ግዛት province

ጉዞት, see ጋዘ

ጊዜያዊ, see ጊዜ

ገዘገዘ *gäzäggäzä* cut with difficulty (of a dull blade), saw

ጕዘጕዘ *gʷäzäggʷäzä* cover the ground with dry grass, scatter grass on the ground, spread hay to make a bed
ጉዝዝ *guzgʷaz* dry grass, leaves or hay which one spreads over the ground

ጋዜጣ *gazeṭa* newspaper
የጋዜጣ ፥ ነጻነት freedom of press
ነጋሪት ፥ ጋዜጣ Official Gazette
ጋዜጠኛ *gazeṭäňňa* journalist, newsman, reporter, correspondent
ጋዜጠኞች *gazeṭäňňočč* press, journalists

ገዘፈ *gäzzäfä* be fat, be stout
ግዙፍ *gəzuf* huge, gross, large, bulky, voluminous (body), tall and fat, immense (building), gigantic, massive, physical (entity)
ግዙፍነት *gəzufənnät* mass (bulkiness), bulk (of elephant)

ጋዥ *gäž*, ጋዢ *gäži* buyer, master, potentate, ruler (see ገዛ)
አገረ ፡ ገዢ governor

ጋየ *gayyä* be set on fire, be consumed by fire
አጋየ *agayyä* put to the torch, consume (of flames), burn off (dry grass from the soil)

ጋያ *gayya* pipe (for smoking)

ገድ *gädd* luck, omen of good fortune
ገደ ፡ ቢስ ill-fated, ill-omened, unlucky, inauspicious

ጉድ *gud* freak, monster, strange, wonderful
ወይ ፡ ጉድ how strange!, what a wonder!, wow! (may imply approval or disapproval)

ጉድ ፡ ጉድ ፡ አለ *gudd gudd alä* flutter about, bustle about

ግድ *gədd* obligation, necessity, compulsion (see ገደደ)
ግድ ፡ ሆነበት *gədd honäbbät* be forced, find something necessary
ግድ ፡ የለም never mind!, it does not matter, I don't mind, there is no harm
ግዴለሽ ፤ ግድ ፡ የለሽ , see below
ግድ ፡ የለኝም *gədd yälläññəm* I don't care
ግድ ፡ የለውም *gədd yälläwəm* he is careless
በግድ *bägədd*, የግድ *yägədd* of necessity, by necessity, necessarily, by force, perforce, without fail
በውድም ፡ በግድም willy-nilly, by hook or by crook (see ውድ)

ጐዳ *gʷädda* damage, injure, harm, hurt, abuse (harm), ruin, impair
ተጐዳ *tägʷädda* be injured, be hit (by a disaster), be infected
ጉዳት *gudat* harm, damage, ruin, loss, injury, disadvantage
ጉጂ , see below
የተጐዳ *yätägʷädda* injured, damaged

የማይጐዳ *yämmayəgʷäda* harmless

ጓዳ *gʷada* back area of Ethiopian round house which is partitioned off from the main area, alcove

ጓድ *gʷadd* company, band (group), gang, team, party, platoon, corps, expedition (scientific)
የሙዚቃ ፡ ጓድ orchestra
የሰላም ፡ ጓድ Peace Corps
ጓደኛ , see below

ገደለ *gäddälä* kill, murder, massacre, slay, put to death
(ራሱን ፡ ገደለ commit suicide)
(ራስን ፡ መግደል suicide)
ተጋደለ *tägaddälä* kill one another, fight, struggle, champion a cause
ገድል , see below
ገዳይ , see below
ግዳይ , see below
ግድያ , see below
ተጋደሎ *tägadlo* crusade, campaign (to fight hunger), battle, mortification
ተጋዳይ *tägaday* champion

ገደል *gädäl* cliff, precipice, abyss, ravine, chasm
ገደል ፡ ገባ fall off a cliff
የገደል ፡ ማሚቶ echo
ገደልማ ፡ ሸለቆ *gädäləmma šäläqo* canyon

ገድል *gädəl* saint's life (usually written in Geez); see ገደለ

*ጋደለ ,አጋደለ *agaddälä* incline (vi.), lean to one side, be lopsided, tilt, slope, tip, incline to do something
ጋደል ፡ ያለ *gadäll yalä* gradual (slope)

ጐደለ *gʷäddälä* be deficient in, be short in, be incomplete, be missing something, lack, get low (water in a river), subside, diminish (vi.), decrease (vi.)
(ጐደለው he lacks)
(የጐደለ in-, as in አስተዋይነት ፡ የጐደለ imprudent, lit. one who lacks prudence)

አጕደለ *agʷäddälä* diminish (vt.), decrease (vt.)

ጕደል *gʷäddäl*, in ከሞላ ፡ ጕደል more or less, by and large, approximately

ጕደሎ, see below

ጕድለት, see below

ጕደሎነት *gʷädälonnät*, ጕዶሎነት *gʷädolonnät*, in ያከል ፡ ጕደሎነት infirmity

†ጕዳይ *gudday* less; affair

ጕደሎ *gʷädälo* deficient, lacking, missing, incomplete, odd (number), not full (see ጕደለ)

እምነት ፡ ጕደሎ dishonest (plan)

አካለ ፡ ጕደሎ invalid, crippled

ግዬለሸ *gəddelläš*, ግድ ፡ የለሸ *gədd yälläš* carefree, careless, mindless, thoughtless, indolent, indifferent, happy-go-lucky (see ግድ, የለሸ)

የግዬለሸ carefree (life)

ግዬለሸነት *gəddelläšənnät*, ግድ ፡ የለ ሸነት *gədd yälläšənnät* neglect (not caring for), carelessness, apathy, indifference, indolence, unconcern

የግዬለሸነት casual

ጕድለት *gudlät* lack, defect, failure, flaw, deficiency, insufficient amount, shortcoming, disability, inaccuracy (see ጕደለ)

ጕደሎነት, see ጕደለ

ገደማ *gädäma* area, location, whereabouts, somewhere about, approximately, roughly, circa, in the neighborhood of

እዚህ ፡ ገደማ hereabouts

ወደ - - - ገደማ toward (near), towards, about

ግድም, see below

ጋደም ፡ አለ *gadämm alä* lie down (to sleep), stretch out (see *ጋደም)

ገዳም *gädam* (pl. ገዳማት *gädamat*) monastery, cloister, convent

የሴቶች ፡ ገዳም convent

*ጋደም, ተጋደም *tägaddämä* lie down, lie

አጋደም *aggaddämä* lay down horizontally

ጋደም ፡ አለ *gadämm alä* recline, repose, stretch out, vi. (on a sofa), lie down

አግድም, see above

አግዳሚ, see above

ግድም *gədəm* area, place, near, around, roughly, approximately (see ገደማ)

ጊዳር *gidär* heifer, calf

ገደበ *gäddäbä* (B) make a dam, dam, harness (a waterfall)

ገደብ, see below

ግድብ *gəddəb* dam, dike, barrage, embankment, bulwark

ገደብ *gädäb* dike, dam, barrier, reservation (restriction), limitations (see ገደበ)

ገደብ ፡ አደረገ stipulate

ገደብ ፡ የሌለው absolute

ጕድባ *gudba* crevasse, breach

ጕዳት, see ጕዳ

ግዬታ *gəddeta* obligation, constraint, condition (stipulation), must (n.), necessity, duty; obligatory, compulsory, mandatory (see ገደ)

በግዬታ ፡ መመልመል conscription (see መለመለ)

የግዬታ obligatory, mandatory, compulsory

ጕዳና *gʷädana* road, avenue

አውራ ፡ ጕዳና highway

(የአውራ ፡ ጕዳና ፡ ባለሥልጣን Highway Authority)

ዋና ፡ ጕዳና thoroughfare, main road

ጕድን *gʷädən* rib, side of the body

*ጕዳኘ, ተጕዳኘ *tägʷädaňňä* befriend, associate

ጓደኛ, see below

ጓደኛ *g^waddäñña* companion, friend, playmate, comrade, ally (see ጓድ, *ጐዳኘ)

ጓደኛ ፡ አበጀ keep company, associate (see በጀ)

ጓደኛ ፡ የሌለው odd (unmatched, unmated)

የሥራ ፡ ጓደኛ *yäsəra*—colleague, coworker

የትምህርት ፡ ቤት ፡ ጓደኛ *yätəmhərt bet*—schoolmate

የክፍል ፡ ጓደኛ *yäkəfəl*—classmate, roommate

የጦር ፡ ጓደኛ ally

ጓደኛነት *g^waddäññannät*, ጓደኝነት *g^waddäññənnät* fellowship (companionship), friendship

ገዳይ *gäday* killer, murderer (see ገደለ)

ነፍስ ፡ ገዳይ murderer, assassin

ነፍስ ፡ ገዳይነት *näfsä gädayənnät* manslaughter, murder

ጉዳይ *gudday* affair, matter, business, occurrence, legal case, problem (see ጐደለ)

ጉዳይ ፡ ይዞኛል *gudday yəzoññal* I am occupied, I am busy (see ያዘ)

ጉዳይ ፡ ፈጻሚ chargé d'affaires (see ፈጸመ)

ባለ ፡ ጉዳይ person who has a case in court or a problem to take up with an official

ጉዳይ *gudday* less (see ጐደለ)

ለአራት ፡ ሩብ ፡ ጉዳይ quarter of four (that is, four less a quarter)

ሦስት ፡ ጉዳይ less three, three too few

ግዳይ *gədday* murder, killing (see ገደለ)

ነፍስ ፡ ግዳይ murder

ግድያ *gədəyya* murder, killing (see ገደለ)

ግድየለሽ, see ግዴለሽ

ገዳደ *gäddädä* be wanting, lack, be necessary, force, oblige

ተገዳደ *tägäddädä* be obligated, be forced, be compelled

አስገዳደ *asgäddädä* force, compel, coerce, obligate, require, constrain, bring pressure on, exact

ግድ, see above

ግዴታ, see above

ግዳጅ, see below

ገዳዳ *gädada* oblique, twisted, distorted

*ጐደደ, ተንጓደደ *täng^waddädä* meander (wander aimlessly), stagger, totter (see also *ገደገደ)

ግዳጅ *gəddaǧ* want, need, obligation, duty, compulsion (see ገደደ)

ግዳጁን ፡ ፈጸመ answer the call of duty

*ገደገደ, ተንገዳገደ *tängädaggädä* stagger, reel (see also *ጐደደ)

ጉድጓድ *gudg^wad* hole, pit, cavity, well, ditch, burrow, depression (see ጐደጐደ)

(የ)ውኃ ፡ ጉድጓድ well of water

የዘይት ፡ ጉድጓድ oil well

ግድግዳ *gədgədda* wall (see also ግርግዳ)

ግድግዳና ፡ ጣሪያ frame of the house

ጐደጐደ *g^wädägg^wädä* sink, subside, sink in (soil, road), become hollow, become deep (hole in the ground)

አጐደጐደ *ag^wädägg^wädä* hollow out, dig out, excavate

ጉድጉድ ፡ ያለ *g^wädg^wädd yalä* concave

ጉድጓዳ *g^wädg^wadda* sunken, hollow, deep (gorge), concave

ጉድጓዳ ፡ ሳሕን bowl, basin

ጉድጓድ, see above

*ጐደጐደ, ተንጐደጐደ *täng^wädägg^wädä* thunder (v.)

ነጐድጓድ thunder (n.)

ገደፈ *gäddäfä* break the fast, err, make a mistake, omit, skip over

ግድፈት *gədfät* error, mistake, lacuna, omission

ግድፍት *gəddəft* a non-fast day

ገደፍ *gädäf*, in እስከ ፡ አፍ ፡ ገደፉ fully

ጉድፍ, see ጐደፈ.

ጐደፈ *gʷäddäfä* be dirty, be ruined (reputation)
አጐደፈ *agʷäddäfä* injure (a reputation), blemish, stain (honor, reputation)
ጉድፍ *gudəf* dirt, rubbish, filth

ግድፈት, see ገደፈ.

ግድፍት, see ገደፈ.

ጐዲፈች *guddifäčča* adoption (of child)
በጐዲፈች ፡ ተቀበለ adopt (a child)
የጐዲፈች adopted (child)

ጎጆ *goǧǧo* small hut made of straw, booth, shack, cottage
ጎጆ ፡ ወጣ set up housekeeping
ጎጆ ፡ ደረጀ set up housekeeping
የወፍ ፡ ጎጆ cage (for birds), nest
ደሳሳ ፡ ጎጆ hovel, miserable shack

ጐጂ *gʷäǧi* harmful, detrimental, inimical (see ጐዳ)
ጐጂነት *gʷäǧinnät* ill effects

*ጋጋ, ተንጋጋ *tängagga* crowd, stampede, make noise (many people walking together); see also *ጓጓ
አንድ ፡ ጋ ፡ ተንጋጋ flock together
ጋጋታ *gagata* rush, haste, din, clamor

ጓጓ *gʷaggʷa* desire, be anxious, be curious, be eager, wish strongly, long, yearn, look forward, be enthusiastic about, crave affection, hunger for (love)
አጓጓ *agʷaggʷa* be a temptation, be tempting, hold out a promise
ጕጕ *guggu* curious, avid, ambitious (eager), desirous
ጕጕት, see below
የሚያጓጓ *yämmiyagʷaggʷa* attractive (offer)

*ጓጓ, ተንጓጓ *tängʷaggʷa* make a noise, be a rumbling noise (see also *ጋጋ)

ጓጓ ፡ አለ *gʷagʷa alä* resound, make a noise
ጓጓታ *gʷagʷata* sound, noise

ጓጐለ *gʷaggʷälä* be lumpy (dough)
ሰውነቴ ፡ ጓጐለ feel stiff, ache all over

*ገገመ, አገገመ *agäggämä* be convalescent, convalesce, recuperate
ገገምታ *gägämta* convalescence
ገገምተኛ *gägämtäñña* convalescent
ገመምተኛ *gämämtäñña* convalescent

ጋገረ *gaggärä* bake bread in the oven
ተጋገረ *tägaggärä* be baked, form a thick layer (of ice)
ጋጋሪ *gagari*, in ዳቦ ፡ ጋጋሪ baker
መጋገሪያ *mägagäriya*, in የዳቦ መጋ ገሪያ oven
ግግር *gəggər* baked

ጕግስ *gugs* polo-type game

ጕጕት *guggut* curiosity, longing, anxiety (see ጓጓ)
በጕጕት impatiently, eagerly

ጕጕት *guggut* owl

ጋጋታ, see ጋጋ

ጓጓታ, see ጓጓ ፡ አለ

ጋጠ *gaṭä* gnaw a bone, graze (vi.), pasture, browse (of cattle), nibble, crop (ሣር ፡ ጋጠ graze)
አጋጠ *agaṭä* graze (vt.)
ግጦሽ, see below

ጋጣ *gaṭa*, ጋጥ *gaṭ* stable, pen (for cattle), stall (for horses)

*ዜጠ, ተዜጠ *tägeṭä* be well-dressed, be embellished, be adorned
አዜጠ *ageṭä* be well-dressed, be decorated
አስዜጠ *asgeṭä* decorate, adorn, embellish, beautify
ዜጥ, see below
የዜጠ *yägeṭä* dressy, fashionable, ornate

ማጌጫ *mageča* adornment

ጌጥ *geṭ* ornament, decoration, adornment (see *ጌጠ)

ጌጥ ፡ የበዛበት *geṭ yäbäzzabbät* colorful

ጌጣጌጥ *geṭageṭ* jewelry, decorative ornament

ገጠመ *gäṭṭämä* fit (vt., vi.), be joined together, be tight (jar lid), join (vi.), match, tally, mingle, be united, deal with (have to do with), engage (the enemy), write poetry
(ችግር ፡ ገጠመው *he met with difficulties)

ተጋጠመ *tägaṭṭämä* meet (of teams), confront (the enemy), encounter, come together, concur, merge (of traffic), grow together (of branches), coincide (of events), articulate (unite by means of joints)
(ፊት ፡ ለፊት ፡ ተጋጠመ *be confronted)

አጋጠመ *aggaṭṭämä* bring together, combine, join, occur by chance, befall

አጋጠመ(ው) *aggaṭṭämä(w)* encounter, experience, meet with, run across, chance on, bump into

ገጣጠመ *gäṭaṭṭämä* reassemble

ተገጣጠመ *tägäṭaṭṭämä* agglutinate, fit together (vi.)

አገጣጠመ *aggäṭaṭṭämä* put together, fit together (vt.), join (vt.), assemble (machinery)

ግጥም, see below

ግጥሚያ, see below

ማገጣጠሚያ *maggäṭaṭämiya* joint (of body, of chair)

አጋጣሚ, see above

ተጋጣሚ *tägaṭami* adversary (contestant)

ግጥም *gäṭäm* poetry, lyrics, poem, verse (see ገጠመ)

የግጥም *yägäṭäm* poetic

የግጥም ፡ አንቀጽ strophe

ግጥሚያ *gäṭmiya* fight, game (competition), contest, match, engagement (fight), encounter, bout (see ገጠመ)

የግጥሚያ ፡ ጥሪ *yägäṭmiya ṭərri* challenge

ገጠር *gäṭär* the environs of a city, suburbs, rural area, countryside, open country

የገጠር rural

ግጦሽ *gäṭoš* pasture, grazing land (see ጋጠ)

የግጦሽ ፡ መሬት grazing land

ጉጠት *guṭät* pliers, forceps, pincers

ጌጣጌጥ, see ጌጥ

ገጨ *gäččä* collide, bump into, hit against, crash into (see also *ገጫገጨ)

ተጋጨ *tägaččä* knock against, hit one another, collide, crash, clash, bump, conflict

አጋጨ *aggaččä* bang (the elbow), clash (vt.), butt
(ከ - - - ጋር ፡ አጋጨ knock against)

ግጭት *gəččət* friction (conflict), discordant view, clash, encounter, crash, smashup, collision

የግጭት ፡ መከላከያ buffer

የሚጋጭ *yämmiggačč* inconsistent (argument)

ግጭት, see above

*ገጫገጨ, ተንገጫገጨ *tängäčaggäčä* clatter (vi.), rattle (vi.), chatter (of teeth), jerk along, bump along (see also ገጨ)

አንገጫገጨ *angäčaggäčä* jolt, rattle (vi.)

ገጽ *gäṣṣ* face (of the earth), surface (of earth, moon), page, side (of paper)

ገጽ ፡ በረከት gift, present

ገፋ *gäffa* push, shove, advance (move forward), be advanced (in age), go on (of time), impel, progress
(ሌሊቱ ፡ ገፍቷል it is getting late)
(በትምህርት ፡ ገፋ be advanced in studies)
(በዕድሜ ፡ ገፋ get on in years)

(ደረቱን ፡ ገፉ he mastered his courage)
ተገፋ tägäffa go forward (of work)
ተጋፋ tägaffa go forward, advance
(vi.), be pushed ahead, be pushed
around, press (push), shove one another, commit acts of violence
(ሥልጣኑን ፡ ተጋፋ he went over his
head)
(ተጋፍቶ ፡ አለፈ tägafto alläfä force
one's way through)
(እየተጋፋ ፡ ሄደ push one's way
through)
ገፋፋ gäfaffa urge on, press strongly, drive, impel, motivate, animate,
put pressure on, goad, prompt,
induce
ገፋ ፡ ቢል gəfa bil at most, at best
ግፍ, see below
ግፊት, see below
ግፊያ, see below
የገፋ advanced (in years)
(በዕድሜ ፡ የገፋ elderly)
ቢገፋ bigäfa at most
ቢገፋ ፡ ቢገፋ at most

ገፍ gäf, in በገፍ in abundance, in
quantity
በገፍ ፡ መኖር affluence

ግፍ gəf violence, injustice, unfairness,
abuse of power, atrocity, wickedness
(see ገፋ)
ግፍ ፡ ዋለ commit evil
ግፍ ፡ ፈጸም commit excesses
በግፍ bägəf violently, unjustly, in
cold blood
የግፍ yägəf iniquitous
የግፍ ፡ ሥራ injustice
ገፈኛ gəfäñña heartless, unfair, unjust

ጐፈሬ gʷäfäre large bushy hairdo

ጐፈር gʷäfär mane of lion

ጉፍታ gufta kerchief, scarf

ግፊት gəffit impulse (of wind), impul-
sion of steam (see ገፋ)
ያየር ፡ ግፊት air pressure (see አየር)

ግፊያ gəffiya crush, n. (people crowded), shoving, elbowing one's way,
pushing with shoulders (see ገፋ)

ጐፈየ gʷäfäyyä be lean (meat), be thin
(ox)
ጉፋየ gufayya lean (meat), thin (animal)

*ገፈገፈ, ተንገፈገፈ tängäfäggäfä have an
aversion to food, be disgusted by
food
አንገፈገፈ angäfäggäfä cause disgust,
arouse disgust, upset

*ጋፈጠ, ተጋፈጠ tägaffäṭä hurl oneself
at (the enemy)
አደጋን ፡ ተጋፈጠ court danger

ገፈፈ gäffäfä strip off (garment, arms,
hide), deprive of, divest, uncover,
skim off, skin, shed, clear away
(smoke)

ጠ

ጠላ ṭälla hate, abominate, abhor, detest, dislike, have a distaste for
ተጣላ täṭalla quarrel, dispute, have a
fight, disagree violently
አስጠላ asṭälla, causative of the
preceding; disgust (vt.), sicken (of
odor)
ጥል, see below
ጠላት, see below
ጥላቻ, see below
አስጠሊ asṭälli abhorrent
የተጠላ yätäṭälla unpopular
የሚያስጠላ yämmiyasṭälla deplorable (order), odious, dreadful

*ጠላ, አጠላ aṭälla shade (vt.)
ጥላ, see below

ጠላ ṭälla native beer

ጣለ ṭalä throw, throw away, throw out,
throw down, discard, drop, fell (a
tree), abandon, lose, repudiate (the
family), shed (the horns), cast off

(መሥረት ፡ ጣለ lay the foundation)
(ቀረጥ ፡ ጣለ impose a tax)
(በረዶ ፡ ጣለ hail, v.)
(ተስፋ ፡ ጣለ(በት) täsfa ṭalä(bbät) he
placed his hopes on him)
(እምነት ፡ ጣለ(በት) he placed his confidence in him)
(ዕቁብ ፡ ጣለ attend the әqqub meeting)
(እንቁላል ፡ ጣለ(ች) lay eggs)
(አደጋ ፡ ጣለ attack by surprise, strike
a blow)
(አደጋ ፡ ላይ ፡ ጣለ expose to danger,
jeopardize, imperil)
(ዝናብ ፡ ጣለ rain, v.)
(ጡት ፡ ጣለ be weaned)
(ጥንቡን ፡ ጣለ hit rock bottom (of
prices)
(ጨርቁን ፡ ጣለ he was stark raving
mad, lit. he threw off his clothes)
አስጣለ asṭalä, causative of the
preceding; rescue
ተጣጣለ täṭaṭalä draw (lots)
ጣል ፡ አደረገ ṭall adärrägä toss, leave
a little bit, throw around the shoulders (a shawl)
የተጣለ yätäṭalä abandoned (child),
forlorn
የሚጥል ፡ በሽታ yämmiṭәl bäššәta epilepsy, fit (n.)

ጥላ ṭәla shadow, shade, umbrella (see
*ጠላ, ጣለለ)
ጥላማ ṭәlamma shady

ጥል ṭәl enmity, hatred, quarrel, brawl,
fight (see ጠላ)
ጥለኛ ṭәläñña person who is not on
speaking terms with someone, antag-
onist

ጠለለ ṭällälä be pure, be clean, be
filtered, be purified
አጠለለ aṭällälä purify, filter, strain
(butter)
ማጥሊያ, see above

ጠለለ ṭällälä shelter, screen off, shade
ተጠለለ täṭällälä take cover, take
shelter (from the rain, sun), seek
refuge

መጠለያ mäṭṭäläya (n.) shed, shelter

ጥሎሽ ṭәloš dowry, money the fiancé
gives the fiancée for her trousseau

ጥላሸት ṭәlašät soot (on pots)

ጠለቀ ṭälläqä dip (bread in sauce),
dunk, dive, plunge, sink (of sun), set
(of sun), submerge (vi.), be deep, be
profound
አጠለቀ aṭälläqä dip (a bucket into
a lake), put on (a sweater, trousers),
wear (a chain around the neck)
(ላብ ፡ አጠለቀው he was drenched
with sweat)
ጠለቅ ፡ አደረገ ṭäläqq adärrägä slip
on (a coat)
ጠለቅ ፡ ያለ ṭäläqq yalä expert, adj.
(advice), serious (book)
ጥልቅ, see below
ጥለቀት ṭәlqät depth
ጥልቅነት ṭәlqәnnät profundity
የጠለቀ yäṭälläqä intimate (knowledge)
[See also ጣልቃ ፡ ገባ, ጥልቅ ፡ አለ]

ጣልቃ ፡ ገባ ṭalqa gäbba meddle, interfere, intervene, break into (a conversation), intrude, pry (see also ጠለቀ,
and ጥልቅ ፡ አለ)
ጣልቃ ፡ ገብ meddler
ጣልቃ ፡ ገብነት intrusiveness, interference

ጥልቅ ṭәlq deep (lake), profound,
penetrating (remark), expert (knowledge), sound (advice), grave
(thought), thorough (study), thoughtful (remark, observation), serious
(book); see ጠለቀ
ጥልቅ ፡ ያልሆነ shallow
በጥልቅ bäṭәlq deeply

ጥልቅ ፡ አለ ṭәllәqq alä intrude, mix in,
cut in, turn up (appear); see also
ጠለቀ and ጣልቃ ፡ ገባ
ጥልቅ ፡ ብዬ ṭәllәqq bәyye busybody

*ጠለቀለቀ, አጥለቀለቀ aṭläqälläqä flood,
inundate, overflow (vt.), wash away

ተጥለቀለቀ *täṭläqälläqä* be flooded, be
overflowing
መጥለቅለቅ *mäṭläqläq*, in የውኃ ፡ መጥ
ለቅለቅ flood (n.)

ጥልቀት *ṭəlqät* depth (see ጠለቀ)
ጥልቀት ፡ ለካ sound (the lake)
ጥልቀት ፡ ያለው—*yalläw* deep
ጥልቀት ፡ የሌለው- shallow
የጀንበር ፡ ጥልቀት sundown

ጥልቅነት *ṭəlqənnät* profundity (see ጠለቀ)

ጠላት *ṭälat* enemy, adversary, foe (see
ጠላ)
የጠላት hostile (territory)
የጠላት ፡ ጊዜ the Italian occupation
ጠላትነት *ṭälatənnät* enmity

ጥለት *ṭəlät* stripe, embroidered fringe
of dress, decorative band

ጥላት *ṭəlat* soot (on pots)

ጥላቻ *ṭəlaččä* hatred, abhorrence, ill
feeling, distaste, dislike, hostility,
animosity, revulsion, antagonism (see
ጠላ)
ጥላቻ ፡ የተመላበት — *yätämällabbät*
hateful (see መላ)
ጥላቻ ፡ ያዘለ —*yazzälä* hostile, inimical (see አዘለ)
የጥላቻ *yäṭəlaččä* hostile (attitude),
inimical

ጥለኛ, see ጥል

ጣልያን *ṭalyan* Italian

*ጠለጠለ, ተንጠለጠለ *tänṭäläṭṭälä* hang
(vi.), swing, vi. (of monkey), dangle,
be suspended
አንጠለጠለ *anṭäläṭṭälä* suspend (a
lamp), hang up
መንጠልጠያ, see above

ጠለፈ *ṭälläfä* grab, entangle, trip, tie
the legs of an animal, kidnap (a girl
to marry her), hijack; embroider
ተጠላለፈ *täṭälalläfä* interlace, vi.
(of branches), interlock (of horns),
intertwine

ጠለፋ *ṭäläfa* abduction, hijacking
ጥልፍ *ṭəlf* embroidery, embroidered,
needlework

ጠማ(ው) *ṭämma(w)* be thirsty, thirst
for, have a thirst for
(ውኃ ፡ ጠማው- he is thirsty for water)
ጥም *ṭəm* thirst
ጥማት *ṭəmat* thirst

ጢም *ṭim* beard, moustache
ባፉ ፡ ጢም ፡ ተደፋ fall on one's
face, fall upside down

ጢም ፡ አለ *ṭimm alä* be crowded to
capacity, be filled to capacity
ጢም ፡ ብሎ ፡ ሞላ *ṭimm bəlo molla*
be filled to capacity, be filled to
the brim

ጣመ *ṭamä* be tasty, taste pleasant,
be of good taste, be savory, satisfy,
content
(ነገሩ ፡ አይጥመኝም *nägäru ayaṭəmäñ-
ñəm* I don't like the way he talks)
ጣም, see below
በጣም *bäṭam* very
ጣዕም, see below
ጥዑም *ṭə'um* mellow (wine)
የማይጥም *yämmayaṭəm* tasteless, drab
(existence), unsatisfactory

ጣም *ṭam* (n.) flavor, taste, savor (see
ጣመ, ጣዕም)

ጥም *ṭəm* thirst; see ጠማ

ጦመ *ṭomä* fast (v.); see also ጾመ
ጦም *ṭom* fast (n.)
ጦሙን ፡ አደረ go without supper

*ጠመለመለ, ተጥመለመለ *täṭmälämmälä*
coil, vi. (of snake), meander (of river),
wriggle (of worm), twist, vi. (of
road), curl (of hair)

ጠመመ *ṭämmämä* be crooked, be
curved, be twisted, be warped, be
deformed
ተጣመመ *täṭammämä* be crooked, be
distorted

አጣመመ *aṭṭammämä* distort (of a mirror distorting the face), twist (vt.), bend (vt.)
ጠማማ *ṭämama* crooked, curved, bent, tortuous (reasoning)

*ጠመረ, አጣመረ *aṭṭammärä* combine (put together), fold (the arms), cross (the arms), join, couple, wed
መስተጻምር *mästäṣamər* conjunction (in grammar)

ጠመቀ *ṭämmäqä* immerse oneself in water; brew beer
አጠመቀ *aṭämmäqä* baptize, christen
ተጠመቀ *täṭämmäqä* be baptized
ጥምቀት, see below

ጥምቀት *ṭəmqät* baptism, Epiphany (Feast of the Immersion); see ጠመቀ
የጥምቀት ፡ በዓል *yäṭəmqät bä'al* Epiphany

ጥምብ, see ጥንብ

ጥማት *ṭəmat* thirst; see ጠማ(ው)

ጠመኔ *ṭämäne* chalk (for blackboard)

ጥሞና *ṭəmona*, in በጥሞና calmly

ጠመንጃ *ṭämänǧa* rifle, gun (see also ጠበንጃ)
(የ)ጠመንጃ ፡ መፍቻ screwdriver

ጠመዝማዛ *ṭämäzmazza* sinuous (see ጠመዘዘ)
ጥምዝምዝ *ṭəməzməz* turn (in the road)

ጠመዘዘ *ṭämäzzäzä* twist, wring (wet clothes)
ተጠማዘዘ *täṭämazzäzä* wind, vi. (of stream), bend, vi. (of stream)
ጥምዝዝ *ṭəmzəz* twisted
ጠምዛዛ *ṭämzazza* tortuous (road), spiral (adj.), winding
መጠምዘዣ *mäṭämzäža* curve, crook (curve), turn (in the road)
የሚጠመዘዝ *yämmiṭṭämäzazzäz* spiral, winding, sinuous
[See also ጠመዝማዛ]

ጠመደ *ṭämmädä* yoke, join up (the oxen)
(ሥራ ጠመደው he is engaged in work)
ተጠመደ *täṭämmädä* be yoked, be involved, be installed (machine)
አጠመደ *aṭämmädä* entrap, set traps, lay snares, ensnare, catch (a fish), install (a machine)
ጥምድ *ṭəmd*, ጥንድ *ṭənd* pair, couple
ጥምድ ፡ በሬ yoke of oxen
ጠማድ *ṭämmad* team (of oxen)
አጥማጅ *aṭmaǧ*, in ዓሣ ፡ አጥማጅ fisherman
ወጥመድ *wäṭmäd* trap for animals, snare

ጠመጠመ *ṭämäṭṭämä* wrap (a scarf around the head or neck), wind (e.g. bandage, turban), tie a package with a string, coil up (vt.)
ተጠመጠመ *täṭämäṭṭämä*, passive of the preceding; be entwined, cling to (a child to his mother)
ጥምጥም ፡ አለ *ṭəmṭəmm alä* curl up
ጥምጥም *ṭəmṭəm* twisted, wrapped around, turban, band for hat

ጠራ *ṭärra* call, call up, name, invite, mention, summon, recite (names)
(ስም ፡ ጠራ take attendance, call the roll)
(ቡና ፡ ጠራ invite to coffee)
(በስልክ ፡ ጠራ n a'ke a telephone call)
ተጠራ *täṭärra*, passive of the preceding; be famous
(ስም ፡ ተጠራ he found recognition)
ጥሪ *ṭərri* call (n.), invitation, summons
ተጠሪ *täṭäri* representative
መጠሪያ, see above
መጥሪያ, see above
አጠራር *aṭṭarar* appellation

ጠራ *ṭärra* be pure, be filtered, be clarified, be clear, brighten, vi. (of sky), clear up (of weather)
አጠራ *aṭärra* purify, make clear, clean, elucidate

ተጣራ *tätarra* be refined (sugar), be purified, be filtered
አጣራ *attarra* purify, filter, distill, clarify, check (figures), ascertain, make sure, clear up (an ambiguity)
ጥሩ, see below
ጥራት, see below
ጥሩነት, see ጥሩ
ማጣሪያ *mattariya* filter (n.)
የጠራ *yätärra* limpid (water), lucid (lake), serene (sky), refined (language), clear (voice, day)
የተጣራ *yatätarra* purified, net (salary), perceptive (analysis)
ያልተጣራ *yaltätarra* impure, crude (oil)

ጡC *tur*, in ነፍስ ፡ ጡC pregnant (see ጠረ)
ጡርነት, in ነፍስ ፡ ጡርነት *näfsä turannät* pregnancy

ጡC *tur* punishment that befalls a wrongdoer
ጡረኛ *turäñña* one who receives the punishment for his wrongdoing

ጣረ *tarä* try very hard, make an effort, labor, toil, be afflicted
ተጣጣረ *tätatarä* endeavor, try again and again, strive for, be in agony
ጣC *tar* death throes
ጣረሞት *tarämot* agony, death throes, apparition, ghost
ጥረት *tärät* labor (effort), application (effort)

ጣራ *tara* ceiling, roof (see also ጣሪያ)

ጥሩ *täru* good, nice, fine (weather), clear (water), perfect (condition); see ጠራ be pure
ጥሩ ፡ አድርጎ well (adv.)
ስም ፡ ጥሩ ፤ ስም ፡ ጥC famous, reputable, prominent, celebrity
ጥሩነት *tärunnät* virtue (good quality), excellence, goodness

ጥሪ, see ጠራ call

ጥራ ፡ ጥሬ ፤ ጥራጥሬ *taratare* cereals, pulses (see ጥሬ)

ጥሬ *tare* raw (meat), green (grain), unripe, crude (vegetables), common (vulgar)
ጥሬ ፡ እቃ raw material
ጥሬ ፡ ገንዘብ cash
ጥራ ፡ ጥሬ ፤ ጥራጥሬ *taratare* cereals

ጥC *tarr* January

ጠረ *torä* care for one's aged parents, provide for someone, support (one's parents); see also ጠወረ
ጡC *tur*, in ነፍስ ፡ ጡC pregnant
ጡረታ, see below
መጠሪያ *mättoriya* pension

ጦC *tor* lance, spear, javelin, war, army
የጦC military (adj.)
የጦC ፡ ኃይል armed forces
የጦC ፡ መርከብ warship
የጦC ፡ መርከቦች fleet
የጦC ፡ መሣሪያ weapon, armament
የጦC ፡ ሚኒስቴC Ministry of War
የጦC ፡ ሜዳ battlefield
የጦC ፡ ስልት strategy, tactics
(የ)ጦC ፡ ሰራዊት army
የጦC ፡ ካሳ war reparations
የጦC ፡ ክፍል army unit
የጦC ፡ ግምባC front (military)
የጦC ፡ ጓደኛ ally
ብሔራዊ ፡ ጦC militia
ክፍለ ፡ ጦC division (army unit)
የምድC ፡ ጦC ground forces
ጦረኛ *toräñña* warrior
ጦርነት, see below

ጠርሙስ *tärmus* glass bottle

ጥሩምባ *trumba* trumpet, auto horn (see also ጥሩንባ)
ጥሩምባ ፡ ነፋ play the trumpet

ጣረሞት *tarämot* death throes, apparition, ghost (see ጣረ, ሞት)

ጠራራ *tärara* blazing (sun), heat of sun
የጠራራ ፡ ፀሐይ midday sun

*ጠራራ, ተንጠራራ *tänṭärarra* stretch,
vi. (to reach a high place), reach up

ጥርስ *ṭərs* tooth, tusk
ጥርስ ፡ አወጣ cut teeth, teethe (see
ወጣ)
ጥርሱን ፡ ነክሶ patiently
የጥርስ ፡ ሐኪም *yäṭərs hakim* dentist
የጥርስ ፡ ሳሙና toothpaste
የዝሆን ፡ ጥርስ ivory

*ጠረቀመ, አጠራቀመ *aṭṭäraqqämä* collect, accumulate (vt.), stockpile,
amass (money)
ተጠራቀመ *tāṭäraqqämä* be collected,
collect (vi.), gather (of many people),
accumulate (vi.), conglomerate
ጥርቃሜ *ṭərəqqami* conglomeration
ማጠራቀሚያ *maṭṭäraqämiya* reservoir

ጠረበ *ṭärräbä* carve, hew (wood, stones)
ጠርብ *ṭärb* board, plank, lumber,
beam (of wood)
መጥረቢያ *mäṭräbiya* hatchet, ax, adze

ጡረታ *ṭuräta* taking care of indigent
parents, retirement (see ጠረ)
ጡረታ ፡ ገባ ፤ ጡረታ ፡ ወጣ retire,
vi. (give up an occupation), be pen-
sioned
ጡረታ ፡ አስገባ pension off, retire (vt.)
የጡረታ ፡ አበል social security, pension

ጥረት, see ጣረ

ጥራት *ṭərat* purity, pureness (see ጠራ
'be pure')

ጠረን *ṭärän* scent (of a person or animal)

ጥሩንባ, see ጥሩምባ

ጥሩነት, see ጥሩ

ጦርነት *ṭorənnät* battle, war, warfare
(see ጦር)
የርስ ፡ በርስ ፡ ጦርነት civil war

ጥርኝ *ṭərəñ* civet cat

ጦረኛ *ṭoräñña* warrior (see ጦር)

ጠረዘ *ṭärräzä* (B) sew together, bind
(a book)
ጠርዝ, see below
ጥራዝ *ṭəraz* volume, binding
ጥራዝ ፡ ነጠቅ *ṭəraz näṭṭäq* dilettante,
semi-learned, superficial, pedantic
ጠራዥ *ṭärraž* bookbinder

ጠርዝ *ṭärz* hem, edge (of plate),
fringe (of leaf), brink (of well),
border (of rug), rim, corner (of box);
see ጠረዘ
የመንገድ ፡ ጠርዝ curb

ጣሪያ *ṭariya* roof, ceiling (see also ጣራ)

ጠረገ *ṭärrägä* sweep, clean, wipe
(dishes, spittle), mop (the forehead), shine (shoes), open a road to,
clear a road to
ጠራጊ *ṭäragi* janitor
(ጫማ ፡ ጠራጊ shoeshine boy)
ጥራጊ *ṭərragi* sweepings, rubbish,
sewage
ጥርጊያ ፡ መንገድ *ṭərgiya mängäd*
cleared and graded (but not paved)
road
መጥረጊያ *mäṭrägiya* broom, sweeper

ጠረጠረ *ṭäräṭṭärä* suspect, mistrust,
doubt, distrust, have suspicions
ተጠራጠረ *tāṭäraṭṭärä* be distrustful
of, doubt, be in doubt about, call
into question, be incredulous of,
wonder (feel a doubt)
አጠራጠረ *aṭṭäraṭṭärä* be unlikely,
be in doubt, raise doubts
ጥርጣሬ *ṭərəṭṭare* distrust, suspicion,
doubt, misgivings
ጥርጥር *ṭərəṭṭər* doubt (n.)
(ያለ ፡ ጥርጥር without question, undoubtedly, unquestionably, doubtless)
ተጠርጣሪ *tāṭärṭari* suspect (n., adj.)
ተጠራጣሪ *tāṭäraṭari* sceptic, scep-
tical, suspicious, distrustful
አጠራጣሪ *aṭṭäraṭari* questionable,
equivocal, doubtful

የማያጠራጥር *yämmayaṭṭäraṭṭər* decided (unquestionable), conclusive
የሚያስጠረጥር *yämmiyasṭäräṭṭər* dubious, suspicious
አይጠረጠርም *ayəṭṭäräṭṭärəm* it is beyond question

ጠረጴዛ *ṭäräppeza* table, desk
የጠረጴዛ ፡ ልብስ tablecloth

ጠረፍ *ṭäräf* coast, shore, bank (of river), frontier, border

ጢስ *ṭis* smoke, fume (see ጢሰ)
የሞርዟ ፡ ጢስ poison gas
ጢሰኛ *ṭisäñña* sharecropper, tenant farmer

ጣሰ *ṭasä* break through (a fence, frontier), pierce through, penetrate (the enemy lines), trespass, breach, violate (the law), infringe, defy
ጥሶ ፡ ገባ *ṭəso gäbba* encroach, break into
መጣስ *mäṭas* transgression, infraction
የማይጣስ *yämmayəṭṭas* inviolable

ጣሳ *ṭasa* tin can
በጣሳ ፡ አሸግ can (food)

ጢሰ *ṭesä* smoke (vi.), emit smoke
አጢሰ *aṭesä* smoke (a cigarette)
ጢስ *ṭis* (n.) smoke, fume
[See also ጨሰ]

ጢሰኛ, see ጢስ

ጦስኝ *ṭosəñ* thyme

ጥሻ *ṭəša*, ጢሻ *ṭiša* thicket, underbrush, bush

ጠቃ *ṭäqqa* beat, knock
ተጠቃ *täṭäqqa*, passive of the preceding; mate (of animals)
አጠቃ *aṭäqqa* attack, assault, commit aggression against, afflict (attack), overpower
(ብቸኝነት ፡ ጠቃው· he is beset with loneliness)
ጥቃት *ṭəqat* assault, attack, oppression

†አጥቂ *aṭqi* aggressor
ማጥቃት *maṭqat* (n.) charge (attack), offensive
የማጥቂያ *yämaṭqiya* offensive, adj. (weapons)

ጥቅል *ṭəqəll* rolled up, parcel, bundle, package, reel, roll, ball (of yarn), spool (see ጠቀለለ)
ጥቅል ፡ ጎመን head of cabbage
ጥቅል ፡ ጸጉር curls
የጥቅል ፡ ስም *yäṭəqəll səm* collective noun

ጠቀለለ *ṭäqällälä* wind, wrap, wrap up, fold, roll up (a rug), envelop, bundle up, pack
ተጠቀለለ *täṭäqällälä* roll, vi. (of cloth), be rolled up, be wrapped, comprise, include (vi.)
አጣቀለለ *aṭṭäqallälä* aggregate (vt.), encompass, cover (a subject), sum up (an idea), generalize, involve (include), lump (put together), compress (into), consolidate (land holdings)
ጥቅልል ፡ አለ *ṭəqləll alä* roll oneself up
ጠቅላላ, see below
ጥቅል, see above
ጠቅላይ, see below
አጠቃላይ, see above
መጠቅለያ *mäṭäqläya* wrapper, package

ጠቅላላ *ṭäqlalla* overall, integral (complete), gross (income), total (entire), general, rough (idea); see ጠቀለለ
ጠቅላላ ፡ ድምር grand total, aggregate, sum total
ጠቅላላ ፡ ጉባኤ General Assembly
ጠቅላላውን *ṭäqlallawən* generally, in general
በጠቅላላ ፡ አነጋገር generally speaking
በጠቅላላው· generally, in general, in the main, all in all, altogether, on the whole, by and large, in sum

ጠቅላይ *ṭäqlay* all-inclusive, that which covers all, that which commands all, principal (adj.); see ጠቀለለ

ጠቅላይ ፣ መምሪያ headquarters
ጠቅላይ ፣ ሚኒስትር premier, prime
minister
ጠቅላይ ፣ ዐቃቤ ፣ ሕግ attorney general
ጠቅላይ ፣ ግዛት province

ጠቀመ ṭäqqämä be beneficial, benefit (vt.), render service, be of use,
profit
ተጠቀመ täṭäqqämä use, make use
of, apply, have the enjoyment of,
benefit (vi.), take advantage of,
derive profit
ጠቃሚ ṭäqami beneficial, advantageous, salutary (useful), valuable
(useful), profitable, productive, helpful (hint), important
ጥቅም, see below
ጠቃሚነት ṭäqaminnät usefulness, utility, importance
ተጠቃሚ täṭäqqami beneficiary
የሚጠቅም yämmiṭäqəm advanta-
geous

ጠቀመ ṭäqqämä darn, stitch (make
stitches in), mend, patch

ጠቄመ ṭäqqʷämä (B) give a hint, tip
off, inform on, intimate, point out,
point at
ጠቋሚ ṭäqqʷami stool pigeon, informer
መጠቌሚያ mäṭäqqʷämiya pointer

ጥቅም ṭəqəm (n.) benefit, use, usefulness, profit, advantage, interest
(in business), value, importance (see
ጠቀመ)
ጥቅም ፣ ቢስ useless
በጥቅም ፣ ላይ ፣ አዋለ bäṭəqəm—
exploit, put to use
ባለ ፣ ጥቅም partner, beneficiary

ጥቅምት ṭəqəmt October

ጠቄረ ṭäqqʷärä be black, turn black,
tan (in the sun), grow dark (see also
ጠቆረቆረ)
አጠቄረ aṭäqqʷärä blacken, darken
(ፊቱን ፣ አጠቄረ have a solemn face)

የጠቄረ yäṭäqqʷärä heavy (skies)
ጥቁር, see below

ጥቁር ṭəqur black, dark (skin), Negro (see ጠቄረ)
ጥቁር ፣ ሰሌዳ blackboard

ጥቀርሻ ṭəqärša soot which has collected on the ceiling or roof

ጠቍርቍር ፣ አለ ṭäqʷärqʷärr alä be
dark (see ጠቄረ)

ጠቀሰ ṭäqqäsä dunk (bread), dip a pen
into ink
አጠቀሰ aṭäqqäsä dip (bread into
the sauce)

ጠቀሰ ṭäqqäsä wink at, gesture, nod,
quote, cite, mention, adduce, motion,
beckon, refer to, allude
ጠቀስ ṭäqqäs, in ሰማይ ፣ ጠቀስ ፣ ሕንጻ
skyscraper
ጥቅስ ṭəqs quotation, citation
(ትእምርተ ፣ ጥቅስ quotation mark)
ጥቅሻ, see below

ጥቅሻ ṭəqša wink, hint (allusion); see
ጠቀሰ wink at

ጥቃቅን ṭəqaqqən diminutive, minor,
miniature (adj.), tiny, finer (points of
a contract)

ጥቂት ṭəqit little, few, some, small
amount
ጥቂት ፣ በጥቂት gradually
ጥቂት ፣ ጊዜ a while
ለጥቂት just, adv. (barely), by a hair
ለጥቂት ፣ አመለጠ he had a narrow
escape
ለጥቂት ፣ ጊዜ for a moment, momentarily, a while

ጥቃት, see ጠቃ

ጠቀጠቀ ṭäqäṭṭäqä trample, tread on,
stuff, press down, pound, scar (of
smallpox), compress
የጠቀጠቀ yäṭäqäṭṭäqä compact
ጠቃጠቆ ṭäqaṭäqo speckle, freckle,
spot

ጠቃጠቆ ፡ አለበት—*alläbbät* be spotty (complexion)

ጥቅጥቅ ፡ አለ *ṭəqṭəqq alä* be dense (fog, forest), be thick (hedge), be luxuriant, be crowded (forest), be heavy (smoke)

ጠባ *ṭäbba* suck, suckle (vi.)
አጠባ(ች) *aṭäbba(čč)* suckle (vt.)
ጣቢ *ṭäbi*, in ጀር ፡ ጣቢ. informer, tattler
ጡት, see below

ጠባ *ṭäbba* become day, dawn
አጥቢያ *aṭbiya* dawn

ጠብ *ṭäb* quarrel, fight, conflict, contention, strife, dissension, state of belligerence
ጠብ ፡ ቄሰቄሰ provoke an argument
ጠብ ፡ ጫረ pick a quarrel
ጠብ ፡ ጫሪ aggressive, trouble maker
(የ)ጠብ ፡ ጫሪነት aggression
ጠብ ፡ ወዳድ belligerent
ጠበኛ, see below

ጠብ ፡ አለ *ṭäbb alä* fall drop by drop, drip, jump down (see also *ጠብ ጠብ)
ጠብታ *ṭäbbəta* drop, speck

ጡብ *ṭub* brick, tile
ጡብ ፡ ገንቢ bricklayer

ጡብ ፡ ጡብ ፡ አለ *ṭubb ṭubb alä* hop about (of birds)

ጥቢ *ṭəbbi* season after the rains

ጠበል *ṭäbäl* mineral water, holy water, monthly ceremony in honor of saints

*ጠበረበረ, አጥበረበረ *aṭbäräbbärä* be glaring (light), blind (of sun), bedazzle

ጠበሰ *ṭäbbäsä* fry, roast (meat, corn), toast, scorch, broil, bake (clay), fire (clay)
ተጠበሰ *täṭäbbäsä* be fired (pots), roast (vi.)

ጥብስ *ṭəbs* roasted, roast, fried, toast
ጠባሳ *ṭäbasa* scar (n.)
መጥበሻ, see above

ጠበቀ *ṭäbbäqä* be firm, be secure, be stuck together, be tightened, be fastened, be stressed (a syllable)
ተጠበቀ *täṭäbbäqä* be geminated (a consonant)
አጠበቀ *aṭäbbäqä* lay emphasis, put emphasis, fasten, tighten
ተጣበቀ *täṭabbäqä* adhere to, be glued, cling to, be stuck together, stick (vi.)
አጣበቀ *aṭṭabbäqä* glue (vt.), stick (glue)
ጥብቆ *ṭəbbəqqo* close-fitting shirt worn by children
ጥብቅ, see below
(ተጠባባቂ *täṭäbabaqi* adhesive)
ማጣበቂያ *maṭṭabäqiya* gum (sticky substance), paste, glue
አጥብቆ, see above
የሚጣበቅ *yämmiṭṭabbäq* cohesive, adherent (sticky)

ጠበቀ *ṭäbbäqä* (B) guard, protect, defend, look after, watch, tend, take care of, maintain, wait for, await, expect, observe (silence, fast, regulations), preserve
(ቃል ፡ ጠበቀ keep one's promise)
(ዠብ ፡ ጠበቀ be on guard duty)
(ጊዜ ፡ ጠበቀ bide one's time)
ተጠበቀ *täṭäbbäqä*, passive of the preceding
(ከ - - - ተጠበቀ abstain)
ተጠባበቀ *täṭäbabbäqä* keep a lookout, await, expect, look forward to something, wait expectantly
ጠባቂ *ṭäbbaqi* guardian, custodian, keeper, attendant
ጠባቂነት *ṭäbbaqinnät* custody
ጠበቃ, see below
ጥበቃ, see below
ተተጠባባቂ *täṭäbabaqi* acting (adj.)

ጠበቃ *ṭäbäqa* attorney, lawyer, advocate, counselor (see ጠበቀ guard)

ጠበቃ ፡ ገዛ hire a lawyer, engage a lawyer
የተከላሽ ፡ ጠበቃ defense attorney
(see ከሰሰ)

ጥብቃ ṭäbbäqa protection, conservation, maintenance, guarding, guard (see ጠበቀ)
የሕዝብ ፡ ጸጥታ ፡ ጥብቃ yähǝzb—Public Security Department
የጤና ፡ ጥብቃ ፡ ሚኒስቴር Ministry of Health
የጽዳት ፡ ጥብቃ yäṣǝdat— sanitation (lit. maintenance of cleanliness)

ጥብቅ ṭǝbq tight, tied, strict, steady (ladder), solid, severe (strict), austere, rigid, rigorous, harsh (judge), stern (teacher), tenacious (grip), drastic (measure), close (examination), deep (secret); see ጠበቀ be firm
ጥብቅ ፡ ያለ ṭǝbbǝqq yalä compact (package)
በጥብቅ bäṭǝbq expressly, tight (adv.), firmly, severely

ጠበበ ṭäbbäbä be narrow, be tight (clothes), be restricted
አጠበበ aṭäbbäbä narrow (vt.), crowd (the room)
ተጣበበ täṭabbäbä be crowded, be jammed
አጣበበ aṭṭabbäbä crowd, jam
ጠበብ ፡ አለ ṭäbäbb alä narrow (vi.)
†ጠባብ ṭäbbab narrow, tight
ጥበት ṭǝbbät constriction (being narrow)
የተጣበበ yätäṭabbäbä cramped (place)

ጠቢብ ṭäbib wise, artisan, metalsmith (see ጥበብ)
የጠቢብ masterly
ጠቢብነት ṭäbibǝnnät wisdom

ጠባብ ṭäbbab narrow, tight (see ጠበበ)
ጠባብ ፡ ሱሪ breeches
እጅ ፡ ጠባብ Ethiopian shirt

ጥበብ ṭǝbäb wisdom, craft, ability, art (skill), technique

ሥነ ፡ ጥበብ fine arts
ዐውደ ፡ ጥበብ encyclopedia
የእጅ ፡ ጥበብ handicraft
ጥበበኛ, see below
[See also ጠቢብ]

ጥበብ ṭǝbäb šämma-dress with multi-colored hems
ጥበብ ፡ የሌለው unembroidered

ጥበበኛ ṭǝbäbäňňa artisan, wise, dexterous (see ጥበብ)
ጥበበኛነት ṭǝbäbäňňannät craftsmanship

ጠብታ ṭäbbǝta (n.) drop, speck (see ጠብ ፡ አለ)

ጠቦት ṭäbbot lamb
የበግ ፡ ጠቦት lamb

ጥበት ṭǝbbät constriction (see ጠበበ)

ጠበንጃ ṭäbänǧa gun, rifle (see also ጠመንጃ)
ጠበንጃ ፡ መፍቻ screwdriver

ጠበኛ ṭäbäňňa pugnacious, quarrelsome, aggressive, person with whom one has a quarrel (see ጠብ)
የጠበኛነት yäṭäbäňňannät combative

ጠባይ ṭäbay nature (character), disposition, conduct (behavior), temperament, character, manners
ልዩ ፡ ጠባይ peculiarity
የአየር ፡ ጠባይ climate, weather

ጣቢያ ṭabiya station, terminal
ባቡር ፡ ጣቢያ railroad station
(የ)ፖሊስ ፡ ጣቢያ police station

ጠብደል ṭäbdäl husky (big and strong)

*ጠበጠበ, ተንጠባጠበ tänṭäbaṭṭäbä trickle (of water), drip, dribble, ooze, fall drop by drop, leak out, be scattered (see also ጠብ ፡ አለ)
አንጠባጠበ anṭäbaṭṭäbä be dripping (of a faucet), drop one by one, make spots on
ነጠብጣብ näṭäbṭab drop (n.), dots

ጥብጣብ *ṭəbṭab* ribbon (for dress), strip of cloth

ጡት *ṭut* breast, nipple, teat, bosom, spout (of coffee pot); see ጠባ
  ጡት : ተወ be weaned
  ጡት : አጠባ adopt a child (see ጠባ)
  ጡት : ጣለ be weaned
  ጡት : አስጣለች wean (see ጣለ)
  የጡት : ልጅ protégé, client (formal relationship)
  የጡት : አባት protector (formal relationship)

ጣት *ṭat* finger
  ሌባ : ጣት index finger
  ትንሽ : ጣት little finger
  አውራ : ጣት thumb
  (የ)መኻል : ጣት middle finger
  የቀለበት : ጣት ring finger
  የእግር : ጣት toe

ጧት ፤ ጥዋት *ṭwat* morning
  ነገ : ጧት tomorrow morning
  ዛሬ : ጧት this morning

ጠና *ṭänna* be strong, be solid, be firm, be resistant (see also ጸና)
  (በዕድሜ : ከጠና : በኋላ late in life)
  ተጠና *täṭänna* be studied, be considered, be under consideration
  አጠና *aṭänna* harden, make strong, reinforce, study, survey (examine)
  አስጠና *asṭänna* help to study, tutor
  አጥናና, see ጸና, አጽናና
  ጠና : ያለ *ṭäna yalä* strong, middle-aged, elderly
  ጥኑ *ṭənu* strong, solid, hard
  ጥናት *ṭənat* vigor, steadfastness, study, consideration, research, survey (a general look)
  በጠና *bäṭänna* seriously (ill)

ጠና *ṭänna*, in ደጅ : ጠና wait at someone's door for favors, court favor
  ደጅ : ጥናት *däǧǧ ṭənat* waiting at someone's door for favors

ጤና *ṭena* health
  ጤና : አይደለም be indisposed

ጤና : አጣ be in poor health
ጤና : ይስጥልኝ *ṭena yəsṭəlləňň* how are you?, good bye! (see ሰጠ)
ለጤና : ጠንቅ insanitary
ለጤናም to your health!
የጤና : ጥበቃ public health
የጤና : ጥበቃ : ሚኒስቴር Ministry of Health
የጤና : ጥበቃ : ኮሌጅ Public Health College
የጤና : ጥበቃ : ዘዴ hygiene
ጤናማ *ṭenamma* healthy (person), in good health
†ጤንነት *ṭenənnät* health
ጤነኛ *ṭenäňňa* healthy (body), sane

ጥና *ṭəna* censer

ጤናማ, see ጤና

ጠነሰሰ *ṭänässäsä* prepare the ingredients of beer, brew (mischief)
  ነገር : ጠነሰሰ brew trouble, brew mischief

ጠንቅ *ṭänq* pernicious, disastrous, harmful, nuisance, evil

ጠነቈለ *ṭänäqʷälä* be a soothsayer, foretell the future, engage in sorcery
  ጥንቈላ *ṭənqʷäla* witchcraft, divination, magic
  ጠንቋይ, see below

*ጠነቀረ, አጠናቀረ *aṭṭänaqqärä* amass, collect (piece by piece), piece together, compose (a speech)
  አጠናቃሪ, see ዜና

*ጠነቀቀ, ተጠነቀቀ *täṭänäqqäqä* be careful, be cautious, take precautions, be prudent, watch out, beware, mind (be careful), be mindful
  አጠናቀቀ *aṭṭänaqqäqä* take care of, settle (affairs), put in order, straighten out matters, complete (one's education, a course), acquire completely
  አስጠነቀቀ *asṭänäqqäqä* admonish, warn, alert, caution

ጠንቀቅ ፧ አለ *ṭänqäqq alä* be on the alert
ጠንቃቃ *ṭänqaqqa* precise, cautious, careful
ጥንቃቄ *ṭanaqqaqe* caution, prudence, attention given something, carefulness, care, precaution
(በጥንቃቄ intently, carefully, cautiously)
ጥንቁቅ *ṭanquq* deliberate (adj.), thorough, careful, meticulous, cautious, circumspect, scrupulous
ተጠንቀቅ *täṭänqäq* attention! (military command)
ተጠንቅቆ *täṭänqaqo* carefully
አጠናቆ *aṭṭänaqqo* completely
ማስጠንቀቂያ *masṭänqäqiya* warning, notice (warning), alert (n.)

ጠንቋይ *ṭänqʷay* magician, wizard, witch doctor (see ጠነቈለ)

ጠነባ *ṭänäbba* stink, putrefy
ጥንብ, see below

ጥንብ *ṭanb* dead body (of an animal), carrion, carcass (see ጠነባ and ጥምብ)
ጥንብ ፧ አንሣ *ṭanb ansa* vulture, buzzard (see ነሣ)
ጥንብ ፧ አንሺ *ṭanb anši* scavenger (see ነሣ)
ጥንቡን ፧ ጣለ hit rock bottom (of prices)

ጥናት, see ጠና

ጥንት *ṭant* beginning, origin, past, former days, ancient times, in olden days, formerly, early, originally (see ወጠነ)
ጥንት ፧ ሁኔታ original circumstances
ጥንት ፧ መሠረት original basis
ጥንት ፧ ነገር essence
ጥንት ፧ ንጥር element (simple substance)
በጥንት *bäṭant* in the beginning, at first
የጥንት *yäṭant* ancient, old, remote, primitive, early (life), antique, archaic

ጥንታዊ *ṭantawi* ancient, former
ጥንታዊነት *ṭantawinnät* antiquity (oldness)

ጡንቻ *ṭunča* muscle
የጡንቻ muscular (ache)
ጡንቻማ *ṭunčamma* muscular (leg)
ጡንቻኛ *ṭunčäňňa* hefty

ጥንቸል *ṭančäl* hare, rabbit

ጤንነት *ṭenännät* health (see ጤና)
ጤንነት ፧ አልተሰማውም he felt bad (see ሰማ)
የጤንነት medical (bulletin)

ጤነኛ *ṭenäňňa* healthy (body), sane (see ጤና)

ጠነከረ *ṭänäkkärä* be hard, be strong, be powerful, be solid, be vigorous, be tough
አጠነከረ *aṭänäkkärä* enforce, reinforce, strengthen, harden, fortify, consolidate (a position), solidify, confirm (strengthen)
ጠንካራ *ṭänkarra* robust, strong, firm, solid, hard, vigorous, tough, sturdy (table), hale
ጥንካሬ *ṭanakkare* strength, toughness
ጠንክሮ *ṭänkaro* hard (adv.)
ጠንካራነት *ṭänkarrannät* stability (of character), fortitude

ጥንዚዛ *ṭanzizza* kind of beetle

ጥንድ, see ጠመደ

ጠነጠነ *ṭänäṭṭänä* wind thread on the spindle
ማጠንጠኛ *maṭänṭäňňa* spool, bobbin, reel

ጥንፍ, see ጽንፍ

ጣዕም *ṭa'am* flavor, taste, good taste, savor (see ጣመ, ጣም)
ጣዕም ፧ ቢስ tasteless, flavorless
ጣዕም ፧ የለውም be insipid, be tasteless, be dull (book)

ጥዑም *ṭə'um* mellow (wine); see ጣመ

ጣዖት *ṭa'ot* idol, deity
ጣዖት ፡ አመለከ practice idolatry
የጣዖት ፡ አምልኮ idolatry

ጥዋ *ṭəwwa* font, chalice, cup (see also
ጽዋ)

*ጠወለወለ, አጥወለወለ *aṭwäläwwälä* nauseate, make one sick (of a motion)
አጥወለወለ(ው) he was airsick, he had
motion sickness

ጠወለገ *ṭäwällägä* wither (vi.), wilt,
fade, droop (of flowers, leaves)

ጠወረ *ṭäwwärä* (B) take care of one's
old indigent relatives (see also ጠረ)

ጣዖስ *ṭawos* pheasant, peacock

ጥዋት, see ጧት

ጢዝ ፡ አለ *ṭizz alä* buzz (of bee),
hum

*ጢዘ , አጢዘ *aṭezä* condense (of vapor)
ጢዛ *ṭeza* dew
የውኃ ፡ መጢዝ condensation

ጣዝማ *ṭazma* bee-like insect, wild honey

ጣይ *ṭay* sun (see also ፀሐይ)

ጠይም *ṭäyyəm* dark brown (person's
complexion)

ጠየቀ *ṭäyyäqä* (B) query, demand, ask,
question, request, require, solicit,
inquire, pay a visit, call on someone
ጠያየቀ *ṭäyayyäqä* quiz, interrogate
ጥያቄ *ṭəyyaqe* question, request, query
(የጥያቄ ፡ ምልክት question mark)
የቃል ፡ ጥያቄ interview
ተጠያቂ *täṭäyyaqi* responsible (liable,
accountable)
መጠየቅ *mäṭṭäyyäq* interrogative (n.)
መጠየቂያ *mäṭṭäyyäqiya* requisition
መጠይቅ *mäṭṭäyyəq* questionnaire

ጠይብ *ṭäyəb* metalsmith, low caste artisan

ጥይት *ṭəyyət* cartridge, bullet, ammunition
ተባራሪ ፡ ጥይት stray bullet (see በረረ)
የውሸት ፡ ጥይት *yäwəšät*—blank
(of bullet)

*ጠጸፈ, ተጠጸፈ *täṭäyyäfä* loathe, despise vehemently, abhor (see also
*ጸየፈ)
አስጠያፊ *asṭäyyafi* nasty (remark,
rumor)

ጠዳ *ṭädda* be clean, be neat (see also
ጸዳ)
ጥዱ *ṭədu* neat, clean

ጣዳ *ṭada* put a kettle or a griddle on
the fire, cook on the griddle
ምጣድ, see above

ጥድ *ṭəd* juniper tree, cedar

*ጠደፈ, ተጣደፈ *täṭaddäfä* hasten (vi.),
dash, hurry (vi.), be in a hurry, be
busy doing something
አጣደፈ *aṭṭaddäfä* hurry (vt.), hasten (vt.), rush (vt.), speed up, accelerate, work feverishly on, assail
(with questions), press (urge)
አጣዳፊ *aṭṭadafi* acute (disease)
ጥድፊያ, see below

ጥድፊያ *ṭədfiya* haste, hurry, rush, feverish activity (see *ጠደፈ)
በጥድፊያ hurriedly

ጠጅ *ṭäǧǧ* mead, hydromel
ጠጅ ፡ ቤት bar where Ethiopian
drinks are served
ወይን ፡ ጠጅ wine

ጥጃ *ṭəǧǧa* calf (young of cow)
የጥጃ ፡ ሥጋ *yäṭəǧǧa səga* veal

ጠጋ *ṭägga* approach, come near to
ተጠጋ *täṭägga* draw close, get near,
approach, advance upon, lean (on a
cushion, on a tree), take shelter
under, seek protection
አስጠጋ *asṭägga* shelter (protect),
harbor (give shelter), lean one thing
against another

ተጠጋጋ *täṭägagga* get close to one
another, be contiguous
(ተጠጋግተው ፡ ቆሙ they huddled
together in a corner)
ጠጋ ፡ ብሎ *ṭäga bəlo* close behind
ጠጋ ፡ አደረገ move closer, edge
nearer
ጥግ, see below
ጥገኛ, see below
ጥገኝነት, see ጥገኛ
መጠጊያ *mäṭṭägiya* resource, refuge,
shelter
የተጠጋጋ *yätäṭägagga* contiguous

ጥግ *ṭəgg* corner, support, protection,
next to, close to, hard by (see ጠጋ)
ጥግ ፡ አደረገ put against
ጥግ ፡ ያዘ take cover
ከ - - - ጥግ ፤ እ - - - ጥግ ፤ በ - - - ጥግ
close to, near to, near, next to, along,
alongside of

ጠገራ *ṭägära* axe, hatchet, wedge used
for splitting wood

ጠጉር *ṭägur* hair (see also ጸጉር)
ጠጉር ፡ አስተካካይ barber, hair dresser
የጠጉር ፡ ማስተካከያ ፡ ቤት barber-
shop
የጠጉር ፡ አሠራር hairdo, headdress
የበግ ፡ ጠጉር wool
ጠጉራም *ṭäguram* hairy

ጠገበ *ṭäggäbä* be satiated, be sated, be
full (from food), be satisfied, be refractory (animal, person), be arrogant, be insolent
አጠገበ *aṭäggäbä* satisfy, satiate
ጥጋብ *ṭəgab* satiety, plenty, arrogance
(የጥጋብ *yäṭəgab* affluent, plentiful)
ጥጋበኛ *ṭəgabäňňa* sated, arrogant
አጥጋቢ *aṭgabi* hearty (meal), satisfactory (result), efficacious, effective,
adequate, convincing, weighty (argument)

ጠገነ *ṭäggänä* (B) repair, treat a fracture or dislocation, patch up, fix,
mend, keep in repair

ጥገና, see below
ጥገነት, see below

ጥገና *ṭəggäna* repair, fixing (see ጠገነ)
ጥገና ፡ ክፍል maintenance shop
ቀዶ ፡ ጥገና operation, surgery (see
ቀደደ)

ጥገነት *ṭəggənnät* cast (for broken
leg), splint (see ጠገነ)

ጥገኛ *ṭəggäňňa* protected, vassal, protec-
torate, dependency (country con-
trolled by another country), client,
affiliate (see ጠጋ)
ጥገኛ ፡ ነፍሳት parasite
ጥገኝነት *ṭəggäňňannät* refuge, asylum,
dependency, vassalage, affiliation,
client status

ጠጣ *ṭäṭṭa* (B) drink, gulp, smoke (cigarettes)
አጠጣ *aṭäṭṭa* give to drink, water
(a plant), irrigate
ጠጪ *ṭäččі* drinker
መጠጥ, see above

ጡጦ *ṭuṭṭo* nipple of baby bottle

ጣጣ *ṭaṭa* complication, problem, trouble, nuisance, mess, affair
ጣጣ ፡ ውስጥ ፡ ገባ get into trouble
ጣጠኛ *ṭaṭäňňa* troublemaker, agitator, complicated (problem)

*ጣጣ, ተንጣጣ *tänṭaṭṭa* fizzle, snap, vi.
(of burning wood), crackle

ጥጥ *ṭəṭ* cotton
ጥጥ ፡ ፍሬ linseed

ጦጣ *ṭoṭa* monkey, ape

ጠጠረ *ṭäṭṭärä* (B) harden, vi. (of cement), become firm (the white of the
egg when fried)
ጥጥር *ṭəṭṭər* solid, n., adj. (not a
liquid)
የጠጠረ *yäṭäṭṭärä* compact (soil)

ጠጠር *ṭäṭär* pebble, gravel

ጠጪ ṭäččī drinker (see ጠጣ)
ጠጪነት ṭäččinnät drunkenness

ጡጫ ṭučča fist, blow with the fist, punch

ጠፋ ṭäffa be lost, go astray, disappear, not show up (for an appointment), vanish, be missing, be lacking, be wanting, be absent, elude (of name), perish, be extinguished, be extinct, go out (of light, fire, electricity), die (of motor), die away (of music, noise), be no longer in existence, be eradicated
(ጠፋ(በት) ṭäffa(bbät), or ጠፋው he lost)
(ስም ፡ ጠፋ be discredited (of a person)
(ስም ፡ ጠፋኝ I forgot his name)
(ሰው ፡ ጠፋ there was no one there)
(ይዞ ፡ ጠፋ yəzo ṭäffa run away with, abscond with)
(አይጠፋም ayṭäfam there is plenty, it is not missing)
አጠፋ aṭäffa exterminate, eradicate, abolish, wipe out, extinguish, turn off (light), blow out, vt. (a candle), ruin, obliterate, erase, efface, deform, spoil, do wrong, commit an offense, destroy, devastate, lose, smear (the reputation), spend, waste (time, money)
(ራሱን ፡ አጠፋ he did away with himself)
(ስም ፡ አጠፋ defame)
(ገንዘብ ፡ አጠፋ squander money)
ጠፍ ፡ መሬት ṭäf märet undeveloped land, wasteland, unclaimed or abandoned land
†ጥፉ ṭəfu bad
ጥፋት, see below
መጥፎ, see above
አጥፊ aṭfi evildoer, vandal, offender
መጥፋት mäṭfat failure, demise
ማጥፋት maṭfat, in ስም ፡ ማጥፋት libel

ጠፋ ṭafa write, patch (garment, tire); see also ጻፈ

መጣፍ mäṭaf book
መጣፊያ mäṭafiya patch (n.)

ጤፍ ṭef millet-like cereal

ጥፉ ṭəfu bad (see ጠፋ)
መልክ ፡ ጥፉ ugly

ጥፊ ṭəffi slap (n.); see ጠፈጠፈ
በጥፊ ፡ መታ slap (v.)
በጥፊ ፡ ጠፈጠፈ slap (v.)

ጦፋ ṭofä rage, fly into a rage, be incensed
በንዴት ፡ ጦፋ fly into a temper

ጧፍ ṭʷaf candle

ጠፈር ṭäfär firmament, universe, space (extra terrestrial)
የጠፈር spatial
የላይኛ ፡ ጠፈር stratosphere (see ላይ)

ጠፍር ṭäfər leather strip, thong

ጥፍር ṭəfər fingernail, claw, hoof

ጥፋት ṭəfat fault, guilt, mistake, ruin, damage, harm, disaster, destruction, loss, ravage, offense, misdeed, misconduct, mishap, wrong (see ጠፋ)
ጥፋት ፡ አጠፋ commit a misdeed (see ጠፋ)
የጥፋት ፡ ውኃ yäṭəfat wəha the flood, the Deluge
ጥፋተኛ ṭəfatäñña guilty, offender, wrongdoer
ጥፋተኛ ፡ አለመሆን innocence
ጥፋተኛነት ṭəfatäññannät guilt

ጣፊያ ṭaffiya spleen, milt

ጣፈጠ ṭaffäṭä be tasty, be sweet, taste sweet, taste good, be delicious, be savory
አጣፈጠ aṭaffäṭä sweeten, flavor, season (improve the flavor), make tasty
ጣፋጭ, see below

ጠፈጠፈ ṭäfäṭṭäfä flatten out, level, smear the wall with manure to fill the gaps, slap repeatedly

(በጥፈ : ጠፈጠፈ slap, v.)
ጠፍጣፋ ṭäfṭaffa flat, level

*ጠፈጠፈ, ተንጠፈጠፈ tänṭäfäṭṭäfä drip,
stream (of sweat), trickle

ጣፋጭ ṭafač sweet, sweets, tasty,
delicious, delicacies (see ጣፈጠ)
ጣፋጭነት ṭafačənnät sweetness

ጨ

ጨሌ čälle glass bead necklace

*ጮለ , አጮለ ačolä smack

ጮሌ čolle prompt, quick, clever,
smart, perspicacious, slick (ingenious), schemer
አፈ : ጮሌ smooth talker, glib

ጨለመ čällämä (B) get dark, be black
(room), be obscure (see also ጨለም
ለም)
አጨለመ ačällämä darken
ጨለማ čälläma obscurity, darkness,
dark (n., adj.)
ጭለማ čəlläma obscurity, darkness

ጨለምለም፡ያለ čälämlämm yalä gloomy,
(corridor); see also ጨለመ
ጭልምልም : ያለ čələmləmm yalä
somber (day)

ጭላት čəlat, in የባሕር : ጭላት gull

ጭላንጭል čəlančəl gleam, glimmer,
spark (of light), ray (of hope)

ጨለጠ čälläṭä (B) drink at one draft,
drink to the last drop, take a gulp
ጭልጥ : አድርጎ : ጠጣ čəllәṭṭ adrәgo
ṭäṭṭa gulp down

ጨለፈ čälläfä (B) take out with a ladle,
ladle out, dip out
ጭልፋ čәlfa ladle, dipper

ጭልፊት čəlfit falcon, hawk

ጫማ čamma shoe, foot (for measurement)

ጫማ : አደረገ put on shoes
ጫማ : ሰፊ shoemaker, cobbler
ጫማ : ጠራጊ shoeshine boy
የጫማ : ማሰሪያ shoelace, shoestring
የጫማ : ማንኪያ shoehorn
የጫማ : ማግቢያ shoehorn
ነጠላ : ጫማ sandal
የቤት : ጫማ slippers
የጎማ : ጫማ rubbers

ጮማ čoma fat (meat), fat animal

*ጨመለቀ , ተጨማለቀ täčämalläqä be
bedraggled (dress), be smeared (face),
be besmirched
አጨማለቀ aččämalläqä smudge
የተጨማለቀ yätäčämalläqä sloppy
(work)

ጨመረ čämmärä (B) add, increase, augment, gain (weight), include, have
some more, gather (speed), raise (the
salary), put into (milk or sugar into
coffee)
ጭማሪ čәmmari increment, increase,
boost (in prices), appendix (of book)
ጭምር čәmmәr added, additional, increase, increment, including, included, in addition
(ምግብ : ጭምር : ነው food is included)
ተጨማሪ täčämmari additional, more
(adj.), extra (adj.), further (adj.)
ተጨማሪ : እቃዎች accessories
(በተጨማሪ in addition, among other
things)
(በተጨማሪ : አለ add in speaking)
መጨመር mäčämmär rise (in prices),
addition

ጨመቀ čämmäqä(B)wring (wet clothes),
squeeze (fruit), compress (squeeze)
ጭማቂ čәmmaqi juice

ጨመተ čämmätä (B) be calm, be tranquil
ጭምት čәmimәt quiet, taciturn, reserved (disposed to keep to oneself)

ጨመደደ čämäddädä crease, vt. (cloth),
wrinkle (vt.)

ተጨማደደ *täčämaddädä* crease (vi.),
be wrinkled (face), shrivel, shrink
አጨማደደ *aččämaddädä* wrinkle (vt.),
crease (vt.), rumple, crush (vt.), con-
tort
የተጨማደደ *yätäčämaddädä* shrunk-
en, shriveled, wrinkled

ጭምጭምታ *čämčämta* rumor
ጭምጭምታ ፡ ሰማ get wind of

ጫረ *čarä* scrape, scribble, rake, scratch,
strike (a match)
(እሳት ፡ ጫረ get fire from a neighbor)
ጫጫረ *čačarä* scrawl, scribble
ጫር ፡ ጫር ፡ አደረገ *čarr čarr adärrägä* stir up
ጫሪ *čari*, in ጠብ ፡ ጫሪ aggressive,
trouble maker
ጫሪነት *čarinnät*, in (የ)ጠብ ፡ ጫሪነት
aggression
ጭረት, see below

ጭራ *čära* hair at the end of the animal's tail, fly swatter, fly whisk
ባለ ፡ ጭራ stringed (instrument)

ጭር ፡ አለ *čärr alä* be deserted (street),
be lonely (road), be solitary (place),
be silent (street), be quiet (place),
be still (place, night)

ጮራ *čorra* ray of the sun, beam of
light

ጨረር *čärär* ray, stream of light
የፀሐይ ፡ ጨረር sunbeam

ጭራሮ *čäraro* small sticks tied together
to make a torch, dry sticks, dead-
wood

ጨረሰ *čärräsä* (B) finish, end, terminate, complete, accomplish, consume,
deplete, exterminate, eat up, use up,
wear out (vt.), exhaust (use up), ruin,
finish off
ጨርሶ *čärräso* through and through,
completely, quite; (with a negative
verb) not at all

(ጨርሶ ፡ በላ eat up)
ጭራሽ, see below
መጨረሻ, see above

ጭራሽ *čärraš* end, altogether, completely, entirely; (with a negative
verb) not at all (see ጨረሰ)
በጭራሽ (with a negative verb) not
at all, absolutely not, never
እስከንጭራሹ *äskännäčärrašu* in perpetuity

ጨረቃ *čäräqa* moon
የጨረቃ lunar
የጨረቃ ፡ ግርዶሽ lunar eclipse

ጨርቅ *čärq* cloth, rag, fabric
ጨርቃ ፡ ጨርቅ *čärqa čärq* cotton
goods, fabrics, textiles
ጨርቁን ፡ ጣለ he was stark raving
mad (lit. he threw off his clothes)

ጨራቅ *čäraq* giant (imaginary being),
monster, man-eater (imaginary figure
in children's tales)

ጮርቃ *čorqa*, ጮርቈ *čorqʷa* nearly ripe
(crops)

ጨረታ *čäräta* tender (n.); see *ጫረተ
የጨረታ ፡ ዋጋ bid (n.)

*ጫረተ, ተጫረተ *täčarrätä* bid (make a
bid)
ጨረታ, see above

ጭረት *čärät* scratch, stroke (in writing),
dash, accent (accent mark); see ጫረ
ንኡስ ፡ ጭረት hyphen

ጨሰ *čäsä* smoke (vi.), fume, smoulder,
seethe, get mad (see also ጢስ)
አጨሰ *ačäsä* cause to smoke, smoke
a pipe or a cigarette
ጭስ *čäs* smoke (n.)
ጨሰኛ *čäsäñña* sharecropper, tenant
farmer (see also ጢሰኛ)

ጩቅ *čuq* miserly, stingy, closefisted

ጭቃ *čäqa* mud, clay, mire (see ጨቀየ)
ጭቃ ፡ ሹም village headman
የጭቃ *yäčäqa* muddy

ጨቅላ čäqla baby

ጨቄነ čäqqʷänä (B) oppress, be cruel, domineer, repress
ጭቄና čəqqʷäna repression, oppression
(የጭቄና ፡ አገዛዝ—aggäzaz tyranny)
ጨዷኝ čäqqʷañ oppressor, harsh, draconic (rules)

ጨቀየ čäqäyyä be muddy, be covered with mud
አጨቀየ ačäqäyyä turn into mire
የጨቀየ yäčäqäyyä muddy
ጭቃ, see below

ጨቀጨቀ čäqäččäqä nag, pester, get into an argument
ተጫቃጨቀ täčäqaččäqä fight (vi.), quarrel, altercate, argue, dispute, squabble
ጭቅጭቅ čəqəččəq argument, dispute, quarrel
ተጨቃጫቂ täčäqačaqi argumentative (person)

ጨቤ čube small dagger

*ጨበረበረ, አጭበረበረ ačbäräbbärä dazzle, swindle, cheat, embezzle, defraud
አጭበርባሪ ačbärbari swindler, crook, imposter, trickster
ማጭበርበር mačbärbär deception, fraud

ጨበጠ čäbbäṭä (B) take possession of, press, clutch, squeeze (the hand), clench (the fist), grab, grasp
ተጨባበጡ täčäbabbäṭu shake hands
(እጅ ፡ ለእጅ ፡ ተጨባበጡ clasp hands, shake hands)
አጨባበጥ ačäbabäṭ grip (n.)
ጨበጣ čäbäṭa, in የጨበጣ ፡ ውጊያ hand-to-hand combat
ጭብጥ čəbbəṭ fistful, handful, bunch
የተጨበጠ yätäčäbbäṭä concrete (adj.), pronounced (opinion)
የማይጨበጥ yämmayəččäbbäṭ elusive, evasive, intangible, abstract

ጨብጡ čäbṭu, ጨብጦ čäbṭo gonorrhea

*ጨበጨበ, አጨበጨበ ačäbäččäbä clap, clap hands, applaud
ተጨበጨበ(ለት) täčäbäččäbä(llät) he was acclaimed (winner)
ጭብጨባ čəbčäba hand clapping, applause

ጫት čat kind of bush whose leaves have a mildly narcotic quality (usually chewed by Muslims and Gallas)

ጫነ čanä load (a mule, truck), burden, pack (mules), put the saddle on, saddle, harness
(ዘውድ ፡ ጫነ wear a crown)
ተጫነ täčanä be loaded, be encumbered, press a button, crush (a box), depress (the gas pedal), predominate over
(ሕዝን ፡ ተጫነ(ው) be broken-hearted)
(ሥራ ፡ ተጫነ(ው) be swamped with work)
ተጫጫነ täčačanä oppress (of weather, sleep)
ተጫጫነ(ው) feel dizzy, be in bad shape
ጫን ፡ አለ čann alä press (a button), press down
ጭነት, see below
ጫኝ ፡ መርከብ čañ märkäb freighter
መጫኛ, see above
የሚጫጫን yämmiččačan drowsy (weather)

ጭን čən thigh, lap
የጭን ፡ ቅልጥም tibia

ጨነቀ čännäqä (B) embarrass, distress
ጨነቀ(ው) čännäqä(w) he is at a loss
ተጨነቀ täčännäqä be embarrassed, have anxiety, be in difficulty, be under stress, be in great straits, show concern, be solicitous, worry (vi.), feel uneasy, take great pains
አስጨነቀ asčännäqä put someone in great difficulty, molest, dismay, distress, give worry, harass

ተጨናነቀ *täčänannäqä* be crowded (of street), be congested (of street), be populous (of city)
አጨናነቀ *aččänannäqä* jam, block up (of cars)
ጭንቅ ፡ አለ *čənnəqq alä* be tense (keyed up)
ጭንቅ *čənq* distress, embarrassment, difficulty, hardship
ጭንቀት *čənqät* disturbance, stress (strain), worry, concern (worry), distress, pressure, anguish
አስጨናቂ *asčännaqi* harrowing
መጨናነቅ *mäččänanäq* congestion (of traffic), jam (traffic)
(የመኪና ፡ መጨናነቅ traffic jam)

ጫንቃ *čanqa* shoulder, shoulder blade

ጭንቅላት *čənqəllat* the top part of the head, skull

ጭንቀት, see ጨነቀ

ጭነት *čənät* cargo, load, burden (carried by pack animals), freight (see ጫነ)
የጭነት ፡ መርከብ *yäčənät*—freighter
የጭነት ፡ መኪና truck, lorry
የጭነት ፡ ከብት pack animal

ጨነገፈ *čänäggäfä* abort (miscarry), go wrong (plan), collapse (plan)
አጨናገፈ *aččänaggäfä* foil, upset, inhibit (growth)

ጭንጫ *čənča* stony ground (usually barren)

ጫኝ, see ጫነ

ጫካ *čakka* woods, forest, jungle
ጫካማ *čakkamma* wooded

ጨከነ *čäkkänä* (B) be cruel, be severe, be harsh, be ruthless, be intrepid
ጭካኔ *čəkkane* cruelty, brutality, savagery (of bandits), atrocity, perseverance
(በጭካኔ ruthlessly, in cold blood)

ጨካኝ *čäkkaň* cruel, ruthless, merciless, tyrannical, brutal

ጨካኝ, see ጨከነ

ጮኸ *čohä* shout in a loud voice, cry (shout), cry out, roar, yell, scream, bark (dog), crack, vi. (of whip); used to refer to most noises uttered by animals
(ዶሮ ፡ ሲጮኸ *doro sičoh* early morning, lit. when the cock crows)
አጮኸ *ačohä* crack, vt. (the whip)
ጮሆ *čoho* loudly, aloud
ጮህ ፡ አለ *čoh alä* raise one's voice
ጮህ ፡ ብሎ loudly, aloud
ጩኸት, see below

ጩኸት *čuhät* scream, shout, yell, cry, noise, roar (of cannon), clamor, howl (see ጮኸ)

ጨዋ *čäwa* urbane, person of free condition (not a slave), person of good breeding, well-behaved, well-bred, well-mannered, gallant, gentleman, layman, illiterate
የጨዋ polite (society), decorous (behavior)
ከጨዋ ፡ ቤተሰብ of good family
ጨዋነት, see below

ጨው *čäw* salt
ጨው ፡ ጨው ፡ አለ *čäw čäw alä* have a salty taste
ጨው ፡ የበዛበት *čäw yäbäzzabbät* salty
የእንግሊዝ ፡ ጨው Epsom salts

ጭው ፡ አለ *čəww alä* ring, v. (of the ears); see also ጭውጭው
ጭው ፡ አለ(በት) *čəww alä(bbät)* feel dizzy
ጭው ፡ ያለ *čəww yalä* dizzy

*ጫወተ, ተጫወተ *täčawwätä* chat, converse, play (a game, a musical instrument)
ተጫወተ(በት) *täčawwätä(bbät)* he played tricks on him

አጫወተ *aččawwätä* amuse someone, entertain, keep someone company, divert, tell stories, talk with someone

ተጨዋወተ *täčäwawwätä* converse

ጨዋታ, see below

ጭውውት, see below

ተጫዋች *täčawač* player, playful, performer (actor), genial (host), sociable

ተጫዋችነት *täčawačǝnnät* good humor

አጫዋች *aččawač* entertainer, jester, referee (in a game)

መጫወቻ *mäččawäča* toy, plaything, game

ጨዋታ *čäwata* play, game, conversation, amusement, entertainment (see *ጫወተ)

ጨዋታ ፡ ያዘ be engaged in conversation

የጨዋታ ፡ ለዛ fascinating conversation

የጨዋታ ፡ ሜዳ playing field

ጨዋነት *čäwannät* politeness, civility, decency, good breeding (see ጨዋ)

የጨዋነት genteel

ጭውውት *čǝwǝwwǝt* conversation, dialogue, chat (see *ጫወተ)

ጭውጭው ፡ አለ *čǝwwǝčǝww alä* chirp (see also ጭው ፡ አለ)

ጫጕላ *čagʷla* nuptial house

ጨንጐራ *čäggʷarra* stomach (of animals, humans), tripe

ጨንጐሬ *čäggʷarre*, in አባ ፡ ጨንጐሬ caterpillar

ጭጋግ *čǝgag* fog, haze, mist

ጭጋግ ፡ የበዛበት—*yäbäzzabbät* foggy

ጭጋጋማ *čǝgagamma* hazy

ጫጫ *čačča* stop growing, become stunted

አጫጫ *ačačča* retard the growth, arrest the growth

*ጫጫ, ተንጫጫ *tänčačča* make a racket, make a loud noise, be noisy (children), squeal, twitter, chirp

ጫጫታ, see below

ጭጭ ፡ አለ *čačč alä* lapse into silence, hush, remain dumb

ጫጩት *čačut* chick

የወፍ ፡ ጫጩት baby bird

ጫጫታ *čačata* noise, chirp, row, commotion (see *ጫጫ)

ጫጫታ ፡ የሚበዛ(በት) — *yämmibäza-(bbät)* noisy

ጨፌ *čäffe* lush grassy land which is slightly marshy

ጫፍ *čaf* extremity, border, tip, edge, hem, top (of mountain), summit, point (of knife)

ጫፍ ፡ ጫፉን along the edge

እ - - - ጫፍ at the top of

ከ - - - ጫፍ from the top of

ወደ - - - ጫፍ to the top of

ጨፈለቀ *čäfälläqä* squash (a bug), crush (beans)

ጨፈረ *čäffärä* (B) assemble in a body (of troops)

ጭፍራ *čǝfra* body of troops, swarm (of bees)

ጨፈረ *čäffärä* (B) dance and sing

ጭፈራ *čǝffära* dance (n.)

ጨፈነ *čäffänä* (B) shut (the eyes), blindfold

በጭፍን *bäčǝffǝn* blindly

የጭፍን *yäčǝffǝn* off the top of one's head (answer)

ዓይኑን ፡ ጨፍኖ—*čäffǝno* fanatically, headlong

ጭፍግግ ፡ ያለ *čǝfgǝgg yalä* muggy

ጰ

ጰንጠቆስጤ *pänṭäqosṭe* Pentecost (see also ቆንጠጰስጤ)

ጸጕሜ *pagʷme* intercalary month (5-10 September); see also ቋጕሜ

ጳጳስ *pappas* bishop
ሊቀ ፡ ጳጳሳት archbishop

ጸ ፤ ፀ

ፀሐይ *ṣ̌ahay* sun (see also ጣይ)
ፀሐይ ፡ ወጣች the sun rose (see ወጣ)
ፀሐይ ፡ ጠለቀች the sun set (see ጠለቀ)
የፀሐይ solar
የፀሐይ ፡ ግርዶሽ solar eclipse (n.)
ፀሐያማ *ṣ̌ahayamma* sunny, bright (day)

ጸሐፊ *ṣ̌ahafi* secretary, scribe, clerk (see ጻፈ)
ጸሐፊ ፡ ትእዛዝ Minister of the Pen
ልዩ ፡ ጸሐፊ private secretary
ቄም ፡ ጸሐፊ calligrapher, scribe
ዋና ፡ ጸሐፊ secretary general

ጽሑፍ *ṣ̌ǝhuf* leaflet, writing (anything written), inscription, article (in a newspaper); see ጻፈ
ሥነ ፡ ጽሑፍ literature, letters
(የሥነ ፡ ጽሑፍ literary)
ዓቢይ ፡ ጽሑፍ lead article

ጽሕፈት *ṣ̌ǝhfät* writing (see ጻፈ)
(የ)ጽሕፈት ፡ ቤት secretariat, office
የጽሕፈት ፡ መሣሪያ stationery (writing materials)
(የ)ጽሕፈት ፡ መሣሪያ ፡ መደብር stationery (store)
የጽሕፈት ፡ መኪና typewriter
አጭር ፡ ጽሕፈት stenography
የቃል ፡ ጽሕፈት dictation
የቄም ፡ ጽሕፈት calligraphy
የእጅ ፡ ጽሕፈት handwriting

ጸሎት *ṣ̌älot* prayer (see ጸለየ)
ጸሎት ፡ መራ conduct the prayers
ጸሎት ፡ አደረሰ pray, recite prayers (see ደረሰ)
የጸሎት ፡ ቤት chapel
የመታሰቢያ ፡ ጸሎት memorial service

ጽላት *ṣ̌ǝllat* tablet of wood or stone kept in the *tabot*, votive stone
ጽላተ ፡ ሙሴ Tablets of the Law

ጸለየ *ṣ̌älläyä* (B) pray, recite prayers
†ጸሎት *ṣ̌älot* prayer
የመጸለያ ፡ ቦታ *yämäṣ̌älläya bota* place of worship

ጸመ *ṣ̌omä* fast (v.); see also ጦመ
ጾም *ṣ̌om* fast (n.), fasting
ጾም ፡ አደረ go without supper

*ፀረረ, ተፃረረ *täṣ̌arrärä* be contradictory, do violence to
የሚፃረር *yämmiṣ̌arrär* contradictory

*ጸበረቀ, አንጸባረቀ *anṣ̌äbarräqä* be glaring, gleam (object), be resplendent, scintillate, sparkle, glitter, shimmer, glisten
ነጸብራቅ *näṣ̌äbraq* glare (n.)
የሚያንጸባርቅ *yämmiyanṣ̌äbarrǝq* glaring, resplendent, brilliant (jewel)

ጾታ *ṣ̌ota* series, order, sex, gender
ተባዕታይ ፡ ጾታ masculine
አንስታይ ፡ ጾታ feminine
የወል ፡ ጾታ common gender

ጸና *ṣ̌änna* be firm, cleave to (a belief), be valid (signature), be binding (contract), be in effect, be in force, be effective (see also ጠና)
(በ - - - ጸና abide by)
ተጸናና *täṣ̌nanna* cheer up (vi.), find solace, take heart (be encouraged)
አጸናና *aṣ̌nanna* give solace, cheer up (vt.), give comfort, console, encourage, sympathise with, reassure
ጽኑ *ṣ̌ǝnu* firm, secure, binding (contract), steadfast, constant, stable (foundation, personality), acute, severe (sentence), durable
(በጽኑ strongly)
ጽናት *ṣ̌ǝnat* stability, tenacity
ጽኑነት *ṣ̌ǝnunnät* strength, firmness
(ሐሳብ ፡ ጽኑነት consistency)
ማጽናኛ, see above

ፀንስ(ች) ṣännäsä(čč) (B) become pregnant, conceive a child
ፅንስ ፡ ሐሳብ ṣənsä hassab theory
ፅንስን ፡ ማስወረድ ṣənsən maswärräd
abortion

ጽናት, see ጸና

ጽኑነት, see ጸና

ጸናጽል ṣänaṣəl sistrum, musical instrument for accompanying songs

ጽንፍ ṣənf (pl. አጽናፍ aṣnaf) border,
edge, extremity, end, peak (of power);
see also ጥንፍ

ጽዋ ṣəwwa font, chalice, cup (see also
ጥዋ)
ጽዋ ፡ አነሣ drink a toast (see ነሣ)

*ጸየፈ, ተጸየፈ täṣäyyäfä (B) loathe, de-
spise vehemently, abhor (see also
*ጠየፈ)
አጸየፈ aṣṣäyyäfä fill with disgust, be
offensive
ጸያፍ ṣäyyaf base (adj.), disgusting,
gross (language), obscene (language)
ጽያፌ ṣəyyafe disgust (n.)

ጸዳ ṣädda be clean, be pure (see also
ጠዳ)
አጸዳ aṣädda clean (the house), clean
up (vt.)
ተጸዳዳ täṣädadda clean up (vi.)
አጸዳዳ aṣṣädadda tidy, clean up (vt.)
ጽዱ ṣədu clean, pure
†ጽዳት ṣədat cleanliness
ማጽጃ masǧa cleanser
መጸዳጃ mäṣṣädaǧa, in የመጸዳጃ ፡ ክፍል
lavatory

ጸደቀ ṣäddäqä be justified, be declared
righteous, be just, be pious, be rati-
fied (of a bill), be valid
አጸደቀ aṣäddäqä ratify (a bill), validate (a passport), approve (a treaty),
endorse, sanction, affirm (confirm)
ጸድቅ ṣadəq (pl. ጸድቃን ṣad(ə)qan)
pious, just, righteous
ጽድቅ ṣədq righteousness
ጽድቅነት ṣədqənnät righteousness

ጽዳት ṣədat cleanliness (see ጸዳ)
የጽዳት ፡ ክፍል yäṣədat — Department of Sanitation
የጽዳት ፡ ጥበቃ sanitation

ጸዳይ ṣäday spring (season of year)

ጸጋ ṣägga grace, virtue (moral excellence), asset, beneficence
ባለጸጋ baläṣägga rich, well-to-do, affluent

ጽጌ ፡ ረዳ ṣəgge räda rose (flower)

ጸጉር ṣägur hair, fur (see also ጠጉር)

ጸጥ ፡ አለ ṣäṭṭ alä be calm, be silent, be
quiet (neighborhood), quiet down
(wind), subside (wind), be tranquil,
be still (lake), be placid (lake), be
smooth (sea), be secure
ጸጥ ፡ አደረገ quell, quash, suppress
(a rebellion)
ጸጥታ, see below

ጸጥታ ṣäṭṭəta (n.) quiet, calm, tranquillity, security, silence, stillness (see
ጸጥ ፡ አለ)
ጸጥታ ፡ አስከበረ keep the peace, restore order (see ከበረ)
ጸጥታ ፡ አስከባሪዎች security forces
(see ከበረ)
በጸጥታ quietly
የጸጥታ ፡ ምክር ፡ ቤት Security Council
የጋራ ፡ ጸጥታ collective security (see
ጋራ)
ጸጥተኛ ṣäṭṭətäňňa quiet (audience)

*ጸጸተ, ተጸጸተ täṣäṣṣätä (B) repent, be
repentant, regret, be sorry
ጸጸት ṣäṣät repentance, regret, remorse, qualm, sorrow
የጸጸት rueful, penitent (expression)

ጻፈ ṣafä write, write down (see also ጣፈ)
(በመኪና ፡ ጻፈ type)
አጻፈ aṣṣafä dictate
ተጻጻፈ täṣaṣafä correspond with one
another
ጽፈት ṣəfät writing

አጸጻፍ *aṣṣaṣaf* manner of writing
(የቃላት ፡ አጸጻፍ spelling, orthography)
[See also ጸሐፈ, ጽሑፍ, ጽሑፈት, መጽ
ሐፍ]

ፈ

ፈላ *fälla* boil (vi.), be effervescent (mineral water), ferment (of beer), be ardent
(ደሙ ፡ ፈላ seethe with anger)
አፈላ *afälla* make to boil, boil (vt.), scald (milk)
ፍል ፡ ውኃ *fəl wəha* hot springs
ማፍያ *mafya* pot, kettle

ፉሎ *fulo* headstall

ፈልም *film* film, movie, screen

ፈለሰ *fälläsä* lose its roots (plant), migrate, emigrate
አፈለሰ *afälläsä* transplant (trees), make to emigrate
አፋለሰ *affalläsä* disrupt (the unity)
ፍልሰታ, see below

ፈለሰመ *fälässämä* philosophize, discuss, invent (see also ፈለሰፈ)

ፍልሰታ *fəlsäta* Assumption (of Mary); see ፈለሰ

ፈለሰፈ *fälässäfä* be a philosopher, make a discovery, invent (a new thing); see also ፈለሰመ
መፈልሰፍ *mäfälsäf* invention
ፈላስፋ *fälasfa* philosopher, inventor
ፈልሳፊ *fälsafi* inventor
ፍልሰፋ *fəlsäfa* discovery, invention
ፍልስፍና, see below

ፍልስፍና *fəlsəfənna* philosophy (see ፈለ
ሰፈ)
ሕግ ፡ ፍልስፍና jurisprudence

ፈላሻ *fälaša* Falasha, Ethiopian of Jewish faith

ፈለቀ *fälläqä* sparkle, gush out (of water, oil), flash (of lightning), spring from, originate
አፈለቀ *afälläqä* produce (ideas), generate (ideas)
[See also *ፈለቀለቀ]

*ፈለቀለቀ, ተፍለቀለቀ *täfläqälläqä* bubble (of water); see ፈለቀ
ፍልቅልቅ *fələqləq* effervescent, ebullient, of cheerful disposition, cheerful

ፈለቀቀ *fäläqqäqä* break loose (vt.)
ፍልቃቂ *fələqqaqi* section (of orange)
መፈልቀቂያ *mäfälqäqiya*, in የብረት ፡ መፈልቀቂያ crowbar

ፈለገ *fällägä* (B) desire, wish, like, want, look for, search for, require, seek, expect, be interested in
አስፈለገ *asfällägä* be imperative, be necessary, be in need of something
አስፈለገ(ው) *asfällägä(w)* need, require, must
ፈለግ *fälläg* trail (of animal), trace, track
ፍለጋ *fəllega* quest, search, need, track, trace
ፍላጎት, see below
ተፈላጊ *täfällagi* required, desirable, necessary, essential
ተፈላጊነት *täfällaginnät* demand, need, necessity
አስፈላጊ *asfällagi* indispensable, necessary, vital
አስፈላጊነት *asfällaginnät* necessity, need, importance

ፍላጎት *fəllagot* (n.) want (need), demand, desire, wish, will, interest (see ፈለገ)
የምግብ ፡ ፍላጎት appetite

ፈለጠ *fällätä* split (wood), cleave, quarry (marble)
ፍልጠት *fəltät* headache
ፈላጭ ፡ ቄራጭ, see below

ፈሲጥ *fäliṭ* style, vogue, mode, fashion, airs, sagacity, fad
ፈሲጣዊ ፡ አነጋገር idiom

ፍላጣ *fəlaṭṭa* arrow (see also ፍላጻ)

ፈላጭ, in ፈላጭ ፡ ቄራጭ *fälač q"äraç* authoritarian, absolute (ruler); see ፈለጠ , ቄረጠ

ፍላጻ *fəlaṣṣa* arrow (see also ፍላጣ)

ፈለፈለ *fäläffälä* shell (beans), husk (corn), hatch, vt. (eggs, chickens), mate (of birds), burrow, bore into, hollow out
ተፈለፈለ *täfäläffälä* be cut out (of rock), hatch, vi. (of chicks, eggs), breed, vi. (of birds), incubate
ፍልፈል *fəlfäl* mole
ፍልፉይ, see below

ፍልፈል *fəlfäl* mole (see ፈለፈለ)

ፎለፎል *foläfol* vivacious

ፍልፉይ *fələffay* pod (of pea); see ፈለ ፈለ

ፋመ *famä* become live coals (fire), get red-hot, become glowing
ተፋፋመ *täfafamä* become coals completely, rage (of battle), be in full swing (of work), come to a head
የተፋፋመ *yätäfafamä* stormy (debate), heated (argument), fierce (battle)
ፍም, see below

ፍም *fəm* embers, hot ashes, coals (see ፋመ)
ፈቱ ፡ ፍም ፡ መሰለ blush

ፋሚሊ *famili*, in የፋሚሊ ፡ አልጋ double bed

ፈራ *färra* fear, be fearful, be afraid, be scared, dread, be frightened
ተፈራ *täfärra* be feared, be respected
አስፈራ *asfärra* frighten, scare, terrify
አስፈራራ *asfärarra* terrify, intimidate, frighten, scare, threaten
ፈሪ *färi* fearful, timid, coward
ፍራቻ *fəračča* fear (n.)
ፈሪነት *färinnät* cowardice
ፍርሃት, see below

አስፈሪ *asfärri* ferocious, fierce (attack), fearful (causing fear), awesome
ማስፈራሪያ *masfärariya* threat
የሚያስፈራ *yämmiyasfärra* scary

*ፈራ , አፈራ *afärra* fructify, produce fruit, yield (fruit, crops), bear fruit, be fertile, be fecund, win (friends, enemies)
ፍሬ, see below

ፌሮ *ferro* cleat

ፍሬ *fəre* fruit, kernel, berry, seed (oil seed), product, result (see *ፈራ)
ፍሬ ፡ ሰጠ bear fruit (speaking of work)
ፍሬ ፡ ቢስ pointless, useless, fruitless, abortive, of no avail, futile
ፍሬ ፡ ነገር essence (of a speech), substance, matter (essence), crux, main point, central idea, gist, summary (of an article)
የሥራ ፡ ፍሬ *yäsəra fəre* output
የብልት ፡ ፍሬ *yäbəllət fəre* testicle
ፍራፍሬ *fərafre* all kinds of fruit
ፍሬያማ *fəreyamma* fruitful

ፍርሃት *fərhat* fright, fear, apprehension, scare (see ፈራ)

ፈረመ *färrämä* (B) sign (a document), endorse (a check)
ተፈራረመ *täfärarrämä* ratify (of both sides)
ፈራሚ *färrami* signatory
ፊርማ *firma* signature

ፎርም *form* form (to fill out), blank

ፎርሙላ *formula* formula (in algebra, chemistry)

ፍርምባ *fərəmba* chest (of animal)

ፎርማጆ *formağo* cheese

ፈረሰ *färräsä* fall apart, fall in ruins, collapse, be demolished, be destroyed, decompose (of flesh), be violated (pact), be abrogated (contract), dissolve, vi. (of a partnership)

አፈረሰ *afärräsä* demolish, destroy, ruin, tear down (a house), cancel, annul, violate (contract, agreement), break (a contract), disband (vt.), dissolve, vt. (a partnership)
ፈረረሰ *färarräsä* be a ruin, fall in ruins, go to ruin, fall to pieces (house)
አፈረረሰ *afärarräsä* wreck, turn to rubble
ፍራሽ *fərraš* remains, ruins
[See also ፍርስርስ, ፍርስራሽ and ፉርሽ]

ፈረስ *färäs* horse, stallion
የፈረስ ፡ ውርንጭላ colt, foal
የፈረስ ፡ ግልገል colt
ፈረሰኛ, see below

ፋርስ *fars* Persian
የፋርስ ፡ ቋንቋ Persian (language)

ፈረሱላ *färäsulla* 17 kilos

ፍርስርስ *fərsrəs* chaos (see ፈረሰ)

ፍርስራሽ *fərəsraš* wreck, rubble, debris, vestige (see ፈረሰ)

ፈረሰኛ *färäsäňňa* horseman, cavalry, cavalryman (see ፈረስ)
ፈረሰኛ ፡ ውኃ water flowing swiftly over a submerged rock
የፈረሰኛነት *yäfäräsäňňannät* equestrian

ፍሬሲዮን *fresiyon* clutch (of car)

ፉርሽ ፡ አደረገ(በት) *furš adärrägä(bbät)* destroy (see ፈረሰ)

ፍራሽ *fərraš* ruins, remains (see ፈረሰ)

ፍራሽ *fəraš* mattress

*ፈረቀ, ተፈራረቀ *täfärarräqä* alternate (vi.), be done alternatively, take turns
አፈራረቀ *affärarräqä* alternate (vt.), do in turns
ተፈራራቂ *täfäraraqi* alternate (adj.)
ፈረቃ *färäqa* turn, interval, alternative

ፍራቻ *fəračča* fear (n.); see ፈራ

ፉርኖ *furno* European-style bread
የፉርኖ ፡ ዱቄት white flour

ፍሬን *fren* brakes
ፍሬን ፡ ያዘ brake (v.), apply the brakes

ፈረንሳዊ *färänsawi* French, Frenchman (see also ፈረንሳይ)
ፈረንሳዊ ፡ አገር France

ፈረንሳይ *färänsay* France, French (see also ፈረንሳዊ)
ፈረንሳይ ፡ አገር France
ፈረንሳይኛ *färänsayəňňa* French (language)

ፈሪነት *färinnät* cowardice (see ፈራ)

ፍራንክ *frank* coin

ፈረንጅ *färänǧ* westerner, foreigner, European, white man
ፈረንጆች *färänǧočč* white people

ፈረከሰ *färäkkäsä* crack, vt. (nuts)
ተፈረካከሰ *täfäräkakkäsä* disintegrate, vi. (of rocks); crush, vi. (break to pieces)
(በቀላሉ ፡ የሚፈረካከስ — *yämmiffäräkakkäs* friable)

ፈረደ *färrädä* dispense justice, judge, render judgment, pronounce sentence
ፈረደለት *färrädällät* he acquitted him, he decided in his favor
ፈረደበት *färrädäbbät* he ruled against him, he condemned him, he found him guilty, he convicted him
ፍርድ, see below
ፍርጅ, see below

ፍሪዳ *f(ə)rida* heifer, bullock

ፍርድ *fərd* judgment, sentence (of court), justice, trial, verdict (see ፈረደ)
ፍርድ ፡ ቤት tribunal, law court, courthouse, court of justice, courtroom
ከፍርድ ፡ ቤት ፡ ቀረበ be arraigned
የፍርድ ፡ ሚኒስቴር Ministry of Justice
የሞት ፡ ፍርድ death sentence, death penalty

የሞት ፡ ፍርድ ፡ ፈረደበት he sentenced
him to death
የይሙት ፡ በቃ ፡ ፍርድ capital punishment
የወታደር ፡ ፍርድ ፡ ቤት court-martial
የጠቅላይ ፡ ንጉሠ ፡ ነገሥት ፡ ፍርድ ፡ ቤት
Supreme Court

ፍርጃ fərǧa punishment by God, disaster, calamity (see ፈረደ)
የእግዚአብሔር ፡ ፍርጃ fate, judgment

ፉርጎ furgo car (of train)

ፈረጠ färräṭä burst (vi.), break open
(vi.)
አፈረጠ afärräṭä squeeze (the pus),
break open (vt.), cut open (a blister),
burst (vt.), bring (the matter) to a
head
ፍርጥ ፡ አለ fərrəṭṭ alä be blunt
(speech), be forthright (reply)
ፍርጥ ፡ አድርጎ fərrəṭṭ adrəgo bluntly, straight out

ፈረፈረ färäffärä break in small pieces,
crumble (vt.), grate (cheese)
ፍርፋሪ fərəffari crumbs, scraps
የተፈረፈረ ፡ እንቁላል yätäfäräffärä
ənqulal scrambled eggs

*ፈረፈረ ፡ ተንፈረፈረ tänfäraffärä flop
around, writhe, thrash about

ፍራፍሬ fərafre all kinds of fruit (see
ፍሬ)

ፈረፋንጎ färäfango fender, bumper

ፈሳ fässa fart, break wind
ፈስ fäs fart (n.)

ፋስ fas axe

ፍስሐ fəssəha happiness, joy

ፈሰሰ fässäsä spill over, be spilled, pour
out (vi.), flow, drain, stream (of
water), empty, vi. (of river); see
also ፍስስ ፡ አለ
(ሐሞቱ ፡ ፈሰሰ his courage failed, he
lost courage)

(ሟሏት ፡ ፈሰሰ overflow)
አፈሰሰ afässäsä make to flow, spill
(vt.), drain (vt.), empty (coffee
grounds), spring a leak, leak (of a
pot), splurge (money)
(አስፋልት ፡ አፈሰሰ lay down a coat
of asphalt)
(ደም ፡ አፈሰሰ shed blood)
(ፍግ ፡ አፈሰሰ spread dung)
ፈሳሽ, see below
ፍሳሽ fəssaš leakage
መፍሰሻ mäfsäša outlet (of a lake)

ፍስስ ፡ አለ fəsəss alä be spilled (see
ፈሰሰ)
ልቡ ፡ ፍስስ ፡ አለ his heart sank
ሰውነቱ ፡ ፍስስ ፡ አለ feel sluggish

ፈሳሽ fäsaš fluid (n.), liquid (n., adj.);
see ፈሰሰ
ፈሳሽ ፡ ውኃ running water

ፍሳሽ fəssaš leakage (see ፈሰሰ)

ፋሲካ fasika Easter
የፋሲካ paschal

ፍስክ fəssək non-fast days

ፋሻ faša bandage, patch (put over a
wound)

ፊሽካ fiška whistle (n.)
ፊሽካ ፡ ነፋ whistle (v.)

ፋሽኮ faško flask

ፋቀ faqä scrape, tan (hide), rub (the
teeth), brush (the teeth), erase, scale
(a fish)
ፋቂ faqi tanner
መፋቂያ, see above
[See also ፈቀፈቀ]

ፎቅ foq story (of a house), floor (story),
upstairs

*ፈቀረ ፡ አፈቀረ afäqqärä adore, love
ፍቅር fəqər love, affection, devotion
ፍቅረኛ fəqräňňa lover, affectionate
ፍቅርተኛ fəqərtäňňa lover
መስተፋቅር mästäfaqər love philtre

ፈቀቅ ፡ አለ *fäqäqq alä* stand aside, get out of the way
ፈቀቅ ፡ አደረገ move aside (vt.)

*ፇቀቀ, ተንፇቀቀ *tänfʷaqqäqä* drag oneself along the ground (crippled person)

ፈቀደ *fäqqädä* allow, permit, grant permission, consent, sanction, approve, authorize, condone, want, wish, desire
ተፈቀደ *täfäqqädä* be permissible, be admissible, be allowable
አስፈቀደ *asfäqqädä* get permission
ፈቃድ, see below

ፈቃድ *fäqad*, ፍቃድ *fəqad* permission, permit, approval, sanction, concession, consent, license, furlough, leave (furlough), will, wish (see ፈቀደ)
በፈቃድ willingly, at will
የፈቃድ ፡ ወረቀት pass, permit, license
መልካም ፡ ፈቃዳቸው ፡ ሆኖ—*fäqädaččäw hono* He having deigned, He condescendingly, He graciously
በገዛ ፡ ፈቃዱ of his own accord
የሕመም ፡ ፈቃድ sick leave
(የ)መንጃ ፡ ፈቃድ driver's license
ፈቃደኛ *fäqadäñña* willing, full of good will, accommodating (obliging)
ፈቃደኛ ፡ ሆነ volunteer (vi.)
ፈቃደኛነት *fäqadäññannät* willingness

ፈቀፈቀ *fäqäffäqä* scrub, scour (a pot); see also ፋቀ
ፍቅፋቂ *fəqəffaqi* shavings, wood chips
መፈቅፈቂያ *mäfäqfäqiya* scraper

ፋብሪካ *fabrika* factory, plant
ባለ ፡ ፋብሪካ manufacturer

ፈታ *fätta* release, untangle, untie, unfasten, dismantle, undo (a knot), free, repudiate (one's wife), divorce, solve, interpret (a dream), explain, decipher (a secret message), guess (a riddle), absolve of sin, give absolution

(ሥራ ፡ ፈታ idle (vi.), be idle, lie idle, be out of work)
ተፋታ *täfatta* divorce one another
አፋታ *affatta* divorce (of a priest pronouncing the divorce)
ፈታታ *fätatta* unwind (a watch), dismount
አፍታታ *aftatta* disentangle a thread, limber, stretch (the legs)
(ሰውነቱን ፡ አፍታታ limber up, exercise)
(እግሩን ፡ አፍታታ stretch one's legs)
ፈት, see below
ፍታት, see below
ፍች ፤ ፍቺ, see below
†መፍቻ *mäfča* key
ይፍታህ *yəftah*, in ዕድሜ ፡ ይፍታህ life imprisonment
[See also ፍትሕ, ፍትሐት, መፍትሔ]

ፈት *fätt* divorced woman (see ፈታ)
ሥራ ፡ ፈት idle, jobless, unemployed
ሥራ ፡ ፈትነት *səra fättənnät* idleness, unemployment

ፉት ፡ አለ *futt alä* sip, drink in little sips

ፊት *fit* face, front, in front of, at first, before
ፊት ፡ ለፊት face to face, in front of, directly opposite, straight across from
ፊት ፡ ሰጠ give in (yield)
ፊት ፡ ቋጠረ frown
ፊቱ ፡ ፍም ፡ መሰለ blush
ፊቱን ፡ ኮሶ ፡ አስመሰለ make a terrible face, grimace (see መሰለ)
በ - - - ፊት ፤ ከ - - - ፊት ፤ እ - - - ፊት in front of, before (time, place)
ከ - - - በፊት in front of, ago, before (time, place)
ከ - - - ፊት ፡ ለፊት in front of, opposite, facing
ከሁሉ ፡ በፊት first of all, beforehand
ከሰዓት ፡ በፊት forenoon
ከዚህ ፡ በፊት before, previously

ወደ ፡ ፊት in the future, later on, forward, ahead
(የወደ ፡ ፊት future (adj.), prospective)
የፊት front (adj.), facial
የፊታቸን ፡ እሑድ yäfitaččən — next Sunday
የፊት ፡ እግር foreleg
የፊት ፡ ዱቄት face powder
የፊት ፡ ጥርስ incisor
የበፊት earlier (adj.)
†ፊተኛ fitäňňa front (adj.), fore
[See also ፊታውራሪ]

ፋታ fata respite, moment of rest, relief (medicine that lessens the pain), lull
(ፋታ ፡ የለውም he is tied down (by work)
ያለ ፡ ፋታ yalä fata without letup, steadily, without a break

ፎቴ fote couch

ፍትሕ fətəh justice, law, judgment, sentence (see ፋታ)
የፍትሕ ፡ ብሔር ፡ ሕግ civil code

ፍትሐት fəthat absolution (see also ፍታት)
ጸሎተ ፡ ፍትሐት funeral ceremony (prior to burial)

ፈተለ fättälä spin, twist together
ፈትል fätəl thread

*ፈተለከ, ተፈተለከ täfätälläkä scoot away, break away (runner), dash off

ፈተሸ fättäšä (B) inspect (baggage), explore, check, search
ፈታሽ fättaš inspector
ፍተሻ fəttäša search, inspection, examination

ፍታት fətat absolution, prayers for the dead (see ፋታ, ፍትሐት)
የፍታት ፡ ጸሎት yäfətat şälot prayer of absolution

ፈተነ fättänä (B) test, try, experiment, examine, put to test, tempt, make an attempt

ፈተና, see below
ፍቱን fətun efficacious (remedy), sure (remedy), tried
ፍቱንነት fətunənnät efficacy

ፈተና fätäna test, trial (test), exam, examination, experiment, temptation (see ፈተነ)
ፈተና ፡ አለፈ pass an exam
ፈተና ፡ ወደቀ fail an exam

ፊተኛ fitäňňa front (adj.), fore (see ፊት)
የፊተኛ yäfitäňňa previous, former

ፊታውራሪ fitawrari general of the vanguard (honorary title); see ፊት, ወረረ

ፈተገ fättägä (B) remove the hulls, rub raw, scrub (pans)

ፎቶግራፍ fotograf photo, picture (photo), shot (photo)
ፎቶግራፍ ፡ አነሣ take a picture (see ነሣ)
ፎቶግራፍ ፡ አንሺ—anši photographer
ፎቶግራፍ ፡ ማንሻ—manša camera
ፎቶግራፍ ፡ አጠበ develop photos

ፈተፈተ fätäffätä crumble up something soft (like bread in a liquid or sauce)
ፍትፍት fətfət bread and pepper sauce mixed together

ፍች fəčč, ፍቺ fəčči interpretation, explanation, solution, meaning, definition, divorce (see ፈታ)
ፍች ፡ ሰጠ define

ፊና fina direction
በየፊናቸው bäyyäfinaččäw in their various ways (directions)

ፋና fana torch, lamp

ፋና fana trace, trail (track)

ፋኖስ fanos lantern, oil lamp, lamp

ፈነቀለ fänäqqälä pull out, rip out
ፈነቃቀለ fänäqaqqälä dislodge (rocks)

ፈንታ fänta, ፋንታ fanta share, portion, turn

በ - - - ፈንታ in place of, instead of

ፍንክች ፦ አለ fənkəčč alä flinch

ፈነዳ fänädda explode (vi.), burst (vi.), blow up, vi. (of powder plant), ignite (of gun powder), blow out (of tire), pop open, erupt (of volcano), be open (of flower), bloom
አፈነዳ afänädda explode (vt.), burst vt. (a balloon), blow up (vt.)
ፈንጇ, see below

ፈነደቀ fänäddäqä be cheerful, be vivacious, exult, be jubilant, be elated
አስፈነደቀ asfänäddäqä elate
ፍንደቃ fəndäqa elation, ecstasy, exaltation

ፈንዲያ fandiya excrement (of horse, donkey, mule)

ፈንጇ fänği explosion, explosive, charge (of dynamite); see ፈነዳ
ፈንጇ ፦ ቀበረ mine (plant a mine)
የፈንጇ ፦ ድምፅ blast (n.)

ፍንጅ, in እጅ ፦ ከፍንጅ ፦ ተያዘ əğğ käfänğ täyazä be caught in the act of, be caught redhanded

ፍንጃል fənğal porcelain cup

ፈነጋለ fänäggälä overturn, overthrow, upset; be a slave dealer
ፈንጋይ, see below

ፈንጋይ fängay, in ባሪያ ፦ ፈንጋይ slave dealer, slave trader (see ፈነጋለ)

ፈንጣ fenṭa grasshopper, cricket

ፈነጠረ fänäṭṭärä spring out, flip out (splinters in chopping wood, cartridges being ejected from a gun)
አስፈነጠረ asfänäṭṭärä project (shells), eject
ተፈናጠረ täfänaṭṭärä ricochet, flip back
(ተፈናጥሮ ፦ ተመለሰ täfänaṭro — spring back)

ፈነጠር ፦ አለ fänṭärr alä emit sparks, stand somewhat apart, be separated, be secluded
ፍንጣሪ fənəṭṭari spark given off by flint, fragment

ፈነጠቀ fänäṭṭäqä project (a beam of light), splash water
ተፈነጠቀ täfänäṭṭäqä radiate (of light), emanate (of light), splash (vi.)
አፈናጠቀ affänaṭṭäqä splash (vt.)
ተፈናጠቀ täfänaṭṭäqä be splashed, be splattered
ፍንጣቂ fənəṭṭaqi spark, splotch (of sauce)

ፈነጠዘ fänäṭṭäzä exult, be merry, revel, be excited and happy
ፈንጠዝ, see below

ፈንጠዝያ fänṭäzəyya, ፈንጠዝያ fänṭäziyya jubilance, exultation, revelry, merrymaking (see ፈነጠዘ)
ፈንጠዝያ ፦ አደረገ make merry, hold revels

ፈንጣጣ fänṭaṭa smallpox

ፍንጢጣ fənṭiṭṭa anus

ፈነጨ fänäččä prance (of horses), gambol, caper, frolic

ፍንጭ fənč inkling, clue, hint, key (to a mystery)

ፈነፈነ fänäffänä smell, sniff (of animal)

ፊኛ fiñña bladder, balloon
የሐሞት ፦ ፊኛ gall bladder

ፈካ fäkka be alight (of face), brighten, vi. (of face), light up, vi. (of face), blossom (of flower)
አፈካ afäkka animate (enliven)

ፉካ fuka hole made in the wall to permit smoke to exit

ፋኩልቲ fakulti faculty (of professors)

ፎከረ fokkärä (B) utter war boasts, narrate one's prowess

ተፎካከረ *täfokakkärä* compete, be in rivalry with one another
ፎከረ *fukkära* boasting, bragging, soldiers' boasting, uttering of war invectives
ፍክክር *fəkəkkər*, ፉክክር *fukəkkər* boasting, competition, rivalry
ተፎካካሪ *täfokakari* rival
ተፎካካሪነት *täfokakarinnät* rivalry

ፋክቱር *faktur* invoice, bill

ፍክክር ፤ ፉክክር, see ፎከረ

ፈወሰ *fäwwäsä* (B) heal, cure
ፈውስ *fäws* medicine, remedy, cure
ፈዋሽነት *fäwwašənnät* medicinal power
የማይፈወስ *yämmayəffäwwäs* incurable

ፈዋሽነት, see ፈወሰ

*ፈዘ, አፈዘ *afezä* joke, jest, mock, make fun of, deride
ፌዝ *fez* joke, jest, mockery, derision
የፌዝ *yäfez* facetious
ፌዘኛ *fezäňňa* one who jokes

ፈዘዘ *fäzzäzä* stare, be glassy (eyes), become dull (of eye), be dazed (by a blow), be in a stupor
አፈዘዘ *afäzzäzä* daze, vt. (of a blow)
(በአስማት ፤ አፈዘዘ bewitch)
ፍዝዝ ፤ አለ *fəzəzz alä* be torpid
ፍዝዝ ፤ አደረገ make listless
ፈዛዛ *fäzaza* feeble (eye)
(ዋዛ ፤ ፈዛዛ aimless pursuit)

ፋይል *fayl* file (record)
ፋይል ፤ ውስጥ ፤ ገባ be filed

ፍየል *fəyyäl* goat
አውራ ፤ ፍየል he-goat
የሜዳ ፤ ፍየል antelope, mountain goat

ፋይዳ *fayda* value, importance

ፊደል *fidäl* letter (of the syllabary), alphabet, script, character (letter)
ፊደል ፤ ለየ master the alphabet
ፊደል ፤ ቆጠረ master the alphabet

ፊደል ፤ አስቆጠረ teach the alphabet (see ቆጠረ)
የፊደል alphabetical
የፊደል ፤ ሰራዊት literacy campaign
የፊደል ፤ ቀጥር spelling

ፈጀ *fäǧǧä* conclude, consume, finish, exterminate, destroy, spend (time), take (time), use up (time, money), burn, vi. (of pepper, of hot coffee)
ተፋጀ *täfaǧǧä* destroy one another, be hot (pepper)
ፈጅ *fäǧǧ*, in ነገረ ፤ ፈጅ representative (in business or legal affairs)
ፍጅት *fəǧǧət* massacre, tumult

ፍግ *fəg* dung, manure
ፍግ ፤ አፈሰሰ spread dung

ፈገገ *fäggägä* smile (v.)
ፈገግ ፤ አለ *fägägg alä* (v.) smile, grin, lighten, vi. (of face)
ፈገግታ *fägägta* smile (n.)

ፈገፈገ *fägäffägä* wipe off (dishes), scrub (pots), scrape one's knee or arm, wear away by rubbing
አፈገፈገ *afägäffägä* draw back, recoil, shrink from, fall back, retreat, give ground, back out
ወደ ፤ ኋላ ፤ አፈገፈገ retreat, withdraw (vi.)

ፎጣ *foṭa* dish cloth, towel
ያንገት ፤ ፎጣ scarf (see አንገት)
የእጅ ፤ ፎጣ napkin

ፈጠረ *fäṭṭärä* create, invent, make up, fabricate (invent), devise (a scheme)
ተፈጠረ *täfäṭṭärä*, passive of the preceding; come into existence, arise (come into being), come up (of a problem), develop, vi. (of a problem)
ፈጣሪ *fäṭari* creator
ፈጠራ *fäṭära* invention, fiction, hoax (የፈጠራ fictitious)
ፍጡር *fəṭur* creature, being (creature)
ፍጥረት, see below
ተፈጥሮ, see above

አፈጣጠር *affäṭaṭär* formation (the way of being formed)

ፍጥረት *fəṭrät* creation, creature, invention (see ፈጠረ)

ሥነ ፡ ፍጥረት science

ፈጠነ *fäṭṭänä* hasten (vi.), go fast, be fast, be quick, be rapid, hurry (vi.), be in a hurry, be prompt, do quickly, speed up (vi.)
ተፋጠነ *täfaṭṭänä* hurry (vi.)
አፋጠነ *affaṭṭänä* speed (vt.), speed up, expedite, quicken, hasten (vt.), accelerate (vt.)
ፈጥኖ *fäṭno* fast (adv.)
ፈጠን ፡ አለ *fäṭänn alä* hustle, make haste, go faster, be brisk
ፈጣን *fäṭṭan* swift, rapid, quick, speedy
ፍጡን ፡ ረድኤት patron saint
ፍጥነት, see below
የተፋጠነ *yätäfaṭṭänä* quick (decision), immediate, speedy, swift

ፍጥነት *fəṭnät* rapidity, hurry, speed, velocity (see ፈጠነ)
ፍጥነት ፡ ጨመረ gather speed, accelerate
በፍጥነት *bäfəṭnät* fast, hurriedly, rapidly, readily, precipitately
የፍጥነት ፡ ልክ speed limit
የተወሰነ ፡ ፍጥነት speed limit (see ወሰነ)

ፈጥኝ, see የፈጥኝ

ፈጠጠ *fäṭṭäṭä* pop (of eyes)
ተፋጠጠ *täfaṭṭäṭä* confront each other
ፍጥጥ ፡ አለ *fəṭäṭṭ alä* pop out (of eyes)
ፍጥጥ ፡ ብሎ ፡ አየ *fəṭäṭṭ bəlo ayyä* stare at

ፈጨ *fäččä* mash (potatoes), grind (grain), reduce to flour, make flour of, mill flour, crush (rocks), powder (sugar)

ተፋጨ *täfaččä* be sharpened (a knife against another knife), rasp, vi. (of file)
አፋጨ *affaččä* grind (the teeth), gnash, chafe (cold hands), clash (swords)
ማፋጨት *maffaččät* friction (rubbing)
†ወፍጮ *wäfčo* grinding slab, mill

*ፉጨ, አፉጨ *af°aččä* whistle (with the mouth or mouth and fingers), hiss, howl (of wind)
†ፉጨት *fuččät* whistling

*ፈጨረጨረ, ተፍጨረጨረ *täfčäräččärä* make frantic efforts, flounder

ፉጨት *fuččät* whistling (see *ፉጨ)
የአደጋ ፡ ፉጨት siren

ፈጸመ *fäṣṣämä* (B) achieve, accomplish, complete, fulfill, perform, settle (vt.), finish, carry out, execute, manage (handle)
ተፈጸመ *täfäṣṣämä*, passive of the preceding; come to an end (of meeting,) end (vi.), be complete, come true
አስፈጸመ *asfäṣṣämä* carry out, get something finished, execute
ፈጸሚ *fäṣṣami*, in ጉዳይ ፡ ፈጸሚ chargé d'affaires
ፈጽሞ *fäṣṣəmo* completely, utterly, entirely; (with a negative verb) not at all, never
ፍጹም *fəṣṣum* perfect, complete, total, absolute, outright (lie)
(በፍጹም certainly, perfectly, absolutely, entirely, completely, quite; (with a negative verb) not at all, not in the least)
ፍጻሜ *fəṣṣame* end, ending, accomplishment, completion, perfection, fulfillment, outcome, result
ፍጹምነት *fəṣṣumənnät* perfection, certitude
አስፈጻሚ *asfäṣṣami* legal executor
አፈጻጸም *affäṣaṣäm* performance, procedure

ፉፉ *faffa* be chubby, thrive (of children), grow fat, become well-developed

የፉፉ *yäfaffa* lusty, plump, chubby

ፏፏቴ *f^waf^wate* falls, waterfall, cataract

ፐ

ፖሊስ *polis* police, policeman
ፖሊስ ፡ ጠቅላይ ፡ መምሪያ police headquarters
የፖሊስ ፡ ሰራዊት police force
(የ)ፖሊስ ፡ ጣቢያ police station

ፕላስተር *plastär* adhesive tape

ፖለቲካ *polätika* politics
የፖለቲካ political
የፖለቲካ ፡ ሰው statesman
የፖለቲካ ፡ ቡድን party (political)

ፕላን *plan* plan

ፖላንድ *poland* Poland
የፖላንድ ፡ ሰው Pole
የፖላንድ ፡ ቋንቋ Polish (language)

ፖም *pom* apple

ፖምፕ *pomp* pump

ፓርላማ *parlama* parliament (see also ፓርላሜንት)

ፓርላሜንት *parlament* parliament (see also ፓርላማ)

ፕሮባ *proba* fitting, n. (by tailor)

ፓርቲ *parti* party (political)

ፕሮቶኮል *protokol* protocol

ፕሬዚዳንት *prezidant* president

ፕሮግራም *program* program

ፕሮፌሶር *profesor* professor

ፕሮፌሽናል *profešənal* professional (player)

ፕሮፓጋንዳ *propaganda* propaganda

ፖስታ *posta* the mails, mail, envelope, letter
ፖስታ ፡ ቤት post office
ፖስታ ፡ አመላላሽ—*ammälalaš* postman (see መለሰ)
የፖስታ ፡ ማጠራቀሚያ ፡ ሣጥን mailbox
(የ)ፖስታ ፡ ሣጥን post-office box
የአየር ፡ ፖስታ airmail
ፖስተኛ *postäňňa* mailman

ፓስፖርት *pasport* passport

ፑደር *pudär* powder (for face)

ፓኮ *pakko* box (of cigars)

ፓኬት *paket* pack (of cigarettes)

ፒጃማ *pižama* pajamas

ፒፓ *pippa* smoking pipe

ENGLISH - AMHARIC

A

a እንድ *and*, or *zero*

abandon ተወ *täwä;* ለቀቀ *läqqäqä;* ጣለ *ṭalä*

abase አዋረደ *awwarrädä*

abate (vt.), see 'lessen'

abbreviate አሳጠረ *asaṭṭärä*

abdicate ዙፋኑን ፡ ለቀቀ *zufanun läqqäqä*

abdomen ሆድ *hod*

abdominal የሆድ *yähod*

abduct ጠለፈ *ṭälläfä*

abhor ጠላ *ṭälla*

abhorrence ጥላቻ *ṭəlačča*

ability (skill) ችሎታ *čəlota;* (talent) ተሰ ጥፖ *täsäṭwo*

abject (wretched) አስቃቂ *assäqqaqi*

abjure ካደ *kadä*

ablaze, be ተንቦገቦገ *tänbogäbbogä;* (be on fire) በእሳት ፡ ተያያዘ *bäʾsat täyayazä*

able (capable) ችሎታ ፡ ያለው *čəlota yalläw*
be able ቻለ *čalä*

abnormal ያልተለመደ *yaltälämmädä;* ከተፈጥሮ ፡ የተለየ *kätäfäṭro yätäläyyä*

aboard, go ～ ተሳፈረ *täsaffärä*

abode መኖሪያ *mänoriya*

abolish አስቀረ *asqärrä;* አጠፋ *aṭäffa*
be abolished ቀረ *qärrä*

abominable አስከፊ *askäffi;* አስቃቂ *assäqqaqi*

abominate ጠላ *ṭälla*

aboriginal የጥንት ፡ ሰው *yäṭənt saw*

abort (miscarry) ጨነገፈ *čänäggäfä;* (fail) ከሸፈ *käššäfä*

abortion ፅንስን ፡ ማስወረድ *ṣənsən maswärräd*

about (concerning) ስለ *səlä;* (approximately) እንደ *and;* ያህል *yahəl;* ወደ *wädä*
he is about to ለ *lä*+imperfect+ ነው *näw*

above (prep.) ከ - - - ላይ *kä - - - lay;* ከ - - - በላይ *kä - - - bäla);* (more than) ከ *kä*
above (adv.) ከላይ *kälay*
above all ከሁሉም፡ ይበልጥ *kähullum yäbälṭ;* ከሁሉም ፡ ይልቅ *kähullum yəläq*

abridge አሳጠረ *asaṭṭärä*

abroad ውጭ ፡ አገር *wəčč agär*

abrupt ድንገተኛ *dəngätäňňa*

abscess እባጭ *əbbač*

absence (being away) መቅረት *mäqrät;* (being without) አለመኖር *alämänor*

absent (v.), ～ oneself ቀረ *qärrä*

absent (adj.) የቀረ *yäqärrä*
be absent (be away) ቀረ *qärrä;* (not exist) አልተገኘም *altägäňňäm*

absolute (complete, certain) ፍጹም *fəṣṣum;* ፍጹም ፡ እርግጠኛ *fəṣṣum ərgaṭäňňa;* (～ authority) ገደብ ፡ የሌለው *gädäb yälelläw*

absolutely በፍጹም *bäfəṣṣum;* ሙሉ ፡ በሙሉ *mulu bämulu;* ከቶ *kätto*

absolution ፍትሐት *fəthat;* ፍታት *fətat;* ስርየት *səryät*
obtain absolution አስተሰረየ *astäsärräyä*

absolve (of sins) ፈታ *fätta;* (of a promise) ሰረዘ(ለት) *särräzä(llät)*

absorb (～ water) መጠጣ *mäṭṭäṭä;* (～knowledge) ያዘ *yazä;* ቀሰመ *qässämä;* (～ one's attention) ማረከ *marräkä*

absorbed, be ～ in ተመሰጠ *tämässäṭä*

abstain (from food, from smoking)
ከ--- ተቄጠበ *kä--- täqʷäṭṭäbä;*
ተጠበቀ *täṭäbbäqä;* (in a vote) ድምፅ፣
አልሰጠም *dəmṣ alsäṭṭäm*

abstract, v. (make a summary) አሳጠረ
asaṭṭärä

abstract, n. (summary) አንጽሮት፣ ጽሑፍ
ahṣərotä ṣəhuf; (not concrete) የነገር፣
ስም *yänägär səm*

abstract (adj.) ረቂቅ *räqiq*

abstraction (absence of mind) ተመስጦ
tämästo; (abstract idea) ረቂቅነት
räqiqənnät

absurd ዘበት *zäbät*

absurdity ዘበት *zäbät*

abundance ብዛት *bəzat;* ሙላት *mulat*
in abundance በጋፍ *bägäf*

abundant ብዙ *bəzu*
be abundant በዛ *bäzza*

abundantly በሰፊው *bäsäffiw*

abuse, v. (mistreat) አጉሳቀለ *aggʷäsaqqʷälä;* (use insulting language)
ሰደበ *säddäbä*

abuse, n. (insulting language) ስድብ
sədəb; (corrupt practice) ተገቢ፣ ያል
ሆነ፣ አድራጎት *tägäbi yalhonä adragot*

abyss ገደል *gädäl*

acacia ግራር *grar*

academy አካዳሚ *akadami*

accede (agree) ተቀበለ *täqäbbälä*

accelerate (hasten) አፋጠነ *affaṭṭänä;*
አጣደፈ *aṭṭaddäfä*

accent, n. (stress) ቅናትና፣ ድፋት *qəna-
tənna dəfat;* (accent mark) ጭረት
* čärät;* (special way of pronouncing)
አነጋገር *annägagär*

accentuate አጐላ *agʷälla*

accept (take) ተቀበለ *täqäbbälä;* (agree)
እሺ፣ አለ *əšši alä*

acceptable, be ተቀባይነት፣ አገኘ *täqäbbayənnät agäññä*

access, have ~ to ለመቅረብ፣ (ለመግ
ባት)፣ ቻለ *lämäqräb (lämägbat) čalä*

accident አደጋ *adäga*
by accident, see 'accidentally'

accidentally እንዳጋጣሚ *əndaggaṭami;*
በድንገት *bädəngät;* ሳይታሰብ *sayəttassäb*

acclaim (v.) የጋላ፣ ስሜት፣ ገለጸ(ለት)
yägalä səmmet gälläṣä(llät)
be acclaimed ተጨበጨበ(ለት) *täčäbäč-
čäbä(llät)*

acclaim, n. (expression of satisfaction)
ሆታ *hota*

acclimatize, see 'accustom'

accommodate (adjust) አስማማ *asmamma;* (have room for, of table) አስቀ
መጠ *asqämmäṭä;* (have room for, of
bedroom) አዘረጋ *azzärägga*

accommodation (lodging) ማረፊያ *maräfiya*

accompany ሸኘ *šäňňä;* አጀበ *aǧǧäbä*

accomplice ግብረ፣ አበር *gəbrä abbär*

accomplish (finish) ፈጸመ *fäṣṣämä;* ጨረሰ
čärräsä; (carry out) አከናወነ *akkänawwänä*

accomplished (adj.) የወጣ(ለት) *yäwäṭṭa-
(llät)*

accomplishment ሥራ *səra;* የሥራ፣ ውጤት
yäsəra wəṭṭet; (completion) ፍጻሜ *fəṣṣame*

accord (vt.) ሰጠ *säṭṭä*

accord (n.) መግባባት *mägbabat;* ስምም
ነት *səmämmənnät*
be in accord ተስማማ *täsmamma*
on his own accord በገዛ፣ ፈቃዱ *bägäzza fäqadu*

accordance, in ~ with እንደ *ändä +*
noun; በ--- መሠረት *bä--- mäsärät*

according to (in agreement) እንደ *ändä;*
በ--- መሠረት *bä--- mäsärät*
according to me እንዴ፣ ከሆነ *ändäne
kähonä*

accordingly በዚያ ፡ መሠረት bäzziya mäsärät; እንደ ፡ ደንብ əndä dänb

accost አነጋገረ annägaggärä

account (v.), ~ for ምክንያት ፡ ሰጠ
məknəyat sättä; ምክንያት ፡ ገለጸ mäknəyat gälläṣä

account, n. (report) መግለጫ mägläča;
(bank deposit) ተቀማጭ ፡ ሒሳብ täqämmač hisab
on account of በ - - - የተነሣ bä - - -
yätänässa; በ - - • ምክንያት bä - - -
məknəyat
on no account በምንም ፡ ምክንያት bämənəm məknəyat
on what account? በምን ፡ ምክንያት
bämən məknəyat
take into account ተመለከተ tämäläkkätä; አመዛዘነ ammäzazzänä

accountable ተጠያቂ täṭäyyaqi; ኃላፊ halafi

accountant ሒሳብ ፡ ዐዋቂ hisab awaqi;
ሒሳብተኛ hisabtäňňa; የሒሳብ ፡ መዝ
ገብ ፡ ያዥ yähisab mäzgäb yaž

accumulate (vt.) ከመረ kämmärä; አከ
ማቸ akkämaččä; አጠራቀመ aṭṭäraqqämä
accumulate (vi.) ተከማቸ täkämaččä;
ተጠራቀመ täṭäraqqämä

accuracy ትክክለኛነት təkəkkəläňňannät;
ትክክል ፡ መሆን təkəkkəl mähon

accurate ትክክለኛ təkəkkəläňňa; ልክ
ləkk

accurately በትክክል bätəkäkkəl

accusation ክስ kəss

accuse (bring a charge against) ከሰሰ
kässäsä; (blame) ወቀሰ wäqqäsä

accused ተከሳሽ täkässaš

accuser ከሳሽ kässaš

accustom አለማመደ allämammädä; አስ
ለመደ aslämmädä

accustomed (adj.) የተለመደ yätälämmädä; ለማዳ lämmada; ልምድ ፡ ያለው
ləmd yalläw

be (get) accustomed ለመደ lämmädä;
ተላመደ tälammädä

ache (v.) አመመ(ው) ammämä(w)

ache (n.) ሕመም həmäm; እመም əmäm

achieve (accomplish) ፈጸመ fäṣṣämä;
ሠራ särra; (attain) አገኘ agäňňä

achievement የሥራ ፡ ክንውን yäsəra kə-
nəwwən

acid (n.) አሲድ asid

acid (adj.) ኮምጣጣ komṭaṭṭa; ሆምጣጣ
homṭaṭṭa

acknowledge (admit as true) አምኖ ፡
ተቀበለ amno täqäbbälä; (~ receipt)
አረጋገጠ arrägaggäṭä

acquaint ገለጸ gälläṣä; አሳወቀ asawwäqä;
አላመደ allammädä
be acquainted with (a thing) ዐወቀ
awwäqä; ተረዳ tärädda; (a person)
ተዋወቀ täwawwäqä; (work) ተላማመደ
tälämammädä
get acquainted with each other ተዋ
ወቀ täwawwäqä

acquaintance ዕውቂያ əwqiya
make acquaintance ተዋወቀ täwawwäqä

acquiesce እሺ ፡ አለ əšši alä

acquire አገኘ agäňňä

acquit በነጻ ፡ ለቀቀ bänäṣa läqqäqä; ፈረደ
(ለት) färrädä(llät)

across (prep.) ከ - - - ባሻገር kä - - - baššagär; ከ - - - ማዶ kä - - - mado
across (adv.) ከዳር ፡ እዳር kädar ədar

act, v. (do) አደረገ adärrägä; (perform
in theater) ተጫወተ täčawwätä

act, n. (action) ድርጊት dərgit; ምግባር
məgbar; ሥራ səra; (division in play)
ጋቢር gäbir

acting, adj. (~ minister) ተጠባባቂ täṭäbabaqi

action ድርጊት dərgit; ሥራ səra; ተግባር
tägbar; (step) እርምጃ ərməǧǧa; (effect) ኃይል hayl
be in action (work) ሠራ särra

active (energetic) ነቁ *nəqu;* (~ member) ሙሉ *mulu;* (~ verb) አድራጊ *adragi*

actively በሙሉ ፡ ልብ *bämulu ləbb*

activity (movement) እንቅስቃሴ *ənqəsəqqase;* (things to do) ተግባር *tägbar*

actor ተዋናይ *täwanay*

actual (real) እውነተኛ *əwnätäñña;* (present) የጊዜ *yägize*

actually በእውነት *bäəwnät;* በውን *bäwən*

acute (severe) ጽኑ *ṣənu;* (keen) ነቁ *nəqu*

adapt አራመደ *arrammädä;* እንዲስማማ ፡ አደረገ *əndismamma adärrägä* adapt oneself ተላመደ *tälammädä*

add (join) ጨመረ *čämmärä;* (sum up numbers) ደመረ *dämmärä;* (say further) በተጨማሪ ፡ አለ *bätäčämmari alä*

addict ሱሰኛ *susäñña*

addiction ሱስ *sus*

addition (summing up) ድምር *dəmmər;* መደመር *mädämmär;* (joining of one thing to another) መጨመር *mäčämmär;* (part added) ቅጥያ *qəṭṭəyya* in addition በተጨማሪ *bätäčämmari* in addition to ከ - - - ሌላ *kä - - -lela;* በ - - - ላይ *bä - - - lay;* ከ - - - በላይ *kä - - - bälay*

additional ተጨማሪ *täčämmari;* ጭምር *čəmmər*

address, v. (~ a meeting) ንግግር ፡ አደረገ *nəgəggər adärrägä;* (~ a letter) አድራሻ ፡ ጻፈ *adrašša ṣafä;* (speak to) አናገረ *annaggärä*

address, n. (of letter) አድራሻ *adrašša;* (speech) ንግግር *nəgəggər;* (skill) ችሎታ *čəlota*

adept ባለሞያ *balämoya*

adequacy ብቁነት *bəqunnät*

adequate (sufficient) በቂ *bäqi;* አጥጋቢ *aṭgabi;* የተማላ *yätämwalla*

adhere (stick) ተጣበቀ *täṭabbäqä*

adherent, n. (supporter) ደጋፊ *däggafi;* ተከታይ *täkättay*

adherent, adj. (sticky) የሚጣበቅ *yämmiṭṭabbäq*

adhesive ተጣባቂ *täṭabaqi*

adjacent ቀጥሎ ፡ ያለ *qäṭṭəlo yalä*

adjective ቅጽል *qəṣṣəl*

adjoin ተዋሰነ *täwassänä*

adjoining የሚቀጥል *yämmiqäṭṭəl;* የሚዋሰን *yämmiwwassän*

adjourn, vt. (~ a meeting) በተነ *bättänä* adjourn, vi. (of meeting) ተበተነ *täbättänä;* ስብሰባ ፡ አበቃ *səbsäba abäqqa*

adjust አስተካከለ *astäkakkälä* adjust oneself ተላመደ *tälammädä*

administer አስተዳደረ *astädaddärä;* አካሄደ *akkahedä*

administration አስተዳደር *astädadär*

administrative ያስተዳደር *yastädadär* administrative assistant ረዳት ፡ አስተዳዳሪ *räddat astädadari*

administrator አስተዳዳሪ *astädadari;* አስኪያጅ *askiyaǧ*

admirable አስደናቂ *asdännaqi;* አስገራሚ *asgärrami;* ድንቅ *dənq;* ግሩም *gərum* be admirable ደነቀ *dännäqä*

admiral የባሕር ፡ ኃይል ፡ ዋና ፡ አዛዥ *yäbahər hayl wanna azzaž*

admiration አድናቆት *adnaqot*

admire አደነቀ *adännäqä*

admissible, be ተፈቀደ *täfäqqädä;* ተቀባይነት ፡ አለው *täqäbbayənnät alläw*

admission (entrance) መግቢያ *mägbiya;* (acknowledging) ማመን *mamän*

admit (let in) አስገባ *asgäbba;* (acknowledge) አመነ *ammänä*

admittance የመግባት ፡ ፈቃድ *yämägbat fäqad*

admonish (rebuke) ገሠጸ *gässäṣä*

admonition ተግሣጽ *tägsaṣ*

adolescence የጉልምስና ፡ የኮረዳነት ፡ ጊዜ *yägulməsənna yäkoräddannät gize* adolescent (male) ጉረምሳ g^wärämsa; (female) ኮረዳ korädda

adopt (accept) ተቀበለ täqäbbälä; (~ a child) በጉዲፈቻ ፡ ተቀበለ bäguddifäčča täqäbbälä

adopted (~ child) የጉዲፈቻ yäguddifäčča

adoption (of child) ጉዲፈቻ guddifäčča

adore (love) አፈቀረ afäqqärä; ወደደ wäddädä; (worship) አመለከ amälläkä; ሰገደ säggädä

adorn አስጌጠ asgeṭä

adornment ጌጥ geṭ

adult ዐዋቂ awaqi

adultery ዝሙት zəmmut
commit adultery ዘማ zämma; አመነ ዘረ amänäzzärä

adulthood አካለ ፡ መጠን ፡ መድረስ akalä mäṭän mädräs

advance, vt. (~ money) በቅድሚያ ፡ ሰጠ bäqədmiya säṭṭä; (~ the time of a meeting) ቀደም ፡ አደረገ qädämm adärrägä

advance, vi. (be ahead) ቀደመ qäddämä; (progress) ተራመደ tärammädä

advance, n. (progress) እርምጃ ərməǧǧa; መሻሻል mäššašal; (movement forward) መግፋት mägfat
in advance በቅድሚያ bäqədmiya; አስ ቀድሞ asqäddəmo; ቀደም ፡ ብሎ qädämm bəlo

advanced, adj. (~ courses) ከፍተኛ käffətäňňa; (~ in years) የገፋ yägäffa

advantage (profit) ጥቅም ṭəqəm; (superiority) ብልጫ bəlča
take advantage of ተጠቀመ(በት) täṭäqqämä(bbät)

advantageous የሚጠቅም yämmiṭäqəm
be advantageous ጠቀመ ṭäqqämä

adventure (bold undertaking) ጀብዱ ǧäbdu

adventurer (adventure seeking) የጀብዱ፡ ሰው yäǧäbdu säw; (schemer) ሞሌ čolle

adventurous (fond of adventure) ደፋር däffar; (risky) ጀብዱ ፡ የበዛበት ǧäbdu yäbäzzabbät

adverb ተውሳክ ፡ ግስ täwsakä gəss

adversary ጠላት ṭälat; ባላጋራ balagara

adverse (~ decision) የሚጎዳ yämmig^wäda; (~ circumstances) ያልተቃና yaltäqanna

adversity መከራ mäkära

advertise አስታወቀ astawwäqä

advertisement የንግድ ፡ ማስታወቂያ yänəgd mastawäqiya

advice ምክር məkər
give advice አማከረ ammakkärä
seek advice ተማከረ tämäkakkärä

advisable, be ተሻለ täšalä; ተገባ tägäbba

advise (give advice) መከረ mäkkärä; አማከረ ammakkärä; (inform) አስታ ወቀ astawwäqä

advisor አማካሪ ammakari

advisory አማካሪ ammakari

advocate (v.) ሰበከ säbbäkä

advocate, n. (in court) ጠበቃ ṭäbäqa

afar ሩቅ ruq

affable ተወዳጅ täwäddaǧ

affair ጉዳይ gudday; ነገር nägär

affect (have an influence on) ተጽዕኖ ፡ አለው täṣə'əno alläw; (~ health) አቃወሰ aqqawwäsä; ጎዳ g^wädda

affection ፍቅር fəqər

affectionate (~ person) ሰው ፡ የሚወድ säw yämmiwädd; (~ nature) ተወዳጅ täwäddaǧ

affianced, be አጨ aččä

affiliation ዝምድና zəmdənna

affinity (relationship) መቀራረብ mäqqäraräb; (similarity) ተመሳሳይነት tämäsasayənnät

affirm (declare) አረጋገጠ arrägaggäṭä

affirmative የአዎንታ yawonta

affix (~ a label) ለጠፈ *läṭṭäfä*

afflict አጠቃ *aṭäqqa*; አሠቃየ *assäqayyä*

afflicted ችግራኛ *čəggəräňňa*

affliction መከራ *mäkära*

affluence ሀብት *habt*

affluent (adj.) ባለጸጋ *baläṣägga*

afford ሰጠ *säṭṭä*; አስገኘ *asgäňňä*

affront (v.) አዋረደ *awwarrädä*

affront (n.) ውርደት *wərdät*

afire, set ~ አቀጣጠለ *aqqäṭaṭṭälä*

aflame, be በእሳት ፡ ተቀጣጠለ *bäəsat täqäṭaṭṭälä*; ተንበለበለ *tänbäläbbälä*

afloat, be ተንሳፈፈ *tänsaffäfä*

afoot በእግር *bägər*

afraid, be ፈራ *färra*; (regret) መሰለ(ው) *mässälä(w)*

after (prep.) ከ - - - በኋላ *kä - - - bähwala*

after (conj.) ከ *kä* + verb + በኋላ *bähwala*

after all መቸም *mäčäm*; ያም ፡ ሆነ ፡ ይህ *yam honä yəh*; የሆነ ፡ ሆኖ *yähonä hono*

afterbirth የእንግዴ ፡ ልጅ *yängəde ləǧ*

afternoon ከሰዓት ፡ በኋላ *käsä'at bähwala*; ከቀትር ፡ በኋላ *käqätər bähwala*

afterwards በኋላ *bähwala*; ኋላ *hwala*; ቀጥሎ *qäṭṭəlo*

again እንደገና *əndägäna*; ሁለተኛ *hulättäňňa*; መልሶ *mälləso*; ደግሞ *dägmo* again and again ደጋግሞ *dägagmo* do again ደገመ *däggämä*

against በ *bä*; (in opposite direction) ከ - - - አንጻር *kä - - - anṣar*; (in opposition) በመቃወም *bämäqqawäm* be against ተቃወመ *täqawwämä*

age (vt.) አሸመገለ *ašämäggälä* age, vi. (of person) አረጀ *aräǧǧä*

age (n.) ዕድሜ *ədme*; (old age) እርጅና *ərǧənna*; (time) ዘመን *zämän* in ages ለብዙ ፡ ዘመናት *läbəzu zämänat*

aged (~ man) ሽማግሌ *šəmagəlle*; (~ woman) አሮጊት *arogit*; (~ wine) የበሰለ *yäbässälä* a boy aged ten ያሥር ፡ ዓመት ፡ ልጅ *yassər amät ləǧ*

agency አገንስ *ažans*; ድርጅት *dərəǧǧət*

agenda አጀንዳ *aǧända*

agent (representative) ወኪል *wäkkil*; (agitator) አነሣሽ *annäsaš*

agglomerate (v.) አደባለቀ *addäballäqä*

aggravate (irritate) አበሳጨ *abbäsaččä*; (make worse) አባሰ(በት) *abasä(bbät)*

aggravation ብስጭት *bəsəččət*

aggression አጥቂነት *aṭqinnät*; የጠብ ፡ ጫሪ ነት *yäṭäb čarinnät*

aggressive ጠብ ፡ ጫሪ *ṭäb čari*; ጠበኛ *ṭäbäňňa*; (energetic) ጥብቅ *ṭəbq*

aggressor ጠብ ፡ ጫሪ *ṭäb čari*; አጥቂ *aṭqi*

aghast, be ከው ፡ አለ *käww alä*

agile ቀልጣፋ *qälṭaffa*

agitate አናወጸ *annawwäṣä*; (~ public opinion) አነሣሣ *annäsassa*; (disturb) አሸበረ *aššäbbärä*

agitation (incitement) ሁከት *hukät*; ማነ ሣሣት *mannäsasat*; (excitement) የመን ፈስ ፡ መረበሽ *yämänfäs märräbäš*

ago ከ - - - በፊት *kä - - - bäfit*; የዛሬ *yäzare* + perfect a long time ago ድሮ *dəro*

agony (great pain) ሥቃይ *səqay*; (final agony) ጣረሞት *ṭarämot*

agree (be of the same mind) ተስማማ *täsmamma*; (consent) ይሁን ፡ አለ *yahun alä*; እሺ ፡ አለ *əšši alä* agree with one (of food) ተስማማ *täsmamma*

agreeable (pleasant) አስደሳች *asdässač*

agreement ስምምነት *səməmmənnät*; ስምም *səməmm*; (correspondence in grammar) መስማማት *mäsmamat* come to an agreement ተስማማ *täsmamma* conclude an agreement ስምምነት ፡ አደረጉ *səməmmənnät adärräga*; ተዋዋለ *täwawalä*

agricultural የእርሻ *yärša*

agriculture ግብርና *gəbrənna*; የርሻ ፡ ተግ ባር *yärša tägbar*
Ministry of Agriculture እርሻ ፡ ሚኒ ስቴር *ərša minister*

ahead ወደፊት *wädäfit*; በቅድሚያ *bäqədmiya*
ahead of ቀደም ፡ ብሎ *qädämm bəlo*; ቀድሞ *qädmo*
be ahead (of) ቀደም *qäddämä*; ላቀ *laqä*
go ahead ቀደም *qäddämä*

aid (v.) ረዳ *rädda*; አገዘ *aggäzä*

aid (n.) እርዳታ *ərdata*
come to one's aid ደረሰ(ለት) *därräsä-(llät)*

aide ረዳት *räddat*

ail ታመመ *tammämä*

ailing በሽተኛ *bäššətäňňa*
be ailing አመመ(ው) *ammämä(w)*

ailment ሕመም *həmäm*; በሽታ *bäššəta*

aim, v. (point a gun) ዓለመ *allämä*; አነጣጠረ *annäṭaṭṭärä*; (intend) አሰበ *assäbä*
be aimed at (of blow, of speech) ተሰነዘረ *täsänäzzärä*; ታሰበ *tassäbä*

aim, n. (aiming) ማነጣጠር *mannäṭaṭär*; (purpose) ዓላማ *alama*; ግብ *gəb*

aimlessly ያላንዳች ፡ ዓላማ *yalandačč alama*

air (v.) አናፈሰ *annaffäsä*

air (n.) አየር *ayyär*; (appearance) መልክ *mälk*; (manner) ሁኔታ *huneta*
take the air ተናፈሰ *tänaffäsä*

airs (manners) ፋሊጥ *faliṭ*
give oneself airs ልታይ ፡ ልታይ ፡ አለ *ləttay ləttay alä*

airborne አየር ፡ ወለድ *ayyär wälläd*

airfield ያውሮፕላን ፡ ጣቢያ *yawroplan ṭabiya*

air force የአየር ፡ ኃይል *yayyär hayl*

air letter የአየር ፡ መልእክት *yayyär mäl'əkt*

airline የአየር ፡ መንገድ *yayyär mängäd*

airmail የአየር ፡ መልእክት *yayyär mäl'əkt*; የአየር ፡ ፖስታ *yayyär posta*

airplane አውሮፕላን *awroplan*; አይሮፕላን *ayroplan*

airport ያውሮፕላን ፡ ማረፊያ *yawroplan maräfiya*

air raid የአየር ፡ ወረራ *yayyär wärära*; የአየር ፡ ጥቃት *yayyär ṭəqat*

aisle መተላለፊያ *mättälaläfiya*

ajar, be ገርበብ ፡ አለ *gärbäbb alä*

akin, be (be related) ተዛመደ *täzammädä*

alarm (v.) አሸበረ *aššäbbärä*; አስደነገጠ *asdänäggäṭä*; አሰጋ *asägga*

alarm, n. (fright) ድንጋጤ *dənəggaṭe*; (warning device) የማስጠንቀቂያ ፡ ደወል *yämasṭänqäqiya däwäl*

alarm clock የሚደውል ፡ ሰዓት *yämmidäwwəl säat*; የሰዓት ፡ ደወል *yäsäat däwäl*

alarming አሳሳቢ *asassabi*; አስጊ *asgi*

alas! ወይኔ *wäyne*; ወዮ *wäyyo*

album የፎቶግራፍ ፡ ማኖሪያ *yäfotograf manoriya*

alcohol አልኮል *alkol*; (liquor) የሚያሰ ክር ፡ መጠጥ *yämmiyasäkkər mäṭäṭṭ*

alcoholic (n.) የአልኮል ፡ ሱሰኛ *yäalkol susäňňa*

alcove ጓዳ *gʷada*

alert (v.) አስጠነቀቀ *asṭänäqqäqä*

alert (n.) ማስጠንቀቂያ *masṭänqäqiya*

alert (adj.) ንቁ *nəqu*

alertness ንቃት *nəqat*; ንቁነት *nəqunnät*

algebra አልጀብራ *alǧebra*

alien (n.) የውጭ ፡ አገር ፡ ዜጋ *yäwəčč agär zega*

alien (adj.) ባዕድ *ba'əd*

alienate አለያየ *alläyayyä;* አራቀ *araqä*

alight, v. (of a bird) አረፈ *arräfä;* (of a person) ወረደ *wärrädä*

align, vt. (~ soldiers) አሰለፈ *assälläfä;* (~ chairs) ደረደረ *däräddärä*
align (vi.) ተሰለፈ *täsälläfä*

alike መሳይ *mäsay;* (in status, age) እኩል *əkkul*
be (look) alike ተመሳሰለ *tämäsassälä*
treat alike ባንድ ፡ ዓይን ፡ አየ *band ayn ayyä*

alimentation አመጋገብ *ammägagäb*

alive በሕይወት ፡ ያለ *bähəywät yallä;* ሕያው *həyaw;* (lively) ንቁ *nəqu*
be alive በሕይወት ፡ አለ *bähəywät allä;* ኖረ *norä*
keep alive (vt.) አቆየ *aqoyyä*

all ሁሉ *hullu*
all along ምንጊዜም *məngizem;* ሁል ጊዜ *hulgize*
all in all በጠቅላላው *bätäqlallaw*
all over በሙሉ *bämulu;* በመላው *bämällaw;* (everywhere) በየቦታው *bäyyäbotaw;* በያለበት *bäyyalläbbät*
at all ምንም *mənəm* + negative verb
be all over (finished) አለቀ *alläqä*
from all over ከየቦታው *käyyäbotaw*
in all በጠቅላላው *bätäqlallaw;* በሙሉ *bämulu*

allay (~ fear) አቃለለ *aqqallälä;* (~ pain) አስታገሠ *astaggäsä*

allegation ቃል *qal;* ነገር *nägär*

allege አለ *alä*

alleged የተባለ *yätäbalä*

allegiance ታማኝነት *tamaňňənnät*
oath of allegiance የታማኝነት ፡ መሐላ *yätamaňňənnät mähalla*

allegory ምሳሌ *məssale*

alleviate (~ pain) አስታገሠ *astaggäsä;* (~ distress) አቃለለ *aqqallälä*

alley ጠባብ ፡ መንገድ *täbbab mängäd*

alliance ኅብረት *həbrät;* ስምምነት *səməm-mənnät*

allied (~ nations) የጦር ፡ ጓደኛ *yätor g°addäňňa;* (related) የሚዛመድ *yäm-mizzammäd*

allocate, see 'allot'

allot ዐደለ *addälä;* መደበ *mäddäbä;* አደላደለ *addäladdälä*

allow (permit) ፈቀደ *fäqqädä;* (make possible) አስቻለ *asčalä*

allowance አበል *abäl;* ልዩ ፡ ወጪ *ləyyu wäči;* የኪስ ፡ ገንዘብ *yäkis gänzäb*

alloy ቅይጥ *qəyyət*

all right እሺ *əšši;* መልካም *mälkam;* ደኅና *dähna*

allude አነሣ *anässa*

allure ስሜት ፡ ሳበ *səmmet sabä*

allusion, make ~ አነሣ *anässa*

ally (v.), ~ oneself ተባበረ *täbabbärä*

ally (n.) ተባባሪ *täbabari;* ጓደኛ *g°addäňňa;* (military ~) የጦር ፡ የቃል ፡ ኪዳን ፡ ጓደኛ *yätor yäqal kidan g°addäňňa*

almighty ኃያል *hayyal*

almond ለውዝ *läwz*

almost ል *lə* + imperfect + ምንም ፡ አል ቀረም *mənəmm alqärräm*

alms ምጽዋት *məṣwat*
give alms መጸወተ *mäṣäwwätä*

alone ብቻ *bäčča;* ለብቻ *läbäčča*

along በ - - - ዳር *bä - - - dar;* በ - - - ጥግ *bä - - - ṭəgg;* በ - - - በኩል *bä - - - bäkkul*
along with ከ - - - ጋር *kä - - - gar;* አብሮ *abro*

alongside ከ - - - ጐን *kä - - - g°änn;* በ - - - ዳርቻ *bä - - - darəčča*

aloof ገለልተኛ *gälältäňňa*
stand aloof ተገሎ ፡ ቆመ *tägällo qomä*

aloofness ገለልተኛነት *gälältäňňannät*

aloud ጮኸ ፡ ብሎ *čok bəlo*

alphabet ፊደል *fidäl*

alphabetical የፊደል *yäfidäl*

alphabetize በፊደል ፡ ተራ ፡ አደረገ *bäfidäl tära adärrägä*

already አስቀድሞ *asqäddəmo;* ዱሮ *duro*

also -ም -*m;* ደግሞ *dägmo;* ደም *dämmo*

altar መሠዊያ *mäsawwiya;* መንበር *mänbär*

alter (vt.) ለወጠ *läwwäṭä*

alteration (change) ለውጥ *läwṭ;* (for clothes) ማስተካከያ *mastäkakäya*

altercate ተጨቃጨቀ *täčäqaččäqä*

altercation ንትርክ *nətərrək*

alternate (vt.) አፈራረቀ *affärarräqä* alternate (vi.) ተፈራረቀ *täfärarräqä*

alternate (n.) ምትክ *mətəkk*

alternate (adj.) ተፈራራቂ *täfäraraqi*

alternative (n., adj.) አማራጭ *ammaräč;* ፈረቃ *färäqa*

although ብ *bə* + imperfect + ም-*m;* ብ *bə* + imperfect + ም ፡ እንኳ-*m ənkʷa*

altitude ከፍታ *käffəta*

altogether (on the whole) በጠቅላላው *bäṭäqlallaw;* (entirely) በፍጹም *bäfəṣṣum*

alumnus የቀድሞ ፡ ምሩቅ *yäqädmo mərruq*

always ሁልጊዜ *hulgize;* ወትሮ *wätro*

amalgamate (vt.) አዋሐደ *awwahadä;* አደባለቀ *addäballäqä*

amass አከማቸ *akkämaččä;* ከመረ *kämmärä;* አጠራቀመ *aṭṭäraqqämä*

amaze አስደነቀ *asdännäqä;* አስገረመ *asgärrämä*
be amazed ተደነቀ *tädännäqä;* ገረ መ(ው) *gärrämä(w)*

amazing የሚያስደነቅ *yämmiyasdännəq;* ግሩም *gərum*
be amazing አስደነቀ *asdännäqä;* ገረመ *gärrämä*

ambassador አምባሳደር *ambasadär*

amber (adj.) ብሩህ ፡ ቢጫ *bəruh biča*

ambiguity አሻሚነት *aššaminnät*

ambiguous አሻሚ *aššami;* ግራ ፡ የሚያገባ *gəra yämmiyagäba;* ግልጽ ፡ ያልሆነ *gəlṣ yalhonä*

ambition ምኞት *məňňot;* ፍላጎት *fəllagot*

ambitious (eager) ጉጉ *guggu;* (~ plan) በጣም ፡ ከፍ ፡ ያለ *bäṭam käff yalä;* ከፍተኛ *käffətäňňa*

ambulance አምቡላንስ *ambulans*

ambush (v.) አደፈጠ *adäffäṭä*

ambush (n.) ደፈጣ *däfäṭa*
lie in ambush አደፈጠ *adäffäṭä*

ameliorate (vt.) አሻሻለ *aššašalä*
ameliorate (vi.) ተሻሻለ *täšašalä*

amen አሜን *amen*

amend አሻሻለ *aššašalä*

amendment የማሻሻያ ፡ ሐሳብ *yämaššašaya hassab*

amends ካሳ *kasa*

amenities ምቾት *məččot*

America አሜሪካ *amerika*

American አሜሪካዊ *amerikawi;* አሜሪካን *amerikan*

Amharic አማርኛ *amarəňňa*

amiable ተወዳጅ *täwäddäǧ*

amicable የወዳጅነት *yäwädaǧənnät*

amidst በ - - - መኻል *bä - - - mähal*

amiss, feel ~ ቅር ፡ አለ(ው) *qərr alä(w)*
be amiss ጐደለ *gʷäddälä*
go amiss ጠፋት ፡ አደረገ *ṭəfat adärrägä*

amity ወዳጅነት *wädaǧənnät*

ammunition ጥይት *ṭəyyət*

amnesty ምሕረት *məhrät*

among በ - - - መሀከል *bä - - - mähakkäl;* መኻል *mähal;* ከ - - - ውስጥ *kä - - - wəsṭ*

amongst በ - - - መሀከል *bä - - - mähakkäl*

amorous, become በፍቅር ፡ ተማረከ *bäfəqər tämarräkä*

amount (v.), ~ to (reach) ደረሰ *därräsä;* አከለ *akkälä;* (be equivalent) ተቈጠረ *täqʷäṭṭärä*

amount, n. (total) መጠን *mäṭän*; (bulk) ብዛት *bəzat*
the whole amount ሁሉ *hullu*

ample (enough) በቂ *bäqi*

amplifier ድምፅ ፡ ማጕያ *dəmṣ magʷya*

amplify አጐላ *agʷälla;* (enlarge on) አብራራ *abrarra*

amputate ቈረጠ *qʷärräṭä*

amulet ክታብ *kətab*

amuse አስደሰተ *asdässätä;* አጫወተ *ač̣č̣awwätä*

amused (~ spectator) የተደሰተ *yätädässätä;* (~ smile) ደስታ ፡ የመላበት *dässəta yämällabbät*

amusement (pleasure) ደስታ *dässəta;* (enjoyment) ጨዋታ *č̣äwata*

amusing የሚያስደስት *yämmiyasdässət;* (causing laughter) አሥቂኝ *assəqiň*

an, see 'a'

analogous ተመሳሳይ *tämäsasay;* መሰል *mässäl*

analogy ማመሳሰል *mammäsasäl;* ተመሳሳይነት *tämäsasayənnät*
draw an analogy አመሳሰለ *ammäsassälä*

analysis (of a situation) ትንተና *təntäna;* (in chemistry) ምርመራ *mərmära*

analyze (~ a situation) ተነተነ *tänättänä*; (in chemistry) መረመረ *märämmärä*

anarchy ግርግር *gərrəgərr*

anatomy (study of anatomy) አናቶሚ *anatomi*; (the physical structure) የሰውነት ፡ አሠራር *yäsäwənnät assärar*

ancestor ቅድመ ፡ አያት *qədmä ayat*
ancestors አባቶች *abbatočč*

ancestral የዘር *yäzär*

ancestry ዘር *zär*; ቅድመ ፡ አያቶች *qədmä ayatočč*

anchor (vt.) መልሕቅ ፡ ጣለ *mälhəq ṭalä*

anchor (n.) መልሕቅ *mälhəq*

ancient (n.) የድሮ ፡ ሰው *yädəro säw*

ancient, adj. (old) አሮጌ *aroge;* (of the past) የጥንት *yäṭənt;* ጥንታዊ *ṭəntawi*

and -ና *-nna*; -ም *-m*

anecdote ተረት *tärät*

angel መልአክ *mäl'ak;* መላክ *mälak*

angelic መልአካዊ *mäl'akawi*

anger (v.) አናደደ *annaddädä;* አስቈጣ *asqʷäṭṭa*

anger (n.) ንዴት *nəddet;* ቁጣ *quṭṭa*
arouse one's anger አስቈጣ *asqʷäṭṭa*

angle (n.) ማእዘን *ma'əzän*
from all angles ከሁሉም ፡ አቅጣጫ *kähullum aqṭač̣č̣a*

angry (~ reply) የቁጣ *yäquṭṭa;* (~ person) የተናደደ *yätänaddädä;* ቁጡ *quṭṭu*
be (become) angry ተናደደ *tänaddädä;* ተቈጣ *täqʷäṭṭa*
make angry, see 'anger' (v.)

anguish ጭንቀት *č̣ənqät*

anguished, be ተጨነቀ *täč̣ännäqä*

angular ማእዘናዊ *ma'əzänawi*

animal እንስሳ *ənsəsa*
domestic animal የቤት ፡ እንስሳ *yäbet ənsəsa*
wild animal አውሬ *awre;* የዱር ፡ አራዊት *yädur arawit*

animate, v. (give life) ሕይወት ፡ ሰጠ *həywät säṭṭä;* (enliven) ድምቀት ፡ ሰጠ *dəmqät säṭṭä*

animate (adj.) ሕይወታዊ *həywätawi*

animated (~ discussion) የተሟሟቀ *yätämʷamʷaqä*

animation የጋለ ፡ ስሜት *yägalä səmmet*

animosity ጥላቻ *ṭəlačča*

ankle ቍርጭምጭሚት *qurč̣əmč̣əmit*

annex, v. (~ a territory) ቀላቀለ *qälaqqälä*; አዋሐደ *awwahadä*

annex (n.) ቅጥያ qəṭṭəyya; ተጨማሪ፡ ሕንጻ täčämmari hənṣa

annihilate ድምጥምጡን ፡ አጠፋ dəməṭ-məṭun aṭäffa; ደመሰሰ dämässäsä

anniversary ያመት ፡ በዓል yamät bä'al

announce (make known) አስታወቀ astawwäqä; አሰማ assämma; አወራ awärra

announcement መግለጫ mägläča; ማስታ-ወቂያ mastawäqiya

announcer ተናጋሪ tänagari; ማስታወቂያ ፡ ተናጋሪ mastawäqiya tänagari

annoy (irritate) አበሳጨ abbäsaččä; (make angry) አናደደ annaddädä

annoyance ብስጭት bəsəččət; ማወክ maw-wäk

annual (n.) ዓመታዊ ፡ መጽሔት amätawi mäṣhet

annual (adj.) ዓመታዊ amätawi; ያመት yamät

annually በያመቱ bäyyamätu

annul ሻረ šarä; አፈረሰ afärräsä

anoint ቀባ qäbba

anonymous ስም ፡ ያልተጻፈበት səm yal-täṣafäbbät

another ሌላ lela

answer (v.) መለሰ mälläsä; መልስ ፡ ሰጠ mäls säṭṭä; (be suitable, fulfill) ጥላ (ለት) molla(llät); አረከ aräkka
answer back መለሰ(ለት) mälläsä(llät)
answer for (be held responsible) በነ ላፊነት ፡ ተጠየቀ(በት) bähalafinnät tä-ṭäyyäqä(bbät)

answer (n.) መልስ mäls; ምላሽ məllaš

ant ጉንዳን gundan

antagonism ጥላቻ ṭəlačča

antecedents (ancestors) ቅድም ፡ አያቶች qədmä ayatočč

antelope ደኵላ däkʷla; የሜዳ ፡ ፍየል yä-meda fəyyäl

anterior የወደፊት yäwädäfit
be anterior ቀደም qäddämä

anthem የሕዝብ ፡ መዝሙር yähəzb mäz-mur

antipathy ጥላቻ ṭəlačča

antiquated ጊዜ ፡ ያለፈ(በት) gize yalläfä-(bbät)

antique የጥንት yäṭənt; ጥንታዊ ṭəntawi

antiquity (times long ago) የጥንት ፡ ጊዜ yäṭənt gize; (oldness, great age) ጥን ታዊነት ṭəntawinnät

antler ቀንድ qänd

anus ፍንጢጣ fənṭiṭṭa; ቂጥ qiṭ

anvil መስፍ mäsf

anxiety (apprehension) ስጋት səgat; (eager desire) ጉጉት guggut

anxious (troubled) የተሸበረ yätäšäbbärä; (eagerly desiring) ጉጉ guggu
be anxious (troubled) ሰጋ sägga; ተሸ በረ täšäbbärä; (eagerly desiring) ጓጓ gʷaggʷa

any (person) ማንም mannəm; ማንኛውም mannəňňawəm; (thing) ምንም mənəm; አንዳች andačč
any other ሌላ lela

anybody ሰው säw; ማንኛውም ፡ ሰው man-nəňňawəm säw
anybody else ሌላ ፡ ሰው lela säw

anyhow ሆኖም honom; እንደምንም ፡ ብሎ əndämənəm bəlo

anyone ሰው säw; ማንኛውም mannəňňa-wəm; ማንም mannəm

anything አንዳች ፡ ነገር andačč nägär; ምንም ፡ ነገር mənəm nägär; ምንም mə-nəm; ምናምን mənamən
anything else ሌላ ፡ ነገር lela nägär
not ... anything ምንም mənəm + neg-ative verb; አንዳችም andaččəm + neg-ative verb
not for anything ለምንም ፡ ነገር ፡ ብሎ lämənəm nägär bəlo

anyway ያም ፡ ሆነ ፡ ይህ yam honä yəh; የሆነ ፡ ሆኖ yähonä hono; ቢሆንም biho-nəm

anywhere የትም *yätəm*
anywhere else ሌላ ፡ ቦታ *lela bota*

apart ተለያይተው *täläyaytäw;* ለየብቻ *läyyäbəčča*
apart from ከ --- በስተቀር *kä --- bästäqär*
be apart (at a distance) ተራራቀ *täraraqä;* (in age) ተበላለጠ *täbälallätä*
keep apart ነጠል ፡ አለ *nättäll alä*
take apart አለያየ *alläyayyä*

apartment አፓርተማ *apartäma*

apathy ግዴለሸነት *gəddelläšənnät*

ape ጦጣ *tota;* ዝንጀሮ *zənǧäro*

apologize ይቅርታ ፡ ጠየቀ *yəqərta täyyäqä;* ይቅርታ ፡ ለመነ *yəqərta lämmänä*

apology ይቅርታ ፡ መጠየቅ *yəqərta mätäyyäq;* ይቅርታ *yəqərta*

apostate ሃይማኖት ፡ የካደ ፡ ሰው *haymanot yäkadä säw*

apostle ሐዋርያ *hawarya*

appall አስደነገጠ *asdänäggätä;* አሰቀቀ *assäqqäqä*

appalling የሚያሰቅቅ *yämmiyassäqqəq;* የሚያሳዝን *yämmiyasazzən*

apparatus መሣሪያ *mässariya*

apparel ልብስ *ləbs*

apparent ግልጽ *gəlş;* የሚታይ *yämmittay*
be apparent ታየ *tayyä*

apparently, relative perfect or imperfect followed by ይመስላል *yəmäslal;* (clearly) በግልጽ *bägəlş*

appeal (vt.) ይግባኝ ፡ አለ *yəgbañň alä*
appeal, vi. (request) ለመነ *lämmänä;* (be attractive) ሳበ *sabä;* ደስ ፡ አለ *däss alä;* ማረከ *marräkä*

appeal (n.) ይግባኝ *yəgbañň;* አቤቱታ *abetuta*

appear ብቅ ፡ አለ *bəqq alä;* ታየ *tayyä;* (be published) ወጣ *wätta;* (seem) መሰለ *mässälä*

appearance (aspect) መልክ *mälk;* (act of appearing) መታየት *mättayät;* ብቅ፡ ማለት *bəqq malät*

make an appearance ብቅ ፡ አለ *bəqq alä*

appease (~anger) አበረደ *abärrädä;* (pacify with concessions) አባበለ *ababbälä*

append አያያዘ *ayyayazä;* ቀጠለ *qättälä*

appendicitis የትርፍ ፡ አንጀት ፡ በሽታ *yätərf anǧät bäššəta*

appendix (of body) ትርፍ ፡ አንጀት *tərf anǧät;* (of a book) ተጨማሪ ፡ መግ ለጫ *täčämmäri mägläča*

appetite የምግብ ፡ ፍላጎት *yäməgəb fəllagot*

applaud አጨበጨበ *ačäbäččäbä;* (praise) አደነቀ *adännäqä*

applause ጭብጨባ *čəbčäba*

apple ቱፋ *tufah;* ፖም *pom*

appliance መሣሪያ *mässariya*

applicable, be ሠራ *särra;* አግባብነት ፡ አለው *agbabənnät alläw*

applicant አመልካች *amälkač*

application (request) ማመልከቻ *mamälkäča;* (manner of using) መጠቀም *mättäqäm;* (putting to use) በሥራ፡ ላይ፡ ማዋል *bäsəra lay mawal;* (effort) ጥረት *tərät;* መትጋት *mätgat*
submit an application አመለከተ *amäläkkätä*

apply, vt. (put to practical use) በሥራ ፡ ላይ ፡ አዋለ *bäsəra lay awalä;* ተጠቀ መ(በት) *tätäqqämä(bbät)*
apply, vi. (make a request) አመለከተ *amäläkkätä;* (be relevant) ጸና *şänna;* አግባብነት ፡ አለው *agbabənnät alläw*

appoint (to an office) ሾመ *šomä*

appointment (date) ቀጠሮ *qätäro;* (office) ሹመት *šumät*
give an appointment ቀጠረ *qättärä*
keep an appointment ቀጠሮ ፡ አከበረ *qätäro akäbbärä*
not keep an appointment ቀጠሮ ፡ አፈ ረሰ *qätäro afärräsä*

apportion አከፋፈለ *akkäfaffälä;* መጠነ *mäṭṭänä;* አደላደለ *addäladdälä*

appraisal ግምት *gəmmət*
make an appraisal ገመተ *gämmätä*

appraise ገመተ *gämmätä*

appreciate (be grateful for) አመሰገነ *amäsäggänä;* (value) ወደደ *wäddädä;* (rise in value) ተወደደ *täwäddädä;* (be aware of) ተገነዘበ *tägänäzzäbä;* ተሰማ (ው) *täsämma(w)*

appreciation (gratitude) ምስጋና *məsgana;* (understanding the value of) አድናቆት *adnaqot;* ስሜት *səmmet*

apprehend (seize) ያዘ *yazä;* (perceive) ተረዳ(ው) *tärädda(w)*

apprehension (understanding) ማወቅ *mawäq;* (fear) ፍርሃት *fərhat;* ስጋት *səgat*
be filled with apprehension በጣም ፡ ሰጋ *bäṭam sägga*

apprehensive, be ሰጋ *sägga*

apprentice ተለማማጅ *tälämamaǧ*

approach, vt. (make proposals to) አነጋገረ *annägaggärä;* (approximate) ደረሰ(በት) *därräsä(bbät)*
approach (vi.) ቀረበ *qärräbä;* ተጠጋ *täṭägga*

approach, n. (coming near) መቃረብ *mäqqaräb;* (way of dealing) ዘዴ *zäde;* አቋም *aqʷam*

appropriate, v. (allot) መደበ *mäddäbä;* (seize) ወሰደ(በት) *wässädä(bbät)*

appropriate (adj.) ተገቢ *tägäbi;* ተስማሚ *täsmami*

approval (consent) ፈቃድ *fäqad;* (act of approving) መስማማት *mäsmamat;* (favorable acceptance) አድናቆት *adnaqot*

approve (agree to) ፈቀደ(ለት) *fäqqädä-(llät);* ተስማማ *täsmamma;* (sanction) አጸደቀ *aṣäddäqä;* (speak well of) አመሰገነ *amäsäggänä*

approximate (v.) ተቃረበ *täqarräbä*

approximate (adj.) በግምት ፡ የሆነ *bägəmmət yähona*

approximately በግምት *bägəmmət;* ከሞላ ፡ ጐደል *kämolla gʷäddäl;* ያህል *yahəl*

approximation ግምት *gəmmət*

April ሚያዝያ *miyazəya*

apron ሸርጥ *šärrəṭ*

apt (~ remark) ተገቢ *tägäbi;* (~ pupil) ንቁ *nəqu*
apt to ሰ *sä* + negative imperfect + አይቀርም *ayqärəm*

aptitude ስጦታ *səṭota;* የተፈጥሮ ፡ ችሎታ *yätäfäṭro čəlota*

Arab ዓረብ *aräb*

Arabia የዓረብ ፡ አገር *yä'aräb agär*

Arabic ዓረብኛ *aräbəňňa*

arbiter አስታራቂ *astaraqi;* ሸምጋሌ *šämagälle*

arbitrary (~ decision) የተገመደለ *yätägämäddälä*

arbitrate አስታረቀ *astarräqä;* ገላገለ *gälaggälä;* ሸመገለ *šämäggälä*

arbitrator, see 'arbiter'

arc ቅስት *qəssət*

arch ቅስት *qəssət*

archaic የጥንት *yäṭənt*

archangel ሊቀ ፡ መላእክት *liqä mäla'əkt*

archbishop ሊቀ ፡ ጳጳሳት *liqä pappasat*

architect ፕላን ፡ የነደፈ *plan yänäddäfä;* መሃንዲስ *mähandis*

architecture (style of building) የሕንጻ ፡ አሠራር *yähənṣa assärar;* (act of designing buildings) የሕንጻ ፡ ጥበብ *yähənṣa ṭəbäb*

archives መዝገብ ፡ ቤት *mäzgäb bet;* ቤተ ፡ መዝገብ *betä mäzgäb*

ardent ጻኑ *ṣänu;* ኀይለኛ *hayläňňa*

ardor የጋለ ፡ ስሜት *yägalä səmmet*

arduous (~ exercise) አድካሚ *adkami;* (~ lesson) በጣም ፡ ከባድ *bäṭam käbbad*

area (surface) ስፋት *səfat;* (region) ቀበሌ *qäbäle;* ስፍራ *səfra;* አካባቢ *akkababi;*

ክፍል ፡ ሀገር *kəflä hagär*
argue (dispute) ተጨቃጨቀ *täčäqaččäqä;*
(~ in court) ተሟገተ *tämʷaggätä*

argument ክርክር *kərəkkər;* ጭቅጭቅ *čə-qəččəq;* (evidence) መረጃ *märräǧa*

argumentative ተጨቃጫቂ *täčäqačaqi*

arid (dry) ደረቅ *däräq;* (uninteresting) የማያስደስት *yämmayasdässət*

aridity ድርቀት *dərqät*

arise (rise up) ተነሣ *tänässa;* (come into being) ተፈጠረ *täfäṭṭärä;* አጋጠመ *aggaṭṭämä*

aristocracy መኳንንት *mäkʷanənt;* መሳ ፍንት *mäsafənt;* ባላባቶች *balabbatočč*

aristocrat ባላባት *balabbat*

arithmetic ሒሳብ *hisab*

ark ታቦት *tabot*
Ark of the Covenant የኪዳን ፡ ታቦት *yäkidan tabot*

arm (vt.) አስታጠቀ *astaṭṭäqä*
arm (vi.) ታጠቀ *taṭṭäqä*

arm እጅ *əǧǧ;* ክንድ *kənd;* (~ of a chair) መደገፊያ *mäddägäfiya*
carry (take) in one's arms አቀፈ *aq-qäfä*
with open arms በደስታ *bädässəta*

armament የጦር ፡ መሣሪያ *yäṭor mässa-riya*

armchair ምቹ ፡ ወምበር *məččʷu wämbär*

armed, be (የጦር) ፡ መሣሪያ ፡ ያዘ *(yäṭor) mässariya yazä*

armed forces የጦር ፡ ኃይል *yäṭor hayl*

armful እቅፍ ፡ ሙሉ *əqqəf mulu*

armistice የጦር ፡ ማቆም ፡ ስምምነት *yäṭor maqom səmämmənät*

armpit ብብት *bəbbət*

arms መሣሪያ *mässariya;* የጦር ፡ መሣሪያ *yäṭor mässariya*
be under arms ለጦርነት ፡ ታጠቀ *läṭo-rənnät taṭṭäqä*
bear arms የጦር ፡ መሣሪያ ፡ ያዘ *yäṭor mässariya yazä*

army ጦር *ṭor;* የጦር ፡ ሰራዊት *yäṭor sä-rawit;* (large number) መዓት *mä'at*

aroma ሽታ *šətta*

around በ - - - ዙሪያ *bä - - - zuriya;* እዚህ *əzzih;* (approximately) ይህል *yahəl;* ገደማ *gädäma*
around here በዚህ ፡ አካባቢ *bäzzih ak-kababi*

arouse (awaken, stir up) ቀሰቀሰ *qäsäq-qäsä;* አስነሣ *asnässa;* (~ suspicion) አሳደረ *asaddärä*

arrange አዘጋጀ *azzägaǧǧä;* አሰናዳ *assä-nadda;* አበጀ *abäǧǧä;* (put in order) ደረደረ *däräddärä;* ደለደለ *däläddälä*

arrest, v. (capture) ያዘ *yazä;* (stop) አቆመ *aqomä*

arrest (n.) እስራት *əssərat*
make an arrest ያዘ *yazä*
be under arrest ተያዘ *täyazä*

arrival መድረስ *mädräs;* መድረሻ *mäd-räša;* መምጣት *mämṭat*

arrive ደረሰ *därräsä;* (succeed) ተሳካ(ለት) *täsakka(llät)*

arrogance እብሪት *əbrit;* ትዕቢት *tə'əbit;* ጥጋብ *ṭəgab*

arrogant እብሪተኛ *əbritäňňa;* ትዕቢተኛ *tə'əbitäňňa*
be arrogant ታበየ *tabbäyä;* ጠገበ *ṭäg-gäbä*

arrow ወስፈንጥር *wäsfänṭər;* (arrow-shaped marker) ቀስት *qäst*

arsenal (for making arms) የመሣሪያ ፡ ፋብሪካ *yämässariya fabrika;* (for storing arms) የጦር ፡ መሣሪያ ፡ ግምጃ ፡ ቤት *yäṭor mässariya gəmǧa bet*

art (fine arts) ኪነ ፡ ጥበብ *kinä ṭäbäb;* (skill) ጥበብ *ṭäbäb;* ዛዴ *zäde*

artery ደም ፡ ቅዳ *däm qəda;* የደም ፡ ሥር *yädäm sər*

article (object) እቃ *əqa;* (section of document) አንቀጽ *anqäṣ;* (~ in newspaper) ጽሑፍ *ṣəhuf;* (grammatical) መስተአምር *mästä'ammər* articulate (v.) በግልጽ ፡ ተናገረ *bägəlṣ tänaggärä*

artifice ዘዴ *zäde*

artificial (made by man) ሰው ፡ ሥራሽ *säw särraš;* (affected) ከልብ ፡ ያልሆነ *käləbb yalhonä*

artillery ከባድ ፡ መሣሪያ *käbbad mässariya*

artisan ጥበበኛ *ṭəbäbäňňa;* ባለ ፡ እጅ *balä əǧǧ*

artist የኪነ ፡ ጥበብ ፡ ሰው *yäkinä ṭäbäb säw;* አርቲስት *artist;* (painter) ሠዓሊ *sä'ali*

as (when) ስ *sə* + imperfect; (because) ስለ *sələ* + verb; ከ *kä* + perfect
as (like) እንደ *əndä*
as far as (prep.) እስከ *əskä*
as far as (conj.) እንደ *əndä* + relative imperfect
as soon as እንደ *əndä* + perfect

ascend ወጣ *wäṭṭa;* (~ the throne) ተቀመጠ *täqämmäṭä*

ascension መውጣት *mäwṭat;* (Christ's ~) ዕርገት *ərgät*

ascent (going up) መውጣት *mäwṭat;* (slope) ዐቀበት *aqäbät;* ዳገት *dagät*

ascertain አረጋገጠ *arrägaggäṭä;* አጣራ *aṭṭarra*

ascetic (n.) መናኝ *männaň;* ባሕታዊ *bahtawi*

ascetic (adj.) የባሕታዊ *yäbahtawi;* የብቃት *yäbəqat*

ash(es) አመድ *amäd*

ashamed, be አፈረ *affärä*

ashore ወደ ፡ ዳርቻ *wädä darəčča*
go ashore ወደ ፡ ባሕር ፡ ጠረፍ ፡ ሄደ *wädä bahər ṭäräf hedä*

ashtray መተርኳሻ *mätärkʷäša*

Asia እስያ *əsya*

aside, ~ from ከ --- በስተቀር *kä --- bästäqär;* ከ - - - ሌላ *kä - - - lela*

sak ጠየቀ *ṭäyyäqä*

asleep, be ተኛ *täňňa;* (be numb, foot) ደነዘዘ(ው) *dänäzzäzä(w)*
fall asleep አንቀላፋ *anqälaffa;* ተኛ *täňňa;* እንቅልፍ ፡ ወሰደው ፡ (ያዘው) *ənqəlf wässädäw (yazäw)*

aspect ሁኔታ *huneta;* መልክ *mälk*
every aspect ከሁሉም ፡ አንጻር *kähullum anṣar*

asphalt አስፋልት *asfalt;* ሬንጅ *renž*

aspiration ምኞት *məňňot*

aspire ተመኘ *tämäňňä;* ጓጓ *gʷaggʷa*

ass (donkey) አህያ *ahəyya;* (behind) ቂጥ *qiṭ*

assail በኃይል ፡ አጠቃ *bähayl aṭäqqa*

assassin ነፍሰ ፡ ገዳይ *näfsä gäday*

assassinate ገደለ *gäddälä*

assault (v.) ደበደበ *däbäddäbä;* አጠቃ *aṭäqqa*

assault, n. (military ~) ጥቃት *ṭəqat;* (~ on a person) ድብደባ *dəbdäba*

assemble (vt.) ሰበሰበ *säbässäbä;* (put together) አጋጠመ *aggaṭṭämä*
assemble (vi.) ተሰበሰበ *täsäbässäbä*

assembly ስብሰባ *səbsäba;* ጉባኤ *guba'e;* (~ of elders) ሸንጎ *šängo*

assent (v.) እሺ ፡ አለ *əšši alä*

assent (n.) ስምምነት *səməmmənnät*

assert (declare positively) ተከራከረ *täkärakkärä;* (insist upon) አረጋገጠ *arrägaggäṭä*

assess ገመተ *gämmätä*

asset ጸጋ *ṣägga;* ጥቅም *ṭəqəm*
assets ንብረት *nəbrät*

assiduity ትጋት *təgat*

assiduous ትጉ *təgu;* ትጉህ *təguh*
be assiduous ተጋ *tägga*

assign (appoint to a duty) መደብ *mäddäbä;* (fix) ወሰነ *wässänä;* (allot) ሰጠ *säṭṭa*

assignment (assigning) ድልድል *dələddəl;* (job to be done) ሥራ *səra;* የተመደበ *yätämädäb*

ለት ፡ ሥራ yätämäddäbällät səra

assist (vt.) ረዳ rädda; አገዘ aggäzä
assist, vi. (be present) ተገኘ tägäňňä

assistance እርዳታ ərdata

assistant ረዳት räddat; ረድእ rädə'

associate (vt.) አዛመደ azzammädä; አያ
ያዘ ayyayazä
associate, vi. (keep company) ተጎዳኘ
tägʷädaňňä; ግንኙነት ፡ ነበረው gənəňňunnät näbbäräw

associate (n.) ተባባሪ täbabari; (in business) ሽርክ šərka

association (society) ማኅበር mahbär;
(companionship) ግንኙነት gənəňňunnät

assort ለየ läyyä

assorted ልዩ ፡ ልዩ ləyyu ləyyu

assume (suppose) ገመተ gämmätä;
(feign) አስመሰለ asmässälä; (take on)
ያዘ yazä; ተቀበለ täqäbbälä

assurance (pledge) ማረጋገጫ marrägagäča; (self-confidence) በራስ ፡ መተማ
መን bäras mättämamän; ሙሉ ፡ እም
ነት mulu əmnät

assure አረጋገጠ arrägaggäṭä

asthma አስማ asma; ቃታ qata
have asthma ቃሰተ qassätä; ቃታ ፡ ያዘ
(ው) qata yazä(w)

astonish አስደነቀ asdännäqä; አስገረመ
asgärrämä
be astonished ተደነቀ tädännäqä; ገረ
መ(ው) gärrämä(w); ተገረመ tägärrämä

astonishment አድናቆት adnaqot

astound, see 'astonish'

astray, go ባከነ bakkänä
lead astray አሳሳተ assasatä

astrology አስትሮሎጂ astroloği; ኮከብ ፡
ቈጣሪ kokäb qʷäṭära

astronomy አስትሮኖሚ astronomi

astute ብልጥ bəlṭ; ጮሌ čolle

asylum ጠጋኝነት ṭəggäňňənnät

at በ bä; ከ kä; እ - - - ላይ ə - - - lay

atheism ክሕደት kəhdät

athlete እስፖርተኛ əsportäňňa

atmosphere ሀዋ hawa

atone ንስሐ ፡ ገባ nəssəha gäbba

atrocious አስቃቂ assäqqaqi

atrocity ግፍ gəf; ጭካኔ čəkkane

attach አሰረ assärä; አያያዘ ayyayazä
be attached to (love) ወደደ wäddädä

attachment (affection) መፈቃቀር mäffä-
qaqär; (contact) ግንኙነት gənəňňunnät

attack (v.) አጠቃ aṭäqqa; (criticize) ነቀፈ
näqqäfä; ዘለፈ zälläfä

attack (n.) ማጥቃት maṭqat; ወረራ wärära

attain አገኘ agäňňä; (reach) ከ - - - ደረሰ
kä - - - därräsä

attempt (n.) ሙከራ mukkära
make an attempt ሞከረ mokkärä; ፈተነ
fättänä

attend (be present) ተገኘ tägäňňä; (accompany) አጀበ aǧǧäbä; (serve) አገለ
ገለ agäläggälä

attendance (presence) መገኘት mäggäňät;
(retinue) አጀብ aǧäb
take attendance ስም ፡ ጠራ səm ṭärra

attendant, n. (guard) ጠባቂ ṭäbbaqi; (servant) አገልጋይ agälgay

attention ስሜት səmmet; መንፈስ mänfäs;
ፍላጎት fəllagot
attract attention ሐሳቡን ፡ ሳበው hassabun sabäw
call (draw) attention to አሳሰበ asassäbä; አመለከተ amäläkkätä; አስገነዘበ
asgänäzzäbä
pay attention አስተዋለ astäwalä; አዳ
መጠ addammäṭä; ሰማ sämma; ልብ
አለ ləbb alä; ልብ ፡ ብሎ ፡ አዳመጠ
ləbb bəlo addammäṭä

attentive ትጉ təgu; ትጉህ təguh; ልባም
ləbbam; አስተዋይ astäway
be attentive አስተዋለ astäwalä

attest መስከረ *mäsäkkärä*

attestation ቃል *qal*; ምስክር *məsəkkər*

attire ልብስ *ləbs*

attitude አስተያየት *astäyayät*

attorney ጠበቃ *ṭäbäqa*
attorney general ጠቅላይ ፡ ዐቃቤ ፡ ሕግ *ṭäqlay aqqabe həgg*

attract (draw to oneself) ሳበ *sabä*; (win the attention) ማረከ *marräkä*

attraction ማራኪነት *marakinnät*

attractive ማራኪ *maraki*; የሚያምር *yämmiyamər*
make attractive አሳመረ *asammärä*

attribute (trait) ባሕርይ *bahrəy*; (mark regarded as a symbol) መለዮ *mälläyyo*

auction ሐራጅ *haraǧ*

audacious ደፋር *däffar*
be audacious ደፈረ *däffärä*

audacity ድፍረት *dəfrät*

audience (people) የተሰበሰበ ፡ ሕዝብ *yätäsäbässäbä həzb*; (viewers) ተመልካች *tämälkač*; (listeners) አድማጭ *admač*; (interview) መገናኛት *mäggänaňät*

auditor (listener) አድማጭ *admač*; (who examines accounts) ተቈጣጣሪ *täqʷäṭaṭari*

auditorium አዳራሽ *addaraš*

augment አበዛ *abäzza*; (~ the pay) ጨመረ *čämmärä*; (~ income) አሳደገ *asaddägä*

august ባለ ፡ ግርማ *balä gərma*

August ነሐሴ *nähase*

aunt አክስት *akəst*

auspices ድጋፍ *dəgaf*

austere (~ person) ጥብቅ *ṭəbq*; (~ look) ኮስታራ *kostarra*; (~ dress) ያለ ዜጣ *yalageṭä*

authentic (~ signature) እውነተኛ *əwnätäňňa*; (~ account) የሚታመን *yämmittammän*

author ደራሲ *därasi*

authoritarian ፈላጭ ፡ ቈራጭ *fälač qʷärač*

authority (power) ሥልጣን *səlṭan*; (permission) ፈቃድ *fäqad*; (expert) ዐዋቂ *awaqi*
authorities ባለ ፡ ሥልጣን *balä səlṭan*

authorization ሥልጣን *səlṭan*

authorize (permit) ፈቀደ *fäqqädä*; (give power) ሥልጣን ፡ ሰጠ *səlṭan säṭṭä*

auto መኪና *mäkina*

autobiography የራስ ፡ የሕይወት ፡ ታሪክ *yäras yähəywät tarik*

automobile መኪና *mäkina*

autonomous (~ nation) ነጻ *näṣa*; (~ department) ራሱን ፡ ችሎ ፡ የሚተዳደር *rasun čəlo yämmittädaddär*

autonomy የራስን ፡ አገዛዝ ፡ ነጻነት *yärasən aggäzaz näṣannät*

autumn መከር *mäkär*; መኸር *mähär*

auxiliary ረዳት *räddat*

avail (v.) ጠቀመ *ṭäqqämä*
avail oneself of ሠራ(በት) *särra(bbät)*

avail (n.) ጥቅም *ṭəqm*
of no avail ፍሬ ፡ ቢስ *fəre bis*
to no avail በከንቱ *bäkäntu*

available, be ተገኘ *tägäňňä*

avalanche ናዳ *nada*

avarice ንፉግነት *nəfugənnät*

avaricious ጨቅ *čuq*; ንፉግ *nəfug*

avenge ተበቀለ *täbäqqälä*

avenue ጐዳና *gʷädana*; (approach) በር *bärr*

average (n., adj.) አማካይ *ammakay*; መሃከለኛ *mähakkäläňňa*; መኻከለኛ *mäkakkäläňňa*; ማእከላዊ *ma'əkälawi*
on an average ከሞላ ፡ ጐደል *kämolla gʷäddäl*

averse, be ~ to ጠላ *ṭälla*

aversion ጥላቻ *ṭəlačča*

avert ዞር ፡ አደረገ *zorr adärrägä*

avid ጉጉ *guggu*

avoid ሸሸ *šäššä;* ከ - - - ራቀ *kä - - - raqä*

avow አመነ *ammänä*

await ተጠባበቀ *täṭäbabbäqä;* ቆየ *qoyyä*

awake (adj.) ንቁ *nəqu*
be awake ነቃ *näqqa;* እንቅልፍ ፡ ለቀ
ቀው *ənqəlf läqqäqäw*
keep awake (vt.) እንቅልፍ ፡ ነሣው *ənqəlf nässaw*
keep (stay) awake (vi.) ነቅቶ ፡ ቆየ *näqto qoyyä*

awaken ቀሰቀሰ *qäsäqqäsä*

award (v.) ሸለመ *šällämä*

award (n.) ሽልማት *šəlləmat*

aware, be ተገነዘበ *tägänäzzäbä;* ተረዳ(ው)
tärädda(w)

away, be ውጭ ፡ ሄደ *wəčč hedä;* (be distant from) ራቀ *raqä*

awe (v.) አስደነቀ *asdännäqä*

awe (n.) አክብሮታዊ ፡ ፍርሃት *akbərota-
wi fərhat*

awesome አስፈሪ *asfärri*

awful አስቃቂ *assäqqaqi;* መጥፎ *mäṭfo;*
አስጠሊ *asṭälli*

awfully ከፉኛ *kəfuňňa;* በጣም *bäṭam*

awhile ለጥቂት ፡ ጊዜ *läṭəqit gize*

awkward (~ person) ገለጃጃ *gälǧaǧǧa;*
(~ time) የማይመች *yämmayəmmäčč*

awl ወስፌ *wäsfe*

awning ገርዶሽ *gərdoš*

ax መጥረቢያ *mäṭräbiya;* (large ax) ምሳር
məssar

azure የጠራ *yäṭärra;* ሰማያዊ *sämayawi*

B

baboon ዝንጀሮ *zənǧäro*

baby ሕፃን *həṣan;* ጨቅላ *čäqla*

baby boy ማሞ *mammo*
baby girl ማሚቱ *mammitu*
new-born baby አራስ ፡ ልጅ *aras ləǧ*

babyhood ሕፃንነት *həṣanənnät*

bachelor ወንደላጤ *wändälaṭṭe*

back, v. (be behind) ከ - - - ጀርባ ፡ ነው
kä - - - ǧärba näw; (support) ደገፈ
däggäfä
back out አፈገፈገ *afägäffägä;* ወደ ፡
ኋላ ፡ አለ *wädä hʷala alä*

back (n.) ጀርባ *ǧärba*
in the back ከ - - - ኋላ *kä - - - hʷala*
take (carry) on one's back አዘለ *azzälä*

back (adj.) የኋላ *yähʷala;* (~ issue of
newspaper) ያለፈ *yalläfä*

back (adv.), ~ and forth ወዲያና ፡ ወ
ዲህ *wädiyanna wädih*
be back ተመለሰ *tämälläsä*

backache የጀርባ ፡ ሕመም *yäǧärba həmäm*

backbone አከርካሪ *akärkari*

background (motive, reason) መነሻ *männäša*
in the background በስተጀርባ *bästäǧärba*
keep in the background አገለለ *agällälä*

backing ድጋፍ *dəgaf*

backward(s) ወደ ፡ ኋላ *wädä hʷala*
be backward ወደ ፡ ኋላ ፡ ቀረ *wädä
hʷala qärrä*

backyard ጓሮ *gʷaro*

bacteria ረቂቃን ፡ ነፍሳት *räqiqan näfsat*

bad ከፉ *kəfu;* መጥፎ *mäṭfo;* (~ language) ጸያፍ *ṣäyyaf*
be bad ባሰ *basä;* ከፋ *käffa*
feel bad ጤንነት ፡ አልተሰማውም *ṭenənnät altäsämmawəm*
go bad ተበላሸ *täbälaššä*
not bad ምንም ፡ አይል *mənəmm ayəl*

badge አርማ *arma;* መለዮ *mälläyyo*

badly (very much) ከፉኛ *kəfuňňa*
be badly off ተቸገረ *täčäggärä*

baffle ግራ ፡ አጋባ *gra aggabba*

bag (purse) ቦርሳ *borsa;* (sack) ዶንያ *donəyya;* ጆንያ *ğonəyya*
leather bag አቆማዳ *aqomada*

baggage ጓዝ *gʷaz;* እቃ *əqa*

bail ዋስትና *wastənna;* የገንዘብ ፡ ዋስ *yägänzäb was*
give bail አዋስ *awasä*

bake (~ bread) ጋገረ *gaggärä;* (~clay) ጠበሰ *ţäbbäsä*

baker ዳቦ ፡ ጋጋሪ *dabbo gagari*

bakery ዳቦ ፡ መጋገሪያ ፡ ቤት *dabbo mägagäriya bet*

balance, vt. (support in a state of equilibrium) ቀጥ ፡ አድርጎ ፡ አቆመ *qätt adrəgo aqomä;* (make equal the debits and credits) አስተካከለ *astäkakkälä*
balance, vi. (of account) ለክ ፡ መጣ *ləkk mätta;* (of scales) ትክክል ፡ ነው *täkəkkəl näw*

balance (n.) ሚዛን *mizan;* (remainder) ቀሪ *qäri*
lose balance ሚዛን ፡ ሳተ *mizan satä*

balcony ሰገነት *sägännät*

bald መላጣ *mälaţa;* ራስ ፡ በራ *rasä bära*
be bald ተመለጠ *tämällätä;* በራ ፡ ሆነ *bära honä*

ball ኳስ *kʷas;* (festivity) የዳንስ ፡ ምሽት *yädans məššət*

balloon ፊኛ *fiňňa*

ballot የምርጫ ፡ ወረቀት *yämərča wäräqät*

bamboo ሻምበቆ *šambäqqo;* ሸመል *šämäl*

ban (v.) አገደ *aggädä*

ban (n.) እገዳ *əggäda*

banal ተራ *tära*

banana ሙዝ *muz*
false banana እንስት *ənsät*

band (for hat) ጥምጥም *ţəmţəm;* (~ of musicians) የሙዚቃ ፡ ጓድ *yämuziqa gʷadd;* (group) ጓድ *gʷadd*

bandage (v.) አሰረ *assärä;* በፋሻ ፡ አሰረ *bäfaša assärä*

bandage (n.) ፋሻ *faša*

bandit ሽፍታ *šəfta;* ወንባዴ *wänbäde*

banditry ውንብድና *wənbədənna*

bang, v. (~ the door) አናጋ *annagga;* (~ the elbow) አጋጨ *aggaččä*

banish አጋዘ *agazä;* ሰደደ *säddädä*

banishment ግዞት *gəzot*

bank (shore) የወንዝ ፡ ዳርቻ *yäwänz daräčča;* ጠረፍ *ţäräf;* (credit firm) ባንክ *bank*

banker ባለ ፡ ባንክ *balä bank*

banknote ገንዘብ *gänzäb;* ብር *bərr*

bankrupt, be ከሰረ *kässärä*

bankruptcy መክሰር *mäksär;* የነግድ ፡ ኪሳራ *yänəgd kisara*

banner (flag) ሰንደቅ ፡ ዓላማ *sändäq alama;* (piece of cloth with writing) የጽሑፍ ፡ ሰሌዳ *yäşəhuf säleda*

banquet የራት ፡ ግብዣ *yärat gəbža;* ድግስ *dəggəs;* ግብር *gəbər*

baptism ክርስትና *krəstənna;* ጥምቀት *ţəmqät*
receive baptism ክርስትና ፡ ተነሣ *krəstənna tänässa*

baptize አጠመቀ *aţämmäqä;* (give a Christian name) የክርስትና ፡ ስም ፡ ሰየመ *yäkrəstənna səm säyyämä*
be baptized ክርስትና ፡ ተነሣ *krəstənna tänässa*

bar (obstruct) አገደ *aggädä;* ዘጋ *zägga;* (forbid) ከለከለ *käläkkälä*

bar, n. (piece of metal) የብረት ፡ ዘንግ *yäbrät zäng;* (bar room) ቡና ፡ ቤት *bunna bet;* (court) ፍርድ ፡ ቤት *fərd bet;* (obstacle) መሰናክል *mäsänakəl*

barbarian አረማኔ *arämäne*

barbarous የጭቈና *yäčəqqʷäna*

barber ጸጉር ፡ አስተካካይ *şägur astäkakay*

barber shop የጸጉር ፡ ማስተካከያ ፡ ቤት
yäṣägur mastäkakäya bet

bare (~ feet, house) ባዶ bado; (naked)
ራቁት raqut
be bare (naked) ተራቀተ täraqqʷätä
lay bare ገላጠ gälläṭä; ገፈፈ gäffäfä

bareback ሌጣ leṭa

barefoot ባዶ ፡ እግሩን bado əgrun

barely ላመል lamäl; በጥቂት bäṭəqit

bargain (v.) ተከራከረ täkärakkärä; ውጣ ፡
ውረዱን፡ተከራከረ wəṭa wərädun täkärakkärä

bargain, n. (something bought cheap)
ጥሩ ፡ ግዢ ṭəru gəži; (agreement) ስም
ምነት səməmmənnät

barge የጭነት ፡ መርከብ yäčənät märkäb

bark (vt.) ላጠ laṭä; መለጠ mälläṭä;
ቀረፈ qärräfä
bark, vi. (of dog) ጮኸ čohä

bark, n. (~ of tree) ቅርፊት qərfit; ልጣጭ
ləṭṭač; (~ of dog) ጩኸት čuhät

barley ገብስ gäbs

barracks የወታደር ፡ ሰፈር yäwättaddär
säfär

barrage ግድብ gəddəb

barrel በርሚል bärmil; በርሜል bärmel

barren (~ woman, cattle) መካን mäkan;
መሃን mähan; (~ soil) ጭንጫ čənča

barricade (v.) ዘጋ zägga

barricade (n.) መከታ mäkäta; መንገድ ፡
መዝጊያ mängäd mäzgiya

barrier ገደብ gädäb; (obstacle) መሰና
ክል mäsänakəl

barring (prep.) ከ kä + negative perfect + በስተቀር bästäqär

barter (v.) ለወጠ läwwäṭä; ተለዋወጠ täläwawwäṭä

barter (n.) የእቃ ፡ መለዋወጥ ፡ ንግድ yäəqa mälläwawäṭ nəgd

base (v.) መሠረተ mäsärrätä

base, n. (foundation) መሠረት mäsärät

base, adj. (morally low) ጸያፍ ṣäyyaf

baseless መሠረት ፡ቢስ mäsärätä bis

basement ምድር ፡ ቤት mədər bet

bashful ዓይናፋር aynaffar; አፋር affar

basic መሠረታዊ mäsärätawi; ዋና wanna;
መደበኛ mädäbäňňa

basically በመሠረቱ bämäsärätu

basin (shallow vessel) ጉድጓዳ ፡ ሳሕን
gʷädgʷadda sahən; (~ of river)
ሸለቆ šäläqo

basis መሠረት mäsärät

basket ቅርጫት qərčat; ሌማት lemat

basketball የቅርጫት ፡ ኳስ yäqərčat kʷas

basket work ስፌት səfet

bastard ዲቃላ diqala

baste ወሰወሰ wäsäwwäsä

bat (v.) ላጋ lägga

bat, n. (bird) የሌሊት ፡ ወፍ yälelit wäf;
(for ball) መለጊያ mäläggiya

batch ከምችት kəməččət

bath የገላ ፡ መታጠቢያ yägäla mättaṭäbiya
take a bath ገላ(ውን) ፡ ታጠበ gäla-
(wən) taṭṭäbä

bathe (vt.) አጠበ aṭṭäbä
bathe (vi.) ገላ ፡ ታጠበ gäla taṭṭäbä

bathing suit የዋና ፡ ልብስ yäwana ləbs

bathrobe የመታጠቢያ ፡ ልብስ yämätta-
ṭäbiya ləbs

bathroom መታጠቢያ ፡ ቤት mättaṭäbiya
bet

bathtub የገላ ፡ መታጠቢያ ፡ ገንዳ yägäla
mättaṭäbiya gända; ባኞ baňňo

battalion (የ)ሻለቃ (yä)šaläqa

batter (n.) ሊጥ liṭ

battery ባትሪ batri

battle (n.) ጦርነት ṭorənnät; ውጊያ wəggiya

battlefield የጦር ፡ ሜዳ yäṭor meda; የጦር
ነት ፡ ሜዳ yäṭorənnät meda

bay (n.) የባሕር ፡ ሰላጤ *yäbahər sällaṭe*

bayonet ሳንጃ *sanǧa*

bazaar መደብር *mädäbbər*

be ሆነ *honä*

beach የባሕር ፡ ዳርቻ *yäbahər darəčča*

bead ዶቃ *doqa*; (~ of sweat) ነጠብጣብ *näṭäbṭab*

beak አፍ *af*

beam (~ of wood) አውታር *awtar*; ጠርብ *ṭärb*; (~ of light) ጮራ *čorra*; ውጋጋን *wəgagan*

bean ባቄላ *baqela*; አደንጓሬ *adängʷarre*

bear, v. (give birth) ወለደች *wällädäčč*; (carry) ተሸከመ *täšäkkämä*; (endure) ታገሠ *taggäsä*; ቻለ *čalä*

bear (n.) ድብ *dəbb*

beard ጢም *ṭim*

bearing (manner) አቋም *aqʷam*; ዛላ *zala*; (relation) ግንኙነት *gənəňňunnät* have bearing on ተመለከተ *tämäläkkätä*

beast አውሬ *awre*; (brutal person) አረ መኔ *arämäne* beasts አራዊት *arawit*

beastly የአውሬነት *yawrennät*

beat (hit) ደበደበ *däbäddäbä*; መታ *mätta*; (defeat) አሸነፈ *aššännäfä* beat up ደበደበ *däbäddäbä*

beating ድብደባ *dəbdäba* suffer a beating ተሸነፈ *täšännäfä*

beautiful ቆንጆ *qonǧo*; ውብ *wəb*; መል ካም *mälkam*; (~ ceremony) የደመቀ *yädämmäqä*; (~ costume) የሚያምር *yämmiyamər*; (~ day) ጥሩ *ṭäru* be beautiful አማረ *amarä*; ተዋበ *täwabä*

beautifully አሳምሮ *asamməro*

beautify አስጌጠ *asgeṭä*

beauty ቁንጅና *qunǧənna*; ውበት *wəbät*

beauty parlor የቁንጅና ፡ ሳሎን *yäqunǧənna salon*

because (conj.) ስለ *səlä* + verb; ምክን ያቱም *məknəyatum* because of ለሱ ፡ ብሎ *lässu bəlo*; ስለ *səlä*; በ - - - ምክንያት *bä - - - məknəyat*

become ሆነ *honä*

becoming, be ተስማማ *täsmamma*; ተገ ባ(ው) *tägäbba(w)*; (look well on) አማረ(ው) *amarä(w)*

bed አልጋ *alga*; (~ of flowers) መደብ *mädäb* go to bed ተኛ *täňňa* lie in bed ተኛ *täňňa* make the bed አልጋ ፡ አነጠፈ *alga anäṭṭäfä* put to bed አስተኛ *astäňňa*

bedbug ትኋን *təhʷan*

bedding ያልጋ ፡ ልብስ *yalga ləbs*

bedridden ያልጋ ፡ ቀራኛ *yalga quraňňa*

bedroom መኝታ ፡ ቤት *mäňňəta bet*

bedspread ያልጋ ፡ ልብስ *yalga ləbs*

bee ንብ *nəb* queen bee የንብ ፡ አውራ *yänəb awra*

beef የበሬ ፡ ሥጋ *yäbäre səga*

beehive ቀፎ *qäfo*

beer ቢራ *bira*; (native ~) ጠላ *ṭälla*

beeswax ሰም *säm*

beetle ጥንዚዛ *ṭənzizza*

befall አጋጠመ *aggaṭṭämä*; ደረሰ(በት) *därräsä(bbät)*

befit ተስማማ *täsmamma*

before (conj.) ሰ *sä* + negative imperfect before, prep. (time) ከ - - - በፊት *kä - - - bäfit*; (place) ፊት ፡ ለፊት *fit läfit* before (adv.) ከዚህ ፡ በፊት *käzzih bäfit*; ከዚህ ፡ ቀደም *käzzih qäddäm*; ቀድሞ *qädmo*

beforehand አስቀድሞ *asqäddəmo*; ከሁሉ ፡ በፊት *kähullu bäfit*

befriend ተጎዳኘ *tägʷadaňňä*; ተወዳጀ *täwädaǧǧä*

beg ለመነ *lämmänä*

beget ወለደ *wällädä*

beggar ለማኝ *lämmaň*

begging ልመና *ləmmäna*

begin (vt.) ጀመረ *ğämmärä;* ወጠነ *wäṭṭänä*

begin (vi.) ተጀመረ *täğämmärä;* ተነሣ *tänässa*

beginner ጀማሪ *ğämmari*

beginning መጀመሪያ *mäğämmäriya;* (act of beginning) አጀማመር *ağğämamär*

begrudge (~ the honor) ቀና *qänna;* (~ the money) ቀጨ(ው) *qäččä(w)*

behalf, in ~ of ስለ *sälä;* ለ *lä*

behave (act well) መልካም ፡ ምግባር ፡ ፈጸመ *mälkam mǝgbar fäṣṣämä;* (act) ሠራ *särra*

behavior (nature) ጠባይ *ṭäbay;* አመል *amäl;* (action) አድራጎት *adragot*

behind ከ - - - ኋላ *kä - - - hʷala;* በ - - - ኋላ *bä - - - hʷala;* ከ - - - በስተኋላ *kä - - - bästähʷala;* ከ - - - ጀርባ *kä - - - ğärba*
be behind ወደ ፡ ኋላ ፡ ቀረ *wädä hʷala qärrä;* (be late) ዘገየ *zägäyyä*

being (creature) ፍጡር *fǝṭur;* (essence) ሀልወና *hälläwǝnna;* ሁኔታ *huneta*

belated የዘገየ *yäzägäyyä*

belch አገሣ *agässa*

belief (opinion) እምነት *ǝmnät;* (religion) ሃይማኖት *haymanot*

believe አመነ *ammänä;* (think) መሰለ *mässälä*
make believe አስመሰለ *asmässälä*

believer አማኝ *amaň*

belittle አንኳሰሰ *ankʷassäsä;* አንቋሸሸ *anqʷaššäšä;* አቃለለ *aqqallälä*

bell ደወል *däwäl;* (small ~) ቃጭል *qaçäl*

belligerent ጠብ ፡ ወዳድ *ṭäb wäddad*

bellow (of ox) አንጐራ *agʷarra*

bellows ወናፍ *wänaf*

belly ሆድ *hod*

bellyache የቁርጠት ፡ ሕመም *yäqurṭät hǝmäm*

belong to (it belongs to him) የሱ ፡ ነው *yässu näw*

belongings ንብረት *nǝbrät;* ጓዝ *gʷaz*

beloved ወዳጅ *wädağ*

below (prep.) ከ - - - በታች *kä - - - bätačč*
below (adv.) ከዚህ ፡ በታች *käzzih bätačč;* ከሥር *käsär;* እግርጌ *ǝgǝrge*

belt ቀበቶ *qäbätto;* መቀነት *mäqännät;* (coffee or wheat belt) ክፍለ ፡ አገር *kǝflä agär*
wear a belt ታጠቀ *taṭṭäqä*

bench አግዳሚ ፡ ወምበር *agdami wämbär;* (legal) ዳኝነት *daňňännät*

bend (vt.) አጐበጠ *agʷäbbäṭä;* አጐነበሰ *agʷänäbbäsä*
bend, vi. (of river) ተጠማዘዘ *täṭämazzäzä;* (of tree) አዘነበለ *azänäbbälä;* ጐነበሰ *gʷänäbbäsä*
bend down አጐነበሰ *agʷänäbbäsä*

bend (n.), ~ in the road መታጠፊያ *mättaṭäfiya*

beneath (prep.) ከ - - - ሥር *kä - - - sär;* በ - - - ሥር *bä - - - sär*
beneath (adv.) ከታች *kätačč;* ከበታች *käbätačč;* እግርጌ *ǝgǝrge*

benediction ቡራኬ *burake;* ምርቃት *mǝrǝqat*
give benediction ባረከ *barräkä;* መረቀ *märräqä*

benefactor ደጋፊ *däggafi*

beneficial ጠቃሚ *ṭäqami*
be beneficial ጠቀመ *ṭäqqämä*

beneficiary ተጠቃሚ *täṭäqami*

benefit (vt.) ጠቀመ *ṭäqqämä*
benefit (vi.) ተጠቀመ *täṭäqqämä*

benefit, n. (advantage) ጥቅም *ṭǝqǝm*

benevolence ቸርነት *qänännät*

benevolent (~ person) በጐ ፡ አድራጊ *bäggo adragi*

benign (~ climate) ተስማሚ *täsmami*

bent, n. (inclination) ተሰጥዎ *täsätwo*

bent (adj.) ጠማማ *ṭämama;* ጕባጣ *gʷäbaṭa;* ጕንብስ *gunbəs*

benumb አደነዛዘ *adänäzzäzä*
be benumbed ደነዘዘ *dänäzzäzä*

bequeath አወረሰ *awärräsä*

bequest (legacy) ውርስ *wərs;* (last will) ኑዛዜ *nuzaze*

bereaved የሞተበት *yämotäbbät;* ሐዘን ተኛ *hazäntäñña*
be bereaved በጣም ፡ አዘነ *bäṭam azzänä*

berry ፍሬ *fəre;* እንጆሬ *ənǧorre*

berserk, see 'haywire'

beseech ለመነ *lämmänä*

beside (prep.) ከ - - ጕን *kä - - - gʷänn;* በ - - - አጠገብ *bä - - - aṭägäb;* ዳር *dar;* ዘንድ *zänd*

besides (prep.) ከ - - - ሌላ *kä - - - lela;* ከ - - - በስተቀር *kä - - - bästäqär;* ከ - - - በቀር *kä - - - bäqär*

besides (adv.) ከዚያም ፡ ሌላ *käzziyam lela;* ከዚያም ፡ በላይ *käzziyam bälay;* ደግሞ *dägmo;* በተቀር *bätäqär*

besiege ከበበ *käbbäbä*

best (adj.) ምርጥ *mərṭ;* ከሁሉ ፡ የተሻለ *kähullu yätäšalä;* የበለጠ *yäbälläṭä;* (~ friend) የቅርብ *yäqərb*
best (adv.) ይበልጥ *yəbälṭ;* ከሁሉ ፡ አብልጦ *kähullu abləṭo*
at best ግፋ ፡ ቢል *gəfa bil*

bestial ያውሬነት *yawrennät*

best man ሚዜ *mize*

bestow (~ an award) ሸለመ *šällämä;* (~ money) ሰጠ *säṭṭä*

bet (v.) ተወራረደ *täwärarrädä*

bet (n.) ውርርድ *wərərrəd*

betray ከዳ *kädda;* (~ confidence) አጠፋ *aṭäffa;* (reveal) ገለጸ(በት) *gälläṣä-(bbät);* አጋለጠ *aggalläṭä*

betrayal ክዳት *kədät;* ክሕደት *kəhdät*

betroth አሳጨ *asaččä*
betrothed (n.) እጮ *əččäu*
be betrothed ታጨ *taččä*

better (v.) አሻሻለ *aššašalä*

better (adj.) የተሻለ *yätäšalä*
be (get) better ተሻለ *täšalä;* (~ after illness) ተሻለ(ው) *täšalä(w)*
feel better ተሻለ(ው) *täšalä(w)*

between በ - - - መካከል *bä - - - mäkakkäl;* በ - - መሀከል *bä - - - mähakkäl;* (from . . . to) ከ - - - እስከ *kä - - - əskä*

beverage መጠጥ *mäṭäṭṭ*

bewail አለቀሰ *aläqqäsä*

beware ተጠነቀቀ *täṭänäqqäqä*

bewilder ግራ ፡ አጋባ *gra aggabba;* አደናገረ *addänaggärä*

bewitch መተት ፡ አደረገ(በት) *mätät adärrägä(bbät)*

beyond (prep.) ከ --- መለስ *kä - - - mälläs;* ከ - - - ባሻገር *kä - - - baššaggär;* ከ - - - ወዲያ *kä - - - wädiya*
beyond (adv.) ወዲያ ፡ ማዶ *wädiya mado*

bias አድልዎ *adləwo*

biased, be አደላ *adälla*

Bible መጽሐፍ ፡ ቅዱስ *mäṣhaf qəddus*

biceps የክንድ ፡ ጡንቻ *yäkənd ṭunča*

bicycle ቢሲክሌት *bisiklet*

bid, v. (invite) ጠራ *ṭärra;* (offer a price) ተጫረተ *täčarrätä;* (order) አዘዘ *azzäzä*

bid (n.) የጨረታ ፡ ዋጋ *yäčäräta waga*

bier ቃሬዛ *qareza*

big ትልቅ *tələq;* (important) ታላቅ *tallaq*

bigness ትልቅነት *tələqənnät*

bile አሞት *amot;* ሐሞት *hamot*

bill (charge for services) ሒሳብ *hisab;* (paper money) ብር *bərr;* (draft of law) የሕግ ፡ ረቂቅ *yähəgg räqiq;* (beak of bird) አፍ *af*

bind አሰረ *assärä;* (~ a book) ጠረዘ *ṭärräzä*

bindery የመጠረዣ ፡ ክፍል *yämäṭṭäräža käfäl*

binding, n. (of book) ጥራዝ *ṭaraz*

binding (adj.) ጽኑ *ṣanu*
be binding ጸና *ṣänna;* ተከበረ *täkäbbärä*

binoculars አቅራቢ ፡ መነጽር *aqrabi mänäṣṣar*

biography የሕይወት ፡ ታሪክ *yähaywät tarik*

biology ባዮሎጂ *bayoloǧi*

bird ወፍ *wäf*

birth ተውልድ *tawladd;* ልደት *ladät;* (being born) መወለድ *mäwwäläd*
give birth to ወለደ *wällädä*

birthday የልደት ፡ ቀን *yäladät qän*
happy birthday! መልካም ፡ ልደት *mälkam ladät*

birthplace (የ)ተውልድ ፡ አገር *(yä)tawladd agär*

biscuit ብስኩት *baskut*

bishop ጳጳስ *pappas*

bit, n. (of bridle) ልጓብ *lagab*

bit, a ~ ትንሽ *tannaš*
bit by bit ትንሽ ፡ በትንሽ *tannaš bätannaš*
not a bit ትንሽም *tannašam* + negative verb
quite a bit በጣም *bäṭam*

bitch ሴት ፡ ውሻ *set wašša*

bite (v.) ነከሰ *näkkäsä;* (of pepper) አቃጠለ *aqqaṭṭälä;* ፈጀ *fäǧǧä;* (of snake) ነደፈ *näddäfä*
bite off ገመጠ *gämmäṭä*

bite (n.) ንክሻ *näkša*
have a bite እህል ፡ ቀመስ *ahal qämmäsä*

biting (~ wind) የሚጋርፍ *yämmiggarraf;* (~ remark) አጥንት ፡ የሚነካ *aṭant yämminäka*

bitter (adj.) መራራ *märara;* (~ hardship) አስቃቂ *assäqqaqi;* (~ words) ክፉ *kafu*
be (taste) bitter መረረ *märrärä*
be bitter about ተማረረ *tämarrärä*

bitterly ተማሮ *tämarro;* አምሮ *amarro;* ክፉኛ *kafuňňa*

bitterness ምረት *marrät*

bizarre ግራ ፡ የሆነ *gra yähonä*

black ጥቁር *ṭaqur*
be (turn) black (color) ጠቆረ *ṭäqqwärä;* (be dark) ጨለመ *čällämä*

blackboard ጥቁር ፡ ሰሌዳ *ṭaqur säleda*

blacken አጠቆረ *aṭäqqwärä*

blacksmith ቀጥቃጭ *qäṭqač;* ባላ ፡ እጅ *balä aǧǧ*

bladder ፊኛ *fiňňa*

blade (of knife) ስለት *sälät;* (of razor) ምላጭ *mälačč;* (of grass) ቅጠል *qaṭäl*

blame, v. (find fault with) ወቀሰ *wäqqäsä;* ነቀፈ *näqqäfä;* ዘለፈ *zälläfä;* (use as an excuse) አመካኘ *ammäkaňňä*

blame (n.) ወቀሳ *wäqäsa;* ነቀፋ *näqäfa;* ዘለፋ *zäläfa*

blameless እንከን ፡ የሌለበት *ankän yälelläbbät*

bland (~ food) ቅመም ፡ የሌለው *qamäm yälelläw*

blank, n. (form) ፎርም *form;* (empty space) ባዶ ፡ ቦታ *bado bota*

blank, adj. (empty) ባዶ *bado*

blanket ብርድ ፡ ልብስ *bard labs*

blare (v.) ጮክ ፡ ብሎ ፡ ነገረ *čok bälo näggärä;* (of trumpet) አምባረቀ *ambarräqä*

blare (n.) ጩኸት *čuhät*

blasphemy የእግዚአብሔር ፡ ስም ፡ በከንቱ ፡ ማንሣት *yägzi'abaher sam bäkäntu mansat*

blast, v. (~ a tunnel) ፈንጂ ፡ በማፈንዳት ፡ አወጣ *fänǧi bämafändat awäṭṭa;* (~ rocks) ፈረካከሰ *färäkak-*

so aswäggädä; (∼ the horn) በጎይል ፡ ነፋ *bähayl näffa*

blast, n. (noise) የፈንጂ ፡ ድምፅ *yäfänği dämṣ*
full blast ሙሉ ፡ በሙሉ *mulu bämulu*

blatant (∼ error) ጉልህ *guləh*

blaze, v. (with light) አሸበረቀ *ašäbärräqä;* (of fire) ተንቀለቀለ *tänqäläqqälä;* ቦግ ፡ አለ *bogg alä*

blaze (n.) ቃጠሎ *qaṭälo*

blazing (∼ sun) ጠራራ *ṭärara*

bleak (∼ weather) ቀፋፊ *qäfafi*

bleat ባ ፡ አለ *ba alä*

bleed ደማ *dämma;* (from the nose) ነሰረ (ው) *nässärä(w)*

blemish (v.) አጉደፈ *agʷäddäfä*

blemish (n.) ጉድለት *gudlät;* እንከን *ənkän*

blend (vt.) ቀየጠ *qäyyäṭä;* ቀላቀለ *qälaqqälä*

blend (n.) ቅይጥ *qəyyəṭ*

bless (of priest) ባረክ *barräkä;* (of father) መረቀ *märräqä;* (of fortune) ዐደለ *addälä*

blessed ቅዱስ *qəddus;* የተባረከ *yätäbarräkä;* ብሩክ *bəruk*

blessing ቡራኬ *burake;* ምረቃ *mərräqa;* በረከት *bäräkät*
give blessing መረቀ *märräqä*
say the blessing ምስጋና ፡ አቀረበ *məsgana aqärräbä*

blind (v.) አሳወረ *asawwärä;* (of sun) አጥበረበረ *aṭbäräbbärä*

blind (n.) መጋረጃ *mäggarä̌ğa*

blind (adj.) ዓይን ፡ ስውር *aynä səwwər;* ዕውር *əwwər*
become (go) blind ታወረ *tawwärä*
be blind ዓይን ፡ የለውም *ayn yälläwəm*

blindly ዓይኑን ፡ ጨፍኖ *aynun čäffəno*

blindness ዕውርነት *əwwərənnät*

blink (∼ the eyes) አርገበገበ *argäbäggäbä;* (∼ flashlight) ብልጭ ፡ ድርግም ፡ አደረገ *bəlläčč dərgəmm adärrägä*

bliss ታላቅ ፡ ደስታ *tallaq dässəta*

blister, form a ∼ ውኃ ፡ ቋጠረ *wəha qʷaṭṭärä*

blizzard ኃይለኛ ፡ ነፋስ *hayläňňa näfas*

block (v.) ዘጋ *zägga;* አገደ *aggädä;* (∼ the view) ከለለ *källälä;* ጋረደ *garrädä*
block up ደፈነ *däffänä;* ወተፈ *wättäfä*

block, n. (of wood) ግንድ *gənd*

blockade መዝጋት *mäzgat*

blond ነጣ ፡ ያለ *näṭa yalä*

blood ደም *däm*
draw blood አደማ *adämma*
in cold blood በግፍ *bägəf;* በጭካኔ *bäčəkkane*

blood money የደም ፡ ዋጋ *yädäm waga;* ጉማ *guma*

blood relative የሥጋ ፡ ዘመድ *yäsəga zämäd*

blood vessel የደም ፡ ሥር *yädäm sər*

bloody (∼ riot) ደም ፡ የሚያፈስስ *däm yämmiyaffässəs*

bloom (v.) አበበ *abbäbä*

bloom (n.) እምቡጥ *əmbuṭ;* አበባ *abäba*

blossom (v.) አበበ *abbäbä*

blossom (n.) አበባ *abäba*

blot (soak up) አመጠጠ *amäṭṭäṭä;* (make a spot) ቀለም ፡ አነጠበ *qäläm anäṭṭäbä*

blot (n.) ነጠብጣብ *näṭäbṭab;* (on character) ጥፋት *ṭəfat*

blotting paper ማምጠጫ ፡ ወረቀት *mamṭäča wäräqät*

blouse ሸሚዝ *šämiz*

blow, vt. (∼ an instrument) ነፋ *näffa*
blow, vi. (of wind) ነፈሰ *näffäsä;* (of dust) ቦነነ *bonnänä;* (of siren) ጮኸ *čohä;* (of fuse) ተቃጠለ *täqaṭṭälä*
blow one's nose ተናፈጠ *tänaffäṭä*
blow on እፍ ፡ አለ *əff alä*
blow out (vt.) አጠፋ *aṭäffa*
blow out (vi.) ጠፋ *ṭäffa*

blow up (vt.) በደማሚት ፡ አፈራረሰ *bädämamit afärarräsä;* (~ tires) ነፉ *näffa*

blow up (vi.) ፈነዳ *fänädda;* (lose temper) በንዴት ፡ ጠፉ *bänəddet ṭofä*

blow (n.) ምት *mət;* ምታት *mətat;* (of a boxer) ቡጢ *buṭṭi*
at one blow በንድ ፡ ጊዜ *band gize*
come to blows ተደባደበ *tädäbaddäbä;* ተማታ *tämatta*

blowout, have a ~ ጎማ ፡ ፈነዳ(በት) *gomma fänädda(bbät)*

blue (~ color) ሰማያዊ *sämayawi;* (gloomy) የተከዘ *yätäkkäzä*

blueprint ንድፍ *nədf*

bluff (v.) አታለለ *attallälä;* አሞኘ *amoňňä*

blunder (v.) ተሳሳተ *täsasatä*

blunder (n.) ስሕተት *səhtät;* ስተት *sətät*

blunt (~ edge) ዳነዝ *dänäz;* (~ point) ዱልዱም *duldum;* (~ speech) ፍርጥ ፡ ያለ *fərrəṭ yalä*
become blunt (edge) ዳነዘ *dännäzä;* (point) ዶለ ዶመ *doläddomä*

bluntly ፍርጥ ፡ አድርጎ *fərrəṭ adrəgo*

blur (v.) አደበዘዘ *adäbäzzäzä*
blurred (~print) ደብዛዛ *däbzazza*

blush አፈረ *affärä*

board, vt. (go on a ship, train) ተሳፈረ *täsaffärä*

board, n. (wood) ሳንቃ *sanqa;* ጠርብ *ṭärb;* (group of persons) ቦርድ *bord*

boarder አዳሪ *adari*

boarding house ምግብና ፡ መኝታ የሚገኝ በት ፡ ስፍራ *məgəbənna mäňňäta yäm-miggäňňəbbät səfra*

boarding school አዳሪ ፡ ትምህርት ፡ ቤት *adari təmhərt bet*

boast (v.) ፎከረ *fokkärä;* ጉራ ፡ ነዛ *gurra näzza;* ተመካ *tämäkka;* ዳነፈ *dänäffa*

boast (n.) ጉራ *gurra;* ትምክሕት *təmkəhət*

boastful, be, see 'boast'

boasting (n.) ፉከራ *fukkära;* ፍክክር *fəkəkkər*

boat መርከብ *märkäb;* (small ~) ጀልባ *ğälba*

bodily (adj.) የሰውነት *yäsäwənnät*

body ገላ *gäla;* ሰውነት *säwənnät;* አካል *akal;* (corpse) ሬሳ *resa;* አስከሬን *askä-ren;* (of persons) ጎድ *gʷadd*
in a body በንድነት *bandənnät*

bodyguard አጃቢ *aǧǧabi*
Imperial Bodyguard የክብር ፡ ዘበኛ *yäkəbər zäbäňňa*

boil, vt. (~ a liquid) አፈላ *afälla;* (~ something in a liquid) ቀቀለ *qäqqälä*
boil (vi.) ፈላ *fälla;* ነፈረ *näffärä*
boil over ገነፈለ *gänäffälä*

boil, n. (swelling) ቡጥንጅ *bugunǧ*

bold (courageous) ደፋር *däffar;* (impudent) ስድ ፡ አደግ *sədd addäg;* (~ statement) የድፍረት *yädəfrät*
be bold ደፈረ *däffärä*

boldness ደፋርነት *däffarənnät;* ድፍረት *dəfrät*

bolt, vt. (fasten) ቀረቀረ *qäräqqärä*
bolt, vi. (dart away) ዳነበረ *dänäb-bärä*
be bolted በቡሎን ፡ ተያያዘ *bäbulon täyayazä*

bolt (n.) መያዣ *mäyaža;* (lock) መቀርቀሪያ *mäqärqäriya*

bomb (v.) በቦምብ ፡ ደበደበ *bäbomb dä-bäddäbä*

bomb (n.) ቦምብ *bomb*

bombard, see 'bomb'

bombardment የቦምብ ፡ ድብደባ *yäbomb dəbdäba*

bond (chain) ሰንሰለት *sänsälät;* (tie) ግን ኙነት *gənäňňunnät*

bondage ባርነት *barənnät*

bone አጥንት *aṭənt*

bonfire ትልቅ ፡ እሳት *təlləq əsat;* (on the holiday of Mäsqäl) ደመራ *dämära*

bonus ጉርሻ *gurša*

bony አጥንታም *aṭəntam*

book, v. (enter on a record) መዝገብ *mäzäggäbä;* (reserve seats) ያዘ *yazä*

book (n.) መጽሐፍ *mäṣhaf*
keep books መዝገብ ፥ ያዘ *mäzgäb yazä*

bookbinder መጽሐፍ ፥ ጠራዥ *mäṣhaf ṭärraž*

bookcase የመጽሐፍ ፥ ሣጥን *yämäṣhaf saṭan*

bookkeeper ሒሳብ ፥ ያዥ *hisab yaž*

booklet ትንሽ ፥ መጽሐፍ *tannaš mäṣhaf*

bookshelf የመጽሐፍ ፥ መደርደሪያ *yämäṣhaf mädärdäriya*

bookstore የመጽሐፍ ፥ መደብር *yämäṣhaf mädäbbar*

boom, v. (of cannons) አንጎ *agʷarra;* (of business) ተስፋፋ *täsfaffa;* ተሟሟቀ *tämʷamʷaqä*

boom, n. (sound) ድንፋት *danfat;* (great increase) መሟሟቅ *mämmʷamʷaq*

boost, v. (lift) ወደ ፥ ላይ ፥ ገፋ *wädä lay gäffa;* (raise prices) አስወደደ *aswäddädä*

boost, n. (in prices) ጭማሪ *čammari*

boot ጫማ *čamma*

booth ዳስ *das;* ጎጆ *goǧǧo*

booty ምርኮ *marko*

border (v.) ተዋሰነ *täwassänä*

border (n.) ጠረፍ *ṭäräf;* ወሰን *wäsän;* ድንበር *danbär;* (of rug) ጠርዝ *ṭärz;* ዘርፍ *zärf*

borderline ድንበር *danbär*

bore, v. (make weary) አሰላቸ *asäläččä;* (make a hole) ሰረሰረ *särässärä;* ነደለ *näddälä*

bored, be ሰለቸ(ው) *säläččä(w)*

boredom መሰልቸት *mäsälčät*

boring አሰልቺ *asälči*
be boring ተሰለቸ *täsäläččä*

borrow (~ money) አበደረ *abäddärä;* (~ object) ተዋሰ *täwasä*

bosom ጡት *ṭut;* ደረት *därät*

bosom friend የልብ ፥ ወዳጅ *yälabb wädağ*

boss (n.) አለቃ *aläqa*

botany የዘርእትና ፥ ያትክልት ፥ ጥናት *yäzar'atanna yatkalt ṭanat*

both ሁለቱ(ም) *hulättu(m)*

bother (vt.) አስቸገረ *asčäggärä;* ነዘነዘ *näzännäzä;* አወከ *awwäkä*
bother (vi.) ተቸገረ *täčäggärä*

bother (n.) ችግር *čaggar*

bottle ጠርሙስ *ṭärmus*

bottom, n. (ground under water) መሬት *märet;* (basis of a matter) ሥረ ፥ ነገር *särä nägär;* መነሾ *männäšo;* (buttocks) ቂጥ *qiṭ*
at bottom በመሠረቱ *bämäsärätu*
at the bottom of ሥር *sär;* እ - - ሥር *a - - - sär*
from top to bottom ከላይ ፥ እስከ ፥ ታች *kälay aska tačč*

bottom, adj. (~ price) የመጨረሻ ፥ ዝቅ ተኛ *yämäčärräša zäqqatäñña;* (~ shelf) ሥረኛ *säräñña*

bough ቅርንጫፍ *qaränčaf*

boulder ትልቅ ፥ ቋጥኝ *tallaq qʷaṭaññ*

bounce (vt.) አነጠረ *anäṭṭärä*
bounce, vi. (of ball) ነጠረ *näṭṭärä;* (of heart) ፈነዳቀ *fänäddäqä*

bound (vi.) ተዋሰነ *täwassänä*

bound, be ~ **for** ሄደ *hedä*

bound, n. (leap) ዝላይ *zällay*

bound(s), n. (area) ክልል *kallal;* (limits) ጽንፍ *ṣanf;* ወሰን *wäsän;* (extent) መጠን *mäṭän*

boundary ድንበር *danbär;* ወሰን *wäsän*

boundless ወሰን ፥ የሌለው *wäsän yälelläw*

bounteous የተትረፈረፈ *yätäträfärräfä*

bountiful ለጋስ *läggas*

bounty ችሮታ *čarota;* ቸርነት *čärannät;* ደግነት *däggannät*

bouquet ያበባ ፥ እቅፍ *yababa aqqaf*

bout ወድድር wədəddər; ግጥሚያ gəṭmiya

bow, v. (bend) ለጠ ፡ አለ läṭṭ alä; (~ to greet) እጅ ፡ ነሣ əǧǧ nässa
bow down ሰገደ säggädä

bow (n.) ቀስት qäst; (of ribbon) የቢራ ቢሮ ፡ ቅርጽ yäbirrabirro qərṣ; (for carding wool) ደጋን dägan

bowels አንጀት anǧät

bowl ጉድጓዳ ፡ ሳሕን gʷädgʷadda sahən

box (v.) በቡጢ ፡ መታ bäbuṭṭi mätta

box, n. (container) ሰንዱቅ sänduq; ሣጥን saṭən; (~ for cigars, matches) ፓኮ pakko; (blow, punch) በቡጢ ፡ መምታት bäbuṭṭi mämtat

boxer ቡጢኛ buṭṭiñña

box office (የ)ቲኬት ፡ መሸጫ (yä)tiket mäšäča

boy ወንድ wänd; ልጅ ləǧ; ወንድ ፡ ልጅ wänd ləǧ

boycott (n.) አድማ adma

boyfriend የከንፈር ፡ ወዳጅ yäkänfär wädaǧ

boyhood ልጅነት ləǧənnät

boy scout እስካውት əskawt

brace (n.) ማስደገፊያ masdäggäfiya

bracelet አምባር ambar

brackets ቅንፍ qənf

brackish ጨው ፡ ጨው ፡ የሚል čäw čäw yämmil

brag ጉራ ፡ ነዛ gurra näzza; ደነፋ dänäffa; ፎከረ fokkärä

braggart ጉረኛ ፡ ሰው gurräñña säw

bragging ድንፋታ dənfata; ጉራ gurra; ፉከራ fukkära

braid (v.) አሸመ aššämä; ጉነጉነ gʷänäggʷänä

braid, n. (of hair) ሹሩባ šurrubba; (ornamental band) ጉንጉን gungun

brain አንጎል angʷäl; ና nala

brake (v.) ፍሬን ፡ ያዘ fren yazä

brake (n.) ፍሬን fren

branch, ~ off ተለያየ täläyayyä; ተገነጠለ tägänäṭṭälä
branch out (of business) ተሰራጨ täsäraččä

branch (n.) ቅርንጫፍ qərənčaf; (of office) ዘርፍ zärf; ቅርንጫፍ qərənčaf

brand, v. (mark by burning) በምልክት ፡ ተኮሰ bämələkkət täkkʷäsä; (label) ቤጠረ qʷäṭṭärä

brand, n. (trade name) ዓይነት aynät; (identifying mark through burning) በመተኮስ ፡ የሚደረግ ፡ ምልክት bämättäkʷäs yämmiddärräg mələkkət

brand-new ፍጹም ፡ አዲስ fəṣṣum addis

brass ነሐስ nähas; መዳብ mädab

brave (v.) ተቋቋመ täqʷaqʷamä

brave, adj. (~ person) ጀግና ǧägna; ደፋር däffar; (~ deed) የጀግንነት yäǧägnənnät

bravery ጀግንነት ǧägnənnät

brawl (v.) ተራበሸ tärabbäšä

brawl (n.) ረብሻ räbša; ጥል ṭəl; አምባጓሮ ambagʷaro

bray አናፋ annaffa

brazen (bold) ነፍረተ ፡ ቢስ hafrätä bis

breach (v.) ጣሰ ṭasä

breach, n. (opening) ጉድባ gudba; (violation) መጣስ mäṭas

bread (of millet) እንጀራ ənǧära; (of wheat) ዳቦ dabbo; (European type) ፉርኖ furno
loaf of bread ዳቦ dabbo

breadth ስፋት səfat

break (vt.) ሰበረ säbbärä; (~ a string) በጠሰ bäṭṭäsä; (~ a habit) ተወ täwä; አስወገደ aswäggädä; (~ a contract) አፈረሰ afärräsä; (~ the law) ጣሰ ṭasä
break (vi.) ተሰበረ täsäbbärä; (of string) ተበጠሰ täbäṭṭäsä
break down (of machine) ተበላሸ täbälaššä; (of bridge) ተደረመሰ tädärämmäsä

break in (a house) ቤቱን ፡ ሰበረ *betun säbbärä;* (~ on a conversation) ጣልቃ፡ገባ *ṭalqa gäbba;* (~ an animal) ገራ *gärra*
break loose አመለጠ *amälläṭä*
break off (vt.) ገነጠለ *gänäṭṭälä;* (~ relations) አቋረጠ *aqqʷarräṭä*
break off (vi.) ተገነጠለ *tägänäṭṭälä*
break out (of fire) ተነሣ *tänässa;* (of disease) ገባ *gäbba;* (escape) አመለጠ *amälläṭä*
break up, vt. (~ boxes) ሰባበረ *säbabbärä;* (~ a meeting) በተነ *bättänä*

break, n. (in relations) ግንኙነት ፡ መቋረጥ *gänäňňunnät mäqqʷäräṭ;* (rest) ዕረ ፍት *əräft;* ፋታ *fata*
take a break ዕረፍት ፡ አደረገ *əräft adärrägä*

breakable ተሰባሪ *täsäbbari*

breakdown ብልሽት *bələššät;* (nervous~) የአእምሮ ፡ ሁከት *yää'məro hukät*

breakfast ቁርስ *qurs*

breast (bosom) ጡት *ṭut;* (chest) ደረት *därät*

breath ትንፋሽ *tənfaš;* እስትንፋስ *əstən-fas*
be out of breath, see 'breathless'
hold one's breath ትንፋሹን ፡ ዋጥ ፡ አደ ረገ *tənfašun waṭṭ adärrägä*
in the same breath ያኔውኑ *yannewnu*

breathe ተነፈሰ *tänäffäsä*

breathing መተንፈስ *mätänfäs*

breathless, be ትንፋሽ ፡ አጠረ(ው) *tənfaš aṭṭärä(w)*

breath-taking, be ልብ ፡ አጠፋ *läbb aṭäffa*

breeches ጠባብ ፡ ሱሪ *ṭäbbab surri*

breed, vt. (~ cattle) አረባ *aräbba;* (give rise to) አስከተለ *askättälä;* አመጣ *amäṭṭa*
breed, vi. (of cattle) ረባ *räbba;* (of birds) ተፈለፈለ *täfäläffälä;* (of rabbits) ተራባ *tärabba*

breeding (of cattle) ማርባት *marbat;* (bringing up) አስተዳደግ *astädadäg*

breeze የነፋስ ፡ ሽውታ *yänäfas šəwwəta;* ለስላሳ ፡ ነፋስ *läslassa näfas*

brew (~ beer) ጠመቀ *ṭämmäqä;* (~ a plot) ጠነሰሰ *ṭänässäsä*

brewery የቢራ ፡ ፋብሪካ *yäbira fabrika*

bribe (v.) በጉቦ ፡ ደለለ *bägubbo dällälä;* ጉቦ ፡ ሰጠ *gubbo säṭṭä*

bribe (n.) ጉቦ *gubbo*

bribery ጉቦ ፡ መብላት *gubbo mäblat*

brick ጡብ *ṭub*

bricklayer ጡብ ፡ ገንቢ *ṭub gänbi;* ግም በኛ *gəmbäňňa*

bridal የሙሽራ *yämušərra*

bride ሙሽራ *mušərra*

bridegroom ሙሽራ *mušərra*

bridesmaid ዳንጋጡር *dängäṭur*

bridge ድልድይ *dəldəy*

bridle, v. (put on a bit) ለጎመ *läggʷämä*

bridle (n.) ልጓም *ləgʷam*

brief አጭር *ač̣č̣ər*
be brief አጠረ *aṭṭärä*
in brief ባጭሩ *bač̣č̣əru*

briefcase ቦርሳ *borsa*

briefly ባጭሩ *bač̣č̣əru*

brigade ብርጌድ *brəged*

brigand ቀማኛ *qämmaňňa;* ወንበዴ *wän-bäde*

bright (~ color) ደማቅ *dämmaq;* (~ sunshine) ብሩህ *bəruh;* (~ fire) ቦግ ፡ ያለ *bogg yalä;* (~ idea) የብሉ *yäbə-ləh;* (~ boy) ብሉህ *bələh;* (~ future) ጥሩ *ṭäru*

brighten, vt. (of colorful object) አደመቀ *adämmäqä;* (of smile) ደስተኛ ፡ አደረገ *dässətäňňa adärrägä*
brighten, vi. (of sky) ጠራ *ṭärra;* (of face) ፈካ *fäkka*

brilliant (~ jewel) የሚያንጸባርቅ *yäm-miyanṣäbarrəq;* (~ color) ደማቅ *dämmaq;* (~ speaker) ድንቅ *dənq;* (~ man) ብሉህ *bələh*

brim (of glass) አፍ *af;* (of hat) ከፈፍ *kəfäf*

bring አመጣ *amäṭṭa;* (~ a person) ይዞ ፡ መጣ *yəzo mäṭṭa*
bring about አስከተለ *askättälä;* አመጣ *amäṭṭa*
bring along ይዞ ፡ መጣ *yəzo mäṭṭa*
bring back መለሰ *mälläsä*
bring down አወረደ *awärrädä;* (~ the price) ቀነሰ *qännäsä*
bring in አገባ *agäbba;* (~ money) አስገኘ *asgäňňä*
bring out (~ a book) አወጣ *awäṭṭa*
bring together አቃረበ *aqqarräbä*
bring up አሳደገ *asaddägä;* (mention) አነሣ *anässa*

brink (of cliff) ጠርዝ *ṭärz;* አፋፍ *afaf*

brisk (~ walk) ፈጠን ፡ ያለ *fäṭänn yalä*

brittle በቀላሉ ፡ የሚሰበር *bäqällalu yämmissäbbär*

broad ሰፊ *säffi;* (~ expanse of plain) ለጥ ፡ ያለ *läṭṭ yalä*
be broad ሰፋ *säffa*

broadcast, v. (by radio) በሬዲዮ ፡ አስተላለፈ *bärediyo astälalläfä;* አሰማ *assämma;* (~ a secret) አሰራጨ *assäraččä*

broadcast (n.) የሬዲዮ ፡ ፕሮግራም *yärediyo program*

broaden (vt.) አሰፋ *asäffa*
broaden (vi.) ሰፋ *säffa*

broad-minded, be አስተያያቱ ፡ ሰፊ ፡ ነው *astäyayatu säffi näw*

broil (vt.) ጠበሰ *ṭäbbäsä*

broke, be ባዶ ፡ ኪሱን ፡ ነው *bado kisun näw*
go broke ከሰረ *kässärä*

broken የተሰበረ *yätäsäbbärä*
be broken ተሰበረ *täsäbbärä*

broker ደላላ *dällala*

bronze ነሐስ *nähas*

brood (vt.) ታቀፈ *taqqäfä*
brood, vi. (think moodily) በሐዘን ፡ ተከዘ *bähazän täkkäzä*

brook ጀረት *ğərät*

broom መጥረጊያ *mäṭrägiya*

broth ሾርባ *šorba;* መረቅ *märäq*

brother ወንድም *wändəmm*

brotherhood (fellowship) ወንድማማችነት *wädəmmamačənnät;* (organization) ያንድነት ፡ ማኅበር *yandənnät mahbär*

brother-in-law ወርሳ *warsa;* አማች *amač*

brotherly የወንድማማችነት *yäwändəmmamačənnät*

brown ቡናማ *bunnamma*

bruise (v.) ሰነበር ፡ አወጣ *sänbär awäṭṭa*

bruise (n.) ሰንበር *sänbär*

brush, v. (~ hair) ቦረሸ *borräšä;* (~ teeth) ፋቀ *faqä*
brush off (~ dust) አራገፈ *arraggäfä*
brush up on ከላለሰ *kälalläsä*

brush (n.) ብሩሽ *bruš;* (brushwood) ጥሻ *ṭäša*

brutal (~ person) ጨካኝ *čäkkaň;* (~ way) የጭካኔ *yäčəkkane*

brutality ጭካኔ *čəkkane*

brute አውሬ *awre*

bubble (v.) ተፍለቀለቀ *täfläqälläqä*

bubble (n.) አረፋ *aräfa*

bucket ባልዲ *baldi*

buckle (v.) ቀለፈ *qʷälläfä*

buckle (n.) ዘለበት *zäläbät*

bud (v.) እምቡጥ ፡ ያዘ *əmbuṭ yazä*

bud (n.) እምቡጥ *əmbuṭ*

budge (vt.) አነቃነቀ *annäqannäqä*
budge (vi.) ተንቀሳቀሰ *tänqäsaqqäsä*

budget ባጀት *bağät*

buffalo ጎሽ *goš*

buffer የግጭት ፡ መከላከያ *yägəččət mäkkälakäya*

bug (n.) ትል *təl;* (bedbug) ትኋን *təhʷan*

build ሠራ *särra*
build up (~ a business) አዳበረ *adabbärä*

building ሕንጻ *hənṣa*

bulb (electric ∼) አምፑል *ampul*; (∼ of a plant) ሥስ *ras*

bulge (vt.) አሳበጠ *asabbäṭä*
bulge (vi.) አበጠ *abbäṭä*; ተወጠረ *täwäṭṭärä*

bulk አብዛኛ *abzaňňa*; (of a container) መጠን *mäṭän*; (of an animal) ግዙፍነት *gəzufənnät*

bulky ግዙፍ *gəzuf*

bull ኮርማ *korma*; አውራ ፡ በሬ *awra bäre* young bull ወይፈን *wäyfän*

bulldozer ቡልዶዘር *buldozär*

bullet ጥይት *ṭəyyət*

bulletin (report) መግለጫ *mägläča*; (notice) ማስታወቂያ *mastawäqiya*; (magazine) መጽሔት *mäṣhet*

bulletin board (የ)ማስታወቂያ ፡ ሰሌዳ *(yä)-mastawäqiya säleda*

bullock ወይፈን *wäyfän*

bulwark ግድብ *gəddəb*

bump (vt.) ገጨት ፡ አደረገ *gäčätt adärrägä*
bump (vi.) ተጋጨ *tägaččä*
bump along ተንገጫገጨ *tängäčaggäčä*
bump into (chance on) አጋጠመ(ው) *aggaṭṭämä(w)*; (collide) ተጋጨ *tägaččä*

bump, n. (swelling) እብጠት *əbṭät*; (raised place) ጉብታ *gubbəta*

bumper ፈረፋንጎ *färäfango*

bumpy አባጣ ፡ ጎርባጣ *abaṭa gʷärbaṭṭa*

bunch (of radishes) ጭብጥ *čəbbəṭ*; (of bananas) ዘለላ *zäläla*

bundle (v.) አሰረ *assärä*; አጨቀ *ačʼčʼäqä*
bundle up ጠቀለለ *ṭäqällälä*

bundle (n.) ጥቅል *ṭəqəll*; እስር *əsər*

buoyancy የመንሳፈፍ ፡ ኃይል *yämänsafäf hayl*

burden (v.) ጫነ *čanä*; (bother) አስቸገረ *asčäggärä*

burden (n.) ሸክም *šäkəm*

beast of burden የጭነት ፡ ከብት *yäčənät käbt*

burdensome ከባድ *käbbad*

bureau (office) ቢሮ *biro*; (table) ጠረጴዛ *ṭäräppeza*

burglar ሰርሳሪ ፡ ሌባ *särsari leba*

burglary ቤት ፡ ሰርሳሪነት *bet särsarinnät*

burial ቀብር *qäbər*; (the burying) መቃብር *mäqbär*

burial grounds የመቃብር ፡ ቦታ *yämäqabər bota*

burn (vt.) አቃጠለ *aqqaṭṭälä*; (of coffee, pepper) ፈጀ *fäǧǧä*; (∼ candles) አበራ *abärra*
burn, vi. (of wood, fire) ነደደ *näddädä*; (of house) ተቃጠለ *täqaṭṭälä*; (of light) በራ *bärra*; (of food) አረረ *arrärä*
burn down (vt.) አቃጠለ *aqqaṭṭälä*
burn down (vi.) ተቃጠለ *täqaṭṭälä*
burn out ጠፋ *ṭäffa*
burn up ተቃጠለ *täqaṭṭälä*

burn (n.) ቃጠሎ *qaṭälo*

burrow (v.) ቈፈረ *qʷäffärä*; ፈለፈለ *fäläffälä*

burrow (n.) ጉድጓድ *gudgʷad*; ጐሬ *gʷäre*

burst (vt.) በጠሰ *bäṭṭäsä*; ሰበረ *säbbärä*; (explode) አፈነዳ *afänädda*
burst (vi.) ፈነዳ *fänädda*; (of ulcer) ፈረጠ *färräṭä*

bury ቀበረ *qäbbärä*

bus አውቶቡስ *awtobus*
bus stop አውቶቡስ ፡ መቆሚያ *awtobus mäqomiya*

bush ቁጥቋጦ *quṭqʷaṭo*

bushy ችፍግ ፡ ያለ *čəffəgg yalä*

business (trade) ንግድ *nəgd*; (matter) ጉዳይ *gudday*; (occupation) ሥራ *səra*; ተግባር *tägbar*

businessman ነጋዴ *näggade*

bustle ተንጐራደደ *tängʷäraddädä*; ጉድ ፡ ጉድ ፡ አለ *gudd gudd alä*

busy (∼ person) ሥራ ፡ የሚበዛበት *səra*

yämmibäzabbät; (~ street) የተጨናነቀ
yätäčänannäqä; ትራፊክ ፡ የሚበዛበት
trafik yämmibäzabbät
be busy ሥራ ፡ ያዘ sǝra yazä; ሥራ ፡
በዛበት sǝra bäzzabbät; (of telephone)
ተያዘ täyazä

but (conj.) ግን gǝn; ነገር ፡ ግን nägär
gǝn; ዳሩ ፡ ግን daru gǝn
but (prep.) ከ - - - በስተቀር kä - - - bästäqär

butcher (v.) አረደ arrädä

butcher (n.) ሉካንዳ ፡ ነጋዴ lukanda näggade; ሥጋ ፡ ሻጭ sǝga šač

butcher shop ሉካንዳ lukanda

butt (stub) ቁራጭ qurraç; (~ of rifle)
ሰደፍ sädäf

butter (v.) ቅቤ ፡ ቀባ qǝbe qäbba

butter (n.) ቅቤ qǝbe

butterfly ቢራቢሮ birrabirro

buttermilk አረራ arera

buttock ቂጥ qiṭ

button (v.) ቆለፈ qwälläfä

button (n.) አዝራር azrar; ቁልፍ qulf; (~
of doorbell) መደወያ mädäwwäya

buy (v.) ገዛ gäzza; (~ grain) ሻመተ
šämmätä

buy (n.) ግዥ gǝžži

buyer ገዢ gäži

buzz, v. (of bee) ጥዝ ፡ አለ ṭazz alä; (of
ear) ጭው ፡ አለ čǝww alä

buzz (n.) ድምፅ dǝmṣ

by (through) በ bä; (near) በ - - - አጠ
ገብ bä - - - aṭägäb; (not later than)
እስከ ǝskä; ከ - - - በፊት kä - - - bäfit
by and by እያደረ ǝyyaddärä
by and large ከሞላ ፡ ጐደል kämolla
gwäddäl
by then እስከዚያ ǝskäzziya

bypass በ - - ጐን ፡ አለፈ bä - - - gwänn
alläfä

C

cab ታክሲ taksi

cabbage የፈረንጅ ፡ ጐመን yäfäränǧ gwämmän

cabin ጎጆ goǧǧo

cabinet (furniture) የቁም ፡ ሳጥን yäqum
saṭǝn; (group of advisors) ካቢኔ kabine

cable (telegram) ቴሌግራም telegram;
(heavy rope) ሽቦ šǝbo

cackle አስካካ askakka

cactus የባሕር ፡ ቁልቋል yäbahǝr qulqwal

cadet እጩ ፡ መኰንን ǝččatu mäkwännǝn

café ቡና ፡ ቤት bunna bet

cage የሽቦ ፡ ቤት yäšǝbo bet; (~ for
bird) የዋፍ ፡ ጎጆ yäwof goǧǧo

cajole አባበለ ababbälä; ዳለለ dällälä

cake ኬክ kek

calamity መቅሠፍት mäqsäft; መዓት mä'at

calculate (count) ቈጠረ qwäṭṭärä; (figure) አሰበ assäbä; አሰላ asälla

calculation ሒሳብ hisab

calendar (table showing the date)
(የ)ቀን፡መቊጠሪያ(yä)qän mäqwṭäriya;
(way of reckoning time) የቀን ፡ አቈጣ
ጠር yäqän aqqwäṭaṭär

calf (young of cow) ጥጃ ṭǝǧǧa; ጊደር gidär; (~ of leg) ባት bat

call (vt.) ጠራ ṭärra; (telephone) ደወለ
däwwälä; (name) ሰየመ säyyämä
call in ጠራ ṭärra; (let in) አስገባ asgäbba
call off ሰረዘ särräzä
call up ደወለ däwwälä

call (n.) ጥሪ ṭǝrri

calligrapher ቁም ፡ ጸሓፊ qum ṣähafi

calligraphy (የ)ቁም ፡ ጽሕፈት (yä)qum
ṣǝhfät

calling (inclination) ዝንባሌ zǝnǝbbale;
(profession) ሙያ muya

callous ርኅሩኄ ፥ የሌለው rəhrahe yälelläw

callus መጅ mäǧ

calm (vt.) አረጋጋ arrägagga
calm down (vt.) አረጋጋ arrägagga;
አበረደ abärrädä
calm down, vi. (of wind) ጸጥ ፥ አለ
ṣäṭṭ alä; (of person) ረጋ ፥ አለ räga
alä

calm (n.) ጸጥታ ṣäṭṭəta; እርጋታ ərgata

calm, adj. (~ person, voice, sea) የረጋ
yärägga
be calm (of sea, voice, weather) ረጋ
rägga; (of person) መንፈሰ ፥ ርጉ ፥ ነው
mänfäsä rəgu näw

calmly በእርጋታ ፤ በርጋታ bärgata; በጥ
ሞና bäṭəmmona

calumniate አማ amma

calumny ሐሜት hamet; አሜት amet

camel ግመል gəmäl

camera ፎቶግራፍ ፥ ማንሻ fotograf manša

camp (v.) ሰፈረ säffärä

camp, n. (military ~) የጦር ፥ ሰፈር yäṭor
säfär; ካምፕ kamp; (~ for summer)
መዝናኛ ፥ ሰፈር mäznaňňa säfär; (faction) ወገን wägän

campaign, n. (military ~) ዘመቻ zämäča; (~ to fight crime) ተጋድሎ tägadlo; (presidential ~) ውድድር wədəd-
där

campus ምድረ ፥ ግቢ mədrä gäbbi

can (~ food) በቆርቆሮ ፥ አሸገ bäqorqorro aššägä

can (be able) ቻለ čalä

can (n.) ጣሳ ṭasa; ቆርቆሮ qorqorro

canal ቦይ boy

cancel (~ an appointment) አፈረሰ
afärräsä; (~ a reservation) ተወ täwä

cancer የነቀርሳ ፥ በሽታ yänäqärsa bäššäta

candid ቅን qən; ግልጥ gəlṭ

candidate እጩ əččü

candle ሻማ šama; ጧፍ ṭʷaf

candy ከረሜላ kärämella

cane (v.) በብትር ፥ መታ bäbəttər mätta

cane (n.) ከዘራ käzära; ሸመል šəmäl;
(reed) ሸምበቆ šambäqqo

canine tooth ክራንቻ kranča; የውሻ ፥ ክራ
ንቻ yäwəšša kranča

canned food የቆርቆሮ ፥ ምግብ yäqorqorro məgəb

cannon መድፍ mädf

canoe ታንኳ tankʷa

canon (code) ሕግ həgg

canopy አጐበር agʷäbär

canteen (bottle) ኮዳ koda; (place for
refreshments) መዝናኛ ፥ ቤት mäznaňňa bet

canvas ሸራ šara

cap, n. (~ for head) ቆብ qob

capability ችሎታ čəlota

capable ችሎታ ፥ ያለው čəlota yalläw
be capable ቻለ čalä

capacity (ability) ችሎታ čəlota; (position, role) ሥልጣን səlṭan; (content)
ይዞታ yəzota
be filled to capacity ጢም ፥ ብሎ ፥ ነው
ṭim bəlo näw
have a capacity of (contain) ያዘ yazä

cape (garment) ካባ kabba; (geographical) ርእስ ፥ ምድር rə'əsä mədər

capital, n. (city) የመናገሻ ፥ ከተማ yä-
männagäša kätäma; ዋና ፥ ከተማ wanna kätäma; (money) ዋና ፥ ገንዘብ wanna gänzäb

capital (adj.) ዓቢይ abiy

capital city, see 'capital'

capital crime በሞት ፥ የሚያስቀጣ ፥ ወን
ጀል bämot yämmiyasqʷäṭṭa wänǧäl

capitalism ካፒታሊዝም kapitalizm

capitalize (~ a letter) በትልቁ ፥ ጻፈ bä-
təlləqu ṣafä

capital letter ትልቅ ፥ ፊደል təlləq fidäl

capital punishment ይሙት ፥ በቃ ፥ ፍርድ
yəmut bäqqa färd

capitol ቤት ፡ መንግሥት *betä mängəst*

capitulate እጅ ፡ ሰጠ *əǧǧ sättä*

captain (of army) ሻምበል *šambäl;* (of plane) ካፒቴን *kapiten;* (of team) የቡ ድን ፡ አባት *yäbudən abbat;* አምበል *ambäl*

captivate ማረከ *marräkä*

captive ምርኮኛ *mərkoňňa*

captivity ምርኮ *mərko;* ምርኮኛነት *mərkoňňannät*

capture (seize) ያዘ *yazä;* ማረከ *marräkä;* (charm) ማረከ *marräkä*

car መኪና *mäkina*

caravan ጉዞ *guzo;* ጓዝ *g*ʷ*az*

carbon paper የካርቦን ፡ ወረቀት *yäkarbon wäräqät*

carcass ሬሳ *resa;* ጥንብ *ṭənb;* ጥምብ *ṭəmb*

card, v. (∼ wool) ነደፈ *näddäfä*

card, n. (playing ∼) ካርታ *karta;* (letter) ካርድ *kard*

cardboard ካርቶን *karton*

cardiac የልብ *yäləbb*

cardinal (adj.) ዐቢይ *abiy*
cardinal number ተራ ፡ ቁጥር *tära quṭər*
cardinal point ዋነኛ ፡ አቅጣጫ *wannäňňa aqṭačča*

care (v.) ፈለገ *fällägä*
care about ወደደ *wäddädä*
care for ጠበቀ *ṭäbbäqä*
I don't care ደንታ ፡ የለኝም *dänta yälläňňəm;* ግድ ፡ የለኝም *gədd yälläňňəm*

care, n. (attention) ጥንቃቄ *ṭənəqqaqe;* (worry) ስጋት *səgat;* (safekeeping) አደራ *adära*
in care of በ - - በኩል *bä - - - bäkkul*
take care of (watch children) ጠበቀ *ṭäbbäqä;* (nurse a sick person) አስታ መመ *astammämä*

career ሥራ *səra;* ቋሚ ፡ ሥራ *q*ʷ*ami səra*

carefree ግድ ፡ የለሽ *gədd yälläš*

careful (cautious) ጥንቁቅ *ṭənquq;* ጠን

ቃቃ *ṭänqaqqa;* (done with care) በጥን ቃቄ ፡ የተሠራ *bäṭənəqqaqe yätäsärra*
be careful ተጠነቀቀ *tätänäqqäqä*

carefully በጥንቃቄ *bäṭənəqqaqe*

careless ቸልተኛ *čälltäňňa;* ግድ ፡ የለሽ *gədd yälläš*
be careless ቸል ፡ አለ *čäll alä;* ቸላ ፡ አለ *čälla alä;* ግድ ፡ የለ(ውም) *gədd yällä-(wəm)*

carelessness ቸልታ *čälləta;* ግድ ፡ የለሽነት *gədd yälläšənnät*

caress ደባበሰ *däbabbäsä*

cargo ጭነት *čənät*

carnal የሥጋ *yäsəga;* ሥጋዊ *səgawi*

carnivore ሥጋ ፡ በል *səga bäll*

carpenter አናጢ *anaṭi;* አናጺ *anaṣi*

carpentry አናጢነት *anaṭinnät*

carpet ምንጣፍ *mənṭaf;* ስጋጃ *səgaǧǧa*

carriage (vehicle) ሰረገላ *särägälla;* (bearing) ዛላ *zala*

carrion ጥንብ *ṭənb;* ጥምብ *ṭəmb*

carrot ካሮት *karot*

carry ተሸከመ *täšäkkämä;* (transport) አጓጓዘ *agg*ʷ*ag*ʷ*azä*
carry away ወሰደ *wässädä*
carry off ወሰደ *wässädä*
carry on ቀጠለ *qäṭṭälä*
carry out (∼ a plan) አከናወነ *akkänawwänä;* ከግብ ፡ አደረሰ *kägəb adärräsä;* ፈጸመ *fäṣṣämä*

cart, horse-drawn ∼ ጋሪ *gari*

carton የካርቱን ፡ ሣጥን *yäkartun saṭən*

cartridge ጥይት *ṭəyyət*

cartridge belt ዝናር *zənnar*

cartridge case ቀለህ *qäläh*

carve (engrave) ቀረጸ *qärräṣä;* (∼ meat) መተረ *mättärä*

case (affair) ጉዳይ *gudday;* (legal ∼) ሙግት *muggət;* (box) ሣጥን *saṭən;* (container) ማኅደር *mahdär*
in case ድንገት *dəngät*
in any case ያም ፡ ሆነ ፡ ይህ *yam honä*

yəh; ምንም ፡ ቢሆን *mənəm bihon;* ለማ
ንኛውም *lämannəññawəm*
in no case በምንም ፡ ምክንያት *bämə-*
nəm məknəyat
in this case እንደዚህ ፡ ከሆነ *əndäzzih*
kähonä

cash, v. (~ a check) መነዘረ *mänäzzärä*

cash (n.) ጥሬ ፡ ገንዘብ *ṭəre gänzäb*

cashier ገንዘብ ፡ ተቀባይ *gänzäb täqäbbay*

cast, v. (throw) ጣለ *ṭalä;* ወረወረ *wä-*
räwwärä; (~ a statue) ቀረጸ *qärräṣä*
cast aside ጣለ *ṭalä*
cast away (~ habits) ተወ *täwä*
cast off ጣለ *ṭalä*

cast, n. (plaster) ጄሶ *ǧesso*

caste ኅብረ ፡ ሰብአዊ ፡ ክፍል *həbrä säb-*
'awi kəfəl

cast iron ብረት *brät*

castle ግምብ *gəmb*

castrate (~ cattle) ሞከተ *mokkätä;* (~
a peıson) ሰለበ *sälläbä*

castrated (calf, goat) ሙክት *mukkət*

casual የግዴለሽነት *yägəddelläšənnät*

casually, be dressed ~ እንደነገሩ ፡ ለበሰ
əndänägäru läbbäsä

casualty ባደጋው ፡ የተጐዳ *badägaw yä-*
täg^wädda; የሞቱና ፡ የቈሰሉ *yämotun-*
na yäq^wässälu

cat ድመት *dəmmät*

catalog (v.) መዘገበ *mäzäggäbä*

catalog (n.) ዝርዝር *zərzər*

catastrophe መቅሠፍት *mäqsäft*

catch ያዘ *yazä;* (~ a ball) ቀለበ *qälläbä;*
(~ fish) አጠመደ *aṭämmädä;* (at-
tract) ማረከ *marräkä;* (understand)
ገባ(ው) *gäbba(w)*

catching (~disease) ተላላፊ *tälalafi*

category ክፍል *kəfəl*

caterpillar አባ ፡ ጫንጎ *abba čägg^warre*

cathedral ካቴድራል *katedral*

Catholic ካቶሊክ *katolik*

cattle ከብት *käbt;* የቀንድ ፡ ከብት *yä-*
qänd käbt

cause (v.) አመጣ *amäṭṭa;* አደረሰ *adär-*
räsä; or expressed by the አ-*a*-stem
or አስ-*as*-stem

cause, n. (reason) ምክንያት *məknəyat;*
ሰበብ *säbäb;* (purpose) ዓላማ *alama*

cauterize ተኩሰ *täkk^wäsä*

caution (v.) አስጠነቀቀ *asṭänäqqäqä*

caution (n.) ጥንቃቄ *ṭənəqqaqe*

cautious ጥንቁቅ *ṭənquq;* ጠንቃቃ *ṭän-*
qaqqa
be cautious ተጠነቀቀ *tätänäqqäqä*

cautiously በጥንቃቄ *bäṭənəqqaqe*

cavalry ፈረሰኛ *färäsäñña*

cave (n.) ዋሻ *wašša*

cavity ጉድጓድ *gudg^wad*

cease (vt.) አቆመ *aqomä*
cease (vi.) ቆመ *qomä;* ተቋረጠ *täq^war-*
räṭä; አበቃ *abäqqa*

ceasefire የተኩስ ፡ ማቆም ፡ ስምምነት *yä-*
täk^ws maqom səmämmənnät

ceaseless የማያቋርጥ *yämmayaqq^warrəṭ*

cede ለቀቀ *läqqäqä*

ceiling ቢላፎን *bilafon;* ጣራ *ṭara*

celebrate (~ holiday) አከበረ *akäbbärä*

celebrated (well known) ዝነኛ *zənnäñña;*
የተመሰገነ *yätämäsäggänä*

celebration (holiday) ባል *bal;* (way of
celebrating) የበዓል ፡ አከባበር *yäbä'al*
akkäbabär

celebrity ስም ፡ ጥሩ *səmä ṭəru;* ዝነኛ ፡
ሰው *zənnäñña säw*

celestial የሰማይ *yäsämay;* ሰማያዊ *sāma-*
yawi

celibate ድንግል *dəngəl;* በብሕትውና ፡
የሚኖር *bäbəhtəwənna yämminor*

cell (small room) ክፍል *kəfəl;* (~ of
human body) ሴል *sel*

cellar ምድር ፡ ቤት *mədər bet*

cement ሲሚንቶ *siminto*

cemetery መቃብር *mäqabər;* መካነ ፡ መቃብር *mäkanä mäqabər*

censor (n.) የሳንሱር ፡ ሹም *yäsansur šum*

censorship ሳንሱር *sansur*

censure (v.) ገሠጸ *gässäṣä*

censure (n.) ተግሣጽ *tägsaṣ*

census የሕዝብ ፡ ቈጠራ *yähəzb qʷäṭära*

cent ሳንቲም *santim*

centenary መቶኛ ፡ ዓመት ፡ በዓል *mätoňňa amät bä'al*

centennial መቶኛ ፡ ዓመት *mätoňňa amät*

center (v.) መሃል ፡ አዋለ *mähal awalä*

center (n.) መሃል *mähal;* መሀከል *mähakkäl;* መካከል *mäkakkäl;* (main point) እምብርት *əmbərt*

centimeter ሴንቲሜትር *sentimetər*

central ማእከላዊ *ma'əkälawi;* አማካይ *ammakay;* (main) ዋና *wanna*
central idea ፍሬ ፡ ነገር *fre nägär*

century መቶ ፡ ዓመት *mäto amät;* ክፍለ ፡ ዘመን *kəflä zämän*

cereal(s) እህል *əhəl;* ጥራጥሬ *ṭəraṭəre*

ceremonial ሥነ ፡ ሥርዓት ፡ ያለው *sənä sər'at yalläw;* የክብረ ፡ በዓል *yäkəbrä bä'al*

ceremony ሥነ ፡ ሥርዓት *sənä sər'at*

certain (some) አንዳንድ *andand;* (sure) እርግጥ *ərgəṭ;* እርግጠኛ *ərgəṭäňňa*
for certain በርግጥ *bärgəṭ*
make certain አረጋገጠ *arrägaggäṭä*

certainly በፍጹም *bäfəṣṣum;* እውነትም *əwnätəm;* በእርግጥ *bärgəṭ*
certainly! እንዴታ *əndeta*

certainty እርግጠኛነት *ərgəṭäňňannät*

certificate የምስክር ፡ ወረቀት *yäməsəkkər wäräqät*

certify አረጋገጠ *arrägaggäṭä;* (state officially) መሰከረ *mäsäkkärä*

certitude እርግጠኛነት *ərgəṭäňňannät*

chaff ገለባ *gäläba;* እብቅ *əbbəq*

chain (v.) በሰንሰለት ፡ አሰረ *bäsänsälät assärä*

chain (n.) ሰንሰለት *sänsälät*

chair (v.) በሊቀ ፡ መንበርነት ፡ መራ *bäliqä mänbärənnät märra*

chair (n.) ወንበር *wänbär;* ወምበር *wämbär*

chairman ሊቀ ፡ መንበር *liqä mänbär*

chairmanship ሊቀ ፡ መንበርነት *liqä mänbärənnät*

chalice ጥዋ *ṭəwwa;* ጽዋ *ṣəwwa*

chalk ጠመኔ *ṭämäne*

challenge, n. (a summons to fight) የግጥሚያ ፡ ጥሪ *yägəṭmiya ṭərri*

chamber ክፍል *kəfəl;* (~ for official occasions) የእንግዳ ፡ መቀበያ ፡ አዳራሽ *yängəda mäqqäbäya addaraš*

chamberlain እልፍኝ ፡ አስከልካይ *əlfəňň askälkay*

Chamber of Deputies የሕግ ፡ መሥሪያ ፡ ምክር ፡ ቤት *yähəgg mäsriya məkər bet*

champion (n.) ሻምፒዮን *šampiyon;* አሸናፊ *aššännafi*

championship አሸናፊነት *aššännafinnät;* አንደኛነት *andäňňannät*

chance (v.), ~ on አጋጠመ(ው) *aggaṭṭämä(w)*

chance (n.) ዕድል *əddəl;* (lottery) እጣ *əṭa*
by chance እንዳጋጣሚ *əndaggaṭami;* በድንገት *bädəngät*
take a chance ዕድል ፡ ሞከረ *əddəl mokkärä*

change (vt.) ለወጠ *läwwäṭä;* ቀየረ *qäyyärä;* (~ money) መነዘረ *mänäzzärä;* (~ from bills to coins) ሸረፈ *šärräfä*
change (vi.) ተለወጠ *täläwwäṭä*

change (n.) ለውጥ *läwṭ;* (~ in money) መልስ *mäls*
for a change ለለውጥ ፡ ያህል *läläwṭ yahəl*
small change ዝርዝር *zərzər*

channel (body of water joining two larger bodies of water) ሰላጤ *sällaṭe;* የባሕር ፡ ወሽመጥ *yäbaḥər wäšmäṭ;* (direction) አቅጣጫ *aqṭačča*

chant (v.) አዜመ *azemä;* ዘመረ *zämmärä*

chant (n.) ዜማ *zema*

chaos ተርምስምስ *tärməsməs;* ፍርስርስ *fərəsrəs*

chap, vt. (~ the skin) አቈረፈደ *aqʷäräffädä*

chapel የጸሎት ፡ ቤት *yäṣälot bet*

chaplain ቄስ *qes*

chapter ምዕራፍ *mə'əraf;* (branch of organization) ቅርንጫፍ *qərənčaf*

char አሳረረ *asarrärä*

character ጠባይ *ṭäbay;* (letter of alphabet) ፊደል *fidäl;* (person in story) ባለ ፡ ታሪክ *balä tarik*

characteristic (n.) መለያ *mälläyya;* ባሕሪይ *bahriy*

characteristic, adj. (usual) የተለመደ *yätälämmädä;* (special) የተለየ *yätäläyyä*

characterize (evaluate) ገመተ *gämmätä*

charcoal ከሰል *käsäl*

charge, v. (ask for payment) አስከፈለ *askäffälä;* (order) አዘዘ *azzäzä;* (~ a battery) ሞላ *molla;* (attack) አጠቃ *aṭäqqa;* (accuse) ከሰሰ *kässäsä*

charge, n. (price) ዋጋ *waga;* (attack) ማጥቃት *maṭqat;* (responsibility) ኃላ ፊነት *halafinnät;* (accusation) ክስ *kəss*
be in charge ኃላፊ ፡ ነው *halafi näw*
free of charge በነጻ *bänäṣa*
take charge of ኃላፊነት ፡ ወሰደ *halafinnät wässädä*

chariot ሰረገላ *särägälla*

charitable በጎ ፡ አድራጊ *bäggo adragi*
be charitable ለገሰ *läggäsä;* ቸርታ ፡ አደረገ *čərota adärrägä*

charity ልግስና *ləggəsənna;* ምጽዋት *məṣwat;* በጎ ፡ አድራጎት *bäggo adragot;* ቸርታ *čərota;* (organization) የበጎ ፡

አድራጎት ፡ ድርጅት *yäbäggo adragot dərəǧǧət*

charm (v.) ማረከ *marräkä*

charm (n.) ውበት *wəbät;* ደግምግነት *dämamənnät;* (talisman) ክታብ *kətab*
charms አስማት *asmat*
have charm ደስ ፡ ደስ ፡ አለ(ው) *däss däss alä(w)*

charming የደስደስ ፡ ያለው *yädässədäss yaläw;* ደስ ፡ የሚል *däss yämmil;* የሚ ያስደስት *yämmiyasdässət*

chart ሰሌዳ *säleda;* ካርታ *karta*

charter (n.) ሕግ ፡ መሠረት *həggä mäsärät*

charwoman ቤት ፡ ጠራጊ ፡ ሴት *bet ṭäragi set*

chase አሳደደ *assaddädä;* አባረረ *abbarärä;* (pursue) ተከታተለ *täkätattälä*
chase away ሰደደ *säddädä;* አባረረ *abbarärä*

chaste ንጹሕ *nəṣuh*

chastity ድንግልና *dəngələnna;* ድንግላዊ ነት *dəngəlawinnät;* ንጽሕና *nəṣhənna*

chat (v.) ተጫወተ *täčawwätä*

chat (n.) ጭውውት *čəwəwwət*

chatter (v.) ለፈለፈ *läfälläfä;* (of teeth) ተንጋጫገጫ *tängäčaggäčä*

chatter (n.) ለፍለፋ *ləfläfa*

chatterbox ለፍላፊ *läflafi*

chauffeur ሾፌር *šofer*

cheap (low in cost) ርካሽ *rəkkaš;* (of poor quality) መናኛ *mänaňňa;* (stingy) ቆጥቋጣ *qʷäṭqʷaṭṭa*

cheat (vt.) አሞኘ *amoňňä;* አታለለ *attalälä;* አጭበረበረ *ačbäräbbärä*

cheater ቀጣፊ *qäṭafi;* አታላይ *attalay*

check, v. (examine) መረመረ *märämmärä;* አጣራ *aṭṭarra;* (mark with check) ምልክት ፡ አደረገ *mäläkkət adärrägä;* (restrain) ጋታ *gätta;* (stop) አገደ *aggädä;* (leave for safekeeping) አስቀመጠ *asqämmäṭä* check off ምልክት ፡ አደረገ *mǝläkkǝt adärrägä*

check, n. (bill) ሒሳብ *hisab;* (draft) ቼክ *ček;* (mark) ምልክት *mǝläkkǝt;* (ticket) ቲኬት *tiket*

checkbook የቼክ ፡ ደብተር *yäček däbtär*

checking account ሒሳብ *hisab*

checkup ምርመራ *mǝrmära*

cheek ጉንጭ *gunč*

cheer (vt.) አደነቀ *adännäqä;* በእልልታና ፡ በጭብጨባ ፡ ተቀበለ *bäǝlǝltanna bäčäbčäba täqäbbälä*
    cheer (vi.) በደስታ ፡ ጮኸ *bädässǝta čohä*
    cheer up (vt.) አበረታታ *abbärätatta;* አጽናና *aṣnanna*
    cheer up (vi.) ተጽናና *täṣnanna*
    cheer up! በርታ *bärta;* አይዞህ *ayzoh*

cheer (n.) ደስታ *dässǝta*
    cheers የደስታ ፡ ጩኸት *yädässǝta čuhät;* እልልታና ፡ ጭብጨባ *ǝlǝltanna čäbčäba*

cheerful (~ room) አስደሳች *asdässač;* (~ person) ፍልቅልቅ *fǝlǝqlǝq;* ደስተኛ *dässǝtäňňa*
    be cheerful ፈነደቀ *fänäddäqä*

cheering ሆታ *hota*

cheese አይብ *ayb;* ፎርማጆ *formaǧo*

chemistry ኬሚስትሪ *kemistri*

cherish (treasure) ከፍተኛ ፡ ዋጋ ፡ ሰጠ *käffǝtäňňa waga säṭṭä;* (care for tenderly) አንከባከበ *ankäbakkäbä*

chess ሰንጠረዥ *sänṭäräž*

chest (part of body) ደረት *därät;* (box) ሰንዱቅ *sänduq;* ሣጥን *saṭǝn*

chest of drawers ባለመሳቢያ ፡ ቁም ፡ ሣጥን *balämäsabiya qum saṭǝn*

chew አኘከ *aňňäkä*
    chew cud አመሰኳ *amäsäkkʷa;* አመነ ዠኸ *amänäžžähä*
    chew off ገመጠ *gämmäṭä*

chewing gum መስቲካ *mästika*

chick ጫጩት *čačut*

chicken ዶሮ *doro*

chicken pox ኩፍኝ *kuffǝňň*

chickpea ሽምብራ *šǝmbǝra*

chief (n.) ሹም *šum;* አለቃ *aläqa*

chief, adj. (principal) ዋና *wanna;* (highest in rank) የበላይ *yäbälay*

chiefly (mostly) አብዛኛው *abzaňňaw;* (mainly) በተላይ *bätäläyy*

child ሕፃን *hǝṣan;* ልጅ *lǝǧ*

childhood ሕፃንነት *hǝṣanǝnnät;* ልጅነት *lǝǧǝnnät;* የልጅነት ፡ ጊዜ *yälǝǧǝnnät gize*

childish እንደ ፡ ሕፃን *ǝndä hǝṣan*

childless መካን *mäkan*

chill (v.) አቀዘቀዘ *aqäzäqqäzä*

chill (n.) ብርድ *bǝrd*

chilly ቀዝቃዛ *qäzqazza*

chimney የጭስ ፡ መውጫ *yäčǝs mäwča*

chin ሸንጉበት *šängʷäbät;* አገጭ *agäč*

china የሸህላ ፡ ሳህን *yäšähla sahǝn*

China ቻይና *čayna*

chip (v.) ሸረፈ *šärräfä*
    chip in አወጣ *awwäṭa*

chip, n. (of cup) ስብርባሪ *sǝbǝrbari;* (of wood) ፍቅፋቂ *fǝqǝffaqi*

chirp (v.) ጭውጭው ፡ አለ *čǝwwǝčäww alä*

chirp (n.) ጫጫታ *čačata*

chisel (v.) ወቀረ *wäqqärä;* ቀረጸ *qärräṣä*

chisel (n.) መቃ *märo*

chocolate ቾኮላታ *čäkolata*

choice (n.) ምርጫ *mǝrča*
    make a choice መረጠ *märräṭä*

choice (adj.) ምርጥ *mǝrṭ*

choir የመዝሙር ፡ ጓድ *yämäzmur gʷadd*

choke (vt.) አነቀ *annäqä*
    choke (vi.) ታነቀ *tannäqä*

choose መረጠ *märräṭä*

choosy መራጭ *märač*

chop (~ wood) ቈረጠ *q^wärräṭä;* ፈለጠ *fälläṭä;* (~ meat) መተረ *mättärä;* ከተፈ *kättäfä*

chopped meat ክትፎ *kətfo*

chore (irksome job) የሚያሰለች ፡ ሥራ *yämmiyasäläčč səra;* (routine job) የዘ ወትር ፡ ሥራ *yäzäwätər səra*

chorus, see 'choir'

christen ክርስትና ፡ አነሣ *krəstənna anäs-sa;* አጠመቀ *aṭämmäqä;* (give a name) የክርስትና ፡ ስም ፡ አለ *yäkrəstənna səm alä*

christening ክርስትና *krəstənna*

Christian ክርስቲያን *krəstiyan*

Christianity ክርስትና *krəstənna*

Christmas ገና *gänna;* ልደት *lədät;* ብር ሃነ ፡ ልደት *bərhanä lədät* merry Christmas! እንኳን ፡ ለብርሃነ ፡ ልደት ፡ አበቃዎት *ənk^wan läbərhanä lədät abäqqawot*

chronic (habitual) ለማደኛ *ləmadäňňa;* (lasting over a long period) ሥር ፡ የሰ ደደ *sər yäsäddädä*

chronicle ዜና ፡ መዋዕል *zena mäwa'əl*

chubby, be ፋፋ *faffa*

chuckle ሣቅ ፡ አለ *saqq alä*

chunk (of meat) ቍራጭ *qurrač;* (of stone) ስባሪ *səbbari*

church ቤተ ፡ ክርስቲያን *betä krəstiyan* go to church ቤተ ፡ ክርስቲያን ፡ ሳመ *betä krəstiyan samä*

churn (v.) ናጠ *naṭä*

churn (n.) መናጫ *mänača*

cigar ሲጋር *sigar*

cigarette ሲጃራ *siǧara;* ሲጋራ *sigara*

cinder አመድ *amäd*

cinema ሲኒማ *sinima*

cinnamon ቀረፋ *qäräfa*

circle, vt. (surround) ከበበ *käbbäbä* circle (vi.) ዞረ *zorä*

circle (n.) ክበብ *kəbäb*

circuit (of city) ዙሪያ *zuriya;* (of the sun) ዑደት *udät*

circular ክብ *kəbb*

circulate, vt. (~ news) አሰራጨ *assäräč-čä;* (~ a letter) አስተላለፈ *astälalläfä* circulate, vi. (move around) ተዘዋወረ *täzäwawwärä;* (of news) ተሰራጨ *tä-säraččä;* ነፈሰ *näffäsä*

circumcise ገረዘ *gärräzä;* ገዘረ *gäzzärä*

circumcision ግርዘት *gərzät;* ግዝረት *gəz-rät*

circumference ክበብ *kəbäb;* ዙሪያ *zuriya*

circumstance ሁኔታ *huneta;* ነገር *nägär;* (incident) አጋጣሚ *aggaṭami* under no circumstances በምንም ፡ ምክ ንያት *bämənəm məknəyat;* በምንም ፡ ዓይነት *bämənəm aynät*

circus ሰርከስ *särkäs*

cistern የውኃ ፡ ማጠራቀሚያ *yäwəha maṭ-ṭäraqämiya*

citation (from Scripture) ጥቅስ *ṭəqs;* (hon-orable mention) የምስጋና ፡ ወረቀት *yäməsgana wäräqät;* (summons to appear in court) መጥሪያ *mäṭriya*

cite ጠቀሰ *ṭäqqäsä*

citizen ዜጋ *zega*

citizenship ዜግነት *zegənnät*

city ከተማ *kätäma*

city dweller ከተሜ *kätäme;* ከተመኛ *kätämäňňa*

city hall ማዘጋጃ ፡ ቤት *mazzägaǧa bet*

civic (of a citizen) ሕዝባዊ *həzbawi;* የዜ ግነት *yäzegənnät;* (of a city) የከተማ *yäkätäma*

civil (~ liberties) ሕዝባዊ *həzbawi;* (po-lite) ትሑት *təhut;* (~ service) ሲቪል *sivil*

civil code የፍትሐ ፡ ብሔር ፡ ሕግ *yäfətha bəher həgg*

civilian ሰላማዊ *sälamawi;* ሲቪል *sivil*

civility ትሕትና *təhtənna;* ጨዋነት *čäwan-nät*

civilization ሥልጣኔ *sələṭṭane*

civilize አሠለጠነ *asäläṭṭänä*

civilized ሥልጡን *sälṭun;* የሠለጠነ *yäsä-läṭṭänä*
be civilized ሠለጠነ *säläṭṭänä*

civil servant የመንግሥት ፡ ሠራተኛ *yä-mängəst särratäňňa*

civil war የርስ ፡ በርስ ፡ ጦርነት *yärs bärs ṭorənnät*

claim, v. (demand) ፈለገ *fällägä;* የኔ ፡ ነው ፡ አለ *yäne näw alä*

claim (n.) ይገባኛል ፡ ማለት *yəggäbbaňňal malät*
file a claim ይገባኛል ፡ ሲል ፡ አመለከተ *yəggäbbaňňal sil amäläkkätä*
lay claim ይገባኛል ፡ አለ *yəggäbbaňňal alä;* የኔው ፡ ነው ፡ አለ *yänew näw alä*

clamor (v.) በጩኸት ፡ አሰማ *bäčuhät assämma*

clamor, n. (uproar) ሁከት *hukät;* (loud noise) ጩኸት *čuhät;* ጋጋታ *gagata*

clan ወገን *wägän;* ጐሳ *gʷäsa*

clandestine የምስጢር *yäməsṭir*

clank ተቃጨለ *täqaččälä*

clap, ~ hands አጨበጨበ *ačäbäččäbä*

clarify (make intelligible) አብራራ *ab-rarra;* (make pure) አነጠረ *anäṭṭärä;* አጣራ *aṭṭarra*

clash (vt.) አጋጨ *aggaččä*
clash (vi.) ተጋጨ *tägaččä;* (contradict) ተቃረነ *täqarränä*

clash (n.) ግጭት *gəččət;* (sound) ድምፅ *dəmṣ*

clasp (v.) ያዘ *yazä*

clasp (n.) መያዣ *mäyaža*

class (v.) መደበ *mäddäbä*

class, n. (studies) ትምህርት *təmhərt;* (grade) ማዕረግ *ma'əräg;* (group of people) የነብረ ፡ ሰብ ፡ ክፍል *yähəbrä säb kəfəl*

classification ድልድል *dələddəl*

classify ለያየ *läyayyä;* ለየብቻ ፡ መደበ *läy-yäbäčča mäddäbä*

classmate የክፍል ፡ ጓደኛ *yäkəfəl gʷad-däňňa*

classroom ክፍል *kəfəl*

clatter (v.) ኳኳ ፡ አለ *kʷakʷa alä;* አን ኳኳ *ankʷakkʷa;* ተንጋጫገጨ *tängäčag-gäčä*

clatter (n.) ውካታ *wəkata;* ኳኳቴ *kʷa-kʷate*

clause (part of agreement) አንቀጽ *an-qäṣ;* (in grammar) ሐረግ *haräg*

clavicle ማጭድ *mačəd*

claw (n.) ጥፍር *ṭəfər*

clay ሸክላ *šäkla;* ሸህላ *šähla*

clean, vt. (~ a room) አጸዳ *aṣädda;* ጠረገ *ṭärrägä;* (by wiping) ወለወለ *wä-läwwälä*
clean up (vi.) ተጸዳዳ *täṣädadda*

clean (adj.) ንጹሕ *näṣuh;* ጽዱ *ṣədu*
be clean ጠለለ *ṭällälä;* ጸዳ *ṣädda*

cleaner የልብስ ፡ ንጽሕና ፡ መስሪያ *yäləbs näṣhənna mäsča*

cleanliness ንጽሕና *näṣhənna;* ጽዳት *ṣə-dat*

cleanser ማጽጃ *maṣ-ǧa*

clear, vt. (remove) አስወገደ *aswäggädä;* (~ the forest) መነጠረ *mänäṭṭärä;* (declare innocent) ነጻ ፡ ለቀቀ *näṣa läqqäqä;* (~ customs) አስመረመረ *asmärämmärä*
clear away (~ dishes) አነሳ *anässa*
clear out (vt.) አጋባ *aggabba*
clear up, vi. (of weather) አበራ *abar-ra;* ጠራ *ṭärra*

clear, adj. (~ water) ጥሩ *ṭäru;* (~ statement) ግልጽ *gəlṣ;* (~ voice, day) የጠራ *yäṭärra*
clear weather ብራ *bərra*

clearance (permission) ፈቃድ *fäqad;* (in the woods) ገላጣ ፡ ቦታ *gälaṭa bota*

clearance sale የማጣሪያ ፡ ሽያጭ *yämaṭṭariya šəyyač*

clearing, n. (of forest) ምንጠር *mənṭər*

clearly ጉልቶ *gʷälto*; በግልጽ *bägəlṣ*

cleave (~ wood) ሰነጠቀ *sänäṭṭäqä*; ፈለጠ *fälläṭä*
cleave to ጸና *ṣänna*

clemency ርኅራኄ *rəhrahe*

clement ርኅሩኅ *rəhruh*; (~ weather) መልካም *mälkam*

clench (~ the fist) ጨበጠ *čäbbäṭä*; (~ the teeth) ነከሰ *näkkäsä*

clergy ቤተ ፡ ክህነት *betä kəhənät*; ክህ ናት *kahənat*

clergyman ካህን *kahən*

clerk (of office) ጸሐፊ *ṣähafi*; (of store) ሻጭ *šač*

clever ብልህ *bələh*; ብልጥ *bəlṭ*

click (vt.) አቃጨለ *aqqaččälä*

click (n.) መቃጨል *mäqqaçäl*

client ደንበኛ *dänbäňňa*

cliff ገደል *gädäl*

climate ያየር ፡ ንብረት *yayyär nəbrät*; ያየር ፡ ጠባይ *yayyär ṭäbay*

climax (n.) ማክተሚያ *maktämiya*

climb ወጣ *wäṭṭa*; (~ a mountain) አዳገተ *addaggätä*

cling (stick) ተጣበቀ *täṭabbäqä*

clinic ክሊኒክ *klinik*

clip, v. (~ hair) ቈረጠ *qʷärräṭä*
clip together አያያዘ *ayyayazä*

clip (n.) አግራፍ *agraf*

clippers መቍረጫ *mäqʷräča*; መቀስ *mäqäs*

clipping (n.) ቍራጭ *qurraç*; ብጣሽ *bəṭṭaš*

cloak (n.) ካባ *kabba*

clock ሰዓት *sä'at*
around the clock ሌት ፡ ተቀን *let täqän*

clod ጓል *gʷal*

clog ወተፈ *wättäfä*; ደፈነ *däffänä*

close (vt.) ዘጋ *zägga*; (~ the eyes) ጨፈነ *čäffänä*; (~ a debate) ደመደመ *dämäddämä*
close (vi.) ተዘጋ *täzägga*; (of a meeting) አበቃ *abäqqa*

close, adj. (~ friend) የቅርብ *yäqərb*
close by በቅርብ *bäqərb*; አጠገብ *aṭägäb*
close to እ - - - ዘንድ *ə - - - zänd*; እ - - - ጋ *ə - - - ga*; ከ - - - ጉን *kä - - - gʷänn*; ከ - - - ጥግ *kä - - - ṭəgg*
be close ተቃረበ *täqarräbä*

closed ዝግ *zəg*

closet (የ)ቁም ፡ ሳጥን *(yä)qum saṭən*

cloth ጨርቅ *čärq*

clothe አለበሰ *aläbbäsä*

clothes ልብስ *ləbs*

clothes hanger የልብስ ፡ መስቀያ *yäləbs mäsqäya*

cloud (n.) ደመና *dämmäna*; ዳመና *dammäna*

cloudy ደመናማ *dämmänamma*

clove ቅርንፉድ *qərənfud*

clown ተራብ *tärrab*; አሥቂኝ ፡ ተዋናይ *assəqiñ täwanay*

club, n. (stick) በትር *bättər*; ዱላ *dulla*; (group of people) ክበብ *kəbäb*

clue ፍንጭ *fənč*

clumsy ቅልጥፍና ፡ የጉደለው *qəlṭəfənna yägʷäddäläw*; ገልጃጃ *gälǧaǧǧa*

cluster (v.), ~ around ከበበ *käbbäbä*

clutch (v.) ጨበጠ *čäbbäṭä*

clutter (v.) ቅጥ ፡ አሳጣ *qəṭṭ asaṭṭa*
be cluttered ተዝረከረከ *täzräkärräkä*

clutter (n.) ምስቅልቅል *məsqəlqəl*

coach (vehicle) ሰረገላ *särägälla*; (of a team) አሠልጣኝ *asälṭañ*

coagulate ረጋ *rägga*

coagulated milk እርጎ *ərgo*

coal ከሰል *käsäl*

coalition ኅብረት *həbrät*

coarse (∼ cloth) ሻካራ *šakkara;* ከርዳዳ *kärdadda;* (∼ behavior) ያልታረመ *yaltarrämä;* (∼ sand) ደቃቃ ፡ ያልሆነ *däqaqa yalhonä*

coast ጠረፍ *ṭäräf;* የባሕር ፡ ዳርቻ *yäbahər daräčča*

coastline ጠረፍ *ṭäräf*

coat, n. (garment) ካፖርት *kabbort;* ኮት *kot*

coax አባበለ *ababbälä;* ተለማመጠ *tälämammäṭä*

cobbler ጫማ ፡ ሰፊ *čamma säfi*

cobweb የሸረሪት ፡ ድር *yäšärärit dər*

cock አውራ ፡ ዶሮ *awra doro*

cockroach በረሮ *bäräro*

coddle አንከባከበ *ankäbakkäbä*

code (rule) ደንብ *dänb;* (for secret messages) የምስጢር ፡ ጽሑፍ *yäməsṭir ṣəhuf*

coerce አስገደደ *asgäddädä*

coffee ቡና *bunna*

coffee bean ቡና *bunna*

coffee grounds የቡና ፡ አተላ *yäbunna atäla*

coffee house ቡና ፡ ቤት *bunna bet*

coffee pot ጀበና *ǧäbäna*

coffin የሬሳ ፡ ሣጥን *yäresa saṭən;* ያስከ ሬን ፡ ሣጥን *yaskären saṭən*

cognate የሚዛመድ *yämmizzammäd*

coherence ቅንብር *qənəbbər*

coherent (logical) የተጣራ *yätäṭarra;* የተ ሳካ *yätäsakka*

cohesive የሚጣበቅ *yämmiṭṭabbäq*

coil (vt.) ጠመጠመ *ṭämäṭṭämä;* ጠቀለለ *ṭäqällälä*
coil, vi. (of snake) ተጥመለመለ *täṭmälämmälä*

coin, v. (mint) አተመ *attämä;* (∼ words) ፈጠረ *fäṭṭärä*

coin (n.) ቤሳ *besa;* ፍራንክ *frank*

coincide (occur at the same time) ተጋ ጠመ *tägaṭṭämä;* (agree) ተስማማ *täsmamma*

coincidence አጋጣሚ *aggaṭami*

cold (n.) ቅዝቃዜ *qəzəqqaze;* ብርድ *bərd;* (illness) ጉንፋን *gunfan*
catch a cold ጉንፋን ፡ ያዘው *gunfan yazä(w)*

cold, adj. (∼ drink) ቅዝቃዛ *qäzqazza;* ባርድ *bärrad;* (∼ wind) ብርዳም *bərdam*
cold weather ብርድ *bärd*
be cold ቀዘቀዘ *qäzäqqäzä;* በረደ *bärrädä*
feel cold ቀዘቀዘው *qäzäqqäzä(w);* በረደው *bärrädä(w)*

colic (የ)ሆድ ፡ ቁርጠት *(yä)hod qurṭät;* ያንጀት ፡ ሕመም *yanǧät həmäm*

collaborate አበረ *abbärä;* ተረዳዳ *tärädadda;* (with the enemy) ተባበረ *täbabbärä*

collaborator ግብረ ፡ አበር *gəbrä abbär*

collapse (v.) ተናደ *tänadä;* ፈረሰ *färräsä;* ተደረመሰ *tädärämmäsä;* (of plan) ተጨ ናገፈ *täčänaggäfä*

collapse (n.) ውድቀት *wədqät*

collar ኮሌታ *kolletta*

colleague የሥራ ፡ ጓደኛ *yäsəra gʷaddäñña*

collect (vt.) ሰበሰበ *säbässäbä;* አከማቸ *akkämaččä*

collection ስብስብ *səbsəb*

collective የጋራ *yägara;* የጋሮሽ *yägarəyyoš*

collective security የጋራ ፡ ጸጥታ *yägara ṣäṭṭəta*

college ኮሌጅ *kolleǧ*

collide (of cars) ተጋጨ *tägaččä;* (of ideas) ተለያየ *täläyayyä*

collision ግጭት *gəččət*

colon (punctuation mark) ድርብ ፡ ሰረዝ *dərrəb säräz;* (large intestine) ትልቅ ፡ አንጀት *təlləq anǧät* colonel ኮሎኔል *kolonel*

colonialism ቅኝ ፡ አገዛዝ *qəňň aggäzaz*

colonize (found a colony) አቀና *aqänna;* ቅኝ ፡ ግዛት ፡ አደረገ *qəňň gəzat adärrägä;* (settle) አሰፈረ *asäffärä*

colony ቅኝ ፡ አገር *qəňň agär;* ቅኝ ፡ ግዛት *qəňň gəzat*

color (v.) ከለር ፡ ቀባ *kälär qäbba*

color (n.) ቀለም *qäläm*

colored (having color) ባለ ፡ ቀለም *balä qäläm*
colored people ነጭ ፡ ያልሆኑ *näčč yalhonu*

colossal በጣም ፡ ትልቅ *bäṭam təlləq*

colt የፈረስ ፡ ውርንጭላ *yäfäräs wərənčəlla*

column ዓምድ *amd;* (of figures) ረድፍ *räd(ə)f*

comb (v.) አበጠረ *abäṭṭärä*

comb (n.) ማበጠሪያ *mabäṭṭäriya;* ሚዶ *mido*

combat (fight) ተዋጋ *täwagga;* (~ a disease) ተከላከለ *täkälakkälä;* (oppose) ተቋቋመ *täqʷaqʷamä*

combat (n.) ውጊያ *wəggiya*

combination ኅብር *həb(ə)r;* ማጣመር *maṭṭamär*

combine አጣመረ *aṭṭammärä;* አቀናበረ *aqqänabbärä;* ቀላቀለ *qälaqqälä;* (~ efforts) አስተባበረ *astäbabbärä*

combustible ነዳጅ *nädaǧ*

come መጣ *mäṭṭa;* (of turn) ደረሰ *därräsä;* (of holiday) ዋለ *walä*
come! ና *na;* fem. ነይ *näy;* pl. ኑ *nu*
come across አገኘ *agäňňä;* አጋጠመ(ው) *aggaṭṭämä(w)*
come apart ተለያየ *täläyayyä*
come back ተመለሰ *tämälläsä*
come down ወረደ *wärrädä*
come in ገባ *gäbba*
come out ወጣ *wäṭṭa*
come to (recover consciousness) ራሱን ፡ (ነፍሱን) ፡ ዐወቀ *rasun (näfsun) aw-*

wäqä; ነፍስ ፡ ዘራ *näfs zärra*

comedy ኮሜዲ *komedi*

comely (~ woman) የደስ ፡ ደስ ፡ ያላት *yädäss däss yalat*

comet ጅራታም ፡ ኮከብ *ǧəratam kokäb*

comfort (v.) አጽናና *aṣnanna*

comfort, n. (physical ease) ምቾት *məččot;* (solace) ማጽናኛ *maṣnaňňa*

comfortable ምቹ *məčču*
be comfortable ተመቸ *tämäččä*
feel comfortable ተዝናና *täznanna*

comical አስቂኝ *assəqiň*

comma ነዓስ ፡ ሰረዝ *nə'us säräz*

command, v. (order) አዘዘ *azzäzä*

command (n.) ትእዛዝ *tə'əzaz*

commander አዛዥ *azzaž;* አዝማች *azmač*

commander-in-chief ዋና ፡ አዛዥ *wanna azzaž*

commandment ትእዛዝ *tə'əzaz*
the Ten Commandments በሥርት ፡ ቃላት ፡ አሪት *ässärtä qalatä orit*

commemorate አከበረ *akäbbärä;* (~ a saint's day) ዘከረ *zäkkärä*

commemoration መታሰቢያ *mättasäbiya;* (of a saint) ዝክር *zəkər*

commence ወጠነ *wäṭṭänä;* ጀመረ *ǧämmärä*

commencement (graduation exercises) የምረቃ ፡ በዓል *yämərräqa bä'al*

commend አመሰገነ *amäsäggänä*

comment (v.) ተቸ *täččä;* አተተ *attätä*

comment (n.) ትችት *təččət*

commentary ሐተታ *hatäta*

commentator ሐተታ ፡ ሰጭ *hatäta säč;* ተቺ *täčči*

commerce ንግድ *nəgd*

commercial የንግድ *yänəgd*

commiserate ሐዘን ፡ ገለጸ(ለት) *hazän gälläṣä(llät)*

commission, v. (give authority) ወከለ *wäkkälä*

commission 300 complement

commission, n. (performing) መፈጸም
mäfäṣṣäm; (percentage of selling
price) ኮሚስዮን *komisyon;* (group
of persons) ኮሚስዮን *komisyon*
be in commission በሥራ ፡ ላይ ፡ ዋለ
bäsəra lay walä
be out of commission ከሥራ ፡ ውጭ ፡
ሆነ *käsəra wəčč honä*

commit ፈጸመ *fäṣṣämä*
commit oneself ቃል ፡ ገባ *qal gäbba*

committee ኮሚቴ *komite;* ደርግ *därg*

common (familiar) የተለመደ *yätälämmädä;* (shared by many people) የጋራ
yägara; (vulgar) ጥሬ *ṭəre*
in common በጋራ *bägara*

commonly ብዙውን ፡ ጊዜ *bəzuwən gize*

commotion ሽብር *šəbbər;* ሁከት *hukata;*
ነውጥ *näwṭ;* ግርግርታ *gərgərta*

communal የኅብረት *yähəbrät*

communicable (∼ disease) ተላላፊ *tälalafi*

communicate, vt. (transmit) አስተላለፈ
astälalläfä
communicate (vi.) ተገናኘ *tägänaňňä*

communication (the coming together)
መገናኘ *mäggänaňa;* (message) መልእ
ክት *mäl'əkt;* (statement) ንግግር *nəgəggər*

communion (sacrament) ቁርባን *qurban*
receive communion ቄረበ *q^wärräbä*

community (place) መንደር *mändär;*
(group of people) ሕዝብ *həzb*

commute ተመላለሰ *tämälalläsä*

compact (∼ bag) የጠቀጠቀ *yäṭäqäṭṭäqä;*
ጥብቅ ፡ ያለ *ṭəbbəqq yalä;* (∼ report)
እጥር ፡ ምጥን ፡ ያለ *əṭṭər məṭṭən yalä*

companion ጓደኛ *g^waddäňňa;* ባልንጀራ
baländära

companionship ጓደኝነት *g^waddäňňannät*

company ጓድ *g^wadd;* (guests) እንግዶች
əngədočč; (military unit) ሻምበል
šambäl; (business firm) ኩባንያ *kubbanəyya*

keep company ጓደኛ ፡ አበጀ *g^waddäň-
ňa abäǧǧä;* አብሮት ፡ ቆየ *abrot qoyyä*
part company ተለያየ *täläyayyä*

comparable ተመሳሳይ *tämäsasay;* ተነጻ
ጻሪ *tänäṣaṣari*
be comparable ተመጣጠነ *tämäṭaṭṭänä*

compare አመሳሰለ *ammäsassälä;* አመዛ
ዘነ *ammäzazzänä;* አነጻጸረ *annäṣaṣṣärä*

comparison ንጽጽር *nəṣaṣṣər*

compartment ክፍል *kəfəl*

compass ኮምፓስ *kompas;* (boundary)
ክልል *kəlləl*

compassion ከፍ ፡ ያለ ፡ ርኅራኄ *käff yalä
rəhrahe;* ሐዘን *hazän;* ምሕረት *məhrät*
have compassion ማረ *marä*

compassionate ርኅሩኅ *rəhruh*
be compassionate ራራ *rarra*

compatible ተስማሚ *täsmami*

compatriot ያገር ፡ ልጅ *yagär ləǧ*

compel አገበረ *agäbbärä;* አስገደደ *asgäddädä*

compensate ካሰ *kasä*

compensation ካሳ *kasa*

compete ተወዳደረ *täwädaddärä;* ተፎካ
ከረ *täfokakkärä*

competence ብቁነት *bəqunnät*

competent ብቁ *bəqu;* ችሎታ ፡ ያለው *čəlota yalläw*

competition ውድድር *wədəddər;* ፉክክር
fəkəkkər

competitor ተወዳዳሪ *täwädadari*

compile አዘጋጀ *azzägaǧǧä*

complain ተናጫነጨ *tänäčannäčä;* አማረረ
ammarrärä; (appeal, petition) አቤት ፡
አለ *abet alä;* አቤቱታ ፡ አቀረበ *abetuta aqärräbä*

complaint (formal charge) ክስ *kəss;* (appeal) አቤቱታ *abetuta;* (dissatisfac-
tion) ቅሬታ *qərreta*

complement (v.) አሟላ *amm^walla*

complement (n.) ማሟያ *mamm^waya*

complete, v. (finish) ጨረሰ *čärräsä;*
ፈጸመ *fässämä;* (make whole) አሞላ
amolla; አሟላ *ammʷalla*

complete (adj.) ሙሉ *mulu;* የተሟላ *yätämʷalla;* ፍጹም *fəssum*
be complete ተፈጸመ *täfässämä;* ተሟላ
tämʷalla

completely ሙሉ ፡ በሙሉ *mulu bämulu;*
ከቶ *kätto;* ጨርሶ *čärrəso;* ጥራሽ *čərraš;* ፈጽሞ *fässəmo*

completion ፍጻሜ *fəssame*

complex (adj.) የተወሳሰበ *yätäwäsassäbä*

complexion መልክ *mälk;* የፊት ፡ ቆዳ *yäfit qoda*

complexity ውስብስብነት *wəsəbsəbənnät*

complicate አማታ *ammatta;* የተወሳሰበ ፡
አደረገ *yätäwäsassäbä adärrägä*

complicated የተረቀቀ *yätäräqqäqä;* የተወ
ሳሰበ *yätäwäsassäbä;* ውስብስብ *wəsəbsəb*

complication ጣጣ *tata;* የተወሳሰበ ፡ ነገር
yätäwäsassäbä nägär

complicity ግብረ ፡ አበርነት *gəbrä abbärənnät*

compliment (v.) አመሰገነ *amäsäggänä*

compliment (n.) ምርቃት *mərrəqat;* ምስ
ጋና *məsgana*
compliments ሰላምታ *sälamta*
pay a compliment አሞገሰ *amoggäsä*

complimentary (∼ remark) የሚያሞግስ
yämmiyamoggəs; (∼ ticket) ነጻ *näsa*

comply እሺ ፡ አለ *əšši alä*

compose (∼ poetry, symphony) ደረሰ
därräsä; (∼ a speech) አጠናቀረ *attä-
naqqärä*

composer የሙዚቃ ፡ ደራሲ *yämuziqa därasi*

composition ድርሰት *dərsät*

composure እርጋታ *ərgata*

compound (n.) አጥር ፡ ግቢ *atər gəbbi;*
ምድረ ፡ ግቢ *mədrä gəbbi;* ቅጥር *qətər*

comprehend (understand) ገባ(ው) *gäb-
ba(w);* (include) ያዘ *yazä*

comprehension ዐውቀት *əwqät*

comprehensive አጠቃላይ *attäqalay*

compress (v.) አመቀ *ammäqä*

comprise ያዘ *yazä*

compromise (v.) ግልግል ፡ አደረገ *gələggəl adärrägä;* ከስምምነት ፡ ደረሰ *käsə-
məmmənnät därräsä*

compromise (n.) ከነ ፡ ይቅር ፡ ከነ ፡ ይቅር ፡
የሚል ፡ ስምምነት *käne yəqər käne yəqər yämmil səməmmənnät*

compulsion ግድ *gədd;* ግዳጅ *gəddağ*

compulsory የግዴታ *yägəddeta*

computation አቄጣጠር *aqqʷätatär*

comrade ጓደኛ *gʷaddäňňa;* ባልንጀራ *ba-
lənğära*

concave ጉድጓዳ *gʷädgʷadda*

conceal ሰወረ *säwwärä;* ሸመቀ *šämmäqä;*
ሸሸገ *šaššägä;* ደበቀ *däbbäqä*

concede (admit) አመነ *ammänä*

conceit ትዕቢት *tə'əbit;* እብሪት *əbrit*

conceited ትዕቢተኛ *tə'əbitäňňa;* እብሪ
ተኛ *əbritäňňa*

conceive አሰበ *assäbä;* ተረዳ(ው) *täräd-
da(w);* (∼ a plan) አመነጨ *amänäččä*
conceive a child ጸነሰ(ች) *sännäsä(čč)*

concentrate (bring together) ሰበሰበ *säbässäbä;* አከማቸ *akkämaččä;* (∼ attention) በሙሉ ፡ አዋለ *bämulu awalä*

concentration (being brought together)
መከማቸት *mäkkämaččät;* (fixed attention) ማስተዋል *mastäwal*

concept ሐሳብ *hassab*

conception (of a plan) ማመንጨት *ma-
mänčät;* (pregnancy) መጸነስ *mäsänäs*

concern, v. (regard, be of interest) ተመ
ለከተ *tämäläkkätä;* (trouble) አሳሰበ
asassäbä
concern oneself (be interested in) ሐሳ
ቡን ፡ አዋለ *hassabun awalä*

concern, n. (objective) ዓላማ *alama;*
(worry) ሐሳብ *hassab;* ጭንቀት *čənqät;*
(business firm) ድርጅት *dərəğğət*

concerned, be አሰበ assäbä

concerning ስለ səlä; ነክ ፡ የሆነ näkk yähonä

concert የሙዚቃ ፡ ትርኢት yämuziqa tər-'it

in concert (together) በኅብረት bähəbrät

concerted የተባበረ yätäbabbärä

concession (right granted) ፈቃድ fäqad; (yielding) ከኔ ፡ ይቅር ፡ ከኔ ፡ ይቅር ፡ ማለት käne yəqər käne yəqər malät; (admitting) ማመን mamän

conciliate, see 'reconcile'

conciliation ዕርቅ ərq; ስምምነት səməmmənnät

concise አጥር ፡ ምጥን ፡ ያለ əṭṭər məṭṭən yalä

conclude (finish) ጨረሰ čärräsä; ደመደመ dämäddämä; (arrive at an opinion) ተረዳ(ው) tärädda(w)

conclusion (end) መጨረሻ mäčärräša; መደምደሚያ mädämdämiya; (decision) ውሳኔ wəssane

draw a conclusion ተገነዘበ tägänäzzäbä

in conclusion በመጨረሻ bämäčärräša

concord ስምምነት səmämmənnät

concordance, in ~ with በ - - - መሠረት bä - - -mäsärät

concrete (n.) ሲሚንቶ siminto

concrete (adj.) የተጨበጠ yätäčäbbäṭä

concubine ዕቁባት əqqubat

concur (agree) ተስማማ täsmamma; (coincide) ተጋጠመ tägaṭṭämä

concurrently ባንድ ፡ ጊዜ band gize

condemn (declare guilty) ፈረደ(በት) färrädä(bbät); (censure) ነቀፈ näqqäfä; አወገዘ awäggäzä

condense አሳጠረ asaṭṭärä

condense to water አጠዘ aṭezä

condition, n. (state) ሁኔታ huneta; አኳኋን akkʷahʷan; (stipulation) ግዴታ gəddeta

on any condition ምንም ፡ ቢሆን mənəm bihon

conditioned, be ተመሠረተ tämäsärrätä

condole አጽናና aṣnanna

condolence የሐዘን ፡ መግለጫ yähazän mägläča

condone ፈቀደ fäqqädä; ችላ ፡ ብሎ ፡ አለፈ čəlla bəlo alläfä

conduce በጀ bäǧǧä

conduct, v. (~ business) አካሄደ akkahedä; (~ electricity) ኤሌክትሪክ ፡ አስተላለፈ elektrik astälalläfä; (~ a symphony) መራ märra

conduct, n. (behavior) አመል amäl; ጠባይ ṭäbay; (action) ምግባር mägbar

conductor (of bus) ቲኬት ፡ ቄራጭ tiket qʷärač; (of orchestra) መሪ märi

confer, vt. (give) ሰጠ säṭṭä

confer, vi. (deliberate) ተማከረ tämakkärä; ተመካከረ tämäkakkärä

conference ስብሰባ səbsäba; ጉባኤ guba'e; (consultation) ምክክር məkəkkər

confess (admit) አመነ ammänä; (~ to a priest) ተናዘዘ tänazzäzä

confession (to a priest) ንስሐ nəssəha; (in court) የእምነት ፡ ቃል yäəmnät qal

go to confession ንስሐ ፡ ገባ nəssəha gäbba

hear confession ናዘዘ nazzäzä

make a confession ተናዘዘ tänazzäzä

confessor የንስሐ ፡ አባት yänəssəha abbat; የነፍስ ፡ አባት yänäfs abbat

confidant ምስጢረኛ məsṭiränña

confide (~ secrets) አካፈለ akkaffälä

confidence (trust) እምነት əmnät; (assurance) ሙሉ ፡ ልብ mulu ləbb; (secret) ምስጢር məsṭir

have confidence አመነ ammänä; ተማመነ tämammänä

confident, adj. (sure) እርግጠኛ ərgəṭäñña

be confident (believe) ተማመነ tämammänä

confidential (~ secretary) ልዩ *ləyyu;* (~ report) ምስጢራዊ *məsṭirawi*

confidentially በምስጢር *bäməsṭir*

confine, v. (limit) ወሰነ *wässänä;* (restrain) አገደ *aggädä;* (keep indoors) አዋለ *awalä;* (imprison) አሰረ *assärä*

confinement (imprisonment) እስራት *əssərat*

confines ክልል *kəlləl*

confirm (approve formally) አጸደቀ *aṣäddäqä*

confirmation (making sure) ማረጋገጫ *marrägagäča;* (rite in the church) የክርስትና ፡ መቀበል ፡ በዓል *yäkrəstənna mäqqäbäl bäal*

confiscate ወረሰ *wärräsä*

conflict (v.) ተቃረነ *täqarränä;* ተጋጨ *tägaččä*

conflict, n. (struggle) ትግል *təgəl;* (battle) ውጊያ *wəggiya;* ጋጭት *gäččət;* (disagreement) ልዩነት *ləyyunnät;* አለመስማማት *alämäsmamat;* አለመግባባት *alämägbabat*

conflicting ተቃራኒ *täqarani*

conform (vi.) ተስማማ *täsmamma*

conformity (agreement) መስማማት *mäsmamat*
in conformity with በ - - - - መሠረት *bä - - - mäsärät*

confound (confuse) አማታ *ammatta;* አደ ባለቀ *addäballäqä*

confront (~ the enemy) ተጋጠመ *tägaṭṭämä*

confuse (of talk) አደናገረ *addänaggärä;* (mix up) አመሳቀለ *ammäsaqqälä;* አማታ *ammatta;* ደባለቀ *däballäqä*

confused ድብልቅ *dəbəlləq*
be confused ግራ ፡ ገባ(ው) *gra gäbba(w)*

confusion ቀውስ *qäws;* ብጥብጥ *bəṭəbbəṭ;* ትርምስ *tərəmməs;* ትርምስምስ *tərməsməs*

congenial (~ roommate) መሳል *mässäl;* (~ host) ተወዳጅ *täwäddağ*

congest (of traffic) አገደ *aggädä;* አጨናነቀ *aččänannäqä*

congestion of the lungs የሳንባ ፡ መታፈን *yäsanba mättafän*

conglomeration ትርቅሚ *tərəqqami*

congratulate እንኳን ፡ ደስ ፡ ያለህ ፡ አለ *ənkʷan däss yaläh alä;* የምስራች ፡ አለ *yäməssərač alä*

congratulations! እንኳን ፡ ደስ ፡ ያለህ *ənkʷan däss yaläh* (masc. sg.)

congregate (vi.) ተሰበሰበ *täsäbässäbä*

congregation (community of men and women) ማኅበር *mahbär;* (gathering of people) ጉባኤ *guba'e*

Congress ምክር ፡ ቤት *məkər bet* congress ስብሰባ *səbsäba;* ጉባኤ *guba'e*

congruent, be ተስማማ *täsmamma*

conjecture (v.) በግምት ፡ ተናገረ *bägəmmət tänaggärä*

conjecture (n.) ማላ ፡ ምት *mala mət;* ይሆ ናል *yəhonal*

conjugate አረባ *aräbba*

conjugation አረባብ *arräbab*

conjunction መጣመር *mäṭṭamär;* (in grammar) መስተፃምር *mästäṣamər*

conjunctivitis ያይን ፡ ማገት ፡ ሕመም *yayn mažät həmäm*

conjure (of a magician) በመታት ፡ አወጣ *bämätät awäṭṭa;* ጕተተ *gʷättätä;* (entreat) ለመነ *lämmänä*

connect (vt.) አያያዘ *ayyayazä;* አገናኘ *aggänaňňä;* (~ a telephone) ቀጠለ *qäṭṭälä*
connect (vi.) ተገናኘ *tägänaňňä*

connection ግንኙነት *gənəňňunnät*
get a connection ተገናኘ *tägänaňňä*
in what connection? በምን ፡ መነሻ *bämən männäša*

conquer አሸነፈ *aššännäfä;* ገዛ *gäzza*

conqueror ድል ፡ አድራጊ. dəl adragi; አሸ
ናፊ aššännafi

conquest (victory) ድል ፡ ማድረግ dəl madräg; (occupancy) መያዝ mäyaz

conscience ኅሊና həllina

conscientious (~ person) ትጉ təgu;
ትጉህ təguh; (~ work) በጥንቃቄ ፡
የተሠራ bäṭənəqqaqe yätäsärra

conscious, be ራሱን ፡ ወቀ rasun awwäqä

consciously ሆን ፡ ብሎ hon bəlo

consciousness ልቡና ləbbuna; ልቦና ləbbona
lose consciousness ሕይወቱን ፡ ሳተ
həywätun satä; ነፍሱን ፡ ሳተ näfsun
satä; ራሱን ፡ ሳተ rasun satä
recover consciousness ራሱን ፡ ወቀ
rasun awwäqä; ነፍሱ ፡ ተመለሰ näfsu
tämälläsä; ነፍስ ፡ ዘራ näfs zärra

conscript ምልምል məlməl

conscription በገዲታ ፡ መመልመል bägəd-
deta mämälmäl

consecrate በስለት ፡ ሰጠ bäsəlät säṭṭä

consecration የምረቃ ፡ ሥነ ፡ ሥርዓት yämərräqa sənä sər'at

consecutive ተከታታይ täkätatay

consensus ስምምነት səmämmənnät

consent, v. (comply) ተስማማ täsmamma; እሺ ፡ አለ əšši alä; (permit) ፈቀደ
fäqqädä

consent, n. (compliance) ስምምነት səmämmənnät; እሽታ əššəta; (permission) ፈቃድ fäqad

consequence የሚያስከትል ፡ ውጤት yäm-
miyaskättəl wəṭṭet
in consequence of በ - - - ምክንያት
bä - - - məknəyat

consequent ያስከተለ yaskättälä

conservation ጥበቃ ṭəbbäqa

conserve (v.) ጠበቀ ṭäbbäqä

consider (regard as) ቆጠረ qʷäṭṭärä; አየ
ayyä; (bear in mind) ተመለከተ tämäläkkätä; አሰበ assäbä

considerable በዛ ፡ ያለ bäza yalä; ብዙ bəzu; (~ distance, skill) ከፍተኛ käffətäňňa

considerably በጣም bäṭam

considerate ለሰው ፡ አሳቢ läsäw assabi
be considerate አሰበ assäbä

consideration (careful thought) ማሰብ
massäb; (thoughtfulness) አሳቢነት
assabinnät
give (take into) consideration ተመለ
ከተ tämäläkkätä; አሰበ assäbä
in consideration of ስለ sälä
not have consideration ግድ ፡ የለውም
gədd yälläwəm

consign (send) ላከ lakä; (set apart) መደበ
mäddäbä; (~ to a guardian) አደራ ፡
ሰጠ adära säṭṭä

consistent ሐሳብ ፡ ጽኑ hassabä ṣənu
be consistent with ተስማማ täsmamma

consolation ማጽናኛ maṣnaňňa

console አጽናና aṣnanna

consolidate (~ a position) አጠነከረ aṭänäkkärä

consonant (n.) ተናባቢ tänababi

consonant, be ~ with ተስማማ täsmamma

conspicuous ጉላ ፡ ያለ gʷäla yalä; ጉልህ
guləh

conspiracy ሴራ sera; አድማ adma; ዱለት
dulät

conspirator አድማኛ admäňňa; ሴረኛ seräňňa

conspire አሰረ aserä; አደመ addämä;
ዶለተ dollätä

constancy ቅንነት qənənnät

constant (ceaseless) የማይቋረጥ yämmayəqqʷarräṭ; (~ friend) ታማኝ tammaň

constantly ሳይቋረጥ sayəqqʷarräṭ; ዘወ
ትር zäwätər; በየጊዜው bäyyägizew

constellation ኅብረ ፡ ኮከብ həbrä kokäb

consternation ድንጋጤ dənəggaṭe
be in consternation ተጨነቀ täčännäqä

constipate ሆድ ፡ አደረቀ *hod adärräqä*

constipation (የ)ሆድ ፡ ድርቀት (*yä*)*hod dərqät*

constitute (appoint) ሾመ *šomä;* (make up) ሆነ *honä*

constitution (law) ሕገ ፡ መንግሥት *həggä mängəst*

constrain (force) አስገደደ *asgäddädä;* (restrain) ገታ *gätta*

constraint ገዶታ *gəddeta*
show constraint አደበ *addäbä*

construct ሠራ *särra*

construction (of building) ሥራ *səra;* (way of building) አሠራር *assärar*

constructive ጠቃሚ *ṭäqami*

construe (interpret) ተረጐመ *täräggʷämä;* (guess) ገመተ *gämmätä*

consul ቆንሲል *qonsil*

consulate ቆንስላ *qonsəla*

consult (with someone) አማከረ *ammakkärä;* (~ one another) ተማከረ *tämakkärä;* ተመካከረ *tämäkakkärä;* (~ a dictionary) ተመለከተ *tämäläkkätä*

consultant አማካሪ *ammakari*

consultation ምክክር *məkəkkər;* ምክር *məkər*

consume (eat) በላ *bälla;* (~ time) አጠፋ *aṭäffa;* ፈጀ *fäǧǧä*

contact (vt.) ግንኙነት ፡ አደረገ *gənəňňunnät adärrägä*

contact (n.) ግንኙነት *gənəňňunnät*
be in contact ተገናኘ *tägänaňňä;* ተጋ ጠመ *tägaṭṭämä*
come into contact, see 'contact' (v.)

contagion ተላላፊ ፡ በሽታ *tälalafi bäššəta*

contagious ተላላፊ *tälalafi*
be contagious ተጋባ *tägabba;* ተላለፈ *tälalläfä*

contain (include) ያዘ *yazä;* አዘለ *azzälä;* (restrain) ገታ *gätta*

container መክተቻ *mäktäča;* ማስቀመጫ *masqämmäča;* መያዣ *mäyaža*

contaminate (~ food) መረዘ *märräzä;* (~ a well) በከለ *bäkkälä;* (desecrate) አረከሰ *aräkkäsä*

contemplate አሰላሰለ *assälassälä;* አሰበ *assäbä*

contemporary (n.) ባንድ ፡ ዘመን ፡ የኖረ *band zämän yänorä*

contemporary, adj. (of the same time) የጊዜ *yägize;* (modern) ዘመን ፡ አመ ጣሽ *zämän amäṭṭaš;* ዘመናዊ *zämänawi*

contempt ንቀት *nəqät*
show contempt ናቀ *naqä;* አቋሸሸ *aqʷaššäšä*

contend (compete) ተወዳደረ *täwädaddärä*

contender ተቀቃኝ *täqänaqaň*

content, be ተደሰተ *tädässätä;* ደስ ፡ አለ(ው) *däss alä(w)*

content, n. (what is contained) ይዞታ *yəzota;* (subject matter) ፍሬ ፡ ነገር *fəre nägär*
contents, table of ~የመጽሐፍ ፡ መውጫ *yämäṣhaf mäwča*

contented በቃኝ ፡ ባይ *bäqqaňň bay*

contention (disputing) ጠብ *ṭäb;* (idea) አስተያየት *astäyayät*

contest, v. (argue against) ተከራከረ *täkärakkärä*

contest (n.) ውድድር *wədəddər;* ግጥሚያ *gəṭmiya*

contestant ተወዳዳሪ *täwädadari*

context የቃል ፡ አገባብ *yäqal aggäbab*

contiguous, be ተጣጋጋ *täṭägagga*

continent አህጉር *ahəgur*

contingent (adj.) ድንገተኛ *dəngätäňňa*
be contingent on ተመሠረተ *tämäsärrätä*

continual የማያቋርጥ *yämmayaqqʷarrəṭ*

continually ወትሮ *wätro;* ያለ ፡ ማቋረጥ *yalä maqqʷaräṭ*

continue ቀጠለ *qäṭṭälä*

continuous, see 'continual'

continuously, see 'continually'

contraband የኮንትሮባንድ ፡ እቃ yäkontroband əqa; ያልተቀረጠበት ፡ እቃ yaltäqärräṭäbbät əqa

contract, vt. (make shrink) አኰማተረ akʷämattärä; (~ a disease) ያዘ(ው) yazä(w)
contract, vi. (shrink) ተኰማተረ täkʷämattörä; (make a contract) ተከ ናተረ täkonattärä

contract (n.) ውል wəl; ኮንትራት kontrat

contractor ሥራ ፡ ተቋራጭ səra täqʷarač

contradict ተቃወመ täqawwämä; (conflict) ተቃረነ täqarränä

contradiction ተቃራኒነት täqaraninnät

contradictory የሚያፋር yämmiṣṣarrär

contrary (~ term) ተቃራኒ täqarani; (~ child) ግርምቢጥ gərəmbiṭ

contrast (vt.) አነጻጸረ annäṣaṣṣärä
contrast (vi.) ተለያየ täläyayyä; ተነ ጻጸረ tänäṣaṣṣärä

contrast (n.) ልዩነት ləyyunnät
in contrast to ከ - - - አንጻር kä - - - anṣar

contribute (~ money) አዋጣ awwaṭṭa

contribution (in money) መዋጮ mäwwaᵤčo; ስጦታ säṭota

control (v.) ተቈጣጠረ täqʷäṭaṭṭärä
control oneself ራሱን ፡ ጋታ rasun gätta

control (n.) ቁጥጥር quṭəṭṭər
keep under control ተቈጣጠረ täqʷäṭaṭṭärä

controller ተቈጣጣሪ täqʷäṭaṭari

controversial አከራካሪ akkärakari

controversy ክርክር kərəkkər; (legal ~) ሙግት muggət

convalesce አገገመ agäggämä

convalescence ገገምታ gägämta

convalescent ገማምተኛ gämämtäňňa; ገገ ምተኛ gägämtäňňa

convene, vi. (gather) ተሰበሰበ täsäbässäbä

convenience ምቾት məččot

convenient ምቹ məčču
be convenient ተመቸ tämäččä; አመቸ amäččä; ተገባ tägäbba

convent የሴቶች ፡ ገዳም yäsetočč gädam

convention (meeting) ስብሰባ səbsäba; (agreement) ስምምነት səməmmənnät; (custom approved) ልማድ ləmad; ባህል bahəl

conventional (of a thing) የተለመደ yätälämmädä; (of a person) ልማድ ፡ አክ ባሪ ləmad akbari

converge (of roads) ተገናኘ tägänaňňä; ተጋጠመ tägaṭṭämä

conversation ጭውውት čəwəwwət; ወሬ wäre
carry on a conversation, see 'converse'

converse (v.) ተወያየ täwäyayyä; ተጫወተ täčawwätä; ተነጋገረ tänägaggärä

convert (change) ለወጠ läwwäṭä; (~ to another religion) አሳመነ asammänä

convey (~ passengers) አጓጓዘ aggʷagʷazä; (~ greetings) አቀረበ aqärräbä

convict (v.) ፈረደ(በት) färrädä(bbät)

convict (n.) የተፈረደበት ፡ ወንጀለኛ yätäfärrädäbbät wänğäläňňa

conviction (belief) እምነት əmnät

convince አረጋገጠ arrägaggäṭä; አሳመነ asammänä; አስረዳ asrädda

convinced, be ተረዳ(ው) tärädda(w)

convocation ስብሰባ səbsäba

convulsed, be (with pain) ተንቀጠቀጠ tänqäṭäqqäṭä; ተንዘፈዘፈ tänzäfäzzäfä

cook (v.) አበሰለ abässälä; ምግብ ፡ ሠራ məgəb särra

cook (n.) ወጥቤት wäṭbet

cookie ብስኩት bəskut

cool (vt.) አቀዘቀዘ aqäzäqqäzä
cool down (off), vt. አበረደ abärrädä
cool down (off), vi. በረደ bärrädä

cool (adj.) ቀዝቃዛ *qäzqazza*
be cool በረደ *bärrädä;* ቀዘቀዘ *qäzäqqäzä*

cooperate ተባበረ *täbabbärä;* ተረዳዳ *tärädadda*

cooperation (help) እርዳታ *ərdata;* (working together) ትብብር *təbəbbər;* መረዳዳት *märrädadat*

cooperative (n.) የኅብረት ፡ ድርጅት *yähəbrät dərəǧǧət*

coordinate, v. (harmonize) አስተባበረ *astäbabbärä*

coordination ትብብር *təbəbbər*

copious በርከት ፡ ያለ *bärkätt yalä*

copper መዳብ *mädab;* ነሐስ *nähas*

copy, v. (make a copy) ገለበጠ *gäläbbäṭä;* ቀዳ *qädda;* (imitate) ቀዳ *qädda*

copy (n.) ቅጂ *qəǧǧi;* ግልባጭ *gələbbač*

cord ሲባጎ *sibago*

cordial የልብ *yäləbb;* ልባዊ *ləbbawi*

cordially ከልብ *käləbb;* በጋለ ፡ ስሜት *bägalä səmmet*

core (of fruit) ውስጥ *wəsṭ;* (of a subject) ፍሬ ፡ ነገር *fre nägär*

cork (n.) ቡሽ *buš*

corkscrew የጠርሙስ ፡ መክፈቻ *yäṭärmus mäkfäča*

corn በቆሎ *bäqqollo;* (on toe) መጅ *mäǧ*

corner (of room) ማእዘን *ma'əzän;* (of street) መታጠፊያ *mättaṭäfiya*

cornerstone የመሠረት ፡ ድንጋይ *yämäsärät dəngay;* (basis) መሠረት *mäsärät*

coronation የዘውድ ፡ በዓል *yäzäwd bäal*

corporal የሥር ፡ አለቃ *yassər aläqa*

corporation ማኅበር *mahbär;* ኩባንያ *kubbanəyya*

corps ጓድ *gwadd*

corpse ሬሳ *resa;* ብድን *bädən*

corpulent ሆዳም *hodam;* ወፍራም *wäfram*

correct, v. (~ mistakes) አረመ *arrämä;* (punish) ቀጣ *qäṭṭa*

correct (adj.) ልክ *ləkk;* ትክክለኛ *təkəkkäläñña;* ዕንበኛ *dänbäñña*

correction እርማት *ərrəmat*

correctly በቅጡ *bäqäṭṭu;* በትክክል *bätəkäkkäl;* በልክ *bäləkk*

correspond (be similar) ተመሳሰለ *tämäsassälä;* (exchange letters) ተጻጻፈ *täṣaṣafä*

correspondence (similarity) ተመሳሳይነት *tämäsasayənnät;* (exchange of letters) የደብዳቤ ፡ መጻጻፍ *yädäbdabbe mäṣṣaṣaf*

correspondent (for a newspaper) ቃል ፡ አቀባይ *qal aqäbbay;* ዜና ፡ አጠናቃሪ *zena aṭṭänaqari*

corridor መተላለፊያ *mättälaläfiya*

corroborate አረጋገጠ *arrägaggäṭä*

corrode ተበላ *täbälla;* ዛጋ *zagä*

corrugated iron ቆርቆሮ *qorqorro*

corrupt (v.) አበላሸ *abbälaššä*

corrupt, adj. (~ person) ምግባረ ፡ ብልሹ *məgbarä bäləššu;* (~ morals) ውድቅ *wədq*

corruption ብልሽት *bäläššət;* እምነትን ፡ ማጉደል *əmnätən magwdäl*

cosmetics መኳኳያ *mäkkwakwaya*

cost, v. (require the expenditure) አወጣ *awäṭṭa;* (cause the loss) ፈጀ *fäǧǧä*

cost (n.) ዋጋ *waga*
costs ወጪ *wäči*
at all costs በምንም ፡ ዓይነት *bämənəm aynät*

costly ውድ *wədd*

costume ልብስ *ləbs*

cot ሸራ ፡ አልጋ *šära alga*

cottage ጎጆ *goǧǧo*

cotton ጥጥ *ṭəṭ*

couch (n.) መከዳ *mäkkädda;* ሶፋ *sofa*

cough (v.) ሳለ *salä*

cough (n.) ሳል *sal*

council ምክር ፡ ቤት *məkər bet;* ሸንጎ *šängo*

counsel (v.) መከረ *mäkkärä*

counsel, n. (advice) ምክር *məkər;* (lawyer) ጠበቃ *ṭäbäqa*
take counsel ተመካከረ *tämäkakkärä;* ተማከረ *tämakkärä*

counselor (lawyer) አማካሪ *ammakari;* ጠበቃ *ṭäbäqa;* (in a camp) ተቄጣጣሪ *täqʷäṭaṭari*

count (v.) ቆጠረ *qʷäṭṭärä;* (be of value) ዋጋ ፡ አለው *waga alläw*
count on ተማመነ(በት) *tämammänä-(bbät);* እምነት ፡ ጣለ *əmnät ṭalä*

count (n.) ቆጠራ *qʷäṭära*

counter (n.) ቲኬት ፡ መሻጫ ፡ ቦታ *tiket mäšäča bota;* (in a bar) ባንኮ *banko*

counteract ተከላከለ *täkälakkälä*

counterattack አጸፋ ፡ መለሰ *aṣäfa mälläsä*

counterfeit (adj.) የውሸት *yäwəšät*

countless ቁጥር ፡ የሌለው *quṭər yälelläw*

country ሀገር *hagär;* አገር *agär;* (countryside) ባላገር *balagär*

countryman (who lives in the country) ባላገር *balagär;* (of one's own country) ያገር ፡ ሰው *yagär säw*

countryside ባላገር *balagär;* አገር ፡ ቤት *agär bet;* ገጠር *gäṭär*

coup አድማ *adma*

couple (n.) ጥምድ *ṭəmd;* (married ～) ባልና ፡ ሚስት *balənna mist*
a couple of አንድ ፡ ሁለት *and hulätt*

coupon ቲኬት *tiket*

courage ጀግንነት *ǧägnənnät;* ጉብዝና *gubzənna*
lose courage ሐሞቱ ፡ ፈሰሰ *hamotu fässäsä*
take courage! አይዞህ *ayzoh;* በርታ *bärta*

courageous ጀግና *ǧägna*

course (direction) አቅጣጫ *aqṭačča;* (way of proceeding) ዛዴ *zäde;* (class) ዓይነት ፡ ትምህርት *aynät təmhərt;* (～ of food) ዓይነት ፡ ምግብ *aynät məgəb*
as a matter of course እንደ ፡ ተለመ ደው *əndä tälämmädäw*
in due course በጊዜው *bägizew;* ጊዜ ፡ ሲደርስ *gize sidärs*
in the course of በ - - - ውስጥ *bä - - - wəsṭ*
of course መቸም *mäčäm;* መቼም *mäčem*
of course! እንዴታ *əndeta*

court, v. (seek to win in marriage) አሽ ኮረመመ *aškorämmämä*

court (～ of house) አጥር ፡ ግቢ *aṭər gäbbi;* (for games) ሜዳ *meda;* (～ of law) ፍርድ ፡ ቤት *färd bet;* (palace) ቤት ፡ መንግሥት *betä mängəst;* ግቢ *gäbbi;* (retinue of a king) ቤት ፡ መን ግሥት *betä mängəst*

courteous ትሑት *təhut*

courtesy ትሕትና *təhtənna*

courthouse ፍርድ ፡ ቤት *färd bet*

courtier ባለምዋል *balämʷal*

court-martial የወታደር ፡ ፍርድ ፡ ቤት *yäwättaddär färd bet*

courtroom ፍርድ ፡ ቤት *färd bet*

courtyard አጥር ፡ ግቢ *aṭər gäbbi*

cousin ያጐት ፡ ልጅ *yaggʷät ləǧ;* ያክስት ፡ ልጅ *yakəst ləǧ*

cover (v.) ከደነ *käddänä;* ሸፈነ *šäffänä;* (travel) ተጓዘ *tägʷazä;* ዘለቀ *zälläqä;* (～ a table) አለበሰ *aläbbäsä;* (～ a mistake) ሸፋፈነ *šäfaffänä*
cover oneself up ለበሰ *läbbäsä*
cover up ደበቀ *däbbäqä*

cover, n. (blanket) የሚደረብ ፡ ልብስ *yämmiddärräb ləbs;* (for pan, box) እፊያ *əffiya;* ከዳን *kädan;* መክደኛ *mäkdäñ-ña;* (for book) ሽፋን *šəfan;* (protection) ተገን *tägän*
take cover ተገን ፡ ያዘ *tägän yazä;* ተጠ ለለ *täṭällälä*

covet ተመኘ tämäňňä; ከፈለ käǧǧälä;
ጐመጀ gʷämäǧǧä

cow ላም lam

coward ቡክን bukkän; ፈሪ färi

cowardice ፈሪነት färinnät

cowherd እረኛ ərräňňa

crab ሸርጣን šärṭan

crack (vt.) ሰነጠቀ sänäṭṭäqä; (~ whip)
አጮኸ ačohä
crack, vi. (of wall) ነቃ näqqa; (of
glass) ተሰነጠቀ täsänäṭṭäqä; (of
whip) ጮኸ čohä

crack, n. (in a wall) ንቃቃት nəqaqat;
ንቅ nəq; (in a plate) ስንጥቅ sənṭəq

cracker (biscuit) ብስኩት bəskut

cradle የሕፃን ፡ አልጋ yähəṣan alga

craft (skill) ጥበብ ṭäbäb; (trade) ሙያ
muya; (slyness) ዘዴ zäde

craftsman ባለሙያ balämuya; ባለ ፡ እጅ
balä əǧǧ

craftsmanship ጥበበኛነት ṭäbäbäňňannät

crafty ብልጥ bəlṭ; ተንኮለኛ tänkʷäläňňa;
ጮሌ čolle

cram አጨቀ ačäqä; አመቀ ammäqä;
ሰከሰከ säkässäkä; (learn hurriedly)
ሸመደደ šämäddäda

cramp, have a~ ሸመቀቀ(ው) šämäqqä-
qä(w)

crank, n. (for motor) ማኑቬል manuvel

cranky ነጭናጫ näčnaččä

crash (vi.) ተሰበረ täsäbbärä; (collide)
ተጋጨ tägaččä; (fall down with great
noise) ተንኳታከተ tänkätakkätä

crash (n.) ግጭት gəččət

crate ሣጥን saṭən

crater (volcanic ~) የእሳት ፡ ገሞራ ፡ እናት
yäəsatä gämora anat; (bomb ~)
ቦምብ ፡ የቦደሰው ፡ መሬት bomb yäbod-
däsäw märet

crave ጐመጀ gʷämäǧǧä; ወደደ wäddädä

crawl, v. (of child) ዳኸ dahä; (of snake)
ተሳበ täsaba

crayon ከለር kälär

crazy እብድ əbd; (~ idea) የማይረባ
yämmayəräba
be crazy አበደ abbädä
drive crazy አሳበደ asabbädä

creak ሲጢጥ ፡ አለ siṭiṭ alä

cream (oily preparation) ቅባት qəbat;
(on milk) ስልባቦት səlbabot

crease (vi.) ተጨማደደ täčämaddädä

create ፈጠረ fäṭṭärä

creation ፍጥረት fəṭrät

creator ፈጣሪ fäṭari

creature ፍጡር fəṭur

credentials የሹመት ፡ ደብዳቤ yäšumät
däbdabbe

credible የሚታመን yämmittammän

credit, n. (time given for payment) ዱቤ
dube; (honor) ዝና zənna; ክብር kəbər
credit association ዕቁብ əqqub

creditor አበዳሪ abäddari; ባለ ፡ ዕዳ balä
əda

creed እምነት əmnät

creek ጅረት ǧərät

creep (of child) ዳኸ dahä; (of vine) ተሳበ
täsaba
creep through ሾለከ šolläkä

crest ጉትዬ guttəyye; (of mountain) ጫፍ
čaf

crevice ስንጥቅ sənṭəq; ንቅ nəq

crew ሠራተኞች särratäňňočč

crib የሕፃን ፡ አልጋ yähəṣan alga; (for
corn) ጐተራ gʷätära

cricket (insect) ፌንጣ fenṭa

crime ወንጀል wänǧäl

criminal ወንጀለኛ wänǧäläňňa
criminal offense የሚያስቀጣ ፡ ወንጀል
yämmiyasqʷäṭṭa wänǧäl

crinkle (vi.) ተጨማደደ täčämaddädä

cripple (v.) ሰነከለ sänäkkälä; አካለ ፡ ጉደሎ ፡ አደረገ akalä gʷädälo adärrägä; (damage) አሰናከለ assänakkälä

cripple (n.) አካለ ፡ ስንኩል akalä sənkul; አካለ ፡ ጉደሎ akalä gʷädälo

crippled, see 'cripple (n.)'

crisis ብጥብጥ bəṭəbbəṭ; አስጊ ፡ ሁኔታ asgi huneta; (financial ∼) ችግር čəggər

crisp ኩርሽም ፡ ያለ kuršəmm yalä

criterion መለኪያ mäläkkiya; መመዘኛ mämäzzäňňa

critic ተቺ täčči

critical (∼ situation) አስጊ asgi; አሳሳቢ asassabi

criticism (analysis) ትችት təččət; (disapproval) ነቀፋ näqäfa; ወቀሳ wäqäsa

criticize ነቀፈ näqqäfä; ገሠጸ gässäṣä; ወቀሰ wäqqäsä; ዘለፈ zälläfä

croak ጮኸ čohä

crocodile አዞ azzo

crook, n. (a bend) መጠምዘዣ mäṭämzäža; (dishonest) አጭበርባሪ ačbärbari

crooked (bent) ጠማማ ṭamama; (dishonest) አጭበርባሪ ačbärbari
be crooked (bent) ጠመመ ṭämmämä; ተጣመመ täṭammämä

crop (n.) ምርት mərt; መክር mäkär; መኸር mähär; ሰብል säbəl; አዝመራ azmära

cross, vt. (∼ a river) ተሻገረ täšaggärä; (∼ a street) አቋረጠ aqqʷarräṭä; (∼ arms) አጣመረ aṭṭammärä
cross oneself አማተበ amattäbä
cross out ሰረዘ särräzä

cross (n.) መስቀል mäsqäl; (result of mixing of breeds) ዲቃላ diqala

cross (adj.) ብስጩ bəsəčču
be cross ተበሳጨ täbäsaččä

crosscut አቋራጭ aqqʷarač

cross-examination መስቀለኛ ፡ ጥያቄ mäsqäläňňa ṭəyyaqe

cross-eyed ሸውራራ šäwrarra

crossing (n.) ማቋረጫ maqqʷaräča

crossroad መስቀለኛ ፡ መንገድ mäsqäläňňa mängäd

crosswalk ማቋረጫ ፡ ሰፍራ maqqʷaräča säfra

crouch አደፋጠ adäffäṭä

crow (v.) ጮኸ čohä

crow (n.) ቁራ qura

crowd, vt. (into a box) አመቀ ammäqä; (of people) ሞላ molla
crowd (vi.) በብዛት ፡ ተሰበሰበ bäbəzat täsäbässäbä

crowd (n.) ሕዝብ həzb; (the common people) ተራ ፡ ሕዝብ tära həzb

crowded ሕዝብ ፡ የበዛበት həzb yäbäzzabbät; የተጣበበ yätäṭabbäbä
be crowded ተጣበበ täṭabbäbä

crown (v.) ዘውድ ፡ ጫነ(ለት) zäwd čanä(llät)
be crowned ዘውድ ፡ ደፋ zäwd däffa

crown ዘውድ zäwd; አክሊል aklil; (of head) አናት anat

Crown Prince አልጋ ፡ ወራሽ alga wäraš

crucifixion ስቅለት səqlät

crucify ሰቀለ säqqälä

crude (∼ person) ባለጌ baläge; (∼ oil) ያልተጣራ yaltäṭarra

cruel (∼ person) ጨካኝ čäkkaň; (∼ war) አሰቃቂ assäqqaqi
be cruel ጨቆ čäqqʷänä; ጨከነ čäkkänä

cruelty ጭካኔ čəkkane

cruise (v.) ተዘዋወረ täzäwawwärä

cruise (n.) የመርከብ ፡ ሽርሽር yämärkäb sərrəsərr

crumb(s) ፍርፋሪ fərəffari

crumble, vt. (∼ bread) ፈረፈረ färäffärä
crumble, vi. (of wall) ተናደ tänadä

crumple (vt.) ጨባበጠ čäbabbäṭä

crunch (vt.) ቁረጣጠመ qʷäräṭaṭṭämä
crunch, vi. (of leaves) ተንኮሻኮሸ tänkʷäšakkʷäšä

crusade (v.) ታገለ *taggälä*

crusade (n.) ተጋድሎ *tägadlo*
Crusade የመስቀል ፡ ጦርነት *yämäsqäl ṭorənnät*

Crusader የመስቀል ፡ ጦርነት ፡ ወታደር *yämäsqäl ṭorənnät wättaddär*

crush (pulverize) ቀጠቀጠ *qäṭäqqäṭä;* አደቀቀ *adäqqäqä;* (~ a rebellion) ደመሰሰ *dämässäsä*

crust ቅርፊት *qərfit*

crutch ምርኩዝ *mərkuz*

crux ፍሬ ፡ ነገር *fre nägär;* ዋና ፡ ነገር *wanna nägär*

cry, v. (weep) አለቀሰ *aläqqäsä;* (shout) ጮኸ *čohä*

cry (n.) ጩኸት *čuhät*

crying (n.) ልቅሶ *ləqso*

cub ግልገል *gəlgäl*

cube (of wood) ቄራጭ *qurräč;* (of sugar) አንኳር *ankʷar*

cubic ኩብ *kub*

cubicle ትንሽ ፡ ክፍል *tənnəš kəfəl*

cubit ክንድ *kənd*
measure by cubits ከነዳ *känädda*

cucumber የፈረንጅ ፡ ዱባ *yäfäränǧ dubba*

cud ምንጥኪ *mənəžžaki*
chew cud አመነዠኸ *amänäžžähä*

cuddle አንካባከበ ፡ አቀፈ *ankäbakbo aqqäfä;* እቅፍ ፡ አደረገ *əqqəf adärrägä*

cue ምልክት *mäläkkət*

cuff link የጅ ፡ ቁልፍ *yäǧǧəge qulf*

culminate ተደመደመ *tädämäddämä*

culprit ወንጀለኛ *wänǧäläňňa*

cult አምልኮ *amləko*

cultivate (~ land) አረሰ *arräsä;* (~ one's mind) አዳበረ *adabbärä*

cultivated (~ land) የታረሰ *yätarräsä*

cultivation ማረስ *maräs;* መትከል *mätkäl*

cultivator አራሽ *araš*

cultural የባህል *yäbahəl*

culture (civilization) ሥልጣኔ *səläṭṭane;* ባህል *bahəl;* (physical ~) ማዳበር *madabär*

cultured ጨዋ *čäwa*

cumin ከሙን *kämun*

cunning ብልጥ *bəlṭ;* ጮሌ *čolle*

cup (n.) ሲኒ *sini;* ስኒ *səni;* ኩባያ *kubbayya;* (as prize) ዋንጫ *wanča*

cupboard ቁም ፡ ሣጥን *qum saṭən*

cupidity ሥሥት *səssət*

cupola ቁብታ *qubbəta*

curable, be ሊድን ፡ የሚቻል *lidən yämmiččal*

curator ጎላፊ *halafi*

curb, v. (one's temper) ገታ *gätta*

curb (n.) የመንገድ ፡ ጠርዝ *yämängäd ṭärz*

curdle ረጋ *rägga*

curds እርጎ *ərgo*

cure (v.) አዳነ *adanä*
be cured ዳነ *danä*

cure, n. (remedy) መድኃኒት *mädhanit;* (solution) መፍትሔ *mäftəhe*

curfew ሰዓት ፡ እላፊ *säat əllafi*

curiosity ጉጉት *guggut;* የማወቅ ፡ ፍላጎት *yämawäq fəllagot;* (something unusual) ብርቅ *bərq*

curious (eager to know) ጉጉ *guggu;* (strange) ልዩ *ləyyu*
be curious ጓጓ *gʷaggʷa*

curl, vi. (of hair) ተጥመለመለ *täṭmäläm-mälä;* (of parchment) ተሸባለለ *täšä-ballälä*

curl (n.) ጥቅል ፡ ጸጉር *ṭəqəll ṣägur*

curly ክርዳዳ *kärdadda*

currency ገንዘብ *gänzäb*

current, n. (of river) ፈረሰኛ ፡ ውኃ *färäsäňňa wəha;* ገስጋሽ ፡ ውኃ *gäsgaš wəha;* (of opinion) አዝማሚያ *azmamiya;* (electric ~) ኮረንቲ *korränti*

current (adj.) ያሁኑ *yahunu;* የጊዜ *yägize*

currently ሰሞኑን *sämonun;* ባሁኑ ፡ ጊዜ *bahunu gize*

curriculum ሥርዓተ ፡ ትምህርት *sər'atä təmhərt*

curse (v.) ረገመ *räggämä;* ተሳደበ *täsaddäbä*

curse (n.) እርግማን *ərgəman;* (evil) መቅ ሠፍት *mäqsäft*

cursed ርጉም *rəgum*

cursive የተቀጣጠለ *yätäqäṭaṭṭälä;* የተያ ያዘ *yätäyayazä*

curtail ቋረጠ(በት) *qʷärräṭä(bbät);* ቀነሰ *qännäsä*

curtain (v.), ~ off ጋረደ *garrädä*

curtain (n.) መጋረጃ *mäggaräǧa*

curve (vt.) አጐበጠ *agʷäbbäṭä* curve (vi.) ታጠፈ *taṭṭäfä*

curve (n.) መጠምዘዣ *mäṭämzäža*

curved (~ back) ጐባጣ *gʷäbaṭa;* (~ road) ጠማማ *ṭämama* be curved (back) ጐበጠ *gʷäbbäṭä;* (road) ጠመመ *ṭämmämä*

cushion ትራስ *təras*

custodian ዐቃቢ *aqqabi;* ጠባቂ *ṭäbbaqi*

custody አዳራ *adära*

custom ልማድ *ləmad;* ባህል *bahəl*

customary የተለመደ *yätälämmädä*

customer ደንበኛ *dänbäñña*

customhouse የጉምሩክ ፡ ቤት *yägumruk bet*

customs (taxes) ጉምሩክ *gumruk;* ቀረጥ *qärät;* (department of customs) ጉም ሩክ *gumruk*

cut ቋረጠ *qʷärräṭä;* (~ grass) ዐጨደ *aččädä;* (reduce) ቀነሰ *qännäsä* cut across አቋረጠ *aqqʷarräṭä* cut down ቋረጠ *qʷärräṭä;* ቀጨ *qäččä* cut off አቋረጠ *aqqʷarräṭä;* ነጠለ *näṭṭälä* cut out ቈረጠ *qʷärṭo awäṭṭa* cut short አቋረጠ *aqqʷarräṭä*

cute የደስ ፡ ደስ ፡ ያለ *yädäss däss yalä*

cycle ዐውድ *awd;* ዑደት *udät*

cyclone ታላቅ ፡ ዓውሎ ፡ ነፋስ *tallaq awlo näfas*

cynical ተጣራጣሪ *täṭäraṭari*

D

daddy! አባባ *abbabba*

dagger ጩቤ *čube*

daily (n.) በየቀኑ ፡ የሚታተም ፡ ጋዜጣ *bäyyäqänu yämmittattäm gazeṭa*

daily (adj.) የቀን *yäqän;* የዕለት *yäəlät;* ዕለታዊ *əlätawi* daily (adv.) ቀን ፡ በቀን *qän bäqän;* ሁል ፡ ቀን *hullə qän;* በየዕለቱ *bäyyä-əlätu*

dainty (~ clothes) ለስላሳ *läslassa;* (~ person) ቅምጥል *qəmṭəl*

dam (v.) ገደበ *gäddäbä*

dam (n.) ግድብ *gəddəb*

damage (v.) አበላሸ *abbälaššä;* ጉዳ *gʷädda*

damage (n.) ብላሽ *bəlaš;* ብልሽት *bələš-šät;* ጉዳት *gudat* damages (paid someone) ካሳ *kasa*

damn (condemn) ኰነነ *kʷännänä;* ፈረደ (በት) *färrädä(bbät)*

damp (adj.) እርጥብ *ərṭəb* be damp ራሰ *rasä;* ረጠበ *räṭṭäbä*

dampness ርጥበት *rəṭbät;* እርጥበት *ərṭəbät*

dance, v. (~ a modern dance) ዳነሰ *dännäsä;* (~ a native dance) ጨፈረ *čäffärä*

dance, n. (modern ~) ዳንስ *dans;* (native ~) ዘፈን *zäfän;* ጭፈራ *čəffära*

dancer ዳናሽ *dännaš;* ዳንሰኛ *dansäñña*

danger አደጋ *adäga*

dangerous አደገኛ *adägäñña*

dangle (vt.) አወዛወዘ awwäzawwäzä;
አንጠለጠለ anṭäläṭṭälä
dangle (vi.) ተወዛወዘ täwäzawwäzä;
ተንጠለጠለ tänṭäläṭṭälä

dare ደፈረ däffärä

daring ደፋር däffar

dark, adj. (without light) ጨለማ čälläma; (~ skin) ጥቁር ṭəqur
be dark ጨለመ čällämä; (of color)
ያልደመቀ yaldämmäqä

darken አጨለመ ačällämä; (~ the skin)
አጠቈረ aṭäqqʷärä

darkness ጭለማ čəlläma

darn ጠቀመ ṭäqqämä

dash, vt. (smash) ከሰከሰ käsäkkäsä
dash, vi. (hurry) ተጣደፈ täṭaddäfä
dash by ተፈትልኮ ፡ አለፈ täfätləko
alläfä
dash off ተጣደፈ täṭaddäfä; ተንደር
ድሮ ፡ ወጣ tändärdəro wäṭṭa

dash (n.) ጭረት čərät

date, v. (mark with a date) ቀኑን ፡ ጻፈ
qänun ṣafä; (escort socially) ተወዳጀ
täwädaǧǧä

date (time) ቀን qän; ጊዜ gize; (appointment) ቀጠሮ qäṭäro; (fruit) ተምር
tämər
be out of date ቀኑ ፡ አለፈ(በት) qänu
alläfä(bbät)
to date እስካሁን əskahun

daughter ሴት ፡ ልጅ set ləǧ

daughter-in-law የልጅ ፡ ሚስት yäləǧ
mist; ምራት mərat

dawn (v.) ነጋ nägga

dawn (n.) ንጋት nəgat; ጎህ goh; (beginning) መክፈቻ mäkfäča
at dawn ጉሀ ፡ ሲቀድ gʷäh siqädd

day ቀን qän; ዕለት ǝlät; (era) ጊዜ gize
day after day ቀን ፡ በቀን qän bäqän;
በየቀኑ bäyyäqänu; ከቀን ፡ ቀን käqän
qän; ዕለት ፡ ዕለት ǝlät ǝlät
day in, day out ነጋ ፡ ጠባ nägga ṭäbba

all day long ሙሉ ፡ ቀን mulu qän;
ቀኑን ፡ ሙሉ qänun mulu
every day በየቀኑ bäyyäqänu
on the same day በዕለት ፡ ቀኑ bä'ə-
lätä qänu
one of these days ሰሞኑን sämonun;
አንድ ፡ ቀን and qän
the following (next) day በማግሥቱ
bämagəstu; በበነጋው bäbänägaw
the other day በቀደም ፡ ዕለት bäqäd-
däm ǝlät
these days ሰሞኑን sämonun

daybreak, at ~ ማለዳ malada; ጎህ ፡
(ጉሀ) ፡ ሲቀድ goh (gʷäh) siqädd

day laborer ሞያተኛ mʷayatäñña

daylight የቀን ፡ ብርሃን yäqän bərhan

daze (of a blow) አፈዘዘ afäzzäzä; (of
news) አደነዘዘ adänäzzäzä
be dazed ፈዘዘ fäzzäzä

dazzle, vt. (blind temporarily) አጭበረ
በረ ačbäräbbärä; (surprise by brilliant performance) አስደነቀ asdännäqä

deacon ዲያቆን diyaqon

dead (n.) ሙት mut

dead (adj.) የሞተ yämotä; (~ plant) የደ
ረቀ yädärräqä; (~ party) በጣም ፡ ቀዝ
ቃዛ bäṭam qäzqazza
be dead ሞታ motä
be dead tired ሙትት ፡ ብሎ ፡ ደከመ
mutətt bəlo däkkämä
fall dead ሙትት ፡ አለ mutətt alä

dead end መውጫ ፡ የሌለው mäwča yälelläw

dead end street መውጫ ፡ የሌለው ፡ መን
ገድ mäwča yälelläw mängäd

deadline የመጨረሻ ፡ ቀን yämäčärräša
qän

deadly የሚገድል yämmigädəl; (~ enemies) የተማረረ yätämarrärä; (~
party) የቀዘቀዘ yäqäzäqqäzä

deaf ደንቆሮ dänqoro
be deaf ደነቈረ dänäqqʷärä

deafen አደነቈረ adänäqqʷärä

deafness ድንቁርና dənqurənna

deal, v. (have contact) ተገናኘ tägänaňňä; ጋጠመ gäṭṭämä; (be concerned
with) ተናገረ tänaggärä; አወሳ awässa
deal in (~ merchandise) ነገደ näggädä
deal with (treat) ያዘ yazä

deal, n. (in business) ንግድ nəgd; መገበ
ያየት mäggäbäyayät; (contract) ውል
wəl
a great deal ብዙ bəzu
transact a deal ተዋዋለ täwawalä

dealer ነጋዴ näggade

dealings አድራጎት adragot; (commercial ~) ይዞታ yəzota

dear (beloved) ተወዳጅ täwäddağ; (expensive) ውድ wədd

dearly በጣም bäṭam

dearth እጥረት əṭrät

death ሞት mot; ዕረፍት əräft
put to death ገደለ gäddälä

death sentence የሞት ፡ ፍርድ yämot fərd

death throes ጣረ ፡ ሞት ṭarä mot

debase, ~ oneself ራሱን ፡ አወረደ rasun
awärrädä

debate (v.) ተከራከረ täkärakkärä
debate with oneself አመነታ amänätta

debate (n.) ክርክር kərəkkər

debt ዕዳ əda; ብድር bəddər

debtor ባለ ፡ ዕዳ balä əda; ተበዳሪ täbäddari

decade ዐሥር ፡ ዓመታት assər amätat

decadence ውድቀት wədqät

decapitate ቀላ qälla

decay, vi. (of fruit) በሰበሰ bäsäbbäsä

deceased ሙት mut; ሟች mʷač
be deceased ሞተ motä

deceit ማታለል mattaläl; እብለት əblät

deceitful አታላይ attalay

deceive አሞኘ amoňňä; ሸፈጠ šäffäṭä;
አታለለ attallälä

December ታህሣሥ tahsas

decent (appropriate) ተገቢ tägäbi; (~
man) ደኅና dähna; ጨዋ čäwa

deception ማጭበርበር mačbärbär

deceptive አሳሳች assasač

decide ቈረጠ qʷärräṭä; ወሰነ wässänä;
(of judge) በየነ bäyyänä; ፍርድ ፡ ሰጠ
fərd säṭṭä

decided adj. (unquestionable) የማያጠራ
ጥር yämmayaṭṭäraṭṭər; (determined)
ቈርጥ qurṭ

decidedly መቶ ፡ በመቶ mäto bämäto

decimate አብዛኛውን ፡ ከፍል ፡ አጠፋ abzaňňawən kəfəl aṭäffa

decipher (~ a message) ፈታ fätta

decision ውሳኔ wəssane; ቍርጥ ፡ ሐሳብ
qurṭ hassab; (of judge) ብይኔ bəyyane

decisive ቈርጥ ፡ ያለ qurräṭ yalä

deck የመርከብ፡መድረክ yämärkäb mädräk

declaration (announcement) መግለጫ
mägläča; ዐዋጅ awağ; (document)
ሰነድ sänäd

declare ዐወጀ awwäğä; (announce) አስ
ታወቀ astawwäqä; ገለጸ gälläṣä

declension እርባታ ərbata

decline (vt.) አልፈቀደም alfäqqädäm;
አልተቀበለም altäqäbbäläm; (~ a
noun) አረባ aräbba
decline (vi.) ቀነሰ qännäsä; ዝቅ ፡ አለ
zəqq alä; እነሰ annäsä

decompose (vt.) ለያየ läyayyä
decompose (vi.) ተለያየ täläyayyä;
(rot) ፈረሰ färräsä

decorate (adorn) አስጌጠ asgeṭä; (give
a medal) ሸለመ šällämä

decoration ጌጥ geṭ; (medal) ሽልማት
šəlləmat

decorative ያጌጠ yageṭä

decrease (vt.) ቀነሰ qännäsä; አሳነሰ asannäsä

decrease (vi.) ተቀነሰ *täqännäsä;* አነሰ
annäsä; ጐደለ *g^wäddälä*

decrease (n.) ቅነሳ *qənnäsa*

decree (v.) ደነገገ *dänäggägä*

decree (n.) ዐዋጅ *awağ;* ድንጋጌ *dənəggage*
issue a decree ዐወጀ *awwäğä*

decrepit ድቅቅ ፡ ያለ *dəqəqq yalä*

dedicate (an installation) መረቀ *märräqä;* (devote) አዋለ *awalä;* (~ a book)
መታሰቢያ ፡ አደረገ *mättasäbiya adärrägä*

deduct ቀነሰ *qännäsä*

deduction ቅናሽ *qənnaš*

deed ሥራ *səra;* ሙያ *muya;* ተግባር *tägbar;* (legal document) ስመርስት *səmä-
rəst*

deem አሰበ *assäbä*

deep (~ lake) ጥልቅ *ṭəlq;* (~ gorge) ጐድ
ጓዳ *g^wädg^wadda;* (~ voice) ወፍራም
wäfram; (~ secret) ጥብቅ *ṭəbq;* (~
sleep) ከባድ *käbbad*

deeply በጥልቅ *bäṭəlq*

deer አጋዘን *agazän*

deface ቅርጽ ፡ አበላሸ *qərṣ abbälaššä*

defamation የስም ፡ ማጥፋት ፡ ወንጀል *yäsəm maṭfat wänğäl*

defame ስም ፡ አጠፋ *səm aṭäffa*

defeat, v. (in battle) ድል ፡ መታ *dəl
mätta;* ድል ፡ አደረገ *dəl adärrägä;*
አሸነፈ *aššännäfä;* (~ a bill) ውድቅ ፡
አደረገ *wədq adärrägä*

defeat (n.) ድል ፡ መሆን *dəl mähon;* መሸ
ነፍ *mäššännäf*

defeated, be ድል ፡ ሆነ *dəl honä;* ተሸ
ነፈ *täšännäfä;* (of a motion) ውድቅ ፡
ሆነ *wədq honä*

defecate አራ *arra;* ሜዳ ፡ ወጣ *meda wäṭṭa;* ቀዘነ *qäzzänä*

defect (v.), ~ to ክድቶ ፡ ገባ *kädto gäbba*

defect (n.) እንከን *ənkän;* ጉድለት *gudlät*

defective የተበላሸ *yätäbälaššä;* ጉድለት ፡
ያለበት *gudlät yalläbbät*

defend (protect) ተከላከለ *täkälakkälä;*
(speak in favor) አስረዳ *asrädda;* (of
a lawyer) ተከራከረ(ለት) *täkärakkärä-
(llät)*

defendant ተከሳሽ *täkässaš*

defense (thing that protects) ተከላከይ
täkälakay; (protection) መከላከያ *mäkkälakäya*
defense attorney የተከሳሽ ፡ ጠበቃ *yä-
täkässaš ṭäbäqa*
Ministry of Defense (የ)መከላከያ ፡
ሚኒስቴር *(yä)mäkkälakäya minister*

defenseless መከላከያ ፡ የሌለው *mäkkälakäya yälelläw*

defensive (n.) መከላከል *mäkkälakäl*

defensive (adj.) የመከላከያ *yämäkkälakäya*

defer አስተላለፈ *astälalläfä*

deference አክብሮት *akbərot*

defiance አለመበገር *alämäbbägär*

defiant እምቢተኛ *əmbitäňňa*

deficiency እጥረት *əṭrät;* ጉድለት *gudlät*

deficient ጐደሎ *g^wädälo;* በቂ ፡ ያልሆነ
bäqi yalhonä
be deficient in ጐደለ *g^wäddälä*

deficit እጥረት *əṭrät;* ኪሳራ *kisara*

define (describe) ወሰነ *wässänä;* (explain) ፍች ፡ ሰጠ *fəčč säṭṭä*

definite ቁርጥ *qurṭ;* ቁርጠኛ *qurṭäňňa;*
የተወሰነ *yätäwässänä*

definite article የተወሰነ ፡ መስተአምር *yätäwässänä mästa'ammər*

definitely በርግጥ *bärgəṭ*

definition ፍች *fəčč*

deform (~ the face) አበላሸ *abbälaššä;*
አጠፋ *aṭäffa;* (~ a person) አካለ ፡
ጐደሎ ፡ አደረገ *akalä g^wädälo adärrägä*

deformity አካለ ፡ ጐደሎነት *akalä g^wädä-
lonnät*

defraud አጭበረበረ *ačbäräbbärä*

defray ከፈለ *käffälä*

defy (∼ the law) ጣሰ *ṭasä*

degrade አዋረደ *awwarrädä;* ዝቅ ፡ አደ
ረገ *zəqq adärrägä*

degree ደረጃ *däräǧa;* (rank given to a
student) ዲግሪ *digri*
by degrees ቀስ ፡ በቀስ *qäss bäqäss*
to a certain degree በመጠኑ *bämäṭänu*

deity አምላክ *amlak*

delay, v. (put off) አቆየ *aqoyyä;* አስተላ
ለፈ *astälalläfä;* (do something late)
አዘገየ *azägäyyä*

delay (n.) መዘግየት *mäzägyät*

delegate (v.) ወከለ *wäkkälä*

delegate (n.) መልእክተኛ *mäl'əktäňňa*

delegation መልእክተኞች *mäl'əktäňňočč*

delete ሰረዘ *särräzä*

deliberate, v. (discuss) ተማከረ *tämakkärä;* ተመካከረ *tämäkakkärä;* (think
over carefully) አሰላሰለ *assälassälä*

deliberate, adj. (careful) ጥንቁቅ *ṭənquq;*
(intentional) ሆን ፡ ብሎ ፡ የተደረገ *hon
bəlo yätädärrägä*

deliberately ሆን ፡ ብሎ *hon bəlo;* ዐውቆ
awqo

deliberation (discussion) ውይይት *wəyəyyət;* (slowness and care) ጥንቃቄ *ṭənəqqaqe*

delicate (∼ situation) በቋፍ ፡ ላይ ፡ ያለ
bäqʷaf lay yallä; (∼ features) ሰል
ካክ ፡ ያለ *sälkäkk yalä*

delicious ጣፋጭ *ṭafač*
be delicious ጣፈጠ *ṭaffäṭä*

delight (vt.) አስደሰተ *asdässätä*
be delighted ደስ ፡ አለ(ው) *däss alä(w);*
ተደሰተ *tädässätä*

delight (n.) ተድላ *tädla;* ደስታ *dässəta*

delightful አስደሳች *asdässač*

delimit ወሰነ *wässänä;* ከለለ *källälä*

delineate (∼ boundaries) ከለለ *källälä;*
ወሰነ *wässänä*

delinquency ወንጀል *wänǧäl;* ጥፋት *ṭəfat;*
ግዳጅ ፡ አለማፈጸም *gəddaǧ alämäfäṣ-
ṣäm*

delinquent (n.) ዱርዬ *durrəyye*

delinquent, adj. (∼ parent) ተግባሩን ፡
የማይፈጽም *tägbarun yämmayəfäṣ-
ṣəm;* (∼ child) ወንጀለኛ *wänǧäläňňa*
become delinquent (bill) ጊዜው ፡ ተላ
ለፈ *gizew tälalläfä*

delirious, become ∼ (rave) አቃዠ(ው)
aqqažžä(w)

delirium ቅዠት *qəžät*

deliver (hand over) አስረከበ *asräkkäbä;*
አሳልፎ ፡ ሰጠ *asalləfo säṭṭä;* አደረሰ
adärräsä; (give birth) ተገላገለች *tägälaggäläčč;* (save from evil) ሰወረ *säwwärä*

delivery ርክክብ *rəkəkkəb;* (of child) መገ
ላገል *mäggälagäl*

delude አታለለ *attallälä;* አጭበረበረ *ačbäräbbärä*
delude oneself ራሱን ፡ አሞኘ *rasun
amoňňä*

deluge (n.) ጐርፍ *gʷärf*

demand (v.) ጠየቀ *ṭäyyäqä;* (require
time) ወሰደ(በት) *wässädä(bbät)*

demand (n.) ፍላጎት *fəllagot;* ተፈላጊነት
täfällaginnät
be in demand ተፈለገ *täfällägä*

demarcate ከለለ *källälä*

demobilize በተነ *bättänä*

democracy ዲሞክራሲ *dimokrasi;* የሕ
ዝብ ፡ ግዛት *yähəzb gəzat*

demolish ናደ *nadä;* አፈረሰ *afärräsä;*
አወደመ *awäddämä;* (∼ a theory)
ውድቅ ፡ አደረገ *wədq adärrägä*
be demolished ፈረሰ *färräsä;* ወደመ
wäddämä

demon ጋኔን *ganen;* ርኩስ ፡ መንፈስ *rəkus mänfäs;* ሰይጣን *säyṭan*

demonstrate, vt. (prove) አስረዳ *asrädda;* (show) አሳየ *asayyä*

demonstrate, vi. (parade) ሰላማዊ ፡
ሰልፍ ፡ አደረገ sälamawi sälf adärrägä

demonstration (proof) ማስረጃ masräǧǧa; (expression) መግለጫ mägläča;
(public display of opinion) ሰላማዊ ፡
ሰልፍ sälamawi sälf; ሰልፍ sälf

demonstrative (~ pronoun) አመልካች
amälkač

demoralize (weaken the spirit) ሞራል ፡
ሰበረ moral säbbärä; ቅስም ፡ ሰበረ qə-
səm säbbärä; (pervert) አበላሸ abbälaššä

demote ሻረ šarä; (degrade) ዘቅ ፡ አደረገ
zəqq adärrägä

den (hideout, burrow) ዋሻ wašša; ጕሬ
gʷäre

denial ክዳት kədat

denote አመለከተ amäläkkätä

denounce (condemn) ወገዘ wäggäzä;
(inform against) አሳበቀ assabbäqä;
ነገረ(በት) näggärä(bbät)

dense, be ጥቅጥቅ ፡ አለ ṭəqṭəqq alä

dentist የጥርስ ፡ ሐኪም yäṭərs hakim

deny (declare not true) ካደ kadä; (refuse) አልተቀበለም altäqäbbäläm

depart (leave) ሄደ hedä; ተጓዘ tägʷazä;
(deviate) ተለየ täläyyä

departed, adj. (dead) ሟች mʷač

department ክፍል kəfəl; (of government) መሥሪያ ፡ ቤት mäsriya bet

department store መደብር mädäbbər

departure መሄድ mähed; መነሻ männäša

depend, ~ on (rely) ተማመነ tämammänä; ተመካ tämäkka; (hinge on) ተመ
ሠረተ tämäsärrätä

dependable ታማኝ tammaňň; ሁነኛ hunäňňa

dependence መመኪያ mämmäkiya

dependency ጥገኛ ṭəggäňňa

dependent, be ~ on ተመሠረተ tämäsärrätä; (rely on) በ - - - ትከሻ ፡ ላይ ፡
ኖረ bä - - - təkäšša lay norä

depict ገለጸ gälläṣä; (of painting) አሳየ
asayyä

deplorable የሚያሳዝን yämmiyasazzən;
አስከፊ askäffi

deplore አዘነ azzänä

deport ካገር ፡ አስወጣ kagär aswäṭṭa
be deported ካገር ፡ ወጣ kagär wäṭṭa

deposit, v. (put) አስቀመጠ asqämmäṭä

deposit, n. (pledge) መያዣ mäyaža;
(custody) አደራ adära; (of mud) ደለል
däläl; (bank account) ተቀማጭ ፡ ገን
ዘብ täqämmač gänzäb

depository ማስቀመጫ masqämmäča

depot ግምጃ ፡ ቤት gəmǧa bet

depraved ነውረኛ näwräňňa; የተበላሸ yätäbälaššä

depreciate ዘቅ ፡ አደረገ zəqq adärrägä

depress (make gloomy) ቀር ፡ አሰኘ qərr
assäňňä; አሳዘነ asazzänä; (lower) አዘ
በጠ azäbbäṭä

depression (low place) ጉድጓድ gudgʷad;
(dullness of trade) ከፉ ፡ ቀን käfu qän
fit of depression ብስጭት bəsəččət;
ተስፋ ፡ መቁረጥ täsfa mäqʷräṭ

deprivation ችጋር čəggar

deprive አስቀረ asqärrä; ከለከለ käläkkälä

depth ጥልቀት ṭəlqät

deputy ምስሌነ məsläne; ምክትል mäkəttəl; እንደራሴ əndärase
deputy minister ምክትል ፡ ሚኒስትር
mäkəttəl ministər

deranged እብድ əbd; አእምሮው ፡ የተና
ወጠ a'mərow yätänawwäṭä

derangement እብደት əbdät

deride አሾፈ ašofä; አፌዘ afezä; አላገጠ
allaggäṭä

derive (acquire) አገኘ agäňňä
be derived (originate) ተወረሰ täwär-
räsä

derogatory የሚነካ yämminäka

descend ወረደ wärrädä; (of a custom)

ሲ.ወርድ ፡ ሲ.ዋረድ ፡ መጣ siwärd siwwarräd mäṭṭa

descent (going downward) ወደ ፡ ታች ፡
መውረድ wädä tačč mäwräd; (downward slope) ቁልቁለት qulqulät; (ancestry) ዘር zär

describe አስረዳ asrädda; ገለጸ gälläṣä

description ገለጻ gäläṣa; መግለጫ mägläča; (kind) ዓይነት aynät

desecrate አረከሰ aräkkäsä

desert (v.) ለቀቀ läqqäqä; ከዳ kädda

desert (n.) ምድር ፡ በዳ mədra bäda

deserted (adj.) ሰው ፡ የሌለበት säw yälelläbbät

deserter ከዳተኛ käddatäňňa

deserve ተገባ(ው) tägäbba(w)

design, v. (~ a bridge) ነደፈ näddäfä;
(~ a plan) አቀደ aqqädä

design, n. (shape) ቅርጽ qərṣ; (plan)
ዓላማ alama

designate (appoint) ሠየመ säyyämä;
(point out) አሳየ asayyä

designer (of clothes) ሞዴል ፡ አውጪ
model awči

desirable (advantageous) የሚመች yäm-
mimmäčč; (pleasing) ደስ ፡ የሚል däss
yämmil

desire (v.) ተመኘ tämäňňä; ጓጓ gʷaggʷa

desire (n.) ምኞት mäňňot; ፍላጎት fälla-
got

desist ተወ täwä

desk ዴስክ desk

desolate (adj.) በዳ bäda

despair (v.) ተስፋ ፡ ቈረጠ täsfa qʷärräṭä; ተስፋ ፡ አጣ täsfa aṭṭa

despair (n.) ተስፋ ፡ መቍረጥ täsfa mäqʷräṭ

desperate (situation) ተስፋ ፡ የሚያስቈ
ርጥ täsfa yämmiyasqʷärrəṭ

despicable የሚናቅ yämminnaq

despise ናቀ naqä; አቃለለ aqqallälä

despite በ bä + imperfect + ም ፡ እንኳ
-m ənkʷa

despondent, be አዝኖ ፡ ተከዘ azno täkkäzä

despot ማን ፡ አለብኝ ፡ ባይ man alläbbäňň bay

dessert ማጣጣሚያ maṭṭaṭamiya

destination መድረሻ mädräša

destined, be (be chosen) ተመረጠ tämär-
räṭä; (bound for) አመራ amärra

destiny (fate) ዕድል əddəl; እጣ əṭa

destitute ምስኪን məskin

destroy አበላሸ abbälaššä; አጠፋ aṭäffa;
አፈረሰ afärräsä
be destroyed (army) አለቀ alläqä;
(by fire) ተቃጠለ täqaṭṭälä

destruction ጥፋት ṭəfat; እልቂት əlqit

destructive ጥፋት ፡ የሚያደርስ ṭəfat yämmiyadärs

detach ነጠለ näṭṭälä; ለያየ läyayyä;
(~ button) በጠሰ bäṭṭäsä; (~ stub)
ገነጠለ gänäṭṭälä; (send on special
duty) መደበ mäddäbä

detachment (standing apart) ገለልተኛ
ነት gälältäňňannät; (of troops) ከፍል
käfäl

detail (v.) ዘረዘረ zäräzzärä

detail (n.) ዝርዝር zərzər

detailed ዝርዝር zərzər

detain (keep in custody) አቆየ aqoyyä;
(delay) አዘገየ azägäyyä

detective ወንጀል ፡ መርማሪ wänǧäl mär-
mari

deteriorate ተበላሸ täbälaššä; ባሰ basä

determination ቁርጥ ፡ ሐሳብ qurṭ hassab;
ቈራጥነት qʷärraṭənnät

determine (decide) ቈረጠ qʷärräṭä; ወሰነ
wässänä; (find out) አወቀ awwäqä

determined (adj.) ሐሳብ ፡ ቈራጥ hassabä
qʷärraṭ
be determined ቈረጠ qʷärräṭä

detest ጠላ ṭälla

detestable አስከፊ *askäffi*

dethrone ከዙፋን ፡ አወረደ *käzufan awär-rädä*

detonate (vi.) ፈነዳ *fänädda*

detonation የፈንጇ ፡ ድምፅ *yäfänği dəmṣ*

detour ዞሮ ፡ መሄድ *zuro mähed*

detrimental, be ~ to ሊጐዳ ፡ ቻለ *ligʷäda čalä*

devastate አጠፋ *aṭäffa;* መዘበረ *mäzäbbärä;* አወደመ *awäddämä*

develop, vt. (~ a country) አበለጸገ *abäläṣṣägä;* (~ muscles, resources) አዳ በረ *adabbärä;* (~ land) አለማ *aläm-ma;* (~ a film) አጠበ *aṭṭäbä*
develop, vi. (of child) አደገ *addägä;* (of country) በለጸገ *bäläṣṣägä;* (of a city) ተስፋፋ *tä sfaffa*

developed, be (land) ለማ *lämma*

development እድገት *ədgät*

deviate ራቀ *raqä*

device (scheme) ዘዴ *zäde;* ስልት *sə lt;* (tool) መሣሪያ *mässariya*

devil ሰይጣን *säyṭan*
poor devil ምስኪን *məskin*

devious ቅን ፡ ያልሆነ *qən yalhonä*
devious ways ተንኮል *tänkʷäl*

devise ፈጠረ *fäṭṭärä*
devise a plan አቀደ *aqqädä*

devoid of (noun) +ቢስ *bis*

devote አዋለ *awalä*

devoted (adj.) ታማኝ *tammaňň*
be devoted to (wholly given to some subject) ብቻ ፡ ተመደበ *bəčča tämäd-däbä;* ተወሰነ *täwässänä;* (love) ወደደ *wäddädä*

devotion (loyalty) ታማኝነት *tammaňňən nät;* (love) ፍቅር *fəqər*

devour (~ food) ጐሰጐሰ *gʷäsäggʷäsä;* (~ gossip) አዳመጠ *addammäṭä*

devout (religious) መንፈሳዊ *mänfäsawi;* ለእግዚአብሔር ፡ ያደረ *läəgziabəher yad-därä;* (~ follower) ታማኝ *tammaňň*

dew ጤዛ *ṭeza*

dexterity ቅልጥፍና *qəlṭəfənna*

dexterous ቀልጣፋ *qälṭaffa;* ጥበበኛ *ṭə bäbäňňa*

diagnosis ምርመራ *mərmära;* የምርመራ ፡ ውጤት *yämərmära wäṭṭet*

diagonal አገናኝ *aggänaň*

diagram ሥዕላዊ ፡ መግለጫ *sə'əlawi mäg-läča*

dial (v.) ደወለ *däwwälä*

dial, n. (of watch) መቊጠሪያ *mäqʷ täri-ya;* (of telephone) ማዞሪያ *mazoriya*

dialect የቋንቋ ፡ ስልት *yäqʷanqʷa sə lt*

dialogue ውይይት *wəyəyyət;* ጭውውት *čəwəwwət*

diameter የከበብ ፡ አጋማሽ ፡ መሥመር *yäkəbäb aggamaš mäsmär*

diamond አልማዝ *almaz*

diarrhea ቅዝን *qəzän;* ተቅማጥ *täqmaṭ*
have diarrhea ቀዘነ *qäzzänä*

diary የቀን ፡ ማስታወሻ *yäqän mastawäša*

dictate አጻፈ *aṣṣafä*

dictation የቃል ፡ ጽሕፈት *yäqal ṣə hfät*

dictator አምባ ፡ ገነን *amba gännän*

diction አነጋገር *annägagär*

dictionary መዝገበ ፡ ቃላት *mäzgäbä qa-lat*

die ሞተ *motä;* አረፈ *arräfä;* (of motor) ጠፋ *ṭäffa*
die down (of fire) ጠፋ *ṭäffa;* (of wind) በረደ *bärrädä*
die out (of custom) ቀረ *qärrä*

diet (n.) ምግብ *məgb*

differ (be unlike) ተለየ *täläyyä;* ተለያየ *täläyayyä;* (disagree) አልተስማማም *altäsmammam*

difference ልዩነት *lə yyunnät;* (disagreement) አለመግባባት *alämägbabat*
have a difference ተከራከረ *täkärak-kärä;* ተለያየ *täläyayyä*

different (not alike) ሌላ *lela;* (distinct,

separate) ልዩ *ləyyu;* የተለያየ *yätälä-yayyä*
be different ተለየ *täläyyä;* ተለያየ *täläyayyä*

differentiate (vt.) ለየ *läyyä;* አለያየ *alläyayyä*

difficult አስቸጋሪ *asčäggari;* ከባድ *käbbad;* (~ time) የመከራ *yämäkära*

difficulty ችግር *čəggər;* አስቸጋሪ ፡ ነገር *asčäggari nägär*
be in difficulty ቸገረ *čäggärä;* ተጨነቀ *täčännäqä*
make difficulties አስቸገረ *asčäggärä*

diffuse (vt.) አስፋፋ *asfaffa;* አሰራጨ *assäračča*
diffuse (vi.) ተሰራጨ *täsäračča*

dig ቆፈረ *qʷäffärä*
dig out ቆፍሮ ፡ አወጣ *qʷäffəro awäṭṭa*
dig up ቆፈረ *qʷäffärä;* መነቀረ *mänäqqärä;* (uproot) ነቀለ *näqqälä*

digest vt. (~ food) አዋሐደ *awwahadä;* አንሸራሸረ *anšäraššärä;* ፈጨ *fäččä;* (absorb mentally) ቀሰመ *qässämä*

digestion የምግብ ፡ መንሸራሸር *yäməgəb mänšärašär*

dignified (adj.) ግርማ ፡ ሞገስ ፡ ያለው *gərma mogäs yalläw*

dignify አስከበረ *askäbbärä*

dignitary መኰንን *mäkʷännən;* ባላ ፡ ሥልጣን *balä səlṭan;* ታላቅ ፡ ሰው *tallaq säw*

dignity (honor) ክብር *kəbər;* (glory) ግርማ *gərma;* (rank) ማዕረግ *ma'äräg*

dike ግድብ *gəddəb*

dilapidated የወደቀ *yäwäddäqä*

dilate (vt.) አሰፋ *asäffa*
dilate (vi.) ሰፋ *säffa*

diligence ትጋት *təgat*

diligent ትጉ *təgu;* ትጉህ *təguh*
be diligent ተጋ *tägga*

dilute አቀጠነ *aqäṭṭänä*

dim (v.) ቀነሰ *qännäsä*

dim (adj.) ደብዛዛ *däbzazza*
get dim (of eyesight) ደከመ *däkkämä;* (of light) ደበዛዘ *däbäzzäzä*

dimensions ውርድና ፡ ስፋት *wərdənna səfat*

diminish (vt.) ቀነሰ *qännäsä;* አሳነሰ *asannäsä*
diminish (vi.) ተቀነሰ *täqännäsä;* አነሰ *annäsä;* ጐደለ *gʷäddälä*

diminution ቅነሳ *qənnäsa*

dine እራት ፡ በላ *ərat bälla*

dingy ቆሸሽ ፡ ያለ *qošäšš yalä*

dining room መብል ፡ ቤት *mäbəl bet;* ምግብ ፡ ቤት *məgəb bet*

dinner ራት *rat;* እራት *ərat*

dip (~ a bucket into the lake) አጠለቀ *aṭälläqä;* (~ bread into sauce) አጠቀሰ *aṭäqqäsä*
dip from (e.g. spring) ቀዳ *qädda*

diploma የምስክር ፡ ወረቀት *yäməsəkkər wäräqät*

diplomacy ዲፕሎማሲ *diplomasi*

diplomatic (of character) ዘዴኛ *zädeňňa;* (in diplomacy) የዲፕሎማሲ *yädiplomasi*

direct, v. (conduct) መራ *märra;* (tell the way to) አሳየ *asayyä;* (order) አዘዘ *azzäzä;* (supervise) ተቈጣጠረ *täqʷäṭaṭṭärä*

direct (adj.) ቀጥተኛ *qäṭṭätäňňa*

direction አቅጣጫ *aqṭačča;* (guidance) መሪነት *märinnät;* (supervision) ተቈጣ ጣሪነት *täqʷäṭaṭarinnät;* (instruction) መመሪያ *mämmäriya*
in which direction? በየት ፡ በኩል *bäyät bäkkul*

directive መምሪያ *mämriya;* መሪ ፡ ቃል *märi qal*

directly በቀጥታ *bäqäṭṭəta*

director ዲሬክተር *diräktär;* አስኪያጅ *askiyağ*
director-general ዋና ፡ ዲሬክተር *wanna diräktär*

directory ማውጫ *mawča;* የስም ፡ ማውጫ *yäsəm mawča*

dirge ሙሾ *mušo*

dirt ቆሻሻ *qošaša;* እድፍ *ədəf;* ጉድፍ *gudəf;* (soil) አፈር *afär*

dirty (adj.) ቆሻሻ *qošaša*
be dirty ቆሸሸ *qoššäšä;* አደፈ *addäfä;* ጐደፈ *gʷäddäfä*

disability (physical) ጉድለት *gudlät*

disable ሰነከለ *sänäkkälä*

disabled ስንኩል *sənkul;* አካለ ፡ ስንኩል *akalä sənkul*

disadvantage ጉዳት *gudat*

disagree አልተስማማም *altäsmammam*

disagreeable ደስ ፡ የማይል *däss yämmayəl*

disagreement አለመግባባት *alämägbabat;* አለመስማማት *alämäsmamat*

disappear ጠፋ *ṭäffa*

disappoint ቅር ፡ አሰኘ *qərr assäňňä*

disappointed, be ቅር ፡ አለ(ው) *qərr alä(w)*

disappointment ቅሬታ *qərreta;* ብስጭት *bəsəččət*

disapprove (oppose) ተቃወመ *täqawwämä;* (have an unfavorable opinion) ነቀፈ *näqqäfä*

disarm (reduce amount of arms) የጦር ፡ መሣሪያ ፡ ቀነሰ *yäṭor mässariya qännäsä;* (take away weapons) መሣሪያ ፡ ገፈፈ *mässariya gäffäfä*

disarmament የጦር ፡ መሣሪያ ፡ ቅነሳ *yäṭor mässariya qənnäsa*

disaster መቅሠፍት *mäqsäft;* መዓት *mä'at;* ጥፋት *ṭəfat*

disastrous አሰቃቂ *assäqqaqi;* አደገኛ *adägäňňa*

disband (vt.) በተነ *bättänä;* አፈረሰ *afärräsä*
disband (vi.) ተበተነ *täbättänä;* ፈረሰ *färräsä*

disburse ከፈለ *käffälä*

discard አስወገደ *aswäggädä;* ጣለ *ṭalä*

discern (distinguish) ለየ *läyyä;* (perceive) ተረዳ *tärädda;* (see) አየ *ayyä*

discerning አስተዋይ *astäway*

discharge, v. (set free) ለቀቀ *läqqäqä;* (~ a cargo) አራገፈ *arraggäfä;* (~ duties) አከናወነ *akkänawwänä;* (~ workers) ከሥራ ፡ አስወጣ *käsəra aswäṭṭa;* (from the army) ረፋተ *räffätä;* አሰናበተ *assänabbätä*

discharge, n. (of gun) መተኩስ *mätäkkʷäs;* (of dynamite) ድምፅ *dəmṣ;* (from army) የመሰናበቻ ፡ ደብዳቤ *yämässänabäča däbdabbe*

disciple ደቀ ፡ መዝሙር *däqqä mäzmur*

disciplinary የቅጣት *yäqəṭat*

discipline (v.) ቀጣ *qäṭṭa*

discipline, n. (order) ሥነ ፡ ሥርዓት *sənä sər'at;* (field of study) ትምህርት *təmhərt*

disclose ገለጸ *gälläṣä;* አወጣ *awäṭṭa*

discomfort (n.) ሥቃይ *səqay*

disconcert አደናገረ *addänaggärä*

disconnect ቈረጠ *qʷärräṭä;* ነቀለ *näqqälä;* ለያየ *läyayyä*

discontent ቅሬታ *qərreta*

discontented, be ቅር ፡ አለ(ው) *qərr alä(w)*

discontinue አቋረጠ *aqqʷärräṭä*

discord (strife) ብጥብጥ *bəṭəbbəṭ;* (disagreement) አለመስማማት *alämäsmamat*

discount, v. (give a reduction) ቅናሽ ፡ አደረገ *qənnaš adärrägä;* (partially disbelieve) በሙሉ ፡ እምና ፡ አልተቀበለም *bämulu amno altäqäbbäläm*

discount (n.) ቅናሽ *qənnaš*

discourage (vt.) ተስፋ ፡ አስቈረጠ *täsfa asqʷärräṭä*
be discouraged ተስፋ ፡ ቈረጠ *täsfa qʷärräṭä*

discouraging, be ተስፋ ፡ አስቈረጠ *täsfa asqʷärräṭä*

discourse (v.) ሰፈ ፡ ነገግር ፡ አደረገ *säffi nəgəggər adärrägä*

discourse (n.) ነገግር *nəgəggər*

discourteous ባለጌ *baläge*

discover (invent) አገኘ *agäňňä;* ፈጠረ *fäṭṭärä;* ፈለሰፈ *fälässäfä;* (find out) ዐወቀ *awwäqä*

discovery (invention) ፍልሰፋ *fəlsäfa;* (act of being discovered) መገኘት *mäggäňät*
make a discovery, see 'discover'

discreet, be (keep a secret) ምስጢር ፡ ጠረ *məsṭir qʷaṭṭärä*

discredit (v.) ዝቅ ፡ አድርጎ ፡ አስገመተ *zəqq adrəgo asgämmätä;* ዋጋ ፡ አሳጣ *waga asaṭṭa*

discrepancy ልዩነት *ləyyunnät;* ተቃራኒነት *täqaraninnät*

discriminate (see the difference) ለየ *läyyä;* (make a distinction) አደላ *adälla*

discrimination (racial ~) የዘር ፡ ልዩነት *yäzär ləyyunnät;* የቀለም ፡ ልዩነት *yäqäläm ləyyunnät*

discuss ተናገረ *tänaggärä;* ተነጋገረ *tänägaggärä;* ተወያየ *täwäyayyä*

discussion ውይይት *wəyəyyət*

disdain (v.) ናቀ *naqä;* አንጓሸሸ *anqʷaššäšä*

disdain (n.) ንቀት *nəqät*

disease በሽታ *bäššəta;* ሕመም *həmäm*

diseased በሽተኛ *bäššətäňňa*

disembark (vi.) ከመርከብ ፡ ወረደ *kämärkäb wärrädä*

disenchant ቅር ፡ አሰኘ *qərr assäňňä*

disengage አላቀቀ *allaqqäqä*

disengagement (disengaging) ማለያየት *malläyayät*

disentangle (~ thread, vine) ፈታ *fätta;* አፍታታ *aftatta;* (~ truth) ለየ *läyyä*

disfigure መልክ ፡ አጠፋ *mälk aṭäffa*

disgrace (v.) አሳፈረ *asaffärä*

disgrace (n.) ነውረት *hafrät;* ነውር *näwr;* ውርደት *wərdät*

disgraceful አሳፋሪ *asaffari*

disguise (v.) ደበቀ *däbbäqä;* አስመሰለ *asmässälä*
disguise oneself as መስሎ ፡ ታየ *mäslo tayyä*

disgust (v.) አስጠላ *asṭälla*

disgust (n.) ጽያፈ *ṣəyyafe*
feel disgust ሰለቸ(ው) *säläččä(w)*

disgusting ጸያፍ *ṣäyyaf*

dish (plate) ሳሕን *sahən;* (food) ምግብ *məgəb*

dishearten ተስፋ ፡ አስቄረጠ *täsfa asqʷärräṭä*
be disheartened ተስፋ ፡ ቄረጠ *täsfa qʷärräṭä*

dishonest (~person) አታላይ *attalay;* ሽፋጭ *šäffäč;* (~ plan) እምነት ፡ ጉደሎ *əmnätä gʷädälo*

dishonor (v.) አዋረደ *awwarrädä*

dishonor (n.) ነውር *näwr;* ውርደት *wərdät*

dishonorable (conduct) አሳፋሪ *asaffari*

disinherit ከውርስ ፡ ነቀለ *käwərs näqqälä;* ከዳ *kadä*

disintegrate (vt.) ገነጣጠለ *gänäṭaṭṭälä*
disintegrate (vi.) ተለያየ *täläyayyä*

disinterested, be (free from bias) አላደላም *aladällam*

disjoint ገነጣጠለ *gänäṭaṭṭälä*

disk (record) ሸክላ *šäkla*

dislike (v.) ጠላ *ṭälla;* አልወደደም *alwäddädäm*

dislike (n.) ጥላቻ *ṭəlačča*

dislocate (of earthquake dislocating buildings) አናጋ *annagga*
be dislocated (shoulder) ወለቀ *wälläqä;* (wrist) ወለም ፡ አለ *wälämm alä*

dislodge (~ rocks) ፈነቃቀለ *fänäqaqqälä;* (~ the enemy) አስለቀቀ *asläqqäqä*

disloyal 323 **dissatisfy**

disloyal ታማኝነት ፡ የጎደለው *tammañ-ñannät yägʷäddäläw*

dismal (∼ weather) ቀፋፊ *qäfafi*

dismantle ፈታታ *fätatta*

dismay (v.) አስጨነቀ *asčännäqä*
be dismayed ተደነገጠ *tädänäggäṭä;* ተጨነቀ *täčännäqä*

dismay (n.) ድንጋጤ *dənaggaṭe;* ተስፋ ፡ መቁረጥ *täsfa mäqʷräṭ*

dismiss አሰወገደ *aswäggädä;* (∼ the class) አሰናበተ *assänabbätä;* (∼ a worker) አሰናበተ *assänabbätä;* ከሥራ ፡ አባረረ *käsəra abbarrärä;* (from office) ሻረ *šarä*

dismount (vi.) ወረደ *wärrädä*

disobedience አለማታዘዝ *alämättazäz*

disobedient የማይታዘዝ *yämmayəttazzäz;* እምቢተኛ *əmbitäñña*

disobey እምቢ ፡ አለ *əmbi alä;* አልታዘዝም ፡ አለ *aləttazzäzəm alä*

disorder ትርምስምስ *tərməsməs;* መዝረክረክ *mäzräkräk;* (riot) ረብሻ *räbša;* (ailment) ሕመም *həmäm*

disorderly (∼ mob) ሕጋ ፡ ወጥ *həggä wäṭṭ;* (∼ person) ልከስከስ *ləkəskəs;* (∼ desk) የተመሰቃቀለ *yätämäsäqaqqälä*

disorganize አቃወሰ *aqqawwäsä*

disown, see 'disinherit'

disparage አንቋሸሸ *anqʷaššäšä*

disparity አለmemጣጠን *alämämmäṭaṭän*

dispatch, v. (send quickly) በፍጥነት ፡ ላከ *bäfəṭnät laka*

dispatch, n. (message) ደብዳቤ *däbdabbe;* (quick action) ቅልጥፍና *qəlṭəfənna*

dispel (∼ the fog) በተነ *bättänä;* (∼ fear) አስወገደ *aswäggädä*

dispensary የሕክምና ፡ ክፍል *yähəkmənna kəfəl*

dispense ዐደለ *addälä*

disperse (vt.) በታተነ *bätattänä*
disperse (vi.) ተበታተነ *täbätattänä*

displace ያለ ፡ በታው ፡ አስቀመጠ *yalä botaw asqämmäṭä*

display (v.) አሳየ *asayyä*

display (n.) ትዕይንት *tə'əyənt;* ማታየት *mättayät*
be on display ታየ *tayyä*

displease አስከፋ *askäffa;* ደስ ፡ አላሰኘም *däss alassäññäm*

displeasure ቅሬታ *qərreta*

dispose, ∼ of (throw away) ጣለ *ṭalä;* (sell) ሸጠ *šäṭä*

disposition (temperament) ባሕሪይ *bahriy;* ጠባይ *ṭäbay;* (inclination) ዝንባሌ *zənəbbale;* (arrangement of soldiers) አመዳደብ *ammädadäb;* (arrangement of chairs) አቀማመጥ *aqqämamäṭ*

dispossess አስለቀቀ *asläqqäqä*

disproportionate ያልተመዛዘነ *yaltämäzazzänä*

disprove ሐሰት ፡ መሆኑን ፡ አስረዳ *hassät mähonun asrädda*

disputable የሚያከራክር *yämmiyakkäräkkär*

dispute (v.) ተጨቃጨቀ *täčäqaččäqä*

dispute (n.) ክርክር *kərəkkər;* ጭቅጭቅ *čəqəččəq;* ጠብ *ṭäb*

disqualify አስቀረ *asqärrä;* ከለከለ *käläkkälä*

disregard (v.) ቸል ፡ አለ *čäll alä;* ቻላ ፡ አለ *čälla alä*

disrespect, show ∼ እንንጠጠ *angʷaṭṭäṭä*

disreputable ወራዳ *wärradda*

disrespectful (person) ባለጌ *baläge;* (attitude) የብልግና *yäbəlgənna*

disrupt (∼ a conference) በጠበጠ *bäṭäbbäṭä;* (∼ the surface of water, the unity of a country) አናወጠ *annawwäṭa*

disruption ብጥብጥ *bəṭəbbəṭ;* ሁከት *hukät*

dissatisfy ቅር ፡ አሰኘ *qərr assäññä*
dissatisfied, be ቅር ፡ ተሰኘ *qərr täsäññä*

disseminate (~ news) አሰራጨ *assärač-čä;* ነዛ *näzza*

dissension ጠብ *ṭäb*

dissent, v. (oppose) ተቃወመ *täqawwämä;* (not agree) አልተስማማም *altäsmammam*

dissent (n.) አለመስማማት *alämäsmamat*

dissident (n.) ተቃዋሚ *täqawami*

dissimilar የተለያየ *yätäläyayyä*

dissimilarity አለመስማማት *alämäsmamat*

dissimulate ሸሸገ *šäššägä;* ደበቀ *däbbäqä*

dissipate (vt.) በተነ *bättänä;* (~ fortune) አባከነ *abakkänä*
    dissipate (vi.) ተበተነ *täbättänä*

dissipated (~ life) ብኩን *bəkun*

dissociate ለየ *läyyä*

dissolute (~ life) የወራዳነት *yäwärraddannät;* (~ person) ምንዝረኛ *mənzəräňňa*

dissolve, vt. (~ salt, sugar) አሟሟ *amʷammʷa;* (~ partnership) አፈረሰ *afärräsä*
    dissolve, vi. (in water) ሟሟ *mʷammʷa;* (of partnership) ፈረሰ *färräsä*

distance ርቀት *rəqät*

distant ሩቅ *ruq*
    be distant ራቀ *raqä*

distaste ጥላቻ *ṭəlačča*

distasteful (~ medicine) ጣዕም ፡ ቢስ *ṭa'əmä bis*

distend ወጠረ *wäṭṭärä*

distill (~ water) አነጠረ *anäṭṭärä;* አጣራ *aṭṭarra*

distinct (different) ልዩ *ləyyu;* የተለያየ *yätäläyayyä;* (clear) ጉልህ *guləh*

distinction (difference) ልዩነት *ləyyunnät;* (honor) ክብር *kəbər;* (excellence) ሊቅነት *liqənnät*

distinctive ልዩ *ləyyu*

distinctly ግልጽ ፡ አድርጎ *gəlṣ adrəgo*

distinguish ለየ *läyyä*

distinguished (adj.) የታወቀ *yätawwäqä*

distort አዛባ *azzabba;* አዛነፈ *azzannäfä;* (of a mirror distorting the face) አጣመመ *aṭṭammämä*

distract, v. (amuse) ጣመ *ṭamä;* (take away one's mind) ሐሳቡን ፡ አዛባ *hassabun azzabba;* ሐሳቡን ፡ ሳበ *hassabun sabä*

distraction (thing that draws away attention) ሐሳብ ፡ የሚስብ ፡ ነገር *hassab yämmisəb nägär*

distress (v.) አሠቃየ *assäqayyä;* አስጨነቀ *asčännäqä*

distress (n.) ሥቃይ *səqay;* ችግር *čəggər;* ጭንቅ *čənq*
    be in distress ጨገረ *čäggärä*

distressing አሳዛኝ *asazzaň*

distribute አከፋለ *akkaffälä*

distribution አከፋፈል *akkäfafäl*

district ቀበሌ *qäbäle;* አውራጃ *awraǧǧa*

distrust (v.) ተጠራጠረ *täṭäraṭṭärä;* አላ መነም *alammänäm*

distrust (n.) ጥርጣሬ *ṭərəṭṭare*

distrustful ተጠራጣሪ *täṭäraṭari*

disturb አወከ *awwäkä;* አስቸገረ *asčäggärä;* (put out of order) አመሰቃቀለ *ammäsäqaqqälä*

disturbance ችግር *čəggər;* ጭንቀት *čənqät;* (political ~) ሁከት *hukät*

ditch ጉድጓድ *gudgʷad*

dive ጠለቀ *ṭälläqä*

diverge (of opinion) ተለያየ *täläyayyä;* (of paths) ተገነጠለ *tägänäṭṭälä*

divergence ልዩነት *ləyyunnät*

diverse የተለያየ *yätäläyayyä*

diversion (change of direction) አቅጣጫ ፡ መለወጥ *aqṭačča mäläwwäṭ;* (pastime) ጊዜውን ፡ የሚያሳልፍበት ፡ ጨዋታ *gizewən yämmiyasalləfəbbät čawata*

divert (turn aside) አቅጣጫ ፡ ለወጠ *aqṭačča läwwäṭä;* (amuse) አስደሰተ *asdässätä;* አጫወተ *ačawwätä*

divide ከፈለ *käffälä;* አካፈለ *akkaffälä;* (separate) ለየ *läyyä*

divination ጥንቄላ *ṭǝnqʷäla;* መነበይ *männäbäy*

divine (v.) ተነበየ *tänäbbäyä*

divine, ∼ kingdom መንግሥተ ፡ ሰማያት *mängǝstä sämayat*
divine scripture ቅዱሳት ፡ መጻሕፍት *qǝddusat mäṣaḥǝft*

divinity መላኮት *mälakot*

divisible ተካፋይ *täkafay*

division (dividing) አከፋፈል *akkäfafäl;* (separation) ልዩነት *lǝyyunnät;* (section) ክፍል *kǝfǝl;* (of army) ክፍለ ፡ ጦር *kǝflä ṭor;* (in arithmetic) ማካፈል *makkafäl*

divorce (v.) ፈታ *fätta*

divorce (n.) ፍች *fǝčč*

divorced (adj.) ፈት *fätt*

divulge (∼ a secret) አወጣ *awäṭṭa*

dizzy, feel ∼ ራሱ ፡ ዞረ *rasu zorä;* ተጫ ጫነ(ው) *täčačanä(w)*

do ሥራ *särra;* አደረገ *adärrägä*

docile ታዛዥ *tazzaž*

dock (n.) የመርከብ ፡ ማራገፊያ *yämärkäb marragäfiya*

doctor (n.) ሐኪም *hakim;* ዶክተር *doktär*

doctrine (of church) ሕግ *hǝgg;* (belief) እምነት *ǝmnät*

document (n.) ሰነድ *sänäd*

dog ውሻ *wǝšša*

dogma ሕግ *hǝgg*

doll አሻንጉሊት *ašangullit*

dollar ብር *bǝrr*

dolorous አሳዛኝ *asazzaň*

domain (estate) ርስት *rǝst;* (territory) ግዛት *gǝzat*

dome ጉልላት *gullǝlat*

domestic (n.) አሽከር *aškär*

domestic (adj.) የቤት *yäbet;* (of one's

own country) የሀገር ፡ ውስጥ *yähagär wǝsṭ*

domesticate አላመደ *allammädä;* ለማዳ ፡ አደረገ *lämmada adärrägä*

domesticated ለማዳ *lämmada*

domicile መኖሪያ *mänoriya*

dominant ከሌላው ፡ የሚልቅ *kälelaw yäm-milǝq;* ጉልቶ ፡ የሚታይ *gʷälto yäm-mittay;* (main) ዋና *wanna*
be dominant ሰፈነ *säffänä*

dominate ገዛ *gäzza*

domination አገዛዝ *aggäzaz*

domineer ጨቄነ *čäqqʷänä*

dominion (territory) ግዛት *gǝzat;* (supreme authority) የበላይነት *yäbäla-yǝnnät*

donate እርዳታ ፡ ሰጠ *ǝrdata säṭṭä;* ረዳ *rädda*

donation እርዳታ *ǝrdata;* ስጦታ *sǝṭota*

done, be (finished) አለቀ *alläqä*

donkey አህያ *ahǝyya*

doom, v. (condemn) ፈረደ(በት) *färrädä-(bbät)*

door መዝጊያ *mäzgiya*
out of doors ደጅ *däǧǧ;* ውጭ *wǝčč*

doorsill ደፍ *däf*

doorstep ደጃፍ *däǧǧaf;* ባራፍ *bärraf*

doorway በር *bärr;* ባራፍ *bärraf;* ደጅ *däǧǧ*

dormitory መኝታ ፡ ቤት *mäňňǝta bet*

dose መጣን *mäṭän*

dossier ፋይል *fayl*

dot, n. (on cloth) ጣቃጠቆ *ṭäqaṭäqo;* (point) ነጥብ *näṭǝb*
on the dot ልክ *lǝkk;* ልክ ፡ በሰዓቱ *lǝkk bäsä'atu*

double, vt. (fold) ዐጠፈ *aṭṭäfä;* (make twice as much) ዕጥፍ ፡ አደረገ *ǝṭǝf adär-rägä*
double (vi.) ዕጥፍ ፡ ሆነ *ǝṭǝf honä*
double up (in pain) ተሸማቀቀ *täšä-maqqäqä;* ተኮራመተ *täkʷärammätä*

double (n.) ዕጥፍ *ətəf*

double, adj. (~ meaning, purpose) ሁለት *hulätt*; (~ door) መንታ *mänta*

double-cross አጭበረበረ *ačbäräbbärä*

doubt (v.)ʾ ጠረጠረ *täräṭṭärä*; ተጠራጠረ *täṭäraṭṭärä*

doubt (n.) ጥርጣሬ *ṭərəṭṭare*; ጥርጥር *ṭə- rəṭṭər*
be in doubt ተጠራጠረ *täṭäraṭṭärä*
beyond doubt, see 'doubtless'
raise doubts አጠራጠረ *aṭṭäraṭṭärä*

doubtful አጠራጣሪ *aṭṭäraṭari*

doubtless ያለ ፡ ጥርጥር *yalä ṭərəṭṭər*

dough ሊጥ *liṭ*; (fermented~) ቡኮ *buko*

dove ርግብ *rəgəb*

down ታች *tačč*

downcast, be አዘነ *azzänä*

downfall ውድቀት *wədqät*

downhill, go~ ቁልቁለቱን ፡ ወረደ *qulqu- lätun wärrädä*
downhill slope ቁልቁለት *qulqulät*

down payment ቀብድ *qäbd*; የመጀመሪያ ፡ ክፍያ *yämäǧämmäriya kəffəya*

downpour ከባድ ፡ ዝናብ *käbbad zənab*

downright ቁርጥ ፡ ያለ *qurrəṭṭ yalä*

downstairs እምድር ፡ ቤት *əmədər bet*

downward ቁልቁል *qulqul*

downwards ወደ ፡ ታች *wädä tačč*

dowry ጥሎሽ *ṭəloš*

doze አንቀላፋ *anqälaffa*

dozen ደርዘን *därzän*

drab (~ clothes) ረጋ ፡ ሠራሽ *räga sär- raš*; (~ existence) የማይጥም *yämma- yəṭəm*

draft, v. (~a bill) አረቀቀ *aräqqäqä*; (into the army) መለመለ *mälämmälä*

draft, n. (of wind) ነፋስ *näfas*; (bill) የሕ ግ ፡ ረቂቅ *yähəgg räqiq*; (of a speech) ረቂቅ *räqiq*; (of bank) ሐዋላ *hawwala*

drag (vt.) ሳበ *sabä*; ጐተተ *gʷättätä*
drag on ተጎተተ *tägʷättätä*

drain, vt. (~ marshland) አደረቀ *adär- räqä*; (~ bathtub) አፈሰሰ *afässäsä*; ውሃ ፡ ለቀቀ *wəha läqqäqä*

drain (n.) የእጣቢ ፡ መውረጃ *yäəṭṭabi mäwräǧa*

drama ቲያትር *tiyatər*; ድራማ *drama*; (story) ታሪክ *tarik*

drape, v. (~a window) ጋረደ *garrädä*; (~a skirt) ሸነሸነ *šänäššänä*

drape (n.) ወፍራም ፡ መጋረጃ *wäfram mäggaräǧa*

drastic (~measure) ጥብቅ *ṭəbq*

draw (drag) ጐተተ *gʷättätä*; ሳበ *sabä*; (~a picture) ሣለ *salä*; (~water) ቀዳ *qädda*; (~lots) ተጣጣለ *täṭaṭalä*; (attract) ማረከ *marräkä*; (~ a sword) መዘዘ *mäzzäzä*; (~a line) አሠመረ *asämmärä*
draw near ተጠጋ *täṭägga*; ተቃረበ *tä- qarräbä*
draw up (~ a plan) ነደፈ *näddäfä*; (~ a program) አዘጋጀ *azzägaǧǧä*; (~ a constitution) አረቀቀ *aräqqäqä*

drawback ዕንቅፋት *ənqəfat*

drawer መሳቢያ *mäsabiya*

drawing ሥዕል *sə'əl*

dread, v. (fear) ፈራ *färra*; ሰጋ *sägga*

dread (n.) ስጋት *səgat*

dreadful አስቃቂ *assäqqaqi*; የሚያስጠላ *yämmiyasṭälla*

dream (v.) አለመ *allämä*

dream (n.) እልም *əlm*; ሕልም *həlm*

dreary ቀፋፊ *qäfafi*; የማያስደስት *yäm- mayasdässət*

dregs (of coffee) አሠር *asär*; አተላ *atä- la*; (of mead) አምቡላ *ambulla*

drench አበሰበሰ *abäsäbbäsä*; አራሰ *arasä*

dress (vt.) አለበሰ *aläbbäsä*
dress (vi.) ለበሰ *läbbäsä*
be all dressed up ሽክ ፡ አለ *šəkk alä*

dress (n.) ልብስ *ləbs*; ቀሚስ *qämis*

dresser (chest of drawers) ባለ ፡ መስታ
ወት ፡ ከመዳኛ balä mästawät kämä-
dino

dressing (bandage) የቁስል ፡ ፋሻ yäqusəl
faša; (sauce for a salad) ማጣፈጫ ma-
ṭafäča

dressmaker ልብስ ፡ ሰፊ ləbs säfi

dribble (of water) ተንጠባጠበ tänṭäbaṭṭäbä

dried (adj.) ደረቅ däräq

drift, v. (of logs) ተንሳፈፈ tänsaffäfä;
(of thoughts) ባከነ bakkänä

drift, n. (direction) አቅጣጫ aqṭačča;
(trend) አዝማሚያ azmamiya

drill, v. (train) ልምምድ ፡ አደረገ ləməmmäd adärrägä; (~ a hole) ሰረሰረ särässärä; በሳ bässa

drill, n. (training) ልምምድ ləməmmäd;
(tool) መሰርሰሪያ mäsärsäriya

drink (v.) ጠጣ ṭäṭṭa

drink (n.) መጠጥ mäṭäṭṭ

drinker ጠጪ ṭäčči

drip ጠብ ፡ አለ ṭäbb alä; ተንጠባጠበ tänṭäbaṭṭäbä; ተንጠፈጠፈ tänṭäfäṭṭäfä

drive, v. (~ a car) ነዳ nädda; (force)
ገፋፋ gäfaffa
drive away አስኬደ askedä; አባረረ abbarrärä
drive out (vt.) አስለቀቀ asläqqäqä

drive, n. (by car) በመኪና ፡ መንሸራሸር
bämäkina mänšäräšär; (forceful effort, energy) ትጋት təgat; የሥራ ፡ መን
ፈስ yäsəra mänfäs; (campaign) ተጋ
ድሎ tägadlo

driver ነጅ näği; (of carriage) ባለጋሪ balägari

driver's license መንጃ ፡ ፈቃድ mänǧa fäqad

driveway መግቢያ ፡ መንገድ mägbiya
mängäd

drizzle (v.) አካፋ akaffa

drizzle (n.) ካፊያ kaffiya

drone, v. (of bees) አነበነበ anäbännäbä

drone (n.) ንብ nəb

drool ለሀጭ ፡ አዝረከረከ lähač azräkärräkä

droop (of flower) ጠወለገ ṭäwällägä; (of
spirit) ደከመ däkkämä

drop (vt.) ጣለ ṭalä; (~ a remark) ጣል ፡
አደረገ ṭall adärrägä; (abandon) ተወ
täwä
drop, vi. (of drops) ነጠበ näṭṭäbä; (of
price) ወደቀ wäddäqä; ዝቅ ፡ አለ zəqq
alä; (of fruit) ረገፈ räggäfä; (of temperature) ቀነሰ qännäsä
drop by (in) ብቅ ፡ አለ bəqq alä; ጎራ ፡
አለ gʷära alä
drop out (of school) ወጣ wäṭṭa

drop (n.) ነጠብጣብ näṭäbṭab; ጠብታ ṭäbbəta; (in prices) ዝቅ ፡ ማለት zəqq
malät

drought ድርቅ dərq

drove መንጋ mänga
come in droves ጎረፈ gʷärräfä
in droves በብዛት bäbəzat

drown (vt.) አሰጠመ asäṭṭämä
drown (vi.) ሰጠመ säṭṭämä; ሰመጠ sämmäṭä

drowse አንጎላጅ angʷälaǧǧä

drowsy (~ weather) የሚያሸልብ yämmiččačan; የሚያንጎላጅ yämmiyan-
gʷälaǧǧ; (person) ያንቀላፋ yanqälaffa

drudgery የማያስደስት ፡ ሥራ yämmayasdässət səra

drug (v.) በመድኃኒት ፡ አደነዛዛ bämädha-
nit adänäzzäzä

drug, n. (medicine) መድኃኒት mädhanit;
(addictive) ሱስ ፡ የሚያሲዝ ፡ መድኃ
ኒት sus yämmiyasiz mädhanit

druggist መድኃኒት ፡ ቀማሚ mädhanit
qämmami

drugstore (የ)መድኃኒት ፡ ቤት (yä)mädha-
nit bet

drum, v. (tap) ደበደበ däbäddäbä; (~ a
drum) ታምቡር ፡ መታ tambur mätta

drum, n. (musical instrument) ከበሮ *kä-bäro;* (small drum) አታሞ *atamo ;* (container) በርሚል *bärmil*
play the drum ከበሮ ፡ መታ *käbäro mätta*

drunk (n.), see 'drunkard'

drunk, be (get) ሰከረ *säkkärä*

drunkard ሰካር *säkkar;* ሰካራም *säkkaram*

drunkenness ስካር *səkar*

dry (vt.) አደረቀ *adärräqä;* (~ dishes) ወለወለ *wäläwwälä*
dry (vi.) ደረቀ *därräqä*

dry (adj.) ደረቅ *däräq;* (~ weather) ድርቅ *dərq*
be dry ደረቀ *därräqä*

dry land የብስ *yäbs*

dryness ድርቀት *dərqät*

dry season በጋ *bäga*

dubious (~ friend) የማይታመን *yämma-yəttammän;* (~ plan) የሚያስጠረጥር *yämmiyasṭärätṭər*

duck (n.) ዳክዬ *dakkəyye*

due(s) ድርሻ *dərša*

due, adj. (proper) ተገቢ *tägäbi*
due to በ - - - ምክንያት *bä - - - məknə-yat;* በ - - - የተነሣ *bä - - - yätänässa*

duke መስፍን *mäsfən*

dull (~ knife) ደነዝ *dänäz;* (~ pencil) ዱልዱም *duldum;* (~ color) ደብዛዝ ፡ ያለ *däbzäzz yalä;* (~ person) ደደብ *däddäb;* (~ game) የሚያሰለች *yämmi-yasäläčč;* (~ book) ጣዕም ፡ የሌለው *ta'əm yälelläw*
be dull (pencil) ዶለደመ *doläddomä;* (knife) ደነዘ *dännäzä;* (be boring) ተሰ ለቸ *täsäläččä*

duly በሚገባ *bämmiggäbba*

dumb (not able to speak) ድዳ *dəda;* (stupid) ደደብ *däddäb*

dumbfounded, be አፉ ፡ ተያዘ *afu täyazä*

dump (v.) ጣለ *ṭalä*

dump (n.) ቆሻሻ ፡ መጣያ *qošaša mäṭṭa-ya;* (of ammunition) ማከማቻ *makkä-mača*

dune ያሸዋ ፡ ክምር *yašäwa kəmmər*

dung ፍግ *fəg*
dried dung (of cow) ኩበት *kubät*

dunk ጠለቀ *ṭälläqä;* (~ bread) ጠቀሰ *ṭäq-qäsä*

dupe (v.) ሸፈጠ *šäffäṭä;* አጭበረበረ *ačbä-räbbärä*

dupe (n.) ተታላይ *tätalay;* ድልል *dəlləl*

duplicate (v.) አባዛ *abbazza*

duplicate (n.) ግልባጭ *gəlbač*
in duplicate ሁለት ፡ ቅጂ *hulätt qəǧǧi*

duplicity አታላይነት *attalayənnät*

durable ጽኑ *ṣənu*
be durable (clothes) በረከተ *bäräkkätä*

during በ - - - ጊዜ *bä - - - gize*

dusk, in the ~ ላይን ፡ ሲያዝ *layn siyəz*

dust (v.) ወለወለ *wäläwwälä*

dust (n.) ትቢያ *təbbiya;* አቧራ *abʷara;* አዋራ *awwara*
turn to dust አመድ ፡ ሆነ *amäd honä*

dusty አቧራማ *abʷaramma*

dutiful (~ person) ታዛዥ *tazzaž;* ቄም ፡ ነገረኛ *qum nägäräñña*

duty (action) ተግባር *tägbar;* (obligation) ግዴታ *gəddeta;* ግዳጅ *gəddaǧ;* (tax) ቀረጥ *qäräṭ*
be on duty ተረኛ ፡ ነው *täräñña näw*
do duty አገለገለ *agäläggälä*

dwarf (n.) ድንክ *dənk*

dwell ኖረ *norä*

dweller ነዋሪ *näwari*

dwelling መኖሪያ ፡ ቤት *mänoriya bet*

dwindle (of food) መነመነ *mänämmänä;* (of water) አጣጣ *aṭṭäṭä*

dye (v.) ነከረ *näkkärä;* ቀለመ *qällämä;* ቀለም ፡ ነከረ *qäläm näkkärä*

dye (n.) መንከሪያ *mänkäriya;* መቅለሚያ *mäqlämiya*

dynamic (∼person) ታታሪ *tatari*

dynamite ደማሚት *dämamit*

dynasty ሥርወ ፡ መንግሥት *sərwä mängəst*

dysentery የተቅማጥ ፡ በሽታ *yätäqmaṭ bäššəta*

E

each እያንዳንድ *əyyandand*
each other እርስ ፡ በርሳቸው *ərs bärsaččäw*

eager ጉጉ *guggu*
be eager ጓጓ *gʷaggʷa*

eagerly በጉጉት *bäguggut*

eagle ንስር *nəsər*

ear ጆሮ *ǧoro;* (of pitcher) እጀታ *əǧǧäta*
ear of corn ራስ *ras*

earlier (adj.) የቀድሞ *yäqädmo;* የበፊት *yäbäfit*
earlier (adv.) ቀደም ፡ ብሎ *qädämm bəlo;* ቅድም *qəddəm*
be earlier ቀደመ *qäddämä*

early, adj. (before the expected time) ቀደም ፡ ያለ *qädämm yalä;* (ancient) የጥንት *yäṭənt*
early, adv. (soon) ቶሎ *tolo;* በጊዜ *bägize;* ቀደም ፡ ብሎ *qädämm bəlo;* (at the beginning) ጥንት *ṭənt;* (in the morning) ማለዳ *maläda*
come early ቀደም ፡ አለ *qädämm alä*
rise early ማለደ *mallädä*

earmark (v.) ለይቶ ፡ አስቀመጠ *läyyəto asqämmäṭä*

earmark (n.) ምልክት *mäləkkət*

earn አተረፈ *atärräfä;* አገኘ *agäňňä*

earnest ቅን *qən*

earring ጉትቻ *gutəčča*

earth መሬት *märet;* ምድር *mədər;* (soil) አፈር *afär*

earthen የሸክላ *yäšäkla*

earthenware ሸክላ *šäkla;* ሸሀላ *šähla;* የሸሀላ ፡ እቃ *yäšähla əqa*

earthly ምድራዊ *mədrawi*

earthquake የመሬት ፡ መንቀጥቀጥ *yämäret mänqäṭqäṭ*

ease, v. (∼pain) አስታገሠ *astaggäsä;* (make easier) አቃለለ *aqqallälä*

ease, n. (life of ∼) ምቾት *məččot*
feel at ease ተዝናና *täznanna;* እንደ ፡ ልቡ ፡ ሆነ *əndä ləbbu honä*

easier, be ቀለለ *qällälä*

easily (without difficulty) በቀላሉ *bäqällalu;* ያለ ፡ ችግር *yalä čəggər*

east (n.) ምሥራቅ *məsraq*

east (adj.) ምሥራቃዊ *məsraqawi*

Easter ፋሲካ *fasika*

eastern የምሥራቅ *yäməsraq;* ምሥራቃዊ *məsraqawi*

easy ቀላል *qällal;* (∼teacher) ልል *ləl*
be easy ቀለለ *qällälä*
take it easy! አትጨነቅ *attaččännäq*

easy chair ምቹ ፡ ወምበር *məčču wämbär*

eat በላ *bälla*

eater, big ∼ ሆዳም *hodam*

eave የቤት ፡ ከፈፍ *yäbet kəfäf*

eavesdrop በስውር ፡ አዳመጠ *bäsəwwər addammäṭä*

ebb, v. (of tide) ሸሸ *šäššä*

ecclesiastic ካህን *kahən*

echo (v.) አስተጋባ *astägabba*

echo (n.) የገደል ፡ ማሚቶ *yägädäl mammito*

eclipse (n.) ግርዶሽ *gərdoš*

economic የኤኮኖሚ *yäekonomi*

economical ቈጣቢ *qʷäṭṭabi*
be economical ቈጠበ *qʷäṭṭäbä*

economics ኤኮኖሚክስ *ekonomiks;* ምጣኔ ፡ ሀብት *mäṭṭane habt*

economize ቈጠበ *q^wäṭṭäbä*

ecstasy ፍንደቃ *fəndäqa*

edge (v.) ከፈፈ *käffäfä*

edge, n. (of town) ዳር *dar;* ዳርቻ *da-räčča;* (of plate) ጠርዝ *ṭärz;* (of cliff) አፋፍ *afaf;* (of knife) ስለት *sälät*

edible የሚበላ *yämmibbälla*

edict ዐዋጅ *awwäǧä*

edifice ሕንጻ *hənṣa*

edit አዘጋጀ *azzägaǧǧä*

edition እትም *əttəm*

editor አዘጋጅ *azzägaǧ*

editorial ርእስ : አንቀጽ *rə'əsä anqäṣ*

educate አስተማረ *astämarä*

educated የተማረ *yätämarä*

education ትምህርት *təmhərt*
receive an education ተማረ *tämarä*
Minister of Education የትምህርት : ሚኒስቴር *yätəmhərt minister*

educational ትምህርት : ነክ *təmhərt näkk*

educator የትምህርት : ሊቅ *yätəmhərt liq*

efface አጠፋ *aṭäffa;* (∼writing) ደመሰሰ *dämässäsä*

effect, v. (bring about) አስከተለ *askättälä;* (accomplish) አከናወነ *akkänawwänä*

effect, n. (result) ውጤት *wəṭṭet;* (force) ኀይል *hayl*
be in effect (rule) ጸና *ṣänna*
go into effect በሥራ : ላይ : ዋለ *bäsəra lay walä*
have an effect ሠራ *särra*
take effect ሠራ *särra*

effective አጥጋቢ *aṭgabi;* ጥሩ : ውጤት : የሚሰጥ *ṭäru wəṭṭet yämmisäṭ;* (∼medicine) ፍቱን *fətun*
be effective ጸና *ṣänna*

effects እቃ *əqa*

effeminate የሴት *yäset;* ሴታ : ሴት *seta set*

efficacious (∼solution) አጥጋቢ *aṭgabi;* (∼remedy) ፍቱን *fətun*

efficiency ቅልጥፍና *qəlṭəfənna*

efficient ቀልጣፋ *qälṭaffa*

effigy ምስል *məsəl*

effort ትግል *təgəl;* ድካም *dəkam;* ጥረት *ṭärät*
make an effort ለፋ *läffa;* ጣረ *ṭarä;* ሞከረ *mokkärä*

effrontery ብልግና *bəlgənna;* ድፍረት *dəf-rät*

egg እንቁላል *ənqulal*
lay an egg እንቁላል : ጣለች *ənqulal ṭaläčč*

eggshell የእንቁላል : ቅርፊት *yäənqulal qərfit*

egoism ራሱን : ብቻ : ወዳድነት *rasun bəč-ča wäddadənnät*

eight ስምንት *səmmənt*
eight o'clock ሁለት : ሰዓት *hulätt sä'at*

eighteen ዐሥራ : ስምንት *asra səmmənt*

eighth ስምንታዊ *səmməntawi*

eighty ሰማንያ *sämanya*

either አንዱም *andum*
either --- or ወይም --- ወይም *wä-yəm --- wäyəm;* ወይም *wäyəm*

eject አስወጣ *aswäṭṭa;* አስፈነጠረ *asfänäṭ-ṭärä*

elaborate (v.) በዝርዝር : አዘጋጀ *bäzərzər azzägaǧǧä*

elaborate, adj. (∼structure) ረቂቅ *räqiq;* (∼preparations) ከፍተኛ : ጥንቃቄ : የሚደረግለት *käffətäňňa ṭənəqqaqe yämmiddärrägəllät*

elapse አለፈ *alläfä;* ተላለፈ *tälalläfä*

elastic (n.) ላስቲክ *lastik*

elastic (adj.) የሚለጠጥ *yämmilläṭṭäṭ*

elate አስፈነደቀ *asfänäddäqä*
be elated ፈነደቀ *fänäddäqä*

elation ፍንደቃ *fəndäqa*

elbow ክርን *kərn*

elder, n. (aged) ሽማግሌ *šämagəlle;* (older person) ታላቅ *tallaq* elder, adj. (～ brother) ታላቅ *tallaq*

elderly በዕድሜ ፡ የገፋ *bäədme yägäffa;* ጠና ፡ ያለ *ṭäna yalä*
elderly woman ባልቴት *baltet*

eldest የበኸር ፡ ልጅ *yäbähər ləǧ*

elect መረጠ *märräṭa*

election ምርጫ *mərča*

electric በኤሌክትሪክ ፡ የሚሠራ *bäelektrik yämmisära*

electric bulb አምፑል *ampul*

electric current ኮረንቲ *korränti*

electrician የኤሌክትሪክ ፡ ሠራተኛ *yäelektrik särratäňňa*

electricity ኤሌክትሪክ *elektrik;* ኮረንቲ *korränti*

electrocuted, be በኮረንቲ ፡ ተገደለ *bäkorränti tägäddälä*

elegant (～ dress) ያሸበረቀ *yašäbärräqä;* (～ furnishings) ያጊያገጠ *yagiyageṭä;* (～ manners) ድንቅ *dənq*

element (single substance) ጥንት ፡ ንጥር *ṭəntä nəṭr;* (essentials) መሠረታዊ ፡ ነገር *mäsärätawi nägär*

elementary (rudimentary) የጀማሪዎች *yäǧämmariwočč*

elementary school አንደኛ ፡ ደረጃ ፡ ትምህ ርት ፡ ቤት *andäňňa däräǧa təmhərt bet*

elephant ዝሆን *zəhon*

elevate (raise in rank or position) ከፍ ፡ አደረገ *käff adärrägä*

elevated, adj. (～ platform) ከፍ ፡ ያለ *käff yalä;* (～ thoughts) ጥልቅ *ṭəlq*

elevation (height) ከፍታ *käffəta;* (raised place) ጉብታ *gubbəta*

elevator አሳንሰር *asansär;* አሳንሱር *asansur;* ኤሌቬትር *elevätər*

eleven አሥራንድ *asrand*
eleven o'clock አምስት ፡ ሰዓት *amməst sä'at*

eligible መመረጥ ፡ የሚችል *mämmäräṭ yämmičəl;* (qualified) ብቁ ፡ የሆነ *bəqu yähonä*

eliminate አስወጣ *aswäṭṭa;* (destroy) አጠፋ *aṭäffa;* (～ difficulties) አስወገደ *aswäggädä*

elite ቁንጮ *qunčo;* ምርጥ ፡ የሆነ *mərṭ yähonä*

elongate አስረዘመ *asräzzämä*

elope ኩብለላ *kʷäbällälä*

eloquence አንደበት ፡ ርቱዕነት *andäbätä rətu'ənnät*

eloquent (～ speaker) አንደበት ፡ ርቱዕ *andäbätä rətu';* (～ speech) የተሳካ *yätäsakka;* (～ plea) ስሜት ፡ የሚነካ *səmmet yämminäka*

else ያለበለዚያ *yaläbäläzziya*

elsewhere ሌላ ፡ ቦታ *lela bota;* ሌላጋ *lelaga*

elucidate አብራራ *abrarra*

elusive, see 'evasive'

emaciate አመነመነ *amänämmänä*
be emaciated መነመነ *mänämmänä;* ከሳ *kässa*

emancipate ነጻ ፡ አወጣ *näṣä awäṭṭa;* አር ነት ፡ አወጣ *arənnät awäṭṭa*

emancipation ነጻ ፡ መውጣት *näṣa mäwṭat*

emasculate ሰለበ *sälläbä*

embankment ግድብ *gəddəb;* ያፈር ፡ ቁልል *yafär qulləl*

embargo ማገጃ *maggäǧa*

embark ተሳፈረ *täsaffärä*

embarrass አሳፈረ *asaffärä;* (disconcert) ቅር ፡ አሰኘ *qərr assäňňä*
be embarrassed አፈረ *affärä;* (be distressed) ተጨነቀ *täčännäqä*

embarrassing (～ question) አሳፋሪ *asaffari;* (～ situation) የሚያስጨንቅ *yämmiyasčännəq*

embarrassment ጭንቅ *čənq*

embassy ኤምባሲ *embasi*

embellish አሳመረ *asammärä;* አስጌጠ *asgeṭä*

ember ፍም *fəm*

embezzle አጭበረበረ ačbäräbbärä; አደራ፣ በላ adära bälla

embezzler አደራ ፣ በላ.ታ adära bällitta; አጭበርባሪ ačbärbari

embitter አመረረ amärrärä; አናደደ annaddädä

emblem አርማ arma

embody (include) ያዘ yazä

embolden አደፋፈረ addäfaffärä

embrace (hug) አቀፈ aqqäfä; (include) ያዘ yazä

embroider ጠለፈ ṭälläfä; (~ a story) ቀባባ qababba

embroidery ጥልፍ ṭəlf

embryo ሽል šəl

emend አሻሻለ aššašalä

emerge ብቅ ፣ አለ bəqq alä

emergency (n.) አስቸኳይ ፣ ሁኔታ asčäkkʷay huneta; አስቸኳይ፣ ጊዜ asčäkkʷay gize
state of emergency, see 'emergency'

emergency (adj.) ያደጋ yadäga

emigrant ስደተኛ səddätäňňa

emigrate ፈለሰ fälläsä; ተሰደደ täsäddädä

emigration ስደት səddät

eminence (elevation) የከፍታ፣ ቦታ yäkäfəta bota; (high standing) ልቀት ləqät

eminent (distinguished) የላቀ yälaqä; ዝነኛ zənnäňňa; (noteworthy) ከፍ፣ ያለ käff yalä

emissary መልእክተኛ mäl'əktäňňa

emit (~ light) አሰራጨ assäraččä; (~ a scream) ለቀቀ läqqäqä

emotion ስሜት səmmet

emotional (appealing to emotion) ስሜ ትን ፣ የሚነካ səmmetən yämminäka; (affected by emotion) ሆዳ ፣ ባሻ hodä bašša

emperor ንጉሥ ፣ ነገሥት nəgusä nägäst

emphasis, lay ~, put ~ አጠበቀ aṭäbbäqä

emphasize (~ the importance of something) አጥብቆ ፣ አሳሰበ aṭbəqo asassäbä; (~ a word) አጋነነ aggannänä

emphatically አጥብቆ aṭbəqo

empire የንጉሥ ፣ ነገሥት ፣ ግዛት yänəgusä nägäst gəzat

employ (~ workers) ቀጠረ qäṭṭärä; (use) ተገለገለ tägäläggälä

employee ሠራተኛ särratäňňa; ተቀጣሪ täqäṭari

employer አሠሪ assärri; ቀጣሪ qäṭari

employment (work) ሥራ səra; (employing) መቅጠር mäqṭär

empower ሥልጣን ፣ ሰጠ səlṭan säṭṭä

empty (vt.) አጋባ aggabba; (drain) ገለ በጠ gäläbbäṭä
empty out ደፋ däffa; አራገፈ arraggäfä

empty, adj. (~ container) ባዶ bado; (~ street) ጭር ፣ ያለ čərr yalä

empty-handed ባዶውን badowən; ባዶ ፣ እጁን bado əǧǧun

enable አስቻለ asčalä

enact (~ a bill) አሳለፈ asalläfä; (~ a part in the theater) በትያትሩ ፣ ውስጥ፣ ሠራ bätəyatru wəsṭ särra

enamored, be (become) ወደደ wäddädä

enchant (delight) መሰጠ mässäṭä; አስደ ሰተ asdässätä; (bewitch) በአስማት ፣ ተበተበ bä'asmat täbättäbä

enchantment ተመሰጦ tämäsṭo

encircle (surround) ከበበ käbbäbä; (go around) ዞረ zorä

enclose (~ a clipping) አያይዞ ፣ ላከ ayyayzo lakä; (fence in) አጠረ aṭṭärä

enclosure ክልል kəlləl; ቅጥር qəṭər; (for cattle) ማጐሪያ magʷäriya; (things enclosed) አባሪ abari

encounter (v.) አጋጠመ(ው) aggaṭṭämä(w)

encounter, n. (fight) ግጥሚያ *gəṭmiya;* ግጭት *gəččət;* (a meeting) መገናኘት *mäggänañät*

encourage አበረታታ *abbärätatta;* አደፋፈረ *addäfaffärä*

encroach ጥሶ ፡ ገባ *ṭəso gäbba*

encumber አስቸገረ *asčäggärä;* ዕንቅፋት ፡ ሆነ *ənqəfat honä*

encumbrance ችግር *čəggər;* ዕንቅፋት *ənqəfat*

encyclopedia ስንክሳር *sənkəsar;* ዐውደ ፡ ጥበብ *awdä ṭəbäb*

end (vt.) ደመደመ *dämäddämä;* ጨረሰ *čärräsä*
end (vi.) አለቀ *alläqä;* ተፈጸመ *täfäṣṣämä*

end (n.) መጨረሻ *mäčärräša;* ማለቂያ *maläqiya;* ማብቂያ *mabqiya;* (of a stick) ጫፍ *čaf;* (purpose) ዋና ፡ ግብ *wanna gəb*
bring to an end አበቃ *abäqqa*
come to an end, see 'end' (vi.)
no end ብዙ *bəzu;* ስፍር ፡ ቁጥር ፡ የሌለው *səfər quṭər yälelläw*
put an end to አቆመ *aqomä*

endanger አደጋ ፡ ላይ ፡ ጣለ *adäga lay ṭalä*

endear ተወዳጅ ፡ አደረገ *täwäddağ adärrägä*

endeavor ተጣጣረ *täṭaṭarä;* ዳከመ *däkkämä*

ended, be አለቀ *alläqä*

ending ፍጻሜ *fəṣṣame*

endless ማለቂያ ፡ የሌለው *maläqiya yälelläw*

endorse (∼ a plan) አጸደቀ *aṣäddäqä;* (∼ a check) ፈረመ *färrämä*

endow (provide with ability) ዐደለ *addälä;* (give money) ችሮታ ፡ አደረገ *čərota adärrägä*

endowment (gift) ስጦታ *səṭota*

endurance ትግሥት *təgəst;* (of pain) መቻል *mäčal*

endure ታገሠ *taggäsä;* ተቋቋመ *täqʷaqʷamä;* ቻለ *čalä*

enemy ጠላት *ṭälat*

energetic ታታሪ *tatari*

energy ጉልበት *gulbät;* ኀይል *hayl*

enfold ጠቀለለ *ṭäqällälä*

enforce (∼ law) አስከበረ *askäbbärä;* (∼ an argument) አጠነከረ *aṭänäkkärä*

engage, vt. (hire) ቀጠረ *qäṭṭärä;* (∼ the enemy) ገጠመ *gäṭṭämä;* (∼ one's time) ወሰደ(በት) *wässädä(bbät);* (∼ attention) ማረከ *marräkä;* ሳበ *sabä*
be engaged (be occupied) ተያዘ *täyazä;* (∼ to marry) አጫ *ačča*

engagement (appointment) ቀጠሮ *qäṭäro;* (promise to marry) መታጨት *mättaçät;* (fight) ግጥሚያ *gəṭmiya*

engaging የሚማርክ *yämmimarrək*

engender ወለደ *wällädä;* (bring about) አስገኘ *asgäññä*

engine ሞተር *motär*

engineer መሃንዲስ *mähandis*

England የእንግሊዝ ፡ አገር *yäəngliz agär*

English (adj.) የእንግሊዝ *yäəngliz;* (language) እንግሊዝኛ *ənglizəňňa*

Englishman እንግሊዝ *əngliz;* እንግሊዛዊ *ənglizawi*

engrave ቀረጸ *qärräṣä*

engraving ቅርጽ *qərṣ*

enigma ምስጢር *məsṭir*

enigmatic ምስጢራዊ *məsṭirawi*

enjoy (have pleasure) ተደሰተ *tädässätä;* ደስ ፡ አለ(ው) *däss alä(w);* (like) ወደደ *wäddädä*

enjoyable አስደሳች *asdässač*

enjoyment ደስታ *dässəta*
have the enjoyment of ተጠቀመ *täṭäqqämä*

enlarge, vt. (widen) አሰፋ *asäffa;* (∼ a photograph) አሳደገ *asaddägä*
enlarge (vi.) ተስፋፋ *täsfaffa*

enlighten አስረዳ *asrädda*

enlist (in the army) መለመለ *mäläm-mälä;* (gain someone's help for a cause) ሳበ *sabä*

enlisted man ተራ ፤ ወታደር *tära wättad-där*

enliven አደመቀ *adämmäqä*

enmity ጥል *ṭəl;* ጠላትነት *ṭälatənnät*

enormity (immensity) ከፍተኛነት *käffə-täññannät;* (extreme in wickedness) አስቃቂነት *assäqqaqinnät;* ግፍና ፤ ጭካኔ *gəfənna čəkkane*

enormous ከፍ ፤ ያለ *käff yalä;* በጣም ፤ ትልቅ *bäṭam təlləq;* (~ animal) በጣም ፤ ግዙፍ *bäṭam gəzuf*

enormously እጅግ *əǧǧəg*

enough በቂ *bäqi*
be enough በቃ *bäqqa*
have enough (food) ጠገበ *ṭäggäbä*

enrage አስቄጣ *asqʷäṭṭa;* አናደደ *annad-dädä*

enraged ቁጡ *quṭṭu*

enrich አበለጸገ *abäläṣṣägä;* (~ the soil) አዳበረ *adabbärä*

enroll (vt.) መዘገበ *mäzäggäbä*
enroll (vi.) ተመዘገበ *tämäzäggäbä*

enshroud ገነዘ *gännäzä*

enslave ባሪያ ፤ አደረገ *bariya adärrägä*

ensnare አጠመደ *aṭämmädä*

ensure አረጋገጠ *arrägaggäṭä*

entail ጠየቀ *ṭäyyäqä*

entangle አወሳሰበ *awwäsassäbä*

enter (vt.) አስገባ *asgäbba;* (record) መዘገበ *mäzäggäbä;* (~ a complaint) አቀረበ *aqärräbä*
enter (vi.) ገባ *gäbba*

enterprise የንግድ ፤ ድርጅት *yänəgd dərəǧǧət*

enterprising ታታሪ *tatari*

entertain (~ guests) አስተናገደ *astänag-gädä;* (amuse) አስደሰት *asdässätä;*

አጫወተ *aččawwätä*

entertainer አጫዋች *aččawač*

entertaining, be አስደሰት *asdässätä*

entertainment (amusement) ጨዋታ *ča-wata;* (treatment of guests) ማስተናገድ *mastänagäd*

enthrone ዙፋን ፤ ላይ ፤ አስቀመጠ *zufan lay asqämmäṭä*

enthusiasm የጋለ ፤ ስሜት *yägalä səmmet*

enthusiastic, be ጋጋ *gʷaggʷa*

enthusiastically በጋለ ፤ ስሜት *bägalä səmmet*

entice አባበለ *ababbälä;* ደለለ *dällälä*

entire መላ *mälla;* ጠቅላላ *ṭäqlalla;* ድፍን *dəfən*

entirely በፍጹም *bäfəṣṣum;* ጭራሽ *čərraš;* ሙሉ ፤ በሙሉ *mulu bämulu*

entitle (give the right) መብት ፤ ሰጠ *mäbt säṭṭä*
be entitled (authorized) ሥልጣን ፤ አለው *səlṭan alläw;* (be called) ተባለ *täbalä*

entomb ቀበረ *qäbbärä*

entrails (የ)ሆድ ፤ እቃ *(yä)hod əqa;* አንጀት *anǧät*

entrance (n.) መግቢያ *mägbiya;* በር *bärr;* ደጅ *däǧǧ;* (entering) መግባት *mägbat*

entrap አጠመደ *aṭämmädä;* (trick) አጎ ባባ *agbabba*

entreat ለመነ *lämmänä;* ተለማመጠ *tälä-mammäṭä*

entreaty ልመና *ləmmäna*

entrench, ~ oneself መሸገ *mäššägä*

entrust (~ care of a child) አደራ ፤ ሰጠ *adära säṭṭä;* (with a task) እምነት ፤ ጣለ (በት) *əmnät ṭalä(bbät)*

entry (entering) አገባብ *aggäbab;* (word in dictionary) የተመዘገበ ፤ ቃል *yätä-mäzäggäbä qal*

enumerate (name one by one) ዘረዘረ *zä-räzzärä*

enunciate (~words) ተናገረ *tänaggärä;*
(~a theory) ገለጸ *gälläṣä*

envelop (cover) ጠቀለለ *ṭäqällälä;* ሸፈነ
šäffänä; (surround) ከበበ *käbbäbä*

envelope አምቦልክ *ambolk;* አንቦልክ *an-*
bolk; ኤንቨሎፕ *envelop*

envenom መረዘ *märräzä*

envious ምቀኛ *məqqäñña;* ቀናተኛ *qänna-*
täñña
be envious ተመቀኘ *tämäqäññä;* ቀና
qänna

environment አካባቢ *akkababi*

environs ዙሪያ *zuriya*

envisage (expect) አሰበ *assäbä;* (visualize) በዓይነ ፡ ኅሊና ፡ አሰበ *bäaynä həl-*
lina assäbä

envoy መልእክተኛ *mäl'əktäñña*

envy (v.) ተመቀኘ *tämäqäññä;* ቀና *qänna*

envy (n.) ምቀኝነት *məqqäññənnät;* ቅናት
qənat

epidemic ተላላፊ ፡ በሽታ *tälalafi bäššəta*

epilepsy የባሪያ ፡ በሽታ *yäbariya bäššəta;*
የሚጥል ፡ በሽታ *yämmiṭəl bäššəta*

Epiphany ጥምቀት *ṭəmqät;* የጥምቀት ፡
በዓል *yäṭəmqät bäal*

episode ምዕራፍ *mə'əraf;* (incident) ድር
ጊት *dərgit*

Epistle መልእክት *mäl'əkt*

epithet የቅጽል ፡ ስም *yäqəṣṣəl səm*

epoch ዘመን *zämän;* (chapter) ምዕራፍ
mə'əraf

equal (v.) አከለ *akkälä;* እኩል ፡ ነው *ək-*
kul näw; ተመጣጠነ *tämäṭaṭṭänä*

equal (n.) እኩያ *əkkuya;* (of the same
status) አቻ *ačča*

equal (adj.) እኩል *əkkul;* ተመጣጣኝ *tä-*
mäṭaṭaň; ትክክል *təkəkkəl*
be equal, see 'equal' (v.)

equality እኩልነት *əkkulənnät*

equalize አስተካከለ *astäkakkälä*

equally በትክክል *bätəkəkkəl*

equate እኩል ፡ አደረገ *əkkul adärrägä;*
አስተካከለ *astäkakkälä*

equator የምድር ፡ መቀነት *yämədər mä-*
qännät

equilibrium (balance) ሚዛን *mizan;*
(evenness of mind) የመንፈስ ፡ እርጋታ
yämänfäs ərgata

equip አስታጠቀ *astaṭṭäqä*
be equipped (soldier) ታጠቀ *taṭṭäqä*

equipment መሳሪያ *mässariya;* (of soldiers) ትጥቅ *təṭq*

equitable (~ decision) ትክክለኛ *təkək-*
kəläñña

equity ትክክለኛነት *təkəkkəläññannät*

equivalence እኩልነት *əkkulənnät*

equivalent ተመጣጣኝ *tämäṭaṭaň;* (in
weight) ተመዛዛኝ *tämäzazaň;* (in
meaning) ተመሳሳይ *tämäsasay*
be equivalent ተመጣጠነ *tämäṭaṭṭänä*

equivocal አጠራጣሪ *aṭṭäraṭari*

era ዘመን *zämän*

eradicate አጠፋ *aṭäffa;* ነቀለ *näqqälä;*
አስወገደ *aswäggädä*

erase (~ a signature) ፋቀ *faqä;* (~
chalk) አጠፋ *aṭäffa*

eraser ላጲስ *lappis*
chalk eraser ማጥፊያ *maṭfiya*

erect, v. (~a monument) አቆመ *aqomä;*
(~a building) ሠራ *särra*
be erected ቆመ *qomä*

erode ሸረሸረ *šäräššärä*

err ሳተ *satä;* ተሳሳተ *täsasatä*

errand መልእክት *mäl'əkt*
errand boy ተላላኪ *tälalaki*
run errands ተላላከ *tälalakä*

erratic ጠባዩ ፡ የሚለዋወጥ *ṭäbayu yäm-*
milläwawwäṭ

erroneous የተሳሳተ *yätäsasatä*

error ስሕተት *səhtät;* ስተት *sətät*

erudite (~ person) ምሁር *məhur;* (~
lecture) የምሁር *yäməhur*

erudition ዕውቀት əwqät

erupt (of volcano) ፈነዳ fänädda; (of battle) በድንገት ፡ ተነሣ bädəngät tänässa; (of skin) ተቄጣ täqʷäṭṭa

escape (v.) አመለጠ amälläṭä; (slip by, a name) ትዝ ፡ አላለ(ውም) təzz alalä-(wəm)

escape (n.) ማምለጫ mamläča

escort (v.) ሸኘ šäňňä; ዐጀበ aǧǧäbä

escort (n.) ዐጀብ aǧäb; ዐጀቢ aǧǧabi

especially በተለይ bätäläyy; ይልቁንም yəlqunəm; ይበልጡንም yəbälṭunəm

espionage ስለላ səlläla

espouse ዳረ darä; (support) ደገፈ däg-gäfä

essay (n.) ድርሰት dərsät

essence መሠረት mäsärät; (substance) ባሕርይ bahrəy; አኳኋን akkʷahʷan; (of a speech) ፍሬ ፡ ነገር fəre nägär

essential (adj.) ዓይነተኛ aynätäňňa; ዋና wanna; ተፈላጊ täfällagi

essentially በመሠረቱ bämäsärätu

establish አቋቋመ aqqʷaqʷamä; መሠረተ mäsärrätä; (~ order) አስከበረ askäbbärä

estate (possession) ርስትና ፡ ንብረት rəstənna nəbrät; (landed property) ርስት rəst

esteem (v.) አከበረ akäbbärä; (consider) ቄጠረ qʷäṭṭärä

esteem, n. (honor) ክብር kəbər; (opinion) ግምት gəmmət

estimate (v.) ገመተ gämmätä; ገመገመ gämäggämä

estimate (n.) ግምት gəmmət

estrange አራቀ araqä; አለያየ alläyayyä

eternal (timeless) የዘላለም yäzälaläm; ዘለዓለማዊ zälä'alämawi; (without stopping) የማያልቅ yämmayalq

eternally ለዘላዓለም läzälä'aläm; ለዘላለም läzälaläm

eternity ዘላዓለማዊ ፡ ሕይወት zälä'aläma-wi həywät; ዘላዓለምነት zälä'aläminnät an eternity ለብዙ ፡ ጊዜ läbəzu gize

ethical (~ behavior) የሐቀኝነት yähaq-qäňňənnät; ግብረ፡ ገባዊ gəbrä gəbbawi ethical behavior ሥነ ፡ ምግባር sənä məgbar

ethics የሥነ ፡ ምግባር ፡ ትምህርት yäsənä məgbar təmhərt

Ethiopia ኢትዮጵያ ityoppəya

Ethiopian (inhabitant) ኢትዮጵያዊ ityop-pəyawi; አበሻ abäša; (~ language) የኢትዮጵያ yäityoppəya

ethnic group ጕሳ gʷäsa

etiquette ሥነ ፡ ምግባር sənä məgbar

eucalyptus ባሕር ፡ ዛፍ bahər zaf

Eucharist ቁርባን qurban

eunuch ጃንደረባ ǧändäräba; ስልብ səlb

euphorbia ቁልቋል qulqʷal

Europe አውሮፓ awroppa

evacuate (~ a building) ለቆ ፡ ወጣ läqqo wäṭṭa; (~ people) አወረደ azzawwärä; ሕዝብ ፡ አስለቀቀ həzb asläqqäqä

evade አመለጠ amälläṭä; (~ a question) አድበሰበሰ adbäsäbbäsä

evaluate አመዛዘነ ammäzazzänä; ገመተ gämmätä; (~ a book) ገመገመ gämäg-gämä

evangelist ወንጌላዊ wängelawi

evangelize ወንጌል ፡ ሰበከ wängel säbbäkä

evaporate (vi.) ተነነ tännänä

evaporation ተን tänn

evasive የማይጨበጥ yämmayəččäbbäṭ

eve ዋዜማ wazema

even (v.) አስተካከለ astäkakkälä
even out አስተካከለ astäkakkälä; ደለ ደለ däläddälä

even, adj. (equal) ትክክል təkəkkəl; እኩል əkkul; (level) ደልዳላ däldalla; ድልድል dəldəl; (~ number) ሙሉ mulu
be even ተካከለ täkakkälä

even (adv.) ስንኳ sankʷa; እንኳ ankʷa; እንኳን ankʷan
even as እንደ andä + perfect
even if ምንም ፡ እንኳ ፡ ብ manam ankʷa ba + imperfect + ም - m
even though ምንም ፡ እንኳ ፡ ብ manam ankʷa ba + imperfect + ም - m; ብ ba + imperfect + እንኳን ankʷan

evening ምሽት maššat; ማታ mata
get evening መሸ mässä
good evening! እንዴት ፡ አመሸህ andet amäššäh (sg. masc.)
spend the evening አመሸ amäššä
this evening ዛሬ ፡ ማታ zare mata

evenly በትክክል bätakakkal; እኩል akkul

event ሁኔታ huneta; ድርጊት dargit; ጉዳይ gudday
at all events የሆነ ፡ ቢሆን yähonä bihon
in any event ምንም ፡ ቢሆን manam bihon

eventually በመጨረሻ bämäčärräša; እያ ደረ ayyaddärä; ውሎ ፡ አድሮ walo adro

ever, gerund of main verb + ያውቃል yawqal (have you ever been in the United States? አሜሪካ ፡ አገር ፡ ሄደህ ፡ ታውቃለህ?); (always) ሁልጊዜ hulgize
ever so much እጅግ ağğag

everlasting (eternal) የዘላዓለም yäzälä'aläm; (that has no end) ማለቂያ ፡ የሌ ለው maläqiya yälelläw

every ማንኛውም mannaññawam; እያንዳ ንድ ayyandand
every now and then አልፎ ፡ አልፎ alfo alfo
every once in a while አልፎ ፡ አልፎ alfo alfo
every one of እያንዳንድ ayyandand
every so often በየጊዜው bäyyägizew

everybody ሁሉ ፡ ሰው hullu säw

everyday (∼clothes) የዘወትር yäzäwätar

everyone ማንም mannam; እያንዳንድ ayyandand

everything ማንኛውም ፡ ነገር mannaññawam nägär

everywhere በየቦታው bäyyäbotaw; በየ ትም bäyätam; በየትም ፡ ቦታ bäyätam bota; በያለበት bäyalläbbät

evict አስወጣ aswäțța; አስወገደ aswäggädä

evidence (n.) መረጃ märräğa; ማስረጃ masräğğa
be in evidence ታየ tayyä

evident ጉልህ gulah; ግልጽ galṣ; የተረጋ ገጠ yätärägaggäṭä

evil (n.) ኃጢአት haṭi'at; ክፋት kafat; (cause of suffering) መቅሠፍት mäqsäft

evil, adj. (∼ person) ክፉ kafu; (∼deed) መጥፎ mäṭfo; (∼ plan) የተንኮል yätänkʷäl

evildoer አጥፊ aṭfi

evil eye ቡዳ buda

evil spirit እርኩስ ፡ መንፈስ arkus mänfäs; ጋኔን ganen

evoke አስከተለ askättälä

evolve (vt.) ፈጠረ fäṭṭärä
evolve (vi.) ቀስ ፡ በቀስ ፡ አደገ qäss bäqäss addägä

ewe ሴት ፡ በግ set bäg

exact (adj.) ልክ lakk; ምጥን mäṭṭan; ትክ ክለኛ takakkaläñña

exacting (∼work) ጥንቃቄ ፡ የሚፈልግ ṭanaqqaqe yämmifälläg; (∼employer) በቃኝ ፡ የማይል bäqqaññ yämmayal

exactitude ርቂቅነት räqiqannät

exactly (precisely) ልክ lakk; በልክ bälakk; (accurately) በትክክል bätakakkal

exaggerate አዳነቀ addannäqä; አጋነነ aggannänä

exalt (praise) አወደሰ awäddäsä; (raise in rank) ክፍ ፡ አደረገ käff adärrägä

examination ፈተና fätäna; (of a witness) ምርመራ marmära

examine ፈተነ fättänä; (look at something closely) መረመረ märämmärä

example 338 execute

example ምሳሌ *məssale;* (person to be imitated) አርአያ *araya*

exasperate አበሳጨ *abbäsaččä*

excavate ቈፈረ *qʷäffärä;* ቈፍሮ ፡ አወጣ *qʷäffəro awäṭṭa*

excavation (act of excavating) ቈፈራ *qʷäfära;* (hole made by excavating) የተቈፈረ ፡ ጉድጓድ *yätäqʷäffärä gudgʷad*

exceed ላቀ *laqä;* በለጠ *bälläṭä*

exceedingly እጅግ *əǧǧəg*

excel ላቀ *laqä;* በለጠ *bälläṭä*

excellence (outstanding ability) ከፍተኛ ፡ ችሎታ *käffətäñña čəlota;* (superior quality) ምርጥነት *mərṭənnät;* ጥሩነት *ṭərunnät*

Excellency, His ~ ክቡር *kəbur*

excellent እጅግ ፡ በጣም ፡ ጥሩ *əǧǧəg bäṭam ṭəru*

except (v.) ወጭ ፡ አደረገ *wäčč adärrägä*

except (prep.) ከ - - - በስተቀር *kä - - - bästäqär;* በቀር *bäqär;* ከ - - በተቀር *kä - - - bätäqär*

exception ወጭ ፡ መሆን *wäčč mähon* with the exception of ከ - - በስተቀር *kä - - - bästäqär* without exception አንድም ፡ ሳይቀር *andəmm sayəqär*

exceptional ወደር ፡ የሌለው *wädär yälelläw;* (~ weather) የተለመደ ፡ አይደለም *yätälämmädä aydälläm*

excerpt ምንባብ *mənbab*

excess (n.) ብልጫ *bəlča;* ትርፍ *tərf* in excess of ከ - - - በላይ *kä - - - bälay* to excess ከማጣን ፡ በላይ *kämäṭän bälay*

excess (adj.) ትርፍ *tərf;* ከተወሰነ ፡ በላይ ፡ የሆነ *kätäwässänä bälay yähonä*

excessive ከማጣን ፡ በላይ ፡ የሆነ *kämäṭän bälay yähonä;* ከልክ ፡ ያለፈ *käləkk yalläfä*

exchange (v.) ለወጠ *läwwäṭä;* (inter-

change) ተለዋወጠ *täläwawwäṭä;* (~ money) መነዛዘረ *mänäzzärä*

exchange(n.) ለውጥ *läwṭ;* ልውውጥ *ləwəwwəṭ;* (of money) ምንዛሪ *mənəzzari;* የገንዘብ ፡ ምንዛሪ *yägänzäb mənəzzari* rate of exchange የምንዛሪ ፡ ዋጋ *yämənəzzari waga;* የምንዛሪ ፡ ሒሳብ *yämənəzzari hisab*

excise ቈርጦ ፡ አወጣ *qʷärṭo awäṭṭa*

excite አሸበረ *aššäbbärä;* ስሜቱን ፡ ቀሰቀሰ *səmmetun qäsäqqäsä* be excited ተሸበረ *täšäbbärä*

excitement (feeling) የጋለ ፡ ስሜት *yägalä səmmet;* (commotion) ሽብር *šəbbər*

exciting ስሜትን ፡ የሚቀሰቅስ *səmmetən yämmiqäsäqqəs*

exclaim (in joy) በደስታ ፡ ተናገረ *bädässəta tänaggärä;* (wondering) በመደነቅ ፡ ጠየቀ *bämäddänäq ṭäyyäqä*

exclamation ድምጽ *dəmṣ;* ጩኸት *čuhät;* (in grammar) ቃለ ፡ አጋኖ *qalä agganno*

exclude (keep out) አስቀረ *asqärrä;* (prevent from entering) ከለከለ *käläkkälä*

exclusion መከልከል *mäkälkäl*

exclusively ብቻ *bəčča*

excommunicate አወገዘ *awäggäzä*

excommunication ውግዘት *wəgzät*

excrement አር *ar;* ዓይነ ፡ ምድር *aynä mədər*

excruciating የሚያሠቃይ *yämmiyassäqay*

excursion ሽርሽር *šərrəšərr*

excuse (v.) ይቅርታ ፡ አደረገ *yəqərta adärrägä* excuse me! ይቅርታ *yəqərta* excuse oneself ይቅርታ ፡ ጠየቀ *yəqərta ṭäyyäqä*

excuse (n.) ምክንያት *mәknəyat* make excuses ምክንያት ፡ ፈጠረ *mәknəyat fäṭṭärä* use as an excuse አመካኘ *ammäkaňňä*

execute ፈጸም *fäṣṣämä;* (~ a plan) በሥራ ፡ ላይ ፡ አዋለ *bäsəra lay awalä*

execution (manner of doing) አሠራር *as-särar;* (death sentence) የሞት ፡ ቅጣት *yämot qäṭat*

executive (n.) አስተዳዳሪ *astädadari;* ባለ፡ ሥልጣን *balä sälṭan*

executive (adj.) ያስተዳደር *yastädadär*

exemplary አርአያነት ፡ ያለው *arayannät yalläw*

exemplify አርአያ ፡ ነው *araya näw*

exempt (v.) ነጻ ፡ አደረገ *näṣa adärrägä*

exempt (adj.) ነጻ *näṣa*

exemption ከ - - ነጻ ፡ ማድረግ *kä - - - näṣa madräg*

exercise (vt.) በልምምድ ፡ አጠነከረ *bälə- məmməd aṭänäkkärä;* (~ horses) አለ ማመደ *allämammädä;* (~ authority) በ - - - ተጠቀመ *bä - - - täṭäqqämä* exercise (vi.) ጅምናስቲክ፡ ሠራ *ğəmnas- tik särra;* (practice) ልምምድ ፡ አደረገ *ləməmməd adärrägä*

exercise, n. (lesson) መልመጃ *mälmäğa;* (training) ልምምድ *ləməmməd;* (gym- nastics) ጅምናስቲክ *ğəmnastik*

exert በ - - - ተጠቀመ *bä - - - täṭäqqämä* exert oneself ጥረት፡ አደረገ *ṭärät adär- rägä*

exertion ልፋት *ləfat;* ድካም *dəkam*

exhale (breathe out) ወደ ፡ ውጭ ፡ ተነፈሰ *wädä wäčč tänäffäsä;* (give off, e.g. odor) አመነጨ *amänäččä*

exhaust, v. (tire) አለፋ *aläffa;* ሙትት ፡ አደረገ *mutətt adärrägä;* (use up) ጨረሰ *čärräsä*

exhaust (n.) ጪስ *čis*

exhausted, be ተዳከመ *tädakkämä;* በድ ካም ፡ ሙትት ፡ አለ *bädəkam mutətt alä;* (used up) አከተመ *akättämä*

exhaustion ድካም *dəkam;* ልፋት *ləfat;* (using up) ማነስ *manäs*

exhaustive የተሟላ *yätäm^walla*

exhibit (v.) አሳየ *asayyä*

exhibit (n.), see 'exhibition'

exhibition ትርእይት *tər'əyt;* ትርኢት *tər- 'it*

exhilarate (of news) ደስ ፡ አሰኘ *däss as- säňňä;* (of weather) አነቃቃ *annäqaqqa*

exhort (urge on) አጥብቆ ፡ አሳሰበ *aṭbəqo asassäbä;* (encourage) አደፋፈረ *addä- faffärä*

exile (v.) አጋዘ *agazä;* ሰደደ *säddädä*

exile (n.) ስደት *säddät;* ግዞት *gəzot;* (per- son who is in exile) ስደተኛ *säddä- täňňa;* ግዞተኛ *gəzotäňňa*

exist (occur) አለ *allä;* ነው *näw;* (live) ኖረ *norä*

existence (life) ኑሮ *nuro;* ሕይወት *həywät;* (the existing) መኖር *mänor* be in existence ሆነ *honä* come into existence ተፈጠረ *täfäṭṭärä*

existent ባሁኑ ፡ ጊዜ ፡ ያለ *bahunu gize yallä*

exit (v.) ወጣ *wäṭṭa*

exit (n.) መውጫ *mäwča*

exorbitant (~ demand) ከመጠን ፡ በላይ ፡ የሆነ *kämäṭän bälay yähonä;* (~ price) በጣም ፡ ውድ *bäṭam wädd*

exotic የባዕድ ፡ አገር *yäbaəd agär;* እንግዳ፡ የሆነ *əngəda yähonä*

expand (vt.) አስፋፋ *asfaffa* expand (vi.) ተስፋፋ *täsfaffa;* (of tire) ተለጠጠ *täläṭṭäṭä;* (of a balloon) ተወ ጠረ *täwäṭṭärä*

expansion (expanding) ማስፋፋት *masfa- fat;* (being expanded) መስፋፋት *mäs- fafat*

expatriate (vi.) አገሩን ፡ ለቆ ፡ ወጣ *agärun läqqo wäṭṭa*

expatriate (n.) የውጭ ፡ አገር ፡ ሰው *yä- wäčč agär säw*

expect, v. (wait) ጠበቀ *ṭäbbäqä;* (sup- pose) አሰበ *assäbä*

expectation ግምት *gəmmət* have expectations ተስፋ ፡ አደረገ *täsfa adärrägä*

expedite አፋጠነ *affaṭṭänä*

expedition (military ~) ዘመቻ zämäča;
(scientific ~) ጉዞ gʷadd
go on a (military) expedition ዘመተ
zämmätä

expel አስወጣ aswätta
be expelled ወጣ wätta

expend ጨረሰ čärräsä

expenditure ወጪ wäči

expense ወጪ wäči

expensive ውድ wadd

experience (v.) አጋጠመ(ው) aggattä-
mä(w)

experience, n. (skill) ልምድ lamd; ልም
ምድ lamammad; (happening) ያጋጠመ፡
ነገር yaggattämä nägär; አጋጣሚ aggatami

experienced (adj.) ልምድ ፡ ያለው lamd
yalläw

experiment (v.) ሞከረ mokkärä; ፈተነ
fättänä

experiment (n.) ሙከራ mukkära; ፈተና
fätäna

expert (n.) ሊቅ liq; ዐዋቂ awaqi

expert, adj. (~ advice, knowledge)
ጠለቅ ፡ ያለ täläqq yalä; ጥልቅ talq;
(~ mechanic) ባለሙያ balämuya

expire (come to an end) ጊዜ ፡ አለቀ gize
alläqä; (die) አረፈ arräfä; (breathe
out) ተነፈሰ tänäffäsä

explain (make clear) አብራራ abrarra;
አስረዳ asrädda; ገለጸ gälläsä

explanation መግለጫ mägläča; ማብራሪያ
mabrariya; ፍቺ fačč; (way of ex-
plaining) አገላለጽ aggälaläs

explanatory የማብራሪያ yämabrariya

explicit ቁርጥ qurt; ግልጽ gals

explode (vi.) ፈነዳ fänädda

exploit, v. (put to use) በጥቅም ፡ ላይ ፡
አዋለ bätaqam lay awalä; (make unfair use for one's own advantage)
የ - - - ጉልበት ፡ ያላግባብ ፡ በላ yä - - -
gulbät yalagbab bälla

exploit, n. (adventurous act) ጀብዱ
ğäbdu

explore እየተዘዋወረ ፡ ጥናት ፡ አደረገ ay-
yätäzäwawwärä tanat adärrägä; (examine thoroughly) ፈተሸ fättäšä

explorer አሳሽ assaš

explosion ፍንጂ fänği; (noise) የፍንጂ ፡
ድምፅ yäfänği damş

explosive(s) ፍንጂ fänği; ደማሚት dämamit

export (v.) ወደ ፡ ውጭ ፡ አገር ፡ ላከ wädä
wäčč agär lakä

export, n. (exporting) ወደ ፡ ውጭ ፡ አገር፡
መላክ wädä wäčč agär mälak; (things
exported) ወደ ፡ ውጭ ፡ አገር ፡ የሚላኩ ፡
ሸቀጦች wädä wäčč agär yämmillaku
šäqätočč

exporter ላኪ laki

expose ገለጠ gällätä; አጋለጠ aggallätä

exposition ኤክስፖዚሲዮን ekspozisiyon

expound አብራራ abrarra

express, v. (~ an opinion) ተናገረ tänaggärä; ገለጸ gälläsä; (reveal) አማለከተ
amäläkkätä
express oneself ሐሳቡን ፡ ገለጸ hassabun gälläsä

express, adj. (explicit) ግልጽ gals; (traveling fast) በራሪ bärari

expression (in words) አባባል abbabal;
መግለጫ mägläča; (face) ፊት fit;
መልክ mälk; (sign) ምልክት mäläkkat

expressly በጥብቅ bätabq; (mainly) በተ
ለይ bätäläyy

expropriate በሕጉ ፡ መሠረት ፡ ወረሰ bä-
haggu mäsärät wärräsä

expulsion ማባረር mabbarär; ማስወጣት
maswättat

exquisite ግሩም garum; በጣም ፡ የሚደነቅ
bätam yämmiddännäq

extant አሁን ፡ ያለ ahun yallä

extend (vt.) ዘረጋ zärägga; (expand) አስ
ፋፋ asfaffa; (~ a visa) አራዘመ aräzzämä

extension (of house) ቅጥያ *qəṭṭəyya;* (being extended) መስፋፋት *mäsfafat;* (of telephone) የውስጥ ፡ መሥመር *yäwəsṭ mäsmär*

extension courses የትርፍ ፡ ጊዜ ፡ ትምህ ርት *yätərf gize təmhərt*

extensive ረጊም *räžžim;* ረጃም *räǧǧim;* ሰፊ *säffi*

extensively በሰፊው *bäsäffiw*

extent መጣን *mäṭän;* (of a place) ስፋት *səfat*
to a certain extent በመጣን *bämäṭän*
to some extent በከፊል *bäkäfil*

exterior (n.) ውጪ *wəčči;* ውጭ *wəčč*

exterior (adj.) የውጭ *yäwəčč*

exterminate ፈጀ *fäǧǧä;* (~ the enemy) ደመሰሰ *dämässäsä;* (~ ants) አጠፋ *aṭäffa*

external የውጭ *yäwəčč*

externally ላይ ፡ ላዩን *lay layun*

extinct የቀረ *yäqärrä;* የጠፋ *yäṭäffa*
be extinct ጠፋ *ṭäffa*

extinguish አጠፋ *aṭäffa*
be extinguished ጠፋ *ṭäffa*

extol አሞገሰ *amoggäsä*

extra, n. (~ workers) ተጨማሪ ፡ ሠራተኛ *täčämmari särratäñña;* (of newspaper) ተጨማሪ ፡ ጋዜጣ *täčämmari gazeṭa*

extra, adj. (additional) ተጨማሪ *täčämmari;* (special) ለዩ *ləyyu;* (remaining) ትርፍ *tərf*
extra (adv.) ከመጣን ፡ በላይ *kämäṭän bälay*

extract (v.) ነቀለ *näqqälä;* (~ oil) አወጣ *awäṭṭa;* (~ passage from a book) መረጠ ፡ አወጣ *märṭo awäṭṭa*

extract (n.) የተውጣጣ ፡ ምንባብ *yätäwṭaṭṭa mənbab*

extraordinary ያልተለመደ *yaltälämmädä;* (special) ለዩ *ləyyu*

extravagance ገንዘብ ፡ አባካኝነት *gänzäb abakaňənnät*

extravagant ገንዘብ ፡ አባካኝ *gänzäb abakaň*

extreme(s), n. ተቃራኒ *täqarani*

extreme, adj. (highest) ከፍ ፡ ያለ *käff yalä;* ኃይለኛ *hayläñña;* (farthest) የመጨ ረሻ *yämäčärräša*

extremely እጅግ ፡ በጣም *əǧǧəg bäṭam*

extremity (the very end) ጫፍ *čaf;* (extreme need) ጭንቅ *čənq*
extremities እጅና ፡ እግሮች *əǧǧənna əgročč*

extricate አላቀቀ *allaqqäqä*

exuberance (high spirits) የተነቃቃ ፡ መን ፈስ *yätänäqaqqa mänfäs*

exuberant (~ crowd) በደስታ ፡ የተሞላ *bädässəta yätämolla;* (~ welcome) በጣም ፡ የጋለ *bäṭam yägalä*

exult ፈነደቀ *fänäddäqä;* ፈነጠዘ *fänäṭ ṭäzä*

exultation ፍንደቃ *fəndäqa;* ፈንጠዝያ *fänṭäzəyya*

eye (v.) አየ *ayyä;* አትኩሮ ፡ ተመለከተ *atkuro tämäläkkätä*

eye (n.) ዓይን *ayn*
keep an eye on ጠበቀ *ṭäbbäqä*
see eye to eye ተስማማ *täsmamma*

eyebrow ሽፋሽፍት *šəfašəft;* ሽፋል *šəfal;* ቅንድብ *qəndäb*

eyeglasses መነጽር *mänäṣṣər;* መነጥር *mänäṭṭər*

eyelash ቅንድብ *qəndäb*

eyelid የዓይን ፡ ሽፋን *yayn šəfan;* የዓይን ፡ ቆብ *yayn qob*

eyesight ዓይን *ayn;* የዓይን ፡ ብርሃን *yayn bərhan*

eyewitness የዓይን ፡ ምስክር *yayn məsək kər*

F

fable ተረት *tärät;* ያፍ ፡ ታሪክ *yaf tarik*

fabric ጨርቅ *čärq*

fabricate (construct) ሠራ *särra;* (invent) ፈጠረ *fäṭṭärä*

face (vt.) ፊቱን ፡ አዞረ *fitun azorä;* (~ the enemy) ገጠመ *gäṭṭämä*
face (vi.) ከ - - - ትዪይ ፡ ነው *kä - - - täyəyy näw*

face (n.) ፊት *fit;* (of earth) ገጽ *gäṣṣ*
face to face ፊት ፡ ለፊት *fit läfit;* ዓይን ፡ ለዓይን *ayn läayn*
fall on one's face ባፉ ፡ ጢሙ ፡ ተደፋ *baf ṭimu tädäffa*

facetious የፌዝ *yäfez*
be facetious አሾፈ *ašofä*

facial የፊት *yäfit*

facilitate አቃለለ *aqqallälä*

facility (skill) ስጦታ *səṭota;* (ease) ቅልጥፍና *qəlṭəfənna*

fact (event) ነገር *nägär;* (truth) እውነት *əwnät*
as a matter of fact እንዲያውም *əndiyawəm*
in fact በውነት *bäwnät;* እንዲያውም *əndiyawəm*

faction ወገን *wägän*

factory ፋብሪካ *fabrika*

faculty (talent) ስጦታ *səṭota;* (staff of teachers) ፋኩልቲ *fakulti*

fade, vi. (of flower) ጠወለገ *ṭäwällägä;* (lose color) ለቀቀ *läqqäqä*

fail, vi. (in exam) ወደቀ *wäddäqä;* (of experiment) ውድቅ ፡ ሆነ *wədq honä;* (of health) ተቀነሰ *täqännäsä;* (of a plan) ሳይሳካ ፡ ቀረ *sayəssakka qärrä;* ከሸፈ *käššäfä;* (of efforts) ከንቱ ፡ ሆና ፡ ቀረ *käntu hono qärrä*

fail to ስ *sə* + negative imperfect

failing, be (eyesight) ደከመ *däkkämä;* (health) ተቀነሰ *täqännäsä*

failure (not succeeding) ያለ ፡ መሳካት *yalä mässakat;* (of health) መታወክ *mättawäk;* (of eyesight) መጥፋት *mäṭfat;* (of motor) መበላሸት *mäbbälašät*

faint (v.) ነፍሱን ፡ ሳተ *näfsun satä;* ነፍ ሱን ፡ አጣ *näfsun aṭṭa;* ሕይወቱን ፡ ሳተ *həywätun satä;* ራሱን ፡ ሳተ *rasun satä*

faint, adj. (~ noise) ቀስስ ፡ ያለ *qəsəss yalä;* (~ hope) የመነመነ *yämänämmänä*

fair (n.) ትርእይት *tər'əyt;* ትርኢት *tər'it*

fair, adj. (~ price) ደኅና *dähna;* (~ judge) ትክክለኛ *täkäkkəläñña;* (~ knowledge) መጠነኛ *mäṭänäñña*

fairly (evenly) በትክክል *bätäkäkkəl;* (moderately) በመጠኑ *bämäṭänu*

fairy tale ተረት *tärät*

faith (religion) ሃይማኖት *haymanot;* (trust) እምነት *əmnät*
have faith አመነ *ammänä*

faithful, n. (believer) ምእመን *mə'əmän*

faithful, adj. (~friend) ታማኝ *tammañ;* (accurate) ትክክለኛ *täkäkkəläñña*
be faithful ታመነ *tammänä*

fake (n.) አባይ *abay*

fall (v.) ወደቀ *wäddäqä;* (of leaves, fruit) ረገፈ *räggäfä;* (of rain) ጣለ *ṭalä;* (of prices) ዝቅ ፡ አለ *zəqq alä;* (of a holiday) ዋለ *walä*
fall apart ፈረሰ *färräsä;* (of stool) ወላለቀ *wälalläqä*
fall back አፈገፈገ *afägäffägä*
fall behind ወደ ፡ ኋላ ፡ ቀረ *wädä hʷala qärrä*
fall down ወደቀ *wäddäqä*
fall off (ring) ወለቀ *wälläqä*
fall out (teeth) ረገፈ *räggäfä;* ወለቀ *wälläqä*

fall (n.) ውድቀት *wədqät;* (season) በልግ *bälg*

fallacious የተሳሳተ *yätäsasatä*

falling star ተወርዋሪ ፡ ኮከብ *täwärwari kokäb*

fallow land እዳሪ *əddari*

falls (waterfall) ፏፏቴ *fʷafʷate*

false (~ alarm) የውሸት *yäwəšät;* (~ idea) የተሳሳተ *yätäsasatä;* (~ friend) ሐሰተኛ *hassätäñña;* (~ hope) ከንቱ *käntu;* (~ statement) የሐሰት *yähassät*

falsehood ሐሰት *hassät*

falsify (dupe) ሸፈጠ *šäffäṭä;* (~ accounts) አማታ *ammatta*

falter (move in an uncertain way) ተደና ቀፈ *tädänaqqäfä;* (hesitate) አወላወለ *awwälawwälä;* አቅማማ *aqmamma;* (speak hesitatingly) ተንተባተብ *täntäbattäbä*

fame ዝና *zənna*

famed የታወቀ *yätawwäqä*

familiar (common) የተለመደ *yätälämmädä;* (intimate) የቅርብ *yäqərb;* (~ face, voice) የሚያውቀው *yämmiyawqäw* be familiar with ወቀ *awwäqä*

familiarize አላመደ *allammädä;* አስተዋ ወቀ *astäwawwäqä* familiarize oneself ተለማመደ *tälämammädä*

family (father, mother, and children) ቤት ፡ ሰብ *betä säb;* (relatives) ዘመድ *zämäd*

famine ረሃብ *rähab;* ችጋር *čəggar*

famished የተራበ *yätäraba*

famous ዝነኛ *zənnäñña;* ስም ፡ ጥሩ *səmä ṭäru;* ስም ፡ ጥር *səmä ṭär;* የታወቀ *yätawwäqä* be famous ታወቀ *tawwäqä*

fan (v.) አራገበ *arraggäbä*

fan (n.) ማራገቢያ *marragäbiya;* ማርገብ ገቢያ *margäbgäbiya;* ነፋስ ፡ መስጫ *näfas mäsča*

fanatic ዓይነን ፡ ጨፍኖ ፡ የሚያምልክ *aynun čäffəno yämmiyamälk*

fancy, v. (imagine) መሰለ(ው) *mässälä(w);* (like) ወደደ *wäddädä*

fancy, n. (imagination) የፈጠራ ፡ ችሎታ *yäfäṭära čəlota;* (notion, whim) ሕልም *həlm*

fancy, adj. (~ clothes) ብልጭልጭ *bələčləč*

fantastic (unbelievable) ጨርሶ ፡ የማይታ መን *čärrəso yämmayəttammän*

fantasy ቅዠት *qəžät*

far ሩቅ *ruq* be (go) far. ራቀ *raqä* that far እስከዚህ *əskäzzih;* ያን ፡ ያህል *yan yahəl*

faraway ሩቅ *ruq*

farce ቀልድ *qäld*

fare (n.) መሳፈሪያ *mässafäriya*

Far East ሩቅ ፡ ምሥራቅ *ruq məsraq*

farewell, bid ~ ተሰናበታ *täsänabbätä*

farm (v.) አረሰ *arräsä*

farm (n.) እርሻ *ərša;* ማሳ *masa*

farmer አራሽ *araš;* ገባሬ *gäbäre*

farming እርሻ *ərša;* ግብርና *gəbrənna*

far-sighted አርቆ ፡ አስተዋይ ፡ የሆነ *arqo astäway yähonä*

fart (v.) ፈሳ *fässa*

fart (n.) ፈስ *fäs*

farther (adj.) የወዲያኛ *yäwädiyaňña* farther (adv.) ራቅ ፡ ብሎ *raqq bəlo*

farthest ከሁሉ ፡ የራቀ *kähullu yäraqä*

fascinate (enchant) ማረከ *marräkä*

fascinated, be (rapt, absorbed) ተመሰጠ *tämässäṭä*

fashion (v.) ሠራ *särra*

fashion, n. (manner) መንገድ *mängäd;* (mode) ሞድ *mod;* ቄንጥ *qenṭ;* ፋሊጥ *fäliṭ*

fast (v.) ጦመ *ṭomä;* ጾመ *ṣomä*

fast (n.) ጦም *ṭom*; ጾም *ṣom*

fast (adj.) ቀልጣፋ *qälṭaffa*; ፈጣን *fäṭṭan*
fast (adv.) ቶሎ *tolo*; ፈጥኖ *fäṭno*; በፍ
ጥነት *bäfäṭnät*
be fast ፈጠነ *fäṭṭänä*; (of watch) ቀደመ
qäddämä
go fast ፈጠነ *fäṭṭänä*

fasten አሰረ *assärä*

fat, n. (of animal) ሞራ *mora*; ሥብ *səb*

fat, adj. (∼person) ወፍራም *wäfram*;
(∼ox) ድልብ *dəlb*; ደንዳና *dändanna*;
(∼meat) ጮማ *čoma*
be fat (person) ወፈረ *wäffärä*; (animal) ሠባ *säbba*; ደለበ *dälläbä*

fatal (causing death) ሞት ፡ ያስከተለ *mot
yaskättälä*

fatality (misfortune) መቅሠፍት *mäqsäft*; (fate) ዕድል *əddəl*

fate ዕድል *əddəl*; እጣ *äṭa*; የግዜር ፡ ፍርጃ
yägzer fərğa

father አባት *abbat*

father confessor, see 'confessor'

father-in-law አማት *amat*; አማች *amač*

fatherland አገር *agär*

fatherly አባታዊ *abbatawi*

fatigue (vt.) አደከመ *adäkkämä*
fatigue (vi.) ደከመ *däkkämä*

fatigue (n.) ድካም *dəkam*

fatten (∼a person) አወፈረ *awäffärä*;
(∼oxen) አሠባ *asäbba*; አደለበ *adälläbä*

faucet ቧምቧ ፡ መክፈቻ *bʷambʷa mäkfäča*

fault ጥፋት *ṭəfat*; (in spelling) ስሕተት
səhtät

faulty (∼education) የተበላሸ *yätäbälaššä*; ብልሽት ፡ ያለበት *bələššət yalläbbät*; (∼logic) ስሕተተኛ *səhtätäñña*;
የተሳሳተ *yätäsasatä*

fauna እንስሳት *ənsəsat*

favor, v. (show preference) አበላለጠ *abbälalläṭä*; (support) ደገፈ *däggäfä*

favor, n. (act of kindness) ውለታ *wəläta*;
(partiality) አድልዎ *adləwo*; (friendly disposition) መልካም ፡ አስተያየት
mälkam astäyayät; ባለኟነት *balämʷalənnät*; (gift) ስጦታ *səṭota*
be in favor of ደገፈ *däggäfä*
court favor ደጅ ፡ ጠና *däğğ ṭänna*
do a favor ውለታ ፡ ዋለ *wəläta walä*
show favor አደላ *adälla*

favorable የሚያመች *yämmiyamäčč*; የሚ
ስማማ *yämmismamma*; (expressing
approval) የሚደግፍ *yämmidäggəf*

favored ባለኟል *balämʷal*; ከሁሉ ፡ የበ
ለጠ ፡ የሚወደድ *kähullu yäbälläṭä
yämmiwwäddäd*

favorite ባለኟል *balämʷal*

favoritism አድልዎ *adləwo*

fear (v.) ፈራ *färra*; (feel concern) ሰጋ
sägga

fear (n.) ፍርሃት *fərhat*; ፍራቻ *färačča*;
ስጋት *səgat*

fearful (showing fear) ፈሪ *färi*; (causing
fear) አስፈሪ *asfärri*
be fearful ፈራ *färra*; ሰጋ *sägga*

fearless ደፋር *däffar*

fearsome አሰቃቂ *assäqqaqi*

feast (v.) ግብር ፡ አበላ *gäbər abälla*;
ድግስ ፡ አበላ *däggəs abälla*

feast (n.) ድግስ *däggəs*; ግብር *gäbər*
give a feast, see 'feast' (v.)

feat ጀብዱ *ğäbdu*

feather ላባ *laba*

feature (n.) መልክ *mälk*; (characteristic)
መለያ *mälläyya*; መለዮ *mälläyyo*

February የካቲት *yäkkatit*

fecund ርቢ *rəbbi*; ወላድ *wällad*

fee ዋጋ *waga*; ገንዘብ *gänzäb*

feeble ደካማ *däkkama*

feeble-minded አእምሮ ፡ ደካማ *a'məro
däkkama*

feed, v. (~ child, chicken) መገበ *mäggäbä;* (~ cattle) አበላ *abälla;* ቀለበ *qälläbä*

feel ተሰማ(ው) *täsämma(w);* (touch cloth) ዳሰሰ *dassäsä;* (~ part of body) ዳበሰ *dabbäsä*
feel for አዘነ(ለት) *azzänä(llät)*

feeling ስሜት *səmmet;* መንፈስ *mänfäs;* (opinion) አስተያየት *astäyayät;* (sympathy) ማሳዘን *masazzän*

feign አስመሰለ *asmässälä*

feigned ከልብ ፡ ያልሆነ *käləbb yalhonä*

feint ቃጣ *qaṭṭa*

fell (a tree) ጣለ *ṭalä*

fellow ሰው *säw*
fellow (adj.) የሥራ ፡ ጓደኛ *yäsəra gʷaddäňňa*
poor fellow! ምስኪን *məskin*

fellowship (companionship) ጓደኝነት *gʷaddäňňannät;* (grant) የመማሪያ ፡ እርዳታ *yämämmariya ərdata*

female (n.) ሴት *set;* አንስት *anəst;* እንስት *ənəst*

female (adj.) የሴት *yäset*

feminine, n. (gender) አንስታይ ፡ ፆታ *anəstay ṣota*

feminine (adj.) የሴት *yäset;* የሴትነት *yäsetənnät*

fence (vt.) አጠረ *aṭṭärä*

fence (n.) አጥር *aṭər*

fencing የሻቦላ ፡ ግጥሚያ *yäšabola gəṭmiya*

fend, ~ for oneself ራሱን ፡ ቻለ *rasun čalä;* ራሱን ፡ ችሎ ፡ ኖረ *rasun čəlo norä*
fend off መከተ *mäkkätä;* ተከላከለ *täkälakkälä*

fender ፈረፋንጎ *färäfango*

ferment, v. (of dough) ቦካ *bokka;* (of beer) ፈላ *fälla*

ferment (n.) እርሾ *əršo;* (political~) ብጥብጥ *bəṭəbbəṭ*

ferocious አስፈሪ *asfärri*

ferocity አውሬነት *awrennät;* አስፈሪ ፡ ሁኔታ *asfärri huneta*

ferry ማሻገሪያ *maššagäriya*

fertile (~ soil) ለም *läm;* ለምለም *lämläm;* (~ cattle) ወላድ *wällad*
be fertile (soil) ለማ *lämma;* ለመለመ *lämällämä;* (cattle) ረባ *räbba*

fertility (of soil) ልምላሜ *ləməllame;* ለምነት *lämənnät;* (of rabbits) መራባት *märrabat*

fertilize አዳበረ *adabbärä*

fertilizer የመሬት ፡ ማዳበሪያ *yämäret madabäriya*

fervent ከፍ ፡ ያለ *käff yalä;* የጋለ *yägalä*

fervor አድናቆት *adnaqot*

fester መገለ *mäggälä;* መግል ፡ ያዘ *mägəl yazä*

festival ባል *bal;* በዓል *bä'al;* የዕለት ፡ በዓል *yäəlät bä'al*

festive የደስታ *yädässəta*

festivity (celebration) ሰነ ፡ በዓል *sänä bä'al;* (merry-making) ጨዋታ *čäwata*

fetch (~ a person) ሄዶ ፡ ጠራ *hedo ṭärra;* (~ an object) ሄዶ ፡ አመጣ *hedo amäṭṭa*

feud ቂም ፡ በቀል *qim bäqäl;* ጠብ *ṭäb*

feudal የባላባት *yäbalabbat*

fever ትኩሳት *təkkusat*
have fever አተኩሰ(ው) *atäkkʷäsä(w)*

feverish ትኩሳት ፡ የሚያመጣ *təkkusat yämmiyamäṭa*
feverish activity ጥድፊያ *ṭədfiya*

few ጥቂት *ṭəqit*
a few ትንሽ *tənnəš;* ጥቂት *ṭəqit*
a few times አንዴ ፡ ሁለቴ *ande hulätte*

fewer አነስ ፡ ያሉ *anäss yalu*

fiancé, fiancée እጮኛ *əččoňňa*

fiber ቃጫ *qačča*

fiction (literary novel) ልብ ፡ ወለድ ፡ ታሪክ *ləbb wälläd tarik;* (something made up) ፈጠራ *fäṭära*

fictitious የፈጠረ yäfätära; በሐሳብ ፡ የተ
ፈጠረ bähassab yätäfättärä

fiddle የፈረንጅ ፡ ማሲንቆ yäfäränğ masinqo

fidelity እምነት əmnät

fidget ተቀነጠነጠ täqʷnätännätä

fief ጉልት gult

field ማሳ masa; ሜዳ meda; መስክ mäsk

fierce (~heat) ኃይለኛ hayläñña; (~
effort) ከፍ ፡ ያለ käff yalä; (~hatred)
የከረረ yäkärrärä; (~dog) ተናካሽ tänakaš

fiery የጋለ yägalä; (~temper) የቁጡ
ነት yäquttunnät

fifteen ዐሥራ ፡ አምስት asra amməst

fifth አምስተኛ amməstäñña; (~order of
the Amharic alphabet) ኃምስ haməs

fifty ኃምሳ hamsa; አምሳ amsa

fig በለስ bäläs

fight (vt.) ተዋጋ täwagga; (~a disease)
ተከላከለ täkälakkälä; (~a habit) አስ
ወገደ aswäggädä
fight (vi.) ተዋጋ täwagga; (of dogs)
ተጣላ tätalla; (of partners) ተጨቃ
ጨቀ täçäqaççäqä

fight, n. (battle) ጠብ täb; (contest) ግጥ
ሚያ gätmiya; (dispute) ጭቅጭቅ
çəqəççəq
have a fight ተጣላ tätalla

fighting ውጊያ wəggiya

figure, v. (make calculation) አሰላ asälla; (think out) በግምት ፡ መሰለ(ው)
bägəmmət mässälä(w)
figure out (~ the costs) አሰላ asälla;
(~a problem) ሠራ särra

figure, n. (number) ቁጥር qutər; ሒሳብ
hisab; (geometrical ~) ቅርጽ qərs;
(illustrative drawing) ሥዕል sə'əl;
(person) ሰው säw; (body) ሰውነት säwənnät; (price) የጠየቀው ፡ ዋጋ yätäy-
yäqäw waga

figure of speech ዘይቤ zäyəbe

file, v. (with a rasp) ሞረደ morrädä;(~
an application) አስገባ asgäbba; (arrange papers) በደንብ ፡ አስቀመጠ bädänb asqämmätä
file out በሰልፍ ፡ ወጣ bäsälf wätta

file, n. (instrument) ሞረድ moräd; (line)
መሥመር mäsmär; (for letters) ፋይል
fayl
keep on file መዘገብ mäzäggäbä

filing መዝገብ ፡ አያያዝ mäzgäb ayyayaz

fill (vt.) ሞላ molla; (~ a need) አሟላ
amʷalla; (~ a position) ያዘ yazä;
(~a prescription) አዘጋጀ azzägaggä
fill (vi.) ሞላ molla
be filled ሞላ molla; ተሞላ tämolla;(of
position) ተያዘ täyazä
fill out ሞላ molla
fill up ሞላ molla

filling station ቤንዚን ፡ ማደያ benzin
maddäya

film (v.) ፊልም ፡ አነሣ film anässa

film (n.) ፊልም film; (thin layer) ሰፈፍ
säfäf

filter (vt.) አጠለለ atällälä; አጣራ attarra

filter (n.) ማጥለያ matläya; ማጣሪያ mattariya

filth ቆሻሻ qošaša; እድፍ ədəf; ጉድፍ gudəf

filthy, be ቆሸሸ qoššäšä; አደፈ addäfä

fin ክንፍ kənf

final የመጨረሻ yämäçärräša

finally በመጨረሻ bämäçärräša; አድሮ
adro; ዞሮ ፡ ዞሮ zoro zoro; ውሎ ፡
አድሮ wəlo adro

finance (v.) ወጪ ፡ ከፈለ wäçi käffälä

finance (n.) የገንዘብ ፡ አያያዝ yägänzäb
ayyayaz
finances የገንዘብ ፡ ይዞታ yägänzäb yəzota

Finance Minister የገንዘብ ፡ ሚኒስትር yägänzäb ministər

financial የገንዘብ yägänzäb

financially በገንዘብ ፡ በኩል bägänzäb bäkkul

find አገኘ agäňňä
find out ዐወቀ awwäqä; ተረዳ(ው) tärädda(w)

fine (v.) ቀጣ qäṭṭa

fine (n.) መቀጫ mäqqäča; መቀጮ mäqqäčo

fine, adj. (good) ማለፊያ maläfiya; (∼ sand) ደቃቃ däqaqa; (thin) ረቂቅ räqiq; (∼pen point) ቀጭን qäččän; (∼ cloth) ስስ säs; (∼weather) ጥሩ ṭäru; (∼manners) የታረመ yätarrämä
feel fine ደኅና ፡ ነው dähna näw

fine arts ሥነ ፡ ጥበብ sänä ṭäbäb

finger ጣት ṭat
index finger ሌባ ፡ ጣት leba ṭat
little finger ትንሽ ፡ ጣት tännäš ṭat
middle finger (የ)መሃል ፡ ጣት (yä)mähal ṭat
ring finger የቀለበት ፡ ጣት yäqäläbät ṭat

fingernail ጥፍር ṭäfär

fingerprint የጣት ፡ አሻራ yäṭat ašara

finish (vt.) ጨረሰ čärräsä; አበቃ abäqqa; ደመደመ dämäddämä
finish (vi.) አለቀ alläqä

finite, be ወሰን ፡ አለ(ው) wäsän allä(w)

fire, vt. (from work) አሰናበተ assänabbätä; ከሥራ ፡ አባረረ käsära abbarrärä
fire, vi. (discharge a weapon) ተኮሰ täkkʷäsä
be fired (of clay) ተጠበሰ täṭäbbäsä; (from work) ተሰናበተ täsänabbätä

fire (n.) እሳት äsat; (a destructive burning) ቃጠሎ qaṭälo; (of weapons) ተኩስ täkʷs
be on fire ተያያዘ täyayazä; በእሳት ፡ ተያያዘ bääsat täyayazä
catch fire በእሳት ፡ ተያያዘ bääsat täyayazä; ተቀጣጠለ täqäṭaṭṭälä
make a fire እሳት ፡ አነደደ äsat anäddädä

put (a pot) on the fire ጣደ ṭadä
put out the fire አጠፋ aṭäffa
set fire to, set on fire አቃጠለ aqqaṭṭälä
start a fire እሳት ፡ አያያዘ äsat ayyayazä

firearm መሳሪያ mässariya

fire department የእሳት ፡ አደጋ ፡ መከላከያ ፡ መሥሪያ ፡ ቤት yääsat adäga mäkkälakäya mäsriya bet

fire engine የእሳት ፡ አደጋ ፡ መኪና yääsat adäga mäkina

fire hazard የእሳት ፡ አደጋ yääsat adäga

fireman የእሳት ፡ አደጋ ፡ ተከላካይ yääsat adäga täkälakay

fireplace ምድጃ mädäǧǧa

firewood ማገዶ magädo

fireworks ርችት räččät

firm (n.) ኩባንያ kubbanäyya; ድርጅት däräǧǧät

firm, adj. (solid) ጽኑ ṣänu; (∼ measures, ground) ጥብቅ ṭäbq; (∼ price) ቁርጥ ፡ ያለ qurräṭṭ yalä
be firm ጠበቀ ṭäbbäqä; ጠና ṭänna; ጸና ṣänna

firmament ሰማይ sämay; ጠፈር ṭäfär

firmly በጥብቅ bäṭäbq; (certainly) በእርግጥ bärgäṭ

first (adj.) የመጀመሪያ yämäǧämmäriya; (in rank) ተቀዳሚ täqäddami; (in class) አንደኛ andäňňa; (∼ prize) ያን ደኛነት yandäňňannät; (in a title of a king) ቀዳማዊ qädamawi; ቀዳማይ qädamay
first (adv.) በመጀመሪያ bämäǧämmäriya
first of all መጀመሪያ ፡ ነገር mäǧämmäriya nägär; ከሁሉ ፡ በፊት kähullu bäfit
be first ቀደመ qäddämä

first aid የመጀመሪያ ፡ እርዳታ ፡ ሕክምና yämäǧämmäriya ärdata häkmänna

first-born በኩር bäkʷär; አንጋፋ angaffa

first-class አንደኛ ፣ ማዕረግ andäñña ma-
'ǝräg

fish (v.) ዓሣ ፣ አጠመደ asa aṭämmädä

fish (n.) ዓሣ asa

fisherman ዓሣ ፣ አጥማጅ asa aṭmaǧ

fishhook መንጠቆ mänṭäqqo

fist ቡጢ buṭṭi; ጡጫ ṭučča

fit, vt. (~ a suit) አስተካከለ astäkakkälä; (put into place) አስገባ asgäbba
fit, vi. (be suitable) ተማቸ tämäččä
fit together (vt.) አገጣጠመ aggäṭaṭṭämä
fit together (vi.) ተገጣጠመ tägäṭaṭṭämä

fit (n.) የሚጥል ፣ በሽታ yämmiṭǝl bäššǝta

fit, adj. (suitable, proper) ተስማሚ täsmami; ተገቢ tägäbi
be fit for ተስማማ täsmamma; ተመቸ
tämäččä

fitting (adj.) ልክ lǝkk; ተገቢ tägäbi;
የሚስማማ yämmismamma

five አምስት ammǝst
five o'clock ዐሥራአንድ ፣ ሰዓት asrand
sä'at

fix (repair) ጠገነ ṭäggänä; (~ supper)
አሰናዳ assänadda; (~ a time) ወሰነ
wässänä; (~ one's eyes on) ተከለ
täkkälä

fixed (adj.) መደበኛ mädäbäñña; የተወ
ሰነ yätäwässänä

flabby ልፍስፍስ lǝfǝsfǝs

flag, v. (of strength) አነሰ annäsä; (of
person, animal) ተዳከመ tädakkämä

flag (n.) ሰንደቅ ፣ ዓላማ sändäq alama;
ባንዴራ bandera

flagellate ገረፈ gärräfä

flagrant ጉልህ gulǝh

flagpole የባንዴራ ፣ መስቀያ yäbandera
mäsqäya

flagstaff, see 'flagpole'

flail መውቂያ mäwqiya

flair ተሰጥዎ täsäṭwo

flamboyant ብላጭላጭ bǝläčläč

flame (v.) በገ ፣ አለ bogg alä

flame (n.) ነበልባል näbälbal; ብርሃን bǝrhan
be in flames በእሳት ፣ ተያያዘ bäǝsat
täyayazä

flammable በቀላሉ ፣ የሚያያዝ bäqällalu
yämmiyyayaz

flank, n. (of body) ሽንጥ šǝnṭ; ወገብ wägäb; (side of anything) ወገን wägän

flap v. (~ wings) አርገበገበ argäbäggäbä

flare (v.), ~ up በገ ፣ አለ bogg alä

flare (n.) ነበልባል näbälbal

flash (vt.) አበራ abärra
flash (vi.) ብላጭ ፣ አለ bǝlläčč alä
flash by ሾ ፣ አለ šǝww alä

flash (n.) ብላጭታ bǝlläčta
in a flash ከመቅጽበት kämäqǝṣbät

flashlight ባትሪ batri

flashy ብላጭላጭ bǝläčläč

flask ኮዳ kodda

flat, adj. (~roof) ለጥ ፣ ያለ läṭṭ yalä;
(~ country) ሜዳማ medamma; (~
dish) ዝርግ zǝrg; (~ place) ደልዳላ
däldalla
fall flat (on the face) ተደፋ tädäffa;
(on the back) ተዘረረ täzärrärä
have a flat tire ጎማ ፣ ተኛ gomma täñña
taste flat እህል ፣ ቅጠል ፣ አይልም ǝhǝl
qǝṭäl ayǝläm

flatly በፍጹም bäfǝṣṣum

flatten (~ iron) ጠፋጠፈ ṭäfäṭṭäfä; (~
the road surface) አስተካከለ astäkakkälä; ደለደለ däläddälä

flatter ሸነገለ šänäggälä; በከንቱ ፣ አወደሰ
bäkäntu awäddäsä; (please) በጣም ፣
አስደሰተ bäṭam asdässätä

flattery ሽንገላ šǝngäla; ከንቱ ፣ ውዳሴ
käntu wǝddase

flavor (v.) አጣፈጠ *aṭaffäṭä*

flavor (n.) ጣም *ṭam;* ጣዕም *ṭaʾəm*

flavoring ማጣፈጫ *maṭṭafäča*

flaw (in glass) ስንጥቅ *sənṭəq;* (in a plan) ጉድለት *gudlät*

flawless እንከን፥የሌለበት *ənkän yälelläbbät*

flax ተልባ *tälba*

flea ቁንጫ *qunəčča*

flee ሸሸ *šäššä*

fleece የበግ ፥ ጸጉር *yäbäg ṣägur*

fleet የጦር ፥ መርከቦች *yäṭor märkäbočč*

flesh (meat) ሥጋ *səga*

fleshy (~ person) ደንዳና *dändanna;* ወፍራም *wäfram;* (of flesh) የሥጋ *yäsəga*

flexible ተለማጭ *tälämmač*

flicker ብልጭ ፥ ድርግም ፥ አለ *bəlləčč dərgəmm alä*

flier (pilot) አውሮፕላን ፥ ነጂ *awroplan näǧi*

flight (flying) በረራ *bärära;* (series of steps) ፎቅ *foq;* (hasty departure) ሽሽት *šəššət* put to flight አሸሸ *ašäššä*

flimsy (~ boat) ደቃቃ *däqaqa;* (~excuse) የማይመስል *yämmayəmäsəl*

flip (~ a coin) ወረወረ *wäräwwärä;* (~ pages of book) በፍጥነት ፥ ገላለጠ *bäfəṭnät gälalläṭä*

flirt (v.) ተዳራ *tädarra*

float (v.) ተንሳፈፈ *tänsaffäfä;* (of rumors) ነፈሰ *näffäsä*

float (n.) መንሳፈፊያ *mänsafäfiya*

flock (v.) ጐረፈ *gʷärräfä*

flock (n.) መንጋ *mänga*

flood (vt.) አጥለቀለቀ *aṭläqälläqä* flood (vi.) ሞላ *molla*

flood (n.) ጐርፍ *gʷärf;* የውኃ ፥ ሙላት *yäwəha mulat* Flood (deluge in the Bible) የጥፋት ፥ ውኃ *yäṭəfat wəha*

floor ወለል *wäläl;* (story) ፎቅ *foq*

flora ዕፀዋት *əṣäwat*

florist አበባ ፥ ሻጭ *abäba šač*

flour ዱቄት *duqet*

flourish, vi. (thrive) ጥሩ ፥ ሆኖ ፥ በቀለ *ṭəru hono bäqqälä;* (reach a high point) በለጸገ *bäläṣṣägä;* (of business) ተስፋፋ *täsfaffa*

flow (v.) ጐረፈ *gʷärräfä;* ፈሰሰ *fässäsä* flow into (of river) ገባ *gäbba*

flower (v.) አበበ *abbäbä*

flower (n.) አበባ *abäba*

flowery (~meadow) አበባማ *abäbamma;* (~speech) ወርቃ ፥ ወርቅ *wärqa wärq*

flu ኢንፍሉዌንዛ *influwenza*

fluctuate ተለዋወጠ *täläwawwäṭä*

fluent, ~speaker አንደበተ ፥ ርቱዕ *andäbätä rətuʾ*

fluently አቀላጥፎ *aqqälaṭfo*

fluid (n.) ፈሳሽ *fäsaš*

fluid, adj. (~situation) የሚዋልል *yämmiwalləl*

flush, vt. (~the toilet) ውኃ ፥ ለቀቀ *wäha läqqäqä* flush (vi.) ፊቱ፥ ደም ፥ መሰለ *fitu däm mässälä*

flute እምቢልታ *əmbilta;* ዋሽንት *wašənt* play the flute ዋሽንት ፥ ነፋ *wašənt näffa*

flutter, vi. (of heart) ትር ፥ ትር ፥ አለ *tərr tərr alä;* (of eyelids) ተርገበገበ *tärgäbäggäbä;* (fly in the breeze) ተውለበለበ *täwläbälläbä*

fly (vi.) በረረ *bärrärä;* (of flag) ተሰቀለ *täsäqqälä;* (of time) ሮጠ *roṭä*

fly (n.) ዝምብ *zəmb;* ዝንብ *zənb*

fly swatter ጭራ *čəra*

foal የፈረስ ፥ ውርንጭላ *yäfäräs wərənčälla*

foam (v.) አረፋ ፥ ወጣ *aräfa wäṭṭa;* (with anger) ዳነፋ *dänäffa*

foam (n.) አረፋ *aräfa;* (on the mouth
of a dog) ለሀጭ *lähač*

fodder ድርቆሽ *dərqoš*

foe ጠላት *ṭälat*

foetus ሽል *šəl*

fog ጉም *gum;* ጭጋግ *čəgag*

foggy (~weather) ጭጋግ ፡ የበዛበት *čəgag yäbäzzabbät*

fold (~ arms) አጣመረ *aṭṭammärä;* (~
clothes, letter) ዐጠፈ *aṭṭäfä;* ዐጣጠፈ
aṭaṭṭäfä
fold up (vt.) ዐጣጠፈ *aṭaṭṭäfä*

-fold (as in two-fold) ዕጥፍ *əṭəf*

folder ማኅደር *mahdär;* ካርታስ *kərtas*

folding chair ታጣፊ ፡ ወምበር *taṭafi wämbär*

foliage ቅጠላ ፡ ቅጠል *qəṭäla qəṭäl*

folk ሰው *säw*
folks ቤተ ፡ ሰቦች *betä säbočč*

folklore ተረትና ፡ ምሳሌ *tärätənna məssale*

folk tale ተረት *tärät*

follow ተከተለ *täkättälä;* ተከታተለ *täkätattälä;* (understand) ገባ(ው) *gäb-
ba(w)*

follower ተከታይ *täkättay*

following (adj.) ተከታይ *täkättay;* የሚ
ቀጥል *yämmiqäṭṭəl*

foment (~rebellion) አነሣሣ *annäsassa*

fond የፍቅር *yäfəqər*
be fond of ወደደ *wäddädä*

food ምብል *mäbəl;* ምግብ *məgəb*
food supplies ቀለብ *qälläb*

fool (vt.) አሞኘ *amoňňä;* አታለለ *attallälä*

fool (n.) ሞኝ *moňň;* ጅል *ğəl*

foolish (~ person) ሞኝ *moňň;* ቂል *qil;*
(~thing) የማይረባ *yämmayəräba;*
(~chatter) ያጅል *yäğəl*
be foolish ቀለለ *qällälä;* ሞኝ ፡ ሆነ
moňň hona

foolishness ሞኝነት *moňňənnät*

foot እግር *əgər;* (measure) ጫማ *čamma;*
(lower part) ሥር *sər*
at the foot of በ - - - ሥር *bä - - - sər;*
ከ - - - ሥር *kä - - - sər*

football የእግር ፡ ኳስ *yäəgər kʷas*

foothold መረጋገጫ *märrägagäča*

footnote የግርጌ ፡ ማስታወሻ *yägərge mastawäša*

footpath የግር ፡ መንገድ *yägər mängäd*

footprint ኮቴ *kotte;* ዱካ *duka*

footstep የግር ፡ ኮቴ *yägər kotte*

for ለ *lä*
be for ደገፈ *däggäfä*

forbid ከለከለ *käläkkälä*

forbidden ክልክል *kəlkəl*

force (v.) አገበረ *agäbbärä;* አስገደደ *asgäddädä*

force (n.) ኃይል *hayl;* ጉልበት *gulbät*
be in force (regulation) ጸና *ṣänna*
by force በግድ *bägədd*

forced (insincere) ካንጋት ፡ በላይ ፡ የሆነ
kangät bälay yähonä

forceful (~ person) ጠንካራ *ṭänkarra;*
(~speech) ኃይለኛ *hayläňňa*

ford መልካ *mälka*

forearm ክንድ *kənd*

forebode መምጣት ፡ አመለከተ *mämṭat
amäläkkätä*

forecast አስቀድሞ ፡ አስታወቀ *asqäddəmo astawwäqä*

forefathers አባቶች *abbatočč*

forefinger ለባ ፡ ጣት *leba ṭat*

forehead ግምባር *gəmbar*

foreign የባዕድ ፡ አገር *yäba'əd agär;*
የውጭ ፡ አገር *yäwəčč agär*

foreign affairs የውጭ ፡ ጉዳይ *yäwəčč
gudday*
Ministry of Foreign Affairs የውጭ ፡
ጉዳይ ፡ ሚኒስቴር *yäwəčč gudday minister*

foreign country የሰው ፡ አገር yäsäw
agär; የባዕድ ፡ አገር yäba'əd agär

foreigner የውጭ ፡ አገር ፡ ሰው yäwəčč
agär säw

foreign minister የውጭ ፡ ጉዳይ ፡ ሚኒ
ስትር yäwəčč gudday ministər

foreign office የውጭ ፡ ጉዳይ ፡ ሚኒስቴር
yäwəčč gudday minister

foreleg የፊት ፡ እግር yäfit əgər

foreman አሠሪ assärri; የሠራተኞች ፡
አለቃ yäsärratäňňočč aläqa

foremost የላቀ yälaqä

forenoon ከሰዓት ፡ በፊት käsäat bäfit

foresee ቀደም ፡ ብሎ ፡ ተገነዘበ qädämm
bəlo tägänäzzäbä

foresight አርቆ ፡ አስተዋይነት arqo astäwayənnät

forest ዱር dur; ጫካ čakka; ደን dänn

foretell ተነበየ tänäbbäyä

forever ለዘላለም läzälaläm; ዘለዓለም zälä'aläm; ሁልጊዜ hulgize

foreword መቅድም mäqdäm

forge, v. (~a chain) ቀጠቀጠ qäṭäqqäṭä; (~a signature) አስመስሎ ፡ ፈረመ
asmässəlo färrämä

forge (n.) ብረት ፡ ማቅለጫ brät maqläča

forget ረሳ rässa; ዘነጋ zänägga

forgetful ልብ ፡ አልባ ləbb alba; ዝንጉ
zəngu

forgive ይቅር ፡ አለ yəqər alä; ይቅርታ ፡
አደረገ yəqərta adärrägä

forgiveness (pardon) ምሕረት məhrät;
(forgiving) ይቅር ፡ ማለት yəqər malät

fork (instrument) ሹካ šukka; (in a tree)
ባላ balla; (in the road) መንታ mänta

forlorn (~kitten) የተጣለ yätäṭalä
feel forlorn ብቸኝነት ፡ ተሰማ(ው) bəččäňňannät täsämma(w)

form, v. (~ a bank) አቋቋመ aqqʷaqʷamä; (~ a coalition) መሠረት
mäsärrätä; (~ habits) አፈራ afärra;
(~ the character) አነጸ annäṣä

form, n. (outward shape) መልክ mälk;
ቅርጽ qərṣ; (mold) ቅርጽ ፡ ማውጫ
qərṣ mawča; (blank) ፎርም form

formal (~agreement) በደንብ ፡ የተጣ
በቀ bädänb yätäṭäbbäqä; (~ dress)
የሥነ ፡ በዓል yäsənä bäal
be formal (in etiquette) ሥነ ፡ ሥር
ዓት ፡ ተከተለ sənä sər'at täkättälä

former የድሮ yädəro; ቀደም ፡ ያለ qädämm
yalä; የቀድሞ yäqädmo; ጥንታዊ ṭəntawi; የፊተኛ yäfitäňňa
former days ጥንት ṭänt

formerly ቀድሞ qädmo; ድሮ dəro; ጥንት
ṭänt

formidable (~task) አዳጋች addagač;
(~opposition) ከፍ ፡ ያለ käff yalä

formula (instructions) መምሪያ mämriya;
(in algebra) ፎርሙላ formula

formulate (~a plan) አዘጋጀ azzägaǧǧä;
(~laws) ደነገገ dänäggägä

forsake ጣለ ṭalä; ተወ täwä

fort ምሽግ məššəg

forth ጀምሮ ǧämməro

forthcoming (~book) በቅርብ ፡ የሚወጣ
bäqərb yämmiwäṭa; (~ trip) ወደፊት ፡
የሚደረግ wädäfit yämmiddärräg

forthright, adj. (~ reply) ፍርጥ ፡ ያለ
fərräṭṭ yalä

forthwith ወዲያው wädiyaw

fortification ምሽግ məššəg

fortify (~ a city) መሸገ mäššägä;
(strengthen the body) አጠነከረ aṭänäkkärä

fortnight ዐሥራ ፡ አምስት ፡ ቀን asrammast
qän

fortress ትልቅ ፡ ምሽግ təlləq məššəg

fortuitous አጋጣሚ aggaṭami

fortunate ዕድለኛ əddäläňňa
be fortunate ዐደለ addälä

fortunately እንደ ፡ ዕድል ፡ ሆኖ əndä əddəl hono; ደግነቱ däggənnätu

fortune (fate) ዕድል əddəl; (wealth) ሀብት
habt

fortuneteller ኮከብ ፡ ቈጣሪ *kokäb qʷätari*

forty አርባ *arba*

forum ሸንጎ *šängo*

forward (v) አስተላለፈ *astälalläfä;* አደ ረሰ *adärräsä;* (send) ላከ *laka*

forward (adj.) የወደፊት *yäwädäfit*

forwards ወደፊት *wädäfit*

fossil ቅሪት ፡ አካል *qərrit akal*

foster (promote) አበረታታ *abbärätatta;* አነቃቃ *annäqaqqa*

foster child የማደጎ ፡ ልጅ *yämadägo ləǧ*

foster father አሳዳጊ *asaddagi*

foster mother አሳዳጊ ፡ እናት *asaddagi ənnat*

foul (v.) በከለ *bäkkälä*

foul, n. (in sport) ጥፋት *ṭəfat*

foul, adj. (~ air) የተበላሸ *yätäbälaššä;* (~ weather) መጥፎ *mäṭfo*

found, v. (establish) ቈረቈረ *qʷäräqqʷä-rä;* አቋቋመ *aqqʷaqʷamä;* (base) መሠ ረተ *mäsärrätä*

foundation መሠረት *mäsärät;* (endowed institution) ድርጅት *dərəǧǧət*
lay the foundation መሠረት *mäsärrä-tä;* መሠረት ፡ ጣለ *mäsärät ṭalä*

founder መሥራች *mäsrač*

foundling ተወልዶ ፡ የተጣለ ፡ ልጅ *täwäldo yätäṭalä ləǧ*

foundry የብረት ፡ ማቅለጫ *yäbrät maqläča*

fountain ምንጭ *mənč*

fountain pen ብዕር *bə'ər*

four አራት *aratt*
four o'clock ዐሥር ፡ ሰዓት *assər sä'at*

fourteen ዐሥራ ፡ አራት *asraratt*

fourth አራተኛ *arattäñña;* (~ order of the Amharic alphabet) ራብዕ *rabə'*
one fourth ሩብ *rub*

fowl አዕዋፍ *a'waf*

fox ቀበሮ *qäbäro*

foxy ተንኮለኛ *tänkʷäläñña*

foyer መተላለፊያ *mättälaläfiya*

fraction (number) ክፍልፋይ *kəfəlfay;* (fragment) ጥቂት ፡ ክፍል *ṭəqit kəfəl*

fracture (n.) ስብራት *səbbərat*

fragile ተሰባሪ *täsäbbari*

fragment (broken part) ስብርባሪ *səbər-bari;* (section) ክፍል *kəfəl*

fragmentary (~ report) ያልተሟላ *yaltä-mʷalla*

fragrance መዓዛ *mä'aza*

fragrant, be ጣፈጠ ፡ መዓዛ ፡ አለው *ṭa-fač mä'aza alläw*

frail (~ person) ደካማ *däkkama;* (~ chair) ተሰባሪ *täsäbbari*

frailty ድካም *dəkam*

frame, v. (~ a picture) መስታወት ፡ ውስጥ ፡ አገባ *mästawät wəsṭ agäbba*

frame, n. (of picture) ክፈፍ *kəfäf;* (of glasses) መያዣ *mäyaža;* (of house) ግድግዳና ፡ ጣሪያ *gədgəddanna ṭariya;* (of a person) አጥንት *aṭənt*
frame of mind መንፈስ *mänfäs*

framework (of a bridge) አውታር *awtar;* (of a house) ግድግዳና ፡ ጣሪያ *gədgəd-danna ṭariya*

France ፈረንሳይ ፡ አገር *färänsay agär;* ፈረንሳይ *färänsay*

frank ግልጽ *gəlṣ;* ቅን *qən;* (~child) የዋህ *yäwwah*

frankly ግልጥ ፡ አድርጎ *gəlləṭṭ adrəgo*

frantic (~ cry) የጩንቀት *yäčənqät*

fraternal የወንድምነት *yäwändəmmənnät*

fraternity (brotherhood) ወንድማማችነት *wändəmmamačännät;* (society) የወን ድማማችነት ፡ ክበብ *yäwändəmmama-čännät kəbäb*

fraternize ተወዳጀ *täwädaǧǧä*

fraud (n.) ሸፍጥ *šäfṭ;* ማጭበርበር *mač-bärbär*

fraudulent የሐሰት *yähassät*

freak ጉድ *gud*

freckle ጠቃጠቆ *ṭäqaṭäqo*

free, v. (~ a slave) አርነት ፡ አወጣ *arənnät awäṭṭa;* (~ a prisoner) ለቀቀ *läqqäqä;* በነጻ ፡ ለቀቀ *bänäṣa läqqäqä;* (make loose) ፈታ *fätta*

free, adj. (having liberty) ነጻ *näṣa;* (empty) ባዶ *bado*
free (adv.) በብላሽ *bäbəlaš;* በነጻ *bänäṣa*
free of charge በነጻ *bänäṣa;* በብላሽ *bäbəlaš*
be free (have time) ጊዜ ፡ አለው *gize alläw;* (of telephone) አልተያዘም *altäyazäm*
become free አርነት ፡ ወጣ *arənnät wäṭṭa*

freeborn ነጻ *näṣa*

freedom ነጻነት *näṣannät;* አርነት *arənnät;* (privileges) መብት *mäbt*

freely (clearly) በግልጽ *bägəlṣ;* (without restriction) እንደልብ *əndäləbb*

freeman የሰው ፡ ልጅ *yäsäw ləǧ;* ነጻ ፡ ሰው *näṣa säw*

freeze (vt.) አቀዘቀዘ *aqäzäqqäzä*
freeze, vi. (of water) ረጋ *rägga;* (of person) ብርድ ፡ አቄረመደ(ው) *bərd aq^wärämmädä(w)*

freezer ማቀዝቀዣ *maqäzqäža*

freezing, be በጣም ፡ በረደ *bäṭam bärrädä*

freight (goods) እቃ *əqa;* (price for transportation) እቃ ፡ ለመላክ ፡ ዋጋ *əqa lämälak waga*

freighter ጫኝ ፡ መርከብ *čäñ märkäb*

French (person) ፈረንሳዊ *färänsawi;* (language) ፈረንሳይኛ *färänsayəñña*

frequent, v. (~ a place) አዘወተረ *azäwättärä*

frequent (adj.) የተደጋገመ *yätädägaggämä*

frequently ብዙ ፡ ጊዜ *bəzu gize;* አዘውትሮ *azäwtəro*

fresh (~ eggs, meat, news) ትኩስ *təkkus;* (~ vegetable) ያልዋለ ፡ ያላደረ *yalwalä yaladdärä;* (~ butter) ለጋ *läga;* (~ fruit) አዲስ ፡ የተቀጠፈ *addis yätäqäṭṭäfä;* (~ air) ንጹህ *nəṣuh;* (~ water) ጠሩ *ṭäru*

friction (rubbing) ማፋጨት *maffaččät;* (disagreement) ግጭት *gəččət*

Friday ዓርብ *arb*

fried (adj.) ጥብስ *ṭəbs*

friend ወዳጅ *wädaǧ*
close friend የቅርብ ፡ ወዳጅ *yäqərb wädaǧ*
become friends ተወዳጀ *täwädaǧǧä*
make friends ወዳጅ ፡ አበጀ ፡ (አፈራ) *wädaǧ abäǧǧä (afärra)*

friendly (amiable) ሰው ፡ ወዳድ *säw wäddad;* (amicable) ወዳጅ *wädaǧ;* የወዳጅነት *yäwädaǧənnät*

friendship ወዳጅነት *wädaǧənnät*

fright ፍርሃት *fərhat*

frighten (vt.) አስፈራ *asfärra*
frighten (vi.) ፈራ *färra*

frightful አስቃቂ *assäqqaqi*

frigid ቀዝቃዛ *qäzqazza*

fringe (of curtain) ዘርፍ *zärf;* (of dress) ጥለት *ṭälät*

fritter ሰባበረ *säbabbärä;* አደቀቀ *adäqqäqä*

frivolous ቧልተኛ *b^waltäñña*

frog እንቁራሪት *ənqurarit*

from ከ *kä;* (because of) በ - - - ምክን ያት *bä - - - məknəyat*

front, n. (of house) ደጃፍ *däǧǧaf;* (military ~) የጦር ፡ ግንባር *yäṭor gənbar*
in front of በ - - - ፊት *bä - - - fit;* ፊት ፡ ለፊት *fit läfit*

front (adj.) የመጀመሪያ *yämäǧämmäriya;* የፊት *yäfit;* ፊተኛ *fitäñña*

frontier ወሰን *wäsän;* ድንበር *dənbär*

front line የጦር ፡ ግንባር *yäṭor gənbar*

frost ውርጭ *wərč*

froth (of milk, on the mouth of a child) አረፋ *aräfa;* (of dog) ለህፅ *lähaç*

frown (v.) ፊት ፡ ጸጠረ *fit qʷaṭṭärä;* ግም ባር ፡ ጸጠረ *gəmbar qʷaṭṭärä*

frown upon ናቀ *naqä*

frozen (∼water) የረጋ *yärägga*

frugal (saving) ቄጣቢ *qʷäṭṭabi;* (∼ supper) ቀላል *qällal*

fruit ፍሬ *fəre*
bear fruit አፈራ *afärra*

fruitful ፍሬያማ *fəreyamma*

fruitless ፍሬ ፡ ቢስ *fəre bis*

frustrate (∼a plan) አከሸፈ *akäššäfä*

fry ጠበሰ *ṭäbbäsä*

frying pan መጥበሻ *mäṭbäša*

fuel ነዳጅ *nädağ*

fugitive (fleeing) ሽሽ *šäši;* የኮበለለ *yäkobällälä*

fulfill ፈጸመ *fäṣṣämä*

fulfillment ፍጻሜ *fəṣṣame*

full (adj.) ሙሉ *mulu*
be full ሞላ *molla;* መላ *mälla;* (be satiated) ጠገበ *ṭäggäbä*
in full በሙሉ *bämulu*

full-grown ዐዋቂ *awaqi*

full time ሙሉ ፡ ቀን፡(ጊዜ) *mulu qän (gize)*

fully ሙሉ ፡ በሙሉ *mulu bämulu;* በሙሉ *bämulu;* መቶ ፡ በመቶ *mäto bämäto*

fumble, ∼for በረበረ *bäräbbärä;* ደባበሰ *däbabbäsä*

fume, v. (give off smoke) ጨሰ *čäsä;* (become angry) ደነፋ *dänäffa*

fume (n.) ጢስ *ṭis*

fumigate ዐጠነ *aṭṭänä*

fun ቀልድ *qäld;* ጨዋታ *čäwata*
have fun ቀለደ *qällädä*
make (poke) fun of አላገጠ *allaggäṭä;* ቀለደ *qällädä;* አሾፈ *ašofä*

function (v.) ሠራ *särra*

function, n. (work) ሥራ *səra;* ተግባር *tägbar;* (purpose) ዓላማ *alama;* (cere-

mony) ሥን ፡ ሥርዓት *sənä sər'at*

functionary ሠራተኛ *särratäňňa*

fund, n. (money set aside) መዋጮ *mäwwaço;* (of knowledge) መጠን *mäṭän*
funds ገንዘብ *gänzäb*

fundamental መሠረታዊ *mäsärätawi*

funeral መቃብር *mäqabər;* ሥርዓት ፡ ቀብር *sər'atä qäbər*

funnel ማጥለያ *maṭläya*

funny አሥቂኝ *assəqiň;* (strange) እንግዳ *əngəda*

fur የውሬ ፡ ጸጉር *yawre ṣägur;* (garment) ባለጸጉር ፡ ልብስ *baläṣägur ləbs*

furious (angry) የተናደደ *yätänaddädä;* (violent) ኃይለኛ *hayläňňa*

furiously በኃይል *bähayl*

furlough ፈቃድ *fäqad*

furnace ምድጃ *mədəǧǧa*

furnish (∼supplies) አቀረበ *aqärräbä;* (∼ an apartment) እቃ ፡ አስገባ *əqa asgäbba*

furnished, be እቃ ፡ አለበት *əqa alläbbät*

furnished room ክፍል ፡ ከነሙሉ ፡ እቃው *kəfəl kännämulu əqaw*

furniture የቤት ፡ እቃ *yäbet əqa*

furor ሁከት *hukät;* ሽብር *šäbbər*

furrow, v. (∼the ground) ተለመ *tällämä;* (wrinkle) አኰማተረ *akkʷämattärä*

furrow, n. (of ground) ትልም *təlm;* (of forehead) መቁጠር *mäqʷaṭär*

further (v.) እንዲስፋፋ ፡ አደረገ *əndisfaffa adärrägä*

further (adj.) ሌላ *lela;* ተጨማሪ *täčämmari*

further, adv. (farther) ወደፊት *wädäfit;* (in addition) ከዚህም ፡ በላይ *käzzihəm bälay;* (more) በይበልጥ *bäyəbälṭ*
further on ወደፊት *wädäfit*

furthermore ከዚህም ፡ በላይ *käzzihəm bälay;* ደግሞ *dägmo*

furtive ሹኮኮ ፡ ያለ šukəkk yalä

furtively በድብቅ bädəbbəq

fury (anger) ንዴት nəddet; (violence) ኃይል hayl

fuse, vt. (combine by melting) አቅልጦ ፡ አያያዘ aqləṭo ayyayazä
fuse, vi. (melt) ቀለጠ qälläṭä; (blend, of ideas) ተዋሐደ täwahadä

fuse (n.) ባልቦላ balbola

fuss (v.) ተነዛነዘ tänäzannäzä
fuss around ተንጋለወደ tängälawwädä

fuss (n.) ትርምስ tərəmməs

fussy ዝብርቅርቅ zəbrəqrəq

fussy, be (person) ተነጫነጨ tänäčannä-čä; (job) ከፍተኛ ፡ ጥንቃቄ ፡ ጠየቀ käffətäñña ṭənəqqaqe ṭäyyäqä

futile ከንቱ käntu; ፍሬ ፡ ቢስ fəre bis

future (n.) መጪ mäči; የወደፊት ፡ ኑሮ yäwädäfit nuro; (tense) የትንቢት ፡ ጊዜ yätənbit gize
in the future ወደ ፡ ፊት wädä fit

future (adj.) መጪ mäči; የወደፊት yäwädäfit

G

gadget መሣሪያ mässariya

gag (make choke) አፈነ affänä

gaiety ተደሳችነት tädässačənnät; ድምቀት dəmqät

gaily በደስታ bädässəta

gain (v.) አገኘ agäñña; አተረፈ atärräfä

gain (n.) ትርፍ tərf

gait አካሄድ akkahed; አረማመድ arrämamäd

gale ዐውሎ ፡ ነፋስ awlo näfas

gall አሞት amot; ሐሞት hamot

gallant (brave) ጀግና ǧägna; (chivalrous) ጨዋ čäwa

gall bladder የሐሞት ፡ ፊኛ yähamot fiñña

gallery (balcony) ሰገነት sägännät; (for exhibit) የሥዕል ፡ አዳራሽ yäsəʿəl addaraš

gallon ጋሎን galon

gallop (v.) ጋለበ galläbä

gallop (n.) ግልቢያ gəlbiya

gamble (v.) ቁማር ፡ ተጫወተ qumar tä-čawwätä

gambler ቁማርተኛ qumartäñña

gambling ቁማር qumar

game (n.) ጨዋታ čäwata; (materials for play) መጫወቻ mäččawäča; (contest) ግጥሚያ gəṭmiya; (wild animals) ያደን ፡ አውሬ yadän awre

gander ወንድ ፡ ዝይ wänd zəyy

gang (n.) ጓድ gʷadd

gangster ወሮበላ wärrobälla

gap (empty place) ባዶ ፡ ቦታ bado bota; (opening) ቀዳዳ qädada

gape አፉን ፡ ከፍቶ ፡ አየ afun käfto ayyä

garage ጋራዥ garaž

garbage ቆሻሻ qošaša

garden (v.) አትክልት ፡ ተከለ atkəlt täkkälä

garden (n.) አታክልት atakəlt; የትክልት ፡ ቦታ yatkəlt bota

gardener አትክልተኛ atkəltäñña

gargle አጉመጠመጠ agʷmäṭämmäṭä

garlic ነጭ ፡ ሽንኩርት näčč šənkurt

garment ልብስ ləbs

garrison (n.) የወታደሮች ፡ የጦር ፡ ሰፈር yäwättaddäročč yäṭor säfär

gas ጋዝ gaz

gasoline ቤንዚን benzin

gasp (v.) ቃተተ qattätä

gas station ቤንዚን ፡ ማደያ benzin mäd-däya

gate መዝጊያ *mäzgiya;* በር *bärr*

gatekeeper በረኛ *bärräñña*

gateway መግቢያ *mägbiya;* በር *bärr*

gather, vt. (∼wood) ለቀመ *läqqämä;* (∼people) ሰበሰበ *säbässäbä;* ከተተ *kättätä;* (∼speed) ጨመረ *čämmärä* gather (vi.) ተሰበሰበ *täsäbässäbä*

gathering ስብሰባ *säbsäba;* ጉባኤ *guba'e*

gaudy, see 'flashy'

gauge, v. (guess) ገመተ *gämmätä;* (measure) ለካ *läkka*

gauge (n.) መለኪያ *mäläkkiya*

gauze ሻሽ *šaš*

gay (∼ voice) የሚያስደስት *yämmiyas-dässət;* (∼ children) ደስ ያለ *däss ya-lä;* (∼ color) ደማቅ *dämmaq*

gaze (v.) አትኩሮ ፡ ተመለከተ *atkʷəro tämäläkkätä*

gazelle አጋዘን *agazän*

gear, n. (equipment) ትጥቅ *təṭq;* (of car) ማርሽ *marš*

gem የከበረ ፡ ድንጋይ *yäkäbbärä dəngay*

geminated, be ተጠበቀ *täṭäbbäqä*

gender ጾታ *ṣota*

genealogy የዘር ፡ አወራረድ *yäzär awwä-raräd;* የዘር ፡ ግንድ *yäzär gənd*

general (n.) ጄኔራል *ǧeneral*

general (adj.) ጠቅላላ *ṭäqlalla;* (∼wel-fare) የሕዝብ *yähəzb*
General Assembly ጠቅላላ ፡ ጉባኤ *ṭäq-lalla guba'e*
in general በጠቅላላው *bäṭäqlallaw*

generalize አጠቃለለ *aṭṭäqallälä;* ጠቅላላ ፡ አስተያየት ፡ ሰጠ *ṭäqlalla astäyayät säṭṭä*

generally (usually) አብዛኛውን ፡ ጊዜ *ab-zaññawən gize;* (widely) በጠቅላላው *bäṭäqlallaw*

generate አስገኘ *asgäñña;* (∼ ideas) አፈለቀ *afälläqä*

generation ትውልድ *təwlədd*

generosity ለጋስነት *läggasənnät;* ልግስ ነት *ləggəsənnät*

generous (∼donor) ለጋስ *läggas;* ቸር *čär*
be generous ለገሰ *läggäsä;* ቸረ *čärä*

genesis ምንጭ *mənč*

genial (∼person) ተጫዋች *täčawač;* (∼greeting) የወዳጅነት *yäwädaǧənnät*

genitals ነፍረተ ፡ ሥጋ *hafrätä səga;* ብልት *bəllət;* አባለ ፡ ዘር *abalä zär*

genius በጣም ፡ ብልህ *bäṭam bələh;* (nat-ural ability) ተሰጥኦ *täsäṭ'o*

gentle ገር *gär;* (∼manners) የደግነት *yä-däggənnät;* (∼horse) ገራም *gärram;* (∼breeze) ለዝብ *ləzzəb;* (∼sound) ለስለስ ፡ ያለ *läsläss yalä;* (∼slope) ዘቅዘቅ ፡ ያለ *zäqzäqq yalä*

gentleman (well-bred) ጨዋ ፡ ሰው *čäwa säw;* (any man) ሰው *säw*
gentlemen ከቡራን *kəburan*

gently (in a gentle way) በርጋታ *bärga-ta;* (gradually) ቀስ ፡ በቀስ *qäss bäqäss*

genuflect ሰገደ *säggädä;* ተንበረከከ *tän-bäräkkäkä*

genuine (∼dollar) እውነተኛ *əwnätäñ-ña;* (∼person) ሐሳብ ፡ ቀና *hassab qänna;* (∼sorrow) ከልብ ፡ የመነጨ *kälbb yämänäččä*

geography ትምህርተ ፡ ምድር *təmhərtä mədər;* ጂኦግራፊ *ǧiografi*

geology ትምህርተ ፡ አለት *təmhərtä alät;* ጂኦሎጂ *ǧiologi*

geometry ጂኦሜትሪ *ǧiometri*

germ(s) ረቂቅ ፡ ሕዋሳት *räqiq həwasat*

German (person) ጀርመን *ǧärmän;* (lan-guage) ጀርመንኛ *ǧärmänəñña*

Germany የጀርመን ፡ አገር *yäǧärmän agär;* ጀርመን *ǧärmän*

germinate በቀለ *bäqqälä*

gerund ቦዝ ፡ አንቀጽ *boz anqäṣ*

gesticulate እጁን ፡ ማነቃነቅ ፡ አበዛ *ǧu-gun mannäqanäq abäzza*

gesture (sign) ምልክት *mǝlǝkkǝt;* (movement of the body, arms) የሰውነት ፡ እንቅስቃሴ *yäsäwǝnnät ǝnqǝsǝqqase*

get (vt.) አገኘ *agäňňä;* (seize) ያዘ *yazä;* (bring) አመጣ *amäṭṭa;* (receive) ደረስ (ው) *därräsä(w);* (understand) ገባ(ው) *gäbba(w)*
get across ተሻገረ *täšaggärä*
get along with ተስማማ *täsmamma;* ተግባባ *tägbabba*
get away አመለጠ *amälläṭä;* (leave) ወጣ *wäṭṭa*
get back ተመለሰ *tämälläsä*
get down ወረደ *wärrädä*
get in ገባ *gäbba*
get off ወረደ *wärrädä*
get out ወጣ *wäṭṭa*
get together ተሰበሰበ *täsäbässäbä*
get up ተነሣ *tänässa*

ghost ጣረሞት *ṭarämot*

giant (of unusual size) ግዙፍ *gǝzuf;* (imaginary being) ጭራቅ *čǝraq*

gift ስጦታ *sǝṭota;* ገጸ ፡ በረከት *gäṣṣä bäräkät;* (talent) ተሰጥዎ *täsäṭwo*

gifted ተሰጥዎ ፡ ያለው *täsäṭwo yalläw*

gigantic ግዙፍ *gǝzuf*

giggle ተንከተከተ *tänkätäkkätä*

ginger ዝንጅብል *zǝnǧǝbǝl*

giraffe ጅራት ፡ ቀጭን *ǧǝratä qäččǝn;* ቀጭኔ *qäččǝne*

gird, ~ oneself ታጠቀ *taṭṭäqä*

girdle (n.) መቀነት *mäqännät*
wear a girdle መቀነት ፡ ታጠቀ *mäqännät taṭṭäqä*

girl ልጃገረድ *lǝǧagäräd;* ሴት ፡ ልጅ *set lǝǧ*

girl friend የከንፈር ፡ ወዳጅ *yäkänfär wädaǧ*

girlhood የልጅነት ፡ ዘመን *yälǝǧǝnnät zämän*

gist ፍሬ ፡ ነገር *fǝre nägär*

give ሰጠ *säṭṭä*
give back መለሰ *mälläsä*

give in (surrender) እጅ ፡ ሰጠ *ǝǧǧ säṭṭä;* (yield) ተበገረ *täbäggärä*
give more ጨመረ *čämmärä*
give out, vt. (distribute) ዐደለ *addälä*
give up ለቀቀ *läqqäqä;* ተወ *täwä*

glacial በርዳማ *bǝrdamma*

glad (~ news) የሚያስደስት *yämmiyasdässǝt*
be glad ደስ ፡ አለ(ው) *däss alä(w);* ተደሰተ *tädässätä*

gladden ደስ ፡ አሰኘ *däss assäňňä*

gladly ደስ ፡ ብሎት *däss bǝlot;* በደስታ *bädässǝta*

glamor ውበት *wǝbät;* ደማቅነት *dämmaqǝnnät*

glance (v.), ~ at መልከት ፡ አደረገ *mälkätt adärrägä;* አየት ፡ አደረገ *ayätt adärrägä*

glance (n.) መልከት ፡ ማለት *mälkätt malät*
at a glance ባንዴ *bande*
throw a glance, see 'glance' (v.)

gland እጢ *ǝṭi*

glare (n.) ነጸብራቅ *näṣäbraq*

glaring (~ light) የሚያንጸባርቅ *yämmiyanṣäbarrǝq;* (~ mistake) በጣም ፡ ጉልህ *bäṭam gulǝh*

glass (the substance) መስታወት *mästawät;* (thing to drink from) ብርጭቆ *bǝrčǝqqo*

glasses መነጽር *mänäṣṣǝr*

gleam, v. (of eyes) አበራ *abärra*

gleam (n.) ብልጭታ *bǝllǝčta;* ጭላንጭል *čǝlančǝl*

glean ለቀመ *läqqämä;* ቃረመ *qarrämä;* ማረረ *marrärä*

glee ደስታ *dässǝta*

glee club የሙዚቃ ፡ ክበብ *yämuziqa kǝbäb*

glib አፈ ፡ ጮሌ *afä čolle*

glide ተንሸራተተ *tänšärattätä*
glide out ሹልክ ፡ ብሎ ፡ ወጣ *šullǝkk bǝlo wäṭṭa*

glimmer (v.) ብልጭ ፡ ብልጭ ፡ አለ bəlləčč bəlləčč alä

glimmer (n.) ጭላንጭል čəlančəl

glimpse (v.), ~at አየት ፡ አለ ayätt alä

glisten አብረቀረቀ abräqärräqä; አንጸባ ረቀ anṣäbarräqä

glitter አሽበረቀ ašäbärräqä; ብልጭ ፡ አለ bəlləčč alä; ተብለጨለጨ täbläčäl läčä

gloat ፈነደቀ fänäddäqä

global ዓለም ፡ አቀፍ aläm aqqäf

globe (earth) መሬት märet; (sphere representing the earth) ሉል lul

gloomy (~day) ቀፋፊ qäfafi; (~corridor) ጨለምለም ፡ ያለ čälämlämm yalä; (depressing) ተስፋ ፡ የሚያስቄርጥ täsfa yämmiyasqʷärräṭ
feel gloomy ቀፈፈ(ው) qäffäfä(w)

glorification ሙገሳ mugäsa

glorify አመሰገነ amäsäggänä; አሞገሰ amoggäsä; ወደሰ wäddäsä

glorious (~event) ያሽበረቀ yašäbärrä qä; (~victory) ታላቅ tallaq; (~day) ብሩህ bəruh

glory (honor) ክብር kəbər; (majesty) ግርማ gərma; (praise) ምስጋና məsgana; ውዳሴ wəddase; (splendor) ውብት wəbät; ታላቅነት tallaqənnät

glossary አጭር ፡ መዝገበ ፡ ቃላት aččər mäzgäbä qalat

glove የጅ ፡ ሹራብ yäǧǧ šurrab; ጓንቲ gʷanti

glow (v.) አበራ abärra

glow (n.) ብርሃን bərhan

glowing (bright) ብሩህ bəruh

glue (v.) አጣበቀ aṭṭabbäqä; በሙጫ ፡ አጣበቀ bämuččä aṭṭabbäqä

glue (n.) ሙጫ muččä; ማጣበቂያ maṭṭa bäqiya

glum, look ~ ቅፍፍ ፡ አለ(ው) qəfəff alä(w)

glutton ሆዳም hodam

gluttony ሆዳምነት hodamənnät

gnash አፋጨ affaččä

gnat ትንኝ tənəňň

gnaw (at a bone) ቄረጣጠመ qʷäräṭaṭṭä mä; ጋጠ gaṭä

go ሄደ hedä; (of train) ተነሳ tänässa; (pass) አለፈ alläfä
go after ተከታተለ täkätattälä
go ahead ቀደመ qäddämä
go around ዞረ zorä
go away ሄደ hedä
go back ተመለሰ tämälläsä
go by አለፈ alläfä
go down ወረደ wärrädä; (of sun) አዘ ቀዘቀ azäqäzzäqä
go forward ተጋፋ tägaffa
go in ገባ gäbba
go on ቀጠለ qäṭṭälä; (of lights) በራ bärra
go on and off ብልጭ ፡ ድርግም ፡ አለ bəlləčč dərgəmm alä
go out ወጣ wäṭṭa; (of lights) ጠፋ ṭäffa
go to and fro ተመላለሰ tämälalläsä
go together (agree) ተስማማ täsmam ma
go under (of ship) ሰጠመ säṭṭämä
go up ወጣ wäṭṭa

goad (v.) ገፋፋ gäfaffa

goal (purpose) ዓላማ alama; (in football) ባር bärr; ግብ gəb; ግብ ፡ ዓላማ gəb alama

goal keeper ግብ ፡ ጠባቂ gəb ṭäbbaqi

goat ፍየል fəyyäl

goatherd እረኛ ərräňňa

goblet ዋንጫ wanča

god አምላክ amlak

God እግዚአብሔር əgzi'abəher; እግዜር əgzer

godchild የክርስትና ፡ ልጅ yäkrəstənna ləǧ

goddess ጣዖት ṭa'ot

godfather የክርስትና ፡ አባት yäkrəstənna abbat

godly የእግዚአብሔር *yäəgzi'abəher*

godmother የክርስትና ፡ እናት *yäkrəstən-na ənnat*

goiter እንቅርት *ənqərt*

gold ወርቅ *wärq*

golden የወርቅ *yäwärq;* ወርቅማ *wärqəm-ma;* ከወርቅ ፡ የተሠራ *käwärq yätä-särra*

goldsmith ወርቅ ፡ ሠሪ *wärq säri*

gong ደወል *däwäl*

good ጥሩ *ṭəru;* ደኅና *dähna;* መልካም *mälkam;* በጎ *bäggo;* ማለፊያ *maläfiya*
be good (valid) አገለገለ *agäläggälä*
a good deal ብዙ *bəzu*
a good many በርከት ፡ ያሉ *bärkätt yalu;* ብዙ *bəzu*
for good እስከ ፡ መጨረሻው *əskä mä-čärräšaw;* እስከነጥራሽ *əskännäčərraš*
a no-good የማያረባ *yämmayəräba*

good afternoon! እንዴት ፡ ዋልክ *əndet walk* (sg. masc.)

goodbye! ጤና ፡ ይስጥልኝ *ṭena yəsṭəl-ləňň;* ደኅና፡ ሁን *dähna hun* (sg. masc.)

good evening! እንዴት ፡ አመሸህ *əndet amäššäh* (sg. masc.)

good-for-nothing, he is ~ አይረባም *ay-räbam*

good-hearted ደግ *dägg*

good-looking መልክ ፡ መልካም *mälkä mälkam;* መልክ ፡ ቀና *mälkä qänna*

good luck! ይቅናህ *yəqnah*

good morning! እንዴት ፡ አደርህ *əndet addärh* (sg. masc.)

good-natured ገር *gär*

goodness ደግነት *däggənnät*

good night! ደኅና ፡ እደር *dähna ədär* (sg. masc.)

goods እቃ *əqa;* ሽቀጣ ፡ ሽቀጥ *šäqäṭa šä-qäṭ*

goose ዝይ *zəyy;* ዝዪ *zəyyi*

gorge ሸለቆ *šäläqo*

gorgeous (~ girl) ውብ *wəb;* የወጣላት ፡ ቆንጆ *yäwäṭṭallat qonǧo;* (~ sunset) ዕዱብ ፡ ድንቅ *əṣub dənq*

Gospel ወንጌል *wängel*

gossip (v.) ወሬ ፡ ቀዳ *wäre qädda;* አወራ *awärra*

gossip (n.) አሉባልታ *alubalta;* ወሬ *wäre*

gourd ቅል *qəl*

govern ገዛ *gäzza;* (determine) ወሰነ *wäs-sänä*

government መንግሥት *mängəst;* (admin-istering) አስተዳደር *astädadär*

governor አገረ ፡ ገዢ *agärä gäži*

Governor General እንዳራሴ *əndärase*

gown ልብስ *ləbs;* ቀሚስ *qämis*

grab ያዘ *yazä;* ጨበጠ *čäbbäṭä*

grace (divine favor) ጸጋ *ṣägga;* (kind-ness) ደግነት *däggənnät;* (elegance of form) ውበት *wəbät;* (clemency) ምሕ-ረት *məhrät*
His Grace ብጹዕነታቸው *bəṣu'ənnä-taččäw*
say grace ምስጋና ፡ አደረሰ *məsgana adärräsä*

graceful (~ person) ለዛ ፡ ያለው *läzza yalläw;* (~ movement) ደስ ፡ ያለ *däss yalä;* ረጋ ፡ ያለ *räga yalä*

gracious ደግ *dägg;* (~ home, manner) የሞቀ *yämoqä;* ሞቅ ፡ ያለ *moqq yalä*
be gracious ምሕረት ፡ አደረገ *məhrät adärrägä*

grade, v. (sort into categories) ለየ *läy-yä;* (~ homework) አረመ *arrämä*

grade (n.) ደረጃ *däräǧa;* (class in school) ክፍል *kəfəl;* (mark) ውጤት *wäṭṭet;* ማርክ *mark*

gradually ቀስ ፡ በቀስ *qäss bäqäss;* እያደረ *əyyaddärä;* ጥቂት ፡ በጥቂት *ṭəqit bä-ṭäqit*

graduate, v. (receive a diploma) ተመረቀ *tämärräqä*

graduate (n.) ምሩቅ *mərruq;* ተመራቂ *tä-märraqi*

graduation (commencement) የምረቃ ፡
በዓል yämərräqa bä'al

graft (n.) ጉቦ gubbo

grain እህል əhəl

grammar ሰዋስው säwasəw

grammatical ሰዋስዋዊ säwasəwawi

granary ጉተራ gʷätära

grand ታላቅ tallaq; (~view) አስደናቂ
asdännaqi

grandchild የልጅ ፡ ልጅ yäləǧ ləǧ

grandeur (of scenery) ውበት wəbät; (of
a ceremony) ታላቅነት tallaqənnät;
(majestic appearance) ግርማ ፡ ሞገስ
gərma mogäs

grandfather አያት ayat; (paternal~)
ያባት ፡ አባት yabbat abbat; (maternal
~) የናት ፡ አባት yännat abbat

grandmother አያት ayat; ሴት ፡ አያት set
ayat

grandson የልጅ ፡ ልጅ yäləǧ ləǧ

grant, v. (give) ሰጠ sättä; (concede, admit) አመነ ammänä

grant (n.) እርዳታ ərdata

granted ከሆነ kähonä

grape ወይን wäyn

grasp ያዘ yazä; ጨበጠ čäbbätä; (understand) ገባ(ው) gäbba(w)

grass ሣር sar

grasshopper ፌንጣ fenṭa

grate, vt. (~cheese) ፈረፈረ färäffärä
grate, vi. (produce a harsh sound)
ሲጢጥ ፡ አለ siṭiṭ alä

grate (n.) የብረት ፡ መክደኛ yäbrät mäk-
dänña

grateful ውለታ ፡ የማይረሳ wəläta yäm-
mayəräsa; (~letter) የምስጋና yäməsgana
be grateful አመሰገነ amäsäggänä

gratify (satisfy) አረካ aräkka; (give
pleasure) አስደሰተ asdässätä

gratifying የሚያስደስት yämmiyasdässət

gratis በብላሽ bäbəlaš

gratitude ውለታ wəläta; ወሮታ wärrota

gratuity ጉርሻ gurša

grave (n.) መቃብር mäqabər

grave, adj. (~mistake) ከባድ käbbad;
(~condition) አስጊ asgi; አሳሳቢ asassabi; (~doubt) ከፍ ፡ ያለ käff yalä
look grave ኮስተር ፡ አለ kostärr alä

gravel ኰረት kʷärät; ጠጠር ṭäṭär

gravely (very badly) ከፉኛ käfuňňa; (in
a sorrowful way) በሐዘን bähazän

gravestone የመቃብር ፡ ድንጋይ yämäqabər dəngay

graveyard መካነ ፡ መቃብር mäkanä mäqabər

gravitation ስበት səbät

gravity (seriousness) አሳሳቢነት asassabinnät; አስጊነት asginnät; (gravitation) ስበት səbät

gravy መረቅ märäq

gray, turn ~ (hair) ሸበተ šäbbätä
gray hair ሸበት šäbät

graze (vt.) አሰማራ assämarra; አጋጠ
agaṭä
graze (vi.) ተሰማራ täsämarra; ሣር ፡
ጋጠ sar gaṭä

grazing ግጦሽ gəṭoš

grease, v. (~the griddle) አሰሰ assäsä;
(~the car) ቅባት ፡ ቀባ qəbat qäbba

grease (n.) ቅባት qəbat

greasy ቅባታም qəbatam

great ትልቅ tələq; ታላቅ tallaq; (~
pain) ጽኑ ṣənu

great-grandchild የልጅ ፡ ልጅ ፡ ልጅ yäləǧ
ləǧ ləǧ

great-grandfather የወንድ ፡ ቅድም ፡ አያት
yäwänd qədmä ayat

great-grandmother የሴት ፡ ቅድም ፡ አያት
yäset qədmä ayat

greatly ያለ ፡ ቅጥ yalä qəṭṭ; በጣም bäṭam

greatness ታላቅነት tallaqännät; ትልቅ
ነት təlləqännät

Greece ግሪክ grik

greed ሥሥት səssət

greedy ሥሥታም səssətam; ስግብግብ səgəbgəb
be greedy ሣሣ sassa; ተስገበገበ täsgäbäggäbä

Greek (person) ግሪክ grik; (language)
የግሪክ : ቋንቋ yägrik qʷanqʷa

green (~color) አረንጓዴ arängʷade;
(~leaves) ለምለም lämläm; (not ripe)
ጥሬ ṭəre; (~ lumber) ያልደረቀ yal-
därräqä

greet ሰላምታ : ሰጠ sälamta säṭṭä; ሰላ
ምታ : አቀረበ sälamta aqärräbä

greeting(s) ሰላም sälam; ሰላምታ sälamta

grenade የጅ : ቦምብ yäǧǧ bomb

griddle ምጣድ məṭad

grief ሐዘን hazän

grievance ቅሬታ qərreta

grieve (vi.) አዘነ azzänä

grieving ሐዘንተኛ hazäntäňňa

grievous (~ news) አሳዛኝ asazzaň; (~
loss) ታላቅ tallaq

grill (v.) ጠበሰ ṭäbbäsä

grill (n.) የብረት : ምድጃ yäbrät mədəǧǧa

grim (~struggle) ጭካኔ : የተሞላበት
čäkkane yätämollabbät; (~ tale) አስ
ቃቂ assäqqaqi; (~determination)
ፍጹም fəṣṣum; የማያዋልዉል yämma-
yawälawwəl
be grim ፈቱን : አኮሰተረ fitun akʷäsättärä

grin (v.) ፈገግ : አለ fägägg alä

grind (~ grain) ፈጨ fäččä; (~ meat)
አደቀቀ adäqqäqä; (~ coffee) ወቀጠ
wäqqäṭä; (~ a knife) ሳለ salä; (~
teeth) አፋጨ affaččä

grindstone መሳያ mäsaya

grip (v.) አጥብቆ : ያዘ aṭbəqo yazä; እንቅ :
አድርጎ : ያዘ ənnəq adrəgo yazä

grip (n.) አያያዝ ayyayaz
come to grips with ተቋቋመ täqʷaqʷamä

groan (v.) አቃሰተ aqassätä

groan (n.) ማቃሰት maqasät

grocer ምግብ : ሻጭ məgəb šäč; ምግብ :
ነጋዴ məgəb näggade

grocery (store) የምግብ : መደብር yäməgəb mädäbbər; (food) የምግብ : ሸቀጣ :
ሸቀጥ yäməgəb šäqäṭa šäqäṭ

groin ብሸሽት bəšəššət

groom, n. (man about to be married)
ሙሽራ mušərra; (who takes care of
horses) ባልደራስ baldäras

groove ቡርቡር burbur

grope ዳሰሰ dassäsä; ዳበሰ dabbäsä

gross (bulky) ግዙፍ gəzuf; (~mistake)
ጉልህ guləh; (~income) ጠቅላላ ṭäqlalla; (~ language) ጸያፍ ṣäyyaf;
(~ manners) ያልታረመ yaltarrämä

grossly ያለ : ቅጥ yalä qəṭ

grotesque (fantastic) አሥቂኝና : አስደ
ናቂ assəqiňənna asdännaqi; (distorted
and odd) አስቀያሚ asqäyyami

grouchy ነጭናጫ näčnačča
be grouchy ተነጫነጨ tänäčannäčä

ground (n.) መሬት märet; (place) ቦታ
bota
grounds (land) ግቢ gəbbi; (of coffee)
አተላ atäla; (reason) ምክንያት məknəyat
gain ground ተቀባይነት : አገኘ täqäbbayənnät agäňňä
give ground አፈጋፈገ afägäffägä
lose ground ድጋፍ : አጣ dəgaf aṭṭa

ground floor ምድር : ቤት mədər bet

ground forces የምድር : ጦር yämədər ṭor

groundless መሠረተ : ቢስ mäsärätä bis

group (n.) ወገን wägän

grove ጫካ čakka

grow, vt. (~roses) ተከለ täkkälä; (soil
growing wheat) አበቀለ abäqqälä;

(farmer growing wheat) ዘራ *zärra;*
(∼ a beard) አሳደገ *asaddägä*
grow, vi. (of children) አደገ *addägä;*
(of grain) በቀለ *bäqqälä;* (of business)
ተስፋፋ *täsfaffa*
grow up አደገ *addägä*

growl (v.) አጕረመረመ *ag^wrämärrämä*

grown-up (n.) ዐዋቂ *awaqi*

growth እድገት *ədgät;* (swelling) እብ
ጠት *əbṭät*

grudge, v. (begrudge) ቅር ፡ አለ(ው) *qərr
alä(w);* ቀና *qänna*

grudge (n.) ቂም *qim;* ቅያሜ *qəyyame*
bear grudge ቂም ፡ ያዘ *qim yazä;* ተቀ
የመ *täqäyyämä*

gruesome አስቀቂ *assäqqaqi*

grumble አጕረመረመ *ag^wrämärrämä*

guarantee, v. (engage to do something)
ቃል ፡ ገባ *qal gäbba;* ቃል ፡ ሰጠ *qal
säṭṭä;* (give guarantee) ዋስትና ፡ ሰጠ
wastənna säṭṭä

guarantee (n.) ዋስ *was;* ዋስትና *wastənna*

guarantor ዋስ *was;* (for a servant)
ተያዥ *täyaž*

guard (v.) ጠበቀ *ṭäbbäqä*

guard (n.) ዘብ *zäb;* ዘበኛ *zäbäňňa;* ጣባቂ
ṭäbbaqi
be on one's guard ተጠነቀቀ *täṭänäqqäqä*
keep guard ጠበቀ *ṭäbbäqä;* ዘብ ፡ ጠ
በቀ *zäb ṭäbbäqä*

guardian ጣባቂ *ṭäbbaqi;* ዘበኛ *zäbäňňa;*
(who has the care of a child) ሞግ
ዚት *mogzit;* ያደራ ፡ አባት *yadära abbat*

guardian angel ወቃቢ ፡ አምላክ *wəqabi
amlak;* ታዳጊ ፡ አምላክ *taddagi amlak*

guardian spirit አድባር *adbar;* ወቃቢ
wəqabi

guerilla የደፈጣ ፡ ተዋጊ *yädäfäṭa täwagi*

guess (v.) በመላ ፡ ዐወቀ *bämäla awwäqä;*

ገመተ *gämmätä;* (think) መሰለ(ው)
mässälä(w)

guess (n.) መላ *mäla;* መላ ፡ ምት *mäla
mət;* ግምት *gəmmət*
make a guess መላ ፡ መታ *mäla mätta*

guest እንግዳ *əngəda*

guidance መሪነት *märinnät;* አመራር *ammärar*

guide (v.) መራ *märra*

guide (n.) መሪ *märi*

guidebook መምሪያ *mämriya;* መግለጫ ፡
መጽሐፍ *mägläča mäṣhaf*

guideline መምሪያ *mämriya*

guile ብልሃት *bəlhat;* ተንኮል *tänk^wäl*

guilt ጥፋት *ṭəfat*

guilty ጥፋተኛ *ṭəfatäňňa*
find guilty ፈረደ(በት) *färrädä(bbät)*

guinea fowl ዠግራ *žəgra*

gulf የባሕር ፡ ሰላጤ *yäbahər sällaṭe*

gull የባሕር ፡ ጭላት *yäbahər čəlat*

gullible ደልል *dälləl*

gully ፈረፈር *färäfär*

gulp, ∼ down (∼ a drink) ጭልጥ ፡ አድ
ርጐ ፡ ጠጣ *čəlləṭ adrəgo ṭäṭṭa;* ተጐ
ነጨ *täg^wänäččä;* (∼ a sob) ዋጥ ፡
አደረገ *waṭ adärrägä*

gulp (n.), at one ∼ ባንድ ፡ ትንፋሽ *band
tənfaš;* ባንዳፍታ *bandafta*
take a gulp, see 'gulp'

gum (sticky substance) ማጣበቂያ *maṭṭabäqiya;* (of teeth) ድድ *dəd*
chewing gum መስቲካ *mästika*

gun ጠብንጃ *ṭäbänǧa;* ጠመንጃ *ṭämänǧa*

gunfire የጠመንጃ ፡ ተኩስ *yäṭämänǧa
täk^ws*

gunpowder ባሩድ *barud*

gurgle, v. (of a bottle) ተንዶቀዶቀ *tän-
doqäddoqä*

gush (v.), ∼ out መነጨ *mänäččä;* ፈለቀ
fälläqä

gust ኃይለኛ ፡ ነፋስ *hayläňňa näfas*

guts (የ)ሆድ ፡ እቃ (yä)hod əqa

gutter አሻንዳ ašända

guttural የጉሮሮ yägurorro

guy ሰው säw; ለጅ ləǧ

gym (building) የሰውነት ፡ ማጠንከሪያ ፡ ክፍል yäsäwənnät maṭänkäriya kəfəl

gymnasium, see 'gym'

gymnastics የሰውነት ፡ ማጠንከሪያ yäsäwənnät maṭänkäriya

H

habit ልማድ ləmad; ልምድ ləmd
adopt habits ለመደ lämmädä

habitable ለመኖሪያ ፡ የሚሆን lämänoriya yämmihon

habitation መኖሪያ mänoriya

habitual የተለመደ yätälämmädä; ልማ ዳዊ ləmadawi; ልማደኛ ləmadäñña

habituated, be ለመደ lämmädä

had, he ～ ነበረው näbbäräw

haggle ተከራከረ täkäräkkärä; ውጣ ፡ ውረ ዱን ፡ ተከራከረ wäṭa wärädun täkärakkärä

haggling የዋጋ ፡ ውጣ ፡ ውረድ yäwaga wäṭa wäräd

hail (v.) በረዶ ፡ ጣለ bärädo ṭalä; (call) ጠራ ṭärra

hail (n.) በረዶ bärädo

hair ጠጉር ṭägur; ጸጉር ṣägur

hairbrush የጸጉር ፡ ብሩሽ yäṣägur bruš

haircut የጸጉር ፡ መቄረጥ yäṣägur mäqʷäräṭ

hairdo የጠጉር ፡ አሠራር yäṭägur assärar

hairdresser ጠጉር ፡ አስተካካይ ṭägur astäkakay

hairy ጠጉራም ṭäguram

hale (adj.) ጠንካራ ṭänkarra; ጤናማ ṭenamma

half ግማሽ gəmmaš; እኩሌታ əkkuleta; (of hour) እኩል əkkul
half a year መንፈቅ mänfäq

half brother ያባት ፡ ልጅ yabbat ləǧ; የእ ናት ፡ ልጅ yännat ləǧ

half-caste ከላስ källäs

half-hearted ከልብ ፡ ያልሆነ käləbb yalhonä

half-heartedly በግማሽ ፡ ልብ bägəmmaš ləbb

half sister ያባት ፡ ልጅ yabbat ləǧ; የእ ናት ፡ ልጅ yännat ləǧ

hall (auditorium) አዳራሽ addaraš; (passageway) መተላለፊያ mättälaläfiya

hallmark መለዮ mälläyyo

hallowed የተቀደሰ yätäqäddäsä

hallway መተላለፊያ mättälaläfiya

halt (vt.) አቆመ aqomä; (～advance of army) አገደ aggädä
halt (vi.) ቆመ qomä; (hesitate in speech) አፉ ፡ ተያዘ afu täyazä

halt (n.), come to a ～ ቆመ qomä

halter ለኮ läko

halve እኩል ፡ ከፈለ əkkul käffälä; ለሁ ለት ፡ ቄረጠ lähulätt qʷärräṭä

hamlet ትንሽ ፡ መንደር tənnəš mändär

hammer (v.) ምስማር ፡ ደበደበ məsmar däbäddäbä; (～metal) ቀጠቀጠ qäṭäqqäṭä

hammer (n.) መዶሻ mädoša

hamper አሰናከለ assänakkälä

hand (v.) አቀበለ aqäbbälä
hand back መለሰ mälläsä
hand down አወረደ awärrädä
hand in (～an application) አገባ agäbba; (～ homework) አስረከበ asräkkäbä
hand out ዐደለ addälä
hand over አቀበለ aqäbbälä; አስረከበ asräkkäbä

hand (n.) እጅ əǧǧ; (of clock) ቄጣሪ qʷäṭari

hand-in-hand (holding hands) እጅ ፡ ለእጅ ፡ ተያይዘው aድ ድ läaደ ድ täyayzäw; (close together) በጉብረት bähabrät

hands up! እጅ ፡ ወደ ፡ ላይ aደ ድ wädä lay

ask for the hand ለጋብቻ ፡ ጠየቀ lägabačča ṭäyyäqä

give someone a hand አገዘ aggäzä

have the upper hand አየለ ayyälä; አሽ ነፈ aššännäfä

lay hands on አገኘ agäňňä

lend a hand ረዳ rädda

on the one hand . . . on the other hand በጎ ፡ በኩል - - - በሌላ ፡ በኩል band bäkkul - - - bälela bäkkul

try one's hand ሞከረ mokkärä

handbag የጅ ፡ ቦርሳ yäǧǧ borsa

handbook የመምሪያ ፡ መጽሐፍ yämämriya mäṣhaf

handcuffs (n.) ካቴና katena

handful እፍኝ affaň; ጭብጥ čabbaṭ

handicap መሰናክል mäsänakal

handicraft የጅ ፡ ሥራ yäǧǧ sǝra; የጅ ፡ ጥበብ yäǧǧ ṭabäb

handiwork የጅ ፡ ሥራ yäǧǧ sǝra

handkerchief መሐረብ mäharräb

handle, v. (people) ያዘ yaza; (affairs) አካሄደ akkahedä

handle, n. (of knife) እጀታ aǧǧäta; (of ax) ዛቢያ zabiya; (of cup) ጆሮ ǧoro; (of suitcase) ማንጠልጠያ manṭälṭäya

handling አያያዝ ayyayaz

handmade በእጅ ፡ የተሠራ bäaǧǧ yätäsärra

handshake እጅ ፡ ለእጅ ፡ መጨባባጥ aǧǧ läaǧǧ mäččäbabäṭ

handsome (~ man) መልክ ፡ ቀና mälkä qänna; መልክ ፡ መልካም mälkä mälkam; (~ mansion) የሚያምር yämmiyamǝr

look handsome አማረ amarä

handwriting የጅ ፡ ጽሕፈት yäǧǧ ṣǝhfät; አጻጻፍ aṣṣaṣaf

handy ባለሙያ balämuya; ቀልጣፋ qälṭaffa; (conveniently located) ምቹ mäčču

come in handy ጠቀመ ṭäqqämä; አገ ለገለ agäläggälä

handyman ባለሙያ balämuya

hang (vt.) ሰቀለ säqqälä

hang, vi. (of lamp) ተንጠለጠለ tänṭäläṭṭälä

hang around ወዲያና ፡ ወዲህ ፡ አለ wädiyanna wädih alä

hang out (~ wash) አሰጣ asäṭṭa; (~ flags) ሰቀለ säqqälä

hang together እንድ ፡ ላይ ፡ ሆኑ and lay honu

hang up ሰቀለ säqqälä; (~ a lamp) አንጠለጠለ anṭäläṭṭälä

hangar ጋራጅ garaǧ

hanger መስቀያ mäsqäya

hanging ስቅለት saqlät

haphazard (~ answer) አፍ ፡ እንዳመጣ ፡ የሚ ስት af andamäṭṭa yämmissäṭṭ; (~ things) ጊዜ ፡ የወለደው gize yäwällädäw

haphazardly ያለ ፡ አቅድ yalä aqd

hapless ምስኪን maskin

happen ሆነ honä; ደረሰ därräsä

happen again ተደገመ tädäggämä

as it happens እንዳጋጣሚ andaggaṭami

what has happened to you? ምን ፡ ሆንክ man honk

happening ድርጊት dargit

happily (joyfully) በደስታ bädässata; ደስ ብሎት däss balot; (fortunately) ደግ ነቱ däggannätu

happiness ደስታ dässata

happy ደስተኛ dässatäňňa

be happy ደስ ፡ አለ(ው) däss alä(w)

happy-go-lucky ግድ ፡ የለሽ gadd yälläš

harass ነዘነዘ näzännäzä; አስጨነቀ asčännäqä

harbor, v. (shelter) አስጠጋ asṭägga; (~ ill will) ያዘ yaza

harbor (n.) ወደብ *wädäb*

hard, adj. (∼ worker, substance) ጠንካራ *ṭänkarra*; (∼ question, language) አስቸጋሪ *asčäggari*; ከባድ *käbbad*; (∼ winter) ከባድ *käbbad*; (∼ times) ከፉ *kǝfu*

hard, adv. (with energy) በርትቶ *bärtǝto*; ጠንክሮ *ṭänkǝro*
hard by ጥግ *ṭǝgg*; ዳር *dar*
hard times ችግር *čǝggǝr*
be hard ጠነከረ *ṭänäkkärä*

harden (vt.) አጠነከረ *aṭänäkkärä*
harden, vi. (of cement) ጠጠረ *ṭäṭṭärä*

hardly በችግር *bäčǝggǝr*; እምብዛም *ǝmbǝzam* + negative verb; ምንም ፡ ያህል *mǝnǝm yahǝl* + negative verb

hardship መከራ *mäkära*; ችግር *čǝggǝr*; ጭንቅ *čǝnq*

hardware ከብረት ፡ የተሠሩ ፡ እቃዎች *käbrät yätäsärru ǝqawoččǝ*

hardworking ብርቱ *bǝrtu*

hardy (∼ soldier) ብርቱ *bǝrtu*; (∼ plant) ድርቅ ፡ የሚችል *dǝrq yämmičǝl*

hare ጥንቸል *ṭǝnčäl*

harken አዳመጠ *addammäṭä*

harm (v.) ጐዳ *gʷädda*

harm (n.) ጉዳት *gudat*; (wrongdoing) ጥፋት *ṭǝfat*
do harm ጐዳ *gʷädda*
there is no harm ግድ ፡ የለም *gǝdd yälläm*

harmful ጠንቅ *ṭänq*; ጐጂ *gʷäǧi*

harmless የማይጐዳ *yämmayǝgʷäda*

harmonious በስምምነት ፡ የሚኖር *bäsǝmǝmmǝnnät yämminor*

harmonize (vt.) አስማማ *asmamma*
harmonize (vi.) ተስማማ *täsmamma*

harmony (agreement) ስምምነት *sǝmǝmmǝnnät*
be in harmony ተስማማ *täsmamma*

harness, v. (∼ a horse) ጨነ *čanä*

harness (n.) የፈረስ ፡ እቃ *yäfäräs ǝqa*

harp በገና *bägäna*
harp player በገና ፡ ደርዳሪ *bägäna därdari*

harsh (∼ judge) ጥብቅ *ṭǝbq*; (∼ climate) መጥፎ *mäṭfo*; (∼ voice) ጐርናና *gʷärnanna*; (∼ words) ኃይለኛ *hayläñña*; (∼ life) አስቸጋሪ *asčäggari*

harshly, treat ∼ አጐሳቈለ *aggʷäsaqqʷälä*

harvest (v.) አመረተ *amärrätä*

harvest (n.) መኸር *mähär*; መከር *mäkär*; አዝመራ *azmära*

hash (v.) ከተፈ *kättäfä*

hash (n.) ክትፎ *kǝtfo*

haste ችኰላ *čǝkkʷäla*; ጥድፊያ *ṭǝdfiya*
make haste ፈጠነ ፡ አለ *fäṭänn alä*

hasten (vt.) አቀለጠፈ *aqäläṭṭäfä*; አጣደፈ *aṭṭaddäfä*; አፋጠነ *affaṭṭänä*
hasten (vi.) ቀለጠፈ *qäläṭṭäfä*; ፋጠነ *fäṭṭänä*; ቸኰለ *čäkkʷälä*; ተጣደፈ *täṭaddäfä*

hastily በችኰላ *bäčǝkkʷäla*

hasty ችኩል *čǝkkul*; (∼ decision) የችኰላ *yäčǝkkʷäla*; በችኰላ ፡ የተደረገ *bäčǝkkʷäla yätädärrägä*

hat ባርኔጣ *barneṭa*

hatch (vt.) ፈለፈለ *fäläffälä*
hatch (vi.) ተፈለፈለ *täfäläffälä*

hatchet መጥረቢያ *mäṭräbiya*

hate (v.) ጠላ *ṭälla*; (dislike) አልወደደም *alwäddädäm*

hate (n.) ጥላቻ *ṭǝlačča*

hateful (∼ remark) ጥላቻ ፡ የተመላበት *ṭǝlačča yätämällabbät*; (∼ crime) አስከፊ *askäffi*

hatred ጥል *ṭǝl*; ጥላቻ *ṭǝlačča*

haughtiness ትዕቢት *tǝ'ǝbit*; እብሪት *ǝbrit*

haughty (∼ person) ትዕቢተኛ *tǝ'ǝbitäñña*; (∼ words) የትዕቢት *yätǝ'ǝbit*
be haughty ታበየ *tabbäyä*

haul (pull) ጐተተ *gʷättätä*; (transport) አጓጓዘ *aggʷagʷaza*

haunch ወገብ *wägäb*

haunt (of ghost) ሰፈረ(በት) *säffärä-(bbät);* (visit persistently) አዘወተረ *azäwättärä*

have አለ-*allä-*with object suffix pronouns (as in አለው *alläw* he has) not have የለ-*yällä-*with object suffix pronouns

haven ማረፊያ *maräfiya;* (for fugitives) መሸሸጊያ *mäššäšägiya*

havoc ጥፋት *ṭəfat;* ሽብር *šəbbər*

hawk ንስር *nəsər;* ጭልፊት *čəlfit*

hay ድርቆሽ *dərqoš*

haywire, be ትርምስምስ፡ አለ *tərməsməss alä* go haywire መላ ፡ ቀጡን ፡ አጣ *mäla qəṭṭun aṭṭa*

hazard (n.) አደጋ *adäga*

hazardous አደገኛ *adägäňňa*

haze ጭጋግ *čəgag*

hazy ጭጋጋማ *čəgagamma*

he እሱ *əssu;* እርሱ *ərsu* He (respect) እርሳቸው *ərsaččäw;* እሳ ቸው *əssaččäw*

head, vt. (lead, guide) መራ *märra;* (~ a department) ሹም ፡ ሆነ *šum honä;* ገላፊ ፡ ሆነ *halafi honä;* (be first) አንደኛ ፡ ሆነ *andäňňa honä* head, vi. (move toward) አመራ *amärra*

head (n.) ራስ *ras;* (of family) አውራ *awra;* (of government) መሪ *märi;* (of a firm) ገላፊ *halafi;* (of a gang) አለቃ *aläqa;* (of a river) ምንጭ *mənč;* (of lettuce) ጥቅል *ṭəqəll* heads or tails ዘውድ ፡ ወይስ ፡ አንበሳ *zäwd wäyəss anbässa* come to a head ተካረረ *täkarrärä;* ተፋ ፈመ *täfafamä* lose one's head ናላው ዞረ *nalaw zorä*

head (adj.) ዋና *wanna*

headache (የ)ራስ ፡ ምታት *(yä)ras mətat;* ፍልጠት *fəlṭät*

heading ርእስ *rə'əs;* አርእስት *ar'əst*

headlight የፊት ፡ መብራት *yäfit mäbrat*

headline አርእስት ፡ ዜና *ar'əstä zena*

headman ጨቃ ፡ ሹም *čəqa šum*

headmaster ዲሬክተር *direktär*

headquarters (of army, police) ጠቅላይ ፡ መምሪያ *ṭäqlay mämriya;* (of an office) ዋና ፡ መሥሪያ ፡ ቤት *wanna mäsriya bet*

headrest ትራስ *təras*

headstrong ሐሳብ ፡ ጋትር *hassabä gəṭṭər*

headwaters ምንጭ *mənč*

heal (vt.) አዳነ *adanä;* አሻረ *ašärä* heal (vi.) ዳነ *danä;* (of a wound) ጠገነ *ṭäggänä;* ሻረ *šarä*

healer መድኃኒተኛ *mädhanitäňňa*

health ጤና *ṭena;* ጤንነት *ṭenənnät* Ministry of Health የጤና ፡ ጥበቃ ፡ ሚኒስቴር *yäṭena ṭəbbäqa minister*

healthful (~food) ጤና ፡ የሚሰጥ *ṭena yämmisäṭ*

healthy (~person) ጤናማ *ṭenamma;* (~body) ጤነኛ *ṭenäňňa;* (~climate) ለ ጤና ፡ የሚስማማ *läṭena yämmismamma*

heap (v.) ከመረ *kämmärä;* ቋለለ *qwällälä* heap up አከማቸ *akkämaččä*

heap (n.) ቁልል *qulləl;* ክምር *kəmmər;* ክምችት *kəməččət* heaps of ብዙ *bəzu*

hear ሰማ *sämma;* (of a judge) አየ *ayyä*

hearing መስማት *mäsmat;* (ability to hear) የመስማት ፡ ችሎታ *yämäsmat čəlota;* (formal meeting) የቀጠሮ ፡ ቀን *yäqäṭäro qän* give a hearing ከርከር ፡ አዳመጠ *kərəkkər addammäṭä*

hearsay (n.) የሰሚ ፡ ሰሚ *yäsämi sämi;* አሉባልታ *alubalta*

hearse የሬሳ ፡ መኪና *yäresa mäkina*

heart ልብ *ləbb;* (innermost part) ውስጥ *wəsṭ;* (center) መካከል *mäkakkäl;* (vi-

tal part) ፍሬ ፡ ነገር *fre nägär*
by heart በቃል *bäqal*
have a heart ርኅሩኅ ፡ ነው *rəhruh näw*
lose heart ተስፋ ፡ ቈረጠ *täsfa qʷärräṭä*
take heart ተጽናና *täṣnanna*
take heart! አይዞህ *ayzoh*

heart attack የልብ ፡ ድካም *yäləbb dəkam*

heartbeat የልብ ፡ ትርታ *yäləbb tərrəta*

heartburn ቃር *qar*

hearten አበረታታ *abbärätatta*

hearth ምድጃ *mädəǧǧa*

heartily ከልብ *käləbb*

heartless አንጀት ፡ የለሽ *anǧät yälläš;*
ግፈኛ *gəfäňňa*

hearty (∼ welcome) ከልብ ፡ የመነጨ *käləbb yämänäččä;* (∼ meal) አጥጋቢ *aṭgabi*

heat (vt.) አሞቀ *amoqä*
heat up (vt.) አሞቀ *amoqä*
heat up (vi.) ጋለ *galä*

heat (n.) ሙቀት *muqät;* (of the sun) የፀ
ሐይ ፡ ሐሩር *yäṣähay harur*

heated, adj. (∼ argument) የጋለ *yägalä;*
የተፋፋመ *yätäfafamä*
be heated (room) ሞቀ *moqä*

heathen አረመኔያዊ *arämäneyawi*

heave, vt. (lift with effort) በስንት ፡ ችግ
ር ፡ አወጣ *bäsənt čəggər awäṭṭa;* (hurl)
በችግር ፡ ወረወረ *bäčəggər wäräwwärä*
heave, vi. (bulge) ጉብ ፡ አለ *gubb alä;*
(rise and fall repeatedly) ከፍ ፡ ዝቅ ፡
አለ *käff zəqq alä*

heaven መንግሥተ ፡ ሰማያት *mängəstä
sämayat*
heavens ሰማይ *sämay*
heavens! አቤት ፡ አቤት *abet abet*
for heaven's sake ስለ ፡ እግዚአብሔር ፡
ብለህ *sälä əgziabəher bäläh*

heavenly የሰማይ *yäsämay*

heavily በኅይል *bähayl*

heavy ከባድ *käbbad;* (∼ expense, taxes)
ከፍ ፡ ያለ *käff yalä;* (∼ cloth) ወፍራም
wäfram; (∼ sleep) ድብን ፡ ያለ *dəbbənn*

yalä; (∼ smoke) ጥቅጥቅ ፡ ያለ *ṭəqṭəqq
yalä;* (∼ drinker) ኀይለኛ *hayläňňa*
be heavy ከበደ *käbbädä*

heavy artillery ከባድ ፡ መሣሪያ *käbbad
mässariya*

Hebrew ዕብራይስጥ *əbrayəsṭ*

hectic የገርጋር *yägərrəgärr*

hedge (vt.) አጠረ *aṭṭärä*
hedge, vi. (avoid being frank) አድበ
ስብሶ ፡ አለፈ *adbäsbəso alläfä*

hedge (n.) የቁጥቋጦ ፡ አጥር *yäquṭqʷaṭo
aṭər*

heed (v.) አደመጠ *adämmäṭä;* ተቀበለ *täqäbbälä*

heed (n.) take ∼ (pay attention) ሰማ
sämma; (be careful) ተጠነቀቀ *täṭänäqqäqä*

heedless የማይጠብቅ *yämmayəṭäbbəq*

heel (n.) ተረከዝ *täräkäz*

hefty (∼ person) ጡንቻኛ *ṭunčäňňa;* (∼
book) በጣም ፡ ትልቅ *bäṭam təlləq*

heifer ጊደር *gidär;* ፍሪዳ *fəridda*

height ርዝመት *rəzmät;* (of a mountain)
ከፍታ *käffəta;* (of man) ቁመት *qumät*

heighten ከፍ ፡ አደረገ *käff adärrägä;* (∼
a fence) አስረዘመ *asräzzämä*

heinous አስቃቂ *assäqqaqi*

heir ወራሽ *wäraš*
legal heir ሕጋዊ ፡ ወራሽ *həggawi wäraš*

heir apparent ሕጋዊ ፡ ወራሽ *həggawi
wäraš*

heirloom ቅርስ *qərs*

hell ገሃነም *gähannäm;* ሲኦል *siol*

hello! ጤና *ṭena;* ይስጥልኝ *yəsṭəlləňň*

helmet የራስ ፡ ቁር *yäras qur*

help (v.) ረዳ *rädda;* አገዘ *aggäzä*
help oneself (to food) ተጋበዘ *tägabbäzä*
help out ረዳ *rädda*

help (n.) እርዳታ *ərdata;* (hired help) ረዳ
ቶች *räddatočč*

helper ረዳት *räddat*

helpful ለመርዳት ፡ ዝግጁ. *lämärdat zəgəǧǧu*
be helpful ረዳ *rädda*

helpless (∼ civilian) መከላከያ ፡ የሌለው *mäkkälakäya yälelläw*
be helpless (weak) ደከመ *däkkämä;*
(have no power) ሥልጣን ፡ የለውም *səlṭan yälläwəm*

hem (v.) ቀመቀመ *qämäqqämä*

hem (n.) ቅምቅማት *qəmqəmat;* ጠርዝ *ṭärz*

hemisphere ክፍለ ፡ ዓለም *kəflä aläm*

hemorrhage የብዙ ፡ ደም ፡ መፍሰስ *yäbəzu däm mäfsäs*

hemorrhoids ያህያ ፡ ኪንታሮት *yahəyya kintarot*

hen ዶሮ *doro*

hence ከ - - - በኋላ *kä - - - bähʷala*

henceforth ከእንግዲህ ፡ ወዲህ *käəngədih wädih*

her የሷ. *yässʷa;* የርሷ. *yärsʷa;* or object suffix pronouns

herald (v.) አበሰረ *abässärä*

herald (n.) አብሳሪ *absari;* ዐዋጅ ፡ ነጋሪ *awaǧ nägari*

herb ዕፅ *əṣ*
herbs ቅጠላ ፡ ቅጠል *qəṭäla qəṭäl*

herbivorous ዕፀ ፡ በል *əṣä bäll*

herd (v.) አጐረ *aggʷärä*

herd (n.) መንጋ *mänga*

herdsman እረኛ *ərräňňa*

here እዚህ *əzzih;* (in this direction) በዚህ፡ በኩል *bäzzih bäkkul*
here is! እነሆ *ənnäho*
here and now አሁኑኑ *ahununu*
here and there አልፎ ፡ አልፎ *alfo alfo*
over here እዚህ ፡ ጋ *əzzih ga*
toward here ወዲህ *wädih*

hereabouts እዚህ ፡ ገደማ *əzzih gädäma*

hereafter ከእንግዲህ *käəngədih*

the hereafter ወዲያኛው ፡ ዓለም *wädiyaňňaw aläm*

hereby በዚህ *bäzzih*

hereditary ሲወርድ ፡ ሲዋረድ *siwärd siwarräd*
be hereditary ከዘር ፡ ተላለፈ *käzär tälalläfä*

heredity ዘር *zär*

herein (in this place) እዚህ ፡ ውስጥ *əzzih wəsṭ;* (in this matter) እዚህ ፡ ላይ *əzzih lay*

heresy መናፍቅነት *mänafəqənnät;* ኑፋቄ *nufaqe*

heretic መናፍቅ *mänafəq*

hereupon በዚህም ፡ ጊዜ *bäzzihəm gize*

heritage ቅርስ *qərs*

hermit መናኝ *männaň;* ባሕታዊ *bahtawi*

hernia ቡቃ *buqa;* ቡአ *buʾa*

hero ባለ ፡ ጀብዱ *balä ǧäbdu;* ጀግና *ǧägna;* (leading character in a story) ባለ ታሪክ *balätarik*

heroic (∼ deed) የጀብዱ *yäǧäbdu;* የጀግንነት *yäǧägnənnät;* (∼ person) ጀግና *ǧägna;* (∼ measures) የድፍረት *yädəfrät*

heroism የጀግንነት ፡ ሙያ *yäǧägnənnät muya*

hers የርሷ. *yärsʷa;* የሷ *yässʷa*

herself, she ∼ ራሷ. *rasʷa;* እርሷ ፡ ራሷ. *ərsʷa rasʷa*
be herself እንደወትሮዋ ፡ ናት *əndäwätrowa nat*
by herself ራሷ. *rasʷa*

hesitant (∼ person) ወላዋይ *wälaway;* አመንች *amänč*

hesitate አመነታ *amänätta;* አቅማማ *aqmamma;* ወላወለ *wälawwälä*

hesitation ማመንታት *mamäntat*

heterogeneous ቅየጥ *qəyyäṭ*

hew ጠረበ *ṭärräbä*
hew off (a branch) መለመለ *mälämmälä*

hiatus ክፍት ፡ ቦታ *kəft bota*

hiccups ስርቅታ *sərəqta*
have the hiccups ሀቅ ፡ አለ(ው) *həqq alä(w)*; ሀቅ ፡ ስርቅ ፡ አለ(ው) *həqq sərq alä(w)*

hidden ስውር *səwwər;* የተደበቀ *yätädäbbäqä;* (~ meaning) የተሰወረ *yätäsäwwärä*

hide (vt.) ሰወረ *säwwärä;* ሸመቀ *šämmäqä;* ሸሸገ *šaššägä;* ደበቀ *däbbäqä*
hide (vi.) ተሸሸገ *täšäššägä;* ተደበቀ *tädäbbäqä*

hide (n.) ቆዳ *qoda*
tanned hide ማስ *mas;* ቁርበት *qurbät*

hide-and-seek ድብብቆሽ *dəbəbbəqoš*

hideaway መደበቂያ *mäddäbäqiya*

hideous (~ crime) አሰቃቂ *assäqqaqi;* (~ face) አስከፊ *askäffi*

hide-out መሸሸጊያ *mäššäšägiya;* መደበቂያ *mäddäbäqiya;* ጐሬ *gʷäre*

hierarchy ባለ ፡ ሥልጣናት *balä səltanat*

high ረዢም *räžžim;* ረጅም *räǧǧim;* (~ office) ከፍተኛ *käffətäňňa;* (~ opinion) ከፍ ፡ ያለ *käff yalä;* (~ fever) ኃይለኛ *hayläňňa;* (~ voice) ቀጭን *qäččən*

highborn ከትልቅ ፡ የተወለደ *kätəlləq yätäwällädä*

highland ደጋ *däga*

highly በጣም *bäṭam*

Highness, His ~ ልዑልነታቸው *lə'ulənnätaččäw*

high-pitched ቀጭን *qäččən*

high priest ሊቀ ፡ ካህናት *liqä kahənat*

high-ranking ከፍተኛ *käffətäňňa*

high school ሁለተኛ ፡ ደረጃ ፡ ትምህርት ፡ ቤት *hulättäňňa däräǧa təmhərt bet*

highway አውራ ፡ ጐዳና *awra gʷädana*

hijack ጠለፈ *ṭälläfä*

hijacking ጠለፋ *ṭäläfa*

hike (v.) ተጓዘ *tägʷaza;* ተንሸራሸረ *tänšäraššärä*

hike (n.) ሽርሽር *šərrəšərr*

hilarious የሚያሥቅ *yämmiyassəq*

hill ኮረብታ *koräbta*
down the hill ቁልቁለቱን *qulqulätun*
up the hill ዳገቱን *dagätun*

hillock ጉብታ *gubbəta*

hillside የኮረብታ ፡ ጐን *yäkoräbta gʷänn;* የተራራ ፡ ጥግ *yätärara ṭəgg*

hilltop የኮረብታ ፡ ጫፍ *yäkoräbta čaf;* አፋፍ *afaf*

hilly ኮረብታማ *koräbtamma*

him እሱን *əssun;* እርሱን *ərsun;* or object suffix pronouns

himself, he ~ ራሱ *rasu*
be himself እንደወትሮው ፡ ነው *əndäwätrow näw*
by himself ብቻውን *bəččawən*

hind የኋላ *yähʷala*

hinder ከለከለ *käläkkälä;* አሰናከለ *assänakkälä*

hindrance ዕንቅፋት *ənqəfat;* መሰናክል *mäsänakəl*

hinge (v.), ~ on ተመሠረተ *tämäsärrätä*

hinge (n.) ማጠፊያ *maṭäfiya*

hint (v.) ጠቀመ *ṭäqqʷämä*

hint, n. (advice) ምክር *məkər;* (allusion) ጥቅሻ *ṭəqša*
give a hint ጠቀመ *ṭäqqʷämä*

hip ሽንጥ *šənṭ;* ወገብ *wägäb*

hippopotamus ጉማሬ *gumarre*

hire, v. (employ) ቀጠረ *qäṭṭärä;* (rent) ተከራየ *täkärayyä*

his የሱ *yässu;* የርሱ *yärsu;* or possessive suffix pronouns

hiss አፏጨ *afʷaččä;* (of air) ቱሽ ፡ አለ *tušš alä*

historian ታሪክ ፡ ጸሐፊ *tarik ṣähafi*

historic ታሪካዊ *tarikawi*

historical (~ event) ታሪካዊ *tarikawi;* (~ costume) የጥንት *yäṭənt*

history ታሪክ *tarik*

hit መታ *mätta;* (~ ball) ለጋ *lägga;*
(smash into something) ከ - - - ጋር ፡
ተጋጨ *kä - - - gar tägaččä*
hit against ጋጨ *gäččä*
hit upon አገኘ *agäññä*

hitch (v.) አሰረ *assärä*

hitch (n.) መሰናክል *mäsänakəl;* እንከን
ənkän

hitherto እስካሁን ፡ ድረስ *əskahun dəräs*

hive (beehive) ቀፎ *qäfo*

hoard (v.) አከማቸ *akkämaččä*

hoarse ጉርናና *gʷärnanna*

hoax ፈጠራ *fäṭära*

hobby የትርፍ ፡ ጊዜ ፡ ማሳለፊያ *yätərf
gize masalläfiya*

hock ቋንጃ *qʷanǧa*

hockey ጋና *gänna*

hodge-podge ትርኪ ፡ ምርኪ *tərki mərki*

hoe (v.) ኰተኰተ *kʷätäkkʷätä*

hoe (n.) ዶማ *doma;* መኰትኰቻ *mäkʷät-
kʷäča*

hog አሳማ *asama*

hoist, v. (~ a flag) ሰቀለ *säqqälä;* (~
a statue) አቆመ *aqomä*

hold (vt.) ያዘ *yazä;* (reserve) ለይቶ ፡ አስ
ቀመጠ *läyyəto asqämmäṭä;* (~ one's
temper) ገታ *gätta;* (~ a meeting) አደ
ረገ *adärrägä*
hold, vi. (endure) ቆየ *qoyyä;* (of a
rule) ሠራ *särra*
hold back አስቀረ *asqärrä;* (~ evidence) ሸሸገ *šäššägä*
hold off ዛሬ ፡ ነገ ፡ ብሎ ፡ ዘገየ *zare
nägä bəlo zägäyyä*
hold out (~ a hand) ዘረጋ *zärägga*
hold up (~ head) ቀና ፡ አደረገ *qäna
adärrägä;* (with gun) አስፈራርቶ ፡ ቀማ
asfärarto qämma; (sustain) ደገፈ *däggäfä*

hold (n.) አያያዝ *ayyayaz;* (influence)
ተጽዕኖ *täṣə'əno*
take hold of ያዘ *yazä*

holdings ንብረት *nəbrät*

hole (n.) ጉድጓድ *gudgʷad;* (of needle)
ቀዳዳ *qädada;* (in an argument) ጉድ
ለት *gudlät*
have a hole ተቀዳደ *täqäddädä*
make a hole in ቀደደ *qäddädä;* በሳ
bässa; ነደለ *näddälä*

holiday ባል *bal;* በዓል *bä'al;* የዓመት ፡
በዓል *yamät bä'al*

holiness ቅዱስነት *qəddusənnät*
His Holiness ብጹዕ *bəṣu'*

hollow (v.), ~ out ቦረቦረ *boräbborä;*
አጉደጉደ *agʷädäggʷädä*

hollow (n.) ጉድጓድ *gudgʷad;* ቡርቡር
burbur

hollow, adj. (~ wall) ክፍት *kəft;* (~
gourd) ባዶ *bado;* (~ tree) የተቦረቦረ
yätäboräbborä; (~ promise) የማይጨ
በጥ *yämmayəččäbbäṭ*
become hollow ጉደጉደ *gʷädäggʷädä*

holy ቅዱስ *qəddus*

Holy Bible መጽሐፍ ፡ ቅዱስ *mäṣhaf qəddus*

Holy Communion ቁርባን *qurban;* ሥጋ ፡
ወደሙ *səga wädämu*
receive Holy Communion ቆረበ *qʷär-
räbä*

Holy Ghost መንፈስ ፡ ቅዱስ *mänfäs qəddus*

Holy Land ቅድስት ፡ አገር *qəddəst agär*

holy of holies ቅድስተ ፡ ቅዱሳን *qəddəstä
qəddusan*

holy orders ሥርዓተ ፡ ቅስና *sər'atä qə-
sənna*

Holy Scripture መጽሐፍ ፡ ቅዱስ *mäṣhaf
qəddus*

holy water ጠበል *ṭäbäl*

homage አክብሮት *akbərot*
pay homage እጅ ፡ ነሣ *əǧǧ nässa*

home (n.) መኖሪያ *mänoriya;* (place
where one was born) ትውልድ ፡ አገር
təwlədd agär

home, adj. (~ town) የተወለደበት yä-täwälläbäbbät
home (adv.) እቤት əbet; ወደ ፡ ቤት wädä bet
at home እቤት əbet
feel at home እንደልቡ ፡ ሲሆን ፡ ቻለ əndäləbbu lihon čalä
get home ገባ gäbba
homeland (የ)ትውልድ ፡ አገር (yä)təwlədd agär
homeless ቤት ፡ የሌለው bet yälelläw
homemade ቤት ፡ የተሠራ bet yätäsärra
homesick, be ናፈቀ naffäqä
hometown የተወለደበት ፡ ከተማ yätäwäl-lädäbbät kätäma
homework የቤት ፡ ሥራ yäbet səra
homily ድርሳን dərsan
homogeneous አንድ ፡ ዓይነት ፡ የሆነ and aynät yähonä; ተመሳሳይ tämäsasay
be homogeneous ተመሳሰለ tämäsas-sälä
homonym ተመሳሳይ tämäsasay
honest (~ person) ሐቀኛ haqqäňňa; ታማኝ tammaňň; ቅን qən; (~ opin-ion) እውነተኛ əwnätäňňa; (~weights) ትክክለኛ təkəkkəläňňa; (~ life) የሐቀኛነት yähaqqäňňannät
honestly በእውነት bäəwnät
honesty ታማኝነት tammaňňənnät; ሐቀኛነት haqqäňňənnät
honey ማር mar
honeycomb የንብ ፡ እንጀራ yänəb ənǧära
honeymoon የጫጉላ ፡ ጊዜ yäčagula gize
honk (vt.) ነፋ näffa
honor (v.) አከበረ akäbbärä; (~ a check) ተቀበለ täqäbbälä
honor (n.) ክብር kəbər; (good name) ስም səm
honor guard የክብር ፡ ዘብ yäkəbər zäb
His Honor ክቡር kəbur
honorable (~ behavior) የሚያስከብር yämmiyaskäbbər; (~ intention) ቅን ፡

የሆነ qən yähonä
honorary የክብር yäkəbər
honored (adj.) የክብር yäkäbər; ክቡር kə-bur
hood ቆብ qob; (of car) ክዳን kədan
hoodlum ዱርዬ durrəyye
hoof ኮቴ kotte
hook, vt. (~ a dress) ቄለፈ qʷälläfä; (~ a fish) በመንጠቆ ፡ ያዘ bämänṭäq-qo yazä
hook. n. (for lamp) መንጠቆ mänṭäqqo; (for coat) ማንጠልጠያ manṭälṭäya; (of telephone receiver) መስቀያ mäsqäya
by hook or by crook በዚህም ፡ ሆነ ፡ በዚያም bäzzihəm honä bäzziyam
hookworm ወስፋት wäsfat
hoot (v.) ጩኸ čohä
hoot (n.) ጩኸት čuhät
not give a hoot ግድ ፡ የለውም gədd yälläwəm
hop ዘለለ zällälä
hop about (of birds) ጡብ ፡ ጡብ ፡ አለ ṭubb ṭubb alä; (of a person) ዘለል ፡ ዘለል ፡ አለ zäläll zäläll alä
hop(s) ጌሾ gešo
hope (v.) ተስፋ ፡ አደረገ täsfa adärrägä
hope (n.) ተስፋ täsfa
give up hope ተስፋ ፡ ቄረጠ täsfa qʷärräṭä
hopeful (~ future) ተስፋ ፡ የሚጣልበት täsfa yämmiṭṭaləbbät; (~ words) ተስፋ ፡ የተመላበት täsfa yätämällabbät
be hopeful ተስፋ ፡ አለ(ው) täsfa allä(w)
hopeless ተስፋ ፡ የሚያስቆርጥ täsfa yäm-miyasqʷärrəṭ
horde መንጋ mänga
horizon አድማስ admas
horizontal አግዳሚ agdami
horn ቀንድ qänd; (wind instrument) መለከት mäläkät; ጥሩምባ ṭrumba
hornet ተርብ tärb

horny የቀንድ yäqänd; (~ hands) ቄር ፋዳ qʷärfadda

horrible (~ sight) የሚያሰቅቅ yämmiyassäqqəq; (~ weather, face) አስከፊ askäffi

horrid (~ behavior) አስከፊ askäffi; (~ climate) መጥፎ mätfo

horrify አሰቀቀ assäqqäqä

horror (of war) ሥቃይ səqay; (fright) ድንጋጤ dənəggaṭe

horse ፈረስ färäs

horseback, on ~ በፈረስ bäfäräs

horseback riding ግልቢያ gəlbiya

horseman ፈረሰኛ färäsäňňa

horsepower የፈረስ ፡ ጉልበት yäfäräs gulbät

horse race የፈረስ ፡ እሽቅድምድም yäfäräs əšqədəmdəm

horseshoe የፈረስ ፡ የብሪት ፡ ኩቴ yäfäräs yäbrät kotte

horticulture የዕፀዋት ፡ አበቃቀል yääṣäwat abbäqaqäl

hose (tube) ቧምቧ bʷambʷa; የውኃ ፡ ቧምቧ yäwəha bʷambʷa; (stocking) የእግር ፡ ሹራብ yäəgər šurrab

hospitable እንግዳ፡ተቀባይ əngəda täqäbbay

hospital ሆስፒታል hospital; ሐኪም፡ቤት hakim bet

hospitality መስተንግዶ mästängədo; እን ግዳ፡ተቀባይነት əngəda täqäbbayənnät show hospitality አስተናገደ astänaggädä

hospitalized, be ሆስፒታል ፡ ገባ hospital gäbba; ሆስፒታል፡ተኛ hospital täňňa

host (v.) ጋበዘ ፡ ነበረ gabäž näbbärä; አስተናገደ astänaggädä

host (n.) አስተናጋጅ astänagaǧ; እንግዳ ፡ ተቀባይ əngəda täqabbay; ጋበዘ gabäž; (heavenly ~) መላእክት mälaəkt

hostage መያዣ mäyaža

hostel ማረፊያ maräfiya

hostess, see 'host'

hostile (~ territory) የጠላት yäṭälat; (~ attitude) የጥላቻ yäṭəlaččä

hostility ጥላቻ ṭəlaččä hostilities ጦርነት ṭorənnät

hot (~ water) ሙቅ muq; (~ weather) ሞቃት moqat; (~ pan) የጋለ yägälä be hot ሞቀ moqä; (of pepper) ተፋጀ täfaǧǧä; (with rage) ጦፈ ṭofä feel hot (of air) ሞቀ moqä

hotel ሆቴል hotel

hot-tempered ግልፍተኛ gəlləftäňňa

hour ሰዓት säʻat, säät; ሳት sat; (any particular time) ጊዜ gize a good hour ሙሉ ፡ ሰዓት mulu säʻat; እንድ ፡ ሰዓት and säʻat for hours ለብዙ ፡ ሰዓት läbəzu säät

hourly (adv.) በየሰዓቱ bäyyäsäʻatu

house (v.) አኖረ anorä be housed አረፈ arräfä

house (n.) ቤት bet; (family) ቤት ፡ ሰብ betä säb around the house ቤቱ ፡ ለቤት bet läbet keep house ቤት ፡ አስተዳደረ bet astädaddärä

household ቤት ፡ ሰብ betä säb

housekeeper የቤት ፡ ቀላቢት yäbet qällabit

housekeeping የቤት ፡ አያያዝ yäbet ayyayaz good housekeeping ባልትና baltənna

housemaid ገረድ gäräd

housewife የቤት ፡ እመቤት yäbet əmmäbet

housework የቤት ፡ ሥራ yäbet səra

housing መኖሪያ mänoriya

hovel ዳሳሳ ጎጆ däsasa goǧǧo

hover አንዣበበ anžabbäbä

how? እንደምን əndämən; እንዴት əndet how እንዴት፡እንዴ əndet əndä + verb how! ምንኛ mənäňňa; እንዴት əndet how come? እንዴት əndet

how far? እስከየት əskäyät
how long? ስንት ፡ ጊዜ sənt gize; ምን ፡ ያህል ፡ ጊዜ mən yahəl gize
how many? ስንት sənt
how much? ስንት sənt; ምን ፡ ያህል mən yahəl
how much! ምንኛ mənəňňa
how often? ስንቴ sənte; ስንት ፡ ጊዜ sənt gize
and how! እንዴታ əndeta

however ነገር ፡ ግን nägär gən; ይሁን ፡ እንጂ yəhun əňgi

howl, v. (of dog) ጮኸ čohä; (of wind) አፏጨ af"ačča

howl (n.) ጩኸት čuhät

huddle (v.) አጐረ agg"ärä
huddle together እፍግፍግ ፡ ብለው ፡ ተቀመጡ əfəgfəgg bəläw täqämmäṭu; (in a corner) ተጠጋግተው ፡ ቆሙ täṭägagtäw qomu

huddle (n.) ቆይታ qoyyəta

hue ቀለም qäläm

hug, v. (hold fast) እቅፍ ፡ አደረገ əqqəff adärrägä; አቅፎ ፡ ያዘ aqfo yazä; (keep close to) ተጠግቶ ፡ ሄደ täṭägto hedä

huge (~ animal) ግዙፍ gəzuf; (~ box) ትልቅ təlləq

hull (v.) ፈለፈለ fäläffälä; ፈተገ fättägä

hull, n. (of almond) ቅርፊት qərfit; (of peanut) ገለባ gäläba; (of ship) አካል akal

hum, v. (of person) እንጐራጐረ ang"äragg"ärä; (of bee) ጥዝ ፡ አለ ṭəzz alä; አነበነበ anäbännäbä

human (n.) ሰው säw

human, adj. (~ body) የሰው yäsäw; (~ liberty) የሰው ፡ ልጅ yäsäw ləğ; (~ rights) ሰብአዊ säb'awi
human being ሰው säw

humane ርኅሩኅ rəhruh; (~ laws) በምሕረት ፡ ላይ ፡ የተመሠረተ bäməhrät lay yätämäsärrätä

humanitarian (n.) በጎ ፡ አድራጊ bäggo adragi

humanitarian (adj.) የበጎ ፡ አድራጎት yäbäggo adragot

humanity የሰው ፡ ልጅ yäsäw ləğ; ሰውሳው; (kindness) ርኅራኄ rəhrahe

humble ትሑት təhut; (~ occupation) ዝቅተኛ zəqqətäňňa; (~ home) አል ባሌ aləbbale

humid እርጥብት ፡ ያለው ərṭəbät yalläw
be humid ረጠበ räṭṭäbä; (of air) ወበቀ wäbbäqä

humidity ወበቅ wäbäq; እርጥብት ərṭəbät

humiliate አዋረደ awwarrädä

humiliation ውርደት wərdät; እፍረት əfrät

humility ትሕትና təhtənna

humor (v.) አጫወተ ač* čawwätä

humor (n.) ቀልድ qäld
be in a bad humor ከፋ(ው) käffa(w)
be in a good humor ደስ ፡ አለ(ው) däss alä(w)
sense of humor ቀልደኛነት qäldäňňannät

humorous አሥቂኝ assəqiň

hump (v.), ~ up (of ground) አበጥ ፡ አለ abäṭṭ alä
hump one's back ጀርባን ፡ ነፋ ṣägurun näffa

hump, n. (of cattle) ሻኛ šaňňa; (of humans) ጀርባ ፡ ላይ ፡ ያለ ፡ ጉብታ ğärba lay yallä gubbəta

hunch (premonition) ግምት gəmmət
have a hunch ተሰማ(ው) täsämma(w)

hunchback ጉብጣ g"äbaṭa

hunchbacked, be ጐበጠ g"äbbäṭä

hundred መቶ mäto

hunger ረኃብ rähab; ራብ rab; ችጋር čəggar

hungry የተራበ yätäräbä
be hungry ራበ(ው) rabä(w)
go hungry ተራበ täräbä

hunt አደነ addänä; (look for) ፈለገ fällägä

hunter አዳኝ *adaň*
hunting አደን *adän*
  go hunting አደነ *addänä*

hurdle (n.) መሰናክል *mäsänakəl*

hurl ወረወረ *wäräwwärä*

hurricane ዐውሎ ፡ ነፋስ *awlo näfas*

hurried (adj.) ችኩል *čəkkul;* የጥድፊያ *yäṭədfiya*

hurriedly በጥድፊያ *bäṭədfiya;* በፍጥነት *bäfəṭnät*

hurry (vt.) አጣደፈ *aṭṭaddäfä;* አፋጠነ *affaṭṭänä*
  hurry (vi.) ቀለጠፈ *qäläṭṭäfä;* ቶሎ ፡ አለ *tolo alä;* ቻኮለ *čäkkʷälä;* ተጣደፈ *täṭaddäfä;* ፈጠነ *fäṭṭänä*
  hurry up! ቶሎ ፡ ና *tolo na;* ቶሎ ፡ በል *tolo bäl*

hurry (n.) ችኮላ *čəkkʷäla;* ፍጥነት *fəṭnät;* ጥድፊያ *ṭədfiya*
  be in a hurry, see 'hurry'

hurt (damage) ጎዳ *gʷädda;* (cause pain) አሳመመ *asammämä*

husband ባል *bal;* ባለቤት *baläbet*

husbandry (farming) እርሻ *ərša;* (of animals) እርባታ *ərbata;* ርቢ *rəbbi*

hush (vi.) ዝም ፡ አለ *zəmm alä;* ጭጭ ፡ አለ *čäčč alä*
  hush! እሽ *əšš*

hush (n.) ጸጥታ *ṣäṭṭəta*

husk (n.) ላንፋ *lanfa*
  strip off the husk ሸለቀቀ *šäläqqäqä;* ፈለፈለ *fäläffälä*

husky (~ voice) ጉርናና *gʷärnanna;* (~ person) ጠብደል *ṭäbdäl*

hustle (v.) ፈጠን ፡ አለ *fäṭänn alä*
  hustle about ወዲያ ፡ ወዲህ ፡ ተርዋርዋጠ *wädiya wädih tärʷarʷaṭä*

hustle and bustle ትርምስ *tərəmməs;* ግር ግር *gärrəgärr*

hut ጎጆ *goǧǧo*

hybrid ክልስ *kəlləs*

hydromel ጠጅ *ṭäǧǧ*

---

hyena ጅብ *ǧəb*

hygiene የጤና ፡ ጥበቃ ፡ ዘዴ *yäṭena ṭəbbäqa zäde*

hymn መዝሙር *mäzmur;* (religious) ቅኔ *qəne*
  compose a hymn ተቀኘ *täqäňňä*
  sing a hymn ዘመረ *zämmärä*

hyphen ንኡስ ፡ ጭረት *nə'us čərät*

hypocrisy ግብዝና *gəbbəzənna*

hypocrite ግብዝ *gəbbəz*

hypothesis መላ ፡ ምት *mäla mət;* ግምት *gəmmət*

I

I እኔ *əne*

ice በረዶ *bärädo*

idea አስተያየት *astäyayät;* አስተሳሰብ *astäsasäb;* ሐሳብ *hassab;* (purpose) ዓላማ *alama*
  have an idea መሰለ(ው) *mässälä(w)*

ideal (n.) ዓይነተኛ ፡ እርኣይ *aynätäňňa araya;* (goal) ዓላማ *alama*

ideal, adj. (~ person) ዓይነተኛ *aynätäňňa;* (~ weather) ተስማሚ *täsmami;* (~ place) የሰጠ *yäsäṭṭä*

idealism የጎልዮ ፡ ኑሮ *yähalləyo nuro*

identical ተመሳሳይ *tämäsasay*
  be identical ተመሳሰለ *tämäsassälä*

identification መታወቂያ *mättawäqiya*

identification card መታወቂያ ፡ ወረቀት *mättawäqiya wäräqät*

identify ለየ *läyyä;* (verify the identity of) እንድ ፡ መሆኑን ፡ አረጋገጠ *and mähonun arrägaggäṭä*

identity (sameness) ተመሳሳይነት *tämäsasayənnät;* (who a person is) ማንነት *mannənnät;* እሱነት *əssunnät*

idiom ፈሊጣዊ ፡ አነጋገር *fäliṭawi annä-gagär*

idiot ደደብ *däddäb*

idle (vi.) ሥራ ፡ ፈታ *sǝra fätta*
idle away አባከነ *abakkänä;* አጠፋ *aṭäffa*

idle, adj. (lazy) ሰነፍ *sänäf;* (not employed) ሥራ ፡ ፈት *sǝra fätt*
be idle (not employed) ሥራ ፡ ፈታ *sǝra fätta;* (loaf) በዘነ *bozzänä*

idleness (laziness) ስንፍና *sǝnfǝnna;* (not being employed) ሥራ ፡ ፈትነት *sǝra fättǝnnät*

idol ጣዖት *ṭa'ot*

idolatrous ጣዖት ፡ አምላኪ *ṭa'ot amlaki*

idolatry የጣዖት ፡ አምልኮ *yäṭa'ot amlǝko*
practice idolatry ጣዖት ፡ አመለከ *ṭa'ot amälläkä*

idolize አመለከ *amälläkä*

if እንደ *ǝndä* + perfect; እንደሆነ *ǝndähonä* + perfect; ብ *bǝ* + imperfect

ignite (vt.) አቃጣጠለ *aqqäṭaṭṭälä;* እሳት ፡ አያያዘ *ǝsat ayyayazä*
ignite (vi.) እሳት ፡ ተያያዘ *ǝsat täyayazä;* (of gun powder) ፈነዳ *fänädda*

ignoble (~man) ወራዳ *wärrada;* (~ defeat) የሚያሳፍር *yämmiyasaffǝr*

ignominious (~act) አሳፋሪ *asaffari;* (~punishment) አዋራጅ *awwaraǧ*

ignorance አለዋቂነት *alawaqinnät;* ድን ቁርና *dǝnqurǝnna*

ignorant አለዋቂ *alawaqi;* ደንቆሮ *dänqoro*

ignore ቸል ፡ አለ *čäll alä;* ችላ ፡ አለ *čǝlla alä*

ill (n.) በሽታ *bäššǝta;* (evil) መቅሠፍት *mäqsäft*

ill (adj.) በሽተኛ *bäššǝtäňňa;* ሕሙም *hǝmum;* ሕመምተኛ *hǝmämtäňňa*
ill feeling ቂም *qim;* ቅያሜ *qǝyyame*
ill luck መጥፎ ፡ አጋጣሚ *mäṭfo aggaṭami*
ill manners ብልግና *bǝlgǝnna*

ill will ክፉ ፡ መንፈስ *kǝfu mänfäs*
be ill አመመ(ው) *ammämä(w)*
fall ill ታመመ *tammämä*
speak ill of ክፉ ፡ አነሣ *kǝfu anässa*
treat ill በደለ *bäddälä*

illegal ሕግ ፡ ወጥ *hǝggä wäṭṭ;* ከሕግ ፡ ውጭ ፡ የሆነ *kähǝgg wǝčč yähona*

illegible የማይነበብ *yämmayǝnnäbbäb*

illegitimate ሕግ ፡ ወጥ *hǝggä wäṭṭ*
illegitimate child ዲቃላ *diqala*

illicit የተከለከለ *yätäkäläkkälä;* ሕጋዊ ፡ ያልሆነ *hǝggawi yalhona*

illiteracy መሃይምነት *mähayyǝmǝnnät*

illiterate መሃይም *mähayyǝm;* መሃይምን *mähayyǝmǝn*

ill-mannered ባለጌ *baläge*

illness ሕመም *hǝmäm;* እመም *ǝmäm*

illogical ከትክክለኛ ፡ አስተሳሰብ ፡ የወጣ *kätǝkǝkkäläňňa astäsasäb yäwäṭṭa*

ill-tempered ቁጡ *quṭṭu*

ill-treat በደለ *bäddälä;* አጐሳቈለ *aggʷäsaqqʷälä*

ill-treatment በደል *bädäl*

illuminate አበራ *abärra;* ብርሃን ፡ ሰጠ *bǝrhan säṭṭä;* (a passage) አብራራ *abrarra*

illusion የተሳሳት ፡ እምነት *yätäsasatä ǝmnät*

illustrate (with drawings) ለመግለጫ ፡ ይሆን ፡ ዘንድ ፡ ሣለ *lämägläča yǝhon zänd salä;* (with an example) አብራራ *abrarra*

illustration ሥዕል *sǝ'ǝl;* (with example) ማብራሪያ *mabrariya*

illustrator ሠዓሊ *sä'ali*

illustrious ገናና *gänana;* ስም ፡ ጥሩ *sǝmä ṭäru*

image ምስል *mǝsǝl;* አምሳል *amsal;* (thing seen in a mirror) መልክ *mälk*

imaginary ሐሳብ ፡ የወለደው *hassab yäwällädäw;* በሐሳብ ፡ የወጣ *bähassab yäwäṭṭa* imagination ዓይነ ፡ ኅሊና aynä həllina; ልብ ፡ ወለድ ləbb wälläd

imagine በሐሳቡ ፡ ፈጠረ bähassabu fäṭṭärä; (think) አሰበ assäbä

imbecile ሞኝ monň; ጅል ǧəl

imitate ቀዳ qädda; (mimic) አስመሰለ asmässälä

imitation ቅጂ qəǧǧi; አምሳይ amsayya; (something not real) ሰው ፡ ሠራሽ säw särraš

immaculate (~clothes) ፍጹም ፡ ንጹሕ fəṣṣum nəṣuh; (~conduct) እንከን ፡ የሌለበት ənkän yälelläbbät

immaterial, be (not consisting of matter) ግዙፍ ፡ አይደለም gəzuf aydälläm; (be unimportant) ግድ ፡ የለውም gədd yälläwəm

immature ያልበሰለ yalbässälä

immeasurable ወሰን ፡ የሌለው wäsän yälelläw

immediate የተፋጠነ yätäfaṭṭänä; ፈጠን ፡ ያለ fäṭänn yalä;(~family, neighbor) የቅርብ yäqərb

immediately አሁኑኑ ahununu; ወዲያው wädiyaw; ወዲያውኑ wädiyawnu; ያኔ ውኑ yannewnu

immense (~room) በጣም ፡ ሰፊ bäṭam säffi; (~building) ግዙፍ gəzuf

immensely እጅግ ፡ በጣም əǧǧəg bäṭam

immerse ነከረ näkkärä
be immersed (in work) ተዋጠ täwaṭä

immigrant ስደተኛ səddätäňňa

immigration ስደት səddät

imminent, be የማይቀር ፡ ነው yämmayəqär näw

immobile, remain~ ቀጥ ፡ ብሎ ፡ ቆመ qäṭṭ bəlo qomä

immodest ትሕትና ፡ የጎደለው təhtənna yägʷäddäläw; (~dress) አስነዋሪ asnäwwari

immoral ከግብረ ፡ ገብነት ፡ ውጭ ፡ የሆነ kägəbrä gäbbənnät wəčč yähonä

immortal ሕያው həyaw

immortality ሕያውነት həyawənnät

immovable (~stubbornness) የማይበገር yämmayəbbäggär
immovable property ቋሚ ፡ ንብረት qʷami nəbrät

immovable, be (of an object) አልተንቀ ሳቀሰም altänqäsaqqäsäm

immovables የማይንቀሳቀስ ፡ ንብረት yämmayənqäsaqqäs nəbrät

immune, be~ to (a disease) ከ---መድን ፡ ነው kä - - - mädən näw

impact ኃይል hayl; (collision) ግጭት gəččət; (influence) ተጽዕኖ täṣə'əno

impair ጎዳ gʷädda

impartial አድልዎ ፡ የሌለበት adləwo yälelläbbät; የማያዳላ yämmayaddalla

impass መውጫ ፡ መንገድ ፡ የሌለበት ፡ ቦታ mäwča mängäd yälelläbbät bota

impassable, be~(of ford) አያሻግርም ayaššäggərəm; (of road) አያስኬድም ayaskedəm

impassive ያለ ፡ ስሜት yalä səmmet

impatience ትዕግሥት ፡ ማጣት təgəst maṭat

impatient, be ትዕግሥት ፡ አጣ təgəst aṭṭa; (be eager) ጓጓ gʷaggʷa

impatiently (eagerly) በጉጉት bäguggut; (not patiently) ትዕግሥት ፡ በማጣት təgəst bämaṭat

impeccable እንከን ፡ የሌለው ənkän yälelläw

impede አገደ aggädä; ከለከለ käläkkälä

impediment መሰናክል mäsänakəl; ዕንቅ ፋት ənqəfat

impel (drive forward) ገፋ gäffa; (force) አስገደደ asgäddädä

impending ሊደርስበት ፡ የሚችል lidärsəbät yämmičəl

impenetrable የማይደረስበት yämmayəddärräsəbbät

imperative (n.) ትእዛዝ ፡ አንቀጽ tə'əzaz anqäṣ

imperceptible በዓይን ፡ የማይታይ bayn yämmayəttay

imperfect (defective) የተበላሸ yätäbäläšša; (~ knowledge) ያልተሟላ yaltämʷalla

imperial የንጉሡ ፡ ነገሥት yänəgusä nägäst
His Imperial Majesty ግርማዊ ፡ ንጉሠ ፡ ነገሥት gərmawi nəgusä nägäst

Imperial Bodyguard የክብር ፡ ዘበኛ yäkəbər zäbäñña

imperialism ኢምፔሪያሊዝም imperiyalizm

imperil አደጋ ፡ ላይ ፡ ጣለ adäga lay ṭalä

imperishable የማይበላሽ yämmayəbbälašš

impertinence ስድነት səddənnät; ብልግና bəlgənna

impertinent (~ person) ስድ ፡ አደግ sədd addäg; (~ remark) የማይገባ yämmayəggäbba

impetuous ችኩል čəkkul

impetus ኃይል hayl

implacable (~ enemies) የምር yämərr; (~ anger) የማይበርድ yämmayəbärd

implement (v.) ሠራ särra; ፈጸመ fäṣṣämä
be implemented በሥራ ፡ ላይ ፡ ዋለ bäsəra lay walä

implement (n.) መሣሪያ mässariya

implicit (~ threat) ውስጣዊ wəsṭawi; ያልተገለጸ yaltägälläṣä

implore ለመነ lämmänä; ተማለለ tämallälä

impolite ባለጌ baläge

import (v.) አስመጣ asmäṭṭa; ከውጭ ፡ አገር ፡ አስመጣ käwəčč agär asmäṭṭa

import, n. (merchandise) ወደ ፡ አገር ፡ ውስጥ ፡ የገባ ፡ እቃ wädä agär wəsṭ yägäbba əqa; (meaning) ፍሬ ፡ ነገር fre nägär

importance ጥቅም ṭəqəm; ጣቃሚነት ṭäqaminnät; አስፈላጊነት asfällaginnät; ዋጋ waga

important (~ matter) ብርቱ bərtu; ከፍተኛ käffətäñña; ከፍ ፡ ያለ käff yalä; (~ person) ታላቅ tallaq
important thing ቁም ፡ ነገር qum nägär
be important አስፈላጊነት ፡ አለው asfällaginnät alläw; ዋጋ ፡ አለው waga alläw

importer አስመጪ asmäčči

impose ጣለ ṭalä
impose on (bother) አስቸገረ asčäggärä; (force) አስገደደ asgäddädä

imposing ግርማ ፡ ያለው gərma yalläw

impossibility የማይቻል ፡ ነገር yämmayəččal nägär

impossible የማይሆን yämmayəhon; የማይቻል yämmayəččal
be impossible ተሳነ täsanä; አልተቻለም altäčäläm

impostor አጭበርባሪ ačbärbari

impotence አለመቻል alämäčal

impotent, be ተሳነ täsanä; ችሎታ ፡ አልነበረውም čəlota alnäbbäräwəm

impoverish አደኸየ adähäyyä
be impoverished ደኸየ dähäyyä

impractical ሊሠራ፡ አይቻልም lisära ayəččaləm

impregnable የማይበገር yämmayəbbäggär

impregnate አጥለቀለቀ aṭläqälläqä

impress (v.) አስደነቀ asdännäqä; አስገረመ asgärrämä; (stamp) ቀረጸ qärräṣä

impression (of heel) ዱካ duka; (of fingerprint) አሻራ ašara; (of seal) መቅረጽ mäqräṣ
be under the impression መሰለ(ው) mässälä(w)

impressive አስደናቂ asdännaqi

imprint (of foot) ዱካ duka; (mark) ምልክት mələkkət

imprison አሰረ *assärä*

imprisonment እስር *əsər;* እስራት *əssərat*

improbable የማይመስል *yämmayəmäsəl*

improper የማይገባ *yämmayəggäbba;* ትክ ክለኛ ፡ ያልሆነ *təkəkkəläňňa yalhonä*

improve (vt.) አሻሻለ *aššašalä* improve (vi.) ተሻለ *täšalä;* ተሻሻለ *tä-šašalä*

improvement መሻሻል *mäššašal*

improvise (~words) ፈጠረ *fäṭṭärä*

imprudent አስተዋይነት ፡ የጐደለው *astä-wayənnät yäg^wäddäläw*

impudence ብልግና *bəlgənna*

impudent ዓይናውጣ *aynawṭa;* ስድ ፡ አደግ *sädd addäg;* ባለጌ *baläge*

impulse (emotion) ስሜት *səmmet;* (of wind) ገፊት *gəffit*

impulsive በስሜት ፡ የሚገፋፋ *bäsəmmet yämiggäfaffa;* ችኩል *čəkkul*

impure ቆሻሻ *qosaša;* ያልተጣራ *yaltäṭarra;* (defiled) ርኩስ *rəkus;* (~air) የተበ ላሸ *yätäbälaššä*

in በ *bä;* እ *ə;* በ - - - ውስጥ *bä - - - wəsṭ;* እ - - - ውስጥ *ə - - - wəsṭ*

inability ያለመቻል *yaläməčal*

inaccessible የማይደረስበት *yämmayəddär-räsəbbät*

inaccuracy (error) ጉድለት *gudlät;* (lack of accuracy) አለመስተካከል *alämästä-kakäl*

inaccurate, be ትክክለኛ ፡ አይደለም *tə-kəkkəläňňa aydälläm*

inaction ስንፍና *sənfənna*

inactive, be አልሰራም *alsärram;* ለገመ *läggämä*

inadequate ያልተሟላ *yaltäm^walla;* ብቁ ነት ፡ የሌለው *bəqunnät yälelläw* be inadequate አይበቃም *aybäqam*

inadvertent (~mistake) ባለማወቅ ፡ የተ ደረገ *balämawäq yätädärrägä*

inadvertently ተሳስቶ *täsasto;* ሳያውቅ *sayawq*

inanimate ግዑዝ *gə'uz*

inapplicable, be አግባብነት ፡ የለውም *ag-babənnät yälläwəm*

inappropriate የማይገባ *yämmayəggäbba* it is inappropriate አይገባም *ayəggäb-bam;* አይሆንም *ayhonəm*

inarticulate (~groan) የማይለይ *yäm-mayəlläyy;* (~speaker) የማይወጣለት *yämmayəwäṭallät*

inattentive ሐሳብ ፡ ብኩን *hassabä bəkun*

inaugural የምረቃ *yämərräqa*

inaugurate መረቀ *märräqä*

inauguration ምረቃ *mərräqa;* (ceremony) የምረቃ ፡ ሥነ ፡ ሥርዓት *yämərrä-qa sänä sər'at*

inborn የተፈጥሮ *yätäfäṭro*

incapable የሥራ ፡ ችሎታ ፡ የሌለው *yä-səra čəlota yälelläw* be incapable of አይችልም *ayčələm*

incapacitate ከለከለ *käläkkälä* be incapacitated ስንኩል ፡ ሆኖ ፡ ቀረ *sənkul hono qärrä*

incarnation ሥጋ ፡ መልበስ *səga mälbäs*

incendiary (~bomb) የእሳት *yäəsat;* (~article) ሕዝብ ፡ የሚያነሣሣ *həzb yäm-miyannäsassa*

incense (v.) አበሳጨ *abbäsaččä* be incensed ጦፈ *ṭofä*

incense (n.) ዕጣን *əṭan*

incentive የሚገፋፋ *yämmigäfaffa*

incertitude እርግጠኛ ፡ አለመሆን *ərgəṭäň-ňa alämähon*

incessantly ያለማቋረጥ *yalämaqq^waräṭ*

inch ኢንች *inč*

incident ድርጊት *dərgit;* አድራጎት *adra-got;* አጋጣሚ *aggaṭami;* (conflict) ግጭት *gəččət*

incidental (~expenses) ልዩ *ləyyu;* (~remark) ቀለል ፡ ያለ *qäläll yalä*

incidentally እንዳጋጣሚ *əndaggaṭami*

incinerate አቃጠለ *aqqaṭṭälä*

incise ወቀረ wäqqärä

incision, make an～በጣ bäṭṭa

incisor የፊት ፡ ጥርስ yäfit ṭərs

incite እነሣሣ annäsassa

inclement (～ruler) ጨዱኝ čäqqʷañ; (～weather) መጥፎ mätfo

inclination (bending) ዶፋ ፡ ቀና ፡ ማድረግ däfa qäna madräg; (preference) ዝንባሌ zənəbbale

incline (vi.) አዘነበለ azänäbbälä; አጋደለ agaddälä
be inclined ዝንባሌ ፡ አለው zənəbbale alläw

include (vt.) አጠቃለለ aṭṭäqallälä; ጨመረ čämmärä

included (adj.) ጭምር čəmmər; አብሮ ፡ የተያያዘ abro yätäyayazä

including እስከነ əskännä; ከነ kännä; ከ - - - ጋር kä - - - gar

incoherent ተከታታይነት ፡ የሌለው täkätatayənnät yälelläw; ያልተያያዘ yaltäyayazä

incombustible የማይቃጠል yämmayəqqaṭṭäl

income ገቢ gäbi

incoming (office holder) አዲስ addis

incomparable ወደር ፡ የሌለው wädär yälelläw

incompatible, be ተስማሚ ፡ አይደለም tässmami aydälläm

incompetent ችሎታ ፡ የሌለው čəlota yälelläw

incomplete ጉደሎ gʷädälo
be incomplete ጉደለ gʷäddälä; የተሟላ ፡ አይደለም yätämʷalla aydälläm

incomprehensible, be አይገባም ayəggäbbam

inconceivable የማይታመን yämmayəttammän; የማይታሰብ yämmayəttassäb

incongruous, be አይስማማም ayəsmammam

inconsiderate ይሉኝታ ፡ ቢስ yəluñta bis

inconsistent ተለዋዋጭ täläwawaç

inconspicuous ዓይን ፡ የማይምርክ ayn yämmayəmərrək

inconvenience (v.) አስቸገረ asčäggärä

inconvenience (n.) ችግር čəggər

inconvenient የማይመች yämmayəmmäčč

incorporate አዋሐደ awwahadä

incorrect ትክክለኛ ፡ ያልሆነ täkäkkäläñña yalhonä

incorrigible የማይታረም yämmayəttarräm

increase (vt.) አበዛ abäzza; (add) ጨመረ čämmärä; (make more) አላቀ alaqä; አበለጠ abälläṭä

increase (n.) ጭማሪ čəmmari

incredible የማይመስል yämmayəmäsəl

increment ጭማሪ čəmmari

incriminate ጥፋተኝነቱን ፡ አመለከተ ṭəfatäññannätun amäläkkätä

incubate ተፈለፈለ täfäläffälä

incumbent ሥልጣኑን ፡ ይዞ ፡ የነበረ səlṭanun yəzo yänäbbärä
be incumbent on (upon) ግዴታው ፡ ነው gəddetaw näw; ተገባሩ ፡ ነው tägbaru näw

incurable የማይፈወስ yämmayəffäwwäs; የማይድን yämmayədən

incursion ወረራ wärära
make an incursion በዘበዘ bäzäbbäzä; ወረረ wärrärä

indebted, be ～to (for help) ባለ ፡ ውለታው ፡ ነው baläwəlätaw näw; (for money) የ - - - ገንዘብ ፡ ነበረብት yä - - - gänzäb näbbäräbbät; ባለ ፡ ዕዳው ፡ ነው balä ədaw näw

indecent (person) ባለጌ baläge; (behavior) የብልግና yäbəlgənna

indecisive, be አወላወለ awwälawwälä

indeed በውነት bäwnät; እውነትም əwnätəm

indefinite (~time) ያልተወሰነ yaltäwässänä; (~ opinion) ግልጽ ፡ ያልሆነ
gəls yalhonä

indefinite article ያልተወሰነ ፡ መስተአ
ምር yaltäwässänä mästä'ammər

indelible (~ ink) የማይለቅ yämmayə-
läqq

indemnity ካሳ kasa

independence ነጻነት näsannät

independent ነጻ näsa
be independent (on one's own) ራሱን ፡
ቻለ rasun čalä

indestructible የማይበላሽ yämmayəbbälašš

indeterminate በትክክል ፡ ያልታወቀ bätəkəkkəl yaltawwäqä

index (measure) መለኪያ mäläkkiya;
(of a book) ማውጫ mawča

index finger ሌባ ፡ ጣት leba ṭat

India ህንድ hənd

indicate አመለከተ amäläkkätä

indication ምልክት mələkkət; (hint)
ፍንጭ fənč

indict ከሰሰ kässäsä

indictment ክስ kəss

indifference ግድ ፡ የለሽነት gədd yälläšənnät

indifferent የግድ ፡ የለሽነት yägədd yälläšənnät
be (remain) indifferent ግድ ፡ የለሽ ፡
ሆነ gədd yälläš honä

indigence ድህነት dəhənnät

indigenous ተወላጅ täwällaǧ

indigent ደኻ däha; የኔ ፡ ቢጤ yäne biṭe

indigestion የምግብ ፡ አለመንሽራሽር yäməgəb alämänšäräšär
give indigestion ሆዱን ፡ ጐረበጠው
hodun gʷäräbbäṭäw

indignant, be ተናደደ tänaddädä

indirect ቀጥተኛ ፡ ያልሆነ qäṭṭətäñña yalhonä

indiscriminate (~action) እጅ ፡ እንዳ
መጣ əǧǧ əndamäṭṭa

indispensable አስፈላጊ asfällagi

indisposed, be ጤና ፡ አይደለም ṭena aydälläm

indisposition (ill health) ሕመም həmäm

indistinct (~noise) የማይለይ yämmayəlläyy; (~ signature) የማይነብብ yämmayənnäbbäb; (~shape) ደብዛዛ däbzazza

individual (n.) ሰው säw

individual (adj.) በነፍስ ፡ ወከፍ bänäfs
wäkäf; የግል yägəll; የራስ yäras

individually በየግል bäyyägəll; አንድ ፡
ባንድ and band

indivisible ሊከፋፈል ፡ የማይችል likkäfaf-
fäl yämmayəčəl

indoctrinate አሳመነ asammänä

indolence ስንፍና sənfənna

indolent ሰነፍ sänäf

indoors እቤት əbet; እቤት ፡ ውስጥ əbet
wəsṭ

induce (persuade) አግባባ agbabba; ገፋፋ
gäfaffa

inducted, be~ (into the army) ተከተበ
täkättäbä

indulgent ላል ləl

industrial የኢንዱስትሪ yäindustri

industrious (~worker) ታታሪ tatari;
(~student) ትጉ təgu

industry ኢንዱስትሪ industri

inebriate አሰከረ asäkkärä

inedible, be አይበላም ayəbbällam

ineffective አጥጋቢ ፡ ያልሆነ aṭgabi yalhonä; የማይረባ yämmayəräba

inefficient (tool) አጥጋቢ ፡ ውጤት ፡ የማ
ይሰጥ aṭgabi wäṭṭet yämmayəsäṭ; (person) ቀልጣፋ ፡ ያልሆነ qälṭaffa yalhonä

ineligible, be (unqualified) ተገቢ ፡ አይ
ደለም tägäbi aydälläm; (not eligible)

መብት ፥ የለውም *mäbt yälläwəm*

inept (∼person) ሙያ ፥ የሌለው *muya yälelläw;* እጅ ፥ የተሳሰረ *əǧǧu yätäsassärä;* (∼ remark) ተገቢ ፥ ያልሆነ *tägäbi yalhonä*

inequality መበላለጥ *mäbbälaläṭ;* አለመስ ተካከል *alämästäkakäl*

inert ግዑዝ *gə'uz*

inevitable የማይጠረጠር *yämmayəṭṭäräṭ-ṭär;* የማይቀር *yämmayəqär*

inexact ትክክል ፥ ያልሆነ *təkəkkəl yalhonä*

inexcusable የማይታለፍ *yämmayəttalläf*

inexhaustible የማያልቅ *yämmayalq*

inexistent, be የለም *yälläm*

inexpensive ርካሽ *rəkaš*

inexperienced የሥራ ፥ ልምድ ፥ የሌለው *yäsəra ləmad yälelläw*

infallible የማይሳሳት *yämmayəssasat*

infamous አስከፊ *askäffi;* ነውረት ፥ ቢስ *hafrätä bis*

infamy ነውር *näwr*

infancy የሕፃንነት ፥ ጊዜ *yähəṣanənnät gize;* ልጅነት *ləǧənnät*

infant ሕፃን *həṣan*

infantile (∼ disease) የልጆች *yälǧočč;* (∼ behavior) የሕፃንነት *yähəṣanənnät*

infantry የእግረኛ ፥ ጦር *yäəgräñña ṭor*

infect መረዝ *märräzä;* (spoil) አበላሸ *abbälaššä*

infection የቁስል ፥ ማመርቀዝ *yäqusəl mamärqäz*

infectious በጅርም ፥ የሚይዝ *bäǧärm yämmiyəz*

inferior, n. (in office) የበታች *yäbätačč*

inferior, adj. (∼ position) ዝቅተኛ *zəqqətäñña;* (∼ quality) መናኛ *mänäñña* be inferior ዝቅ ፥ አለ *zəqq alä*

infest ወረረ *wärrärä*

infidel አረመኔ *arämäne*

infidelity (unfaithfulness) ቃል ፥ ኪዳኑን ፥ ማፍረስ *qal kidanun mafräs*

infiltrate ሰርጎ ፥ ገባ *särgo gäbba*

infiltrator ሰርጎ ፥ ገብ *särgo gäbb*

infinite የማይወሰን *yämmayəwwässän;* መጠን ፥ የሌለው *mäṭän yälelläw*

infinitely ያለ ፥ ቅጥ *yalä qəṭṭ*

infinitive ንኡስ ፥ አንቀጽ *nə'us anqäṣ*

infirm ደካማ *däkkama*

infirmary ክሊኒክ *klinik*

infirmity ያካል ፥ ጉደሎነት *yakal gʷädälonnät*

inflammable ነዳጅ *nädaǧ*

inflammatory የሚያስቄጣ *yämmiyasqʷäṭṭa*

inflate ነፋ *näffa*

inflation (monetary∼) የገንዘብ ፥ ዋጋ ፥ መውረድ *yägänzäb waga mäwräd*

inflect (in grammar) አረባ *aräbba*

inflection (of verb) አረባብ *arräbab*

inflexible ንቅንቅ ፥ የማይል *nəqnəqq yämmayəl;* የማይናወጽ *yämmayənnawwäṣ*

influence (v.) አግባባ *agbabba;* ተጽዕኖ ፥ አለ(ው) *täṣə'əno allä(w)*

influence (n.) ተሰሚነት *täsäminnät;* ተጽ ዕኖ *täṣə'əno*

influential ተደማጭነት ፥ ያለው *tädämmaçənnät yalläw*

inform አስረዳ *asrädda;* አስታወቀ *astawwäqä* inform on አሳበቀ *assabbäqä;* ጠቆመ *ṭäqqʷämä*

informal (∼ discussion) አፈሲዬል ፥ ያል ሆነ *ofisiyel yalhonä;* (∼party) መሳይ *mäsay;* ሥርዓት ፥ ያልተከተለ *sər'at yaltäkättälä;* (∼ dress) የዘወትር ፥ ያ ዛዋተር *yäzäwätər*

information መረጃ *märräǧa;* መግለጫ *mägläça;* (knowledge) የእውቀት ፥ መጠን *yääwqät mäṭän* Ministry of Information የማስታወ

ቂያ ፡ ሚኒስቴር *yämastawäqiya minister*

information desk መረጃ ፡ ክፍል *märräğa kəfəl*

informed, be ዐወቀ *awwäqä*

informer አሳባቂ *assabaqi;* ጠቋሚ *ṭäqqʷami;* ወሬ ፡ አቀባይ *wäre aqäbbay;* ጆሮ ፡ ጠቢ *ğoro ṭäbi*

infraction መጣስ *mäṭas*

infrequently አልፎ ፡ አልፎ *alfo alfo*

infringe ጣሰ *ṭasä*

infuriate አናደደ *annaddädä*

ingenious (~person) ብልሁ *bələh;* (~device) በጣም ፡ የረቀቀ *bäṭam yäräqqäqä*

ingenuity ብልሀነት *bələhənnät*

ingenuous የዋህ *yäwwah*

ingrained ሥር ፡ የሰደደ *sər yäsäddädä*

ingratitude ውለታ ፡ ቢስነት *wəläta bisənnät*

ingredients ቅመማ ፡ ቅመም *qəmäma qəmäm*

inhabit ኖረ *norä*

inhabitant ነዋሪ *näwari*

inhabited, be ሰው ፡ አለበት *säw alläbbät*

inhale አየር ፡ ወደ ፡ ውስጥ ፡ ሳበ *ayyär wädä wəsṭ sabä*

inherent የተፈጥሮ *yätäfäṭro*

inherit ወረሰ *wärräsä*

inheritance ርስት *rəst*

inhospitable አስተናጋጅነት ፡ የጎደለው *astänagağənnät yägʷäddäläw*

inhuman ሰብአዊ ፡ ያልሆነ *säb'awi yalhonä*

inimical ጥላች ፡ ያዘለ *ṭəlaččä yazzälä;* የጥላች *yäṭəlaččä*

iniquity የግፍ ፡ ሥራ *yägəf səra*

initial (n.) የስም ፡ መጀመሪያ ፡ ፊደል *yäsəm mäğämmäriya fidäl*

initial (adj.) የመጀመሪያ *yämäğämmäriya*

initiate ሐሳብ ፡ አመነጨ *hassab amänäččä*

initiative ሐሳብ ፡ የማመንጨት ፡ ችሎታ *hassab yämamänčät čəlota*

inject (give an injection) መርፌ ፡ ወጋ *märfe wägga;* (introduce) ጣልቃ ፡ አስገባ *ṭalqa asgäbba*

injection መርፌ *märfe*
give an injection, see 'inject'

injunction (of father) ትእዛዝ *tə'əzaz;* (of court) የፍርድ ፡ ቤት ፡ ማገጃ *yäfərd bet maggäğa*

injure አቈሰለ *aqʷässälä;* (harm) ጎዳ *gʷädda*

injured የቈሰለ *yäqʷässälä;* ቁስለኛ *qusläňňa*
be injured ቈሰለ *qʷässälä*

injury ቁስል *qusəl*

injustice በደል *bädäl;* የግፍ ፡ ሥራ *yägəf səra*
do injustice በደለ *bäddälä*

ink ቀለም *qäläm*

inland (adj.) ገባ ፡ ያለ *gäba yalä*
inland (adv.) ወደ ፡ መሃል ፡ አገር *wädä mähal agär*

in-laws አማቾች *amatočč*

inlet ትንሽ ፡ ሰላጤ *tənnəš sällaṭe*

inmate (of prison) እስረኛ *əsräňňa;* (of hospital) ነዋሪ ፡ በሽተኛ *näwari bäššətäňňa*

inmost (~desire) የልብ *yäləbb;* (~depth) የመጨረሻ *yämäčärräša*

inn ትንሽ ፡ ሆቴል *tənnəš hotel*

innate የተፈጥሮ *yätäfäṭro*

inner ውስጣዊ *wəsṭawi;* የውስጠኛ *yäwəsṭäňňa*

innermost የመካከለኛ *yämäkakkäläňňa*

innocence ንጹሕ ፡ መሆን *nəṣuh mähon;* ጥፋተኛ ፡ አለመሆን *ṭəfatäňňa alämähon* innocent ንጹሕ *nəṣuh;* ያለ ፡ ነጢአት ፡ የሆነ *yalä haṭiat yähonä;* (without knowledge of evil) የዋህ *yäwwah*

innocuous (~ remark) የማያስከፋ *yämmayaskäffa*
be innocuous (snake) መርዘኛ ፡ አይደ ለም *märzäňňa aydälläm*

innovate (vt.) አሁን ፡ አመጣ *ahun amäṭṭa*

innovation አዲስ ፡ ነገር *addis nägär*

innumerable ቁጥር ፡ ስፍር ፡ የሌለው *quṭar səfər yälelläw*

inoculate ክትባት ፡ አደረገብት *kəttəbat adärrägäbbät*

inoculation ክትባት *kəttəbat*

inoffensive (~ manner) የማያስቀይም *yämmayasqäyyəm*

inopportune የማይመች *yämmayəmmäčč*

inquire ተመራመረ *tämärammärä;* ጠየቀ *ṭäyyäqä*

inquiry ምርመራ *mərmära*

inquisition ምርመራ *mərmära*

inquisitive ተመራማሪ *tämäramari;* ለማ ወቅ ፡ የሚሻ *lämawäq yämmiša*

insane እብድ *əbd;* የአእምሮ ፡ ሕመምተኛ *yäa'məro həmämtäňňa*
be insane አበደ *abbädä*

insanitary ላጢና ፡ ጠንቅ *läṭena ṭänq*

insanity እብደት *əbdät*

insatiable (~ curiosity) የማይረካ *yämmayəräka*
be insatiable ሣሣ *sassa;* አልጠገበም *alṭäggäbäm*

inscribe ቀረጸ *qärräṣä*

inscription ጽሑፍ *ṣəhuf*

insect ተባይ *täbay;* ነፍሳት *näfsat*

insecure የማያስተማምን *yämmayastämammən*

inseparable የማይለያይ *yämmayəlläyayy*

insert አስገባ *asgäbba;* (plug in) ሰካ *säkka*

inside (n.) ውስጥ *wəsṭ*

inside (adj.) የውስጥ *yäwəsṭ*

inside (prep.) በ - - - ውስጥ *bä - - - wəsṭ;* እ - - - ውስጥ *ə - - - wəsṭ*
inside (adv.) በውስጥ *bäwəsṭ;* ከውስጥ *käwəsṭ;* ውስጥ ፡ ለውስጥ *wəsṭ läwəsṭ*

insidious የተንኮል *yätänkʷäl;* ተንኮል ፡ ያዘለ *tänkʷäl yazzälä*

insight አስተዋይነት *astäwayənnät*
get an insight ጠልቆ ፡ ዐወቀ *ṭälqo awwäqä*

insignia አርማ *arma;* መለዮ *mälläyyo*

insignificant (~ role) አነስተኛ *anästäňňa;* (~ details) የማይረባ *yämmayəräba*

insincere (~ opinion) ከልብ ፡ ያልሆነ *käləbb yalhonä;* ካንገት ፡ በላይ ፡ የሆነ *kangät bälay yähonä*

insinuate በአግቦ ፡ ተናገረ *bäagbo tänaggärä*
insinuate oneself into ሹልክ ፡ ብሎ ፡ ገባ *šulləkk bəlo gäbba;* ተለማምጦ ፡ አገኘ *tälämamṭo agäňňa*

insipid, be ጣዕም ፡ የለውም *ṭa'əm yälläwəm*

insist ችክ ፡ አለ *čäkk alä;* ድርቅ ፡ አለ *dərräqq alä*

insistent, be, see 'insist'

insolence ስድነት *səddənnät;* ብልግና *bəlgənna*

insolent ስድ ፡ አደግ *sədd addäg;* ባለጌ *baläge*

insoluble, be (of grease) አልቀለጠም *alqälläṭäm;* (of a mystery) ማወቅ ፡ አል ተቻለም *mawäq altäčaläm;* ፍች ፡ አል ተገኘለትም *fəčč altägäňňällätəm*

insomnia የእንቅልፍ ፡ እጦት *yäənqəlf əṭot*

inspect (~ troops) ጎበኘ *gʷäbäňňa;* (~ baggage) ፈተሸ *fättäšä;* (look carefully over) መረመረ *märämmärä*

inspection ፍተሻ *fəttäša*

inspector ተቆጣጣሪ *täqʷäṭaṭari*

inspiration (stirring of feelings) የሚያነ ሣሣው ፡ መንፈስ *yämmiyannäsassaw mänfäs;* (drawing of air into the lungs) መተንፈስ *mätänfäs*

inspire (arouse to action) ቀሰቀሰ *qäsäqqäsä;* አነሣሣ *annäsassa*

install አቆመ *aqomä;* (~ a telephone) ቀጠለ *qäṭṭälä*

installment (of a story) ተከታታይ ፡ እትም *täkätatay əttəm;* (partial payment) የጊዜ ፡ ክፍያ *yägize kəffəya*

instance (case) ማስረጃ *masräǧǧa;* (example) ምሳሌ *məssale*
for instance ለምሳሌ *läməssale*

instant, at that ~ በዚያን ፡ ጊዜ *bäzziyan gize*
in an instant በንዳፍታ *bandafta;* ከመቅጽበት *kämäqəṣbät*
this instant አሁኑኑ *ahununu*

instantaneous ወዲያውኑ ፡ የሚሆን *wädiyawnu yämmihon*

instantly ወዲያውኑ *wädiyawnu*

instead በሱ ፡ ፈንታ *bässu fänta*
instead of በ - - - ምትክ *bä - - - mətəkk;* በ - - - ፈንታ *bä - - - fänta*

instigate አነሣሣ *annäsassa*

instill አሳደረ *asaddärä*

instinct ተፈጥሮ *täfäṭro;* የተፈጥሮ ፡ ስጦታ *yätäfäṭro səṭota*

institute (n.) ኢንስቲቱት *institut*

institution ድርጅት *dərəǧǧət;* (custom) ልማድ *ləmad*

instruct (inform) አስታወቀ *astawwäqä;* (teach) አስተማረ *astämarä;* (order) አዘዘ *azzäzä*

instruction ማስተማሪያ *mastämariya;* ትምህርት *təmhərt*
instructions (directive) መምሪያ *mämriya;* (order) ትእዛዝ *tə'əzaz*

instructive, be ትምህርት ፡ ሰጠ *təmhərt säṭṭä;* ትምህርት ፡ ተገኘበት *təmhərt tägäňňäbbät*

instructor አስተማሪ *astämari*

instrument መሣሪያ *mässariya*

insubordinate የማይታዘዝ *yämmayəttazzäz*

insubordination አለመታዘዝ *alämättazäz*

insufficient, be አነሰ *annäsä;* በቂ ፡ አልሆነም *bäqi alhonäm*

insular (related to an island) የደሴት *yädäset*

insult (v.) ሰደበ *säddäbä*

insult (n.) ስድብ *sədəb*

insurance የሕይወት ፡ ዋስትና *yähəywät wastənna*
insurance policy የሕይወት ፡ ዋስትና ፡ ውል *yähəywät wastənna wəl*

insure ዋስትና ፡ አስገባ *wastənna asgäbba*

insurgency ዐመፅ *amäṣ*

insurgent ዐመፀኛ *amäṣäňňa*

insurrection ሁከት *hukät;* ዐመፅ *amäṣ*

intact, be ምንም ፡ ጉድለት ፡ የለበትም *mənəm gudlät yälläbbätəm*

intangible የማይዳሰስ *yämmayəddassäs;* ግዑዝ ፡ ያልሆነ *gə'uz yalhonä*

integral (essential) ዓይነተኛ *aynätäňňa;* (entire) ጠቅላላ *ṭäqlalla*

integrate አዋሐደ *awwahadä*

integrity (honesty) ሐቀኝነት *haqqäňňənnät;* (wholeness) አንድነት *andənnät*

intellect ልቡና *ləbbuna;* ልቦና *ləbbona;* አእምሮ *a'məro;* የማሰብ ፡ ችሎታ *yämassäb čəlota*

intellectual (n.) ምሁር *məhur*

intelligence ብልህነት *bələhənnät;* አእምሮ *a'məro;* የማሰብ ፡ ችሎታ *yämassäb čəlota;* (secret information) መርጃ *märräǧa*

intelligent ልባም *ləbbam;* ብልህ *bələh;* ዐዋቂ *awaqi*

intelligible, be (of speech) ጉልቶ ፡ ተሰማ *gʷälto täsämma;* (of response) መረዳት ፡ አላስቸገረም *märrädat alasčäggäräm*

intemperate (~language) ያልተገታ *yaltägätta;* (given to excessive drinking) ከመጣን ፡ በላይ ፡ የሚጣጣ *kämä-ṭän bälay yämmiṭäṭṭa*

intend አሰበ *assäbä;* ዐቀደ *aqqädä*

intended (adj.) የታቀደ *yätaqqädä*
be intended (of a remark) ተሰነዘረ *täsänäzzärä*

intense (∼ heat) ኀይለኛ *hayläňňa*

intensify (∼ effort) አጠነከረ *aṭänäk-kärä*

intensity ኀይል *hayl;* (of anger) ግለት *gälät*

intensive በጥንቃቄ ፡ የተደረገ *bäṭänəqqaqe yätädärrägä*

intent (n.) ዓላማ *alama*

intention አሳብ *assab;* ሐሳብ *hassab;* አሳቢነት *assabinnät*

intentionally ሆን ፡ ብሎ *hon bəlo;* ዐውቆ *awqo*

intently በጥንቃቄ *bäṭänəqqaqe*

intercede አማለደ *ammallädä*

intercession አማላጅነት *ammalaǧənnät*

intercessor አማላጅ *ammalaǧ*

interchange (vt.) አለዋወጠ *alläwawwäṭä;* አቀያየረ *aqqäyayyärä*
interchange (vi.) ተለዋወጠ *täläwawwäṭä*

interconnect (vt.) አስተሳሰረ *astäsassärä*
interconnect (vi.) ተገናኘ *tägänaňňä*

interdict ከለከለ *käläkkälä*

interdiction ማገጃ *maggäǧa*

interest (v.) ፍላጎት ፡ አነሣሣ *fəllagot annäsassa;* (of a book) አስደሰተ *asdässätä*
be interested in ወደደ *wäddädä;* ፈለገ *fällägä;* ፍላጎት ፡ አለው *fəllagot alläw;* ዝንባሌ ፡ አለው *zənəbbale alläw*

interest (n.) ፍላጎት *fəllagot;* (hobby) የሚወደው ፡ ነገር *yämmiwäddäw nägär;* (share) ጥቅም *ṭəqəm;* (money paid on a loan) ወለድ *wälläd*
take an interest in በሙሉ ፡ ልብ ፡ ተካፈለ *bämulu ləbb täkaffälä*

interesting የሚያስደስት *yämmiyasdässət;* አስተያየት ፡ የሚስብ *astäyayät yämmisəb*

interfere (meddle) ጣልቃ ፡ ገባ *ṭalqa gäbba*

interim ጊዜያዊ *gizeyawi*
in the interim በመካከሉ *bämäkakkälu*

interior (n.) ውስጥ *wəsṭ*
Ministry of Interior ያገር ፡ ግዛት ፡ ሚኒስቴር *yagär gəzat minister*

interior (adj.) የመሃል *yämähal;* (domestic) ያገር ፡ ውስጥ *yagär wəsṭ*

interject ወርወር ፡ አደረገ *wärwärr adärrägä*

interjection ቃለ ፡ አጋኖ *qalä agganno*

intermarry ተጋባ *tägabba*

intermediary (n.) አስታራቂ *astarraqi*

intermediary (adj.) መካከለኛ *mäkakkä-läňňa*

intermediate መካከል ፡ ያለ *mäkakkäl yallä*

interminable ማለቂያ ፡ የሌለው *maläqiya yälelläw*

intermingle (vt.) አደባለቀ *addäballäqä*
intermingle (vi.) ተደባለቀ *tädäballäqä*

intermission የዕረፍት ፡ ጊዜ *yäəräft gize*
without intermission ያለ ፡ ፋታ *yalä fata*

intermittently አልፎ ፡ አልፎ *alfo alfo*

intern (v.) አስጠበቀ *asṭäbbäqä*

internal የውስጥ *yäwəsṭ;* ውስጣዊ *wəsṭawi*

international ዓለም ፡ አቀፍ *aläm aqqäf*

internist የውስጥ ፡ አካል ፡ ሐኪም *yäwəsṭ akal hakim*

interpret አስተረጐመ *astäräggʷämä;* (∼ a dream) ፈታ *fätta*

interpretation (of a poem) ትርጓሜ *tərgʷame;* ትርጉም *tərgum;* ፍች *fəčč*

interpreter ትርጓማን *tərǧuman;* አስተርጓሚ *astärgʷami*

interrelate አቀናበረ *aqqänabbärä*

interrogate መረመረ märämmärä; ጠያ
የቀ țäyayyäqä

interrogation ምርመራ mərmära

interrogative pronoun መጠይቅ ፡ ተው
ላጠ ፡ ስም mäțäyyəq täwlaṭa səm

interrupt (cut short) አቋረጠ aqqʷarräṭä

interruption ማቋረጥ maqqʷaräṭ
without interruption ሳያቋርጥ sayaqqʷarrəṭ

intersect ተመሳቀለ tämäsaqqälä; ተላለፈ
tälalläfä

intersection መስቀለኛ ፡ መንገድ mäsqä-
länña mängäd; የመንገዶች ፡ መገናኛ
yämängädočč mäggänaňña

intersperse አልፎ ፡ አልፎ ፡ አስቀመጠ
alfo alfo asqämmäṭä

intertwine (vt.) ታታ tatta
intertwine (vi.) ተመሳቀለ tämäsaqqälä; ተጠላለፈ tätälalläfä

interval ዕረፍት əräft
at intervals አልፎ ፡ አልፎ alfo alfo

intervene (intercede) አማለደ ammallädä; (interfere) በመካከል ፡ ገባ bämä-.
kakkäl gäbba; ጣልቃ ፡ ገባ țalqa gäbba

intervention አማላጅነት ammalağənnät;
ገላጋይነት gälagayənnät

interview (v.) የቃል ፡ ጥያቄ ፡ አቀረበ yäqal
țäyyaqe aqärräbä

interview (n.) የቃል ፡ ጥያቄ yäqal țäyyaqe

intestinal የንጀት yanğät

intestine አንጀት anğät

intimacy የቅርብ ፡ ግንኙነት yäqərb
gənəňňunnät

intimate (v.) ጠቆመ țäqqʷämä

intimate, adj. (∼friend) የቅርብ yäqərb;
(∼knowledge) የጠለቀ yäțälläqä; (∼
details) የምስጢር yäməsṭir

intimidate አስፈራራ asfärarra

into ወደ - - - ውስጥ wädä - - - wəsṭ; ወደ
wädä

intolerable (unbearable) የማይቻል yämmayəččal

intolerance አለመቻቻል alämäččačal

intolerant የሚቃወም yämmiqqawwäm;
የማይቀበል yämmayəqqäbbäl; የማይ
ደግፍ yämmayədäggəf

intonation የቃል ፡ አሰባበር yäqal assä-
babär

intone አዜመ azemä; ዘመረ zämmärä

intoxicate አሰከረ asäkkärä

intransigent ሐሳበ ፡ ግትር hassabä gəttər

intransitive የማይሻገር yämmayəššaggär

intrepid ደፋር däffar

intricate (∼idea) የተወሳሰበ yätäwäsassäbä; (∼design) የረቀቀ yäräqqäqä

intrigue, v. (plot) አሴረ aserä; ዶለተ
dollätä; አደመ addämä; ተመሳጠረ tä-
mäsaṭṭärä; (fascinate) ሳበ sabä; ማረከ
marräkä

intrigue (n.) ሴራ sera; ዱለታ duläta

introduce (insert) ከተተ kättätä; አገባ
agäbba; አስገባ asgäbba; (∼ a bill)
አቀረበ aqärräbä; (∼ people) አስተዋ
ወቀ astäwawwäqä

introduction (of a book) መግቢያ mägbiya

introductory የመግቢያ yämägbiya

intrude ጣልቃ ፡ ገባ țalqa gäbba

intrusion (into a residence) መግባት mägbat; (into a conversation) ጣልቃ ፡
ገብነት țalqa gäbbənnät

intrusive ጣልቃ ፡ ገብ țalqa gäbb

intuition ስሜት səmmet

inundate አጥለቀለቀ aṭläqälläqä

invade ወረረ wärrärä

invader ወራሪ wärari

invalid (n.) አካለ ፡ ስንኩል ፡ ሰው akalä
sənkul säw

invalid, adj. (cripple) ስንኩል sənkul;
አካለ ፡ ስንኩል akalä sənkul; አካለ ፡
ጉደሎ akalä gʷädälo

invalid, be (of document) ውድቅ ፡ ሆነ *wədq honä;* አልጸናም *alṣännam*

invalidate ሻረ *šarä*

invaluable በገንዘብ ፡ የማይገኝ *bägänzäb yämmayəggäňň*

invariable የማይለዋወጥ *yämmayəlläwwäṭ*

invasion ወረራ *wärära*

invent (devise something new) ፈለሰፈ *fälässäfä;* ፈለሰመ *fälässämä;* (make up, fabricate) ፈጠረ *fäṭṭärä*

invention (creation) ፍልሰፋ *fəlsäfa;* (something made up) ፈጠራ *fäṭära*

inventor ፈላስፋ *fälasfa;* ፈልሳፊ *fälsafi*

inventory ዝርዝር *zərzər*

inverse ተቃራኒ *täqarani*

inversion ግልብጥ *gəlbəṭ*

invert ገለበጠ *gäläbbäṭä;* (~a glass) ደፋ *däffa*

invest (~money, time) አዋለ *awalä;* (install in office) ሾመ *šomä;* ሹመት ፡ ሰጠ *šumät säṭṭä*

investigate መረመረ *märämmärä*

investigation ምርመራ *mərmära*

investment ገንዘብ ፡ ማዋል *gänzäb mawal*

invigorate አበረታታ *abbärätatta*

invincible የማይበገር *yämmayəbbäggär*

inviolable የማይጣስ *yämmayəṭṭas*

invisible, be አልታየም *altayyäm*

invitation ጥሪ *ṭərri;* ግብዣ *gəbža;* (written permission) የጥሪ ፡ ወረቀት *yäṭrri wäräqät*

invite ጠራ *ṭärra*
invite in ጋባ ፡ አለ *gəba alä*
invite to a meal ጋበዘ *gabbäzä*

invocation ልመና ፡ ማቅረብ *ləmmäna maqräb*

invoice ፋክቱር *faktur*

invoke ለመነ *lämmänä*

involuntarily ያለ ፡ ውዴታ *yalä wəddeta*

involuntary ያለ ፡ ውዴታው ፡ የተደረገ *yalä wəddetaw yätädärrägä*

involve (require) ጠየቀ *ṭäyyäqä*

involved, be ተወሳሰበ *täwäsassäbä*
be involved in ተካፈይ ፡ ሆነ *täkafay honä;* ገባ(በት) *gäbba(bbät)*

inward (adj.) ውስጣዊ *wəsṭawi*
inward (adv.) ወደ ፡ ውስጥ *wädä wəsṭ*

inwardly ውስጥ ፡ ውስጡን *wəsṭ wəsṭun*

irate የተናደደ *yätänaddädä*

ire ቁጣ *quṭṭa*
arouse ire አስቈጣ *asqʷäṭṭa*

irk ቀር ፡ አሰኘ *qərr assäňňä*

irksome የሚያሰለች *yämmiyasäläčč*

iron (v.) ተኰሰ *täkkʷäsä*

iron (metal) ብረት *brät;* (ironing press) ካውያ *kawəyya*
iron ore የብረት ፡ አፈር *yäbrät afär*

ironical የምጸት *yäməṣṣät*

irony ምጸት *məṣṣät*

irrational (~fear) መሠረት ፡ ቢስ *mäsärätä bis*

irreconcilable ዕርቅ የማይገባው *ərq yämmayəgäbaw*

irrefutable የማይካድ *yämmayəkkad*

irregular (not according to rules) ሕግ ፡ ወጥ *həggä wäṭṭ;* ሥርዓትን ፡ ያልተከተላ *sər'atən yaltäkättälä;* ከተለመደው ፡ የወጣ *kätälämmädäw yäwäṭṭa;* (not even) ወጣ ፡ ገባ *wäṭṭa gäbba*

irrelevant, be አግባብነት ፡ የለውም *agbabənnät yälläwəm;* ግንኙነት ፡ የለውም *gənəňňunnät yälläwəm*

irreligious ሃይማኖት ፡ ቢስ *haymanotä bis*

irreplaceable የማይተካ *yämmayəttäkka*

irresistible (~attack) ለመቋቋም ፡ የማ ይቻል *lämäqqʷaqʷam yämmayəččal*

irresolute ወላዋይ *wälaway*

irresponsible (not to be depended upon) እምነቱን ፡ የማይጠብቅ *əmnätun yämmayəṭäbbəq*

irreverent አክብሮት ፡ የጐደለው *akbərot yägʷäddäläw*

irrevocable የማይሻር *yämmayəššar*

irrigate በመስኖ ፡ አጠጣ *bämäsno aṭäṭṭa*

irrigation መስኖ *mäsno*
irrigation channel መስኖ *mäsno;* ቦይ *boy*

irritable ግልፍተኛ *gəlləftäñña;* ብስጩ *bəsə̣čč̣u*
be irritable ተመረረ *tämärrärä;* ቁጣ ፡ ቁጣ ፡ አለ *quṭa quṭa alä;* (of skin) ተቈጣ *täqʷäṭṭa*

irritate አበሳጨ *abbäsaččä;* አናደደ *annaddädä;* (~ the skin) አስቈጣ *asqʷäṭṭa*

is, he ~ (quality) ነው *näw*
there is አለ *allä*
he is not አይደለም *aydälläm*
there is not የለም *yälläm*

Islam እስላም *əslam;* እስላምና *əslamənna*

island ደሴት *däset*

isolate ከሌሎች ፡ ለየ *käleločč läyyä;* ለይቶ ፡ አኖረ *läyyəto anorä*

isolated (adj.) ገለልተኛ *gälältäñña*
be isolated (of sick children) ከሌሎች ፡ ተገለለ *käleločč tägällälä;* (of a military unit) ተነጠለ *tänäṭṭälä*

isolation ለብቻ ፡ መሆን *läbəčča mähon*

issue, v. (distribute) ዐደለ *addälä;* (publish) አወጣ *awäṭṭa*

issue, n. (matter) ጉዳይ *gudday;* (result) ውጤት *wəṭṭet;* (publication) እትም *əttəm;* (descendants) ዘር *zär*

Italian ኢጣልያን *iṭalyan;* ጣልያን *ṭalyan;* (language) ኢጣልያንኛ *iṭalyanəñña*

Italy ኢጣልያ *iṭalya*

itch, v. (of wound) አሳከከ *asakkäkä;* (of shirt) ኮሰኮሰ *kʷäsäkkʷäsä*

itch (n.) እከክ *əkäk*
have an itch አከከ *akkäkä*

item እቃ *əqa;* (piece of news) ወሬ *ware*

itemize ዘረዘረ *zäräzzärä*

itinerant ተዘዋዋሪ *täzäwawari*

itinerary ጉዞ *guzo*

its የሱ *yässu;* የሷ *yässʷa*

itself ብቻውን *bəččawən*
by itself (alone) ራሱን ፡ ችሎ *rasun čəlo*

ivory የዝሆን ፡ ጥርስ *yäzəhon ṭərs*

ivy ሐረግ *haräg*

J

jab ወጋ *wägga*

jack ክሪክ *krik*

jackal ቀበሮ *qäbäro*

jackass ወዳል ፡ አህያ *wädäl ahəyya*

jacket ጃኬት *ǧaket*

jagged (~ coastline) ወጣ ፡ ገባ *wäṭṭa gäbba;* (~ rock) የሾላ *yäšola*

jail (v.) አሰረ *assärä*

jail (n.) እስር ፡ ቤት *əsər bet;* ወህኒ ፡ ቤት *wähni bet*

jam, v. (place forcibly) ወሸቀ *wäššäqä;* (pack tightly) አጨቀ *aččäqä*
be jammed (crowded) ታጣበበ *tätabbäbä;* (of door, gun) ነከሰ *näkkäsä*

jam, n. (preserve) ማርማላታ *marmälata;* (traffic) የመኪና ፡ መጨናነቅ *yämäkina mäččänanäq;* መተፋፈግ *mättäfafäg*

janitor በረኛ *bärräñña;* ጠራጊ *ṭäragi*

January ጥር *ṭərr*

Japan ጃፓን *ǧapan*

jar, vt. (cause to shake) አነቃነቀ *annäqannäqä;* (cause a shock to) ከው ፡ አደረገ *kəww adärrägä*

jar (n.) ማብረጃ *mabräǧa*

jargon ልዩ ፡ ቋንቋ *ləyyu qʷanqʷa*

jaundice የወፍ ፡ በሽታ *yäwäf bäššəta*

jaw አገጭ *agäč*

jawbone መንጋጋ *mängaga*

jealous ቀናተኛ *qännatäňňa*
  be jealous ቀና *qänna*

jealousy ቅናት *qənat*

jeer (v.) አላገጠ *allaggäṭä;* አሾፈ *ašofä*

jeer (n.) የፌዝ : ሣቅ *yäfez saq*

jeopardize (∼ a chance) አጨናገፈ *ač-čänaggäfä;* (∼ one's life) አደጋ : ላይ : ጣለ *adäga lay ṭalä*

jerk በፍጥነት : ጐታ *bäfəṭnät gätta*

jest (v.) ተሳለቀ *täsalläqä;* አፌዘ *afezä*

jest (n.) ቀልድ *qäld;* ፌዝ *fez*

jester አጫዋች *aččawač*

jet (plane) ጄት : አውሮፕላን *ǧet awroplan;* (of water) ቡልቅታ *bulləqta*

Jew አይሁዳዊ *ayhudawi;* ይሁዲ *yəhudi*

jewel የከበረ : ድንጋይ *yäkäbbärä dəngay*

jeweler አንጥረኛ *anṭəräňňa*

jewelry ዕንቊ *ənqʷ;* ጌጣጌጥ *geṭageṭ*

jingle (vt.) አንቃጨለ *anqaččälä*
  jingle (vi.) ተቅጨለጨለ *täqčäläččälä*

jingle (n.) መቃጨል *mäqqaçäl*

job ሥራ *səra*

jobless ሥራ : ፈት *səra fätt*

jocular (∼ person) ቀልደኛ *qäldäňňa;* (∼ reply) የፌዝ *yäfez*

jocund ሣቂታ *saqqitta*

join (vt.) ቀጠለ *qäṭṭälä;* አገጣጠመ *aggäṭaṭṭämä;* (∼ a couple in marriage) አስተሳሰረ *astäsassärä;* (come into the company) አብሮት : ሄደ *abrot hedä*
  join, vi. (become united) ገጠመ *gäṭṭämä;* ተገናኘ *tägänaňňä;* (participate) ተካፈይ : ሆነ *täkafay honä*

joint, n. (of finger, bamboo) ዐጽቅ *aṣq;* አንጓ *angʷa;* (part where two bones join) መገጣጠሚያ *mäggäṭaṭämiya*

joint (adj.) የጋራ *yägara;* የጋሮሽ *yägarəyyoš*

jointly የጋራቸው *yägaraččäw;* ለጋራው *lägaraw*

joke (v.) ቀለደ *qällädä;* ተዋዛ *täwazza;* አፌዘ *afezä*

joke (n.) ቀልድ *qäld;* ዋዛ *waza;* ፌዝ *fez*

joker ቀልደኛ *qäldäňňa*

jolly (∼ person) ደስተኛ *dässətäňňa;* (∼ time) የደስታ *yädässəta*

jolt አንጋጨገጨ *angäčaggäčä*

jot, ∼ down ጻፈ *ṣafä*

journal መጽሔት *mäṣhet;* (diary) ማስታወሻ *mastawäša*

journalist ጋዜጠኛ *gazeṭäňňa*

journey (v.) ተጓዘ *tägʷazä*

journey (n.) ጉዞ *guzo;* መንገድ *mängäd*
  go on a journey ተጓዘ *tägʷazä*

jovial ደስተኛ *dässätäňňa*

joy ደስታ *dässəta*

joyful ደስተኛ *dässətäňňa*

joyous የሚያስደስት *yämmiyasdässət*

jubilant በደስታ : የተዋጠ *bädässəta yätäwaṭä*
  be jubilant ፈነደቀ *fänäddäqä*

jubilation ፈንጠዝያ *fänṭäzəyya*

jubilee ኢዮቤልዩ *iyobelyu*
  Jubilee Palace (የ)ኢዮቤልዩ : ቤተ : መንግሥት *(yä)iyobelyu betä mängəst*

judge (v.) ፈረደ *färrädä;* ፍርድ : ሰጠ *färd säṭṭä;* (think) መሰለ(ው) *mässälä(w);* ተረዳ(ው) *tärädda(w);* (form an opinion) ገመተ *gämmätä*

judge (n.) ዳኛ *daňňa*

judgment ፍርድ *färd;* (opinion) አስተያየት *astäyayät;* (good sense) አስተዋይነት *astäwayənnät*
  render judgment ፈረደ *färrädä*

judicial (∼ system) የዳኝነት *yädaňňənnät;* (∼ reform) የሕግ *yähəgg;* (∼ mind) አመዛዛኝ *ammäzazaň*

judiciary ሕግ : አውጪ *həgg awči*

judicious (∼ remark) ብልህ *bələh;* (∼ person) ምራቁን : የዋጠ *məraqun yäwaṭä;* አመዛዛኝ *ammäzazaň*

jug ማብረጃ *mabräǧa;* ማንቄርቄሪያ *manqʷärqʷäriya*

juice ጭማቂ *čämmaqi*

July ሐምሌ *hamle*

jumble, ~ up አዝበራርቆ ፡ አስቀመጠ *azbärarqo asqämmäṭä*

jumble (n.) ውጥንቅጥ *wäṭənqəṭ*

jump (v.) ዘለለ *zällälä;* (give a sudden start) ደነበረ *dänäbbärä;* (rise suddenly) ተፍ ፡ ብሎ ፡ ተነሣ *täff bəlo tänässa*
jump in ዘሎ ፡ ገባ *zällo gäbba*
jump up ዘለለ *zällälä*

jump (n.) ዝላይ *zəllay*

junction መገናኛ *mäggänaňňa*

juncture መገናኘት *mäggänaňňät*
at this juncture እዚህ ፡ ላይ *əzzih lay*

June ሰኔ *säne*

jungle ጫካ *čakka*

junior የበታች *yäbätačč;* (~ brother) ታናሽ *tannaš*

juniper ጥድ *ṭəd*

junk (n.) እንቶ ፡ ፍንቶ *ənto fənto;* ትርኪ ፡ ምርኪ *tərki mərki*

juridical ሕጋዊ *həggawi*

jurisdiction ሥልጣን *səlṭan*

jurisprudence ሕግ ፡ ፍልስፍና *həggä fəlsəfənna*

jurist የሕግ ፡ ዐዋቂ *yähəgg awaqi*

just, adj. (righteous) ሐቀኛ *haqqäňňa;* ጻድቅ *ṣadəq;* (~ description) ትክክ ለኛ *täkäkkäläňňa*

just, adv. (exactly) ልክ *ləkk;* (barely) ለጥቂት *läṭəqit;* (a moment ago) ልክ ፡ አሁን *ləkk ahun;* (recently) ገና ፡ አሁን *gäna ahun;* (only) ብቻ *bəčča*
just as እንደ *əndä* + perfect
just so (without purpose) ዝም ፡ ብሎ *zəmm bəlo;* እንዲያው *əndiyaw*

justice ፍትሕ *fətəh;* ትክክለኛ ፡ ፍርድ *täkäkkäläňňa fərd*
Minister of Justice የፍርድ ፡ ሚኒስቴር *yäfərd minister*

dispense justice ፈረደ *färrädä*

justify ተገቢ ፡ አስመሰለ *tägäbi asmässälä;* ምክንያት ፡ አድርጎ ፡ አቀረበ *mək nəyat adrəgo aqärräbä*

juvenile የወጣት *yäwäṭṭat;* የወጣት ፡ ልጆች *yäwäṭṭat ləǧočč*

K

keen (~ mind) ንቁ *nəqu;* (~ edge) ስል *səl;* (~ interest) ከፍ ፡ ያለ *käff yalä*

keep (vt.) ያዘ *yazä;* (retain) አስቀመጠ *asqämmäṭä;* (honor, observe) አከበረ *akäbbärä;* (guard) ጠበቀ *ṭäbbäqä;* (~ a secret) ቋጠረ *qʷaṭṭärä;* (~ house) አስተዳደረ *astädaddärä*
keep apart (vi.) ተገለለ *tägällälä;* ነጠ ል ፡ አለ *näṭäll alä*
keep away (vt.) አራቀ *araqä*
keep back ተከላከለ *täkälakkälä;* ወደ ፡ ኋላ ፡ መለሰ *wädä hʷala mälläsä*
keep from ከለከለ *käläkkälä*
keep in አቆየ *aqoyyä*
keep off (vi.) ገለል ፡ አለ *gäläll alä*
keep out (vt.) አስቀረ *asqärrä*
keep out of ከ - - - ራቀ *kä- - -raqä*
keep up ያዘ *yazä*

keeper ዘበኛ *zäbäňňa;* ጠባቂ *ṭäbbaqi*

keeping, be in ~ with ተስማማ *tä smamma;* ገጠመ *gäṭṭämä*

keepsake ማስታወሻ *mastawäša*

kerchief ሻሽ *šaš;* ጉፍታ *gufta*

kernel ፍሬ *färe*

kerosene ነጭ ፡ ጋዝ *näčč gaz*

kerosene lamp ኩራዝ *kurraz*

kettle ማፈያ *mafəya*

key መክፈቻ *mäkfäča;* መፍቻ *mäfča;* ቁልፍ *qulf;* (clue) ፍንጭ *fənč;* (solution) ፍች *fəčč*

keyhole የቁልፍ ፡ ቀዳዳ *yäqulf qädada*

keystone መሠረት *mäsärät*

kick (v.) ረገጠ *räggäṭä*
kick about ተዘዋወረ *täzäwawwärä*

kick (n.) እርግጫ *ərgəčča*

kid ግልገል *gəlgäl;* (child) ሕፃን *həṣan*

kidnap አፍኖ ፡ ወሰደ *affəno wässädä;* (~ a girl to marry her) ጠለፈ *ṭälläfä*

kidney ኩላሊት *kulalit*

kill ገደለ *gäddälä;* (of a disease) ፈጀ *fäǧǧä;* (of frost) አጠፋ *aṭäffa*

killer ገዳይ *gäday*

kilo ኪሎ *kilo*

kilogram ኪሎግራም *kilogram*

kilometer ኪሎሜትር *kilometər*

kin ዘመድ *zämäd;* ቤተ ፡ ዘመድ *betä zämäd*
next of kin የቅርብ ፡ ዘመድ *yäqərb zämäd*

kind (n.) ዓይነት *aynät*
kind of መሳይ *mäsay;* ቢጤ *biṭe*

kind, adj. (~ person) ደግ *dägg;* (~ act) የደግነት *yädäggənnät*

kindhearted ልብ ፡ ቅን *ləbbä qən;* ርኅሩኅ *rəhruh*

kindle (vt.) አነደደ *anäddädä;* (~ anger) ቀሰቀሰ *qäsäqqäsä*
kindle (vi.) ነደደ *näddädä;* (of eyes, with joy) አበራ *abärra*

kindly (adj.) የደግነት *yädäggənnät*

kindly (adv.) በርኅራኄ *bärəhrahe;* (very much) በጣም *bäṭam*

kindness ደግነት *däggənnät*

kindred (n.) ዘመዶች *zämädočč*

kindred (adj.) የተዛመደ *yätäzammädä;* በዝምድና ፡ የተቀራረብ *bäzəmdənna yätäqärarräbä*

king ንጉሥ *nəgus*
become king ነገሠ *näggäsä*

kingdom መንግሥት *mängəst*

kingly የንጉሥ *yänəgus;* ንጉሣዊ *nəgusawi*

kinship ዝምድና *zəmdənna*

kiss (v.) ሳመ *samä*

kitchen ወጥቤት *wäṭbet;* ማድቤት *madbet*

kite ወላንዳ *wälanda*

kitten የድመት ፡ ግልገል *yädəmmät gəlgäl*

knead ለወሰ *läwwäsä;* አቦካ *abokka*

kneading trough ቡሃቃ *buhaqa*

knee ጉልበት *gulbät*
fall on one's knees ተንበረከከ *tänbäräkkäkä*

kneel ተንበረከከ *tänbäräkkäkä*

knife (v.) በቢላ ፡ ወጋ *bäčube wägga*

knife (n.) ቢላ *billa;* ቢላዋ *billawa*

knit ሠራ *särra*

knob እጀታ *əǧǧäta*

knock (vt.) መታ *mätta*
knock (vi.) በሩን ፡ አንኳኳ *bärrun ankʷakkʷa;* (of engine) ጮኸ *čohä*
knock down መቶ ፡ ጣለ *mätto ṭalä;* (destroy) አፈረሰ *afärräsä*
be knocked out በጣም ፡ ደከመ *bäṭam däkkämä*

knockout መዘረር *mäzzärär*

knoll ጉብታ *gubbəta*

knot (v.) ቋጠረ *qʷaṭṭärä*

knot (n.) ቋጠሮ *qʷaṭäro*
make (tie) a knot ቋጠረ *qʷaṭṭärä*

knotty (~ board) ዓይን ፡ የበዛበት *ayn yäbäzzabbät;* (~ problem) በጣም ፡ አስቸጋሪ *bäṭam asčäggari*

know ዐወቀ *awwäqä;* (recognize) ለየ *läyyä*
I wouldn't know እንጃ *ənǧa*

knowingly ዐውቆ *awqo*

knowledge ዕውቀት *əwqät;* ዐዋቂነት *awaqinnät*
come to one's knowledge ሰማ *sämma*

knowledgeable ዐዋቂ *awaqi*

known ዕውቅ *əwəq*

knuckle ዐጽቅ aṣq

L

label (n.) ምልክት mələkkət

labor, v. (work) ሠራ särra; ለፋ läffa; (exert effort) ጣረ ṭarä

labor (n.) ሥራ sara; የጉልበት ፡ ዋጋ yä-gulbät waga; የሙያተኛ ፡ ዋጋ yämu-yatäñña waga; (effort) ልፋት ləfat; ጥረት ṭärät; (childbirth) ምጥ məṭ

laboratory ቤት ፡ ሙከራ betä mukkära

laborer ሙያተኛ muyatäñña; ሠራተኛ särratäñña

laborious ትጉህ təguh; (~ job) አድካሚ adkami

labor pains ምጥ məṭ; የምጥ ፡ ሕመም yä-məṭ həmäm
have labor pains አማጠ(ች) amaṭä(čč)

lacerate ሰነተረ sänättärä; ቧጠጠ bʷaṭ-ṭäṭä

lack (v.) ቸገረ čäggärä; አጣ aṭṭa

lack (n.) እጥረት əṭrät; እጦት əṭot; ጉድለት gudlät

lacking, be አጣ aṭṭa; ጠፋ ṭäffa
he is lacking in ጉደለው gʷäddäläw; አነሰው annäsäw

ladder መሰላል mäsälal

ladle (v.), ~ out ጨለፋ čälläfä

ladle (n.) ጭልፋ čəlfa

lady ሴት set; ወይዘሮ wäyzäro
ladies ከቡራት kəburat
lady of the house ባለቤት baläbet; እመቤት əmmäbet

lag (v.) ወደ ፡ ኋላ ፡ ቀረ wädä hʷala qärrä

lag, n. (distance) መራራቅ märraraq

lair ጐሬ gʷäre

laity ምእመናን mə'əmänan

lake ሐይቅ hayq

lamb የበግ ፡ ጠቦት yäbäg ṭäbbot

lame (~ leg) ሽባ šəba; (~ man) አን ካሳ ankassa
be lame አነከሰ anäkkäsä

lament (v.) አለቀሰ aläqqäsä; (regret) አዘነ azzänä

lament (n.) ለቅሶ läqso; ልቅሶ ləqso; የሐ ዘን ፡ እንጉርጉሮ yähazän əngurgurro

lamentable በጣም ፡ የሚያሳዝን bäṭam yäm-miyasazzən

lamentation ለቅሶ läqso; ልቅሶ ləqso

lamp መብራት mäbrat; ፋኖስ fanos

lance ጦር ṭor

land (vt.) አሳረፈ asarräfä
land (vi.) አረፈ arräfä; (of passengers) ከመርከብ ፡ ወረደ kämärkäb wär-rädä

land (n.) ምድር mədər; (country) አገር agär; (soil) መሬት märet; (property) ርስት rəst; (dry land) የብስ yäbs

landholder ባለመሬት balämäret

landholding የመሬት ፡ አያያዝ yämäret ayyayaz

landlady ባለቤት baläbet

landlord የቤት ፡ ጌታ yäbet geta

landmark ምልክት mələkkət; (important event) ትልቅ ፡ ምዕራፍ təlləq mə'əraf

landowner ባለመሬት balämäret; ባለርስት balärəst; ርስተኛ rəstäñña

landslide (of earth or rock) ናዳ nada

land tenure የመሬት ፡ ይዞታ yämäret yə-zota

lane የእግር ፡ መንገድ yäəgər mängäd; ጠባብ ፡ መንገድ ṭäbbab mängäd

language ቋንቋ qʷanqʷa

languish (in prison) ማቀቀ maqqäqä
languish for ናፈቀ(ው) naffäqä(w)

lantern ፋኖስ fanos

lap (v.), ~ up ላስ ፡ አደረገ lass adärrägä

lap (n.) ጭን čən

lapel ኰሌታ *kolletta*

lapse, v. (fall into disuse) ተረሳ *tärässa*; (end) አለቀ *alläqä*

larceny ሌብነት *lebənnät*; ስርቆት *sərqot*

large ትልቅ *təlləq*; (~ house) ሰፊ *säffi*; (~ man) ግዙፍ *gəzuf*; (~ family) ብዙ *bəzu*

largely በጠቅላላው *bäṭäqlallaw*

larynx ማንቁርት *manqurt*

lash (v.) ገረፈ *gärräfä*

lash (n.) ጅራፍ *ğəraf*

lassitude ድካም *dəkam*; መታከት *mätakät*

last (v.) ቆየ *qoyyä*; ዘለቀ *zälläqä*; (of clothes) በረከተ *bäräkkätä*

last (adj.) የመጨረሻ *yämäčärräša*

last (adv.) ከሁሉ ፡ መጨረሻ *kähullu mäčärräša*; በመጨረሻ *bämäčärräša* at last በመጨረሻ *bämäčärräša*

lasting ዘላቂ *zälaqi*; የዘለዓለም *yäzälä'aläm*

lastly በመጨረሻ *bämäčärräša*

latch መወርወሪያ *mäwärwäriya*

late (adj.) የመጨረሻ *yämäčärräša*; (no longer living) ሟች *mʷač*
late (adv.) ቆይቶ *qoyyəto*; ዘግይቶ *zägəyto*
it is late (in the morning) ረፈደ *räffädä*; (in the evening) መሸ *mässä*
he is late (in the morning) አረፈደ *aräffädä*; (in the evening) አመሸ *amässä*
be late in coming ዘግይቶ ፡ መጣ *zägəyto mäṭṭa*

lately ሰሞኑን *sämonun*; በቅርቡ *bäqərbu*; ከቅርብ ፡ ጊዜ ፡ ወዲህ *käqərb gize wädih*

later (adv.) ቆይቶ *qoyyəto*; ኋላ *hʷala*
later on ቀጥሎ *qäṭṭəlo*; ወደፊት *wädäfit*; በኋላ *bähʷala*; ከዚያ ፡ በኋላ *käzziya bähʷala*

latest የመጨረሻ *yämäčärräša*; ከቅርቡ ፡ የወጣ *käqərbu yäwäṭṭa*

at the latest ቢዘገይ ፡ ቢዘገይ *bizägäyy bizägäyy*

lather (n.) የሳሙና ፡ አረፋ *yäsamuna aräfa*

latitude (in relation to equator) ኬትሮ ንስ *ketrons*; (freedom of judgment) የሐሳብ ፡ ነጻነት *yähassab näṣannät*

latrine የሰገራ ፡ ቤት *yäsägära bet*; ሽንት፡ ቤት *šənt bet*

laugh ሳቀ *saqä*
laugh at ተሳለቀ *tässälläqä*

laughable አሳቂኝ *assäqiñ*

laughing stock መሳለቂያ *mässaläqiya*

laughter ሳቅ *saq*
burst into laughter ከት ፡ ብሎ ፡ ሳቀ *kätt bəlo saqä*

launch (~ a business) ከፈተ *käffätä*; (~ an attack) ጀመረ *ğämmärä*; (~ a spear) ወረወረ *wäräwwärä*

laundry (clothes) የታጠበ ፡ ልብስ *yätaṭṭäbä ləbs*; (place) ልብስ ፡ አጣቢ ፡ ቤት *ləbs aṭabi bet*; የልብስ ፡ ንጽሕና ፡ መ ስሪ *yäləbs nəṣhənna mäsča*

lavatory የመጸዳጃ ፡ ከፍል *yämäṣṣädaǧa kəfəl*

lavish (adj.) አባካኝ *abakaň*

law ሕግ *həgg*; ፍትሕ *fətəh*; (practice of law) የጥብቅና ፡ ሥራ *yäṭəbqənna səra*; (rules) ደንብ *dänb*
practice law በሕግ ፡ ሥራ ፡ ተሰማራ *bähəgg səra täsämarra*

law court ፍርድ ፡ ቤት *fərd bet*; ችሎት *čəlot*

lawful ሕጋዊ *həggawi*

lawless (~ country) ሕግ ፡ የለሽ *həgg yälläš*; (~ person) ሕግ ፡ የሚጥስ *həgg yämmiṭəs*

lawlessness ሕጓ ፡ ወጥነት *həggä wäṭṭənnät*

lawn የግቢ ፡ መስክ *yägəbbi mäsk*

lawsuit ሙግት *muggət*

lawyer (attorney) ጠበቃ *ṭäbäqa*; (trained in law) የሕግ ፡ ዐዋቂ *yähəgg awaqi* lax (in work) ግድ ፡ የለሽ gədd yälläš; (not strict) ልል ləl be lax ላላ lalla

laxative የሚያስቀምጥ ፡ መድኃኒት yämmiyasqämməṭ mädhanit

lay (v.) አስቀመጠ asqämmäṭä; (~ eggs) ጣለ ṭalä; (~ plans) አወጣ awäṭṭa
lay aside (store) ቄጠበ qʷäṭṭäbä
lay down, vt. (to sleep) አስተኛ astäňňa; (~ rules) አወጣ awäṭṭa; (~ arms) አስረከበ asräkkäbä
lay off ቀነሰ qännäsä
lay open አጋለጠ aggalläṭä

lay (adj.) የተራ ፡ ሰው yätära säw

layer (of sand) ደለል däläl

layman (not an expert) ተራ ፡ ሰው tära säw; (not a clergyman) ማ,ሃይም mähayyəm; መሃይምን mähayyəmən

layout አቀማመጥ aqqämamäṭ

laziness ስንፍና sənfənna

lazy ሰነፍ sänäf; (slow moving) ዝግተኛ zəggətäňňa

lead, v. (guide) መራ märra; (be first) ቀደም qäddämä; (~ a horse) ሳበ sabä; (of a way) አስኪደ askedä
lead toward (a place) አመራ amärra

lead (n., rhymes with 'bead') ቀዳሚነት qädaminnät; (clue) ፍንጭ fənč
take the lead ቀደም qäddämä; ቀዳሚነት ፡ ያዘ qädaminnät yazä

lead (n., rhymes with 'dead') እርሳስ ərsas

leader መሪ märi; (chief) አለቃ aläqa

leadership መሪነት märinnät

leading (~ thought) ዐቢይ abiy; (~ scientist) አውራ awra

leading article ርእስ ፡ አንቀጽ rə'əsä anqäṣ; ዐቢይ ፡ ጽሑፍ abiy ṣəhuf

leaf ቅጠል qəṭäl

leaflet ጽሑፍ ṣəhuf

league ማኅበር mahbär

League of Nations የዓለም ፡ መንግሥታት፡

ማኅበር yäaläm mängəstat mahbär

leak, v. (of pot) አፈሰሰ afässäsä; (of ship) ውኃ ፡ አስገባ wəha asgäbba; (of tire) ተነፈሰ tänäffäsä
leak out (of water) ተጠባጠበ tänṭäbaṭṭäbä; (of a secret) ተሰራጨ täsäraččä

leak (n.) ቀዳዳ qädada; የሚያፈስ ፡ ቀዳዳ yämmiyafäss qädada

lean, v. (slant) ዘመመ zämmämä; (show preference) አዘነበለ azänäbbälä; (rest against) ተደገፈ tädäggäfä; ተጠጋ täṭägga
lean backwards ወደ ፡ ኋላ ፡ ደገፍ ፡ አለ wädä hʷala dägäff alä
lean forward እንገቱን ፡ ብቅ ፡ አደረገ angätun bəqq adärrägä
lean on ተደገፈ tädäggäfä
lean to one side አጋደለ agaddälä
lean out ተጠለጠለ tänṭäläṭṭälä

lean (adj.) ቀጭን qäččən; (~ meat) ጉፋያ gufayya

leap (v.) ዘለለ zällälä

leap (n.) ዝላይ zəllay

leap year ዘመነ ፡ ዮሐንስ zämänä yohannəs

learn ተማረ tämarä; (become informed) ዐወቀ awwäqä; (hear) ሰማ sämma
learn by heart በቃል ፡ ያዘ bäqal yazä

learned (~ person) የተማረ yätämarä; ሊቅ liq; ምሁር məhur

learner ጀማሪ ğämmari

learning ትምህርት təmhərt; (knowledge) ዐዋቂነት awaqinnät

lease (v.) ተከራየ täkärayyä

lease (n.) ክራይ kəray; ኪራይ kiray; (contract) ኮንትራት kontrat

leash (n.) ማሰሪያ masäriya
hold in leash (~ temper) ጋታ gätta

least, at ~ (at the lowest estimate) ቢያ ንስ biyans; (at any rate) ባይሆን bayhon
not in the least በፍጹም bäfəṣṣum

the least ከሁሉ ፡ አነስተኛ *kähullu a-nästäñña*
not the least ፈጽሞ *fäṣṣəmo*

leather ቆዳ *qoda*

leave (vt.) ተወ *täwä;* አስቀረ *asqärrä;*
(~ a job) ለቀቀ *läqqäqä;* (~ home)
ተለየ *täläyyä;* (bequeath) አወረሰ
awärräsä
leave (vi.) ሄደ *hedä;* (of train) ተነሳ
tänässa
leave alone ተወ *täwä*
leave out አስቀረ *asqärrä*

leave, n. (permission) ፈቃድ *fäqad;*
(period of time of permission) ስን
ብት *sənbət*
take leave of one another ተሰናበተ
täsänabbätä

leaven እርሾ *əršo*

lecture ንግግር *nəgəggər*
deliver (give) a lecture ንግግር፡ አደረገ
nəgəggər adärrägä

lecturer ተናጋሪ *tänagari*

ledger መዝገብ *mäzgäb*

leech እልቅት *əlqət*

lees አተላ *atäla*

left (direction) ግራ *gra*

left, be ~ (remain) ቀረ *qärrä;* ተረፈ
tärräfä

left-handed ግራኝ *grañň*

leftover ተራፊ *tərrafi;* የተረፈ ፡ ምግብ
yätärräfä məgəb

leg እግር *əgər*

legacy ቅርስ *qərs*

legal የሕግ *yähəgg;* ሕጋዊ *həggawi;* ሕግ፡
የተከተለ *həgg yätäkättälä;* (~ advisor) የሕግ *yähəgg*

legality ሕጋዊነት *həggawinnät*

legalize ሕጋዊ ፡ አደረገ *həggawi adärrägä*

legation ለጋሲዮን *lägasiyon*

legend አፈ ፡ ታሪክ *afä tarik;*(inscription)
ጽሑፍ *ṣəhuf*

legible የሚነበብ *yämminnäbbäb*

legion ክፍለ ፡ ጦር *käflä ṭor*

legislate ሕግ ፡ አወጣ *həgg awäṭṭa*

legislation ሕግ *həgg;* (enacting of laws)
ሕግ ፡ ማውጣት *həgg mawṭat*

legislative የሕግ *yähəgg*

legislator ሕግ ፡ አውጪ *həgg awči*

legislature የሕግ ፡ አውጪ ፡ ክፍል *yähəgg
awči käfəl*

legitimate ሕጋዊ *həggawi;* (born in wed-lock) ከሕግ ፡ ጋብቻ ፡ የተገኘ *kähəgg
gabəčča yätägäňňä;* (reasonable) በቂ
bäqi

leisure ትርፍ ፡ ጊዜ *tərf gize*

leisurely (adv.) በርጋታ *bärgata;* በዝግታ
bäzəggəta

lemon ሎሚ *lomi*

lend (~ money) አበደረ *abäddärä;* (~
objects) ተዋሰ *täwasä*

length ርዝመት *rəzmät*
at length በሰፊው *bäsäffiw*

lengthen አረዘመ *aräzzämä*

lengthy ረዥም *räžžim;* ረጅም *räǧǧim*

lengthwise ቁም ፡ ለቁም *qum läqum*

lenience ልልነት *lələnnät*

leniency ርህራሄ *rəhrahe*

lenient ልል *ləl*

Lent ሁዳዴ *hudade;* ኩዳዴ *kudade*

lentil ምስር *məssər*

leopard ነብር *näbər*

leper ለምጣም *lämṭam;* ቄማጣ *qʷämaṭa*

leprosy ለምጥ *lämṭ;* ቁምጥና *qumṭənna*

less (adj.) ያነሰ *yannäsä*

less (adv.) ያነሰ *yannäsä*
be less አነሰ *annäsä*

lessen ቀነሰ *qännäsä;* አሳነሰ *asannäsä*

lesser አነስተኛ *anästäñña*

lesson ትምህርት *təmhərt*
give lessons አስተማረ *astämarä*

let (permit) ፈቀደ fäqqädä; (lease) አከ
ራየ akkärayyä
let by አሳለፈ asalläfä
let down አወረደ awärrädä
let go ለቀቀ läqqäqä; ተወ täwä
let in አስገባ asgäbba
let off አወረደ awärrädä; (allow to go
free) ለቀቀ läqqäqä
let out ለቀቀ läqqäqä; (~ a secret)
አወጣ awäṭṭa
let through አሳለፈ asalläfä
let up (of storm) በረድ ፡ አለ bärädd
alä; (of rain) ጋብ ፡ አለ gabb alä

letter ደብዳቤ däbdabbe; (of alphabet)
ፊደል fidäl
letters (literature), see 'literature'

letter box የፖስታ ፡ ማጠራቀሚያ ፡ ሣጥን
yäposta maṭṭäraqämiya saṭən

lettuce ሰላጣ sälaṭa

level (v.) አስተካከለ astäkakkälä; ደለደለ
däläddälä; (raze) አወደመ awäddämä;
(~ criticism) ሰነዘረ sänäzzärä
level off ደለደለ däläddälä

level, n. (position, rank) ደረጃ däräǧa

level (adj.) ደልዳላ däldalla; ጠፍጣፋ ṭäfṭaffa; ለጥ ፡ ያለ läṭṭ yalä
be level ተስተካከለ tästäkakkälä

lexicon መዝገብ ፡ ቃላት mäzgäbä qalat

liability (responsibility) ኃላፊነት halafinnät; (hindrance) መሰናክል mäsänakəl
liabilities (financial) ወጪና ፡ ኪሳራ
wäčinna kisara

liable ተጠያቂ täṭäyyaqi
be liable to ስ sə + negative imperfect + አይቀርም ayqärəm (e.g. he is liable to forget ሳይረሳ፡ አይቀርም saya-
räsa ayqärəm)

liar ዋሾ wašo; ውሸታም wəšätam; ውሽ
ተኛ wəšätäñña

libel (v.) አማ amma

libel (n.) ስም ፡ ማጥፋት səm maṭfat; የስም ፡
ማጥፋት ፡ ወንጀል yäsəm maṭfat wänǧäl

liberal (generous) ለጋስ läggas; (tolerant) የማይቃረን yämmayəqqarrän; (~

donation) በርከት ፡ ያለ bärkätt yalä

liberate ነጻ ፡ አወጣ näṣa awäṭṭa

liberty ነጻነት näṣannät; (privileges)
መብት mäbt

librarian ዐቃቤ ፡ መጻሕፍት aqqabe mäṣaḥəft

library ቤተ ፡ መጻሕፍት betä mäṣaḥəft

license (permission) የፈቃድ ፡ ወረቀት yäfäqad wäräqät

license plate ሰሌዳ säleda; ታርጋ targa

lick ላሰ lasä; (~ a stamp) በምላስ ፡ አረ
ጠበ bäməlas aräṭṭäbä

lid እፊያ əffiya; ክዳን kədan; መክደኛ
mäkdäñña

lie, v. (say a lie) ዋሸ waššä

lie (n.) ውሸት wəšät; ሐሰት hassät

lie, v. (be in a resting position) ተጋደመ
tägaddämä; (be situated, exist) ተገኘ
tägäññä; ነው näw
lie back ተንጋለለ tängallälä
lie down ተጋደመ tägaddämä

lieutenant (የ)መቶ፡ አለቃ (yä)mäto aläqa

life ሕይወት həywät; (way of living) ኑሮ
nuro; (biography) የሕይወት ፡ ታሪክ
yähəywät tarik; (movement, animation) እንቅስቃሴ ənqəssəqase; (energy,
vitality) ንቃት nəqat
bring to life አነቃቃ annäqaqqa
for life ዕድሜ ፡ ልኩን ədme ləkkun
lose one's life ሞተ motä
take (one's) life ራሱን ፡ ገደለ rasun
gäddälä
way of life አኗኗር annʷanʷar

life belt የመንሳፈፊያ ፡ ትጥቅ yämänsa-
fäfiya təṭq

life imprisonment የዕድሜ ፡ ልክ ፡ እስራት
yäädme ləkk əssərat

life insurance የሕይወት ፡ ዋስትና yähəywät wastənna

lifelong የዕድሜ ፡ ልክ yäädme ləkk

lifetime ዕድሜ ədme

lift (v.) አነሣ anässa; (~ the voice) ከፍ ፡

አደረገ *käff adärrägä;* (∼ the spirit)
አነቃቃ *annäqaqqa*
be lifted (of boycott) አበቃ *abäqqa;*
(of restrictions) ተሰረዘ *täsärräzä*
lift up አነሣ *anässa;* (∼ one's eyes)
ቀና ፡ አደረገ *qäna adärrägä*

lift (n.), see 'elevator'

light, vt. (∼ a lamp) አበራ *abärra;* (∼
a pipe, cigarette) ለኰሰ *läkkʷäsä;*
(∼ a fire) አያያዘ *ayyayazä;* አነዳደ *a-
näddädä;* (∼ a match) ጫረ *čarä*
light up (vt.) አበራ *abärra;* ብርሃን ፡
ሰጠ *bärhan sättä*
light up, vi. (of face) ፈካ *fäkka;* (of
eyes) ቁልጭ ፡ አለ *qulläčč alä*

light (n.) ብርሃን *bärhan;* (lamp) መብራት
mäbrat; (match) ክብሪት *kəbrit*
bring to light አስገኘ *asgäññä*
come to light ተገኘ *tägäññä*
put on the light መብራት ፡ አበራ *mäbrat abärra*
put out the light መብራት ፡ አጠፋ *mäbrat aṭäffa*

light, adj. ቀላል *qällal;* (∼ coat) ሰስ
səs; (∼ food) ቀለል ፡ ያለ *qäläll yalä;*
(∼ sentence) አነስ ፡ ያለ *anäss yalä;*
(∼ color) ብሩህ *bəruh*
be light (weight) ቀለለ *qällälä;* (to
see) ብርሃን ፡ ነበረ *bärhan näbbärä*

lighten, vt. (∼ a load) ቀነሰ *qännäsä;*
(∼ a problem) አቃለለ *aqqallälä*
lighten, vi. (of sky) ጠራ *ṭärra;* (of
face) ፈካ *fäkka;* (of lightning) በረቀ
bärräqä; ተብለጨለጨ *täbläčälläčä*

lighter (for cigarettes) ማቀጣጠያ *maqqäṭaṭäya*
lighthearted ግድ ፡ የሌለው *gädd yälelläw*
lighting ብርሃን *bärhan*
lightly (gently) ቀስ ፡ ብሎ *qäss bälo*
lightning መብረቅ *mäbräq*
light switch ማብሪያ *mabriya*
like (vt.) ወደደ *wäddädä;* ፈለገ *fällägä*
like (prep.) እንደ *əndä*
like this እንዲህ *əndih;* እንዲህም *əndi-*
ham; እንዲሁም *əndihum;* እንደዚህ *əndäzzih*
be like መሰለ *mässälä;* ተመሳሰለ *tämäsassälä*
look like መሰለ *mässälä*

likely, adj. (probable) ሊሆን ፡ የሚችል
lihon yämmičäl; (suitable) ምቹ *mäčču*

liken መሰለ *mässälä*

likeness ምሳል *məsəl;* መመሳሰል *mämmäsasäl*

likewise እንዲሁ *əndihu;* እንዲህም *əndi-
ham;* እንደዚሁ *əndäzzihu*

liking, have a ∼ for ወደደ *wäddädä*

limb(s) እጅና ፡ እግር *əǧǧənna əgər;*
(branch) ቅርንጫፍ *qərənčaf*

lime (citrus fruit) ሎሚ *lomi;* (chemical
compound) ኖራ *nora*

limit (v.) ወሰነ *wässänä*

limit, n. (measure) ልክ *ləkk;* መጠን *mäṭän*
limits (frontier) ክልል *kəlləl;* ወሰን
wäsän
within limits በመጠኑ *bämäṭänu*

limited (adj.) የተወሰነ *yätäwässänä*
be limited ወሰን ፡ አለው *wäsän alläw;*
ገደብ ፡ አለው *gädäb alläw*

limitless ወሰን ፡ የሌለው *wäsän yälelläw*

limp (v.) አነከሰ *anäkkäsä*

limp, adj. (∼ cardboard) ላፈስፈስ *ləfəsfəs;* (∼ collar) የተሻሸ *yätäšaššä*
go limp ተዝለፈለፈ *täzläfälläfä*

limpid (∼ water) የጠራ *yäṭärra*

line (v.) አሰመረ *asämmärä*
be lined (of face) ተጨማደደ *täčämaddädä*
line up (vt.) አሰለፈ *assälläfä*

line (n.) መሥመር *mäsmär;* (telephone
∼) የስልክ ፡ መሥመር *yäsəlk mäsmär;*
(row) ረድፍ *rädəf;* (row of persons)
ሰልፍ *sälf;* (descent) ዘር *zär;* (∼ in
poetry) ሐረግ *haräg;* (clothes ∼) ሽቦ
šəbo

all along the line መ·ሉ ፡ በመ·ሉ *mulu bämulu*
form a line ተሰለፈ *täsälläfä*
in line with በ - - - መሠረት *bä - - - mäsärät*

lineage ዘር *zär*

linen (cloth) ሊኖ *lino;* (~ of bed) ያልጋ፡ ልብስ *yalga ləbs*

liner ትልቅ ፡ መርከብ *təlləq märkäb*

linger, ~ about ወዲያ ፡ ወዲህ ፡ አለ *wädiya wädih alä*

linguist የቋንቋ ፡ ዐዋቂ *yäqʷanqʷa awaqi*

lining ገበር *gäbär*

link (v.) አቀናበረ *aqqänabbärä;* አስተሳሰረ *astäsassärä;* አያያዘ *ayyayazä*

link (n.) ማያያዣ *mayayaža*

linseed ተልባ *tälba;* ጥጥ ፡ ፍሬ *ṭəṭ färe*

lion አንበሳ *anbässa*

lip ከንፈር *känfär;* (of cup) አፍ *af*

lipstick የከንፈር ፡ ቀለም *yäkänfär qäläm*

liquefy (vt.) አቀለጠ *aqälläṭä*
liquefy (vi.) ቀለጠ *qälläṭä*

liquid (n.) ፈሳሽ ፡ ነገር *fäsaš nägär*

liquid (adj.) ፈሳሽ *fäsaš*

liquor መጠጥ *mäṭäṭṭ;* አልኮል *alkol*

lisp ተኮላተፈ *täkʷälattäfä*

list (v.) ዘረዘረ *zäräzzärä;* በዝርዝር ፡ ጻፈ *bäzərzər ṣafä*

list (n.) ዝርዝር *zərzər*

listen ሰማ *sämma;* አዳመጠ *addammäṭä*
listen attentively ልብ ፡ ብሎ ፡ አዳመጠ *ləbb bəlo addammäṭä*

listener አድማጭ *admač*

liter ሊተር *litär;* ሊትር *litər;* ሊትሮ *litro*

literacy መጻፍና ፡ ማንበብ *mäṣafənna manbäb*
literacy campaign ተምሮ ፡ ማስተማር *tämro mastämar;* የፊደል ፡ ሰራዊት *yäfidäl särawit*

literally ቃል ፡ በቃል *qal bäqal*

literary የሥነ ፡ ጽሑፍ *yäsənä ṣəhuf*

literate የተማረ *yätämarä*

literature ሥነ ፡ ጽሑፍ *sənä ṣəhuf*

litigant ነጋርተኛ *nägärtäñña*

litigate ተሟገተ *tämʷaggätä*

litigation ሙግት *muggət*

litigious ተሟጋች *tämʷagač*

litter (v.) አቆሻሸ *aqošššäsä;* ረፈረፈ *räfärräfä*
be littered up ተዝረከረከ *täzräkärräkä*

litter, n. (scraps scattered about) ቆሻሻ *qošaša;* ውዳቂ *wəddaqi;* (cot) ቃሬዛ *qareza;* (young born at one time) ግል ገሎች *gəlgäločč*

little ጥቂት *ṭəqit;* (small) ትንሽ *tənnəš;* (unimportant)የማይረባ *yämmayəräba;* አነስተኛ *anästäñña*
a little ትንሽ *tənnəš*
little by little ቀስ ፡ በቀስ *qäss bäqäss;* እያደር *əyyaddär*

liturgy ቅዳሴ *qəddase;* የቤተ ፡ ክርስቲያን ፡ ሥነ ፡ ሥርዓት *yäbetä krəstiyan sənä sər'at*

live (v.) ኖረ *norä;* (maintain oneself) ተዳደረ *tädaddärä*

live (adj.) ነፍስ ፡ ያለው *näfs yalläw*

livelihood መተዳደሪያ *mättädadäriya;* ትዳር *tədar*

lively (alert) ንቁ *nəqu;* (~ party, color) ደማቅ *dämmaq;* (cheerful) ሞቅ ፡ ያለ *moqq yalä;* (~ interest) ከፍ ፡ ያለ *käff yalä*

liven አደመቀ *adämmäqä*
liven up (vi.) ነቃ ፡ አለ *näqa alä*

liver ጉበት *gubbät*

livestock ከብት *käbt*

living (n.) ኑሮ *nuro;* (way of life) አኗኗር *annʷanʷar*
make (earn) a living ተዳደረ *tädaddärä;* ሥርቶ ፡ አደረ *särto addärä*

living (adj.) ሕያው *həyaw;* በሕይወት ፡ ያለ *bähəywät yallä;* (~ language) የሚ ሡ

ራቤት yämmissärrabbät

living conditions የኑሮ ፡ ሁኔታ yänuro huneta

living costs የኑሮ ፡ ውድነት yänuro wəddənnät

living quarters መኖሪያ mänoriya

living room ሳሎን salon

lizard እንሽላሊት ənšəlalit

load (vt.) ጫነ čanä; (~ a gun) አጓረሰ ag^wärräsä

load (n.) ሸከም šäkəm; ጭነት čənät
loads of መዓት mä'at
put on a load አሽከመ aššäkkämä

loaf (v.) በዘነ bozzänä; አውደለደለ awdäläddälä

loaf (n.), ~ of bread ዳቦ dabbo

loafer ሥራ ፡ ፈት səra fätt

loan (v.), see 'lend'

loan, n. (of money) ብድር bəddər; (of objects) መዋስ mäwas

loanword (የ)ትውስት ፡ ቃል (yä)təwəst qal

loathe አንገሸገሸ(ው) angäšäggäšä(w); ተጠየፈ täṭäyyäfä; ተጸየፈ täṣäyyäfä

lobby መተላለፊያ mättälaläfiya

local ያገር ፡ ውስጥ yagär wəsṭ; (~ injury) ባንድ ፡ ቦታ ፡ ላይ ፡ የሆነ band bota lay yähonä

locality ቀበሌ qäbäle

locate (find) ፈልጎ ፡ አገኘ fälləgo agäññä; ደረሰ(በት) därräsä(bbät)
be located ተገኘ tägäññä

location አቀማመጥ aqqämamäṭ

lock (vt.) ቈለፈ q^wälläfä
lock (vi.) ተቈለፈ täq^wälläfä
be locked out ተዘጋ(በት) täzägga(bbät)

lock (n.) መቈለፊያ ፡ ጋን mäq^wälläfiya gan; የቁልፍ ፡ ጋን yäqulf gan; (~ of hair) ዘለላ zäläla
lock, stock and barrel እንዳለ ənḋallä

locker ሣጥን saṭən

locksmith ቁልፍ ፡ ሠራተኛ qulf särratäñña

locomotive ባቡር babur

locust አንበጣ anbäṭa

lodge (vt.) አኖረ anorä; (~ a complaint) አቀረበ aqärräbä
lodge (vi.) ኖረ norä; ሰነበተ sänäbbätä

lodge (n.) የማረፊያ ፡ ጎጆ yämaräfiya goǧǧo

lodger ተከራይ täkäray

lodging መኖሪያ mänoriya; ማደሪያ madäriya

loft ቆጥ qoṭ

lofty ከፍተኛ käffətäñña; (~ manner) ሞቅ ፡ ያለ moqq yalä

log, v. (fell and remove timber) መነጠረ mänäṭṭärä; (enter in the record book) በማስታወሻ ፡ ደብተር ፡ ጻፈ bämastawäša däbtär ṣafä

log, n. (trunk of tree) ግንድ gənd; (record book) ማስታወሻ ፡ ደብተር mastawäša däbtär

logic (sound reasoning) ምርምር mərəmmər; (way of reasoning) አስተሳሰብ astäsasäb; (science of ~) ሎጂክ loǧik

loin ወገብ wägäb

loiter ተንቀዋለለ tänqäwallälä

lone ብቸኛ bəččäñña

loneliness ብቸኝነት bəččäññannät

lonely (~ life) የብቸኝነት yäbəččäññannät; (~ road) ጭር ፡ ያለ čärr yalä; ገለልተኛ gälältäñña

lonesome ብቸኛ bəččäñña
be lonesome for ናፈቀ naffäqä
feel lonesome ብቸኝነት ፡ ተሰማ(ው) bəččäññannät täsämma(w)

long (v.) ጓጓ g^wagg^wa

long (adj.) ረጂም räǧǧim; ረገም räžžim
be long ረዘመ räzzämä

long (adv.) ብዙ ፡ ጊዜ bəzu gize

long ago ድሮ *dəro;* ከብዙ ፡ ጊዜ ፡ በፊት
käbəzu gize bäfit
a long time ብዙ ፡ ጊዜ *bəzu gize*
a long time ago ከብዙ ፡ ጊዜ ፡ በፊት
käbəzu gize bäfit
all day long ቀኑን ፡ ሙሉ *qänun mulu*
how long? ምን ፡ ያህል ፡ ጊዜ *mən yahəl gize*

longing ጉጉት *guggut;* ናፍቆት *nafqot*

longitude ኬክሮስ *kekros*

look (v.) ተመለከተ *tämäläkkätä;* አየ *ayyä;* (appear) መሰለ *mässälä*
look after (watch) ጠበቀ *ṭäbbäqä;*
(follow with the eyes) ባይን ፡ ተከተለ
bayn täkättälä
look alike ተመሳሰለ *tämäsassälä*
look around (search) ዞሮ ፡ ፈለገ *zoro
fällägä*
look at ተመለከተ *tämäläkkätä;* አየ
ayyä; (examine) መረመረ *märämmärä*
look back መለስ ፡ ብሎ ፡ አየ *mäläss
bəlo ayyä*
look for ፈለገ *fällägä*
look into መረመረ *märämmärä*
look like መሰለ *mässälä*
look out ወደ ፡ ውጭ ፡ አየ ፡ (ተመለ
ከተ) *wädä wəčč ayyä (tämäläkkätä)*
look out! ተጠንቀቅ *täṭänqäq*
look through (search) ፈተሸ *fättäšä*
look up (~ words) ተመለከተ *tämäläkkätä;* ፈለገ *fällägä*

look (n.) መልክ *mälk*
looks መልክ *mälk*
have a look አየ *ayyä*

loom (n.) የሸማኔ ፡ እቃ *yäšämmane əqa*

loophole (opening) ቀዳዳ *qädada;*
(means of evasion) ማምለጫ ፡ መንገድ
mamläča mängäd

loose, v. (untie, unfasten) ለቀቀ *läqqäqä;*
(relax) ላላ ፡ አደረገ *lala adärrägä*

loose, adj. (free, not attached) ልቅ *ləqq;*
(~ soil) ልል *ləl;* (~ conduct) ልክስ
ክስ *ləkəskəs;* (~ translation) በጣም ፡
የማይቃረብ *bäṭam yämmayəqqarräb*
be loose ላላ *lalla*

cut loose ቈረጠ *qʷärräṭä*
get loose አመለጠ *amälläṭä;* ጠፋ *ṭäffa*
let (turn) loose ለቀቀ *läqqäqä*

loosen (vt.) አላላ *alalla;* (~ soil) አለሰ
ለሰ *aläsälläsä*
loosen (vi.) ላላ *lalla*

loot (v.) ዘረፈ *zärräfä*

loot (n.) ምርኮ *mərko;* የዘረፈው *yäzär-
räfäw*

lopsided, be አጋደለ *agaddälä*

loquacious ለፍላፊ *läflafi;* ቀባጣሪ *qäba-
ṭari*

lord ጌታ *geta;* (ruler) ሹም *šum;* ፈላጭ ፡
ቈራጭ *fälač qʷärač*

lore ወግ *wäg*

lorry የጭነት ፡ መኪና *yäčənät mäkina*

lose አጣ *aṭṭa;* ጠፋ(በት) *ṭäffa(bbät);*
(waste) አጠፋ *aṭäffa;* (~ the way) ሳተ
satä; (~ the game, in a fight) ተሸ
ነፈ *täšännäfä;* (~ a lawsuit) ተረታ
tärätta
lose (one's) hair ተመለጠ *tämälläṭä*
lose money ከሰረ *kässärä*

loss እጦት *əṭot;* ጥፋት *ṭäfat;* ማጣት *maṭat;* (~ in business, ~ in money)
ኪሳራ *kisara*
be at a loss ግራ ፡ ገባ(ው) *gra gäbba(w)*

lost (adj.) የጠፋ *yäṭäffa;* (~ time) የባ
ከነ *yäbakkänä;* (~ battle) ድል ፡ የሆ
ነበት *dəl yähonäbbät*
be lost ጠፋ *ṭäffa;* (~ in thought)
ተዋጠ *täwaṭä*

lot (piece of ground) መሬት *märet;*
(fate) ዕድል *əddəl;* እጣ *əṭa*
lots of ብዙ *bəzu*
a lot በጣም *bäṭam*
quite a lot ብዙ *bəzu*
cast (draw) lots እጣ ፡ ጣለ *əṭa ṭalä*

lotion ቅባት *qəbat*

lottery ሎተሪ *lotäri*

loud (~ voice) ጉልህ *guləh;* ከፍ ፡ ያለ
käff yalä; (~ laughter) ጮኽ ፡ ያለ
čoh yalä; (~ person) የሚንጫጫ *yäm-*

minčačča; (~ color) ደማቅ *dämmaq*

loudly ጮኸ ፡ ብሎ *čok bəlo*

loudspeaker የድምፅ ፡ ማጕሊያ *yädəmṣ magʷliya*; ድምፅ ፡ ማጕ*ya* dəmṣ magʷya

lounge የእንግዳ ፡ ማረፊያ *yängəda maräfiya*

louse ቅማል *qəmal*

love (v.) ወደደ *wäddädä*

love (n.) ፍቅር *fəqər*
fall in love ፍቅር ፡ ያዘው *fəqər yazäw*

lovely ደስ ፡ የሚል *däss yämmil*; አስደ ሳች *asdässač*

lover ወዳጅ *wädaǧ*; ፍቅረኛ *fəqräñña*

low, adj. (~ mark, ~ position) ዝቅተኛ *zəqqətäñña*; (~ voice) ቀሰስተኛ *qäsästäñña*; ዝቅ ፡ ያለ *zəqq yalä*
low (adv.) ዝቅ ፡ ብሎ *zəqq bəlo*
be low ዝቅ ፡ አለ *zəqq alä*; (of sun) አዘቀዘቀ *azäqäzzäqä*
feel low ከፋ(ው) *käffa(w)*

low country ቆላ *qʷälla*

lower, v. (let descend) አወረደ *awärrädä*; ዝቅ ፡ አደረገ *zəqq adärrägä*; (reduce) ቀነሰ *qännäsä*

lower (adj.) ታችኛ *taččəñña*; (in office) የበታች *yäbätačč*; (~ price) ያነሰ *yannäsä*

lowland ቆላ *qʷälla*

lowly (~ person) ከተራ ፡ የተወለደ *kätära yätäwällädä*; (~ occupation) ወራዳ *wärrada*

loyal ታማኝ *tammaññ*
be loyal ታመነ *tammänä*

loyalty ታማኝነት *tammaññənnät*

lucid (~ lake) የጠራ *yäṭärra*; (~ explanation) ግልጽ *gəlṣ*

luck ዕድል *əddəl*; ገድ *gädd*
good luck! ይቅናህ *yəqnah*

luckily ደግነቱ *däggənnätu*

lucky ዕድለኛ *əddəläñña*
be lucky ዐደለ *addälä*

lucrative ትርፍ ፡ ያለበት *tərf yalläbbät*

luggage ጓዝ *gʷaz*

lukewarm (~ water) ለብ ፡ ያለ *läbb yalä*; (~ reception) ቀዝቃዛ *qäzqazza*

lull እሹሩሩ ፡ አለ *əššururu alä*

lullaby እሹሩሩ *əššururu*

lumber ሳንቃ *sanqa*

luminous (~ room) ብርሃን ፡ የበዛበት *bərhan yäbäzzabbät*; (~ eyes) ብሩህ *bəruh*

lump, vt. (put together) አጠቃለለ *aṭṭäqallälä*
lump, vi. (form into a lump) ጐጐለ *gʷaggʷälä*

lump, n. (of clay) ጐል *gʷal*; (of sugar) አንኳር *ankʷar*; (swelling) እብጠት *əbṭät*
lump sum ባንዴ *bande*; በጠቅላላው *bäṭäqlallaw*

lumpy, be ~ (flour) ጐጐለ *gʷaggʷälä*

lunar የጨረቃ *yäčäräqa*

lunatic እብድ *əbd*

lunch (v.) ምሳ ፡ በላ *məsa bälla*

lunch (n.) ምሳ *məsa*

lung ሳምባ *samba*; ሳንባ *sanba*

lure (v.), ~ into አግባባ *agbabba*; አታሎ ፡ አስገባ *attallo asgäbba*

lurk አደባ *adäbba*; አደፈጠ *adäffäṭä*

luscious ጣፋጭ *ṭafač*

lush (~ grass) ለምለም *lämläm*

lust (for power) ከፍተኛ ፡ ጉጉት *käffə täñña guggut*

luster (of pearls) ማንጸባረቅ *manṣäbaräq*; (of eyes) ድምቀት *dəmqät*

luxurious ምቾትና ፡ ውበት ፡ ያለው *məččotənna wəbät yalläw*

luxury ምቾት *məččot*; ድሎት *dəlot*

lyre ክራር *krar*

M

machine መኪና mäkina

machine gun መትረየስ mäträyyäs

mad እብድ əbd
be mad (crazy) አበደ abbädä; (angry) ጦፋ ṭofä
be mad at ተናደደ tänaddädä

madam ወይዘሮ wäyzäro

madden (cause to become insane) አሳ
በደ asabbädä; (enrage) አናደደ annaddädä

madness እብደት əbdät

magazine (storehouse) መጋዘን mägazän; (publication) መጽሔት mäşhet

magic (n.) መተት mätät; አስማት asmat;
ጥንቈላ ṭənqʷäla; (beauty, charm)
ውበት wəbät

magician ጠንቋይ ṭänqʷay; ቃልቻ qaləčča; አስማተኛ asmatäňña

magnanimity ለጋስነት läggasənnät

magnanimous (generous in forgiving)
ይቅር ፡ ባይ yəqər bay; (kind) ቸር čär

magnet ማግኔት magnet

magnificent ዕጹብ ፡ ድንቅ əşub dənq; አስ
ደናቂ asdännaqi; ግሩም gərum

magnify (make appear larger) አጐላ
agʷälla; አጐልቶ ፡ አሳየ agʷälto asayyä; (exaggerate) አጋነነ aggannänä

magnifying glass ማጉሊያ ፡ መነጽር magʷ-liya mänäşşər

magnitude (size) መጠን mäṭän; (importance) ከፍተኛነት käffətäňňannät

maid ገረድ gäräd

mail (v.) በፖስታ ፡ ላከ bäposta lakä

mail (n.) ፖስታ posta

mail box የፖስታ ፡ ማጠራቀሚያ ፡ ሣጥን
yäposta maṭṭäraqämiya saṭən

mailman ፖስተኛ postäňña

maimed አካለ ፡ ጐደሎ akalä gʷädälo

main (n.), in the~ አብዛኛውን ፡ ጊዜ ab-zaňňawən gize

main (adj.) ዋና wanna

mainland የብስ yäbs

mainly አብዛኛውን ፡ ጊዜ abzaňňawən
gize; ይበልጡን yəbälṭun

maintain (~ a family) አስተዳደረ astä-daddärä; (~ a road) በሚገባ ፡ ጠበቀ
bämmiggäbba ṭäbbäqä; (~ security)
አስከበረ askäbbärä

maintenance (means of support) መተዳ
ደሪያ mättädadäriya

maize የባሕር ፡ ማሽላ yäbahər mašəlla;
በቆሎ bäqqollo

majestic ባለግርማ balägərma; ግርማዊ
gərmawi

majesty (of scenery) ግርማ gərma; (of
a person) ሞገስ mogäs; ግርማ gərma

Majesty, His ~ ግርማዊነታቸው gərma-winnätaččäw
Your Majesty! ግርማዊ ፡ ሆይ gərma-wi hoy; ግርማዊነትዎ gərmawinnätwo

major, n. (in the army) ሻለቃ šaläqa

major (adj.) ዋና wanna; (~ problem)
ከፍ ፡ ያለ käff yalä; (~ war) ትልቅ
təlləq

majority አብዛኞች abzaňňočč; (through
vote) የድምፅ ፡ ብልጫ yädəmş bəlča

make ሠራ särra; አደረገ adärrägä; (earn)
አገኘ agäňňä
make out (understand) ገባ(ው) gäb-ba(w); (see clearly) ለየ läyyä
make up (invent) ፈጠረ fäṭṭärä; (~
a sentence) ሠራ särra; (~ a prescrip-tion) አዘጋጀ azzägaǧǧä
make up with ታረቀ tarräqä

make (n.) ዓይነት aynät

makeup (physical constitution) አቋም
aqʷam; (cosmetics) መኳኳያ mäkkʷakʷaya

malady በሽታ bäššəta

malaria ወባ wäba

male ወንድ wänd; ተባት täbat; ተባዕት
täba'ət; (of animals) አውራ awra

malediction እርግማን ərgəman

malice ተንኮል tänkʷäl

malicious (∼ person) ተንኮለኛ tänkʷäläňňa; (∼ remark) ተንኮል ፣ ያዘለ
tänkʷäl yazzälä

malign (v.) አማ amma

malignant (∼growth) አደገኛ adägäňňa

malt ብቅል bəqəl

man ሰው säw; (male) ወንድ wänd; (husband) ባል bal; (soldier) ወታደር wättaddär
any man ማንም mannəm

manage (vt.) አካሄደ akkahedä; አስተዳ
ደረ astädaddärä; (be able to) ቻለ čalä
manage (vi.) ተዳደረ tädaddärä

management (control, administration)
አመራር ammärar; አስተዳደር astädadär; (those in charge of a business)
አስተዳዳሪዎች astädadariwočč

manager አስተዳዳሪ astädadari; ሥራ ፣
አስኪያጅ sara askiyağ

mandatory የግዴታ yägəddeta

mane ጋማ gamma; (of lion) ጐፈር gʷäfär

maneuvers (of army) ልምምድ ləməmməd

manger ግርግም gərgəm

manhood (adulthood) አካለ ፣ መጠን akalä mäṭän; (manly qualities) ወንድነት
wändənnät

manifest (v.) ገለጸ gälläṣä

manifest (adj.) ግልጽ gəlṣ

manifestation መግለጫ mägläča

manifold (diverse) ልዩ ፣ ልዩ ləyyu ləyyu

manipulate (operate with hands) አንቀ
ሰቀሰ anqäsäqqäsä; (twist to one's
advantage) አማታ ammatta

mankind ሰው säw; የሰው ፣ ልጅ yäsäw
ləğ

manly ወንዳ ፣ ወንድ wända wänd

man-made ሰው ፣ ሠራሽ säw särraš

manner ሁኔታ huneta; ጠባይ ṭäbay; ዓይ
ነት aynät
manners ልማድ ləmad; ባህል bahəl
bad manners ብልግና bəlgənna; መጥ
ፎ ፣ ምግባር mäṭfo məgbar
good manners ጥሩ ፣ ጠባይ ṭäru ṭäbay

mannerly ጨዋ čäwa

manpower ሰው säw

manslaughter ነፍስ ፣ ገዳይነት näfsä gädayənnät

manual (n.) መምሪያ mämriya

manual, adj. (∼skill) የጅ yäğğ; (∼
labor) የጉልበት yägulbät

manufacture (v.) ሠራ särra; (invent)
ፈጠረ fäṭṭärä

manufacturer ባለ ፣ ፋብሪካ balä fabrika

manure ፍግ fəg

manuscript የብራና ፣ መጽሐፍ yäbəranna
mäṣhaf; የእጅ ፣ ጽሑፍ yäğğ ṣəhuf

many ብዙ bəzu; አያሌ ayyale
a great many ብዙ bəzu

map (n.) ካርታ karta

mar (v.) አበላሸ abbälaššä

marble እብነ ፣ በረድ əbnä bäräd

march (v.) ተሰልፎ ፣ ተጓዘ täsälfo tägʷazä; በሰልፍ ፣ ሄደ bäsälf hedä

march (n.) ጉዞ guzo

March መጋቢት mäggabit

mare ባዝራ bazra

margin ኅዳግ həddag
by a narrow margin ለጥቂት läṭəqit

marine (n.) መርከቦች märkäbočč

marine (adj.) የባሕር yäbahər

marital የጋብቻ yägabəčča; የባል yäbal

maritime (~ law) የባሕር yäbahər; (~ district) የባሕር ፡ አዋሳኝ yäbahər awwasañ

mark (v.) ምልክት ፡ አደረገ(በት) mələkkət adärrägä(bbät); (~ examination papers) አረመ arrämä

mark (n.) ምልክት mələkkət; (target) ዒላማ ilama
marks ውጤት wəṭṭet

marked, adj. (clear) ጉልህ guləh; (having a mark) ምልክት ፡ የተደረገበት mələkkət yätädärrägäbbät

marker ምልክት mələkkət

market (n.) ገበያ gäbäya

marketplace ገበያ gäbäya

marmalade ማርመላታ marmälata

marriage ጋብቻ gabəčča; (married life) ትዳር tədar
give in marriage ዳረ dara

married, adj. (~ man) ያገባ yagäbba; (~ woman) የተዳረች yätädaräčč; ያገ ባች yagäbbačč
be married አገባ agäbba
married couple ባለትዳር balätədar
married life ትዳር tədar
newly married ሙሽራ mušərra
newly married couple ሙሽሮች mušärročč

marrow ቅልጥም qəlṭəm

marry (vt.) አገባ agäbba; (give in marriage) ዳረ dara
marry (vi.) አገባ agäbba; (of woman) ባል ፡ አገባች bal agäbbačč

marsh ረግረግ rägräg

marshland ረግረግ ፡ ስፍራ rägräg səfra

martial law ወታደራዊ ፡ ሕግ wättaddärawi həgg

martyr ሰማዕት säma'ət

martyrdom ሰማዕትነት säma'ətənnät

marvel (v.), ~ at ተደነቀ tädännäqä

marvel (n.) ታምር tammər; ተአምር tä-'ammər; ድንቅ dənq

marvelous ድንቅ dənq; ግሩም gərum
be marvelous ደነቀ dännäqä

masculine (n.) ተባዕታይ ፡ ጾታ täba'ətay ṣota

masculine (adj.) የወንድ yäwänd; (in grammar) ተባዕታይ täba'ətay

mash, v. (~ potatoes) ፈጨ fäčča; (~ chickpeas) ለነቀጠ länäqqäṭä

mask (v.) ደበቀ däbbäqä; (~ the face) እንዳይታወቅ ፡ ሸፈነ əndayəttawwäq šäffänä

mask (n.) ሽፋን šäfan

mason አናጢ anaṭi; አናጺ anaṣi; ገምቢ gämbi; ግምበኛ gəmbäňňa

masonry የግምበኝነት ፡ ሥራ yägəmbäňňännät səra

mass (vt.) ሰበሰበ säbässäbä
mass (vi.) ተሰበሰበ täsäbässäbä

mass, n. (large number) ከምር kəmmər; ብዛት bəzat
masses ተራ ፡ ሕዝብ tära həzb

Mass ቅዳሴ qəddase
celebrate Mass ቀደሰ qäddäsä
attend Mass አስቀደሰ asqäddäsä

massacre (v.) ጨደለ gäddälä

massacre (n.) እልቂት əlqit; ፍጅት fəǧǧət

massage (v.) አሸ aššä

massage (n.) መታሸት mättašät

massive (bulky) ግዙፍ gəzuf; (imposing, abundant) ከፍ ፡ ያለ käff yalä; ብዙ bəzu

mast የመርከብ ፡ ምሰሶ yämärkäb məsässo

master, v. (become an expert) ጠንቀቆ ፡ ዐወቀ ṭänqəqo awwäqä

master (n.) ጌታ geta; ጋዥ gäži; (teacher) መምህር mämhər

masterful (domineering) ሥልጣን ፡ የተ

መላበት *səlṭan yätämällabbät;* (expert) ጥበብ ፡ የተመላበት *ṭəbäb yätämällabbät*

masterly የጠቢ.ብ *yäṭäbib*

mastery (skill) ችሎታ *čəlota;* (domination) የበላይነት *yäbälayənnät*

masticate አኘከ *aňňäkä;* አላመጠ *allammäṭä*

mat (n.) ምንጣፍ *mənṭaf*

match (v.) ተመሳሳይ ፡ ሆነ *tämäsasay honä;* ተመሳሰለ *tämäsassälä;* ገጠመ *gäṭṭämä*

match, n. (giving flame) ክብሪት *kəbrit;* (looking alike) ተመሳሳይ *tämäsasay;* (competition) ግጥሚያ *gəṭmiya;* (marriage) ጋብቻ *gabəčča*

mate, v. (of animals) ታጠቀ *taṭṭäqä;* ሰረረ *särrärä*

mate, n. (companion) ጓደኛ *gʷaddäňňa;* (husband or wife) የትዳር ፡ ጓደኛ *yätədar gʷaddäňňa*

material, n. (fabric) ጨርቅ *čärq*

material, adj. (not spiritual) ዓለማዊ *alämawi;* (relating to the body) ሥጋዊ *səgawi;* (important) ጠቃሚ *ṭäqami*

materialize (vt.) ክፍጻሜ ፡ አደረሰ *käfəṣṣame adärräsä*
materialize (vi.) በሥራ ፡ ላይ ፡ ዋለ *bäsəra lay walä*

maternal (motherly) የናት *yännat;* (on the mother's side) በናት ፡ በኩል *bännat bäkkul*

maternity ወላድ ፡ መሆን *wällad mähon*

mathematician የሒሳብ ፡ ዐዋቂ *yähisab awaqi*

mathematics ሒሳብ *hisab*

matrimony ጋብቻ *gabəčča*

matter, v. (be of importance) አስፈላጊ ፡ ነው *asfällagi näw*
it does not matter ግድ ፡ የለም *gədd yälläm*
what does it matter to me? ምን ፡

ቸገረኝ *mən čäggäräňň*

matter (n.) ነገር *nägär;* ጉዳይ *gudday*
as a matter of fact እንዲያውም *əndiyawəm*
in the matter of በ - - - በኩል *bä - - - bäkkul*
no matter what ምንም ፡ ብ *mənəm bə* + imperfect

mattress ፍራሽ *färaš*

mature, vi. (of person) ጎለመሰ *gʷälämmäsä;* (of fruit) በሰለ *bässälä;* (of a plan) ተዓወላ *tämʷalla*

mature, adj. (~mind) የበሰለ *yäbässälä;* (~ age) የጉልምስና *yägulməsənna;* (~ person) ዐዋቂ *awaqi*

maturity (of man) ዕቅም ፡ አዳም *aqmä addam;* (of woman) ዕቅም ፡ ሔዋን *aqmä hewan*
reach maturity, see 'mature' (v.)

maxim ምሳሌ *məssale*

maximum (n.) መጨረሻ *mäčärräša*

maximum (adj.) ከፍተኛ *käffətäňňa*

May ግንቦት *gənbot*

may, expressed by the jussive

maybe ምናልባት *mənalbat*

mayor (of Addis Ababa) ክንቲባ *käntiba;* (of another city) የማዘጋጃ ፡ ቤት ፡ ሹም *yämazzägağa bet šum*

me እኔን *ənen;* or suffix pronoun

mead ጠጅ *ṭäğğ*

meadow መስክ *mäsk*

meager (~ face) የተጎሳቀለ *yätägʷäsaqqʷälä;* (~meal) የማያጠግብ *yämmayaṭägəb;* (~ resources) እጅግም *əğğəgəm*

meal ምግብ *məgəb*

mean, v. (intend) አሰበ *assäbä;* ፈለገ *fällägä;* (signify, denote) ማለት ፡ ነው *malät näw;* (be a sign of) ምልክት ፡ ነው *mələkkət näw*
mean nothing ከምንም ፡ አይቈጠረውም *kämənəm ayqʷäṭräwəm*

mean (n.) አማካኝ ፡ ሐሳብ *ammakaň has-sab*
means (way) መንገድ *mängäd;* (pos-sibilities, wealth) አቅም *aqəm*
by all means በምንም ፡ አኳኋን *bämə-nəm akkʷahʷan*
by means of በ *bä*
by no means በምንም ፡ ዓይነት *bämə-nəm aynät* + negative verb
man of means ባለጸጋ *baläṣägga*

mean, adj. (base, petty) ወራዳ *wärradda;*
(unkind) አስከፊ *askäffi;* (~ dog) ተናካሽ *tänakaš;* (intermediate) መሃከለኛ *mähakkäläňňa;* መካከለኛ *mäkakkä-läňňa;* አማካይ *ammakay*
of mean quality መናኛ *mänaňňa*

meaning ፍች *fəčč;* ትርጉም *tərgum*

meaningful ትርጉም ፡ ያለው *tərgum yal-läw*

meaningless ትርጉም ፡ የሌለው *tərgum yälelläw;* ዋጋ ፡ የሌለው *waga yälelläw*

meantime, in the ~ በማሁሉ *bämähalu;* እስከዚያ ፡ ድረስ *əskäzziya däräs*
for the meantime ለጊዜው *lägizew*

meanwhile እስከዚያ ፡ ድረስ *əskäzziya däräs*

measles ኩፍኝ *kuffəňň*

measure (v.) ለካ *läkka;* (~ grain) ሰፈረ *säffärä;* (~ land) ቀየሰ *qäyyäsä*

measure (n.) ልክ *ləkk;* (unit of meas-uring length) መለኪያ *mäläkkiya;*
(unit of measuring liquids, sugar) መስፈሪያ *mäsfäriya;* (bill) ሕግ *həgg;*
(step) እርምጃ *ərməǧǧa*
beyond measure ከመጠን ፡ በላይ *kä-mäṭän bälay*
in some measure በመጠኑ *bämäṭänu*

measurements ልክ *ləkk*

meat ሥጋ *səga;* (essence) ፍሬ ፡ ነገር *fre nägär*

meaty ሥጋ ፡ የበዛበት *səga yäbäzzabbät*

mechanic መካኒክ *mäkanik*

mechanism መሣሪያ *mässariya*

medal ሜዳይ *meday;* ሽልማት *šälləmat;* ኒሻን *nišan*

meddle ገባ (በት) *gäbba(bbät);* ጣልቃ ፡ ገባ *ṭalqa gäbba*

medial መሃከለኛ *mähakkäläňňa;* መካ ለኛ *mäkakkäläňňa*

mediate ባስታራቂነት ፡ ገባ *bastaraqinnät gäbba*

mediator አማላጅ *ammalaǧ;* አማካይ *am-makay*

medical (~ school) የሕክምና *yähək-mənna;* (~ profession) የሐኪምነት *yähakimənnät;* (~ examination) የጤና *yäṭena;* (~ bulletin) የጤንነት *yäṭe-nənnät*

medicine (drug) መድኃኒት *mädhanit;*
(study of ~) ሕክምና *həkmənna*

medieval የመካከለኛ ፡ ዘመን *yämäkak-käläňňa zämän*

mediocre ተራ *tära*

meditate አሰበ *assäbä;* አወጣ ፡ አወረደ *awäṭṭa awärrädä*

medium (n.) ዘዴ *zäde*
through the medium of በ *bä*

medium (adj.) መካከለኛ *mäkakkäläňňa*

medium-sized መጠነኛ *mäṭänäňňa*

meek የዋህ *yäwwah;* ጐር *gär*

meet (vt.) አገኘ *agäňňä;* (get acquaint-ed) ተዋወቀ *täwawwäqä;* (~ an obli-gation) ፈጸመ *fäṣṣämä*
meet (vi.) ተገናኘ *tägänaňňä;* (assem-ble) ተሰበሰበ *täsäbässäbä;* (to op-pose in competition) ተጋጠመ *tägaṭ-ṭämä*

meeting ስብሰባ *säbsäba;* ጉባኤ *guba'e*
hold a meeting ስብሰባ ፡ አደረገ *säb-säba adärrägä*

melancholy ትካዜ *täkkaze*

mellow, adj. (~ tone) ለዛ ፡ ያለው *läzza yalläw*

melodious ለዛ ፡ ያለው *läzza yalläw*

melody ዜፈን *zäfän;* ዜማ *zema*

melon ሐብሐብ *habhab*

melt, vt. (～ butter, gold) አቀለጠ *aqällätä;* አነጠረ *anäṭṭärä;* (～ sugar in water) አሟሟ *amʷammʷa*

melt, vi. (of butter) ቀለጠ *qällätä;* (of sugar) ሟሟ *mʷammʷa*

member (of body) እጅና ፡ እግር *əǧǧənna əgər;* (of a group) አባል *abal*

membership አባልነት *abalənnät*

memento መታሰቢያ *mättasäbiya*

memoirs የሕይወት ፡ ታሪክ *yähəywät tarik*

memorial (n.) መታሰቢያ ፡ ሐውልት *mättasäbiya hawəlt*
memorial (adj.) የመታሰቢያ *yämättasäbiya*
memorial service የመታሰቢያ ፡ ጸሎት *yämättasäbiya ṣälot*

memorandum ማስታወሻ *mastawäša*

memorize በቃል ፡ አጠና *bäqal aṭänna*

memory (power of remembering) የማስ ታወስ ፡ ችሎታ *yämastawäs čəlota;* (recollection) ትዝታ *təzzəta* from memory በቃሉ *bäqalu* in memory of ለ - - - መታሰቢያ *lä - - - mättasäbiya*

menace (v.) አሰጋ *asägga;* (threaten) ዛተ *zatä*

menace (n.) ዛቻ *začčä*

mend (～ shirt) ጠቀመ *ṭäqqämä;* (～ behavior) አሻሻለ *aššašalä*

menses አደፍ *adäf*

menstruate አደፈ(ች) *addäfä(čč);* አደፍ ፡ ወረዳት *adäf wärrädat*

menstruation አደፍ *adäf*

mental የአእምሮ *yäʾməro*
mental institution የአእምሮ ፡ በሽተ ኞች ፡ ሐኪም ፡ ቤት *yäʾməro bäššä-täňňočč hakim bet*

mentality አስተሳሰብ *astäsasäb;* የአእምሮ ፡ ችሎታ *yäʾməro čəlota*

mention, v. (～ a matter) አነሣ *anässa;* ተናገረ *tänaggärä*

don't mention it! ምንም ፡ አይደል *mə-nəmm aydäll*

menu የምግብ ፡ ዝርዝር *yäməgəb zərzər*

mercenary ቅጥር ፡ ወታደር *qəṭər wät-taddär*

merchandise ሽቀጣ ፡ ሽቀጥ *šäqäṭa šäqäṭ*

merchant ነጋዴ *näggade*

merciful መሃሪ *mähari;* ርኅሩኅ *rəhruh* be merciful ራራ *rarra;* ምሕረት ፡ አለው *məhrät alläw*

merciless ጨካኝ *čäkkaň*

mercury ባዜቃ *bazeqa*

mercy ምሕረት *məhrät* have mercy ማረ *mara*

merely ብቻ *bäčča;* ዝም ፡ ብሎ *zəmm bəlo;* እንዲያው *əndiyaw*

merge, vt. (～ companies) አዋሐደ *aw-wahadä* merge (vi.) ተቀላቀለ *täqälaqqälä;* ተዋ ሐደ *täwahadä;* (of traffic) ተጋጠመ *tägaṭṭämä*

merit (v.) ተገባ(ው) *tägäbba(w)*

merit (n.) መልካም ፡ ሥራ *mälkam səra;* መልካም ፡ ተግባር *mälkam tägbar*

meritorious አስመስጋኝ *asmäsgaň;* ዝና ፡ የሚያተርፍ *zənna yämmiyatärf*

merriment ቡረቃ *burräqa;* ደስታ *dässəta*

merry ደስተኛ *dässətäňňa* Merry Christmas! እንኳን ፡ ለብርሃነ ፡ ልደት ፡ አደረሰህ *ənkʷan läbərhanä lədät adärräsäh* (sg. masc.)

mess (v.), ～ around ተንጎዳጎደ *tän-gʷädaggʷädä* mess up አቃወሰ *aqqawwäsä;* አዘባረቀ *azzäbarräqä*

mess (n.) ቆሻሻ *qošaša;* (disorder) ምስ ቅልቅል *məsqəlqəl;* ውጥንቅጥ *wəṭən-qəṭ;* ዝብርቅርቅ *zəbrəqrəq;* (trouble) ጣጣ *ṭaṭa;* (for soldiers, officers) ምግብ ፡ ቤት *məgəb bet*

message መልእክት *mälʾəkt*

messenger ተላላኪ. tälalaki; መልእክተኛ mäl'əktäñña

messy (~ room) ዝርክርክ zərəkrək; (~ situation) የተበላሸ yätäbälaššä

metal (n.) ብረት brät

metal (adj.) ከብረት ፣ የተሠራ käbrät yätäsärra

metal worker አንጥረኛ anṭräñña

meteor በራሪ ፣ ኮከብ bärari kokäb

meter (unit of measure) ሜትር metər; (measuring instrument) ቴጣሪ qʷäṭari; (in poetry) ምጣኔ məṭṭane

method ዘዴ zäde; መንገድ mängäd

methodical ሥርዓት ፣ ያለው sər'at yalläw; ዘዴ ፣ ያለው zäde yalläw

meticulous ጥንቁቅ ṭənquq

microbe ረቂቅ ነፍሳት räqiq näfsat

microphone ድምፅ፡ማጉያ dəmṣ magʷya

microscope የማጉያ ፣ መነጽር yämagʷya mänäṣṣər

midday ቀትር qätər; እኩለ ፣ ቀን əkkulä qän

middle (n.) መሃል mähal; መካከል mäkakkäl; መሃከል mähakkäl; መንፈቅ mänfäq; አጋማሽ aggamaš
right in the middle መሃል ፣ ለመሃል mähal lämähal

middle (adj.) መሃከለኛ mähakkäläñña; መካከለኛ mäkakkäläñña

middle-aged ጠና ፣ ያለ ṭäna yalä

Middle Ages መካከለኛ ፣ ዘመን mäkakkäläñña zämän

Middle East መካከለኛ ፣ ምሥራቅ mäkakkäläñña məsraq

middleman ደላላ dällala

midget ድንክ dənk

midnight እኩለ ፣ ሌሊት əkkulä lelit

midst, in the ~ of በ - - - መሃከል bä - - - mähakkäl

midwife አዋላጅ awwalağ

might (n.) ኃይል hayl; ጉልበት gulbät

mightily በጣም bäṭam

mighty (adj.) ኃይለኛ hayläñña; (important) ታላቅ tallaq

migrant ተዘዋዋሪ täzäwawari

migrate ፈለሰ fälläsä

migration ከቦታ ፣ ወደ ፣ ቦታ ፣ መዘዋወር käbota wädä bota mäzzäwawär

mild (~ person) ጎር gär; (~ light) ቀላል qällal; (~ tobacco, drink) ለስላሳ läslassa; (~ climate) መካከለኛ mäkakkäläñña

mildew ሻጋታ šagata

mile ማይል mayl

military (n.) የጦር ፣ ሰራዊት yäṭor särawit

military (adj.) የጦር yäṭor; የጦር ፣ ኃይል yäṭor hayl; የወታደር yäwättaddär; ወታደራዊ wättaddärawi

milk (v.) አለበ alläbä

milk (n.) ወተት wätät

mill (v.) ፈጨ fäččä
mill about ተተረማመሰ tätärämammäsä

mill, n. (building containing the mill) ወፍጮ ፣ ቤት wäfčo bet; (machine for grinding) ወፍጮ wäfčo

millenium አንድ ፣ ሺ ፣ ዓመታት and ši amätat

millet ጤፍ ṭef; ማሽላ mašəlla; ዳጉሳ dagussa

million ሚሊዮን miliyon

millstone (upper~) መጅ mäğ; (lower ~) እናት ፣ ወፍጮ ənnat wäfčo

mimic (v.) ቀዳ qädda

mince (~onion, meat) መተረ mättärä; ከተፈ kättäfä

mind, v. (take care of) ጠበቀ ṭäbbäqä; (be careful) ተጠነቀቀ täṭänäqqäqä; (obey) ታዘዘ tazzäzä; (resent) ቅር ፣ አለ(ው) qərr alä(w)

mind you! ልብ ፡ በል ləbb bäl
I don't mind ምን ፡ ከፋኝ män käf-
fañ; ግድ ፡ የለም gədd yälläm
never mind! ግድ ፡ የለም gədd yälläm

mind, n. (intellect) አእምሮ a'məro;
(opinion) ሐሳብ hassab
be of one mind ተስማማ täsmamma
be out of one's mind አበደ abbädä
bear in mind አስታወስ astawwäsä
bring to mind አስታወስ astawwäsä
have in mind አሰበ assäbä
keep in mind አስታወስ astawwäsä
make up one's mind ቈረጠ q°ärräṭä
presence of mind የአእምሮ ፡ እርጋታ
yäa'məro ərgata
set one's mind on ቈረጠ q°ärräṭä
to my mind እንዳነ ändäne; እንዳነ ፡
ከሆነ ändäne kähonä

mindful, be ∼ of ልብ ፡ አለ ləbb alä

mine, n. (of minerals) ማዕድን ma'ədən;
(explosives) ፈንጅ fänği; (source)
ምንጭ mənč

mine (pron.) የኔ yäne

miner የማዕድን ፡ ቈፋሪ yäma'ədən q°äf-
fari

mineral ማዕድን ma'ədən

mineral water ጠበል ṭäbäl

mingle (vt.) አደባለ addabbälä; ቀላቀለ
qälaqqälä; አቀላቀለ aqqälaqqälä
mingle (vi.) ተቀላቀለ täqälaqqälä;
ተደባለቀ tädäballäqä

minimize አቃለለ aqqallälä

minimum (adj.) አነስተኛ anästäñña
a minimum ቢያንስ ፡ ቢያንስ biyans
biyans

minister ሚኒስትር ministər; (of church)
አለቃ aläqa

ministry ሚኒስቴር minister

minor (n.) ለአካለ ፡ መጠን ፡ ያልደረሰ ፡
ሰው läakälä mäṭän yaldärräsä säw

minor, adj. (∼official) ዝቅተኛ zəqqətäñña; (∼injury) ቀላል qällal; (∼
change) አነስተኛ anästäñña

minority በቁጥር ፡ አነስተኛ ፡ የሆነ ፡ ሕዝብ
bäquṭər anästäñña yähonä həzb

minstrel አዝማሪ azmari

minus, prep. (less) ሲቀነስ siqqännäs;
ሲነሣ sinnässa; (without) ያለ yalä

minute (n.) ደቂቃ däqiqa
minutes (of meeting) ቃለ ፡ ጉባኤ qalä guba'e
any minute አሁን ahun
in a minute በቶሎ bätolo
just a minute እስቲ ፡ ቆይ əsti qoyy

minute (adj.) ረቂቅ räqiq; ደቂቅ däqiq;
(∼ instruction) ዝርዝር zərzər

minutely በዝርዝር bäzərzər

miracle ታምር tammər; ተአምር tä'ammər

miraculous ተአምራዊ tä'ammərawi

mire (n.) ማጥ maṭ; ጭቃ čəqa

mirror (vi.) ገለጸ gälläṣä

mirror (n.) መስታወት mästawät; (example) ምሳሌ məssale

misadventure መጥፎ ፡ ዕድል mäṭfo əddəl

misalliance ያላቻ ፡ ጋብቻ yalačča gabəčča

misapprehend በደንብ ፡ አልገባ(ውም) bädänb algäbba(wəm)

misbehave ባለገ ballägä

miscarry (of a woman) አስወረዳት as-
wärrädat; (of a plan) ተጨናገፈ täčänaggäfä

mischief ተንኰል tänk°äl

mischievous የተንኰለኞች yätänk°äläñ-
ñočč

misconduct ጥፋት ṭəfat

misdemeanor አነስተኛ ፡ ወንጀል anästäñña wänğäl

miser ንፉግ näfug

miserable (∼ life) አስቃቂ assäqqaqi;
(∼ meal) መጥፎ mäṭfo; (∼ shack)
ደሳሳ däsasa; (unhappy) ምስኪን məskin; ብስጩ bəsəčču

miserly ሥሥታም sǝssǝtam; ንፉግ nǝfug; ጬቅ čuq

misery መከራ mäkära; ችግር čǝggǝr

misfortune መጥፎ ፡ ዕድል mäṭfo ǝddǝl; መከራ mäkära

misguide አሳሳተ assasatä

mishandle አጕላላ agʷlalla

mishap አደጋ adäga; ጥፋት ṭǝfat

misinform ውሽት ፡ ነገረ wǝšät näggärä

misinterpret በስሕተት ፡ ተረጐመ bäsǝhtät täräggʷämä

misjudge በስሕተት ፡ገመተ bäsǝhtät gämmätä

mislead አሳሳተ assasatä

misleading አሳሳች assasač

misplace ያለ ፡ በታው ፡ አኖረ yalä botaw anorä

misprint የእትም ፡ ስሕተት yäǝttǝm sǝhtät

miss, v. (not find) አጣ aṭṭa; (fail to attend) ቀረ qärrä; (fail to understand) አልገባ(ውም) algäbba(wǝm); (~ the target) ሳተ satä; (be sad at the loss of) ናፈቀ naffäqä

Miss ወይዘሪት wäyzärit

missing, be ጐደለ gʷäddälä; ጠፋ ṭäffa

mission (special task) መልእክት mäl'ǝkt; ተልእኮ täl'ǝko; (purpose) ዓላማ alama; (group of people to carry out an assignment) መልእክተኞች mäl'ǝktäňňočč; (religious ~) ሚሲዮን misyon

missionary የወንጌል ፡ ሰባኪ yäwängel säbaki; ሚስዮናዊ misyonawi

misspell ሲጽፍ ፡ ፊደሉን ፡ አሳሳተ siṣǝf fidälun assasatä

mist ጉም gum; ጭጋግ čǝgag

mistake (n.) ስሕተት sǝhtät; ስተት sǝtät; ጥፋት ṭǝfat
make a mistake ሳተ satä

mistaken, be ሳተ satä; ተሳተ täsatä

Mister, see 'Mr.'

mistranslate አሳስቶ ፡ ተረጐመ assasto täräggʷämä

mistreat በደለ bäddälä; አጕላላ agʷlalla

mistress (of the house) እመቤት ǝmmäbet

mistrust (v.) ተጠራጠረ täṭärattärä

misunderstand በደንብ ፡ አልተረዳም bädänb altäräddam; አልገባ(ውም) algäbba(wǝm)

misunderstanding (mistake as to the meaning) በደንብ ፡ አለመረዳት bädänb alämärrädat; (disagreement) አለመስማማት alämäsmamat; አለመግባባት alämägbabat

misuse (treat badly) አጕሳቄለ aggʷäsaqqʷälä; (use wrongly) ያለ ፡ አግባብ ፡ ተጠቀመ(በት) yalä agbab täṭäqqämä-(bbät)

mitigate አቃለለ aqqallälä; አሻሻለ aššašalä

mix (vt.) ቀላቀለ qälaqqälä; አቀላቀለ aqqälaqqälä
mix, vi. (become blended) ተዋሐደ täwahadä
mix in ጥልቅ ፡ ገባ ṭǝllǝqq gäbba
mix up ደባለቀ däballäqä; (cards) አመሳቀለ ammäsaqqälä

mixture ቅልቅል qǝlǝqqǝl; ድብልቅ dǝbǝllǝq

moan (v.) አቃሰተ aqassätä

mob (n.) ሕዝብ hǝzb; የሚረብሽ ፡ ሕዝብ yämmiräbbäš hǝzb

mobile የሚንቀሳቀስ yämminqäsaqqäs

mobilization የኸተት ፡ ሰራዊት ፡ ትእዛዝ yäkǝtät särawit tǝ'ǝzaz

mobilize አስከተተ askättätä

mock (v.) አላገጠ allaggäṭä; አሾፈ ašofä; አፈዘ afezä

mockery ቀልድ qäld; ዋዛ waza; ፌዝ fez

mode (method) ዘዴ zäde; (fashion) ሞድ mod

model, n. (example) አርአያ araya; (copy) ጥዴል model; (pattern) አብ ነት abənnät

moderate, v. (make less extreme) ለስለ ስ ፡ አደረገ läsläss adärrägä; (preside) በሊቀ ፡ መንበርነት ፡ መራ bäliqä män-bärənnät märra

moderate (adj.) መጠነኛ mäṭänäñña; አማካይ ammakay; (~political views) መካከለኛ mäkakkäläñña

moderately በመጠኑ bämäṭänu

moderation, with ~ በመጠኑ bämäṭänu

moderator የውይይት ፡ መሪ yäwəyəyyət märi

modern የዘመን yäzämän; ዘመናዊ zämä-nawi

modernization ዘመናዊ ፡ ሥልጣኔ zämä-nawi sələṭṭane

modernize ዘመናዊ ፡ አደረገ zämänawi adärrägä

modest (~person) ትሑት təhut; (~income) መጠነኛ mäṭänäñña; (~house) አነስ ፡ ያለ anäss yalä

modesty ትሕትና təhtənna

modify ለወጠ läwwäṭä; (of adjective) ገለጸ gälläṣä

moist እርጥብ ərṭəb
be moist ራሰ rasä; ረጠበ räṭṭäbä

moisten አራሰ arasä; አረጠበ aräṭṭäbä

moisture ርጥበት rəṭbät; እርጥበት ərṭəbät

molar መንጋጋ mängaga

mold, v. (shape) ምስል ፡ ሠራ məsəl sär-ra; (influence) መራ märra; (~ the character) ዐረቀ arräqä

mold, n. (for metal) ቃሊብ qalib; (for cake) ቅርጽ ፡ ማውጫ qərṣ mawča; (on bread) ሻጋታ šagata

moldy, be ሻገተ šaggätä

mole (animal) ፍልፈል fəlfäl

mole (spot on skin), have a~ ማርያም ፡ ሳመችው maryam samäččəw

molest አስጨነቀ asčännäqä; አበሳጨ abbäsaččä

moment ጊዜ gize; ዐለት əlät
a moment ትንሽ tənnəš; ለጥቂት ፡ ጊዜ läṭəqit gize
a moment ago ከጥቂት ፡ ጊዜ ፡ በፊት käṭəqit gize bäfit
at any moment አሁን ፡ ካሁን ahun kahun
at that moment ያኔ yanne
at the moment ለጊዜው lägizew; አሁን ahun
in a few moments ባንድ ፡ አፍታ band afta
in a moment ከመቅጽበት kämäqəṣ-bät; አሁን ahun
just a moment አንድ ፡ ጊዜ and gize

momentarily (for the moment) ለጊዜው lägizew; (for a short time) ለጥቂት ፡ ጊዜ läṭəqit gize

monarch ንጉሠ ፡ ነገሥት nəgusä nägäst

monarchy ንጉሣዊ ፡ አገዛዝ nəgusawi ag-gäzaz

monastery ገዳም gädam

monastic የገዳም yägädam; የመነኮሳት yämänäkʷäsat

monasticism ምንኩስና mənkʷəsənna

Monday ሰኞ säñño

monetary የገንዘብ yägänzäb

money ገንዘብ gänzäb
make money ገንዘብ ፡ አተረፈ gänzäb atärräfä; ገንዘብ ፡ አገኘ gänzäb agäñ-ñä

money order ሐዋላ hawwala

monitor (n.) አለቃ aläqa; የክፍል ፡ አለቃ yäkəfəl aläqa

monk መነኩሴ mänäkʷse
become a monk መነኮሰ mänäk-kʷäsä

monkey ዝንጀሮ zənğäro

monkhood ምንኩስና mənkʷəsənna

monophysitism የተዋሕዶ ፡ ሃይማኖት yä-täwahdo haymanot

monotonous የቸከ yäčäkä; የሚያሰለች yämmiyassäläčč

monster (abnormally misshapen) ጉድ gud; (imaginary creature) ጭራቅ čəraq

monstrous በጣም ፡ አስቃቂ bäṭam assäqqaqi

month ወር wär

monthly (n.) በየወሩ ፡ የሚወጣ ፡ ጋዜጣ bäyyäwäru yämmiwäṭa gazeṭa

monthly (adj.) የወር yäwär

monthly (adv.) በየወሩ bäyyäwäru

monument ሐውልት hawəlt

monumental ታላቅ tallaq

mood ሁኔታ huneta
be in a bad mood ደስ ፡ አላለ(ውም) däss alalä(wəm)
be in a good mood ደስ ፡ ደስ፡አለ(ው) däss däss alä(w)

moody, be ቀፈፈ(ው) qäffäfä(w)

moon ጨረቃ čäräqa
full moon ሙሉ ፡ ጨረቃ mulu čäräqa

mop (n.) መወልወያ mäwälwäya

moral (n.) ሞራል moral
morals ሞራል moral; ግብረ ፡ ገብ gəbrä gäbb

moral, adj. (~ act) የግብረ ፡ ገብ yägəbrä gäbb; (~ support, victory) የመን ፈስ yämänfäs

morality ግብረ ፡ ገብነት gəbrä gäbbənnät

more (adj.) ተጨማሪ täčämmari

more (adv.) አብልጦ abləṭo; ይበልጥ yäbälṭ; ይልቅ yələq
more or less ከሞላ ፡ ጉደል kämolla gʷäddäl; ይብዛ ፡ ይነስ yəbza yənäs
more than ከ - - - በላይ kä - - - bälay; ከ - - - ይልቅ kä - - - yələq; ከ - - - ይበልጥ kä - - - yəbälṭ
more than once ካንድ ፡ ጊዜ ፡ በላይ kand gize bälay
be more than ላቀ laqä
no more ምንም mənəm + negative verb

moreover ከዚያም ፡ ሌላ käzziyam lela; ከዚህም ፡ በላይ käzzihəm bälay; ደግሞ dägmo

morning ጧት ṭʷat
early morning ማለዳ maläda; ዶሮ ፡ ሲጮህ doro sičoh
good morning! እንደምን ፡ አደርክ əndämən addärk (sg. masc.)
the following (next) morning በማግ ሥት bämagəstu
this morning ዛሬ ፡ ጧት zare ṭʷat

morrow, on the ~ በማግሥቱ bämagəstu; በበነጋው bäbänägaw

mortal ሟች mʷač; (~ injury) ከሞት፡የሚ ያደርስ kämot yämmiyadärs; (~ sin) ከባድ käbbad; (~ enemies) ዐርቅ ፡ የ ማይገባው ərq yämmayəgäbaw

mortality ሟችነት mʷačənnät

mortar (for pounding) ሙቀጫ muqäčča; (building material) ሲሚንቶ siminto

mortgage (n.) መያዣ mäyaža; ወለድ ፡ አግድ wälläd aggəd

mosque መስጊድ mäsgid

mosquito የወባ ፡ ትንኝ yäwäba tənəňň

moss (of rock) የደንጊያ ፡ ሽበት yädängiya šäbät; (of water) አረንጓዴ arängʷade

most (of the time) አብዛኛውን abzaňňawən; (very) በጣም bäṭam
most certainly በርግጥ bärgəṭ
most everybody አብዛኞቹ abzaňňočču
most of the time ብዙውን ፡ ጊዜ bəzuwən gize; አብዛኛው ፡ ጊዜ abzaňňaw gize
at most ቢበዛ bibäza
at the most ቢበልጥ bibälṭ; ግፋ ፡ ቢል gəfa bil

mostly (mainly) ይበልጡ yəbälṭu; (most of the time) አብዛኛውን ፡ ጊዜ abzaňňawən gize

moth ነቀዝ näqäz; የእሳት ፡ እራት yäəsat ərat

mother እናት ənnat

mother-in-law አማት amat

motherhood እናትነት ənnatənnät

motherland የትውልድ ፡ አገር yätəwlədd agär

motherly የእናት yäənnat

mother tongue የእናት ፡ ቋንቋ yäənnat qʷanqʷa

motif ዓላማ alama

motion (v.) ምልክት ፡ ሰጠ mələkkət säṭṭä

motion, n. (movement) ንቅናቄ nəqənnaqe; እንቅስቃሴ ənqəsəqqase; (proposal) ሐሳብ hassab
make a motion ሐሳብ ፡ አቀረበ hassab aqärräbä

motionless (adv.) ዝም ፡ ብሎ zəmin bəlo

motivate ገፋፋ gäfaffa

motive ምክንያት məknəyat; መነሻ männäša; (incentive) የሚገፋፋው ፡ ሐሳብ yämmigäfaffaw hassab

motor ሞተር motär

motorcycle ሞተር ፡ ቢሲክሌት motär bisiklet

motto መምሪያ mämriya

mound (small hill) ጉብታ gubbəta; (heap) ክምር kəmmər

mount, vt. (∼a horse) ተቀመጠ täqämmäṭä; (∼a ladder) ወጣ wäṭṭa

mount, n. (mountain) ተራራ tärara; (horse) የኮርቻ ፡ ፈረስ yäkorəčča färäs

mountain ተራራ tärara; ጋራ gara

mountain chain ሸንተረር šäntärär

mountainous ተራራማ täraramma

mourn አለቀሰ aläqqäsä; አዘነ azzänä

mourner ለቀስተኛ läqqästäñña; ሐዘንተኛ hazäntäñña

mournful የሐዘን yähazän; ሐዘን ፡ የተመላ በት hazän yätämällabät

mourning ለቅሶ läqso; ልቅሶ ləqso

mouse አይጥ ayṭ

mouth አፍ af; (of river) መግቢያ mägbiya

mouthful ጉርሻ gurša
take a mouthful ጐረሰ gʷärräsä

movable (∼ property) ተንቀሳቃሽ tänqäsaqaš

move, vt. (change the place) አዘዋወረ azzäwawwärä; ዞር ፡ አደረገ zorr adärrägä; (set in motion) አንቀሳቀሰ anqäsaqqäsä; (prompt) ገፋፋ gäfaffa; (propose) ሐሳብ ፡ አቀረበ hassab aqärräbä; (arouse emotion) ስሜት ፡ ነካ səmmet näkka

move, vi. (change home) ቤት ፡ ለቀቀ bet läqqäqä; (be set in motion) ተሸከረከረ täškäräkkärä; ተንቀሳቀሰ tänqäsaqqäsä; ተነቃነቀ tänäqannäqä; (travel) ተጓዘ tägʷazä; (progress) ተከ ሄደ täkahedä
move around ተዘዋወረ täzäwawwärä
move aside (vt.) ፈቀቅ ፡ አደረገ fäqäqq adärrägä
move aside (vi.) ገለል ፡ አለ gäläll alä; ፈቀቅ ፡ አለ fäqäqq alä
move closer ጠጋ ፡ አደረገ ṭäga adärrägä
move in አዲስ ፡ ቤት ፡ ገባ addis bet gäbba
move out ቤት ፡ ለቀቀ bet läqqäqä
move over ፈቀቅ ፡ አለ fäqäqq alä

move, n. (step) እርምጃ ərməǧǧa; (turn) ተራ tära
make a move ተንቀሳቀሰ tänqäsaqqäsä

movement (political, of army) እንቅስ ቃሴ ənqəsəqqase; (activities) መግ ቢያ ፡ መውጫ mägbiya mäwča

movie ፊልም film; ሲኒማ sinima

moving, see 'exciting'

mow ዐጨደ aččädä

Mr. ሚስተር mistär; (for an Ethiopian) አቶ ato

Mrs. ሚሲዝ misiz; (for an Ethiopian woman) ወይዘሮ wäyzäro

much ብዙ bäzu; እጅግ əǧǧəg; በጣም bätam
be much በዛ bäzza
how much? ስንት sənt; ምን ፡ ያህል mən yahəl
how much! እንዴት əndet; ምንኛ mənäñña
this much ይህን ፡ ያህል yəhən yahəl

mucus ንፍጥ nəft

mud ጭቃ čäqa

muddle አማታ ammatta

muddy የጭቃ yäčäqa; የጨቀየ yäčäqäyyä; ጭቃማ čäqamma
be muddy ጨቀየ čäqäyyä

mule በቅሎ bäqlo

muleteer ለኳሚ läggʷami

multicolored ዝንጉርጉር zəngurgur; ብዙ ፡ ቀለማት ፡ ያለው bäzu qälämat yalläw

multiple ብርከት ፡ ያለ bärkätt yalä; ልዩ ፡ ልዩ ləyyu ləyyu

multiplication table የጊዜ ፡ ቤት yägize bet

multiply (vt.) አበዛ abäzza
multiply (vi.) በዛ bäzza; (of rabbits) ተራባ tärabba; (of a family) ተዋለደ täwallädä

multitude ብዛት bəzat
multitude of በጣም ፡ ብዙ bätam bəzu

mumble አነበነበ anäbännäbä; አጕመተ መተ agʷmätämmätä

mumps ጆሮ ፡ ደግፍ ǧoro däggəf

munch (~parched grain) ቄረጠመ qʷärättämä; (~ a cookie) አላመጠ allammätä

municipality (city hall) ማዘጋጃ ፡ ቤት mazzägaǧa bet; (city) ከተማ kätäma

munitions ትጥቅና ፡ ስንቅ tətqənna sənq

murder (v.) ገደለ gäddälä

murder (n.) ነፍስ ፡ ገዳይነት näfsä gädayənnät; ገዳይ gədday

commit murder ሰው ፡ ገደለ säw gäddälä

murderer ነፍስ ፡ ገዳይ näfsä gäday

murmur, v. (grumble) አጕረመረመ agʷrämärrämä

murmur (n.) ጕሩምሩምታ gurumrumta

muscle ጡንቻ tunča

muscular (~ache) የጡንቻ yätunča; (~ leg) ጡንቻማ tunčamma

muse, see 'ponder'

museum ቤት ፡ መዘክር betä mäzäkkər

mush (food) ንፍሮ nəfro

mushroom እንጉዳይ ənguday

music ሙዚቃ muziqa

musical የሙዚቃ yämuziqa

musician ሙዚቀኛ muziqäñña

Muslim እስላም əslam

muslin ሻሽ šaš

must (v.) ሆነ(በት) honä(bbät); አለ(በት) allä(bbät)

mustache ሪዝ riz

mustard ሰናፍጭ sänafəč

muster ሰበሰበ säbässäbä

musty የሻገተ yäšaggätä

mutate ተለዋወጠ täläwwätä

mute ዲዳ dida; ድዳ dəda

mutilate (cut) ቄራረጠ qʷärarrätä; (spoil) አበላሸ abbälaššä

mutiny (n.) ዐመፅ amäs

mutter (v.) አጕረመረመ agʷrämärrämä

mutter (n.) ጕሩምሩምታ gurumrumta

mutton የበግ ፡ ሥጋ yäbäg səga

mutual የርስ ፡ በርስ yärs bärs; የጋራ yägara

muzzle (v.) አፉን ፡ አሰረ afun assärä

muzzle (n.) አፍ af

my የኔ yäne, or suffix pronoun -ዬ - ye, - e

myself ራሴ *rase*
  by myself (alone) ብቻዬን *bəččayen;*
  (without any help) ራሴ *rase*

mysterious እንግዳ ፡ የሆነ *əngəda yähonä;* ምስጢራዊ *məsṭirawi*

mystery ምስጢር *məsṭir;* (something not understandable) ረቂቅ ፡ ነገር *räqiq nägär*

myth አፈ ፡ ታሪክ *afä tarik*

mythology አፈ ፡ ታሪክ *afä tarik*

N

nag ጨቀጨቀ *čäqäččäqä;* አሰለቸ *asäläččä;* ቸከቸከ *čäkäččäkä;* ነዘነዘ *näzän-näzä*

nail (v.) በምስማር ፡ መታ *bäməsmar mätta*

nail, n. (of metal) ምስማር *məsmar;* (of finger) ጥፍር *ṭəfər*

naive ገራገር *gäragär*

naked ራቁት *raqut* + suffix pronouns (as in ራቁቱን ፡ ነው *raqutun näw* he is naked); (~ eyes) ባዶ *bado*
  be naked ተራቈተ *täraqqʷätä*

nakedness ዕርቃን *ərqan*

name, v. (give a name) ስም ፡ አወጣ *säm awäṭṭa;* (identify, mention) ስም ፡ ጠራ *səm ṭärra;* ስም ፡ ጠቀሰ *səm ṭäqqäsä;* (~ a price) ተናገረ *tänaggärä*
  be named (be appointed) ተሾመ *täšomä;* (be called) ተባለ *täbalä*

name (n.) ስም *säm*
  a good name ዝና *zənna*
  in the name of በ - - - ስም ፡ ሆኖ *bä - - - səm hono*

name giving ስያሜ *səyyame*

namely ይኸውም *yəhäwəm;* ማለት *malät*

namesake ሞክሼ *mokše*

nap (v.) ተኛ *täňňa*

nap (n.) ሽለብታ *šäläbta*

nape of neck ማጅራት *mağrat*

napkin የጅ ፡ ፎጣ *yäǧǧ foṭa*

narcotic የሚያደነዝዝ ፡ መድኃኒት *yäm-miyadänäzzəz mädhanit*

narrate አወራ *awärra;* አወጋ *awägga*

narrative ወግ *wäg;* ታሪክ *tarik*

narrow (vt.) አጠበበ *aṭäbbäbä*
  narrow (vi.) ጠበበ *ṭäbbäbä;* ጠበብ ፡ አለ *ṭäbäbb alä*
  narrow down (vt.) ወሰነ *wässänä*

narrow (adj.) ጠባብ *ṭäbbab;* (~ lane) ቀጭን *qäččən*
  be (get) narrow ጠበበ *ṭäbbäbä*

nasal ያፍንጫ *yafənča*

nasty (~ remark) አስጠያፊ *asṭäyyafi;* (~ medicine, rumor) መጥፎ *mäṭfo;* (~ weather) የቀፈፈ *yäqäffäfä*

nation አገር *agär;* (independent country) መንግሥት *mängəst*

national (n.) ዜጋ *zega*

national (adj.) ብሔራዊ *bəherawi;* የሕዝብ *yähəzb;* (~ dress) የሀገር *yähagär*

national anthem የሕዝብ ፡ መዝሙር *yä-həzb mäzmur*

nationalism ብሔራዊ ፡ ስሜት *bəherawi səmmet*

nationality (citizenship) ዜግነት *zegənnät*

nationalize በመንግሥት ፡ ሥር ፡ አደረገ *bämängəst sər adärrägä*

nationhood መንግሥትነት *mängəstənnät*

native (n.) ተወላጅ *täwälläǧ;* የሀገር ፡ ተወላጅ *yähagär täwälläǧ;* አገሬ *agäre*

native, adj. (~ land) የተውልድ *yätəw-lədd;* (~ custom, dress) የሀገር *yäha-gär*

native country (የ)ተውልድ ፡ አገር *(yä)-təwlədd agär*

native speech, native tongue የእናት ፡ ቋንቋ *yäənnat qʷanqʷa*

natural (inborn, not man-made) የተፈ
ጥሮ yätäfäṭro; (normal, not affected)
የተለመደ yätälämmädä

naturalize የዜግነት ፡ መብት ፡ ሰጠ yäzegǝnnät mäbt säṭṭä

naturally (by nature) በተፈጥሮ bätäfäṭro; (without affectation) እንደ ፡ ተፈ
ጥሮ ǝndä täfäṭro
naturally! (of course) እንዴታ ǝndeta

natural science የተፈጥሮ ፡ ሳይንስ yätäfäṭro sayǝns

nature (natural scenery) ተፈጥሮ täfäṭro; (kind) ዓይነት aynät; (disposition)
ባሕሪይ bahriy; ጠባይ ṭäbay

naught (zero) ዜሮ zero
come to naught ከንቱ ፡ ሆነ käntu
honä

naughty ተንኮለኛ tänkʷäläñña; ባለጌ baläge
be naughty ባለጌ ballägä

nausea, be overcome by ~ አቅለሸለ
ሸ(ው) aqläšälläšä(w)

nauseate አጥወለወለ aṭwäläwwälä

naval የባሕር yäbahǝr; የባሕር ፡ ኃይል
yäbahǝr hayl

navel እምብርት ǝmbǝrt

navy የባሕር ፡ ኃይል yäbahǝr hayl

near (v.) ተቃረበ täqarräbä; ተጠጋ tä
ṭägga

near (adj.) ቅርብ qǝrb
near (prep.) በ - - - - አጠገብ bä - - -
aṭägäb; ዘንድ zänd
be near ቀረበ qärräbä
come near ቀረበ qärräbä; ተቃረበ täqarräbä

nearby (adj.) ባቅራቢያ ፡ የሚገኝ baqrabbiya yämmiggäňň

nearby (adv.) ባካባቢው bakkababiw;
በዚህ ፡ አካባቢ bäzzih akkababi

nearly ለ lä + imperfect + ምንም ፡ አል
ቀረም mǝnǝmm alqärräm

neat ንጹሕ nǝṣuh; ጥዱ ṭǝdu

be neat ጠዳ ṭädda

necessarily በግድ bägǝdd

necessary ተፈላጊ täfällagi; አስፈላጊ asfällagi
be necessary አሻ aššä; ተፈለገ täfällägä

necessity ግድ gǝdd; ግዴታ gǝddeta; ተፈ
ላጊነት täfällaginnät; አስፈላጊነት asfällaginnät; (lack of things needed
for life) ችግር čǝggǝr
in case of necessity አስፈላጊ ፡ በሆነ ፡
ጊዜ asfällagi bähonä gize

neck አንገት angät

necklace ሐብል habl; ያንገት ፡ ጌጥ yangät geṭ; ድሪ dǝri

necktie ከራቫት kravat

need (v.) አስፈለገ(ው) asfällägä(w); ፈለገ
fällägä

need, n. (necessity) ፍላጎት fǝllagot; ተፈ
ላጊነት täfällaginnät; (deprivation)
ችግር čǝggǝr
be in need አስፈለገ(ው) asfällägä(w);
ቸገረ čäggärä
if need be ካስፈለገ kasfällägä

needle መርፌ märfe

needless ተገቢ ፡ ያልሆነ tägäbi yalhonä;
የማይገባ yämmayǝggäbba

needy ችግረኛ čǝggǝräñña; የተቸገረ yätäčäggärä

negation አሉታ aluta

negative (n.) አሉታ aluta; (of electric
current) ሴቴ sete

negative, adj. (~ quality) ያሉታ yaluta;
(~ answer) የእምቢታ yäǝmbita

neglect (v.) ቸል ፡ አለ čäll alä; ቸላ ፡ አለ
čälla alä; (fail to do something) ከ -
- - ቦዘነ kä - - - bozzänä

neglect (n.) ቸልታ čällǝta; ቸል ፡ ባይነት
čäll bayǝnnät; ግድ ፡ የለሽነት gǝdd yälläšǝnnät

neglectful, be ቸላ ፡ አለ čälla alä

negligence, see 'neglect' (n.)

negligent ቸልተኛ čällətäñña

negligible እምብዛም əmbəzam

negotiate ተነጋገረ tänägaggärä

negotiation(s) የስምምነት ፡ ንግግር yäsə-
məmmənnät nəgəggər; ድርድር dərəddər

Negro ሻንቅላ šanqəlla; ጥቁር ṭəqur

neigh አሽካካ aškakka

neighbor (v.) አዋሰነ awwassänä

neighbor (n.) ጉረቤት gʷäräbet

neighborhood ጉረቤት gʷäräbet; (region
near some place) አካባቢ akkababi;
(place, district) ሰፈር säfär; (nearness) ቅርብነት qərbənnät
in the neighborhood of ጋደማ gädäma

neighborly መልካም ፡ ጉረቤት mälkam
gʷäräbet

neither (adj.) ከሁለት ፡ አንዱም kähulätt
andum + negative verb

neither (conj.) --- ም --- ም -m - - m;
neither ... nor ም - - - ም -m - - - m

nephew የወንድም ፡ ልጅ yäwändəmm ləǧ;
የእኅት ፡ ልጅ yäəhət ləǧ

nerve ጅማት ǧəmmat; የደም ፡ ሥር yädäm
sər
get on one's nerves አበሳጨ abbäsaččä; አስጨነቀ asčännäqä

nervous, be (get) ተርበደበደ tärbädäbbädä; ተቀነጠነጠ täqʷnäṭännäṭä;
ተደነጋገጠ tädänäggäṭä

nest (n.) የወፍ ፡ ቤት yäwäf bet; የወፍ ፡
ጎጆ yäwäf goǧǧo

net (n.) መረብ märäb
mosquito net የወባ ፡ ትንኝ ፡ መከላከያ ፡
አጎብር yäwäba tənəňň mäkkälakäya
agʷäbär

net, adj. (~ salary) የተጣራ yätäṭarra

neutral (not taking sides) ገለልተኛ gälältäñña

neutrality ገለልተኛነት gälältäññannät

never ከቶ kätto + negative verb; በጭ
ራሽ bäčərraš + negative verb; ፈጽም

fäṣṣəmo + geruud + አያውቅም ayawqəm
never again ሁለተኛ hulättäñña

nevertheless የሆነ ፡ ሆና yähonä hono;
ሆኖም honom; ቢሆንም bihonəm; ይሁን፡
እንጂ yəhun enǧi

new አዲስ addis; (not accustomed, unfamiliar) እንግዳ əngəda
be new አደሰ addäsä

newcomer አዲስ ፡ መጥ addis mäṭṭ; አዲስ፡
ገብ addis gäbb; መጤ mäṭṭe

newly አዲስ addis; ገና ፡ አዲስ gäna addis

news ወሬ wäre; ዜና zena
give (tell) news አወራ awärra
latest news አዲስ ፡ ወሬ addis wäre;
ትኩስ ፡ ወሬ təkkus wäre

newscast ወሬ wäre

newsman ጋዜጠኛ gazeṭäñña

newspaper ጋዜጣ gazeṭa

New Testament አዲስ ፡ ኪዳን addis kidan

New Year የዘመን ፡ መለወጫ yäzämän
mälläwwäǧa; እንቀጣጣሽ ənqʷəṭaṭaš
happy New Year! እንኳን ፡ ከዘመን ፡
ወደ ፡ ዘመን ፡ አሻገረም ənkʷan käzä-
män wädä zämän aššaggäräwo

next (adj.) የሚመጣ yämmimäṭa; የሚቀ
ጥል yämmiqäṭṭəl
be next ተራኛ ፡ ነው täräñña näw

next (adv.) ቀጥሎ qäṭṭəlo
next to ከ - - - ጥግ kä - - - ṭəgg; ከ -
- - አጠገብ kä - - - aṭägäb

nibble ሻረረፈ šärarräfä; ጋጠ gaṭä

nice (~ day) ጥሩ ṭəru; (~ person) ደግ
dägg; መልካም mälkam

nickname የቅጽል ፡ ስም yäqəṣṣəl səm

niece የወንድም ፡ ልጅ yäwändəmm ləǧ;
የእኅት ፡ ልጅ yäəhət ləǧ

night ሌሊት lelit; ሌት let
night and day ሌት ፡ ተቀን let täqän
good night! ደኅና ፡ እደር dähna ədär
(sg. masc.)
last night ዛሬ ፡ ሌሊት zare lelit; ትላ
ንትና ፡ ማታ təlantənna mata

pass the night አደረ *addärä*
tomorrow night ነገ ፡ ማታ *nägä mata*

nightgown የሌሊት ፡ ልብስ *yälelit ləbs*

nightly ሌሊት ፡ ሌሊት *lelit lelit*

nightmare ቅዠት *qəžät*
have a nightmare ቃዠ *qažžä*

night school ማታ ፡ ተማሪ ፡ ቤት *mata tämari bet*

nightwatch የሌሊት ፡ ዘበኛ *yälelit zäbäňňa*

nimble ቀልጣፋ *qälṭaffa;* (~ mind) ንቁ *nəqu*

nine ዘጠኝ *zäṭäňň*
nine o'clock ሦስት ፡ ሰዓት *sost sä'at*

nineteen ዐሥራ ፡ ዘጠኝ *asra zäṭäňň*

ninety ዘጠና *zäṭäna*

ninth ዘጠነኛ *zäṭänäňňa*

nipple የጡት ፡ ጫፍ *yäṭut čaf;* (of baby bottle) ጡጦ *ṭuṭṭo*

no የለም *yälläm;* አይደለም *aydälläm*
no one ማንም *mannəm* + negative verb

nobility (person of noble rank) መኳን ንት *mäkʷanənt;* (greatness of character) ትልቅነት *təlləqənnät*

noble (n.) መኳንንት *mäkʷanənt*

noble, adj. (~ character) የጨዋ *yäčäwa;* (~ thought) የላቀ *yälaqä*

nobleman መኳንንት *mäkʷanənt;* ባላባት *balabbat*

nobody አንድም *andəm* + negative verb; ማንም *mannəm* + negative verb

nocturnal የሌሊት *yälelit*

nod, v. (bow the head) ደፋ ፡ ቀና ፡ አደ ረገ *däfa qäna adärrägä;* (sway) ተወዛ ወዘ *täwäzawwäzä;* (let the head droop when drowsing) አንጐላጀ *angʷälaǧǧä*

nod (n.) ራሱን ፡ መነቅነቅ *rasun mänäqnäq*

noise ድምፅ *dəmṣ;* (loud ~) ጫጫታ *čačata*
make noise (loud ~) ተንጫጫ *tänčačča;* (slight, strange ~) ድምፅ ፡ ሰጠ *dəmṣ säṭṭä*

noisy ጫጫታ ፡ የሚበዛ(በት) *čačata yammibäza(bbät);* (~ person) ጫጫታ ፡ የሚያበዛ *čačata yämmiyabäza*
be noisy (person) ተንጫጫ *tänčačča;* ጩኸት ፡ አበዛ *čuhät abäzza*

nomad ዘላን *zällan*

nominate (appoint) ሾመ *šomä;* (propose as a candidate) አቀረበ *aqärräbä*

none ማንም *mannəm* + negative verb; አንዱም *andum* + negative verb
none of መኑም *mənum;* አንድ *and* + suffix pronoun + negative verb

nonetheless ዳሩ ፡ ግን *daru gən*

nonsense የማይረባ ፡ ነገር *yämmayəräba nägär*
talk nonsense ላፈላፈ *läfälläfä;* ቀባ ጀረ *qäbaǧǧärä*

nook ሠርጫ *särəčča*

noon ቀትር *qätər;* እኩለ ፡ ቀን *əkkulä qän*
at noon በሰዓት *bäsä'at*

nor -ን *-n* + negative verb

normal የተለመደ *yätälämmädä;* (~ child) እንክን ፡ የሌለው *ənkän yälelläw*

normally ብዙ ፡ ጊዜ *bəzu gize;* አብዛኛ ውን ፡ ጊዜ *abzaňňawən gize*

north ሰሜን *sämen*

northern ሰሜናዊ *sämenawi*

nose አፍንጫ *afənča*

nostril አፍንጫ *afənča*

not, expressed by the negative verb
not a thing ምንም *mənəm* + negative verb
not anybody ማንም *mannəm* + negative verb
not at all በጥራሽ *bäčərraš* + negative verb; ፈጽሞ *fäṣṣamo* + negative verb

notable (n.) ታላቅ ፡ ሰው tallaq säw

note, v. (make a record) ማስታወሻ ፡ አደረገ mastawäša adärrägä; (observe, notice) ተገነዘበ tägänäzzäbä; አስተዋለ astäwalä

note, n. (short letter) አጭር ፡ ደብዳቤ ačč'är däbdabbe; (remark, reminder) ማስታወሻ mastawäša; (paper money) ብር bärr; (in music) ኖታ nota
keep notes በማስታወሻ ፡ ያዘ bämastawäša yazä
take note of አስተዋለ astäwalä; ልብ፡ አደረገ läbb adärrägä

notebook የማስታወሻ ፡ ደብተር yämastawäša däbtär; ደብተር däbtär

noted (renowned) የታወቀ yätawwäqä; የተመሰገነ yätämäsäggänä; ዝነኛ zännäñña

nothing ምንም mənəm + negative verb
nothing doing አይሆንም ayhonəm
nothing else ምንም ፡ ሌላ mənəm lela
for nothing (free of charge) በነጻ bänäṣa; በብላሽ bäbəlaš; (in vain) በከንቱ bäkäntu

notice (vi.) አየ ayyä; ተመለከተ tämäläkkätä; ተረዳ(ው) tärädda(w); (pay attention to) ልብ ፡ አለ läbb alä

notice, n. (written or printed sign) ማስታወቂያ mastawäqiya; (warning) ማስጠንቀቂያ masṭänqäqiya
come to one's notice ሰማ sämma; አወቀ awwäqä
escape one's notice አላስተዋለም alastäwaläm
give notice (inform) አስታወቀ astawwäqä; (warn) አስጠነቀቀ asṭänäqqäqä
take notice of ልብ ፡ አለ läbb alä

noticeable ጉልህ guləh
be noticeable በግልጽ፡ታየ bägələṣ tayyä; ተለይቶ ፡ ታወቀ täläyyəto tawwäqä

notify አስታወቀ astawwäqä; አመለከተ amäläkkätä

notion (idea) ሐሳብ hassab; አስተያየት astäyayät; አስተሳሰብ astäsasäb

notorious የታወቀ yätawwäqä; (famous for some undesirable act) አገር ፡ ያሰ ለቸ agär yasäläččä

notwithstanding ቢሆንም bihonəm; ሆኖም honom

noun ስም səm

nourish መገበ mäggäbä; ቀለበ qälläbä

nourishment ምግብ məgəb

novel (n.) ልብ ፡ ወለድ ፡ መጽሐፍ ፡ (or ታሪክ) ləbb wälläd mäṣhaf (or tarik)

novel (adj.) አዲስ addis

novelist የልብ ፡ ወለድ ፡ ደራሲ yäləbb wälläd därasi

November ኅዳር hədar

novice ጀማሪ ğämmari

now አሁን ahun; (under these circumstances) እንግዲህ əngədih
now and again አልፎ ፡ አልፎ alfo alfo
now and then አልፎ ፡ አልፎ alfo alfo
now then ታዲያ(ስ) tadiya(ss)
by now እስካሁን əskahun
even now አሁንም ahunəm
from now on ካሁን ፡ ጀምሮ kahun ğämməro; ካሁን ፡ አንሥቶ kahun ansəto
just now አሁን ፡ ገና ahun gäna

nowadays ባሁን ፡ ጊዜ bahun gize; በዛሬ፡ ጊዜ bäzare gize

nowhere የትም ፡ ቦታ yätəm bota + negative verb

nozzle የቱቦ ፡ ጫፍ yätubbo čaf

nude ራቁት raqut + suffix pronouns

nuisance ጠንቅ ṭänq; ጣጣ ṭaṭa

null, be ዋጋ ፡ የለውም waga yälläwəm
be null and void ዋጋ ፡ የለውም waga yälläwəm

numb ደንዛዛ dänzazza
be numb ደነዘዘ dänäzzäzä

number (v.) ቈጠረ q''äṭṭärä; ቁጥር ፡ ሰጠ quṭər säṭṭä

number (n.) ቁጥር quṭər; (of a magazine) እትም əttəm
a number of በርከት ፡ ያሉ bärkätt yalu

numeral ቁጥር *quṭər*

numerous ብዙ *bəzu;* በርከት ፡ ያሉ *bär-kätt yalu;* እያሉ *ayyale*
be numerous በዛ *bäzza*

nun መነኩሲት *mänäkʷsit*

nuptial(s) ሰርግ *särg*

nurse, v. (care for in sickness) አስ ታmemመ *astammämä;* (feed at the breast) አጠባች *aṭäbbačč*

nurse (n.) ነርስ *närs;* አስታማሚ *asta-mami;* (who takes care of a young child) ሞግዚት *mogzit*

nursemaid ሞግዚት *mogzit*

nursery (of children) የሕፃናት ፡ ማሳደጊያ *yähəşanat masaddägiya;* (of plants) የችግን ፡ መሸጫ ፡ ቤት *yäčəggən mä-šäča bet*

nursing mother እመጫት *əmmäçat*

nut (fruit) ገውዝ *gäwz;* ለውዝ *läwz;* (of screw) ቡሎን *bulon*

nutrition የምግገብ ፡ ዘደ *yammägagäb zäde*

nutritious መጋቢነት ፡ ያለው *mäggabin-nät yalläw*

O

oar መቅዘፊያ *mäqzäfiya*

oat(s) አጃ *aǧǧa*

oath መሐላ *mähalla*
take an oath መሐላ ፡ ገባ *mähalla gäb-ba;* ማለ *malä*

obedience ታዛዥነት *tazzažənnät*

obedient ታዛዥ *tazzaž*

obelisk ሐውልት *hawəlt*

obese ቦርጫም *borçam;* ወፍራም *wäfram*

obey ታዘዘ *tazzäzä;* (~ the law) አከበረ *akäbbärä*

obituary ዜና ፡ ዐረፍት *zena əräft*

object (v.) ተቃወመ *täqawwämä*

object (n.) እቃ *əqa;* (purpose) ዓላማ *a-lama*
direct object ርቱዕ ፡ ተሳቢ *rətu' täsabi*
indirect object ኢርቱዕ ፡ ተሳቢ *irətu' täsabi*

objection ተቃውሞ *täqawmo*
have (raise) an objection ተቃወመ *täqawwämä*

objectionable የሚያ ያgeñ *yämmayəggäbba*

objective (n.) ዓላማ *alama;* ግብ *gəb*

objective, adj. (real) የሚዳሰስና ፡ የሚታይ *yämmiddassäsənna yämmittayy;* (un-biased) ያልተዛባ *yaltäzabba*

obligate አስገደደ *asgäddädä*

obligation ግድ *gədd;* ግዴታ *gəddeta;* ግዳጅ *gəddaǧ*
be under obligation ግዴታ ፡ አለበት *gəddeta alläbät*

obligatory የግዴታ *yägəddeta*

oblige አስገደደ *asgäddädä*
be obliged ግድ ፡ ሆነበት *gədd honäb-bät*
be obliged to ባለ ፡ ውለታው ፡ ነው *balä wəlätaw näw*

oblique ሰያፍ *säyyaf*

obliterate (destroy) ደመሰሰ *dämässäsä;* አጠፋ *aṭäffa*

oblivion, fall into ~ ተረሳ *tärässa*

oblivious, be ረሳ *rässa;* (inattentive) ግዴ ለውም *gəddellawəm;* ግድ ፡ የለውም *gədd yälläwəm*

oblong ሞላላ *molala*

obnoxious አስጠሊ *asṭälli*

obscene (~ language) ጸያፍ *şäyyaf*

obscure, adj. (~ sound, meaning) ግልጽ ፡ ያልሆነ *gəlş yalhonä;* (~ figure) ደብዛዛ *däbzazza*

obscurity ጭለማ *čəlläma;* ጨለማ *čälläma*
pass into obscurity ተረሳ *tärässa*

observant አስተዋይ *astäway*

observation (watching) መመልከት *mä-mälkät;* (ability to examine) ማስተዋል *mastäwal*

observe (watch carefully) ተመለከተ *tä-mäläkkätä;* (follow closely) ተከታተለ *täkätattälä;* (examine) መረመረ *märämmärä;* (remark) አለ *alä;* (keep, celebrate) አከበረ *akäbbärä;* ጠበቀ *täbbäqä*
be observed (of holiday) ዋለ *walä*

observer ተመልካች *tämälkač;* ታዛቢ *ta-zabi*

obsolescent, be ጊዜ ፡ (ዘመን) ፡ አለፈ(በት) *gize (zämän) alläfä(bbät)*

obsolete ዘመን ፡ ያለፈ(በት) *zämän yal-läfä(bbät)*
be obsolete, see 'obsolescent'

obstacle መሰናክል *mäsänakəl;* ዕንቅፋት *ənqəfat*

obstinate ችኮ *čəkko;* እልኸኛ *əlləhäñña;* ግትር *gəttər*
be obstinate ገተረ *gättärä;* ቻከ *čäkä;* ችክ ፡ አለ *čəkk alä*

obstruct አገደ *aggädä;* ዘጋ *zägga;* (~ the view) ጋረደ *garrädä*

obtain አገኘ *agäññä*

obtuse ጁል *žəl*
form an obtuse angle ገደል ፡ አለ *gä-däll alä*

obverse (of medal) መልክ *mälk;* (of coin) በዘውድ ፡ በኩል *bäzäwd bäkkul*

obvious ግልህ *guləh;* ግልጽ *gəlṣ*

obviously በርግጥ *bärgəṭ;* ፍዱም *fəṣṣum*

occasion (v.) አስነሳ *asnässa*

occasion, n. (particular time or event) ጊዜ *gize;* (chance) ዕድል *əddəl;* ያጋጠ መው ፡ ዕድል *yaggaṭṭämäw əddəl;* (reason) ምክንያት *məknəyat*
on occasion አልፎ ፡ አልፎ *alfo alfo*

occasionally በየጊዜው *bäyyägizew;* አልፎ፡ አልፎ *alfo alfo*

occident ምዕራብ *mə'ərab*

Occident ምዕራባዊ ፡ ክፍለ ፡ ዓለም *mə-'ərabawi kəflä aläm*

occidental ምዕራባዊ *mə'ərabawi*

occupant የሚኖር ፡ ሰው *yämminor säw;* (of an office) የሚሠራ ፡ ሰው *yämmi-sära säw*

occupation (job) ሥራ *səra;* (holding) መያዝ *mäyaz*

occupy ያዘ *yazä;* (live in a house) ኖረ *norä;* (~ time) ፈጀ *fäǧǧä*
be occupied (of a person) ሥራ ፡ ያዘ ወ *səra yazäw;* (of a room) ተያዘ *täyazä*

occur (be found) ተገኘ *tägäññä;* (happen) አጋጠመ *aggaṭṭämä;* ደረሰ *där-räsä;* ሆነ *honä*

occurrence ጉዳይ *gudday;* የሚደርስ ፡ ነገር *yämmidärs nägär*

ocean ውቅያኖስ *wəqyanos*

o'clock ሰዓት *säat*

October ጥቅምት *ṭəqəmt*

oculist ያይን ፡ ሐኪም *yayn hakim*

odd (strange) እንግዳ *2əngəda;* (~ number) ነጠላ *näṭäla;* ጉደሎ *gʷädälo;* (without the rest of a pair) ጓደኛ ፡ የሌለው *gʷaddäñña yälelläw;* (~ jobs) የሆነ ፡ ያልሆነ *yähonä yalhonä*

odds ዕድል *əddəl*
odds and ends ቅራቅንቦ *qəraqənbo;* ጥቃቅን ፡ ነገሮች *ṭəqaqən nägäročč*

odious የሚያስጠላ *yämmiyasṭälla*

odor ሽታ *šətta;* (good ~) መዓዛ *mä'aza*

of ከ *kä;* (belonging to) የ *yä;* (about) ስለ *sələ*

off, be ~ (be interrupted) ተቋረጠ *tä-qʷarräṭä;* (of light) ጠፋ *ṭäffa;* (leave) ሄደ *hedä*
off and on አልፎ ፡ አልፎ *alfo alfo*

offend አስቀየመ *asqäyyämä;* አናደደ *an-naddädä*

offender ጥፋተኛ *ṭəfatäñña;* አጥፊ *aṭfi*

offense (violation of a law) ጥፋት *ṭəfat;* (attack) ማጥቂያ *maṭqiya*

cause offense አስቀየመ *asqäyyämä*
take offense ተቀየመ *täqäyyämä*

offensive (n.) ማጥቃት *maṭqat*

offensive, adj. (~ odor) መጥፎ *mätfo;*
(~ behavior) አስቀያሚ *asqäyyami;*
አስከፊ *askäffi;* (~ weapon) የማጥቂያ
yämaṭqiya

offer, vt. (give) ሰጠ *säṭṭä;* (present) አቀ
ረበ *aqärräbä;* (~ a drink, cigarette)
ጋበዘ *gabbäzä;* (~ advice) አበረከ(ለት)
abärräkä(llät)

offer (n.) ድርድር *dərəddər;* ያቀረበው ፡
ውል *yaqärräbäw wəl*
make an offer (in money) ዋጋ ፡ ነገረ
waga näggärä

offering መሥዋዕት *mäswaət*

office (place of business) መሥሪያ ፡ ቤት
mäsriya bet; ቢሮ *biro;* (post) ሹመት
šumät; (duty) ተግባር *tägbar;* (religious ceremony) የጸሎት ፡ ሥነ ፡ ሥር
ዓት *yäṣälot sənä sər'at*
offices, through the good ~ በ - - -
አማካይነት *bä - - - ammakayənnät*

office boy ተላላኪ *tälalaki*

officer (in the army) መኮንን *mäkʷännən;* (person elected to a position)
ሹም *šum*

official (n.) ባለ ፡ ሥልጣን *balä səlṭan;*
ሹም *šum*

official, adj. (~ visit) የይፋ *yäyəfa;* (~
seal) የመንግሥት *yämängəst*

officially በይፋ *bäyəfa;* በአፊሴል *bäofisel*

offshoot (of tribe) ዝርያ *zərrəyya;* (of
plant) ተቀጥያ *täqäṭṭəyya;* (result)
ውጤት *wəṭṭet*

offspring ዘር *zär;* ዝርያ *zərrəyya*

often ብዙ ፡ ጊዜ *bəzu gize;* ሰርክ *särk*
every so often አልፎ ፡ አልፎ *alfo alfo*
how often? ስንት ፡ ጊዜ *sənt gize*

oh ! ሆይ *hoy*

oil (v.) ቀባ *qäbba*

oil (n.) ዘይት *zäyt*

oil lamp መቅረዝ *mäqräz*

oily (~ rag) ዘይት ፡ የጠጣ *zäyt yäṭäṭṭa;*
(~ hand) በዘይት ፡ የተበከለ *bäzäyt yä-
täbäkkälä*

ointment ቅባት *qəbat*

old (~ thing) አሮጌ *aroge;* (known for
a long time) የቆየ *yäqoyyä;* የድሮ *yädəro;* የጥንት *yäṭənt*
old age ሽምግልና *šəmgələnna;* እርጅና
ərǧənna
old lady ባልቴት *baltet*
old man ሽማግሌ *šəmagəlle;* አረጋዊ
arägawi
old woman አሮጊት *arogit*
become (grow) old ሸመገለ *šämäggälä;* አረጀ *aräǧǧä*
how old are you? ዕድሜህ ፡ ስንት ፡
ነው *ədmeh sənt näw*

olden የድሮ *yädəro*
in olden days ድሮ *dəro;* ጥንት *ṭənt*

older ታላቅ *tallaq*
be older than (person) በዕድሜ ፡ በለጠ
bäədme bälläṭä; (house) ከ - - - አረጀ
kä - - - aräǧǧä
get older አረጀ *aräǧǧä*

old-fashioned (~ ideas) የነፈሰበት *yänäf-
fäsäbbät;* (~ weapons) የድሮ *yädəro*

old maid, be an ~ ቆማ ፡ ቀረች *qoma
qärräčč*

Old Testament ብሉይ ፡ ኪዳን *bəluy kidan*

old-time የድሮ *yädəro*

olive የወይራ ፡ ፍሬ *yäwäyra färe*

olive oil (የ)ወይራ ፡ ዘይት *(yä)wäyra zäyt*

olive tree ወይራ *wäyra*

omen ጋድ *gädd;* የገድ ፡ ምልክት *yägädd
mələkkət*

omit (leave out) አስቀረ *asqärrä;* ገደፈ
gäddäfä; (fail to, neglect) ስ *sə* + negative imperfect + ቀረ *qärrä*

omnipotent ኃያል *hayyal;* (God) ከሃሌ ፡
ኩሉ *kähale kullu*

on ላይ *lay;* እ - - - ላይ *ə - - - lay;* (about)
ስለ *sälä*
on and on ያለማቋረጥ *yalämaqqʷaräṭ*

once (one time) አንዴ *ande;* አንድ ፡ ጊዜ *and gize;* (formerly) ድሮ *dəro;* በቀ ድሞ ፡ ዘመን *bäqädmo zämän*
once in a while አልፎ ፡ አልፎ *alfo alfo*
once in a great while ከስንት ፡ አንዴ *käsənt ande*
once more አንዴ ፡ ደግሞ *ande dägmo;* እንደገና *əndägäna*
once upon a time ከዕለታት ፡ አንድ ፡ ቀን *käəlätat and qän*
at once (at the same time) ባንዴ *bande;* (immediately) አሁኑኑ *ahununu;* ቶሎ *tolo*
this once ያሁኑን ፡ ብቻ *yahunun bəčča*

one (adj.) አንድ *and* and (fem. አንዲት *andit*)
one (pron.) ሰው *säw;* አንድ ፡ ሰው *and säw*
one by one አንድ ፡ ባንድ *and band*
one o'clock ሰባት ፡ ስዓት *säbatt säat*
one of አንድ *and* + suffix pronoun
no one ማንም *mannəm* + negative verb

oneself ራሱ *rasu*
by oneself ያለ ፡ ረዳት *yalä räddat*

onion ሽንኩርት *šənkurt;* ቀይ ፡ ሽንኩርት *qäyy šənkurt*

onlooker ተመልካች *tämälkač*

only ብቻ *bəčča*

onward ወደፊት *wädäfit*

ooze አዠ *ažžä*

open (vt.) ከፈተ *käffätä;* (lay bare) ገለጠ *gällätä*
open (vi.) ተከፈተ *täkäffätä;* (begin) ጀመረ *ğämmärä*

open (adj.) ክፍት *kəft;* (~ wound) ገላጣ *gälata;* (~ road) ግልጽ *gəlş*
in the open (outside the house) ከቤ ት ፡ ውጭ *käbet wəčč*

opening (hole) ቀዳዳ *qädada;* (beginning) መክፈቻ *mäkfäča;* (job vacancy) ክፍት ፡ ቦታ *kəft bota*

openly በግልጽ *bägəlş*

operate, vt. (~ a machine) አንቀሳቀስ *anqäsaqqäsä;* (~ a factory) አካሄደ *akkahedä*
operate, vi. (function) ሠራ *särra;* (perform surgery) ቀዶ ፡ ጠገነ ፡ አደረገ *qäddo təgäna adärrägä*

operation (process of working) ማንቀሳ ቀስ *manqäsaqäs;* (performing) አፈጻ ጸም *affäsaşäm;* (surgery) ቀዶ ፡ ጠገነ *qäddo təgäna*
be in operation በሥራ ፡ ላይ ፡ ዋለ *bäsəra lay walä*

opinion ሐሳብ *hassab;* አሳብ *assab;* አስተ ሳሰብ *astäsasäb;* አስተያየት *astäyayät*

opinionated ሐሳበ ፡ ግትር *hassabä gəttər*

opponent ተቃዋሚ *täqawami;* ተቃራኒ *täqarani;* ባለጋራ *balägara;* (in election) ተወዳዳሪ *täwädadari*

opportune ምቹ *məčču*
be opportune ተመቸ *tämäččä*

opportunist አድር ፡ ባይ *adər bay*

opportunity ዕድል *əddəl;* አጋጣሚ *aggatami*

oppose ተቃወመ *täqawwämä*

opposed, be ~ to ተቃወመ *täqawwämä*

opposite (n., adj.) ተቃራኒ *täqarani*

opposite (prep.) ትይይ *təyəyy;* ከ - - - አን ጻር *kä - - - anşar;* ከ - - - ፊት ፡ ለፊት *kä - - - fit läfit*

opposition ተቃውሞ *täqawmo;* ተቃራኒ ነት *täqaraninnät;* (persons opposing) የተቃዋሚ ፡ ወገን *yätäqawami wägän*

oppress (treat harshly) ጨቈነ *čäqqʷänä;* (of weather, of trouble) ተጫጫነ *tä- čačanä;* አስጨነቀ *asčännäqä*

oppression ጭቈና *čəqqʷäna*

oppressor ጨቋኝ *čäqqʷañ*

optician ያይን ፡ መነጽር ፡ ሻጭ *yayn mä- näşşər šač*

option ምርጫ *mərča*

opulent እጅግ ፡ ሀብታም *əǧǧəg habtam*

or ወይ *wäy;* (in a question) ወይስ *wä-*

yəss; (otherwise) ያለበለዚያ *yaläbäläz-ziya*
or else አለዚያ *aläzziya*

oral (~ examination) የቃል *yäqal;* (~ medicine) የሚዋጥ *yämmiwwaṭ*

orally በቃል *bäqal*

orange ብርቱካን *bərtukan*

oration ንግግር *nəgəggər*

orator ተናጋሪ *tänagari*

orbit ምሕዋር *məhwar*

orchard የተከለ ፡ ቦታ *yätäkəl bota*

orchestra የሙዚቃ ፡ ንድ *yämuziqa g^wadd*

ordain ወሰነ *wässänä;* (order) አዘዘ *az-zäzä;* (to priesthood) ቀሰሰ *qässäsä;* ካነ *kanä*

ordeal ሥቃይ *səqay;* የመከራ ፡ ጊዜ *yä-mäkära gize*

order, v. (command) አዘዘ *azzäzä;* (manage) አጠናቀቀ *aṭṭänaqqäqä*

order, n. (command) ትእዛዝ *tə'əzaz;* (sequence) ተራ *tära;* (proper arrangement) ሥርዓት *sər'at;* (degree) ደረጃ *däräǧa;* (religious organization) የሃይ ማኖት ፡ ማኅበር *yähaymanot mahbär;* (orderly conduct) ጸጥታ *ṣäṭṭəta*
be out of order ተበላሸ *täbälaššä;* አልሠራም *alsärram*
bring to order (~ a riotous crowd) ጸጥ ፡ አደረገ *ṣäṭṭ adärrägä*
in good order በደኅና *bädähna*
in order that ለ *lä* + imperfect; እንድ *ənda* + imperfect; ዘንድ *zänd* preceded by the imperfect
put in order በጥንቃቄ ፡ አከናወነ *bä-ṭənəqqaqe akkänawwänä;* አዘጋጀ *az-zägaǧǧä*

orderly, n. (in a hospital) ረዳት *räddat;* (soldier assigned to an officer) ተላላኪ *tälalaki*

orderly, adj. (~ class) ሥርዓት ፡ የጠበቀ *sär'at yäṭäbbäqä;* (~ desk) በሥርዓት፡ የሆነ *bäsər'at yähonä*

ordinal (~ number) መደበኛ *mädäbäňňa*

ordinance ሥርዓት *sər'at;* ደንብ *dänb;* ድንጋጌ *dənəggage*

ordinarily እንደተለመደው *əndätälämmä-däw*

ordinary የተራ *yätära;* (~ price) የተለ መደ *yätälämmädä*

ore የብረት ፡ አፈር *yäbrät afär*

organ (part of body) አካል *akal;* (musical instrument) አርጋኖን *arganon*

organization ማኅበር *mahbär;* ድርጅት *dərəǧǧət*

organize (~ a party) አዘጋጀ *azzägaǧǧä;* (~ a committee) አቋቋመ *aqq^waq^wa-mä;* (~ work) አቀናበረ *aqqänabbärä;* አደራጀ *addäraǧǧä*

Orient ምሥራቅ *məsraq*

Oriental (n.) የሩቅ ፡ ምሥራቅ ፡ ሰው *yä-ruq məsraq säw*

oriental (adj.) የምሥራቅ *yäməsraq;* ምሥ ራቃዊ *məsraqawi*

orientation (direction) አቅጣጫ *aqṭačča;* (inclination) ዝንባሌ *zənəbbale*

origin መነሻ *männäša;* መነሾ *männäšo;* (former days) ጥንት *ṭənt*

original, n. (of painting) ዋና *wanna;* (of written text) ዋና ፡ ጽሑፍ *wanna ṣəhuf*

original, adj. (first) የመጀመሪያ *yämä-ǧämmäriya;* (former) የቀድሞ *yäqäd-mo;* (novel) አዲስ *addis;* እሱ ፡ የመነ ጨው *əssu yamänäččäw*

originally (at first) በመጀመሪያ *bämä-ǧämmäriya;* ጥንት *ṭənt*

originate (vt.) ለመጀመሪያ ፡ ጊዜ ፡ ፈጠረ *lämäǧämmäriya gize fäṭṭärä*
originate (vi.) መነጨ *mänäččä;* ተነሣ *tänässa*

ornament (n.) ጌጥ *geṭ*

ornate የጌጠ *yägeṭa;* (~ style in writing) የተራቀቀ *yätäraqqäqä*

orphan የሙት ፡ ልጅ *yämut ləǧ;* እናትና ፡ አባት ፡ የሌለው *ənnatənna abbat yä-lelläw* orthography የቃላት ፡ አጻጻፍ yäqalat aṣṣaṣaf

ostensible ግልጽ gəlṣ

ostensibly ላይ ፡ ላዩን lay layun

ostrich ሰጐን säg^wän

other ሌላ lela
any other ሌላ lela
each other እርስ ፡ በርሳቸው ərs bärsaččäw, or reciprocal stem

otherwise (else) ያለበለዚያ yaläbäläzziya; አለዚያ aläzziya; (outside of it) በተረፈ bätärräfä; ካልሆነም kalhonäm

our የኛ yäñña; or - አችን - aččən

ours የኛ yäñña

ourselves ራሳችን rasaččən

oust አስወጣ aswäṭṭa; አስወገደ aswäggädä

out ከ kä
out of ከ - - - ውስጥ kä - - - wəsṭ
out there እዚያ əzziya
be out (be absent) ቀረ qärrä; (be away, be gone) ወደ ፡ ውጭ ፡ ሂደ wädä wəčč hedä; (appear, of a book) ታተሞ ፡ ወጣ tattəmo wäṭṭa

outbreak መነሣት männäsat

outcast ከጎሳረ ፡ ሰብ ፡ ውጭ ፡ የሆነ ፡ ሰው kähəbrä säb wəčč yähonä säw

outcome ውጤት wäṭṭet

outdated, be ዘመኑ ፡ አለፈ zämänu alläfä

outdo በለጠ bälläṭä

outdoor የውጭ yäwəčč

outdoors ውጭ wəčč; ደጅ däǧǧ

outer የውጭ yäwəčč

outfit, n. (equipment) ትጥቅ təṭq; (costume) ልብስ ləbs

outhouse የሰገራ ፡ ቤት yäsägära bet

outing ሽርሽር šərrəšərr

outlast (of clothes) ከ - - - ይልቅ ፡ በረ ከተ kä - - - yələq bäräkkätä

outlaw ሕግ ፡ ወጥ həggä wäṭṭ; ሽፍታ šəfta

outlet (of lake) መፍሰሻ mäfsäša; (electric ~) የኮረንቲ ፡ መሰኪያ yäkorränti mäsäkkiya

outline, v. (~ a plan) ዘረዘረ zäräzzärä; አወጣ awäṭṭa; (draw the outer lines of) ነደፈ näddäfä

outline, n. (drawing) ንድፍ nədf; (line that shows the shape) ቅርጽ qərṣ; (list of main ideas) አርእስት ፡ ጉዳይ ar'əstä gudday; ረቂቅ räqiq

outlook (point of view) አስተያየት astäyayät; (prospect) የወደፊት ፡ ሁኔታ yäwädäfit huneta

outlying ራቅ ፡ ያለ raqq yalä

outmoded ጊዜ ፡ ያለፈ(በት) gize yalläfä(bbät)

out-of-date, see 'outmoded'

output ውጤት wäṭṭet; የሥራ ፡ ፍሬ yäsəra färe

outrage (v.) አናደደ annaddädä; አስቄጣ asq^wäṭṭa

outrageous (~ crime) አስቃቂ assäqqaqi

outright (adj.) ፍጹም fəṣṣum

outright, adv. (direct, openly) ግልጥ ፡ አድርጎ gəlṭ adrəgo; (at once) ወዲያውኑ wädiyawnu; ያኔውኑ yannewnu

outshine አስናቀ asnaqä

outside (n.) ውጭ wəčč

outside (adj.) የውጭ yäwəčč
outside (adv.) ውጪው wäččiw
outside of ከ - - - ሌላ kä - - - lela;
ከ - - - በቀር kä - - - bäqär; (in the exterior) ከ - - - ውጭ kä - - - wəčč
outside of this ከዚህ ፡ ሌላ käzzih lela
at the outside ቢበዛ bibäza

outsider የውጭ ፡ ሰው yäwəčč säw; ባዕድ ba'əd

outskirts ዳር dar; አካባቢ akkababi

outstanding (distinguished) የታወቀ yätawwäqä; (unpaid) እዳ ፡ ያልገባ əǧǧu yalgäbba; ያልተከፈለ yaltäkäffälä
be outstanding (exceptional) ተወዳ ዳሪ ፡ የለውም täwädadari yälläwəm

outstretched የተዘረጋ yätäzärägga

outward (adj.) የውጭ yäwəčč
outward (adv.) ወደ ፡ ውጭ wädä wəčč

outwardly ላይ ፡ ላዩን lay layun

outwear ከ - - - ይልቅ ፡ በረከተ kä - - -
yələq bäräkkätä

outwit አሞኘ amoňňä

oval ሞላላ molala

ovation ከፍ ፡ ያለ ፡ ጭብጨባ käff yalä
čəbčäba

oven ምድጃ mədəǧǧa; (for bread) የዳቦ ፡
መጋገሪያ yädabbo mägagäriya

over (prep.) በ - - - ላይ bä - - - lay;
ከ - - - በላይ kä - - - bälay; (more
than) ከ - - - የበለጠ kä - - - yäbälläṭä
over, adv. (once more) እንደገና əndägäna; (above) ከዚያ ፡ በላይ käzziya
bälay
over and over again ደጋግሞ dägagmo
over here እዚህ əzzih; እዚህ ፡ ጋ əzzih ga
over there እዚያ ፡ ማዶ əzziya mado
be over (finished) አለቀ alläqä; አበቃ
abäqqa

overall ጠቅላላ ṭäqlalla

overcoat ካቦርት kabbort; ካፖርት kapport

overcome (∼ difficulties) አሸነፈ aššännäfä; ተወጣ täwäṭṭa; (render unconscious) ራሱን ፡ እንዲስት ፡ አደረገ rasun əndisət adärrägä

overdo (do too much) ከመጠን ፡ አለፈ
kämäṭän alläfä; (exaggerate) አጋነነ
aggannänä

overdue (of bills) ሳይከፈል ፡ ብዙ ፡ ጊዜ ፡
ሆነው saykäfəl bəzu gize honäw; (of
a schedule being late) ዘገየ zägäyyä

overflow (vt.) አጥለቀለቀ aṭläqälläqä
overflow (vi.) ሞላ molla; ሞልቶ ፡
ፈሰሰ molto fässäsä

overhaul (inspect) መረመረ märämmärä;
(catch up with) ደረሰ(በት) därräsä-
(bbät)

overhear አዳመጠ adammäṭä; ጆሮው ፡
ውስጥ ፡ ጥልቅ ፡ አለ ǧorow wəsṭ ṭəlq
alä

overlap ተደራረበ tädärarräbä

overload ከመጠን ፡ በላይ ፡ ሞላ ፡ (ጫነ)
kämäṭän bälay molla (čänä)

overlook (ignore) አለፈ alläfä; (fail to
see) ሳያስተውለው ፡ ቀረ sayastäwläw
qärrä; (have or give a view over) በ -
- - ጐልቶ ፡ ታየ bä - - - gʷälto tayyä

overnight, adv. (during the night) ባንድ፡
ሌሊት band lelit; (in a very short time)
ባንዴ bande; ባንዳፍታ bandafta
stay overnight አደረ addärä

overpower አሸነፈ aššännäfä; አየለ ayyälä

overrun ወረረ wärrärä

overseas ባሕር ፡ ማዶ bahər mado; ውጭ፡
አገር wəčč agär

oversee ተቈጣጠረ täqʷäṭaṭṭärä

overseer ተቈጣጣሪ täqʷäṭaṭari

overshadow አስናቀ asnaqä

oversight, by ∼ በስሕተት bäsəhtät

overstay ከ - - - ጊዜ ፡ በላይ ፡ ቆየ kä - - -
gize bälay qoyyä

overt ግልጽ gəlṣ

overtake (come upon unexpectedly)
ደረሰ(በት) därräsä(bbät); (catch up)
ቀደመ qäddämä

overthrow ገለበጠ gäläbbäṭä

overtime ሰዓት ፡ እላፊ sä'at əllafi

overturn ገለበጠ gäläbbäṭä; ደፋ däffa

overwhelm በዛ(በት) bäzza(bbät); አሸነፈ
aššännäfä

overwork (n.) የሥራ ፡ ብዛት yäsəra bəzat

owe የ yä + personal pronoun + noun
+ አለበት alläbbät (as in 'he owes me
fifty dollars' የኔ ፡ አምሳ ፡ ብር ፡ አለበት
yäne amsa bərr alläbbät)

owing to በ - - - ምክንያት bä - - - məknəyat

owl ጉጉት *guggut*

own, vt. (possess) ገዛ *gäzza;* አለ(ው) *allä(w)*

own, vi. (confess) አመነ *ammänä*

own (adj.) የራስ *yäras;* የገዛ *yägäzza*
be on one's own ራሱን ፡ ቻለ *rasun čalä*
one's own የራሱ *yärasu*

owner ባለ ፡ ሀብት *balä habt;* ባለቤት *baläbet*

ownership ባለቤትነት *baläbetənnät;* ባለ ፡ ንብረት *balä nəbrät*

ox በሬ *bäre*

P

pace (v.) ወዲያና ፡ ወዲህ ፡ አለ *wädiyanna wädih alä*

pace (n.) እርምጃ *ərməǧǧa*

pacific (people) ሰላምን ፡ የሚወድ *sälamən yämmiwädd;* (~era) የሰላም *yäsälam*

pacify (soothe) አባበለ *ababbälä;* (bring peace) አረጋጋ *arrägagga*

pack, vt. (~into a trunk) ከተተ *kättätä;* (~mules) ጫነ *čanä;* (crowd into) አጨቀ *aččäqä*
pack (vi.) እቃውን ፡ አዘጋጀ *əqawən azzägaǧǧä*
pack up ጠቀለለ *täqällälä*

pack, n. (load) ጭነት *čənät;* (of cigarettes) ፓኬት *paket*

package መጠቅለያ *mäṭäqläya;* ጥቅል *ṭəqəll*

pack animal የጭነት ፡ ከብት *yäčənät käbt*

packhorse አጋሰስ *agasäs*

pact ውል *wəl;* ቃል ፡ ኪዳን *qal kidan;* ኪዳን *kidan*
make a pact ኪዳን ፡ ገባ *kidan gäbba*

paddle (v.) ቀዘፈ *qäzzäfä*

paddle (n.) መቅዘፊያ *mäqzäfiya*

pagan አረማዊ *arämawi*

paganism ጣዖት ፡ ማምለክ *ṭa'ot mamläk*

page (of book) ገጽ *gäṣṣ;* (event worth recording) ምዕራፍ *mə'əraf;* (messenger boy) ተላላኪ *tälalaki*

pagination የገጽ ፡ ቁጥር *yägäṣṣ quṭər*

pail ባልዲ *baldi*

pain (v.) አመመ(ው) *ammämä(w)*

pain, n. (ache) ውጋት *wəgat;* (distress) ሥቃይ *səqay*
pains ድካም *dəkam*
feel a pain in አመመ(ው) *ammämä(w)*
take pains ተጫነቀ *täčännäqä;* ብዙ ፡ ደከመ *bəzu däkkämä*

painful, be አመመ *ammämä;* (be distressing) አስቀጠጠ *asqäṭṭäṭä*

paint, vt. (cover with paint) ቀባ *qäbba;* (draw) ሣለ *salä;* (describe) ገለጸ *gälläṣä*

paint (n.) ቀለም *qäläm*

painter (who paints pictures) ሠዓሊ *sä'ali;* (who paints houses) ቀለም ፡ ቀቢ *qäläm qäbbi*

painting ሥዕል *sə'əl*

pair (n.) ጥምድ *ṭəmd;* ጥንድ *ṭənd*

pajamas ፒጃማ *piǧama*

palace ቤተ ፡ መንግሥት *betä mängəst;* ግቢ *gəbbi*

palate ላንቃ *lanqa*

pale (person) የገረጣ *yägäräṭṭa;* ደብዘዝ ፡ ያለ *däbzäzz yalä*
be pale ገረጣ *gäräṭṭa*

palm (plant) ዘምባባ *zämbaba;* (of hand) መዳፍ *mädaf*

palpate ደባበሰ *däbabbäsä*

palpitate (of heart) ከበሮ ፡ መታ *käbäro mätta*

pamper አሞላቀቀ *ammolaqqäqä*

pamphlet እነስተኛ ፣ መጽሔት anästäňňa mäṣhet

pan መጥበሻ mäṭbäša

pane, window ~ መስታወት mästawät

panel (part of door, of wall) ክፍል kəfəl; (group of speakers) ጓድ gʷadd

panic (vt.) አሸበረ aššäbbärä; አስፈራራ asfärarra

panic (vi.) ተሸበረ täšäbbärä

panic (n.) ሽብር šəbbər; ግርግር gərrəgərr

panic-stricken, be ተሸበረ täšäbbärä

pant (breathe quickly) ቁና ፣ ቁና ፣ ተነፈሰ qunna qunna tänäffäsä; (speak in short gasps) ቁርጥ ፣ ቁርጥ ፣ አለ qurrəṭṭ qurrəṭṭ alä

panther አነር anär; ግስላ gəssəlla

pants ሱሪ surri

papa አባባ abbabba

paper ወረቀት wäräqät; (newspaper) ጋዜጣ gazeṭa; (essay, report) ጽሑፍ ṣəhuf; ድርሰት dərsät

paper clip የወረቀት ፣ መርፌ yäwäräqät märfe

parable ምሳሌ məssale; ተረት tärät

parachute ጃንጥላ ğanṭəla

parade (v.) ተሰለፈ täsälläfä

parade (n.) ሰልፍ sälf

paradise ገነት gännät

paragraph አንቀጽ anqäṣ

parallel, v. (run alongside) ተከትሎ ፣ ሄደ täkättəlo hedä; (be similar to) ተመሳሰለ tämäsassälä

parallel, n. (comparison) ተመሳሳይ tämäsasay
draw a parallel አነጻጸረ annäṣaṣṣärä

parallel, adj. (~ lines) አንዳኝ aggʷadaňň; (similar) የሚመሳሰል yämmimmäsassäl

parallelism ተመሳሳይነት tämäsasayənnät

paralysis መስለል mäsläl

paralyze ሽባ ፣ አደረገ šəba adärrägä; (stop the movement) ዘጋ zägga

paralyzed ሰላላ sälala
be paralyzed ሰለለ sällälä; ሽባ ፣ ሆነ šəba honä; (with fear) ደነ ፣ ሆነ bädən honä; (of traffic) ተዘጋ täzägga

parasite ጥገኛ ፣ ነፍሳት ṭəggäňňa näfsat; (person) ቀላዋጭ qälawaç; በሰው ፣ ትከሻ ፣ የሚኖር bäsäw təkäšša yämminor

parasol ጃንጥላ ğanṭəla; ዣንጥላ žanṭəla

paratrooper ያየር ፣ ወለድ ፣ ወታደር yayyär wälläd wättaddär

parcel (n.) ጥቅል ṭəqəll; (of land) ቁራጭ qurraç

parcel post በፖስታ ፣ የሚላክ ፣ እቃ bäposta yämmillak əqa

parch (roast) ቈላ qʷälla; (dry up) አደረቀ adärräqä

parched grain ቆሎ qollo

parchment ብራና bəranna

pardon, v. (release from penalty) ምሕረት ፣ አደረገ(ለት) məhrät adärrägä(llät); ማረ marä; (forgive) ይቅር ፣ አለ yəqər alä

pardon (n.) ምሕረት məhrät
ask (someone's) pardon ይቅርታ ፣ ጠየቀ yəqərta ṭäyyäqä

pare (peel) ላጠ laṭä

parent ወላጅ wälağ
parents አባትና ፣ እናት abbatənna ənnat

parentage ቤት ፣ ሰብ betä säb

parental የወላጅ yäwälağ

parenthesis ቅንፍ qənnəf

parenthood ወላጅ ፣ መሆን wälağ mähon

parish አጥቢያ aṭbiya; ደብር däbər; (parishoners) የደብር ፣ ሕዝብ yädäbər həzb

park, vt. (~ a car) አቆመ aqomä

park (n.) መናፈሻ männafäša; መናፈሻ ፣ ቦታ männafäša bota

parking place **መኪና ፡ መቆሚያ ፡ ሰፍራ** *mäkina mäqomiya səfra*

parley **ሰብሰባ** *səbsäba*

parliament **ምክር ፡ ቤት** *məkər bet;* **ፓርላማ** *parlama;* **ፓርላሜንት** *parlament*

parlor **ማረፊያ ፡ ክፍል** *maräfiya kəfəl*

parochial (having to do with the parish) **የቤተ ፡ ክህነት** *yäbetä kəhənät;* (limited view point) **በጣም ፡ የተወሰነ** *bätam yätäwässänä*

parrot **በቀቀን** *bäqäqän*

parry **መከተ** *mäkkätä*

parsimonious, see 'stingy'

part (vt.) **አለያየ** *alläyayyä;* **ከፈለ** *käffälä*
part (vi.) **ተለያየ** *täläyayyä*

part (n.) **ክፍል** *kəfəl;* (share) **ድርሻ** *dərša;* (role) **ገላፍነት** *halafinnät;* (in a play) **ቦታ** *bota*
parts (region, place) **አገር** *agär;* **ግድም** *gədəm*
for my part **በኔ ፡ በኩል** *bäne bäkkul;* **በበኩሉ** *bäbäkkule*
for the most part **አብዛኛውን ፡ ጊዜ** *abzaňňawən gize*
in part **በከፊል** *bäkäfil*
on the part of **በ - - - በኩል** *bä - - - bäkkul*
play a part **ቦታ ፡ ያዘ** *bota yazä*
take part in **ተሳተፈ** *täsattäfä;* **ተካፈለ** *täkaffälä*

partake **ተሳተፈ** *täsattäfä;* **ተካፈለ** *täkaffälä*

partial, be ~ to **አደላ** *adälla*

partiality **ዝንባሌ** *zənəbbale*

partially **በከፊል** *bäkäfil*

participant **ተካፋይ** *täkafay*

participate **ተሳተፈ** *täsattäfä;* **ተካፈለ** *täkaffälä*

participation **ሱታፌ** *sutafe*

particle **ቅንጣት** *qənṭat*

particular(s) **ዝርዝር** *zərzər*

particular (adj.) **የተለየ** *yätäläyyä;* **ልዩ** *ləyyu*
be particular **ተጠነቀቀ** *täṭänäqqäqä*
in particular **በተለይ** *bätäläyy*

particularity **የተለየ ፡ ጠባይ** *yätäläyyä ṭäbay*

particularly **በተለይ** *bätäläyy;* **ይበልጡንም** *yəbälṭunəm*

partisan (supporter of a person) **ደጋፊ** *däggafi;* (guerrilla) **የደፈጣ ፡ ተዋጊ** *yädäfäṭa täwagi*

partition (v.) **ከፋፈለ** *käfaffälä*

partition, n. (division) **መከፋፈል** *mäkkäfafäl;* (dividing panel) **የቤት ፡ አካፋይ** *yäbet akkafay*

partly **በከፊል** *bäkäfil*

partner **ሸሪክ** *šärik*

partnership **ሽርክና** *šərkənna*

partridge **ቆቅ** *qoq*

part-time **የትርፍ ፡ ሰዓት** *yätərf sä'at*

party (entertainment) **ግብዣ** *gəbža;* (political ~) **የፖለቲካ ፡ ቡድን** *yäpolätika budən;* (each of the persons in a lawsuit) **ነገርተኛ** *nägärtäňňa;* (group of people) **ጓድ** *gʷadd*

pass, vt. (spend time) **አሳለፈ** *asalläfä;* (hand over) **አቀበለ** *aqäbbälä*
pass (vi.) **አለፈ** *alläfä;* (change from one state to another) **ተለወጠ** *täläwwäṭä;* (of a bill) **ጸደቀ** *ṣäddäqä*
pass around **አስተላለፈ** *astälalläfä*
pass away (go away) **አለፈ** *alläfä;* (die) **አረፈ** *arräfä*
pass by **አለፈ** *alläfä*
pass out (vt.) **ዐደለ** *addälä*

pass, n. (permission) **የይለፍ ፡ ወረቀት** *yäyəläf wäräqät;* **ፈቃድ** *fäqad*

passage (passing) **ማለፍ** *maläf;* (corridor) **መተላለፊያ** *mättälaläfiya;* (trip) **ጉዞ** *guzo;* (from a book) **ምንባብ** *mənbab*
book passage **ቦታ ፡ ያዘ** *bota yazä*

passenger መንገደኛ *mängädäñña;* (on train) ተሳፋሪ *täsafari*

passer-by ጎዳፊ ፣ አግዳሚ *halafi agdami;* መንገደኛ *mängädäñña*

passing, n. (death) ሞት *mot* in passing በነገራ ፣ ላይ *bänägäre lay* passing (adj.) ተላላፊ *tälalafi*

passion ስሜት *səmmet* have a passion for በጣም ፣ ወደደ *bäṭam wäddädä*

passionate የጋለ ፣ ስሜት ፣ ያለው *yägalä səmmet yalläw*

passive (∼person) ተካፋይ ፣ ያልሆነ *täkafay yalhonä;* (∼disposition) የታ ዛዥነት *yätazzažənnät*

passport ፓስፖርት *pasport*

past, n. (past history) የጥንት ፣ ታሪክ *yäṭənt tarik;* (time) ጎዳፊ ፣ ጊዜ *halafi gize;* ጥንት *ṭənt* in the past ከዚህም ፣ በፊት *kässihəm bäfit*

past (adj.) ያለፈ *yalläfä;* (president) የቀ ድሞ *yäqädmo* past (prep.) ከ - - - አለፍ ፣ ብሎ *kä - - - aläff bəlo*

paste (v.) ለጠፈ *läṭṭäfä;* አጣበቀ *aṭṭabbäqä*

paste (n.) ማጣበቂያ *maṭṭabäqiya*

pastime የጊዜ ፣ ማሳለፊያ *yägize masalläfiya*

pastor ካህን *kahən*

pastoral (∼tribe) ከብት ፣ አርቢ *käbt arbi;* (of priest) የቅስና *yäqəssənna*

past tense ጎዳፊ ፣ ጊዜ *halafi gize;* ጎዳፊ ፣ ጊዜያት *halafi gizeyat*

pasture (v.) በላ *bälla;* ለቀመ *läqqämä;* ተሰማራ *täsämarra;* ጋጠ *gaṭä*

pasture (n.) ግጦሽ *gəṭoš*

pat (∼a dog) አሻሸ *ašaššä;* (∼a person) ደባበሰ *däbabbäsä;* ምታ ፣ አደረገ *mäta adärrägä*

patch, v. (a tire) ለጠፈ *läṭṭäfä;* (∼trou-

sers) ጣፈ *ṭafä* patch up (repair) ጠገን ፣ አደረገ *ṭägänn adärrägä*

patch, n. (on tire) ለጥፍ *läṭṭəf;* (on trousers) መጣፊያ *mäṭafiya;* እራፊ *ərrafi;* ድርቶ *dərrito*

paternal አባታዊ *abbatawi*

paternity አባት ፣ መሆን *abbat mähon*

path የእግር ፣ መንገድ *yäəgər mängäd*

patience ትዕግሥት *tə'gəst;* ትግሥት *təgəst;* ታጋሽነት *taggašənnät*

patient, n. (sick person) ሕመምተኛ *həmämtäñña;* በሽተኛ *bäššətäñña*

patient (adj.) ትዕግሥተኛ *tə'gəstäñña;* ቻይ *čay* be patient ታገሠ *taggäsä*

patriarch (of the family) ባለቤት *baläbet;* (of a tribe) ባላባት *balabbat*

patrimony የወረሰው ፣ ሀብት *yäwärräsäw habt*

patriot አርበኛ *arbäñña;* አገሩን ፣ የሚ ወድ ፣ ሰው *agärun yämmiwädd säw*

patriotic ያገር ፣ ፍቅር ፣ ያለበት *yagär fəqər yalläbbät*

patriotism ያገር ፣ ፍቅር *yagär fəqər*

patrol (n.) ቃኚ ፣ ጎድ *qañňi gʷadd*

patron (customer) ደንበኛ *dänbäñña*

patronize (be a regular customer) ደን በኛ ፣ ነው *dänbäñña näw;* (support) ረዳ *rädda*

patron saint ታዳጊ *taddagi*

pattern, n. (of rug) ሐረግ *haräg;* (for dress) ንድፍ *nədf;* (example) ምሳሌ *məssale;* (model) አብነት *abənnät*

paunch ቦርጭ *borč*

pauper የኔ ፣ ቢጤ *yäne biṭe*

pause (v.) ቆም ፣ አለ *qomm alä*

pause, n. (rest) ዕረፍት *əräft;* (brief stop) እልፈት *əlfit*

pave, v. (∼road) አነጠፈ *anäṭṭäfä* be paved ባስፋልት ፣ ተነጠፈ *basfalt tänäṭṭäfä*

pavement የተነጠፈ ፡ መንገድ yätänäṭṭäfä mängäd

paw (n.) መዳፍ mädaf

pawn (v.) አስያዘ asyazä

pawn (n.) መያዣ mäyaža

pay (v.) ከፈለ käffälä; (be profitable)
ጠቀመ ṭäqqämä; (yield a salary) አስ
ገኘ asgäňňa
pay back ብድር ፡ መለሰ bəddər mälläsä; መለሰ mälläsä
pay down በቅድሚያ ፡ ከፈለ bäqədmiya käffälä

pay (n.) ደሞዝ dämoz; ክፍያ kəfəyya

payment (giving of money) መክፈል mäk-
fäl; (that which is paid) ክፍያ kəfəyya

pea አተር atär

peace ሰላም sälam; (agreement to end
a war) የሰላም ፡ ውል yäsälam wəl
be at peace ሰላም ፡ ነው sälam näw
make peace አስታረቀ astarräqä
break the peace ጸጥታ ፡ አደፈረሰ ṣäṭ-
ṭäta adäfärräsä

Peace Corps የሰላም ፡ ጓድ yäsälam
gʷadd

peaceful (calm) ጸጥ ፡ ያለ ṣäṭṭ yalä; (liking peace) ሰላማዊ sälamawi

peach ኮክ kok

peak (of mountain) ጫፍ čaf; (of power) ጽንፍ ṣənf

peanut አችሎኒ oččoloni

pearl ሉል lul

peasant ገባሬ gäbäre

pebble ጠጠር ṭäṭär

peck (pick up) ለቀመ läqqämä; ቄነጠረ
qʷänäṭṭärä; (strike with the beak)
ጠቀመ ṭäqqʷämä

peculiar የተለየ yätäläyyä

peculiarity (strangeness) እንግዳነት əngədannät; (special character) ልዩ ፡ ጠ
ባይ ləyyu ṭäbay

pecuniary የገንዘብ yägänzäb

pedal (n.) መርገጫ märgäča

peddle እያዞረ ፡ ሸጠ əyyäzorä šäṭä

peddler ሱቅ ፡ በደራቴ suq bädäräte; እቃ ፡
አዟሪ əqa azʷari

pedestrian እግረኛ əgräňňa

peek አሾልኮ ፡ አየ ašolləko ayyä

peel (vt.) ላጠ laṭä
peel, vi. (of paint) ተቀረፈ täqärräfä;
(of bark) ተላጠ tälaṭä
peel off ቀረፈ qärräfä

peel (n.) ልጥ ləṭ; ልጣጭ ləṭṭač; ቅርፊት
qərfit; (of orange) ቆዳ qoda

peep, v. (look furtively) ሰርቆ ፡ አየ särqo ayyä; አሾልኮ ፡ አየ ašolləko ayyä;
(chirp) ጩኸ čohä

peer (n.) መሰል mässäl; እኩያ əkkuya;
(of the same status) አቻ ačča

peerless ተወዳዳሪ ፡ የሌለው täwädadari
yälelläw

peg (n.) ችንካር čənkar; ችካል čəkal

pen, n. (for writing) ብዕር bə'ər; (enclosure for cattle) በረት bärät; ማጐሪያ
magʷäriya
Minister of the Pen ጸሐፈ ፡ ትእዛዝ
ṣähafe tə'əzaz

penal የወንጀል yäwänǧäl

penal code የወንጀለኛ ፡ መቅጫ ፡ ሕግ yä-
wänǧäläňňa mäqča həgg

penalize ቀጣ qäṭṭa

penalty ቅጣት qəṭat; መቀጫ mäqqäča;
መቀጮ mäqqäčo

penance ንስሐ nəssəha
do (make) penance ንስሐ ፡ ገባ nəssəha gäbba

pencil እርሳስ ərsas

pencil sharpener መቅረጫ mäqräča

penetrate (enter into) ገባ gäbba; ዘለቀ
zälläqä; (pierce) ጣሰ ṭasä; (find out)
ደረሰ(በት) därräsä(bbät)

peninsula ባሕረ ፡ ገብ ፡ መሬት bahrä
gäbb märet

penitence ንስሐ nəssəha

penitentiary መሀኒ : ቤት *wähni bet;* እስር : ቤት *əsər bet*

penknife ሰንጢ *sänṭi*

penniless ባዶ : እጁን *bado əǧǧun*

penny ሳንቲም *santim;* በሳ *besa*

pension (v.), ~ off ጡረታ : አስገባ *ṭuräta asgäbba*

pension (n.) የጡረታ : አበል *yäṭuräta abäl;* መጦሪያ *mäṭṭoriya*

pensive, be ተከዘ *täkkäzä*

Pentecost (የ)ጴንጠቆስጤ : በዓል *(yä)-qʷänṭäpäsṭe bä'al*

penury ድኽነት *dəhənnät;* ችግረኛነት *čəg-gəräññannät*

people (persons) ሰው *säw;* (persons belonging to a nation) ሕዝብ *həzb;* (family) ቤቶች *betočč*

pepper በርበሬ *bärbärre*

peppery በርበሬ : የበዛበት *bärbärre yä-bäzzabbät*

perceive ተገነዘበ *tägänäzzäbä;* (understand) ገባ(ው) *gäbba(w)*

percent በመቶ *bämäto;* ከመቶ *kämäto;* ከመቶ - - - እጅ *kämäto - - - əǧǧ*

percentage, see 'percent'

perception የመለየት : ችሎታ *yämäläy-yät čəlota*

perceptive (~ person) አስተዋይ *astä-way;* (~analysis) የተጣራ *yätäṭarra*

perch ቆጥ *qoṭ*

perchance ምናልባት *mənalbat* + imperfect + ይሆናል *yəhonal*

percussion ድምፅ *dəmṣ*

per diem የቀን : አበል *yäqän abäl*

perennial (~plant) ካመት : ዓመት : የሚያብብ *kamät amät yämmiyabbəb;* (~ river) ካመት : እስከ : ዓመት : የማ ይደርቅ *kamät əskä amät yämmaya-därq;* (continuous) ዘላቂነት : ያለው *zälaqinnät yalläw*

perfect (v.) ከፍጹምነት : አደረሰ *käfəṣṣu-mənnät adärräsä*

perfect, adj. (without defects) ፍጹም *fəṣṣum;* (exact) ትክክል *təkəkkəl;* (excellent) ጥሩ *ṭəru*

perfection ፍጹምነት *fəṣṣumənnät*

perfectly በፍጹም *bäfəṣṣum;* በትክክል *bätäkäkkəl;* በደንብ *bädänb*

perfidious ሸፍጠኛ *šäfṭäñña*

perfidy ሸፍጥ *šäfṭ*

perforate በሳ *bässa*

perform, vt. (~ a task) ፈጸመ *fäṣṣä-mä;* አከናወነ *akkänawwänä*

performance (carrying out) አፈጻጸም *affäṣaṣäm;* (presentation on a stage) ትርኢት *tər'əyt;*(of an actor) ጨዋታ *čäwata*

performer ተዋናይ *täwanay;* ተጫዋች *täčawač*

perfume, v. (of roses perfuming the air) አወደ *awwädä;* (of a person perfuming the air) ሽቶ : ረጨ *šätto räččä*

perfume (n.) ሽቶ *šätto*

perhaps ምናልባት *mənalbat*

peril አደጋ *adäga*

perilous አደገኛ *adägäñña*

period ዘመን *zämän;* (in school) ከፍለ : ጊዜ *kəflä gize;* (punctuation mark) አራት : ነጥብ *aratt näṭab*

periodical (n.) መጽሔት *mäṣhet*

periodically በየወቅቱ *bäyyäwäqtu*

periphery ዳር *dar*

perish አለቀ *alläqä;* ጠፋ *ṭäffa;* (die) ሞተ *mota*

perishable የሚበላሽ *yämmibbälašš*

perjury በሐሰት : መመስከር *bähassät mä-mäskär*

permanent ቋሚ *qʷami;* ዘላቂ *zälaqi*

permanently ለዘላቂታው *läzäläqetaw;* ለሁል : ጊዜ *lähul gize*

permeate (of rain, water, ideas) ዘለቀ *zälläqä;* (of smell) አወደ *awwädä*

permissible, be ተፈቀደ *täfäqqädä*

permission ፈቃድ *fäqad*
ask permission አስፈቀደ *asfäqqädä*
grant permission ፈቀደ *fäqqädä*

permissive ለል *ləl*

permit (v.) ፈቀደ *fäqqädä*

permit (n.) የፈቃድ ፡ ወረቀት *yäfäqad wäräqät*

pernicious ጠንቅ *ṭänq*

perpetual የማይቋረጥ *yämmayəqqʷarräṭ;* ዘላቂ *zälaqi*

perpetually ያለማቋረጥ *yalämaqqʷaräṭ*

perplex አደናገረ *addänaggärä;* ግራ ፡ አጋባ *gra aggabba*

persecute (harass) አስቸገረ *asčäggärä;* (oppress) አሳቀየ *assäqayyä*

persecution ማሳቀየት *massäqayät*

persevere ተጋ *tägga;* ወደ ፡ ኋላ ፡ አላለም *wädä hʷala alaläm*

persist (keep on) ቀጠለ *qäṭṭälä;* (last) ቆየ *qoyyä*

persistent (~rain) የማይቋረጥ *yämmayəqqʷarräṭ;* (~effort) ያልተቤጠበ *yaltäqʷäṭṭäbä*
be persistent ችክ ፡ አለ *čəkk alä*

person ሰው *säw;* (in grammar) መደብ *mädäb*
in person ራሱ *rasu*

personage ሰው *säw*

personal (~matter, property) የራስ *yäras;* የግል *yägəll;* ግላዊ *gəllawi*

personality ማንነት *mannənnät;* ባሕሪይ *bahriy;* (personage) ሰው *säw*

personally (by oneself) ራሱ *rasu;* (as far as oneself is concerned) በበኩሉ *bäbäkkulu*

personnel ሠራተኞች *särratäňňočč*

perspective አስተያየት *astäyayät;* ሐሳብ *hassab*

perspicacity ልቡና *ləbbuna;* ልቦና *ləbbona;* አስተዋይነት *astäwayənnät*

perspiration ላብ *lab;* ወዝ *wäz*

perspire አላበ(ው) *alabä(w);* ወዛ *wäzza*

persuade አስረዳ *asrädda;* አሳመነ *asammänä;* አግባባ *agbabba*

persuasion (persuading) ማግባባት *mägbabat;* (belief) እምነት *əmnät*

pertinent ተገቢ *tägäbi;* አግባብነት ፡ ያለው *agbabənnät yalläw*

perturb አደናገረ *addänaggärä*

pervade (of smell, odor) አወደ *awwädä;* (of joy) ሰፈነ(በት) *säffänä(bbät)*

perverse (~person) እልኸኛ *əlləhäňňa;* የሰው ፡ ምክር ፡ የማይቀበል *yäsäw məkr yämmayəqqäbbäl;* (~reasoning) የተሳሳተ *yätäsasatä*

pest (plague) ወረርሽኝ *wärräršäňň bäššəta;* (someone who annoys) መሽገር *mäžgär*

pester, see 'nag'

pestilence ቸነፈር *čänäfär*

pestilent (~disease) መርዘኛ *märzäňňa*

pestle መውቀጫ *mäwqäča;* ዘነዛና *zänäzäna*

pet, v. (stroke) ደባበሰ *däbabbäsä;* (treat with special kindness) አንከባከበ *ankäbakkäbä*

pet (n.) ለማዳ ፡ እንስሳ *lämmada ənsəsa;* (child) ብርቅዬ *bərqəyye*

petition (v.) ለመነ *lämmänä;* አቤቱታ ፡ አቀረበ *abetuta aqärräbä*

petition (n.) አቤቱታ *abetuta*

petitioner አመልካች *amälkač*

petrol ቤንዚን *benzin*

petroleum ጋዝ *gaz;* ዘይት *zäyt*

petty (~official) ዝቅተኛ *zəqqətäňňa;* (~detail) የማይረባ ፡ ጥቃቅን *yämmayəräba ṭəqaqən*

pharmacist መድኃኒት ፡ ቀማሚ *mädhanit qämmami*

pharmacy (የ)መድኃኒት ፡ ቤት (yä)mäd-hanit bet

phase (part) ክፍል kəfəl; (stage of development) የእድገት ፡ ደረጃ yäədgät däräǧa; (chapter in history) ምዕራፍ mə'əraf

phenomenon (circumstance that can be observed) ምልክት mələkkət; (something extraordinary) ያልተለመደ ፡ ሁኔታ yaltälämmädä huneta

philanthropy ችሮታ čərota

philosopher ፈላስፋ fälasfa

philosophy ፍልስፍና fəlsəfənna

phone (v.) ስልክ ፡ ደወለ səlk däwwälä

phone (n.) ስልክ səlk

phonetics የድምፅ ፡ ልሳን ፡ ጥናት yädəmṣ ləssan ṭənat

phonograph ሽክላ ፡ ማጫወቻ šäkla mäč-čawäča

photo ፎቶግራፍ fotograf
take a photo ፎቶግራፍ ፡ አነሣ foto-graf anässa

photographer ፎቶግራፍ ፡ አንሺ fotograf anši

phrase (n.) ሐረግ haräg

physical አካላዊ akalawi; (የሰውነት yäsä-wənnät; (∼laws) የተፈጥሮ yätäfäṭro physical labor የጉልበት ፡ ሥራ yägul-bät səra

physician ሐኪም hakim; ዶክተር doktär

physics ፊዚክስ fiziks

physiology የሰው ፡ አካል ፡ ጥናት yäsäw akal ṭənat

piano ፒያኖ piyano

pick, v. (∼flowers) ቀጠፈ qäṭṭäfä; (∼coffee, fruit) ለቀመ läqqämä; (choose) መረጠ märräṭä
pick on ተነኮሰ tänäkkʷäsä
pick out መረጠ märräṭä; መለመለ mälämmälä
pick (someone's) pocket ኪሱ ፡ ሰረቀ(በት) käkisu särräqä(bbät)

pick up ለቀመ läqqämä; (lift) አነሣ anässa

pick, n. (tool) ዶማ doma; መቆፈሪያ mä-qʷäffäriya; (choice) ምርጫ mərča; (crop) አዝመራ azmära

pickaxe, see 'pick' (n.)

pickpocket ኪስ ፡ አውላቂ kis awlaqi

picnic (n.) ሽርሽር šərräšərr

picture, v. (paint) ሣለ salä; (describe) ገለጸ gälläṣä

picture, n. (painting) ሥዕል sə'əl; (description) መግለጫ mägläča; (film) ፊ ልም film; (photo) ፎቶግራፍ fotograf take a picture ፎቶግራፍ ፡ አነሣ fotog-raf anässa

piece ቁራጭ qurrač; (of bread) ቁራሽ qurraš
break to pieces (vi.) እንክትክት ፡ ወጣ ənkətkətt wäṭṭa
fall to pieces (of book) ተገነጣጠለ tägänäṭaṭṭälä; (of house) ፈረረሰ fä-rarräsä; (of car) ውልቅልቁ ፡ ወጣ wə-ləqləqqu wäṭṭa

pier የወደብ ፡ መድራክ yäwädäb mädräk

pierce (of a bullet) ባሳ bässa; (of enemy forces) ጠሰ ፡ ገባ ṭəso gäbba; (of a needle) ወጋ wägga; (of the wind) ዘለቀ ፡ ገባ zälqo gäbba

piercing (∼voice) በጣም ፡ ቀጭን bäṭam qäččən; (∼scream) ጆሮ ፡ የሚበጥስ ǧoro yämmibäṭṭəs; (∼wind) አጥንት ፡ የሚሰብር aṭənt yämmisäbər

piety ሃይማኖታኝነት haymanotäňňannät; ቅድስና qəddəsənna

pig አሳማ asama

pigeon እርግብ ərgəb

pigment, see 'dye'

pile (v.), ∼up ቆለለ qʷällälä; ከመረ kämmärä

pile (n.) ቁልል qulləl; ክምር kəmmər

pilgrim ተሳላሚ täsalami

pilgrimage መሳለም mässaläm
make a pilgrimage ተሳለመ täsallämä

pill ኪኒን *kinin*

pillage (v.) በዘበዘ *bäzäbbäzä;* ዘረፈ *zär-räfä*

pillage (n.) የተዘረፈ ፡ ንብረት *yätäzär-räfä nəbrät;* ዝርፊያ *zərfiya*

pillar ምሰሶ *məsässo;* ዓምድ *amd*

pillow መከዳ *mäkkädda;* ትራስ *təras*

pillowcase የትራስ ፡ ልብስ *yätəras ləbs*

pilot, v. (∼a ship) መራ *märra;* (∼ a plane) ነዳ *nädda*

pilot, n. (of ship) የመርከብ ፡ ነጂ *yämär-käb nägi;* (of plane) አውሮፕላን ፡ ነጂ *awroplan nägi*

pimple ቡጉር *bugur*

pin (n.) የወረቀት ፡ መርፌ *yäwäräqät märfe;* እስፒል *əspil;* (badge) አርማ *arma*

pincers ወረንጦ *wärränṭo;* ጉጠት *guṭät*

pinch (v.) ቈነጠጠ *qʷänäṭṭäṭä*

pinch (n.), take a ∼ ቈነጠረ *qʷänäṭṭärä*

pink (adj.) ሐምራዊ *hamrawi;* ቀላ ፡ ያለ *qäla yalä*

pioneer (n.) አቅኚ *aqñi;* ሰፋሪ *säfari*

pious ሃይማኖተኛ *haymanotäñña*

pipe (musical instrument) ዋሽንት *wašənt;* (to smoke) ጋያ *gayya;* ፒፓ *pipa;* (of water) ቧምቧ *bʷambʷa*

pirate የባሕር ፡ ወንበዴ *yäbahər wän-bäde*

pistol ሽጉጥ *šəgguṭ*

pit (hole) ጉድጓድ *gudgʷad;* (seed of fruit) ፍሬ *fre*

pitch, v. (∼a ball) ወረወረ *wäräwwärä;* (∼a tent) ተከለ *täkkälä*
pitch in ረዳ *rädda*

pitch, n. (of voice) ድምፅ *dəmṣ;* (tar-like substance) ሙጫ *muččo*

pitcher (vessel) ማብረጃ *mabräga;* ማን ቈርቈርያ *manqʷärqʷäriya;* (who throws the ball to the batter) ኳስ ፡ አቀባይ *kʷas aqäbbay*

piteous የሚያሳዝን *yämmiyasazzən*

pitfall ዕንቅፋት *ənqəfat*

pitiful አሳዛኝ *asazzañ*

pitiless, be ርኅራኄ ፡ የለውም *rəhrahe yäl-läwəm*

pity (v.) አዘነ(ለት) *azzänä(llät)*

pity (n.) ሐዘኔታ *hazäneta;* ርኅራኄ *rəh-rahe*
have pity on አዘነ(ለት) *azzänä(llät);* ማረ *marä*
it's a pity ያሳዝናል *yasazzənal*

pivot v. ተሽከረከረ *täškäräkkärä*

pivot, n. (a thing on which some-thing turns) መሽከርከርያ *mäškärkä-riya;* (thing on which something de-pends) መሠረት *mäsärät*

placate አረጋጋ *arrägagga;* ቄጣ ፡ አበረደ *quṭṭa abärrädä*

place (v.) አስቀመጠ *asqämmäṭä;* አኖረ *anorä;* (∼ confidence) ጣለ *ṭalä;* (identify) ትዝ ፡ አለ(ው) *təzz alä(w)*

place (n.) ቦታ *bota;* ስፍራ *səfra;* መካን *mäkan*
any place የትም *yätəm*
in place of በ - - - ፈንታ *bä - - - fänta*
take place ተደረገ *tädärrägä;* ተፈጸመ *täfäṣṣämä*
take the place of ተካ *täkka*

placid (∼lake) ፀጥ ፡ ያለ *ṣäṭṭ yalä*

plague, v. (pester) አሠቃየ *assäqayyä;* አስጨነቀ *asčännäqä*
be plagued ተሠቃየ *täsäqayyä;* (by locusts) ተወረረ *täwärrärä*

plague (n.) ወረርሽኝ ፡ በሽታ *wärräršəñ bäššəta*

plain (n.) ሜዳ *meda*

plain, adj. (∼home) ተራ *tära;* (∼sur-face) ዝርግ *zərg;* (∼food) አልባሌ *aləbbale;* (clear) ጉልህ *guləh;* ግልጽ *gəlṣ;* (homely) የማያምር *yämmayamər*

plainly በጉልህ *bäguləh;* በግልጽ *bägəlṣ*

plaintiff ከሳሽ *käsaš*

plait (v.) ጐነጐነ gʷänäggʷänä

plait (n.) ጉንጉን gungun

plan, v. (devise) አቀደ aqqädä; (intend) አሰበ assäbä

plan, n. (drawing) ፕላን plan; (scheme) አቅድ aqd; እቅድ əqqəd; ዘዴ zäde; (intention) ምኞት mäňňot; ሐሳብ hassab

plane (v.) ላገ lagä

plane, n. (tool used in woodworking) መላጊያ mälagiya; (airplane) አውሮፕ ላን awroplan; (level) ደረጃ däräǧa

plane (adj.) ዝርግ zərg

planet ዓለም aläm

plank ሳንቃ sanqa; ጠርብ ṭärb

plant, v. (∼flowers) ተከለ täkkälä; (∼ wheat) ዘራ zärra; (∼stakes) ቸከለ čäkkälä

plant, n. (trees, herbs) ተክል täkl; (factory) ፋብሪካ fabrika

plantation እርሻ ərša

plaster (v.) ለሰነ lässänä; መረገ märrägä

plaster (n.) ልስን ləssən; ምርጊት mərgit

plate, n. (platter) ሳሕን sahən; ዝርግ ፡ ሳሕን zərg sahən; (illustration) ሥዕል sə'əl

plateau አምባ amba

platform መድረክ mädräk

platoon የመቶ yämäto

platter ሳሕን sahən; ዝርግ ፡ ሳሕን zərg sahən

play (v.) ተጫወተ täčawwätä; (∼the drum) መታ mätta; (∼the trumpet) ነፋ näffa; (∼the harp) ደረደረ däräddärä

play, n. (game) ጨዋታ čäwata; (theatrical performance) ቲያትር tiyatər; (jest) ቀልድ qäld

player ተጫዋች täčawač

playful ተጫዋች täčawač

playground የመጫወቻ ፡ ሜዳ yämäččawäča meda

playing card የመጫወቻ ፡ ካርታ yämäč-čawäča karta

playwright ቲያትር ፡ ደራሲ tiyatər därasi

plea (appeal) ለምና ləmmäna
make a plea ለመነ lämmänä

plead (argue a case in court) ተሟገተ tämʷaggätä; (entreat) ተማጠነ tämaṭṭänä; ለመነ lämmänä; ለምና ፡ አቀረበ ləmmäna aqärräbä; (offer as an excuse) ምክንያት ፡ ሰጠ məknəyat säṭṭä
plead guilty ጥፋተኝነቱን ፡ አመነ ṭəfatäňňannätun ammänä

pleasant ደስ ፡ የሚል däss yämmil; አስ ደሳች asdässač

please (v.) ደስ ፡ አሰኘ däss assäňňä; አስደሰተ asdässätä
please! እባክህ əbakkəh (sg. masc.)
be pleased ደስ ፡ አለ(ው) däss alä(w); ተደሰተ tädässätä

pleasing አስደሳች asdässač
be pleasing ሠመረ sämmärä; ደስ ፡ አለ däss alä

pleasure (n.) ተድላ tädla; ደስታ dässəta; (desire) መልካም ፡ ፈቃድ mälkam fäqad
afford pleasure ደስ ፡ አሰኘ däss assäňňä
take pleasure ተደሰተ tädässätä

pleat (v.) ሸነሸነ šänäššänä

pleat (n.) ሽንሽን šənšən

pledge (v.) ቃል ፡ ገባ qal gäbba; ቃል ፡ ሰጠ qal säṭṭä
pledge allegiance የመሐላ ፡ ቃል ፡ ገባ yämähalla qal gäbba

pledge, n. (solemn promise) መሐላ mähalla; ቃል ፡ ኪዳን qal kidan; (sign of friendship, good will) ማረጋገጫ marrägagäča; ማስታወሻ mastawäša; (something given as a guarantee) መያዣ mäyaža
pledge of allegiance ቃለ ፡ መሐላ qalä mähalla

take the pledge ቃል ፡ ገባ qal gäbba

plenary ሙሉ mulu

plenipotentiary ባለ ፡ ሙሉ ፡ ሥልጣን balä mulu səlṭan

plentiful, be ሞላ molla

plenty ጥጋብ ṭəgab; ብዛት bəzat
plenty of ብዙ bəzu
be plenty በዛ bäzza
have plenty ሞላ(ው) molla(w)
there is plenty of it ሞልቷል moltʷal

pleurisy የሳምባ ፡ በሽታ yäsamba bäššəta

pliant (∼vine) የሚተጣጠፍ yämmittäṭaṭäf; (∼branch, twig) ተወዛዋዥ täwäzawaž; ተለማጭ tälämmaç

pliers መቄንጠጫ mäqʷänṭäça; ጉጠት guṭät

plight መቅሠፍት mäqsäft; መከራ mäkära

plod አዘገመ azäggämä

plot (v.) አሴረ aserä; አደመ addämä; ዶለተ dollätä

plot, n. (conspiracy) ሴራ sera; አድማ adma; ዱለት dulät; (small area of ground) ቀራጭ qurraç; (main story of a novel) ታሪክ tarik

plotter ሴረኛ seräňňa; አድመኛ admäňňa

plow (v.) አረሰ arräsä

plow (n.) ማረሻ maräša

pluck (∼ chicken) ነጨ näççä; (∼ strings of a harp) መታ mätta
pluck out (∼hair) ነጨ näççä

plug (v.) ደፈነ däffänä
plug in ሰካ säkka
plug up ወተፈ wättäfä

plug, n. (piece of material to stop a leak) ውታፍ wətaf; (electric connection) የኮረንቲ ፡ መስኪያ yäkorränti mäsäkkiya

plumber ቧምቧ ፡ ሠራተኛ bʷambʷa särratäňňa

plumbing የቧምቧ ፡ ሥራ yäbʷambʷa səra

plump ደንዳና dändanna; የፋፋ yäfaffa
be plump ደነደነ dänäddänä; ፋፋ faffa

plunder (v.) ዘረፈ zärräfä

plunder (n.) ዘረፋ zäräfa

plunge, vt. (thrust) ጣለ ṭalä; (∼a dagger) ሰካ säkka
plunge (vi.) ጠለቀ ṭälläqä; ዘሎ ፡ ገባ zällo gäbba

plural ብዙ ፡ ቁጥር bəzu quṭər

plus (prep.) ሲደመር siddämmär

pneumonia የሳምባ ፡ ምች yäsamba məčč

pocket (n.) ኪስ kis

pocketbook ቦርሳ borsa

pocketknife ሰንጢ sänṭi

podium መድረክ mädräk

poem ግጥም gəṭəm

poet ባለ ፡ ቅኔ balä qəne

poetic የግጥም yägəṭəm; በግጥም ፡ የተጻፈ bägəṭəm yätäṣafä

poetry ግጥም gəṭəm; (religious ∼) ቅኔ qəne
write poetry ገጠመ gäṭṭämä

point, v. (indicate) አመለከተ amäläkkätä; (aim) ደገነ däggänä
point at አሳየ asayyä
point out አመለከተ amäläkkätä; አስገነዘበ asgänäzzäbä

point, n. (place) ቦታ bota; (tip) ጫፍ çaf; (essence) ፍሬ ፡ ነገር fre nägär; ዋና፡ነገር wanna nägär; (unit of scoring) ነጥብ näṭəb
point by point አንድ ፡ ባንድ and band
at that point ልክ ፡ በዚያን ፡ ጊዜ ləkk bäzziyan gize
at this point እዚህ ፡ ላይ əzzih lay
be on the point of ለ lä + imperfect + ሲል sil
come to the point ፍሬ ፡ ነገር ፡ ተናገረ fre nägär tänaggärä
to a certain point በከፊል bäkäfil
to the point of እስከ əskä + imperfect + ድረስ dəräs

pointed ሹል *šul;* (straight, ears) ቀጥ ፡
ያለ *qäṭṭ yalä*
be pointed ሾለ *šolä*

pointless (blunt) ዱልዱም *duldum;* (having no purpose) ፍሬ ፡ ቢስ ፡ የሆነ *fəre bis yähonä*

point of view አስተያየት *astäyayät;* ሐሳብ *hassab*

poise የርጋታ ፡ መንፈስ *yärgata mänfäs*

poised ረጋ ፡ ያለ *räga yalä*

poison, v. (give poison) መረዘ *märräzä;* መርዝ ፡ አበላ *märz abälla;* (spoil) አበ ላሸ *abbälaššä*

poison (n.) መርዝ *märz*

poison gas የመርዝ ፡ ጢስ *yämärz ṭis*

poisonous መርዛም *märzam;* መርዘኛ *märzäñña;* መርዝነት ፡ ያለው *märzənnät yalläw*

poke (with finger) ወጋጋ *wägagga;* (with elbow) ጐሸመ *gʷäššämä;* (~the fire) ቄሰቀሰ *qʷäsäqqʷäsä*

pole (post, pillar) ምሰሶ *mäsässo;* አጠና *aṭäna;* (either end of the earth's axis) የምድር ፡ ዋልታ *yämədər walta*
North Pole የሰሜን ፡ ዋልታ *yäsämen walta*
South Pole የደቡብ ፡ ዋልታ *yädäbub walta*

police (v.) ተቆጣጠረ *täqʷäṭaṭṭärä*

police (n.) ፖሊስ *polis*

police force የፖሊስ ፡ ሰራዊት *yäpolis särawit*

policeman ፖሊስ *polis*

police station (የ)ፖሊስ ፡ ጣቢያ *(yä)polis ṭabiya*

policy (principle) ዓላማ *alama;* አመራር *ammärar*

polish (v.) ላመጠ *lämmäṭä;* ወለወለ *wäläwwälä;* (~shoes) ጠረገ *ṭärrägä;* (improve) አሻሻለ *aššašalä*

polish (n.) ቀለም *qäläm*

polite ትሑት *təhut;* (~society) የጨዋ *yäčäwa*

politely በትሕትና *bätəhtənna*

politeness ጨዋነት *čäwannät;* ትሕትና *təhtənna*

political የፖለቲካ *yäpolätika*

politics ፖለቲካ *polätika*

poll, n. (voting booth) የምርጫ ፡ ጣቢያ *yämərča ṭabiya;* (voting) የድምፅ ፡ መስ ጠት *yädəmṣ mäsṭät*

pollute መረዘ *märräzä;* (~water) በከለ *bäkkälä*

pollution መበከል *mäbbäkkäl*

pomp ድምቀትና ፡ ሥነ ፡ ሥርዓት *dəmqä-tənna sənä sər'at*

pompous ጉረኛ *gurräñña*

pond ኩሬ *kure*

ponder አሰላሰለ *assälassälä;* አወጣ ፡ አወ ረደ *awäṭṭa awärrädä*

pool ኩሬ *kure*

poor ድሃ *dəha;* (miserable) ምስኪን *məs-kin;* (~district) ችግር ፡ የበዛበት *čəg-gər yäbäzzabbät;* (~food) አሸር ፡ ባ ሸር *ašär bašär;* (~education) በቂ ፡ ያልሆነ *bäqi yalhonä;* (~excuse) የማ ይረባ *yämmayəräba;* (~attendance) አነስተኛ *anästäñña*
be (become) poor ደኸየ *dähäyyä*
of poor quality መናኛ *mänañña*

poorly መጥፎ *mäṭfo;* እንደነገሩ *əndänä-gäru*
feel poorly ጤንነት ፡ አይሰማውም *ṭe-nännät ayəssämmawəm*

pop, vi. (of balloon) ብው ፡ ብሎ ፡ አለ *bäww bəlo alä;* (of cork) ፈነዳ *fä-nädda*
pop in ብቅ ፡ አለ *bəqq alä*
pop open ፈነዳ *fänädda*
pop out (of eyes) ፍጥጥ ፡ አለ *fəṭäṭṭ alä*
pop up ብቅ ፡ አለ *bəqq alä*

pope ሊቀ ፡ ጳጳሳት *liqä pappasat*

popular (of the masses) የሕዝብ *yähəzb;* (~ government) ሕዝቡን ፡ የሚወክል *həzbun yämiwäkəl*

həzbun yämmiwäkkəl; (~ price) **መጠ**
ነኛ *mäṭänäñña;* (~ song) **ዘመናዊ** *zä-*
mänawi; (well liked generally) **የተወ**
ደደ *yätäwäddädä;* **ተወዳጅ** *täwäddaǧ;*
(widespread) **የተዛመተ** *yätäzammätä*

populate **በብዛት ፡ ሰፈረ** *bäbəzat säffärä*

population **ሕዝብ** *həzb;* (number of people) **የሕዝብ ፡ ቁጥር** *yähəzb quṭər*

populous (~ city) **የተጨናነቀ** *yätäčänan-*
näqä

porcelain **የሽ'ኽላ ፡ ሳሕን** *yäšähla sahən*

porch **በረንዳ** *bärända*

porcupine **ጃርት** *ǧart*

pork **ያሳማ ፡ ሥጋ** *yasama səga*

porridge **ገንፎ** *gänfo*

port **ወደብ** *wädäb*

porter **ተሸካሚ** *täšäkkami;* **ኩሊ** *kuli;*
(of hotel) **በረኛ** *bärräñña*

portion (v.) **አከፋፈለ** *akkäfaffälä*

portion (n.) **እጅ** *əǧǧ;* **ከፊል** *käfil*

portrait **ሥዕል** *sə'əl*

portray (make a picture) **ሣለ** *salä;* (describe) **ገለጸ** *gälläṣä*

pose, vt. (place in a certain position)
አስቀመጠ *asqämmäṭä;* (~ a problem)
ፈጠረ *fäṭṭärä*

position (posture) **አቋም** *aqʷam;* **አኳኋን**
akkʷahʷan; (place) **ስፍራ** *səfra;* (job)
ሥራ *səra;* (standing) **ደረጃ** *däräǧa;*
ቦታ *bota;* **ማዕረግ** *ma'əräg;* (way of
thinking) **አቋም** *aqʷam*
be in a position **ቻለ** *čalä*

positive (sure) **እርግጠኛ** *ərgəṭäñña;* (definite) **ቁርጥ ፡ ያለ** *qurrəṭṭ yalä;* (affirmative) **የእሽታ** *yäəššəta;* (constructive) **ጠቃሚ** *ṭäqami;* (electric charge)
ወንዴ *wände*

positively **በርግጥ** *bärgəṭ*

possess **አለ** *allä* with object suffix pronouns (as in **አለው** *alläw* he possesses); (occupy) **ያዘ** *yazä*

possession(s) **ንብረት** *nəbrät;* **ሀብት** *habt;*

(land under control of a government)
ግዛት *gəzat*
come into possession **ባለቤት ፡ ሆነ**
baläbet honä
take possession **ተረከበ** *täräkkäbä*

possessor **ባለቤት** *baläbet*
possessor of **ባለ** *balä*

possibility (chance) **ምርጫ** *mərča;* **መን**
ገድ *mängäd;* (something possible) **የሚ**
ቻል *yämmiččal*

possible **ሊደርስበት ፡ የሚችል** *lidärsəbbät*
yämmičəl
be possible **ተቻለ** *täčalä*

possibly **ምናልባት** *mənalbat*

post, v. (station, assign) **መደበ** *mäddä-*
bä; **አቆመ** *aqomä;* (put into the mail)
ፖስታ ፡ ቤት ፡ አስገባ *posta bet asgäb-*
ba; (display public notice) **ለጠፈ** *läṭ-*
ṭäfä

post, n. (pole) **አጠና** *aṭäna;* **ምሶሶ** *mə-*
sässo; (station) **መደብ** *mädäb;* (job,
position) **ስፍራ** *səfra;* (mail) **ፖስታ**
posta

postage **ቴምብር** *tembər*

postbox **የደብዳቤ ፡ ማጠራቀሚያ** *yädäb-*
dabbe maṭṭäraqämiya

post card **ካርድ** *kard*

posterior (adj.) **ኋለኛ** *hʷaläñña*

posterity **ወደፊት ፡ የሚመጣ ፡ ትውልድ**
wädäfit yämmimäṭa təwlədd

postman **ፖስተኛ** *postäñña*

post offiice **ፖስታ ፡ ቤት** *posta bet*

post office box (የ)**ፖስታ፡ሳጥን** (*yä*)*pos-*
ta saṭən

postpone **አስተላለፈ** *astälalläfä;* **አዘገየ**
azägäyyä

posture **አቋም** *aqʷam*

pot (earthenware container) **ሽክላ** *šäkla;*
(kinds of ~) **ምንቻት** *mənčat;* **ማፈያ**
mafəya; **ማሰሮ** *masäro*

potable **ለመጠጥ ፡ የሚሆን** *lämäṭäṭṭ yäm-*
mihon

potato ድንች dənnəčč
  sweet potato መጣጢስ mäṭaṭis; በጣ
  ጢስ bäṭaṭis
potent (∼medicine) ኃይለኛ hayläñña
potentate ገዢ gäži
potter ሽክላ ፡ ሠሪ šäkla säri
pottery ሽክላ šäkla; ሽህላ šähla; የሽህላ ፡
  እቃ yäšähla əqa
pouch ከረጢት käräṭit
poultry ዶሮ doro
pound (v.) ቀጠቀጠ qäṭäqqäṭä; ወቀጠ
  wäqqäṭä; (∼grain) ሸከሸከ šäkäššäkä
pound, n. (weight) ነጥር näṭr; (money)
  ፓውንድ pawnd
pour, vt. (∼cup of coffee) ቀዳ qädda;
  (∼water on plants) አጠጣ aṭäṭṭa;
  (into a jug) ገለበጠ gäläbbäṭä
  pour, vi. (of water) ፈሰሰ fässäsä;
  (rain heavily) ዶፍ ፡ ወረደ dof wärrädä
  pour out (vt.) አፈሰሰ afässäsä
poverty ድህነት dəhənnät
powder, v. (pulverize) ፈጨ fäččä; ደቄሰ
  däqqʷäsä; ቀጠቀጠ qäṭäqqäṭä; (sprinkle) ነሰነሰ näsännäsä
powder, n. (dry material in fine parti-
  cles) ዱቄት duqet; (for the face) የፊት ፡
  ዱቄት yäfit duqet; ፑዳር pudär; (gunpowder) ባሩድ barud; (explosive) ድማ
  ሚት dəmamit
powdered milk የዱቄት ፡ ወተት yäduqet
  wätät
power ኃይል hayl; (authority) ሥልጣን
  səlṭan; (of argument) ብርቱነት bər-
  tunnät; (electric ∼) ኮረንቲ korränti
powerful ኃያል hayyal; ብርቱ bərtu;
  ኃይለኛ hayläñña; ጠንካራ ṭänkarra;
  (∼voice) ጉልህ guləh
powerless, be ተሳነ täsänä
practical, be በሥራ ፡ ላይ ፡ ዋለ bäsəra
  lay walä
practice, v. (perform repeatedly to
  learn) ለማመደ lämammädä; (work
  at a profession) ሠራ särra

practice, n. (habit) ልማድ ləmad; (repeated performance) ልምምድ ləməmməd; (actual use of something) ገቢር
  gäbir
  be in practice በሥራ ፡ ላይ ፡ ዋለ bäsəra lay walä
practiced (adj.) ሥልጡን səlṭun
prairie የሳር ፡ ሜዳ yäsar meda
praise, v. (glorify) አመሰገነ amäsäggänä; አሞገሰ amoggäsä; ወደሰ wäddäsä;
  (speak favorably of) አደነቀ(ለት) adän-
  näqä(llät)
praise (n.) ሙጋሳ mugäsa; ውዳሴ wäd-
  dase
prance, ∼about ቧረቀ bʷarräqä
prattle ተንተባተበ täntäbattäbä
pray (vi.) ጸለየ ṣälläyä
prayer ጸሎት ṣälot
  offer prayers ጸሎት ፡ አደረገ ṣälot adärrägä
preach ሰበከ säbbäkä
preacher ሰባኪ säbaki
preaching ስብከት səbkät
preamble መግቢያ mägbiya
precarious (∼life) አደገኛ adägäñña
precaution ጥንቃቄ ṭənəqqaqe; (warning)
  ማስጠንቀቂያ masṭänqäqiya
  take precautions ተጠነቀቀ täṭänäqqäqä
precede (happen before in time) ቀደመ
  qäddämä; (be before in rank) በለጠ
  bälläṭä
precedence ቀዳሚነት qädaminnät; ቅድ
  ሚያ qədmiya
  take precedence ቀደመ qäddämä; ቀደ
  ምትነት ፡ አለው qäddämtənnät alläw
preceding ቀዳሚ qädami; ያለፈ yalläfä
precept (rule of conduct) ምክር məkər;
  (maxim) ምሳሌ məssale
precinct ቀበለ qäbäle
  precincts ቅጽር ፡ ግቢ qəṣər gəbbi; (of
  town) ከላል kəllal

precious (costly) ው*ድ wǝdd; የከበረ yäkäbbärä; (highly valued) ጠቃሚ ṭäqami
be precious ከበረ käbbärä

precipice ገደል gädäl

precipitate (bring about) አስከተለ askättälä; (hurl down) አንከባለለ ankäbaläla

precipitately በፍጥነት bäfǝṭnät; በጥድፊያ bäṭǝdfiya

precipitation (haste) ችኮላ čǝkkʷäla

precise (careful) ጠንቃቃ ṭänqaqqa; (accurate) ልክ lǝkk; ትክክለኛ täkäkkäläňňa
at the precise moment ልክ lǝkk

precisely (exactly) ልክ lǝkk; (accurately) በትክክል bätäkäkkǝl

precision ትክክለኛነት täkäkkäläňňannät

preclude አገደ aggädä

predecessor በፊት ፡ በቦታው ፡ የነበረ bäfit bäbotaw yänäbbärä

predestined የታጨ yätaččä

predicate (n.) አንቀጽ anqäṣ

predict ተነበየ tänäbbäyä

prediction ትንቢት tǝnbit

predilection መውደድ mäwdäd
have a predilection for ወደደ wäddädä

predominant የበለጠ yäbälläṭä

predominate አየለ ayyälä

preface (n.) መቅደም mäqdäm; መግቢያ mägbiya

prefer መረጠ märräṭä; (like) ፈለገ fällägä

preference ምርጫ mǝrča
have preference for መረጠ märräṭä
give preference አደላ adälla

prefix (in grammar) ባዕድ ፡ መነሻ ba'ǝd männäša

pregnancy እርግዝና ǝrgǝzǝnna; ነፍስ ፡ ጡርነት näfsä ṭurǝnnät

pregnant እርጉዝ ǝrguz; ነፍሰ ፡ ጡር näfsä ṭur; (~animal) ከብድ käbbad; ክብድ kǝbd
become pregnant አረገዘ(ች) aräggäzä(čč); (animal) ከበደ käbbädä

prejudice (n.) አግባብ ፡ የሌለው ፡ ጥላቻ agbab yälelläw ṭälačča

prelude መግቢያ mägbiya; ዋዜማ wazema

premature, be ጊዜው ፡ ሳይደርስ ፡ ነው gizew saydärs näw

prematurely ያለ ፡ ጊዜው yalä gizew; ያለ ፡ ቀኑ ፡ ቀድሞ yalä qänu qädmo

premium, n. (prize, inducement) ጉርሻ gurša; (payment) ከፍያ käfǝyya
premium (adj.) ከፍተኛ käffätäňňa

preparation መሰናዶ mässänado; ዝግጅት zǝgǝǧǧät

prepare አሰናዳ assänadda; አዘጋጀ azzägaǧǧä; (~a meal) ሠራ särra

prepared ስንዱ sǝnǝddu; ዝግጁ zǝgǝǧǧu
be prepared ተሰናዳ täsänadda; ተዘጋጀ täzägaǧǧä

preponderant ከሁሉ ፡ የበለጠ kähullu yäbälläṭä

preposition መስተዋድድ mästäwadǝd

prerogative የተለየ ፡ መብት yätäläyyä mäbt

prescribe አዘዘ azzäzä

prescription የመድኃኒት ፡ ማዘዣ yämädhanit mazäža

presence መኖር mänor

present, v. (submit) አቀረበ aqärräbä; (give as a gift) ሸለመ šällämä; (~a drama) አሳየ asayyä; (introduce) አስተዋወቀ astäwawwäqä; (~difficulties) አመጣ amäṭṭa
be presented ቀረበ qärräbä

present, n. (gift) ስጦታ säṭota; ገጸ ፡ በረከት gäṣṣä bäräkät; (present tense) ያሁን ፡ ጊዜ yahun gize
at present አሁን ahun; በዘመኑ bäzämänu

make a present of አበረክት *abäräkkätä*

present (adj.) ያሁን *yahun;* ያሁኑ *yahunu*
present! (here!) አቤት *abet*
he is present አለ *allä*

presently (now) አሁን *ahun;* (soon) በቅ ርቡ *bäqərbu*

present tense ያሁን ፡ ጊዜ *yahun gize*

preserve (v.) ጠበቀ *ṭäbbäqä*

preserves የቆርቆሮ ፡ ምግብ *yäqorqorro məgəb*

preside, ～over (act as chairman) በሊቀ ፡ መንበርነት ፡ መረ *bäliqä mänbärənnät märra*

president ፕሬዚዳንት *prezidant*

press, vt. (squeeze) ጨበጠ *čäbbäṭä;* (push) ገፋ *gäffa;* (push a button) ጫን ፡ አለ *čann alä;* (iron) ተኮሰ *täkkʷäsä;* (urge) አጥብቆ ፡ ጠየቀ *aṭbəqo ṭäyyäqä*
press down ጫን ፡ አለ *čann alä*

press, n. (printing) የማተሚያ ፡ መኪና *yämattämiya mäkina;* (newspaper) ጋዜጦች *gazeṭočč*
go to press ታተመ *tattämä*

pressing (urgent) አስቸኳይ *asčäkkʷay;* (important) ብርቱ *bərtu*

pressure, n. (stress) ጭንቀት *čənqät;* (of air) ያየር ፡ ግፊት *yayyär gəffit;* (insistence) መገፋፋት *mägäfafat*
bring pressure on አስገደደ *asgäddädä*

prestige ክብር *kəbər*

presumably ምናልባት *mənalbat*

presume ገመተ *gämmätä*

presumed የሚባል *yämmibbal*

presumptuous ልብ ፡ ሙሉ *ləbbä mulu*

pretend አስመሰለ *asmässälä;* በሐሰት ፡ አለ *bähassät alä*

pretense (excuse) ሰበብ *säbäb;* (false display) ለይምሳል *läyəmsäl*

pretentious አለሁ ፡ አለሁ ፡ ባይ *allähu allähu bay*

pretext ምክንያት *mənəyat;* ሰበብ *säbäb*
use as a pretext አመካኘ *ammäkaňňä*

pretty (adj.) ቆንጆ *qonǧo;* ውብ *wəb*

prevail (succeed) ተሳካ(ለት) *täsakka-(llät);* (predominate) አየለ *ayyälä;* (be dominant) ሰፈነ *säffänä*

prevalence ብዛት *bəzat*

prevalent, be አየለ *ayyälä;* በብዛት ፡ ተገኘ *bäbəzat tägäňňä*

prevent አስቀረ *asqärrä*
prevent from ከ - - - አገደ *kä - - - aggädä;* ከ - - - ከለከለ *kä - - - käläkkälä*

prevention መከላከያ *mäkkälakäya*

preventive (n.) መከላከያ *mäkkälakäya*

previous ቀዳሚ *qädami;* ቀደም ፡ ያለ *qädämm yalä;* የድሮ *yädəro;* የፊተኛ *yäfitäňňa*

previously ቀድሞ *qädmo;* አስቀድሞ *asqäddəmo;* ቀደም ፡ ብሎ *qädämm bəlo;* ከዚህ ፡ በፊት *käzzih bäfit*

price (n.) ዋጋ *waga*
for any price በምንም ፡ ዓይነት *bämənəm aynät*

priceless እጅግ ፡ ውድ *əǧǧəg wädd;* ባለ ፡ ብዙ ፡ ዋጋ *balä bəzu waga*

prick (of needle, thorn) ወጋ *wägga;* (with claws) ቧጠጠ *bʷaṭṭäṭä*

prickle (n.) ጥቃቅን ፡ ሾህ *ṭəqaqən šoh*

prickly እሾሀማ *əšohəmma*

pride ትዕቢት *tə'əbit;* ኩራት *kurat;* (person giving others satisfaction) መኩሪያ *mäkuriya*

priest ቄስ *qes;* ካህን *kahən*
become priest ቀሰሰ *qässäsä*

priesthood ካህነት *kəhanät;* ቅስና *qəssənna;* (priests) ካህናት *kahənat*

priestly የቅስና *yäqəssənna*

primarily (above all) በይበልጥ *bäyəbälṭ;* (principally) በመሠረቱ *bämäsärätu*

primary (preceding) ቀዳሚ *qädami;* (original) መሠረታዊ *mäsärätawi;*

(chief) ዋና wanna

primary school አንደኛ ፡ ደረጃ ፡ ትምህርት ፡ ቤት andäñña däräǧa təmhərt bet

prime (n.) አፍላ afla
prime of life የዕድሜ ፡ አፍላ yäədme afla

prime (adj.) ዋና wanna; በጣም ፡ አስፈላጊ bäṭam asfällagi

prime minister ጠቅላይ ፡ ሚኒስትር ṭäqlay ministər

primer ዐውደ ፡ ንባብ awdä nəbab

primitive (of early days) የጥንት yäṭənt; (simple and crude) ወደ ፡ ኋላ ፡ የቀረ wädä hʷala yäqärrä; (uncivilized) ያልሠለጠነ yalsäläṭṭänä

primogeniture በኩርና bäkʷrənna

prince ለዑል lə'ul
Crown Prince አልጋ ፡ ወራሽ alga wäraš

princess ልዕልት lə'əlt

principal, n. (head of school) ዲረክተር diräktär; (sum of money) ዋና ፡ ገንዘብ wanna gänzäb

principal (adj.) ዋና wanna

principle (rule) ደንብ dänb; መሠረታዊ ፡ ደንብ mäsärätawi dänb; መሠረት ፡ ሐሳብ mäsärätä hassab; (fundamental belief) እምነት əmnät; የሚያምን በት ፡ ነገር yämmiyamənəbbät nägär
as a matter of principle በሕጉ ፡ መሠረት bähəggu mäsärät
in principle በመሠረቱ bämäsärätu

print (v.) አተመ attämä

print (n.) እትም əttəm; ፊደሎች fidäločč; (copy of picture) ቅጂ qəǧǧi; (imprint) አሻራ ašara
be in print ይገኛል yəggäññal
be out of print አለቀ alläqä

printer አታሚ attami

printing እትም əttəm

printing press ማተሚያ ፡ ቤት mattämiya bet

prior ቀደም ፡ ያለ qädämm yalä

priority ቀደምትነት qäddämtənnät; ቀዳሚነት qädaminnät

prison እስር ፡ ቤት əsər bet; ወህኒ ፡ ቤት wähni bet

prisoner እስረኛ əsräñña
prisoner of war ምርኮኛ märkoñña
take prisoner ማረከ marräkä

privacy (seclusion) ለብቻ ፡ መሆን läbəčča mahon; (secrecy) ቁይታ qoyyəta

private (n.) ተራ ፡ ወታደር tära wättaddär

private (adj.) የግል yägəll; (~citizen) ተራ tära
in private ለብቻ läbəčča; በግል bägəll

private secretary ልዩ ፡ ጸሐፊ ləyyu ṣähafi

privation ችግር čəggər

privilege ልዩ ፡ መብት ləyyu mäbt

prize, n. (reward) ሽልማት šəlləmat

probability ይሆናል yəhonal

probable ሊሆን ፡ የሚችል lihon yämmičəl
be probable ስ sə + negative imperfect

probably ምናልባት mənalbat

probe (v.) መረመረ märämmärä

probe (n.) ምርመራ mərmära

problem (matter) ጉዳይ gudday; (difficult issue) ችግር čəggər; ጣጣ ṭaṭa; (in mathematics) ጥያቄ ṭəyyaqe

procedure ሥርዓት sər'at; ሥነ ፡ ሥርዓት sənä sər'at; መንገድ mängäd

proceed ቀጠለ qäṭṭälä

proceeding ነገር nägär
proceedings የሥራ ፡ ውጤት yäsəra wəṭṭet

proceeds ያገኘው ፡ ገንዘብ yagäññäw gänzäb

process (n.) ጉዳይ gudday; (method) ዘዴ zäde
be in the process of በ - - - ላይ ፡ ነው bä - - - lay näw

procession ሰልፍ *sälf*

proclaim (announce, make known) አስ ታወቀ *astawwäqä*; ገለጸ *gälläṣä*; (by a proclamation) ዐወጀ *awwäǧä*

proclamation ዐዋጅ *awaǧ*

procure አገኘ *agäňňä*

prod, v. (poke) ወጋ ፡ ወጋ ፡ አደረገ *wäga wäga adärrägä*; (urge on) ገፋፋ *gäfaffa*

prod (n.) ሹል ፡ ዘንግ *šul zäng*

prodigal ገንዘብ ፡ አባካኝ *gänzäb abakaň*

produce, v. (make) ሠራ *särra*; (bring forth crops) አመረተ *amärrätä*; አበቀለ *abäqqälä*; (bring forward) አቀረበ *aqärräbä*; (bring about) አስገኘ *asgäňňä*

produce (n.) ሀብት *habt*; (of land) የእር ሻ ፡ ሀብት *yäərša habt*; (crop) ምርት *mərt*

product ሀብት *habt*; እቃ *əqa*; (of farm) ምርት *mərt*; (of factory) ውጤት *wəṭṭet*

productive (~ activity) ጠቃሚ *ṭäqami*; (~ business) ትርፍ ፡ ያለበት *tärf yalläbbät*; (~ soil) ለም *läm*; (~ writer) ብዙ ፡ መጽሐፍት ፡ የሚጽፍ *bəzu mäṣahəft yämmiṣəf*

profane (v.) አረከሰ *aräkkäsä*

profane, adj. (secular) ዓለማዊ *alämawi*; (vulgar) የብልግና *yäbəlgənna*

profess (declare) ገለጸ *gälläṣä*; (believe) አመነ *ammänä*

profession ሙያ *muya*

professional, adj. (having to do with a profession) የሙያ *yämuya*; (not amateur) ፕሮፌሽናል *profešənal*

professor መምህር *mämhər*; ፕሮፌሶር *profesor*

proficiency ችሎታ *čəlota*

proficient በቂ ፡ ችሎታ ፡ ያለው *bäqi čəlota yalläw*
be proficient in ሠለጠነ *säläṭṭänä*

profile ጐን *gʷänn*

profit (v.) አተረፈ *atärräfä;* (be advantageous) ጠቀመ *ṭäqqämä*

profit, n. (advantage) ጥቅም *ṭəqəm;* (in business) ትርፍ *tärf*
derive profit ተጠቀመ *täṭäqqämä*
make a profit አተረፈ *atärräfä*

profitable (~ business) ትርፍ ፡ የሚያስ ገኝ *tärf yämmiyasgäňň;* (beneficial) ጠቃሚ *ṭäqami*
be profitable ረባ *räbba*

profound (~ learning) ጥልቅ *ṭəlq;* (~ scholar) ጥልቅ ፡ ዕውቀት ፡ ያለው *ṭəlq əwqät yalläw;* (~ silence) ፍጹም *fäṣṣum;* (~ grief) ከባድ *käbbad*

profuse በጣም ፡ ብዙ *bäṭam bəzu*

profusely ከማጣን ፡ በላይ *kämäṭän bälay*

progeny ዘርይያ *zärrəyya*

prognosis ግምት *gəmmət;* አስተያየት *astäyayät*

program ፕሮግራም *program*

progress, v. (develop) ተኪያሄደ *täkiyahedä;* (improve) እየተሻሻለ ፡ ሄደ *əyyätäšašalä hedä;* ተራመደ *tärammädä*

progress (n.) መሻሻል *mäššašal;* እርምጃ *ərməǧǧa*

progressive (in politics) ተራማጅ *täramaǧ;* ግምባር ፡ ቀደም *gəmbar qäddäm*

prohibit ከለከለ *käläkkälä;* አስቀረ *asqärrä*

prohibition መከልከል *mäkälkäl*

project (n.) አቅድ *aqd;* እቅድ *əqqəd;* ውጥን *wəṭṭən*

prolific ወላድ *wällad*

prologue መቅደም *mäqdäm*

prolong አራዘመ *arrazzämä*

prolonged (adj.) የረዘም ፡ ጊዜ *yäräǧǧim gize*

promenade (v.) ተንሻራሸረ *tänšäraššärä*

prominent (well-known) ስም ፡ ጥር *səmä ṭär;* (~ eyes) የፈጠጠ *yäfäṭṭäṭä;* (~ hump) ጐላ ፡ ያለ *gʷäla yalä*

promiscuous ልክስክስ *ləkəskəs*

promise (v.) ቃል ፡ ሰጠ *qal säṭṭä;* ቃል ፡ ገባ *qal gäbba*

promise (n.) ቃል ፡ ኪዳን *qal kidan;* ተስፋ *täsfa*
make a promise, see 'promise' (v.)
break one's promise አበለ *abbälä*

promised, ~land ምድረ ፡ ተስፋ *mədrä täsfa*

promising ተስፋ ፡ የሚጣልበት *täsfa yämmiṭṭaləbbät;* ተስፋ ፡ ያለው *täsfa yalläw*

promote (~trade) አስፋፋ *asfaffa;* (in rank) አሳደገ *asaddägä;* (bring about) አስከተለ *askättälä*
be promoted የደረጃ ፡ እድገት ፡ አገኘ *yädäräǧa ədgät agäňňa*

promotion የማዕረግ ፡ እድገት *yäma'əräg ədgät;* የሥራ ፡ እድገት *yäsəra ədgät*

prompt (v.) ገፋፋ *gäfaffa;* አነሣሣ *annäsassa*

prompt (adj.) ቀልጣፋ *qälṭaffa*
be prompt ፈጠነ *fäṭṭänä*

promptly (quickly) በፍሎ *bätolo;* ወዲያ ውኑ *wädiyawnu;* (exactly) ልክ *ləkk*

promptness ቅልጥፍና *qəlṭəfənna*

promulgate 0ወጀ *awwäǧä*

prone, be ~ to ዝንባሌ ፡ አለው *zənəbbale alläw*

pronoun ተውላጠ ፡ ስም *täwlaṭä səm*

pronounce (declare) አስታወቀ *astawwäqä;* (utter the sounds) ተናገረ *tänaggärä*

pronunciation አባባል *abbabal;* የቃላት ፡ አነባበብ *yäqalat annäbabäb*

proof መረጃ *märräǧa;* ማስረጃ *masräǧǧa*
put to the proof ፈተነ *fättänä*

prop, ~up ደገፈ *däggäfä*

propaganda ስብከት *səbkät;* ፕሮፓጋንዳ *propaganda*

propagandize ሰበከ *säbbäkä*

propagate አሰራጨ *assäraččä;* አዛመተ *azzammätä*

propel ወደ ፡ ፊት ፡ ገፋ *wädä fit gäffa*

proper (suitable) ምቹ *məčču;* ተገቢ *tägäbi;* (~authorities) አግባብ ፡ ያለው *agbab yalläw*
be proper ተገባ *tägäbba*

properly በሥርዓት *bäsər'at;* በደንብ *bädänb;* በወግ *bäwäg*

proper noun የተጸፃ ፡ ስም *yätäṣäw'o səm*

property ሀብት *habt;* ንብረት *nəbrät;* (land) መሬት *märet;* ርስት *rəst;* (attribute) ጠባይ *ṭabay*

prophecy ትንቢት *tənbit*

prophesy ተነባ *tänäbba;* ተነበየ *tänäbbäyä*

prophet ነቢይ *näbiy*

propitious (~weather) ተስማሚ *täsmami;* (~gods) ቻር *čar*

proportion (n.) ክፍል *kəfəl*
proportions መጠን *mäṭän*
in proportion to ከ - - - ጋር ፡ ሲታይ *kä - - - gar sittay*

proportionate መጠናኛ *mäṭänäňňa*
be proportionate ተመጣጠነ *tämäṭaṭṭänä*

proposal ሐሳብ *hassab;* አሳብ *assab*

propose (suggest) ሐሳብ ፡ አቀረበ *hassab aqärräbä;* (intend) አሰበ *assäbä*

proposition ሐሳብ *hassab*

proprietor ባለቤት *baläbet*

propriety (proper behavior) አገባብ *agäbab;* አግባብ *agbab;* ተገቢነት *tägäbinnät*

prose ስድ ፡ ንባብ *sədd nəbab*

prosecute (continue) ቀጠለ *qäṭṭälä;* (carry out a plan) አከናወነ *akkänawwänä;* (bring suit against) ሕግ ፡ ፊት ፡ አቀረበ *həgg fit aqärräbä*

prosecution (carrying on) አያያዝ *ayyayaz;* ማከናወን *makkänawän;* (conducting of legal action) ክስ *kəss* prosecutor ሕግ ፡ አስከባሪ *həgg askäb-bari;* ቦቃቤ ፡ ሕግ *aqqabe həgg*

prospect, n. (hope) ተስፋ *täsfa;* (chance) ዕድል *əddəl*

prospective የወደፊት *yäwädäfit*

prosper (of country) በለጸገ *bäläṣṣägä;* (succeed) ሰላ *sälla*

prosperity ብልጽግና *bəlṣəgənna;* ልማት *ləmat*

prosperous (~ city) የበለጸገ *yäbäläṣṣägä;* (~ person) ባለጸጋ *baläṣägga;* ሀብታም *habtam;* (~ business) የሚያበላ *yämmiyabäla*

prostitute ሴተኛ ፡ አዳሪ *setäñña adari;* ሽርሙጣ *šärmuṭa*

prostrate, v. (throw down) ገነዳደሰ *gänädaddäsä*
prostrate oneself (before god) ሰገደ *säggädä*

prostrate (adj.), be laid ~ ተዘረረ *täzärrärä*

protect (~ industry) ጠበቀ *ṭäbbäqä;* (~ freedom) ተከላከለ *täkälakkälä*

protection መከላከያ *mäkkälakäya;* ጥበቃ *ṭäbbäqa*
appeal for protection ተማጠነ *tämaṭṭänä*

protector የሚከላከል *yämmikkälakkäl*

protest, v. (object) ተቃወመ *täqawwämä*

protest (n.) ተቃውሞ *täqawmo*

Protestant ፕሮተስታንት *protästant*

protocol ፕሮቶኮል *protokol*

protract አራዘመ *arrazzämä*

protrude (vt.) አወጣ *awäṭṭa*
protrude, vi. (of teeth) ገጠጠ *gäṭṭäṭä*

proud ትዕቢተኛ *tə'əbitäñña;* ኩሩ *kuru*
be proud ኰራ *k^wärra*
be proud of ተመካ *tämäkka*

prove (show that it is true) አረጋገጠ *arrägaggäṭä;* (bring proof) አስረዳ *asrädda;* መሰከረ *mäsäkkärä*

proverb ምሳሌ *məssale*
speak in proverbs መሰለ *mässälä*

provide (give) ሰጠ *säṭṭä;* (furnish) አዘጋጀ *azzägaǧǧä*
provide for ጦረ *ṭorä;* አስተዳደረ *astädaddärä*

providence አርቆ ፡ አስተዋይነት *arqo astäwayənnät*

provident አርቆ ፡ አሳቢ *arqo assabi*

province (division of a country) ጠቅላይ ፡ ግዛት *ṭäqlay gəzat;* (authority) ሥልጣን *səlṭan*

provincial (~ government) የጠቅላይ ፡ ግዛት *yäṭäqlay gəzat;* (~ manners) የባላገርነት *yäbalagärənnät*

provision (providing) ማቅረብ *maqräb;* (stipulation) አንቀጽ *anqäṣ;* ደንብ *dänb;* (plan made beforehand) የወደፊት ፡ እቅድ *yäwädäfit əqqəd*
provisions ስንቅ *sənq*
take provisions for the road ሰነቀ *sännäqä*

provisional ጊዜያዊ *gizeyawi*

provoke (arouse) ቀሰቀሰ *qäsäqqäsä;* አነሳሳ *annäsassa;* አስከተለ *askättälä;* (irritate) አስቈጣ *asq^wäṭṭa*

prowl አደባ *adäbba*

proximity ቅርበት ፡ መሆን *qərbät mähon*

prudence አስተዋይነት *astäwayənnät*

prudent አስተዋይ *astäway;* ቀልባም *qälbam;* አርቆ ፡ የሚያስብ *arqo yämmiyassəb;* ጥንቁቅ *ṭənquq*

prune (a tree) መለመለ *mälämmälä;* ቈጠ ቈጠ *q^wäṭäqq^wäṭä*

pry ጣልቃ ፡ ገባ *ṭalqa gäbba*

psalm መዝሙር *mäzmur*

psaltery መዝሙረ ፡ ዳዊት *mäzmurä dawit*

psychiatry የአእምሮ ፡ ሕክምና *yää'məro həkmənna*

psychology የሥነ ፡ ልቡና ፡ ትምህርት *yäsänä ləbbuna təmhərt*

puberty, see 'maturity'

public (n.) ሕዝብ *həzb*
in public በደባባይ *baddäbabay*

public (adj.) የሕዝብ *yähəzb;* ሕዝባዊ *həz-bawi*
become public በይፋ ፡ ታወቀ *bäyəfa tawwäqä*
make public በግልጽ ፡ አስታወቀ *bägəlṣ astawwäqä*

publication የታተመ ፡ ጽሑፍ *yätattämä ṣəhuf*

publicly (openly) በይፋ *bäyəfa;* በደባባይ *baddäbabay;* (by the public) በሕዝብ ፡ ዘንድ *bähəzb zänd*

public place አደባባይ *addäbabay*

public school የመንግሥት ፡ ትምህርት ፡ ቤት *yämängəst təmhərt bet*

publish (a book) አሳተመ *asattämä*

publisher አሳታሚ *asattami*

puddle የተቋጠረ ፡ ውኃ *yätäqʷaṭṭärä wə-ha*

puff ቁና ፡ ቁና ፡ ተነፈሰ *qunna qunna tä-näffäsä*
puff up (with pride) ተወጠረ *täwäṭṭärä*

pugnacious ጠበኛ *ṭäbäňňa*

pull ሳበ *sabä;* ጐተተ *gʷättätä;* (a tooth) ነቀለ *näqqälä*
pull down (demolish) አፈረሰ *afärrä-sä;* (lower) አወረደ *awärrädä*
pull out (vt.) ነቀለ *näqqälä;* (∼ hair) ነጨ *näččä*
pull out, vi. (of train) ተነሣ *tänässa*
pull up (∼ rocks) ከፍ ፡ አደረገ *käff adärrägä;* (∼ weeds) ነቀለ *näqqälä;* (∼ a chair) ጠጋ ፡ አደረገ *ṭäga adär-rägä*

pulley መዘውር *mäzäwwər*

pulmonary የሳምባ *yäsamba*

pulp ሥጋ *səga*

pulpit መስበኪያ ፡ ስገነት *mäsbäkiya sä-gännät*

pulsate ትር ፡ ትር ፡ አለ *tərr tərr alä*

pulse (n.) የልብ ፡ ትርታ *yäləbb tərrəta*

pulverize (grind to a powder) አደቀቀ *adäqqäqä;* አላመ *alamä;* ደቄሰ *däq-qʷäsä*

pump (n.) ፖምፕ *pomp*

pumpkin ዱባ *dubba*

punch, v. (∼ a ticket) በሳ *bässa;* (box) በቡጢ ፡ መታ *bäbuṭṭi mätta*

punctual ሰዓት ፡ አክባሪ *säat akbari*

punctuate (use periods, commas) ነጥብ ፡ አደረገ *näṭəb adärrägä;* (emphasize) አገነነ *agännänä*

punctuation ሥርዓት ፡ ነጥብ *sər'atä näṭəb*

punctuation mark ሰረዝ *säräz;* ነጥብ *nä-ṭəb*

puncture, v. (of a nail) በሳ *bässa;* (of a needle) ወጋ *wägga*

puncture (n.) ቡኮ *bukko;* ቀዳዳ *qädada*

punish ቀጣ *qäṭṭa*

punishment ቅጣት *qəṭat*

pupil (student) ተማሪ *tämari;* (of eye) የዓይን ፡ ብሌን *yäayn bəlen;* የዓይን ፡ ብሬት *yäayn brät*

puppet አሻንጉሊት *ašangullit*

puppy ቡችላ *buččəlla*

purchase (v.) ገዛ *gäzza*

purchase, n. (the purchasing) መግዛት *mägzat;* (something bought) የተገዛ ፡ እቃ *yätägäzza əqa*

pure ንጹሕ *nəṣuh;* (∼ heart) ቅን *qən;* (∼ language, ∼ metal) የጠራ *yäṭärra*
be pure ጠለለ *ṭällälä;* ጠራ *ṭärra*

purgative የሚያስቀምጥ ፡ መድኃኒት *yäm-miyasqämməṭ mädhanit*

purge, v. (empty the bowels) አስቀመጠ *asqämmäṭä;* (rid of) አስወገደ *aswäg-gädä*

purify አጠለለ *aṭällälä;* አጠራ *aṭärra;* (∼ butter) አነጠረ *anäṭṭärä*

purity (being pure) ንጹሕ ፡ መሆን *nəṣuh mähon;* (innocence) ንጽሕና *nəṣhənna*

purpose (aim) ዓላማ *alama;* (need) ፍላ
ጎት *fəllagot*
on purpose ዐውቆ *awqo;* ሆን ፡ ብሎ
hon bəlo
to no purpose እንዲያው *əndiyaw*

purposely, see 'purpose, on ~'

purr አንኳረፈ *ankʷaräffa*

purse ቦርሳ *borsa*

pursue (follow) ተከታተለ *täkätattälä;*
(chase) አሳደደ *assaddädä;* (harass)
አስቸገረ *asčäggärä*

purulent የሚመግል *yämmimägəl*

pus መግል *mägəl*

push ገፋ *gäffa;* (~ a button) ተጫነ *tä-*
čanä; (urge) ገፋፋ *gäfaffa*
push on ገሰገሰ *gäsäggäsä*

put (set in a certain place) አኖረ *anorä;*
አስቀመጠ *asqämmäṭä;* (insert) አስገባ
asgäbba
put across (explain) አስረዳ *asrädda;*
(place across) አጋደመ *aggaddämä*
put aside አስቀመጠ *asqämmäṭä*
put back መለሰ *mälläsä*
put down አወረደ *awärrädä;* (suppress) ደመሰሰ *dämässäsä*
put forward አቀረበ *aqärräbä*
put into አገባ *agäbba*
put off አስተላለፈ *astälalläfä;* ወዘፈ
wäzzäfä
put on (~ weight) ከብደት ፡ ጨመረ
kəbdät čämmärä; (~ a dress) ለበሰ
läbbäsä; (~ glasses, hat, shoes) አደ
ረገ *adärrägä;* (~ trousers, shirt) አጠ
ለቀ *aṭälläqä*
put out (publish) አወጣ *awäṭṭa;* (extinguish) አጠፋ *aṭäffa*
put together አገጣጠመ *aggäṭaṭṭämä*
put up (~ hands) አነሣ *anässa;* (~
a notice) ለጠፈ *läṭṭäfä*

putrid, be ገማ *gämma*

puzzle (v.) አደናገረ *addänaggärä;* ግራ ፡
አጋባ *gra aggabba*
be puzzled ግራ ፡ ገባ(ው) *gra gäbba(w)*

puzzle (n.) እንቆቅልሽ *ənqoqəlləš*

pyramid ሀረም *haräm*
python ዘንዶ *zändo*

Q

quadrangle አራት ፡ ማእዘን *aratt ma'əzän*

quake (v.) ተንቀጠቀጠ *tänqäṭäqqäṭä*

qualification(s) ችሎታ *čəlota;* ብቁነት *bə-*
qunnät

qualified (having the skills) ብቁ *bəqu;*
(limited, with some reservations) ገደብ፡
ያለው *gädäb yalläw*

qualify (make fit) አበቃ *abäqqa;* (limit
in meaning) ገደብ ፡ አበጀ(ለት) *gädäb*
abäǧǧä(llät)

quality (kind) ዓይነት *aynät;* (excellence)
ጥሩነት *ṭərunnät;* ተመራጭነት *tämär-*
račənnät; (attribute) ችሎታ *čəlota*

quantity መጠን *mäṭän*
quantities of ብዙ *bəzu*
what quantity? ምን ፡ ያህል *mən yahəl*

quarrel (v.) ተጣላ *täṭalla;* ተጫቃጨቀ
täčäqaččäqä

quarrel (n.) ጥል *ṭəl;* ጠብ *ṭäb;* ጭቅጭቅ
čəqəččəq
pick a quarrel ጠብ ፡ ጫረ *ṭäb čarä*

quarrelsome ነጋሪኛ *nägäräňňa;* ጠብኛ *ṭä-*
bäňňa

quarter, n. (one fourth) ሩብ *rub;* (a quarter of a dollar) ስሙኒ *səmuni;* (district) ሰፈር *säfär;* (mercy) ርኅራኄ *rəh-*
rahe
quarters (of soldiers) ሰፈር *säfär;*
(lodging) ማረፊያ *maräfiya*
quarter after three ዘጠኝ ፡ ተሩብ *zä-*
ṭäňň tärub
quarter to three ለዘጠኝ ፡ ሩብ ፡ ጉዳይ
läzäṭäňň rub gudday

queen ንግሥት *nəgəst*

queenly የንግሥት yänəgəst

queer እንግዳ əngəda; የሚገርም yämmigäräm

quench (~ thirst) አረካ aräkka

querulous ነዝናዛ näznazza

query, v. (ask) ጠየቀ țäyyäqä; (feel doubt about) ትክክለኛ ፡ መሆኑን ፡ ተጠ ራጠረ təkəkkəläňňa mähonun täțäraț țärä

query (n.) ጥያቄ țəyyaqe

quest ፈለገ fəlläga

question, vi. (ask) ጠየቀ țäyyäqä; (interrogate) መረመረ märämmärä; (doubt) ተጠራጠረ täțärațțärä

question (n.) ጥያቄ țəyyaqe; (matter to be discussed) ጉዳይ gudday; (doubt) ጥርጣሬ țərəțțare

be beyond question አያጠራጥርም ayațțärațțərəm

beside the question ከአርእስቱ ፡ ውጭ käar'əstu wəčč

without question ያለ ፡ ጥርጥር yalä țərəțțər

questionable አጠራጣሪ ațțärațari

question mark የጥያቄ ፡ ምልክት yäțəyyaqe mələkkət

questionnaire መጠይቅ mäțäyyəq

queue ረድፍ räd(ə)f; ሰልፍ sälf; ተርታ tärta

quick ቀልጣፋ qälțaffa; የተፋጠነ yätäfațțänä; ጮሌ čolle

be quick ፈጠነ fäțțänä; ቶሎ ፡ አለ tolo alä

quicken (vt.) አፋጠነ affațțänä

quickly ቶሎ tolo; በቶሎ bätolo; በፍጥነት bäfəțnät

quick-tempered ቀጠኛ quțțäňňa

quiet (vt.) ዝም ፡ አሰኘ zəmm assäňňa
quiet down ዝም ፡ አለ zəmm alä; (of wind) ጸጥ ፡ አለ șäțț alä; (of excitement) በረደ bärrädä

quiet (n.) ጸጥታ șäțțəta

quiet (adj.) ጸጥተኛ șäțțətäňňa; ዝምተኛ zəmmətäňňa; (~ life) ግርግር ፡ ያልበዛ በት gərrəgərr yalbäzzabbät; (~ colors) ደብዛዛ ፡ ያለ däbzäzz yalä
be quiet ዝም ፡ አለ zəmm alä; (of neighborhood) ጸጥ ፡ አለ șäțț alä

quietly ዝም ፡ ብሎ zəmm bəlo; በጸጥታ bäșäțțəta

quit, v. (leave) ለቀቀ läqqäqä; (give up) ተወ täwä

quite ሙሉ ፡ በሙሉ mulu bämulu; በፍ ጹም bäfəșșum; (to a certain degree) በጣም bäțam

quiver ተንቀጠቀጠ tänqäțäqqäțä

quiz (v.) ጠያየቀ țäyayyäqä

quiz (n.) አጭር ፡ ፈተና ačč̣ər fätäna

quotation ጥቅስ țəqs

quotation mark ትእምርት ፡ ጥቅስ tə'əmərtä țəqs

quote ጠቀሰ țäqqäsä

R

rabbit ጥንቸል țənčäl

rabid (~ dog) እብድ əbd

rabble ለቃሚ ፡ ሕዝብ ləqqami həzb

race, vi. (of horse) ጋለበ galläbä; (of children) ሮጠ rożä; (of car) ከነፋ kännäfä; (participate in a contest) ተሽ ቀዳደመ täšqädaddämä

race, n. (group of people) ዘር zär; (contest) ሩጫ ručč̣a; (of horses) የፈረስ ፡ እሽቅድምድም yäfäräs əšqədəmdəm

race course የሩጫ ፡ መወዳደሪያ ፡ ሜዳ yäručč̣a mäwwädadäriya meda

race track የእሽቅድምድም ፡ ሜዳ yääšqədəmdəm meda

racial የዘር yäzär

racket (disturbing noise) ሁካታ *hukata;* (dishonest way of making a living) ማጭበርበር *maçbärbär;* (of tennis) ራኬት *raket*
make a racket ተንጫጫ *tänçaçça*

radiant (~ sun) ብርሃን ፣ የሚሰጥ *bərhan yämmisäṭ;* (~ color) ደማቅ *dämmaq;* (~ smile) ብሩህ *bəruh*

radiator (for heat) የቤት ፣ ማሞቂያ *yäbet mamoqiya;* (of car) የሞተር ፣ ማቀዝ ቀዣ *yämotär maqäzqäža*

radical, adj. (fundamental) መሠረታዊ *mäsärätawi;* (extreme, in politics) ተራ ማጅ *täramaǧ*

radio ራዲዮ *radiyo;* ራዲዮን *radiyon*

radio station ራዲዮ ፣ ጣቢያ *radiyo ṭabiya*

radish ቀይ ፣ ሥር *qäyy sər*

raft ማንሳፈፊያ *mansafäfiya*

rag ጨርቅ *çärq*
rags ቡትቱ *butətto*

rage, v. (express violent anger) ጦፈ *ṭofä;* (of storm) ባሰ(በት) *basä(bbät)*

rage, n. (violent anger) ንዴት *nəddet*

ragged ቡቱቲም *bututtʷam;* ቡትቱ ፣ የለ በሰ *butətto yäläbbäsä*
ragged clothes ቡትቱ *butətto*

raid (v.) ወረረ *wärrärä;* ዘመተ *zämmätä*

raid (n.) ወራራ *wärara;* ዘመቻ *zämäča*

rail, n. (of railroad) ሐዲድ *hadid;* (horizontal bar) መደገፊያ *mäddägäfiya*

railroad የሐዲድ ፣ መንገድ *yähadid mängäd;* የምድር ፣ ባቡር *yämədär babur*

railroad station (የ)ባቡር ፣ ጣቢያ *(yä)babur ṭabiya*

railway የምድር ፣ ባቡር *yämədər babur;* የባቡር ፣ ሐዲድ *yäbabur hadid*

rain (v.) ዘነበ *zännäbä;* ዘነም *zännämä;* ዝናብ ፣ ጣለ *zənab ṭalä*

rain (n.) ዝናብ *zənab;* ዝናም *zənam*
the rains ክረምት *krämt*

rainbow ቀስተ ፣ ደመና *qästä dämmäna*

raincoat (የ)ዝናብ ፣ ልብስ *(yä)zənab ləbs*

rainy ዝናብ ፣ የሚበዛበት *zənab yämmibäzabbät*
rainy season ክረምት *krämt*

raise, v. (~ children) አሳደገ *asaddägä;* (~ crops) አመረት *amärrätä;* (promote) ከፍ ፣ አደረገ *käff adärrägä;* (~ hand, question) አነሣ *anässa;* (~ money, army) ሰበሰበ *säbässäbä*

raise, n. (in salary) የደሞዝ ፣ ጭማሪ *yädämoz çəmmari;* (promotion) እድገት *ədgät*

raisin ዘቢብ *zäbib*

rake, v. (~ ashes) ጫረ *çarä;* (~ leaves) ሰበሰበ *säbässäbä*

rake (n.) ቅጠል ፣ መጥረጊያ *qəṭäl mäṭrägiya*

rally (vi.) ተሰበሰበ *täsäbässäbä*
rally to ደገፈ *däggäfä*

ram (male sheep) ወጠጤ *wäṭäṭe*

ramble (stroll without purpose) ዙረት ፣ ሄደ *zurät hedä;* (talk without consequence) ቀባጀረ *qäbaǧǧärä;* ዘባረቀ *zäbarräqä*

rampage (n.), go on a ~ (of children) ምስቅልቅሉን ፣ አወጣ *məsqəlqəlun awäṭṭa;* (of army) በዘበዘ *bäzäbbäzä;* ሕዝቡን ፣ ፈጀ *həzbun fäǧǧä*

rampant, be (disease) ተዛመተ *täzammätä*

rampart የምሽግ ፣ ግድግዳ *yäməššəg gədgədda*

ranch (of cattle) ከብት ፣ ማርቢያ ፣ ቦታ *käbt marbiya bota;* ከብት ፣ ማሳማሪያ *käbt massämariya;* (of fruit) እርሻ *ərša*

rancid, be በሳ *bokka*

rancor ቂም *qim;* ቅያሜ *qəyyame*

random, at ~ እንዳገኘ *əndagäňňä*

range, vt. (put in order) ደረደረ *däräddärä*

range (n.) መጠን *mäṭän;* (for cooking) ምድጃ *mədəǧǧa*

cattle range, see 'ranch'

rank, v. (arrange in a row) መደብ *mäd-däbä*
rank above በማዕረግ ፡ በለጠ *bäma'ǝräg bällätä*

rank (n.) ማዕረግ *ma'ǝräg;* ደረጃ *däräǧa*

ransack አምበረበበ *ambäräbbärä*

ransom (v.) ማስለቀቂያ ፡ ገንዘብ ፡ ከፈለ *masläqqäqiya gänzäb käffälä*

ransom (n.) ቤዛ *beza;* ማስለቀቂያ ፡ ገን ዘብ *masläqqäqiya gänzäb*

rap ደበደበ *däbäddäbä*

rapacious (living on prey) አድኖ ፡ የሚ ኖር *adno yämminor;* (greedy) ቄንጿና *qʷänqʷanna*

rapid ቀልጣፋ *qäl̩t̩affa;* ችኩል *čǝkkul;* ፈጣን *fät̩t̩an*

rapidly ቶሎ *tolo;* በፍጥነት *bäfǝt̩nät*

rapture ተመስጦ *tämäst̩o*

rare ብርቅ *bǝrq;* (unusual) ልዩ *lǝyyu;* (strange) እንግዳ *ǝngǝda;* (lightly cooked) በደንብ ፡ ያልበሰለ *bädänb yalbässälä*

rarely አልፎ ፡ አልፎ *alfo alfo;* እምብዛም *ǝmbǝzam* + negative verb; እጅግም *ǝǧǧǝgǝm*

rascal ቀጣፊ *qät̩afi;* ወስላታ *wäslatta*

rash (n.) ሽፍታ *šǝffǝta*
have a rash ሽፍ ፡ አለ *šǝff alä;* ችፍ ፡ አለ *čǝff alä*

rash, adj. (hasty) ችኩል *čǝkkul*

rasp (n.) ምረድ *moräd*

rat አይጥ *ayt̩*

rate, v. (evaluate) ገመተ *gämmätä*

rate (n.) ዋጋ *waga*
at any rate ያም ፡ ሆነ ፡ ይህ *yam hono yǝh*

rather ይልቄንም *yǝlqunǝm;* ይልቅስ *yǝlǝqǝss*
rather than ከ --- ይልቅ *kä - - - yǝlǝq*

ratify (~ a bill) አጸደቀ *aṣäddäqä*

rating የደረጃ ፡ ድልድል *yädäräǧa dǝlǝd-dǝl*

ration (v.) እየመጠነ ፡ አከፋፈለ *ǝyyämät̩-t̩änä akkäfaffälä*

ration (n.) ራሽን *rašǝn*
rations ቀለብ *qälläb*

rational (able to think) አእምሮ ፡ ያለው *a'mǝro yalläw;* (based on reason) በምርምር ፡ የተደረሰበት *bämǝrmǝr yätädärräsäbbät*

rattle (vi.) ካካ ፡ አለ *kʷakʷa alä;* አን ካካ *ankʷakkʷa;* ተንገጫገጨ *tängäčag-gäčä*

rattle (n.) መንቀጫቀጭ *mänqäčaqäč;* (child's toy) የሚቅጨለጨል ፡ መጫ ወቻ *yämmiqčäläččäl mäččawäča*

ravage (destroy) ደመሰሰ *dämässäsä;* (of locust) አወደመ *awäddämä*

rave (talk in a disconnected manner) ቃዠ *qažžä;* (talk with great enthu-siasm) አድንቆ ፡ ተናገረ *adnǝqo tänag-gärä*

raven ቁራ *qura*

ravenous ስግብግብ *sǝgǝbgǝb*

ravine ፋፋ *fafa*

ravish መነጠቀ *mänät̩t̩äqä*

ravishing የሚማርክ *yämmimarrǝk*

raw (~ meat, potatoes) ጥሬ *t̩ǝre;* (~ milk) ያልተፈላ *yaltäfälla;* (~ vege-tables) ያልተቀቀለ *yaltäqäqqälä;* (~ wound) የተላጠ *yätälat̩ä*

raw material ጥሬ ፡ እቃ *t̩ǝre ǝqa*

ray ጮራ *čorra;* ጨረር *čärär*

raze ድምጥምጡን ፡ አጠፋ *dǝmǝt̩mǝt̩un at̩affa*

razor ምላጭ *mǝlačč*

razor blade ምላጭ *mǝlačč*

reach (v.) ደረሰ *därräsä;* (hand over) አቀበለ *aqäbbälä*
reach out እጅን ፡ ዘረጋ *ǝǧǧun zärägga*

read አነበበ *anäbbäbä*

reader (who reads) አንባቢ anbabi;
(schoolbook) የንባብ ፡ መጽሐፍ yänəbab mäshaf

readily በፍጥነት bäfəṭnät

reading ንባብ nəbab

reading room የንባብ ፡ ክፍል yänəbab
kəfəl

ready (adj.) ስንዱ sənəddu; ዝግጁ zəgəǧǧu
be ready ተዘጋጀ täzägaǧǧä; ተሰናዳ
täsänadda; (of dinner) ደረሰ därräsä

real እውነተኛ əwnätäňňa; ትክክል təkəkkəl; (genuine) ደንበኛ dänbäňňa

real estate የማይንቀሳቀስ ፡ ንብረት yämmayənqäsaqqäs nəbrät

reality እውነት əwnät

realize (attain) ከፍጻሜ ፡ አደረሰ käfəṣṣame adärräsä; (be aware) ተረዳ(ው)
tärädda(w); ዐወቀ awwäqä; ተገነዘበ
tägänäzzäbä

really በርግጥ bärgəṭ; በውነት bäwnät

realm ግዛት gəzat

realty, see 'real estate'

reap አመረተ amärrätä; (~ a reward)
አገኘ agäňňä

reappear እንደገና ፡ ብቅ ፡ አለ əndägäna
bəqq alä

rear, vt. (bring up) አሳደገ asaddägä;
(raise up) ቀና ፡ አደረገ qäna adärrägä

rear (n.) ጀርባ ǧärba
in the rear of ከ - - - በስተጀርባ kä - -
bästäǧärba

rear (adj.) የኋለኛ yähʷaläňňa

reason, vi. (argue logically) አስረዳ asrädda; (think logically) ተመራመረ
tämärammärä

reason, n. (motive, pretext) ምክንያት
məknəyat; መነሻ männäša; ሰበብ säbäb; (ability to think) የማሰብ ፡ ኃይል
yämassäb hayl
bring (someone) to reason አግባባ agbabba

for what reason? በምን ፡ የተነሣ bämən yätänässa

reasonable (~ person) አስተዋይ astäway; (~ price) መጣነኛ mäṭänäňňa;
(~ choice) ተገቢ tägäbi

reasoning አስተሳሰብ astäsasäb

reassure አረጋጋጠ arrägaggäṭä

rebate ቅናሽ qənnaš

rebel (v.) ዐመጸ ammäṣä

rebel (n.) ዐመጸኛ amäṣäňňa; አግዳሚ
agdami

rebellion ዐመጽ amäṣ

rebellious (defying authority) ያመጸ yam-
mäṣä; (hard to manage) አትንኩኝ ፡
ባይ attənkuňň bay

rebuke (v.) ወቀሰ wäqqäsä; ዘለፈ zälläfä

rebuke (n.) ወቀሳ wäqäsa; ነቀፌታ näqäfeta; ዘለፋ zäläfa

recalcitrant እምቢተኛ əmbitäňňa; የማይ
ታዘዝ yämmayəttazzäz; (~ cattle) ልግ
መኛ ləgmäňňa

recall (remember) አስታወሰ astawwäsä;
ትዝ ፡ አለ(ው) təzz alä(w)

recant ዐጠፈ aṭṭäfä; ካደ kadä

recapitulate እንደገና ፡ ገለጸ əndägäna gälläṣä

recede ወደ ፡ ኋላ ፡ ሸሸ wädä hʷala šäššä

receipt (written statement) ደረሰኝ därräsäňň
receipts ገቢ gäbi

receive ተቀበለ täqäbbälä; (~ guests)
አስተናገደ astänaggädä

receiver (who receives) ተቀባይ täqäbbay; (of telephone) የስልክ ፡ መነጋገ
ሪያ yäsəlk männägagäriya

recent የቅርብ yäqərb; አዲስ addis; (happening recently) በቅርቡ ፡ የሆነ bäqərbu yähonä

recently ሰሞኑን sämonun; በቅርቡ bäqərbu; በቅርብ ፡ ጊዜ bäqərb gize

receptacle መክተቻ mäktäča

reception (receiving) መቀበል *mäqqäbbäl;* (greeting) አቀባበል *aqqäbabäl;* (formal entertainment) ግብዣ *gəbža*

reception desk የእንግዶች ፡ መቀበያ ፡ ቦታ *yäəngədočč mäqqäbäya bota*

receptionist አስተናጋጅ *astänagağ*

recess, n. (rest) ዕረፍት *əräft;* የዕረፍት ፡ ጊዜ *yäəräft gize*

recession የኢኮኖሚ ፡ ድቀት *yäikonomi dəqät*

recipe (for food) የምግብ ፡ መምሪያ *yäməgəb mämriya;* ያሠራር ፡ መምሪያ *yassärar mämriya*

reciprocal የርስ ፡ በርስ *yärs bärs;* የጋራ *yägara*

reciprocate ዐጸፋ ፡ መለሰ *aṣäfa mälläsä*

recitation ደገማ *dägäma*

recite (~ prayers) ደገመ *däggämä;* (~ a lesson) በቃሉ ፡ ወጣ *bäqalu wäṭṭa*

reckless ግድ ፡ የለሽ *gədd yälläš*

reckon (count, think) አሰበ *assäbä;* (count on) ተማመነ *tämammänä*

reckoning ግምት *gəmmət*

recline ጋደም ፡ አለ *gadämm alä*

recluse መናኝ *männañ*

recognize ዐወቀ *awwäqä;* ለየ *läyyä*

recollect አስታወሰ *astawwäsä*

recollection ትዝታ *təzzəta*

recommend (suggest) አሳሰበ *asassäbä;* ሐሳብ ፡ አቀረበ *hassab aqärräbä;* (write favorably of) ብቁ ፡ መሆኑን ፡ መስከረለት *bəqu mähonun mäsäkkärällät*
recommend to one's care አደራ ፡ ሰጠ *adära säṭṭa*

recommendation (advice) ምክር *məkər;* (written praise) አስተያየት *astäyayät*

recompense, v. (reward) ወሮታውን ፡ ከፈለ *wärrotawən käffälä;* (make amends for) ተካ *täkka;* ካሰ *kasä*

recompense (n.) ካሳ *kasa*

reconcile አስታረቀ *astarräqä;* (bring into agreement) አስማማ *asmamma*
be reconciled ታረቀ *tarräqä*

reconciliation ዕርቅ *ərq*

record, v. (set down in writing) ጻፈ *ṣafä;* መዘገበ *mäzäggäbä*

record, n. (official document) መዝገብ *mäzgäb;* (of student) ሪኮርድ *rikord;* (for phonograph) ሽክላ *šäkla;* የሙዚቃ ፡ ሽክላ *yämuziqa šäkla;* (in sport) ከብረ ፡ ወሰን *kəbrä wäsän*
keep a record of መዘገበ *mäzäggäbä;* መዝገብ ፡ ያዘ *mäzgäb yazä*

recording የተቀዳ ፡ ሙዚቃ *yätäqädda muziqa*

record player ሽክላ ፡ ማጫወቻ *šäkla mäččawäča*

recover, vt. (get back again) አስመለሰ *asmälläsä*
recover, vi. (from illness) ዳነ *danä*

recreation (relaxation) መዝናናት *mäznanat*

recruit, v. (enlist) መለመለ *mälämmälä*

recruit (n.) ምልምል ፡ ወታደር *məlməl wättaddär*

rectangle አራት ፡ ማእዘን *aratt ma'əzän*

rectify አስተካከለ *astäkakkälä*

recuperate ዳነ *danä;* አገገመ *agäggämä*

recur ተቀሰቀሰ(በት) *täqäsäqqäsä(bbät)*

red ቀይ *qäyy*
become red ቀላ *qälla*
be in the red እየከሰረ ፡ ሄደ *əyyäkässärä hedä*

Red Cross ቀይ ፡ መስቀል *qäyy mäsqäl*

redeem (regain possession) አስመለሰ *asmälläsä;* (free) ገንዘብ ፡ ከፍሎ ፡ ነጻ ፡ አወጣ *gänzäb käflo näṣa awäṭṭa;* (save, of Jesus) አዳነ *adanä*

red-handed እጅ ፡ ከፍንጅ ፡ የተያዘ *əğğ käfənğ yätäyazä*

red-hot, be ጋለ *galä*

redouble ዕጥፍ ፡ አደረገ *əṭəf adärrägä*

redress አረመ *arrämä*

reduce, vt. (decrease) ቀነሰ *qännäsä;* (lower in rank) ዝቅ ፣ አደረገ *zəqq adärrägä;* (bring to a situation) አደ ረሰ *adärräsä*
reduce, vi. (in weight) ክብደት ፣ ቀነሰ *kəbdät qännäsä*

reduplicate አባዛ *abbazza*

reed መቃ *mäqa;* ሸምበቆ *šambäqqo*

reek (v.) ከረፋ *käräffa*

reel, v. (stagger) ተግተረተረ *tägtärättärä*

reel, n. (bobbin) መጠቅለያ *mäṭäqläya;* (for film) ጥቅል *ṭəqəll*

refer (direct for information) እንዲመለ ከት ፣ መራ *əndimmäläkkät märra*

referee (in a game) አጫዋች *ačawač*

reference (statement to which attention is directed) መግለጫ *mägläča;* (recommendation) የምስክር ፣ ወረቀት *yäməsəkkər wäräqät;* ያደራ ፣ ወረቀት *yadära wäräqät;* (person who can give information about someone's character) ተጠያቂ *täṭäyyaqi*
make reference to አነሣ *anässa*

refill (~ a pen) አጠጣ *aṭäṭṭa;* (~ a tank) ቤንዚን ፣ ሞላ *benzin molla*

refine (~ oil) አጣራ *aṭṭarra;* (~ manners) አለዘበ *aläzzäbä*

refinery ማጣሪያ *maṭṭariya*

reflect, vt. (show like a mirror) ገለጸ *gälläṣä;* (of mirror) አሳየ *asayyä;* (of glass) አንጸባረቀ *anṣäbarräqä*
reflect, vi. (ponder) አሰበ *assäbä*

reflection (thought) አሳብ *assab*

reform (v.) አሻሻለ *aššašalä*

reform (n.) መሻሻል *mäššašal*

refractory (~ child) እምቢተኛ *əmbitäňňa;* ግትር *gəttər;* (~ ox) ልግመኛ *ləgmäňňa*

refrain (v.) ከ - - - ተቆጠበ *kä - - - täqʷäṭṭäbä*

refrain (n.) አዝማች *azmač*

refresh (of bath) አነቃቃ *annäqaqqa*

refrigerator ማቀዝቀዣ *maqäzqäža*

refuge (place of safety) መጠጊያ *mäṭṭägiya;* (safety) ጥገኝነት *ṭəggäňňənnät*
seek refuge ተጠለለ *täṭällälä*

refugee ስደተኛ *səddätäňňa*

refund (v.) ተካ *täkka;* መለሰ *mälläsä*

refund (n.) ተመላሽ ፣ ገንዘብ *tämällaš gänzäb*

refusal እምቢታ *əmbita;* እምቢ ፣ ማለት *əmbi malät*
give a refusal, see 'refuse'

refuse (v.) እምቢ ፣ አለ *əmbi alä;* or expressed by the negative verb (as in 'he refused to sign' አልፈረመም *alfärrämäm*)

refuse, n. (trash) ቆሻሻ *qošaša;* ውዳቂ *wəddaqi*

refute አስተባበለ *astäbabbälä*

regain (recover) አስመለሰ *asmälläsä;* (reach again) እንደገና ፣ አገኘ *əndägäna agäňňä*

regal ንጉሣዊ *nəgusawi*

regale አስደሰተ *asdässätä*

regalia የክብር ፣ ልብስ *yäkəbər ləbs*

regard, v. (consider) አየ *ayyä;* ቆጠረ *qʷäṭṭärä;* (concern) ተመለከተ *tämäläkkätä*

regard (n.) ዓይን *ayn;* (esteem) ክብር *kəbər*
regards ሰላምታ *sälamta*
have regards (for) አሰበ *assäbä*
in regard to ስለ *sələ*
in that regard እሱ ፣ ላይ *əssu lay*
with regard to በማስታወሻ *bämastawäša;* በ - - - በኩል *bä - - - bäkkul*

regarding ስለ *sələ;* (in respect to) በማ ስታወስ *bämastawäs*

regency እንደራሴነት *əndärasennät*

regent እንደራሴ *əndärase*

regime (system of government) መንግሥት *mängəst*; (period of rule) ዘመን *zämän*

regiment ሬጂመንት *reğimänt*

region ክፍለ ፡ ሀገር *kəflä hagär*; ቀበሌ *qäbäle*

regional የቀበሌ *yäqäbäle*

register (vt.) መዘገበ *mäzäggäbä*
register (vi.) ተመዘገበ *tämäzäggäbä*; (show) ታየ *tayyä*

register (n.) መዝገብ *mäzgäb*

registered letter ሬኮማንዴ *rekomande*

registration (registering) ምዝገባ *məzgäba*

registry ቤት ፡ መዝገብ *betä mäzgäb*; መዝገብ ፡ ቤት *mäzgäb bet*

regret, v. (repent) ተጸጸተ *täşäşşätä*; (be sorry) አዘነ *azzänä*

regret (n.) ጸጸት *şäşät*

regrettable የሚያሳዝን *yämmiyasazzən*

regular, adj. (∼ price) ደንበኛ *dänbäñña*; (∼ habits) የተወሰነ *yätäwässänä*; የተለመደ *yätälämmädä*; (∼ work) ቋሚ *qʷami*; (∼ features) የተስተካከለ *yätästäkakkälä*

regularly ዘወትር *zäwätər*; ያለማቋረጥ *yalämaqqʷaräṭ*; ሳይቋረጥ *sayəqqʷarräṭ*

regulate (adjust) አስተካከለ *astäkakkälä*; (control) ተቆጣጠረ *täqʷäṭaṭṭärä*

regulation (rule) ሥርዓት *sər'at*; ድንጋጌ *dənəggage*; (control) መቆጣጠር *mäqqʷäṭaṭär*

rehearse ተለማመደ *tälämammädä*

reign, v. (rule) ነገሠ *näggäsä*; (prevail) ሰፈነ *säffänä*

reign, n. (supreme rule) አገዛዝ *aggäzaz*; (period of rule) ዘመነ ፡ መንግሥት *zämänä mängəst*

reimburse ተካ(ለት) *täkka(llät)*

rein (of horse) ልጓም *ləgʷam*; ዛብ *zab*

reinforce አጠና *aṭänna*; አጠነከረ *aṭänäkkärä*

reinforcements ተጨማሪ ፡ ጦር *täčämmari ṭor*

reiterate ደጋገመ *dägaggämä*

reject, v. (refuse to take) አልተቀበለም *altäqäbbäläm*; (discard) ጣለ *ṭalä*

rejoice (vt.) አስደሰተ *asdässätä*
rejoice (vi.) ደስ ፡ አለ(ው) *däss alä(w)*; ተደሰተ *tädässätä*

relapse, v. (fall back into illness) አገ ረሸ(በት) *agäräššä(bbät)*

relate (tell) አወራ *awärra*; (associate) አዛመደ *azzammädä*
relate to ተመለከተ *tämäläkkätä*

related, be ተዛመደ *täzammädä*; (connected in some way) ተያያዘ *täyayazä*

relation (narration) የነገረው ፡ ነገር *yänäggäräw nägär*; (relative) ዘመድ *zämäd*; (connection) ግንኙነት *gənəňňunnät*; (family relationship) ዝምድና *zəmdənna*

relative (n.) ዘመድ *zämäd*

relative, adj. (connected) የተያያዘ *yätäyayazä*

relatively በመጠኑ *bämäṭänu*

relax, vt. (∼ efforts) ቀነሰ *qännäsä*; (∼ requirements) አላላ *alalla*
relax (vi.) ተዝናና *täznanna*; ዐረፍት ፡ አገኘ *əräft agäňňä*

relay አስተላለፈ *astälalläfä*

release, v. (set free) ለቀቀ *läqqäqä*; (from vows) ፈታ *fätta*; (from a promise) ማረ *marä*

relegate (turn over) አስተላለፈ *astälalläfä*

relent ላላ *lalla*

relentless (person) ምሕረት ፡ የሌለው *məhrät yälelläw*

relevant አግባብ ፡ ያለው *agbab yalläw*

reliable (∼ source) የታመነ *yätammänä*; (∼ person) ታማኝ *tammaňň*; ሁነኛ *hunäňña*; (∼ firm) እምነት ፡ የሚጣል በት *əmnät yämmiṭṭaləbbät* reliance መመኪያ mämmäkiya

relic ቅርስ qərs

relief (aid) እርዳታ ərdata; (freeing from a pain) ፋታ fata; (person who relieves another from duty) ተቀያሪ täqäyyari; (rest) ዕረፍት əräft; እፎይታ əffoyta

relieve (~ pain) አሻለ aššalä; አስታገሠ astaggäsä; (~ distress) አቃለለ aqqallälä; (release from a post) ቀየረ qäyyärä

religion ሃይማኖት haymanot

religious (~ person) ሃይማኖተኛ haymanotäňňa; (~differences, order) የሃይ ማኖት yähaymanot religious service የጸሎት ፡ ሥነ ፡ ሥርዓት yäṣälot sənä sər'at

relinquish ለቀቀ läqqäqä; ተወ täwä

reluctant, be ፈቃደኛ ፡ አልነበረም fäqadäňňa alnäbbäräm

rely, ~ on አመነ ammänä; ተማመነ tämammänä; እምነት ፡ ጣለ(በት) əmnät ṭalä(bbät); ተመካ tämäkka

remain (be left) ቀረ qärrä; ተረፈ tärräfä; (stay) ቆየ qoyyä

remainder ቀሪ qäri; የቀረ yäqärrä; ትርፍ tərf

remains (of meal) የተረፈ yätärräfä; ት ራፊ tərrafi; (of a dwelling) ፍራሽ färraš; (dead body) አስከሬን askären; ዐጽም aṣəm

remark, v. (notice) አየ ayyä; ተረዳ(ው) tärädda(w); (state, say) ተናገረ tänaggärä

remark (n.) አስተያየት astäyayät

remarkable የሚደነቅ yämmiddännäq

remedy (v.) አሻሻለ aššašalä; መፍትሔ ፡ አገኘ mäftəhe agäňňä

remedy, n. (cure) መድኃኒት mädhanit; (solution) መፍትሔ mäftəhe

remember አስታወሰ astawwäsä; ትዝ ፡ አለ(ው) təzz alä(w)

remembrance ማስታወሻ mastawäša; መታ ሰቢያ mättasäbiya; (remembering) ትዝታ təzzəta

remind አሳሰበ asassäbä; አስታወሰ astawwäsä; አወሳ awässa

reminder ማስታወሻ mastawäša

reminiscence ትዝታ təzzəta

remission (of sins) ምሕረት məhrät

remit (send) ላከ lakä; (pay) ከፈለ käffälä; (~sins) ከ - - - ነጻ ፡ አረደገ kä - - - näṣa adärrägä

remnant ትራፊ tərrafi; የቀረ yäqärrä; (trace) ርዝራዥ rəzərraž

remorse ጸጸት ṣäṣät

remorseless ርኅራኄ ፡ የሌለው rəhrahe yälelläw

remote ሩቅ ruq; (ancient) የጥንት yäṭənt be remote ራቀ raqä

remove አነሣ anässa; (~ ink stains) አስ ለቀቀ asläqqäqä; (~ a bullet) አወጣ awäṭṭa; (from office) አስወጣ aswäṭṭa; (~ a tooth) ነቀለ näqqälä; (~ doubt) አስወገደ aswäggädä

remunerate ዋጋ ፡ ከፈለ waga käffälä

remuneration ዋጋ waga

render (make) አደረገ adärrägä; (give back) መለሰ mälläsä; (translate) ተረ ጎመ täräggʷämä

renegade ከሐዲ kähadi; ከዳተኛ käddatäňňa

renew አደሰ addäsä; አሳደሰ asaddäsä

renounce (disown) ካደ kadä; (give up) በፈቃዱ ፡ ተወ bäfäqadu täwä; (~ the world) መነነ männänä

renovate አደሰ addäsä; አሳደሰ asaddäsä

renown ዝና zənna

renowned የታወቀ yätawwäqä; ዝነኛ zənnäňňa

rent, vt. (hire) ተከራየ täkärayyä; (lease) አከራየ akkärayyä

rent, n. (of room) ክራይ kəray; ኪራይ kiray

reorganize እንደገና ፡ አደራጀ əndägäna addäraǧǧä

repair (v.) ጠገነ ṭäggänä; አበጀ abäǧǧä; ካሰ kasä

repair (n.) ጥገና ṭəggäna

reparations የጦር ፡ ካሳ yäṭor kasa

repay ከፈለ käffälä; (~ a favor) መለሰ mälläsä

repeal ሻረ šarä

repeat (say again) ደገመ däggämä; መላ ለሰ mälalläsä; (recount) አወራ awärra

repeatedly መላልሶ mälalso; ደጋግሞ dägagmo

repel (drive back) መለሰ mälläsä; (disgust) አስከፋ askäffa; (~ water) አላስ ገባም alasgäbbam

repent ተጸጸተ täṣäṣṣätä; ንስሐ ፡ ገባ nəssəha gäbba

repentance ጸጸት ṣäṣät; ንስሐ nəssəha

repetition ድጋሚ dəggami; መድገም mädgäm

replace (put back) መልሶ ፡ አስቀመጠ mälləso asqämmäṭä; (fill the place of) ተካ täkka

replacement ምትክ mətəkk; ተተኪ tätäki

replenish እንደገና ፡ መላ əndägäna mälla

reply (v.) መለሰ mälläsä

reply (n.) መልስ mäls; ምላሽ məllaš

report (v.) አወራ awärra; አስታወቀ astawwäqä; መግለጫ ፡ ሰጠ mägläča säṭṭä; (denounce) አሳበቀ assabbäqä; ነገረ(በት) näggärä(bbät)

report (n.) መግለጫ mägläča; ራፖር rapor; ሪፖርት riport; (rumor) ወሬ wäre

report card የተማሪ ፡ ማመልከቻ yätämari mamälkäča; የምስክር ፡ ወረቀት yäməsəkkər wäräqät

reporter ቃል ፡ አቀባይ qal aqäbbay; ዜና፡ አቀባይ zena aqäbbay

repose (vi.) ጋደም ፡ አለ gadämm alä

repose, n. (peace and quiet) ሰላምና ፡ ጸጥታ sälamənna ṣäṭṭəta; (rest) ዕረ ፍት əräft

reprehensible አስከፊ askäffi

represent (describe) ገለጸ gälläṣä; (act for) ወከለ wäkkälä; (stand for) አመ ለከተ amäläkkätä

representation መግለጫ mägläča

representative, n. (delegate) መልእክተኛ mäl'əktäñña; (agent) ወኪል wäkkil

repress (~ mutiny) ደመሰሰ dämässä sä; (~ a political movement) ጨቆነ čäqqwänä; (~ laughter) ገታ gätta

repression ጭቆና čəqqwäna

reprimand (v.) ወቀሰ wäqqäsä; ገሠጸ gässäṣä

reprimand (n.) ወቀሳ wäqäsa; ግሣጸ gəssaṣe

reprint እንደገና ፡ አተመ əndägäna attämä

reprisal ዐጸፋ aṣäfa
in reprisal ዐጸፋውን aṣäfawən

reproach (v.) ዘለፈ zälläfä; ወቀሰ wäq qäsä

reproach, n. (rebuke) ዘለፋ zäläfa; ወቀሳ wäqäsa

reproduce, vt. (copy) ቀዳ qädda; (show) አሳየ asayyä
reproduce, vi. (produce offspring) ተራባ tärabba

reproduction (copy) ቅጂ qəǧǧi; (producing offspring) መራባት märrabat

republic ሪፑብሊክ republik

repudiate (~ a statement) ካደ kadä

repugnant (~ odor) ገም gəm; (offensive) አስከፊ askäffi

repulse (repel) መለሰ mälläsä; (reject) አረቀ araqä

repulsion, feel ~ for ቀፈፈ(ው) qäffäfä(w)

repulsive ቀፋፊ qäfafi; አስቀያሚ asqäyyami

reputable ስመ ፡ ጥሩ səmä ṭäru

reputation ዝና *zənna;* ስም *səm*

repute ዝና *zənna*

reputed ዕውቅ *əwəq*

request (v.) ለመነ *lämmänä;* ጠየቀ *ṭäyyäqä*

request (n.) ልመና *ləmmäna;* ጥያቄ *ṭəyyaqe*
make a request for ጠየቀ *ṭäyyäqä*

require ጠየቀ *ṭäyyäqä;* (~ time) ፈጀ *fäǧǧä;* (need) አስፈለገ(ው) *asfällägä(w)*

requirement (necessity) አስፈላጊ ፡ ነገር *asfällagi nägär*

requisition (n.) መጠየቂያ *mäṭṭäyyäqiya*

rescind ሻረ *šarä*

rescue (v.) አተረፈ *atärräfä;* አዳነ *adanä*

research (v.) መረመረ *märämmärä*

research (n.) ምርምራ *mərmära;* ጥናት *ṭənat*

resemblance መመሳሰል *mämmäsasäl*

resemble መሰለ *mässälä*

resent ተቀየመ *täqäyyämä;* ቂር አሰኘ(ው) *qərr assäňňä(w)*

resentful, be ቂር ፡ ተሰኘ *qərr täsäňňä*

resentment ቂም *qim;* ቅያሜ *qəyyame;* ቅሬታ *qərreta*

reservation (securing of a place) ቦታ ፡ መያዝ *bota mäyaz;* (secured place) የያዘው ፡ ቦታ *yäyazäw bota;* (restriction) ገደብ *gädäb*

reserve, v. (secure a place) ያዘ *yazä;* (save) ቈጠበ *q*äṭṭäbä;* አስቀመጠ *asqämmäṭä;* (set apart) መደበ *mäddäbä*

reserve, n. (something stored) ተቀማጭ *täqämmač;* መጠባበቂያ *mäṭṭäbabäqiya;* (restraint) ገለልተኝነት *gälältäňňannät*
without reserve በሙሉ ፡ ልብ *bämulu ləbb*

reserved, adj. (restrained) ጭምት *čəmmət*

reservoir ማጠራቀሚያ *maṭṭäraqämiya;* የውሃ ፡ ማከማቻ *yäwəha makkämäča*

reshuffle, n. (of cabinet) ሹም ፡ ሽር *šum šər*

reside ኖረ *norä*

residence (dwelling) መኖሪያ *mänoriya*

resident ተቀማጭ *täqämmač;* ነዋሪ *näwari*

residential የመኖሪያ *yämänoriya*

residue ትርፍ *tərf;* የተረፈ *yätärräfä*

resign ሥራውን ፡ በፈቃዱ ፡ ለቀቀ *särawən bäfäqadu läqqäqä;* (from a club) ወጣ *wäṭṭa*

resignation (from a job) ከሥራ ፡ ለመሰናበት ፡ ያቀረበው ፡ ጥያቄ *käsəra lämässänabät yaqärräbäw ṭəyyaqe;* (quiet submission) ትግሥት *təgəst*

resin ሙጫ *mučča*

resist ተከላከለ *täkälakkälä;* ተቋወመ *täqawwämä*

resistance ተቋውሞ *täqawmo;* መከላከል *mäkkälakäl;* መከላከያ *mäkkälakäya*

resolute ቈራጥ *q*ärraṭ*

resolution (determination) ቈራጥነት *q*ärraṭənnät;* (decision) ቍርጥ ፡ ሐሳብ *qurṭ hassab;* ውሳኔ *wəssane*

resolve, v. (decide) በየነ *bäyyänä;* ወሰነ *wässänä;* (solve) መፍትሔ ፡ አስገኘ *mäftəhe asgäňňä*

resolve (n.) ቈራጥነት *q*ärraṭənnät;* ቍርጠኝነት *qurṭäňňannät*

resort, n. (place for people to go) የመዝናኛ ፡ ቦታ *yämäznaňa bota;* (recourse) ረዳት *räddat;* ምርጫ *mərča*

resound አስተጋባ *astägabba;* ጓጓ ፡ አለ *g*ag*a alä*

resource (resort) መጠጊያ *mäṭṭägiya;* (financial resort) የገቢ ፡ ምንጭ *yägäbi mənč*
resources ሀብት *habt*
natural resources የተፈጥሮ ፡ ሀብት *yätäfäṭro habt*

resourceful ዘዴኛ *zädeňňa*

respect, v. (honor) አከበረ *akäbbärä;* (admire) አደነቀ *adännäqä;* (show consideration for) ጠበቀ *ṭäbbäqä*

respect (n.) አክብሮት *akbərot;* ክብር *kəbər*
respects ሰላምታ *sälamta*
in this respect በዚህ ፡ ረገድ *bäzzih rägäd*
in every respect በመልኩ ፡ በመልኩ *bämälku bämälku;* በማንኛውም ፡ ረገድ *bämannəññawəm rägäd*
in many respects በብዙ ፡ መንገድ *bäbəzu mängäd*

respectable (deserving respect) የተከበረ *yätäkäbbärä;* (~ amount of money) ከፍ ፡ ያለ *käff yalä*

respectful ትሕትና ፡ የተመላበት *təhtənna yätämällabbät;* ክቡር *kəbur*
be respectful toward አከበረ *akäbbärä*

respectfully በአክብሮት *bäakbərot*

respecting (concerning) ስለ *sələ*

respectively እንደ ፡ ቅደም ፡ ተከተላቸው *əndä qədäm täkätälaččäw*

respiration ትንፋሽ *tənfaš*

respite ፋታ *fata*

resplendent, be አንጸባረቀ *anṣäbarräqä;* አሸበረቀ *ašäbärräqä*

respond መለሰ *mälläsä*

response መልስ *mäls*

responsibility ኃላፊነት *halafinnät*

responsible ኃላፊ *halafi;* ተጠያቂ *täṭäyyaqi;* (involving responsibility) ኃላፊነት ፡ ያለበት *halafinnät yalläbbät;* (trustworthy) ታማኝ *tammaňň*
be responsible (be held responsible) በኃላፊነት ፡ ተጠየቀ *bähalafinnät täṭäyyäqä*

rest, vi. (take a rest, relax) አረፈ *arräfä;* እፎይ ፡ አለ *əffoyy alä;* (lie down) ጋደም ፡ አለ *gadämm alä;* (lean) ተደገፋ *tädäggäfä;* (be based) ተመሠረተ *tämäsärrätä;* (be buried) በሰላም ፡ አረፈ *bäsälam arräfä*

rest, n. (repose) ዕረፍት *əräft;* (residue) የቀረ *yäqärrä*
be laid to rest ተቀበረ *täqäbbärä*
take a rest ዕረፍት ፡ አደረገ *əräft adärrägä*

restaurant ምግብ ፡ ቤት *məgəb bet;* ሬስቶራንት *restorant*

restful, be ዕረፍት ፡ ሰጠ *əräft säṭṭä*

restitution (act of being given back) መመለስ *mämmäläs;* (act of making good any loss) ካሳ *kasa;* ምትክ *mətəkk*

restless, get ~ ተቁነጠነጠ *täqᵂnäṭännäṭä*

restoration (of building) እድሳት *əddəsat;* (of independence) መመለስ *mämmäläs*

restore (put back to a former state) አሳደሰ *asaddäsä;* መለሰ *mälläsä;* እንደገና ፡ አደረገ *əndägäna adärrägä*

restrain (~ anger) ጋታ *gätta*

restrict ወሰነ *wässänä*

restriction ገደብ *gädäb;* ቁጥጥር *quṭəṭṭər*

restroom ሽንት ፡ ቤት *šənt bet*

result (v.), ~ from መጣ *mäṭṭa;* ተከተለ *täkättälä*
result in ምክንያት ፡ ሆነ *məknəyat honä;* አስከተለ *askättälä;* አስገኘ *asgäňňä*

result (n.) ውጤት *wəṭṭet;* ፍሬ *färe*

resume (v.) ቀጠለ *qäṭṭälä*

resurrect (~ the dead) አዳነ *adanä*
be resurrected ተነሣ *tänässa*

resurrection ትንሣኤ *tənsa'e*

resuscitate ትንፋሽ ፡ መለሰ *tənfaš mälläsä*

retail (vt.) ቸረቸረ *čäräččärä*

retail (n.) ችርቻሮ *čərəččaro*
retail dealer ችርቻሪ *čärčari*

retain (hold) ያዘ *yazä;* (remember) አስታወሰ *astawwäsä*

retainer (servant) አሽከር *aškär*

retaliate ብድር ፡ መለሰ *bəddər mälläsä;* በቀል ፡ መለሰ *aṣäfa mälläsä*

retaliation በጻፋ *aṣäfa*
in retaliation በጻፋውን *aṣäfawən*

retard (delay) አዘገየ *azägäyyä;* (~progress) ወደ ፡ ኋላ ፡ ጕተተ *wädä hʷala gʷättätä*

retinue በጀብ *ağäb;* የክብር ፡ ተከታዮች *yäkəbər täkättayočč*

retire, vt. (remove from office after a long service) ጡረታ ፡ አስገባ *ṭuräta asgäbba;* (withdraw) አስወገደ *aswäggädä*
retire, vi. (give up an office) ጡረታ ፡ ገባ *ṭuräta gäbba;* (retreat) ተመለሰ *tämälläsä;* (go to bed) ተኛ *täňňa*

retired, adj. (from work) ጡረታ ፡ የወጣ *ṭuräta yäwäṭṭa*
retired life ገላልተኝነት *gälältäňňannät*

retirement ጡረታ *ṭuräta*

retiring (modest) ዓይነፋር *aynaffar;* ዝምተኛ *zəmmətäňňa*

retrace (trace over again) እንደገና ፡ ነደፈ *əndägäna näddäfä*

retract (~ a statement) በጠፈ *aṭṭäfä*

retreat, v. (fall back) አፈገፈገ *afägäffägä;* (go for privacy) ለዕረፍት ፡ ሄደ *läəräft hedä*

retreat, n. (withdrawal) ማፈግፈግ *mafägfäg;* (place for refuge) የማምለጫ ፡ ቦታ *yämamläča bota*

retrieve (regain) አገኘ *agäňňä;* (make good) አረመ *arrämä*

retrogress ተመለሰ *tämälläsä;* (of condition in health) እየባሰ ፡ ሄደ *əyyäbasä hedä*

return, vt. (give back, answer) መለሰ *mälläsä*
return (vi.) ተመለሰ *tämälläsä*

return, n. (coming back) መመለስ *mämmäläs;* (profit) ትርፍ *tərf*
returns ውጤት *wäṭṭet;* የምርጫ ፡ ውጤት *yämrča wäṭṭet*
return ticket የመመለሻ ፡ ቲኬት *yämämmäläša tiket*

in return ልዋጭ *ləwwač;* በበጻፋው *baṣäfaw*

reunion አንድ ፡ ላይ ፡ መገናኘት *and lay mäggäňät*

reunite አንድ ፡ አደረገ *and adärrägä;* አገናኘ *aggänaňňä;* እንደገና ፡ አዋሐደ *əndägäna awwahadä*

reveal (disclose) ገለጸ *gälläṣä;* (~ a secret) አወጣ *awäṭṭa*

revel ፈነጠዘ *fänäṭṭäza*

revelation (revealing of a secret) ማውጣት *mawṭat;* (God's disclosure of Himself) ራእይ *ra'əy*

revelry ፈንጠዝያ *fänṭäzəyya*

revenge (v.) ተበቀለ *täbäqqälä*

revenge (n.) ቂም *qim;* ቅያሜ *qəyyame;* በቀል *bäqäl*

revenue ገቢ *gäbi*

reverberate አስተጋባ *astägabba*

revere በጣም ፡ አከበረ *bäṭam akäbbärä*

reverence (n.) አክብሮት *akbərot;* ክብር *kəbər*
hold in reverence አከበረ *akäbbärä*

reverend አባ *abba*

reverent ሰው ፡ አክባሪ *säw akbari*

reverse, v. (change to the contrary) በተቃራኒው ፡ ለወጠ *bätäqaraniw läwwäṭä;* (revoke) ሻረ *šarä*

reverse, n. (opposite) ተቃራኒ *täqarani;* (defeat) ጉዳት *gudat*

revert ተመለሰ *tämälläsä*

review, v. (~ troops) ጐበኘ *gʷäbäňňä;* (~ a decision, events) መረመረ *märämmärä;* (~ a lesson) ከለሰ *källäsä;* ደገመ *däggämä;* (~ a book) አቃቀር ፡ ጻፈ *aqaqir ṣafä*

review, n. (of army) ሰልፍ *sälf;* (of a book) አቃቀር *aqaqir;* (of events) ምርመራ *mərmära;* (of a lesson) ክለሳ *kəlläsa*
pass in review በሰልፍ ፡ አለፈ *bäsälf alläfä*

revise (change) ለወጠ *läwwäṭä;* (~ the constitution) አሻሻለ *aššašalä*

revision (being revised) መሻሻል *mäššašal*

revival ማንሰራራት *mansärarat* experience a revival አንሰራራ *ansärarra*

revive, vt. (bring back to life) ነፍስ ፡ ዘራ(በት) *näfs zärra(bbät);* (~ a custom) ሕይወት ፡ ሰጠ *həywät säṭṭä;* (~ memories) አስታወሰ *astawwäsä* revive, vt. (of spirit) ተነቃቃ *tänäqaqqa;* (of hope) ታደሰ *taddäsä*

revoke (~ a license) ነጠቀ *näṭṭäqä;* (~ a concession) ሰረዘ *särräzä;* (~ a decision) ሻረ *šarä*

revolt, vi. (rise up against authority) ዐመጸ *ammäṣä;* (of a child against the parents) አሻፈረኝ ፡ አለ *ašaffäräňň alä*

revolt (n.) ዐመፅ *amäṣ*

revolution መሠረታዊ ፡ ለውጥ *mäsärätawi läwṭ;* ሽብር *šäbbər;* (revolving of the earth) መሽከርከር *mäškärkär*

revolutionary (n.) ደመ ፡ ነውጠኛ *dämä näwṭäňňa*

revolutionary, adj. (~ leader) ሞጋደኛ *mogädäňňa;* (causing a great change) ከፍተኛ ፡ ለውጥ ፡ ያመጣ *käffətäňňa läwṭ yamäṭṭa*

revolve (move in a circle) ዞረ *zorä;* ተሽከረከረ *täškäräkkärä;* (occur regularly) ተፈራረቀ *täfärarräqä*

revolver ሽጉጥ *šəgguṭ*

revulsion ጥላቻ *ṭəlačča*

reward, v. (~ loyalty) ወሮታ ፡ ከፈለ *wärrota käffälä*

reward (n.) ወሮታ *wärrota;* ሽልማት *šəlləmat*

rheumatism ቁርጥማት *qurṭəmat*

rhinoceros አውራሪስ *awraris*

rhyme (v.) ቤት ፡ መታ *bet mätta*

rhyme (n.) የቤት ፡ መምቻ *yäbet mämča*

without rhyme or reason ከመሬት ፡ ተነሥቶ *kämäret tänästo;* ያለ ፡ ምክን ያት *yalä məknəyat*

rhythm ውዝዋዜ *wəzəwwaze*

rib ጐድን *gʷädən;* (of umbrella) ሸቦ *šäbo*

ribbon (for hair) ሪቫን *ribän;* (for dress) ጥብጣብ *ṭəbṭab;* (for typewriter) ካር *kärr*

rice ሩዝ *ruz*

rich (~ person) ሃብታም *habtam;* ባለጸጋ *baläṣägga;* (~ soil) ለም *läm;* (~ color) ደማቅ *dämmaq* get rich ከበረ *käbbärä;* በለጸገ *bäläṣṣägä*

riches ሃብት *habt*

rid, get ~ of (a person) ተገላገለ *tägälaggälä;* (of bad habits) አስወገደ *aswäggädä;* ተላቀቀ *tälaqqäqä*

riddle እንቆቅልሽ *ənqoqəlləš*

ride, vt. (~ a motorcycle) ነዳ *nädda;* (~ an equine) ጋለበ *galläbä;* ተቀመጠ *täqämmäṭä*

ride (n.) ጉዞ *guzo*

ridge (chain of hills) ተርተር *tärtär;* (in the ground) ትልም *tələm*

ridicule ተሳለቀ *täsalläqä*

ridiculous (~ person) ሞኝ *moňň;* (~ hat) የሚያስቅ *yämmiyassəq*

rifle ጠበንጃ *ṭäbänǧa;* ጠመንጃ *ṭämänǧa;* ብረት *brät*

rift ስንጥቅ *sənṭəq*

right, n. (privilege) መብት *mäbt;* (opposite of left) ቀኝ *qäňň;* (conservative in politics) ቀኝ ፡ ክፍል *qäňň kəfəl*

right, adj. (proper) ተስማሚ *täsmami;* ተገቢ *tägäbi;* (correct) ልክ *ləkk;* (opposite of left) የቀኝ ፡ እጅ *yäqäňň əǧǧ* you are right እውነትህ ፡ ነው *əwnätəh näw*

right, adv. (opposite of left) ወደ ፡ ቀኝ *wädä qäňň;* (correctly) ልክ *ləkk;* በት

ከከል *bätəkəkkəl;* (directly) በቀጥታ
bäqäṭṭəta
right away አሁኑኑ *ahununu;* ወዲያው
wädiyaw; ወዲያውኑ *wädiyawnu*
right now አሁን *ahun*

righteous ጻድቅ *ṣadəq;* (~ act) መልካም
mälkam

righteousness ጻድቅነት *ṣadəqənnät;* ቅድ
ስና *qəddəsənna*

rightful (~ heir) ሕጋዊ *həggawi;* እውነ
ተኛ *əwnätäñña;* (~ property) በሕግ ፡
የሚገባው *bähəgg yämmiggäbbaw*

rightly (suitably) በሚገባ *bämmiggäbba;*
(correctly) በትክክል *bätəkəkkəl*
rightly or wrongly ልክ ፡ ይሁንም ፡ አይ
ሁን *ləkk yəhunəm ayhun*

right-of-way የቅድሚያ ፡ መንገድ *yäqəd-
miya mängäd*

rigid (~ rule) ጥብቅ *ṭəbq;* (~ stick)
ደረቅ *däräq*

rigorous ጥብቅ *ṭəbq*

rim (of a glass) አፍ *af;* (of eyeglasses)
ከፈፍ *kəfäf;* (of tire) ቸርኬ *čärke*

rind ልጣጭ *ləṭṭač;* ቅርፊት *qərfit*

ring, vt. (~ the bell) ደወለ *däwwälä*
ring (vi.) ደወለ *däwwälä;* (of a doorbell) ተደወለ *tädäwwälä;* (of phone)
ጮኸ *čohä;* (of ears) ጭው ፡ አለ *čəww
alä*

ring, n. (for finger) ቀለበት *qäläbät;* (for
key) ዘለበት *zäläbät;* (of bell) ድምፅ
dəmṣ; (circle) ከበብ *kəbäb*

ring finger የቀለበት ፡ ጣት *yäqäläbät ṭat*

ringleader ቀንደኛ *qändäñña;* የተንኮል ፡
ቀንደኛ *yätänkʷäl qändäñña*

rinse (~ a pot, clothes) አለቀለቀ *aläqälläqä;* (~ the mouth) አጕመጠመጠ
agʷmäṭämmäṭä

riot (v.) በጠበጠ *bäṭäbbäṭä;* ጸጥታ ፡ አደ
ፈረሰ *ṣäṭṭəta adäfärräsä*

riot (n.) ረብሻ *räbša;* ሽብር *šəbbər;* ሁከት
hukät

riotous (~ conduct) ረብሻኛ *räbšäñña;*
(~ crowd) የተራበሸ *yätärabbäšä*

rip (~ cloth) ቀደደ *qäddädä;* (~ a seam)
ተረተረ *tärättärä*
rip off (~ a cover) ገነጠለ *gänäṭṭälä*

ripe የበሰለ *yäbässälä*
be ripe በሰለ *bässälä*

ripen (vt.) አበሰለ *abässälä*
ripen (vi.) በሰለ *bässälä*

rise, v. (get up) ተነሣ *tänässa;* (be high)
ከፍ ፡ አለ *käff alä;* (of sun) ወጣ *wäṭṭa;* (of river) ሞላ *molla;* (of dough)
ኩፍ ፡ አለ *kuff alä*

rise (n.), give ~ to አስነሣ *asnässa;* አስ
ከተለ *askättälä*

risk, ~ one's life አደጋ ፡ ላይ ፡ ጣለ *a-
däga lay ṭalä;* በነፍሱ ፡ ቄረጠ *bänäf-
su qʷärräṭä*

risky አስጊ *asgi*

rite ሥነ ፡ ሥርዓት *sənä sər'at*

ritual (n.) ሥነ ፡ ሥርዓት *sənä sər'at;* የጸ
ሎት ፡ ሥነ ፡ ሥርዓት *yäṣälot sənä sər-
'at*

rival (v.) ተወዳደረ *täwädaddärä;* ተፎካ
ከረ *täfokakkärä*

rival (n.) ተወዳዳሪ *täwädadari;* ተፎካካሪ
täfokakari

rivalry ፉክክር *fəkəkkər;* ተፎካካሪነት *täfokakarinnät;* ውድድር *wədəddər*

river ወንዝ *wänz*

river basin የወንዝ ፡ ሽለቆ *yäwänz šäläqo*

rivet ሪቬት *rivet*

road መንገድ *mängäd;* ጐዳና *gʷädana*

roadblock መሰናከል *mäsänakəl;* መሰ
ከያ *mässänakäya*

roam (of a person) ተንቀዋለለ *tänqäwallälä;* (of animals) ተዘዋወረ *täzäwawwärä*

roar (v.) ጮኸ *čohä;* (of a lion) አገሣ
agässa
roar away ተፈተለከ *täfätälläkä*

roar (n.) ጩኸት *čuhät;* ድምፅ *dəmṣ;* (of a lion) ግሣት *gəsat*

roast, v. (~ meat) ጠበሰ *ṭäbbäsä;* (~ coffee) ቆላ *qʷälla*

roast (n.) ጥብስ ፡ ሥጋ *ṭəbs səga*

roasted grain ቆሎ *qollo*

roasting pan መጥበሻ *mäṭbäša*

rob ሰረቀ *särräqä;* ቀማ *qämma;* ዘረፈ *zärräfä*

robber ቀማኛ *qämmaňňa;* ወንበዴ *wänbäde;* ዘራፊ *zärafi*

robbery ስርቆት *sərqot;* ቀማኝነት *qämmaňňannät;* ዘረፋ *zäräfa*

robe (n.) ልብስ *ləbs;* (imperial ~) ካባ *kabba*

robust ጠንካራ *ṭänkarra*

rock (vt.) አወዛወዘ *awwäzawwäzä;* (~ a baby) እሹሩሩ ፡ አለ *əššururu alä*
rock, vi. (in a chair) ተወዛወዘ *täwäzawwäzä;* (of a boat) ዋለለ *wallälä*

rock (n.) ቋጥኝ *qʷaṭəňň;* አለት *alät*

rocket መንኩራኩር *mänkʷärakʷər*

rocking chair ተወዛዋዥ ፡ ወምበር *täwäzawaž wämbär*

rocky (~ cliff) ቋጥኝ ፡ የበዛበት *qʷaṭəňň yäbäzzabbät;* (~ road) ኩርኩንች *kʷäräkʷänč;* ድንጋያማ *dəngayamma*

rod አርጩሜ *arčumme;* ዘንግ *zäng*

rogue ቀጣፊ *qäṭafi;* ወስላታ *wäslatta*

role ቦታ *bota;* ስፍራ *səfra*

roll, vt. (wrap around) ጠቀለለ *ṭäqällälä;* (~ dough) አድቦለቦለ *adboläbbolä;* (~ a marble, eyes) አንከባለለ *ankäballälä*
roll, vi. (of thunder) አጉረመረመ *agʷrämärrämä;* (of tears) ኮለል ፡ አለ *koläll alä;* (of a ship) ዋለለ *wallälä;* (of a ball) ተንከባለለ *tänkäballälä*
roll up (~ a rug) ጠቀለለ *ṭäqällälä;* (~ a blanket) ዐጣጠፈ *aṭaṭṭäfä*

roll, n. (of thunder) ድምፅ *dəmṣ;* (of wrapping paper) ጥቅል *ṭəqəll;* (small

bread) ድቡልቡል ፡ ዳቦ *dəbulbul dabbo*
rolls (register) መዝገብ *mäzgäb*
call the roll ስም ፡ ጠራ *səm ṭärra*

roller skate መንሸራታች ፡ ጫማ *mänšäratač čamma*

roof ጣራ *ṭara;* ጣሪያ *ṭariya*
roof of the mouth ላንቃ *lanqa*

room (n.) ክፍል *kəfəl;* (space) ስፍራ *səfra;* ቦታ *bota*
room and board ምግብና ፡ መኝታ *məgəbənna mäňňəta*
ladies' room የሴቶች ፡ ሽንት ፡ ቤት *yäsetočč šənt bet*
men's room የወንዶች ፡ ሽንት ፡ ቤት *yäwändočč šənt bet*

roommate ደባል *däbbal;* የክፍል ፡ ጓደኛ *yäkəfəl gʷaddäňňa*

roomy ሰፋ ፡ ያለ *säfa yalä*

rooster አውራ ፡ ዶሮ *awra doro*

root, n. (of tree) ሥር *sər;* (source) ምንጭ *mənč*
take root ሥር ፡ ሰደደ *sər säddädä*

rope (v.) በገመድ ፡ ጠለፈ *bägämäd ṭälläfä*

rope (n.) ገመድ *gämäd*

rosary መቁጠሪያ *mäqʷṭäriya*

rose ጽጌ ፡ ረዳ *ṣəgge räda*

roster መዝገብ *mäzgäb*

rot (vi.) በሰበሰ *bäsäbbäsä*

rotate, vi. (move around) ዞረ *zorä;* ተሽከረከረ *täškäräkkärä;* (change in regular order) ተለዋወጠ *täläwawwäṭä;* ተቀያየረ *täqäyayyärä*

rotation (of office) ተራ *tära*

rote, by ~ በቃል *bäqal*

rotten (decayed) የበሰበሰ *yäbäsäbbäsä;* (corrupt) የተበላሸ *yätäbälaššä*
be rotten በሰበሰ *bäsäbbäsä*

rough (~ surface) ሻካራ *šakara;* (~ road) ኩርኩንች *kʷäräkʷänč;* (~ voice) ጉርናና *gʷärnanna;* (~ times) አስጨናቂ *asčännaqi;* (~ life) ምጿት ፡ የጎደለ *mäččot yägʷäddälä*

rough life, rough times የችግር ፡ ጊዜ
yäčəggər gize
be rough (of surface) ሻከረ šakkärä

roughly (in a rough manner) በጎይል ፡
ቃል bähaylä qal; (approximately)
ከሞላ ፡ ጐደል kämolla gʷäddäl; ያህል
yahəl; በግምት bägəmmət

round (v.) ከብ ፡ አደረገ kəbb adärrägä;
(~ the lips) አሞጠሞጠ amoṭämmoṭä
round up ሰበሰበ säbässäbä

round, n. (in sport) ዙር zur
make the rounds (of watchman) እየ
ተዘዋወረ ፡ ጠበቀ əyyätäzäwawwärä
ṭäbbäqä; (of policeman) ከልል ፡ ቃኘ
kəlləl qaňňä; (of a doctor) እየዞረ ፡ በሽ
ተኞቹን ፡ ጐበኘ əyyäzorä bäššätäňňoč-
čun gʷäbäňňä

round (adj.) ከብ kəbb; ድቡልቡል dəbulbul; እንክብል ənkəbəll; (~ number)
ሙሉ ፡ የተጠጋ mulu yätäṭägga; ሙሉ፡
ቀራቢ mulu qärabi
round (adv.) በሙሉ bämulu; (around)
ዙሪያ zuriya
in round figures በግምት bägəmmət

roundabout ዞረወራ zäwärwärra; የዙሪያ
yäzuriya

round trip ደርሶ ፡ መልስ därso mäls

round trip ticket ደርሶ ፡ መልስ ፡ ቲኬት
därso mäls tiket

rouse (awaken) አስነሳ asnässa; አነቃ a-
näqqa; (stir up) ስሜት ፡ ቀሰቀሰ səmmet qäsäqqäsä

rout (v.) ድል ፡ አድርጎ ፡ በታተነ dəl adrəgo bätattänä

rout (n.) ሽሽት šəššət

route መንገድ mängäd

routine ልማድ ləmad

row (v.) ቀዘፈ qäzzäfä

row, n., rhymes with 'low'; (line) ተርታ
tärta; (of houses) መደዳ mädäda; (of
seats) ረድፍ räd(ə)f
row, rhymes with 'how'; (loud noise)
ጫጫታ čačata; (noisy argument) አም
ባጓሮ ambagʷaro

royal የንጉሥ yänəgus; ንጉሣዊ nəgusawi;
(~ welcome) ከፍ ፡ ያለ käff yalä
His Royal Highness ልዑል lə'ul

royalty (kings and their families) ንጉሣ
ውያን ፡ ቤት ፡ ሰብ nəgusawəyan betä
säb; (position of king) ንጉሥነት nəgusənnät
royalties የደራሲ ፡ ድርሻ yädärasi dərša

rub, vt. አሸ aššä; አሻሸ ašaššä; (polish)
ወለወለ wäläwwälä
rub out ሰረዘ särräzä; ፋቀ faqä

rubber ላስቲክ lastik; ጎማ gomma
rubbers የጎማ ፡ ጫማ yägomma čamma

rubber band ላስቲክ lastik

rubber stamp ማህተም mahtäm

rubbish(trash) ቆሻሻ qošaša; ውዳቂ wəddaqi; ጥራጊ ṭərragi; ጉድፍ gudəf;
(worthless) ምናምን mənamən

rubble ፍርስራሽ fərəsraš
turn to rubble አፈራረሰ afärarräsä;
አማድ ፡ አደረገ amäd adärrägä

rudder መቅዘፊያ mäqzäfiya

rude (not polite) ባላጌ baläge; (roughly
made) እንደነገሩ ፡ የተሠራ əndänägäru
yätäsärra
be rude ባለገ ballägä

rudeness ብልግና bəlgənna

rudiment(s) መሠረታዊ ፡ ደንቦች mäsärätawi dänbočč

rudimentary መጠነኛ mäṭänäňňa

ruffian ወሮበላ wärrobälla

ruffle, n. (of skirt) ዘርፍ zärf

rug ምንጣፍ mənṭaf; ሰጋጃ səgaǧǧa

rugged (~ countryside) ወጣ ፡ ገባ wäṭṭa
gäbba; (~ people) ጠንካራ ṭänkarra

ruin, v. (~ the crop) አጠፋ aṭäffa; (~
health) ጐዳ gʷädda; (~ clothes,
road) አበላሸ abbälaššä; (~ a house)
አፈረሰ afärräsä; (make bankrupt)
አከሰረ akässärä

ruin (n.) ጉዳት gudat; ጥፋት ṭəfat
ruins ፍራሽ fərraš

be (fall) in ruins *ፈረሰ färräsä;* *ፈራረሰ färarräsä*

ruinous *ጉኽ gʷäǧi;* ጥፋት ፡ *የሚያደርስ ṭəfat yämmiyadärs*

rule, v. (govern) *ነገሠ näggäsä;* (make a formal decision) *ፈረደ färrädä;* (make straight lines) *አሠመረ asämmärä*

rule, n. (of law, grammar) *ሕግ həgg;* (conduct) *ደንብ dänb;* (government, authority) *አገዛዝ aggäzaz;* (period of ruling) *ዘመነ ፡ መንግሥት zämänä mängəst*
as a rule *ዘወትር zäwätər*

ruler (who governs) *ገዢ gäži;* (for making lines) *ማሥመሪያ masmäriya*

ruling, n. (of court) *ውሳኔ wəssane*

ruling, adj. (~ class) *የገዢዎች yägäžiwočč;* (~ party) *በሥልጣን ፡ ላይ ፡ ያለ bäsəlṭan lay yallä*

rumble (v.) *አጉረመረመ agʷrämärrämä*

ruminate *አመሰኳ amäsäkkʷa;* *አመነዣከ amänäžžähä*

rummage *ቀሰቀሰ qäsäqqäsä;* *በረበረ bäräbbärä*

rumor (n.) *ወሬ wäre;* *ጭምጭምታ čəmčəmta*

rumple *አጨማተረ aččämattärä*

run, vt. (administer) *አስተዳደረ astädaddärä;* *አካሄደ akkahedä;* (enter in a race) *አስገባ asgäbba*
run (vi.) *ሮጠ roṭä;* (of train) *ሄደ hedä;* (of water) *ፈሰሰ fässäsä;* (of machine, watch) *ሠራ särra;* (of color) *ለቀቀ läqqäqä*
run about *ተርዋርዋጠ tärʷarʷaṭä;* *ወዲያ ፡ ወዲህ ፡ ሮጠ wädiya wädih roṭä*
run across *አጋጠመ(ው) aggaṭṭämä(w)*
run along *ሄደ hedä*
run away *ሸሸ šäššä;* (from home) *ኰበለለ kʷäbällälä*
run into (collide) *ጋጨ gäččä*
run out *ሮጠ ፡ ወጣ roṭo wäṭṭa;* (come to an end) *አለቀ alläqä*

run over (someone) *ረጣ daṭä*

run (n.), in the long ~ *ውሎ ፡ አድሮ wəlo adro;* *የኋላ ፡ ኋላ yähʷala hʷala*

runner (who runs) *ሯጭ rʷač*

running (n.) *ሩጫ ruččä;* (administering) *አስተዳደር astädadär*
be in the running *ተወዳዳሪ ፡ ነው täwädadari näw*

running water *የቧምቧ ፡ ውኃ yäbʷambʷa wəha*

rural *የገጠር yägäṭär*

ruse *ተንኰል tänkʷäl*

rush, vt. (cause to act fast) *አጣደፈ aṭṭaddäfä;* (~ a job) *አቻኰለ aččakkʷälä*
rush (vi.) *ቻኰለ čäkkʷälä;* *ተጣደፈ täṭaddäfä*
rush out *ሮጠ ፡ ወጣ roṭo wäṭṭa*

rush, n. (hurry) *ጥድፊያ ṭədfiya;* (marsh plant) *ጨፈ čäffe*
be in a rush *ቻኰለ čäkkʷälä*

Russia *መስኮብ mäskob;* *ሩሲያ rusiya*

Russian (citizen of Russia) *መስኮባዊ mäskobawi;* (~ language) *መስኮብኛ mäskobəňňa*

rust (v.) *ዛገ zagä*

rust (n.) *ዝገት zəgät*

rustic (~ furniture) *ያገር ፡ ቤት yagär bet;* (~ manners) *የባላገርነት yäbalagärənnät*

rustle (of skirt) *ተንሿሿ tänšʷaššʷa;* (of leaves) *ተንኰሻኰሸ tänkʷäšakkʷäšä*

rusty *የዛገ yäzagä*

ruthless *ጨካኝ čäkkaň*
be ruthless *ጨከነ čäkkänä*

ruthlessly *ያለ ፡ ምሕረት yalä məhrät;* *በጭካኔ bäčəkkane*

rye *አጃ aǧǧa*

S

Sabbath ሰንበት *sänbät;* ቅዳሜ *qədame*

sack ጀንያ *ǧonəyya;* ዶኒያ *doniyya*

sacrament የቁርባን ፡ ሥነ ፡ ሥርዓት *yäqurban sənä sər'at*

sacred ቅዱስ *qəddus;* የተቀደሰ *yätäqäddäsä*

sacrifice (v.) መሥዋዕት ፡ አቀረበ *mäswa'ət aqärräbä;* ሠዋ *säwwa*
sacrifice oneself ራሱን ፡ መሥዋዕት ፡ አደረገ *rasun mäswa'ət adärrägä*

sacrifice (n.) መሥዋዕት *mäswa'ət*

sacrilege የረከሰ ፡ ተግባር *yäräkkäsä tägbar*

sad (~ news) አሳዛኝ *asazzañ*
be sad አዘነ *azzänä;* ተከዘ *täkkäzä*

sadden አሳዘነ *asazzänä*

saddle (v.) ጫነ *čana*

saddle (n.) ኮርቻ *korəčča*
without a saddle ለጣ *leṭa*

sadness ሐዘን *hazän;* ትካዜ *təkkaze*

safe (n.) ካዝና *kazna*

safe (adj.) ደኅና *dähna;* (~ driver) ጥን ቁቅ *ṭənquq;* (reliable) የሚያስተማምን *yämmiyastämammən;* (~ region) ሰ ላም *sälam*
be safe ደኅና ፡ ነው *dähna näw*

safe conduct የይለፍ ፡ ወረቀት *yäyələf wäräqät*

safeguard, n. (against disease) መከላከያ *mäkkälakäya*

safely በደኅና *bädähna*

safety ደኅንነት *dähnənnät*

safety belt የደጋ ፡ ቀበቶ *yadäga qäbätto*

safety pin መርፌ ፡ ቁልፍ *märfe qulf*

sage (n.) ዐዋቂ ፡ ሰው *awaqi säw*

sage, adj. (~person) ብልህ *bələh;* (~ reply) የብልህ *yäbələh*

sail (v.) በመርከብ ፡ ተነሣ *bämärkäb tänässa;* ተጓዘ *tägʷazä*

sail (n.) የመርከብ ፡ ሻራ *yämärkäb šara*

sailor መርከበኛ *märkäbäñña*

saint ቅዱስ *qəddus*

sake, for the ~ of ስለ *sälä;* በንተ *bäntä;* ለ - - - ሲል *lä - - - sil*

salad ሰላጣ *sälaṭa*

salary ደሞዝ *dämoz*

sale ሽያጭ *šəyyač;* (selling at a lower price than usual) የማጣሪያ ፡ ሽያጭ ፡ ጊዜ *yämaṭṭariya šəyyač gize*

salesclerk አሻሻጭ *aššašač*

salesman ሻጭ *šač;* አሻሻጭ *aššašač*

saliva ምራቅ *məraq;* ላህጭ *lähač;* ትፍታ *təffəta*

saloon መጠጥ ፡ ቤት *mäṭäṭṭ bet*

salt (v.) ጨው ፡ ጨመረ *čäw čämmärä*

salt (n.) ጨው *čäw*

salty ጨው ፡ የበዛበት *čäw yäbäzzabbät*

salutary ለጤና ፡ ጥሩ *läṭena ṭaru;* ለጤን ነት ፡ የሚስማማ *läṭenənnät yämmismamma*

salutation ሰላምታ *sälamta*

salute (v.) ሰላምታ ፡ ሰጠ *sälamta säṭṭä;* (by bowing) አጀ ፡ ነሣ *aǧǧ nässa*

salute (n.) ሰላምታ *sälamta*

salvation ደኅንነት *dähnənnät*

salve ቅባት *qəbat*

same, the ~ ያው *yaw*

sample (n.) ላሙና *lamuna;* ናሙና *namuna*

sanctify (consecrate) ባረከ *barräkä;* (cause to be considered sacred) ቅዱ ስ ፡ አደረገ *qəddus adärrägä*

sanction (v.) ፈቀደ *fäqqädä;* ደገፈ *däggäfä*

sanction (n.) ፈቃድ fäqad
sanctions ማገጃ maggäǧa; እገዳ əggäda

sanctity ቅዱስነት qəddusənnät

sanctuary መቅደስ mäqdäs; ቤተ ፡ መቅ
ደስ betä mäqdäs; (refuge and protection) ጥገኝነት ṭəggäňňənnät

sand (n.) አሸዋ ašäwa

sandal የነጠላ ፡ ጫማ yänäṭäla čamma

sandy አሸዋማ ašäwamma

sane ጤነኛ ṭenäňňa

sanitary (free from disease) ንጹሕ nəṣuh; (having to do with health) የጤና፡
አጠባበቅ yäṭena aṭṭäbabäq

sanitation ጽዳት ṣədat
Department of Sanitation የጽዳት ፡
ክፍል yäṣədat kəfəl

sanity አእምሮ a'məro

sap (of plant) ውኃ wəha; ወተት wätät

Satan ሰይጣን säyṭan

satiable, be ～ (of appetite) ረካ räkka

satiate አጠገበ aṭäggäbä
be satiated ጠገበ ṭäggäbä

satiety ጥጋብ ṭəgab

satin አጥላስ aṭlas

satisfaction ደስታ dässəta

satisfactory (～ condition) ደኅና dähna;
(～ reason) በቂ bäqi; (～ results) አጥ
ጋቢ aṭgabi

satisfy (content) አስደሰተ asdässätä; (of
an answer) አጠገበ aṭäggäbä; አስረዳ
asrädda; (～ hunger, needs) አረካ a-
räkka; አጠገበ aṭäggäbä
be satisfied (be content) ደስ ፡ አለ(ው)
däss alä(w); ተደሰተ tädässätä; (be satiated) ጠገበ ṭäggäbä; (of needs, hunger) ረካ räkka

Saturday ቅዳሜ qədame

sauce ሱጎ sugo; ስጎ səgo

saucepan ድስት dəst

saucer ማስቀመጫ masqämmäča

sausage ቋሊማ qʷalima

savage (n.) አረመኔ arämäne

savage, adj. (～ person) ጨካኝ čäkkaň;
አረመኔ arämäne; (～ attack) ኃይለኛ
hayläňňa

savagery አውሬነት awrennät

save, v. (rescue) አዳነ adanä; አተረፈ a-
tärräfä; (～ money) ቆጠበ qʷäṭṭäbä;
(～ a seat) ያዘ yazä

save (prep.) ከ - - - በስተቀር kä - - - bästäqär

savings ተቀማጭ ፡ ገንዘብ täqämmač gänzäb

savings deposit, see 'savings'

savior መድኃኔ mädhane

savor (v.) አጣጣመ aṭṭaṭamä

savor (n.) ጣዕም ṭa'əm; ጣም ṭam

savory, be ጣፈጠ ṭaffäṭä

saw (v.) መገዘ mäggäzä

saw (n.) መጋዝ mägaz

say አለ alä; ነገረ näggärä

saying ምሳሌ məssale

scab ቁርፊት qərfit

scald (burn) አቃጠለ aqqaṭṭälä; (heat to
the boiling point) አፈላ afälla

scale, v. (scrape off) ፋቀ faqä

scale, n. (of fish) ቁርፊት qərfit; (gradu-
ated marking) መለኪያ mäläkkiya
scales ሚዛን mizan
on a large scale በሰፊው bäsäffiw

scalp (n.) አናት anat

scandal ነውር näwr; አሳፋሪ ፡ ነገር asaffari nägär

scant (rare) ብርቅ bərq; (small) አነስ ፡
ያለ anäss yalä

scanty ትንሽ tənnəš; (～ costume) በጣም፡
አጭር bäṭam aččər

scar (n.) ጠባሳ ṭäbasa

scarce ብርቅ bərq
be scarce ጠፋ ṭäffa; በብዛት ፡ አይገኝም
bäbəzat ayyəggäňňəm

scarcely በችግር bäčəggər; እምብዛም əmbəzam + negative verb

scarcity እጥረት əṭrät

scare (vt.) አስፈራ asfärra; አስደነገጠ asdänäggäṭä
be scared ፈራ färra

scare (n.) ፍርሃት fərhat

scarf ያንገት ፥ ልብስ yangät ləbs; ያንገት ፥ ፎጣ yangät foṭa

scary የሚያስፈራራ yämmiyasfärarra

scatter (vt.) በተነ bättänä; በታተነ bätattänä; (~ ashes) ነሰነሰ näsännäsä
scatter (vi.) ተበታተነ täbätattänä

scene (place of action) ስፍራ səfra; ቦታ bota; (incident) ሁኔታ huneta; (division of an act) ትዕይንት tə'əyənt; (scenery) የቲያትር ፥ ትርአይት yätiyatər tər'əyt

scenic ውብ wəb

scent, n. (of flowers) መዓዛ mä`aza; (perfume) ሽቶ šətto; (sense of smell) የማሽተት ፥ ችሎታ yämaštät čəlota

scepter በትረ ፥ መንግሥት bäträ mängəst

sceptic ተጠራጣሪ täṭäraṭari

schedule (v.) ወሰነ wässänä

schedule, n. (of classes) የትምህርት ፥ ቤት ፥ ሰሌዳ yätəmhərt bet säleda; (timetable) የጊዜ ፥ ሰሌዳ yägize säleda

scheme (v.) ዶለተ dollätä; (find a way out of something) ዘዴ ፥ ፈጠረ zäde fäṭṭärä

scheme, n. (plan, design) መላ mäla; አቅድ aqd; ውጥን wəṭṭən; ዘዴ zäde; (plot) ዶለት dulät; (arrangement, layout) ድልድል dələddəl

scholar ሊቅ liq

scholarly (~ person) ምሁር məhur

scholarship (quality of learning) ሊቅነት liqənnät; (grant) የነጻ ፥ ትምህርት ፥ ዕድል yänäṣa təmhərt əddəl

school ትምህርት ፥ ቤት təmhərt bet; ተማሪ ፥ ቤት tämari bet

schooling ትምህርት təmhərt

schoolmate የትምህርት ፥ ቤት ፥ ጓደኛ yätəmhərt bet gʷaddäñña

science ሥነ ፥ ፍጥረት sənä fəṭrät; ሳይንስ sayəns

scientific የሳይንስ yäsayəns

scientist የሳይንስ ፥ ሊቅ yäsayəns liq

scintillate አንጸባረቀ anṣäbarräqä; በረቀ bärräqä

scissors መቀስ mäqäs

scold ነቀፈ näqqäfä; ወቀሰ wäqqäsä

scoop up (~ grain) አፈሰ affäsä; ዘገነ zäggänä; (~ dung) ዛቀ zaqä

scorch ለበለበ läbälläbä; አቃጠለ aqqaṭṭälä
be scorched (food) አረረ arrärä

score, v. (~ a goal) አገባ agäbba

score, n. (in a game) ነጥብ näṭəb; ግብ gəb; (result) ውጤት wəṭṭet; (of music) ስልት səlt; (set of twenty) ሃያ haya
scores of ብዙ bəzu
keep score ቈጠረ qʷäṭṭärä

scorn (v.) አንቋሸሸ anqʷaššäšä; ናቀ naqä

scorn (n.) ንቀት nəqät
feel scorn ናቀ naqä

scorpion ጊንጥ ginṭ

scoundrel ወሮበላ wärrobälla

scour (~ a pot) ፈቀፈቀ fäqäffäqä; (search thoroughly) አሰሰ assäsä

scourge (n.) መቅሠፍት mäqsäft

scout (v.) ቃኘ qaññä

scout, n. (person sent out to get information) አሳሽ assaš; (boy scout) እስካውት əskawt

scramble (v.) አሻማ aššamma

scramble (n.) ሽሚያ šämmiya

scrap, n. (of paper) ብጣሽ bäṭṭaš; ብጭቂ bäččaqi; ቍርጥራጭ qurəṭrač; (of meat) ቍራጭ qurrač
scraps ፍርፋሪ fərəffari

scrape (v.) ፋቀ *faqä;* (~ the skin) ላጠ *laṭä;* (~ the knuckles) ገሸለጠ *gäšälläṭä*
scrape off ፋቀ *faqä*

scraper መፈቅፈቂያ *mäfäqfäqiya*

scratch, vt. (~ the skin with claws) ሟጠጠ *m^waṭṭäṭä;* ሟጨረ *m^waččärä;* ቧጨረ *b^waččärä;* (~ an itching skin) አከከ *akkäkä*
scratch, vi. (of pen) ጫረ *čarä*
scratch out ሰረዘ *särräzä*

scream (v.) ጮኸ *čohä*

scream (n.) ጩኸት *čuhät*

screech ሲጢጥ ፡ አለ *siṭiṭṭ alä*

screen, v. (hide with) ከለለ *källälä;* ጋረደ *garrädä;* (choose) መረጠ *märräṭä*

screen (n.) የሽቦ ፡ ወንፊት *yäšäbo wänfit;* (motion picture) ፊልም *film*

screw (n.) ቡሎን *bulon;* የቅርንፉድ ፡ ምስ ማር *yäqərənfud məsmar*

screwdriver የጠመንጃ ፡ መፍቻ *yäṭämänğa mäfča*

scribe ቀም ፡ ጸሐፊ *qum ṣähafi*

scribble ጫጨረ *čaçarä*

script ፊደል *fidäl*

Scriptures መጽሐፍ ፡ ቅዱስ *mäṣhaf qəddus*

scrub አሸ *aššä;* (~ pots) ፈገፈገ *fägäffägä*

scrutinize በጥንቃቄ ፡ መረመረ *bäṭənəqqaqe märämmärä*

scuffle (v.) ታገለ *taggälä*

scuffle (n.) አምባጓሮ *ambag^waro*

sculptor ቅርጽ ፡ አውጪ *qərṣ awči;* ሐወ ልት ፡ ሠሪ *hawəlt säri*

sculpture ቅርጽ *qərṣ*

scum (of milk) ስልባቦት *səlbabot;* (of water) ሰፈፍ *säfäf;* (worthless people) ልክስክስ ፡ ሰዎች *ləkəskəs säwočč*

scythe ማጭድ *maçəd*

sea ባሕር *bahər*

seal, v. (enclose tightly) አሸገ *aššägä;* (affix a seal to a document) አተመ *attämä;* ማኅተም ፡ አኖረ *mahtäm anorä*

seal (n.) ማኅተም *mahtäm*

seam (n.) ስፌት *səfet;* ዘርፍ *zärf;* (a line where edges join) መጋጠሚያ *mäggaṭämiya*

seaman መርከበኛ *märkäbäñña*

seamstress ልብስ ፡ ሰፊ *ləbs safi*

search (v.) ቀሰቀሰ *qäsäqqäsä;* ፈለገ *fällägä;* ፈተሸ *fättäšä*

search (n.) ፍለጋ *fəlläga;* ፍተሻ *fəttäša*

searchlight ባውዛ *bawza*

seashore የባሕር ፡ ዳር *yäbahər dar*

season (v.) አጣፈጠ *aṭaffäṭä;* ቀመመ *qämmämä*

season (n.) ወራት *wärat;* ወቅት *wäqt*

seasoned (~ troops) ልምድ ፡ ያለው *ləmd yalläw*

seasoning ቅመም *qəmäm*

seat (v.) አስቀመጠ *asqämmäṭä*

seat (n.) መቀመጫ *mäqqämäča;* ወንበር *wänbär;* ወምበር *wämbär;* (in a theater) ቦታ *bota;* (place) ስፍራ *səfra*
have a seat, take a seat ተቀመጠ *täqämmäṭä*

seat belt ያደጋ ፡ ቀበቶ *yadäga qäbätto*

seclude ጋረደ *garrädä*
seclude oneself ራሱን ፡ አገለለ *rasun agällälä*

secluded (~ life) የብቸኝነት *yäbəččäññannät;* (~ place) ገለልተኛ *gälältäñña;* ፈንጠር ፡ ያለ *fänṭärr yalä*

seclusion ገለልተኝነት *gälältäññannät*

second, v. (~ a motion) ደገፈ *däggäfä*

second (n.) ሴኮንድ *sekond*
in just a second አሁኑኑ *ahununu*

second (adj.) ሁለተኛ *hulättäñña;* (~ prize) የሁለተኛነት *yähulättäññannät;* (~ order of the Amharic alphabet) ካዕብ *ka'əb*

Second (with royal names) ዳግማዊ dagmawi

second class መለስተኛ mällästäňňa

second in command ምክትል ፡ አዛዥ məkəttəl azzaž

secondary school ሁለተኛ ፡ ደረጃ ፡ ትምህ ርት ፡ ቤት hulättäňňa däräğa təmhərt bet

second-hand ያገለገለ yagäläggälä

secrecy ምስጢር məstir

secret (n.) ምስጢር məstir
keep a secret ምስጢር ፡ ጠበቀ məstir tabbäqä; ምስጢር ፡ ቄጠረ məstir qwattärä

secret (adj.) ምስጢራዊ məstirawi; (~ hiding place) ስውር səwwər
secret agent ሰላይ sällay

secretariat የጽሕፈት ፡ ቤት yäsəhfät bet

secretary ጸሐፊ sähafi

secretary general ዋና ፡ ጸሐፊ wanna sähafi

secretly በስውር bäsəwwər; በድብቅ bädəbbəq

sect ወገን wägän

section (n.) ክፍል kəfəl; (of town) ሰፈር säfär

sector (military ~) የጦር ፡ ይዞታ yätor yəzota

secular (~ music) ዓለማዊ alämawi; (~ court) የሕዝብ yähəzb; (~ education) ሥጋዊ səgawi

secure, v. (fasten firmly) በደንብ ፡ ዘጋ bädänb zägga; አጥብቆ ፡ አሰረ atbəqo assärä; (protect) ተከላከለ täkälakkälä; (guarantee) በዋስትና ፡ ጠበቀ bäwastənna tabbäqä

secure, adj. (~ life) የማያሰጋ yämma yasäga; (~ foundation) ጽኑ sənu; (~ investment) ኪሳራ ፡ የማያደርስ kisara yämmayadärs
feel secure ያለ ፡ ስጋት ፡ ኖረ yalä səgat norä
keep secure ጠበቀ tabbäqä

security (pledge) መያዣ mäyaža; ዋስትና wastənna; (protection) መከላከያ mäk kälakäya

Security Council የጸጥታ ፡ ምክር ፡ ቤት yäsättata məkər bet

sedentary (~ tribe) ሰፍሮ ፡ የሚኖር säf ro yämminor

sediment ደለል däläl

seduce አሳሳተ assasatä; አባበለ ababbälä

see አየ ayyä; (visit) ጠየቀ tayyäqä
see off ሸኘ šäňňä

seed (v.) ዘራ zärra

seed (n.) ዘር zär
oil seeds የዘይት ፡ ፍሬ yäzäyt fre

seedling ቡቃያ buqayya

seek ፈለገ fällägä; (request) ጠየቀ tay yäqä; (try) ሞከረ mokkärä

seem መሰለ mässälä

seesaw, v. (ride a seesaw) ሚዛን ፡ ተጫ ወተ mizan täčawwätä

seesaw (n.) ሚዛን mizan

seethe (with rage, discontent) ጨሰ čäsä; ተፋፋመ täfafamä

segment ክፋይ kəffay; ብጣሽ bəttaš

segregate ገለል ፡ አደረገ gäläll adärrägä

seize ያዘ yazä; (grasp with the mind) ተረዳ tärädda

seldom እምብዛም əmbəzam + negative verb; ብዙ ፡ ጊዜ bəzu gize + negative verb

select (v.) መረጠ märrätä

select (adj.) ምርጥ mərt; የተመረጠ yätä märrätä

selection ምርጫ mərča

-self ራስ ras- (I myself እኔ ፡ ራሴ əne rase)

self-confidence በራሱ ፡ ላይ ፡ ያለው ፡ እም ነት bärasu lay yalläw əmnät

selfish ራሱን ፡ ወዳድ rasun wäddad

self-supporting, be ራሱን ፡ ቻለ rasun čalä

sell ሸጠ *šäṭä*

semester ወቅት *wäqt*

semicolon ነጠላ ፡ ሰረዝ *näṭäla säräz*

seminar ትምህርታዊ ፡ ጉባኤ *təmhərtawi guba'e*

seminary መንፈሳዊ ፡ ትምህርት ፡ ቤት *mänfäsawi təmhərt bet*

Semite ሴማዊ *semawi*

senate የሕግ ፡ መወሰኛ ፡ ምክር ፡ ቤት *yä-həgg mäwässäñña məkər bet*

send ላከ *lakä;* (~ regards) አቀረበ *aqär-räbä*
send away ሰደደ *säddädä*
send back መልሶ ፡ ላከ *mälləso lakä*
send in አስገባ *asgäbba*

senile የዓጃጃ *yäğağğä*

senior (adj.) የበላይነት ፡ ያለው *yäbäla-yənnät yalläw;* (in age) በዕድሜ ፡ የሚ በልጥ *bäədme yämmibälṭ*

seniority (in service) ያገልግሎት ፡ ዘመን *yagälgəlot zämän*

sensation (feeling) ስሜት *səmmet*

sensational ስሜት ፡ የሚቀሰቅስ *səmmet yämmiqäsäqqəs*

sense, v. (feel) ተሰማ(ው) *täsämma(w);* (understand) ተረዳ(ው) *tärädda(w)*

sense, n. (sensation) ስሜት *səmmet;* (physical, such as smell, taste, etc.) ሕዋስ *həwas;* (meaning) ትርጉም *tərgum*
common sense የተፈጥሮ ፡ ዕውቀት *yä-täfäṭro əwqät*
be out of one's senses አእምሮውን ፡ ሳተ *a'mərowən satä*

senseless, adj. (foolish) የማይረባ *yäm-mayəräba*

sensibility ስሜት *səmmet*

sensible (~ person) አስተዋይ *astäway;* (~ advice) ጠቃሚ *ṭäqami*
be sensible ልብ ፡ ገዛ *ləbb gäzza*

sensitive (irritable) ተናዳጅ *tänadäğ;* የሚ ቄጣ *yämmiqqʷäṭṭa;* (painful) የሚያም *yämmiyamm*
be sensitive to ተሰማ(ው) *täsämma(w)*

sentence (v.) ፈረደ(በት) *färrädä(bbät)*

sentence, n. (in grammar) ዓረፍተ ፡ ነገር *aräftä nägär;* (of court) ፍርድ *färd*
death sentence የሞት ፡ ፍርድ *yämot färd*
pronounce sentence ፈረደ *färrädä*

sentiment (feeling) ስሜት *səmmet;* (belief) አስተያየት *astäyayät*

sentry ዘብ *zäb*

separate (vt.) ለየ *läyyä;* (~ fighting persons) ገላገለ *gälaggälä*
separate (vi.) ተለያየ *täläyayyä*

separate (adj.) ልዩ *ləyyu;* የተለየ *yätä-läyyä*

separately ለየብቻ *läyyäbəčča;* ለብቻ *lä-bəčča*

September መስከረም *mäskäräm*

serene (~ sky) የጠራ *yäṭärra;* (~ sea) ጸጥ ፡ ያለ *ṣäṭṭ yalä*

serf ገባር *gäbbar*

sergeant የኀምሳ ፡ አለቃ *yähamsa aläqa*

series ተራ *tära*

serious (~ person) የምር *yämərr;* ምር ቀኝ ፡ የዋጠ *märaqun yäwaṭa;* (~ situation) አሳሳቢ *asassabi;* አስጊ *asgi;* (~ mistake) ከባድ *käbbad;* (~ difficulty) ከፍ ፡ ያለ *käff yalä;* (~ book) ጠለቅ ፡ ያለ *ṭäläqq yalä*
serious matter ቁም ፡ ነገር *qum nägär*

seriously (ill) በጣና *bäṭänna;* (in earnest) የምር *yämərr;* ከምሩ *kämərru;* ከልብ *käləbb*

seriousness (of situation) አሳሳቢነት *asassabinnät;* አስጊነት *asginnät;* (of crime) ከባድነት *käbbadənnät*

sermon ስብከት *səbkät*

serpent እባብ *əbab*

servant አሽከር *aškär;* አገልጋይ *agälgay*

serve (vt.) አገለገለ *agäläggälä;* (~ food) አቀረበ *aqärräbä;* አሳለፈ *asalläfä* be served (of food) ቀረበ *qärräbä*

service (n.) አገልግሎት *agälgəlot;* (religious ceremony) ቅዳሴ *qəddase*
be of service ረዳ *rädda*
church service ቅዳሴ *qəddase*
render service አገለገለ *agäläggälä;* ጠቀመ *ṭäqqämä*
take service (as a maid) ተቀጠረ *täqäṭṭärä*

service station ቤንዚን ፡ ማደያ *benzin maddäya*

servile አድር ፡ ባይ *adər bay*

servility አድር ፡ ባይነት *adər bayənnät*

servitude ባርነት *barənnät*

session ስብሰባ *səbsäba;* (of court) ችሎት *čəlot;* (class period) ክፍል ፡ ጊዜ *kəflä gize*

set, vt. (place) አስቀመጠ *asqämmäṭä;* (~ the time) ወሰነ *wässänä*
set, vi. (of sun) ገባ *gäbba;* ጠለቀ *ṭälläqä*
set apart (put aside) አስቀመጠ *asqämmäṭä;* (distinguish) ለየ *läyyä*
set aside መደብ *mäddäbä;* አስቀመጠ *asqämmäṭä*
set down አወረደ *awärrädä*
set up አቋቋም *aqqʷaqʷamä*

setback መሰናክል *mäsänakəl;* ዕንቅፋት *ənqəfat*

settle, vt. (~ an argument) አቆመ *aqomä;* ጨረሰ *čärräsä;* (~ affairs) አጠና ቀቀ *aṭṭänaqqäqä;* (~ a business) ፈጸመ *fäṣṣämä;* (~ a country) አቀና *aqänna*
settle, vi. (make one's home) ተቀመጠ *täqämmäṭä;* (come to rest) አረፈ *arräfä;* (come to an agreement) ተስማማ *täsmamma*
be settled (country) ሰው ፡ ሰፈረ(በት) *säw säffärä(bbät)*

settlement (colony) ቅኝ ፡ ግዛት *qəňň gəzat;* (dwelling) መኖሪያ *mänoriya;* ሰፈር *säfär;* (agreement) መስማማት *mäsmamat;* ስምምነት *səməmmənnät*

settler ሰፋሪ *säfari*

seven ሰባት *säbatt*
seven o'clock አንድ ፡ ሰዓት *and säat*

seventeen ዐሥራ ፡ ሰባት *asra säbatt*

seventh ሰባተኛ *säbattäňňa;* (~ order of the Amharic alphabet) ሳብዕ *sabə'*

seventy ሰባ *säba*

sever ነጠለ *näṭṭälä;* ቆረጠ *qʷärräṭä;* (~ relations) አቋረጠ *aqqʷarräṭä*

several (pron.) አንዳንዶቹ *andandoččäu*
several (adj.) አንዳንድ *andand;* አንዳ ዶች *andandočč;* (many) አያሌ *ayyale;* ብዙ *bəzu*

severe (strict) ጥብቅ *ṭəbq;* (~ winter) ኃይለኛ *hayläňňa;* (~ pain) አሰቃቂ *assäqqaqi;* (~ sentence) በርቱ *bärtu;* ጽኑ *ṣənu;* (~ competition) ከፍ ፡ ያለ *käff yalä*

sew ሰፋ *säffa*
sew on (~ a button) ተከለ *täkkälä*

sewage ጥራጊ *ṭərragi;* የቆሻሻ ፡ እጣቢ *yäqošaša äṭṭabi*

sewer ፉካ *fuka*

sewing ስፌት *səfet*

sewing machine የስፌት ፡ መኪና *yäsəfet mäkina*

sex ጾታ *ṣota*

shabby (~ beggar) ቡትቷም *butəttʷam;* (~ clothes) ያለቀ *yalläqä*

shack ደሳሳ ፡ ጎጆ *däsasa goǧǧo*

shackle (n.) የእግር ፡ ብረት *yäəgər brät*

shade, vt. (throw shade) አጠላ *aṭälla;* ጠለለ *ṭällälä*

shade (n.) ጥላ *ṭəla;* (of a window) የሽራ መጋረጃ *yäšära mäggaräǧa*

shadow (n.) ጥላ *ṭəla*

shady ጥላማ *ṭəlamma*

shaft (of spear) ዘንግ *zäng;* እጀታ *əǧǧäta*

shake (vt.) አንቀጠቀጠ *anqäṭäqqäṭä;* (of wind) አወዛወዘ *awwäzawwäzä;* አነቃ ነቀ *annäqannäqä;* (~ the head) ነቀነቀ

näqännäqä; (in a pot) በጠበጠ *bäṭäb-*
bäṭä; (~ the hand) ጨበጠ *čäbbäṭä*
shake (vi.) ተንቀጠቀጠ *tänqäṭäqqäṭä;*
ራዳ *radä;* (of voice) ቁርጥ ፡ ቁርጥ ፡
አለ *qurrəṭ qurrəṭ alä*
shake hands ተጨባበጡ *täčäbabbäṭu*

shaky, be (of bridge) አረገረገ *arägär-*
rägä; (of excuse) አይረባም *ayräbam*

shallow ቅርብ *qərb;* ግልብ *gəlb;* ጥልቅ ፡
ያልሆነ *ṭəlq yalhonä;* (~ dish) ዝርግ
zərg

shambles, be a ~ ተመሰቃቀለ *tämäsä-*
qaqqälä

shame (n.) ነፍረት *hafrät;* እፍረት *əfrät*
bring shame to አሳፈረ *asaffärä*
put to shame አስናቀ *asnaqä;* ዋጋ ፡
አሳጣ *waga asaṭṭa*
what a shame! ያሳዝናል *yasazzənal*
it is a shame ነውር ፡ ነው *näwr näw*

shameful አሳፋሪ *asaffari*

shameless እፍረተ ፡ ቢስ *əfrätä bis*

shape, v. (give form to) ቅርጽ ፡ አበጀ
(ለት) *qərṣ abäǧǧä(llät);* (adjust) አዛ
መደ *azzammädä*

shape (n.) ቅርጽ *qərṣ;* (condition) ሁኔታ
huneta; መልክ *mälk*

share (v.) ተካፈለ *täkaffälä;* ተከፋፈለ
täkäfaffälä

share (n.) ድርሻ *dərša;* ፈንታ *fänta;* (of
stock) አክሲዮን *aksiyon*

sharecropper ጢሰኛ *ṭisäňňa;* ጮሰኛ *čä-*
säňňa

sharp (~ point) ሹል *šul;* (~ edge) ስል
säl; ስለታም *sälätam;* (~ pain) ኃይለኛ
hayläňňa; (~ curve) ድንገተኛ *dəngä-*
täňňa

sharp, adv. (on time) ልክ *ləkk*

sharpen (~ a knife) ሳለ *salä;* አሰላ *asäl-*
la; (~ a pencil) ቀረጸ *qärräṣä;* አሾለ
ašola

shatter ሰባበረ *säbabbärä;* አናጋ *annagga*

shave (vt.) ላጨ *laččä*
shave (vi.) ተላጨ *tälaččä*

shaver ጢም ፡ ምላጭ *ṭim məlačč*

shawl ያንገት ፡ ልብስ *yangät ləbs*

she እሷ *əssʷa;* እርሷ *ərsʷa*

sheaf ነዶ *nädo*

shear (v.) ሸለተ *šällätä;* ቀጠጠ *qäṭṭäṭä*

shears ትልቅ ፡ መቀስ *tälləq mäqäs*

sheath (of sword) ሰገባ *sägäba;* አፎት
afot

shed, v. (~ blood) አፈሰሰ *afässäsä;* (~
skin) ገፋፈ *gäffäfä*

shed (n.) መጠለያ *mäṭṭäläya*

sheep በግ *bäg*

sheet (bedsheet) አንሶላ *ansola;* (of paper) ሉኸ *luh*

shelf መደርደሪያ *mädärdäriya*

shell, v. (~ beans) ፈለፈለ *fäläffälä;*
(bombard) በመድፍ ፡ ደበደበ *bämädf*
däbäddäbä

shell, n. (of nut) ቅርፊት *qərfit;* (of tortoise) ልብስ *ləbs;* (explosives) የመ
ድፍ ፡ ጥይት *yämädf ṭəyyət*

shelter, vt. (give shelter) መጠጊያ ፡ ሰጠ
mäṭṭägiya säṭṭä; (protect) ከለለ *käl-*
lälä; አስጠጋ *asṭägga*

shelter (n.) መጠለያ *mäṭṭäläya;* ተገን *tä-*
gän; መጠጊያ *mäṭṭägiya*
take shelter ተገን ፡ ያዘ *tägän yazä;*
ተጠለለ *täṭällälä*

shepherd እረኛ *ərräňňa*

shield, v. (protect) ተከላከለ *täkälakkälä*

shield (n.) ጋሻ *gašša;* (protection) መከ
ላከያ *mäkkälakäya*

shift (v.) ለወጠ *läwwäṭä;* አዛወረ *azzä-*
wawwärä; (~ a meeting) አሳለፈ *asal-*
läfä
shift, vi. (of wind) አቅጣጫውን ፡ ለወጠ
aqṭäččawən läwwäṭä

shift, n. (of gear) መለወጫ *mälläwäča;*
(group of people working at one
time) ተረኞች *täräňňočč*

shimmer አንጸባረቀ *anṣäbarräqä*

shin ቅልጥም *qəlṭəm*

shine, vt. (~ shoes) ጠረገ *ṭärrägä;* (~ silverware) ወለወለ *wäläwwälä*

shine, vi. (of eyes, sun) አበራ *abärra*

shiny (~ metal) የሚያበረቀርቅ *yämmiyabräqärreq;* (~ day) ፀሐያማ *ṣähayamma*

ship (n.) መርከብ *märkäb*

shipment እቃ *əqa*

shipwreck (n.) የመርከብ ፡ መስጠም *yämärkäb mäsṭäm;* የመርከብ፡ አደጋ *yämärkäb adäga*

shirk ሸሸ *šäššä*

shirt ሸሚዝ *šämiz*

shiver ተንቀጠቀጠ *tänqäṭäqqäṭä*

shock, v. (of action) አሰቀቀ *assäqqäqä;* አስደነገጠ *asdänäggäṭä;* አሸበረ *aššäbbärä;* (of bad language) አሳፈረ *asaffärä*

shock, n. (impact) ኃይለኛነት *hayläňňannät;* (violent disturbance) ድንጋጤ *dənəggaṭe*

shoddy መናኛ *mänaňňa*

shoe ጫማ *čamma*

shoehorn የጫማ፡ማንኪያ *yäčamma mankiya*

shoelace የጫማ ፡ ማሰሪያ *yäčamma masäriya*

shoemaker ጫማ ፡ ሰፊ *čamma säfi*

shoeshine boy ሊስትሮ *listro*

shoot, vt. (fire) ተኮሰ *täkkʷäsä;* (kill) ገደለ *gäddälä;* (~ an arrow) ሰደደ *säddädä;* ወረወረ *wäräwwärä;* (~ pictures) አነሣ *anässa*

shoot (vi.) ተኮሰ *täkkʷäsä*

shoot down ተኩሶ ፡ አወረደ *täkʷso awärrädä*

shoot forth አበበ *abbäbä*

shoot (n.) ቡቃያ *buqayya*

shooting star ተወርዋሪ ፡ ኮከብ *täwärwari kokäb*

shop (v.) ገበየ *gäbäyyä;* ገዛ *gäzza*

shop (n.) ሱቅ *suq*

shopkeeper ባለሱቅ *baläsuq*

shopper ገበያተኛ *gäbäyatäňňa*

shore (n.) ጠረፍ *ṭäräf;* ዳር *dar*

short አጭር *ačč̣ər*
be short አጠረ *aṭṭärä*
be short of አነሰ(ው) *annäsä(w);* አጠረ (ው) *aṭṭärä(w);* ጐደለ(ው) *gʷäddälä(w)*
cut short (shorten) አሳጠረ *asaṭṭärä;* (stop) አቋረጠ *aqqʷarräṭä*
in short ባጭሩ *bačč̣əru*

shortage እጥረት *əṭrät;* ማለቅ *maläq*

short circuit ኮንታክት *kontakt*

shortcoming ጉድለት *gudlät*

short cut አሳባሪ ፡ መንገድ *assabari mängäd;* አቋራጭ *aqqʷaračč̣*
take a short cut አቋረጠ *aqqʷarräṭä*

shorten አሳጠረ *asaṭṭärä*

shorthand አጭር ፡ ጽሕፈት *ačč̣ər ṣəhfät*

shortly በቅርቡ *bäqərbu;* በትንሽ ፡ ጊዜ *bätənnəš gize;* አሁን *ahun*
shortly after (conj.) ወዲያውኑ ፡ እንደ *wädiyawnu əndä* + perfect
shortly afterwards ወዲያው *wädiyaw*

shorts ቁምጣ *qumṭa*

short story አጭር ፡ ታሪክ *ačč̣ər tarik*

short-tempered ግልፍተኛ *gəlləftäňňa*

shot ተኩስ *täkʷs;* (person who shoots) ተኳሽ *täkkʷaš;* (photo) ፎቶግራፍ *fotograf;* (injection) መርፌ *märfe*

shoulder (n.) ትከሻ *təkäšša*

shout (v.) ጮኸ *čohä*

shout (n.) ጩኸት *čuhät*

shove (vt.) ገፋ *gäffa*

shovel (v.) በአካፋ ፡ ዛቀ *bäakafa zaqä;* ቄፍሮ ፡ አወጣ *qʷäffəro awäṭṭa*

shovel (n.) አካፋ *akafa*

shoving ገፊያ *gəffiya*

show (vt.) አሳየ *asayyä;* (reveal) ገለጸ *gälläṣä;* (indicate) አመለከተ *amäläkkätä;* (prove) አሰረዳ *asrädda;* (~ visitors

into the room) አስገባ asgäbba
show (vi.) ታየ tayyä
show (someone) around አስጎበኘ as-gʷäbäňňa
show off ጉራ ፡ ነዛ gurra näzza; ልታይ፡ ልታይ ፡ አለ ləttay ləttay alä
show up (arrive) መጣ mäṭṭa; (appear) ታየ tayyä
show (n.) ትርኢት tər'əyt
for show ለይስሙላ läyəsmulla
shower (n.) ካፊያ kaffiya; (shower bath) የቁም ፡ መታጠቢያ yäqum mättaṭäbiya
take a shower ገላውን ፡ ታጠበ gäla-wən taṭṭäbä
show-off አለሁ ፡ አለሁ ፡ ባይ allähu allähu bay; ጉራኛ gurräňňa
shred ብጫቂ bəččaqi
shrewd ብልጥ bəlṭ; ጮሌ čolle
shriek (v.) ጮኸ čohä
shriek (n.) ድምፅ dəmṣ; ጩኸት čuhät
shrine ቅዱስ ፡ ስፍራ qəddus səfra
shrink (vi.) ተኮማተረ täkʷämattärä; አነሰ annäsä; አጠረ aṭṭärä; ተጨማደደ täčämaddädä
shrink from ሸሸ šäššä; (withdraw) አፈገፈገ afägäffägä
shrivel (vi.) ተኮማተረ täkʷämattärä; ተጨማደደ täčämaddädä
shroud (n.) ከፈን käfän
wrap in a shroud ከፈነ käffänä; ገነዘ gännäzä
shrub ቁጥቋጦ quṭqʷaṭo
shrug ትክሻ ፡ ነቀነቀ täkäšša näqännäqä
shudder (v.) ተንቀጠቀጠ tänqäṭäqqäṭä
shudder (n.) እንቅጥቃጤ ənqəṭṭəqaṭe
shuffle (shift from place to place) እንዲያው ፡ አገላበጠ əndiyaw aggälabbäṭä; (~ cards) በወዘ bäwwäzä
shut ዘጋ zägga; (~ the eyes) ጨፈነ čäffänä
shut off (~ the water) ዘጋ zägga; (~ electricity) ቆረጠ qʷärräṭä; (~ the view) ከለለ källälä
shut up! ዝም ፡ በል zəmm bäl

shutter የሳንቃ ፡ መክፈያ yäsanqa mäk-käläya
shuttle (vt.) አዞዋወረ azzäwawwärä
shuttle (vi.) ተመላለሰ tämälälläsä
shy (adj.) ዓይነፋር aynaffar; አፋር affar
be shy አፈረ affärä
shyness እፍረት əfrät
sick (adj.) በሽተኛ bäššətäňňa; ሕመም ተኛ həmämtäňňa; ሕሙም həmum
be sick ታመመ tammämä
sick leave የሕመም ፡ ፈቃድ yähəmäm fäqad
sickle ማጭድ mačəd
sickly (~ person) በሽተኛ bäššətäňňa
sickness ሕመም həmäm; በሽታ bäššəta
side (v.), ~ with ደገፈ däggäfä
side, n. (of body) ጎን gʷänn; (group, line) ወገን wägän; (aspect) መልክ mälk; (of paper) ገጽ gäṣṣ
side by side ጎን ፡ ለጎን gʷänn lägʷänn
on the side of በ --- በኩል bä --- bäk-kul
the other side ማዶ mado
side (adj.) የጎን yägʷänn
sidewalk የእግር ፡ መንገድ yäəgər mängäd; የእግረኛ ፡ መሄጃ yäəgräňňa mäheǧa
siege, lay ~ to ከበበ käbbäbä
sieve ወንፊት wänfit
sift (separate with a sieve) ነፋ näffa; (sprinkle) ነሰነሰ näsännäsä
sigh (v.) ቁና ፡ ቁና ፡ ተነፈሰ qunna qunna tänäffäsä
sight, v. (see) አየ ayyä; (aim) ዐለመ al-lämä
sight, n. (vision) ዓይን ayn; (spectacle) ትርኢት tər'əyt
catch sight of አየ ayyä
keep out of sight (vi.) ተደበቀ tädäb-bäqä
sightseeing አገር ፡ ማየት agär mayät
sign (v.) ፈረመ färrämä
sign up (enroll) ተመዘገበ tämäzäggäbä

sign (n.) ምልክት mǝläkkǝt; (indicator) መግለጫ mäglǎča; (advertisement) ሰ ሌዳ säleda

signal (v.) አመለከተ amäläkkätä; ምል ክት ፡ አሳየ mǝläkkǝt asayyä

signal (n.) ምልክት mǝläkkǝt; (of traffic) መብራት mäbrat

signature ፊርማ firma

significance ቁም ፡ ነገር qum nägär; ታላ ቅነት tallaqǝnnät

significant (important) ታላቅ tallaq; አስ ፈላጊ asfällagi

signify አመለከተ amäläkkätä

silence (v.) ዝም ፡ አስኘ zǝmm assäňňä; (~ dissent) ደመሰሰ dämässäsä

silence (n.) ዝምታ zǝmmǝta; ጸጥታ šäṭ ṭǝta

silent (~ place) ጭር ፡ ያለ čärr yalä; ጸጥ ፡ ያለ šäṭṭ yalä; (~person)ዝምተኛ zǝm mǝtäňňa; ጸጥተኛ šäṭṭǝtäňňa
be (keep) silent ዝም ፡ አለ zǝmm alä; ጸጥ ፡ አለ šäṭṭ alä

silently ጸጥ ፡ ብሎ šäṭṭ bǝlo

silk ሐር harr

silken (~ robe) ከሐር ፡ የተሠራ käharr yätäsärra; (~ hair) ሐር ፡ የሚመስል harr yämmimäsǝl

silky ሐር ፡ የሚመስል harr yämmimäsǝl

sill ደፍ däf

silly (~ person) ሞኝ moňň; ጅል ǧǝl; (~ behavior) የጅልነት yäǧǝlǝnnät; (~ story) የማይረባ yämmayǝräba

silt ደለል däläl

silver (n.) ብር bǝrr

silver (adj.) የብር yäbǝrr; ከብር ፡ የተሠራ käbǝrr yätäsärra

silversmith አንጥረኛ anṭǝräňňa

silvery ብር ፡ የሚመስል bǝrr yämmimäsǝl

similar መሰል mässäl; መሳይ mäsay; ተመ ሳሳይ tämäsasay
be similar ተመሳሰለ tämäsassälä

similarity መመሳሰል mämmäsasäl; ተመ ሳሳይነት tämäsasayǝnnät

similitude ተመሳሳይነት tämäsasayǝnnät

simmer ተንከተከተ tänkätäkkätä

simple ቀላል qällal; (~clothes) ተራ tä ra; (~ food) መናኛ mänaňňa; (~ de sign) ያልተወሳሰበ yaltäwäsassäbä; (foolish) ቂል qil

simple-minded ሞኝ moňň; ቂል qil

simplicity (naturalness) የዋህነት yäwwa hǝnnät; (of a plan) ቀናነት qännannät

simplify አቃለለ aqqallälä; ቀላል ፡ አደረገ qällal adärrägä

simply (in a clear way) ቀላል ፡ በሆነ ፡ አኳኋን qällal bähona akkʷahʷan; (ab solutely) በፍጹም bäfǝṣṣum; (merely) ብቻ bǝčča

simultaneous, be አንድ ፡ ሆነ and honä

sin (v.) ኃጢአት ፡ ሠራ haṭi'at särra

sin (n.) ኃጢአት haṭi'at

since, conj. (after a time when) ከ kä + perfect + ወዲህ wädih; (because) ስለ sǝlä + verb
since (prep.) ከ - - - ወዲህ kä - - - wä dih; ከ - - - ጀምሮ kä - - - ǧämmǝro
since (adv.) ከዚህ ፡ ወዲህ käzzih wädih
ever since ከዚህ ፡ ወዲያ käzzih wädiya

sincere (~ opinion) ከልብ ፡ የሆነ kälǝbb yähonä; (~ person) ቅን qǝn; ልባ ፡ ቅን lǝbbä qǝn

sincerely ከልብ kälǝbb

sincerity ቅንነት qǝnǝnnät

sinew ጅማት ǧǝmmat

sinful ኃጢአተኛ haṭi'atäňňa

sing ዘፈነ zäffänä; ዘመረ zämmärä; (of birds) ዘመረ zämmärä

singe ለበለበ läbälläbä

singer አዝማሪ azmari; ዛፋኝ zäfaň

single (adj.) አንድ and; (not married) ወንደላጤ wändälaṭṭe
be single (not married) አላገባም ala gäbbam

every single እያንዳንዱ əyyandandu

single-handedly ብቻውን ፡ ሆኖ bäččawən hono

singly (one by one) አንድ ፡ በንድ and band; (alone) ብቻውን bäččawən

singular, n. (in grammar) ነጠላ näṭäla

singular (adj.) እንግዳ ፡ የሆነ əngəda yähonä; ልዩ ፡ የሆነ ləyyu yähonä

sinister ክፉ kəfu; አስጊ asgi

sink (vt.) አስጠመ asäṭṭämä
sink (vi.) ሰመጠ sämmäṭä; ሰጠመ säṭṭämä; (of sun) ጠለቀ ṭälläqä
sink in ጐደጐደ gʷädäggʷädä

sink (n.) እቃ ፡ ማጠቢያ əqa maṭäbiya

sinner ኃጢአ haṭə'; ኃጢአተኛ haṭi'atäñña

sinuous ጠመዝማዛ ṭämäzmazza

sip ማገ magä; ተጐነጨ tägʷänäččä; ፉት፡ አለ futt alä

sir ጌታዬ getaye; ጌቶች getočč

siren የአደጋ ፡ ፉጨት yadäga fuçät

sister እኅት əhət; እት ət

sister-in-law ምራት mərat; ዋርሳ warsa

sistrum ጸናጽል ṣänaṣəl

sit (vi.) ተቀመጠ täqämmäṭä; ቁጭ ፡ አለ quččä alä
sit down ተቀመጠ täqämmäṭä; ቁጭ ፡ አለ quččä alä
sit up (straight) ቀና ፡ ብሎ ፡ ተቀመጠ qäna bəlo täqämmäṭä

site ስፍራ səfra; ቦታ bota

sitting room እንግዳ ፡ ቤት əngəda bet

situate አቋቋመ aqqʷaqqʷamä

situation (location) አቀማመጥ aqqämamäṭ; (circumstances) ሁኔታ huneta; (job) ሥራ səra

six ስድስት səddəst
six o'clock ዐሥራ ፡ ሁለት ፡ ሰዓት asra hulätt sä'at

sixth ስድስተኛ səddəstäñña; (~ order of the Amharic alphabet) ሳድስ sadəs

sixteen ዐሥራ ፡ ስድስት asra səddəst

sixty ስልሳ səlsa

size (v.), ~ up ገመተ gämmätä

size (n.) ልክ ləkk; (of shoe) ቁጥር quṭər; (height) ቁመት qumät; (of room) ስፋት səfat; (of city) ትልቅነት təlləqənnät

sizzle ችስ ፡ አለ čəss alä

skeleton አስከሬን askären; ዐፅም aṣäm

sketch (v.) በንድፍ ፡ አነሣ bänədf anässa

sketch, n. (drawing) ንድፍ nədf

skid ተንሸራተተ tänšärattätä

skill ችሎታ čəlota; ጥበብ ṭäbäb; (profession) ሙያ muya; የጅ ፡ ሥራ yäǧǧ səra

skilled, see 'skillful'

skillful (worker) ባለ ፡ ሙያ balä muya; ቀልጣፋ qälṭaffa; በጅ ፡ ሥራ ፡ የሰለጠነ bäǧǧ səra yäsäläṭṭänä; (work) ልዩ ፡ ሙያ ፡ የሚጠይቅ ləyyu muya yämmiṭäyyəq

skillfully በቅልጥፍና bäqəlṭəfənna

skim (~ the cream) ገፈፈ gäffäfä
skim through (~ a book) ተመለካከተ tämäläkakkätä; ገፈፍ ፡ ገፈፍ ፡ አደረገ gäfäff gäfäff adärrägä

skimp (vt.) አሳነሰ asannäsä

skimpy (~ meal) ለስሙ ፡ ያህል läsəmu yahəl

skin, v. (remove the skin) ቆዳውን ፡ ገፈፈ qodawən gäffäfä
skin off ላጠ laṭä

skin (n.) ቆዳ qoda; (of fruit) ቅርፊት qərfit
sheep skin አጐዛ agʷäza

skinny ከሲታ kässitta; ኮሳሳ kosasa
be skinny ከሳ kässa

skip (vi.) ዘለለ zällälä; (of lambs) ቦረቀ borräqä

skirmish ቀላል ፡ ግጭት qällal gəččät

skirt (n.) ጉርድ ፡ ቀሚስ gurd qämis

skull የራስ ፡ ቅል yäras qäl; ጭንቅላት čənqällat

skull cap ቆብ *qob*

skunk ምጥማጥ *mǝṭmaṭ*

sky ሰማይ *sämay*

skyscraper ሰማይ ፡ ጠቀስ ፡ ሕንጻ *sämay ṭäqqäs hǝnṣa*

slab ቁራጭ *qurrač*

slack, adj. (person) ቻልተኛ *čällǝtäñña;* (~ rope) ልል *lǝl* be slack (of rope) ላላ *lalla;* (of business) ቀዝቀዝ ፡ አለ *qäzqäzz alä;* (of work) ተጐተተ *tägʷättätä*

slacken (vi.) see 'slack, be slack'

slacks ሱሪ *surri*

slam, v. (~ the fist) ደበደበ *däbäddäbä;* (~the door) ዳረገመ *däräggämä;* በኀይል ፡ ዘጋ *bähayl zägga*

slander, v. (backbite) አማ *amma;* (harm the reputation) ስሙን ፡ አጠፋ *sǝmun aṭäffa*

slander (n.) ሐሜት *hamet;* አሜት *amet*

slanderous ስም ፡ የሚያጠፋ *säm yämmiyaṭäfa*

slant (vt.) አዛባ *azzabba;* አደላ *adälla* slant, vi. (tilt) አዘነበለ *azänäbbälä*

slap (v.) በጥፊ ፡ መታ *bäṭǝffi mätta*

slap (n.) ጥፊ *ṭǝffi*

slash በጣ *bäṭṭa;* ቦደሰ *boddäsä*

slate (n.) ጥቁር ፡ ድንጋይ *ṭǝqur dǝngay*

slaughter (v.) አረደ *arrädä*

slaughter (n.) እልቂት *ǝlqit*

slaughterhouse ቄራ *qera*

slave ባሪያ *bariya*

slavery ባርነት *barǝnnät* deliver from slavery አርነት ፡ አወጣ *arǝnnät awäṭṭa*

slave trade የባሪያ ፡ ንግድ *yäbariya nägd*

slave trader ባሪያ ፡ ፈንጋይ *bariya fängay*

slay ገደለ *gäddälä*

sleek ለስላሳ *läslassa*

sleep (vi.) ተኛ *täñña*

sleep (n.) እንቅልፍ *ǝnqǝlf*

sleepy እንቅልፋም *ǝnqǝlfam;* (~ town) ጭር ፡ ያለ *čärr yalä* be sleepy አንቀላፋ *anqälaffa;* እንቅልፍ ፡ እንቅልፍ ፡ አለ(ው) *ǝnqǝlf ǝnqǝlf alä(w)*

sleeve እጅጌ *ǝǧǧǝge*

slender (thin) ቀጭን *qäččǝn;* (scanty) አናስተኛ *anästäñña*

slice (v.) መተረ *mättärä;* ቆረጠ *qʷärräṭä*

slice (n.) ቁራጭ *qurrač*

slide (vi.) ተንሸራተተ *tänšärattätä* slide down ተንሸራ ፡ ቁልቁል ፡ ወረደ *tänšäratto qulqul wärrädä* slide into ሹልክ ፡ ብሎ ፡ ገባ *šullǝkk bǝlo gäbba* slide through (vt.) አሾለከ *ašolläkä*

slide, n. (avalanche) ናዳ *nada;* (of photos) የማይንቀሳቀስ ፡ ፊልም *yämmayǝnqäsaqqäs film*

slight, v. (insult) ቅር ፡ አሰኘ *qǝrr assäññä;* (treat as of little value) ቀም ፡ ነገር ፡ አላለወም *qum nägär alaläwäm*

slight, adj. (small) ትንሽ *tǝnnǝš;* (~ girl) ቀጭን *qäččǝn;* (~ headache) ቀላል *qällal;* (~ lunch) አናስተኛ *anästäñña*

slightly ትንሽ *tǝnnǝš*

slim (adj.) ትንሽ *tǝnnǝš;* ጥቂት *ṭǝqit;* (~ figure) ቀጠን ፡ ያለ *qäṭänn yalä*

slimy ዝለግለግ *zǝlǝglǝg;* ምዝልግልግ *mǝzlǝglǝg*

sling (n.) ወንጭፍ *wänčäf*

slip (vi.) ዳለጠ *dalläṭä;* ተንሸራተተ *tänšärattätä;* አዳጠ(ው) *adaṭä(w);* (enter slyly) ሹልክ ፡ ብሎ ፡ ገባ *šullǝkk bǝlo gäbba* slip away ሹልክ ፡ ብሎ ፡ ወጣ *šullǝkk bǝlo wäṭṭa* slip down ተንሻተተ *tänšattätä;* ተንሻ ፡ ቶ ፡ ወረደ *tänšäratto wärrädä* slip off (vt.) አወለቀ *awälläqä* slip on (~ a coat) ጠለቅ ፡ አደረገ *ṭäläqq adärrägä*

slip one's mind ተረሳ(ው) tärässa(w)
slip out ሹልክ ፡ ብሎ ፡ ወጣ šulləkk
bəlo wätta

slip, n. (of paper) ቁራጭ qurraç; (woman's undergarment) የውስጥ ፡ ልብስ
yäwəsṭ ləbs; (error) ስሕተት səhtät

slipcover ልብስ ləbs

slipper የቤት ፡ ጫማ yäbet čamma

slippery (~ fish) ሙላጭ mulləč; (~
road) የሚያዳልጥ yämmiyadalləṭ
be slippery አዳለጠ adalläṭä; አማለጠ
amʷalläṭä; ሙልጭልጭ ፡ አለ muləč-
ləčč alä

slit (v.), ~ open ቀደደ qäddädä; በጣ
bätta

slit (n.) ቀዳዳ qädada

slogan አርማ arma

slope, v. (of hill) አቀለቀለ aqʷäläqqʷälä

slope, n. (downwards) ቁልቁለት qulqulät; (upwards) ዳገት dagät

sloppy (~ person) ዝርክርክ zərəkrək;
(~ work) የተጨማለቀ yätäčämalläqä

slot ቀዳዳ qädada

slouch ተዝለፍለፍ ፡ ተቀመጠ täzläfləfo
täqämmäṭä

slow (v.), ~ down (vt.) ጐተተ gʷättätä
slow down (vi.) ቀስ ፡ አለ qäss alä;
ዝግ ፡ አለ zəgg alä
slow up ቀስ ፡ አለ qäss alä

slow, adj. (~ worker) ጐታታ gʷätata;
(~ motion) ዝግ ፡ ያለ zəgg yalä
slow (adv.) በዝግታ bäzəggəta
be slow ቀስ ፡ አለ qäss alä; ዝግ ፡ አለ
zəgg alä; (of watch) ወደ ፡ ኋላ ፡ ቀረ
wädä hʷala qärrä; (of market) ቀዘቀዘ
qäzäqqäzä

slowly ቀስ ፡ ብሎ qäss bəlo; ቀስ ፡ በቀስ
qäss bäqäss; በቀስታ bäqässəta; በዝ
ግታ bäzəggəta

sluggish ሰነፍ sänäf

slum ደሳሳ ፡ መኖሪያ däsasa mänoriya;
ቆሻሻ ፡ ሰፈር qošaša säfär

slumber (v.) ተኛ tänña; አንቀላፋ anqälaffa

slumber (n.) እንቅልፍ ənqəlf

slump, see 'slouch'

slur, v. (pronounce indistinctly) ተንተባ
ተበ täntäbattäbä; (harm the reputation of) አዋረደ awwarrädä

slush ማጥ maṭ

sly (~ person) ብልጥ bəlṭ; ተንኮለኛ tän-
kʷälänña; (~ question) ዞር ፡ ያለ zorr
yalä

smack (v.) በጥፊ ፡ መታ bäṭəffi mätta

small ትንሽ tənnəš; ታናሽ tannaš; አነስ
ተኛ anästänña; (~ print) ረቂቅ räqiq
be small አነሰ annäsä

small change ዝርዝር zərzər

smallpox ፈንጣጣ fänṭaṭa

smart (v.) አቃጠለ aqqaṭṭälä

smart (adj.) ጐበዝ gʷäbäz; ብልጥ bəlṭ;
(~ dress) ጥሩ ṭäru

smash (vt.) ሰባበረ säbabbärä
smash (vi.) ተሰባበረ täsäbabbärä; ነካ
ካት näkʷakkʷätä
smash into ከ - - - ጋር ፡ ተጋጨ kä - -
gar tägaččä

smash (n.) ግጭት gəččət

smear (with fat, mud) ቀባ qäbba; (injure the reputation) አጐደፈ agʷäddäfä; አጠፋ aṭäffa

smell (vt.) አሸተተ ašättätä; ሸተተ(ው)
šättätä(w)
smell, vi. (detect by inhaling) አሸተተ
ašättätä; (give off an unpleasant
odor) ሸተተ šättätä; ጋማ gämma
smell good መዓዛ ፡ አለው mä'aza alläw

smell (n.) ሽታ šätta; ክርፋት kərfat;
ጋማት gəmat; (sense of smelling) የማ
ሽተት ፡ ኃይል yämaštät hayl

smelly የሚከረፋ yämmikäräffa

smelt (~ ore) አቀለጠ aqällätä

smile (v.) ሣቅ ፡ አለ saqq alä; ፈገግ fäggägä

smile (n.) ፈገግታ *fägägta*

smith ብረት ፤ ሠራ *brät säri;* ቀጥቃጭ *qäṭqač*

smoke, vt. (~ cigarette) አጤስ *aṭesä;* አጬስ *ačäsä;* ጠጣ *ṭäṭṭa;* (~ fish) በጢ ስ ፤ ዐጠነ *bäṭis aṭṭänä*
smoke (vi.) ጤስ *ṭesä;* ጬስ *čäsä*

smoke (n.) ጢስ *ṭis;* ጭስ *čəs*

smoker ሲጃራ ፤ አጫሽ *siǧara ačaš*

smoking (n.) ማጬስ *mačäs;* ትምባሆ ፤ መጠጣት *təmbaho mäṭäṭṭat*

smoky ጢሳም *ṭisam;* ጢስ ፤ የበዛበት *ṭis yäbäzzabbät*

smooth (v.), ~ out አስተካከለ *astäkakkälä*

smooth (adj.) ለስላሳ *läslassa;* ልስልስ *lasləs;* (~ hair) ሉጫ *lučča;* (~ surface of water) የረጋ *yärägga*
be smooth ለሰለሰ *läsälläsä;* ለዘበ *läzzäbä*

smoothly ዝግ ፤ ብሎ *zəgg bəlo;* ቀስ ፤ ብሎ *qäss bəlo*

smother (vt.) አፍኖ ፤ ገደለ *affəno gäddälä*
smother (vi.) ታፈነ *taffänä*

smuggle በድብቅ ፤ አስገባ *bädəbbəq asgäbba*

smuggler የኮንትሮባንድ ፤ ነጋዴ *yäkontroband näggade*

snack መቆያ *mäqoyya;* መክሰስ *mäksəs*

snag ዕንቅፋት *ənqəfat*

snail ቀንድ ፤ አውጣ *qänd awṭa*

snake እባብ *əbab*

snare (n.) ወጥመድ *wäṭmäd*

snatch መነተፈ *mänättäfä;* መነጨቀ *mänäččäqä;* ነጠቀ *näṭṭäqä*

sneak አደባ *adäbba*
sneak in ሹልክ ፤ ብሎ ፤ ገባ *šulləkk bəlo gäbba*
sneak out ሾለከ *šolläkä;* ሹልክ ፤ ብሎ ፤ ወጣ *šulləkk bəlo wäṭṭa*

sneer, ~ at (look with contempt) በን ቀት ፤ ተመለከተ *bänəqät tämäläkkätä*

sneeze አነጠሰ *anäṭṭäsä*

sniff አነፈነፈ *anäfännäfä*

sniffle ንፍጡን ፤ ማገ *nəfṭun magä*

snipe አድፍጦ ፤ ተኩሶ *adfəṭo täkkwäsä*

sniper የዳፈጣ ፤ አደጋ ፤ ጣይ *yädäfäṭa adäga ṭay*

snore (v.) አኮረፈ *akwärräfä*

snore (n.) ኩርፊያ *kurfiya*

snout አፍንጫ *afənča*

snow (v.) በረዶ ፤ ጣለ *bärädo ṭalä*

snow (n.) በረዶ *bärädo*

snuff (n.) ሱረት *surrät*

so እንዲህ *əndih*
so far (in space) እስከዚህ *əskäzzih;* (in time) እስካሁን *əskahun*
so long! ደኅና ፤ ሁን *dähna hun*
so much ይህን ፤ ያህል *yəhən yahəl*
so that ለ *lə* + imperfect; እንደ *əndə* + imperfect
so then! ታዲያ *tadiya;* እስቲ *əsti;* እን ግዲያስ *əngədiyass*

soak, vt. (in a liquid) ዘፈዘፈ *zäfäzzäfä;* (wet through and through) አራሰ *arasä;* አበሰበሰ *abäsäbbäsä*
soak (vi.) ተዘፈዘፈ *täzäfäzzäfä*
soak up መጠጠ *mäṭṭäṭä*
soaked, get ~ ራሰ *rasä*

so-and-so እከሌ *əkäle;* እገሌ *əgäle*

soap ሳሙና *samuna*

soar (of hawk) አንጋበበ *anžabbäbä;* (of prices) ሰማይ ፤ ወጣ *sämay wäṭṭa*

sob (v.) ተንሰቀሰቀ *tänsäqässäqä;* ተነፈረቀ *tänäfarräqä*

sob (n.) ሲቅ *siq*

sober, adj. (not inebriated) ያልሰከረ *yalsäkkärä*

soccer የእግር ፤ ኳስ ፤ ጨዋታ *yäəgər kwas čäwata*

sociable ተጫዋች *täčawač*

social ማኅበራዊ *mahbärawi;* የኅብረ(ተ) ፤ ሰብ *yähəbrä(tä) säb*

socialism ሶሺያሊዝም *sošiyalizm*

social security የጡረታ ፡ አበል *yäṭuräta abäl*

social studies ኅብረ ፡ ትምህርት *həbrä təmhərt*

social welfare የሕዝብ ፡ በጎ ፡ አድራጎት *yähəzb bäggo adragot*

society (association) ማኅበር *mahbär;* (the people of a particular time and place) ኅብረ(ተ) ፡ ሰብ *həbrä(tä) säb*

sociology ሶሲዮሎጂ *sosiyoloği*

sock የእግር ፡ ሹራብ *yäəgər šurrab*

socket, (electric~) መስኪያ *mäsäkkiya*

sofa ሶፋ *sofa*

soft (~ ground) ልል *ləl;* (~ cushion) ለስላሳ *läslassa;* (~ hide) ልፍ *ləf;* (~ voice) ለስለስ ፡ ያለ *läsläss yalä;* (~ breeze) ቀዝቀዝ ፡ ያለ *qäzqäzz yalä;* (~ light) ደብዛዛ *däbzazza*
have a soft heart ርኅሩኅ ፡ ሆነ *rəhruh honä*

soften አለሰለሰ *aläsälläsä;* (~ hide) አለፋ *aläffa;* (~ a punishment) አላላ *alalla;* (~ the light) ቀነሰ *qännäsä*

soft-hearted ርኅሩኅ *rəhruh*

softly ቀስ ፡ ብሎ *qäss bəlo;* በቀስታ *bäqässəta*

soggy, be ~ (ground) ጨቀየ *čäqäyyä;* (clothes) ራሰ *rasä*

soil, v. (make dirty) አቆሸሸ *aqʷäššäšä*

soil (n.) መሬት *märet;* አፈር *afär;* (country) አገር *agär*

sojourn (v.) ተቀመጠ *täqämmäṭä*

solace, find ~ ተጽናና *täṣnanna*
give solace አጽናና *aṣnanna*

solar የፀሐይ *yäṣähay*

soldier ወታደር *wättaddär*

sole, n. (underside of foot) ውስጥ ፡ እግር *wəsṭ əgər;* (bottom of a shoe) ሶል *sol*

solely ብቻ *bəčča*

solemn (~ voice) ከበድ ፡ ያለ *käbädd*

yalä; (~ festival) ሞገስ ፡ ያለው *mogäs yalläw;* (~ aspect) ረጋ ፡ ያለ *räga yalä*
have a solemn face (of mourners) ፊቱ፡ ጠቆረ *fitu ṭäqqʷärä;* (of a judge) ፊቱ፡ ኮስተር ፡ አለ *fitu kostärr alä*

solemnity (ceremonies) ታላቅ ፡ ሥነ ፡ ሥርዓት *tallaq sənä sər'at*

solicit ጠየቀ *ṭäyyäqä*

solid, adj. (not liquid) ጥጥር *ṭəṭṭər;* (~ chair, ground) ጠንካራ *ṭänkarra;* (~ gold) ድፍን *dəfən;* (~hour) ሙሉ *mulu;* (~ citizen) የሚታመንበት *yämmittammänəbbät*

solidarity መተባበር *mättäbabär;* ኅብረት *həbrät;* አንድነት *andənnät*

solidify (vt.) አጠነከረ *aṭänäkkärä* solidify, vi. (of butter) ረጋ *rägga*

solitary (~ life) የብቸኝነት *yäbəččäňňənnät;* (~ village) ገለልተኛ *gälältäňňa;* (~ person) ብቸኛ *bəččäňňa*

solitude (seclusion) ብቸኛ ፡ መሆን *bəččäňňa mähon;* (of a place) ጭር፡ ማለት *čərr malät*

soluble, be ~ (of sugar) ሟሟ *mʷammʷa*

solution (solving) መፍትሔ *mäftəhe;* ፍች *fəčč;* (dissolving) መሟሟት *mämʷamʷat*

solve (~ a riddle) ፈታ *fätta;* (~ a mathematical problem) ሠራ *särra;* (~ a problem) መፍትሔ ፡ አገኘ *mäftəhe agäňňä*

solvent, be ዕዳውን ፡ ሊከፍል ፡ ቻለ *əda- wən likäfəl čalä*

somber (~ color) ደብዘዝ ፡ ያለ *däbzäzz yalä;* (~day) ጭልምልም፡ ያለ *čələm- ləmm yalä*

some (adj.) አንዳንድ *andand;* አንዳንዶች *andandoč̣č̣;* (~ money) ትንሽ *tənnəš* some of ትንሽ *tənnəš;* ግማሾች *gəm- mašočč* + suffix pronouns

somebody አንድ ፡ ሰው *and säw*

somehow እንደምንም *əndämənəm*
 somehow or other ያም ፡ ሆነ ፡ ይህ
 yam honä yəh; እንደምንም ፡ ብሎ *ən-dämənəm bəlo*

someone ሰው *säw;* አንድ ፡ ሰው· *and säw*
 someone else ሌላ ፡ ሰው· *lela säw*

something አንድ ፡ ነገር *and nägär*
 something or other ምናምን *mənaman*

sometime አንድ ፡ ጊዜ *and gize*

sometimes አንዳንድ ፡ ጊዜ *andand gize;*
 አንዳንዴ *andande*

somewhat ትንሽ *tənnəš*

somewhere አንድ ፡ ቦታ *and bota;* አንዱ ፡
 ጋ *andu ga*
 somewhere about ገደማ *gädäma*
 somewhere else ሌላጋ *lelaga*

son ወንድ ፡ ልጅ *wänd ləǧ*

song (of church) ዜማ *zema;* (secular ∼)
 ዘፈን *zäfän*

son-in-law አማች *amač*

sonorous (∼ voice) ወፈር ፡ ያለ *wäfärr yalä;* (∼ bell) የሚጮኽ *yämmiçoh*

soon በቅርቡ *bäqərbu;* በቅርብ ፡ ጊዜ *bä-qərb gize;* ቶሎ *tolo*
 soon after ወዲያውኑ *wädiyawnu*
 how soon? ምን ፡ ያህል ፡ ጊዜ *mən ya-həl gize*

sooner ቀደም ፡ ብሎ *qädämm bəlo*
 sooner or later ግራም ፡ ነፈሰ ፡ ቀኝ *gəram näffäsä qäňň;* አሁንም ፡ ሆነ ፡
 ሌላ ፡ ጊዜ *ahunəm honä lela gize;* ውሎ ፡
 አድሮ *wəlo adro*

soot (of ceiling) ጥቅርሻ *təqərša;* (of pots)
 ጥላሸት *təlašät;* ጥላት *təlat*

soothe (∼ itching) አስታገሠ *astaggäsä;*
 (∼ a frightened child) አረጋጋ *arrä-gagga*

sorcerer አስማተኛ *asmatäňňa;* ጠንቋይ
 ţänqʷay

sorcery አስማት *asmat*

sordid (squalid) ደሳሳ *däsasa;* (mean and
 base) አስነዋሪ *asnäwwari;* ወራዳ *wär-radda*

sore (n.) ቁስል *qusl*
 have a sore ቁሰለ *qʷässälä*

sore, adj. (∼ part of body) የቁሰለ *yä-qʷässälä;* (∼wound) የበሰበሰ *yäbäsäb-bäsä*
 be sore አመመ *ammämä;* (be offend-ed) ቅር ፡ አለ(ው) *qərr alä(w)*
 get sore ግልፍ ፡ አለ *gəlləff alä*

sorghum ማሽላ *mašəlla;* ዘንጋዳ *zängada*

sorrow (n.) ሐዘን *hazän*

sorrowful (∼ occasion) አሳዛኝ *asazzaň;*
 (∼ person) ያዘነ *yazzänä*
 be sorrowful አዘነ *azzänä*

sorry! ይቅርታ *yəqərta*
 be sorry አዘነ *azzänä*

sort (v.) ለያየ *läyayyä;* ከፈለ *käffälä*

sort (n.) ዓይነት *aynät*
 sort of መሳይ *mäsay;* ቢጤ *biţe*

so-so ምንም ፡ አይል *mənəm ayəl*

soul ነፍስ *näfs*
 not a soul አንድም ፡ ሰው *andəm säw;*
 ማንም *mannəm*

sound, vt. (∼ the trumpet) ነፋ *näffa;*
 (∼public opinion) ገመገመ *gämäggä-mä;* (measure the depth) ጥልቀት ፡ ለካ
 ţəlqät läkka
 sound, vi. (of trumpet) ተነፋ *tänäffa;*
 (seem) መሰለ *mässälä*

sound (n.) ቃል *qal;* ድምፅ *dəmş;* (mean-ing, implication) ሐሳብ *hassab;* (ele-ments composing speech) ህፅ *hohe*

sound, adj. (∼ advice) ጥልቅ *ţəlq;* (∼ mind) ጤፉ *ţäru;* ጤነኛ *ţenäňňa;* (∼ foundation) ጠንካራ *ţänkarra;* (∼ sleep) ድብን ፡ ያለ *dəbbənn yalä;* (∼ argument) በውነት ፡ ላይ ፡ የተመ ሠረተ *bäwnät lay yätämäsärrätä*

soundless, be ድምፅ ፡ የለውም *dəmş yäl-läwəm*

soundly (thoroughly) ሙልጭ ፡ አድርጎ
 mulləčč adrəgo; (wisely) አስቦ *assəbo*

soup ሾርባ *šorba*

sour (adj.) ኮምጣጣ *komṭaṭṭa;* (~ wine) ጕምዛዛ *gʷämzazza*
be sour ኮመጠጠ *kʷämäṭṭäṭä;* (wine) ጕመዘዘ *gʷämäzzäzä*
turn sour (of milk) ኮመጠጠ *kʷämäṭṭäṭä;* (of friendship) ሻከረ *šakkärä*
source ምንጭ *mənč;* (origin) መነሻ *männäšo*
south ደቡብ *däbub*
southern ደቡባዊ *däbubawi*
South Pole ደቡባዊ ፡ ዋልታ *däbubawi walta*
souvenir ማስታወሻ *mastawäša;* መታሰ ቢያ *mättasäbiya*
sovereign (n.) ንጉሥ *nəgus;* አጼ *aṣe*
sovereign (adj.) ራሱን ፡ በራሱ ፡ የሚያስ ተዳድር *rasun bärasu yämmiyastädaddər*
sovereignty (supreme power) ዋና ፡ ሥል ጣን *wanna səlṭan;* (independent political power) ነጻነት *näṣannät*
sow (v.) ዘራ *zärra*
space (n.) ቦታ *bota;* (blank between words) ባዶ ፡ ቦታ *bado bota*
spacious ሰፊ *säffi*
spade (n.) አካፋ *akafa*
Spain እስፓኛ *əspaña*
span (n.) ስንዝር *sənzər;* (period of time) መጠን *mäṭän*
measure by spans ሰነዘረ *sänäzzärä*
spank (v.) መታ *mätta*
spare, v. (show mercy) ምሕረት ፡ አደረገ *məhrät adärrägä;* አተረፈ *atärräfä;* (relieve from something) ከ - - - አዳነ *kä - - - adanä;* (economize) ቆጠበ *qʷäṭṭäbä*
be spared (saved) ተረፈ *tärräfä;* ዳነ *danä*
spare, adj. (scanty) አነስተኛ *anästäñña;* (~ time) ትርፍ *tərf;* (~ tire) ተጠባ ባቂ *täṭäbabaqi*
spare parts መለዋወጫ ፡ እቃ *mäläwawäča əqa*

sparingly በቁጠባ *bäquṭṭäba*
spark (vi.) ብልጭ ፡ ብልጭ ፡ አለ *bälləčč bälləčč alä*
spark (n.) ፍንጣሪ *fənəṭṭari*
make sparks ብልጭ ፡ ብልጭ ፡ አለ *bälləčč bälləčč alä*
sparkle (of water) አንጸባረ ቀ *anṣäbarräqä;* (of eyes) ተብለጨለጨ *täbläčällä čä;* (of fire) ብልጭ ፡ ብልጭ ፡ አለ *bälləčč bälləčč alä;* (with decorations) አሸበረቀ *ašäbärräqä*
spark plug ካንደላ *kandella*
spatial የጠፈር *yäṭäfär*
spatter ረጨ *räččä*
spatula መስቀሰቂያ *mäsäqsäqiya*
speak ነገረ *näggärä;* ተናገረ *tänaggärä*
speak to ተናገረ *tänaggärä*
speaker ተናጋሪ *tänagari*
spear ጦር *ṭor*
special ለዩ *ləyyu;* የተለየ *yätäläyyä*
special delivery ለዩ ፡ መልእክት *ləyyu mäl'əkt*
specialist ለዩ ፡ ባዋቂ *ləyyu awaqi*
specialize, ~ in ለዩ ፡ ችሎታው ፡ ነው *ləyyu čəlotaw näw;* ለዩ ፡ ትምህርቱ ፡ ነው *ləyyu təmhərtu näw*
specially በተለይ *bätäläyy*
species ዓይነት *aynät;* ዘር *zär*
specific (~ purpose) የተወሰነ *yätäwäs sänä;* (~ orders) ለዩ *ləyyu*
specify ወሰነ *wässänä;* ለይቶ ፡ አመለከተ *läyyəto amäläkkätä*
specimen ላሙና *lamuna;* ናሙና *namuna*
speck ጠብታ *ṭäbbəta*
speckle ጠቃጠቆ *ṭäqaṭäqo*
spectacle ትርእይት *tər'əyt;* (impressive sight) ግርማ *gərma*
spectacles መነጽር *mänäṣṣər;* መነጥር *mänäṭṭər*
spectator ተመልካች *tämälkač*

speculate አስቀድሞ ፡ ገመተ asqäddəmo gämmätä; አሰበ assäbä

speech (public talk) ንግግር nəgəggər; (language) ቋንቋ qʷanqʷa; (way of speaking) አነጋገር annägagär

speed (vt.) አፋጠነ affaṭṭänä
speed (vi.) በፍጥነት ፡ ተጓዘ bäfəṭnät tägʷazä
speed up (vt.) አጣደፈ aṭṭaddäfä; አፋ ጠነ affaṭṭänä

speed (n.) ፍጥነት fəṭnät

speed limit የተወሰነ ፡ ፍጥነት yätäwäs- sänä fəṭnät

speedy ፈጣን fäṭṭan

spell (v.) ጻፈ ṣafä; ፊደል ፡ ዘርዝሮ ፡ ተና ገረ fidäl zärzəro tänaggärä

spell, n. (charm) መተት mätät; አስማት asmat
cast a spell በመተት ፡ አሰረ bämätät assärä; በአስማት ፡ ተበተበ bä'asmat täbättäbä
for a short spell ላጭር ፡ ጊዜ ፡ ብቻ laččər gize bəčča

spelling የቃላት ፡ አጻጻፍ yäqalat aṣṣaṣaf
spelling errors የቀለማት ፡ ስሕተት yä- qälämat səhtät

spend (~ money) አወጣ awäṭṭa; (~ time) ፈጀ fäǧǧä; አሳለፈ asalläfä
spend the day ዋለ walä
spend the evening አመሸ amäššä
spend the morning አረፈደ aräffädä
spend the night አደረ addärä
spend some time ሰነበተ sänäbbätä

spendthrift ገንዘብ ፡ አባካኝ gänzäb aba- kaň

sphere ክብ ፡ አካል kəbb akal; (extent of activity) ሙያ muya

spherical እንክብል ənkəbəll; ክብ kəbb; ድቡልቡል dəbulbul

spice (v.) ቅመም ፡ ጨመረ qəmäm čäm- märä

spice (n.) ቅመም qəmäm

spicy ቅመም ፡ የበዛበት qəmäm yäbäzzab- bät

spider ሸረሪት šärärit

spiderweb የሸረሪት ፡ ድር yäšärärit dər

spill (vt.) አፈሰሰ afässäsä; ደፋ däffa
spill over ፈሰሰ fässäsä
be spilled ፈሰሰ fässäsä

spin (~ cotton) ፈተለ fättälä

spinal column አከርካሪ akärkari

spindle እንዝርት ənzərt

spine (of body) አከርካሪ akärkari; (thorn) እሾህ əšoh; ሾህ šoh; ሾክ šok

spinster ያላገባች ፡ ሴት yalagäbbačč set

spiral ጥምዝምዝ ፡ መሠመር ṭəməzməz mäsmär

spirit መንፈስ mänfäs; ዛር zar; ጂን ǧin; (liveliness) ትጋት təgat
be in good spirits ደስ ፡ አለ(ው) däss alä(w)

spiritual መንፈሳዊ mänfäsawi

spit (v.) ተፋ täffa; ትፍ ፡ አለ təff alä; እትፍ ፡ አለ əttəff alä
spit up አስመለሰ asmälläsä

spite (v.) አናደደ annaddädä

spite (n.) ክፋት kəfat; እልህ əlləh
in spite of ብ ba + imperfect + ም-m; እንኳ ənkʷa + imperfect + ም-m

spiteful እልኸኛ əlləhäňňa

spittle ምራቅ məraq; ላሃጭ lähaǧ; እክታ əkkəta

splash (vt.) ውኃ ፡ ረጨ wəha räččä
splash (vi.) ተረጨ täräččä

spleen ጣፊያ ṭafiya

splendid ግሩም gərum; የደመቀ yädäm- mäqä

splendor ውበት wəbät

splinter (n.) ስንጥር sənṭər; ስንጣቂ sənäṭ- ṭaqi

split, vt. (~ wood) ሰነጠቀ sänäṭṭäqä; ፈለጠ fälläṭä; (~ a country) ከፈለ käffälä; (~ profits) ተካፈለ täkaffälä
split up ለያ läyya

split (n.) ስንጥቅ *sənṭəq*; ንቅ *nəq*; (division) መከፋፈል *mäkkäfafäl*

splitting (∼headache) የሚፈልጥ *yämmifälṭ*

splurge አፈሰሰ *afässäsä*

spoil (vt.) አበላሸ *abbälaššä*; (pamper) አሞላቀቀ *ammolaqqäqä*
spoil (vi.) ተበላሸ *täbälaššä*; (of fruit) በሰበሰ *bäsäbbäsä*

spoiled, adj. (∼ child) ሞልቃቃ *molqaqqa*

spokesman ቃል ፡ አቀባይ *qal aqäbbay*

sponge (n.) ሰፍነግ *säfnäg*

sponsor (n.) ደጋፊ *däggafi*

spontaneous በፈቃደኝነት ፡ የተደረገ *bäfäqadäññənnät yätädärrägä*

spool (object on which thread is wound) ድውር *dəwər*; በከራ *bäkära*

spoon ማንካ *manka*; ማንኪያ *mankiya*

spoor ፋና *fana*

sporadic አልፎ ፡ አልፎ ፡ የሚሆን *alfo alfo yämmihon*

sport ስፖርት *sport*; እስፖርት *əsport*

sportsman ስፖርተኛ *sportäňňa*

spot, v. (make spots on) አንጠባጠበ *anṭäbaṭṭäbä*; (∼ the reputation) አበላሸ *abbälaššä*

spot, n. (speckle) ጠቃጠቆ *ṭäqaṭäqo*; ጠብታ *ṭäbbəta*; (mark) ምልክት *mələkkət*; (place) ቦታ *bota*; ስፍራ *səfra*; (blemish) እንከን *ənkän*
in spots አልፎ ፡ አልፎ *alfo alfo*
on the spot (at once) ወዲያውኑ *wädiyawnu*; (at the place mentioned) እዚ ያው *əzziyaw*

spotless ንጹሕ *nəṣuh*

spotlight ባውዛ *bawza*

spotted (∼ animal) ቡራቡሬ *burraburre*; ዝንጉርጉር *zəngurgur*

spouse ሚስት *mist*; ምሽት *məšt*; ባለቤት *baläbet*

spout, n. (of coffee pot) ጡት *ṭut*; (of roof) አሻንዳ *ašända*

sprain ወለም ፡ አለ(ው) *wälämm alä(w)*

sprawl ተዘረጋ *täzärägga*

spray (∼ the garden) ውኃ ፡ አጠጣ *wəha aṭäṭṭa*; ረጨ *räččä*; አርካፈከፈ *arkäfäkkäfa*; አረባረበ *aräbärräbä*

spread, vt. (∼ wings) ዘረጋ *zärägga*; (∼ butter) ቀባ *qäbba*; (∼ a rug) አነጠፈ *anäṭṭäfä*; (∼ disease) አጋባ *aggabba*; (∼ a rumor) ነዛ *näzza*; አዛመተ *azzammätä*; (∼ a new method) አሰራጨ *assäraččä*
spread, vi. (of news) ተነዛ *tänäzza*; (of fire, sickness) ተዛመተ *täzammätä*
spread apart ለያየ *läyayyä*
spread out ዘረጋ *zärägga*; (∼ clothes or grain to dry) አሰጣ *asäṭṭa*

spring (jump) ዘሎ ፡ ተነሣ *zällo tänässa*

spring, n. (season) ጸደይ *ṣädäy*; (source) ምንጭ *mənč*; (of truck) ባሌስትራ *balestra*; (of watch) ሞላ *molla*
hot springs ፍል ፡ ውኃ *fəl wəha*

sprinkle (vt.) ረጨ *räččä*; ውኃ ፡ አርካፈከፈ *wəha arkäfäkkäfä*; (∼ powder) ነሰነሰ *näsännäsä*
sprinkle (vi.) አካፋ *akaffa*

sprinkle (n.) ካፊያ *kaffiya*

sprout (vi.) በቀለ *bäqqälä*

sprout (n.) በቆልት *bäqqolt*

sprouting grain ቡቃያ *buqayya*

spry ንቁ *nəqu*

spume አረፉ *aräfu*

spur, v. (urge on) ገፋፋ *gäfaffa*; (∼ a horse) ኰረኰረ *kʷäräkkʷärä*

spur (n.), on the ∼ of the moment አስ ቀድሞ ፡ ሳያስብ *asqäddəmo sayassəb*

spy (v.) ሰለለ *sällälä*

spy (n.) ሰላይ *sällay*

squabble (n.) ንትርክ *nətərrək*; ጭቅጭቅ *čəqəččəq*

squad ተነጣይ ፡ ጓድ *tänäṭṭay gʷadd*

squadron እስኳድሮን əskʷadron

squalid ደሳሳ däsasa; ቆሻሻ ፡ ያለ qošäšš yalä

squalor መቆሻሻ mäqoššäš

squander አባከነ abakkänä; (ገንዘብ)፥አጠፋ (gänzäb) aṭäffa

square, n. (a plane figure with four equal sides and four right angles) አራት ፡ ማእዘን aratt ma'əzän; (public place) አደባባይ addäbabay

square, adj. (having four equal sides) አራቱም ፡ ጎን ፡ እኩል ፡ የሆነ arattum gʷänn əkkul yähonä square meter ካሬ kare

squash, v. (~ a bug) ጨፈለቀ čäfälläqä; (~ a rebellion) ደመሰሰ dämässäsä

squash, n. (plant) ዱባ dubba

squat ቁጢጥ ፡ አለ quṭiṭṭ alä; ቁጭ ፡ አለ quččč alä

squeak ሲጢጥ ፡ አለ siṭiṭṭ alä

squeal ተንጫጫ tänčačča

squeeze, vt. (~ oranges) ጨመቀ čämmäqä; (~ the hand) ጨበጠ čäbbäṭä; (force by pressing) አመቀ ammäqä

squint ዓይኑን ፡ ጨፈን ፡ አደረገ aynun čäfänn adärrägä; ተንሸዋረረ tänšäwarrärä

squirm (of a worm) ተርመሰመሰ tärmäsämmäsä

squirrel ሽኮኮ šəkokko

stab (v.) ወጋ wägga

stability ጽናት ṣənat; ጠንካራነት ṭänkarrannät

stabilize ወሰነ wässänä

stable (n.) ጋጥ gaṭ; ጋጣ gaṭa

stable, adj. (~ foundation) ጽኑ ṣənu; (~ government) የረጋ yärägga; (~ currency) የማይለዋወጥ yämmayəlläwawwäṭ

stack (v.) ከመረ kämmärä

stack (n.) ክምር kəmmər

stadium እስታድዮም əstadyom

staff, n. (rod) ዘንግ zäng; (group of employees) ሠራተኞች särratäññočč general staff የከፍተኛ ፡ ጦር ፡ መኮን ኖች ፡ መምሪያ yäkäffətäñña ṭor mäkʷännənočč mämriya

stag አጋዘን agazän

stage, n. (platform) መድረክ mädräk; (period of development) ደረጃ därä-ga; (scene of action) ቦታ bota

stagger (vt.) አንገዳገደ angädaggädä stagger (vi.) ተደናቀፈ tädänaqqäfä; ተንገዳገደ tängädaggädä

staggering, adj. (~ blow) የሚያንገዳግድ yämmiyangädaggəd; (~ news) የሚያ ስደነግጥ yämmiyasdänäggəṭ

stagnant (~ water) የረጋ yärägga; የታኘ yätäñña; (~ air) የታፈነ yätaffägä

stagnate ሻተተ šättätä

stain, v. (make dirty) አቈሸሸ aqʷäššä-šä; (~ the reputation) አጐደፈ agʷäd-däfä

stain (n.) ጠብታ ṭäbbəta; ቆሻሻ qošaša; እድፍ ədəf

stained ቆሻሻ ፡ ያለ qošäšš yalä

stair(s) ደረጃ däräga

stairway ደረጃ däräga

stake, n. (post) ካስማ kasma; ዕንጨት ənčät; (interest, share) ድርሻ dərša

stale, be ~ (of bread) ደረቀ därräqä; (of air) ታፈነ taffägä

stalk, n. (of plant) አገዳ agäda

stall (vi.) ዛሬ ፡ ነገ ፡ አለ zare nägä alä; (of motor) ጠፋ ṭäffa

stall, n. (for cows) በረት bärät; (for horses) ጋጣ gaṭa; ጋጥ gaṭ; (for merchandise) መደብ mädäb; ተራ tära

stallion ድንጉላ dəngulla; ፈረስ färäs

stammer ተንተባተበ täntäbattäbä

stammerer ተብታባ täbtabba

stamp, vt. (~ documents) አተመ attä-

mä; (mark, indicate) **መሰከረ(ለት)** *mä-säkkärä(llät)*

stamp, vi. (trample) **ረጋጠ** *räggäṭä;* **በእግሩ ፡ ረገጠ ፡ ረገጠ ፡ አደረገ** *bägru rägäṭṭ rägäṭṭ adärrägä*

stamp out (~ fire) **በእግሩ ፡ አጠፋ** *bägru aṭäffa;* (~ a rebellion) **ደመሰሰ** *dämässäsä*

stamp, n. (official seal) **ማኅተም** *mahtäm;* (for letters) **ቴምብር** *tembər*

stand, vt. (set in an upright position) **አቆመ** *aqomä;* (tolerate) **ታገሠ** *taggäsä*

stand (vi.) **ቆመ** *qomä;* (rise) **ተነሣ** *tänässa;* (remain in force) **እንደጸና ፡ ቆየ** *əndäṣänna qoyyä*

stand aside **ገለለ** *gällälä;* **ዞር ፡ አለ** *zorr alä*

stand by one **ደገፈ** *däggäfä*

stand out **ጐላ** *gʷälla*

stand up **ተነሣ** *tänässa;* (withstand wear) **በረከተ** *bäräkkätä*

stand, n. (booth from which something is sold) **መደብ** *mädäb;* (attitude) **ሐሳብ** *hassab;* **አቋም** *aqʷam*

standard, n. (anything taken as basis for comparison) **ደረጃ** *däräǧa;* (flag) **ሰንደቅ ፡ ዓላማ** *sändäq alama*

standard, adj. (~ weights) **የታወሰነ** *yätäwässänä;* **መደበኛ** *mädäbäňňa;* (~ reference work) **ዋና** *wanna*

standardize **ወሰነ** *wässänä*

standard of living **የኑሮ ፡ ደረጃ** *yänuro däräǧa*

standing, n. (rank) **ደረጃ** *däräǧa*
of long standing **የቆየ** *yäqoyyä*

standing, adj. (~ water) **የረጋ** *yärägga;* (~ order, lamp) **ቋሚ** *qʷami*

standpoint **አቋም** *aqʷam*

standstill, come to a ~ **ተቋረጠ** *täqʷarräṭä*

staple, n. (of food) **ዋና ፡ ምግብ** *wanna məgəb;* (to fasten paper) **የወረቀት ፡ ማያያዣ** *yäwäräqät mayayaža*

star **ኮከብ** *kokäb*

starch (v.) **አሚዶ ፡ አደረገ(በት)** *amido adärrägä(bbät)*

starch (n.) **አሚዶ** *amido*

stare (vi.), ~ at **ፍጥጥ ፡ ብሎ ፡ አየ** *fəṭəṭṭ bəlo ayyä*

start (vt.) **ጀመረ** *ǧämmärä;* (~ a business) **አቋቋመ** *aqqʷaqʷamä;* (~ the motor) **አስነሣ** *asnässa*

start (vi.) **ተጀመረ** *täǧämmärä;* (of fire) **ተነሣ** *tänässa*

start (n.) **መጀመሪያ** *mäǧämmäriya*
from start to finish **ከዳር ፡ እስከ ፡ ዳር** *kädar əskä dar*

starting, ~ today **ከዛሬ ፡ ጀምሮ** *käzare ǧämməro*
starting point **መነሻ** *männäša*

startle (vi.) **ደነበረ** *dänäbbärä;* **ደነገጠ** *dänäggäṭä;* **በረገገ** *bäräggägä*

starvation **ራኅብ** *rähab*

starve (vi.) **ራበ(ው)** *rabä(w);* **ተራበ** *täräbä*

starving **ራኅብተኛ** *rähabtäňňa;* **የተራበ** *yätäräbä*

state, v. (say) **ተናገረ** *tänaggärä;* (present a case) **አቀረበ** *aqärräbä*

state (n.) **አገር** *agär;* (government) **መንግሥት** *mängəst;* (condition) **ይዞታ** *yəzota*
state of affairs **ሁኔታ** *huneta*

stateless **ዜግነት ፡ የሌለው** *zegənnät yälelläw*

stately **ግርማ ፡ ያለው** *gərma yalläw;* **ባለ ፡ ግርማ** *balä gərma*

statement (report) **መግለጫ** *mägläča;* (in court) **ቃል** *qal;* (of a bank) **የሒሳብ ፡ መግለጫ** *yähisab mägläča*

statesman **የፖለቲካ ፡ ሰው** *yäpolätika säw;* **መሪ** *märi*

station (v.) **መደበ** *mäddäbä;* **አቆመ** *aqomä*

station, n. (of bus, radio) **ጣቢያ** *ṭabiya;* (assigned post) **የተመደበለት ፡ ስፍራ** *yätämäddäbällät səfra* stationary, be ~ (of prices) እንዳለ ፡ ቆየ əndallä qoyyä

stationery (writing material) የጽሕፈት ፡ መሣሪያ yäṣəhfät mässariya; (store) የጽሕፈት ፡ መሣሪያ ፡ መደብር yäṣəhfät mässariya mädäbbər

statistics እስታቲስቲክስ əstatistiks

statue ሐውልት hawəlt

stature (height) ቁመት qumät; (moral standing) ክብር kəbər

status (condition) ሁኔታ huneta; (social standing) ቦታ bota; ክብር kəbər

statute ሥርዓት sər'at; ደንብ dänb

staunch (~ friend) የልብ yaləbb

stay (vi.) ቆየ qoyyä; (dwell) አረፈ arräfä; ተቀመጠ täqämmäṭä
stay away ራቅ ፡ አለ raqq alä; ቀረ qärrä
stay behind ኋላ ፡ ቀረ hʷala qärrä

stead, in one's ~ በ - - - ፈንታ bä - - - fänta

steadfast ጽኑ ṣənu

steadily ሳያቋርጥ sayaqqʷarrəṭ; ያለ ፋታ yalä fata

steady, adj. (~ work) ቋሚ qʷami; (~ hand) የማይንቀጠቀጥ yämmayənqäṭäqqäṭ; (~ customer) የዘወትር yäzäwätər

steal ሰረቀ särräqä
steal away ሹልክ ፡ ብሎ ፡ ወጣ šulləkk bəlo wäṭṭa

stealthily በስርቆሽ bäsərqoš

steam (n.) እንፋሎት ənfalot

steam engine በከሰል ፡ የሚሄድ ፡ ባቡር bäkäsäl yämmihed babur

steel ዐረብ ፡ ብረት aräb brät

steep, v. (in water) ዘፈዘፈ zäfäzzäfä; ነከረ näkkärä

steep, adj. (~ stairs) ቀጥ ፡ ያለ qäṭṭ yalä

steer, vt. (~ a ship) መራ märra; (~ a boat) ቀዘፈ qäzzäfä; (~ a car) ነዳ nädda

steer (n.) ሰንጋ sänga; በሬ bäre

steering wheel መሪ märi; የመኪና ፡ መሪ yämäkina märi

stele ሐውልት hawəlt

stem, vt. (~ a flood) አገደ aggädä; (~ the opposition) ጋታ gätta
stem, vi. (originate) መነጨ mänäččä

stem, n. (of flower) ግንድ gənd; (of leaf) አንጓ angʷa

stench ክርፋት kərfat; ግማት gəmat

stenography አጭር፡ጽሕፈት aččər ṣəhfät

step, v. (move) ተራመደ tärammädä; (put the foot down) ረጋጠ räggäṭä
step aside ዞር ፡ አለ zorr alä
step back ወደ ፡ ኋላ ፡ ፈቀቅ ፡ አለ wädä hʷala fäqäqq alä
step down ወረደ wärrädä
step in ገባ gäbba
step off ወረደ wärrädä
step on ረጋጠ räggäṭä
step out ወጣ ፡ አለ wäṭa alä

step, n. (stair) ደረጃ däräğa; (pace, measure) እርምጃ ərməğğa
step by step ቀስ ፡ በቀስ qäss bäqäss
keep step እኩል ፡ ተራመደ əkkul tärammädä
watch one's step ተጠነቀቀ täṭänäqqäqä

stepbrother የእንጀራ ፡ አባቱ ፡ (እናቱ) ፡ ልጅ yäənğära abbatu (or ənnatu) ləğ

stepchild የእንጀራ ፡ ልጅ yäənğära ləğ

stepdaughter የእንጀራ ፡ ልጅ yäənğära ləğ

stepfather የእንጀራ ፡ አባት yäənğära abbat

stepmother የእንጀራ ፡ እናት yaənğära ənnat

stepson የእንጀራ ፡ ልጅ yäənğära ləğ

sterile (~ woman) መካን mäkan; መኻን mähan; (~ cattle) መሲና mäsina; (free from germs) ከነፍሳት ፡ ንጹሕ känäfsat nəṣuh

sterilize ከጀርም ፡ ነጻ ፡ አደረገ käğärm näṣa adärrägä

stern, adj. (~ expression) ኩስተር ፡ ያለ
kʷästärr yalä; (~ person) ጥብቅ *ṭəbq*

stew (n.) ወጥ *wäṭ*

steward (administrator) መጋቢ *mäggabi;*
(of airplane) አስተናጋጅ *astänagaǧ*

stewardess አስተናጋጅ *astänagaǧ*

stick, vt. (pierce) ወጋ *wägga;* (attach)
ለጠፈ *läṭṭäfä;* አጣበቀ *aṭṭabbäqä*
stick, vi. (of glue) አጣበቀ *aṭṭabbäqä;*
(of a door) ነካሰ *näkkäsä*
stick out (vt.) አወጣ *awäṭṭa*
stick to ጸና *ṣänna;* ተከተለ *täkättälä*
be stuck (of glue) ተጣበቀ *täṭabbäqä;*
(of a bone) ተቀረቀረ *täqäräqqärä*

stick (n.) በትር *bättər;* ከዘራ *käzära*

sticky ዝልግልግ *zələgləg*
be sticky (weather) ወበቀ *wäbbäqä*

stiff (~ collar) ደረቅ *däräq;* (~ cover)
ጠንካራ *ṭänkarra*

stiffen (~ resistance) አጠነከረ *aṭänäkkärä*

stifle (suffocate) አፈነ *affänä;* (~ rebellion) ጸጥ ፡ አደረገ *ṣäṭṭ adärrägä*

still, adj. (~ air, water) የረጋ *yärägga;*
(~ house, night) ጭር ፡ ያለ *čərr yalä;*
(~ lake) ጸጥ ፡ ያለ *ṣäṭṭ yalä*
keep still ዝም ፡ አለ *zəmm alä*

still (adv.) አሁንም *ahunəm;* አሁንም ፡
ገና *ahunəm gäna*

stillborn, be ሞቶ ፡ ተወለደ *moto täwäl-
lädä*

stilt ምርኩዝ *mərkuz*

stilted, be ~ (manner) ግትር ፡ ነው *gəttər näw;* (language) ለዛ ፡ የለውም *läzza yälläwəm*

stimulate (~ the interest) ቀሰቀሰ *qäsäqqäsä;* አነሳሳ *annäsassa*

stimulus የሚገፋፋ ፡ ነገር *yämmigäfaffa
nägär*

sting, vt. (of bee) ነደፈ *näddäfä*

stingy ጨቅ *čuq;* ንፉግ *nəfug;* ገብጋባ *gäbgabba*

stink (v.) ሸተተ *šättätä;* ገማ *gämma*

stink (n.) ሽታ *šətta;* ግማት *gəmat*

stipend ቀለብ *qälläb;* አበል *abäl*

stipulate ገደብ ፡ አደረገ *gädäb adärrägä*

stipulation አንቀጽ *anqäṣ;* ገደብ *gädäb*

stir, vt. (excite) አነሳሳ *annäsassa;* (~
a liquid) አማሰለ *ammassälä;* (~ medicine) በጠበጠ *bäṭabbäṭä*

stirrup እርካብ *ərkab*

stitch (v.) ሰፋ *säffa;* ጠቀመ *ṭäqqämä*

stitch, n. (of thread) ክር *kərr;* (made
by a doctor) ሽቦ *šəbo*

stock, n. (race) ዘር *zär;* (cattle) ከብት
käbt; (of gun) ሰደፍ *sädäf;* (supply)
ሻቀጥ *šäqäṭ;* (share in a company)
አክሲዮን *aksiyon*
be out of stock እቃውን ፡ ጨረሰ *əqawən čärräsä*

stock exchange የገበያ ፡ ምንዛሪ *yägäbäya
mənəzzari*

stocking የእግር ፡ ሹራብ *yäəgər šurrab*

stockpile አጠራቀመ *aṭṭäraqqämä*

stocky ዳልዳላ *däldalla*

stoke ቆሰቆሰ *qʷäsäqqʷäsä*

stomach ሆድ *hod*

stomach ache (የ)ሆድ ፡ ቁርጠት *(yä)hod
qurṭät*

stone (v.) በድንጋይ ፡ ወገረ *bädəngay wäggärä*

stone (n.) ዳንጊያ *dängiya;* ድንጋይ *dəngay;* (of fruit) ፍሬ *fre*
precious stone ዕንቁ *ənqʷ*

stony ድንጋያማ *dəngayamma*

stool በርጩማ *bärčumma;* (excrement)
ዓይነ ፡ ምድር *aynä mədər*

stoop አጎነበሰ *agʷänäbbäsä;* ጉንበስ ፡ አለ
gʷänbäss alä; ራሱን ፡ ዝቅ ፡ አደረገ *rasun zəqq adärrägä*

stop (vt.) አቆመ *aqomä;* (restrain, hold
back) አገደ *aggädä*

stop (vi.) ቆመ *qomä;* (of rain) አባራ
abarra
stop off ጐራ ፡ አለ *gʷära alä*
stop up ወተፈ *wättäfä;* ደፈነ *däffänä*

stop (n.) መቆሚያ *mäqomiya;* (stopping) ማቆም *maqom*
bring to a stop አቆመ *aqomä*
come to a stop ቆመ *qomä*
make a stop አረፈ *arräfä*
put a stop to አቆመ *aqomä*

stopper መወተፊያ *mäwättäfiya;* ውታፍ *wəttaf;* ቡሽ *buš*

storage (place for storing) መጋዘን *mägazän;* (keeping in a safe place) መጋ ዘን ፡ ውስተ ፡ ማስቀመጥ *mägazän wəsṭ masqämmäṭ*
put in storage ከተተ *kättätä*

store (v.) አስቀመጠ *asqämmäṭä;* አኖረ *anorä*
store away ከተተ *kättätä*
store up አከማቸ *akkämaččä*

store (n.) መደብር *mädäbbər;* ሱቅ *suq*

storehouse መጋዘን *mägazän;* እቃ ፡ ቤት *əqa bet;* ግምጃ ፡ ቤት *gəmǧa bet*

storekeeper ባለ ፡ ሱቅ *balä suq*

storeroom መጋዘን *mägazän*

stork እርኩም *ərkum*

storm (vi.) ዐውሎ ፡ ነፋስ ፡ ተነሣ *awlo näfas tänässa*

storm (n.) ማዕበል *ma'əbäl;* ዐውሎ ፡ ነፋስ *awlo näfas*

story (account) ተረት *tärät;* ታሪክ *tarik;* (any level of a building) ፎቅ *foq*
tell a story ተረተ *tärrätä*

stout (~ man) ወፍራም *wäfram;* (~ walls) ጥብቅ *ṭəbq*
be (get) stout ወፈረ *wäffärä;* ጠደ *gäzzäfä*

stove ምድጃ *mədəǧǧa*

stow, ~ away ተደብቆ ፡ ሄደ *tädäbbəqo hedä*

straight (adj.) ቀጥ ፡ ያለ *qäṭṭ yalä;* ቀጥ ተኛ *qäṭṭätäňňa;* ትክክል *təkəkkəl;*

(honest) ሐቀኛ *haqqäňňa*
be straight (road) ቀና *qänna;* (line) ቀጥ ፡ አለ *qäṭṭ alä*

straight (adv.) በቀጥታ *bäqäṭṭəta;* (uninterrupted) ሳያቋርጥ *sayaqqʷarrəṭ*
straight across ፊት ፡ ለፊት *fit läfit*
straight ahead በቀጥታ ፡ ወደፊት *bäqäṭṭəta wädäfit*

straighten (~something uneven) አስተ ካከለ *astäkakkälä;* (~ a rod) አቀና *aqänna;* አቃና *aqqanna*
straighten up, vt. (~ room) አዘጋጀ *azzägaǧǧä;* በደንብ ፡ አደረገ *bädänb adärrägä*

straightforward (~ person) ሐሳብ ፡ ቀና *hassabä qänna;* ግልጽ *gəlṣ;* (~ manner) የማያወላውል *yämmayawwälawwəl*

strain, v. (~ the leg) ወለም ፡ አለ(ው) *wälämm alä(w);* (~ butter) አጠለለ *aṭällälä;* (~ the eyes) አፈዘዘ *afäzzäzä;* (~ relations) አሻከረ *aššakkärä*

strain (n.) ጭንቀት *čənqät;* ጣጣ *ṭaṭa*

strained, adj. (~ laughter) ከንጋት ፡ በላይ ፡ የሆነ *kangät bälay yähonä;* (~ voice) የሰለለ *yäsällälä*

strainer ማጥለያ *maṭläya*

strait የባሕር ፡ ወሽመጥ *yäbahər wäšmäṭ*

straits ችግር *čəggər*

strand (n.) ክር *kərr*

stranded ያለ ፡ እርዳታ ፡ የቀረ *yalä ərdata yäqärrä*

strange እንግዳ *əngəda;* (~ behavior) ያልተለመደ *yaltälämmädä;* (~ odor) ልዩ *ləyyu;* የተለየ *yätäläyyä*
feel strange ግራ ፡ ገባ(ው) *gra gäbba(w)*
how strange! ወይ ፡ ጉድ *wäy gud*

stranger እንግዳ *əngəda*

strangle, vt. (choke) አነቀ *annäqä;* (kill by squeezing the throat) አንቆ ፡ ገደለ *anqo gäddälä*

strap (v.) በመጫኛ ፡ አሰረ bämäčaňňa assärä

strap (n.) ጠፍር ṭäfər; (of sandals) ማስ ሪያ masäriya

strategy የጦር ፡ ስልት yäṭor səlt; የጦር ፡ ዘዴ yäṭor zäde

straw (n.) ሣር sar; ኬሻ keša

straw, adj. (~ hat) የኬሻ yäkeša; (~ mattress) የሣር yäsar

stray, v. (of cattle) ተለየ täläyyä; (of thoughts) ባከነ bakkänä

stray, adj. (~ cat) ባለቤት ፡ የሌለው ba-läbet yälelläw; (~ cattle) ልቅ ፡ የሆነ ləqq yähonä; (~ bullet) ተባራሪ täbarari

stream, v. (of water) ፈሰሰ fässäsä; (of tears) ኮለለ ፡ አለ kʷäläll alä; (of crowds) ጐረፈ gʷärräfä

stream (n.) ወንዝ wänz

street መንገድ mängäd

street car ትራም tram

strength ኃይል hayl; ጕልበት gulbät; ብርታት bərtat; ጥንካሬ ṭənəkkare; (of drug) ኃይል hayl

strengthen አበረታ abärätta; አጠነከረ aṭänäkkärä; ጕልበት ፡ ሰጠ gulbät säṭṭä

strenuous (vigorous) ብርቱ bərtu; (requiring exertion) አድካሚ adkami

stress, v. (emphasize) ደጋግሞ ፡ አሳሰበ dägagmo asassäbä

stress ችግር čəggər; (mental ~) ጭንቀት čənqät be under stress ተጨነቀ täčännäqä lay stress (give importance to) ግምት ፡ ሰጠ gəmmət säṭṭä

stretch, vt. (~ a string, hide) ወጠረ wäṭṭärä; (~ a rope) ዘረጋ zärägga; (~ shoes) አሰፋ asäffa; (~ the legs) አፍታታ aftatta
stretch, vi. (of a road) ተዘረጋ täzärägga; (of an empire) ተስፋፋ täsfaffa; (of material) ተሳበ täsabä
stretch out (vt.) ዘረጋ zärägga

stretch out (vi.) ጋደም ፡ አለ gädämm alä

stretcher ቃሬዛ qareza

strew (~ flowers) በተነ bättänä; (~ rushes on the floor) ጐዘጐዘ gʷäzäggʷäzä

strict (~ person) ጥብቅ ṭəbq; (~ diet) የተወሰነ yätäwässänä

stride (v.) ተራመደ tärammädä

stride (n.) እርምጃ ərməǧǧa

strife ጠብ ṭäb

strike, v. (hit) መታ mätta; (~ a match) ጫረ čärä; (cross out) ሰረዘ särräzä; (~ roots) ሰደደ säddädä; (of a disease) ያዘ yazä; (of a thought) ትዝ ፡ አለ(ው) təzz alä(w)
strike, vi. (of lightning) ወደቀ wäddäqä; (stop working) አደመ addämä
strike out ሰረዘ särräzä

strike (n.) የሥራ ፡ ማቆም ፡ አድማ yäsəra maqom adma

striker አድማኛ admäňňa

string, v. (~ beans) ቀነጠሰ qänäṭṭäsä; (~ beads) ሰካ säkka

string, n. (thin cord) ሲባጎ sibago; (of pearls) ድሪ dəri; (of harp) አውታር awtar

stringent (strict) በጣም ፡ ጥብቅ bäṭam ṭəbq

strip, vt. (bark) ላጠ laṭä
strip off (~ clothes) አወላለቀ awälalläqä

strip, n. (of bamboo) ስንጥር sənṭər; (of paper) ብጣሽ bäṭṭaš

stripe መሥመር mäsmär; (fringe of dress) ጥለት ṭälät

striped ዝንጉርጉር zəngurgur; መሥመር ፡ ያለው mäsmär yalläw

strive ደከመ däkkämä; ጥሮ ፡ ሠራ ṭəro särra

stroke, v. (~ the arm) ዳበሰ däbabbäsä; (~ a cat) ዳሰሰ dassäsä

stroke, n. (sound) ድምፅ *dəmṣ;* (a blow) ምት *mət;* ምታት *mətat;* (a sudden attack of illness) የዳም ፡ መርጋት ፡ በሽታ *yädäm märgat bäššəta*
at one stroke ባንዳፍታ *bandafta*

stroll (v.) በእግር ፡ ተንሸራሸረ *bägər tänšäraššärä*

stroll (n.) ሽርሽር *šərrəšərr*

strong (~ man) ብርቱ *bərtu;* ጠንካራ *ṭänkarra;* ጥኑ *ṭənu;* ኃይለኛ *hayläňňa;* (~ tea) ወፍራም *wäfram;* (~ argument) ዓይነተኛ *aynätäňňa*
be strong በረታ *bärätta;* ጠነከረ *ṭänäkkärä;* ጠና *ṭänna*

stronghold ጠንካራ ፡ ምሽግ *ṭänkarra məš-šəg*

strongly በኃይል *bähayl;* አጥብቆ *aṭbəqo*

strophe የግጥም ፡ አንቀጽ *yägəṭəm anqäṣ*

structure (building) ሕንጻ *hənṣa;* (of the human body, of an organization) አቋም *aq"am*

struggle (v.) ታገለ *taggälä*

struggle (n.) ትግል *təgəl*

stub, n. (of ticket) ጉርድ *gurd;* ጉራጅ *gurraǧ;* (of pencil) ቁራጭ *qurraç*

stubborn ችኮ *čəkko;* እልኸኛ *əlləhäňňa;* ሐሳበ ፡ ግትር *hassabä gəttər*
be stubborn ቻከ *čäkä;* ችክ ፡ አለ *čəkk alä;* ገተረ *gättärä*

student ተማሪ *tämari*

studious ጥናት ፡ የሚወድ *ṭənat yämmiwädd*

study (v.) ተማረ *tämarä;* አጠና *aṭänna;* (~ a problem) መረመረ *märämmärä*

study (n.) ትምህርት *təmhərt;* ጥናት *ṭənat;* (investigation, report) ጥናት *ṭənat;* (room) የጥናት ፡ ክፍል *yäṭənat kəfəl*

stuff, v. (~ cotton in the ears) ወተፈ *wättäfä;* (~ clothes in a bag) አጨቀ *aččäqä*

stuff, n. (cloth) ጨርቅ *čärq;* (belongings) እቃ *əqa;* (worthless things) ትርኪ ፡ ምርኪ *tərki mərki*

stuffy (~ hall) የታፈነ *yätaffänä*

stumble (in speech) ተንተባተበ *täntäbattäbä;* (trip) ተደናቀፈ *tädänaqqäfä;* ተሰናከለ *täsänakkälä;* እንቅፋት ፡ መታ(ው) *ənqəfat mätta(w)*

stumbling block እንቅፋት *ənqəfat*

stump (of tree) ጉቶ *gutto*

stumpy ኩሩሩ *kururu*

stun (shock) አስደነበረ *asdänäbbärä;* አስደነገጠ *asdänäggäṭä*
be stunned ከው ፡ አለ *kəww alä*

stupefy (of an attack) አስደነበረ *asdänäbbärä;* (of heat, noise) አደነዘዘ *adänäzzäzä*
be stupefied ከው ፡ ብሎ ፡ ቀረ *kəww bəlo qärrä*

stupendous የሚያስደነ ንቅ *yämmiyasdännəq*

stupid (~ person) ጅል *ǧəl;* ሞኝ *moňň;* ደደብ *däddäb;* (~ conversation) የማ ይረባ *yämmayəräba*

stupidity ጅልነት *ǧələnnät*

stupor, be in a ~ ደነዘዘ *dänäzzäzä*

sturdy ጠንካራ *ṭänkarra*

stutter (v.) ተንተባተበ *täntäbattäbä*

stuttering መንተባተብ *mäntäbatäb*

style ዘዴ *zäde;* ስልት *səlt;* (fashion) ሞድ *mod*

stylish (~ clothing) ቀንጠኛ *qenṭäňňa*

subdue አስገበረ *asgäbbärä;* አሸነፈ *aššännäfä*

subheading ኣርእስት *ar'əst*

subject, v. (bring under control) አስገ በረ *asgäbbärä*
be subjected ተገዛ *tägäzza*

subject, n. (matter) ነገር *nägär;* (course of study) ትምህርት *təmhərt;* (topic) አርእስት *ar'əst;* (citizen) ዜጋ *zega;* (in grammar) ባለቤት *baläbet*

subjection ተገዢነት *tägäžənnät*

subjugate አስገበረ *asgäbbärä*

submarine ሰርጎ ጅ ፡ መርከብ *särg"aǧ märkäb*

submerge (vi.) ጠለቀ ṭälläqä

submissive (humble) ትሑት təhut; (docile) እሺ ፡ ባይ əšši bay

submit, vt. (present) አቀረበ aqärräbä
submit, vi. (yield to) ተገዛ tägäzza
be submitted (bill) ቀረበ qärräbä

subordinate (n.) የበታች yäbätačč

subscribe (money) ሊሰጥ ፡ ቃል ፡ ገባ lisäṭ qal gäbba
subscribe to (a periodical) በማኅበርተኛነት ፡ ገዛ bämahbärtäňňannät gäzza

subscriber የጋዜጣ ፡ ማኅበርተኛ yägazeṭa mahbärtäňňa

subsequent ከጊዜ ፡ በኋላ ፡ የመጣ kägize bähʷala yämäṭṭa

subsequently የኋላ ፡ ኋላ yähʷala hʷala

subside ጐደለ gʷäddälä; (of storm) ጋብ ፡ አለ gabb alä

subsidiary (of a company) ቅርንጫፍ qərənčaf

subsidize የገንዘብ ፡ እርዳታ ፡ አደረገ yägänzäb ərdata adärrägä

subsist (maintain life) በሕይወት ፡ ቆየ bähəywät qoyyä

subsistence ኑሮ nuro; መኖሪያ mänoriya

substance (matter) ነገር nägär; ሥረ ፡ ነገር särä nägär; (essence) መሠረተ ፡ ሐሳብ mäsärätä hassab; ፍሬ ፡ ነገር färe nägär

substantially በመሠረቱ bämäsärätu

substantiate አረጋገጠ arrägaggäṭä

substitute (v.) ተካ täkka

substitute (n.) ምትክ mətəkk

subterfuge ምክንያት mäknəyat; ተንኰል tänkʷäl

subterranean ከመሬት ፡ በታች ፡ የሆነ kämäret bätačč yähona

subtle የረቀቀ yäräqqäqä

subtract ቀነሰ qännäsä

subtraction መቀነስ mäqännäs

suburb ገጠር gäṭär; ከተማ ፡ ዳር kätäma dar

subvention የገንዘብ ፡ እርዳታ yägänzäb ərdata

subversive (መንግሥት) ፡ ተቃዋሚ (mängəst) täqawami

subway መሿለኪያ mäšš waläkiya

succeed, vt. (come directly after) ተተካ tätäkka
succeed, vi. (be successful) ሰላ sälla; ተሳካ(ለት) täsakka(llät)

success የዕድል ፡ መቃናት yäəddəl mäqqanat; የሥራ ፡ መሳካት yäsəra mässakat; መሳካት mässakat

successful (~ person) የተሳካ(ለት) yätäsakka(llät); (~ business) የተሳካ yätäsakka; የሚያዋጣ yämmiyawwaṭṭa
be successful ተሳካ täsakka; ውጤት ፡ አስገኘ wäṭṭet asgäňňä; (person) ተሳካ (ለት) täsakka(llät)

successive ተከታታይ täkätatay

successor ተተኪ tätäki

succumb ተሸነፈ täšännäfä; (die) አረፈ arräfä

such እንዲህ əndih; እንደዚህ əndäzzih
such-and-such እከሌ əkäle

suck (~ the breast) ጠባ ṭäbba; (~ a lemon) መጠጠ mäṭṭäṭä

suckle (vt.) አጠባ(ች) aṭäbba(čč)
suckle (vi.) ጠባ ṭäbba

sudden ያልታሰበ yaltassäbä; ድንገተኛ dəngätäňňa
all of a sudden በድንገት bädəngät

suddenly ወዲያው wädiyaw; ወዲያውኑ wädiyawnu; በድንገት bädəngät

sue (take legal steps) ከሰሰ kässäsä; ክስ ፡ አቀረበ kəss aqärräbä

suffer, vt. (tolerate) ታገሠ taggäsä
suffer (vi.) ተሠቃየ täsäqayyä; (of business) ተዳከመ tädakkämä

suffering (n.) ሥቃይ səqay; ችግር čəggər; መከራ mäkära

suffice በቃ *bäqqa*

sufficient በቂ *bäqi*
be sufficient በቃ *bäqqa*

suffix (in grammar) ባዕድ ፡ መድረሻ *baəd mädräša*

suffocate (vt.) አነቀ *annäqä;* አፈነ *affänä*
suffocate (vi.) ታነቀ *tannäqä;* ታፈነ *taffänä*

sugar ሱኳር *sukkʷar;* ስኳር *səkkʷar*

sugar cane ሸንኩራ ፡ አገዳ *šänkʷära agäda*

suggest (propose) ሐሳብ ፡ አቀረበ *hassab aqärräbä;* (bring to mind) አሳሰበ *asassäbä*

suggestion አስተሳሰብ *astäsasäb;* ያቀረ በው ፡ ሐሳብ *yaqärräbäw hassab*
make a suggestion ሐሳብ ፡ አቀረበ *hassab aqärräbä*

suicide ራሱን ፡ መግደል *rasun mägdäl*
commit suicide ራሱን ፡ ገደለ *rasun gäddälä*

suit, v. (please) አስደሰተ *asdässätä;* (fit) ተስማማ *täsmamma*
suit yourself! እንዳሰኘህ *əndassäňňäh*

suit, n. (set of clothes) ሙሉ ፡ ልብስ *mulu ləbs;* (lawsuit) ክስ *kəss*
bring suit ከሰሰ *kässäsä*
follow suit ተከተለ *täkättälä*

suitable ምቹ *məčču;* ተስማሚ *täsmami;* ተግባቢ *tägbabi*
be suitable ተመቸ *tämäččä;* ተስማማ *täsmamma;* ተግባባ *tägbabba*

suitcase ሻንጣ *šanṭa*

suite (retinue) ተከታዮች *täkättayočč*

suitor (who courts a woman) የሚያሽኮ ረምም *yämmiyaškorämməm*

sulk አኮረፈ *akʷärräfä*

sullen (~child) ያኮረፈ *yakʷärräfä*

sulphur ድኝ *dəňň*

sum (v.), ~up (add into one amount) ደመረ *dämmärä;* (summarize) አጠቃ ለለ *attäqallälä*

to sum up በጭሩ *baččəru*

sum, n. (results obtained by addition) ጠቅላላ ፡ ድምር *ṭäqlalla dəmmər;* (amount of money) ገንዘብ *gänzäb*
in sum በጠቅላላ *bäṭäqlalla*

summarize ፍሬ ፡ ነገሩን ፡ በጭሩ ፡ አቀረበ *fəre nägärun baččəru aqärräbä;* አጠ ቃለለ *attäqallälä*

summary (of an article) ፍሬ ፡ ነገር *fəre nägär*

summer በጋ *bäga*

summit ራስ *ras;* አናት *anat;* ጫፍ *čaf*
summit conference የመሪዎች ፡ ጉባኤ *yämäriwočč guba'e*

summon (call) ጠራ *ṭärra;* (require the presence of someone by a summons) በመጥሪያ ፡ አዘዘ *bämäṭriya azzäzä*

summons መጥሪያ *mäṭriya;* ጥሪ *ṭərri*

sumptuous ድሎት ፡ ያለው *dəlot yalläw*

sun (n.) ፀሐይ *şähay;* (disc of sun) ጀም በር *ğämbär*

Sunday ሰንበት *sänbät;* እሁድ *əhud*
Sunday clothes የከት ፡ ልብስ *yäkətt ləbs*

sundown, see 'sunset'

sunflower ሱፍ *suf*

sunglasses የፀሐይ ፡ መነጽር *yäşähay mänäşşər*

sunny ፀሐያማ *şähayamma*

sunrise የፀሐይ ፡ መውጣት *yäşähay mäwṭat*

sunset የፀሐይ ፡ ጥልቀት *yäşähay ṭəlqät;* የጀምበር ፡ ጥልቀት *yägämbär ṭəlqät*

sunshine የፀሐይ ፡ ብርሃን *yäşähay bərhan*

sunstroke ምች *məčč*

superb ግሩም *gərum*

superficial ጥልቅነት ፡ የሌለው *ṭəlqənnät yälelläw;* (~ mind) ያልበሰለ *yalbässälä*

superficially ላይ ፡ ላዩን *lay layun*

superfluous ለጊዜው ፡ የማያስፈልግ *lägizew yämmayasfälləg*

superintendent ተቈጣጣሪ *täqʷäṭaṭari*

superior, n. (in rank, office) የበላይ *yäbälay;* አለቃ *aläqa*

superior, adj. (~ officer) የበላይ *yäbälay;* (~ mind) የላቀ *yälaqä;* (~ quality) ምርጥ *märṭ*

superiority (mastery) የበላይነት *yäbälayənnät;* መብለጥ *mäbläṭ*

superlative (n.) አበላላጭ ፡ ደረጃ *abbälalaǧ däräǧa*

supersede ተካ *täkka*

superstition አጉል ፡ እምነት *agul əmnät*

superstitious ባጉል ፡ እምነት ፡ የሚያምልክ *bagul əmnät yämmiyamälk*

supervise ተቈጣጠረ *täqʷäṭaṭṭärä*

supervision ተቈጣጣሪነት *täqʷäṭaṭarinnät;* ቁጥጥር *quṭəṭṭər*

supervisor ተቈጣጣሪ *täqʷäṭaṭari*

supper ራት *rat;* እራት *ərat*

supple በቀላሉ ፡ የሚታጠፍ *bäqällalu yämmittaṭṭäf*

supplement (v.) አሟላ *amʷalla*

supplement (n.) ማሟያ *mamʷaya*

supplementary በተጨማሪ ፡ የሚያገለግል *bätäčämmari yämmiyagäläggəl*

supplication ልመና *ləmmäna*

supply (v.) ሰጣ *säṭṭä;* አቀረበ *aqärräbä;* (~ demand) አረካ *aräkka*

supply (n.) እቃ *əqa;* የቤት ፡ ቀለብ *yäbet qälläb*
     supplies (of army) ትጥቅና ፡ ስንቅ *təṭqənna sənq*

support, v. (hold up, prop, uphold) ደገፈ *däggäfä;* (~ one's parents) ጦረ *ṭorä;* (~ one's children) አስተዳደረ *astädaddärä*
     support oneself ራሱን ፡ ቻለ *rasun čalä*

support (n.) መከታ *mäkäta;* ድጋፍ *dəgaf*

suppose መሰለ(ው) *mässälä(w);* ገመተ *gämmätä*
     let's suppose እንበል *ənnəbäl*

supposed (adj.) የተባለ *yätäbalä*

supposition የይምሰል *yäyəmsäl;* ምናልባት *mənalbat;* የይሆናል *yäyəhonal*

suppress (~ a riot) ደመሰሰ *dämässäsä;* አገደ *aggädä;* (~ a smile) አፍኖ ፡ ያዘ *affəno yazä*

suppurate መገለ *mäggälä*

supremacy የበላይነት *yäbälayənnät*

supreme (~ authority) ከፍተኛ *käffətäňňa;* (~ effort) ታላቅ *tallaq*

Supreme Court (of Ethiopia) ጠቅላይ ፡ ንጉሠ ፡ ነገሥት ፡ ፍርድ ፡ ቤት *ṭäqlay nəgusä nägäst fərd bet*

surcharge ተጨማሪ ፡ ዋጋ *täčämmari waga*

sure (certain) እርግጠኛ *ərgəṭäňňa;* (~ friend) ታማኝ *tammaňň;* (~ remedy) ፍቱን *fətun*
     sure! ሙት *mut;* ይሙት *yəmut*
     be sure to እንድ *əndə* + imperfect
     for sure በርግጥ *bärgəṭ*
     make sure አረጋገጠ *arrägaggäṭä*

surely (certainly) በርግጥ *bärgəṭ*
     surely! እንዴታ *əndeta*

surety ዋስ *was;* ዋስትና *wastənna*
     give surety አዋሰ *awasä*

surf የማዕበል ፡ አረፋ *yama'əbäl aräfa*

surface (n.) ገጽ *gäṣṣ*
     on the surface ላይ ፡ ላዩን *lay layun*

surgeon ቀዶ ፡ ጠጋኝ ፡ ሐኪም *qäddo ṭäggaň hakim*

surgery ቀዶ ፡ ጥገና *qäddo ṭəggäna;* ኦፐራሲዮን *operasiyon*

surmount (~ obstacles) ተወጣ *täwäṭṭa;* (of a mountain) በከፍታ ፡ በለጠ *bäkäffəta bälläṭä*

surname የመጫረሻ ፡ ስም *yämäčärräša səm*

surpass በለጠ *bälläṭä;* ላቀ *laqä*

surplus ትርፍ ፡ እቃ tərf əqa; የተረፈ yä-tärräfä

surprise, vt. (cause astonishment) አስደ ነቀ asdännäqä; አስገረመ asgärrämä; (come upon unexpectedly) ደረሰ(በት) därräsä(bbät)
be surprised ተደነቀ tädännäqä; ገረመ (ው) gärrämä(w)

surprise, n. (feeling of surprise) የመደ ነቅ ፡ ስሜት yämäddänäq səmmet; (something unexpected) ያላሰበው ፡ ነገር yalassäbäw nägär
by surprise በድንገት bädəngät
to my surprise ይገርምህ ፡ ብሎ yəgrä-məh bəlo

surprising የሚደንቅ yämmiddännäq

surrender, vt. (~ arms) አስረከበ asräk-käbä
surrender (vi.) እጅ ፡ ሰጠ əǧǧ säṭṭä

surrender (n.) እጅ ፡ መስጠት əǧǧ mästät

surreptitious ስውር səwwər

surround ከበበ käbbäbä

surrounding (adj.) ባካባቢ ፡ ያለ bakka-babi yallä

surroundings አካባቢ akkababi

surveillance መቆጣጠር mäqqʷäṭaṭär

survey, v. (~ the situation) ጠቃቀሰ ṭä-qaqqäsä; (~ land) ቀየሰ qäyyäsä

survey (n.) ጥናት ṭənat; (of land) ቅየሳ qəyyäsa

surveyor ቀያሽ qäyyaš

survival (act of surviving) መትረፍ mät-räf; (thing that survived) ርዝራዥ rə-zərraž

survive (outlive) ተረፈ tärräfä; ዳነ danä; (continue to be) ዛሬም ፡ አለ zaremm alä

suspect (v.) ጠረጠረ ṭäräṭṭärä; (think likely) ገመተ gämmätä

suspect (n.) ተጠርጣሪ täṭärṭari

suspend (~ a lamp) አንጠለጠለ anṭäläṭ-ṭälä; (~ judgment) አዘገየ azägäyyä;

(~ payment) ላጊዜው ፡ አቆመ lägizew aqomä

suspenders ማንጠፍ mangäča

suspicion ጥርጣሬ ṭəräṭṭare
have a suspicion ጠረጠረ ṭäräṭṭärä
arouse suspicion አጠራጠረ aṭṭäraṭṭä-rä; ጥርጣሬ ፡ አሳደረ(በት) ṭəräṭṭare asad-därä(bbät)

suspicious (inclined to distrust) ተጠራ ጣሪ täṭäraṭari; (open to distrust) አጠ ራጣሪ aṭṭäraṭari

sustain (support) ደገፈ däggäfä; (~ the weight) ተሸከመ täšäkkämä; (~ in-juries) ደረሰ(በት) därräsä(bbät)

sustenance ምግብ məgəb; እህል ፡ ውሃ əhəl wəha

swaddle በጨርቅ ፡ ጠቀለለ bäčärq ṭäqäl-lälä

swagger ተንጉራደደ tängʷäraddädä

swallow (vt.) ዋጠ waṭä

swamp (v.) ዋጠ wäṭä
be swamped with work ሥራ ፡ ተጫ ነ(ው) səra täčanä(w)

swamp (n.) ረግረግ rägräg

swampy የረግረግ yärägräg

swarm (vt.) ሞላ molla
swarm (vi.) ጐረፈ gʷärräfä
swarm in ገር ፡ ብሎ ፡ ገባ gärr bəlo gäbba

swarm (n.) ጭፍራ čəfra; መንጋ mänga
swarms of ብዙ bəzu

sway, vt. (shake) አወዛወዘ awwäzaw-wäzä; (influence, move) ማረከ marräkä
sway (vi.) ተወዛወዘ täwäzawwäzä; (lean to one side) አጋደለ agaddälä
be swayed ተሳበ täsabä; ስሜት ፡ ተለ ወጠ səmmet täläwwäṭä

swear (v.) ማለ malä; (use bad words) ተራገመ täraggämä

sweat (v.) አላበ(ው) alabä(w); ወዛ wäzza

sweat (n.) ላብ lab; ወዝ wäz

sweater ሹራብ šurrab

sweep (vt.) ጠረገ *ṭärrägä*
sweep away ጠርጎ ፡ ወሰደ *ṭärgo wässädä*

sweepings ጥራጊ *ṭərragi*

sweet (~tea) ስኳር ፡ ያለበት *səkkʷar yalläbbät;* (~ girl) ደስ ፡ የምትል *däss yämmətəl*
be (taste) sweet ጣፈጠ *ṭaffäṭä*

sweet(s) ከረሜላ *kärämella;* ጣፋጭ *ṭafač*

sweeten አጣፈጠ *aṭaffäṭä*
sweeten with sugar ስኳር ፡ ጨመረ *səkkʷar čämmärä*

sweetheart የከንፈር ፡ ወዳጅ *yäkänfär wädaǧ*

swell (vi.) አበጠ *abbäṭä;* (of river) ሞላ *molla*

swelling እብጠት *əbṭät;* እባጭ *əbbač*

swerve ዞር ፡ አደረገ *zorr adärrägä*

swift ቀልጣፋ *qälṭaffa;* ፈጣን *fäṭṭan*

swiftly በፍጥነት *bäfəṭnät*

swim (v.) ዋኘ *waňňä*

swim (n.) ዋና *wana*

swimmer ዋናተኛ *wanatäňňa*

swimming (n.) ዋና *wana*

swimming pool መዋኛ *mäwaňňa;* የመዋኛ ፡ ስፍራ *yämäwaňňa səfra*

swimsuit የዋና ፡ ልብስ *yäwana ləbs*

swindle (v.) አጭበረበረ *ačbäräbbärä;* አታለለ *attallälä*

swindler ቀጣፊ *qäṭafi;* አታላይ *attalay;* አጭበርባሪ *ačbärbari*

swine አሳማ *asama*

swing (vt.) አወዛወዘ *awwäzawwäzä*
swing, vi. (of pendulum) ተወዛወዘ *täwäzawwäzä;* (on a swing) ጅውጅው ፡ ተጫወተ *ǧəwǧəw täčawwätä*

swing (n.) ጅውጅው *ǧəwǧəw*
be in full swing (of market) ደራ *därra*

swirl ተጥመለመለ *täṭmälämmälä*

switch, v. (whip lightly) ገረረፈ *gärarräfä;* (change) ለወጠ *läwwäṭä;* (exchange) ለዋወጠ *läwawwäṭä*
switch off አጠፋ *aṭäffa*
switch on አበራ *abärra*

switch, n. (of electricity) ማብሪያ ፡ ማጥፊያ *mabriya maṭfiya;* (shoot of tree used as whip) አርጩሜ *arčumme*

swivel ተሽከረከረ *täškäräkkärä*

swollen (~ river) የሞላ *yämolla;* (~ cheek) ያበጠ *yabbäṭä*
be swollen አበጠ *abbäṭä;* (river) ሞላ *molla*

sword ሰይፍ *säyf;* ጎራዴ *gʷärade*

sycamore ወርካ *wärka;* ዋርካ *warka*

syllable ክፍለ ፡ ቃል *kəflä qal*

syllabus ሥርዓተ ፡ ትምህርት *sər'atä təmhərt*

symbol ምሳሌ *məssale;* (in writing) ምልክት *mələkkət*

symbolize ምሳሌ ፡ ነው *məssale näw*

symmetrical ተመዛዣኝ *tämäzazaň*

sympathetic ርኅሩኅ *rəhruh*
be sympathetic to ደገፈ *däggäfä;* ተቀበለ *täqäbbälä*

sympathize (be in agreement) ደገፈ *däggäfä;* (feel compassion) አዘነ(ለት) *azzänä(llät)*

sympathy (a sharing of another's feelings) የሐዘን ፡ ተካፋይ ፡ መሆን *yähazän täkafay mähon*
feel sympathy for አዘነ(ለት) *azzänä(llät)*

symptom ምልክት *mələkkət*

synagogue ምኵራብ *mäkʷrab*

syndicate ማኅበር *mahbär*

synonym ተመሳሳይ *tämäsasay*

syntax አገባብ *aggäbab*

synthetic ሰው ፡ ሠራሽ *säw särraš*

syphilis ቂጥኝ *qiṭṭəň*

syrup ሹሮጥ *šurop*

system ዘዴ zäde; ሥርዓት sər'at

systematic ሥርዓት ፡ ያለው sər'at yalläw

systematize ሥርዓት ፡ አወጣ sər'at awäṭṭa

T

table ጠረጴዛ ṭäräppeza; ገበታ gäbäta
table of contents የመጽሐፍ ፡ ማውጫ yämaṣhaf mawça

tablecloth የጠረጴዛ ፡ ልብስ yäṭäräppeza ləbs

tablespoon የሾርባ ፡ ማንኪያ yäšorba mankiya

tablet ሰሌዳ säleda; (of aspirin) እንክብል ənkəbəll

tableware የገበታ ፡ እቃ yägäbäta əqa

taboo እርም ərm

taciturn ዝምተኛ zəmmətäñña; ጭምት čəmmət

tack, v. (attach) አያያዝ ayyayazä

tackle (~ a problem) ሠራ särra; (seize and throw down) ጠልፎ ፡ ጣለ ṭälfo ṭalä

tact ብልሃት bəlhat

tactics ዘዴ zäde; ስልት səlt; (military ~) የጦር ፡ ስልት yäṭor səlt

tactless ብልሃት ፡ የጐደለው bəlhat yägʷäddäläw

tail (n.) ጭራት ǧərat

tailor ልብስ ፡ ሰፊ ləbs säfi; ሰፊ säfi

take ወሰደ wässädä; (lead) አደረሰ adärräsä; (~ time) ፈጀ fäǧǧä; (~ patience) ጠየቀ ṭäyyäqä; (~ photos) አነሣ anässa; (~ advice) ሰማ sämma; (~ medicine) ዋጠ waṭä; (stand, endure) ታገሠ taggäsä
take! እንካ ənka

take apart አወላለቀ awälalläqä
take away ወሰደ wässädä
take back መለሰ mälläsä
take down አወረደ awärrädä
take in (earn) አገኘ agäññä
take off (~ a coat) አወለቀ awälläqä
take out አወጣ awäṭṭa
take over ተረከበ täräkkäbä; በጃ ፡ አደረገ bäǧǧu adärrägä

tale ታሪክ tarik

talebearer ወሬኛ ፡ ሰው wäreñña säw

talent ተሰጥዎ täsäṭwo

talented ተሰጥዎ ፡ ያለው täsäṭwo yalläw

talisman ከታብ kətab

talk (v.) ተናገረ tänaggärä; ተነጋገረ tänägaggärä; (converse) አወራ awärra; አወጋ awägga
talk back መልስ ፡ ሰጠ mäls säṭṭä
talk one into አግባባ agbabba
talk up በግልጽ ፡ ተናገረ bägəlṣ tänaggärä

talk (n.) ንግግር nəgəggər; (conversation) ጭውውት čəwəwwət; (rumor) ወሬ wäre
deliver (give) a talk ንግግር ፡ አደረገ nəgəggər adärrägä

talkative ለፍላፊ läflafi

tall ረዝም räžžim; ረዥም räǧǧim

tame (v.) ገራ gärra; ለማዳ ፡ አደረገ lämmada adärrägä

tame (adj.) ለማዳ lämmada; ገር gär

tan, vt. (~hide) አለፋ aläffa; ፋቀ faqä
tan, vi. (become brown) ጠቈረ ṭäqʷärä

tangerine መንደሪን mändärin

tangle, v. (~knot) ወሰሰበ wäsassäbä; አመሳቀለ ammäsaqqälä

tank (container for liquids) በርሚል bärmil; (armored vehicle) ታንክ tank

tanker ጫኝ ፡ መርከብ čaň märkäb

tanner ፋቂ faqi

tap (v.) መታ ፡ መታ ፡ አደረገ mäta mäta adärrägä

tape, v. (bind with a band) በማጣበቂያ፥ አያያዘ bämaṭṭabäqiya ayyayazä; (record) በቴፕ ፥ ቀዳ bätep qädda

tape, n. (for a wound) የቁስል ፥ መለጠ ፊያ yäqusəl mäläṭṭäfiya; (magneti ~) ቴፕ tep

tapestry ስጋፃ səgaǧǧa

tapeworm ኮሶ koso

tar (n.) ሬንዥ renž; ቅጥራን qəṭran; ዝፍት zəft

tardy ዳተኛ datäñña; ዘግይቶ ፥ የመጣ zägəyto yämäṭṭa

target (aim) ኢላማ ilama; (purpose) ዓላማ alama

tariff ቀረጥ qäräṭ

tarry (delay) ዘገየ zägäyyä

task ሥራ səra; ተግባር tägbar; ሙያ muya

taste (v.) ቀመሰ qämmäsä
taste good ጣመ ṭamä; ጣፈጠ ṭaffäṭä

taste, n. (sense by which flavor is perceived) የማጣጣም ፥ ችሎታ yämaṭaṭam čəlota; (flavor) ጣም ṭam; ጣዕም ṭa'əm; (liking) ፍላጎት fəllagot

tasteless ጣዕም ፥ ቢስ ṭa'əmä bis

tasty ጣዕም ፥ ያለው ṭa'əm yalläw
be tasty ጣመ ṭamä; ጣፈጠ ṭaffäṭä

tatters ቡትቱ butətto

tattle, ~ on አሳበቀ assabbäqä

tattletale አሳባቂ assabaqi

tattoo (v.) ነቀሰ näqqäsä

tattoo (n.) ንቅሳት nəqqəsat

taut, be (rope) ከረረ kärrärä; ተወጠረ täwäṭṭärä

tavern መሸታ ፥ ቤት mäšäta bet; መጠጥ፥ ቤት mäṭäṭṭ bet

tax (v.) ቀረጠ qärräṭä

tax (n.) ቀረጥ qäräṭ; ግብር gəbər
pay tax ገበረ gäbbärä

taxation ቀረጥ qäräṭ

tax collector ቀረጥ ፥ ተቀባይ qäräṭ täqäbbay

taxi ታክሲ taksi

tea ሻይ šay

teach አስተማረ astämarä

teacher አስተማሪ astämari

teaching መምህርነት mämhərənnät; አስተማሪነት astämarinnät

teacup የሻይ ፥ ሲኒ yäšay sini

teakettle የሻይ ፥ ጀበና yäšay ǧäbäna

team ቡድን budən; (of oxen) ጥምድ ṭəmmad

teapot የሻይ ፥ ጀበና yäšay ǧäbäna

tear (vt.) ቀደደ qäddädä; በጨቀ boččäqä
tear (vi.) ተቀደደ täqäddädä
tear down አፈረሰ afärräsä
tear off ገነጠለ gänäṭṭälä; ነጨ näččä

tear, n. (something torn) ቀዳዳ qädada

tear, n. (of eyes) እንባ ənba

tear gas የሚያስለቅስ ፥ ጢስ yämmiyasläqqəs ṭis

tease አሾፈ ašofä; አቃለደ aqallädä

teaspoon የሻይ ፥ ማንኪያ yäšay mankiya

teat የጡት ፥ ጫፍ yäṭut čaf

technician ቴክኒሺያን teknišiyan

technique ቴክኒክ teknik

tedious, be ሰለቸ säläččä

teem ተሞላ tämolla

teethe ጥርስ ፥ አወጣ ṭərs awäṭṭa

telegram ቴሌግራም telegram

telegraph (v.) ቴሌግራም ፥ አደረገ telegram adärrägä

telephone (v.) ደወለ däwwälä

telephone (n.) ስልክ səlk
telephone operator ስልከኛ səlkäñña; ማዞሪያ mazoriya

tell ነገረ näggärä; ተናገረ tänaggärä; (know, recognize) አወቀ awwäqä
tell apart ለይቶ ፥ አወቀ läyyəto awwäqä

tell on አሳበቀ assabbäqä

teller (in bank) ገንዘብ ፡ ከፋይ gänzäb käfay

temerity ደፋርነት däffarənnät

temper (mood) ጠባይ ṭäbay; (rage) ንዴት nəddet
be in a bad temper ተበሳጨ täbäsaččä
fly into a temper በንዴት ፡ ጦፈ bänəddet ṭofä
lose one's temper ተናደደ tänaddädä

temperament ባሕሪይ bahriy; ጠባይ ṭäbay

temperamental ግልፍተኛ gəlləftäňňa

temperate (~climate) መካከለኛ mäkakkäläňňa; ወይና ፡ ደጋ wäyna däga

temperature ያየር ፡ ሁኔታ yayyär huneta; (fever) ትኩሳት təkkusat

temple ቤት ፡ መቅደስ betä mäqdäs

temporal ዓለማዊ alämawi

temporarily ለጊዜው lägizew

tempt ፈታተነ fätattänä; (persuade) ነፋፈ gäfaffa; (make desire) አስጎመጀ asgʷämäǧǧä

temptation ፈተና fätäna

tempting, be አጓጓ agʷaggʷa

ten ዐሥር assər
ten o'clock አራት ፡ ሰዓት aratt säat

tenacious ጥብቅ ṭəbq

tenacity ጽናት ṣənat

tenant ተከራይ täkäray

tenant farmer ገባር gäbbar; ጭሰኛ čəsäňňa

tend (vt.) ጠበቀ ṭäbbäqä
tend, vi. (be inclined to) ዝንባሌ ፡ አለው zənəbbale alläw

tendency ዝንባሌ zənəbbale

tender, n. (bid) ጨረታ čäräta

tender (adj.) ለስላሳ läslassa; (~leaf) ለምለም lämläm; (~words) የለዘበ yäläzzäbä; (~skin) በቀላሉ ፡ የሚቄጣ bäqällalu yämmiqqʷäṭṭa

tenderhearted ርኅሩኅ rəhruh

tendon ሥር sər; ጅማት ǧəmmat

tense (n.) ጊዜያት gizeyat

tense, adj. (person) የመንፈስ ፡ ጭንቀት ፡ ያለበት yämänfäs čänqät yalläbbät

tension (stretching) መወጠር mäwäṭṭär; (friction) አለመግባባት alämägbabat; (strain) የመንፈስ ፡ ጭንቀት yämänfäs čänqät

tent ድንኳን dənkʷan

tentative ለሙከራ ፡ ያህል ፡ የተደረገ lämukkära yahəl yätädärrägä

tenth ዐሥረኛ asräňňa

tenure ይዞታ yəzota

tepid ለብ ፡ ያለ läbb yalä
be tepid ለብ ፡ አለ läbb alä

term (expression) ቃል qal; (period of time in school) የትምህርት ፡ ወቅት yätəmhərt wäqt; (condition) ውል wəl
be on bad terms ተጣሉ täṭallu
come to terms ተስማሙ täsmammu

terminal, n. (station) ጣቢያ ṭabiya

terminal (adj.) የመጫረሻ yämäčärräša

terminate (vt.) አቋረጠ aqqʷarräṭä; ጨረሰ čärräsä
terminate (vi.) አበቃ abäqqa; አለቀ alläqä

terminus (of bus) ተራ tära; መጫረሻ ፡ ጣቢያ mäčärräša ṭabiya

termite ምሥጥ misṭ; ምስጥ məsṭ

terrace በረንዳ bärända

terrain መሬት märet

terrestrial የመሬት yämäret; ምድራዊ mədrawi

terrible (severe) ኅይለኛ hayläňňa; (bad) መጥፎ mäṭfo; (distressing) በጣም ፡ የሚያሳ g bäṭam yämmiyasäga

terrific ኅይለኛ hayläňňa

terrify አስደነገጠ asdänäggäṭä; አስፈራ asfärra

territory (large area of land) አገር agär; (land under the jurisdiction of a sovereign state) ግዛት gəzat

terror ሽብር šäbbär; ፍርሃት färhat
have a ~ of ፈራ färra

terrorist ዐመፅኛ amäṣäňňa

terrorize አሸበረ aššäbbärä

test (v.) ሞከረ mokkärä; ፈተነ fättänä

test, n. (exam) ፈተና fätäna; (trial) ሙ-
ከራ mukkära

testament ኑዛዜ nuzaze

testicle የብልት : ፍሬ yäbəllət färe

testify መሰከረ mäsäkkärä

testimony የምስክርነት : ቃል yämǝsäk-
kärǝnnät qal; (evidence) ማስረጃ masräğğa

text ጽሑፍ ṣǝhuf; (of a document)
ቃል qal

textbook የመማሪያ : መጽሐፍ yämämmariya mäṣhaf; ማስተማሪያ : መጽሐፍ
mastämariya mäšhaf

textiles ጨርቃ : ጨርቅ čärqa čärq

than ከ kä

thank (v.) አመሰገነ amäsäggänä
thank you! እግዚር : ይመስገን əgzer
yämmäsgän; እግዚር : ይስጥልኝ əgzer
yǝsṭǝlläňň

thankful, be ባለ : ውለታው : ነው balä
wǝlätaw näw

thankless ውለታ : ቢስ wǝläta bis

thanks ምስጋና mǝsgana
thanks to ዕድሜ : ለሱ ǝdme lässu;
በ - - - ምክንያት bä - - - mǝknǝyat

that, adj., pron. (masc.) ያ ya; (fem.)
ያች yačč
that (relative) የ yä + perfect; የም
yämmǝ- (or እም ǝmmǝ-) + imperfect
that (conj.) እንደ ǝndä + perfect or
relative imperfect
that much ያን : ያህል yan yahǝl
that one (masc.) ያኛው yaňňaw; (fem.)
ያች yačč

thatch (v.) ከደነ käddänä

thatch (n.) ከዳን kǝdan

thaw (vt.) አቀለጠ aqälläṭä

thaw, vi. (melt) ሟሟ mʷammʷa

the, masc. -u (after consonant), -w (after vowel); fem. -ዋ -wa, -itu, -itwa

theater ቲያትር tiyatǝr

theft ሌብነት lebǝnnät; ስርቆት sǝrqot

their የነሱ yännässu; የነርሱ yännärsu;
or, object suffix pronoun -አቸው -aččäw

theirs, see 'their'

them እነሱን ǝnnässun; -አቸው -aččäw

theme መልእክት mäl'ǝkt; አርእስት ar'ǝst

themselves ራሳቸው rasaččäw

then (adv.) ቀጥሎ qäṭṭǝlo; ያን : ጊዜ yan
gize; ያኔ yanne; (after that) ከዚያ :
በኋላ käzziya bähʷala
then and there ወዲያው wädiyaw
by then ያኔ yanne
from then on ከዚያን : ጊዜ : ወዲህ käz-
ziyan gize wädih

thence (from that place) ከዚያ käzziya;
(from that time) ከ - - - ወዲህ kä - - -
wädih

thenceforth ከዚያ : ጊዜ : ወዲህ käzziya
gize wädih

theology መንፈሳዊ : ትምህርት mänfäsawi
tǝmhärt

theory ፅንሰ : ሐሳብ ṣǝnsä hassab; ኀልዮ
hallǝyo; ቴዎሪ tewori

there በዚያ bäzziya; እዚያ ǝzziya; እዛ
ǝzza; (on that matter) እዚህ : ላይ əzzih lay
there is አለ allä
there is not የለም yälläm
out there እዚያ ǝzziya
over there እዚያ ǝzziya; እዚያ : ጋ əzziya ga; እዚያ : ማዶ ǝzziya mado
toward there ወደዚያ wädäzziya

thereabouts, or ~ (close to that time)
ወደ wädä; ወይም : ወደዚያ wäyǝm wädäzziya; ጋደማ gädäma; (close to that
place) ወይም : በዚያ : አካባቢ wäyǝm
bäzziya akkababi

thereafter ከዚያ : ወዲህ käzziya wädih

therefore ስለዚህ sǝläzzih

therein እዚያ ፡ ውስጥ *əzziya wəsţ*

thereto ወደዚያ *wädäzziya*

thereupon (immediately after) ያኔ *yanne*

thermometer (for temperature) የትኩሳት ፡ መለኪያ *yätəkkusat mäläkkiya;* (for weather) ተርሞሜትር *tärmometər*

these እነዚህ *ənnäzzih*

they እነሱ *ənnässu;* እነርሱ *ənnärsu*

thick ወፍራም *wäfram;* (~line) ሰፊ *säffi;* (~forest) ጥቅጥቅ ፡ ያለ *ţəqţəqq yalä*
be thick ወፈረ *wäffärä*

thicken (vt.) አወፈረ *awäffärä*
thicken (vi.) ወፈረ *wäffärä*

thicket ጥሻ *ţəša*

thickly ጥቅጥቅ ፡ ብሎ *ţəqţəqq bəlo*

thickness ውፍረት *wəfrät*

thief ሌባ *leba*

thigh ጭን *čən;* ታፋ *tafa*

thin (adj.) ስስ *səs;* ረቂቅ *räqiq;* (~ribbon, man, sauce) ቀጭን *qäččən;* (~crowd) ጥቂት *ţəqit*
be thin ሳሳ *sassa;* ቀጠነ *qäţţänä*
get thin ከሳ *kässa*

thing ነገር *nägär*
things (personal belongings) ጓዝ *g^waz*
among other things በተጨማሪ *bätäčämmari*
not a thing አንድም ፡ ነገር *andəm nägär* +negative verb

think አሰበ *assäbä;* (believe) መሰለ(ው) *mässälä(w)*
think of (remember) ትዝ ፡ አለ(ው) *təzz alä(w)*

third ሦስተኛ *sostäňňa;* (~order of the Amharic alphabet) ሣልስ *saləs;* (of a king or historic person) ሣልሳዊ *salsawi*
a third ሢሶ *siso*
one-third ሦስትያ *sostəyya*

thirst ጥም *ţəm;* ጥማት *ţəmat*

thirsty የጠማ *yäţämma*

be thirsty ጠማ(ው) *ţämma(w)*

thirteen ዐሥራ ፡ ሦስት *asra sost*

thirty ሠላሳ *sälasa*

this (adj., pron.) masc. ይህ *yəh;* fem. ይህች *yəhəčč;* ይች *yäčč*
this much ይህን ፡ ይህል *yəhən yahəl*
this one ይህኛው *yəhəňňaw*

thong መጫኛ *mäčaňňa;* ማሰሪያ *masäriya*

thorn ሾህ *šoh;* ሾክ *šok;* አሾህ *əšoh*

thorny አሾህማ *əšohəmma*

thorough (profound) ጥልቅ *ţəlq;* (careful) ጥንቁቅ *ţənquq*

thoroughfare ዋና ፡ ጉዳና *wanna g^wädana*

thoroughly (carefully) በጥንቃቄ *bäţənəqqaqe;* (in detail) በዝርዝር *bäzərzər*

those (adj., pron.) እነዚያ *ənnäzziya*

though በ *bə* + imperfect + ቅሉ *qəlu*

thought ሐሳብ *hassab;* አሳብ *assab;* (way of thinking) አስተሳሰብ *astäsasäb*

thoughtful (serious) አስተዋይ *astäway;* (considerate of others) ደግ ፡ አሳቢ *dägg assabi*
be thoughtful አሰበ *assäbä*

thoughtless (rash) ግዴለሽ *gəddelläš;* (not thinking of others) ለሰው ፡ የማያስብ *läsäw yämmayassəb*

thousand ሺ *ši;* ሺህ *ših*

thrash ገረፈ *gärräfä;* መታ *mätta*

thread, v. (~ the needle) ከር ፡ አገባ *kərr agäbba;* (~beads) ሰካ *säkka*

thread (n.) ከር *kərr;* ፈትል *fätəl*

threadbare ያለቀ *yalläqä*

threat ዛቻ *začča;* (of war) ሥጋት *səgat*

threaten ዛተ *zatä;* አስፈራራ *asfärarra;* (be a cause of mishap to) አሰጋ *asägga*

three ሦስት *sost*
three o'clock ዘጠኝ ፡ ሰዓት *zäţäňň säat*

thresh ወቃ *wäqqa;* (with oxen) አሄደ *ahedä*

threshing floor አውድማ awdəmma;
ውድማ wədəmma

threshold መጋቢያ mäggabiya

thrifty ቈጣቢ qʷäṭṭabi
be thrifty ቈጠበ qʷäṭṭäbä

thrill (vt.) መንፈስ ፡ አነቃቃ mänfäs annäqaqqa; አስደነቀ asdännäqä
thrill (vi.) በደስታ ፡ ሰሜት ፡ ተነቃ bädässəta səmmet tänäqqa
be thrilled በደስታ ፡ ተዋጠ bädässəta
täwaṭä

thrill (n.) ጥልቅ ፡ የደስታ ፡ ስሜት ṭəlq yädässəta səmmet

thrive (of business) ዳበረ dabbärä; (of
children) ፋፋ faffa

throat ጉሮሮ gurorro

throb በንይል ፡ መታ bähayl mätta

throne ዙፋን zufan
assume the throne ነገሠ näggäsä
succeed to the throne አልጋውን ፡ ወረሰ
algawən wärräsä

throng የተሰበሰበ ፡ ሕዝብ yätäsäbässäbä
həzb

through (prep.) በ - - - በኩል bä - - - bäkkul; (because of) በ - - - ምክንያት
bä - - - məknəyat; (until) እስከ - - -
ድረስ əskä - - - dəräs
through, adv. (directly) በቀጥታ bäqäṭṭəta
through and through ጨርሶ čärrəso
all the way through ከዳር ፡ እስከ ፡ ዳር
kädar əskä dar

throughout (prep.) በ - - - ጊዜ ፡ ሁሉ bä
- - - gize hullu
throughout (adv.) ሙሉ ፡ በሙሉ mulu bämulu; በሙሉ bämulu; (everywhere) በየቦታው bäyyäbotaw; ከዳር ፡
እስከ ፡ ዳር kädar əskä dar

throw ወረወረ wäräwwärä; (bring to the
ground) ጣለ ṭalä
throw away ጣለ ṭalä
throw back ወደ ፡ ኋላ ፡ መለሰ wädä
hʷala mälläsä
throw down ጣለ ṭalä

throw out (discard) ጣለ ṭalä; (eject)
አስወጣ aswäṭṭa
throw up (vomit) አስመለሰ(ው) asmäl-
läsä(w); አስታወከ(ው) astawwäkä(w)

thrust (v.) ወጋ wägga

thumb አውራ ፡ ጣት awra ṭat

thumbtack የወረቀት ፡ ምስማር yäwäräqät
məsmar

thunder (v.) ነጐደ näggʷädä; ተንጐደጐደ
tängʷädäggʷädä; አጐረመረመ agʷrämärrämä

thunder (n.) ነጐድጓድ nägʷädgʷad

thunderbolt መብረቅ mäbräq; ብራቅ bəraq

thunderstorm ነጐድጓድ nägʷädgʷad

Thursday ሐሙስ hamus; አሙስ amus

thus እንዲ əndih; እንዲሁ əndihu; እንዲ
ህም əndihəm; እንደዚህ əndäzzih
thus far እስካሁን əskahun; እዚህ ፡ ድ
ረስ əzzih däräs

tick, n. (cattle tick) መዥገር mäžgär

ticket ቲኬት tiket; (summons) መጥሪያ
mäṭriya
ticket office ቲኬት ፡ መሸጫ tiket mäšäča
ticket seller ቲኬት ፡ ቄራጭ tiket qʷärač
buy tickets ቲኬት ፡ አስቄረጠ tiket
asqʷärräṭä
sell tickets ቲኬት ፡ ቄረጠ tiket qʷärräṭä

tickle ኰረከመ kʷäräkkʷärä

ticklish (risky to handle) አስቸጋሪ asčäggari
be ticklish (feet) ሰቀጠጠ säqäṭṭäṭä

tide ሞገድ mogäd; ማዕበል ma'əbäl
at high tide ማዕበል ፡ ሲነሣ ma'əbäl
sinnässa
at low tide ባሕሩ ፡ ጸጥ ፡ ሲል bahru
ṣäṭṭ sil

tidings ወሬ wäre
glad tidings የምስራች yäməssərač

tidy (v.) አጸዳዳ aṣṣädadda

tidy (adj.) ንጹሕ *nəṣuh*

tie (v.) አሰረ *assärä;* ቀየደ *qäyyädä*
be tied (fastened) ታሰረ *tassärä;*
(make the same score) እኩል ፡ ለኩል ፡
ተለያዩ *əkkul läkkul täläyayyu*

tie, n. (necktie) ክራቫት *kravat;* (connection) ግንኙነት *gənəňňunnät*

tiger ነብር *näbər*

tight (adj.) ጥብቅ *ṭəbq;* (∼shoes) ጠባብ
ṭäbbab; (∼ situation) አስጊ *asgi;* የሚ
ያስጨንቅ *yämmiyasčännəq*
be tight ጠበበ *ṭäbbäbä;* ጠበቀ *ṭäbbäqä*

tight (adv.) በጥብቅ *bäṭəbq;* በጎይል *bähayl*

tighten አጠበቀ *aṭäbbäqä*

tight-fisted ጨቅ *čuq*

tile ጡብ *ṭub*

till (v.) አረሰ *arräsä*

till (prep.) እስከ *əskä;* እስከ *əskä* +noun
+ድረስ *dəräs*

tiller አራሽ *araš*

tilt (vt.) አዘነበለ *azänäbbälä*
tilt (vi.) አጋደለ *agaddälä*

timber ዕንጨት *ənčät*

time (n.) ጊዜ *gize;* ወቅት *wäqt;* (hour,
minutes by the clock) ሰዓት *sä'at*
time after time ደጋግሞ *dägagmo*
time and again መላልሶ *mälalso;* ደጋ
ግሞ *dägagmo*
all the time ሁልጊዜ *hulgize;* ዘወትር
zäwätər
at all times በማንኛውም ፡ ጊዜ *bäman-
nəňňawəm gize*
at any time ምንጊዜም *məngizem*
at one time (earlier) ድሮ *dəro;* (together) ባንድ ፡ ጊዜ *band gize*
at the same time አንድ ፡ ላይ *and lay*
at times አንዳንዴ *andande*
(be) behind the time ወደ ፡ ኋላ ፡ ቀረ
wädä hʷala qärrä
by the time በ *bä* + verb + ጊዜ *gize*
every time ሁልጊዜ *hulgize*
for the time being ለጊዜው *lägizew*

from time to time በየሰዓቱ *bäyyäsä-
atu;* በየጊዜው *bäyyägizew;* አልፎ ፡
አልፎ *alfo alfo*
in no time ባንዳፍታ *bandafta;* ከመቅ
ጽበት *kämäqəṣbät*
in olden times በቀድሞ ፡ ጊዜ *bäqädmo
gize*
on time በሰዓቱ *bäsä'atu;* በጊዜው *bägizew*

timely ከጊዜ ፡ ጋር ፡ ተስማሚ *kägize gar
täsmami*

timetable ፕሮግራም *program;* የጊዜ ፡
ሰሌዳ *yägize säleda*

timid (∼person) ዓይን ፡ አፋር *ayn affar;*
ፈሪ *färi;* (∼animal) ድንጉጥ *dənguṭ*

timidity ፍርሃት *fərhat*

timorous ፈሪ *färi*

tin ቆርቆሮ *qorqorro*

tin can ቆርቆሮ *qorqorro;* ታኒካ *tanika;*
ጣሳ *ṭasa*

tinder እሳት ፡ ማቀጣጠያ *əsat maqqäṭaṭäya*

tinkle ተንቃጨለ *tänqaččälä*

tiny በጣም ፡ ትንሽ *bäṭam tənnäš;* ጥቃ
ቅን *ṭəqaqən*

tip, v. (tilt) አጋደለ *agaddälä;* (give a
small fee for services) ጉርሻ ፡ ሰጠ *gurša sättä*
tip off (give secret information) ሹክ ፡
አለ *šukk alä;* ጠቆመ *ṭäqqʷämä*
tip over (vt.) ደፋ *däffa*
tip over (vi.) ተገለበጠ *tägäläbbäṭä*

tip, n. (point) ጫፍ *čaf;* (a bit of helpful information) ሹክ *šuk;* ጠቃሚ ፡
ወሬ *ṭäqami wäre;* (money given for
services) ጉርሻ *gurša*

tiptoe በእግር ፡ ጣት ፡ ሂደ *bä'əgər ṭat hedä*

tire (vt.) አደከመ *adäkkämä*
tire (vi.) ደከመ *däkkämä*
tire out አለፋ *aläffa*

tire (n.) ጎማ *gomma*

tired (adj.) ደካማ *däkkama*

be tired, get tired ደከመ *däkkämä;* ደከመ(ው) *däkkämä(w)*
grow tired ላፋ *läffa*
be tired of ሰለቸ(ው) *säläččä(w)*

tireless (~worker) የማይታክት *yämmayətakkət;* (~effort) ያልተቋጠበ *yaltäqʷäṭṭäbä*

tiresome አድካሚ *adkami;* (boring) አሰልቺ *asälči*

tithe ዐሥራት *asrat*

title, n. (name of book) አርእስት *ar'əst;* ስም *səm;* (rank) ማዕረግ *ma'əräg;* (right of ownership) መብት *mäbt*

to (toward) ወደ *wädä;* (for) ለ *lä;* (until) እስከ *əskä*

toad ጉርጥ *gurṭ*

toast, v. (brown by heating) ጠበሰ *ṭäbbäsä;* (drink in honor of) ስለ ፡ ጤንነት ፡ ጠጣ *səlä ṭenənnät ṭäṭṭa*

toast, n. (toasted) ጥብስ *ṭəbs*

toaster መጥበሻ *mäṭbäša*

tobacco ትምባሆ *təmbaho*

today ዛሬ *zare;* (in these times) ባሁኑ ፡ ጊዜ *bahunu gize*

toe የእግር ፡ ጣት *yägər ṭat*

together አንድ ፡ ላይ *and lay;* አንድ ፡ ጋ *and ga;* አብሮ *abro;* የሰብሰብ *yäsäbsäb*
together with ከ - - - ጋራ ፡ (ጋር) *kä - - - gara (gar)*

toil (v.) ላፋ *läffa;* ጣረ *ṭarä*

toil (n.) ልፋት *ləfat;* ብርቱ ፡ ሥራ *bərtu səra*

toilet ሽንት ፡ ቤት *šənt bet*

toilet articles መኳኳያ *mäkkʷakʷaya*

tolerance መታገሥ *mättagäs;* ቻይነት *čayənnät*

tolerant ቻይ *čay*

tolerate (endure, put up with) ታገሠ *taggäsä*

toll, n. (tax or fee) የኬላ ፡ ቀረጥ *yäkella qäräṭ;* (loss in number) ጉዳት *gudat*

toll station ኬላ *kella*

tomato ቲማቲም *timatim*

tomb መቃብር *mäqabər*

tombstone የመቃብር ፡ ድንጋይ *yämäqabər dəngay*

tomorrow ነገ *nägä*
the day after tomorrow ከነገ ፡ ወዲያ *känägä wädiya*

tone (of an instrument) ቃና *qana;* (voice) ድምፅ *dəmṣ;* ቃል *qal*

tongs መቄንጣጫ *mäqʷänṭäča*

tongue (organ in the mouth) ምላስ *məlas;* (language) ቋንቋ *qʷanqʷa*
native tongue የናት ፡ ቋንቋ *yännat qʷanqʷa*

tonight ዛሬ ፡ ማታ *zare mata*

tonsil እንጣል *ənṭəl*

too (very) በጣም *bäṭam;* (also) -ም *-m*
too long ብዙ *bəzu*
too much ከመጠን ፡ በላይ *kämäṭän bälay*

tool መሣሪያ *mässariya*

tooth ጥርስ *ṭərs*

toothache የጥርስ ፡ ሕመም *yäṭərs həmäm*

toothbrush የጥርስ ፡ ብሩሽ *yäṭərs bruš*

toothpaste የጥርስ ፡ ሳሙና *yäṭərs samuna*

top, v. (cover the top) ሸፈነ *šäffänä;* (be at the head of) አንደኛ ፡ ወጣ *andäñña wäṭṭa;* (excel) በለጠ *bälläṭä*

top, n. (summit) ራስ *ras;* ጫፍ *čaf;* (cover) ከዳን *kədan;* (child's toy) ጆልቦ *ǧälbo*
from top to bottom ከላይ ፡ እስከ ፡ ታች *kälay əskä tačč*
on top ከላይ *kälay*
on top of በ - - - ላይ *bä - - - lay*

top, adj. (~drawer) ላይኛ *layəñña;* (~speed) ከፍተኛ *käffətäñña;* (~student) ጉብዝ *gʷäbäz*

topic አርእስት *ar'əst*

topple (~a tree) ገነደሰ *gänäddäsä;* (~

an opponent in a fight) ዘረረ zärrärä;
ጣለ ṭalä

torch ችቦ čəbbo

torment (v.) አሠቃየ assäqayyä; (annoy)
አስቸገረ asčäggärä

torment (n.) ሥቃይ səqay

tornado ጎበለኛ ፡ ቧይት hayläňňa bʷayt;
ዓውሎ ፡ ነፋስ awlo näfas

torpid, be ፍዝዝ ፡ አለ fəzəzz alä

torrent ጎርፍ gʷärf; ወራጅ ፡ ውኃ wäraǧ
wəha

torrential ኃይለኛ hayläňňa

torrid በጣም ፡ ሞቃት bäṭam moqqat

tortoise ኤሊ eli

tortuous (~ road) ጠምዛዛ ṭämzazza;
(~reasoning) ጠማማ ṭämama

torture (v.) አሠቃየ assäqayyä

torture, n. (pain) ሥቃይ səqay

toss (throw) ጣለ ፡ አደረጋ ṭall adärrägä;
(cause to roll back and forth) አንገ
ላታ angälatta
toss a coin ዕጣ ፡ አወጣ əṭa awäṭṭa
toss away ወረወረ wäräwwärä

total, v. (amount to) ጠቅላላ ፡ ቁጥራቸው ፡
ነበረ ṭäqlalla quṭraččäw näbbärä;
(add up) ደመረ dämmärä

total (n.) ድምር dəmmər
grand total ጠቅላላ ፡ ድምር ṭäqlalla
dəmmər

total (adj.) ጠቅላላ ṭäqlalla

totality ብዛት bəzat

totally በፍጹም bäfəṣṣum

totter ተንገዳገደ tängädaggädä

touch (vt.) ነካ näkka; (concern) ተመለ
ከተ tämäläkkätä; (mention) አነሣ
anässa; (move) ተሰማ täsämma

touch, n. (sense of touching) የመዳሰስ ፡
ችሎታ yämädasäs čəlota
a touch of ላመል lamäl; ጥቂት ṭəqit
be (get) in touch ግንኙነት ፡ ነበረው
gənäňňunnät näbbäräw; ተገናኘ tägänaňňä

touching (adj.) ልብ ፡ የሚነካ ləbb yämminäka

touching (prep.) ስለ sälä

touchy (~problem) የሚያስቄጣ yämmiyasqʷäṭṭa; የሚያበሳጭ yämmiyabbä-
saččə; (easily offended) ቁጡ quṭṭu; ግል
ፍተኛ gəlləftäňňa

tough (~skin) ጠንካራ ṭänkarra; (~
assignment) ከባድ käbbad; (~meat)
አንጆ anǧo; (~person) የማይበገር yämmayəbbäggär

tour (v.) ጎበኘ gʷäbäňňä; (walk around)
ዞረ zorä

tour (n.) ጉብኝት gubəňňät

tourist ቱሪስት turist; ጎብኚ gʷäbňi

tournament ውድድር wədəddər; ግጥሚያ
gəṭmiya

tow ጎተተ gʷättätä; ሳበ sabä
tow away ጎተቶ ፡ ወሰደ gʷättəto wässädä

toward ወደ wädä; በስተ bästä; (about)
ወደ - - - ገደማ wädä - - - gädäma

towards ወደ - - - ገደማ wädä- - - gädäma

towel ፎጣ foṭa

tower ግንብ gənb

town መንደር mändär

town hall የከተማ ፡ አዳራሽ yäkätäma addaraš

toy (n.) መጫወቻ mäččawäča; አሻንጉ
ሊት ašangullit

trace, v. (draw on transparent paper)
ነደፈ näddäfä; (find) ፈልጎ ፡ አገኘ fälləgo agäňňä

trace (n.) ምልክት mələkkət; (vestige)
ርዝራዥ rəzərraž; (footprint) ዱካ duka; ፈለግ fäläg; ፋና fana

track, n. (path) የእግር ፡ መንገድ yägər
mängäd; (footprint) ዱካ duka; ፈለግ
fäläg; ፋና fana
keep track of ተከታተለ täkätattälä

tractor የእርሻ ፡ መኪና yärša mäkina

trade (v.) ነገደ *näggädä;* (exchange)
ለወጠ *läwwäṭä;* ተለዋወጠ *täläwawwäṭä*

trade (n.) ንግድ *nəgd;* (craft) የእጅ፡ ሥራ
yäǧǧ səra

trade mark የንግድ፡ ምልክት *yänəgd mə-
läkkət*

trader ነጋዴ *näggade*

tradition (convention) ባህል *bahəl*

traditional የባህል *yäbahəl*

traffic (v.), ~in ነገደ *näggädä*

traffic, n. (business) ንግድ *nəgd;* (movement of vehicles) ትራፊክ *trafik;* የመ
ኪናዎች ፡ እንቅስቃሴ *yämäkinawočč
ənqəsəqqase*

traffic jam የመኪና ፡ መጨነቅ *yämäkina
mäččänäq*

tragedy (sad event) አሳዛኝ ፡ መከራ *asazzaň mäkära;* (a play) አሳዛኝ ፡ የሆነ ፡
ቲያትር *asazzaň yähonä tiyatər*

tragic አሳዛኝ *asazzaň*

trail, vt. (follow) ተከታተለ *täkätattälä;*
(pull along) ጐተተ *gʷättätä*
trail behind ኋላ ፡ ኋላ ፡ ሄደ *hʷala hʷala hedä*

trail, n. (path) የእግር ፡ መንገድ *yägər
mängäd;* (track, footprint) ዱካ *duka;*
ፈለግ *fäläg;* ፋና *fana*

train, vt. (educate) አስተማረ *astämarä;*
(give practice in some skill) አሠለጠነ
asäläṭṭänä
train (vi.) ልምምድ ፡ አደረገ *ləməmməd adärrägä*

train (n.) ባቡር *babur*

trained (adj.) የሠለጠነ *yäsäläṭṭänä*

trainer አሠልጣኝ *asälṭaň*

training ትምህርት *təmhərt;* (for some
sport) ማሠልጠን *masälṭän*

trait ባሕሪይ *bahriy*

traitor ከሐዲ *kähadi;* ከዳተኛ *käddatäňňa*

tramp (v.), ~on አራገጠ *arraggäṭä*

tramp (n.) በረንዳ ፡ አዳሪ *bärända adari;*
ዱሪዬ *durriyye*

trample ረገጠ *räggäṭä*

tranquil ጸጥ ፡ ያለ *ṣäṭṭ yalä*
be tranquil ጨመተ *čämmätä;* ጸጥ ፡
አለ *ṣäṭṭ alä*

tranquility ጸጥታ *ṣäṭṭəta*

transact ተገባያየ *tägäbäyayyä*

transaction መገባያየት *mäggäbäyayät*

transfer (vt.) አስተላለፈ *astälalläfä;* አዛ
ወረ *azzawwärä*
transfer (vi.) ተዛወረ *täzawwärä*

transfer (n.) ዝውውር *zəwəwwər*

transform ለወጠ *läwwäṭä*

transformer ኮረንቲ ፡ መለዋወጫ *korränti
mäläwawäča*

transgress (violate) ተላለፈ *tälalläfä;* ጣሰ
ṭasä

transgression መጣስ *mäṭas*

transient (~worker) ጊዜያዊ *gizeyawi*

transition መሸጋገር *mäššägagär*

transitional ጊዜያዊ *gizeyawi*

transitive (~verb) ተሻጋሪ *täšagari*

transitory ኃላፊ *halafi*

translate ተረጐመ *täräggʷämä*

translation ትርጓሜ *tərgʷame*

translator አስተርጓሚ *astärgʷami*

transmit አስተላለፈ *astälalläfä*

transparent ግልጽ *gəlṣ*

transplant (~plants) አዛውሮ ፡ ተከለ *az-
zawro täkkälä;* (~a heart) አዛወረ *azzawwärä*

transport (v.) አመላለሰ *ammälalläsä;* አጋ
ጋዘ *aggʷagʷazä*

transport, n. (ship) የሚያጋጉዝ ፡ መርከብ
yämmiyaggʷagʷəz märkäb; (carrying
of goods, soldiers) ማጋጋዝ *maggʷagʷaz*

transportation (carrying from one place
to another) ማጋጋዝ *maggʷagʷaz;*
(being carried) መጋጋዝ *mäggʷagʷaz*

trap (v.) አጠመደ aṭämmädä; (ambush) አድፍጦ ፡ ያዘ adfəṭo yazä

trap (n.) ወጥመድ wäṭmäd

trash (rubbish) ቆሻሻ qošaša; (worthless) የማይረባ ፡ እቃ yämmayəräba əqa

travel (v.) ተጓዘ tägʷazä
travel about ተዞዋወረ täzäwawwärä

travel (n.) ጉዞ guzo; መንገድ mängäd

traveler መንገደኛ mängädäňňa

traverse አቋረጠ aqqʷarräṭä; ተሻገረ tä-šaggärä

tray ማቅረቢያ maqräbiya; ዝርግ ፡ ሳሕን zərg sahən

treacherous ከዳተኛ käddatäňňa; (~ ground) አታላይ attalay

treachery ክሕደት kəhdät; ክሕዲነት kä-hadinnät; ከዳተኛነት käddatäňňannät

tread (vi.) ተራመደ tärammädä; ሄደ hedä

tread (n.) ኮቴ kotte; (of tire) ጥርስ ṭərs

treason ክሕደት kəhdät; ክሕዲነት kähadinnät

treasonable ከክሕደት ፡ የሚቈጠር käkəhdät yämmiqqʷäṭṭär

treasure (n.) ሀብት habt

treasurer ገንዘብ ፡ ቤት gänzäb bet; ገን ዘቢ ፡ ያዥ gänzäb yaž

treasury (place where funds are kept) ግምጃ ፡ ቤት gəmǧa bet; (funds) ተቀ ማጭ ፡ ገንዘብ täqämmač gänzäb

treat (v.) ያዘ yazä; (~ a customer) አስ ተናገደ astänaggädä; (help toward a cure) አከመ akkämä; (negotiate) ተና ገረ tänaggärä; (~ a subject) ተነተነ tänättänä
treat of ነክ ፡ የሆነ näkk yähonä
treat to (a meal) ጋበዘ gabbäzä

treat (n.) ግብዣ gəbža

treatise ድርሰት dərsät

treatment (manner of dealing) አያያዝ ayyayaz; ማስተዳደር mastädadär; (medical ~) ሕክምና häkmənna

treaty ውል wəl; ስምምነት səməmmən-nät; ቃል ፡ ኪዳን qal kidan

tree ዛፍ zaf

tremble ተንቀጠቀጠ tänqäṭäqqäṭä; ራደ radä; (of voice) ተርገበገበ tärgäbäg-gäbä

tremendous (~ speed) የሚያስገርም yäm-miyasgärrəm; (~ difference) ትልቅ təlləq

tremendously ያለ ፡ ቅጥ yalä qəṭṭ; በጣም bäṭam

trench (irrigation channel) ቦይ boy; (ditch as a protection for soldiers) የመ ከላከያ ፡ ጉድባ yämäkkälakäya gudba

trend አዝማሚያ azmamiya; ዝንባሌ zə-näbbale

trepidation, be filled with ~ ተርበተበተ tärbätäbbätä

trespass ጣሰ ṭasä; ተላለፈ tälalläfä

trial (judgment) ፍርድ fərd; (test) መኩ ራ mukkära; ፈተና fätäna
give a trial ሞከረ mokkärä

triangle ሦስት ፡ ማእዘን sost ma'əzän

triangular ባለ ፡ ሦስት ፡ ማእዘን balä sost ma'əzän

tribal የጐሳ yägʷäsa

tribalism የጐሳ ፡ ልዩነት yägʷäsa ləyyun-nät

tribe ነገድ nägäd; ጐሳ gʷäsa

tribulation መከራና ፡ ችግር mäkäranna čəggər

tribunal ችሎት čälot; ፍርድ ፡ ቤት fərd bet

tributary (of a river) ገባር ፡ ወንዝ gäbbar wänz

tribute (forced payment) ግብር gəbər
pay tribute (taxes) ገበረ gäbbärä; (to someone's memory) በክብር ፡ አስታወሰ bäkəbər astawwäsä

trick ተንኮል tänkʷäl; (skillful act) ትን ግርት təngərt

play tricks ተጫወተ(በት) tāčawwٍätä-
(bbät)

trickle, vi. (of water) ተንጠባጠበ tänṭäbaṭṭäbä

tricky (~politician) ዘዴኛ zädeňňa;
(~question) የሚያሳስት yämmiyasa-
sät

trifle (v.) ቀለደ qällädä

trifle (n.) የማይረባ ፡ ነገር yämmayəräba
nägär; አነስተኛ ፡ ነገር anästäňňa nägär
a trifle ትንሽ tənnəš

trigger (n.) ምላጭ məlaččʼ

trim, v. (~edges) አስተካከለ astäkakkälä; (decorate) አጊያገጠ agiyageṭä

Trinity, Holy~ ሥላሴ səllase

trip, vt. (cause to stumble) አደናቀፈ addänaqqäfä
trip, vi. (stumble) ተደናቀፈ tädänaqqäfä

trip (n.) ጉዞ guzo; መንገድ mängäd

tripe ጨጓራ čäggʷarra

triple (n., adj.) ሦስት ፡ ዕጥፍ sost əṭəf

triplets ሦስት ፡ ልጆች ፡ ባንድ ፡ ጊዜ ፡ የተ
ወለዱ sost ləǧočč band gize yätäwäl-
lädu

triumph, v. (be victorious) ድል ፡ አደረገ
dəl adärrägä; (exalt about victory)
ደነፋ dänäffa

triumph, n. (victory) ድል dəl

trivial ዋጋ ፡ ቢስ waga bis;የማይረባ yämmayəräba

troop (n.) ጭፍራ čəfra
troops ወታደሮች wättaddäročč; ጦር
ṭor

trophy (something captured) ምርኮ mərko; (prize) ሽልማት šälləmat

tropic(s) የሐሩር ፡ አውራጃ yäharur awraǧǧa; ሞቃት፡አገሮች moqqat agäročč

tropical (~climate) ሞቃት moqqat;
(~clothes) ለሙቀት ፡ የሚሆን lämu-
qät yämmihon

trot, v. (of horse) ሶመሶመ somässomä;
ሰገረ säggärä; (of child) ድክድክ ፡ አለ
dəkkədäkk alä

trot (n.) ሶምሶማ somsomma

trouble (vt.) አስቸገረ asčäggärä; አስጨ
ነቀ asčännäqä

trouble (n.) ችግር čəggər
get into trouble ጣጣ ፡ ውስጥ ፡ ገባ
ṭaṭa wəsṭ gäbba
give trouble አስቸገረ asčäggärä
go to any trouble ተቸገረ täčäggärä
look for trouble ጠብ ፡ ያለሽ ፡ ዳቦ ፡
አለ ṭäb yalläš dabbo alä

troublesome አስቸጋሪ asčäggari

trough ገንዳ gända; ግርግም gərgəm
kneading trough ቡሀቃ buhaqa

trousers ሱሪ surri
long trousers ቦላሌ bolale
short trousers ቀምጣ qumṭa

truce በተወሰነ ፡ ጊዜ ፡ ተኩስ ፡ ማቆም bä-
täwässänä gize täkʷs maqom

truck የጭነት ፡ መኪና yäčənät mäkina;
ካሚዮን kamiyon

true እውነተኛ əwnätäňňa; ሐቀኛ haqqäňňa; (~scholar) የተመሰከረ(ለት)
yätämäsäkkärä(llät)
come true ተፈጸመ täfäṣṣämä

truly ከልብ käləbb; በእውነት bäwnät

trumpet ጥሩምባ ṭrumba
play the trumpet ጥሩምባ ፡ ነፋ ṭrumba näffa

trunk (of tree) ግንድ gənd; (of human
body) ወገብ wägäb; (of elephant) ኩ
ንቢ kunbi; (box) ሻንጣ šanṭa; (of car)
የእቃ ፡ ማስቀመጫ yäəqa masqämmäča
trunks ሙታንቲዎች mutantiwočč

trust (v.) አመነ ammänä; ተማመነ tämammänä

trust, n. (firm belief) እምነት əmnät;
(custody) አደራ adära; (company) ድር
ጅት därəǧǧät

trustee ባለ ፡ አደራ balä adära

trusteeship ሞግዚትነት mogzitənnät

trustful ሁሉን ፡ እማኝ *hullun amañ*

trustworthy ታማኝ *tammañ;* ሁነኛ *hunäñña;* ቄም ፡ ነገረኛ *qum nägäräñña*

truth እውነት *əwnät;* ሐቅ *haqq*

truthful ሐቀኛ *haqqäñña;* እውነተኛ *əwnätäñña*

truthfully በእውነቱ *bäwnätu*

try (v.) ሞከረ *mokkärä;* ፈተነ *fättänä;* (examine in a court) አየ *ayyä;* (taste) ቀመሰ *qämmäsä;* (make an effort) ተጣ ጣረ *tätatärä;* ታገለ *taggälä* be tried (in court) ፍርድ ፡ ቤት ፡ ቀረበ *fərd bet qärräbä*

tub ሳፋ *safa*

tube ቱቦ *tubbo;* ላስቲክ *lastik;* (for tire) ከመነዳሪያ *kämänädariya*

tuberculosis የሳምባ ፡ ነቀርሳ *yäsamba näqärsa*

Tuesday ማክሰኞ *maksäñño*

tuft ቁንጮ *qunço*

tug (v.) ጐተተ *gʷättätä*

tugboat ጐታች ፡ ጀልባ *gʷättač ǧälba*

tuition የመማሪያ ፡ ገንዘብ *yämämmariya gänzäb*

tumble (roll about) ተንከባለለ *tänkäballälä;* (perform somersaults) ተገላባ በጠ *tägäläbabbäta* tumble down ዱብ ፡ ዱብ ፡ አለ *dubb dubb alä;* ወደቀ *wäddäqä;* (of a house) ፈረሰ *färräsä*

tumbler (glass) ዋንጫ *wanča*

tumor እብጠት *əbṭät;* ኪንታሮት *kintarot*

tumult ሁካታ *hukata;* ግርግር *gərrəgərr*

tumultuous (~welcome) የጋለ *yägalä;* (~crowd) ከመጠን ፡ በላይ ፡ የሚንጫጫ *kämäṭän bälay yämminčačča*

tune (v.) ቃኘ *qaññä*

tune (n.) ዜማ *zema*

tunnel (n.) መሿለኪያ *mäššʷaläkiya*

turban ጥምጥም *təmṭəm*

turbid ድፍርስ *dəfrəs*

be turbid ደፈረሰ *däfärräsä*

turbulence (noise) ሁካታ *hukata;* (of water) መናወጥ *männawäṣ*

turbulent, be ~ (mob) ሥርዓት ፡ ጐደለ *sər'at gʷäddälä*

turkey የቱርክ ፡ ዶሮ *yäturk doro*

turmoil ግርግር *gərrəgərr*

turn (vt.) አዞረ *azorä;* (~the page) ገለ በጠ *gäläbbäṭä;* (translate) ተረጐመ *täräggʷämä* turn (vi.) ዞረ *zorä;* (of wheel) ተሽከረ ከረ *täškäräkkärä;* (of road) ታጠፈ *taṭṭäfä* turn around (vt.) አዞረ *azorä* turn around (vi.) ዞረ *zorä;* ዞር ፡ አለ *zorr alä* turn away ዞር ፡ አለ *zorr alä* turn back ተመለሰ *tämälläsä* turn down (reject) ሳይቀበለው ፡ ቀረ *sayəqqäbbäläw qärrä;* (refuse) እምቢ ፡ አለ *əmbi alä* turn in, vt. (~ resignation) አቀረበ *aqärräbä;* (give back) አስረከበ *asräkkäbä* turn into (become) ሆነ *honä* turn off (~light) አጠፋ *aṭäffa* turn on አበራ *abärra* turn out well ተሳካ *täsakka;* ተቃና *täqanna;* በጀ *bäǧǧä* turn over (transfer) አስተላለፈ *astälalläfä;* አስረከበ *asräkkäbä;* (invert) ገለበጠ *gäläbbäṭä* turn up (appear) ጥልቅ ፡ አለ *ṭəlləq alä*

turn, n. (in road) መታጠፊያ *mättaṭäfiya;* መጠምዘዣ *mäṭämzaža;* ጥምዝምዝ *ṭəməzməz;* (chance to do something in regular order) ተራ *tära;* ፈረቃ *färäqa* good turn ውለታ *wəläta* in turns ተራ ፡ በተራ *tära bätära* take turns ተራ ፡ ጠበቀ *tära ṭäbbäqä;* ተፈራረቀ *täfärarräqä*

turtle ኤሊ *eli*

turtle dove እርግብ *ərgəb*

tusk ጥርስ *ṭərs*

tutor (v.) አስጠና *asṭänna;* አስተማረ *as-tämarä*

tutor, n. (teacher) አስተማሪ *astämari*

tweezers ወረንጦ *wärränṭo*

twelfth ዐሥራ ፡ ሁለተኛ *asra hulättäñña*

twelve ዐሥራ ፡ ሁለት *asra hulätt*
twelve o'clock ስድስት ፡ ሰዓት *səddəst säat*

twenty ሃያ *haya*

twice ሁለት ፡ ጊዜ *hulätt gize;* ሁለቴ *hulätte*

twig ቀንባጥ *qänbäṭ*

twilight, at ～ ድንግዝግዝ ፡ ሲል *dəngəzgəzz sil*

twin መንታ *mänta*

twine (v.) ጠመጠመ *ṭämäṭṭämä*

twine (n.) ሲባጎ *sibago*

twinkle ብልጭ ፡ አለ *bəlləčč alä*

twirl (vt.) አሽከረከረ *aškäräkkärä*

twist ጠመዘዘ *ṭämäzzäzä;* (～ a rope) ገመደ *gämmädä;* (distort) አጣመመ *aṭṭammämä;* አዛባ *azzabba*

twitter (v.) ተንጫጫ *tänčaččä*

twitter (n.) የወፍ ፡ ጫጫታ *yäwäf čačata*

two ሁለት *hulätt*
two o'clock ስምንት ፡ ሰዓት *səmmənt säat*

type (v.) በመኪና ፡ ጻፈ *bämäkina ṣafä*

type, n. (kind) ዓይነት *aynät;* (typical example) ምሳሌ *məssale;* (letters) ፊደሎች *fidäločč*

typewriter የጽሕፈት ፡ መኪና *yäṣəhfät mäkina*

typhoid ተሰቦ *täsəbo*

typhus ተሰቦ *täsəbo*

typical ዓይነተኛ *aynätäñña*

typing በመኪና ፡ መጻፍ *bämäkina mäṣaf*

typist ታይፒስት *taypist*

tyrannize በጣም ፡ ጨቆነ *bäṭam čäqqʷänä*

tyranny የጭቆና ፡ አገዛዝ *yäčəqqʷäna aggäzaz*

tyrant በጉልበት ፡ አዳሪ *bägulbät adari*

U

udder ጡት *ṭät*

ugly መልክ ፡ ቢስ *mälkä bis;* አስቀያሚ *asqäyyami*

ulcer (external) የቁላ ፡ ቁስል *yäqʷälla qusəl;* (stomach ～) አልሰር *alsär*

ultimate (n.) መጨረሻ *mäčärräša*

ultimate (adj.) የመጨረሻ *yämäčärräša*

ultimately ውሎ ፡ አድሮ *wəlo adro*

ultimatum የመጨረሻ ፡ ማስጠንቀቂያ *yämäčärräša masṭänqäqiya*

ululate እልል ፡ አለ *ələll alä*

umbilical cord እትብት *ətəbt*

umbrella ጃንጥላ *ğanṭəla;* ዣንጥላ *žanṭəla*

umpire ዳኛ *daňňa*

unanimity ሙሉ ፡ ስምምነት *mulu səməmmənnät*

unanimous, be ባንድ ፡ ድምፅ ፡ ነው *band dəmṣ näw*

unanimously ባንድ ፡ ድምፅ *band dəmṣ;* በሙሉ ፡ ድምፅ *bämulu dəmṣ*

unarmed መሣሪያ ፡ ያልያዘ *mässariya yalyazä*

unavoidable የማይቀር *yämmayəqär*

unbearable, be የማይቻል ፡ ነው *yämmayəččal näw*

unbecoming, be ～ (of behavior) ተገቢ ፡ አይደለም *tägäbi aydälläm;* (of clothes) አልተስማማም *altäsmammam*

unbeliever አረመኔ *arämäne*

unbending ግትር gəttər

unceasing የማያቋርጥ yämmayaqqʷarrəṭ

uncertain የማይታወቅ yämmayəttawwäq; ያልተረጋገጠ yaltärägaggäṭä

uncircumcised ወሸላ wäšäla

uncivil ብልግና ፡ የተመላበት bəlgənna yätämällabbät

uncle አጐት aggʷät

unclean ቆሻሻ qošaša; (ritually) ርኩስ rəkus

unconcerned ግድ ፡ የለሽ gədd yälläš

unconscious, be ነፍሱን ፡ ሳተ näfsun satä
be unconscious of አላስተዋለም alastäwaläm

unconsciously ባለማወቅ balämawäq

unconstitutional ሕገ ፡ መንግሥት ፡ የሚ ፃረር həggä mängəst yämmiṣṣarrär

uncouth ስድ sədd

uncover ገለጠ gälläṭä

undecided, be ~ (person) ወላወለ wälaw-wälä; አመነታ amänätta; (question) አልተወሰነም altäwässänäm

undefined ያልተከለለ yaltäkällälä

undeniable የማይካድ yämmayəkkad

under ከ - - - ሥር kä - - - sər; በ - - - ሥር bä - - - sər; ከ - - - ታች kä - - - tačč; ከ - - - በታች kä - - - bätačč; (lower in rank) ከ - - - በታች kä - - - bätačč; (during the time of) በ - - - ጊዜ bä - - - gize

underclothes የውስጥ ፡ ልብስ yäwəsṭ ləbs

underdeveloped, be በልማት ፡ ወደ ፡ ኋላ ፡ ቀረ bäləmat wädä hʷala qärrä

underestimate ዝቅ ፡ አድርጎ ፡ ገመተ zəqq adrəgo gämmätä

undergo (~ an examination) ተደረገ (ለት) tädärrägä(llät); (~ hardships) ደረሰ(በት) därräsä(bbät)

undergraduate የኮሌጁን ፡ ትምህርት ፡ ያል ጨረሰ yäkolleǧun təmhərt yalčärräsä

underground, adj. (~ passage) በመሬት ፡ ውስጥ ፡ ለውስጥ ፡ የሚሄድ bämäret wəsṭ läwəsṭ yämmihed; (~movement) በድብቅ ፡ የሚሠራ bädəbbəq yämmisära; ምስጢራዊ məsṭirawi
underground (adv.) ከመሬት ፡ በታች kämäret bätačč; (by secret methods) በስውር bäsəwwər

undergrowth ቁጥቋጦ quṭqʷaṭo

underhanded, be ተንኮል ፡ አለ(በት) tänkʷäl allä(bbät)

underline (draw a line under) ከሥር ፡ አሠመረ(በት) käsər asämmärä(bbät); (emphasize) ጠቃሚነቱን ፡ አመለከተ ṭäqaminnätun amäläkkätä

undermine (weaken by wearing away the base of) ሸረሸረ šäräššärä; (~ someone's position) አመነመነ(በት) amänämmänä(bbät)

underneath ሥር sər

undernourished, be በደንብ ፡ አልተመገ በም bädänb altämäggäbäm

underpass መሻለኪያ mäššʷaläkiya

underpay ዝቅተኛ ፡ አበል ፡ ከፈለ zəqqətäňňa abäl käffälä

underprivileged ችግረኛ čəggəräňňa

underrate ዝቅ ፡ አድርጎ ፡ ገመተ zəqq adrəgo gämmätä

undershirt ካናቴራ kanatera

understand ገባ(ው) gäbba(w); ተረዳ(ው) tärädda(w); (~ a language) ሰማ sämma

understanding (n.) አእምሮ a'məro; አይ ምሮ ayməro; ብልህነት bələhənnät; (knowledge) ዕውቀት əwqät
come to an understanding ተግባባ tägbabba
reach an understanding ተስማማ täsmamma

undertake (attempt) ጀመረ ǧämmärä; (decide to do) ቆርጦ ፡ ተነሣ qʷärṭo tänässa

undertaking ውጥን *wəṭṭən;* ድርጊት *dər-git*

underwear ሙታንታና ፡ ካናቴራ *mutantanna kanatera*

underworld በወንጀል ፡ ሥራ ፡ የሚኖር *bäwänğäl səra yämminor*

undesirable የማይፈለግ *yämmayəffälläg*

undisciplined ስድ *sədd*

undo (unfasten) ፈታ *fätta*

undoubtedly ያለ ፡ ጥርጥር *yalä ṭərəṭṭər*

undress ልብስ ፡ አወላለቀ *ləbs awälalläqä*

undue ተገቢ ፡ ያልሆነ *tägäbi yalhonä*

unduly ከልክ ፡ በላይ *käləkk bälay*

unearth መሬት ፡ ቆፍሮ ፡ አወጣ *märet qʷäffəro awäṭṭa;* (discover) አገኘ *agäňňä*

uneasy, feel ~ ተጨነቀ *täčännäqä*

unemployed ሥራ ፡ ፈት *səra fätt*

unemployment ሥራ ፡ መታጣት *səra mättaṭat*

unequal የማይመጣጠን *yämmayəmmäṭaṭṭän*
   be unequal to (lack sufficient skill) ብቁ ፡ አልሆነም *bəqu alhonäm*

unequivocal ቁርጥ ፡ ያለ *qurrəṭṭ yalä*

uneven (odd) ጉደሎ *gʷädälo;* (~ ground) ወጣ ፡ ገባ *wäṭṭa gäbba;* ጉርባጣ *gʷärbaṭṭa*

unexpected ያልታሰበ *yaltassäbä*

unexpectedly ሳይታሰብ *sayəttassäb;* በድንገት *bädəngät*

unfailing (~ friend) እውነተኛ *əwnätäňňa*

unfair ገፋኛ *gəfäňňa*
   be unfair ተገቢ ፡ አይደለም *tägäbi aydälläm*

unfairly አላግባብ *alagbab*

unfaltering, be ወደ ፡ ኋላ ፡ አላለም *wädä hʷala alaläm*

unfamiliar የማያውቀው *yämmayawqäw;* እንግዳ *əngəda*

unfasten ፈታ *fätta*

unfavorable (~ decision) ጉጇ *gʷäği*

unfold (~ a map) ገለጠ *gälläṭä;* (~ tablecloth) ዘረጋ *zärägga*

unforeseen ያልታሰበ *yaltassäbä*

unforgettable የማይረሳ *yämmayərrässa*

unfortunate (unlucky) ዕድለ ፡ ቢስ *əddəlä bis;* (unsuitable) ተገቢ ፡ ያልሆነ *tägäbi yalhonä*

unfortunately ከፋቱ *kəfatu*

unfounded, be መሠረት ፡ አልነበረውም *mäsärät alnäbbäräwəm*

unfriendly, be ሰው ፡ አልወደደም *säw alwäddädäm*

unfurnished, be እቃ ፡ አልነበረበትም *əqa alnäbbäräbbätəm*

ungodly (~ man) ከሐዲ *kähadi;* (~ noise) ጆሮ ፡ የሚበጥስ *ğoro yämmibäṭəs*

ungrateful ምስጋና ፡ ቢስ *məsgana bis;* ውለታ ፡ ቢስ *wəläta bis*

unhappily ያሳዝናል *yasazzənal*

unhappy የከፋ *yäkäffa*
   be unhappy አዘነ *azzänä*

unharness አራገፈ *arraggäfä*

unhealthy (sickly) ጤና ፡ የጐደለው *ṭena yägʷäddäläw;* (harmful to health) ሰውነትን ፡ የሚጐዳ *säwənnätun yämmigʷäda*

unhesitatingly ሳያመነታ *sayammänatta*

unification አንድ ፡ ማድረግ *and madräg*

uniform (n.) የደንብ ፡ ልብስ *yädänb ləbs*

uniform (adj.) ተካከለ *täkäkkäl;* እኩል *əkkul*
   be uniform ተካከለ *täkakkälä*

unify አንድ ፡ አደረገ *and adärrägä*

unimportant የሆነ ፡ ያልሆነው *yähonä yalhonäw;* ጥቃቅን *ṭəqaqən;* ቀላል *qällal*

unintelligible (~ writing) የማይነበብ *yämmayənnäbbäb*

uninterrupted, be አልተቋረጠም *altä-q^warräṭäm*

union አንድነት *andənnät;* (being united) መዋሐድ *mäwwahad;* (association of workers) የሠራተኞች ማኅበር *yäsärra-täňňočč mahbär*

unique ተወዳዳሪ ፡ የማይገኝለት *täwädadari yämmayəggäňňəllät*

unison, in~ ተባብረው *täbabräw;* ባንድ ነት *bandənnät*

unit ክፍል *kəfəl;* (military~) የጦር ፡ ክ ፍል *yäṭor kəfəl;* ጓድ *g^wadd;* (standard of measurement) መለኪያ *mäläkkiya*

unite (vt.) አስተባበረ *astäbabbärä;* አዋ ሐደ *awwahadä;* አያያዘ *ayyayazä* unite (vi.) ተባበረ *täbabbärä*

united (adj.) የተባበረ *yätäbabbärä* be united ተባበረ *täbabbärä*

United Nations የተባበሩት ፡ መንግሥታት *yätäbabbärut mängəstat*

United States ዩናይትድ ፡ ስቴትስ *yunay-təd stets;* የተባበሩ ፡ አሜሪካ ፡ መንግሥ ታት *yätäbabbäru amerika mängəstat*

unity አንድነት *andənnät*

universal ዓለም ፡ አቀፍ *aläm aqqäf;* (~ rule) በየትም ፡ ያለ *bäyätəm yallä*

universally በሁሉም ፡ ዘንድ *bähullum zänd*

universe ዓለማት *alämat;* ጠፈር *ṭäfär*

university ዩኒቨርሲቲ *yunivärsiti*

unjust ገፋኛ *gəfäňňa;* ትክክለኛ ፡ ያልሆነ *təkəkkəläňňa yalhonä*

unkind ክፉ *kəfu*

unknown ስሙ ፡ ያልታወቀ *səmu yaltaw-wäqä*
be unknown አልታወቀም *altawwäqäm*

unlawful ሕג ፡ ወጥ *həggä wäṭṭ;* ከሕግ ፡ ውጭ ፡ የሆነ *kähəgg wəčč yähonä;* ከል ከል *kəlkəl*

unleash (~a dog) ፈታ ፡ ለቀቀ *fätto läq-qäqä*

unleavened (~bread) አፍላኛ *aflänňa;* (~dough) ያልቦካ *yalbokka*

unless (conj.) ከ *kä+* negative perfect; ከ - - - በስተቀር *kä - - - bästäqär*

unlikely, be አጠራጠረ *aṭṭäraṭṭärä*

unload አራገፈ *arraggäfä*

unlock ከፈተ *käffätä*

unlucky ዕድለ ፡ ቢስ *əddəlä bis;* ገደ ፡ ቢስ *gäddä bis*

unmannerly ሥርዓተ ፡ ቢስ *sər'atä bis;* ምግባር ፡ የጎደለው *məgbar yäg^wäddä-läw*

unmoved, be~ (not swayed by feelings) ፍንክች ፡ አላለም *fənkəčč alaläm*

unnatural (not true to nature) ከተፈጥሮ ፡ ውጭ ፡ የሆነ *kätäfäṭro wəčč yähona*

unnecessary የማያስፈልግ *yämmayasfäl-ləg;* አስፈላጊ ፡ ያልሆነ *asfällagi yal-honä*

unoccupied (vacant) ባዶ *bado;* (not busy) ሥራ ፡ ፈት *səra fätt*

unofficial አፈሲያል ፡ ያልሆነ *ofisiyäl yal-honä*

unopposed ካላንዳች ፡ ተቃወሞ *kalandačč täqawmo*

unpack (~suitcase) አጋባ *aggabba;* (~clothes) ከሻንጣ ፡ ውስጥ ፡ አወጣ *kä-šanṭa wəsṭ awäṭṭa*

unparalleled, be ወደር ፡ የለውም *wädär yälläwəm*

unpleasant መጥፎ *mäṭfo;* የማያስደስት *yämmayasdässət*

unpopular, be በሕዝብ ፡ ዘንድ ፡ አልተወ ደደም *bähəzb zänd altäwäddädäm;* ተወዳጅ ፡ አይደለም *täwäddäǧ aydälläm*

unprecedented ተደርጎ ፡ የማይታወቅ *tä-därgo yämmayəttawwäq*

unpredictable, be ይሆን ፡ ያህል ፡ ለማለት ፡ አይቻልም *yəhən yahəl lämalät ayəč-čaləm*

unprofessional ለሙያ ፡ ተገቢ ፡ ያልሆነ *lä-muya tägäbi yalhonä*

unprofitable, be ትርፍ ፡ አጣ *tərf aṭṭa*

unqualified, be ~ (unfit) ብቁ ፡ አይደለም bəqu aydälläm; (lacking legal authority) መብት ፡ የለውም mäbt yälläwəm

unquestionable የማይጠረጠር yämmayəṭṭäräṭṭär

unquestionably ያለ ፡ ጥርጥር yalä ṭərəṭṭər

unravel ተረተረ tärättärä; ፈታ fätta

unreal የሕልም yähəlm

unrest ሽብር šəbbər; ሁከት hukät

unrivaled ወደር ፡ የሌለው wädär yälelläw

unroll ዘረጋ zärägga

unruly (~student) በጥባጭ bäṭbač; አዋኪ awwaki; (~behavior) ከሥርዓት ፡ ውጭ ፡ የሆነ käsər'at wəčč yähonä

unsaddle አራገፈ arraggäfä

unsafe አደገኛ adägäňňa

unsanitary, be ንጽሕና ፡ የለውም nəṣhənna yälläwəm

unscrupulous, be ይሉኝታ ፡ የለውም yəluňňəta yälläwəm

unseasonal, be ጊዜው ፡ አይደለም gizew aydälläm

unseat (depose) ከሥልጣን ፡ አወረደ käsəlṭan awärrädä

unseemly, be ተገቢ ፡ አይደለም tägäbi aydälläm

unseen (adv.) ሳይታይ sayəttay

unselfish ለኔ ፡ ብቻ ፡ የማይል läne bəčča yämmayəl

unsettled, be (not decided) ፍጻሜ ፡ አላገኘም fəṣṣame alagäňňäm; (not paid) ተከፍሎ ፡ አላለቀም täkäflo alalläqäm; (not populated) ሰው ፡ አልሰፈረበትም säw alsäffäräbbätəm

unshaken የማይነጋ ፡ የሆነ yämmayənnagga yähonä

unsightly, be ለዓይን ፡ አስቀየም layn asqäyyämä

unsound (~mind) የታወከ yätawwäkä; (~business) በጥሩ ፡ ሁኔታ ፡ ላይ ፡ የማ ይገኝ bäṭəru huneta lay yämmayəggäňň; (~doctrine) መሠረት ፡ የሌለው

mäsärät yälelläw

unsparing ያልተቆጠበ yaltäqʷäṭṭäbä

unspeakable ይህ ፡ ነው ፡ የማይባል yəh näw yämmayəbbal

unstable ተለዋዋጭ täläwawač

unsteady, be ~ (shaky) ተንቀጠቀጠ tänqäṭäqqäṭä; (~ladder) መሬት ፡ አልያዘም märet alyazäm

untangle ፈታ fätta

unthinkable, be ታይቶም ፡ አይታወቅ taytom ayəttawwäq

untie ፈታ fätta

until (prep.) እስከ əskä; እስከ əskä + noun + ድረስ dəräs
until (conj.) እስከ əskə + imperfect

untimely ያለ ፡ ጊዜ yalä gize

untrue, be ውሸት ፡ ነበረ wəšät näbbärä; እውነት ፡ አልነበረም əwnät alnäbbäräm

untruthful ሐሰተኛ hassätäňňa

unused (~space) ክፍት kəft; (~dishes) ያልተጠቀመበት yaltäṭäqqämäbbät

unusual ያልተለመደ yaltälämmädä; ከተለ መደው ፡ የወጣ kätälämmädäw yäwäṭṭa; (strange) እንግዳ əngəda

unusually ከመጠን ፡ በላይ kämäṭän bälay

unveil ገለጠ gälläṭä

unwell, be አልተሻለ(ውም) altäšalä(wəm); ታመመ tammämä

unwholesome (~climate) ለጤና ፡ ጐጂ läṭena gʷäǧi; (~food) መጥፎ mäṭfo

unwind ፈታታ fätatta

unwise, be መኝነት፡ነው moňňənnät näw; ተገቢ ፡ አይደለም tägäbi aydälläm

unworldly ዓለምን ፡ የናቀ alämən yänaqä

unworthy, be ~ of ተገቢ ፡ አይደለም tägäbi aydälläm; አይገባም ayəggäbbam

unwrap ከፈተ käffätä

unwritten በጽሑፍ ፡ ያልሰፈረ bäṣəhuf yalsäffärä

unyielding የማይበገር yämmayəbbäggär

up ከ - - - በላይ kä - - - bälay
up to እስከ əskä; እ ፡ - - - ድረስ ə - - - däräs
up to now እስካሁን əskahun
be up (of sun) ወጣ wätta; (of time, finished) አለቀ alläqä

upbringing አስተዳደግ astädadäg

upgrade በደረጃ ፡ ከፍ ፡ አደረገ bädäräǧa käff adärrägä

upheaval ረብሻ räbša; ብጥብጥ bətəbbət

uphill ዓቀበቱን aqäbätun; ዳገቱን dagätun; ወደ ፡ ላይ wädä lay

uphold (support) ተሸከመ täšäkkämä; (give moral support to) ደገፈ däggäfä; (~the law) አስከበረ askäbbärä

upkeep (of a building) ማደስ maddäs; (of a car) ማስጠገን mastäggän

uplift ቀሰቀሰ qäsäqqäsä

uplifted, be (spirit) ተነቃቃ tänäqaqqa

upon ላይ lay

upper ላይኛ layəňňa; የላይ yälay

uppermost (highest) የመጨረሻ ከፍተኛ yämäčärräša käffətäňňa; (most important) የመጀመሪያ yämäǧämmäriya

upright (straight) ቀጥ ፡ ያለ qätt yalä; (sincere) ልብ ፡ ቅን ləbbä qən
be upright ቀና qänna; ቀጥ ፡ አለ qätt alä

uprising ረብሻ räbša; ዐመፅ amäs

uproar ሁከት hukät; ሁካታ hukata

uproot ነቀለ näqqälä

upset, v. (put in disorder) አመሰቃቀለ ammäsäqaqqälä; አቃወሰ aqqawwäsä; (disturb) አበላጨ abbäsäččä; አሸበረ aššäbbärä; (defeat) ሳይታሰብ ፡ አሸነፈ sayəttassäb aššännäfä

upset, be ተጨነቀ täčännäqä

upside down የዝቅዝቅ yäzəqzəq
be upside down ተዘቀዘቀ täzäqäzzäqä
turn upside down ገለበጠ gäläbbätä

upstairs ፎቅ ፡ ላይ foq lay

upsurge ከፍ ፡ ያለ ፡ እንቅስቃሴ käff yalä ənqəsəqqase

up-to-date ዘመናዊ zämänawi

upward ወደ ፡ ሰማይ wädä sämay; ወደ ፡ ላይ wädä lay; (more than) ከዚያም ፡ በላይ käzziyam bälay

upwards ወደ ፡ ሰማይ wädä sämay
upwards of ከ - - - በላይ kä - - - bälay

urban የከተማ yäkätäma

urge (recommend strongly) በጥብቅ ፡ አሳሰበ bätəbq asassäbä; ገፋፋ gäfaffa
urge on አበረታታ abbärätatta; ገፋፋ gäfaffa

urgency ችኩልነት čəkkulənnät; አስቸኳይነት asčäkkʷayənnät

urgent አስቸኳይ asčäkkʷay

urgently ባስቸኳይ basčäkkʷay

urinate ሸና šänna

urine ሽንት šənt

us (direct object) እኛን əňňan; or suffix -ን -n; (indirect object) ለኛ läňňa

usable, be አገለገለ agäläggälä

usage ልማድ ləmad

use (v.) ተጠቀመ(በት) tätäqqämä(bbät)
use up ጨረሰ čärräsä; ፈጀ fäǧǧä

use (n.) ጥቅም təqəm
be in use ተሠራ(በት) täsärra(bbät); አገለገለ agäläggälä
be of use ጠቀመ täqqämä
be (go) out of use ቀረ qärrä
it's no use ዋጋ ፡ የለውም waga yälläwəm
make use of, see 'use' (v.)
put to use በጥቅም ፡ ላይ ፡ አዋለ bätəqəm lay awalä

used, adj. (~car) የሠራ yäsärra; (~book) ያገለገለ yagäläggälä
be used (serve) አገለገለ agäläggälä
be used to ለመደ lämmädä
be used up አለቀ alläqä

useful ጠቃሚ täqami
be useful ጠቀመ täqqämä; ረባ räbba

usefulness ጠቃሚነት ṭäqaminnät

useless ዋጋ ፡ ቢስ waga bis; ጥቅም ፡ ቢስ ṭəqmä bis; የማይረባ yämmayəräba
be useless አልጠቀመም alṭäqqämäm; ጥቅም ፡ የለውም ṭəqəm yälläwəm

usher (v.) አስተናበረ astänabbärä

usher (n.) አስተናባሪ astänabari

usual የተለመደ yätälämmädä
as usual እንደ ፡ ወትሮው əndä wätrow; እንደተለመደው əndätälämmädäw

usually ባዘቦቱ bazäbotu; አብዛኛውን ፡ ጊዜ abzaňňawən gize; ዘወትር zäwätər

usurer አራጣ ፡ አበዳሪ araṭa abäddari

usurp አላግባብ ፡ ያዘ alagbab yazä

usurper ያላግባብ ፡ ዙፋኑን ፡ የያዘ ፡ ሰው yalagbab zufanun yäyazä säw

usury አራጣ ፡ ማበደር araṭa mabäddär

utensil እቃ əqa

utility (usefulness) ተጠቃሚነት täṭäqaminnät; (public~) ማገልገያ magälgäya

utilize ተጠቀመ(በት) täṭäqqämä(bbät); እጥቅም ፡ ላይ ፡ አዋለ əṭəqəm lay awalä

utmost (n.) የተቻለውን ፡ ያህል yätäčaläwən yahəl
to the utmost እስከ ፡ መጨረሻው ፡ ድረስ əskä mäčärräšaw dəräs

utmost (adj.) ከፍተኛ käffətäňňa

utter, v. (~a cry) አሰማ assämma

utter (adj.) ፍጹም fəṣṣum

utterance (something uttered) የተናገ ረው ፡ ቃል yätänaggäräw qal; (manner of speaking) አነጋገር annägagär

utterly ፈጽሞ fäṣṣəmo

uttermost የሚቻለውን ፡ ሁሉ yämmiččaläwən hullu

uvula እንጥል ənṭəl

V

vacancy (unoccupied position) ክፍት ፡ ቦታ kəft bota; (in a hotel) ያልተያዘ ፡ ክፍል yaltäyazä kəfəl

vacant (~position) ክፍት kəft; (~ chair) ባዶ bado
be vacant አልተያዘም altäyazäm

vacate ለቀቀ läqqäqä

vacation (v.) የዕረፍት ፡ ጊዜ ፡ አሳለፈ yä-əräft gize asalläfä

vacation (n.) ዕረፍት əräft; የዕረፍት ፡ ጊዜ yäəräft gize

vaccinate ከተበ kättäbä

vaccine ክትባት kəttəbat

vacillate ዋለለ wallälä; አወላወለ awwä-lawwälä

vagabond (n.) በረንዳ ፡ አዳሪ bärända adari; ወሮበላ wärroбälla; ዘዋሪ zäwari

vagrant ቀፋፊ qäfafi

vague (~answer) ግልጽ ፡ ያልሆነ gəlṣ yalhona

vain (self-satisfied) ግብዝ gəbbəz; (futile) ከንቱ käntu; ዋጋ ፡ ቢስ waga bis
be vain ኩራ kʷärra; በጣም ፡ ታበየ bäṭam tabbäyä
in vain በከንቱ bäkäntu

valiant (~person) ጀግና ğägna; (~ deed) የጀግንነት yäğägnənnät

valid (binding in court) ሕጋዊ həggawi; (legitimate, acceptable) ተገቢ tägäbi
be valid (signature) ፀና ṣänna

validate (confirm) አረጋገጠ arrägaggä-ṭä; (give official sanction) አጸደቀ aṣäd-däqä

valise ሻንጣ šanṭa

valley ሸለቆ šäläqo

valor ጀብዱ *ǧäbdu;* ጀግንነት *ǧägnənnät*

valuable (object) ከፍ ፡ ያለ ፡ ዋጋ ፡ ያለው *käff yalä waga yalläw;* (~ information) ጠቃሚ *ṭäqami*

valuables ውድ ፡ እቃዎች *wədd əqawočč*

value, v. (estimate) ገመተ *gämmätä;* (consider of importance) ከፍ ፡ ያለ ፡ ዋጋ ፡ ሰጠ *käff yalä waga säṭṭä*

value (n.) ዋጋ *waga;* (importance) ጥቅም *ṭəqəm*

van (truck) የጭነት ፡ መኪና *yäčənät mäkina*

vandal አጥፊ *aṭfi*

vanguard አዝማች ፡ ጦር *azmač ṭor*

vanish ጠፋ *ṭäffa;* እልም ፡ አለ *əlləmm alä*

vanity (conceit) ግብዝነት *gəbbəzənnät;* እብሪት *əbrit;* (lack of value) ከንቱነት *käntunnät*

vanquish ድል ፡ መታ *dəl mätta;* ድል ፡ ነሳ *dəl nässa*

vapor እንፋሎት *ənfalot*

vaporize ተነነ *tännänä*

variable ተለዋዋጭ *täläwawač* be variable ሊለዋወጥ ፡ ቻለ *lilläwawwäṭ čalä*

variant (n.) የተለያየ ፡ መልክ *yätäläyayyä mälk*

variant (adj.) የተለያየ *yätäläyayyä*

variation ልዩነት *ləyyunnät*

varied የተለያየ *yätäläyayyä;* ልዩ ፡ ልዩ *ləyyu ləyyu*

variety ልዩ ፡ ልዩ ፡ ዓይነት *ləyyu ləyyu aynät*

various ልዩ *ləyyu* at various times አልፎ ፡ አልፎ *alfo alfo*

varnish ቀለም ፡ ቀባ *qäläm qäbba*

vary (vt.) ለዋወጠ *läwawwäṭä* vary, vi. (be different) ተለያየ *täläyayyä;* (change) ተለዋወጠ *täläwaw-*

wäṭä

vase ያበባ ፡ ማስቀመጫ *yabäba masqämmäča*

vassal ሎሌ *lole;* ጦገኛ *ṭəggäñña*

vast (~ plain) አውላላ *awlalla;* (~ desert) በጣም ፡ ሰፊ *bäṭam säffi;* (~ sums of money) በጣም ፡ ብዙ *bäṭam bəzu*

vault, n. (arched roof) ባለ ፡ ቀስት ፡ ጣ ሪያ *balä qäst ṭariya*

veal የጥጃ ፡ ሥጋ *yäṭəǧǧa səga*

veer አቅጣጫ ፡ ለወጠ *aqṭaččä läwwäṭä*

vegetables አታክልት *atakəlt;* አትክልት *atkəlt;* ቅጠላ ፡ ቅጠል *qəṭäla qəṭäl*

vegetarian አትክልት ፡ ብቻ ፡ የሚበላ *atkəlt bəčča yämmibäla*

vegetation ሣር ፡ ቅጠል *sar qəṭäl*

vehemence ኃይል *hayl;* ኃይለኛነት *haylän-ñannät*

vehement ኃይለኛ *hayläñña*

vehemently በኃይል *bähayl*

vehicle ተሽከርካሪ *täškärkari*

veil, v. (~ the face) በዓይን ፡ እርግብ ፡ ሸፈነ *baynä ərgəb šäffänä*

veil (n.) ዓይን ፡ እርግብ *aynä ərgəb*

vein የደም ፡ ሥር *yädäm sər*

velocity ፍጥነት *fəṭnät*

velvet አጥላስ *aṭlas;* ከፈይ *käfäy*

vendetta የደም ፡ በቀል *yädäm bäqäl*

vendor ሻጭ *šač*

veneer (thin layer of wood used in veneering) ኮምፐንሳቶ *kompänsato;* ሽፋን *šäfan*

venerable (~ custom) የተቀደሰ *yätäqäddäsä;* (~ appearance) አረጋዊ *arägawi*

venerate አከበረ *akäbbärä;* በታላቅ ፡ አክ ብሮት ፡ ተመለከተ *bätallaq akbərot tämäläkkätä* be venerated ተከበረ *täkäbbärä*

veneration ማክበር *makbär*

vengeance ቂም ፡ በቀል *qim bäqäl*
seek (take) vengeance ተበቀለ *täbäq-qälä*

venom መርዝ *märz*

venomous መርዛም *märzam;* መርዘኛ *mär-zäñña*

vent (n.) የጢስ ፡ ማውጫ *yätis mawča;* የነፋስ ፡ ማስገቢያ *yänäfas masgäbbiya*

ventilate አናፈሰ *annaffäsä*

ventilator የነፋስ ፡ ማስገቢያ *yänäfas mas-gäbbiya*

venture, v. (try) ሞከረ *mokkärä;* (dare) ደፈረ *däffärä;* አደጋ ፡ ላይ ፡ ጣለ *adäga lay tälä*

venture (n.) አደጋ *adäga;* ሙከራ *muk-kära*

venturesome (adventurous) ደፋር *däffar;* (full of risks) አደጋ ፡ ሊያስከትል ፡ የሚችል *adäga liyaskättäl yämmičäl*

veracity ቅንነት *qənənnät;* ትክክለኛነት *täkäkkäläññannät*

veranda በረንዳ *bärända*

verb ግስ *gəss*

verbal (~ agreement) የቃል *yäqal;* (~ translation) የቃል ፡ በቃል *yäqal bäqal*

verbally በቃል *bäqal*

verbatim ቃል ፡ በቃል *qal bäqal*

verbose, be ብዙ ፡ ተናገረ *bəzu tänag-gärä*

verdant ለም *läm;* ለምለም *lämläm*
be verdant ለማ *lämma;* ለመለመ *lä-mällämä*

verdict ፍርድ *fərd;* ውሳኔ *wəssane*

verge ጫፍ *čaf;* ዳር *dar;* አፍ *af*
be on the verge of ለ *lä* + imperfect +ምንም ፡ አልቀረው *mənəmm alqär-räw*

verification ማረጋገጫ *marrägagäča*

verify አረጋገጠ *arrägaggätä*

veritable የታወቀ *yätawwäqä;* እውነተኛ *əwnätäñña*

vermin ተባይ *täbay*

vernacular (everyday speech) ሁል ፡ ጊዜ ፡ የሚነገርበት ፡ ቋንቋ *hul gize yämminnäg-gärəbbät qʷanqʷa*

versatile ሁለ ፡ ገብ ፡ የሆነ *hullä gäbb yä-honä*

verse (poetry) ግጥም *gətəm;* (section of a poem) ቤት *bet*

version (account) ሐተታ *hatäta;* (trans-lation) ትርጉም *tərgum*

vertebra አከርካሪ *akärkari*

vertical ከላይ ፡ ወደ ፡ ታች ፡ ቀጥ ፡ ያለ *kälay wädä tačč qätt yalä*

very በጣም *bätam;* እጅግ ጉጅግ *əǧǧəg*
very much በጣም *bätam*

vessel (boat) መርከብ *märkäb;* (contain-er) እቃ *əqa*

vest ሰደሪያ *sädäriyya*

vested (~ interest) የግል ፡ ጥቅም *yägəll təqəm*
be vested with ተሰጠ *täsättä*

vestibule መተላለፊያ *mättälaläfiya*

vestige (trace) ርዝራዥ *rəzərraž*

vestments ልብስ *ləbs*

vestry እቃ ፡ ቤት *əqa bet*

veteran በጦርነት ፡ ያገለገለ ፡ ሰው *bätorən-nät yagäläggälä säw;* ከዘመቻ ፡ የተ መለሰ *käzämäča yätämälläsä;* (who has had much experience in some position) በ - - - ብዙ ፡ ጊዜ ፡ የቆየ *bä - - - bəzu gize yäqoyyä*

veterinarian የእንስሳት ፡ ሐኪም *yäənsəsat hakim*

veterinary (medicine) የእንስሳት ፡ ሕክምና *yäənsəsat həkmənna*

veto የማገኛ ፡ ድምፅ *yämaggäǧa dəmṣ*

vex አበሳጨ *abbäsaččä*

vexation ብስጭት *bəsəččət*

vexatious ብስጩ *bəsəčču*

vexing, be አበሳጨ *abbäsaččä*

via በ - - - በኩል bä - - - bäkkul

viable (∼plan) ሥራ ፡ ላይ ፡ ሊውል ፡ የሚችል səra lay liwəl yämmičəl

vibrant (resonant) የሚያስተጋባ yämmiyastägabba; (vibrating, as with life, energy) ንቁ nəqu

vibrate (of sound) አስተጋባ astägabba; (of strings) ተርገበገበ tärgäbäggäbä

vicar የደብር ፡ አለቃ yädäbər aläqa; ጳበዝ gäbäz

vice (n.) መጥፎ ፡ አመል mätfo amäl; መጥፎ ፡ ምግባር mätfo məgbar

vice- (deputy) ምክትል məkəttəl

vicinity (surrounding district) አካባቢ akkababi; (nearness) ቅርብነት qərbənnät

vicious (∼criminal) አረመኔ arämäne; (∼dog) ተናካሽ tänakaš; (∼rumor) የተንኮል yätänkʷäl

vicissitudes, ∼of life የኑሮ ፡ ውጣ ፡ ውረድ yänuro wəta wəräd

victim (one who was killed or injured) የሞተ yämotä; የተጎዳ yätägʷädda; ጉዳት ፡ የደረሰ(በት) gudat ፡ yädärräsä(bbät)

victor አሸናፊ aššännafi

victorious አሸናፊ aššännafi; ድል ፡ አድራጊ dəl adragi
be victorious አሸነፈ aššännäfä; ድል ፡ ነሣ dəl nässa; ድል ፡ አደረገ dəl adärrägä

victory ድል dəl
win a victory ድል ፡ ነሣ dəl nässa; ድል ፡ አደረገ dəl adärrägä

victuals ምግብ məgəb; ቀለብ qälläb

vie ተወዳደረ täwädaddärä

view, v. (look at) ተመለከተ tämäläkkätä

view, n. (scenery) ትርኢየት tər'əyt; ትዕይንት tə'əyənt; (opinion) አስተያየት astäyayät

vigil (keeping awake for the purpose of watching) ነቅቶ ፡ መጠባበቅ näqto mättäbabäq; (eve before a religious festival) ዋዜማ wazema
keep a vigil ተጠባበቀ tätäbabbäqä

vigilance ንቃት nəqat

vigilant ንቁ nəqu

vigor ብርታት bərtat; ጉልበት gulbät; ጥናት tənat

vigorous ብርቱ bərtu; ጠንካራ tänkarra

vigorously በብርታት bäbərtat

vile (∼smell) ግም gəm; (∼language) የብልግና yäbəlgənna

vilify ስም ፡ አጎደፈ səm agʷäddäfä

village መንደር mändär

villager መንደርተኛ mändärtäñña

villain ተንኮለኛ tänkʷäläñña

villainy ክፋነት kəfunnät

vindicate (clear of guilt) ነጻ ፡ አወጣ näṣa awäṭṭa; (uphold) ደገፈ däggäfä

vindictive (∼person) ቂመኛ qimäñña; (∼punishment) የበቀል yäbäqäl
be vindictive ቂም ፡ ያዘ qim yazä

vine ሐረግ haräg; ወይን wäyn

vinegar ኮምጣጤ komtatte

vineyard የወይን ፡ ተክል yäwäyn täkəl

violate (∼the law) ጣሰ tasä; (disturb) አደፋረሰ adäfärräsä

violence (disturbance) ሁከት hukät; ብጥብጥ bətəbbət; (intensity) ኃይል hayl
do violence to (damage) አጠፋ(በት) aṭäffa(bbät); ተጓረረ täṣarrärä

violent (∼argument) ኃይለኛ hayläñña; (∼person) ቁጡ quṭṭu

violin ቫዮሊን vayolin

viper እፉኝት əffuññət

virgin (n.) ክብርና ፡ ያለት kəbrənna yallat; ድንግል dəngəl
virgin soil ድንግል ፡ መሬት dəngəl märet

virginity ክብርና kəbrənna; ድንግልና dəngələnna

Virgin Mary ድንግል ፡ ማርያም dəngəl maryam

virile ጉልማሳ gʷälmassa

virtue (excellence) ጥሩነት ṭərunnät; (moral excellence) ጸጋ ṣägga; (merit) ጥቅም ṭəqəm

virtuous ደግ ፡ አድራጊ dägg adragi

virulent (∼ disease) የሚገድል yämmigädəl

virus ቫይረስ vayräs

visa ቪዛ viza

visible የሚታይ yämmittay; ጉልህ guləh
be visible ታየ tayyä

visibly በግልጽ bägəlṣ

vision የማየት ፡ ችሎታ yämayät čəlota; (revelation) ራእይ ra'əy; (broad understanding) አስተያየት astäyayät

visit, v. (∼ a person) ጠየቀ ṭäyyäqä; (∼ a city, museum) ጐበኘ gʷäbäňňä

visit (n.) ጉብኝት gubəňňət
pay a visit ጠየቀ ṭäyyäqä

visitor እንግዳ əngəda; (of a country) ያገር ፡ ጐብኚ yagär gʷäbňi

visual (related to sight) የማያ yämaya

visualize በዓይነ ፡ ሕሊና ፡ አየ baynä həllina ayyä

vital (full of life) ንቁ nəqu; (essential) አስፈላጊ asfällagi

vitality ጥንካሬ ṭənəkkare; ንቁነት nəqunnät

vitamin ቪታሚን vitamin

vivacious ፎለፎል foläfol

vivid (∼ description) ጉልህ guləh; (∼ color) ደማቅ dämmaq

vividly በግልጽ bägəlṣ

vocabulary (glossary) መዝገበ ፡ ቃላት mäzgäbä qalat; (all the words used by a person or group) ቃላት qalat

vocal (∼ organ) ድምጽ ፡ የሚሰጥ dəmṣ yämmisäṭ
be vocal (speak openly) ስሜቱን ፡

በግልጽ ፡ ተናገረ səmmetun bägəlṣ tänaggärä

vocal cords የድምጽ ፡ አውታሮች yädəmṣ awtaročč

vocation (occupation) ሥራ səra; ሙያ muya

vocational የሙያ yämuya

vocational school የሙያ ፡ ትምህርት ፡ ቤት yämuya təmhərt bet; ተግባረ ፡ እድ ፡ ትምህርት ፡ ቤት tägbarä əd təmhərt bet

vociferous (∼ crowd) የሚንጫጫ yämminčačča; (∼ argument) በቁጭት ፡ የተደረገ bäčuhät yätädärrägä

voice (v.) አሰማ assämma

voice (n.) ድምጽ dəmṣ

void (v.) አፈረሰ afärräsä

void (n.) ባዶ ፡ ስፍራ bado səfra

void (adj.) ዋጋ ፡ ቢስ waga bis; የማይጸና yämmayəṣäna
be void አይሠራም ayəsäram

volatile (quick to evaporate) በቀላሉ ፡ የሚተን bäqällalu yämmitänn; (changeable) ተለዋዋጭ täläwawač

volcanic የእሳት ፡ ጋሞራ yäəsatä gämora

volcano እሳተ ፡ ጋሞራ əsatä gämora

volition ፈቃድ fäqad

volleyball የመረብ ፡ ኳስ ፡ ጨዋታ yämäräb kʷas čäwata

voluble ለፍላፊ läflafi

volume (book) መጽሐፍ mäṣhaf; (one of a set of books) ቅጽ qəṣ; (loudness) ድምጽ dəmṣ; (amount) መጠን mäṭän

voluminous (∼ body) ግዙፍ gəzuf; (∼ output) ከፍተኛ käffətäňňa; (∼ report) ሰፊ säffi

voluntarily በገዛ ፡ ፈቃድ bägäzza fäqad

voluntary (∼ action) በገዛ ፡ ፈቃድ ፡ የተደረገ bägäzza fäqad yätädärrägä

volunteer (v.) ፈቃደኛ ፡ ሆነ fäqadäňňa honä

volunteer (n.) ፈቃደኛ *fāqadäňňa;* (of army) ወዶ ፡ ዘማች *wäddo zämač*

vomit አስመለሰ(ው) *asmälläsä(w);* ተፋ *täffa;* አስታወከ(ው) *astawwäkä(w)*

voracious የማይጠግብ *yämmayäṭägǝb*

vote, v. (cast a ballot) መረጠ *märräṭä;* ድምፅ ፡ ሰጠ *dǝmṣ säṭṭä;* (authorize by ballot) ደገፈ *däggäfä*

vote (n.) ድምፅ *dǝmṣ;* የምርጫ ፡ ድምፅ *yämǝrča dǝmṣ* cast votes ድምፅ ፡ ሰጠ *dǝmṣ säṭṭä*

voter መራጭ *märač;* ድምፅ ፡ ሰጭ *dǝmṣ säč*

voting (n.) ምርጫ *mǝrča*

votive offering የስለት ፡ እቃ *yäsǝlät ǝqa*

vouch (guarantee) ተዋሰ *täwasä;* (be responsible for) ኃላፊ ፡ ሆነ *halafi honä*

voucher ደረሰኝ *därräsäňň*

vow, v. (swear) ማለ *malä;* (promise solemnly) ቃል ፡ ኪዳን ፡ ገባ *qal kidan gäbba;* (make a promise to a saint or God) ተሳለ *täsalä*

vow (n.) መሐላ *mähalla;* (of priesthood) ቃለ ፡ መሐላ *qalä mahalla;* (of marriage) ቃል ፡ ኪዳን *qal kidan;* (to a saint) ስለት *sǝlät* take a vow, see 'vow' (v.)

vowel ድምፅ ፡ አናባቢ *dǝmṣ annababi*

voyage (v.) ተጓዘ *tägʷazä*

voyage (n.) ጉዞ *guzo* bon voyage! መልካም ፡ ጉዞ *mälkam guzo;* በደኅና ፡ ግባ *bädähna gǝba* (sg. masc.)

vulgar (coarse) ባለጌ *baläge;* ስድ ፡ አደግ *sǝdd addäg;* (of the common people) ተራ *tära*

vulgarity ስድነት *sǝddǝnnät*

vulnerable ሊጎዳ ፡ የሚችልበት *liggʷädda yämmičǝläbbät*

vulture ጆፈ ፡ አሞራ *ǧoffe amora;* ጥንብ ፡ አንሳ *ṭǝnb ansa*

W

wade (through mud) እየወደቀ ፡ እየተነሣ ፡ ሄዶ *ǝyyäwäddäqä ǝyyätänässa hedä;* (through flood) እየተንቦጫረቀ ፡ ሄዶ *ǝyyätänboçarräqä hedä*

wag ቄላ *qʷälla;* ቆላ *qolla*

wage (v.), ~ war ጦር ፡ አነሣ *ṭor anässa* wage a campaign ዘመቻ ፡ አደረገ *zämäča adärrägä*

wage(s) ደሞዝ *dämoz*

wager (v.) ተወራረደ *täwärarrädä*

wager (n.) ውርርድ *wǝrǝrrǝd*

wagon ሰረገላ *särägälla*

wail, v. (of person) አለቀሰ *aläqqäsä;* ወዮታ ፡ አሰማ *wäyyota assämma*

wail (n.) ልቅሶ *lǝqso*

waist ወገብ *wägäb*

wait (v.) ቆየ *qoyyä;* ጠበቀ *ṭäbbäqä* wait on (of a salesman) አስተናገደ *astänaggädä;* (of a waiter) አቀረበ *aqärräbä*

wait (n.), lie in ~ for አደፈጠ *adäffäṭä*

waiter አሳላፊ *asallafi*

waiting, lady in ~ ደንጋጡር *dängäṭur*

waiting list መቆያ ፡ መዝገብ *mäqoyya mäzgäb*

waiting room ማረፊያ ፡ ክፍል *maräfiya kǝfǝl*

waitress አሳላፊ *asallafi*

waive (give up a claim to) አስቀረ *asqärrä*

wake (vt.) አስነሣ *asnässa;* ቀሰቀሰ *qäsäqqäsä;* አነቃ *anäqqa* wake (vi.) ነቃ *näqqa* wake up (vt.) ቀሰቀሰ *qäsäqqäsä;* አነቃ *anäqqa* wake up (vi.) ተነሣ *tänässa;* ነቃ *näqqa*

wakeful ንቁ *nǝqu*

waken, see 'wake' (vi.)

walk, vt. (take on a walk) አንሻራሸረ
anšäraššärä; (accompany) ሸኘ *šäňňä*
walk, vi. (go on foot) በእግር ፡ ሂደ
bägər hedä; ተራመደ *tärammädä;* (take
a walk) ተንሻራሸረ *tänšäraššärä*
walk back and forth ተንጐራደደ *tän-*
gʷäraddädä
walk in ገባ *gäbba*
walk off with ይዞ ፡ ሂደ *yəzo hedä*
walk out ወጥቶ ፡ ሂደ *wätto hedä*
walk rapidly ገሰገሰ *gäsäggäsä*
walk up ወጣ *wätta*
walk up and down ወዲያ ፡ ወዲህ ፡
ተመላለሰ *wädiya wädih tämälalläsä*

walk (n.) ሽርሽር *šərrəšərr;* (manner
of walking) አረማመድ *arrämamäd;*
(path) የእግር ፡ መንገድ *yägər mängäd*
from all walks of life ትልቅ ፡ ትንሽ ፡
ሳይቀር *təlləq tənnəš sayəqär;* እገሌ ፡
ከእገሌ ፡ ሳይባል ፡ ሁሉም *əgäle käəgäle*
sayəbbal hullum
take a walk ተንሻራሸረ *tänšaraššärä*

walking stick ምርኩዝ *mərkuz*

wall (v.), ∼ in በግንብ ፡ አጠረ *bägənb*
attärä

wall (n.) ገርገዳ *gərgədda;* ግድግዳ *gəd-*
gədda; (of stone) ግምብ *gəmb;* ግንብ
gənb

wallet ቦርሳ *borsa*

wallow ተንከባለለ *tänkäballälä;* ተንደባ
ለለ *tändäballälä*

wallpaper የግድግዳ ፡ ወረቀት *yägədgədda*
wäräqät

wander ተዘዋወረ *täzäwawwärä;* ተንቀዋ
ለለ *tänqäwallälä*
wander in ጐራ ፡ አለ *gʷära alä*
wander off ተንከራተተ *tänkärattätä*

wanderer ዘዋሪ *zäwari*

wane (disappear) ጠፋ *täffa;* (weaken)
እየደከመ ፡ ሂደ *əyyädäkkämä hedä*

want, v. (wish) ፈለገ *ša; fällägä*

want, n. (need) ገዳጅ *gəddaǧ;* ፍላጎት
fəllagot; (lack) እጦት *ətot;* (poverty)
ችግር *čəggər*

be in want ችገረ(ው) *čäggärä(w)*
wanting, be ጠፋ *täffa;* ጐደለ *gʷäddälä*
wanton ለከስከስ *läkəskəs*
war (v.) ተዋጋ *täwagga*
war (n.) ጦር *tor;* ጦርነት *torənnät*
go to war ዘመተ *zämmätä*
make war on ወጋ *wägga*
Ministry of War የጦር ፡ ሚኒስቴር *yä-*
tor minister
war cry ቀረርቶ *qarärto*
ward (v.), ∼ off ተከላከለ *täkälakkälä;*
(with a shield) መከተ *mäkkätä*
ward, n. (division of a hospital) ተራ ፡
ክፍል *tära kəfəl*
warden (of a prison) የወህኒ ፡ ቤት ፡ አለቃ
yäwähni bet aläqa; (officer empow-
ered to enforce law) ተቆጣጣሪ *täqʷä-*
tatari
wardrobe (clothes) የተሟላ ፡ ልብስ *yätä-*
mʷalla ləbs; (closet) የቁም ፡ ሣጥን *yä-*
qum satən
warehouse መጋዘን *mägazän;* ግምጃ ፡ ቤት
gəmǧa bet; እቃ ፡ ቤት *əqa bet*
wares እቃዎች *əqawočč*
warfare ጦርነት *torənnät;* ውጊያ ፡ ማድ
ረግ *wəggiya madräg*
warlike (∼ people) ውጊያ ፡ የሚወድ *wəg-*
giya yämmiwädd; (∼ speech) የጦር ፡
ስሜት ፡ ያዘለ *yätor səmmet yazzälä*
warm (vt.) አሞቀ *amoqä*
warm oneself ሞቀ(ው) *moqä(w)*
warm up (vt.) አሞቀ *amoqä*
warm up, vi. (of a party) ደመቀ *däm-*
mäqä
warm (adj.) ሙቅ *muq;* የሞቀ *yämoqä;*
(∼ climate) ሞቃት *moqqat;* (∼
clothes) የሚሞቅ *yämmimoq;* (∼
welcome) የጋለ *yägalä*
warm weather ሞቃት *moqqat;* ሙቀት
muqät
be warm ሞቀ *moqä*
feel warm ሞቀ(ው) *moqä(w)*

keep warm (vt.) አሞቀ *amoqä*

warmly ከልብ *käləbb;* በጋላ ፡ ስሜት *bä-galä səmmet*

warmonger ጦር ፡ ፈላጊ *ṭor fällagi*

warmth ሙቀት *muqät;* (strong feeling) የጋላ ፡ ስሜት *yägalä səmmet*

warn (caution) አስጠነቀቀ *astänäqqäqä*

warning ማስጠንቀቂያ *mastänqäqiya;* (indication, sign) ምልክት *mələkkət*

warp (vt.) አዛነፈ *azzannäfä*
   warp (vi.) ተዘባ *täzäbba;* ዛባ *zäbba;* (of wood) ተጣመመ *tätammämä*

warp, n. (of woven cloth) ድር *dər*

warrant, v. (guarantee) አረጋገጠ *arrägaggäṭä;* (justify) በቂ ፡ ምክንያት ፡ ሆነ *bäqi məknəyat honä*

warrant, n. (legal authorization) የፍርድ ፡ ቤት ፡ ማዘዣ *yäfərd bet mazäža;* የፍርድ ፡ ቤት ፡ ወረቀት *yäfərd bet wäräqät;* (guarantee) ማረጋገጫ *marrägagäča*

warranty ዋስትና *wastənna*

warrior ጦረኛ *ṭoränňa*

warship የጦር ፡ መርከብ *yäṭor märkäb*

war song ሽለላ *šəlläla*

wart ኪንታሮት *kintarot*

was, I ~ ነበርኩ *näbbärku;* he ~ ነበረ *näbbärä;* she ~ ነበረች *näbbäräčč*

wash, vt. (~ clothes) አጠበ *aṭṭäbä;* (~ face, hands) ታጠበ *taṭṭäbä*
   wash (vi.) ታጠበ *taṭṭäbä*
   wash up ታጠበ *taṭṭäbä*

wash, n. (clothes) የታጠበ ፡ ልብስ *yätaṭṭäbä ləbs*

washing machine የማጠቢያ ፡ መኪና *yämaṭäbiya mäkina*

washroom ማጠቢያ ፡ ቤት *maṭäbiya bet*

wasp ተርብ *tärb*
   wasp nest የተርብ ፡ እንጀራ *yätärb ənǧära*

waste, vt. (~money, time) አባከነ *abakkänä;* አጠፋ *aṭäffa*

waste away መነመነ *mänämmänä*

waste, n. (of time) ማጥፋት *matfat;* (of money) አባካኝነት *abakaňənnät;* (refuse) ቆሻሻ *qošaša*
   go to waste (of talent) በከንቱ ፡ ባከነ *bäkäntu bakkänä;* (of food) ባከነ *bakkänä*

waste (adj.), lay ~ አፈረሰ *afärräsä*
   be laid waste ፈረሰ *färräsä;* ተደመሰሰ *tädämässäsä*

wastebasket ቆሻሻ ፡ መጣያ ፡ ቅርጫት *qošaša mäṭaya qərčat*

wasteful አባካኝ *abakaň*

wasteland ጠፍ ፡ መሬት *ṭäf märet*

wastepaper ቆሻሻ ፡ ወረቀት *qošaša wäräqät*

wastepaper basket የቆሻሻ ፡ ወረቀት ፡ ማጠራቀሚያ ፡ ቅርጫት *yäqošaša wäräqät maṭṭäraqämiya qərčat*

watch, vt. (tend, guard) ጠበቀ *ṭäbbäqä;* (look at) ተመለከተ *tämäläkkätä;* (pay attention to) ተከታተለ *täkätattälä;* (observe) ታዘበ *tazzäbä*
   watch, vi. (be careful) ተጠነቀቀ *täṭänäqqäqä*
   watch out ተጠነቀቀ *täṭänäqqäqä*

watch, n. (person kept to guard) ዘብ *zäb;* (time piece) ሰዓት *säat*
   keep watch over ጠበቀ *ṭäbbäqä*

watchful ንቁ *nəqu;* ንቅ ፡ የሚጠብቅ *näqto yämmiṭäbbəq*
   be watchful for ተጠነቀቀ *täṭänäqqäqä*

watchmaker ሰዓት ፡ ሠሪ *säat säri*

watchman ዘበኛ *zäbäňňa*

watchtower የዘብ ፡ ግንብ *yäzäb gənb*

watchword የይለፍ ፡ ቃል *yäyələf qal*

water (v.) ውኃ ፡ አጠጣ *wəha aṭäṭṭa*

water (n.) ውኃ *wəha*

water closet ሽንት ፡ ቤት *šənt bet*

waterfall ፏፏቴ *fʷafʷate*

waterproof, be ውኃ ፡ አይዘልቀውም *wəha ayzälqäwəm*

watery ውኃማ *wəhamma;* (of eyes) እንባ፡ ያዘለ *ənba yazzälä*

wave, vt. (~ a handkerchief) አርገበገበ *argäbäggäbä;* (~ hands, arms, flag) አውለበለበ *awläbälläbä;* አወዛወዘ *awwäzawwäzä;* (signal) ምልክት ፡ ሰጠ *mələkkət sättä*

wave, vi. (of flags) ተውለበለበ *täwläbälläbä;* (of a person) እጁን ፡ አውለበ ለበ *əǧǧun awläbälläbä;* እጁን ፡ አወዛ ወዘ *əǧǧun awwäzawwäzä* be waved (of hair) ደረጀ ፡ አበጀ *däräǧa abäǧǧä*

wave (n.) ማዕበል *ma'əbäl;* ሞገድ *mogäd* heat wave ሞቃት ፡ ነፋስ *moqqat näfas*

waver አመነታ *amänätta;* አወላወለ *awwälawwälä;* (of voice) ተርገበገበ *tärgäbäggäbä*

wax, v. (polish with wax) ሰም ፡ ቀባ *säm qäbba*

wax (n.) ሰም *säm*

way መንገድ *mängäd;* (means, method) ዘዴ *zäde* ways and means ዘዴ *zäde* way of life አኗኗር *ann"an"ar* way out መውጫ ፡ መንገድ *mäwča män-gäd* by the way ለመሆኑ *lämähonu;* በነገ ሩን ፡ ላይ *bänägäraččən lay;* ለነገሩ *lä-nägäru* by way of በ - - በኩል *bä - - - bäkkul* give way (stand aside) ገለል ፡ አለ *gä-läll alä;* (of army) አፈገፈገ *afägäffä-gä;* (collapse) ተደረመሰ *tädärämmäsä;* ተናደ *tänadä* give way! ዞር ፡ በል *zorr bäl* in a way ባንድ ፡ በኩል *band bäkkul* in no way በምንም ፡ ዓይነት *bämə-nəmm aynät* + negative verb make way for አሳለፈ *asalläfä;* መን ገድ ፡ ለቀቀ *mängäd läqqäqä* on his way እግረ ፡ መንገዱን *əgrä män-gädun* one way or another በዚህም ፡ ሆነ ፡ በዚያ *bäzzihəm honä bäzziya;* ያም ፡ ሆነ ፡ ይህ *yam honä yəh*

that way በዚያ ፡ በኩል *bäzziya bäkkul* this way በዚህ ፡ በኩል *bäzzih bäkkul* what way?, which way? በየት ፡ በኩል *bäyät bäkkul*

waylay አድፍጦ ፡ ዘረፈ *adfəṭo zärräfä*

we እኛ *əňňa*

weak ደካማ *däkkama;* (~ tea, coffee) ቀጭን *qäččən* be weak ደከመ *däkkämä*

weaken (vt.) አደከመ *adäkkämä;* (~ tea) አቀጠነ *aqäṭṭänä* weaken (vi.) ደከመ *däkkämä;* ተዳከመ *tädakkämä*

weakling ዓቅም ፡ ቢስ *aqmä bis;* ደካማ ፡ ሰው *däkkama säw;* ልፍስፍስ ፡ ሰው *ləfəsfəs säw*

weakness ድክም *dəkam;* ደካማነት *däkka-mannät;* (a weak point) ጉድለት *gud-lät* have a weakness for ለ - - - ነፍሱ ፡ ወጣ *lä - - - näfsu wäṭṭa*

wealth ሀብት *habt;* ብልጽግና *bəlṣəgənna;* (abundance of anything) መጠን *mä-ṭän* wealth of ብዙ *bəzu*

wealthy ሀብታም *habtam;* ባለጸጋ *balä-ṣägga*

wean ጡት ፡ አስጣለ(ች) *ṭut asṭālä(čč)* be weaned ጡት ፡ ጣለ *ṭut ṭalä;* ጡት ፡ ተወ *ṭut täwä*

weapon የጦር ፡ መሣሪያ *yäṭor mässariya*

wear, vt. (~ clothes) ለበሰ *läbbäsä;* (~ a hat, a ring) አደረገ *adärrägä;* (~ a belt) ታጠቀ *taṭṭäqä;* (~ a crown) ጫነ *čanä* wear away, vt. (~ rocks) ሻረሻረ *šä-räššärä* wear away (vi.) ተበላ *täbälla* wear off (of paint) ተበላ *täbälla;* (of excitement) በረድ ፡ አለ *bärädd alä* wear out (vt.) ጨረሰ *čärräsä* wear out (vi.) አለቀ *alläqä*

wear, n. (clothing) ልብስ *ləbs;* (damage) ማለቅ *maläq*

for everyday wear የሰርክ *yäsärk*

wearily በድካም ፥ መልክ *bädəkam mälk*

weariness ድካም *dəkam;* መታከት *mätakät*

wearing አድካሚ *adkami*

wearing apparel ልብስ *ləbs*

wearisome አሰልቺ *asälči*

weary, v. (make tired) አደከመ *adäkkämä;* አታከተ *atakkätä;* (bother) አሰ ለቸ *asäläččä*

weary, adj. (tired) ደከማ *däkkama*
be weary, get weary ደከመ *däkkämä;* ታከተ(ው) *takkätä(w)*
be weary of ሰለቸ(ው) *säläččä(w)*

weather (n.) አየር *ayyär;* ያየር ፥ ንብረት *yayyär nəbrät;* ያየር ፥ ሁኔታ *yayyär huneta*
weather conditions ያየር ፥ ሁኔታ *yayyär huneta*

weave (~ cloth) ሠራ *särra;* (of spider weaving a web) አደራ *adärra*

weaver ሸማኔ *šämmane*

web ድር *dər*

wed (join) አጣመረ *aṭṭammärä*
be wed (marry) ተጋባ *tägabba*

wedding ሰርግ *särg;* (wedding ceremony) የሰርግ ፥ (የጋብቻ) ፥ ሥነ ፥ ሥርዓት *yä-särg (yägabəčča) sənä sər'at*
wedding banquet, wedding feast ሰርግ *särg*

wedge (n.) ሽብልቅ *šəbəlləq;* ውሻል *wəš-šal*

Wednesday ሮብ *rob;* ረቡ *räbu;* ረቡዕ *räbu'*

weed (v.) አረመ *arrämä*

weed (n.) አረም *aräm*

week ሳምንት *sammənt*
a week ago ከሳምንት ፥ በፊት *käsam-mənt bäfit*
a week from now ከሳምንት ፥ በኋላ *kä-sammənt bähʷala*

weekday የሥራ ፥ ቀን *yäsəra qän*

weekend የሳምንት ፥ መጨረሻ *yäsammənt mäčärräša;* ቅዳሜና ፥ እሑድ *qədamenna əhud*

weekly (n.) ሳምንታዊ ፥ መጽሔት *sam-məntawi mäṣhet*

weekly (adj.) ሳምንታዊ *samməntawi*

weekly (adv.) በየሳምንቱ *bäyyäsam-məntu*

weep አለቀሰ *aläqqäsä*

weft ማግ *mag*

weigh (vt.) መዘነ *mäzzänä;* (~ words) አመዛዘነ *ammäzazzänä;* መረጠ *märräṭä*
weigh (vt.) መዘነ *mäzzänä*
weigh down ወደ ፥ ታች ፥ አጐበጠ *wä-dä tačč agʷäbbäṭä*
weigh oneself ተመዘነ *tämäzzänä*

weight (the amount a thing weighs) ክብ ደት *kəbdät;* (balance) ሚዛን *mizan;* (piece used in weighing) የሚዛን ፥ ድን ጋይ *yämizan dəngay;* (importance) ዋጋ *waga*
lose weight ክብደት ፥ ቀነሰ *kəbdät qän-näsä*
put on weight ክብደት ፥ ጨመረ *kəb-dät čämmärä*

weighty (heavy) ከባድ *käbbad;* (serious) አሳሳቢ *asassabi*

weird እንግዳ *əngəda*

welcome (v.) ተቀበለ *täqäbbälä;* በደስታ ፥ ተቀበለ *bädässəta täqäbbälä*

welcome (n.) አቀባበል *aqqäbabäl*

welcome, adj. (~ guest) በደስታ ፥ የሚቀ በሉት *bädässəta yämmiqqäbbälut;* (~ news) የሚያስደስት *yämmiyasdässət*
welcome home! እንኳን ፥ ደኅና ፥ ገባህ *ənkʷan dähna gäbbah* (masc. sg.)
you are welcome! አብሮ ፥ ይስጠን *ab-ro yəsṭän*

weld, v. (~ metal) በየደ *bäyyädä;* (unite closely) አስተሳሰረ *astäsassärä*

welder በያጅ *bäyyağ*

welfare (safety) ደኅንነት *dähnənnät;* (aid) በጎ ፥ አድራጎት *bäggo adragot*

well (n.) የውኃ ፡ ጉድጓድ yäwəha gudgʷad; (supply, store) ምንጭ mənč

well (adv., adj.) ደኅና dähna; መልካም
mälkam; በጎ bäggo; ጥሩ ṭəru
well! (interjection) መቻስ mäčäss; ታ
ዲያ tadiya
well over ከ - - የበለጠ kä - - - yäbälläṭä; ከ - - በላይ kä - - - bälay
well then! ታዲያ tadiya; እንግዲያ əngədiya; እኮ əkko
as well as - - - ም - - - ም - - - m - - -
m; እንዲሁም əndihum
get well ተሻለ(ው) täšalä(w); ዳነ danä
go well together ተስማሙ täsmammu
how well? እንዴት əndet
very well ደኅና ፡ አድርጎ dähna adrəgo; (all right) እሺ əšši

well-behaved ጨዋ čäwa

well-being ደኅንነት dähnənnät

well-bred ጨዋ čäwa

well-founded መሠረት ፡ ያለው mäsärät
yalläw

well-known በጣም ፡ የታወቀ bäṭam yätawwäqä

well-mannered ጨዋ čäwa

well-off ሀብታም habtam

well-to-do ሀብታም habtam; ባለጸጋ baläṣägga

west (n.) ምዕራብ mə'ərab

west (adj.) የምዕራብ yämə'ərab

westerly (~ direction) የምዕራብ yämə'ə-
rab; (~ wind) ከምዕራብ ፡ የሚነፍስ
kämə'ərab yämminäfs

western ምዕራባዊ mə'ərabawi

westerner ምዕራባዊ mə'ərabawi; ፈረንጅ
färänǧ

westernization የምዕራባውያን ፡ መንፈስ
yämə'ərabawəyan mänfäs

westernize የምዕራባውያን ፡ መንፈስ ፡ ተከ
ተለ yämə'ərabawəyan mänfäs täkättälä

westward ወደ ፡ ምዕራብ wädä mə'ərab

wet, v. (~clothes) ውኃ ፡ ነከረ wəha näkkärä; (~ hands) አረጠበ aräṭṭäbä;
(of rain) አራሰ arasä; አበሰበሰ abäsäbbäsä

wet (adj.) እርጥብ ərṭəb
be wet ራሰ rasä; ረጠበ räṭṭäbä; በሰ
በሰ bäsäbbäsä

whack አጮለ ačola

whale ዓሣ ፡ ነባሪ asa näbari

wharf የወደብ ፡ መድረክ yäwädäb mädräk

what? ምን mən; ምንድር məndər; ምንድን
məndən; (for time) ስንት sənt
what (relative) የ yä + perfect; የም-
yämmə + imperfect
what! ምንኛ mənäñña; እንዴ ande
what about? -ስ -ss
what for? ለምን lämən
what if ብ bə + imperfect + -ስ -ss
what then? ታዲያ ፡ ምን ፡ ይደረግ tadiya mən yəddäräg
what's more ከዚህም ፡ በላይ käzzihəm
bälay; ከዚህም ፡ ሌላ käzzihəm lela

whatever? ምንድን məndən
whatever (pron., adj.) ምንም mənəm;
ማንኛውም mannəññawəm
whatever happens የሆነ ፡ ቢሆን yähonä bihon

what's-his-name ማነው ፡ ስሙ mannäw
səmu

whatsoever ምንም mənəm

wheat ስንዴ sənde

wheel (n.) መንኮራኩር mänkʷärakʷər;
(of car) ጎማ gomma; (steering wheel)
ማሪ märi

wheelbarrow ኩርኩር kurrəkurr

wheelchair ተሽከርካሪ ፡ ወምበር täškärkari wämbär

wheeze አቃተተ aqattätä

when? መቼ mäče; መቻ mäčä; በምን ፡ ጊዜ
bämən gize; በስንት ፡ ሰዓት bäsənt säat
when በ bä + perfect + ጊዜ gize; ስ
sə + imperfect; ብ bə + imperfect

since when? ከመቼ ፡ ጀምሮ kämäčä
ğämmǝro

whenever? ምን ፡ ጊዜ mǝn gize
whenever በ bä + perfect + ቀጥር qu-
ṭǝr (or ጊዜ gize)

where? የት yät; (where to?) ወዴት wädet; (from where)? ከየት käyät
where else ሌላጋ ፡ የት lelaga yät

whereabout? የት yät

wherefore? ለምን lämǝn

wherein? የት ፡ ላይ yät lay

whereupon? በምን ፡ ላይ bämǝn lay
whereupon በዚያን ፡ ጊዜ bäzziyan gize

wherever የትም ፡ በ yätǝm bǝ + imperfect

whet ሳለ salä

whether (imperfect) + እንደሆነ ǝndähonä

whetstone መሳል mäsal; መሳያ mäsaya

whey አጓት aggʷat

which? ምን mǝn; የቱ yätu; የትኛው yätäññaw
which (relative) የ yä + perfect; የም
yämmǝ + imperfect
which one? የትኛው yätäññaw

whichever, is expressed by the relative
verb; or by የትኛውም ፡ በ yätäñña-
wǝm bǝ + imperfect

while (v.), ~away(time) አሳለፈ asalläfä

while (n.), a while ጥቂት ፡ ጊዜ ṭǝqit gize; ትንሽ tǝnnǝš
a while ago ከጥቂት ፡ ጊዜ ፡ በፊት käṭǝqit gize bäfit
for a long while ለብዙ ፡ ጊዜ läbǝzu
gize
for a while ለጊዜው lägizew; ለጥቂት ፡
ጊዜ läṭǝqit gize
in a little while ከጥቂት ፡ ጊዜ ፡ በኋላ
käṭǝqit gize bähʷala

while (conj.) ስ sǝ + imperfect; በ bä +
perfect

whimper (of child) ተነጫነጨ tänäčannäčä; (of dog) አጉረመረም agʷrämärrämä

whine ተነጫነጨ tänäčannäčä

whip (vt.) ገረፈ gärräfä

whip (n.) አለንጋ alänga; ጅራፍ ğǝraf

whirl (v.) ተሽከረከረ täškäräkkärä

whirlpool አዙሪት azurit; አዝዋሪት azwarit

whirlwind ዐውሎ ፡ ነፋስ awlo näfas

whiskers ሪዝ riz

whisper (v.) ሹክ ፡ አለ šukk alä; አንሾካ
ሾከ anšokaššokä

whisper (n.) ሹክሹክታ šukšukta

whistle, v. (with a whistle) ፈሸካ ፡ ነፋ
fiška näffa; (with the mouth) አፏጨ
afʷaččä

whistle (n.) ፈሸካ fiška

white (n.), ~ of egg ዞፍ zof

white (adj.) ነጭ näčč
white man ነጭ näčč; ፈረንጅ färänğ
white hair ሽበት šǝbät
be white ነጣ nätta
go white ገረጣ gärätta
turn white (hair) ሸበተ šäbbätä

whiten (vt.) አነጣ anätta
whiten (vi.) ነጣ nätta

whitewash (v.) ለቀለቀ läqälläqä; ኖራ ፡
ቀባ nora qäbba; (cover up mistakes)
ተግባር ፡ ሸፋፈነ tägbar šäfaffänä

whitewash (n.) ኖራ nora

whither? ወዴት wädet

who? ማን man; (plural) ማን ፡ ማን man
man; እነማን ǝnnäman
who (relative) የ yä + perfect; የም
yämmǝ + imperfect

whoever የ yä + perfect; የም yämmǝ
+ imperfect; ማንም ፡ ሰው ፡ ይሁን
mannǝm säw yǝhun

whole (n.) ሙሉ mulu
on the whole በጠቅላላው bäṭäqlallaw

whole (adj.) ሙሉ mulu; መላ mälla; የተ
ማላ yätämʷalla

wholeheartedly በሙሉ ፡ ልብ bämulu lǝbb

wholesale (adj.) ጅምላ *ğəmla;* (wide-spread) እጅግ ፡ ከፍ ፡ ያለ *əğğəg käff yalä*
wholesale (adv.) በጅምላ *bäğəmla*
wholesome (~ climate) ለጤና ፡ የሚስ ማማ *läṭena yämmismamma*
wholly ሙሉ ፡ በሙሉ *mulu bämulu;* ሙቶ ፡ በሙቶ *mäto bämäto*
whom? ማንን *mannən*
whooping cough ትክትክ *təkkətəkk*
whose? የማን *yäman*
why? ለምን *lämən;* ለምንድን *läməndən;* ለምንድር *lämindər;* ስለምን *sälämən;* በምን ፡ ምክንያት *bämən məknəyat;* (indirect question) ለምን ፡ እንደ *lämən əndä* + verb
why! እንዴ *ande*
that's why ስለዚህ *säläzzih*
wick ክር *kərr*
wicked ክፉ *kəfu;* መጥፎ *mäṭfo;* (~ deed) የጭካኔ *yäčəkkane*
wickedness ክፋት *kəfat;* ግፍ *gəf*
wickerwork ስፌት *səfet*
wide ሰፊ *säffi*
be wide ሰፋ *säffa*
far and wide ካገር ፡ እስካገር *kagär əskagär*
wide-awake ንቁ *nəqu*
widely (to a wide extent) በሰፊው *bäsäffiw;* (very) በጣም *bäṭam*
widen (vt.) አሰፋ *asäffa*
widen (vi.) ሰፋ *säffa*
widespread ሰፊ *säffi;* (~ belief, view) የተዛመተ *yätäzammätä;* የተሰራጨ *yätäsäraččä*
be widespread በብዛት ፡ ተገኘ *bäbəzat tägäññä;* በሰፊው ፡ አለ *bäsäffiw allä;* ተሰፋፋ *täsfaffa;* (of view) ተሰራጨ *täsäraččä*
widow ባል ፡ የሞተባት ፡ ሴት *balwa yämotäbbat set*
widower ሚስቱ ፡ የሞተችበት ፡ ሰው *mistu yämotäččəbbät säw*

width ስፋት *səfat*
wife ሚስት *mist;* ምሽት *məšt;* ባለቤት *baläbet*
take a wife ሚስት ፡ አገባ *mist agäbba*
wig ሰው ፡ ሠራሽ ፡ ጸጉር *säw särraš ṣägur*
wiggle ተቀነጣጠጠ *täqʷnäṭännäṭä*
wild (~ tribe) አረማኔ *arämäne;* (~ flower) ወፍ ፡ ዘራሽ *wäf zärraš;* (~ child) ያልተገራ *yaltägärra;* (~ horse) የሚዳ *yämeda;* ያልተገራ *yaltägärra;* (~ plan) የማይጨበጥ *yämmayəččäbbäṭ*
wilderness በረሃ *bäräha*
wildlife የዱር ፡ አራዊት *yädur arawit*
wilds ዱር *dur*
wile ብልሃት *bəlhat;* ተንኮል *tänkʷäl*
will, vt. (give by a will) ተናዘዘ *tänazzäzä*
will, vi. (desire) ተመኘ *tämäññä*
will (auxiliary), expressed by the imperfect
will, n. (legal paper) ኑዛዜ *nuzaze;* (determination) ፍላጎት *fəllagot;* (wish) ውዴታ *wəddeta;* ፈቃድ *fäqad*
last will ኑዛዜ *nuzaze*
at will እንደልብ *əndäləbb*
leave (make) a will ተናዘዘ *tänazzäzä*
willful ሐሳበ ፡ ግትር *hassabä gəttər;* ችኮ *čəkko*
willing ፈቃደኛ *fäqadäñña*
willingly ወዶ *wäddo;* በውዴታ *bäwəddeta;* በፈቃድ *bäfäqad*
willingness ውዴታ *wəddeta;* ፈቃደኛነት *fäqadäññannät*
will power ቄራጠነት *qʷärraṭənnät*
willy-nilly በውድም ፡ በግድም *bäwəddəm bägəddəm*
wilt (fade) ጠወለገ *ṭäwällägä;* (lose strength) ጉልበቱ ፡ ፈሰሰ *gulbätu fässäsä*
win (~ a battle) አሸነፈ *aššännäfä;* (~ a case) ረታ *rätta;* (~ a prize) አገኘ *agäññä;* (~ friends) አፈራ *afärra;* (~ the audience) ማረከ *marräkä*

win over አገባባ *agbabba*

wince ተሸመቀቀ *tašämäqqäqä*

wind, vt. (~ turban, bandage) ጠመጠመ *ṭämäṭṭämä;* (~ thread) አጠነጠነ *aṭä-näṭṭänä;* (~ the watch) ሞላ *molla*

wind, vi. (of a road, stream) ተጠማ ዘዘ *täṭämazzäzä*

wind up, vt. (~ yarn) አጠነጠነ *aṭä-näṭṭänä;* (~ a speech) ደመደመ *dä-mäddämä*

wind up, vi. (come to an end) አበቃ *abäqqa*

wind (n.) ነፋስ *näfas;* ንፋስ *nəfas;* (breath) ትንፋሽ *tənfaš*
break wind ፈሳ *fässa*
get wind of ዐወቀ *awwäqä*

winding ጠምዛዛ *ṭämzazza*

windmill የነፋስ ፡ ወፍጮ *yänäfas wäfčo*

window መስኮት *mäskot*

windowpane የመስኮት ፡ መስታወት *yämäs-kot mästawät*

windshield የመኪና ፡ የፊት ፡ መስታወት *yämäkina yäfit mästawät*

windstorm ኀይለኛ ፡ ነፋስ *hayläñña näfas*

windy ነፋሻ *näffaša;* ነፋስ ፡ የሚበዛበት *näfas yämmibäzabbät*

wine ወይን ፡ ጠጅ *wäyn ṭäǧǧ*

wing (n.) ክንፍ *kənf*

wink (vt.) ጠቀሰ *ṭäqqäsä*

wink, vi. (of light) ብልጭ ፡ ድርግም ፡ አለ *bəlləčč dərgəmm alä;* (of a person) በዓይኑ ፡ ጠቀሰ *baynu ṭäqqäsä*

wink (n.) ጥቅሻ *ṭəqša*
in a wink ከመቅጽበት *kämäqəṣbät;* ባንድ ፡ አፍታ *band afta*

winner አሸናፊ *aššännafi*

winning, adj. (in contest) አሸናፊ *aššän-nafi;* (attractive) የሚማርክ *yämmi-marrək*

winnow (~ grain) አነፈሰ *anäffäsä;* አዘራ *azärra;* አበጠረ *abäṭṭärä;* (separate) ለየ *läyyä*

winter ክረምት *krämt*

wipe ማሰሰ *mʷassäsä;* (~ dishes, table) ወለወለ *wäläwwälä*
wipe away, wipe off ጠረገ *ṭärrägä;* (~ tears) ማሰሰ *mʷassäsä*
wipe out (destroy) አወደመ *awäddä-mä;* (~ illiteracy) አጠፋ *aṭäffa*

wire, vt. (bind with metal thread) ሽቦ ፡ አሰረ *šəbo assärä;* (send a message by telegraph) ቴሌግራም ፡ ላከ *telegram lakä*

wire, n. (metal) ሽቦ *šəbo;* (telegram) ቴሌ ግራም *telegram*

wisdom ጥበብ *ṭəbäb*

wisdom tooth በመጨረሻ ፡ የሚበቅል ፡ የመ ንጋጋ ፡ ጥርስ *bämäčärräša yämmibä-qəl yämängaga ṭərs*

wise ብልህ *bələh;* ጠቢብ *ṭäbib;* (learned) ዐዋቂ *awaqi*

-wise (e. g. money-wise) በ - - - በኩል *bä - - - bäkkul*

wish (v.) ተመኘ *tämäňňä;* (want) ፈለገ *fällägä;* ሻ *ša*

wish (n.) ምኞት *mäňňot;* ፍላጎት *fəlla-got*

wishful, ~ thinking የሕልም ፡ እንጀራ *yähəlm ənǧära*

wishy-washy ወላዋይ *wälaway*

wit ቀልድ *qäld;* ቀልደኛነት *qäldäňňannät*
wits አእምሮ *a'məro*
be out of one's wits ግራ ፡ ገባ(ው) *gra gäbba(w)*

witch አስማተኛ *asmatäňňa;* ጠንቋይ *ṭän-qʷay*

witchcraft አስማት *asmat;* ጥንቆላ *ṭän-qʷäla*

witch doctor ጠንቋይ *ṭänqʷay*

with (in the company of) ከ - - ጋራ (ጋር) *kä - - - gara (gar);* (by means of) በ *bä;* (because of) ከ - - - የተነሣ *kä - - - yätänässa;* (in the care of) ለ - - - አደራ *lä - - - adära*

withdraw, vt. (take back) አነሣ *anässa;* ሰረዘ *särräzä;* (remove) አወጣ *awäṭṭa*
withdraw, vi. (retreat) ወደ ፡ ኋላ ፡ እፈ ገፈገ *wädä hʷala afägäffägä;* (from society) ተገለለ *tägällälä*

withdrawn (∼ manner) የገለልተኛነት *yägälältäññannät*

wither, vt. (∼ the face) አጨማደደ *aččämaddädä*
wither, vi. (of plants) ጠወለገ *ṭäwällägä;* (of hope) መነመነ *mänämmänä*

withhold (∼ consent) ከመግለጽ ፡ ተቆ ጠበ *kämägläṣ täqʷäṭṭäbä;* (∼ payment) ያዘ *yazä*

within (prep.) በ - - ውስጥ *bä - - - wəsṭ*
within (adv.) በውስጥ *bäwəsṭ;* ከውስጥ *käwəsṭ*

without, prep. (lacking) አለ *alä;* ያለ *yalä;* (on the outside of) ከ - - - ውጭ *kä - - - wäčč*
without (conj.) ስ *sə* + negative imperfect
without (adv.) ከውጭ *käwäčč;* ከውጭ ፡ በኩል *käwäčč bäkkul*

withstand (endure) ቻለ *čalä;* (resist) ተቋ ቋመ *täqʷaqʷamä;* ተከላከለ *täkälakkälä*

witness (v.) አየ *ayyä*

witness (n.) ምስክር *məsəkkər;* እማኝ *əmmaň;* (proof) ማስረጃ *masräǧǧa*
bear witness መሰከረ *mäsäkkärä*

witty ቀልደኛ *qäldäňňa*

wizard አስማተኛ *asmatäňňa;* ጠንቋይ *ṭänqʷay*

wobble (of a child) ተውተረተረ *täwtärättärä;* (of steering wheel) ተንቀጠቀጠ *tänqäṭäqqäṭä;* ተነቃነቀ *tänäqannäqä*

wobbly, feel ∼ (of legs) ተብረከረከ *täbräkärräkä;* (of chair) ዋዠቀ *wažžäqä*

woe ሐዘን *hazän*
woe to! ወዮ(ለት) *wäyyo(llät)*

woeful (mournful) አሳዛኝ *asazzaň*

wolf ተኵላ *täkʷla*

woman ሴት *set*
woman in childbed አራስ *aras*

womanhood (characteristics typical of a woman) የሴትነት ፡ ባሕርይ *yäsetənnät bahrəy;* (women in general) ሴቶች *setočč*

womankind ሴቶች *setočč*

womanly (∼ person) የሴትነት ፡ ባሕርይ ያላት *yäsetənnät bahrəy yallat*

womb ማኅጸን *mahṣän*

womenfolk ሴቶች *setočč*

wonder, v. (feel surprise) ተደነቀ *tädännäqä;* ተገረመ *tägärrämä;* አስገረመ(ው) *asgärrämä(w);* (be doubtful) ተጠራ ጠረ *täṭäraṭṭärä*

wonder, n. (feeling of wonder) አድናቆት *adnaqot;* (thing or person that causes wonder) አስደናቂ *asdännaqi;* አስገራሚ *asgärrami;* ድንቅ *dənq*
be filled with wonder ተደነቀ *tädännäqä*
work wonders (of a plan) ግሩም ፡ ሆነ *gərum honä;* (of a medicine) ፍቱን ፡ ሆነ *fətun honä*

wonderful ድንቅ *dənq;* አስደናቂ *asdännaqi;* ግሩም *gərum*
be wonderful ዳነቀ *dännäqä;* ገረመ *gärrämä*

wood ዕንጨት *ənčät*
woods ዱር *dur;* ጫካ *čakka;* ደን *dänn*

wooded ጫካማ *čakkamma;* ጫካ ፡ የለበሰ *čakka yäläbbäsä*

wooden የእንጨት *yänčät;* ከእንጨት ፡ የተ ሠራ *känčät yätäsärra*

woody ዛፍ ፡ የለበሰ *zaf yäläbbäsä*

woof ማግ *mag*

wool ሱፍ *suf;* የበግ ፡ ጠጉር *yäbäg ṭägur*

woolen ከሱፍ ፡ የተሠራ *käsuf yätäsärra*

woolens ሱፍ ፡ ልብስ *suf ləbs*

word ቃል *qal;* ነገር *nägär;* (message) መልእክት *mäl'əkt*
word for word ቃል ፡ በቃል *qal bäqal*

give one's word ቃል ፡ ገባ *qal gäbba*
have a word with አነጋገረ *annägag-gärä*
in a word በጭሩ *bäččäru*
take my word! እመነኝ *əmänäññ*
upon my word! ሙት *mut*
wording (choice of words) ቃላትን ፡ መም
ረጥ *qalatən mämräṭ;* (of letter, treaty)
አጻጻፍ *aṣṣaṣaf*
wordy የተንዛዛ *yätänzazza*
work (v.) ሠራ *särra*
work hard በጣም ፡ ጣረ *bäṭam ṭarä*
work out, vt. (~ a problem) ሠራ *sär-ra;* (~ a new method) ፈጠረ *fäṭṭärä*
work (n.) ሥራ *səra;* (of an author)
ጽሑፍ *ṣəhuf*
hard work ልፋት *ləfat*
be out of work ሥራ ፡ ፈታ *səra fätta*
workday የሥራ ፡ ቀን *yäsəra qän;* አዘቦት ፡
ቀን *azäbot qän*
worker ሠራተኛ *särratäñña*
working (adj.) ሠራተኛ *särratäñña*
working man ሠራተኛ *särratäñña*
workman ሠራተኛ *särratäñña*
workmanship አሠራር *assärar*
workshop የመሠሪያ ፡ ቦታ *yämässariya bota*
world ዓለም *aläm;* (people in general)
ሰዎች *säwočč*
worldly ዓለማዊ *alämawi*
world-wide ዓለም ፡ አቀፍ ፡ የሆነ *aläm aq-qäf yähonä*
worm ትል *təl*
worm-eaten, be ~ (of wood) ነቀዘ *näq-qäzä;* (of apple) ተላ *tälla;* ትል ፡ በላው *təl bällaw*
wormy የነቀዘ *yänäqqäzä*
worn (showing signs of wear) ያለቀ *yal-läqä*
worn-out ያለቀ *yalläqä;* ወራጅ *wärraǧ*
be worn-out (of stones) ተበላ *täbälla;*
(of a coat) አረጀ *aräǧǧä;* (of a rug)
አለቀ *alläqä*

worried የተጨነቀ *yätäčännäqä*
worrisome (~ situation) የሚያሰጋ *yäm-miyasäga;* (~parents) የተጨነቀ *yätä-čännäqä*
worry, vt. (annoy) አስቸገረ *asčäggärä;*
አስጨነቀ *asčännäqä;* (cause to be anxious) አሳሰበ *asassäbä*
worry (vi.) አሰበ *assäbä;* ተጨነቀ *tä-čännäqä*
worry (n.) ሐሳብ *hassab;* ስጋት *səgat;*
ጭንቀት *čənqät*
give worry, see 'worry' (v.)
worse የባሰ *yäbasä*
be worse ባሰ *basä;* ከፋ *käffa*
feel worse ባሰ(በት) *basä(bbät)*
get worse ተበላሸ *täbäläššä*
worsen (vt.) አባሰ *abasä*
worsen (vi.) ባሰ *basä*
worship (v.) አመለከ *amälläkä;* ሰገደ *säg-gädä;* (adore) በጣም ፡ ወደደ *bäṭam wäd-dädä*
worship, n. (worshipping) ማምለክ *mam-läk;* (extreme admiration) ክፍተኛ ፡
ክብር ፡ መስጠት *käffətäñña kəbər mäs-ṭät*
house of worship ቤት ፡ መቅደስ *betä mäqdäs*
place of worship የመጸለያ ፡ ቦታ *yä-mäṣälläya bota*
worshipper ምእመን *mə'əmän*
worst (n.) የባሰ *yäbasä*
worst, adj. ከ - - - ሁሉ ፡ በጣም ፡ የከፋ *kä - - - hullu bäṭam yäkäffa*
at worst የቀረው ፡ ቢቀር *yäqärräw bi-qär;* ገፋ ፡ ቢል *gəfa bil*
be worst off ባሰ(በት) *basä(bbät)*
if worst comes to worst የባሰ ፡ ቢብስ *yäbasä bibəs*
worth, n. (value) ምንነት *mənənnät;* ዋጋ *waga;* (merit) ጥቅም *ṭəqəm*
worth (adj.) የሚገባ *yämmiggäbba*
be worth አወጣ *awäṭṭa;* ዋጋ ፡ አለው *waga alläw;* ጠቀመ *ṭäqqämä*

worthless ዋ*ጋ* ፡ ቢስ *waga bis;* ሜና *mäna;* ምናምን *mənamən;* የማይረባ *yämmayə-räba*

worthwhile የሚረባ *yämmiräba*
be worthwhile ዋ*ጋ* ፡ አለው *waga alläw;* ጠቀመ *ṭäqqämä*

worthy ዋ*ጋ* ፡ ያለው *waga yalläw*

would, expressed by the imperfect

wound (v.) አቈሰለ *aqʷässälä*

wound (n.) ቁስል *qusl*

wounded የቈሰለ *yäqʷässälä;* ቁስለኛ *quslänña*
be wounded ቈሰለ *qʷässälä*

wrangle ተጫቃጨቀ *täčäqaččäqä*

wrap (wind around something) ጠመ
ጠመ *ṭämäṭṭämä*
wrap oneself (in a blanket) ለበሰ *läbbäsä;* (in a shawl) ደረብ *därräbä*
wrap up ጠቀለለ *ṭäqällälä*

wrapper መጠቅለያ *mäṭäqläya*

wrapping paper መጠቅለያ ፡ ወረቀት *mäṭäqläya wäräqät*

wrath መዓት *mä'at;* ቁጣ *quṭṭa*

wreath ያበባ ፡ ጉንጉን *yabäba gungun*

wreathe ጐነጐነ *gʷänäggʷänä*

wreck, v. (~ a car) እንክትክት ፡ አደረገ *ənkətkətt adärrägä;* አፈራረሰ *afärarräsä;* (~ a business) አበላሸ *abbälaššä*

wreck, n. (remains of something that has been destroyed) ፍርስራሽ *fərəsraš;* (thing that is destroyed) በግጥ ፡ የተ ሰበረ ፡ ነገር *bägəččət yätäsäbbärä nägär;* (a person in very poor health) ጤና ፡ ያጣ ፡ ሰው *ṭena yaṭṭa säw*
be a nervous wreck ናላው ፡ ዞረ *nalaw zorä*

wrecked የተሰበረ *yätäsäbbärä;* የተጐዳ *yätägʷädda*

wrench (vt.) መነጠቀ *mänäṭṭäqä;* መንጥቆ ፡ ወሰደ *mänṭəqo wässädä*
wrench, vi. (of shoulder) ወለቀ *wälläqä;* (of knee) ወለም ፡ አለ(ው) *wälämm alä(w)*

wrench (n.) ኪያቬ *kiyave*

wrest ነጠቀ *näṭṭäqä*

wrestle ታገለ *taggälä*

wrestler ትግለኛ *təglänña*

wrestling ትግል *təgəl*

wretch (miserable person) ምስኪን *məs-kin;* (contemptible person) እርጉም *ərgum*

wretched (~ person) ምስኪን *məskin;* (~ meal) መጥፎ *mäṭfo*
feel wretched ደጐነነት ፡ አይሰማውም *dähnənnät ayəssämmawəm*

wriggle (of child) ተቀነጠነጠ *täqʷnäṭännäṭä;* (of worm) ተጥመለመለ *täṭmälämmälä*

wring, v. (~ clothes) ጠመዘዘ *ṭämäzzäzä;* ጨመቀ *čämmäqä;* (~ one's hands) አሻሸ *ašaššä*
wring out ጠመዘዘ *ṭämäzzäzä*

wrinkle, vt. (~ clothes) አጨማደደ *aččämaddädä;* (~ the forehead) አኰማ ተረ *akʷämattärä*
wrinkle, vi. (of clothes) ተጨማደደ *täčämaddädä*

wrinkle, n. (of forehead) ሽብሽብ *šəbšəb;* (of dress) የተጨማደደ *yätäčämaddädä*

wrist የጅ ፡ አንጓ *yäǧǧ angʷa*

wrist watch የጅ ፡ ሰዓት *yäǧǧ säat*

write ጻፈ *ṣafä;* (~ novels) ደረሰ *därräsä*
write down, write out ጻፈ *ṣafä*

writer ደራሲ *därasi*

writing (handwriting) ጽሕፈት *ṣəhfät;* ጽፈት *ṣəfät;* (action of writing) መጻፍ *mäṣaf;* (anything that is written) ጽ ሑፍ *ṣəhuf*
writing material የጽሕፈት ፡ መሣሪያ *yäṣəhfät mässariya*

wrong (v.) በደለ *bäddälä*

wrong, n. (which is contrary to right) ስሕተት *səhtät;* (act of injustice) በደል *bädäl*
wrong, adj. (not right) ስሕተተኛ *səh-tätänña;* የተሳሳተ *yätäsasatä;* (unsuit-

able) የማይስማማ *yämmayəsmamma*
be in the wrong ተሳሳተ *täsasatä*
be wrong ተሳተ *täsatä;* ተሳሳተ *täsasatä;* (out of order) ተበላሸ *täbälaššä*
do wrong አሳሳተ *assasatä;* (do something bad) አጠፋ *aṭäffa;* በደለ *bäddälä*
go wrong ተበላሸ *täbälaššä;* not succeed) አልቀና(ውም) *alqänna(wəm)*
wrongdoer ጥፋተኛ *ṭəfatäñña*
wrongdoing መጥፎ ፡ ተግባር *mäṭfo tägbar*
wrongly ተሳስቶ *täsasto*
wrought, be ተሠራ *täsärra*
wrought-up, be ተበሳጨ *täbäsaččä*

Y

yam የስኳር ፡ ድንች *yäsəkkʷar dənnəč*
yard (enclosed space) አጥር ፡ ግቢ *aṭər gəbbi;* (measure) ያርድ *yard*
yarn ሱፍ ፡ ክር *suf kərr;* (story) ወሬ *wäre*
yawn አዛጋ *azzagga*
year ዓመት *amät*
year after year በያመቱ *bäyyamätu*
year by year በያመቱ *bäyyamätu*
year in, year out ከዓመት ፡ ዓመት *käamät amät;* ከዓመት ፡ እስከ ፡ ዓመት *käamät əskä amät*
all year round ዓመቱን ፡ በሙሉ *amätun bämulu*
last year ዓምና *amna*
New Year እንቍጣጣሽ *ənqʷəṭaṭaš*
this year ዘንድሮ *zändəro*
yearbook ዓመታዊ ፡ መጽሔት *amätawi mäṣhet*
yearlong ከዓመት ፡ ዓመት ፡ የሚቆይ *käamät amät yämmiqoyy*
yearly (adj.) የዓመት *yäamät;* ዓመታዊ *amätawi*

yearly (adv.) በያመቱ *bäyyamätu*
yearn ናፈቀ(ው) *naffäqä(w);* (have sympathy) ራራ *rarra*
yearning ናፍቆት *nafqot*
yeast እርሾ *əršo*
yell (v.) ጮኸ *čohä*
yell (n.) ጩኸት *čuhät*
yellow (~color) ብጫ *bəča;* (cowardly) ፈሪ *färi*
yellow fever ብጫ ፡ ወባ *bəča wäba*
yes አዎ *awo;* አዎን *awon;* (agreement) እሺ *əšši*
yesterday ትላንት *təlant;* ትናንት *tənant;* ትላንትና *təlantənna;* ትናንትና *tənantənna*
the day before yesterday ከትናንትና ፡ ወዲያ *kätənantənna wädiya*
yet, adv. (still) ገና *gäna;* አሁንም *ahunəm;* (at some future time) ወደፊት *wädäfit*
yet (conj.) ነገር ፡ ግን *nägär gən*
as yet እስካሁን *əskahun*
not yet ገና ፡ ነው *gäna näw*
yield, vt. (give in return) አስገኘ *asgäñña;* (~ fruit) አፈራ *afärra*
yield, vi. (give in) ተረታ *tärätta;* ተበገረ *täbäggärä;* (assent) ተቀበለ *täqäbbälä;* (surrender) እጅ ፡ ሰጠ *əǧǧ säṭṭä*
yield ground አፈገፈገ *afägäffägä*
yield (n.) ምርት *mərt*
yogurt እርጎ *ərgo*
yoke (v.) ጠመደ *ṭämmädä*
yoke (n.) ቀንበር *qänbär*
yolk የእንቁላል ፡ አስኳል *yänqulal askʷal*
yonder እዚያ *əzziya*
over yonder እዚያ ፡ ማዶ *əzziya mado*
you (subject), masc. sg. አንተ *antä;* fem. sg. አንቺ *anči;* pl. com. እናንተ *ənnantä;* resp. እርስዎ *ərsəwo;* (direct object), masc. sg. -ህ *-h;* fem. sg. -ሽ *-š;* pl. com. -አችሁ *-aččəhu;* resp. -ዎ *-wo;* -ዎት *-wot*

Z

young (of animal) ልጅ *ləǧ*; ግልገል *gəlgäl*; (young man, young people) ወጣት *wäṭṭat*

young (adj.) ልጅ *ləǧ*; ወጣት *wäṭṭat*; (~ nation) ታዳጊ *taddagi*
  young child ሕፃን ፡ ልጅ *həṣan ləǧ*
  young man ልጅ ፡ እግር *ləǧ əgər*; ጕረ ምሳ *gʷärämsa*; ወጣት *wäṭṭat*
  young people ልጅ ፡ እግሮች *ləǧ əgročč*
  young woman ልጅ ፡ እግር ፡ ሴት *ləǧ əgər set*

younger ታናሽ *tannaš*

youngest (child) የመጨረሻ *yämäčärräša*

youngish ልጅ *ləǧ*

youngster ወጣት *wäṭṭat*

your, masc. sg. ያንተ *yantä*; fem. sg. ያንቺ *yanči*; pl. com. የናንተ *yännantä*; resp. የርስዎ *yärsəwo*

yours, see 'your

yourself (subject), masc. sg. አንተ ፡ ራስህ *antä rasəh*; fem. sg. አንቺ ፡ ራስሽ *anči rasəš*; pl. com. እናንተ ፡ ራሳችሁ *ənnantä rasaččəhu*; resp. እርስዎ፡ራስዎ *ərsəwo raswo*

youth, n. (young man) ወጣት *wäṭṭat*; (young people) ወጣቶች *wäṭṭatočč*; (period between childhood and maturity) የወጣትነት ፡ ዘመን *yäwäṭṭatən nät zämän*

youthful (appearance) የወጣትነት *yäwäṭṭatənnät*

zeal ቅንአት *qən'at*

zealot ቀናኢ *qäna'i*

zealous ቀናኢ *qäna'i*
  be zealous ቀና *qänna*

zebra የሜዳ ፡ አህያ *yämeda ahəyya*

zenith የሰማይ ፡ እምብርት *yäsämay əmbərt*

zero (n.) ዜሮ *zero*
  sink to zero ከንቱ ፡ ሆነ *käntu honä*

zest (enthusiasm) የደስታ ፡ መንፈስ *yädässəta mänfäs*; (exciting element, flavor) ድምቀት *dəmqät*; ወዝ *wäz*

zigzag (v.) የተጠማዘዘ ፡ መሥመር ፡ ሠራ *yätäṭämazzäzä mäsmär särra*

zigzag (n.) የተጠማዘዘ ፡ ቅርጽ *yätäṭämazzäzä qərṣ*

zinc ዚንክ *zink*

zip ተፈተለከ *täfätälläkä*
  zip up ዚፐር ፡ ዘጋ *zipär zägga*

zipper ዚፐር *zipär*

zone, v. (divide) ከፈለ *käffälä*

zone, n. (district) ከለል *källäl*; (temperature belt) ከበብ *kəbäb*
  border zone የድንበር ፡ ከለል *yädənbär källäl*

zoo የእንስሳት ፡ መኖሪያ *yänsəsat mänoriya*; የአራዊት ፡ መጠበቂያ *yarawit mäṭäbäqiya*

zoology ዙኦሎጂ *zuoloǧi*

zoom (of airplane) እያጕረመረመ ፡ በረረ *əyyagʷrämärrämä bärrärä*

CORRECTIONS

The reader is advised to transfer the corrections to the indicated pages before using the dictionary.

a (following the page number) = column a
b (following the page number) = column b

P.4a, 1.23, also *həwwa*
1.24, also *hawala*

P.11b, 1.31, cross "or looks"

P.17b, 1.24 *mälläya*

P.27a, 1.4, cross "inebriation"

P.34a, 1.3 *mäkkan*

P.34b, 1.11, also *mäkädda*

P.48b, 1.2 *sällaṭṭe*

P.50a, 1.12 *somsoma*

P.51b, 1.1 bottom *sərqəta*

P.52a, 1.2 *sərqəta*
1.12 *sərrəčča*
1.14 *bäyyäsərrəččaw*
1.3 bottom, cross *sərrəw* and read *sərwä mängəst*

P.84a, 1.22, also *qiṭṭəňň*

P.90b, 1.5 bottom *bərakkʷa*

P.103b, 1.20 read የተባበሩት ፡ መንግ ሥታት

P.108b, 1.10, also *taṭṭafi*

P.109b, 1.22, also *čərčaro*

P.125a, 1.31, also *amakay*

P.146a, 1.3 bottom *iyyobelyu*, also *iyyobelyo*

P.150b, 1.11 *wagämt*

P.151a, 1.1 *maggʷäriya*

P.153a, 1.16, also አጣና *aṭana*

P.169a, 1.33 *wäränṭo*

P.171a, 1.13, also *wašo*
1.15,34, also *wašonnät*
1.21 *wəšal*

P.173a, 1.21 *wəkata*
1.22, also *wäkkäf*

P.176a, 1.4 bottom *wagämt*

P.186b, 1.7 bottom, most normally *yəluňta*

P.198b, 1.5 bottom *dakkəyye*

P.199a, 1.22 *dəwwər*

P.209a, 1.15 *əngurguro*

P.214a, 1.8, read ቃለ ፡ አጋኖ *qalä agganno*

P.225a, 1.23 *ṭəmmona*

P.244b, 1.23 *fäläg*

P.250b, 1.24, most normally ፈንጢጣ *finṭiṭṭa*

P.264b, 1.1 bottom *čokk bəlo*

P.272b, 1.4, also *həwwa*

P.276a, 1.14 *gəžži*

P.277a, 1.1 *sällaṭṭe*

P.280b, 1.10 bottom *čokk bəlo*

P.286b, 1.7 bottom, also *gošš*

P.293a, 1.2 *sällaṭṭe*
1.19 *mälläya*

P.307b, 1.2 bottom, also *mäkädda*

P.326a, 1.23 *kəfəyya*
1.3 bottom, also *hawala*

P.329b, 1.1 bottom *məṭṭane*

P.332b, 1.3 bottom *maggʷäriya*

P.335a, 1.5 *amboləkk, anboləkk*

P.344b, 1.7 bottom *mälläya*

P.362b, 1.19 *sällaṭṭe*

P.367b, 1.22 *fərida*

P.369a, 1.2 *sərqəta*

P.372b, 1.7 *moqqat*

P.380b, 1.13, also *wäkkäf*

P.382b, 1.14 bottom *sällaṭṭe*

P.384a, 1.9 *kəfəyya*

P.389b, 1.17 (*yä*) *iyyobelyu*
1.19 *iyyobelyu*

P.392b, 1.9 *əngurguro*

P.396a, 1.7 bottom, also *waššo*

P.398a, 1.16 *mayyayaža*

P.401a, 1.2 *čokk bəlo*

P.411b, 1.10 bottom, also *hawala*

P.414b, 1.22 *sänafəčč*

P.416b, 1.3 bottom *yälläšənnät*

P.431b, 1.23 *maggʷäriya*

P.435a, 1.7, also *mäkädda*
        1.18 *wäränṭo*

P.445b, 1.16, also *näbiyy*

P.459b, 1.7 bottom, also *čərčaro*

P.463a, 1.6 *qolo*

P.484b, 1.10 bottom *ṭaffiya*

P.485a, 1.18 *dəwwər*

P.487a, 1.2 bottom *mayyayaža*

P.488b, 1.6 bottom *mäkkan*

P.490a, 1.12 *wətaf*

P.497b, 1.2 bottom, also *qiṭṭəňň*

P.509a, 1.6 *yämmiyassassət*

P.509b, 1.4 *somsoma*

P.511a, 1.5 *wäränṭo*

P.515a, 1.19, most normally *yəluňta*

P.526a, 1.12 *wəšal*